The Essential Researcher

THE ESSENTIAL RESEARCHER

MAUREEN CROTEAU AND WAYNE WORCESTER

HarperPerennial

A Division of HarperCollinsPublishers

HarperCollins books may be purchased for educational, business, or sales promotional use. For information, please write: Special Markets Department, HarperCollins Publishers, Inc., 10 East 53rd Street, New York, NY 10022.

FIRST EDITION

Library of Congress Cataloging-in-Publication Data
Croteau, Maureen, 1949–
    The essential researcher / Maureen Croteau, Wayne Worcester. — 1st ed.
       p.   cm.
    ISBN 0-06-271514-3—ISBN 0-06-273040-1 (pbk.)
    1. Handbooks, vade-mecums, etc. I. Worcester, Wayne, 1947–   .
    II. Title.
    AG105.C86   1993
    031.02—dc20   91-58264

93 94 95 96 97 xx/xx 10 9 8 7 6 5 4 3 2 1
93 94 95 96 97 xx/xx 10 9 8 7 6 5 4 3 2 1 (pbk.)

CONTENTS

PART FIVE: SCIENCE, MEDICINE AND TECHNOLOGY

PART SIX: ACCESS TO INFORMATION

PART SEVEN: TECHNICAL VOCABULARIES

PART EIGHT: MATHEMATICS

PART NINE: DISASTERS, U.S. AND FOREIGN

PART TEN: THE JOURNALIST'S NOTEBOOK

PART ELEVEN:
QUICK CENSUS FIGURES

PART TWELVE: RELIGION

PART THIRTEEN: GETTING AROUND

PART FOURTEEN:
POPULAR CULTURE

PART FIFTEEN: SPORTS

FOREWORD

We live in the middle of an information explosion. Books, newspapers, magazines, trade journals and special-interest publications have always demanded the time and attention of people who write for a living. Now there are also fax machines, electronic mail and computer databases, and a plethora of reports, position-papers and newsletters prepared by groups and individuals who have been empowered by desktop publishing.

In theory, this should make the job of nonfiction writing easier. In fact, it often makes it much harder. The blizzard of information can be blinding. We need to get our bearings, to orient ourselves quickly with background information, if we are to find our way. Then we need to be able to map a course to our destination—to get additional, specific, up-to-the-minute information if we need it, and ask the questions that we need to ask. What we need is a guide.

That is what this book attempts to be.

The Essential Researcher gives background information, references and contact information on a wide array of topics: history, law, science, databases, government, Census figures, time zones, fads and sports, to name a few. A researcher in a hurry can learn how to get a passport, whom to call to find out about chemical dumping, how to use trademarks, biographical information about Supreme Court justices, the street names of illegal drugs, the meaning of computer terms and how to convert liters to gallons. *The Essential Researcher* is a book meant to be used. Its goal is to be the reference book that is turned to first, that is used most, that becomes tattered and dog-eared while others remain pristine. It is designed for researchers and writers—whether journalists, business professionals or students—who want to roll up their sleeves and get the job done efficiently and well.

In defining the scope of the book, the authors have drawn on their combined 40 years of experience as reporters, writers, editors and teachers. They have also relied on the advice of colleagues, who have been indulgent in acting as sounding boards and generous in offering advice. In particular, the authors would like to thank Robert Asher, John O. Bailey, Loftus Becker, Linda C. Boutell, Constance L. Chambers, Richard Dujardin, John F. Filhaber, Donna J. Fournier, Mel Goldstein, Paul B. Goodwin, Jr., Col. David C. Gregory, Robert Hamilton, Gail Harkness, Andrew Houlding, Edward Kostiner, John Long, David Markowitz, Karl A. Nieforth, Jon Sandberg and Bud Ward.

The authors also would like to thank four researchers who assisted with the book, Jennifer Hoboth, Laura Osterweis, Susan Blagrave and Dawn Battaglia; our editorial assistant, Patricia Bukowski; our agent, F. Joseph Spieler; and the editorial staff of HarperCollins, particularly Carol Cohen, Maron Waxman and Alison Jahncke.

PART ONE

GOVERNMENT

INTERNATIONAL GOVERNMENT

NATIONS OF THE WORLD

Country: (Region) governmental type; capital; principal languages; area; population; [former name, where applicable]; Embassy: address, telephone.

Afghanistan: (South Asia) Socialist republic; Kabul; Pashtu, Afghan Persian, Turkic languages; 251,773 sq. mi.; 15.9 million; Embassy: 2341 Wyoming Ave. NW, Washington, D.C. 20008, (202) 234-3770.

Albania: (Europe) Socialist republic; Tirana; Albanian, Greek; 11,097 sq. mi.; 3.27 million.

Algeria: (North Africa) Socialist republic; Algiers; Arabic, French, Berber dialects; 919,595 sq. mi.; 25.6 million; Embassy: 2118 Kalorama Rd. NW, Washington, D.C. 20008, (202) 265-2800.

Andorra: (Europe) Semi-independent coprincipality (Spain and France); Andorra la Vella; Catalan, Spanish, French; 180 sq. mi.; 51,400.

Angola: (Africa) Formerly socialist republic, now in transition after civil war; Luanda (UN supervised elections scheduled for fall 1992); Portuguese, Bantu dialects; 481,354 sq. mi.; 8.5 million.

Antigua and Barbuda: (Caribbean) Constitutional monarchy (British) with parliament; St. John's; English, local dialects; 170 sq. mi.; 63,700; Embassy: Suite 4M, 3400 International Dr. NW, Washington, D.C. 20008, (202) 362-5122.

Argentina: (South America) Republic; Buenos Aires; Spanish, English, Italian, German, French; 1,068,302 sq. mi.; 32.3 million; Embassy: 1600 New Hampshire Ave. NW, Washington, D.C. 20009, (202) 939-6400.

Armenia: (Europe) Member of Commonwealth of Independent States, which replaced the USSR; Yerevan; Armenian, Azerbaijani, Russian; 11,490 sq. mi.; 3.3 million.

Australia: (Oceania) Democratic, federal-state system recognizing British monarch as sovereign; Canberra; English, aboriginal languages; 2,966,151 sq. mi.; 16.9 million; Embassy: 1601 Massachusetts Ave. NW, Washington, D.C. 20036, (202) 797-3000.

Austria: (Europe) Republic; Vienna; German; 32,377 sq. mi.; 7.6 million; Embassy: 3524 International Court NW, Washington, D.C. 20008, (202) 895-6700.

Azerbaijan: (Europe) Member of Commonwealth of Independent States, which replaced the USSR; Baku; Azerbaijani, Russian, Armenian; 33,340 sq. mi.; 7 million.

Bahamas: (Caribbean) Independent commonwealth (British); Nassau; English, some Creole; 5,382 sq. mi.; 247,000; Embassy: 2220 Massachusetts Ave. NW, Washington, D.C. 20008, (202) 319-2660.

Bahrain: (Middle East) Emirate; Manama; Arabic, Farsi, Urdu, English; 267 sq. mi.; 520,000; Embassy: 3502 International Dr. NW, Washington, D.C. 20008, (202) 342-0741.

Bangladesh: (South Asia) Presidential/parliamentary system; Dhaka; Bangla, English; 55,598 sq. mi.; 118.4 million; [East Pakistan]; Embassy: 2201 Wisconsin Ave. NW, Washington, D.C. 20007, (202) 342-8372.

Barbados: (Caribbean) Independent commonwealth (British) with parliament; Bridgetown; English; 166 sq. mi.; 262,000; Embassy: 2144 Wyoming Ave. NW, Washington, D.C. 20008, (202) 939-9200.

Belgium: (Europe) Parliamentary democracy under a constitutional monarch; Brussels; Flemish (Dutch), French, German; 11,783 sq. mi.; 9.9 million; Embassy: 3330 Garfield St. NW, Washington, D.C. 20008, (202) 333-6900.

Belize: (Central America) Independent commonwealth (British) with parliament; Belmopan; English, Spanish, Maya, Garifuna; 8,867 sq. mi.; 220,000; [formerly British Honduras]; Embassy: 2535 Massachusetts Ave. NW, Washington, D.C. 20008, (202) 332-9636.

Benin: (Africa) Socialist republic; Porto-Novo; French, Fon, Yoruba, tribal languages; 43,484 sq. mi.; 4.7 million; [Dahomey]; Embassy: 2737 Cathedral Ave. NW, Washington, D.C. 20008, (202) 232-6656.

Bhutan: (South Asia) Monarchy; Thimpu; Dzongkha, Tibetan and Nepalese dialects; 17,954 sq. mi.; 1.5 million.

Bolivia: (South America) Republic; La Paz; Spanish, Quechua, Aymara; 424,164 sq. mi.; 6.7 million; Embassy: 3014 Massachusetts Ave. NW, Washington, D.C. 20008, (202) 483-4410.

Bosnia-Hercegovina: (Europe); Sarajevo; Serbo-Croatian; 19,741 sq. mi.; [Bosnia-Herzegovina is also an accepted spelling].

Botswana: (Africa) Republic; Gaborone; English, Setswana; 224,711 sq. mi.; 1.2 million; [Bechuanaland]; Embassy: 4300 International Dr. NW, Washington, D.C. 20008, (202) 244-4990.

Brazil: (South America) Federal republic; Brasilia; Portuguese, Spanish, English, French; 3,286,488 sq. mi.; 153 million; Embassy: 3006 Massachusetts Ave. NW, Washington, D.C. 20008, (202) 745-2700.

Brunei Darussalam: (Southeast Asia) Sultanate; Bandar Seri Begawan; Malay, English, Chinese;

2,226 sq. mi.; 372,000; Embassy: 2600 Virginia Ave. NW, Washington, D.C. 20037, (202) 342-0159 [Country is commonly called Brunei; Brunei Darussalam is derived from the Malay version, Darussalam Brunei, and is often used in official contexts].

Bulgaria: (Europe) Socialist republic (Communist rule no longer required by constitution); Sofia; Bulgarian; 42,823 sq. mi.; 8.93 million; Embassy: 1621 22d St. NW, Washington, D.C. 20008, (202) 387-7969.

Burkina Faso: (Africa) Military; Ouagadougou; French, tribal languages; 105,870 sq. mi.; 9 million; [Upper Volta]; Embassy: 2340 Massachusetts Ave. NW, Washington, D.C. 20008, (202) 332-5577.

Burma: *See* Myanmar

Burundi: (Africa) Military; Bujumbura; Kirundi, French, Swahili; 10,747 sq. mi.; 5.64 million; Embassy: 2233 Wisconsin Ave. NW, Washington, D.C. 20007, (202) 342-2574.

Byelorussia (Belarus): (Europe) Member of Commonwealth of Independent States, which replaced the USSR; Minsk (which is also the capital of the CIS); Byelorussian, Russian; 80,134 sq. mi.; 10 million.

Cambodia: (Southeast Asia) Government disputed between the National Government of Cambodia (the government-in-exile) and the People's Republic of Kampuchea (which calls itself the State of Cambodia); Phnom Penh; Khmer, French; 69,898 sq. mi.; 6.9 million; [Democratic Kampuchea].

Cameroon: (Africa) Republic; Yaoundé; English, French; 183,569 sq. mi.; 11 million; [French Cameroon]; Embassy: 2349 Massachusetts Ave. NW, Washington, D.C. 20008, (202) 265-8790.

Canada: (North America) Self-governing commonwealth (British) with parliamentary democracy; Ottawa, Ont.; English, French; 3,553,303 sq. mi.; 26.5 million; Embassy: 501 Pennsylvania Ave. NW, Washington, D.C. 20001, (202) 682-1740.

Cape Verde: (Africa) Republic; Praia; Portuguese, Crioulo; 1,557 sq. mi.; 374,000; Embassy: 3415 Massachusetts Ave. NW, Washington, D.C. 20007, (202) 965-6820.

Central African Republic: (Africa) Republic; Bangui; French, Sangho, Arabic, Hunsa, Swahili; 240,535 sq. mi.; 2.8 million; [Central African Empire]; Embassy: 1618 22d St. NW, Washington, D.C. 20008, (202) 483-7800.

Chad: (Africa) Republic; N'Djamena; French, Arabic, Sara, Sango; 486,180 sq. mi.; 5 million; Embassy: 2002 R St. NW, Washington, D.C. 20009, (202) 462-4009.

Chile: (South America) Republic; Santiago; Spanish; 292,132 sq. mi.; 13.08 million; Embassy: 1732

Massachusetts Ave. NW, Washington, D.C. 20036, (202) 785-1746.

China (People's Republic of China): (Far East) Socialist republic; Beijing; Standard Chinese (Putonghua), Mandarin Chinese (based on Beijing dialect) and Yue (Cantonese), Wu (Shanghainese), Minbei (Fuzhou), Minnan (Hokkien-Taiwanese), Xiang, Gan and Hakka dialects; 3,695,500 sq. mi.; 1.11 billion; Embassy: 2300 Connecticut Ave. NW, Washington, D.C. 20008, (202) 328-2500.

Colombia: (South America) Republic; Bogotá; Spanish; 440,831 sq. mi.; 33 million; Embassy: 2118 Leroy Pl. NW, Washington, D.C. 20008, (202) 387-8338.

Comoros: (Africa) Republic; Moroni; Shaafi Islam (Swahili dialect), Malagasy, French; 719 sq. mi.; 460,000; Embassy: 336 E. 45th St., New York, NY 10017, (212) 972-8010.

Congo: (Africa) Socialist republic; Brazzaville; French, many African languages, including Lingala and Kikongo; 132,047 sq. mi.; 2.2 million; [Middle Congo, Brazzaville].

Costa Rica: (Central America) Republic; San José; Spanish, Jamaican dialect of English; 19,730 sq. mi.; 3.03 million; Embassy: 1825 Connecticut Ave. NW, Washington, D.C. 20009, (202) 234-2945.

Côte d'Ivoire: *See* Ivory Coast

Croatia: (Europe) Republic; Zagreb; Serbo-Croatian; 5 million.

Cuba: (Caribbean) Socialist republic; Havana; Spanish; 42,803 sq. mi.; 10.6 million.

Cyprus: (Europe) Republic; Nicosia; Greek, Turkish, English; 3,572 sq. mi.; 708,000; Embassy: 2211 R St. NW, Washington, D.C. 20008, (202) 462-5772.

Czechoslovakia: (Europe) Federal republic; Prague; Czech, Slovak, Hungarian; 49,384 sq. mi.; 15.7 million; Embassy: 3900 Linnean Ave. NW, Washington, D.C. 20008, (202) 363-6315.

Denmark: (Europe) Constitutional monarchy; Copenhagen; Danish, Faeroese, Greenlandic (Eskimo dialect); 16,638 sq. mi.; 5.13 million; Embassy: 3200 Whitehaven St. NW, Washington, D.C. 20008, (202) 234-4300.

Djibouti: (Africa) Republic; Djibouti; French, Arabic, Somali, Afar; 8,958 sq. mi.; 337,000; [French Somalia]; Embassy: 866 United Nations Plaza, New York, NY 10017, (212) 753-3163.

Dominica: (Caribbean) Independent republic within commonwealth; Roseau; English, French patois; 290 sq. mi.; 85,000.

Dominican Republic: (Caribbean) Republic; Santo Domingo; Spanish; 18,680 sq. mi.; 7.2 million; Embassy: 1712 22d St. NW, Washington, D.C. 20008, (202) 332-6280.

Ecuador: (South America) Republic; Quito; Spanish, Quechua, indigenous languages; 106,860 sq. mi.; 10.5 million; Embassy: 2535 15th St. NW, Washington, D.C. 20009, (202) 234-7200.

Egypt: (Africa) Republic; Cairo; Arabic, English, French; 385,229 sq. mi.; 54.7 million; [formerly joined with Syria as United Arab Republic]; Embassy: 2310 Decatur Pl. NW, Washington, D.C. 20008, (202) 232-5400.

El Salvador: (Central America) Republic; San Salvador; Spanish, Nahua; 8,260 sq. mi.; 5.3 million; Embassy: 2308 California St. NW, Washington, D.C. 20008, (202) 265-9671.

Equatorial Guinea: (Africa) Republic; Malabo; Spanish, pidgin English, Fang; 10,831 sq. mi.; 369,000; [Spanish Guinea].

Estonia: (Europe) Republic (declared independence from USSR in August 1991); Tallinn; Estonian, Russian; 17,413 sq. mi.; 1.6 million.

Ethiopia: (Africa) In transition; Addis Ababa; Amharic, Tigrinya, Orominga, Arabic (English widely taught in schools); 483,123 sq. mi.; 51.6 million; [Abyssinia]; Embassy: 2134 Kalorama Rd. NW, Washington, D.C. 20008, (202) 234-2281.

Fiji: (Oceania) Declared a republic by leader of a military coup in 1987; Suva; English, Fijian, Hindustani; 7,095 sq. mi.; 759,000; Embassy: 2233 Wisconsin Ave. NW, Washington, D.C. 20007, (202) 337-8320.

Finland: (Europe) Republic; Helsinki; Finnish, Swedish; 130,559 sq. mi.; 4.97 million; Embassy: 3216 New Mexico Ave. NW, Washington, D.C. 20016, (202) 363-2430.

France: (Europe) Republic (former broad powers of president now shared with prime minister); Paris; French; 210,026 sq. mi.; 56.35 million; Embassy: 4101 Reservoir Rd. NW, Washington, D.C. 20007, (202) 944-6000.

Gabon: (Africa) Republic, with one-party regime since 1964; Libreville; French, Fang, Myene, Bateke, Bapounou (Eschira), Bandjabi; 103,347 sq. mi.; 1.06 million; Embassy: 2034 20th St. NW, Washington, D.C. 20009, (202) 797-1000.

Gambia, The: (Africa) Republic; Banjul; English, Mandinka, Wolof, Fula; 4,361 sq. mi.; 848,000; Embassy: 1355 15th St. NW, Washington, D.C. 20005, (202) 785-1399.

Georgia: (Europe) In transition after declaring independence from USSR (which then was dissolved); Tbilisi; Georgian, Russian, Armenian; 27,000 sq. mi.; 5.5 million.

Germany: (Europe) Federal republic (East and West Germany reunified 1990); Berlin; German; 137,777 sq. mi.; 79.5 million; Embassy: 4645 Reservoir Rd., Washington, D.C. 20007, (202) 298-4000.

Ghana: (Africa) Military; Accra; English, Akan, Moshi-Dagomba, Ewe, Ga; 92,100 sq. mi.; 15.1 million; [Gold Coast]; Embassy: 3512 International Dr. NW, Washington, D.C. 20008, (202) 686-4520.

Gilbert Islands: *See* Kiribati

Greece: (Europe) Presidential parliamentary government; Athens; Greek, English, French; 50,949 sq. mi.; 10.02 million; Embassy: 2221 Massachusetts Ave. NW, Washington, D.C. 20008, (202) 667-3168.

Grenada: (Caribbean) Independent state that recognizes British monarch as chief of state; St. George's; English, French patois; 133 sq. mi.; 84,000; Embassy: 1701 New Hampshire Ave. NW, Washington, D.C. 20009, (202) 265-2561.

Guatemala: (Central America) Republic; Guatemala City; Spanish, 18 Indian dialects; 42,042 sq. mi.; 9 million; Embassy: 2220 R St. NW, Washington, D.C. 20008, (202) 745-4952.

Guinea: (Africa) Republic; Conakry; French, tribal languages; 94,926 sq. mi.; 7.26 million; [French Guinea]; Embassy: 2112 Leroy Pl. NW, Washington, D.C. 20008, (202) 483-9420.

Guinea-Bissau: (Africa) Republic, led by one-party regime since 1974; Bissau; Portuguese, Criolo, many African languages; 10,811 sq. mi.; 999,000; [Portuguese Guinea]; Embassy: 918 16th St. NW, Washington, D.C. 20006, (202) 872-4222.

Guyana: (South America) Republic within the UK commonwealth; Georgetown; English, Amerindian dialects; 83,000 sq. mi.; 765,000; [British Guinea]; Embassy: 2490 Tracy Pl. NW, Washington, D.C. 20008, (202) 265-6900.

Haiti: (Caribbean) Republic; Port-au-Prince; Creole, French; 10,714 sq. mi.; 6.14 million; Embassy: 2311 Massachusetts Ave. NW, Washington, D.C. 20008, (202) 332-4090.

Holy See, The: (Europe) Papacy; Vatican City; Italian, Latin, French; 0.17 sq. mi.; 774; Apostolic Nunciature: 3339 Massachusetts Ave. NW, Washington, D.C. 20008, (202) 333-7121.

Honduras: (Central America) Republic; Tegucigalpa; Spanish, Indian dialects; 43,277 sq. mi.; 5.25 million; Embassy: 3007 Tilden St. NW, Washington, D.C. 20008, (202) 966-7702.

Hungary: (Europe) Republic; Budapest; Hungarian; 35,920 sq. mi.; 10.57 million; Embassy: 3910 Shoemaker St. NW, Washington, D.C. 20008, (202) 362-6730.

Iceland: (Europe) Republic; Reykjavík; Icelandic; 39,679 sq. mi.; 257,000; Embassy: 2022 Connecticut Ave. NW, Washington, D.C. 20008, (202) 265-6653.

India: (South Asia) Federal republic; New Delhi; Hindi, English, many other languages; 1,269,219 sq. mi.; 849.74 million; Embassy: 2107 Massachusetts Ave. NW, Washington, D.C. 20008, (202) 939-7000.

Indonesia: (Southeast Asia) Republic; Jakarta; Indonesian, English, Dutch, local dialects; 735,538 sq. mi.; 190.14 million; [Netherlands East Indies, Dutch East Indies]; Embassy: 2020 Massachusetts Ave. NW, Washington, D.C. 20036, (202) 775-5200.

Iran: (Middle East) Theocratic republic; Teheran; Farsi, Turki, Kurdish, Arabic, English, French; 636,296 sq. mi.; 55.64 million.

Iraq: (Middle East) Nominally a republic, but actually under dictatorial rule; Baghdad; Arabic, Kurdish, Assyrian, Armenian; 169,190 sq. mi.; 18.78 million; Embassy: 1801 P St. NW, Washington, D.C. 20036, (202) 483-7500.

Ireland: (Europe) Republic (six counties in northeast constitute Northern Ireland, which is part of the United Kingdom); Dublin; English, Irish (Gaelic); 26,593 sq. mi.; 3.5 million; Embassy: 2234 Massachusetts Ave. NW, Washington, D.C. 20008, (202) 462-3939.

Israel: (Middle East) Republic; Jerusalem; Hebrew, Arabic, English; 8,302 sq. mi.; 4.4 million; Embassy: 3541 International Dr. NW, Washington, D.C. 20008, (202) 364-5500.

Italy: (Europe) Republic; Rome; Italian, German, French, Slovene; 116,324 sq. mi.; 57.66 million; Embassy: 1601 Fuller St. NW, Washington, D.C. 20009, (202) 328-5500.

Ivory Coast (Côte d'Ivoire): (Africa) Republic; Yamoussoukro (but the United States recognizes Abidjan as the capital); French, Dioula and more than 60 other African languages and dialects; 122,780 sq. mi.; 12.47 million; Embassy: 2424 Massachusetts Ave. NW, Washington, D.C. 20008, (202) 483-2400.

Jamaica: (Caribbean) Independent state in UK commonwealth; Kingston; English, Creole; 4,244 sq. mi.; 2.44 million; Embassy: 1850 K St. NW, Washington, D.C. 20006, (202) 452-0660.

Japan: (Far East) Constitutional monarchy; Tokyo; Japanese; 145,870 sq. mi.; 123.64 million; Embassy: 2520 Massachusetts Ave. NW, Washington, D.C. 20008, (202) 939-6700.

Jordan: (Middle East) Constitutional monarchy; Amman; Arabic, English; 37,738 sq. mi.; 3.06 million; [Transjordan]; 3504 International Dr. NW, Washington, D.C. 20008, (202) 966-2664.

Kazakhstan: (Central Asia) Member of Commonwealth of Independent States, which replaced the USSR; Alma-Ata; Kazakh, Russian, German, Ukrainian; 1,049,155 sq. mi.; 16.5 million.

Kenya: (Africa) Republic within UK commonwealth; Nairobi; English, Swahili, local languages; 219,788 sq. mi.; 24.63 million; [British East Af-

rica]; Embassy: 2249 R St. NW, Washington, D.C. 20008, (202) 387-6101.

Kirgizia (Kyrgystan): (Central Asia) Member of Commonwealth of Independent States, which replaced the USSR; Bishkek; Kirghiz, Russian, Uzbek; 76,460 sq. mi.; 4 million.

Kiribati: (Oceania) Republic; Taraw; English, Gilbertese; 332 sq. mi.; 70,000; [Gilbert Islands].

Korea, North (Democratic People's Republic of Korea): (Far East) Socialist republic; Pyongyang; Korean; 46,540 sq. mi.; 21.29 million; [with South Korea, was Korea].

Korea, South (Republic of Korea): (Far East) Republic with strong executive branch; Seoul; Korean, English; 38,291 sq. mi.; 43.04 million; [with North Korea, was Korea]; Embassy: 2320 Massachusetts Ave. NW, Washington, D.C. 20008, (202) 939-5600.

Kuwait: (Middle East) Nominal constitutional monarchy; Kuwait City; Arabic, English; 6,880 sq. mi.; 2 million; Embassy: 2940 Tilden St. NW, Washington, D.C. 20008, (202) 966-0702.

Laos: (Southeast Asia) Socialist republic; Vientiane; Lao, French, English; 91,400 sq. mi.; 4 million; Embassy: 2222 S St. NW, Washington, D.C. 20008, (202) 332-6416.

Latvia: (Europe) Republic (declared independence from USSR in August 1991); Riga; Latvian, Russian; 24,595 sq. mi.; 2.7 million.

Lebanon: (Middle East) Republic; Beirut; Arabic, French, Armenian, English; 4,036 sq. mi.; 3.3 million; Embassy: 2560 28th St. NW, Washington, D.C. 20008, (202) 939-6300.

Lesotho: (Africa) Constitutional monarchy, independent member of UK commonwealth; Maseru; Sesotho, English, Zulu, Xhosa; 11,720 sq. mi.; 1.71 million; Embassy: 2511 Massachusetts Ave. NW, Washington, D.C. 20008, (202) 797-5533.

Liberia: (Africa) Republic; Monrovia; English, many languages of Niger-Congo language group; 37,743 sq. mi.; 2.63 million; Embassy: 5201 16th St. NW, Washington, D.C. 20011, (202) 723-0437.

Libya: (Africa) Socialist republic; Tripoli; Arabic, Italian, English; 685,524 sq. mi.; 4.22 million.

Liechtenstein: (Europe) Hereditary constitutional monarchy; Vaduz; German, Alemannic dialect; 61.8 sq. mi.; 28,000.

Lithuania: (Europe) Republic (declared independence from USSR in August 1991); Vilnius; Lithuanian, Russian, Polish; 25,170 sq. mi.; 3.7 million.

Luxembourg: (Europe) Constitutional monarchy; Luxembourg-Ville; Luxembourgish, German, French, English; 999 sq. mi.; 383,000; Embassy: 2200 Massachusetts Ave. NW, Washington, D.C. 20008, (202) 265-4171.

Macedonia: (Europe) Republic; Skopje; Serbo-Croatian, Flauvine, Macedonian; 9,925 sq. mi.; 2.03 million.

Madagascar: (Africa) In transition; Antananarivo; French, Malagasy; 224,532 sq. mi.; 11.8 million; [Malagasy Republic]; Embassy: 2374 Massachusetts Ave. NW, Washington, D.C. 20008, (202) 265-5525.

Malawi: (Africa) One-party state; Lilongwe; English, Chichewa, Tombuka; 45,747 sq. mi.; 9.15 million; [Nyasaland]; Embassy: 2408 Massachusetts Ave. NW, Washington, D.C. 20008, (202) 797-1007.

Malaysia: (Southeast Asia) Federal parliamentary democracy with constitutional monarch; Kuala Lumpur; Malay, English, Chinese dialects, Tamil, tribal dialects; 127,320 sq. mi.; 17.5 million; Embassy: 2401 Massachusetts Ave. NW, Washington, D.C. 20008, (202) 328-2700.

Maldives: (Africa) Republic; Male; Divehi, English; 115 sq. mi.; 218,000.

Mali: (Africa) Single-party constitutional government; Bamako; French, Bambara; 471,042 sq. mi.; 8.14 million; [French Sudan]; Embassy: 2130 R St. NW, Washington, D.C. 20008, (202) 332-2249.

Malta: (Europe) Independent parliamentary democracy within UK commonwealth; Valletta; Maltese, English; 122 sq. mi.; 350,000; Embassy: 2017 Connecticut Ave. NW, Washington, D.C. 20008, (202) 462-3611.

Marshall Islands: (Oceania) Republic in free association with U.S. (pact signed 1986); Majuro; English, Malayo-Polynesian dialects, Japanese; 70 sq. mi.; 43,000.

Mauritania: (Africa) Military; Nouakchott; French, Hasaniya Arabic, Toucouleur, Fula, Sarakole; 397,840 sq. mi.; 1.98 million; Embassy: 2129 Leroy Pl. NW, Washington, D.C. 20008, (202) 232-5700.

Mauritius: (Africa) Independent state that recognizes British monarch as chief of state; Port Louis; English, Creole, French, Hindi, Urdu, Hakka, Bojpoori; 788 sq. mi.; 1.07 million; Embassy: 4301 Connecticut Ave. NW, Washington, D.C. 20008, (202) 244-1491.

Mexico: (North America) Federal republic; Mexico City; Spanish; 756,066 sq. mi.; 87.87 million; Embassy: 1911 Pennsylvania Ave. NW, Washington, D.C. 20006, (202) 728-1600.

Micronesia: (Oceania) Constitutional government in free association with U.S. (pact signed 1986); Kolonia; English, Trukese, Pohnpeian, Yapese, Kosrean; 271 sq. mi.; 105,000.

Moldavia (Moldova): (Europe) Member of Commonwealth of Independent States, which replaced the USSR; Kishinev; Moldavian, Russian, Ukrainian; 13,000 sq. mi.; 4.4 million.

Monaco: (Europe) Constitutional monarchy; Monaco; French, English, Italian, Monegasque; 1.21 sq. mi.; 29,000.

Mongolia: (Far East) Socialist republic; Khalkha Mongol, Turkic, Russian, Chinese; 604,250 sq. mi.; 2.18 million; [Outer Mongolia].

Morocco: (Africa) Constitutional monarchy; Rabat; Arabic, Berber dialects, French; 274,461 sq. mi.; 25.61 million; Embassy: 1601 21st St. NW, Washington, D.C. 20009, (202) 462-7979.

Mozambique: (Africa) Socialist republic; Maputo; Portuguese, indigenous languages; 302,739 sq. mi.; 14.56 million; Embassy: 1990 M St. NW, Washington, D.C. 20036, (202) 293-7146.

Myanmar: (South Asia) Republic; Yangon (formerly Rangoon); Burmese; 261,218 sq. mi.; 41.27 million; [Burma]; Embassy: 2300 S St. NW, Washington, D.C. 20008, (202) 332-9044.

Namibia: (Africa) Republic; Windhoek; Afrikaans, German, English, indigenous languages; 317,873 sq. mi.; 1.45 million; [Southwest Africa].

Nauru: (Oceania) Republic; government offices are in Yaren district of the island; Nauruan, English; 8.2 sq. mi.; 9,000; [Pleasant Island].

Nepal: (South Asia) Constitutional monarchy; Kathmandu; Nepali is the official language, 20 other languages are spoken; 56,827 sq. mi.; 19.14 million; Embassy: 2131 Leroy Pl. NW, Washington, D.C. 20008, (202) 667-4550.

Netherlands: (Europe) Constitutional monarchy; Amsterdam; Dutch; 13,103 sq. mi.; 14.93 million; [Holland]; Embassy: 4200 Linnean Ave. NW, Washington, D.C. 20008, (202) 244-5300.

New Zealand: (Oceania) Independent state in UK commonwealth that recognizes British monarch as chief of state; Wellington; English, Maori; 103,883 sq. mi.; 3.29 million; Embassy: 37 Observatory Cir. NW, Washington, D.C. 20008, (202) 328-4800.

Nicaragua: (Central America) Republic; Managua; Spanish, English, Indian; 46,430 sq. mi.; 3.7 million; Embassy: 1627 New Hampshire Ave. NW, Washington, D.C. 20009, (202) 939-6570.

Niger: (Africa) Nominally a republic, with military regimes in power since 1974; Niamey; French, Hausa, Djerma; 489,076 sq. mi.; 7.96 million; Embassy: 2204 R St. NW, Washington, D.C. 20008, (202) 483-4224.

Nigeria: (Africa) Military government; Lagos; English, Hausa, Yoruba, Ibo, Fulani; 351,649 sq. mi.; 118.81 million; Embassy: 2201 M St. NW, Washington, D.C. 20037, (202) 822-1500.

Norway: (Europe) Constitutional monarchy; Oslo; Norwegian, Lapp, Finnish; 125,050 sq. mi.; 4.2 million; Embassy: 2720 34th St. NW, Washington, D.C. 20008, (202) 333-6000.

Oman: (Middle East) Absolute monarchy; Muscat; Arabic, English, Baluchi, Urdu, Indian dialects; 120,000 sq. mi.; 1.45 million; [Muscat]; Embassy: 2342 Massachusetts Ave. NW, Washington, D.C. 20008, (202) 387-1980.

Pakistan: (South Asia) Parliamentary federal republic with strong executive; Islamabad; Urdu, English, Punjabi, Sindhi, Pashtu, Baluchi; 310,403 sq. mi.; 114.64 million; [West Pakistan]; Embassy: 2315 Massachusetts Ave. NW, Washington, D.C. 20008, (202) 939-6200.

Panama: (Central America) Republic; Panama City; Spanish, English; 29,762 sq. mi.; 2.42 million; Embassy: 2862 McGill Terrace NW, Washington, D.C. 20008, (202) 483-1407.

Papua New Guinea: (Oceania) Independent parliamentary state in UK commonwealth that recognizes British monarch as head of state; 715 indigenous languages, English, pidgin English, Motu; 178,704 sq. mi.; 3.82 million; Embassy: 1615 New Hampshire Ave. NW, Washington, D.C. 20009, (202) 745-3680.

Paraguay: (South America) Republic under authoritarian rule; Asunción; Spanish, Guarani; 157,048 sq. mi.; 4.66 million; Embassy: 2400 Massachusetts Ave. NW, Washington, D.C. 20008, (202) 483-6960.

Peru: (South America) Republic; Lima; Spanish, Quechua; 496,225 sq. mi.; 21.9 million; Embassy: 1700 Massachusetts Ave. NW, Washington, D.C. 20036, (202) 833-9860.

Philippines: (Far East) Republic; Manila; Pilipino (based on Tagalog), English; 115,831 sq. mi.; 66.11 million; Embassy: 1617 Massachusetts Ave. NW, Washington, D.C. 20036, (202) 483-1414.

Poland: (Europe) Republic; Warsaw; Polish; 120,727 sq. mi.; 37.77 million; Embassy: 2640 16th St. NW, Washington, D.C. 20009, (202) 234-3800.

Portugal: (Europe) Republic; Lisbon; Portuguese; 33,549 sq. mi.; 10.35 million; Embassy: 2125 Kalorama Rd. NW, Washington, D.C. 20008, (202) 328-8610.

Qatar: (Middle East) Monarchy; Doha; Arabic, English; 4,416 sq. mi.; 490,000; Embassy: 600 New Hampshire Ave. NW, Washington, D.C. 20037, (202) 338-0111.

Romania: (Europe) Republic; Bucharest; Romanian, Hungarian, German; 91,699 sq. mi.; 23.27 million; [Socialist Republic of Romania]; Embassy: 1607 23d St. NW, Washington, D.C. 20008, (202) 232-4747.

Russian Federation: (Europe) Member of Commonwealth of Independent States, which replaced the USSR; Moscow; Russian, Tatar, Ukrainian; 6.6 million sq. mi.; 146 million.

Rwanda: (Africa) Republic in which military leaders hold key positions; Kigali; Kinyarwanda, French, Kiswahili; 10,169 sq. mi.; 7.6 million; Embassy: 1714 New Hampshire Ave. NW, Washington, D.C. 20009, (202) 232-2882.

Saint Kitts and Nevis: (Caribbean) Independent state in UK commonwealth that recognizes British monarch as head of state; Basseterre; English; 101 sq. mi.; 40,000; Embassy: 2100 M St. NW, Washington, D.C. 20037, (202) 833-3550.

Saint Lucia: (Caribbean) Independent state in UK commonwealth that recognizes British monarch as head of state; Castries; English, French patois; 238 sq. mi.; 153,000; Embassy: 2100 M St. NW, Washington, D.C. 20037, (202) 463-7378.

Saint Vincent and the Grenadines: (Caribbean) Independent state in UK commonwealth that recognizes British monarch as head of state; Kingstown; English, French patois; 150 sq. mi.; 113,000.

San Marino: (Europe) Republic; San Marino; Italian; 23.4 sq. mi.; 23,000.

São Tomé and Príncipe: (Africa) Republic; São Tomé; Portuguese; 373 sq. mi.; 125,000; Embassy: 801 2d Ave., New York, N.Y. 10017, (212) 697-4211.

Saudi Arabia: (Middle East) Monarchy; Riyadh; Arabic; 864,869 sq. mi.; 17.11 million; [Arabia]; Embassy: 601 New Hampshire Ave. NW, Washington, D.C. 20037, (202) 342-3800.

Senegal: (Africa) Republic; Dakar; French, Wolof, Pulaar Diola, Mandingo; 74,206 sq. mi.; 7.71 million; Embassy: 2112 Wyoming Ave. NW, Washington, D.C. 20008, (202) 234-0540.

Seychelles: (Africa) Republic; Victoria; English, French, Creole; 175 sq. mi.; 70,000; Embassy: 820 2d Ave., New York, NY 10017, (212) 687-9766.

Sierra Leone: (Africa) Republic with one-party government; Freetown; English, Mende, Temne, Krio; 27,653 sq. mi.; 4.06 million; Embassy: 1701 19th St. NW, Washington, D.C. 20009, (202) 939-9261.

Singapore: (Southeast Asia) Republic with parliamentary system; Singapore; Chinese (Mandarin), English, Malay, Tamil; 240 sq. mi.; 2.72 million; Embassy: 1824 R St. NW, Washington, D.C. 20009, (202) 667-7555.

Slovenia: (Europe) Republic; Ljubljana; Slovenian, Serbo-Croatian; 7,819 sq. mi.; 2.1 million.

Solomon Islands: (Oceania) Independent parliamentary state within UK commonwealth; Honiara; 120 indigenous languages, Melanesian pidgin, English; 10,639 sq. mi.; 335,000; [British Solomon Islands].

Somalia: (Africa) Republic; Mogadishu; Somali, Arabic, Italian, English; 246,201 sq. mi.; 8.42 million.

South Africa: (Africa) Republic; Cape Town is legislative capital, Pretoria is administrative capital, Bloemfontein is judicial capital; Afrikaans, English, Zulu, Xhosa, North Sotho, South Sotho, Tswana; 471,445 sq. mi.; 39.54 million; Embassy:

3051 Massachusetts Ave. NW, Washington, D.C. 20008, (202) 232-4400.

Spain: (Europe) Parliamentary monarchy; Madrid; Spanish, Catalan, Galician, Basque; 194,897 sq. mi.; 39.26 million; Embassy: 2700 15th St. NW, Washington, D.C. 20009, (202) 265-0190.

Sri Lanka: (South Asia) Republic; Colombo; Sinhala, Tamil, English; 24,886 sq. mi.; 17.19 million; [Ceylon]; Embassy: 2148 Wyoming Ave. NW, Washington, D.C. 20008, (202) 483-4025.

Sudan: (Africa) Republic with military government; Khartoum; Arabic, Nubian, Ta Bedawie, dialects of Nilotic, Nilo-Hamitic and Sudanic languages, English; 967,500 sq. mi.; 24.97 million; [Soudan]; Embassy: 2210 Massachusetts Ave. NW, Washington, D.C. 20008, (202) 338-8565.

Surinam: (South America) Republic, with strong governmental role for military; Paramaribo; Dutch, English, Sranan Tongo (also called Taki-Taki), Hindi, Suriname Hindustani, Javanese; 63,037 mi.; 397,000; [Dutch Guiana]; Embassy: 4301 Connecticut Ave. NW, Washington, D.C. 20008, (202) 244-7488.

Swaziland: (Africa) Monarchy; Mbabane; English, Siswati; 6,704 sq. mi.; 779,000; Embassy: 4301 Connecticut Ave. NW, Washington, D.C. 20008, (202) 362-6683.

Sweden: (Europe) Constitutional monarchy; Stockholm; Swedish, Lapp, Finnish; 170,250 sq. mi.; 8.4 million; Embassy: 600 New Hampshire Ave. NW, Washington, D.C. 20037, (202) 944-5600.

Switzerland: (Europe) Federal republic; Bern; German, French, Italian, Romansh; 15,943 sq. mi.; 6.74 million; Embassy: 2900 Cathedral Ave. NW, Washington, D.C. 20008, (202) 745-7900.

Syria: (Middle East) Republic that has been under left-wing military control since 1963; Damascus; Arabic, Kurdish, Armenian, Aramaic, Circassian, French, English; 71,043 sq. mi.; 12.48 million; [previously joined with Egypt as United Arab Republic]; Embassy: 2215 Wyoming Ave. NW, Washington, D.C. 20008, (202) 232-6313.

Tadzhikistan: (Central Asia) Member of Commonwealth of Independent States, which replaced the USSR; Dushanbe; Tadzhik, Uzbek, Russian; 55,240 sq. mi.; 4.8 million.

Taiwan (Republic of China): (Far East) One-party dominates, although other parties now may legally be formed; Taipei; Mandarin Chinese, Taiwanese and Hakka dialects; 13,900 sq. mi.; 20.54 million.

Tanzania: (Africa) Republic; Dar es Salaam; Swahili, English, indigenous languages; 342,102 sq. mi.; 25.97 million; [United Republic of Tanganyika and Zanzibar]; Embassy: 2139 R St. NW, Washington, D.C. 20008, (202) 939-6125.

Thailand: (Southeast Asia) Constitutional monarchy; Bangkok; Thai, English; 198,115 sq. mi.; 55.11 million; [Siam]; Embassy: 2300 Kalorama Rd. NW, Washington, D.C. 20008, (202) 483-7200.

Togo: (Africa) One-party republic; Lomé; French, Ewe, Mina, Dagomba, Kabyè; 21,925 sq. mi.; 3.67 million; [French Togo]; Embassy: 2208 Massachusetts Ave. NW, Washington, D.C. 20008, (202) 234-4212.

Tonga: (Oceania) Constitutional monarchy; Nuku'alofa; Tongan, English; 289 sq. mi.; 101,000; [Friendly Islands].

Trinidad and Tobago: (Caribbean) Parliamentary democracy; Port of Spain; English, Hindi, French, Spanish; 1,980 sq. mi.; 1.34 million; Embassy: 1708 Massachusetts Ave. NW, Washington, D.C. 20036, (202) 467-6490.

Tunisia: (Africa) Republic; Tunis; Arabic, French; 63,170 sq. mi.; 8.09 million; Embassy: 1515 Massachusetts Ave. NW, Washington, D.C. 20005, (202) 862-1850.

Turkey: (Middle East) Republican parliamentary democracy; Ankara; Turkish, Kurdish, Arabic; 300,948 sq. mi.; 56.7 million; Embassy: 1714 Massachusetts Ave. NW, Washington, D.C. 20036, (202) 387-3200.

Turkmenistan (Turkmenia): (Central Asia) Member of Commonwealth of Independent States, which replaced the USSR; Ashkhabad; Turkmen, Russian, Uzbek, Kazakh; 186,400 sq. mi.; 3.5 million.

Tuvalu: (Oceania) Independent republic, special member of UK commonwealth; Funafuti (atoll); Tuvaluan, English; 10 sq. mi.; 9,100; [Ellice Islands].

Uganda: (Africa) Republic; Kampala; English, Luganda, Swahili, Bantu and Nilotic languages; 76,084 sq. mi.; 17.96 million; [British East Africa]; Embassy: 5909 16th St. NW, Washington, D.C. 20011, (202) 726-7100.

Ukraine: (Europe) Member of Commonwealth of Independent States, which replaced the USSR; Kiev; Ukrainian, Russian; 231,990 sq. mi.; 51.7 million.

Union of Soviet Socialist Republics: (Europe) [The USSR was dissolved in December 1991. The following information describes the country at that time.] Communist state; Moscow; Russian, more than 200 other languages; 8,599,228 sq. mi.; 290.93 million; [Russia]. [*See* Armenia, Azerbaijan, Byelorussia, Estonia, Georgia, Kazakhstan, Kirgizia, Latvia, Lithuania, Moldavia, Russian Federation, Tadzhikistan, Turkmenistan, Ukraine, Uzbekistan]

United Arab Emirates: (Middle East) Federation of seven sheikhdoms (Abu Dhabi, Dubai, Sharjah, Ajman, Fujairah, Ras al-Khaimah and Umm al-Qaiwain) with some powers delegated to UAE central government and others retained by member sheikhdoms; Abu Dhabi; Arabic, Hindi, Ursu, Farsi, English; 30,000 sq. mi.; 2.25 million; [Trucial States]; Embassy: 600 New Hampshire Ave. NW, Washington, D.C. 20037, (202) 338-6500.

United Kingdom: (Europe) Constitutional monarchy; London; English, Welsh, Scottish form of Gaelic; 94,249 sq. mi.; 57.36 million; Embassy: 3100 Massachusetts Ave. NW, Washington, D.C. 20008, (202) 462-1340.

United States: (North America) Federal republic; Washington, D.C.; English, Spanish, many other languages among ethnic minorities; 3,540,939 sq. mi.; 248.7 million.

Uruguay: (South America) Republic; Montevideo; Spanish; 68,037 sq. mi.; 3 million; Embassy: 1919 F St. NW, Washington, D.C. 20006, (202) 331-1313.

Uzbekistan: (Central Asia) Member of Commonwealth of Independent States, which replaced the USSR; Tashkent; Uzbek, Russian, Kazakh, Tadzhik, Tatar; 172,741 sq. mi.; 20 million.

Vanuatu: (Oceania) Republic; Port Vila; Bislama, English, French; 4,707 sq. mi.; 165,000; [New Hebrides].

Vatican City: *See* Holy See, The

Venezuela: (South America) Republic; Caracas; Spanish, Indian dialects; 352,144 sq. mi.; 19.7 million; Embassy: 2445 Massachusetts Ave. NW, Washington, D.C. 20008, (202) 342-2214.

Vietnam: (Southeast Asia) Socialist republic; Hanoi; Vietnamese, French, Chinese, English, Khmer, ethnic languages; 127,246 sq. mi.; 66.17 million.

Western Sahara: (Africa) Disputed (legal status is unresolved as independence is challenged by Morocco); El Aaiun; Hassaniya Arabic, Moroccan Arabic; 102,703 sq. mi.; 192,000; [Spanish Sahara].

Western Samoa: (Oceania) Constitutional monarchy under tribal chief; Apia; Samoan, English; 1,093 sq. mi.; 186,000; Embassy: 1155 15th St. NW, Washington, D.C. 20005, (212) 599-6196.

Yemen: (Middle East) Republic; San'a; Arabic; 207,286 sq. mi.; 9.45 million; [previously North Yemen was known as the Yemen Arab Republic and South Yemen was known as the People's Democratic Republic of Yemen]; Embassy: 600 New Hampshire Ave. NW, Washington, D.C. 20037, (202) 965-4760.

Yugoslavia: (Europe) Federation of Serbia and Montenegro, torn by factional and ethnic differences; Belgrade; Serbo-Croatian; Slovene, Macedonian, Albanian, Hungarian; 39,438 sq. mi.; 10.41 million; Embassy: 2410 California St. NW, Washington, D.C. 20008, (202) 462-6566.

Zaire: (Africa) Republic with strong president; Kinshasa; French, English, Lingala, Swahili, Kingwana, Kikongo, Tshiluba; 875,525 sq. mi.; 36.58 million; [Congo Free State, Belgian Congo, Democratic Republic of the Congo]; Embassy: 1800 New Hampshire Ave. NW, Washington, D.C. 20008, (202) 234-7690.

Zambia: (Africa) Republic; Lusaka; English, many indigenous languages; 285,994 sq. mi.; 8.11 million; [Northern Rhodesia]; Embassy: 2419 Massachusetts Ave. NW, Washington, D.C. 20008, (202) 265-9717.

Zimbabwe: (Africa) Parliamentary democracy; Salisbury; English, ChiShona, Si Ndebele; 149,293 sq. mi.; 10.39 million; [Southern Rhodesia]; Embassy: 1608 New Hampshire Ave. NW, Washington, D.C. 20009, (202) 332-7100.

INTERNATIONAL ORGANIZATIONS

Arab League: The Arab League (formally the League of Arab States) was formed in 1945 to coordinate the political activity and protect the sovereignty of member states. Each member has one vote in the League's council. Only unanimous votes are binding. Members were split over Iraq's invasion of Kuwait in August 1990. (Iraq and Kuwait are both members of the Arab League.) Bahrain, Djibouti, Egypt, Kuwait, Lebanon, Morocco, Oman, Qatar, Saudi Arabia, Somalia, Syria, and the United Arab Emirates voted to condemn Iraq. The other members—Algeria, Jordan, Libya, Mauritania, the Palestine Liberation Organization, Sudan, Tunisia, and Yemen—were generally pro-Iraq. Headquarters: Tunis. It also maintains an office at 1100 17th St. NW, Washington, D.C. 20036, (202) 265-3210.

Association of Southeast Asian Nations: ASEAN was established in 1967 to strengthen regional cohesion and self-reliance, and emphasize economic, social and cultural cooperation and development. It supported the anti-Communist position in the Vietnam War and is generally considered pro-Western. Members are: Brunei Darussalam, Indonesia, Malaysia, the Philippines, Singapore and Thailand. Headquarters: ASEAN Secretariat, Jakarta, Indonesia.

Commonwealth of Nations: The Commonwealth is a cooperative, consultative association of Great Britain, the independent countries that were once part of the British Empire, and their dependencies. Government heads meet every one to three years for consultation, but their decisions are not binding. Initially, all members had to hold allegiance to the British monarch. As British possessions gained independence, the organization dropped that requirement. Instead, independent members must recognize the monarch only as symbolic head of the Commonwealth (although some continue to recognize the monarch as head of state). Independent members are: Antigua and Barbuda*, Australia*, the Bahamas*, Bangladesh, Barbados*, Belize*, Botswana, Brunei, Canada*, Cyprus, Dominica, Gambia, Ghana, Grenada*, Guyana, India, Jamaica*, Kenya, Kiribati, Lesotho, Malawi, Malaysia, Maldives, Malta, Mauritius*, Nauru, New Zealand*, Nigeria, Pakistan, Papua New Guinea*, Saint Kitts and Nevis*, Saint Lucia*, Saint Vincent and the Grenadines*, Seychelles, Sierra Leone, Singapore, Solomon Islands*, Sri Lanka, Swaziland, Tanzania, Tonga, Trinidad and Tobago, Tuvalu*, Uganda, the United Kingdom of Great Britain and Northern Ireland*, Vanuatu, Western Samoa, Zambia and Zimbabwe. Nauru and Tuvalu are special members. Various colonies and protectorates are also part of the Commonwealth. Headquarters: London. (* Recognizes British monarch as head of state.)

European Community: The EC is a group of three organizations that share membership: the European Economic Community (EEC or Common Market), the European Coal and Steel Community and the European Atomic Energy Community (Euratom). The term "Common Market" is often improperly applied to the EC, as well as to the EEC. The goal of the EC is to integrate members' economies, coordinate social development and foster political union. The structure consists of a Council of Ministers, a Commission, a European Parliament and a Court of Justice. Members are: Belgium, Denmark, France, Germany, Greece, Ireland, Italy, Luxembourg, the Netherlands, Portugal, Spain and the United Kingdom. Turkey is an associate member and 60 nations in Africa, the Caribbean and the Pacific are affiliates. Headquarters: Brussels. The EC maintains a press and public affairs office at 2100 M St. NW, Washington, D.C. 20037, (202) 862-9510.

European Free Trade Association: The EFTA was established in 1959 to promote free trade among member nations in western Europe. Members are: Austria, Iceland, Norway, Sweden, Switzerland and Finland. Headquarters: Geneva.

Group of Seven (G-7): G-7 represents the seven leading industrial countries—Great Britain, France, Canada, Germany, Italy, Japan and the United States. It coordinates economic and commercial activities and offers aid to other nations.

Nonaligned Movement: Members of the Nonaligned Movement are countries that, theoretically, have not been aligned with either the United States or the USSR. In fact, many of them have had ties to one of the superpowers. Members, most of whom are from Asia, Africa and Latin America, meet to discuss policy and areas of common interest. With the USSR dissolved and the Cold War over, the group is reexamining its goals. Members are: Afghanistan, Algeria, Angola, Argentina, Bahrain, Bangladesh, Barbados, Belize, Benin, Bhutan, Bolivia, Botswana, Burkina Faso, Burundi, Cameroon, Cape Verde, Central African Republic, Chad, Comoro Islands, Congo, Cuba, Djibouti, Ecuador, Egypt, Equatorial Guinea, Ethiopia, Gabon, Gambia, Ghana, Grenada, Guinea, Guinea-Bissau, Guyana, India, Indonesia, Iran, Iraq, Israel, Ivory Coast, Jamaica, Jordan, Kenya, Kuwait, Laos, Lebanon, Lesotho, Liberia, Libya, Madagascar, Malawi, Malaysia, Maldives, Mali, Malta, Mauritania, Mauritius, Morocco, Mozambique, Nepal, Nicaragua, Niger, Nigeria, North Korea, Oman, Pakistan, Panama, Peru, Qatar, Rwanda, Saint Lucia, São Tomé and Príncipe, Saudi Arabia, Senegal, Seychelles, Sierra Leone, Singapore, Somalia, South Africa, Sri Lanka, Sudan, Surinam, Swaziland, Syria, Tanzania, Togo, Trindad and Tobago, Tunisia, Uganda, United Arab Emirates, Yemen, Yugoslavia, Vietnam, Zaire, Zambia and Zimbabwe. Headquarters: None.

North Atlantic Treaty Organization: NATO was formed in 1949 to deter potential Soviet aggression in Europe. Its primary role is defense, although members also consider economic, scientific, cultural and environmental issues. NATO members agree that "an armed attack against one or more of them . . . shall be considered an attack against them all" under Article 5 of the North Atlantic Treaty. NATO has a military force, the major element of which is Allied Command Europe. Its headquarters is in Brussels. (There is also an Atlantic and Channel force.) The North Atlantic Council is NATO's chief policymaking board. It meets in Brussels. Each member provides a permanent representative to the group. These ambassadorial-level representatives meet at least once a week. Foreign ministers meet twice a year, and heads of state meet occasionally. The Secretary General chairs the sessions. Members are: Belgium, Canada, Denmark, France, Germany, Greece, Iceland, Italy, Luxembourg, the Netherlands, Norway, Portugal, Spain, Turkey, the United Kingdom, and the United States. Headquarters: Brussels.

Organization for Economic Cooperation and Development: The OECD was originally set up in 1948 as the Organization for European Economic Cooperation to help rebuild Europe after World War II. In 1961, when reconstruction was completed, it became the OECD, an international group that seeks financial growth and stability among its members and seeks to promote world trade, employment and improved living standards. Members are: Australia, Austria, Belgium, Canada,

Denmark, Finland, France, Germany, Greece, Iceland, Ireland, Italy, Japan, Luxembourg, the Netherlands, New Zealand, Norway, Portugal, Spain, Sweden, Switzerland, Turkey, the United Kingdom and the United States. Yugoslavia is a special member. Headquarters: Paris. It maintains an office at 2001 L St. NW, Washington, D.C. 200361, (202) 785-6323.

Organization of African Unity: The OAU was established in 1963 to defend the independence and territorial integrity of member states, to promote development and to coordinate policy in areas of common interest, including welfare, defense and foreign affairs. It is opposed to colonialism. Members are: Algeria, Angola, Benin, Botswana, Burkina Faso, Burundi, Cameroon, Cape Verde, Central African Republic, Chad, Comoros, Congo, Djibouti, Egypt, Equatorial Guinea, Ethiopia, Gabon, Gambia, Ghana, Guinea, Guinea-Bissau, Ivory Coast, Kenya, Lesotho, Liberia, Libya, Madagascar, Malawi, Mali, Mauritania, Mauritius, Morocco, Mozambique, Niger, Nigeria, Rwanda, São Tomé and Príncipe, Senegal, Seychelles, Sierra Leone, Somalia, Sudan, Swaziland, Tanzania, Togo, Tunisia, Uganda, Zaire, Zambia and Zimbabwe. Headquarters: Addis Ababa, Ethiopia.

Organization of American States: The OAS is concerned with settling disputes and maintaining peace in the Western Hemisphere. It also fosters economic cooperation and implements the Rio Treaty, a regional security agreement that went into effect in 1948. In case of armed attack or any other threat to peace, the foreign ministers of member nations meet to determine appropriate action. Members are: Antigua, Argentina, Bahamas, Barbados, Belize, Bolivia, Brazil, Chile, Colombia, Costa Rica, Cuba, Dominica, the Dominican Republic, Ecuador, El Salvador, Grenada, Guatemala, Guyana, Haiti, Honduras, Jamaica, Mexico, Nicaragua, Panama, Paraguay, Peru, Saint Kitts and Nevis, Saint Lucia, Saint Vincent, Surinam, Trinidad and Tobago, the United States, Uruguay and Venezuela. Headquarters: 17th St. and Constitution Ave. NW, Washington, D.C. 20006, (202) 458-3841.

Organization of Petroleum Exporting Countries: OPEC was created in 1960 in response to price cuts by U.S. and European oil companies. Its goal is to maintain or increase oil prices by negotiation and by setting oil production quotas for member nations to prevent an oversupply. Members are: Algeria, Ecuador, Gabon, Indonesia, Iran, Iraq, Kuwait, Libya, Nigeria, Qatar, Saudi Arabia, United Arab Emirates and Venezuela. Headquarters: Vienna.

Warsaw Treaty Organization: The Warsaw Pact was dissolved on April 1, 1991. For 35 years, it had established a military alliance between the USSR and its Eastern European satellites, and had kept the smaller countries under Soviet control. Formed in 1955 as a counterpart to the North Atlantic Treaty Organization, it became less important as the Cold War ended. When the Eastern European countries began breaking away from Soviet influence in 1989, it became moribund. Members were Bulgaria, Czechoslovakia, Hungary, Poland, Romania and the USSR. The headquarters was in Moscow.

UNITED NATIONS

The United Nations is an intergovernmental body established after World War II to promote peace and international cooperation and to promote economic and social development. It was designed as a more effective replacement for the League of Nations, an international peacekeeping organization that had been ineffectual in preventing World War II. The charter establishing the United Nations was signed by representatives of 50 nations on June 26, 1945. (Poland, which signed on Oct. 15, is also considered a founding member.)

The United Nations Headquarters is a 16-acre site in New York City along the East River, between 42d and 48th streets. It includes the General Assembly and Secretariat buildings and a library. The mailing address is: United Nations, New York, NY 10017. Other offices are in buildings nearby. The UN also has permanent offices in Geneva (United Nations, Palais des Nations, 1211 Geneva 10, Switzerland) and Vienna (United Nations International Centre, A-1400 Vienna, Austria). The UN's International Court of Justice is in the Netherlands (International Court of Justice, Peace Palace, 2517 KJ, The Hague, The Netherlands).

Business is conducted in six official languages: Arabic, Chinese, English, French, Russian and Spanish. All major documents are translated into each language, as are all meetings of the General Assembly, the Security Council and the Economic and Social Council.

There are six principal organs of the UN: the General Assembly, the Security Council, the Secretariat, the Economic and Social Council (ECOSOC), the International Court of Justice (ICJ) and the Trusteeship Council.

The **General Assembly** is a forum for discussion of world peace, human rights, the environment and health issues. Each member nation has one vote. Although the body cannot legislate or compel members to take specific actions, its recommendations carry considerable weight as a reflection of international opinion. The General Assembly is also responsible for overall supervision of UN activities. The General Assembly usually meets from the third Tuesday of September through December, although committees and other subsidiary groups work throughout the year. Frequently there are special sessions or conferences dealing with specific topics. If there is a threat to world peace, the General Assembly can be convened in 24 hours. Many matters can be determined by a simple majority vote. Some important issues require a two-thirds vote. Among those issues are recommendations relating to maintaining peace and security, election of the nonpermanent members of the Security Council, election of the members of the ECOSOC, suspension or expulsion of members, and budgetary issues.

The **Security Council** is the only UN organ that can make decisions that member governments are obligated to carry out. (The other organs act by recommendation only.) Under the UN's charter, all member nations agree to carry out the decisions of the Council. The Council investigates situations that may threaten world peace and makes recommendations concerning resolution. It may send observers or peacekeeping forces to areas of conflict, direct collective military involvement and decide on ceasefire measures. There are five permanent members: China, France, Russia, the United Kingdom and the United States. Ten other members are elected by the General Assembly for two-year terms. The members are: Spain (1994), New Zealand (1994), Venezuela (1993), Brazil (1994), Djibouti (1994), Morocco (1993), Hungary (1993), Japan (1993), Cape Verde (1993) and Pakistan (1994). Their terms end on December 31 of the year indicated. Decisions regarding procedural matters require agreement of at least nine members. Decisions on substantive issues require agreement of at least nine members, including all permanent members. The negative vote of one permanent member acts as a veto. (An abstention does not count as a veto.) Nations that are not UN members, or that are not members of the Security Council, may be asked to participate in deliberations that affect them.

The **Secretariat** serves the other UN organs and agencies by providing studies, information and facilities, by administering peacekeeping operations, and by organizing conferences on international problems. It is headed by the Secretary General, who is elected by the General Assembly for a five-year term. The Secretary General cannot be from one of the permanent-member nations of the Security Council. Those who have held the post have been: Trygve Lie of Norway, 1946–52; Dag Hammarskjold of Sweden,

1953–61; U Thant of Burma, 1961–71; Kurt Waldheim of Austria, 1972–81; Javier Pérez de Cuéllar of Peru, 1982–91; Boutros Boutros-Ghali of Egypt, 1992—.

The **Economic and Social Council** coordinates the economic and social work of the UN and its specialized agencies. It makes recommendations to the General Assembly and initiates activities concerning human rights, world trade, natural resources, education, health and development, social welfare, science, technology and other economic and social issues. The council has 54 members, one-third of whom are elected each year by the General Assembly for three-year terms. Each member has one vote. Voting on all issues is by simple majority.

The **International Court of Justice** decides cases submitted to it by member states and issues opinions requested by the General Assembly, the Security Council or other specialized UN agencies. The Court, which meets in The Hague, Netherlands, consists of 15 judges elected by the General Assembly and the Security Council for nine-year terms. Each judge must be from a different country. Jurisdiction is based on the consent of the parties. Although there is no appeal, parties may apply for revision of a judgment within 10 years if there is a change in a decisive factor. If a party refuses to perform its obligations called for under a judgment, the other party may take the issue before the Security Council. The court deals with a wide variety of issues, including territorial rights, maritime rights, sovereignty and the rights of individuals to asylum.

The **Trusteeship Council** supervises the administration of trust territories. It consists of representatives of states that administer trust territories, representatives of permanent members of the Security Council and enough other members so that representation is divided between administering and nonadministering states. Originally, the Trusteeship Council oversaw 11 territories. The only one remaining is Palau, a chain of islands in the western central Pacific Ocean that is a trust territory of the United States.

In addition to the six main organs of the UN, there are many programs that have been created by the General Assembly and report to it through the Economic and Social Council. There are also independent, self-governing agencies that work with the UN and each other through the Economic and Social Council. Membership in the self-governing agencies is separate from UN membership.

The UN-sponsored programs are:

• United Nations Centre for Human Settlements (Habitat), P.O. Box 30030, Nairobi, Kenya, which promotes housing, especially in developing nations.

• International Research and Training Institute for the Advancement of Women (INSTRAW), Calle César Nicolas Penson, 102-A, Santo Domingo, Dominican Republic, which promotes the role of women.

• United Nations Conference on Trade and Development (UNCTAD), Place des Nations, 1211 Geneva 10, Switzerland, which formulates, mediates and coordinates trade agreements and policies, with emphasis on developing nations.

• United Nations Development Programme, 1 United Nations Plaza, New York, NY 10017, which coordinates all development projects of the UN.

• United Nations Environment Programme, P.O. Box 30552, Nairobi, Kenya, which monitors the environment and encourages sound practices. Its programs include Earthwatch, an international monitoring program that also operates a computerized, international referral service and the International Register of Potentially Toxic Chemicals.

• United Nations Population Fund (UNFPA), 1 United Nations Plaza, New York, NY 10017, which aids population programs in developing countries and promotes understanding of population factors.

• Office of the United Nations High Commissioner for Refugees (UNHCR), Place des Nations, 1211 Geneva 10, Switzerland, which provides food, clothing and shelter for refugees and works with governments to ensure their safety.

• United Nations Children's Fund (UNICEF), UNICEF House, 3 UN Plaza, New York, NY 10017, which provides community-based nutrition, health, sanitation and education services for children in developing countries.

• United Nations Institute for Training and Research (UNITAR), 801 UN Plaza, New York, NY 10017, which trains members of the UN's permanent missions.

• United Nations University, Toho Seimei Building, 15-1, Shibuya 2-chome, Shibuya-ku, Tokyo 150, Japan, which is an international community of scholars conducting research concerning peace, economics, energy, resources, food, biotechnology, poverty and social development. It has no campus or faculty, although it operates research centers in Finland and Ivory Coast.

• World Food Council (WFC), Via delle Terme di Caracalla, 00100, Rome, Italy, which works with developing nations to plan and adopt strategies for food production and distribution.

• World Food Programme (WFP), Via Cristoforo Colombo, 426, 00145 Rome, Italy, which provides food to development agencies and during emergencies. It also operates land-use projects. It is a joint program of the UN and the Food and Agriculture Organization, an independent, UN-related organization (See below).

• United Nations Disaster Relief Organization, Place des Nations, 1211 Geneva 10, Switzerland, which acts as a clearinghouse for information and donations for relief efforts and promotes disaster planning and prevention.

The independent, specialized agencies that operate through the UN are:

• International Atomic Energy Agency (IAEA), Vienna International Centre, P.O. Box 100, A-1400 Vienna, Austria, which fosters the development of peaceful uses of nuclear energy and aids in the international exchange of information. It differs from the other specialized agencies in that it reports directly to the General Assembly, not the Economic and Social Council.

• International Labour Organisation, 4, rue des Morillons, CH-1211 Geneva 22, Switzerland, which promotes policies and programs to improve working and living conditions.

• Food and Agriculture Organization of the United Nations (FAO), Via delle Terme di Caracalla, 00100 Rome, Italy, which seeks to increase farm, forest and fishery production. It cosponsors the World Food Programme.

• United Nations Educational, Scientific and Cultural Organization (UNESCO), 7, Place de Fontenoy, 75007 Paris, France, which promotes education through teacher training, school building and textbook development. It also seeks to preserve world cultural treasures, including books and art.

• World Health Organization (WHO), 20, avenue Appia, 1211 Geneva 27, Switzerland, which works with governments, other UN agencies and nongovernmental organizations to solve and prevent health problems.

• The World Bank, 1818 H St. NW, Washington, D.C. 20433, a group of three institutions: the International Bank for Reconstruction and Development (which provides loans and guidance to developing countries), the International Finance Corporation (which promotes the flow of private capital to investments in member countries) and the International Development Association (an affiliate of the International Bank for Reconstruction and Development that lends money to poor countries on more favorable terms than the Bank can provide).

• International Monetary Fund (IMF), 700 19th St. NW, Washington, D.C. 20431, which provides economic management advice to members and provides financial assistance to member nations who are having balance-of-trade difficulties.

• International   Civil   Aviation   Organization

(ICAO), 1000 Sherbrooke St. West, Suite 400, Montreal, Quebec H3A 2R2, Canada, which promotes safer air travel.

• Universal Postal Union (UPU), Weltpoststrasse 4, Berne, Switzerland, which promotes the smooth international exchange of mail.

• International Telecommunication Union (ITU), Place des Nations, 1211 Geneva 20, Switzerland, which coordinates the use of radio frequencies and communications satellites, and develops telecommunication equipment and policies.

• World Meteorological Organization (WMO), 41, avenue Giuseppe-Motta, 1211 Geneva 20, Switzerland, which promotes the international exchange of weather information.

• International Maritime Organization (IMO), 4 Albert Embankment, London SE1 SR, England, which seeks to improve international shipping, maritime safety and marine pollution control.

• World Intellectual Property Organization (WIPO), 34, chemin des Colombettes, 121 Geneva 20, Switzerland, which promotes international cooperation concerning copyright, trademark and patent enforcement.

• International Fund for Agricultural Development (IFAD), Via del Serafico 10, 00142 Rome, Italy, which lends money for agricultural development programs in developing countries.

• United Nations Industrial Development Organization (UNIDO), Wagramerstrasse 5, Vienna XXII, Austria, which promotes industrialization in developing countries by providing technical assistance and training programs.

CONTACTS AND REFERENCES:

Information: Public Inquiries Unit, UN, Room GA-57, New York, NY 10017, (212) 963-4475. Press information, (212) 963-7160.

Publications: UN Sales, UN, Room DC2-853, New York, NY 10017, (212) 963-8302.

Database: United Nations Information Service (UNISER), Global Education Motivators Inc., Chestnut Hill College, Chestnut Hill, PA 19118-2695, (215) 248-1150.

UNITED NATIONS MEMBER NATIONS

MEMBERS 1992

Member	Date Joined
Afghanistan	1946
Albania	1955
Algeria	1962
Angola	1976
Antigua and Barbuda	1981
Argentina	1945
Armenia	1992
Australia	1945
Austria	1955
Azerbaijan	1992
Bahamas	1973
Bahrain	1971
Bangladesh	1974
Barbados	1966
Belgium	1945
Belize	1981
Benin	1960
Bhutan	1971
Bolivia	1945
Bosnia-Hercegovina	1992
Botswana	1966
Brazil	1945
Brunei Darussalam	1984
Bulgaria	1955
Burkina Faso	1960
Burundi	1962
Byelorussian Soviet Socialist Republic	1945
Cambodia	1955
Cameroon	1960
Canada	1945
Cape Verde	1975
Central African Republic	1960
Chad	1960
Chile	1945
China[1]	1945
Colombia	1945
Comoros	1975
Congo	1960
Costa Rica	1945
Croatia	1992
Cuba	1945
Cyprus	1960
Czechoslovakia	1945
Denmark	1945
Djibouti	1977
Dominica	1978
Dominican Republic	1945
Ecuador	1945
Egypt[2]	1945
El Salvador	1945
Equatorial Guinea	1968
Estonia	1991
Ethiopia	1945
Fiji	1970
Finland	1955
France	1945
Gabon	1960
Gambia	1965
Germany (Federal Republic of)	1973
Ghana	1957
Greece	1945
Grenada	1974
Guatemala	1945
Guinea	1958
Guinea-Bissau	1974
Guyana	1966
Haiti	1945

Honduras	1945	Rwanda	1962	
Hungary	1955	Saint Kitts and Nevis	1983	
Iceland	1946	Saint Lucia	1979	
India	1945	Saint Vincent and the Grenadines	1980	
Indonesia	1950	Samoa	1976	
Iran (Islamic Republic of)	1945	San Marino	1992	
Iraq	1945	São Tomé and Príncipe	1975	
Ireland	1955	Saudi Arabia	1945	
Israel	1949	Senegal	1960	
Italy	1955	Seychelles	1976	
Ivory Coast	1960	Sierra Leone	1961	
Jamaica	1962	Singapore[4]	1965	
Japan	1956	Slovenia	1992	
Jordan	1955	Solomon Islands	1978	
Kazakhstan	1992	Somalia	1960	
Kenya	1963	South Africa	1945	
Kuwait	1963	South Korea	1991	
Kyrgyzstan	1992	Spain	1955	
Lao People's Democratic Republic	1955	Sri Lanka	1955	
Latvia	1991	Sudan	1956	
Lebanon	1945	Surinam	1975	
Lesotho	1966	Swaziland	1968	
Liberia	1945	Sweden	1946	
Libyan Arab Jamahiriya	1955	Syrian Arab Republic[2]	1945	
Liechtenstein	1990	Tajikistan	1992	
Lithuania	1991	Thailand	1946	
Luxembourg	1945	Togo	1960	
Madagascar	1960	Trinidad and Tobago	1962	
Malawi	1964	Tunisia	1956	
Malaysia	1957	Turkey	1945	
Maldives	1965	Turkmenistan	1992	
Mali	1960	Uganda	1962	
Malta	1964	Ukrainian Soviet Socialist Republic	1945	
Marshall Islands	1991	United Kingdom of Great Britain and N. Ireland	1945	
Mauritania	1961			
Mauritius	1968	United Arab Emirates	1971	
Mexico	1945	United Republic of Tanzania[5]	1961	
Micronesia	1991	United States	1945	
Moldova	1992	Uruguay	1945	
Mongolia	1961	Uzbekistan	1992	
Morocco	1956	Vanuatu	1981	
Mozambique	1975	Venezuela	1945	
Myanmar	1948	Vietnam	1977	
Namibia	1990	Yemen, Republic of	1947	
Nepal	1955	Zaire	1960	
Netherlands	1945	Zambia	1964	
New Zealand	1945	Zimbabwe	1980	
Nicaragua	1945			
Niger	1960			
Nigeria	1960			
North Korea	1991			
Norway	1945			
Oman	1971			
Pakistan	1947			
Panama	1945			
Papua New Guinea	1975			
Paraguay	1945			
Peru	1945			
Philippines	1945			
Poland	1945			
Portugal	1955			
Qatar	1971			
Romania	1955			
Russia[3]	1945			

1. In 1971, the General Assembly voted to recognize the People's Republic of China as "the only legitimate representative of China" and to expel the representatives of Chiang Kai-shek.

2. Egypt and Syria were original UN members in 1945. When the two were united as the United Arab Republic in 1958, the new country became a single member. When Syria resumed its independence in 1961, it and Egypt returned to their status as separate members.

3. When the Union of Soviet Socialist Republics dissolved in December 1991, Russia assumed its role. The USSR was a charter member in 1945.

4. Singapore became a member after gaining its independence in 1965. (It had been represented as part of Malaysia since 1963.)

5. Tanganyika became a member in 1961; Zanzibar in 1963. The two united in 1964.

U.S. GOVERNMENT

PRESIDENTIAL POWERS

The powers of the president are specified in Article II of the Constitution. [*See* U.S. Constitution and Amendments, page 49]

The president is commander-in-chief of the armed forces, is the head of executive departments, and may grant reprieves and pardons (although he may not revoke impeachments).

He shares some responsibilities with Congress. He has the power to make treaties, provided the Senate concurs by a two-thirds majority. He nominates ambassadors, public ministers, consuls and judges of the Supreme Court but needs the consent of the Senate to appoint them. (If the Senate is in recess, the president may fill vacancies temporarily.) The president must report to the Congress on the state of the union and advise Congress. He may convene either or both houses of Congress on "extraordinary occasions" and may adjourn them. He receives ambassadors and other public ministers. He ensures that laws are executed and commissions officers. The 25th Amendment (1967) requires the president (with the consent of Congress) to fill vice presidential vacancies. [*See* Vice Presidential Succession, below]

When bills are passed by both houses of Congress, they are sent to the president for his approval. He may veto them. When a bill is vetoed, it is returned to the house that originated it. Congress may override the president's veto by a two-thirds vote of both houses. If the president does not sign a bill within 10 days, it becomes law (just as if he had signed it) as long as Congress is still in session. If Congress adjourns during those 10 days, and the president fails to sign the bill, it does not become law. This is known as a pocket veto.

Although the broad powers of the presidency are defined by the Constitution, they are also affected by court precedent, the philosophy of the current president and his political influence and ability. The balance between the powers of Congress and the powers of the president is constantly in flux.

Abraham Lincoln was one of the earliest presidents to claim special war powers, based on his interpretation of the Constitutional provisions that make the president commander-in-chief and require him to ensure faithful execution of laws. To discharge these responsibilities, he unilaterally suspended the writ of habeas corpus, expanded the army, blockaded southern ports and appropriated Treasury funds for the prosecution of the war. Under ordinary circumstances, all of these actions would have required prior Congressional approval. Lincoln acted first and got approval later. Later presidents interpreted their war powers more narrowly, but the war-power concept had been well established.

Under Article I, Section 8 of the Constitution, only Congress has the power to declare war. Congress and the president often differ, though, on what constitutes a war. As commander-in-chief, the president can deploy military forces. At what point does that deployment become war and require authorization by Congress? The question remains unresolved, but precedent indicates that the president can wield great power. Neither the Korean War nor the Vietnam War was declared by Congress.

Because of the magnitude of the Vietnam War, and the fact that Pres. Lyndon B. Johnson used his authority to conduct the war without the approval of Congress, the War Powers Act was enacted in 1973. It requires a president to notify Congress within 48 hours if he sends U.S. forces to a hostile area without a declaration of war. The forces may remain no longer than 90 days unless Congress approves.

Presidents have also claimed to have "executive privilege," a right that is not specifically stated in the Constitution, that entitles them to keep certain documents and information secret from the public and from Congress. In 1973, Richard M. Nixon claimed executive privilege when he refused to release subpoenaed tape recordings of conversations held in his office that were relevant to prosecution of the Watergate break-in case. The Supreme Court ruled in 1974 that Nixon's "executive privilege" did not excuse him from answering a subpoena in a criminal trial. He released the tapes—with one infamous 18-minute gap. The extent of a president's executive privilege has not been fully determined.

PRESIDENTIAL SUCCESSION

Under the Constitution, the vice president replaces the president if he dies, becomes incapacitated, resigns or is disqualified from office. Article II gives Congress the right to determine the line of succession after the vice president. In 1947, Congress determined the present order. Cabinet members are listed in the order in which their departments were established. When a department is removed or added, the order changes automatically. The successor must be a U.S. citizen and at least 35 years old to assume the presidency. The successor to the presidency serves as long as the president is disabled, or until another election is held.

The 25th Amendment to the Constitution, added in 1967, specifies conditions for determining incapacity of the president. The president may declare his incapacity by writing to the President Pro Tempore of the Senate and the Speaker of the House. The vice president then becomes "acting president" until the president gives written notification that he is no longer incapacitated. If the president is unable or unwilling to declare his incapacity, it may be done by the vice president and a majority of the cabinet (or some other body designated by Congress). To resume his role, the president must notify the President Pro Tempore and the Speaker of the House that he is no longer incapacitated. If the vice president and a majority of the cabinet disagree with the president's assessment, they have four days in which to notify the President Pro Tempore of the Senate and the Speaker of the House that they believe him to be incapable of resuming of powers and duties. The issue is then determined by Congress. If they determine by a two-thirds vote that he is incapacitated, the vice president remains acting president.

The order of succession is:

1 Vice president
2 Speaker of the House
3 President Pro Tempore of the Senate
4 Secretary of State
5 Secretary of the Treasury
6 Secretary of Defense
7 Attorney General
8 Secretary of the Interior
9 Secretary of Agriculture
.10 Secretary of Commerce
11 Secretary of Labor
12 Secretary of Health and Human Services
13 Secretary of Housing and Urban Development
14 Secretary of Transportation
15 Secretary of Energy
16 Secretary of Education
17 Secretary of Veteran Affairs

Vice Presidential Succession

Until the 25th Amendment to the Constitution was passed in 1967, there was no provision for filling the office of vice president if it became vacant. It sometimes remained empty, increasing the possibility that the Speaker of the House would succeed to the presidency. The amendment now requires that the president name a nominee for the office, who then must be confirmed by a majority of both houses of Congress. Two vice presidents have been appointed in this way. Pres. Richard M. Nixon chose Gerald R. Ford after Spiro Agnew resigned in 1973. When Nixon resigned in 1974 and Ford became president, he named Nelson A. Rockefeller.

FEDERAL DEPARTMENTS AND AGENCIES CONTACT INFORMATION

Executive Offices:

Office of the President: 1600 Pennsylvania Ave. NW, Washington, D.C. 20500; (202) 456-1414; daily schedule, (202) 456-2343.
  Chief of staff; (202) 456-6797.
  Press secretary; (202) 456-2100.
Office of the Vice President: Old Executive Office Bldg., 17th St. and Pennsylvania Ave. NW, Washington, D.C. 20500; (202) 456-2326.
  Press secretary; (202) 456-7034.
Office of the First Lady: 1600 Pennsylvania Ave. NW, Washington, D.C. 20500; (202) 456-2957.
  Press secretary; (202) 456-7136.

Executive Agencies:

Council of Economic Advisers: (202) 395-5042.
Council on Environmental Quality: (202) 395-5080.
National Security Council: (202) 456-2255.
Office of Management and Budget: (202) 395-4840.
Office of Science and Technology Policy: (202) 456-7116.
Office of U.S. Trade Representative: (202) 395-3204.

Cabinet-level Departments:

Agriculture Department: 14th St. and Independence Ave. SW, Washington, D.C. 20250; locator, (202) 720-8732; information, (202) 720-2791.
  Divisions: Agricultural Stabilization and Conservation Service; Animal and Plant Health Inspection Service; Commodity Credit Corp.; Extension Service; Farmers Home Administration; Federal Grain Inspection Service; Food and Nutrition Service; Food and Safety Inspection Service; Foreign Agricultural Service; Forest Service; Rural Electrification Administration; Soil Conservation Service.
Commerce Department: Main Commerce Bldg., 14th St. and Constitution Ave. NW, Washington, D.C. 20230; locator, (202) 482-2000; press information, (202) 482-4901; public information, (202) 482-3263.
  Divisions: Bureau of Export Administration; Census Bureau; Economic Development Administration; Minority Business Development Agency; National Institute of Standards and Technology; National Oceanic and Atmospheric Administration; Patent and Trademark Office; Technology Administration; U.S. Travel and Tourism Administration.
Defense Department: The Pentagon, Washington, D.C. 20301; switchboard, (703) 545-6700; defense

news, (703) 695-0192; armed forces news, (703) 697-5131; public information, (703) 697-5737.

Divisions: Air Force Department; Army Department; Navy Department.

Education Department: 400 Maryland Ave. SW, Washington, D.C. 20202; locator, (202) 708-5366; information, (202) 401-1576.

Divisions: Educational Research and Improvement; Elementary and Secondary Education; Postsecondary Education; Special Education and Rehabilitative Services; Vocational and Adult Education.

Energy Department: 1000 Independence Ave. SW, Washington, D.C. 20585; locator, (202) 586-5000; information, (202) 586-5806 (press), (202) 586-5575 (public).

Divisions: Economic Regulatory Administration; Energy Information Administration; Federal Energy Regulatory Commission.

Health and Human Services Department: 200 Independence Ave. SW, Washington, D.C. 20201; locator, (202) 619-0257; information, (202) 245-6343 (press), (202) 245-6867 (public).

Divisions: Administration for Children, Youth, and Families; Alcohol, Drug Abuse, and Mental Health Administration; Family Support Administration; Food and Drug Administration; Health Care Financing Administration; Health Resources and Services Administration; National Institutes of Health; Office of Human Development Services; Public Health Service; Social Security Administration.

Housing and Urban Development Department: HUD Bldg., 451 7th St. SW, Washington, D.C. 20410; locator, (202) 708-1422; information, (202) 708-0980 (press), (202) 708-1420 (public).

Divisions: Community Planning and Development; Fair Housing and Equal Opportunity; Government National Mortgage Association (Ginnie Mae); Federal Housing Commissioner; Policy Development and Research; Public and Indian Housing.

Interior Department: Main Interior Bldg., 1849 C St. NW, Washington, D.C. 20240; locator, (202) 208-3100; information, (202) 208-3171.

Divisions: Bureau of Indian Affairs; Bureau of Land Management; Bureau of Mines; Bureau of Reclamation; Minerals Management Service; National Park Service; U.S. Fish and Wildlife Service; U.S. Geological Survey.

Justice Department: Main Justice Bldg., 10th St. and Constitution Ave. NW, Washington, D.C. 20530; locator, (202) 514-2000; information, (202) 514-2007.

Divisions: Antitrust Division; Bureau of Prisons; Civil Division; Civil Rights Division; Criminal Division; Drug Enforcement Administration; Envi-

ronment and Natural Resources Division; Federal Bureau of Investigation; Foreign Claims Settlement Commission of the United States; Immigration and Naturalization Service; Office of Justice Programs; Tax Division; U.S. Marshals Service; U.S. Parole Commission.

Labor Department: 200 Constitution Ave. NW, Washington, D.C. 20210; locator, (202) 219-4000; information, (202) 219-7316.

Divisions: Bureau of Labor Statistics; Employment and Training Administration; Employment Standards Administration; Labor-Management Standards; Mine Safety and Health Administration; Occupational Safety and Health Administration; Pension and Welfare Benefits Administration.

State Department: Main State Bldg., 2201 C St. NW, Washington, D.C. 20520; locator, (202) 647-3686; information, (202) 647-2492 (press), (202) 647-6575 (public).

Divisions: Bureau of Consular Affairs; Bureau of Economic and Business Affairs; Bureau of Intelligence and Research; Bureau of International Organization Affairs; Bureau of Oceans and International Environmental and Scientific Affairs; Bureau of Politico-Military Affairs; Foreign Service; Office of Protocol.

Transportation Department: 400 7th St. SW, Washington, D.C. 20590; locator, (202) 366-4000; information, (202) 366-5580.

Divisions: Federal Aviation Administration; Federal Highway Administration; Federal Railroad Administration; Maritime Administration; National Highway Traffic Safety Administration; Research and Special Programs Administration; Saint Lawrence Seaway Development Corp.; U.S. Coast Guard; Urban Mass Transportation Administration.

Treasury Department: Main Treasury Bldg., 1500 Pennsylvania Ave. NW, Washington, D.C. 20220; locator, (202) 622-2000; information, (202) 622-2960.

Divisions: Bureau of Alcohol, Tobacco, and Firearms; Bureau of Engraving and Printing; Comptroller of the Currency; Internal Revenue Service; Office of Thrift Supervision; U.S. Customs Service; U.S. Mint; U.S. Secret Service.

Veterans Affairs Department: 810 Vermont Ave. NW, Washington, D.C. 20420; locator, (202) 233-4010; information, (202) 233-2741.

Divisions: Health Services and Research Administration; Veterans Benefits Administration.

Selected Federal Agencies

Agency for International Development: (A division of the U.S. International Development Cooperation Agency) Main State Bldg., 2201 C St. NW, Washington, D.C. 20520; locator, (202) 663-1449; information, (202) 647-4274 (press), (202) 647-1850 (public).

Central Intelligence Agency: Langley, VA (mailing address, Washington, D.C. 20205); information, (703) 482-7676.

Commission of Fine Arts: Judiciary Square, 441 F St. NW, Washington, D.C. 20001.

Commission on Civil Rights: 1121 Vermont Ave. NW, Washington, D.C. 20425; locator, (202) 376-8177; information, (202) 376-8312.

Commodity Futures Trading Commission: 2033 K St. NW, Washington, D.C. 20581; locator, (202) 254-6387; information, (202) 254-8630.

Consumer Product Safety Commission: 5401 Westbard Ave., Bethesda, MD (mailing address: Washington, D.C. 20207); locator, (301) 504-0100; information, (301) 504-0580.

Environmental Protection Agency: 401 M St. SW, Washington, D.C. 20460; locator, (202) 260-2090; information, (202) 260-4355 (press), (202) 260-4454 (public).

Equal Employment Opportunity Commission: 1801 L St. NW, Washington, D.C. 20507; locator, (202) 663-4264; information, (202) 663-4900.

Farm Credit Administration: 1501 Farm Credit Dr., McLean, VA 22102; locator, (703) 883-4000; information, (703) 883-4056.

Federal Communications Commission: 1919 M St. NW, Washington, D.C. 20554; information, (202) 632-5050 (press), (202) 632-7000 (public).

Federal Deposit Insurance Corp.: 550 17th St. NW, Washington, D.C. 20429; locator, (202) 393-8400; information, (202) 898-6996.

Federal Election Commission: 999 E St. NW, Washington, D.C. 20463; locator, (202) 219-3440; information, (202) 219-4155 (press), (202) 219-3420 (public).

Federal Emergency Management Agency: 500 C St. SW, Washington, D.C. 20472; locator, (202) 646-2500; information, (202) 646-4600.

Federal Housing Finance Board: 1777 F St. NW, Washington, D.C. 20006; information, (202) 408-2500.

Federal Labor Relations Authority: 500 C St. SW, Washington, D.C. 20424; locator, (202) 382-0751.

Federal Maritime Commission: 1100 L St. NW, Washington, D.C. 20573; information, (202) 523-5707.

Federal Mediation and Conciliation Service: 2100 K St. NW, Washington, D.C. 20427; locator, (202) 653-5300; information, (202) 653-5290.

Federal Reserve System, Board of Governors: 20th and C Sts. NW, Washington, D.C. 20551; locator,

(202) 452-3419; information, (202) 452-3204 (press), (202) 452-3215 (public).

Federal Trade Commission: 6th St. and Pennsylvania Ave. NW, Washington, D.C. 20580; locator, (202) 326-2000; information, (202) 326-2180 (press), (202) 326-2222 (public).

General Accounting Office: 441 G St. NW, Washington, D.C. 20548; locator, (202) 275-5067; information, (202) 275-2812.

General Services Administration: 18th and F Sts. NW, Washington, D.C. 20405; locator, (202) 501-1082; information, (202) 501-1231 (press), (202) 501-0705 (public).

Government Printing Office: 732 N. Capitol St. NW, Washington, D.C. 20401; information, (202) 783-3238.

Interstate Commerce Commission: 12th St. and Constitution Ave. NW, Washington, D.C. 20423; locator, (202) 927-7119; information, (202) 927-5350 (press), (202) 927-7252 (public).

National Aeronautics and Space Administration: 600 Independence Ave. SW, Washington, D.C. 20546; locator, (202) 358-0000; information, (202) 453-8400.

National Credit Union Administration: 1776 G St. NW, Washington, D.C. 20456; locator, (202) 682-9600; information, (202) 682-9650.

National Foundation on the Arts and the Humanities:

National Endowment for the Arts: 1100 Pennsylvania Ave. NW, Washington, D.C. 20506; information, (202) 682-5570 (press), (202) 682-5400 (public).

National Endowment for the Humanities: 1100 Pennsylvania Ave. NW, Washington, D.C. 20506; information, (202) 606-8438.

National Labor Relations Board: 1717 Pennsylvania Ave. NW, Washington, D.C. 20570; locator, (202) 254-8064; information, (202) 632-4950.

National Railroad Passenger Corp. (Amtrak): 60 Massachusetts Ave. NE, Washington, D.C. 20002; switchboard, (202) 906-3000; information, (202) 906-3860 (press), (202) 906-2121 (consumer relations/complaints).

National Science Foundation: 1800 G St. NW, Washington, D.C. 20550; locator, (202) 357-5000; information, (202) 357-9498.

National Transportation Safety Board: 490 L'Enfant Plaza East SW, Washington, D.C. 20594; locator, (202) 382-6725; information, (202) 382-6600.

Nuclear Regulatory Commission: 11555 Rockville Pike, Rockville, MD (mailing address: Washington,

D.C. 20555); switchboard, (301) 492-7000; information, (301) 504-2240.

Occupational Safety and Health Review Commission: 1825 K St. NW, Washington, D.C. 20006; information, (202) 634-7943.

Office of Personnel Management: 1900 E St. NW, Washington, D.C. 20415; locator, (202) 606-2424; information, (202) 606-1800.

Office of Special Counsel: 1120 Vermont Ave. NW, Washington, D.C. 20005; information, (202) 653-7188.

Panama Canal Commission: 2000 L St. NW, Washington, D.C. 20036.

Peace Corps: 1990 K St. NW, Washington, D.C. 20526; locator, (202) 606-3886; information, (202) 606-3010.

Securities and Exchange Commission: 450 5th St. NW, Washington, D.C. 20549; locator, (202) 272-3100; information, (202) 272-2650.

Selective Service System: 1023 31st St. NW, Washington, D.C. 20435; locator, (202) 724-0820; information, (202) 724-0790.

Small Business Administration: 409 3d St. SW, Washington, D.C. 20416; locator, (202) 205-6600; information, (202) 205-6740.

U.S. Information Agency: 301 4th St. SW, Washington, D.C. 20547; locator, (202) 619-4700; information, (202) 619-4355.

U.S. International Development Cooperation Agency: *See* Agency for International Development.

U.S. International Trade Commission: 500 E St. SW, Washington, D.C. 20436; locator, (202) 205-2651; information, (202) 205-1819 (press), (202) 205-1000 (public).

U.S. Postal Service: 475 L'Enfant Plaza SW, Washington, D.C. 20260; locator, (202) 268-2020; information, (202) 268-2156 (press), (202) 268-2284 (public).

CABINET MEMBERS, PRESIDENTIAL ADVISERS, SELECTED FEDERAL AGENCY HEADS*
Cabinet Members:

Secretary of Agriculture: Mike Espy
Secretary of Commerce: Ron Brown
Secretary of Defense: Les Aspin
Secretary of Education: Richard W. Riley
Secretary of Energy: Hazel O'Leary

*List includes presidential nominees, subject to Congressional approval as of January 22, 1993.

Secretary of Health and Human Services: Donna Shalala
Secretary of Housing and Urban Development: Henry Cisneros
Secretary of the Interior: Bruce Babbitt
Secretary of Labor: Robert Reich
Secretary of State: Warren Christopher
Secretary of Transportation: Federico Pena
Secretary of the Treasury: Lloyd Bentsen
Secretary of Veterans Affairs: Jesse Brown

CHIEF OF STAFF:

Thomas F. "Mack" McLarty

Presidential Advisers, Executive and Federal Agency Heads (selected):

Assistant to the President for Economic Policy: Robert E. Rubin
Environmental Protection Agency: Carol Browner, administrator
National Security Adviser: Anthony Lake
Office of Management and Budget: Leon Panetta
Surgeon General: Joycelyn Elders
U.S. Trade Representative: Mickey Kantor

ELECTED OFFICIALS

FEDERAL ELECTED OFFICIALS
Executive Branch

President: William Jefferson Clinton (born William Jefferson Blythe 4th), Democrat, Arkansas. Born Aug. 19, 1946 in Hope, Ark., to Virginia Kelley and William Jefferson Blythe 3d, who had died three months earlier. Adopted by mother's second husband, Roger Clinton, when he was 15 years old. B.A. in international affairs from Georgetown University (1968), Rhodes Scholar at Oxford University (1968–70), law degree from Yale University (1973), law teacher at University of Arkansas at Fayetteville (1973–76). Directed Texas campaign of Democratic presidential candidate George McGovern (1972), managed Arkansas campaign of Democratic presidential candidate Jimmy Carter (1976). Defeated in first political campaign (1974) by incumbent Rep. John Paul Hammerschmidt (R—Ark). Ran unopposed for Arkansas attorney general (1976). Elected Arkansas governor (1978). Defeated for re-election (1980). Practiced law (1981–82). Re-elected governor (1982) when the term was extended from two years to four. Re-elected twice more (1986, 1990). Defeated Republican incumbent George Bush for the presidency (1992). Married a fellow Yale law student, Hillary Rodham (1975). Daughter, Chelsea, born 1980. Contact: Office of the President, The White House, 1600 Pennsylvania Ave., Washington, D.C. 20500, (202) 456-1414.

Vice President: Albert Arnold Gore Jr., Democrat, Tennessee. Born March 31, 1948, in Washington, D.C., to Pauline and Albert Arnold Gore Sr. (who served 32 years as Democratic Congressman and Senator from Tennessee). B.A. in government from Harvard (1969), served as a journalist in the Army, including a tour in Vietnam (1969–71), worked as reporter for the *Tennessean* newspaper in Nashville (1971–76), opened livestock and tobacco farm in Carthage, Tenn. (1973). Won House seat once held by his father (1976). Re-elected (1978, 1980, 1982). Elected to Senate (1984, 1990). Unsuccessful in attempt to win Democratic presidential nomination (1988). Wrote best-selling book, *Earth in the Balance: Ecology and the Human Spirit* (1992). Elected vice president (1992). Married Mary Elizabeth "Tipper" Aitcheson (1970). Four children: Karenna, Kristen, Sara and Albert Arnold Gore 3rd. Contact: Office of the Vice President, Old Executive Office Building, 17th St. and Pennsylvania Ave. NW, Washington, D.C. 20500, (202) 456-2326.

Legislative Branch
SENATE

Senate Partisan Committees:

(All addresses are Washington, D.C. 20510 unless otherwise indicated)

Democratic Policy Committee: S-118 The Capitol, (202) 224-5551.

Democratic Steering Committee: S-309 The Capitol, (202) 224-3735.

Democratic Senatorial Campaign Committee: 430 S. Capitol St. SE, Washington, D.C. 20003, (202) 224-2447.

National Republican Senatorial Committee: 425 Second St. NE, Washington, D.C. 20002, (202) 675-6000.

Republican Committee on Committees: 487 Russell Building, (202) 224-6253.

Republican Policy Committee: 347 Russell Building, (202) 224-2946.

Senate Standing Committees:

(All addresses are Washington, D.C. 20510)

Committee on Agriculture, Nutrition and Forestry: 328 A Russell Senate Office Building, (202) 224-2035.

Committee on Appropriations: S-128 The Capitol; also 128 Dirksen Senate Office Building, (202) 224-3471.

Committee on Armed Services: 228 Russell Senate Office Building, (202) 224-3871.

Committee on Banking, Housing and Urban Affairs: 534 Dirksen Senate Office Building, (202) 224-7391.

Committee on Commerce, Science and Transportation: 254 Russell Senate Office Building, (202) 224-5115.

Committee on Energy and Natural Resources: 364 Dirksen Senate Office Building, (202) 224-4971.

Committee on Environment and Public Works: 458 Dirksen Senate Office Building, (202) 224-6176.

Committee on Finance: 205 Dirksen Senate Office Building, (202) 224-4515.

Committee on Foreign Relations: 446 Dirksen Senate Office Building, (202) 224-3953.

Committee on Governmental Affairs: 340 Dirksen Senate Office Building, (202) 224-4751.

Committee on the Judiciary: 224 Dirksen Senate Office Building, (202) 224-5225.

Committee on Labor and Human Resources: 428 Dirksen Senate Office Building, (202) 224-5375.

Committee on Rules and Administration: 311 Russell Senate Office Building, (202) 224-6352.

Committee on Small Business: 428 A Russell Senate Office Building, (202) 224-5175.

Committee on Veterans Affairs: 414 Russell Senate Office Building, (202) 224-9126.

Senate Select Committees:

(All addresses are Washington, D.C. 20510)

Special Committee on Aging: G-31 Dirksen Senate Office Building, (202) 224-5264.

Select Committee on Ethics: 220 Hart Senate Office Building, (202) 224-2981.

Select Committee on Indian Affairs: 838 Hart Senate Office Building, (202) 224-2251.

Select Committee on Intelligence: 211 Hart Senate Office Building, (202) 224-1700.

Joint Committees of Congress:

(All addresses are Washington, D.C. 20510, unless otherwise noted)

Joint Economic Committee: G-01 Dirksen Senate Office Building, (202) 224-5171.

Joint Committee on Taxation: 1015 Longworth House Office Building, Washington, D.C. 20515, (202) 225-3621.

Joint Committee on the Library: 103 Annex 1, Washington, D.C. 20515, (202) 226-7633.

Joint Committee on Printing: 818 Hart Senate Office Building, (202) 224-5241.

THE 102D CONGRESS OF THE UNITED STATES

Senators: (political party, next election date)

Alabama: Howell Thomas Heflin, D, 1996; Richard Craig Shelby, D, 1998

Alaska: Ted Stevens, R, 1996; Frank H. Murkowski, R, 1998

Arizona: Dennis DeConcini, D, 1994; John Stuart McCain, R, 1998

Arkansas: Dale Bumpers, D, 1998; David Hampton Pryor, D, 1996

California: Diane Feinstein, D, 1998; Barbara Boxer, D, 1998

Colorado: Ben Nighthorse Campbell, D, 1998; Hank Brown, R, 1996

Connecticut: Christopher J. Dodd, D, 1998; Joseph I. Lieberman, D, 1994

Delaware: William Victor Roth, Jr., R, 1994; Joseph R. Biden, Jr., D, 1996

Florida: Robert Graham, D, 1998; Connie Mack III, R, 1994

Georgia: Samuel Augustus Nunn, D, 1996; Paul Coverdell, R, 1998

Hawaii: Daniel K. Inouye, D, 1998; Daniel Kahikina Akaka, D, 1996

Idaho: Dirk Kempthorne, R, 1998; Larry Craig, R, 1996

Illinois: Carol Moseley Braun, D, 1998; Paul Simon, D, 1996

Indiana: Richard Green Lugar, R, 1994; Daniel R. Coats, R, 1998

Iowa: Charles Ernest Grassley, R, 1998; Thomas R. Harkin, D, 1996

Kansas: Robert Dole, R, 1998; Nancy Landon Kassebaum, R, 1996

Kentucky: Wendell Hampton Ford, D, 1998; Mitch McConnell, R, 1996

Louisiana: J. Bennett Johnston, Jr., D, 1996; John B. Breaux, D, 1998

Maine: William S. Cohen, R, 1996; George J. Mitchell, D, 1994

Maryland: Paul Spyros Sarbanes, D, 1994; Barbara A. Mikulski, D, 1998

Massachusetts: Edward M. Kennedy, D, 1994; John Kerry, D, 1996

Michigan: Donald W. Riegle, Jr., D, 1994; Carl M. Levin, D, 1996

Minnesota: David F. Durenberger, R, 1994; Paul Wellstone, DFL, 1996

Mississippi: Thad Cochran, R, 1996; Trent Lott, R, 1994

Missouri: John Claggett Danforth, R, 1994; Christopher Samuel "Kit" Bond, R, 1998

Montana: Max Baucus, D, 1996; Conrad Burns, R, 1994

Nebraska: J. James Exon, D, 1996; Joseph Robert Kerrey, D, 1994

Nevada: Harry M. Reid, D, 1998; Richard H. Bryan, D, 1994

New Hampshire: Judd Gregg, R, 1998; Robert C. Smith, R, 1996

New Jersey: Bill Bradley, D, 1996; Frank R. Lautenberg, D, 1994

New Mexico: Pete V. Domenici, R, 1996; Jeff Bingaman, D, 1994

New York: Daniel Patrick Moynihan, D, 1994; Alfonse M. D'Amato, R, 1998

North Carolina: Jesse Alexander Helms, R, 1996; Lauch Faircloth, R, 1998

North Dakota: Kent Conrad, D, 1994; Byron Dorgan, D, 1998

Ohio: John Herschel Glenn, Jr., D, 1998; Howard M. Metzenbaum, D, 1994

Oklahoma: David Lyle Boren, D, 1996; Donald Lee Nickles, R, 1998

Oregon: Mark O. Hatfield, R, 1996; Robert William Packwood, R, 1998

Pennsylvania: Harris Wofford, D, 1994; Arlen Specter, R, 1998

Rhode Island: Claiborne Pell, D, 1996; John H. Chafee, R, 1994

South Carolina: James Strom Thurmond, R, 1996; Ernest F. Hollings, D, 1998

South Dakota: Larry Pressler, R, 1996; Thomas Andrew Daschle, D, 1998

Tennessee: James Ralph Sasser, D, 1994; Bob Kruger, D, Special Election: May 1993; Harlan Mathews, D, 1994

Texas: special election to fill vacancy; Phil Gramm, R, 1996

Utah: Robert Bennett, R, 1998; Orrin Grant Hatch, R, 1994

Vermont: Patrick Leahy, D, 1998; James M. Jeffords, R, 1994

Virginia: John W. Warner, R, 1996; Charles S. Robb, D, 1994

Washington: Patrick Murray, D, 1998; Slade Gorton, R, 1994

West Virginia: Robert Carlyle Byrd, D, 1994; John D. Rockefeller IV, D, 1996

Wisconsin: Russell Feingold, D, 1998; Herbert H. Kohl, D, 1994

Wyoming: Malcolm Wallop, R, 1994; Alan K. Simpson, R, 1996

HOUSE OF REPRESENTATIVES

House Partisan Committees:

(All addresses are Washington, D.C. 20510, unless otherwise indicated)

Democratic Congressional Campaign Committee: 430 S. Capitol St. SE, Washington, D.C. 20003, (202) 863-1500.

Democratic Personnel Committee: B343 Rayburn House Office Building, (202) 225-4068.

Democratic Steering and Policy Committee: H-324 The Capitol, (202) 225-8550.

National Republican Congressional Committee: 320 First St. SE, Washington, D.C. 20003, (202) 479-7000.

Republican Committee on Committees: H-230 The Capitol, (202) 225-0600.

Republican Policy Committee: 1616 Longworth House Office Building, (202) 225-6168.

Republican Research Committee: 1622 Longworth House Office Building, (202) 225-0871.

House Standing Committees:

(All addresses are Washington, D.C. 20515)

Committee on Agriculture: 1301 Longworth House Office Building, (202) 225-2171.

Committee on Appropriations: H-218 The Capitol, (202) 225-2771.

Committee on Armed Services: 2120 Rayburn House Office Building, (202) 225-4151.

Committee on Banking, Finance and Urban Affairs: 2129 Rayburn House Office Building, (202) 225-7057.

Committee on Budget: House Annex 1, (202) 226-7234.

Committee on Education and Labor: 2181 Rayburn House Office Building, (202) 225-4527.

Committee on Energy and Commerce: 2125 Rayburn House Office Building, (202) 225-2927.

Committee on Foreign Affairs: 2170 Rayburn House Office Building, (202) 225-5021.

Committee on Government Operations: 2157 Rayburn House Office Building, (202) 225-5051.

Committee on House Administration: H-326 The Capitol, (202) 225-2061.

Committee on Interior and Insular Affairs: 1324 Longworth House Office Building, (202) 225-2761.

Committee on the Judiciary: 2138 Rayburn House Office Building, (202) 225-3951.

Committee on Merchant Marine and Fisheries: 1334 Longworth House Office Building, (202) 225-4047.

Committee on Post Office and Civil Service: 309 Cannon House Office Building, (202) 225-4054.

Committee on Public Works and Transportation: 2165 Rayburn House Office Building, (202) 225-4472.

Committee on Rules: H-312 The Capitol, (202) 225-9486.

Committee on Science, Space and Technology: 2321 Rayburn House Office Building, (202) 225-6375.

Committee on Small Business: 2361 Rayburn House Office Building, (202) 225-5821.

Committee on Standards of Official Conduct (Ethics Committee): HT-2 The Capitol, (202) 225-7103.

Committee on Veterans Affairs: 335 Cannon House Office Building, (202) 225-3527.

Committee on Ways and Means: 1102 Longworth House Office Building, (202) 225-3625.

House Select Committees:

(All addresses are Washington, D.C. 20515)

Select Committee on Intelligence: H-405 The Capitol, (202) 225-4121.

Select Committee on Aging: 712 Annex 1, (202) 226-3375.

Select Committee on Children, Youth and Families: H2-385 House Annex 2, (202) 226-7660.

Select Committee on Hunger: 507 House Annex 2, (202) 226-5470.

Select Committee on Narcotics Abuse and Control: 234 House Annex 2, (202) 226-3040.

Joint Congressional Committees:

See entry under Senate listing above

Representatives: (district, political party)

Alabama: H.L. "Sonny" Callahan, 1st, R; Terry Everett, 2d, R; Glen Browder, 3d, D; Tom Bevill, 4th, D;

Robert "Bud" Cramer, 5th, D; Spencer Bachus, 6th, R; Earl Hilliard, 7th, D

Alaska: Don Young, at large, R

Arizona: Sam Coppersmith, 1st, D; Ed Pastor, 2d, D; Bob Stump, 3d, R; Jon Llewelyn Kyl, 4th, R; James Thomas Kolbe, 5th, R; Karan English, 6th, D

Arkansas: Blanche Lambert, 1st, D; Ray Thornton, 2d, D; Tim Hutchinson, 3d, R; Jay Dickey, 4th, R

California: Dan Hamburg, 1st, D; Wally Herger, 2d, R; Vic Fasio, 3d, D; John T. Doolittle, 4th, R; Robert T. Matsui, 5th, D; Lynn Woolsey, 6th, D; George Miller, 7th, D; Nancy Pelosi, 8th, D; Ronald V. Dellums, 9th, D; Bill Baker, 10th, R; Richard Pombo, 11th, R; Tom Lantos, 12th, D; Fortney H. "Pete" Stark, 13th, D; Anna Eshoo, 14th, D; Norman Y. Mineta, 15th, D; Don Edwards, 16th, D; (vacant; special election May 1993); Gary Condit, 18th, D; Richard Lehman, 19th, D; Calvin Dooley, 20th, D; William Thomas, 21st, R; Michael Huffington, 22d, R; Elton Gallegly, 23d, R; Anthony Charles Beilenson, 24th, D; Howard McKeon, 25th, R; Howard Lawrence Berman, 26th, D; Carlos J. Moorhead, 27th, R; Dave Dreier, 28th, R; Henry A. Waxman, 29th, D; Xavier Becerra, 30th, D; Matthew G. Martinez, 31st, D; Julian C. Dixon, 32d, D; Lucille Roybal-Allard, 33d, D; Esteban Edward Torres, 34th, D; Maxine Waters, 35th, D; Jane Harman, 36th, D; Walter Tucker, 37th, D; Steve Horn, 38th, R; Edward Royce, 39th, R; Jerry Lewis, 40th, R; Jay Kim, 41st, R; George E. Brown, Jr., 42d, D; Kenneth Calvert, 43d, R; Al McCandless, 44th, R; Dana Rohrabacher, 45th, R; Robert K. Dornan, 46th R; C. Christopher Cox, 47th, R; Ron Packard, 48th, R; Lynn Schenck, 49th, D; Bob Filner, 50th, D; Randy "Duke" Cunningham, 51st, R; Duncan Hunter, 52d, R

Colorado: Patricia Scott Schroeder, 1st, D; David E. Skaggs, 2d, D; Scott McKinnis, 3d, D; Wayne Allard, 4th, R; Joel Hefley, 5th, D; Dan L. Schaefer, 6th, D

Connecticut: Barbara Bailey Kennelly, 1st, D; Samuel Gejdenson, 2d, D; Rosa DeLauro, 3d, D; Christopher Shays, 4th, R; Gary Franks, 5th, R; Nancy Lee Johnson, 6th, R

Delaware: Michael N. Castle, at large, R

Florida: Earl Dewitt Hutto, 1st, D; Pete Peterson, 2d, D; Corrine Brown, 3d, D; Tillie Fowler, 4th, R; Karen Thurman, 5th, D; Cliff Stearns, 6th, R; John Mica, 7th, R; Bill McCollum, 8th, R; Michael Bilirakis, 9th, R; C.W. "Bill" Young, 10th, R; Sam M. Gibbons, 11th, D; Charles Canady, 12th, R; Dan Miller, 13th, R; Porter Goss, 14th, R; Jim Bacchus, 15th, D; Tom Lewis, 16th, R; Carrie Meek, 17th D; Ileana Ros Lehtinen, 18th, R; Harry A. Johnston 2d, 19th, D; Peter Deutsch, 20th, D; Lincoln Diaz-

Balart, 21st, R; E. Clay Shaw Jr., 22d, R; Alcee L. Hastings, 23rd, D

Georgia: Jack Kingston, 1st, R; Sanford Bishop, 2d, D; Mac Collins, 3d, R; Jon Linder, 4th, R; John R. Lewis, 5th, D; Newton Leroy Gingrich, 6th, R; George "Buddy" Darden, 7th, D; James Roy Rowland, 8th, D; Nathan Deal, 9th, D; Don Johnson, 10th, D; Cynthia McKinney, 11th, D

Hawaii: Neil Abercrombie, 1st, D; Patsy T. Mink, 2d, D

Idaho: Larry LaRocco, 1st, D; Michael Crapo, 2d, R

Illinois: Bobby Rush, 1st, D; Melvin J. Reynolds, 2d, D; William O. Lipinski, 3d, D; Luis V. Gutierrez, 4th, D; Dan Rostenkowski, 5th, D; Henry John Hyde, 6th, R; Cardiss Collins, 7th, D; Philip M. Crane, 8th, R; Sidney R. Yates, 9th, D; John Edward Porter, 10th R; George E. Sangmeister, 11th, D; Jerry F. Costello, 12th, D; Harris W. Fawell, 13th, R; John Dennis Hastert, 14th, R; Thomas Ewing, 15th, R; Donald Manzullo, 16th, R; Lane Evans, 17th, D; Robert H. Michel, 18th, R; Glenn Poshard, 19th, D; Richard J. Durbin, 20th, D

Indiana: Peter J. Visclosky, 1st, D; Philip Riley Sharp, 2d, D; Tim Roemer, 3d, D; Jill Long, 4th, D; Steve Buyer, 5th, R; Daniel L. Burton, 6th, R; John T. Myers, 7th, R; Frank McCloskey, 8th, D; Lee H. Hamilton, 9th, D; Andrew Jacobs, Jr., 10th, D

Iowa: James A.S. Leach, 1st, R; Jim Nussle, 2d, R; Jim Ross Lightfoot, 3d, R; Neal Edward Smith, 4th, D; Fred Grandy, 5th, R

Kansas: Charles Patrick Roberts, 1st, R; Jim Slattery, 2d, D; Jan Meyers, 3d, R; Daniel Robert Glickman, 4th, D

Kentucky: Tom Barlow, 1st, D; William Huston Natcher, 2d, D; Romano Louis Mazzoli, 3d, D; Jim Bunning, 4th, R; Harold Dallas Rogers, 5th, R; Scott Baesler, 6th, D

Louisiana: Robert L. Livingston, Jr., 1st, R; William J. Jefferson, 2d, D; W.J. "Billy" Tauzin, 3d, D; Cleo Fields, 4th, D; James McCrery, 5th, R; Richard Hugh Baker, 6th, R; James A. Hayes, 7th, D

Maine: Thomas H. Andrews, 1st, D; Olympia J. Snowe, 2d, R

Maryland: Wayne T. Gilchrest, 1st, R; Helen Delich Bentley, 2d, R; Benjamin Louis Cardin, 3d, D; Albert Wynn, 4th, D; Steny Hamilton Hoyer, 5th, D; Roscoe Bartlett, 6th, R; Kweisi Mfume, 7th, D; Constance Albanese Morella, 8th, R

Massachusetts: John Olver, 1st, D; Richard E. Neal, 2d, D; Peter Blute, 3d, R; Barney Frank, 4th, D; Martin Meehan, 5th, D; Peter Torkildsen, 6th, R; Edward J. Markey, 7th, D; Joseph Patrick Kennedy II, 8th, D; John Joseph Moakley, 9th, D; Gerry Eastman Studds, 10th, D

Michigan: Bart Stupak, 1st, D; Peter Hoekstra, 2d, R; Paul B. Henry, 3d, R; Dave Camp, 4th, R; James

Barcia, 5th, D; Frederick S. Upton, 6th, R; Nick Smith, 7th, R; M. Robert Carr, 8th, D; Dale E. Kildee, 9th, D; David E. Bonior, 10th, D; Joseph Knollenberg, 11th R; Sander M. Levin, 12th, D; William David Ford, 13th, D; John J. Conyers, Jr., 14th, D; Barbara-Rose Collins, 15th, D; John D. Dingell, Jr., 16th, D

Minnesota: Timothy J. Penny, 1st, D; David Minge, 2d, D; James Ramstad, 3d, R; Bruce F. Vento, 4th, D; Martin Olav Sabo, 5th, D; Rod Grams, 6th, D; Collin C. Peterson, 7th, D; James L. Oberstar, 8th, D

Mississippi: Jamie L. Whitten, 1st, D; Michael Espy, 2d, D; G.V. "Sonny" Montgomery, 3d, D; Mike Parker, 4th, D; Gene Taylor, 5th, D

Missouri: William L. Clay, Sr., 1st, D; James Talent, 2d, R; Richard A. Gephardt, 3d, D; Isaac Newton "Ike" Skelton IV, 4th, D; Alan Wheat, 5th, D; Pat Danner, 6th, D; Melton D. Hancock, 7th, R; William Emerson, 8th, R; Harold L. Volkmer, 9th, D

Montana: Pat Williams, at large, D

Nebraska: Douglas Kent Bereuter, 1st, R; Peter D. Hoagland, 2d, D; William Barrett, 3d, R

Nevada: James H. Bilbray, 1st, D; Barbara F. Vucanovich, 2d, R

New Hampshire: William Zeliff, 1st, R; Richard Nelson Swett, 2d, D

New Jersey: Robert E. Andrews, 1st, D; William John Hughes, 2d, D; H. James Saxton, 3d, R; Christopher H. Smith, 4th, R; Marge Scafati Roukema, 5th, R; Frank Pallone, Jr., 6th, D; Bob Franks, 7th, R; Herbert Klein, 8th, D; Robert G. Torricelli, 9th, D; Donald M. Payne, 10th, D; Dean A. Gallo, 11th, R; Richard Zimmer, 12th, R; Robert Menendez, 13th, D

New Mexico: Steven Schiff, 1st, R; Joseph Richard Skeen, 2d, R; Bill Richardson, 3d, D

New York: George J. Hochbrueckner, 1st, D; Rick Lazio, 2d, R; Peter King, 3d, R; David Levy, 4th, R; Gary L. Ackerman, 5th, D; Floyd H. Flake, 6th, D; Thomas J. Manton, 7th, D; Jerrold Nadler, 8th, D; Charles E. Schumer, 9th, D; Edolphus Towns, 10th, D; Major R. Owens, 11th, D; Nydia Velazquez, 12th, D; Susan Molinari, 13th, R; Carolyn Maloney, 14th, D; Charles B. Rangel, 15th, D; Jose E. Serrano, 16th, D; Eliot L. Engel, 17th, D; Nita M. Lowey, 18th, D; Hamilton Fish, Jr., 19th, R; Benjamin A. Gilman, 20th, R; Michael R. McNulty, 21st, D; Gerald B.H. Solomon, 22d, R; Sherwood Boehlert, 23d, R; John McHugh, 24th, R; James T. Walsh, 25th, R; Maurice Hinchey, 26th, D; L. William Paxon, 27th, R; Louise Slaughter, 28th, D; John J. LaFalce, 29th, D; Jack Quinn, 30th, R; Amory Houghton, Jr., 31st, R

North Carolina: Eva Clayton, 1st, D; Itimous Thaddeus "Tim" Valentine, Jr., 2d, D; H. Martin Lancaster, 3d, D; David Eugene Price, 4th, D; Stephen Lybrook Neal, 5th, D; John Howard Coble, 6th, R; Charles Grandison Rose III, 7th, D; W.G. "Bill" Hefner, 8th, D; J. Alex McMillan III, 9th, R; Thomas Cass Ballenger, 10th, R; Charles H. Taylor, 11th, R; Melvin Watt, 12th, D

North Dakota: Earl Pomeroy, at large, D

Ohio: David Mann, 1st, D; Willis D. "Bill" Gradison, Jr., 2d, R; Tony P. Hall, 3d, D; Michael G. Oxley, 4th, R; Paul E. Gillmor, 5th, R; Ted Strickland, 6th, D; David L. Hobson, 7th, R; John A. Boehner, 8th, R; Marcy Kaptur, 9th, D; Martin Hoke, 10th, R; Louis Stokes, 11th, D; John R. Kasich, 12th, R; Sherrod Brown, 13th, D; Thomas C. Sawyer, 14th, D; Deborah Pryce, 15th, R; Ralph S. Regula, 16th, R; James A. Traficant, Jr., 17th, D; E. Douglas Applegate, 18th, D; Eric Fingerhut, 19th, D

Oklahoma: James M. Inhofe, 1st, R; Michael L. Synar, 2d, D; William Brewster, 3d, D; Dave McCurdy, 4th, D; Ernest Jim Istook, 5th, R; Glenn English, 6th, D

Oregon: Elizabeth Furse, 1st, D; Robert R. Smith, 2d, R; Ron Wyden, 3d, D; Peter A. DeFazio, 4th, D; Michael Kopetski, 5th, D

Pennsylvania: Thomas M. Foglietta, 1st, D; Lucien Blackwell, 2d, D; Robert A. Borski, 3d, D; Ron Klink, 4th, D; William F. Clinger, Jr., 5th, R; Tim Holden, 6th, D; Wayne Curtis Weldon, 7th, R; Jim Greenwood, 8th, R; E.G. "Bud" Shuster, 9th, R; Joseph M. McDade, 10th, R; Paul Edmund Kanjorski, 11th, D; John P. Murtha, Jr., 12th, D; Marjorie Mezvinsky, 13th, D; William J. Coyne, 14th, D; Paul McHale, 15th, D; Robert Smith Walker, 16th, R; George W. Gekas, 17th, R; Richard Santorum, 18th, R; William Goodling, 19th, R; Austin J. Murphy, 20th, D; Thomas J. Ridge, 21st, R

Rhode Island: Ronald K. Machtley, 1st, R; John F. Reed, 2d, R

South Carolina: Arthur Ravenel, Jr., 1st, R; Floyd D. Spence, 2d, R; Butler Derrick, 3d, D; Bob Inglis, 4th, R; John M. Spratt, Jr., 5th, D; James Clyburn, 6th, D

South Dakota: Timothy Peter Johnson, at large, D

Tennessee: James Henry Quillen, 1st, R; John J. "Jimmy" Duncan, Jr., 2d, R; Marilyn Lloyd, 3d, D; Jim Cooper, 4th, D; Bob Clement, 5th, D; Barton Jennings Gordon, 6th, D; Donald Kenneth Sundquist, 7th, R; John S. Tanner, 8th, D; Harold Eugene Ford, 9th, D

Texas: Jim Chapman, 1st, D; Charles Nesbitt Wilson, 2d, D; Sam Johnson, 3d; R; Ralph M. Hall, 4th, D; John Wiley Bryant, 5th, D; Joe Linus Barton, 6th, R; W.R. "Bill" Archer, 7th, R; Jack Fields, 8th, R; Jack B. Brooks, 9th, D; James Jarrell "Jake" Pickle, 10th, D; Chet Edwards, 11th, D; Preston M. "Pete"

Geren, 12th, D; Bill Sarpalius, 13th, D; Greg Laughlin, 14th, D; E. "Kika" de la Garza, 15th, D; Ronald D'Emory Coleman, 16th, D; Charles W. Stenholm, 17th, D; Craig Washington, 18th, D; Larry Ed Combest, 19th, R; Henry B. Gonzalez, 20th, D; Lamar S. Smith, 21st, R; Thomas Dale DeLay, 22d, R; Henry Bonilla, 23d, R; Martin Frost, 24th, D; Michael A. Andrews, 25th, D; Richard Keith Armey, 26th, R; Solomon P. Ortiz, 27th, D; Frank Tejeda, 28th, D; Gene Green, 29th, D; Eddie Bernice Johnson, 30th, D

Utah: James V. Hansen, 1st, R; Karen Shepherd, 2d, D; William Orton, 3d, D

Vermont: Bernard Sanders, at large, I

Virginia: Herbert H. Bateman, 1st, R; Owen B. Pickett, 2d, D; Robert C. Scott, Jr., 3d, D; Norman Sisisky, 4th, D; Lewis Franklin Payne, Jr., 5th, D; Robert Goodlatte, 6th, R; Thomas Bliley, Jr., 7th, R; James P. Moran, Jr., 8th, D; Frederick C. Boucher, 9th, D; Frank R. Wolf, 10th, R; Leslie Byrne, 11th, D

Washington: Maria Cantwell, 1st, D; Al Swift, 2d, D; Jolene Unsoeld, 3d, D; Jay Inslee, 4th, D; Thomas S. Foley, 5th, D; Norman D. Dicks, 6th, D; James A. McDermott, 7th, D; Jennifer Dunn, 8th, R; Mike Kreidler, 9th, D

West Virginia: Alan B. Mollohan, 1st, D; Robert E. Wise, Jr., 2d, D; Nick Joe Rahall II, 3d, D

Wisconsin: Les Aspin, 1st, D; Scott L. Klug, 2d, R; Steven Craig Gunderson, 3d, R; Gerald D. Kleczka, 4th, D; Thomas Barrett, 5th, D; Thomas E. Petri, 6th, R; David R. Obey, 7th, D; Toby Roth, 8th, R; F. James Sensenbrenner, Jr., 9th, R

Wyoming: Craig Thomas, at large, R

REFERENCES AND CONTACTS:

Washington Information Directory 1991–1992, Congressional Quarterly Inc., 1414 22d St. NW, Washington, D.C. 20037.

Almanac of Federal PACs, Edward Zuckerman, Amward Publications Inc., Washington, D.C., annual.

Addresses for Representatives: The Honorable . . . , House Office Building, Washington, D.C. 20515. (There are three House office buildings [Cannon, Longworth and Rayburn]. You do not need to distinguish among them when writing to a Representative.)

Addresses for Senators: Senator . . . , Senate Office Building, Washington, D.C. 20510. (There are three Senate office buildings [Dirksen, Hart and Russell]. You do not need to distinguish among them when writing to a Senator.)

Telephone number for Representatives and Senators: All can be reached through the Capitol switchboard, (202) 224-3121.

STATE GOVERNMENT INFORMATION

Alabama: 501 Dexter Ave., Montgomery, AL 36130, (205) 242-8000

Alaska: 333 Willoughby Ave., Juneau, AK 99801, (907) 465-2111

Arizona: 1700 W. Washington St., Phoenix, AZ 85007, (602) 542-4900

Arkansas: 1 State Capitol Mall, Little Rock, AR 72201, (501) 682-3000

California: 601 Sequoia Pacific Blvd., Sacramento, CA 95814, (916) 322-9900

Colorado: 1525 Sherman St., Denver, CO 80203, (303) 866-5000

Connecticut: 30 Kennedy St., Hartford, CT 06106, (203) 566-2211

Delaware: Legislative Hall, Dover, DE 19901, (302) 739-4000

District of Columbia: City Hall, Washington, D.C. 20004, (202) 727-1000

Florida: Larson Bldg., Tallahassee, FL 32301, (904) 488-1234

Georgia: 330 Capitol Ave. SW, Atlanta, GA 30334, (404) 656-2000

Hawaii: State Capitol, Honolulu, HI 96813, (808) 586-2211

Idaho: 650 W. State St., Boise, ID 83702, (208) 334-2411

Illinois: 501 S. 2d St., Rm. 176, Springfield, IL 62706, (217) 782-2000

Indiana: 100 N. Senate Ave., Indianapolis, IN 46204, (317) 232-1000

Iowa: E. 10th & Grand Ave., Des Moines, IA 50319, (515) 281-5011

Kansas: 915 SW Harrison St., Topeka, KS 66612, (913) 296-0111

Kentucky: Capitol Annex, Rm. 52, Frankfort, KY 40601, (502) 564-2500

Louisiana: 7389 Florida Blvd., Rm. 300, Baton Rouge, LA 70806, (504) 342-6600

Maine: 100 State St., Augusta, ME 04333, (207) 582-9500

Maryland: 80 Calvert St., Rm. 105, Annapolis, MD 21401, (301) 974-3431

Massachusetts: 1 Ashburton Pl., Boston, MA 02108, (617) 727-7030

Michigan: P.O. Box 30026, Lansing, MI 48909, (517) 373-1837

Minnesota: 50 Sherburne Ave., Rm. G18B, St. Paul, MN 55155, (612) 296-6013

Mississippi: 239 N. Lamar St., Jackson, MS 32901, (601) 359-1000

Missouri: 301 W. High St., Jefferson City, MO 65101, (314) 751-2000

Montana: Mitchell Bldg., Rm. 219, Helena, MT 59620, (406) 444-2511

Nebraska: State Capitol, Lincoln, NE 68509, (402) 471-2311

Nevada: 406 E. 2d St., Carson City, NV 89710, (702) 885-5000

New Hampshire: 107 N. Main St., Concord, NH 03301, (603) 271-1110

New Jersey: John Finch Plaza, Trenton, NJ 08625, (609) 292-2121

New Mexico: 810 San Mateo Ave., Santa Fe, NM 87503, (505) 827-4011

New York: Empire State Plaza, Concourse Level, Albany, NY 12242, (518) 474-2121

North Carolina: 116 W. Jones St., Raleigh, NC 27603, (919) 733-1110

North Dakota: State Capitol Bldg., Bismarck, ND 58505, (701) 224-2000

Ohio: 65 E. State St., Columbus, OH 43266, (614) 466-2000

Oklahoma: 6601 N. Broadway, Oklahoma City, OK 73116, (405) 521-1601

Oregon: 1225 Ferry St., Salem, OR 97310, (503) 378-3131

Pennsylvania: 8102 Transportation Bldg., Harrisburg, PA 17125, (717) 787-2121

Rhode Island: 610 Mt. Pleasant Ave., Providence, RI 02908, (401) 277-2000

South Carolina: 1026 Sumpter St., Columbia, SC 29201, (803) 734-1000

South Dakota: 500 E. Capitol Ave., Pierre, SD 57501, (605) 773-3011

Tennessee: 334 Cordell Hall, Rm. C-3, Nashville, TN 37219, (615) 741-3011

Texas: 201 E. 14th St., Austin, TX 78701, (512) 463-4630

Utah: 1226 State Office Bldg., Salt Lake City, UT 84114, (801) 538-3000

Vermont: State Administration Bldg., Montpelier, VT 05602, (802) 828-1110

Virginia: 109 Governor St., Richmond, VA 23219, (804) 786-0000

Washington: 11th Ave. & Columbia St., Olympia, WA 98504, (206) 753-5000

West Virginia: State Capitol Bldg., Charleston, WV 25305, (304) 558-3456

Wisconsin: 41 N. Mills St., Madison, WI 53715, (608) 266-2211

Wyoming: 200 W. 24th St., Cheyenne, WY 82002, (307) 777-7220

GOVERNORS (POLITICAL PARTY)

Alabama: Harold Guy Hunt, R
Alaska: Walter Hickel, I
Arizona: J. Fife Symington III, R
Arkansas: Bill Clinton, D
California: Pete Wilson, R
Colorado: Roy R. Romer, D
Connecticut: Lowell P. Weicker, Jr., I
Delaware: Tom Carper, D
Florida: Lawton Chiles, D
Georgia: Zell Miller, D
Hawaii: John D. Waihee, D
Idaho: Cecil D. Andrus, D
Illinois: Jim Edgar, R
Indiana: Evan Bayh, D
Iowa: Terry E. Branstad, R
Kansas: Joan Finney, D
Kentucky: Brereton C. Jones, D
Louisiana: Charles "Buddy" Roemer, R
Maine: John R. McKernan, Jr., R
Maryland: William Donald Schaefer, D
Massachusetts: William Weld, R
Michigan: John Engler, R
Minnesota: Arne Carlson, R
Mississippi: Kirk Fordice, R
Missouri: Mel Carnahan, D
Montana: Marc Racicot, R
Nebraska: Ben Nelson, D
Nevada: Robert Miller, D
New Hampshire: Steve Merrill, R
New Jersey: James J. Florio, D
New Mexico: Bruce King, D
New York: Mario M. Cuomo, D
North Carolina: Jim Hunt, Jr., D
North Dakota: Edward Schafer, R
Ohio: George V. Voinovich, R

Oklahoma: David Walters, D
Oregon: Barbara Roberts, D
Pennsylvania: Robert D. Casey, D
Rhode Island: Bruce G. Sundlun, D
South Carolina: Carroll A. Campbell, Jr., R
South Dakota: George S. Mickelson, R
Tennessee: Ned R. McWherter, D
Texas: Ann Richards, D

Utah: Mike Leavitt, R
Vermont: Howard L.G. Dean, D
Virginia: L. Douglas Wilder, D
Washington: Mike Lowry, D
West Virginia: Gaston Caperton, D
Wisconsin: Tommy G. Thompson, R
Wyoming: Michael J. Sullivan, D

MAYORS OF 50 LARGEST U.S. CITIES*

Rank	City, State	Mayor	Term	Next election
1	New York, N.Y.	David N. Dinkins	4 years	November 1993
2	Los Angeles, Calif.	Tom Bradley	4 years	June 1993
3	Chicago, Ill.	Richard M. Daley	4 years	April 1995
4	Houston, Tex.	Bob Lanier	2 years	November 1993
5	Philadelphia, Pa.	Edward Rendell	4 years	November 1995
6	San Diego, Calif.	Susan Golding	4 years	November 1996
7	Detroit, Mich.	Coleman A. Young	4 years	November 1993
8	Dallas, Tex.	Steve Bartlett	2 years	November 1993
9	Phoenix, Ariz.	Paul Johnson	4 years	October 1993
10	San Antonio, Tex.	Nelson Wolff	4 years	April 1995
11	San Jose, Calif.	Susan Hammer	4 years	June 1994
12	Indianapolis, Ind.	Stephen Goldsmith	4 years	November 1995
13	Baltimore, Md.	Kurt L. Schmoke	4 years	November 1995
14	San Francisco, Calif.	Frank Jordan	4 years	November 1995
15	Jacksonville, Fla.	Ed Austin	4 years	May 1995
16	Columbus, Ohio	Greg Lashutka	4 years	November 1995
17	Milwaukee, Wis.	John Norquist	4 years	April 1996
18	Memphis, Tenn.	Willie Herenton	4 years	October 1995
19	Washington, D.C.	Sharon Pratt (Dixon) Kelly	4 years	November 1994
20	Boston, Mass.	Raymond L. Flynn	4 years	November 1995
21	Seattle, Wash.	Norman Rice	4 years	November 1993
22	El Paso, Tex.	William S. Tilney	2 years	May 1993
23	Nashville, Tenn.	Phil Bredesen	4 years	August 1994
24	Cleveland, Ohio	Michael R. White	4 years	November 1993
25	New Orleans, La.	Sidney J. Barthelemy	4 years	February 1994
26	Denver, Colo.	Wellington Webb	4 years	May 1995
27	Austin, Tex.	Bruce Todd	3 years	April 1994
28	Fort Worth, Tex.	Kay Granger	2 years	May 1993
29	Oklahoma City, Okla.	Ronald J. Norick	4 years**	March 1994
30	Portland, Oreg.	Vera Katz	4 years	November 1996
31	Kansas City, Mo.	Emanuel Cleaver	4 years	April 1995
32	Long Beach, Calif.	Ernie Kell	4 years	April 1994
33	Tucson, Ariz.	George Miller	4 years	November 1995
34	St. Louis, Mo.	Vincent C. Schoemehl, Jr.	4 years	April 1993
35	Charlotte, N.C.	Sue Myrick	2 years	November 1993
36	Atlanta, Ga.	Maynard Jackson	4 years	October 1993
37	Virginia Beach, Va.	Meyera E. Oberndorf	4 years	May 1996
38	Albuquerque, N. Mex.	Louis E. Saavedra	4 years	October 1993
39	Oakland, Calif.	Elihu Mason Harris	4 years	November 1996
40	Pittsburgh, Pa.	Sophie Masloff	4 years	November 1993
41	Sacramento, Calif.	Joseph Serna, Jr.	4 years	November 1996
42	Minneapolis, Minn.	Donald M. Fraser	4 years	November 1993
43	Tulsa, Okla.	Rodger Randle	4 years	April 1993
44	Honolulu, Hawaii	Frank F. Fasi	4 years	November 1996
45	Cincinnati, Ohio	Dwight Tillery	2 years	November 1993
46	Miami, Fla.	Xavier L. Suarez	4 years	November 1993
47	Fresno, Calif.	Karen Humphrey	4 years	March 1993
48	Omaha, Nebr.	P.J. Morgan	4 years	May 1993
49	Toledo, Ohio	John McHugh	2 years	November 1994
50	Buffalo, N.Y.	James D. Griffith	4 years	November 1993

Ranked by population, 1990 Census.
** Term of current mayor is three years, but normal term is four.

PART TWO

POLITICS

POLITICAL TERMINOLOGY

anarchism: The philosophy that government is intrinsically bad and should be abolished, by violent means if necessary, because it interferes with individual freedoms.

authoritarianism: Unquestioned and complete rule by a leader whose underlings support and help sustain control.

blue laws: Legislation banning commerce, usually on Sunday, for religious reasons.

blue sky laws: A general reference to laws and regulations aimed at preventing fraud in the sale of securities and land.

communism: An extension or evolutionary development of socialism characterized by dictatorial control, communal ownership of all property, the absence of class distinctions, equal distribution of all goods and services, and the primacy of the state.

conservatism: A political philosophy typified by preference for moderate change and maintenance of the status quo—for example, the maintaining of traditional values and limited government involvement in socioeconomic affairs.

economic determinism: The philosophy that economic concerns are at the root of all human behavior and historical developments.

electoral college: The constitutionally founded body that officially elects the president. [*See* Presidential Electoral Process, page 42]

federalism: The sharing of power between a strong central government and an assemblage of lesser governmental units, such as the relationship between the U.S. federal government in Washington, D.C., and the governments of the 50 states.

filibuster: Long speeches intended to obstruct passage of a bill, particularly in the U.S. Senate.

gerrymandering: The drawing or redrawing of legislative district boundaries in such a way as to benefit the dominant or incumbent political party. The term evolved in 1811 when Massachusetts Gov. Elbridge Gerry created a voting district that resembled the shape of a salamander.

Gramm-Rudman-Hollings Act: Commonly referred to as "Gramm-Rudman," this is the 1985 law requiring that the federal deficit be lowered incrementally until balance is achieved. The law was intended to balance the budget by 1991, but the target year later was changed to 1997.

isolationism: The notion that a nation's best interests are served by minimizing its foreign involvements. Though the philosophy has been popular at various points in U.S. history, modern communications, commerce and balances of power make the idea unrealistic in the 20th century.

liberalism: Typically, a political philosophy that favors change in the status quo, the development of individual freedoms, and governmental responsibility for social welfare.

libertarianism: A political philosophy that favors minimal government involvement in the affairs of its citizens.

Marxism: A political philosophy, based on the works of Karl Marx and Friedrich Engels, that portrays all of history as a class struggle.

McCarthyism: Sensational, indiscriminate and irresponsible anti-Communism. The term derives from the name of Sen. Joseph R. McCarthy, R-Wisc., who gained power and notoriety in the early 1950s by publicly charging a wide assortment of people and groups, from movie actors to Army generals, with being Communists or Communist-influenced.

nationalism: A political philosophy embodying a sense of national consciousness and patriotism, but implying a narrow, chauvinistic concern that puts the country's welfare and interests above any international interest.

neoconservatism: A pragmatic, liberal-oriented political philosophy embracing the notion that government should have a major role in social welfare but should not impinge on personal behavior and values or restrict free enterprise.

nepotism: The practice of using the authority of public office—whether elective or appointive—to hire, appoint or otherwise favor relatives of the officeholder.

nihilism: A philosophy that espouses a belief in literally nothing, and that advocates the destruction of all existing political, economic and social institutions.

patronage: An official's power to confer benefits such as appointments, honors, jobs or contracts on political supporters. Patronage is the traditional method that officeholders use to affirm, maintain or extend political control.

political action committee (PAC): An organization established to raise funds for political purposes. The Federal Election Commission regulates the activities of PACs.

populism: A political ideology that stresses and promotes the interests and well-being of the poor and working classes against those of the powerful and wealthy.

pork barrel: Government action or legislation geared

to currying favor for a particular politician; typically, the arbitrary award of a federal public works project that will bring economic advantage to a particular legislator's district.

protectionism: The policy of protecting domestic interests and industries by imposing taxes, tariffs, quotas or regulations restricting the importation of competing goods and services; the opposite of a free trade policy.

socialism: A political system in which production, trade and service delivery are owned or controlled by the government, rather than by private individuals. The government is directly responsible for the welfare of its citizens, who all share in the work and benefits of the system.

sunset law: A general characterization of laws or legal provisions geared to ending a program or regulation on a predetermined date unless the measure is specifically reenacted.

sunshine law: Used generally, the term encompasses laws, statutes or regulations requiring that the instruments of government, from documents to meetings and hearings, be subjected to public scrutiny. When used specifically, the term usually refers to requirements that government business meetings be held in public and that specific, advance notice of the meetings be published.

totalitarianism: A system of governance that invests all power and social control in a ruling elite that allows no opposition and uses secret police to maintain dominance.

POLITICAL SCANDALS

U.S. POLITICAL SCANDALS SINCE 1923

(Unless otherwise noted, dates in boldface indicate the year in which the scandal was brought to public attention.)

Teapot Dome (1923)
Pres. Warren G. Harding's secretary of the interior, Albert Fall, accepts interest-free loans and $260,000 in bribes, allowing Mammoth Oil Co. an exclusive lease to federal oil reserves in Teapot Dome, Wyo., and allowing a principal of Pan-American Oil Co. a similar lease to federal oil reserves in Elk Hills and Buena Vista, Calif.

Jimmy Walker (1932)
The dapper mayor of New York City resigns amid three politically inspired formal investigations into charges of misfeasance, malfeasance and negligence of his duties. The charges were generally unfounded.

Alger Hiss (1948)
Alger Hiss, former temporary Secretary General of the United Nations and adviser to Pres. Franklin D. Roosevelt, is dragged into public disgrace by charges that he was a former member of the Communist party who had helped pass state secrets to the Soviet Union. The charges, which were never substantiated, are leveled by *Time* magazine editor Whittaker Chambers before the House Committee on Un-American Activities. Committeeman Richard M. Nixon is Hiss's most vigorous interrogator.

Julius, Ethel Rosenberg (1950)
FBI Director J. Edgar Hoover charges American Communist party members Julius and Ethel Rosenberg with passing the secret of the atomic bomb to Soviet agents. The Rosenbergs are tried in 1951 and executed in 1953, still proclaiming their innocence.

Richard M. Nixon/Checkers Speech (1952)
Charges surface in the 1952 presidential campaign that Republican candidate Dwight D. Eisenhower's vice presidential running mate, Richard M. Nixon, has maintained a secret and illegal slush fund for political purposes. In a live, televised speech Sept. 23, 1952, Nixon clearly and completely explains his legitimate use of the fund and asks to remain on the GOP ticket. In the speech, he refers poignantly to his family's black-and-white spaniel, "Checkers," as a political gift, but tells viewers he will allow his young daughter to keep the dog. The speech is well-received, and Nixon goes on to serve for eight years as Eisenhower's vice president.

Joseph McCarthy (1954)
U.S. Sen. Joseph R. McCarthy, R-Wisc., is formally censured by his colleagues (Dec. 2) but only after he waged a self-serving and notoriously irresponsible five-year campaign to ferret out alleged Communists and Communist sympathizers from American government, industry, the military and society in general. McCarthy's Senate Subcommittee on Investigations took advantage of Cold War fears and entrenched political animosities to ruin or sully the reputations of hundreds of people.

Robert G. "Bobby" Baker (1963)
The former secretary and protégé of Vice Pres. Lyndon B. Johnson resigns amid a swirl of charges that he has used his position for illicit financial gain. He is tried in 1967, found guilty of numerous improprieties—from theft and tax evasion to conspiracy to defraud the government—and sent to prison.

Thomas J. Dodd (1967)
On June 23, the distinguished U.S. Democratic Senator from Connecticut becomes the sixth person in Senate history to be formally censured by his colleagues. Dodd is chastised for diverting testimonial and campaign contributions to his own use.

Adam Clayton Powell, Jr. (1967)
One of the most influential political and civil rights leaders in the nation, Rep. Adam Clayton Powell, Jr., D-N.Y., is denied his seat in the 90th Congress and later stripped of his seniority and fined $25,000 for improper use of government funds. In 1969's 91st Congress, his seat is restored and the U.S. Supreme Court rules the expulsion unconstitutional.

Chappaquiddick (1969)
Sen. Edward M. Kennedy, D-Mass, is enveloped in scandal July 18, 1969, when the car he is driving home from a party on Martha's Vineyard goes off Dike Bridge on Chappaquiddick Island into a tidal pool, drowning his passenger, Mary Jo Kopechne. Kennedy says he tried in vain to save the young woman, but offers no excuse for not reporting the accident until the following day. He later pleads guilty to leaving the scene of an accident.

Watergate (1972–74)
See section entitled The Watergate Scandal on page 38.

Spiro T. Agnew (1973)
In the summer of 1973, as the Watergate scandal is enveloping the Nixon administration, a federal grand jury charges Vice Pres. Spiro T. Agnew with

bribery, conspiracy, tax fraud and extortion. The charges arise from his tenure as former Baltimore county executive and governor of Maryland. Agnew is allowed to plead no contest to the income-tax evasion charge and he resigns the vice presidency in disgrace.

Wilbur D. Mills (1974)

The scandalous private life of Arkansas Democrat Wilbur D. Mills, the powerful, long-time chairman of the House Ways and Means Committee, becomes his undoing on Oct. 7, 1974, when a passenger in his car, stripper Fanne Fox, jumps into the waters of the Tidal Basin in Washington, D.C., and is arrested with Mills and a masseuse friend. Mills is reelected to his House seat a month later, but in December resigns his committee chairmanship. In 1975, he leaves politics.

Wayne L. Hayes (1976)

The long political career of U.S. Rep. Wayne L. Hayes, D-Ohio, comes to an ignominious end when in late May his jilted mistress, Elizabeth Ray, explains publicly that Hayes put her on the federal payroll strictly for sexual favors. Hayes is broken by the scandal and resigns Sept. 1.

Abscam (1980)

Thirty-one public officials, including a U.S. senator, six U.S. representatives, and the mayor of Camden, N.J., are named in an FBI sting operation nicknamed Abscam (for Arab scam), charging that they traded political influence for cash. Indicted, and later found guilty on related charges, are: Sen. Harrison A. Williams, Jr., D-N.J.; U.S. Representatives Michael O. Meyers, D-Pa.; John M. Murphy, D-N.Y.; John W. Jenrette, Jr., D-S.C., Raymond F. Lederer, D-Pa.; Richard Kelly, R-Fla.; Frank Thompson, Jr., D-N.J. and Camden mayor Angelo J. Errichetti.

Iran-Contra Affair (1986)

A story in the Lebanese magazine *Al Shiraa* on Nov. 4, 1986, says the Reagan administration sold arms to Iranian moderates in hopes of influencing the release of American hostages in Lebanon, and then, despite a Congressional ban against support, used cash from the arms deals to finance secretly the activities of anti-Communist *contra* rebels in Nicaragua.

The secret activities had been going on since early 1984, while President Reagan was unsuccessfully fighting Congress for support of the Nicaraguan rebels and publicly maintaining a hard-line stand against any form of negotiation with Middle East terrorists.

Continuing disclosures of high-level government involvement in the affair severely undermine the government's credibility and suggest that, at best,

President Reagan is isolated and out of touch with the activities of his own administration. He eventually admits that he approved the arms sales and the diversion of funds, but denies any wrongdoing, including trying to trade arms for hostages.

Law suits, grand jury inquiries and congressional investigations stretch well into 1992 at an estimated minimum cost of more than $30 million.

On June 16, 1992, one day before the expiration of the statute of limitations, Caspar W. Weinberger, Secretary of Defense from 1981 to 1987, is indicted on five counts of perjury, lying to Congress and obstructing justice. Weinberger, the highest-ranking Reagan administration official directly touched by the scandal, says he will plead not guilty to all counts.

Seven people pleaded guilty to scandal-related charges: Carl R. "Spitz" Channell, a conservative fund-raiser; Richard R. Miller, public relations executive and fund-raiser; Robert C. "Bud" McFarlane, National Security Adviser (1983–85); Richard V. Secord, arms dealer and retired Air Force major; Albert Hakim, arms dealer; Alan D. Fiers, arms dealer and retired chief of the CIA's Central American Task Force; Elliott Abrams, Assistant Secretary of State for Inter-American Affairs (1985–89).

Marine Lt. Col. Oliver L. North, National Security Staff Deputy Director for Political–Military Affairs (1981–86), is convicted of three charges, but the case against him eventually is dismissed.

Vice Admiral John M. Poindexter, National Security Adviser (1985–86), is convicted of five charges, but all are later reversed.

The Bush administration blocked prosecution of Joseph F. Fernandez, former CIA station chief in Costa Rica, and charges were dropped.

By the end of 1992, it seems the scandal probe will stretch well beyond the tenure of lame duck President George Bush. Thomas G. Clines, a former CIA official, is appealing his conviction. Cases are pending against Weinberger, Clair E. George, the CIA's retired chief of covert operations, and Duane R. Clarridge, former chief of the CIA's European division.

On December 24, 1992, President Bush pardons Weinberger, McFarlane, Feirs, Abrams, George, and Clarridge, calling some of the men patriots and proclaiming that it is "time for the country to move on."

Independent counsel Lawrence E. Walsh is outraged. He says he will now investigate President Bush's role in the scandal, and charges that the Iran-contra coverup "has now been completed."

Gary Hart (1987)

Sen. Gary Hart, D-Colo., a front-runner for the presidential nomination, withdraws from the campaign after reports of an extramarital affair with model Donna Rice. He renews his bid in December, but quits the race for good in March of 1988.

Mario Biaggi (1987–88)

U.S. Rep. Mario Biaggi, D-N.Y., one of the most decorated policemen in New York City history and a popular long-time Congressman, is fined and sentenced to prison for influence-peddling involving Brooklyn politician Meade Esposito. Less than a year later, in the fall of 1988, Biaggi is convicted on federal racketeering charges in connection with the sudden, multimillion-dollar growth of a small Bronx machine shop called the Wedtech Corporation, for which he helped secure government contracts. Wedtech went bankrupt in 1986. Biaggi resigns his House seat in August 1988.

Savings-and-Loan Scandal (1989)

Phoenix millionaire Charles Keating, Jr.'s American Continental Corporation files for bankruptcy protection (April 13). The action renders worthless more than $250 million in bonds sold by American Continental's wholly owned thrift institution, Lincoln Savings and Loan Company of Irvine, Calif. The federal government takes over the Lincoln S&L a day later. National attention focuses on Keating's activities. The failure of the conservative Republican's Lincoln S&L turns out to be only one of the most spectacular examples of a rapidly emerging pattern of S&L failures.

The Reagan administration's deregulation of savings and loan institutions and banks earlier in the decade had inadvertently opened the door to abuse. What had been anticipated was aggressive and healthy competition and enhanced returns for savers; at first, that's what seemed to result. Then, in the late 1980's, the national economy began to sag. Real estate values sharply declined in many parts of the country, particularly the Southwest. Borrowers began to default on their loans, leaving many federally insured banks and savings and loan institutions insolvent or teetering precariously. Lawsuits and government investigations began to uncover a pattern of high-risk investment and loan practices, political favoritism and flagrant profiteering.

The eventual cost of the government's takeovers runs into many billions of dollars; the cost of bailing out Lincoln S&L, alone, exceeds $1.6 billion, making it one of the most expensive taxpayer-financed bailouts in history. On Sept. 19, 1990, Charles Keating and his business associates are indicted for securities fraud and charged with duping investors into buying junk bonds without sufficiently explaining the risks.

On Nov. 15, 1990, the Senate Ethics Committee opens hearings into the conduct of "The Keating Five": Senators Alan Cranston, D-Calif.; Dennis DeConcini, D-Ariz.; John Glenn, D-Ohio; John McCain, R-Ariz. and Donald W. Riegle, Jr., D-Mich. The senators are accused of taking more than $1.3 million from Keating to intercede with bank examiners who were investigating the rapid growth of the Lincoln S&L.

On Feb. 27, 1991, the Senate Ethics Committee mildly criticizes the actions of Glenn and McCain; recommends no action against Riegle and DeConcini, though their conduct "appeared" improper; but finds "substantial credible evidence" of misconduct by Cranston. The senator is reprimanded before the full Senate on Nov. 20, 1991, for "improper and repugnant" dealings with Keating.

On Dec. 4, 1991, a California Superior Court jury finds Keating guilty of 17 of the 18 fraud-related charges against him. Days later, before he can be sentenced, Keating and other principals of Lincoln S&L are charged in a 77-count federal indictment for racketeering, bank and securities fraud and conspiracy. Additional lawsuits against Keating and his associates were pending in 1992.

BCCI, Bank of Credit and Commerce International (1991)

Led by the Bank of England, bank regulators in 62 countries shut down the offices and operations of the Bank of Credit and Commerce International (July 5), charging fraud on an unprecedented scale. The bank was founded in Pakistan in 1972, incorporated in Luxembourg and headquartered in London. As the complex scandal unfolds, BCCI and its vast network of shell companies and holding operations emerges as the financial heart of international schemes involving money-laundering, drug and arms deals, secret CIA operations, revolutions and the looting of national treasuries. Implicated in the scandal is former Presidential adviser and Defense Secretary Clark M. Clifford, chairman of First American Bankshares Inc., one of many companies controlled by BCCI. Clifford proclaims his innocence, telling Congressional investigators he was unaware of BCCI's secret stake in First American, and that he was duped by BCCI officials. Clifford and his protégé and former law partner Robert A. Altman, who served with him at the head of First American, resign from the corporation in August 1991. In mid-December, BCCI pleads guilty to U.S. fraud charges. By then, claims against the bank total more than $200 billion. On July 29, 1992, grand juries indict Clifford, Altman and others for conspiracy, conspiracy to commit fraud, bribe-taking and falsifying business records.

House Bank Scandal, "Rubbergate" (1991)

The General Accounting Office, an investigative arm of Congress, reports Sept. 18, 1991, that current and former members of the U.S. House of Representatives wrote more than 8,300 bad checks on their House bank accounts during the fiscal year ending June 30, 1990, and that 581 of the overdrafts were issued in amounts exceeding $1,000. Unlike commercial banks, the private House bank routinely honored checks drawn against insufficient funds, posted no interest on account balances, charged no interest or penalty fees for bounced checks and used money from other clients' accounts to cover them. The effect was to make the basic House checking account a potentially open-ended line of credit for any lawmaker who wanted one, and many did.

The House Ethics Committee reports March 11, 1992, that 355 current and former House members had written nearly 20,000 bad checks, some of them for several thousands of dollars.

On March 14, about two weeks before the House Ethics Committee begins naming names at Congress' behest, the Associated Press publicly identifies most of the worst offenders.

The top five offenders in the 39 months between July 1, 1988 and Oct. 3, 1991, were former Democrat Tommy Robinson (R-Ark.), with 996 bounced checks; Robert J. Mrazek (D-N.Y.), with 920; Robert W. Davis (R-Mich.), with 878; former Rep. Doug Walgren (D-Pa.), with 858, and Ronald V. Dellums (D-Calif.), with 851.

The largest overdrafts were written by former California Democratic U.S. Representatives Douglas Bosco and Tony Coelho. Bosco was on top with an overdraft of $75,723; he wrote 124 bad checks. Coelho, who wrote 316 bad checks, ranked second with an overdraft of $60,625.

The scandal loses its partisan edge quickly. On March 17, 1992, three members of President Bush's Cabinet admit to having written bad checks when they were members of the House: Defense Secretary Dick Cheney, 21 bad checks; Agriculture Secretary Edward Madigan, 49 bad checks and Labor Secretary Lynn Martin, 16 bad checks.

The scandal figures prominently in the retirements of several members of Congress and further tarnishes voters' opinions of incumbent officeholders. A national poll April 3 shows that 76 percent of the public blames "both parties equally."

THE WATERGATE SCANDAL

The Watergate scandal begins when five men are charged with breaking into the Democratic National Committee headquarters at the Watergate office building in Washington, D.C. (June 17, 1972). The men are: James W. McCord (a former CIA official), Bernard L. Barker (alias Frank Carter), Frank Angelo Fiorini (alias Edward Hamilton), Eugenio L. Martinez (alias Gene Valdes) and Raul Godoy (alias V.R. Gonzales). They and two former White House aides—G. Gordon Liddy and E. Howard Hunt—are indicted on charges of burglary, conspiracy and wiretapping (Sept. 1972).

Nixon is reelected, defeating Democratic Sen. George S. McGovern by a landslide (Nov. 7, 1972).

Federal District Court Judge John J. Sirica proffers leniency in exchange for additional information, which encourages some of Nixon's aides (including Jeb Stuart Magruder) to talk to federal prosecutors. Members of the CIA and the Committee to Re-elect the President (CRP) are implicated.

Liddy and McCord are convicted of breaking into and illegally wiretapping Democratic headquarters (Jan. 30, 1973). The five others who had been indicted with them had already pleaded guilty. The Senate sets up an investigative subcommittee, headed by Sen. Sam Ervin, Jr., D-N.C. (Feb. 1973).

Acting FBI Director L. Patrick Gray resigns after revelations that he had destroyed Watergate documents (April 27, 1973). White House chief of staff H.R. Haldeman, White House counsel John W. Dean III and John Ehrlichman, the chief presidential adviser on domestic affairs, resign (April 30, 1973). Attorney General Richard G. Kleindienst also resigns, saying that he cannot be involved in the Watergate investigation because some of his friends have become suspects (April 30, 1973).

The *Washington Post* wins a Pulitzer Prize for its Watergate investigation, conducted by reporters Carl Bernstein and Bob Woodward (May 1973).

Financier Robert Vesco and former Cabinet members John Mitchell and Maurice Stans are indicted in connection with $200,000 in illegal campaign contributions to Nixon's reelection campaign (May 10, 1973).

Archibald Cox, a Harvard Law School professor, is sworn in as special Watergate prosecutor (May 25, 1973). John Dean testifies before the Senate subcommittee and implicates Haldeman, Ehrlichman, Nixon, Mitchell and others in a cover-up aimed at separating Nixon from the Watergate break-in (June 25–29, 1973). Cox and the Senate subcommittee subpoena tapes of conversations in the Oval Office (July 23, 1973). Nixon refuses to give up the tapes, citing executive privilege, and appeals through the courts. On Oct. 19, 1973, he offers to give Cox a summary of the tapes. Cox refuses the offer, setting the stage for what has become known as the Saturday Night Massacre. Nixon tells Attorney General Elliot Richardson to fire Cox. Richardson refuses and resigns. Deputy Attorney General William Ruckelshaus refuses and is fired. Solicitor General Robert Bork fires Cox (Oct. 20, 1973).

Vice President Spiro T. Agnew resigns and pleads no contest to charges that he failed to pay taxes on payments made to him by contractors while he was governor of Maryland (Oct. 10, 1973). Gerald R. Ford is appointed vice president (Oct. 12, 1973).

Leon Jaworski replaces Cox as special prosecutor (Nov. 1, 1973) and continues to demand tapes. Rose Mary Woods, Nixon's personal secretary, testifies that she accidentally erased five minutes of one of the subpoenaed tapes (Nov. 23, 1973). An additional gap of 13½ minutes is not explained.

Nixon releases edited transcripts of the tapes (April 30, 1974). Sirica subpoenas additional tapes; Nixon refuses. The Supreme Court rules in United States v. Richard M. Nixon that Nixon must turn over the tapes because they do not deal with national security (July 24, 1974).

John Ehrlichman and three White House "plumb-ers" are convicted of conspiring to violate the civil rights of Dr. Lewis Fielding, who had been Daniel Ellsberg's psychiatrist, by breaking into his office in an attempt to gather damaging information concerning Ellsberg, who had leaked the Pentagon papers to the press (July 12, 1974).

The House Judiciary Committee recommends that Nixon be impeached on charges of obstruction of justice, abuse of presidential powers, and trying to impede the impeachment process by defying committee subpoenas (July 27–30, 1974).

Nixon releases three tapes (Aug. 5, 1974). The tapes indicate that he was involved in the Watergate cover-up from the start. With impeachment imminent, Nixon becomes the first president to resign from office (Aug. 9, 1974). President Gerald R. Ford grants him an unconditional pardon for all federal crimes that he "committed or may have committed" while in office (Sept. 8, 1974).

TRADITIONAL VOTING BLOCS

Social and physical mobility have made voting blocs less important than they once were. Northerners move to the South. Children of working-class parents get educations and take up middle-class professions. Traditions in voting, like other traditions, are open to change and sometimes are discarded.

Both the Democratic and the Republican parties are broad-based, with substantial support from diverse segments of society. Still, some blocs of voters tend to align more with one party than the other. In some cases, this alignment can be quite pronounced. The strongest example is black voters, who overwhelmingly have voted Democratic since 1964. In the 1984 presidential election, for example, when the popular vote was 42 percent Democratic and 56 percent Republican, the vote among blacks was 91 percent Democratic and 9 percent Republican. In 1988, the same wide margins applied. The Democrats got 47 percent of the total popular votes, but 92 percent of black votes.

This allegiance to the Democratic party represents an historical about-face for black voters. For 60 years after the Civil War, blacks were predominantly members of the Republican party, supporting the party of Abraham Lincoln and the Reconstruction Congress. Southern whites were predominantly Democratic. Blacks shifted to the Democratic party during the Depression and the New Deal, when the Democrats' social and economic policies were perceived as being better for them, many of whom were in low-income households. In the 1964 election between Republican Barry Goldwater and Democrat Lyndon B. Johnson, civil rights became a compelling issue. The Democrats, perceived as more liberal than the Republicans, widened their margin of support among black voters.

The transition of blacks from the Republican to the Democratic party made the South a Democratic stronghold. White Southerners had been Democrats since the Civil War, rejecting the party of Lincoln and the Reconstruction Congress. They had voted for Democratic presidential candidates repeatedly and overwhelmingly, with one significant exception. In 1928 New York Governor Al Smith became the first Catholic presidential candidate, and religion became a major issue. Southern whites, who were predominantly Protestant, voted for Republican Herbert Hoover. With that exception, however, the South was overwhelmingly Democratic territory through the 1950s.

Since then, there has been a shift. As Northerners have moved South, and as education and job status have changed, party alignment has begun to shift. The middle class in the South is following the path of the middle class elsewhere and is becoming more Republican. The working class, particularly the black working class, remains strongly Democratic.

The process of change in the South—in which blacks have moved from the Republican to the Democratic party, and whites are beginning to move in the opposite direction—epitomizes the volatile nature of voting blocs. It also symbolizes the interaction of factors that affect voting patterns. Voting behavior depends on the times, the economy, the candidates and the many characteristics that make us who we are—our race, religion, income and region, as well as factors such as education and social status. There is no such thing as a typical black voter or white voter or blue-collar voter or Catholic voter or Southern voter. We are all amalgams of many characteristics that affect the way we vote.

Keeping that in mind, it is easy to see why voting blocs are not static or easy to define. Traditionally, Democrats and Republicans have drawn their strongest support from among certain groups, but this is by no means predictive of how votes will be cast in future elections. For party strategists, much depends upon the degree to which traditional areas of support can be retained and new areas gained. In the past, Republican support has been strongest among: white Protestants, white-collar workers, nonunion members, people in middle- and upper-class households, people with college educations and people in the Plains and Mountain states. Democratic support has been strongest among: Catholics, Jews, blacks, Southerners, blue-collar workers and labor union members. Recently some new trends have begun to emerge. Republicans are gaining support among white Southerners, Catholics, Asian-Americans, Cuban-Americans and lower-income people. Democrats are gaining support among middle-class voters, certain professionals (such as those in the communications industries, universities and foundations), women and Mexican-Americans. The process of social, economic and political evolution continues.

U.S. POLITICAL PARTIES

American Party of the United States
P.O. Box 597
Provo, UT 84603
(801) 374-5717, (800) 456-8683

Communist Party of the U.S.A.
235 W. 23d St.
New York, NY 10011
(212) 989-4994

Conservative Party
486 78th St.
Ft. Hamilton Station, NY 11209
(718) 921-2158

Democratic Party
National headquarters: 430 S. Capitol St. SE
Washington, D.C. 20003
(202) 863-8000

International Green Party
P.O. Box 3413
Fullerton, CA 92631
(714) 526-2482

LaRaza Unida Party
483 5th St.
San Fernando, CA 91340
(818) 365-6534

Libertarian Party
1528 Pennsylvania Ave. SE
Washington, D.C. 20003-3116
(202) 543-1988

National States Rights Party
P.O. Box 4063
Marietta, GA 30061

National Unity Party
P.O. Box 106
Timonium, MD 21093

New Party
8319 Fulham Ct.
Richmond, VA 23227
(804) 266-7400

Populist Party of America
P.O. Box 1989
Ford City, PA 16226
(412) 763-1225

Progressive Labor Party
231-E W. 29th St., Rm. 502
New York, NY 10001
(212) 629-0002

Prohibition Party
Prohibition National Committee
P.O. Box 2635
Denver, CO 80201
(303) 572-0646

Republican Party
National headquarters: 310 First St. SE
Washington, D.C. 20003
(202) 863-8500

Socialist Labor Party
914 Industrial Ave.
Palo Alto, CA 94303
(415) 494-1532

Socialist Party U.S.A.
516 W. 25th St., Rm. 404
New York, NY 10001
(212) 691-0776

Socialist Workers Party
14 Charles La.
New York, NY 10014
(212) 675-3820,
(212) 242-5530

PRESIDENTIAL ELECTORAL PROCESS

In the United States, nearly all elections are direct: voters cast their ballots directly for candidates. The candidate who gets the majority of the votes, or a sufficient plurality, wins. (A plurality is the margin of votes by which a candidate outdistances other candidates in elections in which three or more people are running.) There is one significant exception, however. Presidential elections are indirect: voters cast their ballots for electors, who then vote for a presidential candidate.

In many states, the names of the electors do not appear on the ballot. The names of the candidates to whom they are pledged appear, instead. Nevertheless, it is the electors who are chosen by popular vote, not the president and vice president.

The electors, who are nominated by political parties, are pledged to specific candidates, but they are not legally obligated to follow that promise. In fact, the drafters of the Constitution intended that electors would vote independently. They did not foresee that political parties would grow so strong that electors would become not independent voters but pledged representatives. The election process was intended to assemble a knowledgeable group, chosen by popular vote, to make an informed choice. Congress was given the authority to settle cases in which no candidate receives a majority of electoral votes.

Although electors are not required to follow their pledges, they nearly always do. Occasionally, however, an elector will switch, either as a protest or to honor a local politician. In six of the last nine elections, one elector has switched his vote.

The Constitution grants each state a number of electors equal to its number of U.S. senators and representatives. The Twenty-third Amendment also allots three electors to the District of Columbia. To win the presidency and vice presidency, the candidates must receive a majority—270—of the 538 electoral votes.

If no presidential candidate receives a majority of electoral votes, the House of Representatives then chooses from among the three leading candidates. In this voting, each state Congressional delegation has one vote. The winner must receive a majority of votes. If no vice presidential candidate receives a majority of electoral votes, the Senate chooses from among the two leading candidates.

The House of Representatives has chosen the president twice—in 1800 and 1824. In 1800, Thomas Jefferson and his running mate, Aaron Burr, received the same number of votes. Originally, the Constitution called for the leading vote-getter to be president and the runner-up to be vice president. The electors, who were pledged to both candidates on the ticket, had no way of showing their preference for the presidency. The House resolved the tie in Jefferson's favor and the Twelfth Amendment was added to the Constitution, which provides for the separate elections of president and vice president. In the 1824 election, Andrew Jackson received 99 electoral votes, John Quincy Adams 84, William Crawford 41 and Henry Clay 37. Clay threw his support to Adams, who was elected by a one-vote majority.

The electoral process in the states is essentially a winner-take-all system. In every state except Maine, the candidate who receives a plurality of the popular vote gets all of the electoral votes. In Maine, two of its four electoral votes go to the winner of the statewide plurality, and one electoral vote goes to the winner in each of the two Congressional districts. Although in theory Maine's vote could be split, in practice all four votes have gone to one candidate.

Because a candidate does not need a majority of the popular vote to win all of a state's electoral votes, and because it is the electoral votes that count, a candidate can win the popular vote nationwide but still not win the election. In fact, in three cases the winner of the popular vote did not win the election. In 1824, Andrew Jackson won a plurality of the popular vote in the 18 states that chose electors by popular ballot. (In the six remaining states, electors were chosen by the state legislature.) The election, decided in the House of Representatives, went to John Quincy Adams. In 1876, Samuel J. Tilden was the popular vote winner, but the election went to Rutherford B. Hayes when he was awarded disputed electoral votes from Oregon and three southern states. In 1888, Grover Cleveland won a plurality of the popular vote, but lost in the electoral college to Benjamin Harrison.

The present process gives an advantage to states with a large number of electoral votes, and to large cities in those states. Candidates are likely to pay more attention to those areas, on the grounds that they represent more electoral votes. Reforms of the electoral process have been proposed often. They include replacing the process with a direct popular vote, awarding candidates a number of electors proportionate to their percentage of the popular vote, choosing electors by Congressional districts, and adding two at-large electors from each state. Congress has not felt compelled to change the process, however. Since 1888, the winner of the popular vote has also been the winner of the electoral vote. In fact, the winners have received more resounding victories in the electoral college than from the populace. And the states with the largest number of electoral votes also have the largest number of votes in Congress, giving them an edge in maintaining the status quo.

POLITICAL CAMPAIGN SLOGANS

Campaigns for the nation's highest office often have generated slogans, mottoes, epithets or catch words and phrases. Not all of them are memorable, but some remain long after the candidate is gone. Here is a sampling.

William Jennings Bryan
1900 Democratic presidential campaign:
"Liberty, Justice And Humanity"
"The Constitution And The Flag, One And Inseparable, Now And Forever"
1908 Democratic presidential campaign:
"Let The People Rule"
"Shall The People Rule?"

Jimmy Carter
1976 Democratic presidential campaign:
"Leadership For A Change"

Grover Cleveland
1884 Democratic presidential campaign:
"A Public Office Is A Public Trust"

Calvin Coolidge
1924 Republican presidential campaign:
"Let Well Enough Alone"
"A Man Of Character"
"Keep Cool With Coolidge"
"Coolidge Of Course"
"Coolidge And Dawes/Full Dinner Pail" (Charles G. Dawes)
"Coolidge And Prosperity"
"Deeds—Not Words"
"Courage, Confidence And Coolidge"

Thomas E. Dewey
1944 Republican presidential campaign:
"Dewey Or Don't We?"
"Time For A Change"
1948 Republican presidential campaign:
"Save What's Left"
"Clean House With Dewey"
"Dewey The Racket Buster—New Deal Buster"
"4-H Club: Help Hustle Harry Home" (Harry S. Truman)

Dwight D. Eisenhower
1952 Republican presidential campaign:
"I Like Ike"
"Had Enough?"
"Vote Right With Dwight"
"For The Love Of Ike Vote Republican"
"Crime, Corruption, Communism And Korea"
"Dem-Ike-Crats For Eisenhower"
"Peace And Power With Eisenhower"

"Make The White House The Dwight House"
"Let's Clean House With Ike And Dick" (Richard M. Nixon)
1956 Republican presidential campaign:
"Don't Bump A Good Man Out Of The White House"
"I'm Safe With Ike"
"We Still Like Ike"

Millard Fillmore
1856 Whig presidential campaign:
"The Union Now, The Union Forever"

Gerald R. Ford
1976 Republican presidential campaign:
"Betty's Husband For President In '76"

John C. Frémont
1856 Republican presidential campaign:
"Free Kansas And The Union"
"Free Soil, Free Men, Free Speech, And Frémont"
1864 Radical Republican presidential campaign:
"Free Speech. Free Press. Frémont"

Barry Goldwater
1964 Republican presidential campaign:
"Au H20" (on golden yellow bumper stickers)
"In Your Heart You Know He's Right"
"What's Wrong With Being Right?"
"Goldwater For President—Victory Over Communism"
"A Choice For A Change"
"A Choice—Not An Echo"
"I'm Extremely Fond of Barry"

Warren G. Harding
1920 Republican presidential campaign:
"Back To Normalcy"
"Let's Be Done With Wiggle And Wobble"
"Steady America"
"Think Of America First"

William Henry Harrison
1840 Whig presidential campaign:
"Tippecanoe And Tyler Too" (reference to Harrison as victor in 1811 Battle of Tippecanoe and to running mate John Tyler)

Herbert Hoover
1928 Republican presidential campaign:
"A Chicken In Every Pot, A Car In Every Garage"
"You Never Had It So Good"
"Help Hoover Help Business"

"Who But Hoover?"
1932 Republican presidential campaign:
"Hoover And Happiness"
"Prosperity Is Just Around The Corner"
"Hold On To Hoover"
"Play Safe With Hoover"
"Don't Swap Horses—Stand By Hoover"
"The Worst Is Past"
"It Might Have Been Worse"

Charles Evans Hughes
1916 Republican presidential campaign:
"Fear God And Take Your Own Part"

Hubert H. Humphrey
1968 Democratic presidential campaign:
"Who But Hubert?"
"HHH—The Happy Warrior"
"Nixon And Spiro" = "Zero" (Richard M.
   Nixon and Spiro T. Agnew)

Andrew Jackson
1832 Democratic presidential campaign:
"The Union Must And Shall Be Preserved"

Lyndon B. Johnson
1964 Democratic presidential campaign:
"In Your Guts You Know He's Nuts" (reference
   to opponent Barry Goldwater)
"Goldwater in 1864"
"Hari-kari With Barry"
"Help Barry Stamp Out Peace"
"All The Way With LBJ"
"Let Us Continue"
"LBJ For The USA"

John F. Kennedy
1960 Democratic presidential campaign:
"All The Way With J.F.K."
"If I Were 21, I'd Vote For Kennedy"
"Leadership For The '60's"
"Nix On Nixon"
"On The Right Track With Jack"
"Let's Back Jack"

Alf Landon
1936 Republican presidential campaign:
"Let's Get Another Deck"

Abraham Lincoln
1860 Republican presidential campaign:
"A House Divided Against Itself Cannot Stand"
"Abraham Lincoln/Honest Abe Of The West"
"The Constitution And The Union, Now And For-
   ever"
"Millions For Freedom, Not One Cent For Slav-
   ery"
"Free Land, Free Speech And Free Men"
1864 Republican presidential campaign:

"Don't Swap Horses In The Middle Of The
   Stream"

Eugene McCarthy
1968 Democratic presidential nomination campaign:
"Give The Presidency Back To The People"
"Keep Clean with Gene"

George McGovern
1972 Democratic presidential campaign:
"Come Home, America"
"Make America Happen Again"
"Peace, Jobs, And McGovern"

Richard M. Nixon
1960 Republican presidential campaign:
"The Nation Needs Richard M. Nixon"
"Vote Republican—The Party Of Lincoln"
"Click With Dick"
"My Pick Is Dick"
"No Substitute For Experience"
1968 Republican presidential campaign:
"The 'I' In Nixon Stands For Integrity"
"Nixon's The One"
"The New Nixon"
"Bring Us Together"
"Forward Together"
1972 Republican presidential campaign:
"Nixon Now More Than Ever"
"Four More Years"
"Stand Pat With Nixon"
"The Nation Needs Fixin' With Nixon"

James K. Polk
1844 Democratic presidential campaign:
"Fifty-four Forty Or Fight" (reference to dispute
   between the United States and Great Britain
   over the northern boundary of the Oregon Territory)

Franklin D. Roosevelt
1932 Democratic presidential campaign:
"America Calls Another Roosevelt"
"In Hoover We Trusted, Now We Are Busted"
"The New Deal"
"Throw The Spenders Out"
"Roosevelt Or Ruin"
"Roosevelt And Recovery"
"Out Of The Red With Roosevelt"
"Return The Country To The People"
"Roosevelt—Friend Of The People"
"Down With Hoover"
"Happy Days Are Here Again"
"Roosevelt And Repeal" (anti-Prohibition)
1936 Democratic presidential campaign:
"Where Were You In '32?"
"He Saved America"

"Remember Hoover?"
1940 Democratic presidential campaign:
"Repeat With Roosevelt Or Repent With Willkie"
"Two Good Terms Deserve Another"
"Safe On Third"
"Wall Street Wears A Willkie Button, America Wears A Roosevelt Button"
1944 Democratic presidential campaign:
"Three Good Terms Deserve Another"
"Go 4th To Win The War" (reference to bid for fourth term)
"Vote Straight Democratic: Protect America"
"We Are Going To Win The War And The Peace That Follows"

Theodore Roosevelt
1904 Republican presidential campaign:
"Stand Pat"
"The Big Stick" (Speak Softly And Carry A Big Stick)
1912 Progressive/Bull Moose presidential campaign:
"A Square Deal All Around"
"Pass Prosperity Around"

Alfred E. Smith
1928 Democratic presidential campaign:
"The Happy Warrior"
"Al Smith—Up From The Street"

Adlai Stevenson
1952 Democratic presidential campaign:
"We're Madly For Adlai"
"Vote Gladly For Adlai"
"All The Way With Adlai"
1956 Democratic presidential campaign:
"Adlai and Estes Are The Bestes" (Estes Kefauver)
"Adlai Likes Me"

Harry S. Truman
1948 Democratic presidential campaign:
"Give 'Em Hell Harry"
"Phooey On Dewey"
"Tried And True Truman"

"60 Million People Working—Why Change?"
"Don't Let Them Take It Away"
"Truman Fights For Human Rights"
"The Won't-Do Congress Won't Do"

George C. Wallace
1968 American Independent Party presidential campaign:
"Segregation Now, Segregation Tomorrow, Segregation Forever"
"Let The People Speak"
"If You Liked Hitler, You'll Love Wallace" (anti-Wallace and his vice presidential running mate Curtis C. LeMay)

Wendell L. Willkie
1940 Republican presidential campaign:
"Win With Willkie"
"Willkie Or Bust"
"The American Way With Willkie"
"Roosevelt For Ex-President"
"All I Have Left Is A Vote For Willkie"
"No More Fireside Chats"
"Perhaps Roosevelt Is All You Deserve"
"We Don't Want Eleanor Either" (First Lady Eleanor Roosevelt)
Willkie in reference to President Roosevelt's bid for an unprecedented third term:
"No Man Is Good Three Times"
"Washington Wouldn't, Grant Couldn't, Roosevelt Shouldn't"
"We Want Willkie—Third Term Means Dictatorship"
"No Fourth Term Either"
"No Crown For Roosevelt"
"No Franklin The First"

Woodrow Wilson
1912 Democratic presidential campaign:
"Win With Wilson"
1916 Democratic presidential campaign:
"He Kept Us Out Of War"
"He Proved The Pen Mightier Than The Sword"
"War In The East! Peace In The West! Thank God For Wilson"
"The Man Of The Hour—Woodrow Wilson"

PART THREE

LAW

THE LAW OF THE LAND

U.S. CONSTITUTION AND AMENDMENTS

PREAMBLE

We the People of the United States, in Order to form a more perfect Union, establish Justice, insure domestic Tranquility, provide for the common defence, promote the general Welfare, and secure the Blessings of Liberty to ourselves and our Posterity, do ordain and establish this Constitution for the United States of America.

ARTICLE I

Section 1. All legislative Powers herein granted shall be vested in a Congress of the United States, which shall consist of a Senate and House of Representatives.

Section 2. [1] The House of Representatives shall be composed of Members chosen every second Year by the People of the several States, and the Electors in each State shall have the Qualifications requisite for Electors of the most numerous Branch of the State Legislature.

[2] No Person shall be a Representative who shall not have attained to the Age of twenty five Years, and have been seven Years a Citizen of the United States, and who shall not, when elected, be an Inhabitant of that State in which he shall be chosen.

[3] Representatives and direct Taxes shall be apportioned among the several States which may be included within this Union, according to their respective Numbers, which shall be determined by adding to the whole Number of free Persons, including those bound to Service for a Term of Years, and excluding Indians not taxed, three fifths of all other Persons. The actual Enumeration shall be made within three Years after the first Meeting of the Congress of the United States, and within every subsequent Term of ten Years, in such Manner as they shall by Law direct. The Number of Representatives shall not exceed one for every thirty Thousand, but each State shall have at Least one Representative; and until such enumeration shall be made, the State of New Hampshire shall be entitled to chuse three, Massachusetts eight, Rhode Island and Providence Plantations one, Connecticut five, New York six, New Jersey four, Pennsylvania eight, Delaware one, Maryland six, Virginia ten, North Carolina five, South Carolina five, and Georgia three.

[4] When vacancies happen in the Representation from any State, the Executive Authority thereof shall issue Writs of Election to fill such Vacancies.

[5] The House of Representatives shall chuse their Speaker and other Officers; and shall have the sole Power of Impeachment.

Section 3. [1] The Senate of the United States shall be composed of two Senators from each State, chosen by the Legislature thereof, for six Years; and each Senator shall have one Vote.

[2] Immediately after they shall be assembled in Consequence of the first Election, they shall be divided as equally as may be into three Classes. The Seats of the Senators of the first Class shall be vacated at the Expiration of the Second Year, of the second Class at the Expiration of the fourth Year, and of the third Class at the Expiration of the sixth Year, so that one third may be chosen every second Year; and if Vacancies happen by Resignation, or otherwise, during the Recess of the Legislature of any State, the Executive thereof may make temporary Appointments until the next Meeting of the Legislature, which shall then fill such Vacancies.

[3] No Person shall be a Senator who shall not have attained to the Age of thirty Years, and been nine Years a Citizen of the United States, and who shall not, when elected, be an Inhabitant of that State for which he shall be chosen.

[4] The Vice President of the United States shall be President of the Senate, but shall have no Vote, unless they be equally divided.

[5] The Senate shall chuse their other Officers, and also a President pro tempore, in the Absence of the Vice President, or when he shall exercise the Office of President of the United States.

[6] The Senate shall have the sole Power to try all Impeachments. When sitting for that Purpose, they shall be on Oath or Affirmation. When the President of the United States is tried, the Chief Justice shall preside: And no Person shall be convicted without the Concurrence of two thirds of the Members present.

[7] Judgment in Cases of Impeachment shall not extend further than to removal from Office, and disqualification to hold and enjoy any Office of honor, Trust, or Profit under the United States: but the Party convicted shall nevertheless be liable and subject to Indictment, Trial, Judgment, and Punishment, according to Law.

Section 4. [1] The Times, Places and Manner of holding Elections for Senators and Representatives, shall be prescribed in each State by the Legislature thereof; but the Congress may at any time by Law make or alter such Regulations, except as to the Places of chusing Senators.

[2] The Congress shall assemble at least once in

every Year, and such Meeting shall be on the first Monday in December, unless they shall by Law appoint a different Day.

Section 5. [1] Each House shall be the Judge of the Elections, Returns, and Qualifications of its own Members, and a Majority of each shall constitute a Quorum to do Business; but a smaller Number may adjourn from day to day, and may be authorized to compel the Attendance of Absent Members, in such Manner, and under such Penalties as each House may provide.

[2] Each House may determine the Rules of its Proceedings, punish its Members for disorderly Behavior, and, with the Concurrence of two thirds, expel a Member.

[3] Each House shall keep a Journal of its Proceedings, and from time to time publish the same, excepting such Parts as may in their Judgment require Secrecy; and the Yeas and Nays of the Members of either House on any question shall, at the Desire of one fifth of those Present, be entered on the Journal.

[4] Neither House, during the Session of Congress, shall, without the Consent of the other, adjourn for more than three days, nor to any other Place than that in which the two Houses shall be sitting.

Section 6. [1] The Senators and Representatives shall receive a Compensation for their Services, to be ascertained by Law, and paid out of the Treasury of the United States. They shall in all Cases, except Treason, Felony and Breach of the Peace, be privileged from Arrest during their Attendance at the Session of their respective Houses, and in going to and returning from the same; and for any Speech or Debate in either House, they shall not be questioned in any other Place.

[2] No Senator or Representative shall, during the Time for which he was elected, be appointed to any civil Office under the Authority of the United States, which shall have been created, or the Emoluments whereof shall have been increased during such time; and no Person holding any Office under the United States, shall be a Member of either House during his continuance in Office.

Section 7. [1] All Bills for raising Revenue shall originate in the House of Representatives; but the Senate may propose or concur with Amendments as on other Bills.

[2] Every Bill which shall have passed the House of Representatives and the Senate, shall, before it becomes a Law, be presented to the President of the United States; If he approve he shall sign it, but if not he shall return it, with his Objections to the House in which it shall have originated, who shall enter the Objections at large on their Journal, and proceed to reconsider it. If after such Reconsideration two thirds of that House shall agree to pass the Bill, it shall be sent together with the Objections, to the other House, by which it shall likewise be reconsidered, and if approved by two thirds of that House, it shall become a Law. But in all such Cases the Votes of both Houses shall be determined by yeas and Nays, and the Names of the Persons voting for and against the Bill shall be entered on the Journal of each House respectively. If any Bill shall not be returned by the President within ten Days (Sundays excepted) after it shall have been presented to him, the Same shall be a Law, in like Manner as if he had signed it, unless the Congress by their Adjournment prevent its Return in which Case it shall not be a Law.

[3] Every Order, Resolution, or Vote, to Which the Concurrence of the Senate and House of Representatives may be necessary (except on a question of Adjournment) shall be presented to the President of the United States; and before the Same shall take Effect, shall be approved by him, or being disapproved by him, shall be repassed by two thirds of the Senate and House of Representatives, according to the Rules and Limitations prescribed in the Case of a Bill.

Section 8. [1] The Congress shall have Power To lay and collect Taxes, Duties, Imposts and Excises, to pay the Debts and provide for the common Defence and general Welfare of the United States; but all Duties, Imposts and Excises shall be uniform throughout the United States:

[2] To borrow money on the credit of the United States;

[3] To regulate Commerce with foreign Nations, and among the several States, and with the Indian Tribes;

[4] To establish an uniform Rule of Naturalization, and uniform Laws on the subject of Bankruptcies throughout the United States;

[5] To coin Money, regulate the Value thereof, and of foreign Coin, and fix the Standard of Weights and Measures;

[6] To provide for the Punishment of counterfeiting the Securities and current Coin of the United States.

[7] To Establish Post Offices and Post Roads;

[8] To promote the Progress of Science and useful Arts, by securing for limited Times to Authors and Inventors the exclusive Right to their respective Writings and Discoveries;

[9] To constitute Tribunals inferior to the supreme Court;

[10] To define and punish Piracies and Felonies committed on the high Seas, and Offenses against the Law of Nations;

[11] To declare War, grant Letters of Marque and Reprisal, and make Rules concerning Captures on Land and Water;

[12] To raise and support Armies, but no Appro-

priation of Money to that Use shall be for a longer Term than two Years;

[13] To provide and maintain a Navy;

[14] To make Rules for the Government and Regulation of the land and naval Forces;

[15] To provide for calling forth the Militia to execute the Laws of the Union, suppress Insurrections and repel Invasions;

[16] To provide for organizing, arming, and disciplining, the Militia, and for governing such Part of them as may be employed in the Service of the United States, reserving to the States respectively, the Appointment of the Officers, and the Authority of training the Militia according to the discipline prescribed by Congress;

[17] To exercise exclusive Legislation in all Cases whatsoever, over such District (not exceeding ten Miles square) as may, by Cession of particular States, and the Acceptance of Congress, become the Seat of the Government of the United States, and to exercise like Authority over all Places purchased by the Consent of the Legislature of the State in which the Same shall be, for the Erection of Forts, Magazines, Arsenals, dock-Yards, and other needful Buildings:—And

[18] To make all Laws which shall be necessary and proper for carrying into Execution the foregoing Powers, and all other Powers vested by this Constitution in the Government of the United States, or in any Department or Officer thereof.

Section 9. [1] The Migration or Importation of Such Persons as any of the States now existing shall think proper to admit, shall not be prohibited by the Congress prior to the Year one thousand eight hundred and eight, but a Tax or duty may be imposed on such Importation, not exceeding ten dollars for each Person.

[2] The privilege of the Writ of Habeas Corpus shall not be suspended, unless when in Cases of Rebellion or Invasion the public Safety may require it.

[3] No Bill of Attainder or ex post facto Law shall be passed.

[4] No capitation, or other direct, Tax shall be laid, unless in Proportion to the Census or Enumeration herein before directed to be taken.

[5] No Tax or Duty shall be laid on Articles exported from any State.

[6] No Preference shall be given by any Regulation of Commerce or Revenue to the Ports of one State over those of another; nor shall Vessels bound to, or from, one State be obliged to enter, clear, or pay Duties in another.

[7] No money shall be drawn from the Treasury, but in Consequence of Appropriations made by Law; and a regular Statement and Account of the Receipts and Expenditures of all public Money shall be published from time to time.

[8] No Title of Nobility shall be granted by the United States: And no Person holding any Office of Profit or Trust under them, shall, without the Consent of the Congress, accept of any present, Emolument, Office, or Title, of any kind whatever, from any King, Prince, or foreign State.

Section 10. [1] No State shall enter into any Treaty, Alliance, or Confederation; grant Letters of Marque and Reprisal; coin Money; emit Bills of Credit; make any Thing but gold and silver Coin a Tender in Payment of Debts; pass any Bill of Attainder, ex post facto Law, or Law impairing the Obligation of Contracts, or grant any Title of Nobility.

[2] No State shall, without the Consent of the Congress, lay any Imposts or Duties on Imports or Exports, except what may be absolutely necessary for executing its inspection Laws: and the net Produce of all Duties and Imposts, laid by any State on Imports or Exports, shall be for the Use of the Treasury of the United States; and all such Laws shall be subject to the Revision and Control of the Congress.

[3] No State shall, without the Consent of Congress, lay any Duty of Tonnage, keep Troops, or Ships of War in time of Peace, enter into any agreement or Compact with another State, or with a foreign Power, or engage in War, unless actually invaded, or in such imminent Danger as will not admit of delay.

ARTICLE II

Section 1. [1] The executive Power shall be vested in a President of the United States of America. He shall hold his Office during the Term of four Years, and, together with the Vice President, chosen for the same Term, be elected, as follows:

[2] Each State shall appoint, in such Manner as the Legislature thereof may direct, a Number of Electors, equal to the whole Number of Senators and Representatives to which the State may be entitled in the Congress; but no Senator or Representative, or Person holding an Office of Trust or Profit under the United States, shall be appointed an Elector.

[3] The Electors shall meet in their respective States, and vote by Ballot for two Persons, of whom one at least shall not be an Inhabitant of the same State with themselves. And they shall make a List of all the Persons voted for, and of the Number of Votes for each; which List they shall sign and certify, and transmit sealed to the Seat of the Government of the United States, directed to the President of the Senate. The President of the Senate shall, in the Presence of the Senate and House of Representatives, open all the Certificates, and the Votes shall then be counted. The Person having the greatest Number of Votes shall be the President, if such Number be a Majority of the whole Number of Electors appointed; and if there be more than one who have such Majority, and

have an equal Number of Votes, then the House of Representatives shall immediately chuse by Ballot one of them for President; and if no Person have a Majority, then from the five highest on the List the said House shall in like Manner chuse the President. But in chusing the President, the Votes shall be taken by States the Representation from each State having one Vote; A quorum for this Purpose shall consist of a Member or Members from two thirds of the States, and a Majority of all the States shall be necessary to a Choice. In every Case, after the Choice of the President, the Person having the greater Number of Votes of the Electors shall be the Vice President. But if there should remain two or more who have equal Votes, the Senate shall chuse from them by Ballot the Vice President.

[4] The Congress may determine the Time of chusing the Electors, and the Day on which they shall give their Votes; which Day shall be the same throughout the United States.

[5] No person except a natural born Citizen, or a Citizen of the United States, at the time of the Adoption of this constitution, shall be eligible to the Office of President; neither shall any Person be eligible to that Office who shall not have attained to the Age of thirty-five Years, and been fourteen Years a Resident within the United States.

[6] In case of the removal of the President from Office, or of his Death, Resignation or Inability to discharge the Powers and Duties of the said Office, the Same shall devolve on the Vice President, and the Congress may by Law provide for the Case of Removal, Death, Resignation or Inability, both of the President and Vice President, declaring what Officer shall then act as President, and such Officer shall act accordingly, until the Disability be removed, or a President shall be elected.

[7] The President shall, at stated Times, receive for his Services, a Compensation, which shall neither be increased nor diminished during the Period for which he shall have been elected, and he shall not receive within that Period any other Emolument from the United States, or any of them.

[8] Before he enter on the Execution of his Office, he shall take the following Oath or Affirmation: "I do solemnly swear (or affirm) that I will faithfully execute the Office of President of the United States, and will to the best of my Ability, preserve, protect and defend the Constitution of the United States."

Section 2. [1] The President shall be Commander in Chief of the Army and Navy of the United States, and of the militia of the several States, when called into the actual Service of the United States; he may require the Opinion, in writing, of the principal Officer in each of the Executive Departments, upon any Subject relating to the Duties of their respective Of-

fices, and he shall have Power to grant Reprieves and Pardons for Offenses against the United States, except in Cases of Impeachment.

[2] He shall have Power, by and with the Advice and consent of the Senate to make Treaties, provided two thirds of the Senators present concur; and he shall nominate, and by and with the Advice and consent of the Senate, shall appoint Ambassadors, other public Ministers and Consuls, Judges of the supreme Court, and all other Officers of the United States, whose Appointments are not herein otherwise provided for, and which shall be established by Law; but the Congress may by Law vest the Appointment of such inferior Officers, as they think proper, in the President alone, in the Courts of Law, or in the Heads of Departments.

[3] The President shall have Power to fill up all Vacancies that may happen during the Recess of the Senate, by granting Commissions which shall expire at the End of their next Session.

Section 3. He shall from time to time give to the Congress Information of the State of the Union, and recommend to their Consideration such Measures as he shall judge necessary and expedient; he may, on extraordinary Occasions, convene both Houses, or either of them, and in Case of Disagreement between them, with Respect to the Time of Adjournment, he may adjourn them to such Time as he shall think proper; he shall receive Ambassadors and other public Ministers; he shall take Care that the Laws be faithfully executed, and shall Commission all the Officers of the United States.

Section 4. The President, Vice President and all civil Officers of the United States, shall be removed from Office on Impeachment for, and Conviction of, Treason, Bribery, or other high Crimes and Misdemeanors.

ARTICLE III

Section 1. The judicial Power of the United States, shall be vested in one supreme Court, and in such inferior Courts as the Congress may from time to time ordain and establish. The Judges, both of the supreme and inferior Courts, shall hold their Offices during good Behaviour, and shall, at stated Times, receive for their Services a Compensation, which shall not be diminished during their Continuance in Office.

Section 2. [1] The judicial Power shall extend to all Cases, in Law and Equity, arising under this Constitution, the Laws of the United States, and Treaties made, or which shall be made, under their Authority; —to all Cases affecting Ambassadors, other public Ministers and Consuls; —to all Cases of admiralty and maritime Jurisdiction; —to Controversies to which the United States shall be a Party; —to Controversies between two or more States; —between a State and Citizens of another State; —between Citizens of different States; —between Citizens of the same State claiming Lands under the Grants of different States, and between a State, or the Citizens thereof, and foreign States, Citizens or Subjects.

[2] In all Cases affecting Ambassadors, other public Ministers and Consuls, and those in which a State shall be a Party, the supreme Court shall have original Jurisdiction. In all the other Cases before mentioned, the supreme Court shall have appellate Jurisdiction, both as to Law and Fact, with such Exceptions, and under such Regulations as the Congress shall make.

[3] The trial of all Crimes, except in Cases of Impeachment, shall be by Jury; and such Trial shall be held in the State where the said Crimes shall have been committed; but when not committed within any State, the Trial shall be at such Place or Places as the Congress may by Law have directed.

Section 3. [1] Treason against the United States, shall consist only in levying War against them, or, in adhering to their Enemies, giving them Aid and Comfort. No Person shall be convicted of Treason unless on the Testimony of two Witnesses to the same overt Act, or on Confession in open Court.

[2] The Congress shall have Power to declare the Punishment of Treason, but no Attainder of Treason shall work Corruption of Blood, or Forfeiture except during the Life of the Person attainted.

ARTICLE IV
Section 1. Full Faith and Credit shall be given in each State to the public Acts, Records, and judicial Proceedings of every other State. And the Congress may by general Laws prescribe the Manner in which such Acts, Records and Proceedings shall be proved, and the Effect thereof.

Section 2. [1] The Citizens of each State shall be entitled to all Privileges and Immunities of Citizens in the several States.

[2] A Person charged in any State with Treason, Felony, or other Crime, who shall flee from Justice, and be found in another State, shall on demand of the executive Authority of the State from which he fled, be delivered up, to be removed to the State having Jurisdiction of the Crime.

[3] No Person held to Service or Labour in one State, under the Laws thereof, escaping into another, shall, in Consequence of any Law or Regulation therein, be discharged from such Service or Labour, but shall be delivered up on Claim of the Party to whom such Service or Labour may be due.

Section 3. [1] New States may be admitted by the Congress into this Union; but no new State shall be formed or erected within the Jurisdiction of any

other State; nor any State be formed by the Junction of two or more States, or Parts of States, without the Consent of the Legislatures of the States concerned as well as of the Congress.

[2] The Congress shall have Power to dispose of and make all needful Rules and Regulations respecting the Territory or other Property belonging to the United States; and nothing in this Constitution shall be so construed as to Prejudice any Claims of the United States, or of any particular State.

Section 4. The United States shall guarantee to every State in this Union a Republican Form of Government, and shall protect each of them against Invasion; and on Application of the Legislature, or of the Executive (when the Legislature cannot be convened) against domestic Violence.

ARTICLE V
The Congress, whenever two thirds of both Houses shall deem it necessary, shall propose Amendments to this Constitution, or, on the Application of the Legislatures of two thirds of the several States, shall call a Convention for proposing Amendments, which, in either Case, shall be valid to all Intents and Purposes, as part of this Constitution, when ratified by the Legislatures of three fourths of the several States, or by Conventions in three fourths thereof, as the one or the other Mode of Ratification may be proposed by the Congress; Provided that no Amendments which may be made prior to the Year One thousand eight hundred and eight shall in any Manner affect the first and fourth Clauses in the Ninth Section of the first Article; and that no State, without its Consent, shall be deprived of its equal Suffrage in the Senate.

ARTICLE VI
[1] All Debts contracted and Engagements entered into, before the Adoption of this Constitution shall be as valid against the United States under this Constitution, as under the Confederation.

[2] This Constitution, and the Laws of the United States which shall be made in Pursuance thereof; and all Treaties made, or which shall be made, under the Authority of the United States, shall be the supreme Law of the Land; and the Judges in every State shall be bound thereby, any Thing in the Constitution or Laws of any State to the Contrary notwithstanding.

[3] The Senators and Representatives before mentioned, and the Members of the several State Legislatures, and all executive and judicial Officers, both of the United States and of the several States, shall be bound by Oath or Affirmation, to support this Constitution; but no religious Test shall ever be required as a Qualification to any Office or public Trust under the United States.

ARTICLE VII

The Ratification of the Conventions of nine States shall be sufficient for the Establishment of this Constitution between the States so ratifying the Same.

AMENDMENT I [1791]

Congress shall make no law respecting an establishment of religion, or prohibiting the free exercise thereof; or abridging the freedom of speech, or of the press; or the right of the people peaceably to assemble, and to petition the Government for a redress of grievances.

AMENDMENT II [1791]

A well regulated Militia, being necessary to the security of a free State, the right of the people to keep and bear Arms, shall not be infringed.

AMENDMENT III [1791]

No Soldier shall, in time of peace be quartered in any house, without the consent of the Owner, nor in time of war, but in a manner to be prescribed by law.

AMENDMENT IV [1791]

The right of the people to be secure in their persons, houses, papers, and effects, against unreasonable searches and seizures, shall not be violated, and no Warrants shall issue, but upon probable cause, supported by Oath or affirmation, and particularly describing the place to be searched, and the persons or things to be seized.

AMENDMENT V [1791]

No person shall be held to answer for a capital, or otherwise infamous crime, unless on a presentment or indictment of a Grand Jury, except in cases arising in the land or naval forces, or in the Militia, when in actual service in time of War or public danger; nor shall any person be subject for the same offence to be twice put in jeopardy of life or limb; nor shall be compelled in any criminal case to be a witness against himself, nor be deprived of life, liberty, or property, without due process of law; nor shall private property be taken for public use, without just compensation.

AMENDMENT VI [1791]

In all criminal prosecutions, the accused shall enjoy the right to a speedy and public trial, by an impartial jury of the State and district wherein the crime shall have been committed, which district shall have been previously ascertained by law, and to be informed of the nature and cause of the accusation; to be confronted with the witnesses against him; to have compulsory process for obtaining witnesses in his favor, and to have the Assistance of Counsel for his defence.

AMENDMENT VII [1791]

In Suits at common law, where the value in controversy shall exceed twenty dollars, the right of trial by jury shall be preserved, and no fact tried by jury, shall be otherwise re-examined in any Court of the United States, than according to the rules of the common law.

AMENDMENT VIII [1791]

Excessive bail shall not be required, nor excessive fines imposed, nor cruel and unusual punishments inflicted.

AMENDMENT IX [1791]

The enumeration in the Constitution, of certain rights, shall not be construed to deny or disparage others retained by the people.

AMENDMENT X [1791]

The powers not delegated to the United States by the Constitution, nor prohibited by it to the States, are reserved to the States respectively, or to the people.

AMENDMENT XI [1798]

The Judicial power of the United States shall not be construed to extend to any suit in law or equity, commenced or prosecuted against one of the United States by Citizens of another State, or by Citizens or Subjects of any Foreign State.

AMENDMENT XII [1804]

The Electors shall meet in their respective states and vote by ballot for President and Vice-President, one of whom, at least, shall not be an inhabitant of the same state with themselves; they shall name in their ballots the person voted for as President, and in distinct ballots the person voted for as Vice-President, and they shall make distinct lists of all persons voted for as President, and of all persons voted for as Vice-President, and of the number of votes for each, which lists they shall sign and certify, and transmit sealed to the seat of the government of the United States, directed to the President of the Senate; —The President of the Senate shall, in the presence of the Senate and House of Representatives, open all the certificates and the votes shall then be counted; —The person having the greatest number of votes for President, shall be the President, if such number be a majority of the whole number of Electors appointed; and if no person have such majority, then from the persons having the highest numbers not exceeding three on the list of those voted for as President, the House of Representatives shall choose immediately, by ballot, the President. But in choosing the President, the votes shall be taken by states, the representation from each state having one vote; a quorum for this purpose shall consist of a member or members from two-thirds of the states, and a majority of all states shall be necessary to a choice. And if the House of Representatives shall not choose a President whenever the right of choice shall devolve upon them before the fourth day of March next following, then the Vice-President shall act as President, as in the case of the death or other constitutional disability of the President. —The person having the greatest number of votes as Vice-President, shall be the Vice-President, if such number be a majority of the whole number of Electors appointed, and if no person have a majority, then from the two highest numbers on the list, the Senate shall choose the Vice-President; a quorum for the purpose shall consist of two-thirds of the whole number of Senators, and a majority of the whole number shall be necessary to a choice. But no person constitutionally ineligible to the office of President shall be eligible to that of Vice-President of the United States.

AMENDMENT XIII [1865]
Section 1. Neither slavery nor involuntary servitude, except as a punishment for crime whereof the party shall have been duly convicted, shall exist within the United States, or any place subject to their jurisdiction.

Section 2. Congress shall have power to enforce this article by appropriate legislation.

AMENDMENT XIV [1868]
Section 1. All persons born or naturalized in the United States, and subject to the jurisdiction thereof, are citizens of the United States and of the State wherein they reside. No State shall make or enforce any law which shall abridge the privileges or immunities of citizens of the United States; nor shall any State deprive any person of life, liberty, or property, without due process of law; nor deny to any person within its jurisdiction the equal protection of the laws.

Section 2. Representatives shall be apportioned among the several States according to their respective numbers, counting the whole number of persons in each State, excluding Indians not taxed. But when the right to vote at any election for the choice of electors for President and Vice President of the United States, Representatives in Congress, the Executive and Judicial officers to a State, or the members of the Legislature thereof, is denied to any of the male inhabitants of such State, being twenty-one years of age, and citizens of the United States, or in any way abridged, except for participation in rebellion, or other crime, the basis of representation therein shall be reduced in the proportion which the number of such male citizens shall bear to the whole

number of male citizens twenty-one years of age in such State.

Section 3. No person shall be a Senator or Representative in Congress, or elector of President and Vice President, or hold any office, civil or military, under the United States, or under any State, who having previously taken an oath, as a member of Congress, or as an officer of the United States, or as a member of any State legislature, or as an executive or judicial officer of any State, to support the Constitution of the United States, shall have engaged in insurrection or rebellion against the same, or given aid or comfort to the enemies thereof. But Congress may by a vote of two-thirds of each House, remove such disability.

Section 4. The validity of the public debt of the United States, authorized by law, including debts incurred for payment of pensions and bounties for services in suppressing insurrection or rebellion, shall not be questioned. But neither the United States nor any State shall assume or pay any debt or obligation incurred in aid of insurrection or rebellion against the United States, or any claim for the loss or emancipation of any slave; but all such debts, obligations and claims shall be held illegal and void.

Section 5. The Congress shall have power to enforce, by appropriate legislation, the provisions of this article.

AMENDMENT XV [1870]
Section 1. The right of citizens of the United States to vote shall not be denied or abridged by the United States or by any State on account of race, color, or previous condition of servitude.

Section 2. The Congress shall have the power to enforce this article by appropriate legislation.

AMENDMENT XVI [1913]
The Congress shall have power to lay and collect taxes on incomes, from whatever source derived, without apportionment among the several States, and without regard to any census or enumeration.

AMENDMENT XVII [1913]
[1] The Senate of the United States shall be composed to two Senators from each State, elected by the people thereof, for six years; and each Senator shall have one vote. The electors in each State shall have the qualifications requisite for electors of the most numerous branch of the State legislatures.

[2] When vacancies happen in the representation of any State in the Senate, the executive authority of such State shall issue writs of election to fill such vacancies: Provided, That the legislature of any State may empower the executive thereof to make temporary appointments until the people fill the vacancies by election as the legislature may direct.

[3] This amendment shall not be so construed as to affect the election or term of any Senator chosen before it becomes valid as part of the Constitution.

AMENDMENT XVIII [1919]

Section 1. After one year from the ratification of this article the manufacture, sale, or transportation of intoxicating liquors within, the importation thereof into, or the exportation thereof from the United States and all territory subject to the jurisdiction thereof for beverage purposes is hereby prohibited.

Section 2. The Congress and the several States shall have concurrent power to enforce this article by appropriate legislation.

Section 3. This article shall be inoperative unless it shall have been ratified as an amendment to the Constitution by the legislatures of the several States, as provided in the Constitution, within seven years from the date of the submission hereof to the States by the Congress.

AMENDMENT XIX [1920]

[1] The right of citizens of the United States to vote shall not be denied or abridged by the United States or by any State on account of sex.

[2] Congress shall have power to enforce this article by appropriate legislation.

AMENDMENT XX [1933]

Section 1. The terms of the President and Vice President shall end at noon on the 20th day of January, and the terms of Senators and Representatives at noon on the 3d day of January, of the years in which such terms would have ended if this article had not been ratified; and the terms of their successors shall then begin.

Section 2. The Congress shall assemble at least once in every year, and such meeting shall begin at noon on the 3d day of January, unless they shall by law appoint a different day.

Section 3. If, at the time fixed for the beginning of the term of the President, the President elect shall have died, the Vice President elect shall become President. If the President shall not have been chosen before the time fixed for the beginning of his term, or if the President elect shall have failed to qualify, then the Vice President elect shall act as President until a President shall have qualified; and the Congress may by law provide for the case wherein neither a President elect nor a Vice President elect shall have qualified, declaring who shall then act as President, or the manner in which one who is to act shall be selected, and such person shall act accordingly until a President or Vice President shall have qualified.

Section 4. The Congress may by law provide for the case of the death of any of the persons from whom the House of Representatives may choose a President whenever the right of choice shall have devolved upon them, and for the case of the death of any of the persons from whom the Senate may choose a Vice President whenever the right of choice shall have devolved upon them.

Section 5. Sections 1 and 2 shall take effect on the 15th day of October following the ratification of this article.

Section 6. This article shall be inoperative unless it shall have been ratified as an amendment to the Constitution by the legislatures of threefourths of the several States within seven years from the date of its submission.

AMENDMENT XXI [1933]

Section 1. The eighteenth article of amendment to the Constitution of the United States is hereby repealed.

Section 2. The transportation or importation into any State, Territory, or possession of the United States for delivery or use therein of intoxicating liquors, in violation of the laws thereof, is hereby prohibited.

Section 3. This article shall be inoperative unless it shall have been ratified as an amendment to the Constitution by conventions in the several States, as provided in the Constitution, within seven years from the date of the submission hereof to the States by the Congress.

AMENDMENT XXII [1951]

Section 1. No person shall be elected to the office of the President more than twice, and no person who has held the office of President, or acted as President, for more than two years of a term to which some other person was elected President shall be elected to the office of President more than once. But this Article shall not apply to any person holding the office of President when this Article was proposed by the congress, and shall not prevent any person who may be holding the office of President, or acting as President, during the term within which this Article becomes operative from holding the office of President or acting as President during the remainder of such term.

Section 2. This article shall be inoperative unless it shall have been ratified as an amendment to the Constitution by the legislatures of three-fourths of the several States within seven years from the date of its submission to the States by the Congress.

AMENDMENT XXIII [1961]

Section 1. The District constituting the seat of Government of the United States shall appoint in such manner as the Congress may direct:

A number of electors of President and Vice President equal to the whole number of Senators and Representatives in Congress to which the District would be entitled if it were a State, but in no event more than the least populous state; they shall be in addition to those appointed by the states, but they shall be considered, for the purposes of the election of President and Vice President, to be electors appointed by a state; and they shall meet in the District and perform such duties as provided by the twelfth article of amendment.

Section 2. The Congress shall have power to enforce this article by appropriate legislation.

AMENDMENT XXIV [1964]

Section 1. The right of citizens of the United States to vote in any primary or other election for President or Vice President, for electors for President or Vice President, or for Senator or Representative in Congress, shall not be denied or abridged by the United States or any State by reason of failure to pay any poll tax or other tax.

Section 2. The Congress shall have power to enforce this article by appropriate legislation.

AMENDMENT XXV [1967]

Section 1. In case of the removal of the President from office or of his death or resignation, the Vice President shall become President.

Section 2. Whenever there is a vacancy in the office of the Vice President, the President shall nominate a Vice President who shall take office upon confirmation by a majority vote of both Houses of Congress.

Section 3. Whenever the President transmits to the President pro tempore of the Senate and the Speaker of the House of Representatives his written declaration that he is unable to discharge the powers and duties of his office, and until he transmits to them a written declaration to the contrary, such powers and duties shall be discharged by the Vice President as Acting President.

Section 4. Whenever the Vice President and a majority of either the principal officers of the executive departments or of such other body as Congress may by law provide, transmit to the President pro tempore of the Senate and the Speaker of the House of Representatives their written declaration that the President is unable to discharge the powers and duties of his office, the Vice President shall immediately assume the powers and duties of the office as Acting President.

Thereafter, when the President transmits to the President pro tempore of the Senate and the Speaker of the House of Representatives his written declaration that no inability exists, he shall resume the powers and duties of his office unless the Vice President and a majority of either the principal officers of the

executive department or of such other body as Congress may by law provide, transmit within four days to the President pro tempore of the Senate and the Speaker of the House of Representatives their written declaration and the President is unable to discharge the powers and duties of his office. Thereupon Congress shall decide the issue, assembling within fortyeight hours for that purpose if not in session. If the Congress, within twenty-one days after receipt of the latter written declaration, or, if Congress is not in session, within twenty-one days after Congress is required to assemble, determines by two-thirds vote of both Houses that the President is unable to discharge the powers and duties of his office, the Vice President shall continue to discharge the same as Acting President; otherwise, the President shall resume the powers and duties of his office.

AMENDMENT XXVI [1971]

Section 1. The right of citizens of the United States, who are eighteen years of age or older, to vote shall not be denied or abridged by the United States or by any State on account of age.

Section 2. The Congress shall have power to enforce this article by appropriate legislation.

AMENDMENT XXVII [1992]

No law varying the compensation for the services of senators and representatives shall take effect until an election of representatives shall have intervened.

LANDMARK SUPREME COURT CASES

Cases are presented in chronological order.

Marbury v. Madison, 1 Cranch 137 (1803). For the first time, the court found an act of Congress to be unconstitutional, establishing the foundation for the doctrine that the Supreme Court is the ultimate authority on what is law under the Constitution.

Martin v. Hunter's Lessee, 1 Wheaton 304 (1816). Held that the Supreme Court has power to review judgments of state courts on cases involving federal laws.

McCulloch v. Maryland, 4 Wheaton 316 (1819). Affirmed the concept of broad federal powers by interpreting the Constitution as giving Congress not only specifically enumerated powers, but also the "implied powers" necessary to carry out its duties.

Trustees of Dartmouth College v. Woodward, 4 Wheaton 518 (1819). Held that state charters to corporations are contracts, and that the contract clause of the Constitution applies to them as to other contracts.

Gibbons v. Ogden, 9 Wheaton 1 (1824). Held that Congress has the authority to regulate all commercial intercourse among states, not just interstate travel.

Dred Scott v. Sandford, 19 Howard 393 (1857). Held that descendants of slaves were not citizens, that the Missouri Compromise was unconstitutional and that Congress could not forbid slavery in new territories.

Ex parte Milligan, 4 Wallace 2 (1866). Held that martial law must be confined to "the theater of active military operations" and that civilians could not be tried in military courts if civil courts remained open. Limited the war powers of the president.

Munn v. Illinois, 94 U.S. 113 (1877). Held that Illinois could set maximum rates for grain storage because states have the right to regulate businesses that affect the public interest.

Civil Rights Cases, 109 U.S. 3 (1883). (Five cases tried together.) Declared much of the Civil Rights Act of 1875 unconstitutional. Held that racial discrimination by private individuals was beyond federal control, even in inns and other public accommodations.

United States v. E.C. Knight Company, 156 U.S. 1 (1895). Severely limited the scope of the Sherman Antitrust Act (1890) by holding that it did not apply to conspiracies to monopolize manufacturing.

Plessy v. Ferguson, 163 U.S. 537 (1896). Held that states could require racial segregation, as long as facilities were "equal but separate."

Northern Securities Company v. United States, 193 U.S. 197 (1904). Held that the Sherman Antitrust Act could be applied to a conspiracy to monopolize interstate commerce.

Lochner v. New York, 198 U.S. 45 (1905). Held that a state law limiting work hours was an illegal interference in the right to form a contract.

Standard Oil Co. of New Jersey et al. v. United States, 221 U.S. 1 (1911). Dissolved John D. Rockefeller's Standard Oil Trust because attempts to exclude or crush rivals caused an "unreasonable" restraint of trade.

Schenck v. United States, 249 U.S. 47 (1919). Upheld the authority of the federal Espionage Act (1917) to restrain free speech during wartime. Held that a person who encouraged draft resistance during a war could be convicted under the act if he represented "a clear and present danger," which Congress had a right to prevent.

Schechter Poultry Corp. v. United States, 295 U.S. 495 (1935). Struck down the National Industrial Recovery Act (1933), which allowed industries to regulate themselves, because it improperly delegated legislative powers to private individuals.

National Labor Relations Board v. Jones & Laughlin Steel Corp., 301 U.S. 1 (1937). Expanded the ability of the federal government to regulate commerce.

Upheld federal laws protecting unions and barring "unfair labor practices" because they pertained to the "stream of commerce." Held that companies that sell goods and receive materials through interstate trade are, therefore, subject to federal regulation.

West Coast Hotel Co. v. Parrish, 300 U.S. 379 (1937). Ruled that states could set minimum wages, effectively overruling Lochner v. New York, 198 U.S. 45 (1905).

West Virginia Board of Education v. Barnett, 319 U.S. 624 (1943). Reversed an earlier ruling that had required Jehovah's Witnesses to abide by a state law requiring them to salute the flag, despite a religious belief that forbid it. In this case, also involving Jehovah's Witnesses, the court ruled that the First Amendment protected "the right of silence" as well as of speech.

Korematsu v. United States, 323 U.S. 214 (1944). Upheld a presidential order requiring the evacuation of 120,000 persons of Japanese ancestry from the West Coast, and their internment in camps in the interior of the country, due to "military necessity" during World War II. The only basis for their internment was their ancestry. About 70,000 were American citizens.

Youngstown Sheet & Tube Co. v. Sawyer, 343 U.S. 579 (1952). Restricted presidential power. Held that President Harry S Truman's seizure of steel mills during the Korean War was unconstitutional. Truman had seized the mills to keep them operating, despite a strike.

Brown v. Board of Education of Topeka, Kansas, 347 U.S. 483 (1954), 349 U.S. 294 (1955). Held that racial segregation of public schools is unconstitutional. Effectively overruled the "separate but equal" standard of Plessy v. Ferguson, 163 U.S. 537 (1896).

Roth v. United States, 354 U.S. 476 (1957). Held that obscenity is not protected speech under the First Amendment. Defined obscenity as that which "appeals to prurient interest" of an "average person, applying contemporary community standards."

Mapp v. Ohio, 367 U.S. 643 (1961). Held that the federal rule excluding the use of illegally obtained evidence in criminal trials should be applied to the states because it was based on the Constitution's guarantee of a fair trial.

Engel v. Vitale, 370 U.S. 421 (1962). Held that a state-sponsored program of school prayer was unconstitutional, even though the prayer was voluntary.

Gideon v. Wainwright, 372 U.S. 335 (1963). Held that a defendant in a felony case who could not afford to hire a lawyer must be provided with one because qualified counsel is "fundamental" to a fair trial. Clarence Earl Gideon, who had been denied free counsel in Florida, was retried and acquitted. In a later case, the requirement was extended to all cases that might result in imprisonment, not just felonies.

Abington Township v. Schempp, 374 U.S. 203 (1963). Struck down a Pennsylvania statute that required verses from the Holy Bible to be read each day in public schools.

Heart of Atlanta Motel, Inc. v. United States, 379 U.S. 241 (1964). Upheld the portion of the Civil Rights Act of 1964 that forbids racial discrimination in public accommodations such as hotels, restaurants and theaters.

New York Times v. Sullivan, 376 U.S. 254 (1964). Established a new libel standard for public officials, which made it more difficult for them to recover damages in libel cases. Held that they could recover damages for defamatory falsehoods about their official conduct or fitness for office only if they could prove that the falsehoods were published with "actual malice." Defined actual malice as publishing with "knowledge" of falsehood "or with reckless disregard" of whether the statement was false or not.

Griswold v. Connecticut, 381 U.S. 479 (1965). Struck down a state law that forbid the use of contraceptive devices. Held that the law was an unconstitutional intrusion into a married couple's right of privacy.

Miranda v. Arizona, 384 U.S. 436 (1966). Overturned the kidnap and rape conviction of Ernesto Miranda because his confession was obtained without counsel and without advising him that he had a right to remain silent. The court held that before police interrogate an individual they must inform him that he has the right to remain silent, that any statement he makes may be used as evidence against him, that he has the right to have a lawyer present, and that if he cannot afford a lawyer, one will be appointed to represent him.

Swann v. Charlotte-Mecklenburg Board of Education, 402 U.S. 1 (1971). Upheld a federal court ruling requiring school busing to end segregation.

New York Times Co. v. United States, 403 U.S. 713 (1971). President Richard M. Nixon had obtained restraining orders prohibiting the *New York Times* and the *Washington Post* from publishing the Pentagon Papers, documents that showed government duplicity in the Vietnam War. The court held that the restraining orders were improper because the Nixon administration had not met the "heavy burden" of justification necessary to inflict "prior restraint" upon the press.

Furman v. Georgia, Jackson v. Georgia, Branch v. Texas, 408 U.S. 238 (1972). Held state death penalty laws unconstitutional on the grounds that they inflicted "cruel and unusual punishment" because they were imposed discriminatorily and arbitrarily. After the ruling, many states redrafted laws to attempt to solve the constitutional problem.

Roe v. Wade, 410 U.S. 113 (1973). Held that state laws prohibiting abortion in the first two trimesters of pregnancy were an unconstitutional invasion of a woman's right to privacy.

United States v. Nixon, 418 U.S. 683 (1974). Held that secret tape recordings made in the office of Pres. Richard M. Nixon were subject to subpoena for the Watergate trial. Rejected Nixon's contention that such records were protected from disclosure by executive privilege.

Woodson v. North Carolina, 428 U.S. 280 (1976). Found unconstitutional a law that required a mandatory death sentence for all first-degree murder convictions and that allowed no discretion in sentencing. Reached a similar decision in Roberts v. Louisiana, 428 U.S. 325 (1976) and Green v. Oklahoma, 428 U.S. 907 (1976).

Gregg v. Georgia, 428 U.S. 153 (1976). Upheld a state statute that permitted some jury discretion in imposing the death penalty but that attempted to minimize the likelihood that the death penalty would be imposed arbitrarily or discriminatorily. Reached a similar decision in Jurek v. Texas, 428 U.S. 262 (1976) and Proffitt v. Florida, 428 U.S. 242 (1976).

University of California v. Bakke, 438 U.S. 265 (1978). Held that a university may consider race and ethnic background as factors in considering applicants for admission, but may not establish fixed quotas.

Richmond Newspapers, Inc. v. Virginia, 448 U.S. 555 (1980). Held that the press and the public have the right of access to criminal trials. Held that the public can be banned only when no alternative will guarantee a fair trial.

Bowers v. Hardwick, 478 U.S. 186 (1986). Held that the constitutional right to privacy does not protect homosexual relations, even between consenting adults in their own homes. Upheld Georgia's law against sodomy.

United States v. Salerno, 481 U.S. 739 (1987). Held that a federal law permitting pretrial detention is not unconstitutional when applied to a suspect who is considered dangerous to the community.

Texas v. Johnson, 491 U.S. 490 (1989). Held that a state cannot punish someone for desecrating the flag during a peaceful demonstration because of the First Amendment guarantee of freedom of expression.

Webster v. Reproductive Health Services, 491 U.S. 397 (1989). Upheld a Missouri law barring the use of public facilities or employees for abortions and requiring doctors to test the viability of any fetus believed to be more than 20 weeks old.

Cruzan v. Missouri Department of Health,* U.S.

(1990), 88-1503. Held that family members can be barred from removing life-support equipment from a persistently comatose patient if that patient had not made his or her wishes known conclusively.

Ohio v. Akron Center for Reproductive Health,* U.S. (1990), 88-805. Held that a state may require that one parent be notified when an unmarried girl seeks an abortion.

Arizona v. Fulminante,* U.S. (1991), 89-839. Held that the use of a coerced confession does not automatically invalidate a conviction. Held that the admission of an involuntary confession in a criminal trial may be "harmless error."

California v. Acevedo,* U.S. (1991), 89-1690. Broadened the authority of police officers to search bags and other containers found in cars. Held that police can search such containers if they have probable cause to believe that drugs or other illegal items are inside, whether or not they have probable cause to search the car.

Barnes v. Glen Theater,* U.S. (1991), 90-26. Held that states may ban nude dancing to protect "order and morality." Upheld an Indiana law requiring female dancers to wear pasties and g-strings.

SUGGESTED REFERENCES:

Encyclopedia of the American Constitution, Leonard W. Levy, editor, Macmillan, 1990 (supplement, 1991).

Guide to the Supreme Court, Elder Witt, Congressional Quarterly Inc., 1990.

The Supreme Court Yearbook, Joan Biskupic, Congressional Quarterly Inc., 1991.

* For recent cases, complete citations are not available until books are printed. For those cases, the court number is given.

FEDERAL COURT SYSTEM

SUPREME COURT OF THE UNITED STATES

The Supreme Court consists of one Chief Justice and eight Associate Justices appointed by the president and confirmed by the Senate. The number of justices, which is established by Congress, has been unchanged since 1869. The court's powers are outlined in Article III, Sections 1 and 2, of the U.S. Constitution. The court has original jurisdiction in cases affecting ambassadors, other public ministers and consuls and in cases in which a state is a party (although this authority is limited, somewhat, by the 11th Amendment). The court has appellate jurisdiction over all federal courts and over state supreme courts on matters of federal law or Constitutional issues. Although the court is obligated to hear certain appeals, most come to it on a writ of certiorari. Such a writ asks the court to review a lower court's decision. The court may grant certiorari or refuse, as it sees fit, with no explanation. The affirmative vote of four justices is needed to grant certiorari. Refusing to grant certiorari does not mean that the Supreme Court is affirming the lower court's decision. It means merely that the justices choose not to hear the case. This may be for many reasons, one of which is that the case does not present an issue substantial enough for the court's review.

The court's yearly sessions begin on the first Monday of October and usually continue until the end of June, although a term sometimes continues into July. Special sessions can be called if needed. During its session, the court usually devotes two weeks of each month to oral arguments of cases, and spends two weeks in recess doing research and writing opinions. Before cases are decided they are discussed by the justices in a closed conference. At the conference, the Chief Justice presents his view of a case, elicits the opinions of the other justices and takes a vote. If the Chief Justice is in the majority, he assigns the writing of the opinion. If he is not, the most senior member of the majority group assigns the writing of the opinion. Any justice is free to write a concurring or dissenting opinion. All opinions (including concurring opinions and dissents) are circulated among the justices for comment before final drafts are presented. Decisions are announced from the bench, as they become available. The justice who has written the majority opinion reads or summarizes it.

Suggested contact:

Supreme Court of the United States, 1 First St. NE, Washington, D.C. 20543, (202) 479-3000. Information on new cases and the status of pending cases is available from the office of the clerk, (202) 479-3037. Other information is available from the public information office, (202) 479-3211.

Current Supreme Court Justices

William Hubbs Rehnquist

Born in Milwaukee, Wisc., Oct. 1, 1924; Army Air Force, World War II; Stanford University B.A. (1948); Harvard University M.A. in political science (1950); Stanford University LL.B. (1952); law clerk to U.S. Supreme Court Justice Robert H. Jackson, 1952–53; law practice in Arizona, 1953–69, active in Republican politics; Assistant U.S. Attorney General, Office of Legal Counsel, 1969–71; nominated Associate Justice by Richard M. Nixon, Oct. 21, 1971; confirmed Dec. 10, 1971; nominated Chief Justice by Ronald Reagan, June 17, 1986; confirmed Sept. 17, 1986; succeeded Chief Justice Warren Burger, who retired; married 1953; widowed 1991; two daughters, one son.

Byron Raymond White

Born in Fort Collins, Colo., June 8, 1917; University of Colorado B.A. (1938); professional football player (known as "Whizzer" White) for the Pittsburgh Pirates, 1938; Rhodes Scholar, Oxford University, 1939; professional football player (Detroit Lions), 1940–41; U.S. Navy in World War II; Yale Law School LL.B. (1946); law clerk, Chief Justice Fred M. Vinson, 1946–47; law practice in Colorado, 1947–60; elected to National Football Hall of Fame (1954); led national volunteer group in presidential campaign of John F. Kennedy; U.S. Deputy Attorney General, 1961–62; nominated Associate Justice by John F. Kennedy, March 30, 1962; confirmed April 11, 1962; married 1946; one son, one daughter.

Harry Andrew Blackmun

Born in Nashville, Ill., Nov. 12, 1908; Harvard College B.A. (1929); Harvard Law School LL.B. (1932); clerk for John Sanborn, U.S. Court of Appeals for the Eighth Circuit, 1932–33; law practice in Minneapolis, 1934–50 (also taught part-time at St. Paul College of Law and University of Minnesota Law School, 1941–47); resident counsel, Mayo Clinic, Rochester, Minn., 1950–59; judge in U.S. Court of Appeals, Eighth Circuit, 1959–70; nominated Associate Justice by Richard M. Nixon, April 14, 1970; confirmed May 12, 1970; married 1941; three daughters.

JUSTICES OF THE SUPREME COURT

Justice	Dates	Appointed By
*John Jay	1789–95	George Washington
*John Rutledge[1]	1789–91, '95	George Washington
William Cushing	1789–1810	George Washington
James Wilson	1789–98	George Washington
John Blair	1789–96	George Washington
James Iredell	1790–99	George Washington
Thomas Johnson	1791–93	George Washington
William Paterson	1793–1806	George Washington
Samuel Chase	1796–1811	George Washington
*Oliver Ellsworth[2]	1796–99	George Washington
Bushrod Washington	1798–1829	John Adams
Alfred Moore	1799–1804	John Adams
*John Marshall	1801–35	John Adams
William Johnson	1804–34	Thomas Jefferson
H. B. Livingston	1806–23	Thomas Jefferson
Thomas Todd	1807–26	Thomas Jefferson
Joseph Story	1811–45	James Madison
Gabriel Duval	1811–35	James Madison
Smith Thompson	1823–43	James Monroe
Robert Trimble	1826–28	John Quincy Adams
John McLean	1829–61	Andrew Jackson
Henry Baldwin	1830–44	Andrew Jackson
James M. Wayne	1835–67	Andrew Jackson
*Roger B. Taney	1836–64	Andrew Jackson
Philip P. Barbour	1836–41	Andrew Jackson
John Catron	1837–65	Andrew Jackson
John McKinley	1837–52	Martin Van Buren
Peter V. Daniel	1841–60	Martin Van Buren
Samuel Nelson	1845–72	John Tyler
Levi Woodbury	1845–51	James K. Polk
Robert C. Grier	1846–70	James K. Polk
Benjamin R. Curtis	1851–57	Millard Fillmore
John A. Campbell	1853–61	Franklin Pierce
Nathan Clifford	1858–81	James Buchanan
Noah H. Swayne	1862–81	Abraham Lincoln
Samuel F. Miller	1862–90	Abraham Lincoln
David Davis	1862–77	Abraham Lincoln
Stephen J. Field	1863–97	Abraham Lincoln
*Salmon P. Chase	1864–73	Abraham Lincoln
William Strong	1870–80	Ulysses S. Grant
Joseph P. Bradley	1870–92	Ulysses S. Grant
Ward Hunt	1872–82	Ulysses S. Grant
*Morrison R. Waite	1874–88	Ulysses S. Grant
John Marshall Harlan	1877–1911	Rutherford B. Hayes
William B. Woods	1880–87	Rutherford B. Hayes
Stanley Matthews	1881–89	James A. Garfield
Horace Gray	1881–1902	Chester A. Arthur
Samuel Blatchford	1882–93	Chester A. Arthur
Lucius Q. C. Lamar	1888–93	Grover Cleveland
*Melville W. Fuller	1888–1910	Grover Cleveland
David J. Brewer	1889–1910	Benjamin Harrison
Henry B. Brown	1890–1906	Benjamin Harrison
George Shiras	1892–1903	Benjamin Harrison
Howell E. Jackson	1893–95	Benjamin Harrison
*Edward D. White[3]	1894–1921	Grover Cleveland
Rufus W. Peckham	1895–1910	Grover Cleveland
Joseph McKenna	1898–1925	William McKinley
Oliver W. Holmes	1902–32	Theodore Roosevelt
William R. Day	1903–22	Theodore Roosevelt

JUSTICES OF THE SUPREME COURT

Justice	Dates	Appointed By
William H. Moody	1906–10	Theodore Roosevelt
Horace H. Lurton	1910–14	William H. Taft
Charles Evans Hughes[4]	1910–16	William H. Taft
Willis Van Devanter	1910–37	William H. Taft
Joseph R. Lamar	1911–16	William H. Taft
Mahlon Pitney	1912–22	William H. Taft
James C. McReynolds	1914–41	Woodrow Wilson
Louis O. Brandeis	1916–39	Woodrow Wilson
John H. Clarke	1916–22	Woodrow Wilson
*William Howard Taft	1921–30	Warren G. Harding
George Sutherland	1922–38	Warren G. Harding
Pierce Butler	1922–39	Warren G. Harding
Edward T. Sanford	1923–30	Warren G. Harding
*Harlan F. Stone[5]	1925–46	Calvin Coolidge
*Charles Evans Hughes[4]	1930–41	Herbert Hoover
Owen J. Roberts	1930–45	Herbert Hoover
Benjamin N. Cardozo	1932–38	Herbert Hoover
Hugo L. Black	1937–71	Franklin D. Roosevelt
Stanley Reed	1938–57	Franklin D. Roosevelt
Felix Frankfurter	1939–62	Franklin D. Roosevelt
William O. Douglas	1939–75	Franklin D. Roosevelt
Frank Murphy	1940–49	Franklin D. Roosevelt
James F. Byrnes	1941–42	Franklin D. Roosevelt
Robert H. Jackson	1941–54	Franklin D. Roosevelt
Wiley Rutledge	1943–49	Franklin D. Roosevelt
Harold H. Burton	1945–58	Harry S. Truman
*Frederick M. Vinson	1946–53	Harry S. Truman
Tom C. Clark	1949–67	Harry S. Truman
Sherman Minton	1949–56	Harry S. Truman
*Earl Warren	1953–69	Dwight D. Eisenhower
John Marshall Harlan	1955–71	Dwight D. Eisenhower
William J. Brennan, Jr.	1956–90	Dwight D. Eisenhower
Charles E. Whittaker	1957–62	Dwight D. Eisenhower
Potter Stewart	1958–81	Dwight D. Eisenhower
Byron R. White	1962–	John Kennedy
Arthur J. Goldberg	1962–65	John Kennedy
Abe Fortas	1965–69	Lyndon Johnson
Thurgood Marshall	1967–91	Lyndon Johnson
*Warren E. Burger	1969–87	Richard Nixon
Harry A. Blackmun	1970–	Richard Nixon
Lewis F. Powell Jr.	1972–87	Richard Nixon
*William Rehnquist[6]	1971–	Richard Nixon
John P. Stevens	1975–	Gerald Ford
Sandra D. O'Connor	1981–	Ronald Reagan
Antonin Scalia	1986–	Ronald Reagan
Anthony M. Kennedy	1987–	Ronald Reagan
David H. Souter	1990–	George Bush
Clarence Thomas	1991–	George Bush

1. Served as Chief Justice in 1795, but was never confirmed by Senate.
2. Chief Justice 1796–1800.
3. Nominated as Chief Justice in 1910 by William Howard Taft.
4. Resigned to run for President. Appointed Chief Justice in 1930.
5. Nominated as Chief Justice in 1941 by Franklin D. Roosevelt.
6. Nominated as Chief Justice in 1986 by Ronald Reagan.

* Chief Justice. Served complete term as Chief Justice unless otherwise indicated.

John Paul Stevens

Born in Chicago, Ill., April 20, 1920; University of Chicago B.A. (1941); U.S. Navy, 1941–44; Northwestern University School of Law J.D. (1947); clerk for Justice Wiley Rutledge, 1947–49; law practice in Chicago, 1949–70; judge, U.S. Court of Appeals, Seventh Circuit, 1970–75; nominated Associate Justice by Gerald Ford, Nov. 28, 1975; confirmed Dec. 17, 1975; married 1942; three daughters, one son; divorced 1979; married 1980.

Sandra Day O'Connor

Born in El Paso, Tex., March 26, 1930; Stanford University B.A. (1950); Stanford University Law School LL.B. (1952); Deputy County Attorney, San Mateo, Calif., 1952–53; civilian lawyer for U.S. Army, Frankfurt, Germany, 1954–57; Assistant Attorney General, Arizona, 1965–69; Arizona state senator, 1969–75; state Senate majority leader, 1972–74; judge, Maricopa County Superior Court, 1974–79; judge, Arizona Court of Appeals, 1979–81; nominated Associate Justice by Ronald Reagan, Aug. 19, 1981; confirmed Sept. 21, 1981; married 1952; three sons.

Antonin Scalia

Born in Trenton, N.J., March 11, 1936; Georgetown University A.B. (1957); Harvard University LL.B. (1960); law practice in Cleveland, 1960–67; taught University of Virginia Law School, 1967–71; general counsel, White House Office of Telecommunications Policy, 1971–72; chairman, Administrative Conference of the United States, 1972–74; head, Justice Department's Office of Legal Counsel, 1974–77; taught University of Chicago Law School, 1977–82; judge, U.S. Court of Appeals, District of Columbia, 1982–86; nominated Associate Justice by Ronald Reagan, June 17, 1986; confirmed Sept. 17, 1986; married 1960; nine children.

Anthony McLeod Kennedy

Born in Sacramento, Calif., July 23, 1936; Stanford University A.B. (1958); Harvard Law School LL.B. (1961); California Army National Guard, 1961; law practices in San Francisco and Sacramento, 1961–75; taught McGeorge School of Law, University of the Pacific, 1965–88; judge, U.S. Court of Appeals, Ninth Circuit, 1975–88; nominated Associate Justice by Ronald Reagan, Nov. 11, 1987, after his first selection, Robert H. Bork, was rejected by the Senate and his second choice, Douglas H. Ginsburg, withdrew after admitting that he smoked marijuana while a law professor; confirmed Feb. 3, 1988; married 1963; two sons, one daughter.

David Hackett Souter

Born in Melrose, Mass., Sept. 17, 1939; Harvard College B.A. (1961); Rhodes Scholar, Oxford University, 1961–63; Harvard University Law School LL.B.

(1966); law practice in Concord, N.H., 1966–68; Assistant N.H. Attorney General, 1968–71; Deputy N.H. Attorney General, 1971–76; N.H. Attorney General, 1976–78; Associate Justice N.H. Superior Court, 1978–83; Associate Justice, N.H. Supreme Court, 1983–1990; judge, U.S. Court of Appeals, First Circuit, 1990; nominated Associate Justice by George Bush, July 23, 1990; confirmed Oct. 2, 1990.

Clarence Thomas

Born in Savannah, Ga., June 23, 1948; Holy Cross College B.A. (1971); Yale Law School LL.B. (1974); office of the Missouri Attorney General (1974–77); private practice (1977–79); legislative assistant to U.S. Senator John Danforth (1979–81); head of civil rights division of Department of Education (1981–82); head of Equal Employment Opportunities Commission (1982–90); judge, U.S. Court of Appeals, District of Columbia Circuit, 1990–91; nominated Associate Justice by George Bush, July 1, 1991; confirmed by a 52–48 vote, Oct. 15, 1991, after a televised Senate hearing concerning allegations that he had sexually harassed Anita Hill when she worked for him as a lawyer at the Department of Education and the Equal Opportunity Commission.

OTHER FEDERAL COURTS
Federal District Courts

The district courts are the basic trial courts in the federal system. They are divided into civil and criminal divisions. Each state, the District of Columbia, the commonwealth of Puerto Rico and each territory has at least one district court. Large states are divided into as many as four subdistricts, with a district court in each.

ALABAMA: Northern, 1729 5th Ave. N., Birmingham, AL 35203, (205) 731-1701. Middle, P.O. Box 711, Montgomery, AL 36101, (205) 223-7308. Southern, 113 St. Joseph's St., Mobile, AL 36602, (205) 690-2371.

ALASKA: 222 West 7th Ave. #4, Anchorage, AK 99513, (907) 271-5568.

ARIZONA: 230 N. 1st Ave., Phoenix, AZ 85025, (602) 379-3342.

ARKANSAS: Eastern, P.O. Box 869, Little Rock, AR 72203, (501) 324-5351. Western, P.O. Box 1523, Fort Smith, AR 72902, (501) 783-6833.

CALIFORNIA: Northern, 450 Golden Gate Ave., San Francisco, CA 94102, (415) 556-3031. Eastern, 650 Capitol Mall, Sacramento, CA 95814, (916) 551-2615. Central, 312 N. Spring St., Los Angeles, CA 90012, (213) 894-3533. Southern, 940 Front St., San Diego, CA 92189, (619) 557-5600.

COLORADO: 1929 Stout St., Denver, CO 80294, (303) 844-3157.

CONNECTICUT: 141 Church St., New Haven, CT 06510, (203) 773-2140.

DELAWARE: 844 N. King St., Box 18, Wilmington, DE 19801, (302) 573-6170.

DISTRICT OF COLUMBIA: 333 Constitution Ave. NW, Washington, D.C. 20001, (202) 273-0555.

FLORIDA: Northern, 110 E. Park Ave., Tallahassee, FL 32301, (904) 942-8826. Middle, P.O. Box 53558, Jacksonville, FL 32201, (904) 232-2320. Southern, 301 North Miami Ave., Miami, FL 33128-7788, (305) 536-4131.

GEORGIA: Northern, 75 Spring St. SW, Atlanta, GA 30335, (404) 331-6886. Middle, P.O. Box 128, Macon, GA 31202, (912) 752-3497. Southern, P.O. Box 8286, Savannah, GA 31412, (912) 652-4281.

HAWAII: P.O. Box 50129, Honolulu, HI 96850, (808) 541-1300.

IDAHO: Box 039, Federal Bldg., Boise, ID 83724, (208) 334-1361.

ILLINOIS: Northern, 219 S. Dearborn St., Chicago, IL 60604, (312) 435-5684. Central, P.O. Box 315, Springfield, IL 62701, (217) 492-4020. Southern, U.S. Courthouse, 750 Missouri Ave., East St. Louis, IL 62201, (618) 482-9371.

INDIANA: Northern, 204 S. Main St., South Bend, IN 46601, (219) 236-8260. Southern, 46 E. Ohio St., Indianapolis, IN 46204, (317) 226-6670.

IOWA: Northern, 101 1st St. SE, Cedar Rapids, IA 52401, (319) 364-2447. Southern, U.S. Courthouse, East, 1st and Walnut sts., Des Moines, IA 50309, (515) 284-6248.

KANSAS: 401 N. Market, Wichita, KS 67202, (316) 269-6491.

KENTUCKY: Eastern, P.O. Drawer 3074, Lexington, KY 40596, (606) 233-2503. Western, 601 W. Broadway, Louisville, KY 40202, (502) 582-5156.

LOUISIANA: Eastern, 500 Camp St., New Orleans, LA 70130, (504) 589-4471. Middle, P.O. Box 1991, Baton Rouge, LA 70821, (504) 389-3950. Western, 500 Fannin St., Shreveport, LA 71101, (318) 676-4273.

MAINE: 156 Federal St., Portland, ME 04112, (207) 780-3356.

MARYLAND: 101 West Lumbard Ave., Baltimore, MD 21202, (301) 962-2600.

MASSACHUSETTS: Post Office and Courthouse Building, Boston, MA 02109, (617) 223-9152.

MICHIGAN: Eastern, 231 W. Lafayette St., Detroit, MI 48226, (313) 226-7060. Western, 452 Federal Building, 110 Michigan NW, Grand Rapids, MI 49503, (616) 456-2381.

MINNESOTA: 514 U.S. Courthouse, 110 S. 4th St., St. Paul, MN 55401, (612) 348-1821.

MISSISSIPPI: Northern, P.O. Box 727, Oxford, MS 38655, (601) 234-1971. Southern, 245 E. Capital St., Jackson, MS 39201, (601) 965-4439.

MISSOURI: Eastern, 1114 Market St., St. Louis, MO 63101, (314) 539-2315. Western, 811 Grand Ave., Kansas City, MO 64106, (816) 426-2811.

MONTANA: 316 N. 26th St., Billings, MT 59101, (406) 657-6366.

NEBRASKA: P.O. Box 129 DTS, Omaha, NE 68101, (402) 221-4761.

NEVADA: 200 S. Third St., Las Vegas, NV 89155, (702) 455-4011.

NEW HAMPSHIRE: P.O. Box 1498, Concord, NH 03302, (603) 225-1423.

NEW JERSEY: P.O. Box 419, Newark, NJ 07102, (201) 645-3730.

NEW MEXICO: 500 Gold SW, Albuquerque, NM 87103, (505) 766-2851.

NEW YORK: Northern, 445 Broadway, P.O. Box 1037, Albany, NY 12201, (518) 472-5651. Southern, 40 Foley Sq., New York, NY 10007, (212) 791-0108. Eastern, 225 Cadman Plaza East, Brooklyn, NY 11201, (718) 330-7671. Western, 68 Court St., Buffalo, NY 14202, (716) 846-4211.

NORTH CAROLINA: Eastern, P.O. Box 25670, Raleigh, NC 27611, (919) 856-4370. Middle, P.O. Box V-1, Greensboro, NC 27402, (919) 333-5347. Western, 60 Court Plaza, Asheville, NC 28801, (704) 255-4702.

NORTH DAKOTA: P.O. Box 1055, Bismarck, ND 58502-1055, (701) 222-6690.

OHIO: Northern, 201 Superior Ave., Cleveland, OH 44114, (216) 522-4356. Southern, 85 Marconi Blvd., Columbus, OH 43215, (614) 469-5835.

OKLAHOMA: Northern, 333 W. 4th St., Tulsa, OK 74103, (918) 581-7796. Eastern, P.O. Box 607, Muskogee, OK 74401, (918) 687-2471. Western, 200 NW 4th, Oklahoma City, OK 73102, (405) 231-4792.

OREGON: 620 SW Main St., Portland, OR 97205, (503) 326-5412.

PENNSYLVANIA: Eastern, 601 Market St., Philadelphia, PA 19106, (215) 597-7704. Middle, North Washington Ave. and Lyndon St., Scranton, PA 18501, (717) 347-0205. Western, 7th and Grant St., Pittsburgh, PA 15219, (412) 644-3528.

PUERTO RICO: San Juan, PR 00904, (809) 766-6484.

RHODE ISLAND: 1 Exchange Terrace, Providence, RI 02903, (401) 528-5100.

SOUTH CAROLINA: 1845 Assembly St., Columbia, SC 29201, (803) 765-5816.

SOUTH DAKOTA: 400 S. Phillips Ave., Sioux Falls, SD 57102, (605) 330-4447.

TENNESSEE: Eastern, P.O. Box 2348, Knoxville, TN 37901, (615) 545-4228. Middle, 801 Broadway St., Nashville, TN 37203, (615) 736-5498. Western, 167 N. Main St., Memphis, TN 38103, (901) 544-3315.

TEXAS: Northern, 1100 Commerce St., Dallas, TX

75242, (214) 767-0787. Southern, P.O. Box 61010, Houston, TX 77208, (713) 250-5500. Eastern, 211 W. Ferguson St., Tyler, TX 75702, (903) 592-8195. Western, 655 E. Durango St., San Antonio, TX 78206, (512) 229-6550.

Utah: 350 S. Main St., Salt Lake City, UT 84101, (801) 524-5160.

Vermont: P.O. Box 945, Burlington, VT 05402, (802) 951-6301.

Virginia: Eastern, 200 S. Washington St., Alexandria, VA 22320-2449, (703) 557-5131. Western, P.O. Box 1234, Roanoke, VA 24006, (703) 982-4661.

Washington: Eastern, P.O. Box 1493, Spokane, WA 99210-1493, (509) 353-2150. Western, 1010 5th Ave., Seattle, WA 98104, (206) 553-5598.

West Virginia: Northern, P.O. Box 1518, Elkins, WV 26241, (304) 636-1445. Southern, P.O. Box 2546, Charleston, WV 25329, (304) 342-5154.

Wisconsin: Eastern, 517 E. Wisconsin Ave., Milwaukee, WI 53202, (414) 297-3372. Western, P.O. Box 432, Madison, WI 53701, (608) 264-5156.

Wyoming: P.O. Box 727, Cheyenne, WY 82003, (307) 772-2145.

Territorial District Courts:

Guam: Agana, GU 96910, (671) 472-7411.
Virgin Islands: Charlotte Amalie, St. Thomas, VI 00801, (809) 774-8310.

U.S. Courts of Appeals

Courts of Appeals are intermediary federal appellate courts created to relieve the burden on the U.S. Supreme Court. There are 11 geographically divided circuits, one District of Columbia circuit and a federal circuit. The Federal Circuit Court of Appeals is a specialized appeal court. It reviews decisions concerning international trade, patent infringement and copyright. It also hears appeals from district courts in cases in which the U.S. government is a defendant.

Circuit for the District of Columbia: Chief Judge Patricia M. Wald, 500 Indiana Ave. NW, Rm. 6000, Washington, D.C. 20001, (202) 879-2770, Circuit Justice William H. Rehnquist.

Federal Circuit: Chief Judge Helen W. Nies, 717 Madison Pl. NW, Washington, D.C. 20439, (202) 633-6550, Circuit Justice William H. Rehnquist.

First Circuit (Maine, New Hampshire, Massachusetts, Rhode Island, Puerto Rico): Chief Judge Stephen Breyer, Boston, MA 02109, (617) 223-9049, Circuit Justice David Souter.

Second Circuit (Vermont, Connecticut, New York): Chief Judge James Oakes, 40 Foley Sq., New York, NY 10007, (212) 791-0982, Circuit Justice Clarence Thomas.

Third Circuit (New Jersey, Pennsylvania, Delaware, the Virgin Islands): Chief Judge Dolores K. Sloviter, U.S. Courthouse, 601 Market St., Philadelphia, PA 19106, (215) 597-2995, Circuit Justice David Souter.

Fourth Circuit (Maryland, West Virginia, Virginia, North Carolina, South Carolina): Chief Judge Sam J. Ervin III, U.S. Courthouse, 10th & Main sts., Richmond, VA 23219, (804) 771-2213, Circuit Justice William H. Rehnquist.

Fifth Circuit (Mississippi, Louisiana, Texas): Chief Judge Henry A. Politz, 600 Camp St., New Orleans, LA 70130, (504) 589-6514, Circuit Justice Antonin Scalia.

Sixth Circuit (Ohio, Michigan, Kentucky, Tennessee): Chief Judge Gilbert S. Merritt, 538 U.S. Post Office & Courthouse, Cincinnati, OH 45202, (513) 684-2953, Circuit Justice John Paul Stevens.

Seventh Circuit (Indiana, Illinois, Wisconsin): Chief Judge William J. Bauer, Chicago, IL 60604, (312) 435-5850, Circuit Justice John Paul Stevens.

Eighth Circuit (Minnesota, Iowa, Missouri, Arkansas, North Dakota, South Dakota): Chief Judge Donald Lay, 1114 Market St., St. Louis, MO 63101, (314) 744-9800, Circuit Justice Harry A. Blackmun.

Ninth Circuit (California, Oregon, Nevada, Montana, Washington, Idaho, Arizona, Alaska, Hawaii, Guam, Northern Mariana Islands): Chief Judge J. Clifford Wallace, San Francisco, CA 94101, (415) 744-9800, Circuit Justice Sandra Day O'Connor.

Tenth Circuit (Colorado, Wyoming, Utah, Kansas, Oklahoma, New Mexico): Chief Judge Monroe G. McKay, 1929 Stout St., Denver, CO 80294, (303) 844-3157, Circuit Justice Byron R. White.

Eleventh Circuit (Georgia, Florida, Alabama): Chief Judge Gerald B. Tjoflat, 56 Forsyth St., Atlanta, GA 30303, (404) 331-5724, Circuit Justice Anthony M. Kennedy.

Special Federal Courts

U.S. Claims Court: 717 Madison Pl. NW, Washington, D.C. 20005, (202) 219-9657. Has jurisdiction over monetary claims against the United States that are based on acts of Congress or the Constitution.

U.S. Court of International Trade: 1 Federal Plaza, New York, NY 10007, (212) 264-2800. Has jurisdiction over civil cases involving federal import laws in which the United States is a defendant.

U.S. Court of Military Appeals: 450 E St. NW, Washington, D.C. 20442-0001, (202) 272-1448. Final appeals court for court-martial convictions for all armed services.

Temporary Emergency Court of Appeals: 801 Pennsylvania Ave. NW, Washington, D.C. 20004, (202) 535-3390. Has jurisdiction over appeals from district courts concerning economic stabilization and energy conservation laws.

U.S. Court of Veterans' Appeals: 625 Indiana Ave. NW, Washington, D.C. 20004, (202) 501-5970. Reviews decisions of the Boards of Veterans' Appeals.

U.S. Tax Court: 400 2d St. NW, Washington, D.C. 20217, (202) 606-8754. Hears disputes concerning Internal Revenue Service decisions on income, estate, gift and personal holding company taxes.

COMMONLY CITED FEDERAL LAWS

This listing gives highlights of some commonly cited federal laws. For specifics, refer to the laws themselves in the United States Code (U.S.C.) or in the United States Code Annotated (U.S.C.A.). Citations for laws list the title number first, the source and then the section. For example, 20 U.S.C.A. §1231g refers to Title 20, section 1231g, found in the United States Code Annotated. The U.S.C. and the U.S.C.A. use the same numbering system. Although U.S.C. is the standard citation, citations below are for the U.S.C.A. because that compendium gives additional explanatory material that is useful to researchers. Both the U.S.C. and the U.S.C.A. are updated regularly by "pocket" parts inserted in the back of each book. Researchers should check those sections for updates.

Age Discrimination in Employment Act of 1967 (29 U.S.C.A. §621 et seq.). Prohibits job discrimination against people more than 40 years old. Prohibits age discrimination in job advertisements. The law applies to city and state governments and to organizations that have 20 or more employees and participate in interstate commerce. Age can be used as a job criterion only when the employer can show that it is a Bona Fide Occupational Qualification. In many cases, the law prohibits mandatory retirement based on age. There are many exceptions, however, including executives, firefighters and police.

Americans With Disabilities Act of 1990 (42 U.S.C.A. §12101 et seq., 47 U.S.C.A. §§ 152, 221, 225, 611). Prohibits discrimination against the disabled in employment, public accommodations, transportation and telecommunications. The act applies to anyone with a physical or mental impairment that "substantially limits one or more of the major life activities." Employers are prohibited from segregating the disabled from other workers, from using employment tests that screen out the disabled and from using standards that effectively discriminate against the disabled. The law requires employers to make "reasonable accommodations" for disabled workers, including making work areas accessible, modifying work schedules and providing braille devices and interpreters for the hearing impaired. The employer may avoid providing "reasonable accommodations" if he can show that doing so would cause "undue hardship" in that it would require "significant difficulty or expense." The employment aspects of the law are being phased in. For businesses with 25 or more employees, they took effect in 1992. For businesses with 15

to 24 employees, the date is 1994. Businesses with fewer than 15 employees are exempt. The employment section of the law is enforced by the Equal Employment Opportunities Commission. The public transportation section of the law requires that public bodies purchasing or leasing new buses, trains or taxis must make sure that they are accessible to people with disabilities, including those in wheelchairs. New terminals and stations also must be made accessible. Major existing commuter train stations must be accessible within three years (although extensions of up to 30 years may be granted if renovations would be extraordinarily expensive). Within five years, all commuter and intercity trains must have at least one car that is accessible to the physically disabled. The public accommodations portion of the law requires hotels, restaurants, theaters, stadiums, museums, libraries, schools, banks and hospitals to build or remodel facilities so that they are free of architectural and communications barriers. Businesses must comply only if that is possible "without much difficulty or expense." The telecommunications portion of the law requires telephone companies to provide relay operators for the hearing impaired who use telecommunications equipment. (The equipment transmits printed text to an operator, who acts as an intermediary.)

Bankruptcy Reform Act of 1978 (11 U.S.C.A. §101 et seq.). There are several forms of bankruptcy outlined by the Bankruptcy Reform Act. Three common types are identified by the chapters in which they are found: Chapter 7, Chapter 11 and Chapter 13. Under Chapter 7 (straight bankruptcy), all nonexempt assets are sold and the proceeds are split among creditors. Most debts are discharged. Some, such as taxes and child support, remain. In many cases, the home may be kept. The car may be kept if it is necessary for work and if arrangements are made to pay off any lien against it. Under Chapter 13 (wage earner's bankruptcy), the debtor proposes a plan for repaying all or a percentage of debts. Payments are made from disposable income over three to five years. Home, car and other assets are kept if the court-approved plan is carried out successfully. Chapter 11 (reorganization) is used primarily by businesses. Creditors' claims are frozen while the company's management or a trustee devises a plan to discharge the company's debts. The court-approved plan can modify or forgive debts, provide for mergers, takeovers or new capital, or dispose of assets. The law was amended in

1984 to restructure the bankruptcy court system and to modify some liberal provisions of the 1978 act concerning consumer bankruptcy. Specific property exemptions vary from state to state.

Buckley Amendment (20 U.S.C.A. §1232 g). Gives parents the right to see children's school records. Also gives students over age 18 the right to see their own records. Forbids the release of records to others without the consent of parents or the student, if he or she is over 18. Says that schools that have ongoing policies that do not keep students' grades confidential are not eligible for federal funds.

Civil Rights Act of 1964 (42 U.S.C.A. §2000 a et seq.). Prohibits job discrimination based on race, color, religion, sex or national origin. Bans discrimination in public accommodations connected with interstate commerce, including hotels, restaurants and theaters. (The Civil Rights Act of 1968 extended this protection to housing and real estate.) The Civil Rights Act of 1964 established the Equal Employment Opportunity Commission to enforce the job portion (Title VII) of the law.

Clayton Act. *See* Sherman Antitrust Act

Consumer Credit Cost Disclosure Act. *See* Truth in Lending Act

Consumer Credit Protection Act. *See* Truth in Lending Act, Fair Credit Reporting Act

Consumer Leasing Act of 1976 (15 U.S.C.A. §§ 1601, 1640, 1667 to 1667e). Requires the lessor to disclose information allowing the consumer to compare the costs and terms of leases.

Copyright Act. *See* Part X, Copyright, page 418.

Emergency Planning and Community Right-to-Know Act of 1986. *See* Part V, Common Toxic Chemicals, page 206.

Equal Credit Opportunity Act (15 U.S.C.A. §1691 et seq.). Prohibits a credit grantor from using age, race, color, national origin, sex, religion, marital status or receipt of public aid to prohibit a consumer from receiving credit. The factors also may not be used to discourage application for a loan or to alter the terms or amount of the loan. The grantor's legitimate standards must be applied uniformly to assess creditworthiness.

Equal Employment Opportunity Act (42 U.S.C.A. 2000e et seq.). An amendment to the Civil Rights Act of 1964 (q.v.), it increased the authority of the Equal Employment Opportunity Commission and extended the discrimination provisions of the Civil Rights Act to state and local governments, labor organizations with 15 or more employees, and employment agencies.

Equal Pay Act of 1963 (29 U.S.C.A. §206). An amendment to the Fair Labor Standards Act (q.v.), it provides that women and men who work for the same enterprise under similar conditions must receive equal pay for work that requires equal or similar effort, skill and responsibility.

Ethics in Government Act (2 U.S.C.A. §701 et seq.). Seeks to eliminate conflict of interest by former federal executive branch employees. Prohibits certain activities in their next jobs. The prohibitions vary depending upon the person's role in government. It bars top government officials from lobbying their former agencies for a year after leaving their government job.

Fair Credit Billing Act (15 U.S.C.A. §1601 et seq.). Establishes procedures to correct errors in a credit account, and prevents damage to a credit rating while a dispute is being settled.

Fair Credit Reporting Act (15 U.S.C.A. §1601 et seq.). (Also known as the Consumer Credit Reporting Act; part of the Consumer Credit Protection Act.) The Fair Credit Reporting Act protects consumers against the circulation of inaccurate credit information and sets procedures for credit reporting agencies. Under the law, consumers have the right to be told the name and address of credit agencies that prepared reports used to deny credit, insurance or employment or to increase the cost of credit or insurance. If requested, the credit agencies must disclose the nature and substance of information (except medical) used in their reports. The information must be provided for free if it is requested within 30 days of adverse outcomes caused by the reports. In other cases, the information must be provided for a reasonable fee. Consumers are entitled to learn who has received credit reports on them in the last six months (or two years, if employment is at issue). They have the right to have incomplete or incorrect information investigated and to have errors corrected in their files and made known to those to whom the credit reporting agency has made reports. If a dispute between consumers and reporting agencies cannot be resolved, consumers have the right to have their version placed into the files.

Fair Debt Collection Practices Act (15 U.S.C.A. §1692 et seq.). Prohibits debt collectors from using abusive practices. The debt collector must communicate with the debtor at a reasonable time, and not at the debtor's place of employment. If the debtor indicates refusal to pay, the collector cannot continue to communicate with him, although the collector can take legal action.

Fair Employment Practices Act (42 U.S.C.A. §2000e et seq.). The portion of the Civil Rights Act of 1964 (q.v.) that deals with employment.

Fair Housing Act (42 U.S.C.A. §3601 et seq.). Title VIII of the Civil Rights Act of 1968. Prohibits housing discrimination by real estate firms and homeowners on the basis of race, religion, gender, color or national origin. Amendments in 1988 extend this protection to the handicapped. It gives tenants the right to modify existing apartments and requires that all new multifamily housing must be adaptable for the handicapped. There are many exceptions to both the act and the amendments.

Fair Labor Standards Act (29 U.S.C.A. §§201–219). Sets standards for minimum wages, overtime pay, equal pay, record-keeping and child labor. The Wage and Hour Division enforces the law with respect to private, state and local government employees and certain federal employees. The Office of Personnel Management enforces the act with respect to most federal employees.

Family Education Rights and Privacy Act. *See* Buckley Amendment

Federal Election Campaign Act (2 U.S.C.A. §431 et seq., 437c). Requires candidates for federal office and national political committees to file financial reports with the Clerk of the House of Representatives, the Secretary of the Senate and the Federal Election Commission (which was established to oversee the law). The law prohibits contributions from the treasuries of corporations, labor unions and national banks, from government contractors, and from foreign nationals who are not permanent residents of the United States. It also prohibits cash contributions totaling more than $100 per person per campaign, contributions made by one person in the name of another, and contributions in excess of prescribed maximum amounts. In general, an individual can give a maximum of $1,000 per candidate per election, and a committee can give a maximum of $5,000. (An individual can give no more than $25,000 to all federal candidates in one year. There is no limit for committees.) The law also limits spending in presidential primaries and elections. It provides matching funds for candidates in presidential primaries, once they have raised at least $5,000 in each of 20 states. The law provides full financing for major-party presidential candidates. Candidates of minor parties (or unaffiliated candidates) are eligible for reimbursement if they receive 5 percent or more of the vote.

Freedom of Information Act. *See* Freedom of Information, page 295.

Hatch Act (18 U.S.C.A. §594 et seq.). Restricts the political activities of federal employees and of state employees whose positions are federally funded. Employees are prohibited from serving as delegates to political party conventions, from soliciting or handling political contributions, from being officers of political clubs, from electioneering, from speaking to partisan meetings, and from running for elective political office (with some exceptions).

Job Training Partnership Act (29 U.S.C.A. §1501 et seq.). Provides for job training programs to be jointly controlled by local officials and private industry in areas designated by the governor of each state.

National Labor Relations Act (29 U.S.C.A. §151 et seq.). (Also called the Wagner Act. The Labor-Management Relations Act [Taft-Hartley Act] is an amendment.) Governs the labor-management relations of firms that participate in interstate commerce (except railroads and airlines). The law guarantees employees the right to form unions, to choose representatives and to bargain collectively. The National Labor Relations Board enforces these provisions and prohibits unfair practices by unions.

Occupational Safety and Health Act of 1970 (29 U.S.C.A. §651 et seq.). Requires employers to meet specified standards to provide a safe workplace. Established the Occupational Safety and Health Administration to develop standards, issue regulations, determine compliance, issue citations and propose penalties.

Privacy Act of 1974. *See* Part X, Privacy Law, page 415.

Rehabilitation Act of 1973 (29 U.S.C.A. §701 et seq.). Prohibits discrimination against the handicapped by the federal government, its contractors and subcontractors, and by programs that receive federal funds.

Sherman Antitrust Act (15 U.S.C.A. §301 et seq.). Passed in 1890 to combat business monopoly and maintain competition, it makes monopoly and restraint of trade illegal. It sets criminal fines (up to $50,000) and allows injured parties to sue for three times the actual damage inflicted. In 1914, the Federal Trade Commission Act established the FTC to investigate alleged violations and issue cease and desist orders. (A 1938 amendment extended the FTC's purview to include "unfair or deceptive acts or practices" in commerce, whether or not they are related to competition.) The Clayton Act of 1914 (and subsequent amendments) prohibits exclusive dealing contracts, tying arrangements and mergers when they substantially lessen competition or create the effect of a monopoly. Under the Robinson-Patman Act of 1936, price discrimination is illegal under the same circumstances.

Social Security Act (42 U.S.C.A. §301 et seq.). The law was passed in 1935 to provide retirement benefits. It created the Social Security Administration (within the federal Department of Health, Education and Welfare) to administer programs. The law's scope has been widened many times by amendments. It now includes survivor, disability and health insurance benefits, as well as public assistance and health and welfare provisions. The Supplemental Security Income program, which became effective in 1974, provides monthly income for physically or mentally disabled persons with limited assets and income. Medicare, which became effective in 1966, provides medical insurance coverage for persons aged 65 and over.

Superfund Amendments and Reauthorization Act of 1986, Title III. *See* Part V, Common Toxic Chemicals, page 206.

Taft-Hartley Act. *See* National Labor Relations Act

Truth in Lending Act (15 U.S.C.A. §1601 et seq.). (Also known as the Consumer Credit Cost Disclosure Act; part of the Consumer Credit Protection Act.) The Truth in Lending Act requires creditors to tell credit applicants the finance charge (total dollar cost) and the annual percentage rate. The information must be provided in writing, before a loan is made. The law also gives borrowers three business days to change their minds and cancel an agreement when their home is used as security for the loan. It also limits liability when credit cards are stolen. The maximum liability for each card is $50. The owner of the card is not liable for any charges made after the credit card company has been notified of the loss of the card.

Wages and Hours Act. *See* Fair Labor Standards Act

SUGGESTED REFERENCE:

To find the citations for laws that are not listed here, refer to *Shepard's Acts and Cases by Popular Names, Federal and State*, Shepard's/McGraw-Hill, 1986, (updated quarterly).

The Guide to American Law, vols. 1–12, West Publishing Co., 1985 (with annual supplements).

PART FOUR

HISTORY

AMERICAN HISTORY

IMPORTANT DATES IN AMERICAN HISTORY

For detailed information, see related entries in the chapters on American History, World History, Wars and Armed Conflicts, and Aviation

1492: Christopher Columbus discovers the New World.

1565: Spaniards found St. Augustine, Fla.

1607: First permanent English settlement founded at Jamestown, Va., by Capt. John Smith.

1609: Henry Hudson sails into New York harbor; Samuel de Champlain explores Lake Champlain.

1619: Virginia establishes House of Burgesses, first representative assembly in North America.

1620: Pilgrims found Plymouth Colony in Massachusetts.

1626: Peter Minuit buys Manhattan Island for the Dutch from Indians.

1660: British pass Navigation Act regulating colonial commerce.

1675–76: New England colonists fight Indians in King Philip's War (named for chief of Wampanoag Indians, King Philip).

1689–1763: French and Indian Wars; a series of campaigns between England and France over territory in North America; the wars included King William's War (1688–97), Queen Anne's War (1702–13), King George's War (1744–48), the French and Indian War (1754–63).

1692: Nineteen executed for witchcraft in Salem, Mass.

1704: The first successful colonial newspaper, *The Boston News-Letter*, begins publication.

1735: John Peter Zenger, relying on truth as defense, acquitted of libeling governor, establishes freedom of press.

1764: British Sugar Act taxes lumber, food, molasses and rum in colonies.

1765: British Stamp Act taxes colonial newspapers, legal documents and other printed materials.

1767: British Townshend Acts tax glass, painter's lead, paper and tea in colonies.

1770: British troops kill five civilians in the Boston Massacre (March 5).

1773: Colonists protest tea tax by dumping tea from East India Co. ships into Boston Harbor during Boston Tea Party (Dec. 16).

1774: Britain's "Intolerable Acts" limit Massachusetts' self-rule, close Boston Harbor; First Continental Congress meets in Philadelphia, protests Intolerable Acts (Sept. 5–Oct. 26).

1775: Revolutionary War begins when British meet Colonists at Lexington and Concord, Mass. (April 19).

1776: Declaration of Independence approved by Second Continental Congress (July 4).

1781: Americans defeat British at Yorktown, Va., last major battle of Revolutionary War.

1783: Treaty of Paris ends Revolutionary War.

1787: U.S. Constitution written at Constitutional Convention in Philadelphia.

1789: George Washington chosen first President.

1791: Bill of Rights goes into effect.

1803: Louisiana Purchase from France doubles nation's size.

1812–14: War of 1812 fought with Britain; "Star Spangled Banner" written by Francis Scott Key (1814) as he watches attack on Fort McHenry.

1820: Missouri Compromise allows slavery in Missouri but not in other areas west of the Mississippi River and south of Missouri; temporarily ends slavery dispute.

1823: Monroe Doctrine opposes European intervention in Western Hemisphere.

1831: Nat Turner leads slave revolt in Virginia.

1836: Texans besieged at Alamo; Texas declares independence from Mexico.

1845: Texas admitted to United States (Dec. 29).

1846–48: Mexican War; victory expands U.S. territory in West.

1848: Discovery of gold in California starts Gold Rush.

1850: Compromise of 1850 attempts to settle slavery dispute by admitting California as a free state, and Utah and New Mexico as territories without a decision on their status.

1854: Kansas-Nebraska Act lets settlers resolve slavery issue, fuels dispute over slavery.

1861: Southern states secede, set up Confederate States of America; Civil War begins.

1862: Homestead Act grants free farmland to settlers.

1863: Abraham Lincoln issues Emancipation Proclamation.

1865: Robert E. Lee surrenders to Ulysses S. Grant at Appomattox Court House, Va. (April 9); Civil War ends; Abraham Lincoln shot by John Wilkes Booth, dies the next morning (April 15); 13th Amendment, abolishing slavery, takes effect (Dec. 18).

1867: United States buys Alaska from Russia.

1869: Transcontinental railroad completed (May 10).

1876: Col. George A. Custer and 264 soldiers die at

Battle of the Little Big Horn, Mont., in Sioux Indian War (June 25).

1881: Pres. James A. Garfield shot (July 2); dies (Sept. 19).

1888: Four hundred die in Great Blizzard in eastern U.S. (March 11–14).

1889: In Johnstown, Pa., at least 2,209 die in flood (May 31).

1890: Battle of Wounded Knee, S. Dak., marks last major battle between Indians and troops (Dec. 29); Ellis Island (New York) opens as immigration depot; Sherman Antitrust Act enacted.

1896: U.S. Supreme Court approves "separate but equal" segregation doctrine in Plessy v. Ferguson.

1898: Spanish American War frees Cuba from Spain.

1901: Pres. William McKinley shot (Sept. 6); dies (Sept. 14).

1903: Wright brothers complete first successful airplane flight near Kitty Hawk, N.C. (Dec. 17).

1906: San Francisco earthquake and fire kill 503 (April 18–19).

1913: 16th Amendment gives federal government power to levy income tax.

1917–18: United States fights in World War I.

1920: 18th Amendment prohibits sale of alcoholic beverages; 19th Amendment gives suffrage to women.

1927: Charles A. Lindbergh makes first solo flight across Atlantic Ocean.

1929: Stock market crash marks start of Great Depression (Oct. 29).

1933: Pres. Franklin D. Roosevelt institutes New Deal programs; Prohibition ends (Dec. 5).

1941: Japan attacks Pearl Harbor, Hawaii, leaving 2,300 dead (Dec. 7).

1941–45: U.S. fights in World War II.

1945: United States becomes charter member of United Nations.

1950: United States fights in Korean War; U.S. Sen. Joseph R. McCarthy begins campaign against officials and private citizens he accuses of having ties to Communism.

1954: Supreme Court rules segregation of public schools unconstitutional in Brown v. Board of Education (May 17).

1957: Arkansas Gov. Orval Faubus calls out National Guard to keep black students from entering all-white Central High School in Little Rock (Sept. 4); federal court orders removal of National Guard (Sept. 21).

1958: U.S. joins space race by launching satellite, Explorer 1 (Jan. 31).

1959: Alaska becomes 49th state (Jan. 3); Hawaii becomes 50th state (Aug. 21).

1960: U-2 spy plane shot down in Soviet Union (May 1).

1961: United States severs relations with Cuba (Jan. 3); Cuba repulses U.S.-backed Bay of Pigs invasion aimed at overthrowing Premier Fidel Castro (April 17).

1962: Lt. Col. John H. Glenn, Jr., becomes first American to orbit Earth (Feb. 20); Soviet Union removes missiles from Cuba; James Meredith becomes first black student at University of Mississippi after troops end riots (Oct. 1).

1963: In Washington, D.C., 200,000 people demonstrate for equal civil rights for blacks (Aug. 28); Pres. John F. Kennedy assassinated by Lee Harvey Oswald in Dallas, Tex. (Nov. 22).

1964: Congress passes omnibus civil rights bills banning discrimination in jobs, voting, public accommodations, etc. (June 29); Congress passes Tonkin Resolution authorizing military action in Vietnam (Aug. 2).

1965: United States sends combat troops to Vietnam; 34 die in riots in Watts section of Los Angeles (Aug. 11–16).

1968: Civil rights leader Martin Luther King, Jr., assassinated in Memphis, Tenn., by James Earl Ray (April 4); U.S. Sen. Robert F. Kennedy (D-N.Y.) shot by Sirhan Sirhan in Los Angeles (June 5), dies the next day (June 6); riots disrupt Democratic National Convention (Aug. 29).

1969: Astronaut Neil A. Armstrong becomes the first man to walk on the moon (July 20); 250,000 march on Washington, D.C., to protest Vietnam War (Nov. 15).

1970: Four students die at Kent State University in Ohio when National Guardsmen fire into crowd during a war protest (May 4).

1972: Five men arrested for breaking into Democratic National Committee offices in the Watergate complex in Washington, D.C. (June 17).

1973: U.S. Supreme Court rules that states may not prevent abortions in the first six months of pregnancy in Roe v. Wade (Jan. 22); Vietnam peace pacts signed (Jan. 27); Vice Pres. Spiro T. Agnew resigns due to charges of tax evasion (Oct. 10).

1974: Richard M. Nixon becomes first president to resign (Aug. 9).

1979: An accident at Three Mile Island nuclear reactor near Middletown, Pa., causes part of the uranium core to melt, increasing concern about safety of nuclear power (March 28).

1982: The Equal Rights Amendment is defeated after a 10-year battle for ratification by the states.

1983: Marines join peacekeeping force in Beirut, where Moslem terrorists kill 240 of them (Oct. 23); U.S. invades Grenada (Oct. 25), and the Marxist regime is deposed.

1986: The space shuttle *Challenger* explodes, killing six astronauts and Christa McAuliffe, a teacher

(Jan. 28); Pres. Ronald Reagan denies clandestine trading of arms for hostages in Iran-*Contra* scandal (November).

1987: The stock market crashes (Oct. 19).

1988: U.S.S. *Vincennes* in Persian Gulf shoots down Iranian passenger jet by mistake, killing 290 (July 3); Pan Am Boeing 747 crashes in Lockerbie, Scotland, due to bomb, killing 259 on board and 11 on ground (Dec. 21).

1989: *Exxon Valdez* supertanker runs aground, causing massive oil spill in Alaska (March 24); earthquake hits San Francisco Bay area (Oct. 17); U.S. invades Panama (Dec. 20), forcing Manuel Noriega out of power.

1990: Former President Ronald Reagan testifies that he approved covert arms sales to Iran and aid to Nicaraguan *contras* (Feb. 22); U.S. and international coalition begin arms build-up in Saudi Arabia and Persian Gulf in preparation for war with Iraq (Aug. 3).

1991: Air war begins against Iraq (Jan. 17); U.S.-led coalition begins ground war against Iraq (Feb. 24); ceasefire declared (Feb. 28).

1992: Democratic Arkansas Gov. Bill Clinton wins the presidency in a three-way race with incumbent George Bush and Texas billionaire Ross Perot, an independent candidate (Nov. 3). U.S. troops land in Mogadishu, Somalia, in an effort to help millions of starving civilians victimized by drought and warring clans (Dec. 8).

THE DECLARATION OF INDEPENDENCE

In Congress, July 4, 1776.
A Declaration by the Representatives of the United States of America.
In General Congress Assembled.

When in the Course of human Events, it becomes necessary for one People to dissolve the Political Bands which have connected them with another, and to assume among the Powers of the Earth, the separate and equal Station to which the Laws of Nature's God entitle them, a decent Respect to the Opinions of Mankind requires that they should declare the causes which impel them to the Separation.

We hold these Truths to be self-evident, that all Men are created equal, that they are endowed by their Creator with certain unalienable Rights, that among these are Life, Liberty, and the Pursuit of Happiness — That to secure these Rights, Governments are instituted among Men, deriving their just Powers from the Consent of the Governed, that whenever any Form of Government becomes destructive of these Ends, it is the Right of the People to alter or to abolish it, and to institute new Government, laying its Foundations on such Principles, and organiz-

ing its Powers in such Form, as to them shall seem most likely to effect their Safety and Happiness. Prudence, indeed, will dictate that Governments long established should not be changed for light and transient Causes; and accordingly all Experience hath shewn, that Mankind are more disposed to suffer, while Evils are sufferable, than to right themselves by abolishing the Forms to which they are accustomed. But when a long Train of Abuses and Usurpations, pursuing invariably the same Object, evinces a design to reduce them under absolute Despotism, it is their Right, it is their Duty, to throw off such Government, and to provide new Guards for their future Security. Such has been the patient Sufferance of these Colonies; and such is now the Necessity which constrains them to alter their former Systems of Government. The History of the present King of Great-Britain is a History of repeated Injuries and Usurpations, all having in direct Object the Establishment of an absolute Tyranny over these States. To prove this, let Facts be submitted to a candid World.

He has refused his Assent to Laws, the most wholesome and necessary to the public Good.

He has forbidden his Governors to pass Laws of immediate and pressing Importance, unless suspended in their Operation till his Assent should be obtained; and when so suspended, he has utterly neglected to attend them.

He has refused to pass other Laws for the Accommodation of large Districts of People, unless those People would relinquish the Right of Representation in the Legislature, a Right inestimable to them, and formidable to Tyrants only.

He has called together Legislative Bodies at Places unusual, uncomfortable, and distant from the Depository of their public Records, for the sole Purpose of fatiguing them into Compliance with his Measures.

He has dissolved Representative Houses repeatedly, for opposing with manly Firmness his Invasions on the Rights of the People.

He has refused for a long Time, after such Dissolutions, to cause others to be elected; whereby the Legislative Powers, incapable of Annihilation, have returned to the People at large for their exercise; the State remaining in the mean time exposed to all the Dangers of Invasion from without, and Convulsions within.

He has endeavoured to prevent the Population of these States; for that Purpose obstructing the Laws for Naturalization of Foreigners; refusing to pass others to encourage their Migrations hither, and raising the Conditions of new Appropriations of Lands.

He has obstructed the Administration of Justice, by refusing his Assent to Laws for establishing Judiciary Powers.

PRESIDENTS OF THE UNITED STATES

Name	Party	Years in Office	State	Born–Died	Election Opponent (main)
George Washington	Fed.	1789–97	Va.	1732–99	unopposed
John Adams	Fed.	1797–1801	Mass.	1735–1826	Thomas Jefferson (Dem.-Rep.)
Thomas Jefferson	Dem.-Rep.	1801–9	Va.	1743–1826	1800, John Adams (Fed.); 1804, Charles Pinckney (Fed.)
James Madison	Dem.-Rep.	1809–17	Va.	1751–1836	1808, Charles Pinckney (Fed.); 1812, DeWitt Clinton (Fed.)
James Monroe	Dem.-Rep.	1817–25	Va.	1758–1831	1816, Rufus King (Fed.); 1820, John Q. Adams (Dem.-Rep.)
John Quincy Adams	Dem.-Rep.	1825–29	Mass.	1767–1848	Andrew Jackson, William Crawford, Henry Clay (all Dem.-Rep.)
Andrew Jackson	Dem.	1829–37	Tenn.	1767–1845	1828, John Q. Adams (Nat.-Rep.); 1832, Henry Clay (Nat.-Rep.)
Martin Van Buren	Dem.	1837–41	N.Y.	1782–1862	William Henry Harrison (Whig)
William Henry Harrison	Whig	1841	Ohio	1773–1841[1]	Martin Van Buren (Dem.)
John Tyler	Whig	1841–45	Va.	1790–1862	succeeded Harrison
James Knox Polk	Dem.	1845–49	Tenn.	1795–1849	Henry Clay (Whig)
Zachary Taylor	Whig	1849–50	La.	1784–1850[1]	Lewis Cass (Dem.)
Millard Fillmore	Whig	1850–53	N.Y.	1800–74	succeeded Taylor
Franklin Pierce	Dem.	1853–57	N.H.	1804–69	Winfield Scott (Whig)
James Buchanan	Dem.	1857–61	Penn.	1791–1868	John C. Frémont (Rep.)
Abraham Lincoln	Rep.	1861–65	Ill.	1809–65[2]	1860, Stephen A. Douglas, John Breckinridge (both Dem.); 1864, George B. McClellan (Dem.)
Andrew Johnson	Dem.	1865–69	Tenn.	1808–75	succeeded Lincoln
Ulysses Simpson Grant	Rep.	1869–77	Ohio	1822–85	1868, Horatio S. Seymour (Dem.); 1872, Horace Greeley (Liberal Rep.-Dem.)
Rutherford B. Hayes	Rep.	1877–81	Ohio	1822–93	Samuel J. Tilden (Dem.)
James Abram Garfield	Rep.	1881	Ohio	1831–81[2]	Winfield S. Hancock (Dem.)
Chester Alan Arthur	Rep.	1881–85	N.Y.	1829–86	succeeded Garfield
Grover Cleveland	Dem.	1885–89	N.Y.	1837–1908	James G. Blaine (Rep.)
Benjamin Harrison	Rep.	1889–93	Ind.	1833–1901	Grover Cleveland (Dem.)
Grover Cleveland	Dem.	1893–97	N.Y.	1837–1908	Benjamin Harrison (Rep.)
William McKinley	Rep.	1897–1901	Ohio	1843–1901[2]	William J. Bryan (Dem.-Pop.)
Theodore Roosevelt	Rep.	1901–09	N.Y.	1858–1919	1900, William Jennings Bryan (Dem.); 1904, Alton B. Parker (Dem.)
William Howard Taft	Rep.	1909–13	Ohio	1857–1930	William J. Bryan (Dem.)
Woodrow Wilson	Dem.	1913–21	N.J.	1856–1924	1912, Theodore Roosevelt (Progressive), William Taft (Rep.); 1916, Charles Hughes (Rep.)

He has made Judges dependent on his Will alone, for the Tenure of their Offices, and the Amount and Payment of their Salaries.

He has erected a Multitude of new Offices, and sent hither Swarms of Officers to harass our People, and eat out their Substance.

He has kept among us, in Times of Peace, Standing Armies, without the consent of our Legislatures.

He has affected to render the Military independent of and superior to the Civil Power.

He has combined with others to subject us to a Jurisdiction foreign to our Constitution, and unacknowledged by our Laws; giving his Assent to their Acts of pretended Legislation:

For quartering large Bodies of Armed Troops among us;

For protecting them, by a mock Trial, from Punishment for any Murders which they should commit on the Inhabitants of these States;

PRESIDENTS OF THE UNITED STATES

Name	Party	Years in Office	State	Born–Died	Election Opponent (main)
Warren Gamaliel Harding	Rep.	1921–23	Ohio	1865–1923[1]	James M. Cox (Dem.)
Calvin Coolidge	Rep.	1923–29	Mass.	1872–1933	succeeded Harding; 1924, John W. David (Dem.)
Herbert Clark Hoover	Rep.	1929–33	Calif.	1874–1964	Alfred E. Smith (Dem.)
Franklin D. Roosevelt	Dem.	1933–45	N.Y.	1882–1945[1]	1932, Herbert Hoover (Rep.); 1936, Alfred M. Landon (Rep.); 1940, Wendell L. Willkie (Rep.); 1944, Thomas E. Dewey (Rep.)
Harry S Truman[4]	Dem.	1945–53	Mo.	1884–1972	succeeded Roosevelt; 1948, Thomas E. Dewey (Rep.)
Dwight David Eisenhower	Rep.	1953–61	Kans.	1890–1969	1952, Adlai E. Stevenson (Dem.); 1956, Adlai E. Stevenson (Dem.)
John Fitzgerald Kennedy	Dem.	1961–63	Mass.	1917–63[2]	Richard M. Nixon (Rep.)
Lyndon Baines Johnson	Dem.	1963–69	Tex.	1908–73	succeeded Kennedy; 1964, Barry M. Goldwater (Rep.)
Richard Milhous Nixon	Rep.	1969–74[3]	Calif.	1913–	1968, Hubert H. Humphrey (Dem.); 1972, George S. McGovern (Dem.)
Gerald Rudolph Ford	Rep.	1974–77	Mich.	1913–	succeeded Nixon
Jimmy (James) Carter	Dem.	1977–81	Ga.	1924–	Gerald R. Ford (Rep.)
Ronald Reagan	Rep.	1981–89	Calif.	1911–	1980, Jimmy Carter (Dem.); 1984, Walter F. Mondale (Dem.)
George Bush	Rep.	1989–93	Texas	1924–	1988, Michael S. Dukakis (Dem.)
William J. Clinton	Dem.	1993–	Ark.	1946–	George Bush (Rep.), Ross Perot (Ind.)

[1.] Died of natural causes while in office.
[2.] Assassinated.
[3.] Resigned.
[4.] Harry Truman had no middle name, only an initial. The use of a period after the initial is optional. He professed no preference.

VICE PRESIDENTS OF THE UNITED STATES

Name/Inauguration		Name/Inauguration		Name/Inauguration	
John Quincy Adams	1789	Andrew Johnson	1865	Charles Curtis	1929
Thomas Jefferson	1797	Schuyler Colfax	1869	John Nance Garner	1933
Aaron Burr	1801	Henry Wilson	1873	Henry Agard Wallace	1941
George Clinton	1805	William A. Wheeler	1877	Harry S. Truman[4]	1945
Elbridge Gerry	1813	Chester A. Arthur	1881	Alben W. Barkley	1949
Daniel D. Tompkins	1817	Thomas A. Hendricks	1885	Richard M. Nixon	1953
John C. Calhoun	1825	Levi P. Morton	1889	Lyndon B. Johnson	1961
Martin Van Buren	1833	Adlai E. Stevenson	1893	Hubert H. Humphrey	1965
Richard M. Johnson	1837	Garret A. Hobart	1897	Spiro T. Agnew	1969
John Tyler	1841	Theodore Roosevelt	1901	Gerald R. Ford	1973
George M. Dallas	1845	Charles W. Fairbanks	1905	Nelson A. Rockefeller	1974
Millard Fillmore	1849	James S. Sherman	1909	Walter F. Mondale	1977
William R. King	1853	Thomas R. Marshall	1913	George Bush	1981
John C. Breckinridge	1857	Calvin Coolidge	1921	Dan Quayle	1989
Hannibal Hamlin	1861	Charles G. Dawes	1925	Albert A. Gore, Jr.	1993

For cutting off our Trade with all Parts of the World;

For imposing Taxes on us without our Consent;

For depriving us, in many Cases, of the Benefits of Trial by Jury;

For transporting us beyond Seas to be tried for pretended Offences;

For abolishing the free System of English Laws in a neighbouring Province, establishing therein an arbitrary Government, and enlarging its Boundaries, so as to render it at once an Example and fit Instrument for introducing the same absolute Rule into these Colonies;

For taking away our Charters, abolishing our most

valuable Laws, and altering fundamentally the Forms of our Governments;

For suspending our own Legislatures, and declaring themselves invested with Power to legislate for us in all Cases whatsoever.

He has abdicated Government here, by declaring us out of his Protection and waging War against us.

He has plundered our Seas, ravaged our Coasts, burnt our Towns, and destroyed the Lives of our People.

He is, at this Time, transporting large Armies of foreign Mercenaries to compleat the Works of Death, Desolation, and Tyranny, already begun with circumstances of Cruelty and Perfidy, scarcely paralleled in the most barbarous Ages, and totally unworthy the Head of a civilized Nation.

He has constrained our fellow Citizens taken Captive on the high Seas to bear Arms against their Country, to become the Executioners of their Friends and Brethren, or to fall themselves by their Hands.

He has excited domestic Insurrections amongst us, and he has endeavoured to bring to the Inhabitants of our Frontiers, the merciless Indian Savages, whose known Rule of Warfare, is an undistinguished Destruction, of all Ages, Sexes and Conditions.

In every stage of these Oppressions we have Petitioned for Redress in the most humble Terms: Our repeated Petitions have been answered only by repeated injury. A Prince, whose Character is thus marked by every act that may define a Tyrant, is unfit to be the Ruler of a free People.

Nor have we been wanting in Attentions to our British brethren. We have warned them from Time to Time of Attempts by their Legislature to extend an unwarrantable Jurisdiction over us. We have reminded them of the Circumstance of our Emigration and Settlement here. We have appealed to their native Justice and Magnanimity, and we have conjured them by the Ties of our common Kindred to disavow these Usurpations, which, would inevitably interrupt our Connections and Correspondence. They too have been deaf to the Voice of Justice and of Consanguinity. We must, therefore, acquiesce in the Necessity, which denounces our Separation, and hold them, as we hold the rest of Mankind, Enemies in War, in Peace, Friends.

We, therefore, the Representatives of the United States of America, in General Congress, Assembled, appealing to the Supreme Judge of the World for the Rectitude of our Intentions, do, in the Name, and by the Authority of the good People of these Colonies, solemnly Publish and Declare, That these United Colonies are, and of Right ought to be, Free and Independent States; that they are absolved from all Allegiance to the British Crown, and that all political Connection between them and the State of Great-Britain, is and ought to be totally dissolved; and that as Free and Independent States, they have full Power to levy War, conclude Peace, contract Alliances, establish Commerce, and to do all other Acts and Things which Independent States may of right do. And for the support of this Declaration, with a firm Reliance on the Protection of our divine Providence, we mutually pledge to each other our Lives, our Fortunes, and our sacred honor.

Signed by Order and in Behalf of the Congress,
   John Hancock, President
   Attest.
Charles Thomson, Secretary

[SIGNERS OF THE DECLARATION OF INDEPENDENCE]

New Hampshire:
John Hancock
Josiah Bartlett
William Whipple
Matthew Thornton

Massachusetts-Bay:
Samuel Adams
John Adams
Robert Treat Paine
Elbridge Gerry

Rhode-Island and Providence, &c.:
Stephen Hopkins
William Ellery

Connecticut:
Roger Sherman
Samuel Huntington
William Williams
Oliver Wolcott

New-York:
William Floyd
Philip Livingston
Francis Lewis
Lewis Morris

New-Jersey:
Richard Stockton
John Witherspoon
Francis Hopkinson
John Hart
Abraham Clark

Pennsylvania:
Robert Morris
Benjamin Rush
Benjamin Franklin
John Morton
George Clymer
James Smith
George Taylor
James Wilson
George Ross

Delaware:
Caesar Rodney
George Read
Thomas McKean [his name was added later, probably in 1781]

Maryland:
Samuel Chase
William Paca
Thomas Stone
Charles Carroll

Virginia:
George Wythe
Richard Henry Lee
Thomas Jefferson
Benjamin Harrison
Thomas Nelson, Jr.
Francis Lightfoot Lee
Carter Braxton

North-Carolina:
William Hooper
Joseph Hewes
John Penn

South-Carolina:
Edward Rutledge
Thomas Heyward, Jr.
Thomas Lynch, Jr.
Arthur Middleton

Georgia:
Button Gwinnett
Lyman Hall
George Walton

THE GETTYSBURG ADDRESS

(Delivered by Pres. Abraham Lincoln at the dedication of a national cemetery at Gettysburg, Pa., Nov. 19, 1863. The cemetery was the site of the battle that marked the turning point in the Civil War on July 1–3, 1863.)

Four score and seven years ago our fathers brought forth on this continent, a new nation, conceived in Liberty, and dedicated to the proposition that all men are created equal. Now we are engaged in a great civil war, testing whether that nation or any nation so conceived and so dedicated, can long endure. We are met on a great battle-field of that war. We have come to dedicate a portion of that field, as a final resting place for those who here gave their lives that this nation might live. It is altogether fitting and proper that we should do this. But, in a larger sense, we can not dedicate—we can not consecrate—we can not hallow—this ground. The brave men, living and dead, who struggled here, have consecrated it, far above our poor power to add or detract. The world will little note, nor long remember what we say here, but it can never forget what they did here. It is for us the living, rather, to be dedicated here to the unfinished work which they who fought here have thus far so nobly advanced. It is rather for us to be here dedicated to the great task remaining before us—that from these honored dead we take increased devotion to that cause for which they gave the last full measure of devotion—that we here highly resolve that these dead shall not have died in vain—that this nation, under God, shall have a new birth of freedom—and that government of the people, by the people, for the people, shall not perish from the earth.

WORLD HISTORY

GEOLOGIC TIMELINE

When dealing with geologic time, all numbers are approximate. Experts frequently differ on the lengths of particular periods and epochs as new scientific information causes theories to be revised and adjusted.

13 to 20 billion years ago: Universe is created.

10 billion years ago: Galaxies begin to form.

11.9 billion years ago: Stars begin to shine.

8 billion years ago: Interstellar cloud forms that will eventually contract to form the Solar System. A nebula collapses, forming the Sun (6 billion years ago). Earth forms (4.7 billion years ago).

4.5 to 4 billion years ago: Earth assumes its present structure: inner core, mantle, outer crust and atmosphere.

3.4 billion to 3 billion years ago: Microscopic life forms (bacteria and nonphotosynthetic blue-green algae) develop on Earth.

2.9 billion years ago: Early photosynthetic organisms appear.

600 million years ago: Soft-bodied invertebrates appear.

Paleozoic Era: The Paleozoic Era began 570 million years ago and lasted 325 million years. During this time, life forms developed on Earth, starting with simple invertebrate marine creatures and ending with reptiles and mammal-like reptiles. There are six periods within the Paleozoic Era, the earliest being the Cambrian Period. History before this era is, therefore, known as Pre-Cambrian.

Period	Began	Lasted	Events
Cambrian	570 million years ago	65 million years	Protozoans, trilobites proliferate in oceans.
Ordovician	505 million years ago	67 million years	Snails, jawless fish and other invertebrates develop.
Silurian	438 million years ago	30 million years	Sea scorpions, corals, fish with jaws develop. Plants proliferate on land.
Devonian	408 million years ago	48 million years	Fish proliferate, including lungfish and sharks; starfish develop. First insects appear.
Carboniferous	360 million years ago	74 million years	Beds of vegetation, which will become modern-day coal deposits, are laid down in swampy forests. Insects and amphibians develop. Reptiles appear.
Permian	286 million years ago	41 million years	Early finbacked reptiles, mammal-like reptiles appear.

Mesozoic Era: The Mesozoic Era began 245 million years ago and lasted 179 million years. It is commonly known as the Age of the Reptiles, when dinosaurs roamed the earth. They evolved during the era and were extinct at the end of it. The Mesozoic Era includes three periods.

Period	Began	Lasted	Events
Triassic	245 million years ago	37 million years	Marine reptiles (including plesiosaurs and ichthyosaurs) develop late in the period, as do crocodiles and small dinosaurs (terrestrial reptiles).
Jurassic	208 million years ago	64 million years	Sea-going reptiles proliferate; large dinosaurs develop, as do flying reptiles (pterosaurs).
Cretaceous	144 million years ago	78 million years	Dinosaurs and other reptiles prevailed on Earth. Mammals, ancient birds, modern fish and snakes were also abundant. By the end of the period, the dinosaurs were extinct, perhaps in part because of their inability to adapt to a changing environment.

Cenozoic Era: The Cenozoic Era is the modern era. It began 66 million years ago. It is marked by the development of modern plants and animals, including man. It is divided into two periods, the Tertiary and the Quaternary. The Tertiary Period comprises five epochs: Paleocene, Eocene, Oligocene, Miocene and Pliocene. The Quarternary Period comprises two periods: Pleistocene and Holocene.

Period	Epoch	Began	Lasted	Events
Tertiary	Paleocene	66 million years ago	8.6 million years	Early primates, horses, kangaroos, rodents develop.
"	Eocene	57.4 million years ago	21.2 million years	Whales, penguins, bats, camels, elephants, dogs, cats develop.
"	Oligocene	36.2 million years ago	12.9 million years	Deer, pigs, monkeys appear.
"	Miocene	23.3 million years ago	18.4 million years	Seals, dolphins, early apes appear.
"	Pliocene	4.9 million years ago	3.3 million years	Apes diversify, early hominids appear, including *Homo habilis*. Mammoths appear.
Quarternary	Pleistocene	1.6 million years ago	1.6 million years	Four major ice ages, separated by meltings, occur. At the end of the last ice age, the glaciers that cover North America and Eurasia melt, shaping present topography. Mammoths, saber-toothed tigers become extinct. Man evolves.
"	Holocene	10,000 years ago	10,000 years	Modern humans, animals and present plants exist.

B.C. (Before Christ)

10,000–4500 B.C.: Cities develop from agricultural settlements. First walled cities, pottery, use of metals appear.

4500–3001 B.C.: City-state developed by Sumerians in Tigris and Euphrates valleys. **First phonetic writing** used. Earliest date on Egyptian calendar (4236 B.C.). Earliest date on Jewish calendar (3760 B.C.). Earliest date in Mayan chronology (3372 B.C.).

3000–2001 B.C.: Rule of Pharaohs begins in Egypt. First Egyptian pyramid (Cheops) built. Great Sphinx of Giza built. Papyrus used by Egyptians. First iron objects manufactured.

2000–1501 B.C.: Bronze Age begins in Europe (c. 2000 B.C.). **Egypt enslaves Israelites.** King Hammurabi of Babylon develops oldest code of laws. Code of Hammurabi establishes criminal laws, lines of inheritance. **Stonehenge erected** in England. Shang dynasty founded in China (1760 B.C.).

1500–1001 B.C.: Tutankhamen rules in Egypt. **Moses leads Israelites out of slavery** in Egypt, into Canaan. Moses receives the Ten Commandments. Greeks destroy Troy (1193 B.C.) during the **Trojan War.** Iron Age begins in Asia (c. 1400 B.C.). Chou dynasty begins in China (1122 B.C.). Saul becomes first king of Israel (1002 B.C.); he is defeated by the Philistines.

1000–901 B.C.: Hebrews establish Jerusalem as capital of Israel (1000 B.C.). David is king of Israel and Judah, with Jerusalem as capital (1000 to 960 B.C.). After his death, his son, Solomon, replaces him as king (960 to 925 B.C.). Kingdom is divided into Israel and Judah (935 B.C.). Works begins on Old Testament. In Sierra Nevada and California, Pinto Indians build huts of wood, reeds and loam.

900–801 B.C.: Carthage founded by Phoenicians (815 B.C.). The *Iliad* and the *Odyssey*, ascribed to the Greek poet Homer, are written.

800–701 B.C.: First Olympic Games are held in Greece (776 B.C.). **Rome is founded** (c. 753 B.C.). Celts move into England.

700–601 B.C.: Byzantium established by Greeks. **Acropolis begun in Athens.** Chinese philosopher Lao-Tse, founder of Taoism, is born (604 B.C.).

600–501 B.C.: King Nebuchadnezzar II of Babylon builds empire, holds Jews captive, creates Hanging Gardens of Babylon. **Democracy established in Athens. Buddha is born** (563 B.C.). Confucius is born (551 B.C.).

500–401 B.C.: Greeks defeat Persians. Sparta defeats Athens in **Peloponnesian Wars.** Sophocles (496–406 B.C.). writes Greek dramas. Hippocrates, the Father of Medicine, is born in Greece (460 B.C.).

400–301 B.C.: The first five books of the Old Testament take their final form. **Philip of Macedon conquers Greece,** is assassinated. His son, Alexander the Great, succeeds him. Greek philosopher Socrates is tried and executed (399 B.C.). His student, Plato, writes *Apologia* in his defense (396 B.C.). Euclid establishes tenets of geometry. The philosopher **Aristotle teaches and writes in Greece.** Chandragupta founds first empire in India.

300–201 B.C.: Rome defeats Carthage in the First Punic War (264–241 B.C.) and dominates Mediterranean. Archimedes, the Greek mathematician, develops fundamental theories. In the Second Punic War (219–201 B.C.) the Carthaginian general **Hannibal crosses the Alps** and reaches the gates of Rome. He retreats and is defeated. Ch'in Dynasty begins in China (221 B.C.). **The Great Wall of China**

is begun (c. 215 B.C.) when convicts are used to link pieces of older walls.

200–101 B.C.: In the Third Punic War (149–146 B.C.) Rome destroys Carthage. **Rome dominates Europe.** The Venus de Milo sculpture is created (c. 140 B.C.).

100–1 B.C.: Julius Caesar (100–44 B.C.) invades Britain, conquers Gaul. **Cleopatra VII becomes last queen of Egypt.** Herod becomes Roman governor of Judea. **Caesar murdered** by conspirators Brutus and Cassius Longinus. Caesar's nephew, Octavian, defeats Mark Antony and Cleopatra, establishes Roman empire as Emperor Augustus.

1–1000 A.D. (Anno Domini)

1–100 A.D.: **Jesus Christ is born** (date is estimated at between 4 B.C. and 7 A.D.). Jesus Christ crucified (c. 30 A.D.). Followers establish Christian communities in eastern Mediterranean. Paul of Tarsus spreads teachings to Asia Minor, Greece, Rome (30–60 A.D.). **Romans begin persecution of Christians.** After Great Fire of Rome (64 A.D.) Emperor Nero uses Christians as scapegoats, kills Sts. Peter and Paul. Jews revolt against Rome (66–70 A.D.). Jerusalem is destroyed (70 A.D.). Romans build Colosseum (71–80 A.D.). **Mt. Vesuvius erupts** (79 A.D.), destroying Pompeii. Chinese produce first paper made from plant fibers (c. 100 A.D.).

101–200 A.D.: Hadrian rules Rome (117–138 A.D.), codifies Roman law, builds Hadrian's Wall between England and Scotland. Judea becomes Palestine as Jewish revolt (132–135 A.D.) is suppressed. **Jews are banned from Jerusalem** and dispersion (Diaspora) begins (135 A.D.). Barbarians invade Roman Empire from the northeast (161–180 A.D.).

201–300 A.D.: In North America, **the Golden Age of Mayan civilization begins** (c. 250 A.D.). Mayans begin building temples in Central America.

301–400 A.D.: Constantine the Great becomes Roman emperor (306 A.D.). He becomes Christian (312 A.D.) and legalizes Christianity in the Roman Empire (313 A.D.). He founds Constantinople (now Istanbul) on the site of Greek Byzantium (330 A.D.). **Roman Empire is permanently divided** (395 A.D.). Rome becomes capital in the West, Constantinople in the East.

401–500 A.D.: Visigoths plunder Rome (410 A.D.). Attila becomes leader of the Huns (433 A.D.). **The Vandals destroy Rome** (455 A.D.). Western Roman Empire is overthrown (476 A.D.) and Odoacer, German chief, becomes first king of Italy.

501–600 A.D.: Justinian, emperor of the Eastern Roman Empire, conquers Italy, North Africa and southeastern Spain (527–565 A.D.). **Illuminated**

manuscripts are produced in monasteries in northern Europe (c. 530 A.D.).

601–700 A.D.: **Mohammad begins preaching** in Mecca (612 A.D.). His followers (Muslims) begin Holy War in Medina (622 A.D.). **Islam founded.** Mohammad dies (632 A.D.). Arabs conquer Syria, Palestine, Egypt and North Africa (by 680 A.D.).

701–800 A.D.: **Feudalism begins in western Europe.** Arabs invade Spain, southern France (711 A.D.). Muslim advance into Europe is stopped (732 A.D.) by Franks at Battle of Poitiers. **Charlemagne** becomes sole king of the Franks (771 A.D.) after the death of his brother. Later crowned emperor by Pope Leo III in Rome (800 A.D.). **Vikings begin raids on Britain** and the coast of Europe (780 A.D.). Anglo-Saxon epic poem **Beowulf** written by unknown poet (c. 800 A.D.).

801–900 A.D.: Danish Vikings invade France and Germany (843 A.D.). Frankish kingdom ends. Swedish Vikings invade Russia (862 A.D.). **The Eastern Church and the Roman Church separate** (867–890 A.D.). Norwegians establish a colony in Iceland (872 A.D.). Alfred the Great defeats the Danes, rules southern England (878–899 A.D.).

901–1000 A.D.: German King Otto I conquers central Europe, is crowned Holy Roman Emperor (962 A.D.). Edgar of Wessex becomes the first king of England (973 A.D.). **Eric the Red (a Norseman) establishes a colony in Greenland** (982–986 A.D.). His son, **Leif Ericsson, discovers Vinland on the coast of Newfoundland** (c. 1000) and starts a colony there. **The Chinese invent gunpowder.**

1001–1992

Please see additional sections of chapter entitled Wars and Armed Conflict, page 119, for separate chronological overviews of the American Revolution, the Civil War, World War I, World War II, the Korean War, the Vietnam War and the War in the Persian Gulf. See pages 112–114 for the dissolution of the USSR.

1001–1100: Danes (under King Knut or Canute) assume control in England (1013–42). Chinese print with movable type (c. 1040). **Duncan, the king of Scotland, is murdered by Macbeth** (1040), who succeeds him as king. Macbeth is defeated by Malcolm and Siward of Northumbria at Dunsinane (1054). **William the Conqueror of Normandy takes control of England with victory at Battle of Hastings** (1066), where he defeats England's last Saxon king (Harold II). He is crowned King William I. In 1095, Pope Urban II calls for war to take the Holy Land from the Moslems. In **the First**

Crusade (1096–99) French and Norman peasants, who are filled with religious fervor but ill prepared, are annihilated when they reach Asia Minor. They are followed by armies, who defeat the Turks in Constantinople on their way to free the Holy Land. In 1099 the crusaders take Jerusalem. Timbuktu becomes the cultural center of western Africa (c. 1100).

1101–1200: In **the Second Crusade** (1147–49), the forces of King Louis VII of France and Emperor Conrad III attack Damascus but accomplish little. In England, Oxford University is founded (c. 1167). A church-state struggle for power ends when **Henry II orders the execution of Archbishop Thomas Becket** (1170). Jerusalem is retaken by Saladin, the sultan of Turkish Syria and Egypt (1187). **The Third Crusade** (1189–92) fails militarily, but a three-year truce between Saladin and King Richard I of England gives Christians access to Jerusalem. In America, **the Mayan civilization collapses** in Central America and **the Inca civilization begins its rise** in Peru (c. 1200).

1201–1300: **The Fourth Crusade** (1202–4) stops at Constantinople en route to Jerusalem, sacking the city and establishing the Latin Empire of Constantinople. This assault by one Christian force against another does much to discredit the Crusades and destroys one of their purported goals—to reconcile the Latin and Greek churches. **The Children's Crusade** fails dismally as French and German children die, are captured or are sold into slavery during an unsuccessful attempt to reach the Holy Land (1212). The Mongol leader **Genghis Khan invades China** (1214), conquers Persia (1218) and invades Russia (1223). In England, barons force King John to sign **the Magna Carta,** which limits royal power (1215). **The Fifth Crusade** tries but fails to take Egypt (1218–21). The Emperor Frederick II leads the **Sixth Crusade** against the Pope's wishes (1228–29) and retakes Jerusalem. The Moslems reclaim Jerusalem (1244), which remains under their control until 1917. In China, the Mongol leader **Kublai Khan** rules (1260–94). The Greek army recaptures Constantinople, restoring the Byzantine Empire (1261). **The Eighth Crusade,** led by Louis IX of France and Prince Edward of England, reaches Tunis but is a military failure. King Edward I conquers Wales (1276–84) and Scotland (1285–1307). In Turkey, Osman I founds the Ottoman dynasty (1290–1326). The Italian explorer **Marco Polo travels to China, India, Sumatra and Persia** (1271–95).

1301–1400: In Africa, the Mali Empire reaches its apex (1307–32). The Italian poet **Dante begins** *The Divine Comedy* (1307). Scotland regains independence (1314). **The Renaissance begins in Italy** (c. 1325). **Aztecs establish a capital city** on the site of the present Mexico City (c. 1325). **The Hundred Years' War** (1337–1453) for control of France begins when King Edward III of England claims the French throne. **Bubonic plague (Black Death),** probably spread by returning Crusaders, kills at least 25 million people in Europe (1347–51). **Great Schism** (1378–1415) divides Europe as rival popes (Urban VI in Rome and Clement VII in Avignon, France) fight for control of the Roman Catholic Church. **Geoffrey Chaucer writes** *The Canterbury Tales* (1387–1400).

1401–1500: **Henry V defeats the French at Agincourt** and captures Paris (1415–20). **Joan of Arc leads the French** against the English (1428). She is victorious at Orléans (1429), is later captured (1430) and burned at the stake (1431). **The Hundred Years' War ends** when the French defeat the English at Castillon (1453). In Germany, the printer **Johann Gutenberg develops molds to cast individual letters of type** in metal (1438). His first books are printed (c. 1450). In Tibet, **the first Dalai Lama is recognized as the high priest of Buddhism** (c. 1447). The Medicis make Florence an arts center (c. 1450). The Byzantine Empire ends when the Turks capture Constantinople (1453). In England, nobles clash for power in the **War of the Roses** (1455–85). Ivan the Great becomes the first czar of Russia (1462). In Milan, **Leonardo da Vinci paints** *The Last Supper* (1497). An age of exploration unfolds: **Bartolomeu Dias of Portugal rounds the Cape of Good Hope** at the southern tip of Africa (1488); **Columbus, sponsored by Ferdinand and Isabella of Spain, discovers the Bahamas** (1492); in later trips, he sights Dominica, Jamaica, Puerto Rico, Honduras and Panama (1493–1504); **John Cabot discovers Newfoundland** while seeking a northwest sea route to India (1497–98); **Vasco da Gama of Portugal reaches the west coast of India** after sailing around Africa (1498). The Italian explorer **Amerigo Vespucci explores the coast of South America** (1499–1501).

1501–1600: **Leonardo da Vinci paints the** *Mona Lisa* (c. 1503). St. Peter's Church is begun in Rome (1506). Completion takes 120 years and includes the work of Michelangelo, da Vinci and Raphael. Henry VIII is crowned in England (1509). The cleric **Martin Luther begins the Reformation in Germany** when he posts his 95 theses denouncing church abuses on a church door in Wittenberg (1517). In Mexico, **Hernán Cortez defeats the Aztecs and seizes Mexico for Spain** (1519–21). Ferdinand Magellan of Portugal sets out to circumnavigate the globe (1519). He is killed, but one of his ships completes the voyage (1522). **Martin Luther is excommunicated** (1520). **The coast of New England and New York is explored by Giovanni de Verrazzano,** an Italian sailing under the French flag. Troops of the Holy Roman Empire attack Rome and imprison the pope (Clement VII), marking the end of the Italian Renaissance. **Reformation begins in England** when Henry VIII makes himself head of the English church, after having been excommunicated by the Pope. **Sir Thomas Moore is executed** as a traitor when he refuses to recognize the king as the head of the church (1535). **Jacques Cartier, the French explorer, sails up the St. Lawrence River in Canada** (1535). Henry VIII executes his second wife, Anne Boleyn (1536). **Nicolaus Copernicus, a Polish scholar, publishes his theory that the Earth revolves around the Sun,** in contradiction of church teaching (1543). The Council of Trent holds meetings to define Catholic dogma and affirm the authority of the Pope (1545–63). Queen Mary I restores Roman Catholicism in England (1553). Queen Elizabeth I is crowned (1558) and restores Protestantism. She establishes Anglican Church of England. **William Shakespeare (1564–1616) produces his first plays** (c. 1590). British dramatist **Christopher Marlowe** (1564–93) and poet **Edmund Spenser** (c. 1552–99) write. In the Netherlands, **Pieter Breughel** (1525–69) paints both religious and nonreligious subjects, often with humorous touches. **Peter Paul Rubens** (1577–1640) begins his work, ushering in the golden age of Flemish painting. Queen Elizabeth I orders **Mary, Queen of Scots, executed** for treason (1587). **The Spanish Armada is defeated by the English** (1588). Galileo (see below) experiments with falling objects (1590).

1601–1700: The English East India Company is formed to develop overseas trade (1600). **Jamestown, Va., is founded by the English** (1607). Samuel de Champlain founds a French colony at Quebec (1609). The King James Version of the Bible is published in England (1611). European Protestants revolt against Catholic domination in **The Thirty Years' War** (1618–48). **The Pilgrims sail from Plymouth, England (Sept. 6, 1620), and arrive off the Massachusetts coast** in November. They land at Plymouth Rock (Dec. 16, 1620). **Manhattan Island purchased from Indians for $24 worth of goods by Peter Minuit,** director-general of the Dutch West India Company, who founds New Amsterdam (1626). The Italian astronomer **Galileo Galilei** (1564–1642) is accused of heresy after affirming Copernicus's theory that the Sun, not the Earth, is the center of the universe (1632). He renounces his view, after being imprisoned and being threatened with torture. In England, attempts to curb the power of the Crown and the Church leads to Civil War (1642–46). **Oliver Cromwell defeats the Royalists** (1646). Charles I offers concessions after Parliament demands reforms. He is tried for treason and beheaded (1649). Cromwell is named Lord Protector. When he dies (1658) the government collapses. Parliament restores the monarchy under Charles II (1660). In North America, **the British capture New Amsterdam from the Dutch and rename it New York** (1664). The English physicist **Isaac Newton publishes his laws of motion and the theory of gravity** in *Philosophiae naturalis principia mathematica* (1687). The **Great Plague** kills 75,000 in London (1665). A year later, the **Great Fire** burns 450 acres in the city (Sept. 2–9, 1666). James II, a Catholic, becomes King of England (1685) and **British Protestants, fearing religious domination, precipitate Glorious Revolution.** Parliament invites Prince William of Orange (a Protestant grandson of Charles I) to return to England from Holland and ascend the throne (1688). James II flees to France. William III and his wife, Mary, are crowned. In France, Louis XIV revokes religious freedom for Protestants, thousands of whom flee (1685). **Peter the Great becomes Czar of Russia** (1689–1725), builds its military power and introduces many Western influences. **In Ireland, the former King James II stages a Catholic rebellion and is defeated by King William III at the Battle of the Boyne** (1690). Adolescent girls act as though they are possessed, perhaps as a prank, and touch off mass hysteria **in Salem, Mass. Fourteen women and six men are executed as witches.** The girls blame a slave, Tituba, who is beaten until she confesses. Other accusations follow (1692). Four years later, the jurors at the witchcraft trials apologize.

1701–1750: **The War of the Spanish Succession begins** (1701), marking the last attempt of France's Louis XIV to extend his rule in Europe. The war (called Queen Anne's War in America) involves widespread territorial disputes and the right of succession to the Spanish throne, which Louis XIV claims for his grandson after the death of Spain's Charles II. England, Holland and the Holy Roman Empire declare war on France to prevent it from becoming too strong in Europe and to limit its growing commercial power in North America, Asia and Africa (1702). **The United Kingdom of Great Britain is formed** when England, Wales and Scotland are joined by an act of Parliament (1707). **The War of the Spanish Succession ends** with the Peace of Utrecht (1714), which permits Louis's grandson (Philip V) to become King of Spain, with the understanding that the French and Spanish crowns will never be merged. The British Empire emerges as a major force when France surrenders Newfoundland, Nova Scotia and the Hudson Bay territory. Britain also gets Gibraltar and Minorca from Spain, along with rights to the lucrative West African slave trade.

Daniel Defoe publishes *Robinson Crusoe*, considered to be the first true English novel (1719). In Germany, **Johann Sebastian Bach** completes the *Brandenburg Concertos* (1721). **Jonathan Swift**, the Irish poet, publishes *Gulliver's Travels* (1726). In New York, **John Peter Zenger is accused of libel.** Zenger, the editor of the *New-York Weekly Journal*, is accused of libeling New York Royal Gov. William Cosby. Imprisoned, he continues publication by slipping instructions to his wife through a hole in his cell door. The Philadelphia lawyer Andrew Hamilton uses a novel defense—that Zenger should not be convicted of libel because what he printed was true. The judge (whose appointment by Cosby had been criticized by Zenger) insists that truth cannot be a defense. The jury, however, acquits Zenger after an impassioned speech by Hamilton. The verdict lays the foundation for freedom of the press in America (1735). In Sweden, the botanist **Carolus Linnaeus** publishes *Systema Naturae*, which presents an orderly system for classifying plants and animals (1735). The **War of the Austrian Succession begins** when Prussia's **Frederick the Great** seizes Silesia from Austria (1740). Britain supports Austria against France, Spain and Prussia in a war that is fought in Europe, India and North America. In Dublin, the *Messiah*, by the German composer **George Frederick Handel,** is performed for the first time (1742). The Treaty of Aix-la-Chapelle ends the War of the Austrian Succession (1748). Austria loses Silesia, but territorial boundaries in North America remain unchanged. In London, **Henry Fielding** publishes *Tom Jones* (1749).

1751–1800: **The Seven Years' War (called the French and Indian War in America) begins** (1756) when Austria tries to regain Silesia. Austria fails. Other European nations are drawn into the conflict. In America, this marks the final round of battles between France and England for control of colonies. British sea forces destroy the French fleet. **The British general James Wolfe captures Quebec (1759), defeating Gen. Louis Joseph de Montcalm on the Plains of Abraham.** Wolfe and Montcalm die in the battle. The Treaty of Paris ends the war (1763) and marks a decisive victory for the British. France loses all of its holdings on the mainland of North America: French possessions in Canada and east of the Mississippi River go to Britain; Louisiana goes to Spain. Britain also gets most of France's holdings in India, giving it dominance there.

In France, *L'Encyclopédie* is written (1751–66), under the direction of the philosopher **Denis Diderot,** and with entries by some of the leading philosophers of the day, including **Voltaire, Jean-Jacques Rousseau** and the **baron de Montesquieu.** The book is an important milestone in **the Enlightenment,** an age in which Western intellectuals turn from a religion-based view of the world to one based on empiricism. The Austrian **Franz Joseph Haydn** (1732–1809) composes symphonies. The Scottish craftsman **James Watt invents a new type of steam engine** (c. 1765) that is much more efficient than earlier models, an important step in **Britain's Industrial Revolution.**

[*See* The American Revolution, page 119]

Hawaii is discovered by Capt. James Cook (1778). Russians settle the Aleutian Islands (1785). In Europe, **Wolfgang Amadeus Mozart** composes his first major opera, *The Marriage of Figaro* (1786).

France, the prime ally of the United States during the Revolutionary War, is engulfed in problems of its own. Its involvement in the American Revolution has been expensive, and it lacks the industrial and commercial ability to profit significantly from trade with the United States. Britain, which produces goods familiar to Americans, remains a strong trading partner. In addition, France's support of the American Revolution was based on its hatred for England, not on its sympathy for populist government, which French royalty finds abhorrent. The populist movement gains momentum in France as commoners, the bourgeoisie, protest rule by the two privileged classes, the nobility and the clergy. In response, Louis XVI convenes the States-General (May 5, 1789), a French national assembly in which clergy, nobles and commoners are represented by separate bodies. The States-General had not been convened since 1614. The Third Estate (commons) joins some of the clergy and a few nobles in seeking political and social reforms that far exceed the authority of the States-General. In defiance of the king, they declare themselves the National Assembly (June 17, 1789), and vow to establish a constitution. Louis XVI yields and legalizes the Assembly. A popular force in the reform movement, Jacques Necker, the Director General of Finances and Minister of State, is dismissed by Louis XVI. **Necker's dismissal incites a Paris mob to storm the Bastille** (July 14, 1789), a fortress and prison that had become a symbol of oppression because of its rumored use by the Crown for arbitrary and secret imprisonment. **The attack marks the start of the French Revolution.** Louis XVI reinstates Necker, who resigns a year later (1790). The National Assembly abolishes feudal privileges (1789) and drafts a constitution (1791) that creates a limited monarchy and an elected, unicameral legislature (the Legislative Assembly). The preamble to the constitution is the Declaration of the Rights of Man and Citizen. The king attempts to flee, but is seized at Varennes (June 21, 1791) and forced to return to Paris and accept the new constitution.

In the United States, **the Bill of Rights** is ratified (1791). In Scotland, **James Boswell** publishes *The Life of Johnson* (1791).

A coalition of European nations—Austria, Prussia, Britain, the Netherlands and Spain—fights to restore the French nobility (1792–97). This war (the **War of the First Coalition**) begins a series of wars with France and other European nations that lasts for more than 20 years and increases France's influence in Europe.

In France, the republican Girondists and the extreme Jacobins and Cordeliers gain control of the Legislative Assembly. "Liberty, equality, fraternity" becomes a rallying cry. **Rumors of treason by King Louis XVI and Queen Marie Antoinette spur the lower classes to action. They storm the royal palace of the Tuileries** (August 1792). The Assembly suspends the king and orders a convention to draw up another constitution. Hundreds of royal prisoners are killed by mobs (Sept. 2–7, 1792). The Assembly abolishes the monarchy (Sept. 21, 1792), sets up the First Republic and tries the king for treason. **Louis XVI is executed** (January 1793). Marie Antoinette's 8-year-old son (Louis XVII) is taken from her. She is tried by a revolutionary tribunal and guillotined (Oct. 16, 1793). Louis XVII becomes the titular King of France after his father's death, but he remains imprisoned until his death about two years later. (Legends of his escape inspire several impostors to claim that they are the "lost dauphin.") The execution of Louis XVI leads to royalist uprisings, which are followed by the **Reign of Terror, directed by Maximilien Robespierre,** the leader of the Jacobins. He dominates the Committee of Public Safety, which is created (April 6, 1793) to rule the nation and root out counterrevolutionaries. The committee and the Revolutionary Tribunal reign supreme. Thousands are arrested for treason and guillotined. When the pace of executions increases in June 1794, popular discontent grows. The Reign of Terror ends when Robespierre is arrested, tried and guillotined (July 28, 1794). The third French constitution establishes the **Directory** government (1795), in which France is ruled by five men chosen by the legislature. The Directory government is corrupt and inept, characterized by internal schemes, runaway inflation and bankruptcy. **Napoleon Bonaparte overthrows the Directory** (Nov. 9–10, 1799), aided by revolutionaries who have become disillusioned with it. The Consulate government is established. Bonaparte becomes First Consul. The appearance of republican rule is maintained temporarily, but Napoleon is virtually a dictator. He works to end civil strife, forming alliances with powerful factions throughout France. He also centralizes the nation's bureaucracy and grants amnesty to thousands of émigrés, provided they take a loyalty oath. This allows many of the nation's elite to return and assume important positions in society.

In the United States, **Eli Whitney invents the cotton gin,** which reduces human labor and increases productivity in the cotton industry (1793). Farmers in Pennsylvania object to liquor taxes in the **Whiskey Rebellion.** This challenge to the authority of the federal government is crushed by a show of force, without bloodshed (1794). In England, the country physician Edward Jenner performs the **first successful vaccination against smallpox** after 20 years of experiments (1796).

In Haiti, the **slave revolt led by Toussaint l'Ouverture** forces French troops from the island (1796–1802). France's Napoleon Bonaparte conquers Rome and Egypt (1798), then Italy (1800). The English poet **Samuel Taylor Coleridge** publishes *The Rime of the Ancient Mariner* and **William Wordsworth** publishes *Tintern Abbey* (1798). In the U.S., the federal capital moves from Philadelphia to Washington, D.C.

1801–25: **Parliamentary act unites Britain and Ireland** (1801); **Catholics are excluded from voting.** In France, Napoleon increases the nation's influence by defeating Austria and acquiring land in Italy and Germany (1801). He signs an agreement with Pope Pius VII that allows French Catholics to practice their religion but gives Napoleon great influence over the Church, which further strengthens his position as leader (1801). In North America, the United States makes the **Louisiana Purchase,** buying from France 800,000 square miles of land bounded by the Mississippi River, the Rocky Mountains, the Gulf of Mexico and the Canadian border. The U.S. pays about $15 million (1803).

In France, **Napoleon becomes emperor** (1804), symbolic of his quest for absolute power, which had been cloaked in concern for the people and for domestic tranquility. He systematizes French law under the Code Napoleon, which asserts two fundamental rights: equality of all citizens before the law, and security of wealth and private property. The latter is important to the lower class, some of whom purchased lands confiscated from the Church and the nobility. In fact, France under Napoleon becomes increasingly oppressive as free expression is restricted and political foes are jailed. Napoleon appoints a minister of police, Joseph Fouché, who keeps thousands of citizens under surveillance. **Haiti declares its independence** from France (1804), becoming the first black nation to free itself from European rule.

In the U.S., former Treasury Secretary **Alexander Hamilton is killed in a duel with Vice President Aaron Burr,** the outgrowth of a political feud (1804). **Meriwether Lewis** and **William Clark** explore and map the Louisiana Territory and the Pacific Northwest (1804–6). **Robert Fulton** makes his first successful steamboat trip, from New York City to Albany, on the *Clermont* (1807).

Britain, Austria, Russia and Sweden join forces to limit the expansion of Napoleon's empire in Europe. **Lord Nelson** virtually annihilates a fleet of French and Spanish at Trafalgar, protecting England from the possibility of invasion (Oct. 21, 1805). Napoleon defeats Austrian and Russian forces at the Battle of Austerlitz (1805). French armies occupy Rome and Spain (1808). **Napoleon's army invades Russia** four years later (June 1812). By winter, they are forced to retreat, suffering one of the greatest military defeats in history. About 500,000 of his 600,000 soldiers die, including many forces volunteered by his allies, Austria and Prussia. When Napoleon refuses to accept concessions that would reduce France to its historic size and end fighting, Austria and Prussia desert Napoleon and side with Russia, Great Britain, Sweden and Portugal in the War of Liberation. **Napoleon is defeated and forced to abandon his throne** (April 4, 1814). He is exiled to Elba, off the coast of Italy, where he is allowed to live with some dignity and ample money. The Bourbon King Louis XVIII assumes the French throne.

While Great Britain has been battling Napoleon in Europe, it has also been fighting a war in America. In **1812**, the **U.S. declares war on Great Britain,** sparked by interference with American trade and the impressment of American seamen (whom British naval officers repeatedly "mistake" for deserters from the Royal Navy). The war is also sparked by the War Hawks, Congressmen from the West and South who believe British agents in Canada are inciting Indians to slaughter American settlers in the Northwest Territory. In New England, the war is unpopular, even among ship owners, and states refuse to send their militias to fight. American attacks on Canada (designed to prevent the possibility of British invasion of the Northwest Territory) fail. Detroit is surrendered to the British (Aug. 16, 1812). The U.S. frigate *Constitution* (also known as **Old Ironsides** because of its thickly tim-

bered hull) sinks the British frigate *Guerrière* off the Massachusetts coast and takes prisoners (Aug. 19, 1812), the first of many American maritime victories. The British blockade the coast (1813), but American privateers are able to slip through. They capture 1,700 British merchant vessels by the end of the war. Although Americans suffer repeated defeats on land, their success on water continues when **Capt. Oliver H. Perry defeats a British flotilla on Lake Erie** (Sept. 10, 1813). "We have met the enemy, and they are ours," Perry reports to Gen. William H. Harrison. Harrison promptly sweeps the British from Detroit and defeats the British and their Indian allies at the Battle of the Thames in Canada (Oct. 5, 1813). **Tecumseh,** Britain's most important Indian ally, is killed in the battle. The **British capture Washington, D.C.** (Aug. 24, 1814), burning the Capitol, the White House and other public buildings. The British leave Washington for Baltimore (Aug. 25–26, 1814), but the Maryland militia repels the land attack, and **Fort McHenry** withstands a heavy naval bombardment. **Francis Scott Key,** an American, is held on a British ship after attempting to obtain the release of a prisoner. He watches the attack on Fort McHenry through the night, and sees "by the dawn's early light" that the American flag's "broad stripes and bright stars" are still flying. He begins jotting down a poem recording the battle, **"The Star-Spangled Banner"** (Sept. 14, 1814). U.S. and British representatives meeting in Ghent, Belgium, accept terms of a treaty (Dec. 24, 1814). The treaty restores boundaries that existed before the war and make no mention of impressment or trading rights. Unaware that a peace treaty has been signed, **British troops attack the forces of Maj. Gen. Andrew Jackson at New Orleans** and are repulsed. The British lose 2,000; the Americans 13. The U.S. Senate ratifies the **Treaty of Ghent** (Feb. 16, 1815), marking the official end of the war.

Napoleon escapes from Elba (February 1815) and sails to France, where he marches on Paris with a small group of French officers and soldiers. Louis XVIII flees and Napoleon takes command, but his rule is short-lived. After a hundred days, **Napoleon is defeated at Waterloo** by British troops led by the Duke of Wellington. Napoleon is imprisoned on St. Helena, a rocky island off the western coast of Africa (June 18, 1815).

Spain begins to lose control in South America when **Simón Bolívar** claims independence for Venezuela (1817).

In the U.S., slavery comes to the center of the national stage for the first time when Missouri seeks to become a state, with a constitution that permits slavery. Northerners wishing to curtail slavery suggest a compromise: Missouri will not be able to import slaves, but will be able to retain its slaves until they are age 25, at which time they will be freed. The proposal fuels dissension between the North and the South, which has a stronger economic tie to slavery. House Speaker Henry Clay effects a compromise. Maine will be admitted as a free state and Missouri will be admitted as a slave state, to maintain the balance between slave and free states. However, the rest of the land in the Louisiana Purchase (north of 36° 30') will be "forever free." Congress approves the **Missouri Compromise** (March 1820).

Peru, Guatemala, Panama, Santo Domingo and Mexico declare themselves independent of Spain (1821). In the U.S., Pres. James Monroe, fearful of Spanish efforts to regain territory, declares the **Monroe Doctrine** (1823), warning European nations not to interfere in the Western Hemisphere.

Greece proclaims independence from Turkey (1822). Turkey invades Greece.

1826–50: Russia declares war on Turkey (1828). France and Britain side with Greece. **Turkey accepts Greek independence** (1829). In France, Charles X rescinds the reforms of Louis XVIII, censoring the press and limiting the voting rights of the middle class. Revolt is swift. In three days of fighting, his government is toppled (1830) and his cousin, Louis Philippe, Duke of Orléans, ascends the throne.

In the U.S., **Joseph Smith founds the Mormon Church** (1830). **Nat Turner leads a successful slave rebellion** in Virginia (Aug. 21–23, 1831). Turner, a literate man and a religious fanatic, serves as a preacher to other slaves. He believes he has been ordained by God to lead slaves out of bondage. He and several others kill his master and the master's family while they sleep. Then he leads 60 others on a two-day rampage that leaves 55 whites dead, including 24 children. He hides from the state militia for six weeks before being captured. He and 16 companions are tried and hanged in November. Fear of similar revolts causes Southern states to enact codes that severely limit the movement of Negroes and forbid their education.

In Texas, American settlers seek to gain independence from Mexico. When **Gen. Antonio López de Santa Anna becomes dictator of Mexico** (1834), American settlers set up their own republican government in Texas and mobilize forces. Texans take the Mexican stronghold of San Antonio (Dec. 9, 1835). Santa Anna assembles an army of about 3,000, returns to San Antonio (Feb. 22, 1836) and lays siege to an old mission building, **the Alamo,** where 200 Texas freedom fighters are garrisoned. Santa Anna tells them to surrender. Their leaders, **William Travis** and **James Bowie,** refuse. For nearly two weeks, the Texans repel repeated attacks. Finally, the Mexicans storm the mission (March 6, 1836) and capture it after bloody, hand-to-hand combat. Travis, Bowie and **Davy Crockett** all die in the assault. Six weeks later, **Sam Houston defeats Santa Anna at San Jacinto, winning independence for Texas** (April 21, 1836). He is elected president of the Republic of Texas.

The American inventor **Samuel Colt patents the revolver** (1836). **Pres. William Henry Harrison,** 68, seeking to maintain his image as a war hero, delivers his lengthy inaugural address without hat or coat, despite bitter temperatures (March 4, 1841). He catches a cold, which leads to pneumonia. Exactly one month after his inauguration, **he becomes the first U.S. president to die in office** (April 4, 1841). His vice president, John Tyler, succeeds him. **Samuel F.B. Morse patents the telegraph** (1844). He sends his first message from Baltimore to Washington, D.C.

In Ireland, the failure of the potato crop causes widespread famine (1846–51). The United States declares war on Mexico and annexes California and New Mexico (1846). The Mormon leader **Brigham Young** attempts to stem panic that spreads in the Church of Jesus Christ of the Latter-day Saints following the murder of **Joseph Smith** by a lynch mob in 1844. Convinced that the church needs to be separated from American society to survive, he leads its members from their homes in Illinois to the Great Salt Lake Desert of Utah, along what becomes known as the **Mormon Trail** (1846).

In France, the government of Louis Philippe comes under attack after it refuses to consider electoral reform. **Popular revolt forces him to resign** (Feb. 24, 1848). A provisional republic is proclaimed. The right to vote, which had been severely restricted, is given to every adult male. Ideologies clash as peasants and the middle and upper classes attempt to rule together. **A class war erupts in Paris** (June 1848) in which 10,000 are killed or injured. **Louis Napoleon, grandson of Napoleon Bonaparte, is elected president of the French Republic** (Dec. 10, 1848).

The U.S.–Mexico War ends when **Mexico gives up its claims to Texas, California, Arizona, New Mexico, Utah and Nevada** (1848). A treaty with Great Britain sets the boundary of the Oregon Territory at the 49th parallel (1848). **Karl Marx** and **Friedrich Engels** publish the *Communist Manifesto* (1848).

The Gold Rush begins in California (1849) after flakes of gold are discovered in the water at Sutter's Mill near San Francisco. Before the rush, California's population was less than 15,000. By the end of 1849, arrival of the so-called **Forty-Niners** brings the total to more than 100,000. Although a few miners make fortunes, most fail. Within five years, the rush is exhausted.

California seeks to become a state, without slavery. This rekindles smoldering dissension between the North and South. Sen. **Henry Clay,** old and infirm, offers a compromise: California is to be admitted as a free state; New Mexico and Utah are to be organized as territories, with their residents deciding on slavery later; the slave trade (but not slavery) is to be abolished in Washington, D.C.; and the **Fugitive Slave Act** sets federal penalties for aiding a slave's escape and requires that runaway slaves be returned. The **Compromise of 1850 is approved,** but it only temporarily calms the storm between North and South. The **Underground Railroad,** a secret network of escape routes for slaves that has been operating since about 1812, becomes even more heavily traveled as abolitionists defy the Fugitive Slave Act and help slaves escape to free states and territories. **Harriet Tubman,** who escapes slavery in 1849, returns to the South 19 times to lead 300 others out of servitude, earning the nickname "Moses."

1851–75: Herman Melville publishes *Moby Dick* (1851). **Harriet Beecher Stowe publishes *Uncle Tom's Cabin; or, Life Among the Lowly*** (1851–52) in installments in the *National Era,* an abolitionist newspaper. The novel (also published in book form in 1852) portrays the cruel existence of slaves, stirring antislavery sentiment in the North in the years before the Civil War. The characters—including the kindly old slave Uncle Tom, the brutal slave driver Simon Legree and Eliza, a mulatto slave who is chased by dogs as she crosses a frozen river—become permanent literary references. The book, which is widely read and produced as a play, has such an impact that years later, when Abraham Lincoln meets Mrs. Stowe, he reportedly says to her, "So you're the little woman who wrote the book that made this great war."

In France, Louis Napoleon declares himself the Emperor Napoleon III (1852). Scottish medical missionary **David Livingstone discovers Victoria Falls** (1855). In the **Crimean War,** Britain, France and Sardinia successfully assist Turkey in repelling Russian advances (1853–56). The war is particularly remembered for the bloody allied victory at **Balaklava,** immortalized by **Alfred Lord Tennyson** in *The Charge of the Light Brigade.* The English nurse **Florence Nightingale** organizes a group of 38 nurses to care for the sick and wounded during the war (1854). By war's end, she has become a heroine.

In the United States, the **Kansas-Nebraska Act** (May 30, 1854) creates two new territories and permits their residents to decide, before admission as states, whether they will be slave or free. This effectively repeals the Missouri Compromise of 1820 and paves the way toward civil war. **The Republican Party is formed** (1854) by Whigs, Free-Soilers and northern Democrats, united by antislavery sentiment and anger over the Kansas-Nebraska Act. **Henry David Thoreau** publishes *Walden* (1854). In the **Dred Scott** case, the U.S. Supreme Court rules that the Missouri Compromise was unconstitutional because Congress has no right to limit slavery in the territories (1857). Scott, a slave, had been taken to Illinois and Wisconsin, a free state and territory. When he returned to Missouri, a slave state, he sued for his freedom on the basis of his residence in a free state and territory. In addition to finding the Missouri Compromise unconstitutional, the court ruling states that blacks "as beings of an inferior order" have "no rights a white man was bound to respect." The ruling further inflames antislavery sentiment in the North. Scott, whose situation was used as a test case by his owner, who no longer favored slavery, is freed several days after the decision. A series of historic debates takes place between Sen. **Stephen A. Douglas** of Illinois and **Abraham Lincoln,** a little-known Republican lawyer from Illinois, as they compete for a Senate seat. The seven debates (Aug. 21–Oct. 15, 1858) in Illinois spotlight the growing divisiveness of the slavery issue. Lincoln, who opposes slavery, says the nation will have to decide the issue once and for all because "this government can not endure permanently half slave and half free." Douglas, while not defending slavery, argues that each state and territory should be able to decide the question for itself. Douglas wins the Senate seat, but Lincoln is cast into the national spotlight.

John Brown, an abolitionist, and 21 followers seize the U.S. arsenal at **Harpers Ferry,** Va. (now West Virginia), in a plan to liberate slaves through armed intervention (Oct. 16, 1859). The arsenal is retaken the next morning by **Robert E. Lee.** Brown is tried and hanged (Dec. 2, 1859). He is viewed by some as a martyr, even though his zealotry had earlier led him to direct the slaughter of five proslavery men, claiming that he was guided by the hand of God.

Work begins on the Suez Canal (1859). The English naturalist **Charles Darwin** publishes *Origin of Species,* which sets forth the principles of evolution and natural selection (1859). The British philosopher and economist **John Stuart Mill** publishes *On Liberty* (1859). In Russia, the Czar Alexander II frees 10 million male serfs and their families (1861).

In the U.S., Abraham **Lincoln is elected presi-**

dent (1860) with a minority of the popular vote. [See Civil War and Reconstruction, page 120] In Europe, Prussia conquers Austria and other German states in the **Seven Weeks' War** (1866). Prussia's ally, Italy, gets Venice.

The **British North America Act establishes the Dominion of Canada** (1867). **Russia sells Alaska to the United States** for $7.2 million (1867). The purchase, negotiated by Secretary of State William Henry Seward, is known as "Seward's Folly" because Alaska is considered to be a nearly worthless frozen wasteland.

In Spain, **Queen Isabella II** is overthrown (1868).

In the United States, **the 14th Amendment, which grants civil rights to Negroes,** is ratified (1868). The Central Pacific and the Union Pacific railroads complete construction of the **first transcontinental railroad,** joining their lines at Promontory Point, Utah (May 10, 1869), spurring development of the American West.

The 15th Amendment to the Constitution, which prohibits states from denying voting rights due to race, is ratified (1870). [See Civil War and Reconstruction, page 120]

As a result of the **Franco-Prussian War** (1870–71), France becomes a republic and Italy gains Rome, which becomes its capital.

Sir Henry Morton Stanley, a British explorer and journalist, is sent by the *New York Herald* to locate the Scottish explorer **David Livingstone in Africa** (1871). He greets him ("Dr. Livingstone, I presume?") and joins him on a journey to the north end of Lake Tanganyika.

1876–1900: In the U.S., **Lt. Col. George Custer and his troops are killed at Little Bighorn** in the Dakota Territory by Sioux and Cheyenne Indians led by Sitting Bull and Crazy Horse (June 25, 1876). Custer, ignoring reports from his scouts, attacks the Indians rather than waiting for reinforcements. He and his troops, who are greatly outnumbered, are slaughtered in what becomes known as Custer's Last Stand. For the Indians, however, the victory is short-lived. An 1868 treaty, which had given the Black Hills of Dakota to the Sioux forever, was repeatedly violated after gold was found in the area. Advancing whites had sought to place the Indians on reservations. Little Bighorn was the Indians' greatest victory, but their last. Unable to supply a large force, the Cheyenne and Sioux scatter in small bands and are hunted down or driven into Canada by the U.S. Army.

Pres. James A. Garfield is shot by Charles Guiteau as he enters a Washington, D.C., train station (July 2, 1881). Guiteau, a demented lawyer who had been rejected for a federal patronage job, fires two shots; one grazes Garfield's arm and one strikes him in the back. **Garfield dies** Sept. 19, 1881. Guiteau is convicted and hanged (June 30, 1882).

American corporations begin to form trusts to monopolize their industries. The **Standard Oil Trust** (1882) leads the way, controlling 90 percent of the nation's petroleum industry. Its success inspires other company directors to follow suit, raising public concern about the concentration of power. The **Sherman Antitrust Act** (1890) outlaws trusts and other business arrangements that restrain interstate or foreign commerce.

The bold Apache warrior **Geronimo surrenders** to U.S. troops for the last time (1886). Geronimo, chief of a band of Mexican Apaches known as the Chiricahuas, had led numerous raids in northern Mexico and the U.S. border area. By 1876, he and his followers had been captured and confined to a reservation at San Carlos, Ariz. They escaped repeatedly and conducted more raids. Greatly outnumbered, he is forced to surrender in 1886. He is imprisoned in Florida, then resettled in Oklahoma. In 1909 he dies of pneumonia.

The **Brooklyn Bridge** and the **Metropolitan Opera House** are completed in New York City (1883). The **Statue of Liberty** is dedicated (Oct. 28, 1886). The 151-foot statue, financed by the French and American people to commemorate their revolutions and their friendship, was designed by French sculptor Frédéric Auguste Bartholdi, who proposed the project. For immigrants, it comes to symbolize freedom. A sonnet by Emma Lazarus (a Russian Jewish immigrant) is engraved at its base. The sonnet concludes: ". . . Give me your tired, your poor,/ Your huddled masses yearning to breathe free,/ The wretched refuse of your teeming shore./ Send these, the homeless, tempest-tost to me,/ I lift my lamp beside the golden door!"

Sir Arthur Conan Doyle publishes his first Sherlock Holmes story, "A Study in Scarlet" (1887).

In 1889, the federal Indian Bureau becomes concerned about a "Ghost Dance" religion that is spreading among Plains Indians on government reservations. It orders that the leaders of the movement be rounded up. The Sioux Chief **Sitting Bull** (who had been reduced to touring with Buffalo Bill Cody's Wild West Show in 1885), is suspected of being a leader. He is arrested and killed in a scuffle with Indian police (Dec. 15, 1890). His followers are halted (Dec. 28, 1890) and ordered to surrender their arms the next morning. In the turmoil, shots are fired and 200 Indian men, women and children are killed. About 30 soldiers are killed, some by their own crossfire. **Sioux warriors are massacred by U.S. cavalry at Wounded Knee Creek** near Pine Ridge, S. Dak. (Dec. 29, 1890), marking the last incident of the Indian Wars, which had begun in 1609 and continued sporadically ever since, fueled by the white man's desire for land.

Louisiana becomes the last of the Confederate states to enact a law that requires railroads to provide "equal but separate accommodations for the white and colored races" (1890). This was to become the test case for other **Jim Crow Laws**—state laws designed to maintain racial segregation. The laws, which began even before the Civil War, are named after a popular minstrel show character, a black beggar. In **Plessy v. Ferguson, the U.S. Supreme Court rules that requiring "separate but equal accommodations" is a "reasonable" use of state power,** allowing the Jim Crow laws to stand. The "separate but equal" doctrine remains in effect until it is overturned by the court in Brown v. Board of Education of Topeka in 1954.

The end of the 19th century is a time of invention and discovery. **Alexander Graham Bell transmits the first telephone message** (March 10, 1876) when he summons his assistant from another room in his Boston workshop: "Mr. Watson, come here; I want you." **Thomas Edison invents the phonograph** (1877) **and the first practical incandescent electric light** (1879) in his workshop in Menlo Park, N.J. In Germany, **Gottlieb Daimler and Karl Benz produce the first successful automobile** (1887). **Edison perfects the Kinetoscope,** the first motion picture machine (1893). The Italian physicist **Guglielmo Marconi develops radio** when he sends long-wave signals over a mile (1895). German physicist **Wilhelm Roentgen discovers X-rays** (1895). In Paris, **Marie and Pierre Curie discover radium** and determine its properties (1898).

Britain, Germany, France and Italy compete to colonize Africa (1881–98).

In France, **Capt. Alfred Dreyfus is accused of supplying French military documents to the Germans.** Due in part to anti-Semitism, Dreyfus, an Alsatian Jew, is accused, convicted and sentenced to life imprisonment (1894). In 1898 it is learned that much of the evidence against him had been fabricated by a French intelligence officer. His cause polarizes French society, uniting and bringing to power the French left wing. He later receives a presidential pardon.

In England, Victoria celebrates her Diamond Jubilee, marking 60 years as queen (1897). Her reign (which lasts until her death in 1901) has seen the rise of industrialism at home and imperialism abroad. Her marriage to her first cousin, Prince Albert, and the marriages of their nine children have linked the royal family to Russia, Germany, Greece, Denmark and Romania.

In Cuba, rebellion erupts against Spanish rule (1895) and the U.S. sympathizes. American sentiments are inflamed by sensationalistic reporting in **William Randolph Hearst**'s *New York Journal* and **Joseph Pulitzer**'s *New York World*, which are in a circulation war. They compete with sensational stories, gimmicks and comics. When the *Journal* lures the popular "Yellow Kid" comic strip from the *World*, the rivalry becomes known as the Battle of the Yellow Kids. The so-called **"yellow journalism"** greatly exaggerates Spanish abuses in Cuba, pushing the U.S. along the path to war. When Cubans loyal to Spain riot in Havana against the U.S. (January 1898), the battleship *Maine* is dispatched to protect American lives and property. When **the *Maine* is blown up in Havana harbor** (Feb. 15, 1898), the press blames Spain, although evidence is lacking. Hearst personally captains a press boat off Cuba and issues as many as 40 extra editions a day. Congress is exhorted to "remember the *Maine*" by declaring war. It obliges (April 25, 1898). A U.S. naval squadron led by **Com. George Dewey defeats a Spanish fleet in Manila harbor** in the Philippines (May 1, 1898). U.S. troops, including the **Rough Riders** (organized by **Theodore Roosevelt**), win land battles, including the **Battle of San Juan Hill** (July 1, 1898). Santiago is captured (July 17, 1898) and an armistice is signed (Aug. 12, 1898). **Cuba becomes free, but under U.S. guidance. Spain cedes Puerto Rico and Guam to the U.S., and surrenders the Philippines** for $20 million.

In China, increasing Western and Japanese influence leads the **Empress Tz'u-hsi** to encourage her followers to expel foreigners. In **the Boxer Uprising** (1898–1900), her followers (the Boxers) besiege Westerners and Chinese Christians in Peking (June 1900). An international force of British, French, Russian, U.S., German and Japanese troops ends the siege (Aug. 1900).

1901–25: A treaty ends the **Boer War** (1899–1902), a struggle over English imperialism in South Africa. The Boers (South African inhabitants of Dutch or French Huguenot descent) accept British rule, but bitterness continues. The country becomes a dominion of England, the Union of South Africa (1910).

Pres. William McKinley is shot in the chest and abdomen by Leo Czolgosz, an anarchist, while visiting the Pan-American Exposition in Buffalo, N.Y. (Sept. 6, 1901). Eight days later he dies.

In the **Russo-Japanese War,** Japan gains control of Korea and the approaches to Manchuria (1904–5). Russia's loss, which reveals the corruption and incompetence of the regime of Czar Nicholas II, sets the stage for revolution. The Russian Revolution of 1905 begins in January, when troops fire on a crowd of workers who are on their way to present a petition to the czar. "Bloody Sunday" leads to months of confrontations throughout Russia. The czar grants basic civil liberties and provides for a parliament (a duma), but then ruthlessly suppresses the revolutionary movement.

In San Francisco, an earthquake and three-day fire leave 500 dead (April 18–20, 1906). A nationwide **financial panic** (1907) causes a run on banks. Many close due to insufficient funds.

Austria annexes Bosnia and Herzegovina (in west-central Yugoslavia) in 1908.

In China, a revolution (1911–12) overthrows the Manchu dynasty. A republic is established and the revolutionary **Sun Yat-sen** is elected provisional president. He resigns in favor of Yuan Shih-kai, who becomes increasingly dictatorial. Sun revolts against Yuan and becomes president of a self-proclaimed national government (1921). In 1924, he begins accepting help from Chinese Communists and the USSR.

In the **First Balkan War** (1912), Serbia, Greece and Bulgaria take Macedonia from the Ottoman Empire. Serbia then quarrels with Bulgaria about how the spoils of the First Balkan War are to be divided, resulting in the **Second Balkan War** (1913). Austria intervenes (1913) and forces Serbia to give up Albania. The move delights Balkan nationalists, who want independence for each of the Balkan states. The leaders of the Austro-Hungarian Empire are concerned by the response because they fear that their multinational empire may be split. In this tense atmosphere, the heir to the Austrian and Hungarian thrones, **Archduke Ferdinand, is assassinated with his wife, Sophie,** by Bosnian revolutionaries (June 28, 1914) during a visit to Sarajevo, the capital of Bosnia. The assassination leads rival alliances into **World War I.**

A U.S. Senate investigation (1922–23) of the so-called **Teapot Dome Scandal** reveals that Albert B. Fall, Secretary of the Interior under Warren G. Harding, secretly leased oil reserves at Teapot Dome, Wyo., and Elk Hills, Calif., for personal gain. Fall was later convicted of accepting bribes (Nov. 1, 1929). [*See* World War I, page 122]

1926–50: **General strike in Great Britain** shuts down coal mines, transportation, the press and foundries for 12 days (May 1926). **Charles A. Lindbergh makes first successful solo flight nonstop from New York to Paris** (May 21, 1927). **Nicola Sacco and Bartolomeo Vanzetti executed** (Aug. 23, 1927) in Massachusetts for slayings during a payroll holdup in 1920. Their case had become an international cause because of claims that the men, Italian-born anarchists, were convicted because of their political beliefs. **Kellogg-Briand Treaty,** out-

lawing war, signed by United States, France, Great Britain, Germany and 11 other nations (Aug. 27, 1928). **Alexander Fleming discovers penicillin** (1928). Seven Chicago mobsters slain by rivals in **Valentine's Day Massacre** (Feb. 14, 1929). Stock market plunges on **Black Tuesday** (Oct. 29, 1929), signaling the start of the **Great Depression** (1929–33), which is felt worldwide. In the United States, the Depression follows the boom years of the **Roaring Twenties.** It is fueled by easy credit, speculation and overproduction of goods and agricultural products, which cannot be sold at a profit. Black Tuesday is an indicator of the nation's economic chaos, not its cause. By 1932, 44 percent of the nation's banks have failed and unemployment has risen from 1.5 million to 15 million. In the 1932 Presidential election, Franklin D. Roosevelt defeats the incumbent Herbert C. Hoover by promising to help "the forgotten man at the bottom of the economic pyramid." His **New Deal** programs (1933–41) bolster the banks, offer help to industry, farmers and labor, and provide aid and job programs for the unemployed. In August 1935, Congress passes the **Social Security Act,** providing a comprehensive system of old-age and unemployment insurance.

In Germany, the **Nazis come to power** (1932). [*See* World War II, page 125] In the United States, **Prohibition** is repealed (1933). **The son of Charles A. and Anne Morrow Lindbergh is kidnapped and killed** (1932). Bruno Richard Hauptmann is arrested (1934), convicted (1935) and executed (1936). The **Dionne quintuplets** are born in Canada (May 28, 1934).

In England, **King Edward VIII abdicates** the throne to marry Wallis Warfield Simpson, an American seeking a divorce from her second husband (1936). **In Spain, civil war begins** (1936). The Fascist forces of Francisco Franco overthrow the Loyalists, with the help of Germany and Italy (1939).

Amelia Earhart disappears in the Pacific. Earhart, the first woman to fly across the Atlantic, was on a round-the-world flight with her navigator, Frederick J. Noonan (1937).

In the United States, the first network television broadcast occurs when station WRGB in Schenectady, N.Y., rebroadcasts a program from NBC in New York City (Feb. 1, 1940).

[*See* World War II, page 125] The **charter for the United Nations is signed,** establishing operating rules; 51 nations are members of the peacekeeping body (1945). In Germany, World War II Allies hold **war crimes trial in Nuremberg** (Nov. 1945–Oct. 1946). Twelve Nazi leaders (including one tried in absentia) are sentenced to hang; seven imprisoned;

three acquitted. (Hermann Goering commits suicide two hours before he and the others are to be executed on Oct. 15, 1946.) Winston Churchill warns of an **"Iron Curtain"** that divides the capitalist, democratic Western nations and the Communist bloc (1946). The nations become increasingly estranged in the wake of World War II, facing each other in an economic and political **Cold War.** The status of Berlin, which had been partitioned at the end of World War II, is a major issue in the Cold War. In 1948 and 1949, **the Western powers conduct a massive airlift to supply West Berlin** during a Soviet land and water blockade.

The United Nations recommends that Palestine be split into an Arab state and a Jewish state (Nov. 29, 1947). The resolution sparks immediate warfare between Arab guerrillas and Israelis. **The state of Israel is founded** (May 14, 1948). The new nation is attacked by Palestine Arab forces and troops from Jordan, Iraq, Lebanon and Syria in the First Palestinian War. The fighting continues until January 1949. When fighting ceases, Israel has annexed 1,930 sq. mi. more than the 4,983 sq. mi. that had been allocated under the U.N. resolution.

Communists seize control of Czechoslovakia (Feb. 1948). **Hideki Tojo and 23 others are tried as war criminals** and convicted (Nov. 12, 1948); seventeen receive life sentences, Tojo and six others are hanged (Dec. 23, 1948). **Alger Hiss,** a former State Department official, is convicted of perjury after denying that he helped **Whittaker Chambers** transmit secret documents to the Russians (1950). **Mao Zedong** becomes the first chairman of the Communist People's Republic of China.

Sen. Joseph R. McCarthy, R-Wisc., begins a campaign against Communists, who he alleges have infiltrated the State Department and other high government positions (Feb. 1950). His groundless accusations, which eventually extend to the Army, fuel a campaign against "subversives" that injures many and makes him a celebrity. **Two Puerto Rican nationalists attempt to assassinate President Truman.** One assailant and a presidential guard are killed in the gunfire (Nov. 1, 1950).

[*See* Korean War, page 135]

1951–60: **Julius and Ethel Rosenberg are sentenced to die** for passing top-secret data about nuclear weapons to the USSR (March 1951). Despite appeals and claims that the trial was influenced by the Cold War political climate, they are executed on June 19, 1953.

Edmund Hillary of New Zealand and Tenzing Norkay of Nepal become the first men to reach the peak of Mt. Everest (May 29, 1953). **Soviet tanks crush an anti-Communist uprising in East Berlin** (June 17, 1953).

Four Puerto Rican nationalists fire at Congressmen from the spectator gallery of the House (March 1, 1954). Five Congressmen are wounded. **Sen. Joseph R. McCarthy, R-Wisc., heads the Senate Permanent Committee on Investigations,** which holds public hearings based on half-truths, unsubstantiated accusations and innuendo (1954). The hearings draw the ire of Senate Democrats, some Republicans, the Army and the press, including CBS commentator Edward R. Murrow. On Dec. 2, 1954, **the Senate condemns McCarthy for conduct unbecoming a senator.**

In Vietnam, **French-held Dien Bien Phu falls to the Communist Viet Minh** (May 7, 1954). [*See* Vietnam War, page 136]

U.S. Supreme Court rules unanimously in **Brown v. Board of Education of Topeka** that segregation of public schools is unconstitutional (May 17, 1954). It sets aside the earlier "separate but equal" standard.

For the first time, **schoolchildren are inoculated against poliomyelitis,** using vaccine developed by Dr. Jonas E. Salk (1954).

After nearly 10 years of Allied occupation, **West Germany becomes a sovereign state** (May 5, 1955). The **Warsaw Pact** establishes a defense alliance among Albania, Bulgaria, Czechoslovakia, East Germany, Hungary, Poland, Romania and the Soviet Union (May 14, 1955).

Argentine President Juan Perón is ousted by a military junta (Sept. 19, 1955). He is exiled to Paraguay.

In Montgomery, Ala., **Rosa Parks defies a state segregation law when she refuses to give up her seat at the front of a bus to a white person** (Dec. 1, 1955). A bus boycott begins, under the direction of the Rev. Martin Luther King, Jr. (Dec. 5, 1955). Supreme Court rules that segregation in public transportation is unconstitutional (Nov. 13, 1956).

Egypt seizes control of the Suez Canal from French and British interests (July 26, 1956). Israel attacks Egypt's Sinai Peninsula, marking the start of the Suez-Sinai War (Oct. 29, 1956). British and French invade Egypt at Port Said (Nov. 5, 1956). The U.N., at the urging of the United States, forces a ceasefire in Egypt (Nov. 6, 1956).

Soviet troops, planes and tanks crush anti-Communist rebellion in Hungary, destroying much of Budapest (Nov. 1956).

Arkansas Gov. Orval Faubus calls out National Guard to keep black students from entering all-white Central High School in Little Rock, in defiance of federal law (Sept. 4, 1957). A federal court order removes the National Guard (Sept. 21, 1957) but does not end violent protests. President Eisenhower sends 1,000 troops to enforce segregation (Sept. 24, 1957). Nine black students enter the school (Sept. 25, 1957).

The Soviet Union launches **Sputnik,** the first man-made satellite, into Earth orbit (Oct. 4, 1957). Its satellite launched Nov. 3, 1957, contains a dog, Laika. The United States launches its first satellite, **Explorer 1**, on Jan. 31, 1958.

Vice Pres. Richard M. Nixon and his wife, Pat, are booed, stoned and spat upon during a tour of Latin America as angry crowds protest U.S. dominance in the area (May 1958). In China, Chairman Mao Zedong launches his **Great Leap Forward,** a program to promote industrial growth (1958).

Thousands of severe birth defects are linked to the drug **thalidomide,** used widely in Europe as a sleeping pill and to treat morning sickness. Thousands of babies are born with flipper-like arms and legs and other serious deformities (1958).

Cuban President Fulgencio Batista is overthrown by revolutionaries led by Fidel Castro (Jan. 1, 1959). The **Dalai Lama escapes to India** as Chinese forces occupy Tibet (March 1959).

In the U.S., **TV quiz show scandal erupts** after a contestant says he was given an answer on *The $64,000 Question.* Producer admits to Congress that several shows have been rigged for years, prompting investigation of television standards (1959). Throughout the American South, **blacks hold sit-ins at segregated lunch counters,** demanding that they be served.

An American U-2 spy plane is shot down over the Soviet Union (May 1, 1960). The pilot, Francis Gary Powers, is sentenced to prison for 10 years. He is released in 1962 in exchange for a Soviet spy. **Israelis capture Adolph Eichmann,** who directed the murder of millions of Jews during World War II (1960). Eichmann, who had been living in Argentina, is taken to Israel, where he is tried (1961) and executed (1962).

Belgium grants independence to the Congo (now Zaire) (June 30, 1960). **Cuban leader Fidel Castro seizes American-owned property** (Aug. 7, 1960). Vice Pres. Richard M. Nixon and Sen. John F. Kennedy meet in the first televised debate between presidential contenders (Sept. 26, 1960).

1961–70: **The United States severs diplomatic relations with Cuba** (Jan. 3, 1961). **The Soviet Union puts a man, Yuri Gagarin, in orbit around the Earth** for the first time (April 12, 1961). **The birth control pill goes on sale** in the United States (1961). President Kennedy establishes the **Peace Corps,** to help developing nations (March 1, 1961).

Anti-Castro exiles invade Cuba's Bay of Pigs (April 17, 1961). The landing, covertly supported by the United States, is a fiasco, ignites interna-

tional tensions and fosters ties between Cuba and the Soviet Union. It sets the stage for the **Cuban missile crisis,** a major Cold War confrontation. After the Bay of Pigs, the USSR begins building missile launching sites in Cuba. President Kennedy demands withdrawal of the missiles (Oct. 22, 1962) and blockades Cuba. On Oct. 28, 1962, Soviet Premier Nikita Khrushchev agrees to dismantle the launching sites.

Berlin Wall is built by East Germans to stop residents from fleeing (Aug. 13, 1961). **France grants independence to Algeria** (July 3, 1962).

James Meredith becomes the first Negro to attend the University of Mississippi (Oct. 1, 1962), after violent protests by whites. President Kennedy sends federal troops to enforce law prohibiting segregation. In May 1963, he sends troops to Alabama to quell racial violence there.

President Kennedy expresses support for the people of West Berlin, who live surrounded by Communist countries. In a speech at the Berlin Wall, he declares, "Ich bin ein Berliner" (I am a Berliner).

British Secretary of War John Profumo resigns (June 5, 1963) after being charged with having had sex with a prostitute, Christine Keeler, who was also having an affair with a Soviet naval officer.

In Washington, D.C., **more than 200,000 people participate in a peaceful civil rights demonstration.** The Rev. Martin Luther King, Jr., delivers his famous "I have a dream" speech (Aug. 28, 1963).

Pres. John F. Kennedy, 46, is assassinated as he rides in a motorcade in Dallas (Nov. 22, 1963). He is rushed to Parkland Memorial Hospital, where he dies due to massive head and neck wounds, without regaining consciousness. Texas Gov. John B. Connally, Jr., riding in the same open limousine as President and Mrs. Kennedy, is wounded in the chest, ribs and arm. Within two hours of Kennedy's death, **Lyndon B. Johnson is sworn in** as president. The ceremony is held in the presidential jet at Love Field in Dallas as Mrs. Kennedy watches, wearing a blood-stained pink suit.

Within hours of the assassination, **Lee Harvey Oswald, 24, is arrested for the murder.** Oswald kills Dallas Policeman J.D. Tippit while resisting arrest. He is accused of shooting the president from the sixth floor of the Texas School Book Depository, using a mail-order rifle with a telescopic sight. Oswald is an ex-Marine who had once defected to the Soviet Union and been active in pro-Communist causes.

On Nov. 24, 1963, **Dallas nightclub owner Jack Ruby kills Oswald** in the basement of the Dallas jail, while Oswald is being transferred to another facility. Ruby is convicted of murder and sentenced to die (1964). His conviction is overturned (1966). He dies while awaiting a new trial (1967).

A special investigative commission, headed by Chief Justice Earl Warren, determines that Oswald acted alone (1964). Fourteen years later, however, a U.S. House of Representatives select committee concludes that Kennedy "was probably assassinated as the result of a conspiracy" (1978).

Three civil rights workers are murdered in Mississippi (June 21, 1964). The men—James E. Chaney, 21, who is black, Michael Schwerner, 24, and Andrew Goodman, 21, both of whom are white—are reported missing June 21, 1964, after having been held by local police on a speeding charge. President Johnson orders an FBI search for the men. Their bodies are found Aug. 4, 1964, buried on a farm outside Philadelphia, Miss. In 1967, seven Ku Klux Klan members are convicted of conspiracy in connection with the murders.

The **Civil Rights Act of 1964** prohibits racial discrimination in employment, public accommodations, publicly owned facilities, unions and federally funded programs. **The Rev. Martin Luther King, Jr., and more than 2,600 others are arrested in Selma, Ala.,** during demonstrations against voter registration rules (Feb. 1965). On March 28, 1965, **25,000 civil rights demonstrators march from Selma, Ala., to Montgomery,** the state capital, led by Dr. King. **Race riots in the Watts section of Los Angeles** leave 34 dead, more than 1,000 injured and $175 million worth of fire damage (Aug. 11–16, 1965).

A malfunction at an Ontario power plant cuts off electrical power to 24 million people in nine northeastern states and parts of Canada (Nov. 9, 1965).

Mao Zedong launches the Great Proletarian Cultural Revolution in China (1966–69) to renew the country's revolutionary fervor. He recruits youth for the Red Guard, which attacks so-called bourgeois elements in education, culture and the bureaucracy. The Red Guard, supported by the army, attacks anyone it accuses of having capitalist ties, influences or thoughts.

Three American astronauts—Virgil I. "Gus" Grissom, Edward H. White 2d and Roger B. Chaffee—die as a flash fire engulfs their spacecraft during a launch simulation (Jan. 27, 1967).

Israel defeats its Arab enemies in the Six-Day War (June 5–10, 1967). They capture the Sinai Peninsula, the Old City of Jerusalem, the Gaza Strip, the east bank of the Suez Canal and the Golan Heights.

Race riots sweep across the United States (summer 1967). In the largest, in Detroit, 7,000 National Guardsmen are sent in to help end the fires and looting. **Dr. Christiaan N. Barnard and other South African surgeons perform the first successful heart transplant** (Dec. 3, 1967). The patient, Louis Washkansky, dies 18 days later.

North Korea seizes the U.S. Navy intelligence ship *Pueblo* off the coast of North Korea and holds the 83 crew members as spies (Jan. 23, 1968). They are released after 11 months of captivity.

The Rev. Dr. Martin Luther King, Jr., is assassinated at the Lorraine Motel in Memphis, Tenn. (April 4, 1968). James Earl Ray pleads guilty to the slaying and is sentenced to 99 years in prison. **Sen. Robert F. Kennedy, D-N.Y., is fatally wounded** at the Ambassador Hotel in Los Angeles while claiming victory in the California Democratic presidential primary (June 5, 1968). He dies 20 hours later. Sirhan Bishara Sirhan, a 25-year-old Palestinian Arab, is convicted of the crime. He testifies he hated Kennedy for supporting Israel.

Czechoslovakia is invaded by the Soviet Union and other Warsaw Pact nations (Aug. 20, 1968). Alexander Dubcek, leader of the Communist Party in Czechoslovakia, is forced to give up his democratic reforms and adopt Soviet policies.

Protesters against the Vietnam War disrupt the Democratic national convention in Chicago (Aug. 1968). Hundreds of police, many swinging nightsticks, charge demonstrators as they march to the convention center. Seven men are alleged to have planned the riot by protesters. The defendants—David Dellinger, Rennie Davis, Thomas Hayden, Abbie Hoffman, Jerry Rubin, John Froines and Lee Weiner—become known as the Chicago Seven. Their convictions are overturned because Judge Julius Hoffman waited too long to impose sentence.

A human walks on the moon for the first time (July 20, 1969). Neil A. Armstrong steps on the surface first, followed by Edwin E. Aldrin, Jr. While they land, the third member of the Apollo 11 team, Michael Collins, orbits the moon in the command ship.

Mary Jo Kopechne dies when a car driven by Sen. Edward M. Kennedy, D-Mass., plunges off a bridge on Chappaquiddick Island in Massachusetts. Kennedy pleads guilty to leaving the scene of the accident, gets a two-month suspended sentence (July 1969). **The Woodstock Music and Art Fair draws as many as 500,000 rock music fans** to a farm near Woodstock, N.Y., where they camp, listen to music, and share drugs and peaceful sentiments (Aug. 15–17, 1969). Four months later, the spirit of harmony is broken when **a free concert by the Rolling Stones erupts into violence in Altamont, Calif.** and four people die.

Actress Sharon Tate, three house guests and a

neighbor are brutally murdered in Beverly Hills, Calif. (Aug. 8, 1969). Tate, wife of movie director Roman Polanski, was eight months pregnant. The next night, Leno and Rosemary LaBianca are murdered at their nearby home. Charles Manson and three female members of his commune (Susan Atkins, Leslie Van Houten and Patricia Krenwinkel) are convicted of the murders (1971).

1971–80: **The 26th Amendment to the U.S. Constitution lowers the voting age to 18** (June 30, 1971). The first installment of the **Pentagon Papers** is published in the *New York Times* (June 13, 1971). The papers, secret Pentagon documents leaked to the paper by Daniel Ellsberg, reveal the covert history of the Vietnam War. The Department of Justice has the publication halted, citing national security. The U.S. Supreme Court rules in New York Times Company v. United States (1971) that the government's reasons are not sufficient to justify limiting the freedom of expression guaranteed under the 1st Amendment.

[*See* Vietnam War, page 136]

The **U.N. admits the People's Republic of China** and expels Nationalist China (Oct. 25, 1971). President Nixon makes a historic eight-day visit to Communist China (Feb. 1972).

Alabama Gov. George C. Wallace is shot at a political rally in Laurel, Md., by Arthur H. Bremer (May 15, 1972). Wallace, who had been campaigning for the Democratic presidential nomination, is left paralyzed.

[*See* The Watergate Scandal, page 38]

At **the Olympic Games in Munich 11 Israeli athletes are killed** by eight Arab terrorists (Sept. 5, 1972). Black September guerrillas break into the Israelis' building, kill two coaches and take nine athletes hostage. Israel rejects demands that Palestinian prisoners be released in exchange for the hostages. After 18 hours in the Israelis' building, the hostages and their captors are flown by helicopter to the Munich airport, where a plane is waiting. In an exchange of gunfire between the terrorists and German sharpshooters, four of the guerrillas, a German police officer and all nine hostages are killed. In retaliation, Israel conducts air raids on Lebanon and Syria.

Pres. Richard M. Nixon wins re-election, defeating Democratic Sen. George S. McGovern, who carries only Massachusetts and the District of Columbia (Nov. 7, 1972).

In **Roe v. Wade, the Supreme Court rules in a 7–2 decision that states cannot prohibit or restrict a woman's right to abortion in the first three months of pregnancy.** In the second three months, it rules, states may regulate abortions "in ways that are reasonably related to maternal health"

(Jan. 21, 1973).

In Chile, military leaders seize control of the government, killing Pres. Salvador Allende (Sept. 11, 1973). Gen. Augusto Pinochet Ugarte becomes president. Pinochet remains in power until Patricio Aylwin Azocar takes office in March 1990, ending 17 years of military dictatorship.

Egypt and Syria, backed by the Soviet Union, invade Israel on Yom Kippur (Oct. 6, 1973). Israel, supported by the U.S., drives back the Syrians and crosses the Suez Canal into Egypt. Fighting ends Oct. 24.

Vice Pres. Spiro T. Agnew resigns, pleading nolo contendere (no contest) to charges that he evaded tax on payments made to him by contractors while he was governor of Maryland (Oct. 10, 1973). **Gerald R. Ford is appointed vice president** (Oct. 12, 1973) and sworn in (Dec. 6, 1973).

Patricia (Patty) Hearst is kidnapped by the Symbionese Liberation Army (Feb. 4, 1974). She and members of the SLA are captured by FBI agents (Sept. 18, 1975). She is accused of adopting her captors' radical beliefs and helping them rob a bank. She is convicted of bank robbery (March 20, 1976).

Pres. Richard M. Nixon resigns due to the Watergate scandal (Aug. 9, 1974). Gerald R. Ford becomes president. He chooses former New York governor Nelson A. Rockefeller as his vice president. [*See* The Watergate Scandal, page 38]

The *Mayaguez*, a U.S. merchant ship, is seized by Cambodian forces in the Gulf of Siam (May 12, 1975). The U.S. attacks Tang Island, where the *Mayaguez* is being held. The hostages are released.

Pres. Gerald R. Ford is the object of two assassination attempts in 17 days. Lynette "Squeaky" Fromme, a follower of Charles Manson, points a pistol at him in Sacramento (Sept. 5, 1975). Sara Jane Moore fires a gun at him in San Francisco (Sept. 22, 1975). Ford is not injured.

In Argentina, a military junta deposes Isabel Perón (March 24, 1976), who had succeeded to the presidency after the death of her husband, Juan, in 1974.

Israeli commandos raid the airport at Entebbe, Uganda, and release 103 hostages held by pro-Palestinian hijackers (July 3, 1976).

Legionnaire's Disease kills 29 people, many of whom attended an American Legion convention in Philadelphia (August 1976). The cause of the mysterious, flu-like illness is later traced to a bacterium.

A nuclear-nonproliferation pact, curbing the spread of nuclear weapons, is signed by the U.S., the USSR and 13 other nations (Sept. 21, 1977). **The U.S. Senate ratifies an agreement that**

would turn over the **Panama Canal to Panama** on Dec. 31, 1999 (April 18, 1978).

The first "test-tube baby" is born (July 25, 1978). Louise Brown is the daughter of Lesley and John Brown, a British couple, who were treated by Doctors Robert G. Edwards and Patrick Steptoe. The mother's egg was united with the father's sperm in a laboratory dish, then implanted in the mother.

Pope Paul VI dies (Aug. 6, 1978). **His successor, Pope John Paul I, dies after 34 days in office** (Sept. 28, 1978). He is succeeded by Karol Cardinal Wojtyla of Poland, who becomes Pope John Paul II (Oct. 16, 1978).

Israeli Prime Minister Menachem Begin and Egyptian President Anwar el-Sadat meet at Camp David, using Pres. Jimmy Carter as an intermediary, and complete the outline of a peace plan (Sept. 1978).

In Guyana, 911 followers of the Rev. Jim Jones's cult commit suicide or are killed at the People's Temple (Nov. 18, 1978). Most die after drinking a combination of Kool-Aid and cyanide at the urging of Jones. The deaths are sparked by the ambush of U.S. Rep. Leo J. Ryan and four others who had come to investigate the cult, which had lured hundreds of Americans to the Guyanan jungle. When Jones learns that some of Ryan's party had escaped, he orders the suicides.

San Francisco Mayor George Moscone and Supervisor Harvey Milk, the city's first acknowledged gay official, are shot to death in City Hall by Dan White, a self-styled defender of morality (Nov. 27, 1978).

In Iran, opposition forces Muhammad Reza Shah Pahlevi and his family to flee the country (Jan. 16, 1979). The exiled religious leader Ayatollah Ruhollah Khomeini returns to Iran and takes control (Feb. 1, 1979). The new government nationalizes local and foreign-owned businesses. The U.S. Embassy in Teheran is invaded and staff members are taken hostage (Nov. 4, 1979). In return for the hostages' release, the Iranians demand that the United States promise to stay out of Iran's affairs, release $8 billion in frozen assets and cancel damage claims. A raid by the United States fails to free the hostages in April. On Jan. 20, 1981, the 52 hostages are released after 444 days in captivity. In return, the United States agrees to most of Iran's demands.

An accident at the Three Mile Island nuclear power plant in Pennsylvania releases small amounts of radioactivity (March 28, 1979). A problem with the cooling system of one of the reactors caused overheating and a partial meltdown of the uranium core. Thousands are evacuated from the area during the 12 days required to stabilize the situation.

Nicaraguan President Anastasio Somoza Debayle resigns, flees to Miami (July 17, 1979) and is replaced by a government led by Sandinista rebels. Somoza and two aides are later assassinated in Asunción, Paraguay (Sept. 17, 1980).

The Soviet Union invades Afghanistan (Dec. 1979) and orchestrates the overthrow of Hafizullah Amin (Dec. 27, 1979). He is replaced by Babrak Karmal, who is more pro-Soviet. The Soviet Union continues to fight rebel forces throughout Afghanistan for nine years. When the Soviet Union withdraws its last troops (Feb. 15, 1989), civil war erupts.

Soviet nuclear physicist and political dissident Andrei Sakharov is exiled from Moscow to Gorki with his wife, Yelena Bonner, after speaking out against the Soviet presence in Afghanistan and for human rights (Jan. 22, 1980). They will be allowed to return to Moscow on Dec. 23, 1986, as part of Soviet leader Mikhail S. Gorbachev's new policy of "glasnost," or openness. Glasnost is linked to Gorbachev's plan for "perestroika," a political and economic restructuring.

The results of Abscam, a two-year FBI sting operation, are made public (Feb. 2, 1980). FBI agents, posing as an Arab sheik and his aides, had offered bribes to government officials in exchange for political favors. Abscam (short for Arab scam) results in the conviction of seven members of Congress and five other public officials on bribery, conspiracy and related charges. Sen. Harrison Williams, D-N.J., and Reps. John Jenrette, D-S.C., Richard Kelly, R-Fla., Raymond Lederer, D-Pa., John Murphy, D-N.Y., Michael Myers, D-Pa., and Frank Thompson, D-N.J., are convicted. Critics accuse the FBI of entrapment. In 1982, a Senate panel will criticize the FBI's tactics but conclude that the agency had not violated civil rights.

Mount St. Helens volcano erupts in Washington (May 18, 1980). The volcano, which had been dormant since 1857, leveled 120 sq. mi. and left 15 people dead and 40 missing.

The Iran-Iraq War begins when Iraq invades Iran (Sept. 22, 1980), the result of rivalry between the two countries for control of the Persian Gulf area. Iraq seeks control of the Shatt-al-Arab waterway that divides the countries. In June 1982, Iraq withdraws troops from many regions, after meeting heavy resistance. In 1984, Iraq attacks commercial ships in the Persian Gulf, as part of an economic campaign against Iran. Iran attacks ships carrying war matériel to Iraq and its allies. The war has the potential for a major international confrontation: Iraq buys arms from France and the USSR and gets financial aid from Kuwait and other Arab states;

Iran is backed by Syria and Libya. The United States, officially neutral, gives aid to Iraq and secretly sells weapons to Iran. On May 27, 1987, an Iraqi missile hits the U.S.S. *Stark*, which had been in the Persian Gulf protecting shipping lanes. The strike, apparently an accident, kills 37 sailors. The incident causes the United States to increase its presence in the Gulf. A UN-sponsored ceasefire plan takes effect on Aug. 20, 1988, after an estimated 1 million deaths. On Aug. 15, 1990, Iraq's Saddam Hussein gives up all that he had won in eight years of war, in the hope that Iran would not side with the United States in the new Persian Gulf War. [*See* The Persian Gulf War, page 140]

Three American nuns and a lay worker are found shot to death in El Salvador (Dec. 4, 1980). As a result, American aid is withheld, which forces a crisis in the military-civilian junta government. Exiled Pres. José Napoleón Duarte is allowed to return and take control. Five members of El Salvador's National Guard are convicted of the crime (May 24, 1984). **Former Beatle John Lennon is shot to death** by a crazed fan, Mark David Chapman, outside the Dakota apartment building in New York City (Dec. 8, 1980).

1981–85: **Nation welcomes 52 American hostages released from Iran** after 444 days in captivity (Jan. 25, 1981). **Pres. Ronald Reagan, Press Secretary James Brady and two law enforcement officers are wounded** outside the Hilton Hotel in Washington, D.C. (March 30, 1981). Brady, the most seriously injured, is left paralyzed by a head wound. Reagan recovers fully after surgery for a chest wound. The assailant, John W. Hinckley, Jr., 27, says that he had been trying to impress an actress, Jodie Foster. He is found not guilty by reason of insanity (June 21, 1982).

Pope John Paul II is wounded by a Turkish terrorist as he rides in an open car in St. Peter's Square (May 13, 1981). **Prince Charles and Lady Diana Spencer are wed** in St. Paul's Cathedral in London in a ceremony broadcast around the world (July 29, 1981).

Aerial walkways collapse, killing 111 people in the Hyatt Regency Hotel in Kansas City (July 17, 1981). **Air traffic controllers go on strike nationwide** (Aug. 3, 1981).

Egyptian Pres. Anwar el-Sadat is assassinated by soldiers during a military parade in Cairo (Oct. 6, 1981).

The Polish government outlaws the Solidarity labor party and political movement (Dec. 1981).

AT&T ends an eight-year antitrust suit by agreeing to divest itself of 22 Bell Telephone operating systems (Jan. 8, 1982).

An Air Florida jet taking off from Washington's National Airport crashes into a bridge over the Potomac River, killing 78, six of whom were on the bridge in rush-hour traffic (Jan. 13, 1982).

Argentine troops seize the Falkland Islands, a British Crown Colony that Argentina had long claimed as its own (April 2, 1982). The British mount a massive sea, air and land attack until the Argentines surrender (June 14, 1982). **Israel invades Lebanon** in an attack aimed at the Palestine Liberation Organization (June 1982).

The Equal Rights Amendment fails to win ratification by the states (June 30, 1982). **An artificial human heart is successfully implanted for the first time** (Dec. 2, 1982). Dr. William C. DeVries heads the surgical team at the University of Utah Medical Center in Salt Lake City that implants the Jarvik-7 artificial heart, named for its developer, Dr. Robert K. Jarvik. The patient, Barney B. Clark, a retired dentist, lives 112 days after surgery.

Benigno S. Aquino, Jr., is slain in Manila (Aug. 21, 1983). Aquino had been the political rival of Philippine Pres. Ferdinand E. Marcos. **A South Korean jetliner strays into Soviet airspace and is shot down** (Sept. 1, 1983). All 269 on board are killed, including 61 Americans. The Soviet Union claims the plane, en route from New York to Seoul, was on a spy mission.

A terrorist attacks the U.S. Marine headquarters in Beirut with a truck filled with explosives, killing 241 Marine and Navy personnel (Oct. 23, 1983).

U.S. and Caribbean allies invade Grenada (Oct. 25, 1983) at the request of the Organization of Eastern Caribbean States after the Grenadian Prime Minister and several cabinet members were executed by pro-Cuban Marxists. Americans living in Grenada are evacuated and order is restored by Nov. 2, 1983.

The U.S. Senate votes to stop federal funds from being used to mine Nicaraguan harbors (April 10, 1984), which had been ordered by Pres. Ronald Reagan. **José Napoleón Duarte, a moderate backed by U.S. funds, is elected president of El Salvador** (May 11, 1984).

Indian Prime Minister Indira Gandhi is shot to death by two Sikh bodyguards (Oct. 31, 1984). After her death, fighting between Sikhs and Hindus claims at least 1,000 lives. Her son, Rajiv Gandhi, succeeds her as prime minister.

Toxic gas leaks from a Union Carbide insecticide plant in Bhopal, India, killing more than 3,500 and injuring 200,000 (Dec. 3, 1984). Union Carbide claimed that a disgruntled Indian employee released the methyl isocyanate gas. The Indian government claimed that plant design and maintenance were poor. The Indian Supreme

Court later orders the American company to pay $470 million in damages (Feb. 14, 1989).

Shiite Moslem gunmen capture a TWA jet with 133 on board after it takes off from Athens (June 14, 1985). Navy diver Robert Stethem is killed on the first day. Other passengers are released gradually as the hijackers direct the plane to shuttle between Beirut and Algiers. The two hijackers demand that Israel release more than 700 Shiite and Palestinian prisoners. Israel does not comply. The United States moves warships to the area and prepares for a commando raid. The gunmen surrender on the seventeenth day (June 30, 1985).

PLO terrorists hijack the Italian cruise ship *Achille Lauro* as it leaves Alexandria, Egypt (Oct. 7, 1985). An American, Leon Klinghoffer, is shot to death. The hijackers demand the release of prisoners by Israel. They surrender Oct. 9, when Egypt offers them free passage out of the country. The plane carrying the hijackers out of Egypt is intercepted by U.S. Navy jets and forced to land in Italy, but the leader of the hijackers escapes.

Pres. Ronald Reagan signs the Gramm-Rudman bill, which requires that the federal deficit be eliminated (Dec. 12, 1985).

Palestinian Abu Nidal terrorists kill 19 and wound more than 100 in grenade and machine gun attacks in the Rome and Vienna airports (Dec. 30, 1985). Both attacks occur at the checkout counters of the El Al Israeli Airlines.

1986: **Pres. Ronald Reagan freezes Libyan assets in the United States,** accusing Libyan leader Moammar Khadafy of supporting international terrorism, including the raids on the Rome and Vienna airports (Jan. 8, 1986). U.S. planes attack alleged terrorist centers in Libya (April 1986).

The space shuttle *Challenger* **explodes moments after liftoff** at Cape Canaveral, Fla., killing all six astronauts and Christa McAuliffe of Concord, N.H., who was to have been the first schoolteacher in space (Jan. 28, 1986). Millions watched the disaster on television. [*See* Milestones in Space: Manned Flights, page 240]

Haitian Pres. Jean-Claude "Baby Doc" Duvalier flees to France, ending 28 years of dictatorship by him and his father (Feb. 7, 1986). **Ferdinand Marcos flees the Philippines** after 20 years as president (Feb. 26, 1986). He is succeeded by Corazon Aquino, widow of Benigno Aquino, a Marcos opponent who had been murdered. Marcos and his wife, Imelda, settle in Hawaii. In 1988, they are indicted on U.S. fraud and racketeering charges stemming from the corruption of their administration. Marcos dies of kidney, lung and heart ailments (Sept. 28, 1989). His wife is later acquitted on charges that she and her husband took $200 million from the Philippine treasury and spent it on art, jewels and New York City real estate (July 2, 1990). Adnan M. Khashoggi is acquitted of charges that he helped her conceal her involvement.

Swedish Prime Minister Olaf Palme is shot to death while walking home from a movie (Feb. 28, 1986).

A major accident at the Chernobyl nuclear plant in the Soviet Union produces increased radiation levels through Eastern Europe and Scandinavia (April 26, 1986). Even five years after the disaster, the death toll was unknown. The Soviet government says that 31 people died. Others claim that the toll could be anywhere between 250 and 10,000. Millions of people live within the 52,000 sq. mi. that the government says were hit by radioactive fallout. The long-term effects on them are unknown. The government blamed the steam explosion that led to the disaster on human error. Many experts also blame the reactor's design.

Secret White House arms sales to Iran are revealed (Nov. 1986). Pres. Ronald Reagan is accused of trying to exchange the arms for American hostages held in Lebanon, in contradiction to his stated policy, and of using some of the money from the sales to aid *contra* rebels in Nicaragua, in defiance of a Congressional ban. He acknowledges that he approved the sales, but denies that he tried to exchange arms for hostages. Initially, he denies that he had detailed knowledge of the diversion of funds to the *contras,* but he later admits that the idea was his. He dismisses White House National Security Adviser Adm. John Poindexter and his aide, Marine Lt. Col. Oliver North. Senate and House committees later conducted televised hearings on the Iran-*Contra* affair (May–Aug. 1987), while a special prosecutor conducted a separate investigation. Poindexter's predecessor as National Security Adviser, Robert McFarlane, pleads guilty to withholding information from Congress concerning secret aid to the *contras.* He is fined $20,000 and given two years' probation. North, Poindexter, Richard V. Secord (a retired Air Force major general) and Albert Hakim (an Iranian businessman) are indicted on a variety of charges, including conspiracy to defraud the federal government (March 1988). The prosecution accepts plea bargains from Secord and Hakim. North is convicted on three of 12 criminal counts; he is fined $150,000 and given a three-year suspended sentence (July 1989). His verdict is later overturned by an appeals court that found defects in the trial procedure. Poindexter is convicted on five counts of deceiving Congressional investigators (April 7, 1990). He is sentenced to six months in prison.

Ivan Boesky, accused of insider trading on Wall Street, agrees to plead guilty to an unspecified criminal count, pay a $100 million fine and return profits (Nov. 14, 1986).

1987: The Rev. Jim Bakker resigns from his popular PTL (Praise the Lord) television ministry as a result of an extramarital sex scandal (March 19, 1987). He claims that he was "wickedly manipulated" by former friends into having sex with a woman in Florida in December 1980, and that he later paid blackmail money to protect his ministry and his wife, Tammy. He is defrocked as a minister by the Assemblies of God and is indicted on charges of illegally diverting millions of dollars of church donations to his own use. He is convicted on 24 counts of fraud and conspiracy, sentenced to 45 years in prison and fined $500,000. He will be eligible for parole in 10 years.

Democrat Gary Hart withdraws from the campaign for the presidential nomination due to reports that Hart, who is married, was conducting an affair with a 27-year-old model, Donna Rice (May 8, 1987). He rejoins the race in December but quits again in March.

The presidents of Costa Rica, Nicaragua, Honduras, Guatemala and El Salvador sign a peace agreement (Aug. 7, 1987). The agreement calls for each nation to arrange a ceasefire with rebels, hold elections and restore freedom of the press.

The Los Angeles area is struck by a severe earthquake, which kills six and injures 100 (Oct. 1, 1987).

The stock market crashes, plunging a record 508 points to 1,738.74 (Oct. 19, 1987). Analysts blame budget and trade deficits, rising interest rates, unrest in the Persian Gulf and computerized trading programs, which generated a huge volume of trades when the market began to decline.

The Supreme Soviet legislature approves a transfer of power from the Communist Party to a popularly elected legislative body, the Congress of People's Deputies (Dec. 1, 1988). The reform, orchestrated by Mikhail S. Gorbachev, is viewed as a step toward democratization, and as an effort by Gorbachev to broaden his base of popular support.

Pres. Ronald Reagan and Soviet leader Mikhail S. Gorbachev sign an arms-reduction agreement that calls for the dismantling of all missiles in the 300- to 3,400-mile range (Dec. 8, 1987).

1988: Panamanian strongman Gen. Manuel Noriega is indicted by the U.S. Justice Department on charges that he helped the Medellin drug cartel in exchange for bribes and kickbacks (Feb. 4, 1988). The cartel is alleged to be responsible for most of the cocaine smuggled into the United States.

The U.S. Navy missile cruiser *Vincennes* **shoots down an Iran Air passenger jet in the Persian Gulf** (July 3, 1988). All 290 on board die. The crew mistook the plane for an Iranian jet fighter. The Defense Department says the incident was caused by a young crew under battle stress.

Gen. Augusto Pinochet relinquishes control of Chile after his defeat in a plebiscite (Oct. 6, 1988).

An earthquake in Soviet Armenia leaves 60,000 dead and 500,000 homeless (Dec. 7, 1988).

A Pan Am jetliner crashes in Lockerbie, Scotland, killing all 259 on board and 11 on the ground (Dec. 21, 1988). The plane, Pan Am flight 103 from London to New York, was destroyed by a bomb hidden in a cassette player by Libyan terrorists.

The prominent Wall Street investment firm of Drexel Burnham Lambert Inc. agrees to plead guilty to six felony counts and pay $650 million in penalties (Dec. 21, 1988). The charges include mail fraud, wire fraud and securities fraud in connection with insider trading between 1984 and 1986. Most of the charges were connected with their dealings with financier Ivan Boesky.

1989: U.S. Navy F-14 jets shoot down two Libyan MiG-23 warplanes in the Mediterranean, 70 miles off the coast of Libya (Jan. 4, 1989). The U.S. claims the planes showed "clear hostile intent." Libya claims they were not armed.

Iran's Ayatollah Ruhollah Khomeini calls for the death of Salmon Rushdie, the Indian author of the novel *The Satanic Verses*, due to the book's alleged insults to the Muslim religion (Feb. 14, 1989). He offers a $1 million reward for his murder. The publisher, Viking Penguin, refuses to halt publication or distribution, despite threats, demonstrations and book-store bombings.

The last Soviet troops leave Afghanistan after nine years of war (Feb. 15, 1989). The civil war in Afghanistan continues.

The Senate refuses to confirm the nomination of former Senator John Tower as defense secretary, amid claims that Tower has a drinking problem (March 9, 1989).

The tanker *Exxon Valdez* **runs aground and dumps 10.9 million gallons of oil in Alaska's Prince William Sound** (March 24, 1989). The spill, which cannot be contained, pollutes hundreds of square miles of Alaskan waters and hundreds of miles of coastline, becoming the largest spill in U.S. history. At the time of the accident, the tanker was being piloted by a third mate instead of its captain, Joseph Hazelwood. The National Transportation Safety Board finds that Hazelwood had an unacceptably high level of alcohol in his blood at the time of the accident.

The first multicandidate elections are held in the Soviet Union (March 26, 1989). The members of the new Congress of People's Deputies include dissidents such as Boris Yeltsin and Andrei Sakharov. The 2,500-member group elects Gorbachev president.

The Polish government and the union Solidarity sign an accord providing for free elections (April 5, 1989). In the elections, held on June 4, Solidarity becomes the majority party, making Poland the only fully democratic Eastern European nation.

Chinese students begin prodemocracy meetings, marches and protests (April 15, 1989). In Beijing, the students converge on Tienanmen Square. The government demands that the protests end (April 20, 1989). The students refuse, and gain the support of teachers, journalists and many other adults. Hundreds of thousands take part in the protests in Beijing, which are broadcast around the world and become increasingly embarrassing to the Chinese government. On May 20, martial law is declared, but troops are reluctant to act against the 1 million people who are protesting peacefully in Beijing. On May 29, the students build a statue resembling the Statue of Liberty in Tienanmen Square. On June 4, thousands of protesters are attacked in Tienanmen Square by army troops and tanks, who shoot some of the unarmed protesters even as they are fleeing. The death toll is probably in the thousands—perhaps as many as 5,000. Estimates vary widely as the government attempts to minimize its actions. The government, led by Zhao Zhiang, ignores international condemnation of the massacre and clamps down on the prodemocracy movement. Protesters are tracked down, arrested and jailed or executed. The foreign press is banned.

Explosion in turret of U.S.S. *Iowa* kills 47 sailors. Navy alleges that the explosion may have been set, perhaps by a sailor who was upset because of the end of a friendship or a homosexual liaison (April 19, 1989).

In Panama, democratic candidates led by Guillermo Endarra sweep an election, but Gen. Manuel Noriega falsifies records and declares Carlos Duque president-elect (May 7, 1989). After opposition, Noriega declares the election void on May 10. An Organization of American States report declares the Noriega government "devoid of constitutional legitimacy" (Nov. 1989). In mid-December, Noriega declares that Panama and the United States are at war. Pres. George Bush sends troops to Panama to oust Noriega after a U.S. soldier is killed (Dec. 20, 1989). Noriega flees and takes refuge in the residence of the Papal Nuncio in Panama City. On Jan. 3, 1990, he surrenders to U.S. troops and is flown to Miami to face trial on drug trafficking charges. Guillermo Endara becomes president.

Solidarity candidates win a decisive majority of parliamentary seats in the first free election in Poland in four decades (June 4, 1989). In August 1990, a coalition government is formed when Communist Pres. Wojciech Jaruzelski chooses a Solidarity member, Tadeusz Mazowiecki, as prime minister.

House Speaker James C. Wright, Jr., D-Tex., resigns from Congress amid charges of unethical conduct (June 30, 1989).

In Lebanon, Hezbollah terrorists release a videotape purporting to show that U.S. Marine Lt. Col. William R. Higgins has been hanged (July 31, 1989). The terrorists had warned that Higgins would be killed unless Hezbollah leader Sheikh Abdul Karim Obeid was released by his Israeli captors. (The Israelis had kidnapped Obeid in July so that they could use him to barter for the release of Israelis held by Lebanon.)

The savings-and-loan industry gets a $166 billion bailout from the federal government. Pres. George Bush signs the bailout bill into law Aug. 9, 1989. The law provides immediate bailout funds and tighter regulation of the industry, particularly junk bond investments. The industry had been hurt by bad loans, poor administration, inadequate regulation and fraud.

The San Francisco Bay area is hit by the second-most powerful earthquake in U.S. history (Oct. 17, 1989). The quake, measuring 7.1 on the Richter scale, kills 67, injures 3,000 and causes nearly $6 billion in damages. Many of the victims die when a section of the upper level of the Bay Bridge crashes to the level below.

In Czechoslovakia, riot police attack 10,000 prodemocracy demonstrators in Prague (Oct. 28, 1989). Despite the use of force, the protests continue. On Oct. 24, 1989, key Communist government leaders resign in response. On Oct. 28, 1989, an agreement is reached to include noncommunists in the government by Dec. 3, 1989. On Dec. 29, the parliament elects as interim president Vaclav Havel, a dissident writer who had been jailed repeatedly for his prodemocracy views.

East Germany opens its borders, eliminating the Berlin Wall as a barrier (Nov. 9, 1989). Thousands gather on both sides of the wall, which had divided the city for 28 years, for an all-night celebration. Within a week, 3 million East Germans visit West Germany. The opening of the wall follows several months of antigovernment protests and a government shake-up in East Germany. The Brandenburg Gate in Berlin is opened on Dec. 22, 1989, in Berlin, signifying unrestricted travel for all Germans.

The Palestine National Council proclaims the formation of a Palestinian state, led by Yasir Arafat (Nov. 15, 1989). It also accepts two UN resolutions that provide a basis for negotiations of the Arab-Israeli homeland dispute.

The Soviet Union, troubled by factionalism and ethnic unrest since its formation, faces the secession of several republics (late 1989). In the Caucasus region, Armenia declares its independence on Aug. 23, 1989, and Azerbaijan declares itself sovereign on Sept. 23, 1989. The Soviet Union denounces both moves and declares martial law in parts of both regions. In the Baltic Republics, nationalist sentiment grows after the Soviet Union admits that it annexed Estonia, Latvia and Lithuania before World War II. Previously, the USSR had alleged that the republics joined the union willingly.

New York hotel queen Leona Helmsley is sentenced to four years in prison and fined $7.1 million for tax fraud (Dec. 12, 1989).

In Romania, Communist party boss Nicolae Ceausescu is driven from power after he vows that Romania would resist the tide of democratization. He and his wife flee Bucharest by helicopter as private citizens and soldiers clash in the streets (Dec. 22, 1989). The Ceausescus are captured (Dec. 23, 1989), hastily tried and executed by firing squad (Dec. 25, 1989). The next day, Ion Iliescu is named interim president.

1990: **In the Soviet Union, the movement toward independence gains momentum in several republics.** Lithuania declares its independence on March 11, 1990. The Soviet Union replies with a show of force and cuts off oil and natural gas supplies. After several weeks, Lithuania agrees to postpone independence. The Soviet government agrees to work on procedures for secession of republics. Estonia declares its independence on March 30, 1990, but does not name a date for secession. On May 4, 1990, Latvia issues an equivocal statement of independence. The movement toward independence, bolstered by Soviet President Mikhail Gorbachev's democratization policies of 1989 and by longstanding ethnic and political differences, continues throughout 1990, including Ukraine, Moldavia, and the Uzbek, Turkmen, Tadzhik and Kirghiz republics, all of which declare their sovereignty. The movement even extends to the Russian Soviet Federative Socialist Republic—the largest of the Soviet Union's 15 union republics. In July 1990, the republic's parliament elects Boris Yeltsin president of the Russian Republic. Yeltsin is a strong opponent of Gorbachev's plan to reform the nation's economy and political system. After his election, Yeltsin resigns from the Communist party, calls for a rapid transition to a market economy and seeks more authority for the individual republics and less for the Union.

Plans to unify East and West Germany move quickly. In free elections in East Germany, a Christian Democratic coalition gets 48 percent of the votes, Social Democrats get 22 percent and the Democratic Socialists (the former Communist party) gets 16 percent. Lothar de Maizière, a Christian Democrat, is chosen as prime minister. In February 1990, East Germany, West Germany and the four postwar occupying powers—Great Britain, France, the United States and the Soviet Union—agree on reunification talks. The depressed East German economy makes speedy reunification with prosperous West Germany imperative. The East German Ostmark currency is replaced by the West German Deutsche Mark on July 1, in a one-for-one exchange. On Sept. 12, Great Britain, France, the United States and the Soviet Union relinquish all occupation rights. On Oct. 2, East and West Germany are united as the German Republic.

The Yugoslavian Communist party votes to relinquish its monopoly on political power, permitting a multiparty system (Jan. 22, 1990).

As part of a movement toward ending apartheid in South Africa, African National Congress leader Nelson Mandela is freed after 27 years in prison (Feb. 11, 1990). He is elected president of the ANC. He and South Africa Pres. Frederik W. de Klerk begin discussions of a new constitution. Mandela's release is seen by his supporters as an opportunity to take control of black politics, which has been split into several factions. Hundreds are killed as factions fight for control. In a tour of the United States, Mandela is greeted as a hero (June 1990). When he addresses Congress, he is given three standing ovations (June 26, 1990).

Former Pres. Ronald Reagan testifies at the trial of his former National Security Adviser, John M. Poindexter (Feb. 16, 1990). He admits in federal court in Los Angeles that he was responsible for the part of the Iran-*Contra* affair that supported Nicaraguan rebels and attempted to trade weapons for American hostages. He claims, though, that he didn't tell Poindexter to break the law, did not know how much his aides were helping the *contras* and didn't remember details of many of the decisions. On June 11, 1990, Poindexter is convicted of five felonies, including conspiring to deceive Congress, and is sentenced to six months in prison.

In Nicaragua, incumbent Pres. Daniel Ortega Saavedra, a Sandinista, is defeated by Violeta Barrios de Chamorro, the candidate of a 14-party coalition (Feb. 25, 1990).

Namibia gains independence after 75 years of South African rule (March 20, 1990).

In Romania, Ion Iliescu (a former Communist serving as interim president) wins 85 percent of

the vote in the presidential election (May 20, 1990). Anti-Communist protests continue despite the fact that the Communist party no longer is officially in control. During the summer, protesters are beaten and killed by officially sanctioned goon squads.

An earthquake measuring 7.3 on the Richter scale leaves 40,000 dead in northwest Iran (June 21, 1990).

In Liberia, Pres. Samuel K. Doe is captured and killed by Prince Johnson and his rebel forces after 10 months of civil war during which thousands of civilians were slaughtered by the forces of Doe, Johnson and Charles Taylor, as the three factions vied for power (Sept. 10, 1990).

The civil war in Nicaragua ends when 100 top *contra* **fighters turn over their arms to Pres. Violeta Barrios de Chamorro** (June 28, 1990). The ceremony marks the end of demobilization, which had been overseen by a UN force.

Iraqi troops invade Kuwait and overthrow the government (Aug. 2, 1990). The UN Security Council orders a trade and financial embargo on Iraq and the occupied area of Kuwait, which significantly limits Iraq's market for oil (Aug. 6, 1990). UN troops, later supported by multinational forces, are sent to Saudi Arabia to protect it from invasion by Iraq. A U.S. naval blockade prohibits oil exports and all imports other than food. Iraqi Pres. Saddam Hussein rounds up Westerners and sends them to Iraqi military, oil production and industrial sites, to use them as human shields. OPEC agrees to increase oil production to make up for the loss caused by the embargo of Iraq (Aug. 29, 1990). [*See* The Persian Gulf War, page 140]

Solidarity Chairman Lech Walesa is elected president of Poland (Dec. 9, 1990).

1991: [*See* The Dissolution of the USSR, page 112]

Rhode Island Gov. Bruce Sundlun declares bank emergency, closes 45 privately insured banks and credit unions until federal insurance for $1.7 billion in deposits can be arranged (Jan. 1, 1991). **Federal government seizes the Bank of New England and two affiliates after withdrawals of more than $1 billion in two days** (Jan. 5, 1991).

[*See* The Persian Gulf War, page 140]

President Bush, in state of the union message, promises victory in Persian Gulf and over domestic economic problems (Jan. 29, 1991).

Father Jean-Bertrand Aristide becomes Haiti's first democratically elected president in 186 years (Feb. 7, 1991). He is later overthrown by a military coup (Sept. 30, 1991).

A videotape shot by an amateur shows four police officers in Los Angeles beating and kicking a handcuffed suspect as other officers watch (March 3, 1991). The suspect, Rodney Glen King, had been stopped for speeding; it did not appear as though he was resisting arrest.

High school teacher Pamela Smart of Exeter, N.H., is sentenced to life in prison for her role in plotting with a 15-year-old student, who was also her lover, to kill her husband (March 22, 1991). Gregory Smart was shot to death by the boy, William Flynn, in May 1990.

The Supreme Court rules that a coerced or involuntary confession may be "harmless error" and does not automatically invalidate a conviction (March 26, 1991).

Soviet Union ends its role as Eastern European military watchdog; Warsaw Pact ends (March 31, 1991).

President Bush is hospitalized after suffering shortness of breath while jogging (May 4, 1991). He is diagnosed as having Graves' disease, a treatable thyroid condition.

In South Africa, **Winnie Mandela is convicted** of being an accessory after the fact and is sentenced to six years in prison in connection with an assault on four youths who were kidnapped and taken to her home in 1988; one of the boys was found dead nearby (May 13, 1991).

Rajiv Gandhi, former prime minister of India, is assassinated as he campaigns to regain the post and strengthen the Congress Party (May 21, 1991). Gandhi and 14 others are killed when a bomb explodes in a crowd. Gandhi, 46, was the son of Prime Minister Indira Gandhi, who was assassinated in 1984.

Supreme Court upholds, 5–4, federal regulations that prohibit federally funded clinics from discussing abortion with patients (May 23, 1991).

NATO agrees to cut U.S. forces in Europe by 50 percent (May 28, 1991).

Mt. Pinatubo erupts in the Philippines (June 10, 1991). [*See* Part IX: Disasters, U.S. and Foreign, page 375]

Boris Yeltsin elected president of Russian Republic (June 12, 1991). Meets with President Bush in Washington (June 20, 1991). [*See* The Dissolution of the USSR, page 112]

South African Pres. F. W. de Klerk repeals last apartheid law (June 17, 1991).

The world's largest brokerage house, Nomura Securities Co. of Tokyo, admits that it improperly compensated big clients for $120 million in losses and that its executive vice president gave $150 million in financing to a member of a prominent crime family as part of a stock scheme (June 21, 1991). Nikko Securities admits it compensated clients for $122 million in losses.

Yugoslavia begins to disintegrate as two of its six republics, Slovenia and Croatia, proclaim in-

dependence (June 25, 1991). The Slovenia militia defeats the Yugoslav army, forcing it to withdraw from Slovenia by early July. In August, **Croatia faces opposition from within as Serbian rebels try to seize control of the ethnically Serbian area, seeking to make it part of Serbia.** The Serbs hold about one-third of the region. They are aided in part by the Yugoslav army, which is about 70 percent Serbian. Fighting escalates throughout the year.

President Bush announces that he will nominate Clarence Thomas to replace Thurgood Marshall as an Associate Justice of the Supreme Court (July 1, 1991).

Eight nations, led by the Bank of England, shut down operations of Bank of Credit and Commerce International, alleging fraud that includes false accounts, hidden deposits, shell companies, secret loans and kickbacks (July 5, 1991). BCCI allegedly was trying to cover losses of several billion dollars. Bank regulators say BCCI, with major operations in London and backed by Arab oil money, secretly acquired two U.S. banking companies, First American Bankshares Inc. in Washington and Independence Bank in California. [*See* Political Scandals, page 35]

President Bush lifts trade sanctions against South Africa due to progress in abolition of apartheid (July 10, 1991).

A coup attempts to overthrow Soviet President Mikhail Gorbachev while he is on vacation in the Crimea (July 19, 1991). It fails two days later. [*See* The Dissolution of the USSR, page 112]

Milwaukee police arrest Jeffrey Dahmer, believed to have killed 17 people in 13 years. Dahmer confesses to drugging, strangling and dismembering victims. Human heads and body parts are found in his apartment after a would-be victim escapes and calls police (July 22, 1991).

In Lebanon, **British television journalist John McCarthy is freed by pro-Iranian militants** who had held him hostage since April 17, 1986 (Aug. 8, 1991). Hours later, a French aid worker, Jerome Leyraud, is kidnapped in Beirut by a fringe group that objects to the release of Westerners. Leyraud is freed Aug. 11 in Beirut, as is Edward Tracy, an American book salesman who had been held hostage since Oct. 21, 1986.

The Yugoslavian province of Macedonia proclaims independence, following the lead of Slovenia and Croatia (Sept. 9, 1991).

Israel releases 51 Arab prisoners after it gets confirmation that an Israeli soldier missing in Lebanon since 1983 is dead (Sept. 11, 1991). The soldier's body is returned to Israel (Sept. 13, 1991). British hostage Jack Mann, 77, is released in Beirut (Sept. 24, 1991). He had been held captive since Dec. 5, 1989.

Federal appeals court dismisses case against Oliver North for his role in Iran-*Contra* affair. (He had been convicted of falsifying and destroying documents, accepting an illegal gratuity and aiding and abetting the obstruction of Congress.) Judge Gerhard A. Gesell of U.S. District Court, Washington, D.C., rules that his case had been tainted by Congressional testimony that North had given under promise of immunity (Sept. 16). [*See* Political Scandals, page 35]

An audit of the House Bank shows that hundreds of House members have written checks for amounts exceeding their account balances (Sept. 1991). [*See* Political Scandals, page 35]

In a nationally televised address, **President Bush announces that the U.S. will eliminate short-range nuclear arms** from American bases in Europe and Asia and from all naval vessels because Soviet invasion of Western Europe is "no longer a realistic threat" (Sept. 27, 1991).

The Senate Judiciary Committee begins hearings on confirmation of Clarence Thomas as Supreme Court Associate Justice (Sept. 10, 1991). Thomas, a prominent black conservative, avoids giving any indication of his feelings on key issues, including abortion. He denies ever having discussed Roe v. Wade. **Thomas's conservative background and his "bootstrap" approach to minority advancement draw criticism** from numerous groups, including the NAACP, NOW, the Leadership Conference on Civil Rights, the National Abortion Rights League, the Alliance for Justice and People for the American Way. **The Judiciary Committee sends the nomination to the Senate with no recommendation,** after a 7–7 vote (Sept. 27, 1991). The Senate vote, scheduled for Oct. 8, is delayed when a story in *Newsday* of New York charges that the Judiciary Committee had considered allegations of sexual harassment against Thomas, but had not made them public (Oct. 6, 1991). **Anita Hill, a law professor at the University of Oklahoma, claims that Thomas had sexually harassed her** when she served as his assistant at the Department of Education and the Equal Employment Opportunity Commission in the early 1980s. **The Judiciary Committee reconvenes to hear testimony concerning the allegations** (Oct. 11, 1991). Thomas vehemently denies the allegations. Hill calmly maintains that her account is accurate. The hearings are televised live, getting a larger share of the ratings than the major league baseball playoffs. **By a 52–48 vote, the Senate votes to confirm Thomas** (Oct. 15, 1991).

Crazed gunman drives pickup truck through

window of Luby's Cafeteria in Killeen, Tex., and opens fire with high-powered pistol. George Hennard kills 22 customers and employees before killing himself (Oct. 16, 1991).

U.S. Navy apologizes to the family of Gunner's Mate 2d Class Clayton Hartwig, whom it had once accused of triggering a battleship turret explosion that killed 47 people (including Hartwig). Navy says the cause of the explosion may never be known (Oct. 17, 1991).

Fire sweeps through hills above San Francisco Bay, killing 24, destroying 3,000 houses and apartments and causing more than $5 billion in damages (Oct. 19–20, 1991). [See Part IX: Disasters, U.S. and Foreign, page 375]

American mathematics professor Jesse Turner, 44, is released by the Islamic Jihad for the Liberation of Palestine (Oct. 22, 1991). He had been held hostage since Jan. 24, 1987.

Dr. Jack Kevorkian, a retired pathologist, assists two women in their suicides by providing devices and medical knowledge. He oversees the deaths of Marjorie Wantz, 58, and Sherry Miller, 43, in a cabin in a state park in Michigan (Oct. 23, 1991). Wantz suffered from a painful but not terminal pelvic disease; Miller was paralyzed by multiple sclerosis.

Bosnia-Herzegovina becomes the fourth Yugoslavian republic to declare independence (Oct. 15, 1991).

Mideast peace talks begin in Madrid (Oct. 30, 1991). The historic talks between Arabs and Israelis seek to end 40 years of hostilities. President Bush and Soviet President Mikhail Gorbachev call for compromise. A second round of talks begins Dec. 11, 1991, with little progress made.

Hostages Terry Waite and Thomas Sutherland are released in Lebanon (Nov. 18, 1991). Waite, an envoy of the Church of England, was kidnapped Jan. 20, 1987, while on a mission seeking the release of Western hostages. Sutherland, the agriculture dean of American University, had been kidnapped June 10, 1986.

Senate Ethics Committee reprimands Sen. Alan Cranston, D-Calif., for "improper and repugnant" conduct in accepting campaign donations from Charles H. Keating, Jr., former owner of Lincoln Savings and Loan. Cranston had intervened with thrift regulators on behalf of the S&L (Nov. 20, 1991). [See Political Scandals, page 38]

U.S. closes Clark Air Base in the Philippines, which had been damaged by eruption of Mt. Pinatubo in June (Nov. 26, 1991).

In Lebanon, Joseph Cicippio, acting comptroller of American University in Beirut, is freed (Dec. 2, 1991). He had been kidnapped Sept. 12, 1986, by the Revolutionary Justice Organization. Alann Steen, 52, an American communications professor at Beirut University College, is freed (Dec. 3, 1991). He had been kidnapped Jan. 24, 1987. Terry Anderson, 44, chief Middle East correspondent for the Associated Press, is freed by the Islamic Jihad (Dec. 4, 1991). Anderson had been abducted March 16, 1985.

William Kennedy Smith is acquitted of charge that he raped a woman at his family's estate in West Palm Beach, Fla. (Dec. 11, 1991). The woman claimed that she met Smith (and his uncle, Sen. Edward M. Kennedy) at a nightclub, and that she later gave Smith a ride home. Smith claimed that they engaged in consensual sexual acts on the beach and lawn. The woman claimed that Smith threw her onto the lawn and raped her. The trial was broadcast live.

1992: President Bush tours Japan in an attempt to win trade concessions (Jan. 7–9, 1992). He faints at a state dinner in Tokyo (Jan. 8, 1992) due to a stomach virus. Bush calls the trip a success. Critics, including the chairmen of the Big Three auto makers who accompanied him, say that the concessions he won were not adequate.

The military seizes power in Algeria (Jan. 11, 1992). Military leaders force Pres. Chadli Bendjedid to resign, cancel elections and declare a state of emergency.

In El Salvador, the government and rebels belonging to the Farabundo Marti National Liberation Front (FMLN) sign a peace treaty ending 12 years of civil war (Jan. 16, 1992). The treaty follows 21 months of talks mediated by the United Nations. The war claimed 75,000 lives and pitted the rightist government (supported by the United States) against the leftist rebels (supported by the former Soviet Union, Cuba and the Sandinista National Liberation Front in Nicaragua).

The European Community recognizes Croatia and Slovenia as independent republics, separate from Yugoslavia, as the country continues to break apart in a civil war based on ethnic and regional identities and interests (Jan. 15, 1992).

Arkansas Gov. Bill Clinton, a contender for the Democratic presidential nomination, faces allegations of extramarital affairs, including a long-term one with Gennifer Flowers, a former Arkansas government employee (Jan. 1992). Clinton calls the claims, which were first published in a supermarket tabloid (the Star), "totally bogus."

One of the country's largest retailers, R.H. Macy & Co., files for bankruptcy (Jan. 27, 1992), reflecting difficulties in the retail industry due to the economic recession. Trans World Airlines Inc. files for bankruptcy (Jan. 31, 1992). The action follows similar filings by Pan American World Airlines, Continental Airlines Holdings Inc., America West Airlines, Braniff International Corp., Eastern Air Lines Inc. and Midway Airlines Inc. in the last year. (Midway, Eastern and Pan Am shut down.)

The United States begins forcibly returning Haitian refugees to their homeland from the U.S. processing center at the Guantanamo Bay Naval base in Cuba (Feb. 1, 1992). The refugees had begun fleeing Haiti after a coup ousted Pres. Jean-Bertrand Aristide on Sept. 30, 1991. The Bush administration claims that most of the refugees left for economic, not political, reasons, and that repatriation would discourage others from undertaking the hazardous sea voyage. Opponents, including the UN high commissioner for refugees, express concern for the safety of the returned refugees. Later, President Bush orders the Coast Guard to intercept the refugees at sea and return them to Haiti (May 24, 1992), saying that the processing center at Guantanamo Bay is overcrowded and that the 600-mile journey from Haiti is too dangerous for the refugees in their ill-equipped boats.

In Venezuela, rebel soldiers stage an unsuccessful coup attempt (Feb. 2, 1992) in response to concerns about rampant inflation, a widening gap between the wealthy and the poor, and the government's inability to deal with widespread corruption. The attack is repulsed by soldiers loyal to Pres. Carlos Andres Perez.

Former world heavyweight boxing champion Mike Tyson is convicted of raping Desiree Washington (Feb. 10, 1992), an 18-year-old contestant in the Miss Black America pageant in Indianapolis in 1991. Tyson was a judge of the beauty contest. He is sentenced to six years in prison and fined $30,000.

Serial killer Jeffrey L. Dahmer is sentenced in Milwaukee County Court to 15 consecutive life terms for the murders of 15 men and boys, whom he dismembered and, in some cases, cannibalized, between 1978 and 1991 (Feb. 17, 1992). He had confessed to those murders and to two others. (In one of those cases, police lack enough evidence to charge him. In the other case, in Ohio, he later pleads guilty to aggravated murder.)

William Aramony, president of United Way of America, quits amid allegations of mismanagement (Feb. 27, 1992). The charity undertakes an internal investigation. It releases a report (April 3, 1992) that alleges haphazard financial arrangements, possible law violations and lavish spending on travel and personal items by Aramony, who had been paid a $390,000 annual salary. Aramony denies the allegations.

Texas businessman **Ross Perot enters the presidential race** when he announces on the *Larry King Live* talk show that he would run for the office if voters petitioned to get him on the ballot (March 16, 1992). Perot's "outsider" candidacy is so attractive to voters that he is soon outpacing Pres. George Bush and Democratic front-runner Bill Clinton in the polls.

South African whites, by a 68.6-to-31.2 percent margin, endorse a plan to negotiate an end to white-minority rule (March 17, 1992). In the referendum, open only to whites, voters support the efforts of Pres. F. W. de Klerk to negotiate with the black majority for a new, nonracial constitution.

Hotel magnate Leona Helmsley, 71, is sentenced to four years in prison for cheating the government out of millions of dollars in taxes (April 1, 1992). Her 83-year-old husband, Harry, also had been indicted but had been ruled incompetent to stand trial due to ill health.

The Group of Seven major industrial countries (the U.S., Germany, Japan, Great Britain, France, Italy and Canada) announces a one-year, $24 billion aid package for Russia (April 1, 1992).

Edith Cresson, France's first female premier, resigns (April 2, 1992). Her 11 months in office were marked by record-low ratings in opinion polls, ongoing financial scandals in government and an unemployment rate of nearly 10 percent. She is replaced by Finance Minister Pierre Beregovoy.

John Gotti, reputed leader of the Gambino crime family, is convicted in U.S. District Court in Brooklyn of all charges in a 13-count federal indictment charging him with racketeering, murder, extortion, illegal gambling, obstruction of justice and tax fraud. (April 2, 1992). Codefendant Frank (Frankie Locs) Locasio is convicted of seven of eight charges, including racketeering and murder. Three earlier trials had ended in acquittal, which caused Gotti to become known as the "Teflon Don."

The United States recognizes the independence of Croatia, Slovenia and Bosnia-Herzegovina from Yugoslavia (April 7, 1992). The European Community, which had already recognized Croatia and Slovenia, recognizes the independence of Bosnia-Herzegovina (April 7, 1992). Fighting continues throughout Yugoslavia and the newly independent republics as Serbs, Croats and Muslims battle for territory and recognition.

Peruvian Pres. Alberto K. Fujimori seizes authoritarian power (April 5, 1992). He dissolves the National Congress, censors the press, arrests political rivals and suspends parts of the constitution. He says the measures are needed to stop drug traffickers and attacks by rebels.

At a press conference, **tennis champion Arthur Ashe announces that he has the AIDS virus** (April 8, 1992). Ashe assails the press for raising the issue, which he had hoped to keep private. (The newspaper *USA Today* had asked him to comment on rumors that he had the AIDS virus.) Ashe says that he became infected from a blood transfusion after heart surgery in 1983.

British Prime Minister John Major is re-elected (April 9, 1992), the fourth consecutive victory for the Conservatives.

Former Panamanian strongman **Gen. Manuel Noriega is convicted** in U.S. District Court in Miami of eight counts of racketeering, drug trafficking and money laundering (April 9, 1992). He is acquitted of charges of importing and distributing cocaine. Noriega had been accused of accepting millions of dollars from Colombia's Medellin drug cartel in exchange for allowing Panama to be used as a center for drug trafficking to the United States.

Riots erupt in Los Angeles after a California Superior Court in suburban Simi Valley acquits four white Los Angeles police officers of charges arising from the March 1991 beating of a black motorist, Rodney G. King (April 29, 1992). (The jury deadlocked on one count against one of the officers.) The beating had been videotaped by a nearby resident and had been broadcast widely. It showed police officers repeatedly kicking King and beating him with their batons as he lay on the ground. Looting, random violence and arson fires break out across the predominantly black and Hispanic South Central area of Los Angeles. Mayor Tom Bradley declares a local state of emergency. Gov. Pete Wilson calls out the National Guard. A three-day rampage leaves 60 dead and thousands injured. More than 5,500 fires are reported. Damages are estimated at $785 million.

A Constitutional amendment barring Congress from enacting mid-term pay raises is ratified when Michigan becomes the 38th state to approve it (May 7, 1992). The amendment, passed by Congress in 1789, included no deadline for ratification.

Fidel V. Ramos is elected president of the Philippines (May 11). Ramos is the first president to take power peacefully since Ferdinand Marcos in 1965.

Six of the 11 countries in the Commonwealth of Independent States sign a mutual security treaty (May 15, 1992). The signers are the presidents of Russia, Kazakhstan, Belarus, Armenia, Turkmenistan and Uzbekistan. Factional differences and unrest prevent the presidents of the Ukraine, Tajikistan, Moldova, Azerbaijan and Kyrgystan from attending the summit.

The European Community imposes a trade embargo on Yugoslavia (May 27, 1992) in an attempt to stop fighting in Bosnia-Herzegovina. Serbian militias and guerrillas from Yugoslavia (a federation of Serbia and Montenegro) have occupied most of Bosnia and hold the capital, Sarejevo, under siege. Savage attacks on civilians have been reported. **The UN Security Council imposes a trade embargo on Yugoslavia** (May 30, 1992) and freezes the country's foreign assets. Russia and China abstain from the vote. The sanctions are supported by the remaining 13 member nations.

The UN-sponsored Earth Summit draws representatives of 178 nations to Rio de Janeiro for the largest conference ever on the environment (June 3–14, 1992). The European Community and 153 countries sign treaties aimed at slowing global warming and protecting biological diversity. The United States signs the global warming treaty after forcing negotiators to drop target dates for reductions in carbon dioxide emissions. The United States does not sign the biological diversity treaty, which pledges protection of endangered species and cooperation in genetic and biological technology. U.S. delegates cite concerns about financing and intellectual property rights.

The U.S. Supreme Court rules that the U.S. may prosecute criminal suspects whom it has kidnapped from foreign countries (June 15, 1992). The case, U.S. v. Alvarez Machain, concerns a Mexican doctor who was a suspect in the murder of a U.S. Drug Enforcement Administration agent. When Mexico refused to extradite him for trial, he was kidnapped by bounty hunters paid by the DEA.

The United States and Russia announce a strategic arms limitation agreement (June 16, 1992) that calls for sweeping reductions in the number of nuclear warheads on long-range missiles. The announcement comes on the first day of a two-day summit meeting in Washington, D.C., between Russian President Boris Yeltsin and President Bush. Yeltsin addresses a joint session of Congress (June 17, 1992), seeking financial aid for Russia and the other republics of the former Soviet Union. Yeltsin and President Bush sign accords pledging economic, scientific and military cooperation.

Former Defense Secretary Casper W. Weinberger is indicted (June 16, 1992). He is accused of obstructing a Congressional inquiry into the Iran-*Contra* arms scandal.

Fidel V. Ramos is declared the winner of the Philippine presidential elections (June 16, 1992) after a month-long vote count.

Forty-six black residents are slain in an attack on the South African township of Boipatong (June 17, 1992). Most are women, children or old people.

Survivors claim that Zulu men invaded the town, attacking with rifles, axes and knives. The African National Congress claims that the government is guilty of complicity, which Pres. F. W. de Klerk denies.

The last Western hostages in Lebanon are freed by Shiite guerrillas (June 17, 1992). German relief workers Heinrich Struebig and Thomas Kemptner had been kidnapped May 16, 1989.

The U.S. Supreme Court overturns a "hate-crimes" ordinance that makes it a crime to engage in speech or actions that are inflammatory due to racist, sexist or otherwise bigoted content (June 22, 1992). In R.A.V. v. St. Paul (Minn.) the court rules that the city's ordinance infringed on the right of free expression. The case concerned a teenager who had been convicted of burning a cross on the lawn of a black family.

Navy Secretary H. Lawrence Garrett III resigns due to complaints concerning the Navy's handling of the Tailhook sex-abuse scandal (June 26, 1992). The Navy initially had failed to prosecute suspects, although an investigation had found that 26 women had been sexually abused at the September 1991 convention of the Tailhook Association, a private organization of Navy and Marine Corps fliers.

Kidnapped Exxon executive is found dead (June 27, 1992). Sidney Reso's body is found in a shallow grave in New Jersey. Arthur D. and Irene J. Seale are accused of kidnapping him in April and seeking $18.5 million in ransom.

Algerian President Mohammed Boudiaf is assassinated during a speech at a cultural center (June 29, 1992).

Gov. Bill Clinton of Arkansas accepts the Democratic nomination for the presidency (July 16, 1992) at the party's convention (July 13–16, 1992) in New York City. Tennessee Sen. Al Gore accepts the vice presidential nomination. **Texas billionaire Ross Perot withdraws from the race** (July 16, 1992). Perot, who had been running as an independent candidate, said that public support for a "revitalized" Democratic party would make it impossible for him to win the election outright. A three-way race might mean that no candidate would win a majority, in which case the winner would be determined by the House of Representatives. Perot said that would be "disruptive to the country." Polls had indicated that Perot's popularity was falling.

In Czechoslovakia, the Slovak National Council declares the sovereignty of the Slovak republic (July 17, 1992). Czechoslovakian Pres. Vaclav Havel, who opposes the separation of the Czech and Slovak republics, resigns (July 20, 1992).

The 25th Summer Olympic Games open in Barcelona, Spain (July 25, 1992). South Africa, which had been excluded for 32 years because of its apartheid policy, is allowed to take part. Athletes from the new nations that were formerly part of the Soviet Union join forces as the Unified Team. They include representatives of the 11 republics of the Commonwealth of Independent States and Georgia.

Washington, D.C., lawyers **Clark M. Clifford and Robert A. Altman are indicted in connection with the Bank of Credit & Commerce International scandal** on state and federal charges of conspiracy, bribe-taking, falsifying business records and scheming to commit fraud (July 29, 1992). They deny the allegations. Both were officers of first American Bankshares Inc., which was under the control of BCCI.

In South Africa, 4 million blacks go on strike to urge the government to accept black majority rule (Aug. 3–4, 1992). Black businesses are closed, public transportation is disrupted, some industries are brought to a standstill and schoolchildren stay home during the protest.

A federal grand jury indicts four white, Los Angeles police officers on charges of violating the civil rights of Rodney G. King, a black motorist whom they beat in March 1991 (Aug. 5, 1992). Three of the officers had been acquitted of state charges in April and the fourth was scheduled for retrial. The decisions had sparked riots in Los Angeles and other cities in April.

The United States, Canada and Mexico agree to a 15-year, free-trade pact, the North American Free Trade Agreement (Aug. 12, 1992). The pact will eliminate tariffs and other trade and investment restrictions. It must be signed by the three heads of state and ratified by the three legislatures before it takes effect.

The UN Security Council authorizes the use of military force to permit the delivery of food and medicine to embattled Bosnia-Hercegovina and condemns the Serbian policy of "ethnic cleansing" (Aug. 13, 1992). Heavy shelling had made the delivery of relief supplies dangerous, and had caused the UN to suspend flights for four days earlier in the month.

Attorney General William P. Barr rejects a request from the House Judiciary Committee to appoint a special prosecutor to investigate the role of the Bush Administration in supplying aid to Iraq before the Persian Gulf War (Aug. 10, 1992). The committee had claimed that the Justice Department would not be able to conduct an unbiased investigation because of political conflict of interest. Barr replied that the committee's request was, in itself, politically motivated. Bush had repeatedly denied that his administration knew that Iraq had been diverting U.S. funds for agricultural aid to military uses. In July, he had called the allegations "pure, gut American politics."

The XXV Summer Olympic Games end in Barcelona, Spain (Aug. 16, 1992). The Unified Team (representatives of the 11 republics of the Commonwealth of Independent States and Georgia) wins the most gold medals, 112. The U.S. is second with 108, and Germany is third with 82.

President George Bush and Vice President Dan Quayle are renominated (Aug. 20, 1992) at the Republican National Convention in Houston's Astrodome.

President Bush orders an emergency airlift of food to Somalia, where more than one million people are starving due to a civil war and drought (Aug. 14, 1992). UN peace-keeping forces are sent to prevent looting and make sure that international humanitarian relief efforts can reach the starving population (Sept. 14, 1992).

Hurricane Andrew devastates southern Florida (Aug. 24, 1992) and causes substantial damage to parts of Louisiana (Aug. 25–26, 1992). In Florida, 13 people die, 250,000 are left homeless and damages are estimated as high as $20 billion. One person is killed in Louisiana. U.S. troops are sent to Florida to deliver food, water and medical supplies, set up tent cities and maintain order (Aug. 28, 1992).

Czechoslovakian leaders agree to dissolve the federation between the Czech and Slovak republics as of Jan. 1, 1993, creating separate nations (Aug. 26, 1992).

Hurricane Iniki strikes the western Hawaiian islands (Sept. 11, 1992), killing three people and causing damages estimated at $1 billion.

In Peru, police capture Abimael Guzman Reynoso, leader of the Shining Path guerrilla movement that has fought the government for 12 years (Sept. 12, 1992). He is convicted of treason and sentenced to life in prison (Oct. 7, 1992).

French voters narrowly approve the European Community's Treaty on European Union that would create a common currency and strengthen cooperation on defense and foreign trade (Sept. 20, 1992). The treaty, which had been negotiated in Maastricht, the Netherlands, in 1991, requires ratification by all 12 EC members. France became the fourth nation to ratify, joining Greece, Ireland and Luxembourg.

The United Nations expells Yugoslavia because of its role in the war in Bosnia-Hercegovina (Sept. 22, 1992). Yugoslavia is the first sitting member of the UN to be expelled.

Acting Navy Secretary Sean C. O'Keefe announces that three admirals will be punished for improper handling of the Tailhook scandal (Sept. 24, 1992). More that 20 women, including military officers, claimed that they had been sexually abused by aviators at a convention of the Tailhook Association in Las Vegas in 1991. The admirals are accused of failing to properly investigate the incident. Two admirals are asked to retire; one is relieved of his post and reassigned.

Brazilian President Fernando Collor de Mello is impeached on charges that he profited from kickbacks set up by his former campaign treasurer (Sept. 29, 1992).

Texas billionaire Ross Perot rejoins the presidential race as an independent candidate (Oct. 1, 1992). His running mate is retired Admiral James B. Stockdale. The three presidential candidates meet in a series of debates in St. Louis, Mo. (Oct. 11, 1992), Richmond, Va. (Oct. 15, 1992) and East Lansing, Mich. (Oct. 19, 1992). The vice presidential candidates debate in Atlanta, Ga. (Oct. 13, 1992).

In Mozambique, the warring factions in the nation's 16-year civil war sign a peace accord (Oct. 4, 1992). The leftist government and, the rightist Mozambique National Resistance guerrilla movement agree to disband their armies and surrender their arms to UN peacekeepers. The war had claimed 600,000 lives.

Five American nuns are shot to death in Liberia (between Oct. 20 and 31, 1992). Two of the nuns were believed to have been killed by rebel forces while trying to rescue a child wounded in the country's civil war (Oct. 20, 1992). The other three nuns were believed to have been killed several days later.

A Paris court convicts three French health officials of knowingly allowing blood products tainted with the AIDS virus to be used in transfusions (Oct. 23, 1992). Although untainted blood was available from other countries in early 1985, the officials continued to permit the use of tainted blood until the fall, when a French method of purification was developed.

Arkansas Gov. Bill Clinton is elected president (Nov. 3, 1992), winning 32 states, 370 electoral votes and 43 percent of the popular vote. George Bush wins 18 states, 168 electoral votes and 38 percent of the popular vote. Ross Perot, who fails to take any states, wins 19 percent of the popular vote.

Democrats retain control of Congress (Nov. 3, 1992). After a runoff and a special election, they keep their previous majority of 57 seats in the Senate. They lose nine House seats, leaving them with

258 to the Republicans' 176. (One seat is held by an independent.) **The number of women in Congress increases.** Four are added in the Senate, bringing the total to six. In the House, the number grows from 28 to 47. **The ethnic makeup of the House changes,** with the number of blacks increasing from 25 to 38 and the number of Hispanics from 10 to 17.

Neo-Nazism and rightist attacks against foreigners and immigrants increase in Germany, resulting (Nov. 23, 1992) in the worst incidence of violence since re-unification, a firebombing in which a Turkish woman and her two daughters are killed. Authorities try to defuse the problem with a law restricting immigration.

Venezuela's president, Carlos Andrés Pérez, survives the second coup attempt (Nov. 27, 1992) in 10 months. More than 230 are killed in the revolt. Pérez vows to remain in office until a successor is elected next year.

The United Nations Security Council approves United States-led military intervention to ensure that relief supplies reach Somalia (Dec. 3, 1992), which has been destroyed by famine and clan fighting since the collapse of the government in January 1991. More than 300,000 people have died, and an estimated 1.5 million are reported in imminent danger of starvation. President Bush dispatches 28,150 U.S. troops (Dec. 4, 1992).

Hindu militants destroy a 16th century mosque (Dec. 6, 1992), plunging India once again into a religious and political crisis. Hindus and Muslims riot throughout northern cities and towns the next day; at least 1,200 people are killed.

U.S. troops land in Mogadishu, Somalia, (on Dec. 8, 1992) beginning Operation Restore Hope, an attempt to aid millions of starving civilians victimized by drought, civil war and years of political unrest.

In England, **Prime Minister John Major announces that Prince Charles and Princess Diana will separate** but that succession to the throne will not be affected (Dec. 9, 1992).

President George Bush pardons former Defense Secretary Caspar Weinberger and five other former government officials involved in the Iran-Contra investigation (Dec. 24, 1992).

Czechoslovakia splits peacefully into two countries as the year ends (Dec. 31, 1992), becoming Slovakia and the Czech Republic at midnight.

THE DISSOLUTION OF THE USSR

When 1991 began, the Soviet Union was moving toward change, led by Pres. Mikhail Gorbachev. The country, beset by serious economic problems and factional differences, was re-examining its role in the world community, and the economic and political foundations of its existence. Change came with breathtaking speed.

By year's end, Gorbachev was out of a job. The Union of Soviet Socialist Republics was no more. It had been replaced, instead, by the Commonwealth of Independent States, a loose confederation of 11 of the 15 republics that had made up the USSR. (One republic, Georgia, remained unaligned. The three Baltic states—Lithuania, Latvia and Estonia—had established themselves as independent countries.)

The 11 republics that had joined the CIS sought to establish their roles there. Russia, the largest of the republics, assumed a great deal of influence under the leadership of Boris Yeltsin, but the other republics also sought power and position. As they struggled for identity, some republics even changed their names: Byelorussia became Belarus; Moldavia became Moldova; Turkmenia became Turkmenistan; Kirgizia became Kyrgystan.

The change that swept the Soviet Union in 1991 gained momentum gradually, starting with Gorbachev's public recognition in 1985 that the old system was not working:

1985: **Mikhail Sergeyevich Gorbachev (1931–) named General Secretary of Communist party** after death of Konstantin Chernenko (March 11, 1985). The party supports his platform of "**perestroika,**" restructuring of the system. Gorbachev meets with Pres. Ronald Reagan in Geneva; agrees to eliminate medium- and short-range nuclear missiles (Nov. 1985).

1986: **Anatoly Sharansky, a Jewish dissident imprisoned for his activism, is released** as part of a spy swap (Feb. 11, 1986). After widespread international appeals, **Gorbachev ends internal exile of physicist Andrei Sakharov,** a human-rights activist and winner of the Nobel Peace Prize.

1987: Gorbachev vows to destroy stockpiles of chemical weapons (April 10, 1987). He meets with Prime Minister Margaret Thatcher in London and President Reagan in Washington. **Gorbachev signs treaty to eliminate medium-range nuclear missiles** (Dec. 1987).

1988: **Gorbachev elected president of the legislature,** the Supreme Soviet (Oct. 1, 1988). The old Supreme Soviet is dissolved and is replaced by a larger Congress of People's Deputies, designed to provide more popular participation, and a new, smaller Supreme Soviet (Nov. 29, 1988). **Gorbachev calls for a new world order in an address to the United Nations** (Dec. 7, 1988). He returns to USSR early due to massive earthquake in Armenia, which draws international aid.

1989: **Last troops are removed from Afghanistan, ending an expensive, demoralizing, nine-year war** (Feb. 15, 1989). Communist regimes are swept from power in Eastern Europe. USSR declines to intervene (March 6, 1989). Gorbachev removes 110 old-line government leaders and replaces them with appointees sympathetic to his reform goals (April 25, 1989). **Gorbachev convinces the Congress of People's Deputies that the country needs a new form of government with a strong presidency. He is elected president** (May 25, 1989).

1990: **Prodemocracy rallies in Moscow attract 300,000** (Feb. 4, 1990). Gorbachev urges the Communist Party Central Committee to embrace a multiparty system. Gorbachev reelected president by Congress of People's Deputies (March 15, 1990). **Gorbachev rival Boris Yeltsin becomes president of Russia, the largest and most influential republic in the USSR** (May 29, 1990). The 28th **Communist Party Congress relinquishes the party's total control** of the country (July 15, 1990). **Gorbachev wins Nobel Peace Prize for his role in ending the Cold War** (Oct. 15, 1990). Foreign Minister Eduard Shevardnadze resigns, warning that Gorbachev is seeking dictatorial power (Dec. 20, 1990).

1991: **Soviet troops seize Latvia's main publishing house** in Riga six days after Latvia announces plans to become independent (Jan. 2, 1991). Soviet Defense Ministry begins sending troops to Estonia, Latvia, Lithuania, Georgia, Armenia, Moldavia and Ukraine in an attempt to enforce the draft and to catch deserters (Jan. 7, 1991). **More than 100 Soviet military vehicles enter Vilnius, the capital of Lithuania,** in an attempt to round up draft dodgers. Young people, particularly in Lithuania and Georgia, have been ignoring the draft as an indication of anti-Soviet sentiment. Soviet troops storm the press center and civilian militia building in Vilnius (Jan. 11, 1991). They seize the state broadcast center, declare a curfew, ban public gatherings, search civilians and ban tape recorders and television cameras. **Violence erupts, leaving 15 dead** (Jan. 13, 1991). **In Riga, Latvia, commandos of the Soviet Interior Ministry raid the Latvian Interior Ministry, leaving five people dead** in a 90-minute gun battle (Jan. 20, 1991). **More than 100,000 demonstrators in Moscow protest the Latvian bloodbath and call for Gorbachev's resignation.** In response to Moscow's crackdown on Latvia and Lithuania, the European Parliament delays a much-needed $1 billion in food aid and $550 million in technical assistance (Jan. 22, 1991).

The Soviet government begins joint military and police patrols throughout the country in an attempt to maintain order (Feb. 1, 1991). Several republics resist. **Lithuanians vote 9-to-1 for independence** (Feb. 9, 1991). A rally by 30,000 soldiers in Moscow supports Gorbachev (Feb. 23, 1991). The next day, 40,000 marchers demand his resignation.

Latvia and Estonia vote for independence (March 3, 1991). In Moscow, more than 100,000 demonstrators march to oppose Gorbachev's proposed referendum on national unity, and to support Boris Yeltsin, the influential president of the Russian Republic. **In a referendum, Soviet citizens support Gorbachev's call for "preservation of the USSR"** as a renewed federation of equal, sovereign republics. Six of the nation's 15 republics boycott the vote (March 17, 1991). In Moscow, 100,000 demonstrators gather in defiance of Gorbachev's ban on public gatherings (March 28).

In Minsk, Byelorussia, thousands of workers demand wage increases and call for Gorbachev's resignation (April 4, 1991). A month earlier, striking coal miners in Kazakhstan and Ukraine had held similar protests. **Gorbachev demands a year-long moratorium on strikes, and faster movement toward a market economy** (April 9, 1991). The next day, thousands of workers in Minsk gather to protest Gorbachev's proposal. Gorbachev meets with Japan's Prime Minister Toshiki Kaifu in an attempt to encourage aid and investment in the USSR (April 16, 1991).

Trying to end a potentially paralyzing strike, **the Soviet government agrees to demands of strikers, transferring control of Siberian coal industry to the Russian Republic** (May 6, 1991). Soviet troops and Azerbaijan police attempt to disarm villages along the Armenian border, where residents are fighting for control of an ethnic enclave. **In two weeks of fighting, 48 Armenians are killed** in several confrontations, including an air attack on the village of Paravakar (May 8, 1991). **To preserve the dying economy, 13 of the 15 Soviet republics agree to an emergency plan** to ban strikes and increase wages and productivity (May 16, 1991). The headquarters of the leading anti-Communist, pro-Yeltsin group is bombed in Moscow (May 16, 1991). Moldavia, Georgia, Armenia, Estonia, Latvia and Lithuania form the Assembly of National Fronts to coordinate their activities as they proceed with their plans to secede (May 26, 1991).

The Russian Republic holds its first direct presidential election, choosing Boris Yeltsin from a field of six candidates (June 12, 1991). Yeltsin visits Washington, meets President Bush and members of Congress (June 19–20, 1991).

In a major change from traditional government monopoly, **Soviet parliament approves legislation allowing private ownership of industry** (July 1,

1991). Representatives of the Group of Seven largest industrialized countries consider Gorbachev's plea for loans and grants to save the failing Soviet economy. They agree to provide technical, but not financial, assistance in helping the USSR move toward a market economy (July 7, 1991). **Russian President Boris Yeltsin bans Communist party from workplaces** (July 20, 1991). Gorbachev says he will fight Yeltsin's ban. The Communist party, at Gorbachev's request, approves a new charter that seeks to align it with democratic reforms.

With the Cold War virtually dead, **President Bush and President Gorbachev sign a treaty agreeing to reduce long-range nuclear weapons** (July 31, 1991).

Politically conservative military forces attempt coup against Gorbachev two days before he is to sign pact giving increased powers to the republics (Aug. 18, 1991). Gorbachev and his family are held at their vacation home in the Crimea. In Moscow, popular Russian President Boris Yeltsin rallies citizens against the military coup and urges them to refrain from violence. Hundreds of thousands rally to his cause and join him outside the Russian Parliament, in defiance of a military curfew. **The unpopular coup collapses** under the weight of Yeltsin's opposition (Aug. 21, 1991). Gorbachev returns to Moscow. The Speaker of the Soviet Parliament, Anatoly Lukyanov, is accused of orchestrating the coup; he resigns. Yeltsin blames Communist party for the coup. The party is outlawed in Latvia and Lithuania (Aug. 22, 1991). Latvia, Lithuania and Estonia declare their long-anticipated independence (Aug. 1991). **Gorbachev resigns as General Secretary of the Communist party and bans it from any official government role** (Aug. 24, 1991). Ukraine declares independence (Aug. 24, 1991). The declaration is ratified overwhelmingly by residents on Dec. 1.

The Soviet Union recognizes the independence of the Baltic states—Estonia, Latvia and Lithuania (Sept. 6, 1991). **Armenia declares its independence** (Sept. 23, 1991).

The Soviet Parliament opens, but only seven of the 15 original republics are represented. Gorbachev pleads that some form of national unity can be maintained (Oct. 20, 1991).

The leaders of Russia, Byelorussia, Kazakhstan, Azerbaijan, Kirghizia, Tadjikistan and Turkmenia agree to form a new political union, tentatively called the Union of Sovereign States (Nov. 13, 1991). In Moldavia, two ethnic enclaves vote for independence and a third votes to merge with Romania (Dec. 1, 1991). On the same day, **Ukrainian residents vote overwhelmingly for independence.**

Gorbachev tries to win support for his Union Treaty, which would bind the republics together in voluntary cooperation. He appeals to the republics to preserve the union, predicting warfare and a "catastrophe for all mankind" if it disintegrates (Dec. 3, 1991).

The leaders of the nation's three most powerful republics—Russia, Byelorussia and Ukraine—meet in a hunting lodge for two days to discuss economic cooperation and unity (Dec. 7–8, 1991). **The leaders, who represent nearly three-quarters of the Soviet Union's population, agree to form the Commonwealth of Independent States** (Dec. 8, 1991). By year's end, 11 of the 15 former Soviet republics had joined. (Latvia, Lithuania and Estonia retained their independent status. Georgia remained uncommitted.) CIS members declare the USSR no longer exists (Dec. 21, 1991). **In a televised address, Gorbachev resigns** (Dec. 25, 1991).

BRITISH SOVEREIGNS

House of Cerdic:

Egbert	827–839
Ethelwulf	839–858
Ethelbald	858–860
Ethelbert	860–866
Ethelred I	866–871
Alfred the Great	871–899
Edward the Elder	899–925
Athelstan	925–940
Edmund I	940–946 (assassinated)
Edred	946–955
Edwy	955–959
Edgar	959–975
Edward the Younger	975–978 (assassinated)
Ethelred II (the Unready)	978–1016
Edmund II (Ironside)	1016

House of the Skjoldungs or of Denmark:

Canute the Great	1016–35
Harold I	1035–40
Hardicanute	1040–42

House of Cerdic:

Edward the Confessor	1042–66

House of Godwin:

Harold II	1066 (killed at the Battle of Hastings)

House of Normandy:

William I (the Conqueror)	1066–87
William II (Rufus)	1087–1100
Henry I	1100–35
Stephen	1135–54

House of Anjou or Plantagenet:	
Henry II	1154–89
Richard I	1189–99
John	1199–1216
Henry III	1216–72
Edward I	1272–1307
Edward II	1307–27 (deposed)
Edward III	1327–77
Richard II	1377–99 (deposed, killed)

House of Lancaster:	
Henry IV	1399–1413
Henry V	1413–22
Henry VI	1422–61 (deposed)

House of York:	
Edward IV	1461–70

House of Lancaster:	
Henry VI (again)	1470–71

House of York:	
Edward IV (again)	1471–83
Edward V	April–June 1483 (killed in tower)
Richard III	1483–85

House of Tudor:	
Henry VII	1485–1509
Henry VIII	1509–47
Edward VI	1547–53
Jane Grey	1553 (9 days)
Mary I	1553–58
Elizabeth I	1558–1603

House of Stuart:	
James I	1603–25
Charles I	1625–49 (beheaded)

Commonwealth and Protectorate:	
Council of State	1649–53
Oliver Cromwell (protector)	1653–58
Richard Cromwell (protector)	1658–59

House of Stuart:	
Charles II	1660–85
James II	1685–88 (fled)

House of Orange:	
William III, Mary II	1689–94
William III alone	1694–1702

House of Stuart:	
Anne	1702–14

House of Hanover:	
George I	1714–27
George II	1727–60
George III	1760–1820
George IV	1820–30
William IV	1830–37
Victoria	1837–1901

House of Saxe-Coburg-Gotha:	
Edward VII	1901–10

House of Windsor:	
George V	1910–36
Edward VIII	1936 (abdicated after 325 days)
George VI	1936–52
Elizabeth II	1952–

BRITISH PRIME MINISTERS

Sir Robert Walpole	1721–42
Earl of Wilmington	1742–43
Henry Pelham	1743–54
Duke of Newcastle	1754–56
Duke of Devonshire	1756–57
Duke of Newcastle	1757–62
Earl of Bute	1762–63
George Grenville	1763–65
Marquess of Rockingham	1765–66
William Pitt the Elder (Earl of Chatham)	1766–68
Duke of Grafton	1768–70
Frederick North (Lord North)	1770–82
Marquess of Rockingham	1782
Earl of Shelburne	1782–83
Duke of Portland	1783
William Pitt the Younger	1783–1801
Henry Addington	1801–4
William Pitt the Younger	1804–6
William Wyndham Grenville (Baron Grenville)	1806–7
Duke of Portland	1807–9
Spencer Perceval	1809–12
Earl of Liverpool	1812–27
George Canning	1827
Viscount Goderich	1827–28
Duke of Wellington	1828–30
Earl Grey	1830–34
Viscount Melbourne	1835–41
Sir Robert Peel	1841–46
Lord John Russell (later Earl)	1846–52
Earl of Derby	1852
Earl of Aberdeen	1852–55
Viscount Palmerston	1855–58
Earl of Derby	1858–59
Viscount Palmerston	1859–65
Earl Russell	1865–66
Earl of Derby	1866–68
Benjamin Disraeli	1868
William E. Gladstone	1868–74
Benjamin Disraeli	1874–80
William E. Gladstone	1880–85
Marquess of Salisbury	1885–86
William E. Gladstone	1886
Marquess of Salisbury	1886–92
William E. Gladstone	1892–94
Earl of Rosebery	1894–95
Marquess of Salisbury	1895–1902
Arthur James Balfour, first Earl of Balfour	1902–5
Sir Henry Campbell-Bannerman	1905–8

Herbert Henry Asquith, first Earl of Oxford and Asquith	1908–16
David Lloyd George, first Earl of Dwyfor	1916–22
Andrew Bonar Law	1922–23
Stanley Baldwin, first Earl Baldwin of Bewdley	1923–24
James Ramsay MacDonald	1924
Stanley Baldwin, first Earl Baldwin of Bewdley	1924–29
James Ramsay MacDonald	1929–35
Stanley Baldwin, first Earl Baldwin of Bewdley	1935–37
Arthur Neville Chamberlain	1937–40
Sir Winston Leonard Spencer Churchill	1940–45
Clement Richard Attlee, first Earl Attlee	1945–51
Sir Winston Leonard Spencer Churchill	1951–55
Anthony Eden, first Earl of Avon	1955–57
Harold Macmillan	1957–63
Sir Alec Douglas-Home	1963–64
Harold Wilson	1964–70
Edward Heath	1970–74
Harold Wilson	1974–76
James Callaghan	1976–79
Margaret Thatcher	1979–90
John Major	1990–

FRANCE'S HEADS OF STATE

Carolingian Dynasty:

Pépin the Short	751–768
Charlemagne	768–814
(ruled with brother, Carloman)	768–771
Louis the Pious	814–840
Charles II the Bald	843–877
Louis II	877–879
Louis III	879–882
Carloman	879–884
Karl III, Holy Roman Emperor	884–887
Eudes	888–898
Charles III the Simple	893–923
Robert I	922–923
Raoul	923–936
Louis IV	936–954
Lothair	954–986
Louis V	986–987

Capetian Kings:

Hugh Capet	987–996
Robert II	996–1031
Henri I	1031–60
Philippe I	1060–1108
Louis VI	1108–37
Louis VII	1137–80
Philippe II (Auguste)	1180–1223
Louis VIII	1223–26
Louis IX, Saint	1226–70
Philippe III	1270–85
Philippe IV	1285–1314
Louis X	1314–16
Jean I	1316
Philippe V	1316–22
Charles IV	1322–28

House of Valois:

Philippe VI	1328–50
Jean II	1350–64
Charles V	1364–80
Charles VI	1380–1422
Charles VII	1422–61
Louis XI	1461–83
Charles VIII	1483–98
Louis XII	1498–1515
François I	1515–47
Henri II	1547–59
François II	1559–60
Charles IX	1560–74
Henri III	1574–89

House of Bourbon:

Henri IV	1589–1610
Louis XIII	1610–43
Louis XIV (the Sun King)	1643–1715
Louis XV	1715–74
Louis XVI	1774–93

First Republic:

Robespierre	1792–94
The Directory	1795–99
Barras	1795–99
Rewbell	1795–99
La Révellière-Lepeaux	1795–99
Carnot	1795–97
Letourneur	1795–97
Barthélémy	1797
Merlin	1797–99
François	1797
Sièyes	1799
Gohier	1799
Roger Ducos	1799
Moulin	1799
The Consulate	1799–1804
First Consul: Napoléon	1799–1804
Second Consul: Sièyes	1799–1800
Cambaceres	1800–4
Third Consul: Ducos	1799–1800
Le Brun	1800–4

House of Bonaparte:

Napoléon I (abdicated); returned in 1815 for the Hundred Days rule	1804–14

House of Bourbon (restored):

Louis XVIII	1814–24
Charles X (abdicated)	1824–30

House of Bourbon-Orléans:

Louis Philippe (abdicated)	1830–48

Second Republic:

Louis Napoléon Bonaparte (president)	1848–52

House of Bonaparte:

Napoléon III (abdicated)	1852–70

Presidents of the Third Republic:

Adolphe Thiers	1871–73
Marshal MacMahon	1873–79
Jules Grevy	1879–87
Sadi Carnot (assassinated)	1887–94
Jean Casimir-Périer	1894–95
François Félix Faure	1895–99
Emile Loubet	1899–1906
Armand Fallières	1906–13
Raymond Poincaré	1913–20
Paul Deschanel	1920
Alexandre Millerand	1920–24
Gaston Doumergue	1924–31
Paul Doumer (assassinated)	1931–32
Albert Lebrun	1932–40

Chief of the French State:

Marshal Pétain	1940–44

Head of the Provisional Government:

Charles de Gaulle	1944–47
(had been head of the French Resistance from 1940–44)	

Presidents of the Fourth Republic:

Vincent Auriol	1947–53
René Coty	1953–58

Presidents of the Fifth Republic:

Charles de Gaulle	1958–69
Georges Pompidou	1969–74
Valéry Giscard d'Estaing	1974–81
François Mitterand	1981–

SPANISH RULERS

Houses of Aragon and Castille:

Ferdinand II of Aragon and Isabella I of Castille	1479–1504
Ferdinand II and Joanna the Mad	1504–6

House of Hapsburg:

Charles I (Holy Roman Emperor Charles V)	1516–56
Philip II	1556–98
Philip III	1598–1621
Philip IV	1621–65
Charles II	1665–1700

House of Bourbon:

Philip V	1700–abdicated 1724
Luis	Jan.–Aug. 1724
Philip V (again)	1724–46
Ferdinand VI	1746–59
Charles III	1759–88
Charles IV	1788–1808
Ferdinand VII	1808

House of Bonaparte:

Joseph Bonaparte	1808–13

House of Bourbon (restored):

Ferdinand VII (again)	1813–33
Isabella II	1833–68
interregnum	1868–70

House of Savoy:

Amadeo	1870–73

First Spanish Republic: 1873–74

House of Bourbon (restored):

Alfonso XII	1874–85
Maria Cristina	1885–86
Alfonso XIII	1886–abdicated 1931

Second Spanish Republic: 1931–39

Fascist Dictatorship:

Gen. Francisco Franco	1939–75

House of Bourbon (restored):

Juan Carlos I	1975–

RUSSIAN RULERS
Czars of the Russian Empire

House of Rurik:

Ivan III, the Great (proclaimed himself czar, 1480)	1462–1505
Vassili III	1505–33
Ivan IV, the Terrible	1533–84
Fyodor I	1584–98

House of Godunov:

Boris	1598–1605
Fyodor II	1605
interregnum	1605–13

House of Romanov:

Michael	1613–45
Alexis	1645–1776
Fyodor III	1676–82
Ivan V	1682–89
Sophia (regent)	1682–89
Peter I, the Great	1682–1725
Catherine I	1725–27
Peter II	1727–30
Anne	1730–40
Ivan VI	1740–41
Elizabeth	1741–62
Peter III	1762
Catherine, the Great	1762–96
Paul	1796–1801
Alexander I	1801–25
Nicholas I	1825–55
Alexander II	1855–81
Alexander III	1881–94
Nicholas II (abdicated due to revolution; he and family were murdered by Bolsheviks in 1918)	1894–1917

Provisional Government:
Premiers:

Prince Georgi Lvov, Alexander Kerensky	1917

Leaders of the USSR

Premiers:
(The premier is the chairman of the Council of Ministers. The position was eliminated in 1990, during a government reorganization.)

Vladimir Ilyich Ulyanov Lenin	1917–24
Aleksei Rykov	1924–30
Vyacheslav M. Molotov	1930–41
Joseph Stalin	1941–53
Georgi M. Malenkov	1953–55
Nikolai A. Bulganin	1955–58
Nikita S. Krushchev	1958–64
Aleksei N. Kosygin	1964–80
Nikolai Tikonov	1980–85
Nikolai I. Ryzhkov	1985–90

Presidents:
(The president is the chairman of the Presidium of the Supreme Soviet.)

Mikhail Kalinin	1923–46
Nikolai Shvernik	1946–53
Kliment Voroshilov	1953–60
Leonid Brezhnev	1960–64
Anastas Mikoyan	1964–65
Nikolai Podgorny	1965–77
Leonid Brezhnev	1977–82
Yuri Andropov	1983–84
Konstantin Chernenko	1984–85
Andrei Gromyko	1985–88
Mikhail Gorbachev*	1988–91

* Resigned Dec. 25, 1991, after dissolution of USSR. *See* The Dissolution of the USSR, page 112.

CHINESE DYNASTIES AND HEADS OF STATE
Dynasties

The Five Sovereigns (Legendary Epoch)	2697–2205 B.C.
Hsia Dynasty	2205–1766 B.C.
Shang or Yin Dynasty	1766–1122 B.C.
Chou Dynasty	1122–255 B.C.
Ch'in Dynasty	255–206 B.C.
Han Dynasty	206 B.C.–220 A.D.
Six Dynasties period	220–589 A.D.
Sui Dynasty	589–618 A.D.
T'ang Dynasty	618–907 A.D.
Wu Tai (The Epoch of the Five Dynasties)	907–960 A.D.
The Sung Dynasty	960–1279 A.D.
Yüan (Mongol) Dynasty	1279–1368 A.D.
Ming Dynasty	1368–1644 A.D.
Ch'ing (Manchu) Dynasty	1644–1912 A.D.

Heads of State (1911 to present)
REPUBLIC OF CHINA

Sun Yat-sen (provisional president)	1911–12
Yuan Shi-Kai (provisional, then president)	1912–16
Li Yuan-hung (president)	1916–17
Feng Kuo-chang (president)	1917–18
Hsu Shih-chang (president)	1918–22
Li Yuan-hung (president)	1922–23
Ts'ao K'un (president)	1923–24
Chiang Kai-shek (president)	1928–32
Lin Sen (president)	1932–43
Chiang Kai-shek (president)	1943–49

COMMUNIST PEOPLE'S REPUBLIC

Mao Zedong	1949–76
Hua Guofeng	1976–78
Ye Chien-ying	1978–81
Deng Xiaoping	1981–89
Jiang Zemin	1989–

WARS AND ARMED CONFLICT

THE AMERICAN REVOLUTION

For the British, the colonies in North America were becoming increasingly troublesome in the mid-1700s. Though they offered important trade and territorial possibilities, they were also expensive to defend, and increasingly headstrong. In 1763, Britain issued an edict limiting western expansion in North America, which added to tensions concerning regulation of commerce and taxation. The conflict increased as Britain tried to assert its control over the colonies, and the colonies sought to run their own affairs.

In 1764, Parliament passed the **Currency Act,** which prohibited the colonies from printing their own money. It also passed the **Sugar Act,** placing a tax on sugar. The colonies protested both measures.

Defending the colonies during the Seven Years' War had been costly. Britain, trying to recoup some of its loss, continued its plan to increase taxes in the colonies. The **Stamp Act** of 1765 levied taxes (indicated by stamps) on many commercial and legal documents, including diplomas, newspapers, marriage licenses, almanacs and pamphlets. The colonists, protesting the taxes on the grounds that the colonies were not represented in Parliament, began a boycott of British goods. Parliament repealed the Stamp Act in 1766 due to protests from British merchants, who feared a loss of business. It did not accept the colonists' argument that there should be no taxation without representation, however.

A year later, Parliament passed the **Townshend Act,** which established duties on certain colonial imports, including lead, paper and tea. Colonists, spurred by leaders including Samuel Adams of Massachusetts, protested. The British sent troops to the colonies. On March 5, 1770, British soldiers, baited by an angry Boston crowd, fired at the demonstrators, killing several. This incident came to be known as the **Boston Massacre.**

Parliament again backed down, repealing all taxes except the one on tea. Colonists protested the **British Tea Act** (1773), which granted a special tax exemption to the British East India Company, allowing it to sell tea at bargain rates in the colonies, undercutting the business of established colonial dealers. In Massachusetts, colonists dressed as Indians protested at the **Boston Tea Party** by dumping East India Company tea into Boston Harbor (Dec. 16, 1773). The protest was followed by recriminations by Parliament, which the colonists called the **Intolerable Acts** (1774). The acts temporarily closed the port of Boston, reduced the self-government of the Massachusetts colony, allowed royal officials to transfer certain legal cases to England for trial, and established rules under which British soldiers could take over inns and empty buildings for quarters.

The colonies joined in protest, coordinating their efforts through the Committees of Correspondence. The **First Continental Congress,** representing 12 colonies (all but Georgia) met in Philadelphia in 1774. Representatives drafted a Declaration of Rights and Grievances, which it sent to King George III. Both the British and the colonists hoped to be able to patch up their differences, but both prepared for armed conflict.

The royal governor of Massachusetts, Gen. Thomas Gage, sent British soldiers to seize military supplies stored by the colonists at Concord, Mass. Alerted by Paul Revere and William Dawes, the Minutemen faced British soldiers at **Lexington and Concord** on April 19, 1775, marking the start of the American Revolution, the "shot heard round the world."

The **Second Continental Congress** met in Philadelphia in May 1775, with John Hancock as president, and considered ways to appease the king, but also began to raise an army. On June 17, 1775, British troops defeated the Americans in Boston at the **Battle of Bunker Hill,** the first major battle of the Revolution. Although the patriots lost the battle, they continued to press their war against the British troops. In March 1776, the British troops, under the command of Sir William Howe, were forced to leave Boston. Until the end of the Revolution, New England continued primarily under American control.

The Second Continental Congress assumed legislative, executive and judicial powers. Thomas Paine published *Common Sense* (1776), an influential and widely circulated pamphlet attacking the theory of monarchy and calling for self-government. On July 4, 1776, colonial representatives signed the **Declaration of Independence** [*See* The Declaration of Independence, page 77], written largely by Thomas Jefferson. State governments with new written constitutions were set up, replacing the Crown's colonial governments.

After a failed southern campaign, the British turned their attention to the middle states. Sir William Howe took New York City in the Battle of Long Island on Aug. 27, 1776. George Washington's forces escaped across the East River. They defeated the Hessians (German mercenaries) at Trenton, N.J., on Dec. 26, 1776, and the British at Princeton, N.J., on Jan. 3, 1777. Howe gained an important victory when he captured Philadelphia on Sept. 27, 1777. A month later, American regulars and militiamen were victorious at Saratoga, N.Y., forcing Sir John Burgoyne to surrender his command on Oct. 17, 1777.

On Nov. 15, 1777, the Continental Congress completed the **Articles of Confederation** and sent them to the states for ratification. The articles formally established the powers of the Continental Congress. In a debate concerning whether there should be a strong or weak central government, the weak central government faction prevailed. States, not the national government, would be allowed to levy taxes and regulate commerce. Although it had no tax power, the national government would be able to make treaties, declare war, raise military forces, issue currency and float loans.

George Washington and his forces suffered through the winter of 1777–78 at **Valley Forge,** Pa., while Howe and his troops spent the winter in Philadelphia.

France, still smarting from Britain's victory in the Seven Years' War, formally recognized American independence in 1778. Even before then, the French secretly had supplied guns and gunpowder. The British sent the colonies a plan for reconciliation but, bolstered by France's public support, the colonies rejected it.

The British evacuated Philadelphia in June 1778 and turned their attention to the South. They captured Savannah, Ga., in December 1778, and Charleston, S.C., in May 1780. Two months later, Count Jean Baptiste de Rochambeau arrived in Newport, R.I., with 6,000 troops. On Sept. 23, 1780, the British spy Major John André was captured and revealed a plot by **Benedict Arnold** to surrender West Point to the British. Arnold escaped, but André was hanged as a spy on Oct. 2, 1780.

After their success in Charleston, Lord Cornwallis's troops pressed north through the Carolinas, winning several battles, then being defeated at the Battle of King's Mountain in North Carolina on Oct. 7, 1780. Cornwallis moved his remaining troops to Yorktown, Va., by August 1781, where they were caught between a French fleet and George Washington's ground forces, strengthened by some of Rochambeau's troops. **Cornwallis surrendered,** a decisive victory for the colonies, on Oct. 19, 1781.

Although the British still held New York, Charleston and Savannah, they had suffered significant losses, and the war had become increasingly unpopular in Great Britain, especially after France (and later Spain) aligned with the colonies. By 1782, Britain was willing to recognize the independence of the United States of America. A preliminary **peace agreement** was signed on Nov. 30, 1782; the final document was signed in Paris on Sept. 3, 1783.

Florida, which had been held by the English since 1763, was returned to Spain. The **Constitution of the United States** was drafted in 1787 and ratified in 1788. **George Washington** was elected president by unanimous vote of the Electoral College in 1789.

CIVIL WAR AND RECONSTRUCTION

Prelude to War: The issue of slavery had been divisive to the nation for decades. The Missouri Compromise of 1820 [*See* Important Dates in American History, page 75; World History, page 82] was the first attempt to put the issue to rest, by specifying that some states would be slave states and others free. But when California sought to be admitted to the Union as a free state, without slaves, the balance was threatened. The Compromise of 1850 [*See* 1001–1992, page 84] provided a temporary calm, but **the slavery issue was too explosive to be contained.** The Southern states, with an economy that was dependent upon slave labor, saw the practice as normal and necessary. Elsewhere, sentiment had turned against slavery. Harriet Beecher Stowe's novel, *Uncle Tom's Cabin; or Life Among the Lowly*, had done much to inflame antislavery sentiment in the 1850s. [*See* 1001–1992, page 84]

The conflict took center stage during **election debates between Abraham Lincoln and Stephen A. Douglas** in 1858. The men, who were seeking a U.S. Senate seat in Illinois, personified the nation's dilemma. Douglas, while not condoning slavery, argued that each state should be able to choose for itself. Lincoln, who opposed slavery, said that "this government can not endure permanently half slave and half free." Lincoln lost that election, but he gained national prominence, which helped him in his next campaign, for the presidency.

When **Lincoln was elected president,** reaction was swift. Before he was inaugurated on March 4, 1861, **seven Southern states seceded.** The states—South Carolina, Mississippi, Florida, Alabama, Georgia, Louisiana and Texas—formed the Confederate States of America, with Jefferson Davis as president.

The War: In response, Lincoln sent federal troops to augment forces at Fort Sumter, S.C. On April 12, 1861, Confederate Gen. Pierre G.T. **Beauregard fired on Fort Sumter,** marking the first hostilities of the Civil War. The fort surrendered to Beauregard on April 13, 1861.

In the spring of 1861, **Virginia, Arkansas, Tennessee and North Carolina left the Union,** completing the 11-state Confederacy. The Civil War arose not only out of the slavery issue, but also due to disagreement over whether states could secede, and to economic and political disputes between the agrarian South and the increasingly industrialized North.

Union naval forces blockaded Southern ports beginning in April 1861. Gen. Beauregard defeated Union Gen. Irvin McDowell at the **first Battle of Bull Run** (near Manassas, Va.), the first major battle of the Civil War, on July 21, 1861. Confederate Gen. Thomas J. Jackson got the nickname "Stonewall" at Bull Run for his firm stand.

More than 100,000 troops were engaged in the **Battle of Shiloh,** fought near Pittsburgh Landing, Tenn., April 6–7, 1862. Union Gen. Ulysses S. Grant was victorious, but losses were heavy on both sides. Union Capt. David G. **Farragut took New Orleans** on May 1, 1862. The Union Army under Gen. George B. McClellan tried unsuccessfully to capture **Richmond, Va.,** by invading a peninsula between the York and James rivers between April and July 1862. The Union Army was successful at **Yorktown, Norfolk and Fair Oaks,** where Confederate Gen. Joseph E. Johnston was wounded. His successor, Gen. Robert E. Lee, forced McClellan to retreat from the peninsula after a brilliant seven-day campaign.

At the **second Battle of Bull Run** the Confederate generals Stonewall Jackson and Robert E. Lee routed Union forces, who retreated to Washington, D.C., Aug. 29–30, 1862. Stonewall Jackson took the federal arsenal at **Harpers Ferry,** W.Va., on Sept. 15, 1862. The arsenal was abandoned on Sept. 20, 1862, and Union troops returned on Sept. 22.

The **Battle of Antietam,** Md., was the bloodiest one-day battle of the Civil War. Robert E. Lee failed in his first attempt to invade the North. Each side suffered more than 2,000 deaths and 9,000 injuries on Sept. 17, 1862.

Abraham Lincoln issued a preliminary version of the **Emancipation Proclamation** on Sept. 22, 1862; it became effective Jan. 1, 1863. It freed only those slaves in areas controlled by the Confederacy, "as a fit and necessary war measure for suppressing said rebellion." It was designed to deplete Southern manpower and to gain political support abroad. The Confederacy did not accept the Proclamation as law, and it did not apply to the four Union states in which slavery was legal (Delaware, Maryland, Missouri and Kentucky). As a result, its real effect was negligible.

The North suffered a major defeat at the **Battle of Fredericksburg,** Va., on Dec. 13, 1862, ending Gen. Ambrose Burnside's drive on Richmond. More than 12,000 of Burnside's men were killed or wounded, more than double the casualties suffered by the South. Congress passed the **nation's first conscription act** on March 3, 1863. Military service could be avoided by paying $300 or providing a substitute. Confederate Gen. Robert E. Lee won his greatest victory at the **Battle of Chancellorsville,** Va., May 1–4, 1863, 50 miles southwest of Washington, D.C.

Stonewall Jackson, accidentally wounded by his own men, died eight days after the battle.

The **Gettysburg campaign** of June and July 1863 marked the turning point of the war. After his victory at Chancellorsville, Lee crossed the Potomac into Pennsylvania and engaged Union troops at Harrisburg and Chambersburg. His forces met those of Union Gen. George G. Meade west of Gettysburg, Pa., in the biggest battle of the war, fought July 1–3, 1863. After initial success, Lee ordered Gen. George E. Pickett to attack the center of the Union forces. The assault, known as **Pickett's charge,** was disastrous. Of Pickett's 4,800 men, 3,393 were killed or wounded. In total at Gettysburg, there were 30,000 Confederate and 23,000 Union casualties.

At **Vicksburg,** Miss., Confederate troops surrendered to Gen. Ulysses S. Grant on July 4, 1863, after a three-month campaign, thereby losing control of the Mississippi River.

In New York City, **antidraft riots** erupted July 13–16, 1863, leaving 1,000 dead or wounded before federal troops restored order.

At **Chickamauga,** Tenn., Confederate troops under Gen. Braxton Bragg defeated Union forces, which retreated to Chattanooga, Tenn. (Sept. 19–20, 1863).

Abraham Lincoln delivered the **Gettysburg Address** at ceremonies dedicating the Gettysburg battlefield as a national cemetery on Nov. 19, 1863. The battlefield was still strewn with debris from the battle. Lincoln's speech, which took only about two minutes, was over so quickly that a photographer did not have time to take his picture. It followed a two-hour speech by the orator Edward Everett. Reaction in newspapers was mixed. One, in reporting the ceremony, remarked only, "We will skip over the silly remarks of the President." Another said that his remarks "will live among the annals of man." [See The Gettysburg Address, page 81]

At **Chattanooga,** Tenn., Union reinforcements under Gen. Grant captured Confederate positions, causing Confederate troops to flee to Georgia (Nov. 23–25, 1863).

Abraham **Lincoln was re-elected** in 1864.

The Battle of the Wilderness, May 5–6, 1864, ended indecisively. Fought in thick forest near Chancellorsville, Va., the troops of Robert E. Lee and Ulysses S. Grant both suffered heavy losses.

Adm. David Farragut defeated a Confederate fleet in **Mobile Bay** (Aug. 5–23, 1864).

Union Gen. William Tecumseh **Sherman captured Atlanta** on Sept. 2, 1864. He **burned the city** on Nov. 15, 1864, and set off, with 60,000 men, to **march to the sea,** cutting a path of devastation. He captured Savannah on Dec. 21, 1864, then turned north through South Carolina.

On March 2, 1865, Gen. Robert E. Lee asked Gen.

Ulysses S. Grant for a conference to settle differences between the North and South. Lincoln refused, demanding surrender before discussion.

At Petersburg, Va., Gen. Lee tried to break through the Union line but was beaten back on March 25, 1865. Lee recommended that Richmond, Va., the capital of the Confederacy, be evacuated. Confederate Pres. Jefferson Davis and his cabinet fled on April 2, 1865, before Gen. **Grant took Richmond. Lee surrendered to Grant at the courthouse at Appomattox, Va., on April 9, 1865, ending the war.**

On April 14, 1865, **Abraham Lincoln was shot by John Wilkes Booth** as he watched a comedy, *Our American Cousin*, at Ford's Theater in Washington, D.C. Booth, an actor and a Confederate sympathizer, entered Lincoln's unguarded theater box shortly after 10 P.M. and shot the president in the head at point-blank range. He leaped to the stage, shouting, "Sic semper tyrannis! The South is avenged!" He broke his leg in the fall, but managed to escape.

Lincoln was taken to a home across the street, where he died at 7:22 the next morning. Secretary of State William Henry Seward was seriously injured in the attack, but recovered.

On April 26, 1865, **Booth was cornered in a barn in Virginia, which was set afire. He died of a gunshot wound,** fired either by one of the troops surrounding the barn or by himself. Nine other persons were convicted of conspiracy. Four were jailed and four were hanged. The ninth, Dr. Samuel A. Mudd, received a life sentence but was pardoned in 1869. He had set Booth's broken leg, not realizing that Booth was Lincoln's assassin.

After the War: In the South, **Reconstruction** (1865–77) began as Pres. Andrew Johnson considered how to allow the physically and economically devastated Confederate states to rejoin the Union. He suggested lenient terms, similar to those proposed by Lincoln. They were rejected by the Republican-dominated Congress, which had mixed motives.

Several Southern states had enacted Black Codes, perpetuating the master-slave relationship. The Republicans were concerned about the welfare of freed slaves, who were denied the right to freely choose for whom they would work; many of them petitioned Congress for help. The Republicans were also concerned that readmission of the Southern states would flood Congress with Southern Democrats, eliminating Republican control, unless blacks were given the vote. Over President Johnson's veto, Congress enacted a law repudiating the Black Codes. It also passed the **14th Amendment to the Constitution,** which granted full citizenship to all persons born or naturalized in the United States, in 1866. (The amendment was ratified in 1868.)

Over presidential vetoes, Congress passed the four **Reconstruction Acts** (1867–68), which divided the former Confederate states into five military districts and gave district commanders the power to organize new governments, control voting and registration, and appoint and remove state officials.

The Republican governments in the South were composed of freed Negroes, Carpetbaggers from the North and Scalawags (sympathetic Southern whites). They enacted progressive social and civil-rights legislation, but were also characterized by widespread greed and corruption.

The **15th Amendment to the Constitution,** which prohibits states from denying voting rights due to race, was ratified in 1870.

WORLD WAR I

War began in Europe in August 1914, with Britain, France and Russia allied against Germany and Austria-Hungary. Americans were committed to neutrality, although President Wilson's cabinet was generally pro-British. When **Germany invaded Belgium,** a small, neutral nation, American sentiment began to turn.

Belgium resisted valiantly, but unsuccessfully. The French counterattack at the **Battle of the Marne** (Sept. 6–12, 1914) halted the Germans and **established a line of trench warfare on the Western Front that lasted three years.** The battle line extended from the North Sea, through eastern France to the border of Switzerland.

Britain blockaded Germany, which prevented neutral nations from trading with Germany, and even interrupted trade among neutral nations on the grounds that the goods might eventually reach Germany. The **United States protested the trade restrictions,** but the protests became milder as the war progressed and American sympathy for Britain increased. Germany also blocked trade to the Allies, but U.S. reaction was less sanguine because Germany enforced its ban with U-boats.

By February 1915, the British blockade had caused serious food shortages in Germany. In response, the **Germans established a war zone around the British Isles,** warning that all merchant vessels in the zone would be sunk without warning. Pres. Woodrow Wilson maintained that Americans had the right to safe travel on the seas, and that if Americans were injured, Germany would be held accountable.

On May 7, 1915, a **German U-boat sank the British liner *Lusitania* off the coast of Ireland,** claiming 1,198 lives, including 128 Americans. The sinking enraged the American public, and President Wilson was urged to seek a declaration of war. An apology from Germany, the offer of financial reparations and a promise to end unrestricted submarine warfare eased the situation temporarily, although American neutrality had become more a formality than an actuality.

In September 1915, President Wilson allowed private loans to the warring nations. In the next 18 months, Americans invested more than $2 billion in the bonds of the Allied powers. Much of the American investment returned to the U.S. in the form of orders for food and supplies. The U.S. underwent an economic boom, which tied it even more closely to the Allies.

Early in 1916, **President Wilson tried to negotiate a peace,** but his attempts failed. He **won re-election,** using the slogan, "He kept us out of war," but the nation gradually prepared for combat. A military recruitment drive was started, reserve corps for officers and enlisted troops were established, construction of naval vessels was accelerated, and the Council on National Defense was set up to prepare the economy for war. In November 1916, President Wilson made one more unsuccessful bid for a negotiated "peace without victory."

On Jan. 31, 1917, Germany announced that it would immediately resume unrestricted submarine warfare, in an effort to break Britain by cutting off its supplies. Three days later, the **U.S. broke off diplomatic relations with Germany.** When the so-called Zimmerman note became public in March, war became inevitable. The coded message from German Foreign Secretary Arthur Zimmerman urged Mexico to wage war against the U.S. in exchange for financial support. (The U.S. had been at odds with Mexico since 1910, when its new revolutionary government had appropriated American-owned properties in Mexico. In 1916, when guerrilla leader Pancho Villa and his bandit army made raids across the U.S. border, President Wilson had ordered U.S. troops to pursue him in Mexico, in the Mexican Border Campaign.) Although Mexico did not accept Zimmerman's proposal, Wilson realized that the United States was being drawn into the war and could no longer remain neutral.

The push toward war was propelled by the sinking of three American merchant ships on March 18, and by England's claim that its supplies were so low that its survival was threatened. It was also aided by a revolution in Russia, which made that country a more attractive ally: Czar Nicholas II had been overthrown by a socialist government (which proved to be short-lived) that pledged democratic reform.

President Wilson told Congress that the time had come to declare war, in order to make the world "safe for democracy." The **United States declared war** against Germany on April 6, 1917. It declared war on Austria-Hungary on Dec. 7.

The U.S. introduced a naval convoy system, which cut shipping losses dramatically, and laid a mine barrier across the North Sea. Congress passed a **Selective Service Act** (May 18, 1917) that required all men between the ages of 21 and 30 to register for military service. (The ages later were expanded to include men 18 to 45 years old.) The act, which for the first time gave local civilian boards the responsibility of classifying and drafting registrants, also provided for conscientious objectors for the first time.

To pay for the war, the U.S. borrowed as never before. Of the $36 billion that was spent on the war, one-third was raised through taxes and the rest through **bond drives.** The Council of National Defense, in charge of guiding the **wartime economy,** directed agencies that increased production of merchant vessels, conserved food through "wheatless Mondays" and "meatless Tuesdays" and conserved fuel through "gasless days." In addition, privately owned rail lines were placed under federal control, and exporters were licensed in an attempt to keep American goods out of enemy hands. One of these agencies, the War Industries Board under the direction of Wall Street financier Bernard M. Baruch, exercised vast control over the economy. It supervised supplying the armed forces, fixed many prices, allocated scarce materials and coordinated Allied purchasing.

In June 1917 and May 1918, **Congress passed two espionage acts** that severely limited civil liberties. The acts were used to silence pacifists, socialists and others opposed to U.S. involvement. Some 1,500 dissenters were prosecuted for offenses that ranged from interfering with the draft to merely using "disloyal . . . or abusive language about the form of government."

Public support of the war effort, already high and now shielded from dissent, was further fueled by the Committee on Public Information, a group formed by President Wilson to rally support through a **propaganda campaign.** Some 75,000 speakers (called "four-minute men") were dispatched to movie houses and other public-gathering spots to deliver patriotic addresses. Newspaper stories and editorials, planted by the committee, spurred anti-German sentiment. The public reacted predictably: German-Americans were taunted and abused, German books were removed from libraries, and vigilantes crushed dissent with threats of violence. The day he asked for a declaration of war, President Wilson had told a friend, "Once lead this people into war, and they'll forget there ever was such a thing as tolerance." His prediction proved true, due partly to his own actions.

Americans expected a speedy victory, but they

were disappointed. In the early spring of 1917, the battle line of the Western Front was virtually as it had been three years earlier. Two lines of trenches and fortifications faced each other, separated by no-man's land. Repeatedly since 1914, the Germans, English or French had tried to advance their positions, but each time they had been stopped, often with heavy losses. In the spring of 1917, the French tried again and were pushed back, but this time the loss of life was so great and the cause seemed so futile that some French soldiers mutinied.

Meanwhile, another ally, **Russia, was facing rebellion at home.** In November 1917, **the provisional government, which had pledged democratic reform, fell to the Bolsheviks.** In March, the **Bolsheviks made peace with Germany,** allowing it to redeploy hundreds of thousands of troops to the Western Front. While **Germany gained strength on the Western Front,** the **Allies were forced to cut back.** Italy, which had joined the Allied cause, had suffered serious losses when it faced the German-Austrian army in the Italian Alps. The Allies were forced to transfer some of their much-needed troops from the Western Front to Italy to help in that country's defense.

When **Americans joined the war in France** (June 26, 1917), the Allied position was precarious at best. By the end of the year, 180,000 American troops were in France and more were promised. For Germany, the time had come to attempt to break through and seize Paris, before more American troops were in place.

President Wilson proposed his Fourteen Points, a peace plan that would revise the map of Europe along historically established national lines (Jan. 8, 1918). It would also establish an association of nations (the **League of Nations**) that would maintain peace through conciliation, mediation and arbitration. The **Germans, convinced that a spring offensive would bring victory, were not interested in conciliation.** Instead, **they began a massive drive northeast of Paris.** They advanced slowly, getting to within 56 miles of Paris in May. American troops repelled the Germans at Montdidier, then captured Cantigny (May 28, 1918). Nine days later, they attacked the Germans at Belleau Wood, a stronghold of machine guns and artillery. The Germans were forced to flee after a weeklong offensive, but at significant cost to the Americans. More than half of the U.S. troops had been killed or injured.

In mid-June the Germans tried again to break through the line northeast of Paris. Unsuccessful there, they then made a desperate effort at the **Second Battle of the Marne.** They attacked on both sides of the city of Rheims, pelting the Allies with artillery shells before dispatching their troops to try once again to break through the line. After several days, the Germans stopped.

On July 15 they tried again. Three days later they were again stopped, then forced to retreat. **The Allies, greatly reinforced by 550,000 American troops under Gen. John J. Pershing, pushed the Germans farther back,** taking their fortification at St. Mihiel on the Meuse River. Despite opposition from Pershing, who wanted to press forward to the German stronghold of Metz, the overall Allied commander, Marshal Ferdinand Foch, then shifted the Americans west through **the Argonne Forest.** The action was aimed at retaking the French city of Sedan and cutting the main German supply route, a rail line between Sedan and Metz. It was the **bloodiest battle of the war.** The offensive began with artillery barrages on Sept. 26, 1918, and ended in victory 40 days later, but at a terrible cost. Of the 1.2 million U.S. troops involved, 177,000 were killed, wounded or captured.

By early November, **German forces were in full retreat. Kaiser Wilhelm II was forced to abdicate,** and a provisional government made peace overtures. At 5 A.M. on Nov. 11, 1918, representatives of the German and Allied armies met in a railway car in the Compiègne Forest and signed an **armistice agreement.** In four years of war, tens of millions of soldiers had been killed or wounded, or had died of disease. Among the Americans, 53,500 died in battle and more than 63,000 died of disease or accidents. Another 200,000 were injured.

On June 28, 1919, German representatives signed the **Treaty of Versailles,** a compromise agreement forged by 27 Allied nations and satisfying no one. The principal negotiators were President Wilson, Lloyd George of England, Georges Clemenceau of France and Vittorio Orlando of Italy. The treaty required Germany to admit sole guilt for the war, dismantle most of its army and pay $15 billion to the Allies. It also stripped Germany of Alsace-Lorraine and its colonies in Africa, Asia and the Pacific. Most important for Wilson, who had sought a more conciliatory agreement, it **established the League of Nations** to promote international peace and cooperation.

Wilson's vision of a world peacekeeping body, which he had envisioned in his Fourteen Points, was not popular at home, however. Keeping peace would have meant defending foreign borders when they were threatened. Further, the United States would have lost the ability to act unilaterally. The Republican-controlled Congress refused to commit the nation to league membership. Wilson, a Democrat with little leverage, would not compromise. On March 19, 1920, **the Senate refused to ratify the Treaty of Versailles, dooming the League of Nations.**

Germany was left in economic turmoil, due in part to the large reparations it was forced to pay. The economy undermined attempts at democracy made by the postwar Weimar Republic, and gave the Nazis the opportunity to come to power. **The stage was set for World War II.**

WORLD WAR II

Prelude to War: **The settlement of World War I had left Germany demoralized and economically devastated.** The worldwide economic downturn at the end of the 1920s hit Germany particularly hard and eroded confidence in the Weimar Republic, which had administered a fragile democracy in Germany since the war. The country was ripe for Adolf Hitler, a power-hungry party leader who promised better times while asserting German superiority and blaming the country's problems on Jews and Communists.

Hitler had tried to seize control in late 1923. The Weimar Republic seemed poised for collapse and Hitler attempted an armed takeover in Munich. His poorly planned assault was crushed in less than a day, and he was sentenced to prison. The trial gained publicity for him, however, and the prison term (he served less than a year of a five-year sentence) gave him time to revise his strategy. **In prison, he dictated his biography,** *Mein Kampf* **(My Struggle), which defined his guiding principles: space and race.** Germany's future lay in conquering more territory and eliminating inferior human beings from the culture, he wrote; only then could the country, home of a master race, fulfill its destiny. He had also learned an important lesson from his failed takeover. If he was to gain control, it would have to be through political channels, not force.

From 1924 to 1929 Hitler worked at building the National Socialist German Workers' party (the Nazi party). By 1928, he had 100,000 loyal followers. They won 12 seats in the Parliament (the Reichstag), working against the government from within.

When the Great Depression struck in 1929, bankruptcies and unemployment soared, further weakening the position of the government. Hitler promised the nation economic salvation. In 1930, the Nazis won 107 seats in Parliament, becoming the second largest political party. **As the economy worsened, with 43 percent of the work force unemployed by 1932, Hitler's rhetoric intensified and the Nazis became the dominant party in the Reichstag.** The two other leading parties, the Social Democrats and the Communists, were so committed in their opposition to each other that they could not work together to oppose the Nazis. Hitler used his political power to make friends in high places: the military and big

business. On Jan. 30, 1933, Hitler was named chancellor (chief minister) by Pres. Paul von Hindenburg.

Hitler immediately called for a new election, in which he expected the Nazis to take control. When they gained only 44 percent of the votes, he promptly outlawed the Communist party and arrested its Reichstag representatives. **With the significant opposition out of the way, the Nazis in the Reichstag pushed through the Enabling Act, which gave Hitler dictatorial powers.**

All parties other than the Nazi party were outlawed, which left the Reichstag under Hitler's control. Nazis were placed in top bureaucratic positions, and a party bureaucracy was developed that acted as a second government. Labor, educational and cultural organizations were all under Nazi control. Books that did not meet Nazi ideological standards were burned. All that Hitler needed was the loyalty of the German military, and he devised a way to gain that.

Before the takeover, the Nazis had used their militant branch, the storm troopers, to attack Communists and Jews. There were now 3 million storm troopers—rowdy, brown-shirted thugs—who expected to be rewarded by Hitler. The German military was wary of them, which Hitler knew. Hitler's propagandists spread rumors of a storm-trooper conspiracy to grab power, although no such plan existed. Hitler ordered his personal guard, the SS, to put an end to the "conspiracy." On June 30, 1934, the SS arrested about 1,000 storm-trooper leaders, and executed them without benefit of trial. President Hindenburg sent Hitler a telegram of congratulations. **The German army pledged its allegiance to Hitler.** The SS, under the leadership of Heinrich Himmler, and the Gestapo (the party police) were free to carry out Hitler's will without fear of reprisal.

Jews had already been the object of attacks and economic reprisal, as they were forced from their jobs and their homes. In 1935 they were also deprived of German citizenship, which caused many to flee. **The attacks on Jews escalated, with synagogues, businesses and homes looted and destroyed.** By 1938, a quarter of Germany's 500,000 Jews had fled the country. Soon emigration was no longer an option. [*See* The Holocaust, page 132]

Hitler, who had promised better economic times, put the unemployed to work building highways, public buildings and housing. He also rebuilt the army, which had been limited to 100,000 men under the Treaty of Versailles at the end of World War I. Unemployment vanished, business prospered, but wages were stagnant. Still, Hitler had many supporters. And those who did not support him—the Communists, the Social Democrats, some high-ranking army officers and Protestant and Catholic clergy—were silenced.

When Hitler first sought to expand Germany's territory he might have been stopped by other European nations, but they were not eager to undertake another war like the Great War (World War I). **Britain adopted a policy of appeasement,** not realizing that there was no end to what Hitler would demand. In 1936, when **Hitler marched into the Rhineland** (a region bordered by Germany on the east and Switzerland, France, Belgium and the Netherlands on the west), England did nothing to stop him. The occupation of the ethnically German area did not seem outrageous to the British. And France would not act without the support of Britain.

In Italy, the Fascist dictator Benito Mussolini believed that he had found something of a kindred spirit in Hitler. After all, Hitler had supported Italy when it had expanded its influence in Africa by taking over Ethiopia. He did not know that Hitler had secretly supplied arms to Ethiopia, to make the conflict more dramatic and a Nazi alliance more attractive. **Italy and Germany became aligned, forming the so-called Rome-Berlin Axis, in 1936. Japan, which was trying to expand its influence in Asia, joined them.** The three countries, despite many cultural differences, were united by their poor economic conditions, by their lack of faith in the effectiveness of democratic government, and by their perception that expansion held the key to prosperity and influence. (Hungary and Romania joined the Axis in 1940. Bulgaria joined in 1941.)

In March 1938, Hitler annexed Austria. He then threatened to invade Czechoslovakia, claiming that German minorities had been mistreated there. Great Britain and France, fearing that war on the Continent was imminent, arranged a meeting with Hitler and Mussolini in September 1938. **Great Britain and France agreed to allow Germany to control the Sudetenland** (a 10,000-sq.-mi. area of Czechoslovakia that bordered Germany), in the hope of appeasing Hitler and avoiding war. British Prime Minister Neville Chamberlain said that the Munich Conference would result in "peace in our time." He and Premier Edouard Daladier of France had seriously underestimated Hitler's appetite for *lebensraum* (living space).

Within weeks of signing the agreement, Hitler was planning to annex all of Czechoslovakia. On March 15, Czech Pres. Emil Hácha met with Hitler in Berlin in an attempt to avoid a takeover. Hitler and his aides harassed the elderly Hácha until he fainted. Then they revived him with drugs and compelled him to sign a document that would make Czechoslovakia a German protectorate.

In March 1939, Hitler seized the rest of Czecho-slovakia and a port in Lithuania. He then demanded that Poland give him the Polish Corridor (a strip of land between Prussia and Germany that connected Poland with the Baltic Sea) and the port of Danzig (Gdańsk). France and Great Britain had promised to protect Poland if it were attacked, but assistance seemed militarily impossible. The Soviet Union was in a much better position to help, but the Poles opposed having Communist forces on their soil. Instead, the Soviet Union signed a nonaggression pact with Germany, its enemy, leaving Poland without an effective military ally.

War in Europe: **On Sept. 1, 1939, Hitler's forces invaded Poland, marking the start of a global war that would eventually be fought in Europe, the coast of North Africa, the central and southwest Pacific, China, Burma and Japan and involve all of the major world powers.** The Allies included: Australia, Belgium, Canada, China, Denmark, France, Greece, India, the Netherlands, New Zealand, Norway, Poland, the USSR, the Union of South Africa, the United Kingdom, the United States and Yugoslavia. The Axis powers included Bulgaria (which later joined the Allies), Finland, Germany, Hungary, Italy (which later joined the Allies), Japan and Romania.

On Sept. 3, Great Britain and France declared war on Germany. On Sept. 17, Russian troops invaded Poland. By the end of the month, the country had been partitioned between Germany and the Soviet Union.

The Soviet Union annexed the Baltic countries of Latvia, Lithuania and Estonia after first forcing them to allow Soviet military bases on their soil. The USSR made the same demands on Finland but was refused. **The Soviet Union invaded Finland in November 1939** and fought for more than three months before overpowering the greatly outnumbered Finns.

April 9, 1940, Germany attacked Denmark and Norway. Denmark was vanquished in a day. Norway, supported by French and British troops, lost much of its territory early, and gave up its final port in June. **Germany invaded the Low Countries—Belgium, the Netherlands and Luxembourg—on May 10, 1940.** The countries were strategically important because they could provide easy military access to France. Great Britain and France came to their defense, but German forces were far superior in numbers, tanks and air power. On May 13, 1940, Queen Wilhelmina of the Netherlands fled to England. The next day her army surrendered. As the British and French tried to protect key Belgian positions in the north, the Germans attacked through Luxembourg into southeastern Belgium, cutting off the French and British supply lines and putting themselves in an excellent position to enter France.

The French had felt fairly secure behind the Maginot Line, a line of fortifications along France's border with Germany. The Germans had managed to circle around the Line, however, and pressed on toward the English Channel. In Belgium, the Germans met decreasing resistance; on May 28, King Leopold II surrendered. **The British Expeditionary Force (BEF) in Belgium led a retreat to Dunkirk, France,** a port on the English Channel, where the Royal Navy and civilian ships ferried more than 300,000 British, French and Belgian troops to England.

The German panzer (armored) divisions made fast work of the French army, which was unprepared to fight tanks. The Germans were helped by Italian forces, which entered southern France on June 10, 1940. **Germany took Paris on June 14, 1940,** and Premier Paul Reynaud resigned. The new premier, Marshal Henri Philippe Pétain, asked Germany for peace terms. On June 21, 1940, an armistice was signed.

Under the terms of the agreement, three-fifths of France was placed under German control. The rest ostensibly was free, although it was under German influence. Its government was established at Vichy, a resort city in central France, under the leadership of Marshal Pétain and Pierre Laval.

French General Charles de Gaulle had escaped to England, where he established the Free French resistance movement.

When France fell, the impact was felt worldwide. Japan was able to advance into French Indochina (now Cambodia, Laos and Vietnam). Great Britain braced for invasion, and Prime Minister Winston Churchill appealed to the United States for help. The United States shipped guns and ammunition to Great Britain, and prepared for war.

Britain's greatest military strength was the Royal Air Force (RAF). German Field Marshal Hermann Goering planned to draw the RAF into battle over Great Britain, destroy the RAF and then invade. **The German Luftwaffe (air force) began its attack on Great Britain in August 1940 and continued for three months. During the Battle of Britain, many British cities were severely damaged, and thousands of civilians died.** In London alone, more than 12,000 civilians died in the *blitzkrieg* (lightning war). Eventually, however, the RAF was able to repel the Luftwaffe, which suffered heavy losses.

While Germany was attacking England, **Italy attacked British holdings in Africa.** It succeeded in British Somalia (now Somalia), the Sudan and Kenya. The real prize for Mussolini, however, was to be Egypt, with its strategic position on the Mediterranean and its Suez Canal. **In September 1940, Italian forces invaded Egypt.** They were routed by the British. Within six months, the British had taken 130,000 prisoners and were driving into Libya, which

was under Italian control. In response, **Hitler sent one of his best generals, Erwin Rommel, and Germany's desert fighters, the Afrika Korps.** Rommel (nicknamed "the Desert Fox" by the British) quickly repelled the British from Libya and pushed into Egypt before being stopped at Tobruk by British and Australian forces.

In October 1940, while the fighting raged in Africa, Mussolini took on another adversary, Greece. Italian troops invaded Greece through Albania, expecting to meet little resistance from Greek forces, who were poorly armed. Instead, they were defeated, proving themselves no match for the Greek forces at fighting in mountainous terrain. The Greek victory was short-lived, however. **On April 6, 1941, Germany invaded Greece and Yugoslavia. Within the month, both countries had been conquered.** The Germans followed up with an air strike against the Greek island of Crete, forcing British troops stationed there to flee to Egypt.

Meanwhile, the Germans were fomenting revolt in Iraq. After World War I, Iraq had come under British rule. Although it had since gained its independence, economic and political ties—and resentments—remained. Germany fanned the embers into an anti-British war, which the British were able to put down within a month. The British then continued their success in Syria, where Germany had attempted to set up a base of operations.

The setbacks suffered by Germany in late 1940 caused Hitler to delay, but not cancel, one of his most ambitious plans. **On June 22, 1941, German troops invaded the Soviet Union,** intent on sweeping a path to Moscow and establishing European superiority for Germany. Hitler had planned to start the campaign in May, and he underestimated what the delay would cost him militarily. German troops faced Russian soldiers who were better equipped than they had anticipated, and they faced severe supply problems, an early winter and a lack of momentum. **By early November, the Germans had reached and taken Leningrad (St. Petersburg), which they held for two years.** The snow and cold left them greatly incapacitated, however, and a 10-week armored campaign against Moscow failed miserably.

Meanwhile, the Germans were also suffering a serious defeat in North Africa, where Rommel had been pushed back to Libya by the British.

At the start of the war, England had attempted to blockade Germany to prevent it from obtaining supplies by sea, but the action had produced little effect. **In 1940, Germany began a blockade of Great Britain,** which had the potential to devastate the island nation. Germany's goal was to block Great Britain's prime trading routes, with the United States and Canada, in the Atlantic. **During the blockade, which** came to be known as the Battle of the Atlantic, the Germans attacked merchant vessels with battleships (including the *Bismarck*) and U-boats (submarines).

The United States, though still officially neutral, came to Great Britain's aid. It sent 50 destroyers (in exchange for leases on military bases) and joined in air and sea patrols. One American military ship, the *Reuben James*, was sunk.

Meanwhile, the relationship between the United States and Japan had become increasingly strained. Pres. Franklin D. Roosevelt had stopped the sale of scrap iron and steel to Japan in 1940, which greatly limited its offensive capabilities. Later he expanded the prohibition to include all strategic materials. When Japan moved into southern Indochina in 1941, Roosevelt responded by freezing all Japanese assets in the United States.

The U.S. Joins the War: **On Sunday morning, Dec. 7, 1941, Japanese warplanes attacked the U.S. military base in Pearl Harbor, Hawaii.** While most of the island slept, the planes attacked, sinking or seriously injuring five U.S. battleships, including the *Arizona*, and 14 smaller ships. At Hickam and Wheeler airfields, 80 naval aircraft and 97 army aircraft were destroyed. In less than two hours, more than 2,400 sailors, soldiers and civilians had been killed; 1,300 had been injured.

On Dec. 8, 1941, Congress declared war on Japan. In his address to Congress, President Roosevelt called Dec. 7, 1941, a date "which will live in infamy." Three days later, **Italy and Germany declared war on the United States, and Congress adopted a resolution recognizing a state of war against them.**

Japan wanted to take over Malaya (now part of Malaysia), Hong Kong, Burma, the islands of Java, Sumatra and Borneo, the Philippines, New Guinea, the Celebes and the Solomon Islands. **While attacking Pearl Harbor, the Japanese had also attacked the Philippines, Malaya and Hong Kong. The next day it attacked American bases in Guam and Wake Island. On Dec. 10, 1941, Japanese forces invaded the northern island of Luzon in the Philippines.** They captured Manila, the capital, and pushed into other islands. American and Filipino troops, led by Gen. Douglas MacArthur, withdrew to the Bataan peninsula. The island fortress of Corregidor remained under American control.

Hong Kong fell to the Japanese within weeks. Singapore, at the southern tip of Malaya, held out until Feb. 15, 1942.

The Japanese were also attacking the islands of the Netherlands East Indies. The Allies suffered an important defeat when the Japanese inflicted heavy losses on an American fleet in the Battle of the Java Sea from Feb. 27 to March 1, 1942. Java soon fell. By summer, Sumatra also was under Japanese control.

On the Bataan peninsula, American and Filipino troops suffered from fever and hunger throughout the winter of 1942, with little hope of assistance. With defeat imminent, MacArthur was reassigned to Australia. When he left, he vowed, "I shall return." MacArthur was replaced by Lt. Gen. Jonathan M. Wainwright. **On April 9, 1942, Bataan was taken by the Japanese.** Wainwright and about 3,500 soldiers and nurses withdrew to Corregidor, where they held on until May.

For the 37,000 captured at Bataan, the horror was just beginning. **The Bataan Death March began at dawn on April 10.** American and Filipino prisoners were forced to march 85 miles in six days, with only one meal of rice to sustain them. The soldiers, sick, exhausted and starving, were beaten along the way. More than 5,200 Americans and many more Filipinos died before reaching a Japanese concentration camp.

Japan was also making progress in Burma. It had forced Thailand to sign an alliance, after occupying Bangkok, and was using Thailand as a base from which to attack Burma. **By the end of 1942, Japan had occupied all of Burma and was moving toward India.** The British navy sent forces to defend the Bay of Bengal.

Throughout late 1941 and early 1942, the Allies suffered significant losses. In mid-April, however, the tide began to turn. American bombers from the aircraft carrier *Hornet* stung Tokyo and other Japanese cities with surprise raids. The raids, under the direction of Col. James H. Doolittle, caused the Japanese to divert some of their forces to guarding their home front.

From May 4 to May 8, 1942, American and Japanese naval forces faced each other in the Battle of the Coral Sea, northeast of Australia. Although both sides sustained heavy losses, the battle was a clear victory for the U.S., which battered the Japanese fleet with air attacks. The U.S. lost a carrier, a destroyer and a tanker. Japan lost seven warships. For the first time, it was forced to turn back.

For the Japanese, an even more devastating loss was to follow. **During the Battle of Midway, from June 4 to June 6, 1942, American forces prevented the Japanese from taking Midway Island in the Central Pacific.** The Japanese lost four aircraft carriers, two large cruisers, three destroyers and more than 300 planes. In addition, three battleships and four cruisers were heavily damaged. The United States lost an aircraft carrier (the *Yorktown*), a destroyer and 150 planes. The battle gave the United States superiority in the Pacific, and dealt Japan a blow from which it was unable to recover.

Japan's heavy losses also prevented it from pursuing an offensive in the Aleutian Islands, the only part of North America invaded in World War II. Several islands were occupied on June 14, but Japan could not follow up successfully and was driven out by American forces.

After the Battle of Midway, the next goal for the Allies was to eliminate Japan's strength in the South Pacific. **On Aug. 7, 1942, U.S. Marines landed at Guadalcanal in the Solomon Islands,** where the Japanese were building an air base. The battle, which included some of the bloodiest fighting of the war, continued on land and sea until the Allies gained a victory in February 1943.

Meanwhile, the Japanese were also making inroads in New Guinea, having landed 11,000 troops near Port Moresby. Success at Port Moresby would give them a base from which to attack Australia. Australian and American troops turned back the Japanese after months of jungle warfare.

While the Allies were making progress in the Pacific, the British were suffering temporary reversals in North Africa. Rommel, having recovered from his earlier defeat, struck again at the British in Libya and managed to push them back 350 miles. In May 1942, British forces were pushed all the way to El Alamein in Egypt. The British, under Lt. Gen. Bernard Law Montgomery, resupplied their forces and waited for an opportunity. On Oct. 23, Montgomery's forces attacked. Within three months, Rommel's forces had been pushed back 1,400 miles and had suffered 59,000 casualties.

To divert German forces from the Soviet Union, the Allies sought to move the war to a new front. Because the British opposed any new front in Europe, the Allies settled on French North Africa, which was under control of the Vichy government. **On Nov. 8, 1942, Lt. Gen. Dwight D. Eisenhower led an American and British force into Algiers, Oran and Casablanca.** After mild opposition, the Vichy forces went over to the Allies. In retaliation, **Germany occupied all of France** and amassed troops in Tunisia.

During 1942, Great Britain and the United States bombed centers of the German defense industry, including Essen, Cologne and Düsseldorf. **Still, Hitler was able to attack the Caucasus, an oil-rich area of southern Russia, and Stalingrad** (now Volgagrad). He got to the Caucasus through the Crimean peninsula, attacking its southern port of Sevastopol in July. By August, his forces had taken all of the peninsula and had advanced to the foothills of the Caucasus.

Stalingrad was an important city that Hitler vowed to take at any cost. He planned to deplete the Russian army by causing it to defend Stalingrad against repeated attacks. By early November, he had reduced much of the city to rubble, but he had not accomplished his goal. The Russians managed a counterattack that left Hitler's forces surrounded and hopeless. When **the Germans surrendered in January 1943, they had lost more than 200,000 men.**

In North Africa, the battle became centered in Tunisia. Rommel had been forced into southern Tunisia by Montgomery's forces and the Americans were attacking the Germans in northern Tunisia. Rommel waged a surprise attack against the Americans, then against the British, and was repelled. By April, his forces were virtually surrounded. **On May 12, 1942, the Axis forces in North Africa surrendered.**

On July 10, 1942, the Allied forces began their invasion of Europe at Sicily. The forces included U.S. troops led by Gen. George S. Patton, British troops led by Field Marshal Montgomery, and French and Canadian forces. Sicily was used as a stepping-stone to the Italian mainland. The invasion, and the imminent fall of Sicily, caused dissent throughout Italy. On July 25, Mussolini was imprisoned by his own countrymen after having been forced to resign. (On Sept. 12 he was rescued by German commandos and formed a puppet government in northern Italy.)

The Allies crossed the Strait of Messina and invaded southern Italy on Sept. 3, 1943. Five days later, the Italian government surrendered to the Allies, but the Germans continued to fight. On Sept. 9, American, British, Dutch, French and Polish forces landed at Salerno, on Italy's southwestern coast, and met severe opposition. By Oct. 1, the Allies had managed to take Naples. On Oct. 13, the new Italian government, under the leadership of Pietro Badoglio, declared war on Germany.

On Jan. 22, 1944, Allied troops landed at Anzio, about 30 miles south of Rome. Their goal was to cut the Germans' lines of communication, help other Allied forces push north, and capture Rome. They met little resistance at the beachhead, but by the time they were 10 miles inland, the Germans managed to amass a strong counterforce. Instead of moving swiftly into Rome as the Allies had hoped, they were stalled for nearly five months.

Meanwhile, the Allied forces under MacArthur had made important advances in the Southwest Pacific, crossing the islands like stepping-stones. In the Central Pacific, naval forces under Adm. Chester W. Nimitz began to advance on the Gilbert Islands. On Nov. 20, 1943, they landed on Tarawa and Makin islands, the Japanese strongholds in the Gilberts. Makin offered little resistance, but more than 3,500 Marines were killed or wounded before Tarawa was taken.

In January 1944, American forces overtook key Japanese positions in the Marshall Islands in the Central Pacific. They followed those victories with others at the Japanese naval base of Truk in the Caroline Islands and at Saipan in the Marianas. The Americans captured the Admiralty Islands in the

Southwest Pacific in March 1944 and advanced through New Guinea from April through July.

Meanwhile in Europe, Allied bombers were conducting bombing raids aimed at cutting German supply lines. The attack continued from March to May, seriously restricting Germany's ability to supply its front-line troops and forcing it to begin to pull back. (The Allies also began bombing Berlin on March 6, dropping more than 2,000 tons of bombs on the German capital.) **On May 18, 1944, British troops were able to take Monte Cassino in Italy. On June 4, 1944, Allied forces entered Rome.**

The Germans were also suffering losses in the Soviet Union. **In January 1944, Russian troops were able to free Leningrad,** which had been held by the Germans for more than two years, and continued to push the Germans back. By spring, most German troops were out of the Soviet Union, and Russians were pushing into the Balkans and Poland.

In Burma, the British succeeded in capturing Rangoon from the Japanese on May 3, 1944. Taking the capital city allowed them to open up the Burma Road for trade. The Japanese occupation of Burma in 1941 had stopped trade over the road, eliminating one of China's main supply routes. During 1943 and 1944 the Allies had succeeded in retaking part of northern Burma and establishing an alternative route, but it was longer and more circuitous.

The Allies had long planned for a massive invasion of western Europe. **On June 6, 1944 (D-Day), American and British forces landed at Normandy, France,** just across the Channel from England. It was the largest amphibious operation in history.

Two months of preparatory bombing raids already had destroyed bridges, rail lines and airfields near the battle site. Just after midnight on June 6, one British and two American airborne battle units parachuted in to complete the preparations for the naval invasion by cutting communication lines and blocking river and beach escape routes.

At dawn on D-Day, Allied troops landed on the beaches. British and Canadian forces covered the left flank. The Americans landed at the center of the area, at a spot dubbed Omaha Beach in the plan, and at the north, at an area called Utah Beach. More than 5,000 ships transported the troops and equipment across the Channel.

The landing went fairly smoothly for the British and Canadians, and for the Americans at Utah Beach. At Omaha Beach, however, the troops came under heavy crossfire from the Germans, positioned in hills above the beach.

Within eight days of the invasion, the Normandy beachhead had been secured by the Allies. Reinforcements and supplies were arriving on schedule, and landing strips had been established. On June 27,

Cherbourg became the first major French port to be taken by the Allies. On July 19, the British took Caen.

In June, Hitler launched his new "miracle weapon," V-1 rockets, aimed at England. The jet-propelled, pilotless bombs each carried a ton of explosives. Thousands died in England before the Allies seized German launching pads in Normandy. (In September, Hitler launched a new version, the V-2, from northeast Germany. The rockets, aimed at London and Antwerp, carried the same payload as the V-1s but were much faster, making them nearly impossible to detect.)

After the British took Caen, the Americans headed south, toward Brittany, but were met by strong German forces at Saint-Lô. On July 18, after a bloody battle, the Americans took the city. This victory allowed the Americans and the British to advance into Brittany, and toward Le Mans and Paris. The Germans tried to hold on in the east, but they were trapped by Allied forces at Falaise, where they lost 25,000 men. On Aug. 15, American forces landed on the southern coast of France. They advanced 140 miles in eight days. By this time, most German troops in France were in defeat; those that were not were being routed.

On Aug. 25, 1944, the German commander Gen. Dietrich von Choltitz surrendered to French Gen. Jacques-Philippe Leclerc. Paris was liberated. Gen. Charles de Gaulle, leader of the Free French movement, led the triumphant procession into the city.

The Allies continued to make progress in Europe, until a gasoline shortage in late August temporarily stopped them from getting vital supplies. The delay slowed their advance toward the German border and gave the German army a chance to regroup.

On July 20, 1944, Hitler was wounded and some of his aides were killed when a bomb exploded in his headquarters. The leaders of the plot to kill Hitler, including two of Hitler's top military leaders, were rounded up and killed. Marshal Rommel, who was suspected of participation, committed suicide at Hitler's order.

During the summer of 1944, the Russians drove the Germans from Lithuania, Latvia and Estonia and defeated weak German forces in Romania. In August, Romania and Bulgaria withdrew from the war, and German troops began to leave Greece. On Oct. 13, 1944, Allied troops freed Athens.

From Sept. 17 to 27, British and American forces waged an airborne invasion of Holland, but were unsuccessful. Troops were dropped behind German lines to seize five bridges across the Rhine River, including the key Arnhem Bridge. The attack went badly from the beginning, as the Allies faced much greater resistance than they had expected.

To keep their troops supplied, the Allies had to

clear the approaches to Antwerp, which had been blocked by Germany. They worked at that task through the fall, while Allied troops made their first advances onto German soil. Aachen, Germany, fell to the Americans on Oct. 21. By late November, Antwerp harbor had been cleared and the Allied supply lines were once again open.

The Allies were trying to advance to the Rhine River, from where they hoped to be able to seize the Ruhr. By December, both sides had suffered significant losses, and Hitler was amassing forces. On Dec. 10, 1944, he had assembled 250,000 troops opposite the Americans in the Ardennes Forest of Belgium.

On Dec. 16, 1944, the Germans began a surprise attack (the Battle of the Bulge) along the 80-mile American front. The Germans broke through in two places and headed deeper into Belgium. The battle, called the Battle of the Bulge because of its shape on a map, was planned by Hitler himself. Initially, the Allies had underestimated the size of the attack, interpreting it as only a local operation. Their forces were surrounded or forced back at several sites. Not until the skies cleared on Dec. 22 were they able to make significant gains. Then their air forces were able to pinpoint German armored units and trains and destroy many of them.

The Germans, greatly weakened by the air attacks, fought on until late January 1945. The Allies won a significant victory, but at significant cost. There were nearly 77,000 American casualties. For Germany, however, the results were even worse: 120,000 men were killed, injured or taken prisoner and 1,600 airplanes and 700 tanks were lost.

While the tide was turning in Europe, Gen. Douglas MacArthur was making good on his promise to return to the Philippines. On Oct. 20, 1944, American troops landed at Leyte island. The Americans defeated the Japanese fleet at the battle of Leyte Gulf from Oct. 23 to 26. After the battle, the Japanese fleet no longer posed a serious threat to the Allies. The Americans lost three battleships and three destroyers. The Japanese, who used kamikaze (suicide) planes for the first time in this battle, lost three battleships, four carriers, 10 cruisers and nine destroyers. From Leyte in the south, the Americans were able to expand their progress in the Philippines. In early January 1945, they landed 70,000 troops in the north, away from the Japanese concentrations in Manila and Bataan. From there, they were able to overtake the Japanese in Manila and Corregidor, which was liberated in February. During the campaign to retake the Philippines, the Americans suffered more than 60,000 casualties. More than 300,000 Japanese died. In addition, Japan lost half of its remaining naval fleet and 7,000 planes.

After the victory in the Philippines, the Allies planned to take an island air base off the coast of Japan, which they could use as a base for their attack on the Japanese mainland. The target was Iwo Jima, although Formosa, Okinawa, Tokyo and other air bases also were attacked. **On Feb. 19, 1945, 60,000 Marines landed on Iwo Jima,** backed up by the U.S. Navy's Fifth Fleet. They met little resistance on the beach, but the Japanese awaited on the high ground. By the time the fighting ended in mid-March, the Americans had suffered nearly 20,000 casualties.

On April 1, 1945, American soldiers and Marines landed on Okinawa, which was to be the last island stepping-stone before Japan. In the first few days, resistance was light. Nearly 100,000 Japanese troops were stationed in coral and limestone fortifications in the southern part of the island, however, and efforts to blast them out with artillery or air power were nearly futile. On April 6, 400 Japanese planes attacked the American fleet. Kamikaze pilots, each flying a plane with a one-ton warhead, made 21 direct hits. The Japanese also sent out the remnants of their navy, which was severely disabled. Even with their military forces severely weakened, the Japanese were proving to be extremely tenacious.

In Europe, meanwhile, the Allies were making steady progress toward Germany. In late 1944 and the spring of 1945, Russian troops had advanced through Hungary, East Prussia, Poland and Upper Silesia. By mid-February, they were within 60 miles of Berlin. The Americans approached from the west and crossed the Rhine at Remagen on March 7, seriously eroding the German position on the east bank. By March 29, the Americans had taken Frankfurt. In early April they encircled the heavily industrialized Ruhr region, trapping German troops. After two weeks of ground and air attacks, the 325,000 German troops surrendered.

With Germany's defeat imminent, **the leaders of the three major powers met from Feb. 4 to Feb. 11, 1945, at Yalta in the Soviet Union to discuss the postwar structure of Europe.** Roosevelt, Churchill and Stalin agreed that Germany would be occupied by four powers—the U.S., Great Britain, the Soviet Union and France. They also agreed to a conference to set up the United Nations, and that Poland would have representative government. The Soviet Union consented to join the war against Japan, in return for the right to occupy eastern Europe.

The Russians attacked Berlin on April 17. By April 25 they had the city surrounded. **Hitler, who had chosen to remain in his command bunker in Berlin, killed himself and his longtime mistress, Eva Braun, on April 30, 1945.** (He and Braun had been married the day before.) Other key military advisers, including his propaganda minister, Paul Joseph Goebbels, also killed themselves.

In Italy, the German army surrendered to the Allies on April 28. On the previous day, **Italian partisans had held a hasty trial for Mussolini, his mistress and 11 aides, who had tried to escape to Switzerland. They were shot to death, then hanged** by their heels in a public square in Milan.

Before Hitler killed himself, he named Adm. Karl Doenitz as his successor. On May 4, Doenitz offered to surrender all of his forces in northern Germany, the Netherlands and Denmark. Field Marshal Montgomery accepted his offer the next day. On May 7, a **ceasefire agreement was signed** at Rheims, France. **The Allies designated May 8 as V-E (Victory in Europe) Day.**

The war in the Pacific continued, however, with the Allies fighting for control of Okinawa until June 1945. The Allied victory was extremely costly. The toll for the Americans was 12,520 troops killed or missing, 36 ships sunk and 763 planes destroyed. For the Japanese, there were 110,000 dead, 16 ships sunk and 7,800 planes destroyed.

In the spring of 1945 the Americans began bombing Japan's main cities. The raids escalated through July, with thousands of B-29s dropping thousands of tons of incendiary bombs on Tokyo, Yokohama, Nagoya, Kobe, Osaka and other cities. In May and June, Emperor Hirohito sought a resolution short of unconditional surrender but was rebuffed.

Meanwhile, the Americans were developing a dangerous new weapon. While the heads of the Allied nations were preparing to meet in Potsdam, Germany, to discuss the postwar organization of Europe, the United States was testing the first atomic bomb at White Sands, New Mexico.

Pres. Harry S Truman learned during the Potsdam Conference (July 17–Aug. 2, 1945) that the test had been successful, but it was not a topic of discussion. He, Stalin and Churchill set up a council of foreign ministers to prepare peace treaties, plan the government of postwar Germany and decide on reparations. (Churchill, whose government was defeated in the British election, was replaced by the new prime minister, Clement Attlee, after July 28.) The Allies also agreed to try Nazi leaders as war criminals.

On July 26, the Allied leaders offered Japan a surrender plan. Japan refused because the plan did not deal with the future status of the emperor.

At 8:15 A.M. on Aug. 6, 1945, a B-29 dropped an atomic bomb on Hiroshima. The bomb destroyed more than four sq. mi. of the city and left more than 71,000 people dead or missing. (The plane, the *Enola Gay*, was piloted by Col. Paul W. Tibbets, Jr.)

The Russians, who had held back from war with the Japanese, declared war on Aug. 8 and began to invade Manchuria, Korea and southern Sakhalin. **On Aug. 9, 1945, the United States dropped an atomic bomb on Nagasaki.** About 40,000 people were killed, and one-third of the city was devastated.

On Aug. 14, 1945, Japan surrendered. **The war officially ended on Sept. 2, 1945, with the formal surrender of Japan aboard the U.S. battleship *Missouri* in Tokyo Bay.** The day was designated V-J (Victory over Japan) Day by the Allies.

THE HOLOCAUST

Prelude to the Holocaust: Anti-Semitism had a long history. For centuries Jews had been denounced as the murderers of Christ. **In Germany after World War I, anti-Semitism grew in fertile ground.** The nation had been **demoralized by the Treaty of Versailles,** which stripped it of territory, wealth and much of its army. The worldwide **economic depression** of the 1930s only worsened the situation. The Jews became convenient scapegoats.

Long excluded from traditional occupations in rural areas, Jews had gravitated toward jobs in commerce, finance and journalism in cities. They were better assimilated in Germany than in any other country in Europe. But many were liberal, at a time when conservative sentiment was strong.

In *Mein Kampf* (My Struggle), Hitler vocalized the hatred and mistrust of Jews and blamed them for the nation's problems. His message fell on receptive ears. In public statements, his message became stronger. In 1939, as German armies invaded Poland, Hitler vowed that no Jew would survive.

Before the start of the war, Jews had already been stripped of many basic rights. The **Nuremberg Laws** of 1935 forbid Germans to do business with Jews and to marry them. Subsequent laws added more restrictions in an **attempt to force Jews out of Germany.** Some did flee, but most believed that their homeland would not follow Hitler's lead indefinitely.

Violence Begins: On the night of Nov. 9–10, 1938, Hitler's war against the Jews took an alarming turn. In carefully orchestrated anti-Semitic riots in Berlin, **synagogues were destroyed, businesses and homes owned by Jews were looted and burned,** 20,000 Jews were imprisoned, and 90 people were killed. Thousands of stores' windows were smashed. The night became known as *Kristallnacht*, Night of Broken Glass.

After the start of the war in 1939, **Jews were stripped of their property and possessions, prohibited from emigrating, forced into ghettos and used as slave labor.** In the ghettos they faced overcrowding, poverty, disease and starvation. Those who survived were rounded up, crowded into freight cars and shipped to **concentration camps,** where forced labor, malnutrition, disease, brutality and shooting killed hundreds of thousands more. As of Sept. 19, 1941, **all**

Jews were required to identify themselves by wearing the Star of David sewn to the left breast of their clothing.

The "Final Solution": When Germany attacked the Soviet Union in June 1941, **strike squads killed Soviet Jews on sight.** At the **Babi Yar ravine** in Kiev, 33,771 Jews were machine-gunned between Sept. 29 and 30, 1941. The massacre represented efficiency to the Nazis, who were searching for the "final solution of the Jewish question." Part of the solution, they determined, lay in **transforming the concentration-camp system into a death-camp system.** Keeping prisoners was not efficient; killing them in production-line fashion was. Death would no longer be a by-product; it would become the only product.

By 1942, death camps had been set up all over German-occupied Europe for annihilation of Jews, Slavs, Gypsies, political dissidents, the mentally handicapped and others the Nazis found inferior. At the camps, the strongest 10 percent were kept as slave labor. The others went quickly to their deaths, often in gas chambers disguised as showers. Others were killed by electrocution, phenol injections, flamethrowers, hand grenades and execution squads. Their bodies were cremated—after their gold teeth, clothes and hair had been removed for use in the war effort. By the end of the war, the names of the camps had become synonymous with inhumanity: Dachau, Buchenwald and Bergen-Belsen in Germany, and Auschwitz (the German spelling of Oswiecim), Chełmno and Treblinka in Poland, among others.

Resistance: For the Jews, vastly outnumbered and with few weapons, the act of survival was, in itself, an act of resistance. Many hid, sometimes for years. Others fled, often with the help of sympathetic non-Jews. Some defied or attacked their persecutors, and were killed in the process.

The **Warsaw Ghetto uprising** of April 1943 came to symbolize the Jews' fight for freedom. In 1942, there had been 500,000 people living in the ghetto. With promises of relocation, thousands were lured onto freight trains for trips to death camps. By the morning of April 19, 1943, only 60,000 people remained in the ghetto, and they knew where the trains were going.

When Nazis began searching the ghetto house by house, rounding up the remaining inhabitants, the Jews resisted with their pitiful arsenal of handguns, rocks and knives. The battle lasted 28 days. Hundreds of German SS troopers—and more than 56,000 Jews—were killed in the battle before the Nazis' flamethrowers, tanks, mortars and machine guns silenced the uprising. A similar uprising took place at Treblinka in August 1943, but with similar results.

While the major nations of the world fought a global war over territory, the European Jews were left largely to fend for themselves. There were brave exceptions—non-Jews who hid Jews or helped them escape. One, the **Swedish diplomat Raoul Wallenberg, is credited with saving as many as 20,000 Hungarian Jews** by providing them with Swedish passports. The Danish people undertook the most successful rescue, smuggling their entire Jewish community to safety in Sweden, despite German occupation. Still, there was little hope of help for the millions of Jews whose lives were at stake. The Allies heard reports of the death camps by the spring of 1942, but offered no rescue attempts while they continued the prosecution of the war. Christian churches offered little help, except in Scandinavia and the Netherlands.

At War's End: When Allied troops entered the death camps at the end of the war, they were witnesses to inhumanity on a scale that is nearly beyond imagination. At Buchenwald, the slave laborers who had managed to cling to life lay stacked in wooden bunks, barely able to raise their heads or to brush away maggots from their eyes. Those who could talk told of prisoners who were used as human guinea pigs for sadistic medical experiments, and of others who were forced to dig their own graves. At Dachau, Allied troops found 200,000 malnourished, mistreated prisoners from countries throughout Europe. At Bergen-Belsen, there were 13,000 unburied corpses.

Hitler had lost his battle with the Allies—but not before he had come sickeningly close to achieving his "final solution" of eliminating all of the Jews in Europe. **By the end of the war, Hitler's regime had murdered 6 million Jews in Germany and other countries under his control.** Only 2 million survived the Holocaust.

WORLD WAR II NAMES THAT MADE THE NEWS

Bradley, Omar Nelson (1893–1981): American five-star general; led U.S. First Army in invasion of Normandy (1944).

Chamberlain, Neville (1869–1940): British prime minister 1937–40; architect of an appeasement policy toward Hitler.

Churchill, Sir Winston Leonard Spencer (1874–1965): British statesman, soldier, winner of Nobel Prize in literature; as prime minister during the war (1940–45), he inspired his people and the Allies with his oratory and steadfast opposition to Hitler; also prime minister from 1951 until his retirement in 1955.

de Gaulle, Charles (1890–1970): French general and statesman; fled to London in 1940 and organized the Free French forces; provisional president of France (1945–46); later became president (1959–69).

Doolittle, James Harold (1896–   ): American general who led the first air attack on Tokyo. Later, he was a commander of the Eighth Air Force in the European and Pacific theaters. He had also sunk a German battleship in World War I and was an award-winning racing pilot. His involvement in the war did much to boost American morale.

Eichmann, Adolf (1906–62): German Nazi in charge of the Gestapo's Jewish pogrom; directed the deportation and murder of millions of Jews in concentration camps; escaped to Argentina at the end of the war but was found and abducted by Israeli agents in 1960; tried in Israel for war crimes; hanged.

Eisenhower, Dwight David (1890–1969): U.S. commander of the European theater of operations (1942); Supreme Commander of the Allied Expeditionary Force (1943–45); Army Chief of Staff (1945–48); a five-star general, his war record helped propel him to the presidency (1953–61).

Goebbels, Paul Joseph (1897–1945): An early follower of Hitler; became propaganda minister in 1933, controlling radio, press, movies and theater; conducted propaganda campaign against the Jews; killed himself and his family after Germany's defeat.

Goering, Hermann Wilhelm (1893–1946): An early follower of Hitler, he founded and led the Gestapo (secret police) until 1936; directed the air war (1937–43); at Nuremberg trials after the war, sentenced to death for war crimes; hanged himself before he could be executed.

Hess, Rudolf (1894–1987): An early follower of Hitler, he was captured by the British in 1941 after his plane crash-landed in Scotland; he may have been on a mission to negotiate peace with England. After the war he was tried as a war criminal in Nuremberg and sentenced to life imprisonment; at age 93 he strangled himself with an electric cord in Spandau Prison, West Germany.

Himmler, Heinrich (1900–1945): An early follower of Hitler, he led the Gestapo (secret police) from 1936 to 1945; he directed the deaths of millions in labor and concentration camps; directed Germany's domestic affairs; killed himself with poison after being captured by the British in 1945.

Hirohito (1901–89): Emperor of Japan (1926–89); in 1946 a new constitution left him with only ceremonial duties.

Hitler, Adolf (1889–1945): German dictator; founder of National Socialist (Nazi) party (1920); his book *Mein Kampf*, a treatise on anti-Semitism and world domination, became the guide for the Nazi party; after gaining political position, he took control of the country by crushing opposition; sought to make Germany the dominant world power by force,

and by the elimination of Jews, Gypsies and others he considered inferior to his "master race." When defeat was imminent, he committed suicide.

MacArthur, Douglas (1880–1964): American five-star general; commander of the Allied forces in the Southwest Pacific.

Marshall, George Catlett (1880–1959): American five-star general, Army Chief of Staff (1939–45); as Secretary of State (1947–49) directed European Recovery Plan; efforts to restore postwar Europe won him Nobel Peace Prize (1953).

Mengele, Josef (1911–79?): A Nazi medical doctor at Auschwitz concentration camp who assisted in the murder of 4 million people, mostly Jews; his medical "experiments" on prisoners, including children, resulted in countless maimings and deaths; nicknamed the "Angel of Death," escaped to Paraguay after the war; in 1985, the United States, West Germany and Israel attempted to hunt him down; skeletal remains, identified as his, were found in a grave outside São Paulo, Brazil; an Austrian couple living in the area, who admitted they had sheltered him, said he had died in 1979 in a swimming accident.

Montgomery, Bernard Law (1887–1976): British field marshal revered for his victory at El Alamein in North Africa, where he defeated Erwin Rommel, Germany's best general; commanded forces in Normandy and in northern Germany.

Mountbatten, Louis Francis Albert Victor Nicholas (1900–1979): British admiral; directed commando raids in Europe; commander of Allied forces in Burma (1943–45).

Mussolini, Benito (1883–1945): Italian dictator, founded National Fascist party (1921); signed alliance with Nazi Germany (1939); sought to expand into Greece and North Africa by force; military efforts failed; dismissed, jailed by king, but protected by Germans; executed by Italian partisans in the last days of the war in Europe.

Nimitz, Chester William (1885–1966): American five-star admiral; commanded U.S. Pacific fleet.

Patton, George Smith, Jr. (1885–1945): American general; commander of the Third Army in its campaigns in France (1944) and Germany (1945); his brilliant record as a military leader was marred by an incident in 1943, when he slapped a soldier suffering from battle fatigue.

Pétain, Henri Philippe (1856–1951): Head of the Fascist-oriented Vichy Government put in place by the Germans after their conquest of France in 1940; after the war he was tried by his countrymen and sentenced to death, but his sentence was commuted to life imprisonment.

Rommel, Erwin (1891–1944): German field marshal; commander of the Afrika Korps in the North African campaign (1941–43), he was nicknamed "the

Desert Fox" for his military cunning; committed suicide on Hitler's orders, after having been implicated in a plot to kill Hitler.

Roosevelt, Franklin Delano (1882–1945): 32nd president of the United States (1933–45); sent military and financial aid to England before U.S. joined the war; after the attack on Pearl Harbor (Dec. 7, 1941), obtained a declaration of war from Congress; directed the U.S. war effort; conferred with Allied leaders; worked for establishment of U.N.; died suddenly of a cerebral hemorrhage (April 12, 1945) as the war was winding down.

Stalin, Joseph Vissarionovich (1879–1953): Revolutionary, head of the USSR (1924–53); unsuccessfully sought alliances with Great Britain and France against Nazi Germany in the 1930s; in 1939, signed a nonaggression pact with Germany; aligned with the Allies after invasion by Germany; as premier, directed his nation's war effort.

Tojo, Hideki (1884–1948): Japanese general, prime minister (1941–44); directed Japan's military efforts; approved attack on Pearl Harbor; was tried by Allies as a war criminal; executed.

Tokyo Rose: Tokyo Rose was the name given by American soldiers in the Pacific to a group of women who broadcast music and enemy propaganda from Japan. One woman, an American named Iva Ikuki Toguri D'Aquino, was convicted of treason in 1949, although she claimed to have been forced to make the broadcasts. Imprisoned for seven years, she was later granted a presidential pardon.

Truman, Harry S (1884–1972): vice president (1945), 33rd president of the United States (1945–52); became president upon the death of Franklin D. Roosevelt, weeks before the end of the war in Europe; made the controversial decision to drop atomic bombs on Hiroshima (Aug. 6, 1945) and Nagasaki (Aug. 9, 1945), spurring Japan's surrender (Aug. 14, 1945).

KOREAN WAR

The Korean War (1950–53) had its beginnings in the settlement of World War II. Korea had been a Japanese colony from 1910 to 1945. When Japan surrendered, the Allies agreed that Korea should be democratically governed. Until that could be accomplished, **the Soviet Union would take control of Korea north of the 38th parallel and the United States would take charge of the south.** The Soviet Union and the United States were to work together to set up a commission to form a provisional government for Korea.

The two superpowers soon disagreed, however, on which political groups should be included in the formation of the provisional government. The United States, which had become a leader among Western nations opposed to what was viewed as the Soviet Union's worldwide expansionist intent, did not trust the Soviet Union's motives in Korea. The Soviet Union, in these early days of the Cold War, was no more trusting of the United States.

What had begun as a temporary dividing line became a permanent boundary. To the north was the Democratic People's Republic of Korea (also called the Korean People's Republic or KPR), led by the revolutionary Kim Il-Sung and supported by the Soviet Union and the Communist forces in China. To the south was the Republic of Korea (ROK), led by the conservative Syngman Rhee and supported by the United States.

In August 1948, three months after Rhee's election, **the United States recognized South Korea as an independent state.** In September 1948, **the northern KPR claimed authority over the entire country.** Following the plan outlined at the end of World War II, the U.S. removed its troops from South Korea in 1949. When Secretary of State Dean Acheson outlined a U.S. "defensive perimeter" in the Far East, he excluded South Korea, which was supposed to be in charge of its own affairs. To North Korea, the south seemed ready for reunification—by force.

On June 25, 1950, at 4 o'clock on a rainy morning, **the North launched a major attack against the South.** KPR troops, using Russian-made tanks, crossed the 38th parallel, attacking with an artillery barrage and groundfire. Extensive military skirmishes followed. The Korean War had begun.

Rhee, who had little defense against the well-equipped Soviet-backed KPR, turned to the United States and the United Nations for help. On June 27, 1950, **the UN Security Council agreed to help South Korea.** It was able to act because the Soviet Union, which had veto power, was boycotting the Council to protest the exclusion of Communist China from U.N. membership.

North Korean forces moved rapidly in the first days of the war. They had already overtaken the capital of South Korea, Seoul, and were racing toward the key southern port of Pusan in an attempt to complete their conquest before UN forces could arrive. **On June 30, 1950, the first American troops arrived in South Korea as part of the UN effort.** Although 17 nations joined in the UN effort, most of the forces and equipment were from the United States and South Korea. Gen. Douglas MacArthur was named Supreme Commander of the U.N. forces.

The North Korean forces had a military advantage as the U.S. and other U.N. troops assembled. By early September 1950, **MacArthur's forces were contained in the Pusan area**, on the far southern coast of South Korea. On Sept. 15, however, **MacArthur directed a** bold strike behind enemy lines, an amphibious landing at Inchon (on the northwest coast of South Korea) that cut the enemy's supply lines. The **North Korean troops were forced to retreat. MacArthur's forces pursued them north of the 38th parallel.**

The invasion of North Korea meant trouble for the UN forces. As **MacArthur's troops advanced through North Korea, approaching the border of Communist China,** Chinese leader Mao Zedong repeatedly warned that the Chinese would attack if the advance toward the Manchurian border region continued. The warnings were given little credence. On Nov. 26, 1950, some **200,000 Chinese Communist soldiers crossed the Yalu River, entered North Korea and joined the war.**

The UN forces were driven back. The Communist forces regained the North Korean capital of Pyongyang, then crossed the 38th parallel and recaptured Seoul on Jan. 4, 1951. By spring the **U.N. forces were able to push the enemy back across the 38th parallel,** but soon the war became a virtual stalemate, despite furious attacks and counterattacks.

MacArthur wanted to bomb supply depots in China. President Truman, fearful that such an attack would escalate into a world war, refused to approve MacArthur's plan. The 70-year-old general, who had distinguished himself as one of the nation's greatest military leaders and who had an ego to match his accomplishments, would not accept the President's decision. **MacArthur chose to bring his plan to the public, threatening China** and seeking to force the president into agreement. When he refused the president's order to remain silent on the subject, **Truman dismissed him** on April 11, 1951, which resulted in a political uproar in which ultraconservatives called for Truman's impeachment.

MacArthur returned to a hero's welcome. In an address to Congress, he recalled the words of an old military ballad, "Old soldiers never die, they just fade away." With tears in his eyes, he continued, "and I, like the old soldier of the ballad, I now close my military career and just fade away, an old soldier who tried to do his duty as God gave him the light to see that duty."

A **Senate investigation of the incident supported Truman's decision to dismiss MacArthur. Gen. Matthew B. Ridgway replaced MacArthur as commander in Korea.**

In June 1951, the UN forces announced that they were ready to take part in peace talks, which had been proposed by the Soviet Union. The talks began in July but seemed to be at an impasse. The fighting continued.

The unproductive talks became an important issue in the 1952 U.S. presidential campaign. In December 1952, President-elect Dwight D. Eisenhower went to Korea to attempt to break the stalemate, in fulfillment of a campaign promise. The breakthrough did not come until March 1953, however, when the Communists agreed to a UN plan to exchange sick and wounded prisoners.

An **armistice was signed** on July 27, 1953, at Panmunjom, North Korea. The **agreement called for a ceasefire and for establishment of a demilitarized zone (DMZ) between North and South Korea** in the area of the 38th parallel. More than 200 armistice violations were noted between 1953 and 1959.

After three years of war, nearly 25,000 American deaths, more than 1 million South Korean deaths and more than 1 million Communist deaths, neither side could claim any political gain.

VIETNAM WAR

Prelude to War: The Vietnam War was the first major military defeat for the United States, and a victory for Communist-led insurgents. It had a profound effect not only in Southeast Asia, but also in the United States, where the protests, political impact and economic repercussions were felt for years. By the end of the conflict, North Vietnam had been severely injured, South Vietnam was devastated and the United States was sharply divided by its role in a war that, to many, seemed unnecessary and impossible to win. Unlike returning veterans of other wars, Vietnam vets often were greeted not with gratitude but with accusations and contempt. The wounds were deep and hard to heal.

Although the United States did not officially enter the Vietnam War until 1961, **U.S. involvement had roots reaching back to the final days of World War II.** At that time, operatives of the Office of Strategic Services (a U.S. intelligence agency) parachuted into what was then called Indochina to help the anti-Japanese forces there, the Vietminh, led by Ho Chi Minh.

The U.S. wanted to expel the Japanese and to allow the area to rule itself. When the Japanese surrendered in August 1945, France sought to reclaim Indochina, which it had colonized in the 19th century and had ruled before the war. The United States refused to help.

From 1945 to 1954, **France fought to regain control of Indochina** from the Communist-led Vietminh, which included many non-Communist nationalists. The Vietminh were backed by China and the Soviet Union. Meanwhile, the **U.S. had itself become involved in a war to stop Communist expansion in Asia, the Korean War,** which led it to change its position. In 1950 the U.S. sent France $2 billion in military aid, but refused to send troops unless Great Britain agreed to send an equal number. Unable to continue to fight alone, **France surrendered** at Dienbienphu on May 7, 1954.

Great Britain, the Soviet Union, the United States, France and Communist China participated in the peace talks in Geneva, along with the newly recognized segments of Indochina: North Vietnam, South Vietnam and Cambodia. In July 1954, the conference **agreed to divide North and South Vietnam along the 17th parallel until reunification elections could be held.** Ho Chi Minh's Communist regime would rule the North from Hanoi; Ngo Dinh Diem's government would rule the South from Saigon. The Geneva Accords called for the reunification election to be held in July 1956 (although that provision was not signed by South Vietnam or the United States).

The pact did little to resolve Vietnam's problems. Some of Ho Chi Minh's troops remained in the South, where they terrorized villages and trained local guerrilla fighters, the Viet Cong, for the day when they would retake the South. Ngo Dinh Diem, meanwhile, was becoming oppressive himself. He limited freedom of religion, filled local offices with his appointees and initiated an "agrarian reform" that returned land to landlords, virtually guaranteeing that peasants would rebel. He also refused to hold the 1956 elections that had been called for by the Geneva peace agreement, claiming that free balloting was impossible because of repression in the North, violating the Geneva Accords. The U.S. continued to back Diem with both military and non-military aid. In May 1960, **Pres. Dwight D. Eisenhower increased the number of U.S. military advisers in South Vietnam** to the maximum allowed by the Geneva Accords: 685.

Officially, the position of the United States was that it was helping South Vietnam to resist Communist forces from the North. In fact, until the mid-1960s, much of Diem's opposition came from insurgents in the South, reacting to his oppressive regime.

In December 1960, a month before Pres. John F. Kennedy was inaugurated, **the Communists announced that they had formed the National Front for the Liberation of South Vietnam to overthrow the Diem government in Saigon.** The group used the initials NLF, from the French spelling of its name. They followed the announcement with increased guerrilla activities, particularly in the heavily populated Mekong Delta. **Diem sought help from President Kennedy, who responded with money, troops and matériel. By 1962, the U.S. had 10,000 "military advisers" (who bore a strong resemblance to combat troops) in South Vietnam.**

In response to attack, the **Diem government became increasingly oppressive.** It curbed the press and threw hundreds of non-Communist insurgents into prison. By mid-1963, militant Buddhists had launched an attempt to topple Diem's regime, which discriminated against them in favor of Diem's fellow Catholics. In protest, **some Buddhist nuns and monks soaked themselves with gasoline and burned themselves to death** in the streets of Saigon. In June 1963, a news photo of the self-immolation of an elderly Buddhist monk, Quang Due, helped shift U.S. opinion against Diem. On Nov. 1, 1963, the **Diem regime was overthrown in a coup directed by officers of the Army of South Vietnam (ARVN), with the covert assistance of the United States.** Gen. Duong Van Minh became the leader of South Vietnam. After a power struggle, Nguyen Van Thieu became president of South Vietnam in 1965.

When President Kennedy was assassinated (Nov. 22, 1963), the task of supplying an anti-Communist victory in Vietnam fell to Pres. Lyndon B. Johnson. He also faced an election in 1964, in which his **Republican opponent, Barry Goldwater, berated the Kennedy-Johnson administration for its leniency toward North Vietnam, and called for the tactical use of nuclear weapons.** Johnson portrayed Goldwater as trigger-happy, ready to drop a nuclear bomb on North Vietnam at any moment. Goldwater maintained that he had no such intent. Johnson escalated the war using conventional weapons.

On Aug. 6, 1964, **two U.S. destroyers were reported to have been attacked by the North Vietnamese in separate instances in Tonkin Harbor.** (A Senate investigation four years later raised questions about whether both attacks had actually occurred, or whether a minor second incident had been exaggerated for dramatic effect by the Johnson administration.) On the day of the purported attack, **President Johnson ordered retaliatory air strikes** against North Vietnam. At his request, **Congress passed the Tonkin Gulf Resolution (Aug. 7, 1964) enabling Johnson to "take all necessary measures" in Vietnam.**

In November, President Johnson won re-election in one of the biggest landslides in history. He then further escalated the war, telling the U.S. ambassador to Saigon, "I am not going to lose Vietnam. I am not going to be the president who saw Southeast Asia go the way China went."

The bombing of the North after the Tonkin Gulf incident had set a precedent. American forces were clearly changing roles, from being "advisers" to being combatants. **President Johnson approved massive air strikes on North Vietnam and on Viet Cong strongholds in the South.** A Viet Cong attack on the Pleiku air base in February 1965 brought on intensified bombing by the U.S. By the end of 1965, there were more than 180,000 American troops in Vietnam. A year later, there were 385,000. **At the peak of U.S. involvement, in March 1969, there were 543,000 American troops in Vietnam.**

The U.S. escalation was paralleled by changes in the Viet Cong's conduct of the war. Until 1965, the Viet Cong had conducted a classic guerrilla war in South Vietnam, relying on local troops and supplies. **After 1965, the North Vietnamese army and the Viet Cong received increasing amounts of military aid from China and the Soviet Union.** The increased capability was most dramatically demonstrated in the **Tet Offensive** of January and February 1968. During Tet, the Buddhist New Year period, the Viet Cong and the North Vietnamese army staged a massive, coordinated attack against about 120 South Vietnamese targets. **The U.S. Tan Son Nhut air base, the former imperial capital city of Hue and 36 provincial capitals were all hit. In Saigon, the U.S. Embassy compound was invaded and held for six hours.** Although the Communist attack was repelled, the Viet Cong and the North Vietnamese had convincingly demonstrated their considerable strength, and the impossibility of South Vietnam defending itself without U.S. assistance.

In the U.S., military involvement in Vietnam was becoming increasingly unpopular. Universities became a center of activism, beginning with the first "teach-in" in March 1965 at the University of Michigan in Ann Arbor. **Students for a Democratic Society and other campus groups held protests at colleges across the nation.** Young men burned their draft cards. More than 200,000 young men were charged with draft evasion, and 8,750 of those were convicted. At Columbia University in New York City, students led by Mark Rudd took over the campus and held a dean hostage for 24 hours in April 1968. On May 18, 1970, the nation was stunned when **National Guardsmen fired into a crowd of student protesters at Kent State University in Ohio, killing four** and wounding eight. The students had been protesting against the invasion of Cambodia by U.S. and South Vietnamese forces.

Protests were not limited to college campuses. Massive rallies were held in Washington, D.C., in late 1966 and 1967. In November 1969, an antiwar protest drew 250,000 to Washington.

The nature of the war inspired protest. The guerrilla fighters were difficult to distinguish from the general population, which led to civilian casualties, often inadvertently but sometimes through negligence or worse. The most tragic example was the **My Lai massacre** of March 16, 1968, when more than 300 unarmed civilians were killed by a U.S. Army infantry unit.

The Americans, under the command of Capt. Ernest L. Medina and Lt. William L. Calley, Jr., were brought by helicopter into the area, which had long been a rebel stronghold. Expecting a military assault, **the troops lashed out at whomever they found in the hamlet of My Lai, primarily women, children and old men.** Some were herded into ditches and shot. The My Lai massacre became infamous due to the efforts of Ronald Ridenhour, a Vietnam veteran who forced the Army to hold an official inquiry, and Seymour M. Hersh, who won a Pulitzer Prize in 1970 for reporting the story. Several members of Calley's Charley Company were charged in connection with the My Lai killings, but only Calley was convicted. In March 1971, he was found guilty of slaying at least 22 civilians. (He was sentenced to life at hard labor, which was later reduced to 20 years, then further reduced to 10 years.) The members of Bravo Company, who killed civilians in the nearby hamlet of My Khe while Charley Company was attacking My Lai, were never prosecuted.

The My Lai episode added to growing American disenchantment with the war effort, which had already been criticized for its effect on civilians and the countryside. If guerrillas were difficult to identify in face-to-face combat, they were impossible to identify from the air. **Napalm bombing,** meant to burn guerrillas from their strongholds, killed thousands of civilians. And the planned destruction of the ecological system, with napalm and with **herbicides,** wreaked considerable hardship on civilians, many of whom lost their homes and their livelihoods. One herbicide, **Agent Orange,** has been blamed for health problems, including cancer, among the Vietnamese, American veterans and their children. The defoliation was supposed to separate the civilians from the guerrillas by causing the civilians to flee toward the protection of the ARVN and the U.S. military. The effect was that 4 million South Vietnamese, about one-quarter of the population, became refugees and the forests and agricultural areas were devastated. Air strikes against North Vietnam destroyed much of its transportation and industry, and evidence began to build that civilian targets such as schools and hospitals also were hit.

Faced with the growing opposition to the war among Americans, and the Communist show of strength in the Tet offensive, President Johnson made a decision. On March 31, 1968, in a nationally televised address, **Johnson announced that the United States would stop bombing North Vietnam north of the 20th parallel. He also announced that he would not run for reelection,** stating that there was "division in the American house" and that he "should not permit the Presidency to become involved in the partisan divisions that are developing." A poll showed that only 26 percent of those questioned approved of his handling of the war. In addition, the cost of the war prevented him from fulfilling his promise of a Great Society, which included increased aid to education and his War on Poverty.

On May 13, 1968, **peace talks began in Paris,** punctuated by squabbles over such things as the shape of the bargaining table. On Oct. 31, **President Johnson announced an end to all bombing,** hoping to speed the talks. The first talks occurred on Jan. 25, 1969, shortly after the inauguration of Pres. Richard M. Nixon, who had campaigned on the promise of "peace with honor."

On June 8, 1969, President Nixon met on Midway Island with South Vietnamese dictator Nguyen Van Thieu to tell him that the United States planned to withdraw troops gradually, and that the South Vietnamese would have to take over. **The United States began a gradual troop withdrawal, but still remained very much involved in the war.** In 1970 and 1971 the U.S. even joined the South Vietnamese in attacks on Communist strongholds in neighboring Cambodia and Laos. (In Cambodia, pro-American Lon Nol had ousted the neutralist government of Prince Norodom Sihanouk. The Communist-led Khmer Rouge then quickly took over many of Cambodia's western provinces, which prompted the attack by South Vietnam and the United States. Laos was attacked because the North Vietnamese were increasing their use of supply routes there, the so-called Ho Chi Minh Trail.) **Nixon argued that attacks on Cambodia and Laos would help hasten the day when all American troops would be able to leave South Vietnam.** His critics claimed that he was widening the war, and demanded that he set a date for total withdrawal.

Public suspicion was fueled by the release of the Pentagon Papers, a secret Defense Department report supplied to the press by Daniel Ellsberg, a former Pentagon consultant. The report, which was 7,000 pages long, detailed the behind-the-scenes history of the Vietnam War. It showed that the U.S. had plans to bomb North Vietnam as early as 1964, and that it knew about plans to overthrow its supposed ally, Diem. In short, the report showed that what the public had been told about the war had often been incomplete or misleading. **The *New York Times* began publishing articles based on the papers** on June 13, 1971. Two days later the **Department of Justice obtained a temporary restraining order** to prevent the *Times* from publishing further installments, claiming that publication of classified information endangered national security. On June 18, the *Washington Post* **began publishing its own series based on the report.** It, too, became a defendant.

On June 30, 1971, the Supreme Court, in a 6–3 decision, refused to grant a permanent restraining order, stating that the Nixon administration had not shown sufficient cause to justify prior restraint of publication. In 1973, Ellsberg and an associate, Anthony Russo, Jr., were tried on charges of espionage, theft and conspiracy. The charges were dismissed when the judge learned that the office of Ellsberg's psychiatrist had been burglarized by the so-called White House "plumbers" in an attempt to gain damaging information against him.

Although the peace talks were not very fruitful, **President Nixon speeded up American withdrawal** from the increasingly unpopular war. By the end of 1971, the number of American troops was down to 156,800.

On March 30, 1972, **the North Vietnamese took advantage of their increasingly favorable military position by crossing the demilitarized zone (DMZ) and attacking the Central Highlands** of the South and the Cambodian border. The **United States responded by bombing North Vietnam and mining Haiphong Harbor,** North Vietnam's primary supply port.

Neither side won outright victory. North Vietnam gained territory, but suffered severe losses. South Vietnam, with substantial help from the United States, was able to maintain its government.

While the fighting continued, the United States and North Vietnam held secret peace talks in Paris. The United States was represented by Henry Kissinger (a foreign-policy adviser who later became Secretary of State) and North Vietnam was represented by Le Duc Tho, a member of the Politburo. On May, 8, 1972, **President Nixon announced that he would be willing to withdraw all U.S. troops from South Vietnam within four months of an internationally supervised ceasefire,** leaving North and South Vietnam to negotiate their own political settlement. On Oct. 8, 1972, **the North Vietnamese accepted the proposal.**

When Nixon faced reelection in November 1972, reports from Kissinger indicated that peace was at hand. After his victory, however, peace seemed as elusive as ever. **During December 1972 and early January 1973 the U.S. resumed heavy bombing** of North Vietnamese cities.

By late January 1973, **Kissinger and Le Duc Tho managed to devise an agreement that both North and South Vietnam, and their allies, would accept.** The plan, signed on Jan. 27, 1973, called for the U.S. to withdraw its troops while American prisoners of war were being released. On March 29, 1973, **the last U.S. troops left South Vietnam.** Two days later, 590 American POWs were released. **An international force supplied by neutral nations was to police the ceasefire,** until North and South Vietnam could reach a political settlement. **The process of political negotiation broke down irrevocably in 1974,** however, when Nguyen Van Thieu refused to allow a Council of National Reconciliation to be elected in the South. He asserted that voting in areas controlled by the Viet Cong would not be free. **The North built up its military forces and the South made sporadic raids** into Communist-controlled villages. The **fighting escalated** until, in early 1975, the North Vietnamese undertook major attacks in the Central Highlands, causing Thieu's forces to retreat. In April, **Thieu resigned and the new government surrendered to the enemy.**

Estimates indicate that **nearly 2 million Vietnamese, including civilians, were killed during the war,** and 4 million more were wounded.

The cost to the United States also was staggering. In dollar terms the war was very expensive—$164 billion—making it second only to World War II. In human terms, the losses are incalculable.

By the end of the war, **more than 47,000 Americans had died in combat, and over 10,000 had died of other war-related causes,** including accidents and disease. More than 153,000 Americans had been wounded seriously; another 150,000 received less serious wounds that did not require hospital care. Others came home with drug problems. Some began a long journey to self-destruction, fueled by a potent mixture of futility, atrocity, fear, anger and despair. More than 2,000 never came home at all. They were listed as Missing in Action, their fates unknown.

THE PERSIAN GULF WAR

At 2 A.M. on **Aug. 2, 1990, Iraq invaded its neighbor Kuwait,** quickly overthrew its government, and took control of its oil fields and capital, Kuwait City. Iraqi troops immediately began pressing farther south toward Kuwait's border with Saudi Arabia, where the largest oil deposits in the world would be within striking distance.

The international community was startled by the invasion, though **it was entirely in keeping with the bellicose policies of Iraqi leader Saddam Hussein.** He had a reputation for ruthlessness and prided himself as a latter-day Nebuchadnezzar, a reincarnation of the ancient Babylonian king who destroyed Jerusalem in 587 B.C. Saddam, too, wanted to conquer, unite and rule the Middle East as an Arab world.

Only months earlier, he had narrowly won a costly and bloody eight-year war with Iran, Iraq's neighbor to the east and its traditional rival for dominance and influence. Saddam had gained control of the strategic Shatt-Al-Arab waterway, but little else. **Declining world oil prices, industrial damage, depressed trade and the direct, staggering cost of the** war with Iran had left Iraq with a huge national deficit.

Saddam turned his attentions south toward Kuwait with a series of demands. Kuwait had loaned him $10 billion to help finance the long war with Iran; he demanded that Kuwait forgive the loan and pay billions of dollars on the grounds that Kuwait's overproduction of oil while Iraq was at war was part of "an imperialist Zionist plan" to force a decline in world prices that had cost Iraq billions of dollars in lost revenue. Saddam also charged that Kuwait had stolen nearly $2.5 billion worth of oil from the fields at Rumaila, which span Kuwait's disputed border with Iraq. Saddam insisted, too, that Kuwait had stretched that border nearly 45 miles to the north. He demanded that Kuwait give up its part of the Rumaila fields and grant Iraq a long-term lease on two strategically situated islands, Bubiyan and Warbah, in the northern end of the Persian Gulf at the mouth of the Shatt-Al-Arab. The two Kuwaiti islands were now all that stood in the way of Iraq's unrestricted access to Gulf shipping lanes. On Aug. 1, 1990, Saddam began moving thousands of his troops to the Kuwaiti border. The Emir of Kuwait fled to safety inside Saudi Arabia only hours before Iraqi troops overran his Sief palace.

International response was immediate. **The United Nations imposed a sweeping trade embargo. U.S. Pres. George Bush condemned the invasion as "naked aggression," ordered all Iraqi and Kuwaiti assets in the United States frozen, and dispatched a battle group of aircraft carriers to the Gulf.**

Under the direction of Gen. Colin Powell, Chairman of the Joint Chiefs of Staff, the United States on Aug. 7, 1990, launched **Operation Desert Shield,** a defensive operation that quickly became the largest deployment of U.S. military personnel and armament since the Vietnam War.

National anxiety, fed by memories of Vietnam, rose quickly. President Bush pledged on Nov. 30, 1990, that his administration would not repeat the mistakes of Vietnam. No key U.S. player in the developing drama seemed to symbolize the administration's resolve more than four-star Army Gen. H. Norman Schwarzkopf, Commander-in-Chief of U.S. forces in the Persian Gulf theater. A highly decorated Vietnam War veteran, Schwarzkopf was a soldier by temperament, vocation and training, and he promised that, if need be, he would use all the firepower he could muster.

The U.N.'s international embargo began to take its toll on Iraq as the rapid military buildup continued, but Saddam only hardened his stand. He announced that he was annexing Kuwait and that all foreigners, except diplomats, in both countries were now his "guests" and were forbidden to leave. Later, Saddam said he would remove all Western foreign nationals to military and industrial sites as "human shields" against potential allied bombings, and he called on all Moslems to join him in a holy war. Despite the region's history of increasing animosity toward the West as the great enemy of Islam, Saddam's plea was all but ignored.

On Aug. 25 the U.N. Security Council authorized the allied armada in the Persian Gulf to use force if necessary to ensure the continued effectiveness of the blockade against Iraq.

On Nov. 29 the U.N. Security Council voted 12 to 2 on Resolution 678, which authorized the use of force ("all necessary means") against Iraq if it did not withdraw from Kuwait on or by Jan. 15, 1991. Yemen and Cuba opposed the resolution; China abstained.

On Dec. 6, Saddam announced he would release U.S. hostages.

Congress began formal debate on the issue of war or peace on Jan. 10, and on Jan. 12 it authorized President Bush to use force against Iraq. The resolution, which was written chiefly by Rep. Stephen J. Solarz (D-N.Y.), passed in the House of Representatives by a vote of 250 to 183, with 164 Republicans and 86 Democrats voting in favor; 179 Democrats, three Republicans and one Independent opposing. The Senate voted in favor of the Solarz Resolution 52 to 47; 42 Republicans and 10 Democrats voted for the measure, 45 Democrats and 2 Republicans against.

The Congressional action was the first of its kind in more than 26 years. Not since Aug. 7, 1964, when Congress passed the Tonkin Gulf Resolution, had a U.S. president been authorized to go to war.

Saddam's threats remained uncompromisingly fierce. Iraqis would win, he said, because Western forces would not be able to withstand the horror of losing 10,000 soldiers in a single battle, "the mother of all battles." He would, he said, burn the oil fields of Kuwait and turn the Middle East into a graveyard for anyone who opposed him. He said he intended to see Saudi Arabia's King Fahd "rot in hell." He warned that he would annihilate "the poisonous nest in Tel Aviv."

As the world nervously counted down the hours to the Jan. 15 deadline, **the military forces arrayed for battle in the Middle East reached enormous proportions.** Allied operations were based on an assessment that Iraq had deployed roughly 540,000 regular troops, including eight battle-hardened divisions of Saddam's elite Republican Guard. Behind them were nearly 500,000 mobilized reserves. No less worrisome was the specter of Iraq's using its stores of chemical and biological weapons, about 3,000 tons of hydrogen cyanide, nerve gas and mustard gas.

Equally disturbing was the knowledge that **Saddam Hussein had been working for several years to develop a nuclear capability,** and now was believed to be near his goal. By war's end, however, it was clear that the Pentagon had vastly overestimated the size and preparedness of Iraqi opposition. Saddam was at least a year away from having a nuclear warhead, and his troop totals appeared to have been on the order of 250,000.

United States armed forces arrayed against Saddam totaled about 540,000, and international coalition forces swelled allied ranks by Jan. 15 to well over 700,000 troops.

At midnight Jan. 15, 1991, the U.N. deadline quietly expired. The Persian Gulf War began one day later, 6:35 P.M. Jan. 16, 1991, Eastern Daylight Time; 2:35 A.M. Jan. 17, Gulf time. The very first operation, perhaps the most critical of the entire Gulf war, was carried out by the U.S. Air Force's top commando unit, the First Special Operations Wing. Commando helicopters destroyed Saddam's early-warning stations and opened a hole in Iraqi radar through which the allies' main air assault could begin.

U.S. Navy warships launched the first of 52 Tomahawk land-attack missiles at heavily guarded telecommunications and command centers in Baghdad. More than 1,000 sorties were launched against key Iraqi installations in the first 24 hours of the campaign.

At 6:35 P.M. Jan. 16, 1991, Cable News Network's reporters in Iraq—Bernard Shaw, John Holliman and Peter Arnett—broke the news that war had begun in the Persian Gulf, and began reporting live from the Al-Rashid Hotel in Baghdad. Moments later, Presidential spokesman Marlin Fitzwater read an announcement in Washington, D.C., from President Bush: "The liberation of Kuwait has begun. In conjunction with the forces of our coalition partners, the United States has moved, under the code name of Operation Desert Storm, to enforce the mandates of the United Nations Security Council. As of seven o'clock P.M., Eastern Standard Time, Operation Desert Storm forces were engaging targets in Iraq and Kuwait."

Saddam responded quickly with the first of what would be a total of 86 missile shots, 40 at Israel and 46 at Saudi Arabia. One Israeli citizen died in the attacks, and 239 others were wounded. In Dhahran, Saudi Arabia, however, **an Iraqi Scud rocket destroyed a U.S. Army barracks,** killing 28 soldiers and wounding 80.

The United States redoubled its efforts to knock out Iraqi missile-launching sites and immediately supplied Israel with Patriot antimissile defense systems, interceptor rockets designed to blow up incoming missiles. Israeli losses were minimal.

Less than one week into the air campaign, after more than 12,000 missions, allied forces claimed total air superiority. Before the air war was over, coalition pilots were flying an average of 2,850 sorties per day. By war's end, the number of allied sorties totaled 109,876.

Statistics concerning the war are imprecise and contradictory even now. Estimates of the total weight of bombs dropped on Iraq and Kuwait, for example, have varied from 88,500 tons to nearly 142,000 tons. Either figure translates to an intensity of bombing unrivaled in military history. **Desert Storm may well be remembered as the first campaign in which the impact of conventional bombs approached that of low-level nuclear weapons.**

Tight control over the media and periodic briefings by Pentagon officials and U.S. Central Command in Riyadh, Saudi Arabia, helped keep world attention focused on the precision of the military's high-tech weaponry. Though laser- and computer-guided bombs made up only about 10 percent of the bombs dropped on Iraq and Kuwait, the weapons were hailed by the military as uncannily accurate. The effect of the claim was to temporarily allay critics' fears of heavy allied losses and of victimized, untargeted civilian populations.

Long after the end of the war, the U.S. military was slow to reveal damage done by bombs that missed their targets, but it was begrudgingly clear that the "smart" bombs were not nearly as accurate as U.S. officials had alleged. In fact, carpet-bombing by B-52s had done the most damage.

The U.S. military controlled the media's reporting. Reporters were forced to work through pools guided and censored by the military. CNN's Peter Arnett earned accolades and brickbats for staying behind in Baghdad. His work, though cleared by Iraqi censors, was the only reporting from Baghdad after all other foreign correspondents had left.

Iraqi officials said that 1,591 civilians died in the war and that thousands more were wounded. International concern was blunted by outrage over evidence that once inside Kuwait Saddam's troops had carried out a "scorched-earth policy"; Iraqi soldiers raped, tortured and killed Kuwaiti citizens, destroyed cultural and governmental sites and pillaged national treasures.

Early in the war, **on Jan. 22, Saddam's troops began setting fire to Kuwaiti oil wells.** By war's end 600 of the nation's 1,000 oil wells were ablaze. Three days after the well fires began, on Jan. 25, Iraqi saboteurs opened up release valves at Kuwait's Sea Island Terminal, a supertanker loading dock, dumping an estimated 1.2 million gallons of crude oil into the Persian Gulf. The act was universally decried as ecological terrorism.

In the weeks that followed, intelligence reports to the Pentagon indicated that allied bombing had left enemy troop morale low, air power nil, radar protection nonexistent and internal communications severely crippled. Coalition forces had created a clear advantage. **On Feb. 22, President Bush told Saddam he had until noon of the following day to get out of Kuwait unconditionally.** The ground war began only hours after the deadline expired: 8 P.M. in Washington, D.C., Feb. 23; 4 A.M. Saudi time, Feb. 24.

Six U.S. Navy SEALS slipped ashore in occupied Kuwait and set off enough explosive charges to simulate the start of an amphibious landing. The feint drew parts of two Iraqi troop divisions to the coast while the real assault began far inland.

U.S., Saudi, Egyptian, French and Syrian airborne and armored units raced north along the 300-mile Kuwait border with Saudi Arabia to establish bases for rapidly advancing ground forces. Coalition troops attacked the double line of Iraqi defenses in the south. Tanks and armored carriers fitted with bulldozer blades swept over miles of trenches, burying hundreds and thousands of enemy soldiers where they stood. Meanwhile, the ground forces that were stretched out along the western flank wheeled eastward in a huge arc, a tactic Schwarzkopf later likened to "a Hail Mary play" in football. Coalition forces cut off the Republican Guard, and blocked the retreat of Iraqi forces to the west and northwest.

Iraqi forces were routed. Remnants of the Republican Guard retreated to the north, and Iraqi soldiers surrendered by the thousands. On nationwide television Feb. 27, President Bush announced that combat operations would end at midnight, exactly 100 hours after they began.

On March 1, U.S. soldiers raised the American flag outside the U.S. Embassy in Kuwait City. Kuwait's leader, Emir Shaikh Jabir al-Ahmad al-Jabir al-Sabah, did not return for another two weeks.

On March 3, Iraqi military leaders accepted strong coalition terms for ending the war. Saddam Hussein remained in power, but somewhat precariously. Iraq was torn apart by the war. Kurdish rebels in northern Iraq and Shiite Moslems in the southern part of the country tried, in vain, to overthrow the stricken regime. Thousands of impoverished and starving Kurdish refugees fled into the mountains of northern Iraq. U.S. and coalition forces airlifted emergency relief supplies to them while diplomatic efforts got under way to establish a safe zone for the refugees.

The cost of Iraq's reconstruction was estimated at more than $100 billion, and the country was roughly $70 billion in debt. Saddam's nuclear-development efforts were set back a decade, and the nation was weakened militarily. The war had cost Iraq more than half of its air force, nearly 40 percent of its artillery and almost half of its tank force. British estimates put Iraq's manpower losses at about 30,000 dead and 100,000 wounded. Estimates by the U.S. Defense Intelligence Agency were nearly three times higher. Actual losses probably never will be known.

Kuwaiti ministers estimated that reconstruction of their emirate would take at least $40 billion and several years.

In the end, the Persian Gulf War proved to be one of history's fastest, most intense and lopsided military engagements. The *Washington Post* reported that 304 Americans died in the war, 296 men and 8 women. Of that number, 122 were killed in action, at least 10 by "friendly" fire.

Time magazine reported that 357 Americans were wounded and that casualties among other coalition forces totaled 77 dead and 830 wounded.

President Bush's popularity in the aftermath of the war soared. In a Gallup Poll of American voters, he reached an approval rating of 85 percent, a full point higher than Pres. Franklin D. Roosevelt in World War II.

Throughout the long pullout of U.S. troops from the Middle East, soldiers returned to outstretched arms and massive victory celebrations. The biggest were held in Washington, D.C., and New York City on June 10. The count of celebrants in the nation's capital was put at more than 800,000, but New York's turnout dwarfed that; crowd estimates ranged from 1.5 million to more than 4 million. New York City Mayor David N. Dinkins was proud. "This," he said, "was the mother of all parades."

NECROLOGY OF MAJOR PUBLIC FIGURES, JAN. 1, 1960–DEC. 31, 1992

Abbott, William "Bud": 78; comedian, Abbott and Costello team; April 24, 1974.

Abernathy, Ralph: 64; civil-rights activist, protégé of Dr. Martin Luther King, Jr.; April 17, 1990.

Abrams, Creighton: 59; military commander; Sept. 4, 1974.

Acheson, Dean: 78; Secy. of State, 1949–53; a chief architect of Cold War policy; Oct. 12, 1971.

Acuff, Roy: 89; gentleman showman, singer and fiddler; the "king of country music" with Nashville's Grand Ole Opry for 54 years; best known for his songs, "Wabash Cannonball," "The Great Speckled Bird" and "Night Train to Memphis"; Nov. 23, 1992.

Adams, Ansel: 82; landscape photographer, American West; April 23, 1984.

Adams, Harriet: 89; author of *Nancy Drew, Hardy Boys, Tom Swift, Jr.* books; March 27, 1982.

Adamson, George: 83; environmentalist, gained fame after his wife Joy wrote *Born Free* and *Living Free;* Aug. 20, 1989.

Adler, Stella: 91; actress and renowned acting teacher who defined The Method School and taught and influenced such stars as Marlon Brando and Robert DeNiro; Dec. 21, 1992.

Addams, Charles: 76; cartoonist of the macabre for *The New Yorker* for five decades; Sept. 29, 1988.

Adenauer, Konrad: 91; West German leader; April 19, 1967.

Aiken, Conrad: 84; writer, critic; Aug. 17, 1973.

Ailey, Alvin: 58; choreographer who broadly influenced popularity of modern dance; Dec. 1, 1989.

Alcorn, Hugh Meade, Jr.: 84; Republican National Committee chairman during the Eisenhower administration; Jan. 13, 1992.

Alexis, Patriarch of Moscow and All the Russias: 92; April 17, 1970.

Allen, George: 72; one of the National Football League's legendary coaches; Dec. 31, 1990.

Allen, Gracie [Mrs. George Burns]: 58; comedian, Aug. 28, 1964.

Allen, Irwin: 75; producer of big-budget disaster films including *The Towering Inferno* and *The Poseidon Adventure;* Nov. 2, 1991.

Allen, Peter: 48; songwriter and entertainer best-known for "Arthur's Theme," "I Go To Rio," "Quiet Please (There's A Lady On Stage)"; June 18, 1992.

Allison, Fran: 81; star of "Kukla, Fran and Ollie" television show of the 1940s and '50s; June 13, 1989.

Allman, Duane: 24; rock singer, guitarist; Oct. 29, 1971.

Alzado, Lyle: 43; star defensive end, played 15 seasons in the National Football League—eight with the Denver Broncos, three with the Cleveland Browns and four with the Oakland Raiders—retiring after the 1985 season; May 14, 1992.

Andrews, Dana: 83; soft-voiced Southern actor whose film career as a leading man extended from the 1940s into the early 1970s in such movies as *Laura, The Ox-Bow Incident,* and *The Best Years of Our Lives;* Dec. 17, 1992.

Andrews, Roy Chapman: 86; naturalist; March 11, 1960.

Andropov, Yuri: 69; Soviet leader, ex-head of KGB; Feb. 9, 1984.

Antoon, A.J.: 47; director of Pulitzer Prize–winning play *That Championship Season* and numerous productions for the New York Shakespeare Festival; Jan. 22, 1992.

Arbus, Diane: 49; American photographer; July 26, 1971.

Arden, Eve: 78; stage and screen actress best known as the warm-hearted, wisecracking star of "Our Miss Brooks" on radio and television; Nov. 12, 1990.

Arendt, Hannah: 69; German-American philosopher; Dec. 4, 1975.

Arlen, Harold: 80; blues, pop composer; April 23, 1986.

Armstrong, Henry: 75; only professional boxer ever to hold three world titles at same time; Oct. 24, 1988.

Armstrong, Louis "Satchmo": 71; gravel-voiced master of jazz trumpet; July 6, 1971.

Arno, Peter: 64; American cartoonist; Feb. 22, 1968.

Arthur, Jean: 90; U.S. actress, starred in *Mr. Smith Goes to Washington;* June 19, 1991.

Ashcroft, Dame Peggy: 83, British stage, film and television actress; won Academy Award for *A Passage to India;* June 14, 1991.

Ashley, Laura: 60; British designer; Sept. 17, 1985.

Asimov, Isaac: 72; one of the most prolific writers in history and one of the most respected in science fiction; author of more than 400 books; introduced "robotics" to the vernacular; April 6, 1992.

Astor, John Jacob, 5th [Lord of Hever]: 85; U.S.-born British press baron, former publisher of *The Times of London;* July 19, 1971.

Astor, Lady Nancy: 84; first woman in British House of Commons; May 2, 1964.

Atkinson, Brooks: 90; *New York Times* drama critic for 31 years; Jan. 13, 1984.

Attlee, Clement: 84; British Labor party leader; Oct. 8, 1967.

Atwater, Lee: 40, hard-hitting presidential campaign strategist and chairman of Republican National Committee; March 29, 1991.

Auden, W.H.: 66; English poet; Sept. 28, 1973.

Backus, Jim: 76; voice of cartoon character Mr. Magoo, played marooned millionaire on television's "Gilligan's Island"; July 3, 1989.

Bacon, Francis: 82; controversial but exalted artist whose works featured twisted, translucent but disturbing and eerily realistic forms; April 28, 1992.

Bailey, Pearl: 72; singer, actress, entertainer for more than six decades; Aug. 17, 1990.

Baker, Josephine: 68; model of 1920s hedonism, led a host of black Americans to Paris in search of artistic freedom; April 12, 1975.

Balanchine, George: 78; choreographer; April 30, 1983.

Baldwin, James: 63; civil-rights spokesman, essayist, novelist (*The Fire Next Time*); Dec. 1, 1987.

Baldwin, Roger: 97; a founder of American Civil Liberties Union; Aug. 26, 1981.

Balfa, Dewey: 65; proud fiddler largely responsible for popularization of Cajun music; June 17, 1992.

Ball, Lucille: 77; actress, comedian best known for title role in television's "I Love Lucy"; April 26, 1989.

Bankhead, Tallulah: 65; actress; Dec. 12, 1968.

Barber, "Red" (Walter Lanier): 84; pioneering and folksy play-by-play radio announcer for professional baseball; probably best remembered as the voice of the old Brooklyn Dodgers. In a career that spanned 33 years, Barber became known for unswerving fairness. He was a weekly commentator on National Public Radio from 1981 until his death; Oct. 22, 1992.

Barber, Samuel: 70; American composer; Jan. 23, 1981.

Barbie, Klaus: 77; Nazi war criminal ("Butcher of Lyons") who may have been responsible for murdering 10,000 people in France during World War II; Sept. 25, 1991.

Barnet, Charlie: 77; U.S. bandleader and saxophone virtuoso; Sept. 4, 1991.

Barth, Karl: 82; Swedish theologian; Dec. 9, 1968.

Bartholomew, Freddie: 67; one of the most popular child movie actors of the 1930s and, after Shirley Temple, the highest paid; starred in *Captains Courageous, David Copperfield, Little Lord Fauntleroy*; Jan. 23, 1992.

Baruch, Bernard M.: 94; financier, philanthropist, adviser to presidents; June 20, 1965.

Basie, Count: 79; jazz pianist, Big Band leader; April 26, 1984.

Batista, Fulgencio: 71; Cuban ex-dictator; Aug. 6, 1973.

Bavier, Frances: 86; actress known for role as Aunt Bee on television's "Andy Griffith Show"; Dec. 6, 1989.

Baxter, Anne: 62; movie, television actress; Dec. 12, 1985.

Bearden, Romare: 75; black-American painter; March 11, 1988.

Beaton, Cecil: 76; British designer, photographer; Jan. 18, 1980.

Beck, C.C.: 79; cartoonist, created *Captain Marvel*; Nov. 22, 1989.

Beckett, Samuel: 83; Irish playwright whose innovative work profoundly influenced drama; Nobel Prize for Literature, 1969 (*Waiting for Godot*); Dec. 29, 1989.

Begin, Menachem: 78; fiery former Israeli prime minister who, with Egyptian Pres. Anwar Sadat, won the 1978 Nobel Peace Prize for securing a peace treaty with Egypt; March 9, 1992.

Begley, Ed: 69; character actor; April 28, 1970.

Behan, Brendan: 41; Irish playwright; March 20, 1964.

Bellamy, Ralph: 87, U.S. actor renowned for portrayal of Franklin D. Roosevelt on stage, screen and television; Nov. 29, 1991.

Bellmer, Hans: 73; German painter, sculptor; Oct. 19, 1975.

Belushi, John: 33; comic actor, rose to stardom on "Saturday Night Live"; March 5, 1982.

Ben-Gurion, David: 87; Israel's first premier; Dec. 1, 1973.

Benny, Jack: 80; comedian, television star; Dec. 21, 1974.

Benton, Thomas Hart: 85; American regionalist painter; Jan. 19, 1975.

Bergalis, Kimberly: 23; AIDS victim who contracted disease from her dentist; weeks before her death, she pleaded with Congress for mandatory testing of health care workers and patients; Dec. 8, 1991.

Bergman, Ingrid: 67; actress; Aug. 29, 1982.

Berkeley, Busby: 79; American choreographer; March 14, 1976.

Berlin, Irving: 101; American composer, wrote "White Christmas"; Sept. 22, 1989.

Berne, Dr. Eric: 60; psychiatrist, author (*Games People Play*); July 15, 1970.

Bernstein, Leonard: 72; premier American composer, conductor and pianist; Oct. 14, 1990.

Bettelheim, Bruno: 86; psychologist who pioneered

in treatment of childhood mental disturbances; March 13, 1990.

Bigart, Homer: 83; U.S. journalist, winner of two Pulitzer Prizes, renowned for coverage of World War II, Korean War and beginning of Vietnam War; April 16, 1991.

Birnbaum, Stephen: 54; U.S. travel writer; creator and editor of *Birnbaum Travel Guide* series; Dec. 20, 1991.

Black, Hugo L.: 85; retired Supreme Court justice, Sept. 24, 1971.

Blake, Amanda: 60; actress best known as Miss Kitty on television's "Gunsmoke"; Aug. 17, 1989.

Blake, Eubie: 100; ragtime musician; Feb. 12, 1983.

Blakey, Art: 71; "Thunder," influential, innovative jazz drummer, leader of Jazz Messengers band; Oct. 16, 1990.

Blanc, Mel: 81; voice of cartoon characters such as Bugs Bunny, Woody the Woodpecker; July 10, 1989.

Bloom, Allan: 62; University of Chicago professor of political philosophy whose best-selling 1987 book *The Closing of the American Mind* decried modern universities' reliance on relevance rather than the traditional "great books" of Western culture as curricula guideposts; Oct. 7, 1992.

Bohr, Niels: 77; Danish scientist, developed the modern concept of the atom; Nov. 18, 1962.

Boll, Heinrich: 68; German writer; July 16, 1985.

Bolling, Richard: 74; Democratic Congressman from Missouri, 1948–81; April 21, 1991.

Booth, Shirley: 94; broadly talented stage, screen and television actress best known for her role as an irrespressible maid on the 1961–66 TV comedy series "Hazel" for which she won two Emmy awards; Oct. 16, 1992.

Boumedienne, Houari: 46; President of Algeria; Dec. 27, 1978.

Bourke-White, Margaret: 67; pioneer photojournalist; Aug. 27, 1971.

Bow, Clara: 60; actress, known as "The It Girl"; Sept. 26, 1965.

Boyington, Gregory "Pappy": head of World War II's Black Sheep Squadron; Jan. 11, 1988.

Bradley, Omar Nelson: 88; World War II hero, last five-star general; April 8, 1981.

Brandt, Willy: 78; German statesman, Federal Chancellor of West Germany from 1969 to 1974, whose work to heal the Cold War division of Europe earned the Nobel Peace Prize in 1971. As a Social Democrat, he became a symbol of reconciliation and tolerance and a force that paved the way for the reunification of his country; Oct. 8, 1992.

Braque, Georges: 81; French painter, exponent of Cubism; Aug. 31, 1963.

Bratby, John: 64; prolific British artist who pioneered the "Kitchen Sink School" of painting, which focused on commonplace items; July 20, 1992.

Brel, Jacques: 49; Belgian songwriter; Oct. 10, 1978.

Breton, André: 70; French poet, literary theorist; Sept. 28, 1966.

Brezhnev, Leonid: 75; leader of Soviet Union; Nov. 10, 1982.

Brodkin, Herbert: 77; producer, assaulted television taboos with provocative dramas, documentaries; Oct. 29, 1990.

Brook, Alexander: 81; American realist painter; Feb. 26, 1980.

Broyard, Anatole: 70; *New York Times* editor, book critic; Oct. 11, 1990.

Bruce, Lenny: 39; American comedian; Aug. 3, 1966.

Brundage, Avery: 87; president of Olympic Committee for 20 years; May 8, 1975.

Bryant, Bear: 69; legendary football coach of University of Alabama; Jan. 26, 1983.

Brynner, Yul: 65; Broadway star, movie actor; Oct. 10, 1985.

Buber, Martin: 87; Jewish philosopher, theologian; June 13, 1965.

Buck, Pearl S.: 80; novelist, winner of 1932 Pulitzer Prize for Fiction (*The Good Earth*); in 1938, Nobel Prize for Literature; March 6, 1973.

Buñuel, Luis: 82; Spanish film director; July 29, 1983.

Burke, Billie: 84; musical, film star, widow of Flo Ziegfeld; May 14, 1970.

Burpee, David: 87; founder, mail-order seed catalogue; June 25, 1980.

Burton, Richard: 58; British movie, theater actor; Aug. 5, 1984.

Busch, Niven: 88, U.S. author of *Duel in the Sun;* Aug. 25, 1991.

Bush, Dorothy: 91; mother of former President George Bush, who credited her as the source of his competitive spirit and appreciation of athletics and teamwork; Nov. 19, 1992.

Butterfield, Paul: 44; Chicago blues harmonica player; May 4, 1987.

Byington, Spring: 72; stage, film, TV actress (*December Bride*); Sept. 7, 1971.

Cage, John: 79; influential avante-garde composer and pioneer in experimental music; his work often incorporated the sounds of everyday life; Aug. 12, 1992.

Cagney, James: 86; vaudeville dancer, movie actor; March 20, 1986.

Cain, James M.: 85; novelist (*The Postman Always Rings Twice*); Oct. 27, 1977.

Calder, Alexander: 77; American sculptor; Nov. 11, 1976.

Caldwell, Erskine: 84, novelist of South (*Tobacco Road*); April 12, 1987.

Callas, Maria: 53; celebrated opera singer; Sept. 16, 1977.

Camus, Albert: 70; Algerian-born existentialist author; Nobel Prize for Literature, 1957; (*The Stranger*); Jan. 4, 1960.

Cantor, Eddie: 72; entertainer famous for comedy on stage, movies, radio, television; Oct. 10, 1964.

Capote, Truman: 59; novelist, short-story and nonfiction writer (*In Cold Blood*); Aug. 25, 1984.

Capp, Al: 70; cartoonist, creator of "L'il Abner" comic strip; Nov. 5, 1979.

Capra, Frank: 94, Italian-born American film director; winner of three Academy Awards; films included *It Happened One Night, Mr. Deeds Goes to Town, Meet John Doe, Mr. Smith Goes to Washington* and *It's a Wonderful Life;* Sept. 3, 1991.

Capucine [Germaine Lefebvre]: 57; French actress popular in 1960s movies; March 17, 1990.

Carlson, Chester Floyd: 62; inventor of Xerox; Sept. 19, 1968.

Carmichael, Hoagy: 82; composer, "Stardust"; Dec. 27, 1981.

Carnera, Primo: 60; Italian ex-boxing champ; June 29, 1967.

Carpenter, Karen: 33; American pop singer; Feb. 4, 1983.

Carson, Rachel: 56; biologist; book *Silent Spring* started national debate on pesticides; April 14, 1964.

Carswell, G. Harrold: 72; former federal appeals court judge whose nomination to the U.S. Supreme Court by Pres. Richard M. Nixon in 1970 was bitterly and successfully fought by the Senate; July 31, 1992.

Carter, Billy: 51; brother of ex-president; Sept. 25, 1988.

Carvel, Tom: 84; founder of Carvel ice cream chain; produced the first soft ice cream; Oct. 21, 1990.

Carver, Raymond: 50; poet and short-story writer (*Near Klamath*); Aug. 2, 1988.

Casals, Pablo: 73; Spanish cellist; Oct. 22, 1973.

Casey, William J.: 73; former Central Intelligence Agency director; May 6, 1987.

Cassavetes, John: 59; movie actor, director; Feb. 3, 1989.

Ceausescu, Nicolae: 71; ruler of Romania for 24 years; Dec. 25, 1990.

Cerf, Bennett A.: 73; book publisher, TV personality ("What's My Line?"); Aug. 27, 1971.

Chagall, Marc: 97; influential modern painter, engraver; March 28, 1985.

Chandler, A.B. "Happy": 92; Kentucky governor (1935–39, 1955–59) and Senator (1939–44); major-league baseball commissioner (1944–51) who brought black players into major leagues; June 15, 1991.

Chanel, Gabrielle "Coco": 87; French couturiere; Jan. 10, 1971.

Chaney, Lon, Jr.: 67; American actor, horror films; July 13, 1973.

Chapin, Harry: 38; folk musician; July 16, 1981.

Chaplin, Charlie: 88; comic actor, silent films; Dec. 25, 1977.

Chaplin, Lady Oona: 66; widow of Charlie Chaplin; daughter of American playwright Eugene O'Neill; born in U.S., she became a British citizen after her husband was denied entry into the U.S. in 1952 because of alleged Communist associations; Sept. 27, 1991.

Chayefsky, Paddy: 58; American dramatist; Aug. 1, 1981.

Cheever, John: 70; short-story writer, novelist (*The Wapshot Chronicle*); June 18, 1982.

Chernenko, Konstantin: 73; Soviet leader; March 10, 1985.

Chevalier, Maurice: 83; dapper French singer, actor, star of musical comedies and numerous movies, including *Love in the Afternoon* and *Gigi;* Jan. 1, 1972.

Chiang Kai-Shek: 87; Nationalist Chinese leader, last of WWII Big Four Allies; April 5, 1975.

Chichester, Sir Francis: 71; British yachtsman, first to sail solo around the world; Aug. 26, 1972.

Christie, Dame Agatha: 85; British author known for suspense novels (*And Then There Were None*); Jan. 12, 1976.

Chrysler, William P.: 79; prominent art collector, son of auto tycoon; Sept. 17, 1988.

Chou En-lai: *See* Zhou Enlai

Churchill, Sir Winston: 90; British statesman, world leader; Jan. 24, 1965.

Clark, General Mark: 87; last of top five Army commanders in WWII; April 16, 1984.

Clarke, Mae: 81; Broadway and Hollywood actress who appeared in 85 films; best known as the gun moll who had a grapefruit pushed in her face by James Cagney in the 1931 movie *Public Enemy;* April 29, 1992.

Clay, Gen. Lucius: 80; leader of Berlin airlift; April 16, 1978.

Clemente, Roberto: 38; Hall of Fame outfielder for Pittsburgh Pirates; Dec. 31, 1972.

Clift, Montgomery: 45; actor; July 23, 1966.

Cobb, Ty: 74; "The Georgia Peach," first baseball player elected to Hall of Fame; July 17, 1961.

Cocteau, Jean: 74; avant-garde playwright; Oct. 11, 1963.

Cohn, Roy S.: 58; chief counsel to Sen. Joseph McCarthy in 1950s; Aug. 2, 1986.

Cole, Nat "King": 45; singer; Feb. 15, 1965.

Coles, Charles "Honi": 81; elegant and widely acclaimed virtuosic tap dancer; teacher of black dance and its history; Nov. 12, 1992.

Coltrane, John: 40; jazz saxophonist; July 17, 1967.

Compton, Arthur H.: 69; physicist, 1927 Nobel Prize winner; developed A-bomb; March 15, 1962.

Conant, James: 84; chemist, educator, Harvard president for 20 years; Feb. 11, 1978.

Condon, Eddie: 67; American jazz guitarist; Aug. 4, 1973.

Conigliaro, Tony: 45; "Tony C"; star 1960s Red Sox baseball player whose career ended when he was hit in the face by a pitch; Feb. 24, 1990.

Connolly, Maureen "Little Mo": 34; tennis star; June 21, 1969.

Connors, Chuck: 71; former professional basketball and baseball player who achieved stardom in the role of Lucas McCain, "The Rifleman," one of television's most popular weekly Westerns from 1958 to 1963; Nov. 10, 1992.

Conte, Silvio O.: 69; Republican Congressman from Massachusetts, beginning his 17th term at time of death; Feb. 8, 1991.

Convy, Bert: 57; U.S. actor and game-show host; July 15, 1991.

Coogan, Jackie: 69; actor; March 1, 1984.

Cooke, Sam: 29; singer, songwriter, pioneer in soul and rhythm-and-blues music; Dec. 11, 1964.

Cooke, Terence Cardinal: 61; leader of Roman Catholic Archdiocese of New York; Oct. 6, 1983.

Cooper, Gary: 60; Hollywood movie actor, leading man; May 13, 1961.

Copland, Aaron: 90; America's best-known composer of classical music; Dec. 2, 1990.

Coughlin, Charles: 88; radio priest of the 1930s; Oct. 27, 1979.

Coward, Sir Noël: 73; British playwright, actor; March 26, 1973.

Cowley, Malcolm: 90; critic, writer, poet; March 27, 1989.

Crawford, Broderick: 75; movie, television actor; April 26, 1986.

Crawford, Joan: 73; movie star; May 10, 1977.

Croce, Jim: 31; folk-rock singer, songwriter and guitarist; Sept. 20, 1973.

Crosby, Harry "Bing": 73; singer, actor; Oct. 14, 1977.

Cugat, Xavier: 90; Spanish bandleader, popularized rumba and Latin-American music in U.S.; Oct. 27, 1990.

Cukor, George: 83; American film director; Jan. 24, 1983.

Cullen, Bill: 70; popular television game-show host for more than three decades; July 7, 1990.

Cummings, E.E. (Edward Estlin): 67; American poet; Sept. 3, 1962.

Cummings, Robert: 82; debonair star of early television's "Bob Cummings Show," and an actor in more than 100 movies; Dec. 2, 1990.

Curtis, King [Curtis Ousley]: 36; blues and soul musician; Aug. 14, 1971.

Cushing, Richard Cardinal: 75; retired head of Boston Archdiocese, confidante of the Kennedy family; Nov. 2, 1971.

Daley, Richard: 74; mayor of Chicago from 1955 until his death; Dec. 20, 1976.

Dalí, Salvador: 84; flamboyant Surrealist artist, sculptor, writer, film maker; Jan. 23, 1989.

Daly, John Charles, Jr.: 77; U.S. journalist, host of TV game show "What's My Line?", ABC executive; Feb. 25, 1991.

Dante, Nicholas: 49; U.S. dancer, co-author of *A Chorus Line;* of AIDS; May 21, 1991.

D'Aubuisson, Roberto: 48; charismatic leader of El Salvador's political right wing and alleged organizer of death squads that killed thousands of Salvadorans; Feb. 20, 1992.

David, Elizabeth: 78; one of the most influential food writers of the 20th century, her *Book of Mediterranean Food* helped popularize the use of simple spices in otherwise bland European cuisines; May 22, 1992.

Davies, Marion: 64; American film actress, protégée of William Randolph Hearst; Sept. 22, 1961.

Davis, Bette: 81; actress, major movie star for five decades; Oct. 6, 1989.

Davis, Miles: 65; U.S. jazz trumpet virtuoso; Sept. 28, 1991.

Davis, Sammy, Jr.: 64; singer, dancer, actor who went to work in vaudeville when he was three and was an American entertainment icon for 60 years; May 16, 1990.

Day, Dennis: 71; Irish tenor and foil for Jack Benny; June 22, 1988.

de Beauvoir, Simone: 78; writer (*The Second Sex*); April 14, 1986.

de Chirico, Giorgio: 90; Italian Surrealist painter; Nov. 20, 1978.

Dean, Dizzy: 63; baseball pitcher; July 11, 1974.

Dearden, John Cardinal: 80; ex-Archbishop of the Roman Catholic Archdiocese of Detroit, leading liberal voice in church; Aug. 1, 1988.

de Gaulle, Charles: 79; retired president of France; Nov. 9, 1971.

Delacorte, George T.: 97, U.S. publisher (Delacorte Press, Dell Publishing) and philanthropist; May 4, 1991.

Dempsey, Jack: 87; heavyweight champion boxer; May 31, 1983.

De Valera, Eamon: 92; former prime minister, president, statesman, Republic of Ireland; Aug. 29, 1975.

Dennis, Sandy: 54; actress; won 1966 Academy Award as best supporting actress in *Who's Afraid of Virginia Woolf?;* starred in *The Out of Towners* and *Up the Down Staircase;* March 2, 1992.

Dewey, Thomas E.: 68; three-time governor of New York, twice GOP candidate for president; March 16, 1971.

Dewhurst, Colleen: 67; U.S. stage, film and television actress (two Tonys, two Emmys), renowned for portrayal of Eugene O'Neill characters; Aug. 22, 1991.

Diefenbaker, John G.: 83; former prime minister of Canada; Aug. 16, 1979.

Dietrich, Marlene: 90; sultry German-born actress whose diverse roles on stage and screen made her an international star for more than four decades; May 6, 1992.

Dinesen, Isak: 77; author (*Out of Africa*); Sept. 7, 1962.

Disney, Walt: 65; creator of Mickey Mouse, other cartoon characters; Dec. 15, 1966.

Dodd, Thomas J.: 64; ex-Senator (D-Conn.); May 24, 1971.

Doe, Samuel K.: 38; president of Liberia; Sept. 10, 1990.

Doenitz, Grand Adm. Karl: 89; Hitler's hand-picked successor; Dec. 25, 1980.

Dos Passos, John: 74; novelist of post WWI generation (*U.S.A.*); Sept. 28, 1970.

Douglas, Virginia O'Hanlon: 81; her 1897 letter to *New York Sun* prompted famous editorial, "Yes, Virginia, there is a Santa Claus"; May 13, 1971.

Douglas, William O.: 81; Supreme Court justice; Jan. 19, 1980.

Dr. Seuss: *See* Geisel, Theodore Seuss

Duarte, José Napoleón: 64; former president of El Salvador; Feb. 23, 1990.

Dubcek, Alexander: 70; popular Czechoslovak leader who tried to reform communism in his country in 1968 only to have his "Prague Spring" movement crushed by Soviet-led Warsaw Pact troops; Nov. 7, 1992.

Duchamp, Marcel: 81; French painter, Cubist and a founder of Dadaism; Oct. 1, 1968.

Duff, Howard: 76; movie, radio, television actor for more than 40 years; July 9, 1990.

Duncan, Donald F.: 79; repopularized the yo-yo; parking-meter fortune; May 15, 1971.

Dunne, Irene: 91; movie actress popular in 1930s and 1940s; Sept. 4, 1990.

Du Pont, Henry Belin: 71; industrialist; April 13, 1970.

Dupree, "Champion" Jack: 81; New Orleans jazz pianist; innovator known for "barrelhouse" style; famous in Europe in the 1960s; Jan. 21, 1992.

Durant, Will: 96; historian, philosopher, co-author of *The Story of Civilization;* Nov. 7, 1981.

Durante, Jimmy: 86; comedian; Jan. 29, 1980.

Durocher, Leo "The Lip": 86; baseball player, manager prone to spirited exchanges with umpires; teams won three pennants (Brooklyn Dodgers and N.Y. Giants, twice) and World Series (N.Y. Giants); Oct. 7, 1991.

Durrell, Lawrence: 78; British poet, novelist (*The Alexandria Quartet*); Nov. 7, 1990.

Duvalier, François "Papa Doc": 61; President-for-Life of Haiti; April 22, 1971.

Eames, Charles: 71; architect, designer; Aug. 21, 1978.

Eden, Sir Anthony: 79; British statesman; Jan. 14, 1977.

Edgarton, Harold "Doc": 86; MIT professor who invented electronic flash; Jan. 4, 1990.

Edward the VIII, Duke of Windsor: 77; in 1936, became the only British sovereign to voluntarily relinquish the crown; married American socialite Wallis Simpson; May 28, 1972.

Edwards, Douglas: 73; television's first news anchorman; Oct. 13, 1990.

Eisenhower, Mamie: 82; ex-first lady; Nov. 1, 1979.

el-Sadat, Anwar: 62; Egyptian leader; assassinated; Oct. 6, 1981.

Eldridge, Roy "Little": 78; jazz trumpeter; Feb. 26, 1989.

Eliot, T.S. (Thomas Sterns): 76; US and English poet, playwright and critic; one of the dominant figures in modern literature (*Prufrock and Other Observations, The Wasteland, Murder in the Cathedral*); won 1948 Nobel Prize for Literature; Jan. 4, 1965.

Elliott, Denholm: 70; actor on stage, screen and television who won numerous awards, primarily for supporting roles. His career spanned 47 years and ranged from Shakespearean plays to modern comedy; Oct. 6, 1992.

Enriquez, Rene: 58; actor known for role in television's "Hill Street Blues"; March 23, 1990.

Epstein, Brian: 32; discovered the Beatles in a Liverpool club; Aug. 27, 1967.

Ernst, Max: 84; German-born French painter; April 1, 1976.

Evans, Bill: 51; American jazz pianist; Sept. 15, 1980.

Evans, Gil: 75; jazz composer-arranger second only to Duke Ellington in importance; March 20, 1988.

Evans, Walker: 71; photographer (*Let Us Now Praise Famous Men*); April 10, 1975.

Evers, Medgar: 37; civil-rights leader and field secretary for the National Association for the Advancement of Colored People; his murder in Jackson, Miss., touched off riots throughout the South; June 12, 1963.

Exley, Frederick: 63; author whose first novel, *A*

Fan's Notes, won critical acclaim and earned him a cult following; June 17, 1992.

Faisal: 70; king of Saudi Arabia; March 25, 1975.

Farouk: 45; ex-king of Egypt; March 17, 1965.

Farrell, James T.: 75; novelist (*Studs Lonigan* trilogy); Aug. 21, 1979.

Faulkner, William: 64; Southern novelist, one of most important figures in American literature (*The Sound and the Fury, As I Lay Dying*); won 1949 Nobel Prize for Literature; Pulitzer Prizes for Fiction in 1955 (*A Fable*); in 1963 (*The Reivers*); July 6, 1962.

Fenwick, Millicent: 82; former four-term Republican congresswoman from New Jersey known, to her disgruntlement, for her trademark pipe-smoking but best remembered for her high ethical standards and stylish, outspoken manner; Sept. 16, 1992.

Ferber, Edna: 80; playwright, novelist (*Show Boat*); April 16, 1968.

Ferrer, José: 80; popular stage, screen and television actor, won 1950 Academy Award Best Actor for *Cyrano de Bergerac,* in which he also starred on Broadway; Jan. 26, 1992.

Ferrari, Enzo: 90; Italian entrepreneur, designed Ferrari race car; Aug. 14, 1988.

Fiedler, Arthur: 84; conductor of Boston Pops Orchestra; July 10, 1979.

Field, Virginia: 74; actress in more than 30 movies in the 1930s and 1940s; Jan. 2, 1992.

Finch, Peter: 60; British actor; Jan. 14, 1977.

Fisher, Mary Frances Kennedy (M.F.K.): 83; one of the world's most prominent food writers, hailed both for her prose and culinary wisdom (*The Physiology of Taste* and *The Gastronomical Me*); June 22, 1992.

Fleming, Ian: 56; creator of fictional spy James Bond, Agent 007; Aug. 12, 1964.

Fleming, Sir Arthur: 79; British engineer, pioneer in radar technology; Sept. 14, 1960.

Flexner, Stuart Berg: 62; lexicographer, editor, author (*I Hear America Talking*); Dec. 3, 1990.

Flippen, Jay C.: 70; comedian, character actor; Feb. 3, 1971.

Fodor, Eugene: 85; author of best-selling travel guides; Feb. 18, 1991.

Fogarty, Tom: 48; guitarist, cofounder of Creedence Clearwater Revival rock band; Sept. 6, 1990.

Fonda, Henry: 77; actor; Aug. 12, 1982.

Fontanne, Lynn: 96; stage actress; July 30, 1983.

Fonteyn, Margot: 71; British ballerina who gained fame for her roles in *Sleeping Beauty* and *Swan Lake* with the Royal Ballet; partner with Rudolf Nureyev; Feb. 21, 1991.

Forbes, Malcolm: 70; wealthy, ostentatious publisher of *Forbes* magazine; Feb. 24, 1990.

Ford, Henry II: 70; head of Ford Motor Co., grandson of its founder; Sept. 29, 1987.

Ford, John: 78; movie director famed for Westerns; Aug. 31, 1973.

Ford, Tennessee Ernie "Ol' Peapicker": 72; U.S. country singer ("Sixteen Tons"); host of popular network television show in the 1950s and '60s; Oct. 17, 1991.

Foreman, John: 67; movie producer best known for *Butch Cassidy and the Sundance Kid, Prizzi's Honor* and *The Life and Times of Judge Roy Bean;* Nov. 20, 1992.

Forester, C.S.: 66; British writer of Capt. Horatio Hornblower series; April 2, 1966.

Forster, E.M.: 91; British novelist (*A Passage to India*); June 7, 1970.

Fosse, Bob: 60; director, choreographer for theater, movies; Sept. 24, 1987.

Foucault, Michel: 57; French philosopher, cultural historian; June 25, 1984.

Foxx, Redd: 68; U.S. comedian, actor; father on popular television series "Sanford and Son" (1972–77); Oct. 11, 1991.

Franchi, Sergio: 57; popular tenor, nightclub performer; May 1, 1990.

Franciscus, James: 57; U.S. television actor; July 8, 1991.

Franco, Generalissimo Francisco: 72; ruler of Spain 36 years; Nov. 20, 1975.

Frankfurter, Felix: 82; ex-Supreme Court justice; Feb. 22, 1965.

Franz Josef II: 83; ruler of Liechtenstein; Nov. 13, 1989.

Fromm, Erich: 79; psychoanalyst, philosopher (*The Art of Loving*); March 18, 1980.

Frost, Robert: 88; four-time Pulitzer Prize–winning poet; Jan. 29, 1963.

Fuller, Buckminister: 87; eclectic inventor, conceived geodesic dome; July 1, 1983.

Funk, Casimir: 83; Polish-American biochemist, coined term "vitamin"; Nov. 20, 1967.

Furillo, Carl: 66; baseball star of Brooklyn Dodgers; immortalized in Roger Kahn's *The Boys of Summer;* Jan. 21, 1989.

Gable, [William] Clark: 59; popular movie actor; one of the most enduring leading men in American cinema—starring in such films as *It Happened One Night, Mutiny on the Bounty, Gone With the Wind, Run Silent, Run Deep, The Misfits;* Nov. 16, 1960.

Gagarin, Yuri: 34; Soviet astronaut, first man in space; March 27, 1968.

Gaines, William M.: 70; a founder and publisher of *Mad* magazine, one of the first general-circulation magazines to broadly and persistently lampoon mass culture; June 3, 1992.

Galento, Tony: 69; heavyweight boxer known as

"Two-Ton," knocked down Joe Louis; July 22, 1979.

Gallo, Joseph: 43; organized-crime figure known as "Crazy Joe"; April 7, 1972.

Gann, Ernest: 81, U.S. author of adventure novels (*The High and the Mighty, Twilight for the Gods, Fate Is the Hunter*); Dec. 19, 1991.

Garbo, Greta: 84; stunning 1930s actress whose popularity and aura of mystery long outlasted her reign in movies; April 15, 1990.

Gardenia, Vincent: 71; character actor with a long career on stage, television and in numerous hit movies such as *Bang the Drum Slowly* and *Moonstruck;* Dec. 9, 1992.

Gardner, Ava: 67; seductive, popular actress, Hollywood star for four decades; Jan. 25, 1990.

Gardner, Erle Stanley: 80; author of *Perry Mason* novels; March 11, 1970.

Gardner, John: 49; American poet, critic, novelist (*The Sunlight Dialogues*); Sept. 14, 1982.

Garland, Judy: 47; singer, actress; June 22, 1969.

Garner, Erroll: 60; jazz pianist, composed "Misty"; Jan. 2, 1977.

Garner, John Nance: 98; vice president under FDR; Nov. 7, 1967.

Garrison, Jim: 70; controversial former District Attorney of New Orleans who startled the world in 1967 with assertions that the U.S. government, the military, the mob, politicians and spies—and not Lee Harvey Oswald alone—assassinated President John F. Kennedy. Though vehemently disputed, Garrison's charges have gained considerable credibility. His role in the investigation of the assassination was the focus of the popular 1991 movie *J.F.K.;* Oct. 21, 1992.

Gary, Romain: 66; French novelist, ex-diplomat; Dec. 2, 1980.

Gaye, Marvin: 44; singer, songwriter, musician; April 1, 1984.

Geisel, Theodore Seuss: 87; author of widely read children's books, including *The Cat in the Hat, Green Eggs and Ham, How the Grinch Stole Christmas* and *The Lorax;* creator of cartoon character Gerald McBoing Boing; winner of three Academy Awards; Sept. 26, 1991.

Genet, Jean: 76; French poet, playwright, novelist; April 15, 1986.

Genovese, Vito: 71; U.S. Mafia boss; Feb. 14, 1969.

Getty, J. Paul: 83; billionaire, symbol of oil, wealth, power; June 6, 1976.

Getz, Stan: 64; U.S. jazz musician (11 Grammys); renowned for tenor saxophone stylings; June 6, 1991.

Ghandi, Rajiv: 46; former prime minister of India (1984–89) assassinated during reelection campaign; he had succeeded his mother, Indira Ghandi, as prime minister after her assassination; May 21, 1991.

Gibb, Andy: 30; singer, The Bee Gees; March 9, 1988.

Gilbert, Billy: 77; comedian noted for his sneeze; Sept. 23, 1971.

Gillars, Mildred E.: 87; nicknamed "Axis Sally" for her Nazi radio broadcasts; June 25, 1988.

Gimbel, Bernard: 81; department store magnate; Sept. 29, 1966.

Gleason, Jackie: 67; comedy actor, television and movies; June 24, 1987.

Gobel, George: 71; comedian known for deadpan delivery; Feb. 24, 1991.

Goddard, Paulette: 78; movie actress who personified Hollywood glamour in the 1930s and '40s; April 23, 1990.

Godfrey, Arthur: 80; radio, television entertainer; March 16, 1983.

Goldberg, Arthur J.: 81; former Secretary of Labor, Supreme Court justice, U.N. ambassador; Jan. 20, 1990.

Goldberg, Rube: 87; whimsical cartoonist noted for zany inventions; Dec. 7, 1971.

Goldmark, Peter Carl: 71; inventor of the long-playing record; Dec. 7, 1977.

Goldwyn, Samuel: 91; film producer; Jan. 31, 1974.

Gomez, Vernon "Lefty": 79; Hall of Fame pitcher for N.Y. Yankees; Feb. 17, 1989.

Gomulka, Wladyslaw: 76; Polish Communist leader; Sept. 2, 1982.

Goodman, Benny: 77; jazz clarinetist, bandleader, "King of Swing"; June 13, 1986.

Goodman, Martin: 84; founder and publisher of Marvel Comics, creators of such comic book heroes as Spiderman and Captain America; June 6, 1992.

Goodson, Mark: 77; television producer who created such game shows as "What's My Line?," "To Tell the Truth," and "The Price Is Right"; helped establish the texture of modern television; Dec. 18, 1992.

Gordon, Dexter: 67; jazz tenor saxophonist famous in the 1940s, later an actor; April 25, 1990.

Gordon, Ruth: 89; movie, theater actress; Aug. 28, 1985.

Goren, Charles: 90; U.S. contract bridge player who helped popularize the game in the 1940s and '50s; April 3, 1991.

Gottlieb, Adolph: 71; American painter; March 4, 1974.

Gould, Glenn: 50; Canadian pianist; Oct. 4, 1982.

Graham, Martha: 96, U.S. dancer, choreographer whose work shaped modern dance throughout much of the century; April 1, 1991.

Grange, Harold "Red": 87; football running back for University of Illinois and Chicago Bears in 1920s and '30s; known as "the Galloping Ghost"; Jan. 28, 1991.

Grant, Cary: 80; movie actor, matinee idol; Nov. 30, 1986.

Grasso, Ella: 61; ex-governor of Connecticut; Feb. 5, 1981.

Graves, Robert: 90; British poet; Dec. 7, 1985.

Graziano, Rocky: 71; world middleweight boxing champion, focus of 1956 movie *Somebody Up There Likes Me;* May 22, 1990.

Greene, Graham: 86; British author whose work included probing novels about man in the modern world, thrillers, plays, travel books and criticism; April 3, 1991.

Greene, Lorne: 71; star of television's "Bonanza"; Sept. 11, 1987.

Gromyko, Andrei: 79; former Soviet foreign minister; July 2, 1989.

Gropius, Walter: 86; German architect, founded Bauhaus school of design; July 5, 1969.

Groves, Lt. Gen. Leslie: 73; headed secret development of atomic bomb in WWII; July 13, 1970.

Gruenberg, Louis: 79; American composer, opera *Emperor Jones;* June 9, 1964.

Guard, Dave: 56; original member of Kingston Trio folksinging group; March 22, 1991.

Guggenheim, Harry F.: 80; founder of Long Island, N.Y., *Newsday;* Jan. 22, 1971.

Guggenheim, Peggy: 81; international arts patron, collector; Dec. 23, 1979.

Guimarães, Ulysses: 76; veteran Brazilian congressman known as the "grandfather" of the nation's democracy; Oct. 12, 1992.

Gunther, John: 68; author, *Inside U.S.A.*, five similar books; May 29, 1970.

Guston, Philip: 67; American painter; June 7, 1980.

Guthrie, A.B.: 90; U.S. author of historical Western fiction; won Pulitzer Prize for *The Way West;* April 26, 1991.

Guthrie, Woodrow Wilson "Woody": 55; folk singer; Oct. 3, 1967.

Habib, Philip C.: 72; top troubleshooter for the State Department, played a key role in U.S. policy decisions involving Vietnam, the Middle East and the Philippines; May 25, 1992.

Hahn, Otto: 89; German physicist, pioneer in nuclear fission; July 28, 1968.

Halas, George: 88; founder professional football; Oct. 31, 1983.

Hale, Alan, Jr.: 71; movie and television actor best known as "the Skipper" on television's "Gilligan's Island"; Jan. 2, 1990.

Haley, Alex: 70; author of *The Autobiography of Malcolm X* and winner of 1977 Pulitzer Prize for *Roots: The Saga of an American Family*, which traced a family's saga from Africa to slavery in America and freedom; book became an international bestseller in 37 languages and the basis for a 1977 ABC television miniseries which drew more than 130 million viewers; Feb. 10, 1992.

Haley, Bill: 53; American rock star with Comets; Feb. 9, 1981.

Halston [Roy Halston Frowick]: 57; fashion designer, influenced women's dress in the 1970s; March 26, 1990.

Hammarskjöld, Dag: 56; Swedish diplomat, economist and author (*Markings*), secretary general of the United Nations (1953–61); winner of Nobel Peace Prize, 1961; Sept. 18, 1961.

Hammer, Armand: 92; founder of Occidental Petroleum Corp. and renowned art collector; Dec. 10, 1990.

Hammerstein, Oscar: 65; lyricist, master of musicals; Aug. 23, 1960.

Hand, Learned: 89; distinguished jurist; often referred to as the tenth justice of the U.S. Supreme Court; served longest term, 52 years, as federal judge in District Court and Circuit Court of Appeals; Aug. 18, 1961.

Hansberry, Lorraine: 34; noted black playwright; Jan. 12, 1965.

Harriman, Averell: 94; adviser to four presidents; ex-governor of New York; July 26, 1986.

Harrington, Michael: 61; a leading U.S. socialist spokesman, author (*Poverty in America*); July 31, 1989.

Harrison, Rex: 82; British stage, movie actor best known as Professor Henry Higgins in *My Fair Lady;* June 1, 1990.

Hart, Moss: 57; writer, director for theater and films; Dec. 20, 1961.

Hawkins, Coleman: 64; jazz saxophonist; May 19, 1969.

Hawks, Howard: 81; American film director; Dec. 26, 1977.

Hayakawa, S.I.: 85; iconoclastic former U.S. Senator from California and president of San Francisco State University; semantics professor and author; known for his trademark tam-o-shanter; Feb. 27, 1992.

Hayes, George "Gabby": 83, comical sidekick of cowboy favorite Hopalong Cassidy, acted in scores of Westerns; Feb. 9, 1969.

Haynesworth, Clement F., Jr.: 77; U.S. judge, controversial Supreme Court nominee; Nov. 22, 1989.

Hays, Wayne L.: 77; ex-Ohio congressman best known for scandalous relationship with staff member; Feb. 10, 1989.

Hayward, Susan: 56; Hollywood actress; March 14, 1975.

Hayworth, Rita: 68; actress, known as "the Love Goddess"; May 15, 1987.

Heflin, Van: 60; film, stage star; July 23, 1971.

Heidegger, Martin: 86; German philosopher; May 26, 1976.

Heifetz, Jascha: 86; world-renowned violinist; Dec. 10, 1987.

Heinlein, Robert A.: 80; science fiction writer (*Stranger in a Strange Land*); May 8, 1988.

Heinz, John: 52, Republican congressman and senator from Pennsylvania (1976–91); died in a midair collision of private plane and helicopter which was flying near the plane to check for possible problem with landing gear; April 4, 1991.

Heisenberg, Werner Karl: 74; German physicist, 1932 Nobel Prize winner in physics, discovered the "uncertainty principle," introducing the element of chance into modern physics; Feb. 1, 1976.

Hellman, Lillian: 79; playwright (*The Children's Hour*); June 30, 1984.

Hemingway, Ernest: 61; most famous U.S. novelist and short-story writer of his generation; Nobel Prize for Literature, 1954; July 2, 1961.

Hendrix, Jimi: 27; American rock guitarist; Sept. 18, 1970.

Henie, Sonja: 57; Norwegian figure skater; Oct. 12, 1969.

Henreid, Paul: 84; actor and director best known for his role as the stoic resistance fighter in the 1942 classic movie *Casablanca;* March 29, 1992.

Henson, Jim: 53; puppeteer, creator of the Muppets; May 16, 1990.

Herman, Woody: 74; Big Band leader; Oct. 29, 1987.

Heywood, Eddie: 73; jazz pianist, composer, popular 1940s band leader; Jan. 2, 1989.

Hill, Benny: 67; internationally popular British comedian, dubbed "King Leer" by British tabloids; April 20, 1992.

Hilton, Conrad: 91; hotel magnate; Jan. 4, 1979.

Hirohito: 87; former Emperor of Japan; Jan. 7, 1989.

Hitchcock, Alfred: 80; director, television and movie suspense films; April 29, 1980.

Hoffa, Jimmy: 61; American labor leader; July 30, 1975.

Hofstadter, Richard: 54; historian; Oct. 24, 1970.

Holden, William: 62; movie actor; Nov. 16, 1981.

Holloway, Sterling: 87; movie and television actor best-known for his work as the unique raspy voices of Walt Disney's animated characters Winnie the Pooh, the snake, Kaa, in *The Jungle Book*, the Cheshire cat in *Alice in Wonderland*, and Messenger Stork in *Dumbo;* Nov. 22, 1992.

Holm, Hanya: 99; masterful, pioneering choreographer of modern dance and Broadway musicals; Nov. 3, 1992.

Holman, Carl: 69; civil-rights leader, president of National Urban Coalition; Aug. 9, 1988.

Hondo, Soichiro: 84; Japanese automaker; turned his motorcycle company (Honda) into an international automaking giant; Aug. 5, 1991.

Hoover, Herbert Clark: 90; 31st president of the United States, from 1928 to 1932; Oct. 20, 1964.

Hoover, J. Edgar: 77; directed Federal Bureau of Investigation for 48 years; May 2, 1972.

Hopper, Hedda: 75; queen of Hollywood gossip; Feb. 1, 1966.

Hornsby, Rogers: 66; one of baseball's greatest right-handed hitters; Jan. 5, 1963.

Horowitz, Vladimir: 85; the most celebrated pianist of the 20th century; Nov. 5, 1989.

Horton, Edward Everett: 83; comic character actor; Sept. 29, 1970.

Houseman, John: 86; movie, television actor, producer, director; Oct. 31, 1988.

Howard, Trevor: 71; British actor; Jan. 7, 1988.

Hubbard, L. Ron: 74; founder of Scientology; Jan. 27, 1986.

Hubbell, Carl: 85; New York Giants pitcher nicknamed "the Meal Ticket"; Nov. 21, 1988.

Hudson, Rock: 59; movie, television actor; Oct. 2, 1985.

Hughes, Howard: 70; billionaire recluse; April 5, 1976.

Humphrey, Hubert: 66; Democrat senator, vice president under LBJ; Jan. 13, 1978.

Huntley, Chet: 62; anchor for "NBC Nightly News"; March 20, 1974.

Hurok, Sol: 85; impresario; March 5, 1974.

Huston, John: 81; actor, movie director; Aug. 28, 1987.

Hutton, Barbara: 66; Woolworth heiress; May 11, 1979.

Huxley, Aldous: 69; British essayist, novelist (*Brave New World*); Nov. 22, 1963.

Huxley, Sir Julian: 87; British scientist, author, humanist; Feb. 24, 1975.

Inge, William: 60; Midwestern playwright; June 10, 1973.

Ireland, Jill: 54; British-born television, movie actress, wrote candidly of her bout with cancer; May 18, 1990.

Ireland, John: 78; stage, screen and television actor; appeared in more than 200 movies; March 21, 1992.

Irwin, James B.: 61; astronaut who walked on the moon in 1971; later founded interdenominational evangelical group; Aug. 8, 1991.

Jackson, Mahalia: 71; Gospel singer; Jan. 26, 1972.

Jackson, Shirley: 45; American writer (*The Lottery*); Aug. 8, 1965.

Jaffe, Sam: 93; movie, theater, television actor; March 24, 1984.

Jagger, Dean: 87; U.S. character actor; won Academy Award for supporting role in *Twelve O'Clock High;* Feb. 5, 1991.

Jarrell, Randall: 51; American poet; Oct. 15, 1965.

Jaspers, Karl: 86; German existentialist philosopher; Feb. 26, 1969.

Jepson-Young, Peter: 35; physician known to millions of Canadian television viewers as "Dr. Peter," whose numerous 3-minute "AIDS Diaries" helped fight stereotypes and misunderstanding associated with the deadly disease; Nov. 15, 1992.

Jiang Quing: 77; Chinese political leader during Cultural Revolution; widow of Mao Zedong; served life imprisonment as part of The Gang of Four; death reported to be suicide; May 14, 1991.

Joffrey, Robert: 57; founder, artistic director of Joffrey Ballet; March 25, 1988.

John Paul I, Pope [Albino Luciani]: 65; died after 34 days as pontiff; Sept. 30, 1978.

John XXIII, Pope [Angelo Giuseppe Roncalli]: 81; known for his ecumenism, he was one of the Roman Catholic Church's best-loved pontiffs in modern times; June 3, 1963.

Johnson, Lyndon B.: 64; 36th president of the United States; Jan. 22, 1973.

Jones, Brian: 26; guitarist with Rolling Stones; July 3, 1969.

Jones, James: 55; WWII novelist (*From Here to Eternity*); May 9, 1977.

Jones, Spike: 52; entertainer, band leader; May 1, 1964.

Joplin, Janis: 27; blues and rock star; Oct. 4, 1970.

Jorgensen, Christine: 62; man who underwent first sex-change operation, 1952; May 13, 1989.

Jung, Carl C.: 85; pioneer in modern analytic psychiatry; June 6, 1961.

Kaiser, Henry: 85; American industrialist; Aug. 24, 1967.

Karloff, Boris: 81; actor known for role as Frankenstein monster; Feb. 3, 1969.

Kasavubu, Joseph: 56; first president of the Republic of the Congo (Zaire); March 24, 1969.

Kaufman, George S.: 71; dramatist, critic for *New York Times;* June 2, 1961.

Kaufman, Judge Irving R.: 81; U.S. federal judge who became nationally known in 1951 for sentencing Ethel and Julius Rosenberg to death after their conviction for conspiring to pass information about the U.S. atomic bomb to the Soviets; Feb. 1, 1992.

Kaye, Danny: 74; comedian, entertainer, stage and movies; March 3, 1987.

Keaton, Buster: 70; silent-movie actor; Feb. 1, 1966.

Keller, Helen: 87; deaf, blind since 18 months of age, pioneer advocate for the handicapped; June 1, 1968.

Kelly, Jack: 65; actor who played cardshark Bart Maverick in the popular television series "Maverick" from 1957 to 1962; also a former mayor of Huntington Beach, Calif., where he served as a City Councilman for the past 10 years; Nov. 7, 1992.

Kendricks, Eddie: 52; former lead singer with the Temptations, one of the top male vocal groups of the 1960s; Oct. 5, 1992.

Kennedy, Arthur: 75; stage actor and character in more than 70 movies; Jan. 5, 1990.

Kennedy, John F.: 46; 35th president of the United States; Nov. 22, 1963.

Kennedy, Joseph P.: 81; patriarch of political dynasty, former ambassador to Great Britain; Nov. 18, 1969.

Kennedy, Robert: 42; U.S. senator, ex-attorney general; June 6, 1968.

Kenyatta, Jomo [Kamau Johnstone]: 86; Kenyan nationalist leader; Aug. 22, 1978.

Kerouac, Jack: 46; hero of Beat Generation, writer (*On the Road*); Oct. 21, 1969.

Khomeini, Ayatollah Ruhollah: 89; long-exiled cleric, spiritual leader of Iran; June 6, 1989.

Khrushchev, Nikita S.: 77; flamboyant premier of Soviet Union 1953–64; Sept. 11, 1971.

Kilpatrick, William: 93; philosopher, father of progressive education; Feb. 13, 1965.

King, Albert: 69; legendary blues guitarist who influenced such modern rock musicians as Eric Clapton; Dec. 21, 1992.

King, Rev. Dr. Martin Luther, Jr.: 39; civil-rights leader; April 4, 1968.

Kinison, Sam: 38; controversial shock comedian; April 11, 1992.

Kinski, Klaus: 65, Polish-born film actor; Nov. 23, 1991.

Kirsten, Dorothy: 82; Soprano prima donna best known for roles in lyric operas for more than 30 years with New York's Metropolitan Opera; after 1983, active supporter of Alzheimer's disease research; Nov. 18, 1992.

Klemperer, Otto: 88; German conductor; July 6, 1973.

Kline, Franz: 51; American Abstract Expressionist painter; May 13, 1962.

Knopf, Alfred A.: 91; publisher; Aug. 11, 1984.

Kokoschka, Oscar: 93; Austrian painter, printmaker; Feb. 22, 1980.

Kopechne, Mary Jo: 28; drowned when car driven by Sen. Edward M. Kennedy plunged off bridge; July 30, 1969.

Kostelanetz, André: 78; popular American composer; Jan. 14, 1980.

Kosygin, Aleksei: 75; Soviet premier 1964–80; Dec. 18, 1980.

Kroc, Ray A.: 81; founder of McDonald's fast foods and owner, San Diego Padres baseball team; Jan. 14, 1984.

L'Amour, Louis: 80; prolific author of Western novels (*Hondo*); June 10, 1988.

Land, Edwin H.: 81; U.S. scientist, inventor of Polaroid Land camera; March 1, 1991.

Landon, Alf: 100; 1936 GOP presidential nominee; Oct. 12, 1987.

Landon, Michael: 54; U.S. actor best known for work in "Bonanza," "Little House on the Prairie" and "Highway to Heaven" television series; July 1, 1991.

Lang, Fritz: 85; German film director; Aug. 2, 1976.

Lange, Dorothea: 70; American documentary photographer; Oct. 11, 1965.

Lanson, Snooky: 76; popular singer, regular on "Your Hit Parade" in the 1950s; July 2, 1990.

Laughton, Charles: 63; character actor; Dec. 15, 1962.

Laurel, Stan: 74; comedian of the Laurel and Hardy team; Feb. 23, 1965.

Le Corbusier [Charles-Edouard Jeanneret-Gris]: 77; Swiss architect; Aug. 27, 1965.

Le Duc Tho: 79; Vietnamese diplomat, negotiated Paris peace talks with U.S. that led to U.S. troop withdrawal; Oct. 13, 1990.

Lean, David: 83; British director (*Bridge on the River Kwai, Lawrence of Arabia*) whose films won 28 Academy Awards; April 16, 1991.

Lee, Gypsy Rose: 56; legendary burlesque queen; April 27, 1970.

Lefebvre, Archbishop Marcel: 85; French prelate who opposed Second Vatican Council reforms; excommunicated in 1988 for defying papal authority; March 26, 1991.

Leigh, Vivien: 53; actress, known for role as Scarlett O'Hara in *Gone With the Wind;* July 8, 1967.

LeMay, Gen. Curtis E.: 83; leading advocate of strategic air power; running mate with George Wallace in 1968 presidential campaign; Oct. 1, 1990.

Lemnitzer, General Lyman L.: 89; World War II hero, U.N. commander in Korea; head, Joint Chiefs of Staff; Nov. 12, 1988.

Lennon, John: 40; British rock star, songwriter with the Beatles; Dec. 8, 1980.

Leopold, Nathan: 66; 1924 thrill killer; Aug. 29, 1971.

Lerner, Max: 89; liberal columnist, author, passionate supporter of education and the rights of Jews throughout the world; June 5, 1992.

Levine, Joseph E.: 81; film producer; July 31, 1987.

Lewis, C.S.: 64; Christian scholar, writer; Nov. 22, 1963.

Lewis, Joe E.: 69; nightclub comedian; June 4, 1971.

Lewis, Robert Q.: 71; U.S. radio disc jockey who became a frequent host on early television game, quiz and variety shows; Dec. 11, 1991.

Liberace [Wladziu Valentino]: 57; bejeweled, flamboyant pianist; Feb. 4, 1987.

Lie, Trygve: 72; first Secretary General of UN; Dec. 30, 1968.

Lindbergh, Charles A.: 72; aviator, first nonstop solo flight across Atlantic; Aug. 26, 1974.

Lindner, Richard: 76; American artist; April 16, 1978.

Lippmann, Walter: 85; political commentator; Dec. 14, 1974.

Liston, Charles "Sonny": 38; former world heavyweight boxing champ; Jan. 5, 1971.

Little, Cleavon: 53; stage and screen actor best known for his role as a black sheriff hired to save a redneck town in the 1974 movie comedy *Blazing Saddles;* won the 1970 Tony Award for best actor in the musical *Purlie;* Oct. 22, 1992.

Lloyd, Harold: 77; bespectacled comedy star of silent films; March 8, 1971.

Lodge, Henry Cabot: 82; diplomat; Feb. 26, 1985.

Loewe, Frederick: 86; composer, wrote such scores as *My Fair Lady;* Feb. 14, 1988.

Logan, Joshua L.: 79; director of Broadway hits such as *South Pacific* and *Mister Roberts;* July 12, 1988.

Lombardi, Vince: 57; legendary football coach of Green Bay Packers; Sept. 3, 1970.

Lombardo, Guy: 75; American bandleader; Nov. 5, 1977.

Lon Nol: 72; ex-leader of Cambodia; Nov. 17, 1985.

Lopat, Eddie: 73; left-handed pitching star for the New York Yankees; figured in five World Series titles from 1949 to 1953; June 15, 1992.

Lorre, Peter: 59; Hollywood actor; March 23, 1964.

Louis, Joe: 67; longest reigning heavyweight champion boxer (11 years, 8 months); April 12, 1981.

Lowenstein, Allard: 51; former Congressman, civil rights, antiwar leader known for 1968 "Dump Johnson" movement; March 14, 1980.

Luce, Clare Boothe: 84; playwright, editor, diplomat, politician; Oct. 9, 1987.

Luce, Henry: 68; magazine magnate, founded *Time, Fortune, Sports Illustrated;* Feb. 28, 1967.

Luciano, Salvatore "Lucky": 64; ruled U.S. Mafia; Jan. 26, 1962.

Lumumba, Patrice: 35; deposed first prime minister of the Congo; Feb. 12, 1961.

Lund, John: 81; actor, leading man in numerous films of the 1940s and '50s; May 10, 1992.

MacArthur, Douglas: 84; Army general who led Allied victory over Japan in World War II; April 5, 1964.

MacDonald, John D.: 70; prolific mystery, short-story writer, creator of Travis McGee series; Dec. 28, 1986.

Macmillan, Harold: 92; British ex-prime minister; Dec. 29, 1986.

MacMurray, Fred: 83; U.S. actor in films (*Double Indemnity*) and television ("My Three Sons"); Nov. 5, 1991.

Maddow, Ben: 83; prolific screenwriter, novelist and photography critic best known for his collaboration with John Huston on the screenplay for the 1950 movie *The Asphalt Jungle;* Oct. 9, 1992.

Malamud, Bernard: 71; short-story writer, novelist (*The Natural*); March 18, 1986.

Malcolm X [Malcolm Little]: 39; Black Muslim leader; Feb. 21, 1965.

Malraux, André: 75; writer, politician, war hero; Nov. 23, 1976.

Mangiapane, Sherwood: 79; bass player long known by aficionados of New Orleans jazz; Jan. 23, 1992.

Mansfield, Jayne: 34; actress, pin-up queen; June 29, 1967.

Mantovani, Anunzio Paolo: 74; conductor of popular orchestras; March 29, 1980.

Mao Zedong: 82; Communist Chinese leader; Sept. 9, 1976.

Maravich, Pete: 40; leading college basketball scorer; Jan. 5, 1988.

March, Frederic: 77; American actor; April 14, 1975.

Marciano, Rocky: 45; boxer, only heavyweight champ to retire undefeated; Aug. 31, 1969.

Marcos, Ferdinand: 72; former president of Philippines, exiled since 1986 in Honolulu; Sept. 29, 1989.

Marcuse, Herbert: 81; Marxist philosopher; July 29, 1979.

Marley, Bob: 36; most influential star of Jamaican reggae music; May 11, 1981.

Martin, Billy: 61; baseball player, fiery manager of N.Y. Yankees five times; Dec. 25, 1989.

Martin, Kiel: 39; television actor, a star of "Hill Street Blues"; Dec. 31, 1990.

Martin, Mary: 76; long-reigning Broadway musical star, best known for her roles in *South Pacific* and *Peter Pan;* Nov. 3, 1990.

Martinez Marquez, Guillermo: 91; one of the most prominent Cuban-born journalists of the 20th century; Feb. 29, 1992.

Marvin, Lee: 63; television ("M Squad"), movie actor (*Cat Ballou, The Dirty Dozen*); Aug. 29, 1987.

Marx, Harpo: 70; the silent blond-wigged member of the Marx Brothers comedy team; Aug. 28, 1964.

Marx, Julius "Groucho": 77; movie television comedian; Aug. 19, 1977.

Maserati, Ettore: 96; founder of internationally famous Italian sports and race car company; Aug. 4, 1990.

Mason, James: 75; British actor, more than 100 movies; July 27, 1984.

Maugham, W. Somerset: 91; writer (*Of Human Bondage*); Dec. 16, 1965.

Maxwell, Robert: 68; British publishing tycoon whose $2 billion global publishing empire included the *Daily Mirror* of London and the *New York Daily News;* his nude body was found floating near his $21 million yacht off the coast of Tenerife, Canary Islands; initial autopsy results indicated he died of a heart attack; Nov. 5, 1991.

Mays, Carl: 79; N.Y. Yankees pitcher threw ball that killed Cleveland Indians batter Ray Chapman in 1920; April 4, 1971.

McCarthy, Mary: 77; columnist, critic, novelist (*The Group*); Oct. 25, 1989.

McClintock, Barbara: 90; pioneering geneticist, winner of the 1983 Nobel Prize for Physiology/Medicine for her discovery of mobile genetic elements, "jumping genes"; Sept. 2, 1992.

McCrea, Joel: 84; movie actor in more than 90 films, mostly Westerns; Oct. 20, 1990.

McCullers, Carson: 50; novelist (*The Heart Is a Lonely Hunter*); Sept. 29, 1967.

McGowan, William G.: 64; telecommunications entrepreneur who led the drive to break up American Telephone & Telegraph Company's monopoly over U.S. telephone service; a founder of MCI Communications Corp.; June 8, 1992.

Mead, Margaret: 76; anthropologist, author (*Coming of Age in Samoa*); Nov. 15, 1978.

Meany, George: 85; president of AFL-CIO for nearly 25 years; Jan. 10, 1980.

Meir, Golda: 80; Israel's first woman prime minister; Dec. 8, 1978.

Menninger, Karl: 96; leading psychiatrist; July 18, 1990.

Mercer, Johnny: 66; songwriter ("That Old Black Magic"); June 25, 1976.

Mercury, Freddie: 45; British lead singer of rock group Queen; died of AIDS one day after announcing he had the disease; Nov. 24, 1991.

Merman, Ethel: 75; musical comedy star for four decades; Feb. 15, 1984.

Merrill, Gary: 74; movie and Broadway actor; March 5, 1990.

Messiaen, Olivier: 83; prolific, distinctive and influential French composer whose work reflected a mystical faith and love of nature; best known for "Quartet for the End of Time"; April 27, 1992.

Mies van der Rohe, Ludwig: 83; one of the great figures of 20th-century architecture; Aug. 17, 1969.

Mikoyan, Anastase: 82; Soviet statesman; Oct. 21, 1978.

Milestone, Lewis: 84; film director; Sept. 25, 1980.

Miller, Henry: 87; novelist (*Tropic of Cancer*); Jan. 7, 1980.

Miller, Roger: 56; quirky Country and Western singer and prolific songwriter, most popular in the 1960s and 1970s; career rebounded in the mid-1980s when his musical score for the hit Broadway musical *Big River* won a Tony Award; Oct. 25, 1992.

Mills, Herbert: 77; member of Mills Brothers singing group, made 2,246 records since 1930s; April 14, 1989.

Mills, Wilbur D.: 82; Democrat and long-time chairman of the House Ways and Means Committee who wrote much of the federal tax code and helped shape Social Security; May 2, 1992.

Mindszenty, Jozsef Cardinal: 83; exiled primate of Hungary; May 6, 1975.

Mingus, Charles: 56; American innovator in jazz; Jan. 5, 1979.

Miró, Joan: 90; Spanish Surrealist painter; Dec. 25, 1983.

Mitchell, John N.: 75; convicted for Watergate role while President Nixon's Attorney General; Nov. 9, 1988.

Molotov, Vyacheslav: 95; Soviet ex-Foreign Minister; Nov. 8, 1986.

Monk, Thelonius: 64; jazz pianist, composer; Feb. 17, 1982.

Monroe, Marilyn: 36; American film star; Aug. 5, 1962.

Montand, Yves: 70; Italian-born, French-reared actor and singer; movies included *Let's Make Love, Grand Prix* and *On a Clear Day You Can See Forever*; Nov. 9, 1991.

Montgomery, Field Marshal Bernard Law: 88; British World War II hero; March 24, 1976.

Moravia, Alberto: 82; prolific and popular Italian novelist (*Two Women*); Sept. 26, 1990.

Morley, Robert: 84; British playwright and character actor whose career spanned more than five decades in movies and television; June 3, 1992.

Morrison, Jim: 27; lead singer, The Doors; July 3, 1971.

Moses, Grandma [Anna Mary Robertson]: 101, folk artist; Dec. 13, 1961.

Motherwell, Robert: 76; U.S. artist whose work helped define Abstract Expressionism; July 16, 1991.

Mountbatten, Lord Louis: 79; World War II sea battle strategist; last British Viceroy in India; Aug. 27, 1979.

Muggeridge, Malcolm: 87; prolific British journalist and social critic; Nov. 14, 1990.

Muhammad, Elijah: 79; American spiritual leader of Black Muslims; Feb. 25, 1975.

Mumford, Lewis: 94; social critic, philosopher and author (*The City in History*); Jan. 26, 1990.

Munson, Thurman: 32; New York Yankees catcher; Aug. 2, 1979.

Murphy, Audie: 46; movie actor, most decorated soldier of World War II; May 28, 1971.

Murphy, George L.: 89; Hollywood singer and dancer who appeared in 55 movies from the 1930s to the 1950s and then served one term (1964–70) as a Republican U.S. senator from California; May 3, 1992.

Murray, Arthur: 95; U.S. teacher of ballroom dancing who built an empire of franchised dance studios and mail-order instruction, based in part on the popularity of his television program in the 1950s; March 3, 1991.

Murrow, Edward R.: 56; CBS newsman; April 23, 1965.

Myrdal, Gunnar: 89; Swedish economist, sociologist, student of U.S. race relations; May 17, 1987.

Nabokov, Vladimir: 78; novelist (*Lolita*); July 2, 1977.

Nagurski, Bronislaw "Bronko": 81; legendary Pro Football Hall of Fame running back with Chicago Bears; Jan. 7, 1990.

Nance, Jim: 49; running back for the American Football League's old Boston Patriots; set rushing record of 1,458 yards in 1966; June 15, 1992.

Nash, Ogden: 68; poet noted for humorous light verse; May 19, 1971.

Nasser, Gamal Abdel: 52; Egyptian leader; Sept. 28, 1970.

Negri, Pola: 87; exotic silent-film star; Aug. 1, 1987.

Nehru, Jawaharlal: 74; Prime Minister of India; May 28, 1964.

Nelson, Ricky: 45; singer, a star of 1950s TV show, "The Adventures of Ozzie and Harriet"; Dec. 31, 1985.

Nemerov, Howard: 71; U.S. poet laureate, 1988–90; winner of Pulitzer Prize, National Book Award; July 5, 1991.

Nesbit, Evelyn: 83; American actress, figured in infamous 1906 scandal as mistress of millionaire architect Stanford White, who was shot by her jealous husband Harry K. Thaw; Jan. 18, 1967.

Nevins, Allan: 80; historian, biographer; March 5, 1971.

Newman, Alfred: 68; Hollywood composer, conductor, won eight Academy Awards; Feb. 18, 1970.

Newton, Huey: 47; cofounder of the 1960s Black Panther Party; Aug. 22, 1989.

Niebuhr, Reinhold: 78; Protestant theologian; June 1, 1971.

Nielsen, A.C.: 83; inventor of the Nielsen ratings; June 3, 1980.

Nimitz, Adm. Chester: 80; commander Pacific Fleet in WWII; Feb. 20, 1966.

Nin, Anaïs: 73; writer (*Diary of Anaïs Nin*); Jan. 14, 1977.

Niven, David: 73; British actor; July 29, 1983.

Nkrumah, Kwame: 62; first president of Ghana; March 27, 1972.

Noyce, Robert N.: 62; scientist and inventor whose microchip revolutionized computers; June 3, 1990.

Nurmi, Paavo: 76; Finnish long-distance runner; Oct. 2, 1973.

O'Brien, Lawrence: 73; former Democratic National Committee chairman, Postmaster General; commissioner, National Basketball Association; Sept. 28, 1990.

O'Connor, Flannery: 39; Southern novelist (*Wise Blood*); Aug. 3, 1964.

O'Connor, Msgr. William L.: 84; founder of California's best-known home for troubled youths, the Hanna Boys center, which came to be known as the "Boy's Town of the West"; Dec. 30, 1991.

O'Faoláin, Sean: 91; Irish novelist, biographer, playwright, short-story writer; April 20, 1991.

O'Hara, Frank: 40; American poet, art critic; July 25, 1966.

O'Hara, John: 65; novelist (*Appointment in Samarra*); April 11, 1970.

O'Keeffe, Georgia: 98; influential artist, American Southwest; March 6, 1986.

Oberon, Merle: 68; movie actress; Oct. 23, 1979.

Odets, Clifford: 57; dramatist of the Depression; Aug. 15, 1963.

Olav V: 87; king of Norway (1957–91); Jan. 17, 1991.

Olivier, Sir Laurence: 82; Shakespearean actor; July 11, 1989.

Onassis, Aristotle: 69; Greek shipping magnate, married Jacqueline Kennedy; March 15, 1975.

Oppenheimer, Robert: 62; American physicist, pioneer in atom bomb research; Feb. 18, 1967.

Orbison, Roy: 52; rock 'n' roll singer; Dec. 6, 1988.

Oswald, Lee Harvey: 24; accused assassin of President Kennedy; Nov. 24, 1963.

Owens, Jesse: 66; U.S. track star, four gold medals, 1936 Olympics; March 31, 1980.

Page, Geraldine: 63; theater, movie actress; June 13, 1987.

Pahlevi, Mohammed Reza: 60; Shah of Iran; July 27, 1980.

Paige, Leroy "Satchel": 75; first black baseball pitcher in American League; June 8, 1982.

Paley, William S.: 89; founder of CBS; Oct. 26, 1990.

Palme, Olaf: 59; Prime Minister of Sweden; Feb. 28, 1986.

Papandreou, George: 80; three-time premier of Greece, Nov. 1, 1968.

Papp, Joseph: 70; U.S. theater producer who brought 17 productions to Broadway, including *A Chorus Line, The Pirates of Penzance, Drood, That Champi-*onship Season and *Two Gentlemen of Verona;* brought Shakespearean plays to New York's Central Park; Oct. 31, 1991.

Parker, Dorothy: 74; humorist and short-story writer; June 7, 1967.

Parks, Bert: 77; song-and-dance man and TV game-show host best known as emcee of the annual Miss America Pageant for 25 years, from 1956 to 1980, and then in a return appearance in 1990; Feb. 2, 1992.

Parnis, Mollie: 87; fashion designer for the wealthy and famous; July 18, 1992.

Parrish, Maxfield: 95; American painter; March 30, 1966.

Pasternak, Boris: 70; Russian poet and novelist; Nobel Prize for Literature, 1958; (*Doctor Zhivago*); May 29, 1960.

Pasternak, Joe: 89; Hungarian-born producer of Hollywood films; Sept. 13, 1991.

Paul VI, Pope [Giovanni Battista Montini]: 80; pontiff of the Roman Catholic Church; Aug. 6, 1978.

Paul, Alice: 92; militant in fight for women's suffrage; July 9, 1977.

Payne, John: 77; movie actor, leading man in 1940s, '50s movies such as *Miracle on 34th Street;* Dec. 6, 1989.

Peckinpah, Sam: 58; film director; Dec. 28, 1984.

Penney, J.C.: 95; founder of department store chain; Feb. 12, 1971.

Pepper, Claude: 88; Florida congressman, champion of the elderly; May 30, 1989.

Percy, Walker: 74; novelist (*The Moviegoer*); May 10, 1990.

Perelman, Sidney Joseph: 75; humorist, essayist, screenwriter; Oct. 17, 1979.

Perkins, Anthony: 60; stage and screen actor best known for his film portrayal of psychopath Norman Bates in Alfred Hitchcock's 1960 classic thriller *Psycho* and its three less successful sequels; Sept. 12, 1992.

Perón, Juan Sosa: 78; president of Argentina; July 1, 1974.

Philby, H.A.R. "Kim": 76; notorious British double agent who fled to Soviet Union; May 14, 1988.

Piaf, Edith: 47; Parisian street singer; Oct. 11, 1963.

Piaget, Jean: 84; noted child psychologist; Sept. 16, 1980.

Picasso, Pablo: 92; century's greatest modern artist, exponent of Cubism; April 8, 1973.

Pickford, Mary: 96; silent-film actress, "America's Sweetheart"; May 29, 1979.

Picon, Molly: 94; international star of Yiddish theater and Broadway whose career spanned nearly eight decades; April 6, 1992.

Plath, Sylvia: 30; US poet; her 1962 novel *The Bell Jar* won wide acclaim, but is best known for her poetry, published after her suicide; *Ariel* (1965); *The Collected Poems* (1981), which won the 1982 Pulitzer Prize for Poetry; Feb. 11, 1963.

Podgorny, Nikolai: 79; Soviet statesman; Jan. 11, 1983.

Pollock, Charles: 86; Abstract painter, educator, brother of Jackson; May 8, 1988.

Pollock, Lee Krasner: 75; Abstract Expressionist painter; June 19, 1984.

Pompidou, Georges: 62; president of France; April 2, 1974.

Pons, Lily: 71; French coloratura soprano; Feb. 13, 1976.

Porter, Cole: 71; American composer, lyricist; Oct. 15, 1964.

Porter, Eliot: 88; influential landscape photographer; Nov. 2, 1990.

Porter, Katherine Anne: 90; short-story writer, novelist (*Ship of Fools*); Sept. 18, 1980.

Porter, Sylvia: 77; U.S. financial writer, syndicated columnist; June 5, 1991.

Post, Emily: 86; grande dame of etiquette; Sept. 25, 1960.

Poulenc, Francis: 64; French composer; Jan. 30, 1963.

Pound, Ezra: 87; poet; Nov. 1, 1972.

Pousette-Dart, Richard: 76; acclaimed artist whose work in the late 1940s helped dramatize the emerging importance of American Abstract Expressionist painters; Oct. 25, 1992.

Powell, Adam Clayton: 63; controversial Harlem congressman; March 4, 1972.

Preminger, Otto: 80; American film producer, director; April 23, 1986.

Presley, Elvis: 42; "The King" of American rock 'n' rollers; Aug. 16, 1977.

Presser, Jackie: 61; president of Teamsters, nation's largest union; July 9, 1988.

Priestley, J.B.: 89; prolific British novelist, essayist, playwright; Aug. 15, 1984.

Princess Grace of Monaco [Grace Kelly]: 52; former movie actress; Sept. 10, 1982.

Pucci, Emilio: 78; leading Italian fashion designer known for colorful and bold designs and "Palazzo pajama" pants; Nov. 29, 1992.

Pyne, Joe: 44; acerbic TV talk-show host; May 23, 1970.

Quayle, Sir Anthony: 76; leading British actor, producer; Oct. 20, 1989.

Radner, Gilda: 42; comedian, member of "Saturday Night Live" cast of 1970s; May 20, 1989.

Rains, Claude: 77; British actor; May 30, 1967.

Rand, Ayn: 76; novelist (*The Fountainhead*); March 6, 1982.

Rankin, Jeannette: 92; pacifist, first woman in Congress; May 18, 1973.

Ransom, John Crowe: 86; poet, critic; July 3, 1974.

Rathbone, Basil: 75; British actor best known for Sherlock Holmes radio, movie portrayals; July 21, 1967.

Ray, Aldo: 64; U.S. film actor (*Battle Cry, The Naked and the Dead*); March 27, 1991.

Ray, Johnnie: 63; popular 1950s singer ("Cry"); Feb. 24, 1990.

Ray, Man: 86; American photographer, Dadaist painter; Nov. 18, 1976.

Ray, Satyajit: 70; prolific, versatile and critically acclaimed Indian film maker; April 23, 1992.

Rayburn, Sam: 79; Speaker of the House for 17 years; Nov. 16, 1961.

Reasoner, Harry: 68, U.S. television journalist, news anchor well known for work on "60 Minutes"; Aug. 6, 1991.

Redding, Otis: 26; soul singer; Dec. 10, 1967.

Reed, Carol: 44; pioneer TV "weather girl"; June 4, 1970.

Reed, Robert: 59; popular television actor best known for his portrayal of Mike Brady, patriarch of "The Brady Bunch"; May 12, 1992.

Remarque, Erich Maria: 72; German-born novelist (*All Quiet on the Western Front*); Sept. 25, 1970.

Remick, Lee: 55; U.S. stage, television, film actress (*Days of Wine and Roses*); July 2, 1991.

Rennie, Michael: 62; movie, television star; June 10, 1971.

Renoir, Jean: 84; French film director; Feb. 13, 1979.

Reuther, Walter P.: 62; president, United Auto Workers; May 9, 1970.

Rhee, Syngman: 90; first president of South Korea; July 19, 1965.

Richardson, Sir Ralph: 80; British actor; Oct. 10, 1983.

Richardson, Tony: 63; British director of Oscar-winning film *Tom Jones* and others, including *The Loneliness of the Long-Distance Runner, Look Back in Anger, The Entertainer* and *A Taste of Honey;* Nov. 14, 1991.

Richter, Charles: 85; American seismologist; Sept. 30, 1985.

Rickenbacker, Capt. Eddie: 82; American WWI flying ace; July 24, 1973.

Rickover, Adm. Hyman: 86; father of nuclear Navy; July 8, 1986.

Rivers, Rep. L. Mendel: 65; D-S.C., head of House Armed Services Committee; Dec. 28, 1971.

Rizzo, Frank: 70; law-and-order Philadelphia police commissioner (1967–71) and mayor (1971–79) who drew praise and criticism for his hardline approach; July 16, 1991.

Rizzo, Jilly: 75; longtime friend and confidante of singer Frank Sinatra; May 6, 1992.

Roach, Hal: 100; writer, director and producer who

pioneered in American film comedy as a creative force behind Laurel and Hardy, Our Gang, Will Rogers, Harold Lloyd, *Topper*, "The Amos and Andy Show," "Public Defender," "My Little Margie" and "The Life of Riley"; Nov. 2, 1992.

Robeson, Paul: 77; singer, actor; Jan. 23, 1976.

Robinson, Edward G.: 79; American actor; Jan. 26, 1973.

Robinson, Jackie: 53; baseball great, first black player in majors; Oct. 24, 1972.

Robinson, Sugar Ray: 67; 25-year career as prizefighter, won middleweight title five times; April 12, 1989.

Rockefeller, John D., Jr.: 86; philanthropist, one of the world's richest men; May 11, 1960.

Rockefeller, Nelson A.: 70; former vice president, four times governor of New York; Jan. 26, 1979.

Rockwell, Norman: 84; illustrator, known for his *Saturday Evening Post* magazine covers; Nov. 8, 1978.

Roddenberry, Gene: 70; TV producer and writer who created "Star Trek" series; Oct. 24, 1991.

Roethke, Theodore: 55; American poet; Aug. 1, 1963.

Roosevelt, Eleanor: 77; ex-first lady, reformer, U.N. envoy; Nov. 7, 1962.

Rose, David: 80; popular composer for movies and television; Aug. 23, 1990.

Rossellini, Roberto: 71; Italian film director; June 3, 1977.

Rothko, Mark: 66; pioneer of Abstract Expressionist painting; Feb. 25, 1970.

Rubinstein, Arthur: 95; one of the century's greatest pianists; Dec. 20, 1982.

Ruby, Jack: 56; Dallas nightclub owner who shot and killed Lee Harvey Oswald; Jan. 3, 1967.

Rudd, Hughes: 71; veteran journalist and commentator for CBS and ABC television; former co-anchor of CBS "Morning News" program, 1973–77; Oct. 13, 1992.

Rupp, Adolph: 76; American basketball coach; Dec. 10, 1977.

Russell, Bertrand: 97; philosopher, mathematician, essayist; Nobel Prize for Literature, 1950; (*Mysticism and Logic*); Feb. 2, 1970.

Russell, Bill: 87; jazz historian and composer known for recording of early live jazz performances; Aug. 9, 1992.

Rustin, Bayard: 74; pacifist, civil-rights activist; Aug. 24, 1987.

Ryan, Cornelius: 53; Irish-American writer, WWII chronicles (*The Longest Day, A Bridge Too Far*); Nov. 24, 1974.

Sakharov, Andrei: 68; Soviet nuclear physicist, leading proponent of perestroika; Dec. 14, 1989.

Salazar, Antonio de Oliveira: 81; dictator of Portugal for 36 years; July 27, 1970.

Salerno, Anthony "Fat Tony": 80; former boss of New York's powerful Genovese crime family; rated by *Fortune* magazine in 1986 as the wealthiest, most powerful and influential man in the Mafia; July 27, 1992.

Salk, Lee: 65; popular child psychologist who taught common-sense parenting; pioneered research on infant heartbeat sounds, sudden infant death syndrome and the impact of early experience on later behavior; May 2, 1992.

Salmi, Albert: 62; theater, movie and television actor; April 23, 1990.

Sandburg, Carl: 89; poet, biographer (*Abraham Lincoln, The War Years*); July 22, 1967.

Sanger, Margaret: 82; early champion of birth control; Sept. 6, 1966.

Saroyan, William: 72; playwright, novelist (*The Human Comedy*); May 5, 1981.

Sartre, Jean-Paul: 74; French philosopher; Nobel Prize for Literature, 1964; April 15, 1980.

Sato, Eisaku: 74; ex-premier of Japan; June 2, 1975.

Saud, King: 67; king of Saudi Arabia; Feb. 23, 1969.

Schneider, Romy: 43; actress; May 29, 1982.

Schumacher, E.F.: 62; American comic actor; Sept. 8, 1977.

Schuman, William: 81; American composer, two-time winner of the Pulitzer Prize, founding president of New York's Lincoln Center and president of the Juilliard School; Feb. 15, 1992.

Schweitzer, Albert: 90; humanitarian, musician; Sept. 4, 1965.

Scopes, John T.: 70; his teaching of evolution led to 1925 "Monkey Trial" in Dayton, Tenn.; Oct. 21, 1970.

Seberg, Jean: 40; actress; Sept. 8, 1979.

Segovia, Andrés: 94; classical guitarist; June 3, 1987.

Selassie, Haile: 83; last emperor in 3,000-year-old Ethiopian monarchy; Aug. 27, 1975.

Sellers, Peter: 54; comedian, famed as Inspector Clouseau in *Pink Panther* movies; July 23, 1980.

Selznick, David O.: 63; American film producer (*Gone With the Wind*); June 22, 1965.

Sennett, Mack: 80; film pioneer, popularized slapstick comedy in the United States, directed Charlie Chaplin; Nov. 5, 1960.

Serkin, Rudolph: 88; Austrian-born concert pianist; May 8, 1991.

Sevareid, Eric: 79; erudite and eloquent newscaster, a pioneer of incisive commentary on radio and television, primarily for CBS; July 9, 1992.

Sexton, Anne: 45; American poet; Oct. 4, 1974.

Shannon, Del: 50; popular 1950s songwriter, singer ("Runaway"); Feb. 9, 1990.

Shawn, William: 85; longtime editor of *The New Yorker* whose work and support nourished the careers of some of the country's best writers, among them E.B. White, James Baldwin, James Thurber and John Updike; Dec. 8, 1992.

Sheeler, Charles: 81; American painter, industrial landscapes; May 7, 1965.

Sheppard, Dr. Samuel H.: 46; osteopath freed in second trial for first wife's murder; April 6, 1970.

Shostakovich, Dimitri: 68; Soviet composer; Aug. 10, 1975.

Shuster, Joseph: 78; artist who, with writer Jerry Siegel, created the comic book hero, Superman, for DC Comics in 1938; Aug. 2, 1992.

Signoret, Simone: 64; French actress; Sept. 30, 1985.

Sikorsky, Igor: 83; aviation pioneer who developed first practical helicopter; Oct. 26, 1972.

Simenon, Georges: 86; most widely published author of century; Sept. 4, 1989.

Sims, Zoot: 59; American jazz saxophonist; March 23, 1985.

Sinclair, Upton: 90; American novelist (*The Jungle*); Nov. 25, 1968.

Singer, Isaac Bashevis: 87; Polish-born writer (U.S. resident) who fled Holocaust; evocative work expressed Jewish experience and culture; winner of Nobel Prize for Literature (1978); July 24, 1991.

Sirica, John J.: 88; federal judge who presided over the Watergate trials that led to the fall of Richard M. Nixon's presidency; Aug. 14, 1992.

Skinner, B.F.: 86; behavioral psychologist, author (*Walden Two*); Aug. 18, 1990.

Snelling, Richard A.: 64; Republican governor of Vermont (1977–85, 1991); Aug. 13, 1991.

Snow, C.P.: 75; British novelist, physicist, civil servant; July 1, 1980.

Snyder, Mitch: 46; social activist, advocate for the homeless; July 6, 1990.

Somoza, Anastasio Debayle: 55; deposed president of Nicaragua; Sept. 17, 1980.

Somoza, Luis Debayle: 44; ex-president, Nicaragua; April 13, 1967.

Sopwith, Sir Thomas: 101; British aircraft pioneer, designer of Sopwith Camel, shot down infamous Red Baron of Germany in WWI; Jan. 27, 1989.

Speck, Richard: 49; imprisoned mass murderer who stabbed and strangled eight student nurses in their Chicago apartment in 1966; of heart attack; Dec. 5, 1991.

Speer, Albert: 76; official architect of Nazi Germany's Third Reich; Sept. 1, 1981.

Spencer-Churchill, Baroness Clementine (of Chartwell): 92; widow of Sir Winston Churchill; Dec. 12, 1977.

Spiegel, Sam: 82; film producer; Dec. 31, 1985.

St. Jacques, Raymond: 60; movie and television actor; Aug. 27, 1990.

Stanwyck, Barbara: 82; movie, television star typically cast as strong-willed woman; Jan. 20, 1990.

Steinbeck, John: 66; novelist; Nobel Prize for Literature, 1962; (*The Grapes of Wrath*); Dec. 20, 1968.

Stengel, Casey: 85; garrulous baseball wizard, New York Yankees, Mets; Sept. 29, 1975.

Steptoe, Dr. Patrick: 74; pioneer in test-tube baby technology; March 12, 1988.

Stevens, Inger: 35; actress; television's "Farmer's Daughter"; April 30, 1970.

Stevenson, Adlai E. II: 65; presidential candidate, ambassador to United Nations; July 14, 1965.

Still, Clyfford: 75; Abstract Expressionist painter; June 24, 1980.

Stirling, Sir James Frazer: 66; leading modernist architect renown for his designs of school and museum buildings; June 25, 1992.

Stokowski, Leopold: 95; conductor; Sept. 13, 1977.

Stone, I.F.: 81; journalist famed as muckraker; June 18, 1989.

Stone, Irving: 86; biographical novelist (*Lust for Life*); Aug. 26, 1989.

Stotz, Carl: 82; founded Little League baseball in 1939 in Williamsport, Pa., but severed ties with his creation in 1955 over commercialization; June 4, 1992.

Stout, Rex: 88; American detective novelist, created Nero Wolfe; Oct. 27, 1975.

Stravinsky, Igor: 88; influential composer noted for avant-garde orchestral and ballet works; April 6, 1971.

Sukarno, Ahmed: 69; Indonesian independence leader in 1949, deposed as president in 1967; June 21, 1970.

Sullivan, Ed: 72; CBS variety-show host; Oct. 13, 1974.

Sulzberger, Arthur Hays: 77; *New York Times* owner; Dec. 11, 1968.

Sulzberger, Iphigene Ochs: 97; directed the *New York Times* for more than 70 years; Feb. 26, 1990.

Summerson, Sir John: 87; Britain's preeminent architectural historian; Nov. 10, 1992.

Sutherland, Graham: 76; British portrait painter, Feb. 17, 1980.

Swanson, Gloria: 84; movie actress; April 4, 1983.

Syms, Sylvia: 74; nightclub jazz singer long hailed by her colleagues as one of the best; May 10, 1992.

Tamayo, Rufino: 91; Mexican artist whose paintings evoke folk heritage; June 24, 1991.

Tayback, Vic: 60; actor best known as Mel on television's "Alice"; May 25, 1990.

Taylor, Robert: 57; movie actor; June 8, 1969.

Taylor, William: 53; tough-minded head of the Federal Deposit Insurance Corporation who oversaw the 1990–91 taxpayer-financed cleanup of the Savings and Loan industry; Aug. 20, 1992.

Terry-Thomas: 78; British comedian known for gap-toothed smile; Jan. 8, 1990.

Thant, U: 65; Burmese educator, third Secretary General of United Nations; Jan. 25, 1974.

Thomas, Danny: 79; comedian, star of TV show "Make Room for Daddy," founder of and prominent fundraiser for St. Jude Children's Research Hospital; Feb. 6, 1991.

Thomas, Ryan: 10; AIDS victim, infected by blood transfusion at birth, who won federal court battle in 1986 to allow him to remain in kindergarten; Nov. 28, 1991.

Thompson, Dorothy: 66; American foreign correspondent, columnist; Jan. 31, 1961.

Thornton, Willie Mae "Big Mama": 57; blues singer; July 25, 1984.

Thurber, James: 66; American humorist; Nov. 2, 1961.

Tierney, Gene: 70; U.S. actress (*Laura, Leave Her to Heaven, Belle Starr, Heaven Can Wait, A Bell for Adano, The Ghost and Mrs. Muir*); Nov. 6, 1991.

Tito, Josip Broz: 87; Yugoslavia's independent-minded President-for-Life; May 8, 1980.

Tolkien, J.R.R.: 81; British writer (*The Lord of the Rings*); Sept. 2, 1973.

Toomer, Jean: 72; Harlem writer (*Cane*); March 30, 1967.

Tower, John G.: 65; Republican Senator from Texas (1961–85); nomination as Secretary of Defense was rejected by Senate in 1990 after bitter hearing with political overtones; died in commuter plane crash; April 5, 1991.

Townsend, Francis Everett: 93; American physician, activist for Social Security; Sept. 1, 1960.

Toynbee, Arnold: 86; historian, Western civilization; Oct. 22, 1975.

Tracy, Spencer: 67; movie actor, leading man in more than 70 films; June 10, 1967.

Trilling, Lionel: 70; American critic, educator, novelist; Nov. 6, 1975.

Truffaut, François: 52; director New Wave movies; Oct. 21, 1984.

Truman, Harry S.: 88; 33rd president of the United States; Dec. 26, 1972.

Truman, Bess: 97; former first lady of United States; Oct. 18, 1982.

Tse-tung, Mao: *See* Mao Zedong.

Tshombe, Moise: 49; Congo independence leader; June 29, 1969.

Tucker, Richard: 60; leading tenor with Metropolitan Opera for 30 years; Jan. 8, 1975.

Tucker, Sophie: 78; singer; Feb. 8, 1966.

Ulbricht, Walter: 80; former head of German Democratic Republic; Aug. 1, 1973.

Valachi, Joseph: 66; underworld figure, first used term "Cosa Nostra" in Senate testimony in 1963; April 3, 1971.

Van Cleef, Lee: 64; movie actor, usually a villain; Dec. 16, 1989.

Vanderbilt, Harold S.: 86; yachtsman, financier; July 4, 1970.

Vaughan, Sarah: 66; immensely popular jazz singer for nearly 50 years; April 3, 1990.

Vaughan, Stevie Ray: 35; musician, composer, blues guitarist; Aug. 27, 1990.

Ventura, Charlie: 75; premier jazz tenor saxophonist during the Big Band Era; Jan. 17, 1992.

Vicious, Sid: 21; punk rocker; Feb. 2, 1979.

Vincent, Gene: 36; rock star of 1950s; Oct. 12, 1971.

Visconti, Luchino: 69; Italian film director; March 17, 1976.

Von Braun, Wernher: 65; German rocket scientist; June 16, 1977.

Wagner, Robert F.: 80; mayor of New York (1954–65); Feb. 12, 1991.

Walker, Aaron "T-Bone": 64; American blues guitarist; March 16, 1975.

Walker, Nancy: 69; comedic actress best known for her role as the mother of Rhoda Morgenstern on television's "Mary Tyler Moore Show" and its spin-off, "Rhoda"; March 25, 1992.

Wallace, DeWitt: 91; founder of *The Reader's Digest*; March 30, 1981.

Wallace, Henry A.: 77; liberal politician, vice president under FDR; Nov. 18, 1965.

Wallace, Irving: 74; best-selling U.S. author (*The Chapman Report*); June 29, 1990.

Wallace, Lila: 94; philanthropist, cofounder of *The Reader's Digest*; May 8, 1984.

Walter, Bruno: 85; German-American conductor, founder of Salzburg Festival; Feb. 17, 1962.

Walton, Sam: 74; business pioneer whose focus on low prices and customer service built Wal-Mart into the nation's largest retail chain; April 5, 1992.

Wang, An: 70; Chinese-American inventor, founded Wang Laboratories, computer company; March 24, 1990.

Warhol, Andy: 56; pop artist; Feb. 23, 1987.

Warren, Earl: 83; ex-Chief Justice of the United States; July 9, 1974.

Warren, Robert Penn: 84; first U.S. poet laureate; Sept. 15, 1989.

Washington, Harold: 65; the first black mayor of Chicago (1983–87), and one of the nation's most visible symbols of urban black power; Nov. 25, 1987.

Waters, Ethel: 76; Broadway actress, singer; Sept. 1, 1977.

Waters, Muddy [McKinley Morganfield]: 68; American blues singer, guitarist; April 30, 1983.

Waugh, Evelyn: 62; British satirical novelist (*Brideshead Revisited*); April 10, 1966.

Wayne, John: 72; "The Duke," star of epic Western movies; June 11, 1979.

Weber, Max: 80; Russian-American painter; Oct. 4, 1961.

Weidman, Charles: 73; pioneer in American modern dance; July 15, 1975.

Weissmuller, Johnny: 79; swimming star, played Tarzan in movies; Jan. 20, 1984.

Welch, Robert: 85; founder of the John Birch Society; Jan. 7, 1985.

Welk, Lawrence: 89; irrepressible bandleader whose wholesome, middle-of the-road "champagne music" entertained national television audiences for 27 years; May 17, 1992.

Welles, Orson: 70; pioneering radio dramatist, movie actor, director *Citizen Kane;* Oct. 12, 1985.

Wells, Mary: 49; pop music star best known for early 1960s hits "My Guy," "You Beat Me to the Punch," and "Two Lovers"; July 26, 1992.

West, Dottie: 59; U.S. country singer; of injuries suffered in auto accident; Sept. 4, 1991.

West, Jessamyn: 81; short-story writer, novelist (*The Friendly Persuasion*); Feb. 23, 1984.

West, Mae: 87; American actress, sex symbol of 1930s movies (*She Done Him Wrong, I'm No Angel);* Nov. 22, 1980.

White, E.B.: 86; essayist, author of children's books (*Charlotte's Webb*); Oct. 1, 1985.

White, Ryan: 18; AIDS victim and advocate for understanding, compassionate treatment of AIDS victims; April 8, 1990.

White, Theodore H.: 71; journalist known for *The Making of the President* books; May 15, 1986.

Whiteman, Paul: 76; "The Jazz King"; Dec. 29, 1967.

Wilder, Thornton: 78; author, playwright (*Our Town*); Dec. 30, 1975.

Wilkins, Roy: 80; civil-rights activist, led NAACP; Sept. 8, 1981.

Williams, Tennessee: 72; leading playwright (*A Streetcar Named Desire*); Feb. 25, 1983.

Williams, William Carlos: 79; physician and poet; March 4, 1963.

Wilson, Edmund: 77; critic, historian, novelist and journalist; June 12, 1972.

Wilson, Teddy: 73; American jazz pianist; Aug. 1, 1986.

Winchell, Walter: 74; father of the gossip column; Feb. 20, 1972.

Wolf, Howling [Chester Burnett]: 65; American blues vocalist; Jan. 10, 1976.

Wood, Natalie: 43; movie actress; Nov. 29, 1981.

Wright, H. Dudley: 71; American industrialist and philanthropist; Jan. 20, 1992.

Wright, Richard: 52; literary spokesman for black America, novelist (*Black Boy*); Nov. 29, 1960.

Wrigley, Philip K.: 82; chairman of chewing gum company, owner of Chicago Cubs baseball team; April 12, 1977.

Wyler, William: 79; film director; July 27, 1981.

Yawkey, Jean R.: 83; majority owner of the Boston Red Sox baseball team and the only woman ever to serve on the board of directors of the Baseball Hall of Fame; Feb. 26, 1992.

York, Sgt. Alvin C.: 76; World War I infantry hero, Medal of Honor; Sept. 2, 1964.

York, Dick: 63; stage, screen and television actor best known for his role as a high-strung advertising executive on the ABC sitcom "Bewitched"; Feb. 20, 1992.

Young, Whitney M.: 49; civil-rights leader, executive director, Urban League; March 11, 1971.

Zanuck, Darryl F.: 76; film producer; Dec. 22, 1979.

Zhou Enlai: 78; Prime Minister of China beginning 1949; Jan. 8, 1976.

Zukor, Adolph: 103; founder of Paramount movie empire; June 10, 1976.

PART FIVE

SCIENCE, MEDICINE AND TECHNOLOGY

CHEMISTRY

THE ELEMENTS

Elements are substances that cannot be reduced to simpler substances by ordinary means. They are composed of **atoms,** which are made up of **protons** (positively charged electrical particles) and **neutrons** (with a neutral charge), which form a central **nucleus,** and **electrons** (negatively charged particles), which travel around the nucleus. The **atomic number** is the number of protons in the nucleus. The mass number is the number of protons and neutrons in the nucleus. The atomic weight is the average weight of an atom of the element.

Although each element has a specific number of protons and electrons, the number of neutrons may vary. When an element exists in several forms, with different numbers of neutrons, those forms are known as **isotopes.** For example, there are three isotopes of hydrogen: protium (which, unlike other elements, has no neutrons), deuterium (which has one neutron) and tritium (which has two neutrons).

Ninety elements are found in nature. There are also 18 **synthetic elements,** which have been created in nuclear laboratories by bombarding other elements with radioactive particles. Synthetic elements are also called artificial elements; because they all have atomic numbers greater than uranium's (92), they are also known as the transuranium elements.

Radioactive elements are elements in which the nuclei decompose (decay) naturally, transforming themselves into other, more stable elements. During the decay, energy and radioactive particles are released.

Rare earth metals are elements that commonly occur together in minerals and are difficult to separate because of their chemical similarities. Although they were once believed to be uncommon, they are not.

THE ELEMENTS

Element (Atomic number)	Symbol	Type	Date of discovery
actinium* (89)	Ac	metal	1899
aluminum (13)	Al	metal	1825
americium* (95)	Am	metal/synthetic	1944
antimony (51)	Sb	metal	known since ancient times
argon (18)	Ar	gas	1894
arsenic (33)	As	nonmetal	1250
astatine* (33)	At	nonmetal/synthetic	1940
barium (56)	Ba	metal	1808
berkelium* (97)	Bk	metal/synthetic	1949
beryllium (4)	Be	metal	1798
bismuth (83)	Bi	metal	1753
boron (5)	B	nonmetal	1808
bromine (35)	Br	liquid nonmetal	1826
cadmium (48)	Cd	metal	1817
calcium (20)	Ca	metal	1808
californium* (98)	Cf	metal/synthetic	1949
carbon (6)	C	nonmetal	known since ancient times
cerium (58)	Ce	rare earth	1803
cesium (55)	Cs	metal	1860
chlorine (17)	Cl	gas	1774
chromium (24)	Cr	metal	1797
cobalt (27)	Co	metal	1735
copper (29)	Cu	metal	known since ancient times
curium* (96)	Cm	metal/synthetic	1944
dysprosium (66)	Dy	rare earth	1886
einsteinium* (99)	Es	synthetic	1952
erbium (68)	Er	rare earth	1843
europium (63)	Eu	rare earth	1896
fermium* (100)	Fm	metal/synthetic	1953
fluorine (9)	F	gas	1886

Element (Atomic number)	Symbol	Type	Date of discovery
francium* (87)	Fr	metal	1939
gadolinium (64)	Gd	rare earth	1880
gallium (31)	Ga	metal	1875
germanium (32)	Ge	metal	1886
gold (79)	Au	metal	known since ancient times
hafnium (72)	Hf	metal/synthetic	1923
helium (2)	He	gas	1895
holmium (67)	Ho	rare earth	1878
hydrogen (1)	H	gas	1766
indium (49)	In	metal	1863
iodine (53)	I	nonmetal	1811
iridium (77)	Ir	metal	1804
iron (26)	Fe	metal	known since ancient times
krypton (36)	Kr	gas	1898
lanthanum (57)	La	rare earth	1839
lawrencium* (103)	Lr	metal/synthetic	1961
lead (82)	Pb	metal	known since ancient times
lithium (3)	Li	metal	1817
lutetium (71)	Lu	rare earth	1907
magnesium (12)	Mg	metal	1808
manganese (25)	Mn	metal	1774
mendelevium* (101)	Md	metal/synthetic	1955
mercury (80)	Hg	liquid metal	known since ancient times
molybdenum (42)	Mo	metal	1778
neodymium (60)	Nd	rare earth	1885
neon (10)	Ne	gas	1898
neptunium* (93)	Np	metal/synthetic	1940
nickel (28)	Ni	metal	1751
niobium (41)	Nb	metal	1801
nitrogen (7)	N	gas	1772
nobelium* (102)	No	metal/synthetic	1958
osmium (76)	Os	metal	1804
oxygen (8)	O	gas	1774
palladium (46)	Pd	metal	1803
phosphorus (15)	P	nonmetal	1669
platinum (78)	Pt	metal	1735
plutonium* (94)	Pu	metal/synthetic	1940
polonium* (84)	Po	metal	1898
potassium (19)	K	metal	1807
praseodymium (59)	Pr	rare earth	1885
promethium* (61)	Pm	rare earth	1945
protactinium* (91)	Pa	metal	1917
radium* (88)	Ra	metal	1898
radon* (86)	Rn	gas	1900
rhenium (75)	Re	metal	1925
rhodium (45)	Rh	metal	1803
rubidum (37)	Rb	metal	1861
ruthenium (44)	Ru	metal	1844
samarium (62)	Sm	rare earth	1879
scandium (21)	Sc	metal	1879
selenium (34)	Se	nonmetal	1817
silicon (14)	Si	nonmetal	1824
silver (47)	Ag	metal	known since ancient times
sodium (11)	Na	metal	1807
strontium (38)	Sr	metal	1790
sulfur (sulphur) (16)	S	nonmetal	known since ancient times
tantalum (73)	Ta	metal	1802

Element (Atomic number)	Symbol	Type	Date of discovery
technetium* (43)	Tc	metal/synthetic	1937
tellurium (52)	Te	metal	1782
terbium (65)	Tb	rare earth	1843
thallium (81)	Tl	metal	1861
thorium* (90)	Th	metal	1828
thulium (69)	Tm	rare earth	1879
tin (50)	Sn	metal	known since ancient times
titanium (22)	Ti	metal	1791
tungsten (74)	W	metal	1783
unnilennium* (109)	Une	metal/synthetic	1982
unnilhexium* (106)	Unh	metal/synthetic	1974
unnilpentium* (105) (called nielsbohrium in the C.I.S., rutherfordium [symbol: Rf] in the U.S.)	Unp	metal/synthetic	1970
unnilquadium* (104 (called kurchatovium in the C.I.S., hahnium [symbol: Ha] in the U.S.)	Unq	metal/synthetic	1969
unnilseptium* (107)	Uns	metal/synthetic	1981
uranium* (92)	U	metal	1789
vanadium (23)	V	metal	1830
xenon (54)	Xe	gas	1898
ytterbium (70)	Yb	rare earth	1907
yttrium (39)	Y	rare earth	1794
zinc (30)	Zn	metal	1746
zirconium (40)	Zr	metal	1789

* radioactive element

COMMON CHEMICALS

Chemical	Formula	Description
acetic acid	CH_3COOH	essential component of vinegar
acetone	CH_3COCH_3	solvent
acetylene (ethyne)	$HC{\equiv}CH$	gas; explosive
aluminum sulfate	$Al_2(SO_4)_3$	used in dyeing, foam fire extinguishers, water purifying
ammonia	NH_3	pungent gas used in chemical processes
benzene	C_6H_6	used in drugs, dyes, plastics, etc.; toxic, carcinogenic
carbon dioxide	CO_2	odorless gas; produced by animal respiration
carbolic acid (See phenol)		
carbonic acid	H_2CO_3	weak acid
carbon monoxide	CO	odorless, poisonous gas; in car exhaust fumes
ethanol (ethyl alcohol)	CH_3CH_2OH	grain alcohol
formaldehyde (methanal)	$HCHO$	poisonous gas with strong odor
glucose (dextrose)	$C_6H_{12}O_6$	sugar found in fruits, honey
hydrochloric acid (muriatic acid)	HCl	strong acid used in industry
hydrocyanic acid	HCN	(See hydrogen cyanide)
hydrofluoric acid	HF	used to etch glass

Chemical	Formula	Description
hydrogen cyanide	HCN	poisonous; used in gas chambers. (Sodium cyanide [NaCN] pellets are dropped in water, releasing HCN gas.)
hydrogen peroxide	H_2O_2	disinfectant; bleach
isopropyl alcohol	$CH_3CHOHCH_3$	rubbing alcohol
lactose	$C_{12}H_{22}O_{11}$	milk sugar
magnesium hydroxide	$Mg(OH)_2$	antacid; milk of magnesia
maltose	$C_{12}H_{22}O_{11}$	malt sugar
methane	CH_4	swamp gas; combustible, explosive; from decaying organic matter
methanol (methyl alcohol)	CH_3OH	wood alcohol
nitric acid (aquafortis)	HNO_3	corrosive, poisonous liquid
nitroglycerin	$CH_2NO_3CHNO_3CH_2NO_3$	Highly unstable oil; medically, used as a vasodilator. Mixed with a stabilizing substance, it is used as an explosive in dynamite.
oxygen (atmospheric)	O_2	component in the air (roughly 20 percent) which sustains animal life
ozone	O_3	formed in stratosphere; blocks harmful radiation from reaching earth; irritant; component of certain types of smog
phenol (carbolic acid, hydroxybenzene, oxybenzene, phenylic acid)	C_6H_5OH	used in plastic production; toxic; disinfectant
potassium permanganate	$KMnO_4$	bleaching agent; laboratory chemical
propane	$CH_3CH_2CH_3$	gas, fuel
propenol (allyl alcohol, propenyl alcohol)	$CH_2=CHCH_2OH$	used in chemical manufacture
prussic acid	HCN	(See hydrogen cyanide)
saltpeter (potassium nitrate)	KNO_3	used as a fertilizer, food additive; mixed with sulfur and charcoal it becomes gunpowder.
silica (silicon dioxide)	SiO_2	quartz; chief ingredient in glass
sodium bicarbonate (sodium hydrogen carbonate)	$NaHCO_3$	bicarbonate of soda; baking soda
sodium chloride	NaCl	common salt
sodium cyanide	NaCN	poisonous powder used in extracting certain metals; produces hydrogen cyanide [HCN] gas when added to water; used in gas chambers
sodium hydroxide	NaOH	lye; caustic soda
sucrose	$C_{12}H_{22}O_{11}$	cane, beet, maple sugar
sulfuric acid	H_2SO_4	common industrial chemical; corrosive; toxic
TNT (trinitrotoluene)	$CH_3C_6H_2(NO_2)_3$	explosive
toluene	$C_6H_5CH_3$	used in manufacture of chemicals, explosives; toxic
water	H_2O	covers 70 percent of earth

COMMON ILLEGAL DRUGS

(Includes drugs commonly abused but legally produced.)

A: *See* amphetamines

A-bomb: A smokable mixture of marijuana and heroin.

Acapulco gold: *See* marijuana

ace: *See* marijuana

acid: *See* LSD

adam: *See* analogs of amphetamines and methamphetamines

aerosol sprays: *See* inhalants

African black: *See* marijuana

Alice B. Toklas: A chocolate brownie with marijuana as an ingredient. [*See* marijuana]

amies: *See* amyl nitrite

amoeba weed: The common garden herb parsley soaked in phencyclidine (PCP), dried and smoked as a cigarette. [*See* phencyclidine]

amphetamines: These are much-abused, synthetic, central nervous system stimulants. Until recent years, amphetamines were prescribed routinely, in pill or capsule form, as aids to dieting and overcoming mental depression and fatigue. Amphetamine is the parent compound of the much stronger, more widely abused drug, methamphetamine. Amphetamine was first synthesized in 1887 and used medically in the United States for the first time in 1927 as a stimulant and nasal decongestant. In the early 1930s, the drug was sold as Benzedrine tablets and inhalers. During the war years of the 1940s, amphetamines were supplied routinely to U.S., British, Japanese and German soldiers to combat exhaustion. Concentrated abuse was not noted until the 1950s, when U.S. soldiers in Japan and Korea mixed heroin with amphetamines to create intravenous "speedballs." In the United States, long-haul truck drivers and depressed, dieting homemakers were the primary abusers of amphetamines until the 1960s, when the drug's ability to produce euphoria and a heightened sense of confidence made it more generally popular. Abuse continued through the 1970s and grew dramatically through the 1980s. Considered together, abuse of various forms of amphetamine and methamphetamine throughout the world probably outranks use of cocaine today. Excessive use of amphetamines may cause dizziness, malnutrition, severe anxiety, paranoia, psychological dependence, impaired coordination, hallucinations and sleeplessness. Street names, which encompass references to some methamphetamines, include A, AMT, bam, beans, bennies, biphetamines, black beauties, black mollies, brain ticklers, brownies, bumblebees, cartwheels, chalk, chicken powder, crank, Christmas trees, copilots, crossroads, cross tops, crystal, dexies, diet pills, dolls, double cross, eye-openers, fives, footballs, forwards, hearts, ice, jam, jellybeans, leapers, lid poppers, lightning, meth, pep pills, purple hearts, rippers, sparkle plenties, sparklers, speed, splash, sweets, tens, thrusters, truck drivers, uppers, uppies, ups, wake-ups, water, white crosses. [*See* crank, crystal, ice, methamphetamines; also Common Prescription and Nonprescription Drugs, page 191]

AMT: *See* amphetamines

amyl nitrite: A heart stimulant and vasodilator discovered in 1857, amyl nitrite is used medically to lower blood pressure, primarily in treatment of patients suffering from angina pectoris. The clear yellowish liquid is sold in small, cloth-covered ampules which are broken and inhaled; the drug's street names, poppers or snappers, derive from the sound of the breaking ampule. The drug acts within 30 seconds and produces a brief euphoria. Drug abusers value amyl nitrite for its purported ability to intensify orgasm, but the drug has undesirable side effects, including dizziness, vomiting, nausea and, because amyl nitrite relaxes smooth muscles, involuntary passing of urine and feces. Long-term use may cause brain or liver damage. Slang references include amies, amys, pearls, poppers, snappers. [*See* Common Prescription and Nonprescription Drugs, page 191]

amys: *See* amyl nitrite

Amytal: This barbiturate, sold under the brand name Amytal, has a hypnotic, sedative effect that lasts approximately five hours. Pills are manufactured in colors that vary with the pill's drug content, from light green (15 mg.), to yellow (30 mg.), orange (50 mg.) and pink (100 mg.) [*See* barbiturates]

Amytal Sodium: More commonly abused than Amytal, this sedative depressant contains the barbiturate amobarbitol in 60- and 180-mg. sizes. Street names are based on the two-tone blue color of the capsules: blue angels, blue heavens, bluebirds, blue bullets, blue devils, blue dolls, blue tips, blues. [*See* barbiturates]

anabolic steroids: Abuse of these powerful compounds, which are closely related to the male hormone testosterone, has been increasingly prevalent among body builders and athletes since the

1950s because the drugs significantly enhance body weight and muscle strength. The drugs' side effects, however, are numerous and varied. Regular use may cause acne, sterility and impotence. The drugs also may cause liver, kidney and heart damage. Some users also have profound psychological reactions ranging from severe depression and paranoia to wildly aggressive behavior dubbed "roid rage." Steroids sold on the street usually are made by illegal labs or imported from Europe or Mexico.

analogs of amphetamines and methamphetamines: These analogs, chemical variants concocted from a parent compound, are generally classified as hallucinogenic. They include a broad assortment of drugs—from STP, the powerful psychedelic street drug of the '60s, to MDMA, or Ecstasy, the supposedly mellow designer drug of the '80s. All are used primarily for their ability to produce a rush of euphoria, and all pose a risk of neurochemical damage. Although the MDAs, methylene dioxamphetamines, achieved a new popularity with the white middle class in the last decade, they are not new drugs; some were first produced in the early 1960s. MDMA, or Ecstasy, actually dates to 1914. Street names of MDAs include MDMA (Adam, E, Ecstasy, Essence, X, XTC), MDE, MDM, M&M, STP, PMA, 2,5-DMA, TMA, DOM, DOB, EU4IA, EVE. Some are white powders that can be snorted, injected or smoked. Others are ingested as capsules or tablets. Any of these analogs may cause blurred vision, chills, faintness, nausea, anxiety, depression and paranoia. [*See* designer drugs, MDMA]

analogs of fentanyl: These are wildly addicting, extremely powerful narcotic designer drugs known variously as China white, Persian white, Tango and Cash, goodfella, and synthetic heroin. By making minor alterations to the molecular structure of fentanyl, a synthetic anesthetic used regularly in major surgery in the United States since 1972, underground chemists have produced white-powder street drugs that appear identical to heroin. They are used in the same way, but are from 20 to 40 times stronger and as much as 7,000 times more powerful than morphine. One thousandth of a milligram of China white, for example, which was among the earliest of the fentanyl analogs to appear, can induce euphoria; 300 micrograms, a quantity approximating one one-hundred thousandth of an aspirin-sized tablet, may kill novices, or "chippers," occasional users who haven't developed a tolerance. There are at least 200 known analogs of fentanyl, and experts say countless more may be possible. Designer fentanyl is even available in grades; one accommodates shooters; another, snorters. The analogs diminish pain, relax muscles and produce euphoria, but also may cause nausea, drowsiness, slurred speech, depressed breathing and diminished blood pressure, resulting in death. Some cocaine users addict themselves to fentanyl analogs as a way to ease themselves down after snorting and freebasing. Other drug users end up taking fentanyl analogs unknowingly because dealers sometimes use it to cut heroin and cocaine. Still others intentionally smoke "juice," a mixture of fentanyl analogs and cocaine. By 1992, abusers in New York were wearing skin patches containing fentanyl, enough for a steady high of up to three days. The patches are legally manufactured for use by cancer patients. [*See* blue thunder, China white, designer drugs, good fella, Persian white, synthetic heroin, Tango and Cash]

analogs of meperidine: These designer narcotics often are sold as synthetic heroin. Actually, they are potent derivatives of meperidine hydrochloride, the strong painkiller marketed as Demerol, but their white-powder form allows them to be passed off as heroin. They include MPPP, another heroin substitute, and the deadly neurotoxins PEPAOP and MPTP, better known as "new heroin." These drugs are snorted or injected, and may cause irreparable brain damage. [*See* designer drugs, MPPP, MPTP, PEPAOP, synthetic heroin]

analogs of phencyclidine: There are at least 30 designer derivatives of the unique and ubiquitous drug phencyclidine, PCP. All of them are psychoactive, and more powerful and less predictable than their notorious parent compound. Among the best known analogs are TCP, PCC, PCE, and PCPY. They are usually white powder in form, and can be eaten, smoked or injected. At best, they cause hallucinations and illusions and impair the user's perceptions; at worst, convulsions, heart and lung failure or permanent damage to the brain and nervous system. [*See* designer drugs, phencyclidine]

angel dust: *See* phencyclidine

angel/angel's trumpet: *See* datura

animal trank: *See* phencyclidine

Aunt Mary: *See* marijuana

aurora borealis: *See* phencyclidine, tetrahydrocannabinol

baby: *See* marijuana

bador: Aztec term for morning glory seeds. [*See* hallucinogens, morning glory]

bad seed: *See* peyote

bale: *See* marijuana

bam: *See* amphetamines

bangers: Any drug that acts as a depressant.

bank bandit pills: *See* barbiturates

barbiturates: These commonly prescribed and widely abused sedatives depress the user's central nervous system, reduce blood pressure and decrease heart and respiratory activity. In small doses, barbiturates relieve tension and anxiety and induce mild euphoria. Large doses induce drowsiness, and sleep. The most widely abused barbiturates—Amytal, Nembutal, Seconal, Tuinal and their related compounds—take effect in 20 to 45 minutes and last five to six hours. Suicides and accidental deaths due to barbiturate overdoses are very common, particularly when barbiturates are ingested with alcohol, since both are central nervous system depressants. Barbiturates, which were first synthesized in 1864 and have been widely prescribed in the United States since the 1930s, also are popular among abusers of other drugs. Heroin addicts often substitute heavy barbiturate doses when they can't get heroin. Other drug users commonly fall into an up-down pattern of abuse, using amphetamines as stimulants and barbiturates as depressants. The risk of physical addiction to barbiturates is high, because with heavy use tolerance develops steadily. Barbiturate withdrawal symptoms can be more severe than the symptoms of withdrawal from morphine or heroin, and the process may take several months. Street names include bank bandit pills, barbs, beans, black beauties, block busters, blue angels, brain ticklers, candy, courage pills, dolls, downers, downs, F-40, G.B., goofballs, goofers, gorilla pills, King Kong pills, nebbies, nemish, nimbies, peanuts, phennies, phenos, pink ladies, pinks, purple hearts, rainbows, red birds, red bullets, red devils, red dolls, red lillies, reds, seccy, seggie, sleepers, stumblers, yellow bullets, yellow jackets, yellows. [See Amytal, Amytal Sodium, Nembutal, Seconal, Tuinal; see also Barbiturates in chapter entitled Common Prescription and Nonprescription Drugs, page 191]

barbs: See barbiturates

barn: See amphetamines

barrels: See LSD

base: See freebase

baseball: See freebase

basing: Using cocaine freebase.

beans: See amphetamines, barbiturates, mescaline

beast: See LSD

beats: See LSD

belladonna: The ancients used tinctures from the root and leaves of this plant, known historically as deadly nightshade, as a sedative in small doses and a poison in large doses. The ancient Romans also used belladonna as a cosmetic; the drug causes dilation of the pupils, which the Romans considered a mark of beauty. The name belladonna, in fact, is from the Italian meaning "beautiful lady." The plant is a member of the potato family and contains the powerful alkaloids atropine, hyoscyamine and scopolamine. Ingestion of less plant material than what is commonly found in a marijuana cigarette can induce coma and death. Tinctures of belladonna still are prescribed today in treatment of some stomach disorders.

benny, bennies: See benzedrine

benz: See benzedrine

benzedrine: This central nervous system stimulant was first synthesized in 1927 and by 1932 was in common use as a decongestant inhalant. In World War II, German, Japanese and American soldiers were issued benzedrine in their survival kits as a way to counteract fatigue. The drug has been widely prescribed as an aid to dieting, narcolepsy and the treatment of alcoholism and depression. The risk of psychological dependence on benzedrine is high, so the drug has been more judiciously prescribed in recent years. Street names include bennies, benz, peaches, roses, whites. [See amphetamines]

bernice: See cocaine

bernies: See cocaine

big bag: See heroin

big C: See cocaine

big chief: See mescaline, peyote

big D: See LSD

big H: See heroin

big M: See morphine

biphetamine: This drug, which is a central nervous system stimulant, combines amphetamine and dextroamphetamine. It has been widely used, and abused, as an aid to weight control. Common references include black beauties, blackbirds, black mollies. [See amphetamines]

birdie powder: See morphine

black beauties: See amphetamines, barbiturates, biphetamine

black gunion: A very potent, black marijuana from Africa or Jamaica. [See marijuana]

black mollies: See biphetamine

black pills: See opium

black Russian: See hashish

black stuff: See opium

blackbirds: See biphetamine

black tar: See heroin

blast: See phencyclidine

blanco: Spanish for heroin. [See heroin]

block busters: See barbiturates

blotter: Blotter paper impregnated with LSD. [See LSD]

blow: See cocaine

blue acid: See LSD

blue angels: See Amytal Sodium, barbiturates

bluebirds: See Amytal Sodium

blue bullets: See Amytal Sodium

blue cheer: *See* LSD

blue devils: *See* Amytal Sodium

blue dolls: *See* Amytal Sodium

blue heaven: *See* LSD

blue heavens: *See* Amytal Sodium

blue mist: *See* LSD

blues: *See* Amytal Sodium, numorphan

blue star: *See* LSD

blue thunder: Heroin that surfaced in New York early in 1990, suspected of being cut with the potent synthetic tranquilizer called fentanyl. [*See* analogs of fentanyl, heroin]

blue tips: *See* Amytal Sodium

blue velvet: A mixture of codeine, tripelennamine (antihistamine) and terpin hydrate elixir (turpentine derivative high in alcohol content). Mild euphoric and sedative effects.

bo: Street slang for marijuana. [*See* marijuana]

bolsa: Spanish for heroin sold in a pouch or bag. [*See* heroin]

bolt: *See* butyl nitrite

bomb: *See* heroin

bombita: Spanish for "little bomb"; a solution of cocaine or heroin mixed with amphetamine to maximize the high and minimize depression.

boo: *See* marijuana

bouncing powder: *See* cocaine

boy: *See* heroin

brain ticklers: *See* amphetamines, barbiturates

brick: *See* marijuana

broccoli: *See* marijuana

brother: *See* heroin

brown: Heroin from Mexico, where dilution with brown milk sugar gives the drug its telltale color. [*See* heroin]

brown dots: *See* LSD

brownies: Usually Dexedrine timed-release capsules, which have brown caps. [*See* amphetamines]

brown mixture: *See* opium

brown rocks: Heroin in granular form cut to 50 percent strength for smoking. [*See* heroin]

brown stuff: *See* opium

brown sugar: *See* brown, heroin

bud: Street slang for marijuana. [*See* marijuana]

bufotenine: A hallucinogenic substance derived from the skin of toads as well as several plant species and the mushroom *Amanita muscaria*. A snuff called cohoba or yopo, which is popular in parts of South and Central America and Haiti, contains bufotenine. The drug's impact is similar to LSD, though milder and shorter in duration. [*See* hallucinogens]

bullet: *See* butyl nitrite

bumblebees: *See* amphetamines

burese: An obsolete reference to cocaine. [*See* cocaine]

bush: *See* marijuana

businessman's special: *See* DMT

buttons: Small protuberant growths on the surface of the peyote cactus. [*See* mescaline, peyote]

butyl nitrite: Classified as a volatile inhalant, butyl nitrite has many of the same properties as amyl nitrite and is similarly abused as a way to produce a brief but intense euphoria and to intensify orgasm. Butyl nitrite may lower blood pressure and cause headaches, vomiting, nausea and, because it relaxes smooth muscles, involuntary passing of urine and feces. Long-term use may cause brain or liver damage. Street names include bolt, bullet, and climax. Head shops and mail order outlets sell the inhalant in small bottles as room freshener called Locker Room, Rush, and Jac-Aroma.

C: *See* cocaine

caapi: A hallucinogenic tea brewed from a vine native to Brazil and Colombia.

caballo: Spanish for horse, a reference to heroin. [*See* heroin]

cactus: *See* mescaline, peyote

California sunshine: *See* LSD

Canadian black: Marijuana of a characteristic dark color grown in Canada. [*See* marijuana]

candy: *See* barbiturates

cannabis: *See* marijuana

canned sativa: *See* hashish

canned stuff: Opium packages for smoking. [*See* opium]

cap: *See* LSD

carga: A Spanish term for heroin. [*See* heroin]

cartwheels: Round amphetamine pills marked with a cross, which makes them resemble a wheel. [*See* amphetamines]

cat: *See* heroin

chalk: Amphetamine tablets that are easily crumbled. [*See* amphetamines]

charas: An Indian name for hashish, the powerful and pure resin extracted from the flowering top of the female marijuana plant, *Cannabis sativa*. [*See* hashish]

charge: *See* marijuana

Charles: An obsolete reference to cocaine. [*See* cocaine]

Charlie: *See* cocaine

chicharra: Puerto Rican slang for a shared cigarette of marijuana and tobacco.

chick: *See* heroin

chicken powder: *See* amphetamines

chief: *See* LSD

China white: Originally the street name for the highest-grade heroin in Southeast Asia, China white has become synonymous with alpha-methyl fentanyl, a powerful synthetic narcotic that first surfaced as a heroin lookalike in Orange County,

Calif., in December 1979 and spread along the West Coast. After a rash of more than a hundred overdoses in 1980, the drug faded from popularity, but around 1988 it resurfaced in Pennsylvania. [*See* analogs of fentanyl, designer drugs, Persian white]

Chinese red: Brown heroin, usually from Mexico. [*See* heroin]

chiva: *See* heroin

chloral hydrate: This is the famous nonbarbiturate sedative behind the "Mickey Finn" knockout potion that bad guys have been slipping good guys for years. The name, in fact, dates back to a Chicago barkeep who was notorious for using knockout drops in the 1890s. A few drops of liquid chloral hydrate in alcohol produces acute intoxication. The drug is also known as joy juice or knockout drops; the drink, a torpedo or a Mickey.

chocolate chips: *See* LSD

Christmas trees: *See* Dexamyl

cocaine: Cocaine, an alkaloid drug found in the leaves of the coca plant, has been known as a drug since the time of the Incas. Long before the first white men arrived in Peru in the 1500s, Inca priests and members of the aristocracy chewed the leaves of the coca plant because they believed the mild euphoria that resulted helped them to understand religious truths. The conquering Spaniards banned the use of cocaine in religious ceremonies, but allowed Inca plantation workers to use the drug, partly as incentive to work and partly because cocaine helped prolong physical endurance and diminish hunger.

Pure cocaine, in white crystalline powder form, was first isolated from the leaves of the coca plant in the 1850s by the German chemist Albert Niemann. European society soon came to value the drug as a stimulant and medicine. In Paris, Angelo Mariani infused coca leaves into wine and created his "Vin Coca Mariana," a drink that became popular throughout 19th-century Europe. Psychiatrist Sigmund Freud used cocaine and cited the drug's value in the treatment of depression, morphine addiction, eating disorders and alcoholism. In *Über Coca*, Freud wrote: "The psychic effect of cocaine consists of exhilaration and lasting euphoria which does not differ from normal euphoria of a healthy person.... Absolutely no craving for further use of cocaine appears after the first or repeated taking of the drug." His advocacy was short-lived. By 1885, evidence of addiction and mounting cocaine overdose deaths prompted Dr. Albrecht Erlenmeyer to warn his colleagues against using cocaine to cure morphine addiction. Freud followed suit.

By the early 1900s, some form of cocaine was a primary ingredient in numerous potions and many patent medicines that were readily available from doctors and druggists. Meanwhile, a new soft drink called Coca-Cola had been quickly growing in popularity since its introduction in 1886, and it, too, contained an extract of cocaine. America's first cocaine epidemic had begun. With the Pure Food and Drug Act of 1906, the federal government finally banned interstate shipment of all food and soda water containing cocaine.

Eight years later, in 1914, the Harrison Narcotics Act formally identified cocaine as a narcotic, and in 1922 Congress banned importation of coca leaves and cocaine. In 1932, the Uniform Narcotic Drug Act imposed stiff criminal penalties for possession of cocaine. The drug's popularity diminished greatly in the decades that followed, but it surged back into prominence in the 1960s, a watershed decade for drug use in the United States.

Despite law enforcement's focus on cocaine traffic, use of the drug spread dramatically through the 1970s and especially the 1980s, particularly among young, relatively affluent users who could afford cocaine at high prices. One of every 100 Americans—2.2 million people—were hard-core cocaine addicts by 1990, according to a May 1990 report by the U.S. Senate Judiciary Committee; 7 percent of youths, 28 percent of young adults and 9 percent of older adults said they had used cocaine at least once. Despite U.S. interdiction efforts and intensified crackdowns among cooperating governments, anywhere from 60 to 100 tons of cocaine is smuggled into the United States every year, mostly from South America. Colombia alone supplies more than half of the world's illicit cocaine supply. According to the Justice Department, annual cocaine sales in the United States amount to $29 billion.

Traditionally, cocaine in white powder form is shaped into a "line" and "snorted," quickly inhaled into the nostrils, from a small coke spoon or through a straw or rolled piece of paper such as currency. The drug passes quickly through the mucous membranes and into the bloodstream, stimulating the central nervous system and yielding a short-lived but intense euphoria. Cocaine in solution is sometimes injected for greater impact. Regular use of the drug, according to scientists, creates a true and overpowering physiologic addiction. Prolonged use may cause nervousness, delirium, impotence, malnutrition, anemia, and deterioration of nasal cartilage. Withdrawal symptoms include extreme paranoia, depression, fatigue, insomnia, irritability and formication, the "coke-bug" phenomenon in which users believe that ants are crawling under their skin.

Cocaine-related deaths, generally caused by

heart-rhythm disturbances, convulsions, hemorrhages or respiratory collapse, rose through the 1980s. By the latter part of the decade, it appeared that high market prices for cocaine (anywhere from $25,000 to $35,000 per kilo), rising public sentiment and the continued attention of law enforcement and the media had, at least for the moment, helped reduce the incidence of cocaine abuse among all populations in the United States, especially among the middle and upper classes. Then the introduction of cocaine in a less expensive, smokable form, crack cocaine, made the drug more readily available to a much broader and lower-income segment of the nation's population. Use quickly blossomed into epidemic proportions.

Street names for cocaine include Bernice, bernies, big C, blow, bombita, bouncing powder, burese, C, Charles, Charlie, coke, Corrine, dream, dust, eight-ball (reference to an eighth-ounce of cocaine), first line, flake, fly, girl, gold dust, heaven, heaven dust, her, incentive, jam, Jim Jones (marijuana cigarette laced with cocaine and soaked in PCP), joy powder, lady, lady snow, nose candy, nose powder, paradise, poison, powder, primo (marijuana cigarette laced with cocaine), rock, sniff, snow, snowbirds, spacebase, stardust, sugar, toot, toots, white, white lady, white powder, white stuff. [*See* crack, freebase]

cococaine: *See* fake coke

codeine: This natural alkaloid of opium was discovered in 1832. The drug can be extracted from the juices of the unripened pod of the white-flowering poppy, but quantities are so small that codeine is most often synthesized instead. Though derived from morphine, codeine is only about one-sixth to one-tenth as powerful. As a narcotic painkiller, codeine has been most useful as a cough-suppressing agent in cough syrups. In very large doses, the drug relieves minor pain, produces a mild euphoria or drowsiness and may include constipation and nausea as side effects. The drug is considered only mildly addictive. Instances of outright addiction to codeine are, in fact, relatively rare. The phosphate form of codeine is usually a component of elixirs; codeine sulfate is manufactured in tablet form. The slang reference to the latter includes fours, schoolboys and pops. [See: Common Prescription and Nonprescription Drugs, page 191]

climax: *See* butyl nitrite

cohoba: Hallucinogenic snuff made in Trinidad from a plant called piptadenia. [*See* bufotenine]

coke: *See* cocaine

Colombian: Marijuana from Colombia. [*See* marijuana]

colum: Marijuana from Colombia. [*See* marijuana]

contact lens: *See* LSD

copilots: Dexedrine tablets. [*See* amphetamines, Dexedrine]

Corrine: *See* cocaine

courage pills: General reference to barbiturates. [*See* barbiturates]

crack: This is a smokable form of cocaine, a cream-colored, rough-shaped pellet or "rock" made by adding ammonia or sodium bicarbonate to a water solution of cocaine hydrochloride; crack is the precipitate. The drug usually is smoked in a pipe over a continuous heat source, such as a butane lighter. The euphoria from the drug is intense but brief, lasting only about five minutes, but street prices range from $10 to $30 for a quarter-gram rock, making it much more accessible to a broader range of people—facts that help account for the wildfire growth of the drug's popularity since its introduction in the mid-1980s. Also contributing to crack's appeal is the fact that it is possible to consume more of it at one time than cocaine. Cocaine powder, by comparison, constricts the blood vessels in nasal passages when the drug is snorted, thereby limiting the amount a user can ingest; there is no such threshold for crack, and the desire to regain the initial euphoria is overpowering. The name crack comes from the crackling sound the drug makes when smoked. [*See* cocaine, freebase]

crank: On the East Coast of the United States, crank generally refers to a blend of smokable heroin and crack that produces an intense but calm euphoria with minimal post-use depression. In the West and Southwest, "crank" is more apt to mean powdered methamphetamine, a synthetic nervous system stimulant. This latter form of crank grew in popularity in the mid-1980s as a homegrown alternative to cocaine, especially among blue-collar and poor drug users. By the latter part of the decade, illegal crank labs had proliferated throughout the rural West, where biker gangs controlled much of the drug's production and distribution. Crank is off-white or brownish in color and is generally sold in eighth-ounce packages called eightballs. When dissolved and taken intravenously, crank can produce a high that lasts six to eight hours and is followed by a period of psychosis that may last more than twice as long. [*See* methamphetamine]

crap: *See* heroin

crossroads: *See* amphetamines

cross-tops: Benzedrine. [*See* amphetamines, Benzedrine]

crystal: *See* ice, methamphetamine

crystal meth: *See* ice, methamphetamine

crystal methedrine: *See* ice, methamphetamine

cubes: Cubes of sugar treated with LSD. [*See* LSD]

cupcakes: *See* LSD

cura: A heroin injection; Spanish for cure. [*See* heroin]

D: *See* LSD

dagga: Marijuana from South Africa. [*See* marijuana]

datura: Several species of this narcotic hallucinogenic drug, which has been used for centuries as a poison, are known; the most common is *Datura stramonium*, a member of the potato family. Drug users dry and smoke the plant's leaves. Street names include angel, angel's trumpet, devil's apple, devil's weed, Jamestown weed, jimson weed, stinkweed, thorn apple. [*See* hallucinogens]

dawamesk: This is a small, aromatic, North African cake made of marijuana or hashish, sugar, orange juice, cardamom, cinnamon, cloves, nutmeg, musk and pine and pistachio nuts. French literati of the 1840s—among them Victor Hugo, Honoré de Balzac, Alexandre Dumas, Charles Baudelaire, Gérard de Nerval and Théophile Gautier—introduced marijuana and hashish to Europe at their club in Paris, Club des Hachichins, by serving members dawamesk.

deadly nightshade: *See* belladonna

deeda: *See* LSD

Demerol: *See* meperidine hydrochloride

designer drugs: By tinkering with the chemical composition of known drugs, underground chemists are able to easily and inexpensively produce analogs, closely related drugs that often are many times more powerful than the compounds from which they were derived. In theory, a good chemist can custom-make, or design, a drug to suit his customers' desires. In reality, quality control is nonexistent and so is testing of the drug. The result often is disaster or death.

The term "designer drug" was coined by Gary Henderson, professor of pharmacology at the University of California at Davis, in reference to the development in 1979 of alpha-methyl fentanyl, the illegal and potent heroin substitute known as China white.

Originally, underground chemists' new drugs also were designed to be technically legal, at least for a while. Until the federal Drug Enforcement Administration could test, identify and schedule the new drugs as controlled substances, neither the makers nor takers of the drugs had broken the law. Late in 1984, largely in response to the sudden popularity of designer drugs, Congress gave the DEA emergency powers that streamlined the so-called drug scheduling process. The Anti-Drug Abuse Act of 1986 went a step further. The act made all analogs of all controlled substances as illegal as their parent compounds. Still, by the time investigators even hear of a new drug, it usually has done plenty of damage on the street.

Researchers and law enforcement specialists agree that the proliferation of designer drugs could represent one of the most dangerous and vexing trends in drug abuse; dangerous because no one knows the true effect of the drugs until they actually are used; vexing because kitchen chemists seem able to produce new drugs whenever the need arises. [*See* analogs of amphetamines and methamphetamines, analogs of fentanyl, analogs of meperidine, analogs of phencyclidine, China white, MPTP]

DET: Diethyltriptamine is a synthetic hallucinogenic drug similar to DMT, though more powerful and longer-lasting—two or three hours, compared with 30 to 60 minutes. [*See* DMT, hallucinogens]

devil's apple: *See* datura

devil's weed: *See* datura

Dexamyl: An amphetamine and barbiturate stimulant made by Smith, Kline & French Laboratories and sold as elixir, green tablets or slow-release green-and-white capsules. Commonly known as dexies or Christmas trees. In Great Britain, the drug is sold as Drinamyl and known on the street for its color in tablet form as purple hearts or French blues.

Dexedrine: This is the brand name of dextroamphetamine sulfate, a powerful amphetamine made by Smith, Kline & French Laboratories. The drug has been widely prescribed as an aid to weight control. It is sold as elixir, pale orange tablets or slow-release brown, orange and white capsules. The drug has been widely abused and is addictive. The most common slang references are copilots or dexies. [*See* amphetamine]

dexies: *See* amphetamine, Dexamyl, Dexedrine

diet pills: *See* amphetamines

Dilaudid: A derivative of morphine that is approximately five times more powerful than its parent compound. Sold as small white pills, oval-shaped tablets, rectal suppositories, cough syrup and ampules for injection. Known as dillies, footballs.

dillies: *See* Dilaudid

djamba: Brazilian for marijuana. [*See* marijuana]

djoma: African for marijuana. [*See* marijuana]

DMT: This is dimethyltryptamine, which is similar to the hallucinogenic psilocybin. Its immediate effects are comparable to LSD but much shorter in duration, lasting less than an hour. Slang references include businessman's special or lunchtime special. [*See* hallucinogens]

d-lysergic acid diethylamide tartrate 25: *See* LSD

DOA: A street name for phencyclidine, PCP, after the phrase "dead on arrival." [*See* phencyclidine]

DOB: *See* analogs of amphetamines and methamphetamines, designer drugs

dogie: *See* heroin

dolls: *See* amphetamines, barbiturates

dolly: Street name for Dolophine, methadone. [*See* dolophine hydrochloride]

Dolophine (dolophine hydrochloride): Dolophine is a trade name for methadone, a synthetic narcotic developed in World War II by Nazi chemists when the Allied naval blockade of Germany prevented importation of opium. The chemists named the drug after their leader, Adolf Hitler. Dolophine was first used in the United States in the late 1940s. The drug is addicting and slightly more powerful than morphine, but poses less severe withdrawal problems.

Since the 1960s, Dolophine has been widely used to detoxify and stabilize heroin addicts. The drug produces a longer-lasting euphoria than heroin, blocks the effect of the illegal narcotic and decreases the addict's cravings. Because methadone is taken orally, the addict's intravenous drug use may end, curtailing the risk of infections and exposure to diseases such as hepatitis and AIDS. Because methadone is available legally, the addict may break the cycle of criminal activity and association that usually accompanies heroin addiction. Methadone is subject to abuse, but controlled application of the drug still is generally held to be the most successful alternative to heroin addiction. Street reference is "dolly." [*See* heroin]

DOM: This is dimethoxy-methylamphetamine, more commonly known as the powerful synthetic hallucinogen STP. [*See* STP]

dome: A capsule-like form of LSD. [*See* LSD]

doobie: *See* marijuana

doojee: *See* heroin

dope: *See* marijuana

dots: The standard, minute dosage of LSD; actually microdots of the drug. [*See* LSD]

double cross: *See* amphetamines

downers: *See* barbiturates

downs: *See* barbiturates

dream: *See* cocaine

dreamer: *See* morphine

drinamyl: *See* dexamyl

dry high: *See* marijuana

duby: *See* marijuana

duji: *See* heroin

dust: *See* cocaine

ecstasy: *See* analogs of amphetamines and methamphetamines, designer drugs, MDMA

eightballs: An eighth-ounce package of crank or cocaine. [*See* cocaine, crank]

eighth: *See* heroin

electric Kool-Aid: *See* LSD

elephant: *See* phencyclidine

emm: *See* morphine

essence: *See* analogs of amphetamines and methamphetamines, designer drugs, MDMA

EU4IA: *See* analogs of amphetamines and methamphetamines, designer drugs, MDMA

EVE: *See* analogs of amphetamines and methamphetamines, designer drugs, MDMA

eye openers: *See* amphetamines

fake coke: These cocaine substitutes—generally synthetic local anesthetics—can be as harmful as cocaine itself. They include "the caines": Lidocaine, Novocaine, Pontocaine, Procaine, and Tetracaine, and often are advertised as legal cocaine available by mail order. Users risk collapsed blood vessels, diminished blood pressure, and heart damage. Street names include cococaine, Florida snow, snowcaine, supercaine, toot and ultracaine.

fatty: A thick marijuana cigarette. [*See* marijuana]

fentanyl: *See* analogs of fentanyl

F-40: Seconal, the brand name of secobarbitol, a widely abused barbiturate. [*See* barbiturates, Seconal]

first line: *See* cocaine

fives: Amphetamines in 5-mg. tablets. [*See* amphetamines]

flake: *See* cocaine

flash: *See* LSD

flea powder: *See* heroin

Florida snow: *See* fake coke

flowers: *See* marijuana

fly: *See* cocaine

flying saucers: A variety of morning glory seeds. [*See* hallucinogens, morning glory]

footballs: *See* amphetamines, Dilaudid

forwards: *See* amphetamines

fours: Tablets of Tylenol and codeine, numbered one through four for their potency. [*See* codeine]

freebase: Cocaine users say that a freebase high is cocaine euphoria at its most intense. The smoking of cocaine began in the 1970s, when Peruvian users found that the paste produced in the processing of coca leaves, although riddled with dangerous impurities, could be smoked. Cocaine, in its standard street form, must be converted from its hydrochloride state to an alkaloid before it can be smoked. The process of freebasing is dangerous, involving the heating of cocaine with a flammable solvent or with baking soda and ether. The purified cocaine is then smoked in a special pipe or added to a tobacco or marijuana cigarette. Street references to freebase cocaine include freebase, base, spacebase, baseball, white tornado, snowflake. [*See* cocaine]

freebase rocks: *See* crack

freeze: *See* ice

French blues: *See* dexamyl

Frisco speedball: A mixture of heroin, cocaine and LSD.

full moon: A large piece of peyote, usually about four inches in diameter, representing the entire top of the cactus. [*See* peyote]

gage: *See* marijuana

gangster: *See* marijuana

garbage: *See* heroin

gangster pills: *See* barbiturates

gauge: *See* marijuana

GHB: This is gamma hydroxybutyric acid, a drug that didn't emerge as a problem until late 1990 after more than 30 people in California, Florida and Georgia became seriously ill after taking it. GHB was sold in powdered or granular form by health food stores, gyms and fitness centers as an aid in strength training, body building, and weight loss and as a replacement for L-tryptophan, a food additive taken off the market earlier in the year. Head shops and some mail order houses also sold GHB as a "legal psychedelic." In Europe, the drug has been used in combination with some anesthetics. When the FDA issued its order in November 1990, GHB was being evaluated in government-approved studies for the treatment of narcolepsy. The FDA linked use of the drug to cases of severe nausea and vomiting, respiratory problems, seizures and coma. GHB also is called sodium oxybate and gamma hydroxybutyrate sodium. [*See* L-tryptophan]

ghost: *See* LSD

ghostbusters: Freebase cocaine combined with phencyclidine. [*See* cocaine, freebase, phencyclidine]

giggleweed: *See* marijuana

girl: *See* cocaine

glass: *See* ice

godfather: Heroin that surfaced in New York early in 1990, suspected of being cut with the potent synthetic tranquilizer fentanyl. [*See* analogs of fentanyl, heroin]

God's flesh: *See* sacred mushrooms

God's medicine: *See* morphine

gold: Reference to Acapulco gold, a high-grade marijuana. [*See* marijuana]

gold dust: *See* cocaine

golden leaf: Reference to Acapulco gold, a high-grade marijuana. [*See* marijuana]

goma de mota: *See* hashish

goodfella: Heroin that surfaced in New York early in 1990, suspected of being cut with the potent synthetic tranquilizer fentanyl. [*See* analogs of fentanyl, heroin]

good stuff: *See* heroin

goofballs: Pills combining a combination of barbiturates and amphetamines.

goofers: This is a slang word used in reference to barbiturates or amphetamines.

gorilla pills: *See* barbiturates, Tuinal

grass: *See* marijuana

green: An inferior grade of marijuana from Mexico; sometimes called Mexican green. [*See* marijuana] Also may be used in reference to ketamine hydrochloride in its crystalline powder form. [*See* ketamine hydrochloride]

green dragon: *See* LSD

grefa: Spanish for marijuana. [*See* marijuana]

greta: *See* marijuana

grifa: *See* marijuana

griffo: *See* marijuana

grillo: *See* marijuana

grunt: *See* marijuana

gungeon (also ganga, ganja, gunga, gunja): These are names for potent marijuana from Jamaica or Africa. In the United States and Great Britain, these terms are most commonly associated with Rastafarianism, a religious and cultural movement that originated in Jamaica in the 1930s. Rastafarians, who have strongly influenced reggae music, regard Africa as the holy land and the late emperor of Ethiopia, Haile Selassie I, as their deliverer. The name Rastafarianism derives from Selassie's original name, Ras Tafari Makonnen. [*See* marijuana]

gunk: *See* morphine

H: *See* heroin

hallucinogens: Though many different drugs may induce auditory or visual hallucinations, the term hallucinogen is generally taken to mean a specific category of mind-altering drugs in which LSD, mescaline, peyote, psilocybin, marijuana and tetrahydrocannabinol-related compounds predominate.

Hallucinogenic drugs have been used in many parts of the world for more than 4,000 years, primarily in religious ceremonies. Hallucinogens such as LSD rose to popularity with the growth of the drug culture in the United States during the 1960s. Widespread use has declined greatly since the late '70s. Reactions to hallucinogens vary, depending on the dose and the user. This class of drugs tends to distort users' perceptions of time and space and may cause sensory crossovers; sight, for example, may be perceived as sound. Some images may be kaleidoscopic. Some users react to such sensory confusion with profound panic and anxiety, a "bad trip," and flashbacks may recur weeks or even months later. [*See* Hawaiian wood rose, ibogaine, LSD, marijuana, mescaline, morning glory, nutmeg, peyote, psilocybin, phencyclidine, sacred mushrooms, STP]

hard stuff: *See* heroin

harry: *See* heroin

hash: *See* hashish

hashish: This is the very potent, resinous extract of the female hemp plant, *Cannabis sativa*, from which virtually all forms of marijuana derive. Hashish is made by scraping resin from the plant or by boiling resin-covered parts of the plant in a solvent to extract the resin as a precipitate. It is the resin that contains tetrahydrocannabinol, THC, the active hallucinogen in cannabis. The resin is shaped into small lumps or cakes for smoking or eating. Liquid hashish, a distillate of the plant's parts, is much more powerful than even the resin—though potency of marijuana in all forms is dramatically affected by variety and growing conditions. Generally, the darker the color of the hashish, the higher is its THC content and, hence, its potency. Most hashish in the United States comes from Morocco, Afghanistan, Pakistan, Lebanon and Nepal. In the United States, hashish users most often smoke, rather than ingest, the drug dosage, so that intoxication can be more precisely controlled. The name hashish originates from Hasan-ibn-al-Sabbah, leader of a terrorist sect of Shiite Moslems in 11th-century Persia known as Hashishi. The word assassin also evolved from his name. Modern street names for hashish include black Russian, canned sativa, charas, goma de mota, hash, Lebanese, mahjuema, and soles. [*See* liquid hashish]

hashish oil: *See* hashish, liquid hashish

Hawaiian wood rose: A plant native to Asia and Hawaii with seeds that produce effects similar to LSD when eaten. The seeds of the baby Hawaiian wood rose are more powerful in this regard than the variety commonly known as large Hawaiian wood rose. [*See* hallucinogens, LSD]

hawk: *See* LSD

hay: *See* marijuana

haze: *See* LSD

H-caps: *See* heroin

hearts: *See* amphetamines

heaven: *See* cocaine

heaven dust: *See* cocaine

heavenly blues: Name of a popular variety of morning glory seeds. [*See:* hallucinogens, morning glory]

hemp: *See* marijuana

Henry: *See* heroin

her: *See* cocaine

herb: *See* marijuana

heroin: This well-known and powerful narcotic was first isolated from morphine in 1874 and then produced commercially in 1898 by Germany's Bayer Company. Bayer marketed the drug as a better pain reliever and cough suppressant than morphine and as offering relief from the symptoms of morphine and opium withdrawal. One of the new drug's most promising features was the fact that it appeared to be nonaddictive. Nearly 12 years passed before the medical world realized what thousands of people knew already: Heroin was at least as addictive as morphine. Authorities estimated that by 1910 the number of heroin addicts in the United States ranged from a half-million to one million. The Harrison Narcotics Act of 1914 taxed the manufacture, importation and distribution of heroin in an effort to discourage doctors from prescribing the drug. Ten years later, in 1924, manufacture of heroin was outlawed in the U.S. and control became the province of law enforcement authorities. So much heroin already had been manufactured for medical use that it took more than 20 years to deplete the nation's stocks. In fact, it took until 1956 for all remaining supplies of legally synthesized heroin in the United States to be surrendered by pharmacies and manufacturers. By then, illegal use of heroin was widespread; it had become the drug of choice among users of opiates. Prohibition had enhanced the value of the drug on the black market, and its reduced bulk compared with morphine and its increasing profitability made smuggling easier and highly lucrative. Until 1973, most heroin sold in the United States was derived from Southeast Asian opium that was converted to heroin in labs around Marseilles, France—the so-called French Connection—and then moved on the black market. Mexico, Iran, Afghanistan, Pakistan, India, Burma, Laos and Thailand are among the major sources of heroin today. There are an estimated 700,000 heroin addicts in the United States.

The effects of heroin vary widely, depending on the amount and frequency of use. When reasonably pure, heroin is a white powder. It can be snorted or smoked or mixed with a liquid and swallowed, but injection is most common because it produces the greatest intensity of feeling. The drug depresses the central nervous system and creates euphoria, and a sense of well-being as well as lethargy and drowsiness. Side effects range from constipation and nausea to diminished appetite and sex drive. Tolerance to heroin develops rapidly, and stronger, more frequent doses, "fixes," are needed to recreate the original euphoria and stave off withdrawal symptoms: restlessness, tremors, irritability, cramps, muscle pain and spasm, sweating, runny nose, nausea, vomiting, diarrhea and shortness of breath. Death from heart arrhythmia is a possibility during withdrawal. Though heroin-related deaths often are called overdoses, more often deaths actually amount to acute reactions to the combination of the drug with alcohol, barbiturates or any of a number of substances that are commonly used to "cut" the heroin before sale. Increasingly, heroin packets are found to include an extraordinarily potent synthetic drug called fentanyl, which dramatically increases the risk of overdose. [*See* analogs of fentanyl]

Since 1965, detoxification centers have had some success treating heroin addicts on maintenance programs revolving around regular use of methadone, an addicting heroin substitute. Methadone (dolophine hydrochloride) produces a longer-lasting euphoria than heroin, blocks the effect of the illegal narcotic and decreases the addict's cravings. Because methadone is taken orally, the addict's intravenous drug use may end, curtailing the risk of infections and exposure to diseases such as hepatitis and AIDS. Because methadone is available legally, the addict may break the cycle of criminal activity and association that usually accompanies heroin addiction. While methadone, too, is subject to abuse, controlled use of the drug generally is considered to be the most successful alternative to heroin addiction.

Street names for heroin include big bag, big H, black tar, blanco, blue thunder, bolsa, boy, bomb, brother, brown, brown rocks, brown sugar, caballo, carga, cat, chick, Chinese red, chiva, crap, cura, dogie, doojee, duji, dust, eighth, flea powder, garbage, godfather, goodfella, good stuff, H, hard stuff, harry, H-caps, henry, him, horse, hombre, jones, joy powder, junk, Mexican mud, mojo, muzzle, pack, poison, powder, pure, red chicken, red rock, scag, smack, stuff, tecata, thing, white boy, white junk, white stuff. [*See* Dolophine, morphine, opium]

heroin substitute: Depending on context, the term may be used to describe any narcotic drug that resembles heroin in form and effect, from methadone to designer drugs. [*See* designer drugs, Dolophine, heroin]

him: *See* heroin
hocus: *See* morphine
hog: *See* phencyclidine
hombre: *See* heroin
homegrown: *See* marijuana
hop: *See* opium
horse: *See* heroin
hydrocarbons: *See* inhalants
hyoscine: *See* scopolamine
ibogaine: A hallucinogenic stimulant derived from the roots of some plants native to Africa, Asia and South America. [*See* hallucinogens]

ice: Law enforcement officials began the 1990s fearing that this smokable form of methamphetamine would replace crack as the U.S. epidemic drug of the decade. Though ice has been known for more than 10 years in major cities from San Diego to New York, only in Hawaii has its abuse reached extensive proportions. Ice looks like crystal candy or rock salt, and is smoked in a glass pipe. The drug is manufactured easily and the euphoria it induces lasts from four to six hours, compared with crack's 20- or 30-minute high. For drug users ice is a more productive investment, but its aftermath is far worse. Users may experience irregular heartbeat, convulsions, severe depression, impaired speech, hallucinations and delusions. Chronic abuse can produce permanent brain damage and behavior resembling paranoid schizophrenia. Street names include crystal, crystal meth, crystal methedrine, freeze, glass, quartz. [*See* methamphetamine]

incentive: *See* cocaine
Indian hay: *See* marijuana
Indian hemp: *See* marijuana
inhalants: Sometimes referred to as deliriants, inhalants have been used and abused for thousands of years. It was common long ago to inhale the vapors of burning spices and herbs, for example, in certain religious ceremonies. Anesthetic gases such as chloroform, ether and nitrous oxide, discovered in the 18th century, were used recreationally long before they were used medicinally; inhalant parties were popular in the 19th century. Most inhalant abuse today involves either volatile hydrocarbons—distillates of petroleum or natural gas such as benzene, kerosene or gasoline—or organic solvents such as toluene, naphtha, carbon tetrachloride, acetone and cyclohexane. The latter abound in everyday household products—from varnish, lacquer, thinners and nail polish removers to glues, cements, cleaning solutions and aerosols. All inhalants quickly reach the lungs and bloodstream, and in small doses most produce a mild euphoria and light-headedness. Some inhalants depress the central nervous system, so heavy users risk respiratory collapse. High doses and prolonged abuse of some inhalants may induce nausea, headache, vomiting, nosebleeds, violent behavior, unconsciousness, and ultimately may damage the liver, kidneys, blood, bone marrow, heart, brain or chromosomes. [*See* amyl nitrite, butyl nitrite, nitrous oxide]

intsaga: In Africa, a word for marijuana. [*See* marijuana]
intanfu: In Africa, a word for marijuana. [*See* marijuana]
J: A joint, a marijuana cigarette. [*See* marijuana]

Jac-Aroma: Trade name of a room spray commonly abused as an inhalant. [*See* butyl nitrite, inhalants]

jam: *See* amphetamines, cocaine

Jamestown weed: *See* datura

Jane: As in Mary Jane, marijuana. [*See* marijuana]

jay smoke: *See* marijuana

Jim Jones: A marijuana joint laced with cocaine and soaked in PCP. [*See* cocaine, marijuana, PCP]

jimson weed: *See* datura

jelly beans: *See* amphetamines

joint: A marijuana cigarette. [*See* marijuana]

Jones: *See* heroin

joy juice: *See* chloral hydrate

joy powder: *See* cocaine, heroin

Juanita: Mexican for marijuana. [*See* marijuana]

juice: A smokable mixture of fentanyl analogs and cocaine. [*See* analogs of fentanyl]

junk: *See* heroin

ketamine hydrochloride: A fast-acting general anesthetic that was first used during the Vietnam War. Users heat liquid ketamine to produce a fine powder called "green" that is sprinkled on tobacco or marijuana and smoked for its effect as a depressant and hallucinogen. Slang reference is Vitamin K.

kibbles and bits: Street slang for a minute amount of cocaine or crumbs of crack cocaine. [*See* cocaine, crack]

kick sticks: Marijuana cigarettes. [*See* marijuana]

kif: In Africa, a word for marijuana. [*See* marijuana]

killer, killer weed: Used in reference to very powerful marijuana or marijuana that has been laced with phencyclidine, PCP. [*See* marijuana, phencyclidine]

kilter: *See* marijuana

King Kong pills: *See* barbiturates

KJ: *See* phencyclidine

knockout drops: *See* chloral hydrate

L: *See* LSD

lady: *See* cocaine

lady snow: *See* cocaine

laudanum: The Swiss alchemist and physician Phillippus Aureolus Paracelsus dissolved powdered opium in alcohol in 1541 to create a tincture he called laudanum, the first medicinal form of opium. Laudanum was used widely through the 19th century to relieve pain, manage dysentery, sedate nervous, traumatized or upset patients, and control coughing. [*See* opium]

laughing gas: *See* nitrous oxide

leapers: *See* amphetamines

Lebanese: *See* hashish

lid poppers: *See* amphetamines

lightning: *See* amphetamines

liquid hashish: A very powerful distillation of marijuana plant material that is added in small amounts to tobacco, food or alcohol. [*See* hashish]

locker room: *See* butyl nitrite

loco: *See* marijuana

loveboat: *See* phencyclidine

lovely: *See* phencyclidine

LSD: D-lysergic acid diethylamide tartrate 25. In 1943, a Swiss research chemist named Dr. Albert Hofmann accidentally ingested a minute amount—four-millionths of a gram—of a substance he and his partner, W.A. Stoll, had first distilled from ergot, a rye fungus, five years earlier. He was startled by the effect, which he described as "fantastic visions," and to be certain of its cause later took a much larger dose. His account of the experience was among the first formal descriptions of an acid trip. In the 1950s, the Central Intelligence Agency and the U.S. Army secretly used unsuspecting soldiers and civilians to test the drug's usefulness in brainwashing and chemical warfare. Meanwhile, a small group of psychiatrists and psychologists experimented briefly with LSD as a treatment for psychoses. Beyond those forays, no one showed much interest in LSD until Aldous Huxley rekindled public interest in psychedelic experiences with his book *The Doors of Perception* in 1954. Huxley's experience was based on the use of mescaline, which was not readily available. LSD, by comparison, could be derived from lysergic acid in a laboratory and it was much more powerful. The counterculture of the 1960s eagerly embraced LSD after zealous researchers, among them Harvard psychologist Timothy Leary, declared the powerful but nonaddicting drug a key to religious experience, insight and the creative self.

LSD in minute amounts causes hallucinations, heightens the user's senses, distorts time and can cause synesthesia—sensory crossovers in which a user may, in effect, "see" music and "hear" colors. LSD can unlock a user's deeply repressed memories, fears and anxieties, cause physical imbalance, severe nausea and vomiting, panic attacks and damaging psychotic episodes. Some evidence also links LSD with chromosome damage. Good trip or bad, a typical LSD experience lasts 12 to 14 hours, and "flashbacks," hallucinogenic recurrences, may occur later at any time.

Most of LSD's street names reflect its various forms: blotter acid, or tabs, small paper squares that have been soaked in LSD and, often, decorated with cartoon characters; cubes, sugar cubes containing LSD; microdot, tiny pellets of powder; windowpane, small gelatinous chips, and many others, including acid, barrels, beast, Big D, blue acid, blue cheer, blue heaven, blue mist, blue star, brown dots, California sunshine, cap, chief, chocolate chips, contact lens, cubes, cupcakes, D, deeda, domes, dots, electric Kool-Aid, flash, ghost, green dragon, hawk, haze, L, lysergide, mellow yellows, orange cubes, orange wedges, orange sunshine, paper acid, peace, pellets, pink owsley, purple haze, red dragon, red pyramid, royal blue, sacrament, strawberries, strawberry fields, sugar cubes, sunshine, tabs, ticket, twenty-five, wedges, white lightning, window pane, yellow. [*See* hallucinogens]

L-tryptophan: An amino acid occurring naturally in many foods, including meat and dairy products, L-tryptophan was used as a food supplement, sleep aid and for depression and weight control throughout the 1980s. Presuming the drug was safe, many people also took L-tryptophan supplements for insomnia, premenstrual syndrome, and stress reduction. Late in 1989, the Federal Drug Administration linked L-tryptophan to a rare, debilitating and sometimes fatal blood disorder called eosinophilia-myalgia syndrome, EMS. The disease is characterized by muscle pain so excruciating that patients often need hospitalization just to be given intravenous morphine. If left untreated, complete paralysis or severe damage to the heart, lungs and other organs can result. By March 1990, the Federal Drug Administration had recalled all L-tryptophan but some protein supplements, infant formulas, and special dietary foods in which small amounts are needed for nutrient fortification. By then, more than 1,400 cases of EMS had been confirmed, 19 people had died of the disease, and new cases were being reported to the Centers for Disease Control at the rate of 50 to 100 a month. Authorities suspect the cause of the epidemic may not be L-tryptophan itself but a contaminant in the product. Tracking the poison is extraordinarily difficult because all L-tryptophan sold in the U.S. is made in Japan by as many as six different manufacturers, each using a different procedure.

ludes: *See* methaqualone

lunchtime special: *See* DMT

lysergide: *See* LSD

M: *See* morphine

macon: In West Africa, a word for marijuana. [*See* marijuana]

maconha: In Brazil, a word for marijuana. [*See* marijuana]

magic mushrooms: *See* sacred mushrooms

mahjeuma: A concentrated form of hashish. [*See* hashish]

majoon, majoun, ma'jun: Indian words for marijuana. [*See* marijuana]

m and m: *See* analogs of amphetamines and methamphetamines, designer drugs

marijuana: Throughout the world, only alcohol, caffeine and nicotine are more commonly abused than marijuana, and in the United States, no other illegal drug is more popular. Marijuana is the dried upper section—flowering top, stems and leaves—of the Indian hemp plant, *Cannabis sativa*, a four- to eight-foot-tall leafy, herbaceous annual that grows wild in many parts of the world but best in hot, dry climates. Tetrahydrocannabinol (THC) is the psychoactive ingredient that gives users of marijuana a feeling of mild euphoria and reduced inhibitions. The drug is sometimes eaten or added to food, but is most commonly inhaled by smoking as a cigarette, or joint, or in a pipe.

Traditionally, Jamaican, South American and Southeast Asian marijuanas were considered the most powerful strains because they contained a high percentage of THC. In recent years, U.S.-grown marijuana has risen in popularity. This is partly due to the painstaking cultivation of sinsemilla, the flowering top of the unpollinated and seedless female marijuana plant. Prized for its potency, sinsemilla can have a THC content roughly triple that of most marijuana.

Some researchers believe chronic marijuana use may result in a psychological reliance on the drug's sedative and euphoric effects. For that reason, they see marijuana as a gateway to harder drugs. Current research focuses on the residual effects of marijuana consumption and the relationship between marijuana smoking and respiratory diseases, including lung cancer, since most users draw the smoke deep into their lungs. Those who argue for legalization, chiefly members of the National Organization for the Repeal of Marijuana Laws (NORML), suggest that marijuana is, if not entirely harmless, then at least no worse than alcohol.

Another group, the Alliance for Cannabis Therapeutics (ACT), has unsuccessfully pressed the government to reclassify marijuana so that it may be more readily prescribed as medicine. The drug is known to reduce the nausea and vomiting associated with some AIDS and cancer chemotherapies, and also has been shown to be beneficial to some victims of multiple sclerosis and glaucoma. The government, however, has approved the medical use of marijuana in only a handful of cases.

Marijuana has had hundreds of names, owing to its having been known as a drug since approximately 2737 B.C. Street references have included: Acapulco gold, ace, African black, Alice B. Toklas (marijuana cooked in a brownie), Aunt Mary, baby, bale, black gunion, bo, bomb, boo, brick, broccoli, bud, bush, Canadian black, cannabis, charge, Colombian, dagga, dawamesk, djamba, djoma, doobie, dope, dry high, duby, fatty, flowers, gage, ganga, gangster, ganja, gauge, giggleweed, gold, golden leaf, grass, green, grefa, greta, grifa, griffo, grillo, grunt, gunga, gungeon, gunja, hay, hemp, herb, homegrown, Indian hay, Indian hemp, intsaga, intanfu, J, Jane, jay smoke, joint, Juanita, kick sticks, kif, killer, killer weed, kilter, loco, macon, maconha, Mary, Mary Ann, Mary Jane, Mary Warner, Mary Weaver, meserole, Mexican brown, Mexican green, Mexican locoweed, M.J., mooca, moota, mooters, mootie, mota, mother, mu, muggles, muta, number, Panama gold, Panama red, pod, poke, pot, primo (marijuana cigarette laced with cocaine), ragweed, rainy day woman, red dirt, reefer, roach, root, rope, sinsemilla, smoke, snop, stick, Sweet Lucy, tea, Texas tea, twist, weed, wheat, yerba, Zacatecas purple.

Mary, Mary Ann, Mary Jane, Mary Warner, Mary Weaver: Obsolete references to marijuana. [*See* marijuana]

mash Allah: *See* opium

MDA: *See* analogs of amphetamines and methamphetamines, designer drugs

MDM: *See* analogs of amphetamines and methamphetamines, designer drugs

MDMA: This is Ecstasy, the so-called mellow drug, or the LSD of the '80s, which actually dates to 1914, when the drug was created. A mildly hallucinogenic stimulant, MDMA was used very little until psychotherapists dusted it off in the 1970s and started prescribing it for patients to stimulate empathy and insight. MDMA's reputed mildness and acceptance by health professionals, not to mention its having names such as Ecstasy and Essence, helped make the drug appealing. By 1985, MDMA was a favored recreational drug. Researchers have proven since that MDMA may cause liver damage, psychosis, heart problems and brain damage. Other names for the drug include Adam, E, EU41A, Eve, M and M, MDM, X and XTC. [*See* analogs of amphetamines and methamphetamines, designer drugs]

mellow yellows: *See* LSD

meperidine hydrochloride: This synthetic opiate, more commonly known by its trade name, Demerol, commonly is prescribed as a painkiller and sedative. It is one of the most widely used drugs in hospitals, particularly as an anesthetic in childbirth. Prolonged use of the drug leads to physical dependence. [*See* analogs of meperidine]

mescaline: This is the primary alkaloid in the peyote cactus and one of the earliest hallucinogens to be identified formally—in 1886 by the German pharmacologist Louis Lewin. The drug is derived from the small mescal buttons atop the cactus. Mescaline resembles LSD in its effect, but is milder and, unlike peyote, is not as apt to make the user nauseated. There is little demand for the drug. Street references include beans, big chief, buttons, cactus, cactus buttons, mesc, mescal, moon, and topi.

meserole: An outdated reference to marijuana that derives from the name of a 1940 jazz musician and marijuana peddler from Harlem, Mezz Mezzrow. [*See* marijuana]

meth: *See* methamphetamine

methadone: *See* Dolophine

methamphetamine: This white crystalline derivative of amphetamine is much stronger than its parent compound, and law enforcement authorities expect that this stimulant, in its various forms, is becoming the illegal drug of choice in the '90s. It is generally one-third to one-half of the price of cocaine, more readily available because it can be made synthetically in underground labs, and longer-lasting—four- to six-hour highs compared with less than an hour for cocaine. Methamphetamine originated with the amphetamine group of drugs in the 1930s as an aid in the treatment of narcolepsy. The German army in World War II gave soldiers methamphetamine, Methedrine pills, to combat fatigue. Thereafter, the drug also was prescribed as a short-term appetite suppressant, and for years it also was commonly used by long-haul truck drivers. The drug's ability to produce euphoria and a heightened sense of confidence rekindled its popularity in the '60s. Psychological dependence develops rapidly, driven by a desire to regain and perpetuate euphoria and a distorted sense of well-being. Prolonged use can produce profound behavioral changes—intense panic, aggressiveness and auditory and visual hallucinations. Users may develop a drug-induced psychosis that mirrors paranoid schizophrenia. Methamphetamine is taken in pill form (Methedrine), inhaled, injected or smoked. Street names are speed, crank, crystal meth, crystal methedrine, ice, glass, quartz, freeze. [*See* crank, ice]

methaqualone: This hypnotic sedative was developed in India in 1951 as an antimalarial drug and introduced in the United States in the mid-1960s for use in the treatment of anxiety and insomnia. Doctors believed the drug was not addictive and prescribed it widely until the early 1970s when it gained a solid foothold among drug abusers for its alleged ability to induce a sense of mellowness and enhance sexual gratification. In fact, the drug seems to have approximately the same effect on the central nervous system as alcohol. Tolerance develops quickly, and overdoses were numerous during the peak of the drug's popularity. By the 1980s, abuse of the drug was so common in the United States that it was taken off the market. Lookalike capsules now are made in Colombia and sold in the United States. Trade names include Biphetamine T, Optimil, Parest, Qs, Quaalude, Quacks, Quads, Somnafax and Sopor. Street names include ludes and soapers, or sopors.

Methedrine: A brand name of methamphetamine. [*See* methamphetamine]

methyl fentanyl: *See* analogs of fentanyl

Mexican brown: A better grade marijuana from Mexico. [*See* marijuana]

Mexican green: An inferior grade marijuana from Mexico. [*See* marijuana]

Mexican locoweed: Generally, a southwestern U.S. reference to marijuana. [*See* marijuana]

Mexican mud: *See* heroin

Mexican mushrooms: *See* sacred mushrooms

Mexican red: Illicit Seconal imported from Mexico. [*See* Seconal]

Mickey, Mickey Finn: *See* chloral hydrate

microdots: *See* LSD

Mike: A microdot of LSD. [*See* LSD]

mini-bennies: Benzedrine. [*See* amphetamines]

mini-whites: *See* amphetamines

Miss Emma: *See* morphine

Miss Morph: *See* morphine

M.J.: *See* marijuana

mojo: A probable reference to voodoo magic that translates, in drug parlance, to hard drugs, i.e., morphine, heroin or cocaine.

mooca: *See* marijuana

moocah: *See* morphine

moon: *See* peyote

moota: *See* marijuana

mooters, mootie: *See* marijuana

morning glory: The seeds of this common and pretty garden flower contain hallucinogens similar to LSD. With other hallucinogens, they have been used in certain Native American rituals and religious ceremonies in Mexico and the Southwest United States for hundreds of years. The ancient Aztecs of Central Mexico were the first to use morning glory seeds as hallucinogens, and their word "ololiuqui" is still used in general reference to all varieties of the flower's seeds. Modern manufacturers say they routinely coat the seeds with a substance that will induce nausea. The seeds are known commercially by the names of the flowers they produce—Heavenly Blues, Flying Saucers, Pearly Gates and Wedding Bells. [*See* hallucinogens]

morph: *See* morphine

morphine: A German pharmacist named Frederick W. Serturner was the first to isolate morphine from opium, around 1803. He named the drug after Morpheus, the Greek god of dreams and sleep. The drug was not actually used in medicine until the 1820s, and then it became popular quickly as a painkiller,

a panacea and also as a cure for opium addiction, which, of course, it was not. Morphine was widely available and liberally prescribed by doctors through the 1850s. During the Civil War the drug was a priceless asset in the treatment of casualties, but the result was a U.S. population of morphine addicts that was estimated to number about 400,000.

Heroin was first isolated from morphine in 1874, and in the next several decades, the new drug's potency and availability on the black market established it as the drug of choice among drug abusers. As controls tightened, the use of morphine gradually slipped back to the realm of medicine. The drug was not completely synthesized in the laboratory until 1952, and is very rarely found on the illegal market today. Morphine remains the most powerful pain-relieving medication known. Its effects last longest when taken orally, but injection produces almost immediate relief. Regular use leads quickly to tolerance and physical and psychological dependence. An overdose produces respiratory depression severe enough to cause coma and death. Slang references to morphine have included big M, birdie powder, dreamer, Emm, God's medicine, gunk, hocus, M, Miss Emma, Miss Morph, morph, moocah, morpho, morphy, white stuff. [*See* heroin, opium]

morpho: *See* morphine

morphy: *See* morphine

mota: *See* marijuana

mother: *See* marijuana

MPPP: A designer narcotic and a heroin substitute derived from meperidine. [*See* analogs of meperidine, designer drugs, MPTP]

MPTP: This is the infamous analog of meperidine known as "new heroin," a designer drug and a powerful neurotoxin that first surfaced in Bethesda, Md., in 1979. It was the accidental byproduct of a drug user's attempt to make the heroin substitute MPPP. He injected himself with his designer drug concoction and later developed symptoms of Parkinson's disease—uncontrollable tremors, drooling and paralysis, hallmarks of irreversible brain damage. MPTP was not formally identified until 1982, after the same unlikely symptoms struck young heroin users in San Jose, Calif., and investigators tracked the source of the drug to a home laboratory. [*See* analogs of meperidine]

mu: *See* marijuana

mud: *See* heroin

muggles: *See* marijuana

mushrooms: *See* sacred mushrooms

muta: *See* marijuana

muzzle: *See* heroin

nebbies: *See* barbiturates, Nembutal

Nembutal: The trade name of a much-abused sedative containing the barbiturate pentobarbitol. Commonly known as nebbies, nemmies, nemish, nimby, yellow bullets, yellow dolls, yellow jackets, yellows. [*See* barbiturates]

nemmies: *See* barbiturates, Nembutal

nemish: See barbiturates, Nembutal

nimbies: *See* barbiturates, Nembutal

new heroin: *See* analogs of meperidine, designer drugs, MPTP

nitrous oxide: The English theologian and scientist Joseph Priestly discovered nitrous oxide in 1776, but nearly a hundred years passed before it actually was used, with other agents, as an anesthetic in minor surgery. Nitrous oxide has been used in dentistry and oral surgery in this country for years. The drug is commonly known as laughing gas for its ability to induce hilarity, giddiness and hallucinations, but prolonged inhalation can depress breathing and cause coma and death. The gas is available in 8-gram metal cylinders called whippets.

nose candy: *See* cocaine

nose powder: *See* cocaine

number: *See* marijuana

numorphan: As a pain reliever, this semisynthetic derivative of morphine is nearly 10 times more powerful than its parent compound. The drug can be physically and psychologically addicting. It is sold as a solution, for injection, and as suppositories or pills; the latter are known popularly as blues.

nutmeg: A couple of spoonfuls of this common household spice dissolved in hot water and swallowed induces a mild euphoria, the effect of myristicin and elemicin, two hallucinogenic substances that are part of the spice. The fact that the user also has to put up with dizziness, nausea and vomiting makes abuse generally unappealing.

O: *See* opium

ololiuqui: *See* morning glory

op: *See* opium

opium: The air-dried juice from the unripened pod of the oriental poppy, *Papaver somniferum*, is gathered and formed into cakes for hardening and processing into this granddaddy of all narcotics. The opium poppy probably originated in Asia Minor. Opium was known in Mesopotamia and Assyria in 5000 B.C., and was used as an anesthetic by Egyptian physicians in 1500 B.C. The opium poppy was imported to China from India and the Middle East some time in the 7th century. Throughout the Middle East, opium was in use by the year 1200 as a medicine and an intoxicant. The Swiss alchemist and physician Phillippus Aureolus Paracelsus dissolved powdered opium in alcohol in 1541 to create a tincture he called laudanum, one of the first medicinal forms of opium used in the West. Laudanum was used throughout the 19th century as a sedative, cough suppressant, pain killer and an aid in the control of dysentery. Another tincture of opium, paregoric, which included camphor and alcohol, was used well into the 20th century to sedate teething infants and control diarrhea. Opium and its tinctures diminished as targets of abuse as its purer and more powerful derivatives, morphine and later heroin, gained popularity. Slang references include black pills, black stuff, brown mixture, brown stuff, canned stuff, hop, mash Allah, O, op, tar.

orange cubes: *See* LSD

orange wedges: *See* LSD

orange sunshine: *See* LSD

pack: *See* heroin

Panama gold: Variety of marijuana from Panama known for its potency. [*See* marijuana]

Panama red: Variety of marijuana from Panama known for its potency. [*See* marijuana]

paper acid: A reference to the way LSD is sold, in microdot doses on blotting paper. [*See* LSD]

paradise: *See* cocaine

paregoric: This tincture of opium, alcohol and camphor was first prepared in the early 18th century. Well into the 20th century mothers used paregoric to lessen infants' pain in teething, put them to sleep and control diarrhea. Paregoric is considered an old-fashioned drug today, but is still available by prescription. [*See* opium]

PCE: *See* analogs of phencyclidine, designer drugs

PCP: *See* phencyclidine

PCPY: *See* analogs of phencyclidine, designer drugs

peace: *See* LSD, phencyclidine

peace pill: *See* phencyclidine

peaches: Benzedrine tablets. [*See* amphetamines, benzedrine]

peanuts: *See* barbiturates

pearls: *See* amyl nitrite

pearly gates: The name of a popular variety of morning glory seeds. [*See* hallucinogens, morning glory]

pellets: Capsules of LSD. [*See* LSD]

PEPAOP: A designer drug first cousin of new heroin, or MPTP, the analog of meperidine which is known to cause irreparable brain damage resulting in symptoms mimicking Parkinson's disease. [*See* analogs of meperidine, designer drugs, MPTP]

pep pills: *See* amphetamines

Persian white: A powerful heroin substitute with a name intended to conjure up images of high-grade heroin from the Middle East. [*See* analogs of fentanyl, China white, designer drugs, synthetic heroin]

peyote: A small spineless cactus native to parts of

Mexico that is noteworthy for the hallucinogenic quality of its crown, or button, which is cut, dried and eaten or brewed in water to make a tea. The ancient Aztecs used peyote in religious ceremonies, and the practice is an integral part of the religious observances of some tribes today. Nearly half of the states allow the sacramental use of hallucinogens by organized congregations such as the Native American Church. Peyote contains eight active alkaloids, but it is primarily mescaline that produces the kaleidoscopic hallucinations associated with the drug. References include bad seed, big chief, buttons, cactus, full moon, P, peyotl, topi. [*See* hallucinogens]

peyotl: *See* peyote

phencyclidine: This unique drug is the only known psychoactive that affects all of the brain's neurotransmitters at the same time, making phencyclidine a depressant, a stimulant, an anesthetic and a hallucinogen. The immediate effect on the user is unpredictable, at best, and the health risks are major, ranging from slurred speech to organic brain dysfunction, convulsions, coma, panic attacks, psychotic reactions, flashbacks and heart and lung failure. Phencyclidine can be snorted, eaten or injected, but is most often smoked in cigarettes, called super kools or sherms. Phencyclidine is sometimes used in combination with marijuana or cocaine, and has shown up with cocaine in a freebase form known as ghostbusters or spacebase. The drug debuted in a Los Angeles lab in 1965 and was used as an animal tranquilizer until it was found to be too dangerous. Thereafter, the illicit use of phencyclidine spread throughout the country and the world. Street names include amoeba weed (parsley soaked in PCP), angel dust, animal trank, aurora borealis, blast, DOA, elephant, hog, Jim Jones (marijuana and cocaine cigarette laced with PCP), killer weed, KJ, loveboat, lovely, PCP, peace, Peace pill, rocket fuel, sherm (cigarette laced with PCP), supergrass, super kools (tobacco cigarette laced with PCP), superweed, tic tac, whack.

phennies: *See* barbiturates
phenos: *See* barbiturates
pink ladies: *See* barbiturates
pink owsley: *See* LSD
pinks: *See* barbiturates, Seconal
PMA: *See* analogs of amphetamines and methamphetamines, designer drugs
poison: *See* cocaine, heroin
poppers: *See* amyl nitrite
pod: *See* marijuana
poke: *See* marijuana
pops: *See* codeine
pot: *See* marijuana

powder: *See* cocaine, heroin
primo: Marijuana joint laced with cocaine. [*See* cocaine, marijuana]
psilocybin: *See* hallucinogens, sacred mushrooms
pure: *See* heroin
purple haze: *See* LSD
purple hearts: *See* amphetamines, barbiturates, Dexamyl
Q's: For Quaaludes. [*See* methaqualone]
Quaaludes: *See* Methaqualone
quacks, quads: For Quaaludes. [*See* methaqualone]
quartz: *See* ice
ragweed: *See* marijuana
rainbows: *See* Tuinal
rainy day woman: A marijuana cigarette. [*See* marijuana]
red apples: *See* barbiturates, Seconal
red birds: *See* barbiturates, Seconal
red bullets: *See* barbiturates, Seconal
red chicken: Chinese heroin. [*See* heroin]
red devils: *See* barbiturates, Seconal
red dirt marijuana: Marijuana growing wild. [*See* marijuana]
red dolls: *See* barbiturates, Seconal
red dragon: *See* LSD
red lillies: *See* barbiturates, Seconal
red pyramid: *See* LSD
red rock: Granular Chinese heroin. [*See* heroin]
reds: *See* barbiturates, Seconal
reds and blues: *See* Tuinal
reefer: *See* marijuana
rippers: *See* amphetamines
roach: The butt of a marijuana cigarette. [*See* marijuana]
rock: *See* cocaine, crack
rocket fuel: *See* phencyclidine
root: *See* marijuana
rope: *See* marijuana
roses: Benzedrine tablets. [*See* benzedrine]
royal blue: *See* LSD
rush: *See* butyl nitrite
sacrament: *See* LSD
sacred mushrooms: Any of a number of hallucinogenic mushrooms used sacramentally for centuries by some Indian cultures in Mexico, the American Southwest and Central America. The mushrooms are eaten; the effect is similar to that of mescaline or LSD, due to the presence of the alkaloid psilocybin, a fast-acting hallucinogen that's more powerful than mescaline but generally less powerful than LSD. Common references include magic mushrooms, Mexican mushrooms, mushrooms, shrooms. [*See* hallucinogens]
scag: *See* heroin
schmack: A general reference to drugs; from the Yiddish.

schoolboy: *See* codeine

scopolamine: A nonbarbiturate sedative and muscle relaxant occurring naturally in henbane and certain plants of the potato family, including datura and belladonna. The drug has been known since ancient times and used in potions and poisons. Scopolamine also has been used in interrogation as a so-called truth serum, because it induces a state similar to hypnosis. Scopolamine is used occasionally as a tranquilizer and is a common ingredient in certain nonprescription sleep aids. Toxic doses cause death by paralysis, coma and respiratory failure. The drug also is known as hyoscine.

seccy, seccies: *See* Seconal

secobarbitol: *See* Seconal

Seconal: The brand name of the fast-acting sedative secobarbitol, a commonly abused barbiturate. The drug is known as seccy or seccies, seggy or seggies, but more commonly as F-40, pinks, red apples, red birds, red bullets, red devils, red dolls, red lillies or reds—after the bright red color of the pills. [*See* barbiturates]

seggy, seggies: *See* Seconal

sherms: Slang name for a tobacco cigarette laced with PCP; also called super kools. [*See* phencyclidine]

shrooms: *See* sacred mushrooms

sinsemilla: The flowering top of the female marijuana plant, stripped of its leaves and unpollinated, has a tetrahydrocannabinol (THC) concentration approximately five times higher than normal. Marijuana grown, cultivated and properly harvested in this fashion is referred to as sinsemilla and prized for its potency. [*See* marijuana]

sleepers: *See* barbiturates

smack: *See* heroin

smoke: *See* marijuana

snappers: *See* amyl nitrite

sniff: *See* cocaine

snop: *See* marijuana

snow: *See* cocaine

snowbird(s): *See* cocaine

snowcaine: *See* fake coke

snowflake: *See* freebase

soapers: *See* methaqualone

soles: *See* hashish

sopors: *See* methaqualone

spacebase: Freebase cocaine combined with phencyclidine. [*See* cocaine, freebase, phencyclidine]

sparkle plenties: Reference to amphetamines derived from a *Dick Tracy* comic strip character named Sparkle Plenty. [*See* amphetamines]

sparklers: *See* amphetamines

speed: *See* amphetamines, methamphetamines

speedball: A blend of smokable heroin and crack. The combination produces an intense euphoria, but a calmer reaction and post-use depression is minimized. On the East Coast of the United States, the drug is often referred to as crank. [*See* crack, crank, heroin]

splash: *See* amphetamines

star dust: *See* cocaine

steroids: *See* anabolic steroids

stick: *See* marijuana

stinkweed: *See* datura

STP: The origin of STP, dimethoxy-methamphetamine—and its name—is still a mystery. It may have been first adopted by California motorcycle gangs who named it after the popular motor oil additive STP—Scientifically Treated Petroleum. Another story identifies the name as the creation of Harvard psychologist and drug guru Timothy Leary: STP—"serenity, tranquility and peace." Some people believe STP actually was an experimental drug synthesized by Dow Chemical Co., and that the formula for it was leaked or stolen. Regardless, STP is unique. The drug is similar to amphetamine and mescaline, but more powerful than either. STP's effects mimic LSD, but last much longer—three or four days, according to some users—as opposed to eight or ten hours. STP was first reported in the chemical literature in 1964, but did not reach public attention until the spring of 1967 when drug users in San Francisco began displaying psychotic reactions to the drug. [*See* DOM, hallucinogens]

strawberries: *See* LSD

strawberry fields: *See* LSD

stuff: *See* heroin

stumblers: *See* barbiturates

sugar: *See* cocaine

sugar cubes: *See* LSD

sunshine: *See* LSD

supercaine: *See* fake coke

super grass: Generally PCP. [*See* phencyclidine]

super kools: Cigarettes laced with PCP. [*See* phencyclidine]

superweed: *See* phencyclidine

sweet Lucy: *See* marijuana

sweets: *See* amphetamines

synthetic heroin: A dealer's "synthetic heroin" is much more likely to be one of the more powerful designer drugs that are masqueraded as heroin substitutes. Heroin can be produced from scratch in a laboratory, but the process is expensive and yield is low. [*See* analogs of fentanyl, analogs of meperidine, China white, designer drugs, MPPP, MPTP, Persian white]

tabs: Reference to small tabs of paper impregnated with LSD. [*See* LSD]

T and B: This is a pill that combines the antihistamine pyribenzamine with Talwin, a moderately powerful synthetic opiate that has about one-third the potency of morphine. The pills sometimes are called "T's and blues" after the color of the 50-mg. tablet.

Tango and Cash: This mixture of heroin and the extraordinarily potent synthetic tranquilizer fentanyl surfaced early in 1990 in New York, New Jersey and Connecticut and quickly accounted for at least 17 overdose deaths. [*See* analogs of fentanyl, designer drugs, heroin]

tar: *See* opium

tea: *See* marijuana

tecata: *See* heroin

tens: Amphetamines in 10-mg. tablets. [*See* amphetamines]

tetrahydrocannabinol: This resinous hallucinogen, actually delta-9-tetrahydrocannabinol, is the active ingredient in cannabis, or marijuana; the higher the concentration, the more potent the marijuana. It is commonly known by its initials, THC. Aurora borealis is an occasional slang reference. [*See* hashish, marijuana]

Texas tea: *See* marijuana

Thai stick: Powerful, seedless marijuana from Vietnam and Thailand that is sold in bundles resembling sticks. [*See* marijuana, sinsemilla]

THC: *See* tetrahydrocannabinol

thing: *See* heroin

thorn apple: *See* datura

thrusters: *See* amphetamines

thumb: A fat marijuana cigarette. [*See* marijuana]

ticket: *See* LSD

tic tac: *See* phencyclidine

topi: *See* peyote

truck drivers: *See* amphetamines

TMA: A synthetic hallucinogen derived from mescaline that is more powerful than its parent compound but less potent than LSD. [*See* analogs of amphetamines and methamphetamines, designer drugs]

tooies: *See* Tuinal

toot: *See* fake coke

topi: *See* peyote

torpedo: General reference to an alcoholic drink laced with knockout drops. [*See* chloral hydrate]

tuies: *See* Tuinal

Tuinal: A hypnotic sedative that combines the barbiturates amobarbitol and secobarbitol, Amytal and Seconal, respectively. Slang references, based on the name and the blue and orange color of the capsules, are rainbows, reds and blues, tooies, tuies. [*See* Amytal, barbiturates, Seconal]

twist: *See* marijuana

twenty-five: A shorthand reference to the full and formal name of LSD—d-lysergic acid diethylamide tartrate 25. [*See* LSD]

2,5-DMA: *See* analogs of amphetamines and methamphetamines, designer drugs

ultracaine: *See* fake coke

uppers, uppies, ups: *See* amphetamines

vipe: *See* marijuana

vitamin K: *See* ketamine hydrochloride

vitamin Q: *See* methaqualone

wake-ups: *See* amphetamines

wallbangers: *See* methaqualone

water: Amphetamine, especially methamphetamine. [*See* amphetamines]

Wedding Bells: Name of a popular variety of morning glory seeds. [*See* hallucinogens, morning glory]

wedges: *See* LSD

weed: *See* marijuana

whack: *See* phencyclidine

wheat: *See* marijuana

whippets: *See* nitrous oxide

white: *See* cocaine

white boy: *See* heroin

white crosses: *See* amphetamines

white junk: *See* heroin

white lady: Cocaine or heroin. [*See* cocaine, heroin]

white lightning: *See* LSD

white powder: *See* cocaine

whites: *See* benzedrine

white stuff: *See* heroin, morphine

white tornado: *See* freebase

window pane: *See* LSD

X: *See* analogs of amphetamines and methamphetamines, designer drugs, MDMA

XTC: *See* analogs of amphetamines and methamphetamines, designer drugs, MDMA

yellow: *See* LSD

yellow bullets: *See* barbiturates, Nembutal

yellow dolls: *See* barbiturates, Nembutal

yellow jackets: *See* barbiturates, Nembutal

yellows: *See* barbiturates, Nembutal

yerba: *See* marijuana

yopo: *See* Bufotenine

Zacatecas purple: A potent, purple-seeded marijuana from Zacatecas, a state in central Mexico. [*See* marijuana]

SUGGESTED REFERENCES AND CONTACTS:

Drug Abuse: An Introduction, Howard Abadinsky. Chicago: Nelson-Hall Inc., 1989.

Encyclopedia of Drug Abuse, Evans, O'Brien, Cohen and Fine. New York: Facts On File, 2nd ed., 1990.

Narcotics and Drug Abuse A to Z. Jamaica, N.Y.: Croner Publications, Inc., 1991 (updated quarterly).

Pathway Society, 1659 Scott Blvd. No. 30, Santa Clara, CA 95050, (408) 244-1834. Staff will answer reporters' inquiries on street drugs and narcotics abuse.

National Clearinghouse for Alcohol and Drug Information, P.O. Box 2345, Rockville, MD 20852, (301) 468-2600. Provides publications; has recent information on illegal drugs and alcohol abuse.

Drug Enforcement Administration, Washington, D.C. 20537-0001, (202) 307-1000. Handles inquiries from reporters and offers booklets about drugs and drug enforcement. The booklet *Drugs of Abuse* provides clear factual information about illegal drugs, side effects and regulation. Every June, the DEA also publishes *The NNICC Report*, the annual report of the National Narcotics Intelligence Consumers Committee, which provides clear and factual country-by-country information on the production of illegal drugs and their supply to the United States.

American Council for Drug Education, 204 Monroe St., Rockville, MD 20850, (301) 294-0600. Publishes booklets and brochures with information about street drugs, abuse, treatment and prevention.

National Institute on Drug Abuse, 5600 Fisher's Lane, Room 10A39, Rockville, MD 20857, (301) 443-6245 (press information). Answers reporters' questions about drugs and drug abuse.

PRESCRIPTION AND NONPRESCRIPTION DRUGS

DRUG RANKINGS

TOP 50 PRESCRIPTION DRUGS DISPENSED BY U.S. COMMUNITY PHARMACIES/1991*

Rank	Product	Marketer
1	Amoxil	Beecham
2	Premarin	Wyeth-Ayerst
3	Zantac	Glaxo Pharmaceuticals
4	Lanoxin	Burroughs Wellcome
5	Xanax	Upjohn
6	Synthroid	Boots
7	Ceclor	Lilly
8	Seldane	Merrell Dow
9	Procardia	Pfizer
10	Vasotec	Merck Sharp & Dohme
11	Cardizem	Marion
12	Tenormin	ICI Pharmaceuticals
13	Naprosyn	Syntex
14	Dyazide	Smith Kline & French
15	Ortho-Novum 7/7/7	Ortho
16	Capoten	Squibb
17	Calan	Searle
18	Prozac	Dista
19	Tagamet	Smith Kline & French
20	Augmentin	Beecham
21	Proventil	Schering
22	Mevacor	Merck Sharp & Dohme
23	Lopressor	Geigy
24	Ventolin	Allen & Hanbury's
25	Cipro	Miles
26	Provera	Upjohn
27	Trimox	Apothecon
28	Micronase	Upjohn
29	Dilantin	Parke-Davis
30	Amoxicillin	Biocraft
31	Tylenol w/codeine	McNeil
32	Lasix	Hoechst-Roussel
33	Ortho-Novum	Ortho
34	Voltaren	Geigy
35	Darvocet-N	Lilly
36	Polymox	Apothecon
37	Triphasil	Wyeth-Ayerst
38	Halcion	Upjohn
39	Vicodin	Knoll
40	Theo-Dur	Schering
41	Inderal	Wyeth-Ayerst
42	Lopid	Parke-Davis
43	Coumadin	Dupont
44	Ibuprofen	Boots
45	Feldene	Pfizer
46	Diabeta	Hoechst-Roussel
47	Glucotrol	Roerig
48	Lo/Ovral	Wyeth-Ayerst
49	Micro-K	Wyeth-Ayerst
50	Hismanal	Janssen

* Rankings are based on new and refill prescriptions, all strengths.
Compiled by Pharmaceutical Data Services, Scottsdale, Ariz.
[For descriptions of drugs, *see* below, Common Prescription and Nonprescription Drugs]

COMMON PRESCRIPTION AND NONPRESCRIPTION DRUGS

This listing includes drugs that have been identified by Pharmaceutical Data Services of Scottsdale, Ariz., as being among the 50 most frequently dispensed prescription drugs. It also contains common nonprescription drugs (such as aspirin), drugs that are sometimes in the news because they relate to mental or emotional conditions, drugs that are noteworthy because they are new, controversial or subject to abuse, and descriptions of drug types.

Brand names are capitalized. Generic names are lower-cased.

Accutane: *See* isotretinoin
acetaminophen: analgesic
    Acetaminophen is a painkiller that is available without prescription, either by its generic name or under more than 25 brand names (including Anacin-3, Panadol, Liquiprin and Tylenol). It is often combined with other nonprescription drugs (such as caffeine) or with prescription drugs (such as codeine).
acyclovir: antiviral
    Acyclovir is used to treat herpes, shingles, cold sores and chicken pox. Some research has also indicated that it may prolong the life of AIDS patients by controlling cytomegalovirus, which is associated with AIDS.
Adapin: *See* doxepin
adrenocorticosteroid hormones (adrenocorticoids)
Adrenocorticosteroid hormones are drugs that are similar to hormones produced naturally by the adrenal glands. The naturally occurring hormones affect many physiological conditions, including fluid balance, body temperature and reaction to

191

inflammation. Adrenocorticoids are used to augment the body's hormone production, either when production is low or when the physical demands of illness require extraordinarily high levels of the hormones. They are used to treat a variety of disparate illnesses, including endocrine and rheumatic disorders, asthma, certain cancers, certain gastrointestinal disorders and respiratory diseases. Their antiinflammatory effect is useful in the treatment of arthritis, dermatitis and poison ivy. They can depress the immune system. [See prednisone]

albuterol: bronchodilator

Often prescribed in inhalant form to relieve wheezing and shortness of breath caused by lung diseases, including asthma. Also available as tablet, syrup and injection. Brand names include Proventil and Ventolin.

alcohol: central nervous system depressant

The form of alcohol used in alcoholic beverages is ethanol (also known as ethyl alcohol or grain alcohol). It is the only form suitable for human consumption. Denatured alcohol, used in industry, is ethanol to which toxic substances have been added. Isopropyl alcohol is used in automobile antifreeze and as rubbing alcohol. It can be fatal if swallowed. Methanol (also called methyl alcohol or wood alcohol) is used as a solvent and in antifreeze. It is extremely poisonous and can be fatal in relatively small amounts. Ingesting even tiny amounts can cause blindness. Prolonged exposure of the skin to the liquid, or inhalation of the fumes, can also cause blindness.

Ethanol depresses the central nervous system. It impairs perception, judgment, coordination and alertness and reduces anxiety and inhibition. It causes drowsiness and, in high doses, can even cause unconsciousness or death. Heavy, long-term use can damage the brain, liver and heart. Alcohol is physically and psychologically addictive, although some people may be more predisposed to addiction than others. Genetics may play a role in the disease, as do familial, cultural and psychological factors.

Alcoholism is defined as drinking to such a degree that major parts of one's life (such as work, relationships, health and safety) are seriously and repeatedly affected. A person may be an alcoholic even though he or she does not drink all day or every day.

Alcoholism is widely regarded as a chronic disease. Those who are physically dependent on alcohol may experience delirium tremens (delirium, trembling, hallucinations and/or seizures) upon withdrawal. Delirium tremens can be fatal, even with hospital care.

Treatment includes peer and psychological counseling, support groups such as Alcoholics Anonymous, antianxiety drugs to reduce withdrawal symptoms, and use of disulfiram (Antabuse), a drug that causes an extremely unpleasant reaction to alcohol, including headache and nausea. [See disulfiram]

alprazolam: sedative/hypnotic

Alprazolam is a prescription drug used to treat anxiety and symptoms of anxiety associated with depression. It is one of a group of drugs called benzodiazepines, all of which are central nervous system depressants. The group includes diazepam (brand name Valium), chlordiazepoxide (Librium) and flurazepam (Dalmane), among many others. Alprazolam is sometimes abused for its sedative effect. An overdose of alprazolam, or taking it with other benzodiazepines or alcohol, can cause unconsciousness or death. It is known commonly by its brand name, Xanax.

Alurate: See barbiturates

Alzapam: See lorazepam

amantadine: antiparkinsonism medication/antiviral

Amantadine is a prescription drug used to treat the symptoms of Parkinson's disease, a degenerative brain disorder that produces trembling lips and hands, rigidity, body tremors and a shuffling gait. Amantadine is believed to increase the level of dopamine, a brain chemical that is low in patients with Parkinsonism. It improves muscle control and decreases rigidity.

Amantadine is also used to prevent or treat respiratory infections caused by the influenza type A virus. It is not effective against other types of viruses. Brand names include Symadine and Symmetrel.

Amaphen: See butalbital

Amitril: See amitriptyline

amitriptyline: antidepressant

Amitriptyline is a tricyclic antidepressant. Brand names include Amitril, Elavil, Emitrip, Endep and Enovil. [See antidepressants]

amobarbital: See barbiturates

amoxapine: antidepressant

Amoxapine is one of a group of prescription drugs known as tricyclic antidepressants that are believed to relieve the symptoms of mental depression by increasing the levels of certain chemicals used to transmit nerve signals in the brain. It is available under the brand name Asendin.

Amoxil: See amoxicillin

amoxicillin: antibiotic

Amoxicillin, a type of penicillin, is used to treat a variety of bacterial infections, particularly those of the middle ear, upper and lower respiratory tracts and urinary tract. It is available under a variety of brand names, the most common of which are Amoxil, Trimox and Polymox. It is also available combined with clavulanic acid, which prevents the amoxicillin from breaking down in the body. The combination is available under the brand name Augmentin.

amphetamines: central nervous system stimulants

Amphetamines are prescribed to treat children with Attention Deficit Disorder because they increase attention or decrease restlessness in these children, who have difficulty concentrating. Use of amphetamines for this purpose has become somewhat controversial, amid claims that the drugs are sometimes prescribed when other treatment, including counseling, might be more appropriate. Amphetamines are also used to treat narcolepsy. They were formerly frequently prescribed to aid weight loss, but this use is no longer recommended because they are highly addictive and are prone to abuse. Amphetamine drugs include: amphetamine (available generically), dextroamphetamine (available generically and under the brand names Dexedrine, Ferndex, Oxydess II and Spancap No. 1) and methamphetamine (available under the brand names Desoxyn and Desoxyn Gradumet). [*See* amphetamines in chapter entitled Common Illegal Drugs, page 171]

amyl nitrite: antianginal

Amyl nitrite is used as an inhalant to relieve the pain of angina. It relaxes blood vessels, which increases the supply of blood and oxygen to the heart and eases the heart's workload. It is packaged in cloth-covered glass capsules, which can be crushed with the fingers when needed. Pain relief can be felt in from one to five minutes. Amyl nitrite capsules are also sold illegally as "poppers" and are used for a brief "high." [*See* antianginals; *see also* amyl nitrite, illegal drugs, chapter entitled Common Illegal Drugs, page 171)

Amytal: *See* barbiturates

analgesics Analgesics are medications that relieve pain but do not cause a loss of consciousness. They include nonprescription drugs (such as aspirin and acetaminophen) and prescription drugs (such as codeine).

Antabuse: *See* disulfiram

antianginals Angina is chest pain caused by an insufficient supply of blood (and, therefore, oxygen) to the heart. The heart, like any muscle, requires oxygen to function properly. Antianginal drugs increase the oxygen supply. They include vasodilators (like nitroglycerin), calcium channel blockers (like nifedipine) and beta-adrenergic blocking agents (like nadolol). [*See* amyl nitrite, beta-andrenergic blocking agents, calcium channel blockers, nifedipine, nitroglycerin (systemic), nitroglycerin (topical)]

antibiotics Antibiotics are used to treat bacterial infections. They interfere with the growth of bacteria by interrupting the bacteria's normal biochemical functions. Louis Pasteur laid the foundation for the development of antibiotics in the mid-19th century when he showed that one microorganism can kill another. Use of antibiotics became widespread during World War II, when penicillin and streptomycin were mass-produced for the first time. Antibiotics, which were initially produced from molds and other microorganisms, can now also be produced synthetically. They are not effective against viruses. [*See* penicillins]

anticholinergics Anticholinergic drugs slow the action of the bowel and decrease stomach action. They are used to relieve bowel spasms.

antidepressants Antidepressants are used to relieve the symptoms of mental depression, which can include sleep disturbances, loss or gain of weight, listlessness, inability to concentrate or make decisions, despondency and thoughts of suicide. Major mental depression (as opposed to ordinary, transient feelings of sadness) is believed to be caused by a chemical imbalance within the brain. The imbalance has been attributed to genetic factors, emotional stress or a combination of both. Drug therapy seeks to establish a normal level of the brain chemicals, called neurotransmitters, that transmit nerve impulses.

One group of antidepressants, called tricyclics because of the three rings in their chemical structure, affect the levels of the neurotransmitters norepinephrine or serotonin in the brain. Another group, the monoamine oxidase (MAO) inhibitors, block the action of monoamine oxidase, which results in higher levels of the neurotransmitters norepinephrine and serotonin. Tricyclics include imipramine (brand name Tofranil) and amitriptyline (Elavil). MAO inhibitors include tranylcypromine (brand name Parnate). Tricyclics and MAO inhibitors may cause drowsiness. Patients receiving MAO inhibitors must avoid wine or aged cheese, which contain chemicals that can cause adverse reactions. They are also in danger of developing high blood pressure.

In 1988, the federal Food and Drug Administration approved the use of another prescription drug, fluoxetine (brand name Prozac), for the treatment of depression. Fluoxetine appears to have fewer side effects than tricyclics or MAO inhibitors. It increases the level of serotonin in the brain, a neurotransmitter related to a feeling of well-being. [*See* amitriptyline, fluoxetine, imipramine, tranylcypromine, trimipramine]

antihistamines Antihistamines are drugs used to treat or prevent the symptoms of hay fever and other allergies. They counter the effects of histamine, a chemical released by the body during an allergic reaction. Some are also used to prevent motion sickness. Because some cause drowsiness as a side effect, they are sometimes used as a sleep aid. They are available in prescription and nonprescription varieties, under scores of brand names. [See chlorpheniramine, dimenhydrinate, diphenhydramine, terfenadine]

antihypertensives Antihypertensives are used to treat high blood pressure (hypertension), which can damage the brain, eyes, heart or kidneys if left untreated. The drugs work in several ways. Some block nerve impulses that cause arteries to constrict. Others slow the heart rate and ease the force of contraction. Others reduce the body's level of aldosterone, a hormone that raises blood pressure. They are frequently prescribed with diuretics. They are available under many brand names, the most common of which is Vasotec. [See diuretics]

aprobarbital: See barbiturates

Asendin: See amoxapine

aspirin: analgesic/anti-inflammatory

Aspirin is a common nonprescription drug used to reduce mild to moderate pain, fever and inflammatory conditions. Because it also reduces the risk of blood clots, it is used as a preventive measure by patients who are at risk of suffering heart attacks or small strokes. It is often combined with other nonprescription drugs (such as caffeine in the brand-name product Anacin) and with prescription drugs (such as codeine or oxycodone). It can cause stomach irritation. Brand names include Bayer, Easprin, Ecotrin, Empirin and Measurin. [See codeine, oxycodone]

astemizole: antihistamine

Astemizole is used to treat allergic conditions such as hay fever and hives. It is often prescribed for patients who cannot tolerate the drowsiness that other types of antihistamines can cause. It is available under the brand name Hismanal. [See antihistamines]

atenolol: beta-adrenergic blocking agent

Atenolol is prescribed to treat high blood pressure and angina. It is available under the brand name Tenormin. [See beta-adrenergic blocking agents]

Ativan: See lorazepam

Augmentin: See amoxicillin

Aventyl: See nortriptyline

azidothymidine: See AZT

AZT: anti-AIDS drug

AZT is the primary drug approved by the Federal Drug Administration to combat Acquired Immune Deficiency Syndrome directly. It is not a cure for the disease, but has been shown to slow its progress, and may even delay onset of symptoms. It was identified as a possible AIDS medication in 1985 and became widely available in mid-1987, six years after the first AIDS cases were diagnosed.

AZT (also known as zidovudine and azidothymidine) is produced by Burrough Wellcome Co., Research Triangle Park, N.C., which has exclusive rights. The drug can cost patients $5,000 to $10,000 per year, which has raised concern about its availability to patients who have little or no insurance.

The Human Immunodeficiency Virus (HIV), which causes AIDS, reduces the number of a type of white blood cell. Because white blood cells fight infection, this leaves the body vulnerable to opportunistic infections and cancers, which can cause the patient's death. Drug therapies and research attempt to help patients in one of three ways: by bolstering the immune system (using drugs such as interferon and interleukin); by treating the opportunistic infections and cancers; and by attacking the HIV virus itself.

According to the Centers for Disease Control, more than 70,000 Americans had died of AIDS by early 1990. Because of the gravity of the problem, research is proceeding rapidly and new drugs are constantly undergoing testing and clinical trials. [See interferon, interleukin]

Barbased: See barbiturates

Barbita: See barbiturates, phenobarbital

barbiturates Barbiturates are so named because they are derived from barbituric acid. They are central nervous system depressants that have a tranquilizing effect in low doses. In higher doses they cause sleep, and in still higher doses they act as anticonvulsants and anesthetics. They are often prescribed as sleeping pills. When used to relieve insomnia, they become ineffective within several weeks, prompting some users to increase doses. Taking large doses of barbiturates, or mixing barbiturates with alcohol or other central nervous system depressants, can cause unconsciousness or death. Barbiturates include amobarbital (brand name Amytal), apropbarbital (Alurate), butabarbital (Barbased, Butalan, Buticaps, Butisol and Sarisol No. 2), mephobarbital (Mebaral), metharbital (Gemonil), pentobarbital (Nembutal), phenobarbital (Barbita, Luminal and Solfoton), secobarbital (Novosecobarb and Seconal), secobarbital and amobarbital combination (Tuinal) and talbutal (Lotusate).

Barbiturates are also used in certain states as a method of legal execution. A lethal dose is administered to the prisoner through an intravenous tube in the arm.

Benadryl: *See* diphenhydramine

benzotropine: anticholinergic/antiparkinsonism agent Benzotropine is a prescription drug used to improve muscle control and decrease stiffness in patients with Parkinson's disease. It is also used to control adverse reactions to certain medications, including some tranquilizers. [*See* anticholinergics]

beta-adrenergic blocking agents Beta-adrenergic blocking agents (commonly called beta blockers) are used to lower blood pressure and relieve angina (chest pain). Some are also used to treat migraine headaches and irregular heartbeats. They work by blocking beta receptors—areas of body cells that respond to chemical stimulation. Stimulating the beta receptors causes the heart to beat faster and harder, among other effects. Beta blockers prevent this stimulation, which reduces the work the heart must do. [*See* antianginals, atenolol, metoprolol, propranolol]

birth control pills Oral contraceptives are usually a combination of an estrogen and a progestin. Some pills contain only a progestin, however. The pills work by changing the hormone levels in a woman's body, which prohibits pregnancy. Although they are safe for most users, the risk of adverse side effects increases after age 35, especially among smokers. Side effects include weight gain, headaches, nausea and blood clots. They are available under many brand names, the most common of which are Lo/Ovral, Ortho-Novum, Ortho-Novum 7/7/7, and Triphasil. [*See* estrogens, progestins]

brand name drugs Brand names are registered trademarks held by drug companies to distinguish their products from the chemically equivalent products produced by other companies. Often there are many brand names for the same drug. For example, Deltasone, Liquid Pred, Merticorten, Orasone and Panasol are all brand names for the drug prednisone. When a company develops and patents a drug, it gains the exclusive right to market that drug until its patent expires. While the patent is in effect, the drug is available only under one brand name. When the patent expires, other companies are free to sell the drug under their own brand names or under its generic name. [*See* generic drugs]

brompheniramine: antihistamine Brompheniramine is a common ingredient in many over-the-counter allergy remedies. It appears under many brand names, including Chlorphed, Diamine and Dimetane. [*See* antihistamines]

Buspar: *See* buspirone

buspirone: antianxiety agent Buspirone is a prescription drug used to treat anxiety disorders. It is commonly available under the brand name Buspar.

Butalan: *See* barbiturates

butabarbital: *See* barbiturates

butalbital: barbiturate Butalbital is a prescription drug that frequently is combined with pain relievers such as acetaminophen, aspirin, codeine and hydrocodone. Caffeine is sometimes added as well. Common brand names for combination forms include Amaphen, Fioricet, Fiorinal, Medigesic Plus, Phrenilin and Sedapap. [*See* barbiturates]

Buticaps: *See* barbiturates

Butisol: *See* barbiturates

caffeine: stimulant Caffeine is a mild stimulant found naturally in coffee beans, tea leaves and cola nuts. It can also be produced synthetically. In large amounts, or in people who are particularly sensitive, it can cause insomnia, heart irregularities and anxiety. It is found in both prescription and over-the-counter drugs. It broadens bronchial airways, which makes it useful in treating asthma, and it decreases blood flow to the brain, which makes it useful in treating migraine headaches. It frequently is combined with analgesics, such as aspirin, because it increases their effectiveness.

Calan: *See* verapamil

calcium channel blockers Calcium channel blockers are prescribed to reduce chest pain (angina). They relax blood vessels by slowing the flow of calcium to muscle cells. The decreased calcium causes blood vessels to dilate, which increases the supply of blood and oxygen carried to the heart. [*See* antianginals]

Calm X: *See* dimenhydrinate

Capoten: *See* captopril

captopril: antihypertensive Captopril, a prescription drug, dilates blood vessels, which lowers blood pressure. It is available under the brand name Capoten. [*See* antihypertensives]

carbamazepine: anticonvulsant Carbamazepine is a prescription drug used to treat seizure disorders and to relieve neuralgia (nerve pain). Brand names include Epitol and Tegretol.

Cardizem: *See* diltiazem

Ceclor: *See* cefaclor

cefaclor: antibiotic Cefaclor is a cephalosporin antibiotic used to treat a wide variety of bacterial infections, including those of the middle ear, urinary tract and respiratory tracts. It is available under the brand name Ceclor.

chlordiazepoxide: sedative/hypnotic

Chlordiazepoxide is a prescription drug used to treat nervousness, anxiety and alcohol withdrawal. It is one of a group of drugs called benzodiazepines, all of which are central nervous system depressants. The group includes diazepam (brand name Valium) and flurazepam (Dalmane), among many others. This drug, when used improperly or for long periods, has the potential for abuse. When taken in excess, or with other central nervous system depressants (including alcohol, other sedatives, tranquilizers and narcotics), it can cause unconsciousness or death. Brand names include Libritabs, Librium, Lipoxide, Mitran, Reposans and Sereen. It is also available in combination with other drugs. Chlordiazepoxide and amitriptyline (available under the brand name Limbritol) are used to treat mental depression accompanied by anxiety. Chlordiazepoxide and clidinium (available under the brand names Clindex, Clinoxide, Clipoxide, Librax and Lidox) are used to calm the digestive system and reduce stomach acid. [See sedatives]

chlorpheniramine: antihistamine

Chlorpheniramine is a common ingredient in many over-the-counter allergy remedies. It appears under many brand names, including Chlor-Trimeton and Teldrin. [See antihistamines]

chlorpromazine: tranquilizer

Chlorpromazine was the first drug widely prescribed for the treatment of mental disorders. It is used to relieve the symptoms of psychosis, the manic phase of manic-depressive disorder and severe behavioral problems in children. It is also sometimes used to treat tetanus, relieve anxiety before surgery and to control severe hiccups and vomiting. Brand names include Sonazine, Thorazine and Thor-Prom. [See tranquilizers]

cimetidine: gastric acid inhibitor

Cimetidine is a prescription drug used to treat duodenal and gastric ulcers and other digestive disorders. It reduces the amount of acid produced by the stomach. It is available under the brand name Tagamet.

Cipro: See ciprofloxacin

ciprofloxacin: antibiotic

Ciprofloxacin is a prescription drug used to treat a wide variety of bacterial infections. It is available under the brand name Cipro. [See antibiotics]

clorazepate: sedative/hypnotic

Clorazepate is a prescription drug used to relieve anxiety and treat seizures and alcohol withdrawal. It is one of a group of drugs called benzodiazepines, all of which are central nervous system depressants. The group includes diazepam (brand name Valium), chlordiazepoxide (Librium) and flurazepam (Dalmane), among many others. It

has the potential for abuse and can cause unconsciousness or death if used in excess or with other central nervous system depressants, including alcohol or tranquilizers. It is available under the brand name Tranxene. [See sedatives]

cocaine: local anesthetic

Cocaine, which is widely used as an illegal drug, has a legal use as well. When applied to the skin (in areas such as the nose, mouth or throat) it causes numbing. It is used for surgery or to permit pain-free examination. It is used only under the direct supervision of a physician. It is not available to patients as a prescription drug.

codeine: analgesic/cough suppressant

Codeine is a narcotic, available only by prescription, that acts on the central nervous system to relieve mild to moderate pain and to suppress coughing. It is frequently combined with other medications, such as expectorants or aspirin. Codeine, like morphine, is derived from opium. It is addictive, causing physical and psychological dependence. Withdrawal symptoms include muscle aches, diarrhea, nausea, vomiting, shivering, trembling, runny nose, irritability and sleep disorders.

Coumadin: See warfarin

cyclosporin: immunosuppressant

Cyclosporin is used by organ transplant patients to help prevent rejection of the organ. Normally, the body's immune system rejects foreign matter. This is a protective mechanism that allows the body to fight infection. This same process can cause the body to reject transplanted kidneys or livers or hearts, however. Cyclosporin suppresses the activity of the immune system, allowing the body to accept the foreign organ. As a side effect, it also decreases the body's ability to fight infection.

Dalmane: See flurazepam

Darvocet-N: See propoxyphene

Demerol: See meperidine

Depo-Provera: See medroxyprogesterone

deprenyl: antiparkinsonism medication

Deprenyl appears to slow the progress of Parkinson's disease in some patients in the early stages of the disease. When used with the drug levodopa (l-dopa) it has produced moderate improvement in some patients with more advanced disease. Deprenyl was approved by the Food and Drug Administration in October 1989. Outside of research studies, it may be used only in combination with standard levodopa therapy.

DES: See diethylstilbestrol

desipramine: antidepressant

Desipramine is one of a group of prescription drugs known as tricyclic antidepressants that are believed to relieve the symptoms of mental depression by increasing the levels of certain chemicals used to transmit nerve signals in the brain. Brand names include Norpramin and Pertofrane.

DiaBeta: *See* glyburide

diazepam: sedative/hypnotic

Diazepam is a prescription drug used to treat anxiety, seizures, muscles spasms and alcohol withdrawal. It is one of a group of drugs called benzodiazepines, all of which are central nervous system depressants. The group includes chlordiazepoxide (Librium) and flurazepam (Dalmane), among many others. It has the potential for abuse and can cause unconsciousness or death if used in excess or with other central nervous system depressants, including alcohol or tranquilizers. Brand names include Valium and Vazepam. [*See* sedatives]

diclofenalac: nonsteroidal anti-inflammatory

Diclofenalac is used to relieve the pain, swelling and stiffness of rheumatoid arthritis and osteoarthritis. It is also prescribed for menstrual cramps. It is available under the brand name Voltaren.

diethylpropion: appetite suppressant

Diethylpropion is prescribed to help dieters by temporarily suppressing appetite. It can help some patients start a diet, but its effectiveness lasts only a few weeks. Brand names include Tenuate and Tepanil.

diethylstilbestrol: estrogen

Diethylstilbestrol (DES) is a synthetic estrogen that is used in hormone replacement therapy and in birth control pills. In very high doses, it is also used as a so-called "morning-after pill." It can prevent pregnancy if taken within three days of intercourse. The federal Food and Drug Administration has never approved it for this use, but the fact that it is a legally available drug allows doctors to prescribe it as they see fit. It is often prescribed for rape victims who fear that they may become pregnant. (Pills that combine estrogen and progesterone are also sometimes used for this purpose, in extremely high doses.) The long-term effects of DES, when used in this way, are unknown.

DES has been shown to be linked to an increased incidence of cancer in the daughters of women who took it during pregnancy. It was prescribed frequently from the late 1940s to the mid-1960s to prevent miscarriage and other problems associated with pregnancy. DES daughters are at higher risk of cancer of the vagina and cervix. Some also have structural abnormalities of the uterus, which may interfere with pregnancy. Mothers and daughters who have been affected by DES have formed groups to provide information and support in many states. [*See* estrogens]

digoxin: digitalis medicine

Digoxin is one of a group of medications that were derived originally from the foxglove plant (*Digitalis purpurea*). The drugs are used to treat heart failure and irregular heartbeats. They slow the pulse and increase the strength of heart contractions. The drugs include digoxin (available under the brand name Lanoxin), deslanoside (brand name Cedilanid-D) and digitoxin (brand name Crystodigin). They are sometimes improperly prescribed for weight reduction. Because of their cardiac effect, they can be extremely dangerous when improperly prescribed.

Dilantin: *See* phenytoin

Dilaudid: *See* hydromorphone

diltiazem: calcium channel blocker

Diltiazem is a prescription drug used to prevent angina. It is available under the brand name Cardizem. [*See* calcium channel blockers]

dimenhydrinate: antihistamine

Dimenhydrinate is a common ingredient in over-the-counter preparations for the prevention of motion sickness. Brand names include Calm X, Dramamine and Motion-Aid.

diphenhydramine: antihistamine

Diphenhydramine is a common ingredient in many over-the-counter allergy and sleep remedies. In its syrup form it is used to calm coughing. It appears under many brand names, including Benadryl, Benylin Cough, Compoz, Nervine Nighttime Sleep-Aid, Nytol with DPH and Sominex. [*See* antihistamines]

disulfiram: antialcoholic

Disulfiram is prescribed to help patients overcome alcohol abuse problems by discouraging them from drinking. They experience extremely unpleasant side effects if they drink while taking the drug. Side effects can include nausea and vomiting, headache, profuse sweating, weakness, flushing, blurred vision, dizziness, confusion, fast heartbeat and chest pain. It is available under the brand name Antabuse.

diuretics Diuretics, commonly called water pills, are used to decrease the amount of water and salt in the body. As a result, they are also useful in lowering blood pressure. They are often used in combination with antihypertensives, drugs used to treat high blood pressure. Most diuretics work on the kidneys, causing them to increase output. They are available under many brand names, the most common of which is Dyazide. [*See* antihypertensives]

doxepin: antidepressant

Doxepin is one of a group of prescription drugs known as tricyclic antidepressants that are believed to relieve the symptoms of mental depression by increasing the levels of certain chemicals used to transmit nerve signals in the brain. Brand names include Adapin and Sinequan.

Dramamine: *See* dimenhydrinate

Durapam: *See* flurazepam

Dyazide: *See* diuretics

Elavil: *See* amitriptyline

enalapril: *See* antihypertensives

ergoloid mesylates: anti-Alzheimer medication

Ergoloid mesylates (available under the brand name Hydergine) is the only medication specifically approved for the treatment of Alzheimer's disease. It is also used to treat changes in mood, memory and behavior caused by circulatory problems to the brain. A study in the *New England Journal of Medicine* (August 1990) questioned its effectiveness in the treatment of Alzheimer's disease, however. It is supposed to reduce memory loss and other symptoms of dementia that accompany the disease. The study, by researchers at the University of Colorado, concluded that it was useless as an Alzheimer's drug, and in some cases made the disease worse. The five-year study was paid for by the drug's manufacturer, Sandoz Pharmaceuticals Corp. of East Hanover, N.J.

estrogens Estrogens are hormones that regulate the menstrual cycle and sexual development in females. They are prescribed to augment the natural supply of estrogens when the body does not produce enough of its own, as in menopause. They are also used to treat certain types of breast cancer in men and women, to treat certain types of prostate cancer in men and to help prevent bone weakening (osteoporosis) in women after menopause. They are used in birth control pills, combined with progesterone. The generic names include chlorotrianisene, diethystilbestrol, estradiol, conjugated estrogens, esterified estrogens, estrone, estropipate, ethinyl estradiol and quinestrol. Estrogens are available under dozens of brand names, the most common of which is Premarin. [*See* birth control pills, progestins]

Etrafon: *See* perphenazine

Feldene: *See* piroxicam

Fioricet: *See* butalbital

Fiorinal: *See* butalbital

fluoxetine: antidepressant

Fluoxetine is a prescription drug used to treat mental depression. In many patients it causes loss of appetite as a side effect. Because of this, it is sometimes prescribed as a weight-reducing aid. Its effects in this regard are not uniform or permanent, however. In fact, some patients gain weight while taking this drug. It is available under the brand name Prozac. Some patients have claimed that they experienced unprompted rages while taking the drug, becoming violent with themselves or others. In August 1991, the Food and Drug Administration rejected a request to ban the drug, saying that data did not prove a link between the drug and violent behavior. The request for the ban had come from a group affiliated with the Church of Scientology. [*See* antidepressants]

flurazepam: sedative/hypnotic

Flurazepam is a prescription drug used to treat insomnia. It is one of a group of drugs called benzodiazepines, all of which are central nervous system depressants. The group includes diazepam (brand name Valium) and chlordiazepoxide (Librium), among many others. When taken in excess or with other central nervous system depressants (including alcohol and tranquilizers), it can cause unconsciousness or death. Brand names include Dalmane and Durapam.

Foscavir: AIDS drug

Foscavir is used to treat cytomegalovirus retinitis, a viral infection that causes blindness in AIDS patients. It was approved by the Food and Drug Administration Sept. 27, 1991. Astra Pharmaceuticals of Sweden makes the drug.

furosemide: diuretic/antihypertensive

Furosemide is a prescription drug used to lower blood pressure and reduce fluid accumulation in the body. It is available under several brand names, the most common of which is Lasix. [*See* antihypertensives, diuretics]

ganciclovir: AIDS drug

Ganciclovir is used to treat cytomegalovirus retinitis, a viral infection that causes blindness in AIDS patients.

gemfibrozil: lipid-lowering drug

Gemfibrozil lowers the level of cholesterol and triglycerides in the blood. It is available under the brand name Lopid.

generic drugs Generic drugs are medications sold under a chemical name instead of a brand (or trade) name. They are supposed to be chemically equivalent to the brand-name product. The same drug may be available in both generic and brand-name forms. For example, amoxicillin is the generic name for a common antibiotic. It is also available as Amoxil, Larotid, Polymox, Trimox, Utimox and Wymox. All are registered brand names that are owned by different manufacturers and are used to distinguish their amoxicillin from that produced by other companies. Generic drugs are often less expensive than their brand-name counterparts because they do not have the advertising and promotional expenses of the brand-name products.

Although generic and brand-name drugs are supposed to be chemically equivalent, there has been some controversy concerning that issue. In 1989, the federal Food and Drug Administration reported that it had uncovered serious manufacturing flaws among several large manufacturers of generic drugs. The FDA also said the companies had circumvented the proper testing and evaluation process. [*See* brand name drugs]

glipizide: oral antidiabetic

Glipizide, which reduces the amount of sugar in the blood, is used to treat diabetes that cannot be controlled by diet alone. It is effective against diabetes that occurs in adulthood (known as non-insulin-dependent diabetes mellitus or maturity-onset diabetes or Type II diabetes). It is not effective against juvenile-onset diabetes. It is available under the brand name Glucotrol. [*See* insulin]

Glucotrol: *See* glipizide

glyburide: oral antidiabetic

Glyburide, which reduces the amount of sugar in the blood, is used to treat diabetes that cannot be controlled by diet alone. It is effective against diabetes that occurs in adulthood (known as non-insulin-dependent diabetes mellitus or maturity-onset diabetes or Type II diabetes). It is not effective against juvenile-onset diabetes. Brand names include DiaBeta and Micronase. [*See* insulin]

Halcion: *See* triazolam

Haldol: *See* haloperidol

haloperidol: tranquilizer

Haloperidol is a major tranquilizer used to treat psychosis, the manic phase of manic-depressive disorder, severe behavioral problems in children and Tourette's syndrome (a rare neurological disorder characterized by involuntary utterances, movements and tics). It is available under the brand name Haldol. [*See* tranquilizers]

Hismanal: *See* astemizole

hydrocodone: narcotic

Hydrocodone is used to relieve pain and to quiet coughing. It is used in dozens of prescription pills and cough syrups, combined with a variety of antihistamines, expectorants, decongestants and analgesics. It is available under a variety of brand names, the most common of which is Vicodin, a hydrocodone and acetaminophen combination. [*See* narcotics]

hydromorphone: narcotic

Hydromorphone is a prescription drug used to relieve moderate to severe pain. It is available under the brand name Dilaudid. [*See* narcotics]

ibuprofen: analgesic/anti-inflammatory

Ibuprofen is a painkiller that also reduces inflammation. It is available as an over-the-counter drug or, in greater strength, as a prescription. It is used to relieve mild pain of many types and to relieve the inflammation of arthritis, gout, bursitis and tenonitis. It is also used to treat menstrual pain. Over-the-counter brand names include Advil, Haltran, Ibuprin, Medipren, Midol 200, Nuprin, Pamprin-IB and Trendar. Prescription brand names include Ifen, Motrin and Rufin.

imipramine: antidepressant

Imipramine is a tricyclic antidepressant. It is also used to treat bedwetting in children. Brand names include Janimine, Tipramine and Tofranil.

Inderal: *See* propranolol

insulin: antidiabetic

Insulin is a hormone produced by the islets of Langerhans in the pancreas. It is used to reduce the level of glucose (sugar) in the blood. When the body does not produce enough insulin, the resulting chemical imbalance can cause serious effects, including kidney disease, blindness, circulatory problems and even death. Some diabetic patients are able to regulate their glucose level through diet or oral antidiabetic drugs. When this is not possible, they must receive injections of insulin. The drug cannot be taken in pill form because stomach acid destroys its effect. It is effective in the treatment of juvenile-onset and adult-onset diabetes.

interferon The drug interferon is a synthetic version of a type of protein produced by the body to fight infections and tumors. It is used to treat certain kinds of cancer and genital warts, and has been used to treat AIDS patients. [*See* AZT]

interleukin The drug interleukin is a synthetic version of a natural protein that is important in blood production and the body's immune system. It is used to treat certain kinds of cancer and has been used to treat AIDS patients.

ipecac: emetic

Ipecac causes vomiting. It is a nonprescription syrup used to treat drug overdoses or poisoning.

isotretinoin: anti-acne medication

Isotretinoin is taken orally for severe, cystic acne that has not responded to other therapy. It can cause serious birth defects when taken by pregnant women. A Food and Drug Administration epidemiologist has estimated that nearly 1,000 babies have been born with birth defects since 1982 due to the drug. The manufacturer, Roche Dermatologics division of Hoffmann-LaRoche, has claimed that the FDA estimate is greatly overstated.

Lanoxin: *See* digoxin

Lasix: *See* furosemide

levodopa: antiparkinsonism medication

Levodopa is a prescription drug used to treat the symptoms of Parkinson's disease, a degenerative brain disorder that produces trembling lips and hands, rigidity, body tremors and a shuffling gait. Levodopa is converted in the body to dopamine, a brain chemical that is low in patients with Parkinsonism. Brand names include Dopar and Larodopa.

levothyroxine: thyroid hormone

Levothyroxine is prescribed to replace or augment natural thyroid hormones when they are lacking due to disease or surgery. Thyroid hormones regulate the body's metabolic rate. It is available under several brand names, the most common of which is Synthroid.

Librium: *See* chlordiazepoxide

lithium: mood stabilizer

Lithium is a prescription drug used to control the manic phase of bipolar disorder (also called manic-depressive illness). Manic-depressive patients have severe mood swings, from extreme excitement in the manic phase to despair in the depressive phase.

Lo/Ovral: *See* birth control pills

Lopid: *See* gemfibrozil

Lopressor: *See* metoprolol

lorazepam: sedative/hypnotic

Lorazepam is a prescription drug used to treat anxiety and the anxiety that is associated with depression. It is one of a group of drugs called benzodiazepines, all of which are central nervous system depressants. The group includes diazepam (brand name Valium), chlordiazepoxide (Librium) and flurazepam (Dalmane), among many others. When taken in excess, or with other central nervous system depressants (including alcohol) it can cause unconsciousness or death. Brand names include Alzapam, Ativan and Loraz. [*See* sedatives]

lovastatin: cholesterol-lowering agent

Lovastatin is used, with a dietary program, to reduce the level of fat in the blood. It is available under the brand name Mevacor.

loxapine: antipsychotic

Loxapine is prescribed to relieve symptoms of mental illnesses, including psychosis. It acts by blocking certain chemicals that transmit nerve signals in the brain. It is available under the brand name Loxitane.

Loxitane: *See* loxapine

medroxyprogesterone: hormone

Medroxyprogesterone is a synthetic version of the female hormone progesterone. It is used to treat abnormal menstrual bleeding, painful menstruation and lack of menstruation. It is available under several brand names, the most common of which is Provera.

The brand name Depo-Provera has been mentioned frequently in the press because of its use as a treatment for male sex offenders. It, like other female hormones, has been prescribed in an effort to decrease sex drive. This practice is sometimes called "chemical castration," although the effects are not permanent. The drug's effectiveness, and the civil-rights implications of its use, are controversial issues. [*See* progestins]

Mellaril: *See* thioridazine

meperidine: analgesic

Meperidine is a narcotic used to relieve moderate to severe pain. Brand names include Demerol and Pethadol. [*See* narcotics]

mephobarbital: *See* barbiturates

metharbital: *See* barbiturates

methadone: analgesic

Methadone is a narcotic used to relieve moderate to severe pain. It is also prescribed for narcotics addicts, to prevent or minimize withdrawal symptoms when they discontinue their use of illegal drugs. When they are free of illegal drugs, they must then break their physical and psychological dependence on methadone, or continue to take maintenance doses of methadone for the rest of their lives. It is available under the brand names Dolophine and Methadose.

methylphenidate: stimulant

Methylphenidate is a central nervous system stimulant used to treat Attention Deficit Disorder in children (hyperactivity). It decreases restlessness in children who are overactive and cannot concentrate for appropriate amounts of time. It is also prescribed for patients who have narcolepsy (sudden attacks of deep sleep or an uncontrollable desire to sleep). It is available under the brand name Ritalin.

metoprolol: beta-adrenergic blocking agent

Metoprolol is used to treat high blood pressure and angina and to prevent additional heart attacks in heart attack patients. It is available under the brand name Lopressor. [*See* beta-adrenergic blocking agents]

Mevacor: *See* lovastatin

Micro-K: *See* potassium chloride

Micronase: *See* glyburide

minoxidil (systemic): antihypertensive

Minoxidil is prescribed in pill form to lower high blood pressure. It is available under the brand name Loniten. [*See* antihypertensives]

minoxidil (topical): hair-growth stimulant

When a 2-percent solution of minoxidil is applied to the scalp it stimulates hair growth in some men who are balding. It is not effective in all men. The hair remains only as long as treatments last. It is a prescription drug, available under the brand name Rogaine.

moricizine: antiarrhythmic

Moricizine is used to treat heartbeat irregularities, which are blamed for hundreds of thousands of deaths each year. The drug was developed in the Soviet Union in 1964. It is the first Soviet drug licensed by a U.S. pharmaceutical company and approved by the Food and Drug Administration. Du Pont received federal approval to market the drug in June 1990. The Soviet government will get royalties of 4 percent of sales. It is available under the brand name Ethmozine.

morphine: analgesic

Morphine is a narcotic prescribed to relieve moderate to severe pain. Brand names include MS Contin, MSIR, RMS and Roxanol. [See narcotics]

Naprosyn: See naproxen

naproxen: analgesic/anti-inflammatory

Naproxen is a prescription painkiller that also reduces inflammation. It is used to relieve mild pain of many types and to relieve the inflammation of arthritis, gout, bursitis and tenonitis. It is also used to treat menstrual pain. Brand names include Anaprox and Naprosyn.

narcotics Narcotics are strong painkillers that also affect mood and behavior. They include codeine, morphine, opium, meperidine, methadone and their derivatives. All narcotics are addictive. Although they have many medical uses, they are also the subject of considerable abuse. The street drug heroin is a derivative of morphine. Medically, narcotics are used to lessen pain, to induce sleep and to treat diarrhea. Overdoses can cause respiratory failure and death. [See Common Illegal Drugs, page 171]

Navane: See thiothixene

Nembutal: See barbiturates

nicotine Nicotine is an extremely poisonous chemical that is found in tobacco. Two or three drops of the pure substance can be fatal to an adult if placed on the tongue. Only about one-fiftieth of that amount reaches the bloodstream from smoking a cigarette. Nicotine can be habit-forming, which means that giving up smoking requires more than changing habits. It requires physical readjustment as well. People who try to quit smoking experience irritability, headaches, fatigue and insomnia as a result of nicotine withdrawal. Nicotine gum and transdermal patches are available by prescription to help smokers through withdrawal by allowing them to taper off their daily "dose" of nicotine.

nifedipine: calcium channel blocker

Nifedipine is a prescription drug used to treat angina. It is available under several brand names, the most common of which is Procardia. [See antianginals, calcium channel blockers]

nitroglycerin (systemic): antianginal

Nitroglycerin is used to treat angina (chest pain). It dilates the blood vessels, which increases the oxygen supply to the heart. It is available in several forms. Tablets that are placed under the tongue are effective quickly and are used to relieve pain after it has started. Oral spray also is used in this way. Tablets and capsules that are swallowed are slower acting. They are used to prevent pain. The drug is available under many brand names, including Klavikordal, Niong, Nitro-Bid Plateau Caps, Nitrolingual and Nitrospan. [See antianginals, nitroglycerin (topical)]

nitroglycerin (topical): antianginal

Nitroglycerin ointment and patches are applied to the skin to prevent angina (chest pain). The medication is absorbed through the skin. Like systemic nitroglycerin, it dilates the blood vessels and increases the oxygen supply to the heart. It is not fast-acting. It is available under many brand names, including Deponit, Nitrodisc, Nitro-Dur, Nitrol and Transderm-Nitro. [See antianginals, nitroglycerin (systemic)]

Norplant: birth-control implant

Norplant consists of six matchstick-size plastic capsules that are implanted in the upper arm. They release a synthetic progesterone (levonorgestrel) which acts as a contraceptive. The implants, which are inserted under local anesthetic in a doctor's office, are effective for five years.

nortriptyline: antidepressant

Nortriptyline is one of a group of prescription drugs known as tricyclic antidepressants that are believed to relieve the symptoms of mental depression by increasing the levels of certain chemicals used to transmit nerve signals in the brain. Brand names include Aventyl and Pamelor.

oral contraceptives: See birth control pills

Ortho-Novum: See birth control pills

Ortho-Novum 7/7/7: See birth control pills

oxazepam: sedative/hypnotic

Oxazepam is a prescription drug used to relieve anxiety, including that associated with depression or alcohol withdrawal. It is one of a group of drugs called benzodiazepines, all of which are central nervous system depressants. The group includes diazepam (brand name Valium), chlordiazepoxide (Librium) and flurazepam (Dalmane), among many others. When taken in excess, or with other central nervous system depressants (including alcohol), it can cause unconsciousness or death. It is available under the brand name Serax.

oxycodone: analgesic

Oxycodone is a narcotic prescribed to relieve moderate to severe pain. It is available under the brand name Roxicodone. It is available combined with acetaminophen, under the brand names Percocet and Tylox. It is also available combined with aspirin, under the brand names Codoxy and Percodan. [See narcotics]

Pamelor: See nortriptyline

penicillins: antibiotics

Penicillins are antibiotics that fight a wide range of bacterial infections by damaging the bacteria's cell walls, preventing them from growing or multiplying. They are not effective against viruses, fungi or parasites. Although consumers often speak of "penicillin" as though there were only one such drug, there are actually many penicillins. The different varieties are used to treat different types of bacterial infections. They include amoxicillin, ampicillin, antibiotics, carbenicillin, cloxacillin, dicloxacillin, penicillin G and penicillin V.

pentazocine: analgesic

Pentazocine is a narcotic prescribed to relieve moderate to severe pain. It is combined with naloxone to prevent abuse. Naloxone has no effect when pentazocine is taken in the prescribed pill form. If it is converted to a liquid and injected, however, the naloxone blocks the action of pentazocine in the bloodstream. It is available under the brand name Talwin NX. [*See* narcotics]

pentobarbital: *See* barbiturates

Percocet: *See* oxycodone

Percodan: *See* oxycodone

perphenazine: tranquilizer

Perphenazine is prescribed to relieve the symptoms of psychosis, the manic phase of manic-depressive disorder and serious behavioral problems in children. It is available under the brand name Trilafon. When combined with amitriptyline, a tricyclic antidepressant, it is used to treat anxiety and depression. The combination is available under the brand names Etrafon and Triavil. [*See* amitriptyline, tranquilizers]

Pethadol: *See* meperidine

phenmetrazine: anorectic

Phenmetrazine is an appetite suppressant. It is prescribed to help patients establish new eating patterns during the first few weeks of dieting. It is effective only for approximately three to 12 weeks. It is available under the brand name Preludin.

phenobarbital: sedative/anticonvulsant/hypnotic

Phenobarbital is a barbiturate, one of a group of drugs that depress the activity of the central nervous system. It is prescribed to relieve anxiety, to control convulsive seizures and to cause sleep. Phenobarbital, like other barbiturates, can be habit-forming. It is available under the brand names Barbita, Luminal and Solfoton. [*See* barbiturates]

phenytoin: anticonvulsant

Phenytoin is prescribed to control epilepsy. It is available under several brand names, the most common of which is Dilantin.

Phrenilin: *See* butalbital

piroxicam: analgesic/anti-inflammatory

Piroxicam is prescribed to relieve the pain and inflammation caused by certain types of arthritis, gout, bursitis and tendinitis. It is available under the brand name Feldene.

Polymox: *See* amoxicillin

potassium chloride: potassium replacement

Potassium chloride is prescribed to prevent or treat potassium deficiency, which often is caused by diuretics. It is available under a variety of brand names, the most common of which is Micro-K.

prazepam: sedative/hypnotic

Prazepam is prescribed to relieve anxiety. It is one of a group of drugs called benzodiazepines, all of which are central nervous system depressants. The group includes diazepam (brand name Valium), chlordiazepoxide (Librium) and flurazepam (Dalmane), among many others. When taken in excess, or with other central nervous system depressants (including alcohol), it can cause unconsciousness or death. It is available under the brand name Centrax. [*See* sedatives]

prednisone: adrenocorticosteroid hormone

Prednisone is prescribed to treat a variety of illnesses, including asthma, certain cancers, blood diseases, endocrine imbalances, rheumatic disorders, eye disorders, respiratory diseases, severe allergic reactions, inflammations (including arthritis and skin rashes), and gastrointestinal disturbances. Brand names include Deltasone, Liquid Pred, Meticorten, Orasone, Panasol-S, Prednicen-M and Sterapred. [*See* adrenocorticosteroid hormones]

Preludin: *See* phenmetrazine

Premarin: *See* estrogens

Procardia: *See* nifedipine

prochlorperazine: tranquilizer/antiemetic

Prochlorperazine is prescribed to relieve the symptoms of psychosis, the manic phase of manic-depressive illness and severe behavioral problems in children. It is also used to treat nausea and vomiting. It is available under the brand name Compazine.

progestins Progestins are hormones that regulate the menstrual cycle and, with estrogen, are necessary for the development of milk-producing glands. They are prescribed to regulate the menstrual cycle, to treat endometriosis (a disorder of the uterus) and to treat certain types of breast, kidney and uterine cancer. They are also used in birth control pills, either alone or combined with an estrogen. The progestins include hydroxyprogesterone, medroxyprogesterone, megestrol, norethindrone, norethindrone acetate, norgestrel and progesterone. [*See* birth control pills, estrogens]

progesterone: *See* progestins

propoxyphene: analgesic

Propoxyphene is a narcotic prescribed to relieve mild to moderate pain. Brand names include Darvon, Dolene and Doxaphene. When combined with acetaminophen it is available under the brand name Darvocet-N. [*See* narcotics]

propranolol: beta-adrenergic blocking agent

Propranolol is used to treat high blood pressure, angina and irregular heartbeats. It is also used to prevent migraine headaches and to prevent additional heart attacks in heart attack patients. It is available under the brand name Inderal. [*See* antianginals, beta-adrenergic blocking agents]

Proscar: anti-prostate-enlargement drug

Proscar is used to reduce enlargement of the prostate gland. Approved for use in the United States in 1992, it is the first drug of its type. Produced by Merck & Co., it is marketed only under the Proscar trade name. (The generic name is finasteride.) It is used as an alternative to surgery in some patients.

protriptyline: antidepressant

Protriptyline is one of a group of prescription drugs known as tricyclic antidepressants that are believed to relieve the symptoms of mental depression by increasing the levels of certain chemicals used to transmit nerve signals in the brain. It is commonly available under the brand name Vivactil.

Proventil: *See* albuterol

Provera: *See* medroxyprogesterone

Prozac: *See* fluoxetine

ranitidine: anti-ulcer medication

Ranitidine limits the amount of acid produced by the stomach. It is used to treat duodenal (intestinal) and gastric (stomach) ulcers.

Restoril: *See* temazepam

Retin-A: *See* tretinoin

Ritalin: *See* methylphenidate

Rogaine: *See* minoxidil (topical)

RU-486 (mifepristone): abortifacient, antiprogestin

RU-486 is a pill that induces abortion within the first five weeks of pregnancy. The pill causes the uterine lining to slough off, expelling the embryo. The French government has approved its sale, but it is not available in the United States. Abortion opponents have protested its use, which has discouraged the company that invented and manufactures the drug from marketing it in other countries. In fact, the manufacturer, Group Roussel Uclaf, temporarily suspended its sale in France in 1988 due to objections from activists. The suspension was quickly overruled by the French government, which stated that the drug had become "the moral property of women." Abortion opponents in the United States have threatened to boycott any company that produces the drug.

Research into development of the drug was co-sponsored by the French government and the World Health Organization. Although WHO has confirmed that RU-486 is safe and effective, it has not pressed Roussel to market it in other countries. Some American researchers have claimed that opponents have limited their ability to obtain the drug for research on its usefulness in cancer treatment and as a contraceptive.

scopolamine: antiemetic

Scopolamine is a prescription drug used to prevent vomiting due to motion sickness. It is applied behind the ear in a patch, which releases a continuous dose of the drug for three days. It is available under the brand name Transderm-Scop.

secobarbital: sedative/hypnotic

Secobarbital is a barbiturate, one of a group of drugs that depress the activity of the central nervous system. It is prescribed to relieve anxiety and sleeplessness. Secobarbital, like other barbiturates, can be habit-forming. It is available under the brand name Seconal. [*See* barbiturates]

Seconal: *See* secobarbital

sedatives Sedatives are drugs that are used to calm activity in the central nervous system. They are used to treat anxiety or to induce sleep. Sedatives used to cause sleep are called "hypnotics."

Seldane: *See* terfenadine

Serax: *See* oxazepam

Sereen: *See* chlordiazepoxide

Sinequan: *See* doxepin

Slo-bid: *See* theophylline

Slo-Phyllin: *See* theophylline

Sodium Pentothal Sodium Pentothal is the brand name of a fast-acting barbiturate that is injected before surgery to cause sleep. It can also be used to cause a trance-like state, during which patients may be able to recall suppressed memories. This use has led to its inaccurate nickname, "truth serum." Its generic name is thiopental sodium.

Sofarin: *See* warfarin

Solfoton: *See* phenobarbital

Sominex: *See* diphenhydramine

Somophyllin-T: *See* theophylline

Sonazine: *See* chlorpromazine

Stelazine: *See* trifluoperazine

Sterapred: *See* prednisone

sulfacytine: *See* sulfonamide antibiotics

sulfadiazine: *See* sulfonamide antibiotics

sulfamethiazole: *See* sulfonamide antibiotics

sulfonamide antibiotics (sulfa drugs) Sulfa drugs, which are derived from the chemical sulfanilamide, were the first systemic drugs to successfully combat bacterial infections in humans. The advent of other, more widely effective antibiotics has decreased their use. They still are used frequently to treat urinary-tract infections, ulcerative colitis and streptococcal infections, however. They are available under a variety of generic and brand names, including sulfacytine (brand name Renoquid), sulfadiazine (Microsulfon), sulfamethiazole (Proklar, Thiosulfil Forte), sulfamethoxazole (Gamazole, Gantanol, Urobak) and sulfisoxazole (Gantrisin, Gulfasin, Lipo-Gantrisin).

Symadine: *See* amantadine
Symmetrel: *See* amantadine
Synthroid: *See* levothyroxine
Tagamet: *See* cimetidine
talbutal: *See* barbiturates
Talwin NX: *See* pentazocine
Tenormin: *See* atenolol
Tenuate: *See* diethylpropion
temazepam: sedative/hypnotic

Temazepam is a prescription drug used to treat insomnia. It is one of a group of drugs called benzodiazepines, all of which are central nervous system depressants. The group includes diazepam (brand name Valium), chlordiazepoxide (Librium) and flurazepam (Dalmane), among many others. An overdose of temazepam, or combining it with other central nervous system depressants such as alcohol, can cause unconsciousness or death. It is available under the brand name Restoril.

Tepanil: *See* diethylpropion
terfenadine: antihistamine

Terfenadine is a prescription drug used to relieve allergy symptoms. It is available under the brand name Seldane. It is often prescribed for patients who cannot tolerate the drowsiness that other types of antihistamines can cause. [*See* antihistamines]

thalidomide

Thalidomide, a sleeping pill and sedative, was popular in 46 countries from the mid-1950s to 1961. Then it was recognized as the cause of severe birth defects. Thousands of children (estimates go as high as 12,000) were born with deformed or missing limbs because their mothers had taken the supposedly safe drug during their pregnancies. Most of the children were born in West Germany, where the drug was manufactured. The drug had not been approved for use in the United States because the federal Food and Drug Administration feared side effects unrelated to the birth defects. Although the United States was spared, photos of children with missing or flipper-like arms and legs appeared in newspapers and on television news programs throughout the country, arousing considerable sympathy and concern.

Thalidomide still has a medical use—as a treatment for leprosy—but is available only through special programs of the U.S. Public Health Service. The Food and Drug Administration has not approved it for general use. The original manufacturer in West Germany stopped producing it in 1985 because of fear of legal liability. The U.S. Public Health Service, which has used thalidomide for 20 years to treat leprosy patients and has found it effective and safe, has made its own supply for several years. (It is not given to women in their childbearing years.) There has been some interest in producing it commercially in the United States, but extensive testing would be required before that could become a reality.

theophylline: bronchodilator

Theophylline relaxes the muscles of the bronchi (breathing tubes), which relieves spasms and makes breathing easier. It is prescribed for patients with asthma, bronchitis, emphysema and other lung diseases. It is available under many brand names, the most common of which is Theo-Dur.

Theo-Dur: *See* theophylline
thioridazine: tranquilizer

Thioridazine is prescribed to relieve the symptoms of psychosis, the manic phase of manic-depressive illness and severe behavioral problems in children. It is available under the brand names Mellaril and Millazine. [*See* tranquilizers]

thiothixene: antipsychotic

Thiothixene is prescribed to treat mental illness, including psychosis. It is available under the brand name Navane.

Thorazine: *See* chlorpromazine
Thor-Prom: *See* chlorpromazine
Tipramine: *See* imipramine
Tofranil: *See* imipramine
Toradol: anesthetic

Toradol, which was marketed in the United States for the first time in the summer of 1990, is a nonaddictive painkiller. It is administered by injection to treat acute pain. Unlike other strong painkillers, it does not act as a narcotic on the central nervous system. Instead, it reduces the production of prostaglandins, chemical substances that transmit the pain message when tissues are injured.

tranquilizers

Tranquilizers work on the central nervous system to relieve emotional agitation. Major tranquilizers, such as chlorpromazine (brand name Thorazine), are used to ease the symptoms of psychosis, including agitation, delusions and anxiety. Minor tranquilizers are used to reduce anxiety and nervousness.

Transderm-Scop: *See* scopolamine
tranylcypromine: antidepressant

Tranylcypromine is a MAO inhibitor. It is available under the brand name Parnate. [*See* antidepressants]

Tranxene: *See* clorazepate

trazodone: antidepressant

Trazodone is prescribed to relieve the symptoms of mental depression. Brand names include Desyrel, Trazon and Trialodine. [*See* antidepressants]

Trazon: *See* trazodone

tretinoin: acne preparation

Tretinoin is approved by the federal Food and Drug Administration as a treatment for acne. The cream has also been touted as a "cure" for wrinkles caused by prolonged exposure to the sun. Some physicians prescribe it for this purpose, although there is disagreement about its effectiveness. It is available under the brand name Retin-A.

Trialodine: *See* trazodone

Triavil: *See* perphenazine

triazolam: sedative/hypnotic

Triazolam is prescribed to treat insomnia. It is one of a group of drugs called benzodiazepines, all of which are central nervous system depressants. The group includes diazepam (brand name Valium), chlordiazepoxide (Librium) and flurazepam (Dalmane), among many others. An overdose, or taking triazolam and other central nervous system depressants (including alcohol), can cause unconsciousness or death. It is available under the brand name Halcion. It was banned in Great Britain in 1991 due to concerns about side effects, including memory loss and depression. In the United States, Upjohn Co. agreed to package the pills in smaller amounts, with stronger warnings, as a reminder that the drug is for short-term use only. [*See* sedatives]

trifluoperazine: tranquilizer

Trifluoperazine is a major tranquilizer prescribed to treat the emotional symptoms of psychosis, the manic phase of manic-depressive disorder and severe behavioral problems in children. Brand names include Stelazine and Suprazine.

trimipramine: antidepressant

Trimipramine is a tricyclic antidepressant. It is commonly available under the brand name Surmontil.

Trimox: *See* amoxicillin

Triphasil: *See* birth control pills

Tylenol: *See* acetaminophen

Tylox: *See* oxycodone

Valium: *See* diazepam

Vasotec: *See* enalapril

Vazepam: *See* diazepam

Ventolin: *See* albuterol

verapamil: calcium channel blocker/antihypertensive

Verapamil is a prescription drug used to treat angina and high blood pressure. Brand names include Calan and Isoptin. [*See* antianginals, antihypertensives, calcium channel blockers]

Vicodin: *See* hydrocodone

Vivactil: *See* protriptyline

Voltaren: *See* diclofenalac

warfarin: anticoagulant

Warfarin is prescribed for patients with certain heart, lung and blood vessel conditions. It decreases the blood's clotting ability, which helps to prevent clots from forming and blocking blood vessels, causing strokes, heart attacks and other problems. It is available under several brand names, the most common of which is Coumadin.

Xanax: *See* alprazolam

Zantac: *See* ranitidine

zidovudine: *See* AZT

COMMON TOXIC CHEMICALS

GUIDE TO INVESTIGATING CHEMICAL HAZARDS

A federal law enacted in 1986 makes more information available about hazardous chemicals than ever before. How a company stores its hazardous chemicals, what chemicals that company routinely releases or releases accidentally, and how it treats chemical effluent is all public information. The information alone does not tell a story, however.

Chemicals that are harmless in some contexts can be injurious in others. Sodium chloride, which is common table salt, may be harmless when sprinkled on popcorn but toxic at high concentrations in baby formula. An axiom of toxicology is that "the dose makes the poison." The method, frequency and duration of exposure are also important, as are environmental conditions and the presence of other chemicals.

Whether writing about industrial, home, or farm use of chemicals, the nonexpert must be able to identify the issues, know the available sources of information, and be able to ask the questions that will elicit well-informed answers from experts. There are three important issues: What is the potential for harm? What can be learned from public reports? Who are the experts, and what do they say?

1. What is the potential for harm? Because of the exposure variables mentioned above, this is not always an easy question. The federal government has identified as many as 500,000 products containing chemicals that may have health risks. This means that they could be dangerous under certain conditions. The government has singled out about 1,100 chemicals as either Extremely Hazardous Substances, Hazardous Substances or Toxic Chemicals and has made them subject to special reporting provisions. For quick guidance concerning a chemical's potential for harm, it makes sense to see whether it is one of those 1,100 chemicals. [See Hazardous Substances and Toxic Chemicals, page 209] The fact that a chemical is on the list does not mean that any exposure to it will be harmful, or that any release into the environment will be cataclysmic. But the fact that it is on the list should raise questions. (The fact that a chemical is not on the list does not mean that it is entirely harmless: A cup of table salt dumped into a municipal water supply would not have a noticeable effect, but a cup dumped into a fishbowl would kill the fish.) The list should be used as a signal, not a conclusion.

Library reference sources can provide useful background information. [See Contacts and References, below] So many factors can alter a chemical's effects, however, that experts usually must be consulted. To discuss the effects of the chemical with an expert, it is important to know the following information: the name of the chemical (one chemical may be known by several names, so it is useful to know the chemical's Identifying Chemical Abstract number as well), the amount of chemical, the duration of the release or exposure, the surrounding environmental conditions (temperature, wind direction, weather conditions, etc.), how humans or animals may have been exposed (skin contact, inhalation, ingestion), how the chemical would affect individuals with particular vulnerabilities, such as asthma, and whether other chemicals were present.

2. What public reports should be available? In 1986, federal legislation dramatically increased the amount of information that industry must make public concerning chemicals it uses, stores and releases. The federal Emergency Planning and Community Right-to-Know Act (also known as Title III of the Superfund Amendments and Reauthorization Act of 1986, or SARA) was a reaction to a devastating chemical accident in Bhopal, India. (More than 2,500 people died and tens of thousands were injured when a cloud of methyl isocyanate gas escaped from the Union Carbide plant there on Dec. 4, 1984.) The law requires states and communities to plan for chemical accidents, and requires industry to provide the information necessary for them to do so.

The law has four major components: Emergency Planning (Sections 301–303), Emergency Release Notification (Section 304), Hazardous Chemical Reporting (Sections 311–312) and Toxic Chemical Release Reporting and Inventory (Section 313).

Emergency Planning (Sections 301–303): Each state must have a State Emergency Response Commission (SERC) that oversees Local Emergency Planning Committees (LEPCs). The committees collect information supplied by industry and make it available to the public. Each LEPC must study the reports for its region and other chemical dangers not subject to the reporting requirements, and develop plans to respond to chemical emergencies. Emergency planning focuses on a list of more than 350 chemicals designated by the U.S. Environmental Protection Agency as Extremely Hazardous Substances. The list includes a "threshold planning quantity" for each substance. When that quantity or more is present in any manufacturing plant, warehouse, hospital, farm, small business or other facility the LEPC and the SERC must be notified. (Federal facilities are exempt from the requirement.) Those records are public.

Emergency Release Notification (Section 304): When an Extremely Hazardous Substance or one of more than 700 so-called Hazardous substances is released in an amount that exceeds a specified minimum, LEPCs and SERCs must be notified immediately. The initial report may be verbal. A written report, which is a public record, must be made within 30 days and include: the chemical name; location of release; whether the chemical is on the Extremely Hazardous Substances list; how much has been released; time and duration of the release; whether the chemical was released into the air, water or soil; possible health risks and necessary medical attention; proper emergency precautions (such as evacuation); and the name of a contact person.

Hazardous Chemical Reporting (Sections 311–312): This component of the law applies to broad categories of chemicals, present in as many as 500,000 products. All companies must report the amounts, locations and possible effects of such substances if they are present in specified quantities. They must keep Material Safety Data Sheets on file for each of the designated substances, and these sheets must be available to employees. The data sheets must include information on the chemical's properties, possible short-term or long-term health hazards, fire hazard and other hazards. The data sheets, or a list of MSDS chemicals, are public records and must be submitted to the LEPCs, the SERC and the local fire department. They are public records. Companies must also submit annual inventories of these chemicals to the LEPCs, SERCs and local fire departments. The inventories also are available to the public.

Toxic Chemical Release Reporting and Inventory (Section 313): Manufacturing plants with 10 or more employees that release one of more than 300 specified chemicals or compounds must file annual reports concerning the releases. They must also report any of the chemicals that they have transported to off-site waste facilities. The reports must include: the names of the chemicals released; the amount that went into the air, water or land; the amount transported for off-site disposal; the method of on-site waste treatment; and the efficiency of the treatment. The reports are submitted to EPA headquarters in Washington, D.C., each July 1 and to the state environmental, health or emergency response agency that works with the SERC. The EPA compiles these reports into a database (the Toxic Release Inventory, or TRI), which is available on-line through the National Library of Medicine, on microfiche and as custom printouts.

Although many manufacturing companies have had to report air, water or soil pollution information to a variety of state and federal agencies for years, the advantage of this system is that reports of releases are recorded in one location that is readily available to the public. The information can be viewed and sorted by various criteria, including company name, zip code, geographic location, chemical name and waste treatment methods. A researcher could discover, for example, how much of a specified chemical a national company reported released from its various plants around the country, or what chemicals were reported released into a local lake, or what waste treatment methods were reported by state companies, or how effective the treatment methods were estimated to be.

Although the federally mandated reports are a useful starting point, they have limitations. Their usefulness depends on the accuracy of the original data submitted by the companies, and that is difficult to judge. In some cases (such as the TRI database), the figures reported are merely company estimates. The accuracy of the estimates cannot be guaranteed. Even when exact figures are required, there is no way to be sure that every business is accurate in its measurements or truthful in its statements. The TRI figures are always at least six months out of date because they are submitted July 1 for the preceding calendar year. They cannot indicate whether a new problem has developed or an old problem has been solved. The TRI figures also do not indicate whether all of the releases occurred on one day, or whether they were gradual releases throughout the year. In addition to these problems, the reports also do not cover all chemical users. Federal government facilities are exempt from the regulations, and private use of chemicals (for purposes such as lawn care) is not covered.

3. Who are the experts, and what do they say? The best place to begin is often the Local Emergency Planning Committee. The LEPC must include representatives of all of the following groups: elected state and local officials; law enforcement, civil defense, firefighting, first aid, health, local environmental and transportation agencies; hospitals; broadcast and print media; community groups; and facilities subject to Emergency Planning and Community Right-to-Know Act requirements. The committee should have good information about industrial and other chemical uses in its area and about environmental conditions, and it should have an up-to-date emergency plan for dealing with accidents. The expertise of committee members makes the LEPC especially useful. The LEPC can be located through the State Emergency Response Committee, which appoints the local groups, or through municipal officials. The SERC is a good source for statewide information.

When covering chemical hazards, professional opinion often differs, especially when long-term effects are an issue. For this reason, it is important to obtain a variety of responsible opinions. When a company is involved, it is important to get the company's opinion of the hazard. (This may be supplemented with Material Safety Data Sheets which the company may have submitted to the LEPC, SERC and local fire department.) Colleges and universities, state and federal government agencies, industry associations, and environmental groups may also provide good sources of expertise.

SUGGESTED REFERENCES AND CONTACTS:

For Toxic Release Inventory data:
   U.S. Environmental Protection Agency
   P.O. Box 70266
   Washington, D.C. 20024-0266
   Attention: TRI Public Inquiry
For technical and regulatory information:
   U.S. Environmental Protection Agency, 401 M St. SW, Washington, D.C. 20460; toxic substances library, (202) 260-2331; Emergency Planning and Community Right-to-Know Information Hotline, (800) 535-0202 between 8:30 A.M. and 7:30 P.M. Eastern time.
Occupational Safety and Health Administration, Health Standards Division, 200 Constitution Ave. NW, Washington, D.C. 20210; statistician, (202) 219-7105.

State Emergency Response Commissions:

Alabama: (205) 260-2700
Alaska: (907) 790-4900
Arizona: (602) 231-6326
Arkansas: (501) 374-1202
California: (916) 262-1750
Colorado: (303) 293-1723
Connecticut: (203) 566-3180
Delaware: (302) 834-4531
District of Columbia: (202) 727-6161
Florida: (904) 488-1472
Georgia: (404) 656-4863
Hawaii: (808) 586-4249
Idaho: (208) 334-3263
Illinois: (312) 886-6236
Indiana: (317) 241-4336
Iowa: (515) 281-3231
Kansas: (913) 296-1690
Kentucky: (502) 564-2380
Louisiana: (504) 925-6113
Maine: (207) 289-4080 [in-state, (800) 452-8735
Maryland: (301) 486-4422
Massachusetts: (508) 820-2000
Michigan: (517) 373-8481

Minnesota: (612) 643-3000
Mississippi: (601) 960-9973
Missouri: (314) 634-2436
Montana: (406) 444-3948
Nebraska: (402) 471-2186
Nevada: (702) 687-4240
New Hampshire: (603) 271-2231
New Jersey: (609) 882-2000
New Mexico: (505) 827-9223
New York: (518) 457-9996
North Carolina: (919) 733-3867
North Dakota: (701) 224-2111
Ohio: (614) 644-2260
Oklahoma: (405) 271-8056
Oregon: (503) 378-3473
Pennsylvania: (717) 783-8150
Rhode Island: (401) 277-3039
South Carolina: (803) 734-0425
South Dakota: (605) 773-3231
Tennessee: (615) 741-0001
Texas: (512) 465-2138
Utah: (801) 535-5467
Vermont: (802) 244-8721
Virginia: (804) 225-2513
Washington: (206) 493-2787
West Virginia: (304) 348-5380
Wisconsin: (608) 266-3232
Wyoming: (307) 777-7566

State TRI Contacts:

Alabama: (205) 271-7931
Alaska: (907) 465-2600
Arizona: (602) 231-6326
Arkansas: (501) 682-4541
California: (916) 322-2793
Colorado: (303) 692-3300
Connecticut: (203) 566-4856
Delaware: (302) 737-4791
District of Columbia: (202) 727-6161
Florida: (904) 488-1472
Georgia: (404) 656-6905
Hawaii: (808) 586-4249
Idaho: (208) 334-3263
Illinois: (312) 886-6236
Indiana: (317) 241-4336
Iowa: (515) 281-3231
Kansas: (913) 296-1690
Kentucky: (502) 564-2380
Louisiana: (504) 342-5633
Maine: (207) 289-4080
Maryland: (301) 631-3806
Massachusetts: (617) 292-5982
Michigan: (517) 373-8481
Minnesota: (612) 643-3000
Mississippi: (601) 960-9973
Missouri: (314) 526-3349

Montana: (406) 444-6911
Nebraska: (402) 471-2186
Nevada: (702) 687-4240
New Hampshire: (603) 271-2231
New Jersey: (609) 292-6714
New Mexico: (505) 827-9222
New York: (518) 457-4107
North Carolina: (919) 733-3867
North Dakota: (701) 224-3300
Ohio: (614) 889-7150
Oklahoma: (405) 521-2481
Oregon: (503) 378-4040
Pennsylvania: (717) 783-2071
Rhode Island: (401) 277-2808
South Carolina: (803) 734-0428
South Dakota: (605) 773-3296
Tennessee: (615) 741-0001
Texas: (512) 463-7727
Utah: (801) 536-4100
Vermont: (802) 828-2886
Virginia: (804) 225-2513
Washington: (206) 296-3830
West Virginia: (304) 348-5380
Wisconsin: (608) 266-3362
Wyoming: (307) 777-7566

Environmental Protection Agency and Federal Emergency Management Agency Regional Offices:

Region 1 (Connecticut, Maine, Massachusetts, New Hampshire, Rhode Island, Vermont): Boston, (617) 565-4502 (EPA); (617) 223-9565 (FEMA).

Region 2 (New Jersey, New York, Puerto Rico, Virgin Islands): New York, (212) 264-2515 (EPA); (212) 225-7208 (FEMA).

Region 3 (Delaware, Maryland, Pennsylvania, Virginia, West Virginia, District of Columbia): Philadelphia, (215) 597-9800 (EPA); (215) 931-5528 (FEMA).

Region 4 (Alabama, Florida, Georgia, Kentucky, Mississippi, North Carolina, South Carolina, Tennessee): Atlanta, (404) 347-3931 (EPA); (404) 853-4454 (FEMA).

Region 5 (Illinois, Indiana, Michigan, Minnesota, Ohio, Wisconsin): Chicago, (312) 353-2000 (EPA); (312) 408-5524 (FEMA).

Region 6 (Arkansas, Louisiana, New Mexico, Oklahoma, Texas): Dallas, (214) 655-2270 (EPA); Denton, Texas, (817) 898-9137 (FEMA).

Region 7 (Iowa, Kansas, Missouri, Nebraska): Kansas City, Kansas, (913) 551-7000; Kansas City, Missouri, (816) 283-7011 (FEMA).

Region 8 (Colorado, Montana, North Dakota, South Dakota, Utah, Wyoming): Denver, (303) 293-1723 (EPA); (303) 235-4923 (FEMA).

Region 9 (Arizona, California, Hawaii, Nevada, Northern Mariana Islands, American Samoa, Guam): San Francisco, (415) 744-1500 (EPA); (415) 923-7187 (FEMA).

Region 10 (Alaska, Idaho, Oregon, Washington): Seattle, (206) 553-1200 (EPA); Bothell, Washington, (206) 487-4600 (FEMA).

Environmental, Business and Public Service Organizations:

Environmental Health Center, National Safety Council, 1019 19th St. NW, Suite 401, Washington, D.C. 20036; (202) 293-2270.

Friends of the Earth, 218 D St. SE, Washington, D.C. 20003; (202) 544-2600.

National Wildlife Federation, 1400 16th St. NW, Washington, D.C. 20036; (202) 797-6800.

Natural Resources Defense Council, 1350 New York Ave. NW, Washington, D.C. 20006; (202) 783-7800.

Chemical Manufacturers Association, 2501 M St. NW, Washington, D.C. 20037; (202) 887-1100.

National Association of Manufacturers, 1331 Pennsylvania Ave. NW, Washington, D.C. 20004; (202) 637-3000.

BOOKS AND PERIODICALS:

Chemicals, the Press and the Public: A Journalist's Guide to Reporting on Chemicals in the Community. Environmental Health Center Division of National Safety Council, 1019 19th St. NW, Suite 401, Washington, D.C. 20036, (202) 293-2270.

Dangerous Properties of Industrial Materials (3 vols.), N. Irving Sax and Richard J. Lewis. New York: Van Nostrand Reinhold Co., 7th ed., 1988.

Environment Writer, a monthly newsletter for reporters published by the Environmental Health Center Division of National Safety Council, 1019 19th St. NW, Suite 401, Washington, D.C. 20036, (202) 293-2270.

Hawley's Condensed Chemical Dictionary, N. Irving Sax and Richard J. Lewis. New York: Van Nostrand Reinhold Co., 11th ed., 1987.

Pocket Guide to Chemical Hazards. National Institute for Occupational Safety and Health Publications, 4676 Columbia Parkway, Cincinnati, OH 45226, (513) 533-8287, (800) 356-4674.

HAZARDOUS SUBSTANCES AND TOXIC CHEMICALS

The following chemicals are subject to reporting under the federal Emergency Planning and Community Right-to-Know Act (also known as Title III of the Superfund Amendments and Reauthorization Act of 1986, or SARA). The chemicals in bold type are classified as Extremely Hazardous Substances under Section 302 of the act. They are the focus of emergency planning because they can be acutely toxic when released in sufficient amounts. The other chemicals are classified as hazardous substances under Section 304 of the act or as toxic chemicals under Section 313. In addition to the chemicals listed here, Sections 311 and 312 of the act require reporting of any workplace chemicals that can pose physical or health hazards. The definition is so broad that it encompasses as many as 500,000 products.

This list should be used only to help identify potential chemical hazards. These chemicals are not inherently unsafe in all uses. Concentration, method of use and storage, mode and extent of human exposure, combination with other chemicals, and environmental factors all affect safety. Those factors must be weighed by experts. [*See* Guide to Investigating Hazardous Chemicals (above)]

Acenaphthene
Acenaphthylene
Acetaldehyde
Acetaldehyde, trichloro-
Acetamide
Acetic acid
Acetic anhydride
Acetone
Acetone cyanohydrin
Acetone thiosemicarbazide
Acetonitrile
Acetophenone
2-Acetylaminofluorene
Acetyl bromide
Acetyl chloride
1-Acetyl-2-thiourea
Acrolein
Acrylamide
Acrylic acid
Acrylonitrile
Acrylyl chloride
Adipic acid
Adiponitrile
Aldicarb
Aldrin
Allyl alcohol
Allylamine
Allyl chloride
Aluminum (fume or dust)
Aluminum oxide (fibrous forms)
Aluminum phosphide
Aluminum sulfate
2-Aminoanthraquinone
4-Aminoazobenzene
4-Aminobiphenyl
1-Amino-2-methylanthraquinone
Aminopterin
4-Aminopyridine

Amiton
Amiton oxalate
Amitrole
Ammonia
Ammonium acetate
Ammonium benzoate
Ammonium bicarbonate
Ammonium bichromate
Ammonium bifluoride
Ammonium bisulfite
Ammonium carbamate
Ammonium carbonate
Ammonium chloride
Ammonium chromate
Ammonium citrate, dibasic
Ammonium fluoborate
Ammonium fluoride
Ammonium hydroxide
Ammonium nitrate (solution)
Ammonium oxalate
Ammonium picrate
Ammonium silicofluoride
Ammonium sulfamate
Ammonium sulfate (solution)
Ammonium sulfide
Ammonium sulfite
Ammonium tartrate
Ammonium thiocyanate
Ammonium vanadate
Amphetamine
Amyl acetate
iso-Amyl acetate
sec-Amyl acetate
tert-Amyl acetate
Aniline
Aniline,2,4,6-trimethyl-
o-Anisidine
p-Anisidine
o-Anisidine hydrochloride
Anthracene
Antimony
Antimony compounds
Antimony pentachloride
Antimony pentafluoride
Antimony potassium tartrate
Antimony tribromide
Antimony trichloride
Antimony trifluoride
Antimony trioxide
Antimycin A
ANTU
Aroclor 1016
Aroclor 1221
Aroclor 1232
Aroclor 1242
Aroclor 1248

Aroclor 1254
Aroclor 1260
Arsenic
Arsenic acid
Arsenic compounds
Arsenic disulfide
Arsenic pentoxide
Arsenic trioxide
Arsenic trisulfide
Arsenous oxide
Arsenous trichloride
Arsine
Asbestos (friable)
Auramine
Azaserine
Azinphos-ethyl
Azinphos-methyl
Aziridine
Aziridine, 2-methyl
Barium
Barium compounds
Barium cyanide
Benz [c] acridine
Benzal chloride
Benzamide
Benzamide,3,5-dichloro-N-(1,1-dimethyl-2-
    propynyl)
Benz [a] anthracene
Benzenamine, 3 (trifluoromethyl)-
Benzene
Benzene, 1 (chloromethyl)-4-nitro-
Benzene, m-dimethyl-
Benzene, o-dimethyl-
Benzene, p-dimethyl-
Benzenearsonic acid
Benzeneethanamine, alpha, alpha-dimethyl
Benzenesulfonyl chloride
Benzenethiol
Benzidine
Benzimidazole, 4, 5-dichloro-2 (trifluoromethyl)-
Benzo [b] fluoranthene
Benzo [k] fluoranthene
Benzoic acid
Benzotrichloride
Benzonitrile
Benzo [ghi] perylene
Benzo [a] pyrene
p-Benzoquinone
Benzotrichloride
Benzoyl chloride
Benzoyl peroxide
Benzyl chloride
Benzyl cyanide
Beryllium
Beryllium chloride
Beryllium compounds

Beryllium fluoride
Beryllium nitrate
alpha-BHC
beta-BHC
delta-BHC
Bicyclo[2.2.1]heptane-2-carbonitrile,   5-chloro-6-
    ((((methyl amino)carbonyl) oxy)imino)-, (1s-(1-
    alpha, 2-beta, 4-alpha, 5-alpha, 6E))-
2-2'-Bioxirane
Biphenyl
Bis (2-chloroethoxy) methane
Bis (2-chloroethyl) ether
Bis (chloromethyl) ether
Bis (2-chloro-1-methylethyl) ether
Bis (chloromethyl) ketone
Bis (2-ethylhexyl) adipate
Bis (2-ethylhexyl) phthalate
Bitoscanate
Boron trichloride
Boron trifluoride
Boron trifluoride compound with methyl ether (1:1)
Bromadiolone
Bromine
Bromoacetone
Bromochlorodifluoromethane [Halon 1211]
Bromoform
Bromomethane
4-Bromophenyl phenyl ether
Bromotrifluoromethane [Halon 1301]
Brucine
1, 3-Butadiene
2-Butene, 1, 4-dichloro-
iso-Butyl acetate
sec-Butyl acetate
tert-Butyl acetate
Butyle acetate
Butyl acrylate
n-Butyl alcohol
sec-Butyl alcohol
tert-Butyl alcohol
Butylamine
iso-Butylamine
sec-Butylamine
tert-Butylamine
Butyle benzyl phthalate
1,2-Butylene oxide
n-Butyle phthalate
Butyraldehyde
Butyric acid
iso-Butyric acid
Cacodylic acid
Cadmium
Cadmium acetate
Cadmium bromide
Cadmium chloride
Cadmium compounds

Cadmium oxide
Cadmium stearate
Calcium arsenate
Calcium arsenite
Calcium carbide
Calcium chromate
Calcium cyanamide
Calcium cyanide
Calcium dodecylbenzenesulfonate
Calcium hypochlorite
Camphechlor
Camphene, octachloro-
Cantharidin
Captan
Carbachol chloride
Carbamic acid, methyl-, 0-(((2,4-dimethyl1-1, 3-di-
    thiolan-2-YI)   methylene)amino)-
Carbaryl
Carbofuran
Carbon disulfide
Carbonic difluoride
Carbon tetrachloride
Carbonyl sulfide
Carbophenothion
Catechol
CFC-11
CFC-114
CFC-115
CFC-12
Chloramben
Chlorambucil
Chlordane
Chlorfenvinfos
Chlorinated benzenes
Chlorinated ethanes
Chlorinated naphthalene
Chlorinated phenols
Chlorine
Chlorine dioxide
Chlormephos
Chlormequat chloride
Chloraphazine
Chloroacetaldehyde
Chloroacetic acid
2-Chloroacetophenone
Chloralkyl ethers
p-Chloroaniline
Chlorobenzene
Chlorobenzilate
p-Chloro-m-cresol
Chlorodibromomethane
Chloroethane
Chloroethanol
Chloroethyl chloroformate
2-Chloroethyl vinyl ether
Chloroform

Chloromethane
Chloromethyl ether
Chloromethyl methyl ether
2-Chloronaphthalene
Chlorophacinone
2-Chlorophenol
Chlorophenols
4-Chlorophenyl phenyl ether
Chloroprene
3-Chloroproprionitrile
Chlorosulfonic acid
Chlorothalonil
4-Chloro-o-toluidine, hydrochloride
Chloroxuron
Chlorpyrifos
Chlorthiophos
Chromic acetate
Chromic acid
Chromic chloride
Chromic sulfate
Chromium
Chromium compounds
Chromous chloride
Chrysene
C.I. acid green 3
C.I. basic green 4
C.I. basic red 1
C.I. direct black 38
C.I. direct blue 6
C.I. direct brown 95
C.I. disperse yellow 3
C.I. food red 5
C.I. food red 15
C.I. solvent orange 7
C.I. solvent yellow 3
C.I. solvent yellow 14
C.I. solvent yellow 34
C.I. vat yellow 4
Cobalt
Cobalt compounds
Cobalt,   ((2,2'-(1,2-ethanediylbis   (nitrilomethyli-
    dyne))   bis(6-fluorophenolato)) (2-)-n,n',o,o')-
Cobalt carbonyl
Cobaltous bromide
Cobaltous formate
Cobaltous sulfamate
Coke oven emissions
Colchicine
Copper
Copper compounds
Copper cyanide
Coumaphos
Coumatetralyl
Creosote
p-Cresidine
m-Cresol

o-Cresol
p-Cresol
Cresol (mixed isomers)
Crimidine
Crotonaldehyde
Crotonaldehyde, (E)-
Cumene
Cumene hydroperoxide
Cupferron
Cupric acetate
Cupric acetoarsenite
Cupric chloride
Cupric nitrate
Cupric oxalate
Cupric sulfate
Cupric sulfate, ammoniated
Cupric tartrate
Cyanide compounds
Cyanides (soluble salts and complexes)
Cyanogen
Cyanogen bromide
Cyanogen chloride
Cyanogen iodide
Cyanophos
Cyanuric fluoride
Cyclohexane
Cyclohexanone
Cycloheximide
Cyclohexylamine
2-Cyclohexyl-4,6-dinitrophenol
Cyclophosphamide
2,4-D
2,4-D acid
2,4-D esters
Daunomycin
DBCP
DDD
DDE
DDT
DDT and metabolites
Decaborane (14)
Decabromodiphenyl oxide
DEHP
Demeton
Demeton-s-methyl
Dialifor
Diallate
2,4-Diaminoanisole
2,4-Diaminoanisole sulfate
4,4'-Diaminodiphenyl ether
Diaminotoluene
2,4-Diaminotoluene
Diaminotoluene (mixed isomers)
Diazinon
Diazomethane
Dibenz [a,h] anthracene

Dibenzofuran
Dibenz [a,i] pyrene
Diborane
1,2-Dibromo-3-chloropropane
1,2-Dibromoethane
Dibromotetrafluoroethane [Halon 2402]
Dibutyl phthalate
Dicamba
Dichlobenil
Dichlone
Dichlorobenzene
o-Dichlorobenzene
1,2-Dichlorobenzene
1,3-Dichlorobenzene
1,4-Dichlorobenzene
Dichlorobenzene (mixed isomers)
3,3'-Dichlorobenzidine
Dichlorobenzidine
Dichlorobromomethane
Dichlorodifluoromethane [CFC-12]
1,2-Dichloroethane
1,1-Dichloroethane
1,2-Dichloroethylene
1,1-Dichloroethylene
Dichloroethyl ether
Dichloroisopropyl ether
Dichloromethane
Dichloromethyl ether
Dichloromethylphenyl-silane
2,4-Dichlorophenol
2,6-Dichlorophenol
Dichlorophenylarsine
Dichloropropane
Dichloropropane-dichloropropene (mixture)
1,1-Dichloropropane
1,2-Dichloropropane
1,3-Dichloropropane
2,3-Dichloropropene
2,2-Dichloropropionic acid
1,3-Dichloropropylene
Dichlorotetrafluoroethane [CFC-114]
Dichlorvos
Dicofol
Dicrotophos
Dieldrin
Diepoxybutane
Diethanolamine
Diethylamine
Diethylarsine
Diethyl carbamazine citrate
Diethyl chlorophosphate
Di(2-ethylhexyl) phthalate
Diethyl-p-nitrophenyl phosphate
Diethyl phthalate
o-o-Diethyl o-pyrazinyl phosphorothioate
Diethylstilbestrol

Diethyl sulfate
Digitoxin
Diglycidyl ether
Digoxin
Dihydrosafrole
Diisopropylfluorophosphate
Dimefox
Dimethoate
3,3'-Dimethoxybenzidine
Dimethyl phosphoro-chloridothioate
Dimethylamine
4-Dimethylaminoazobenzene
Dimethylaminoazobenzene
n-n-Dimethylaniline
7,12-Dimethylbenz[a] anthracene
3,3'-Dimethylbenzidine
Dimethylcarbamyl chloride
1,1-Dimethyl hydrazine
2,4-Dimethylphenol
Dimethyl phthalate
Dimethyl sulfate
Dimethyldichlorosilane
Dimethylhydrazine
Dimethyl-p-phenylenediamine
Dimetilan
Dinitrobenzene (mixed isomers)
m-Dinitrobenzene
o-Dinitrobenzene
p-Dinitrobenzene
Dinitrocresol
4,6-Dinitro-o-cresol
4,6-Dinitro-o-cresol and salts
Dinitrophenol
2,4-Dinitrophenol
2,5-Dinitrophenol
2,6-Dinitrophenol
Dinitrotoluene (mixed isomers)
2,4-Dinitrotoluene
2,6-Dinitrotoluene
3,4-Dinitrotoluene
Dinoseb
Dinoterb
Di-n-octyl phthalate
n-Dioctylphthalate
1,4-Dioxane
Dioxathion
Diphacinone
1,2-Diphenylhydrazine
Diphenylhydrazine
Diphosphoramide, octamethyl-
Dipropylamine
Diquat
Disulfoton
Dithiazanine iodide
Dithiobiuret
o-o-Diethyl s-methyl dithiophosphate

Diuron
Dodecylbenzenesulfonic acid
2,4-D, salts and esters
Emetine, dihydrochloride
Endosulfan
alpha-Endosulfan
beta-Endosulfan
Endosulfan and metabolites
Endosulfan sulfate
Endothall
Endothion
Endrin
Endrin aldehyde
Endrin and metabolites
Epichlorohydrin
Epinephrine
EPN
Ergocalciferol
Ergotamine tartrate
Ethanesulfonyl chloride, 2-chloro
Ethane, 1,1,1,2-tetrachloro
Ethanimidothioic acid, N-[[(methylamino) carbon-
yl] oxy]-, methyl ester
Ethanol, 1,2-dichloro-, acetate
Ethanol, 2-ethoxy-
Ethion
Ethoprophos
2-Ethoxyethanol
Ethyl acetate
Ethyl acrylate
Ethylbenzene
Ethylbis (2-chloroethyl) amine
Ethyl carbamate
Ethyl chloride
Ethyl chloroformate
Ethyl cyanide
Ethyl ether
Ethyl methacrylate
Ethyl methanesulfonate
Ethylene
Ethylene dibromide
Ethylene fluorohydrin
Ethylene oxide
Ethylenebisdithiocarbamic acid, salts and esters
Ethylenediamine
Ethylenediamine-tetraacetic acid (EDTA)
Ethylene dichloride
Ethylene glycol
Ethyleneimine
Ethylene thiourea
Ethylthiocyanate
Famphur
Fenamiphos
Fenitrothion
Fensulfothion
Ferric ammonium citrate

Ferric ammonium oxalate
Ferric chloride
Ferric fluoride
Ferric nitrate
Ferric sulfate
Ferrous ammonium sulfate
Ferrous chloride
Ferrous sulfate
Fluenetil
Fluometuron
Fluoranthene
Fluorene
Fluorine
Fluoroacetamide
Fluoracetic acid
Fluoroacetic acid, sodium salt
Fluoroacetyl chloride
Fluorouracil
Fonofos
Formaldehyde
Formaldehyde cyanohydrin
Formetanate hydrochloride
Formic acid
Formothion
Formparanate
Fosthietan
Freon 113
Fuberidazole
Fumaric acid
Furan
Furan, tetrahydro-
Furfuarl
Gallium trichloride
D-Glucose, 2-deoxy-2-[[(methylnitrosoamino)-
  carbonyl] amino]-D-
Glucose
Glycidylaldehyde
Glycol ethers
Guanidine, N-methyl-N'-nitro-N-nitroso-
Guthion
Haloethers
Halomethanes
Halon 1211
Halon 1301
Halon 2402
Heptachlor
Heptachlor and metabolites
Heptachlor epoxide
Hexachlorobenzene
Hexachloro-1,3-butadiene
Hexachlorobutadiene
Hexachlorocyclopent-adiene
Hexachlorocyclohexane (gamma isomer)
Hexachloroethane
Hexachloronaphthalene
Hexachlorophene

Hexachloropropene
Hexaethyl tetraphosphate
Hexamethylenediamine, N,N'-dibutyl-
Hexamethylphosphoramide
Hydrazine
Hydrazine, 1,1-dimethyl-
Hydrazine, 1,2-diethyl-
Hydrazine, 1,2-dimethyle-
Hydrazine, 1,2-diphenyl-
Hydrazine sulfate
Hydrazobenzene
Hydrochloric acid
Hydrocyanic acid
Hydrofluoric acid
Hydrogen chloride (gas only)
Hydrogen cyanide
Hydrogen fluoride
Hydrogen peroxide (conc. > 52%)
Hydrogen selenide
Hydrogen sulfide
Hydroperoxide, 1-methyl-1-phenylethyl-
Hydroquinone
Indeno (1,2,3-cd) pyrene
Iron, pentacarbonyl-
Isobenzan
Isobutyl alcohol
Isobutryaldehyde
Isobutyronitrile
Isocyanic acid, 3,4-dichlorophenyl ester
Isodrin
Isofluorphate
Isophorone
Isophorone diisocyanate
Isoprene
Isopropanolamine dodecylbenzene sulfonate
Isopropyl chloroformate
Isopropyl alcohol (mfg-strong acid process)
Isopropylmethylpyra-zolyl dimethyl-carbamate
Isosafrole
5-(Aminomethyl)-3-isoxazolol
Kepone
Lactonitrile
Lasiocarpine
Lead
Lead compounds
Lead acetate
Lead arsenate
Lead chloride
Lead fluoborate
Lead fluoride
Lead iodide
Lead nitrate
Lead phosphate
Lead stearate
Lead subacetate
Lead sulfate

Lead sulfide
Lead thiocyanate
Leptophos
Lewisite
Lindane
Lithium chromate
Lithium hydride
Malathion
Maleic acid
Maleic anhydride
Maleic hydrazide
Malononitrile
Maneb
Manganese
Manganese compounds
Manganese, tricarbonyl methylcyclopenta-dienyl
MBI
MBOCA
Mechlorethamine
Melphalan
Mephosfolan
Mercaptodimethur
Mercuric acetate
Mercuric chloride
Mercuric cyanide
Mercuric oxide
Mercuric sulfate
Mercuric thiocyanate
Mercurous nitrate
Mercury
Mercury compounds
Mercury fulminate
Methacrolein diacetate
Methacrylic anhydride
Methacrylonitrile
Methacryloyl chloride
Methacryloyloxyethyl isocyanate
Methamidophos
Methanamine, N-methyle-N-nitroso-
Methanesulfonyl fluoride
Methanol
Methylpyrilene
Methidathion
Methiocarb
Methomyl
Methoxychlor
2-Methoxyethanol
Methoxyethylmercuric acetate
Methyl acrylate
Methyl 2-chloroacrylate
Methyl bromide
Methyl chloride
Methyl chloroform
Methyl chloroformate
3-Methylcholanthrene
4,4'-Methylenebis (2-chloroaniline)

4,4'-Methylenebis (N,N-dimethyl) benzenamine
Methylenebis (phenyl isocyanate)
Methylene bromide
Methylene chloride
4,4'-Methylenedianiline
Methyl ethyl ketone (MEK)
Methyl ethyl ketone peroxide
Methyl hydrazine
Methyl iodide
Methyl isobutyl ketone
Methyl isocyanate
Methyl isothiocyanate
Methyl mercaptan
Methylmercuric dicyanamide
Methyl methracrylate
Methyl parathion
Methyl phenkapton
Methyl phosphonic dichloride
Methyl tert-butyl ether
Methyl thiocyanate
Methylthiouracil
Methyltrichlorosilane
Methyl vinyl ketone
Metolcarb
Mevinphos
Mexacarbate
Michler's ketone
Mitomycin C
Molybdenum trioxide
Monochloropenta-fluoroethane [CFC-115]
Monocrotophos
Monoethylamine
Muscimol
Mustard gas
Naled
Naphthalene
Naphthenic acid
1,4-Naphthoquinone
alpha-Naphthylamine
beta-Naphthylamine
Nickel
Nickel ammonium sulfate
Nickel carbonyl
Nickel chloride
Nickel compounds
Nickel cyanide
Nickel hydroxide
Nickel nitrate
Nickel sulfate
Nicotine
Nicotine and salts
Nicotine sulfate
Nitric acid
Nitric oxide
Nitrilotriacetic acid
p-Nitroaniline

5-Nitro-o-anisidine
Nitrobenzene
4-Nitrobiphenyl
Nitrocyclohexane
Nitrofen
Nitrogen dioxide
Nitrogen mustard
Nitroglycerin
Nitrophenol (mixed isomers)
m-Nitrophenol
p-Nitrophenol
2-Nitrophenol
4-Nitrophenol
Nitrophenols
2-Nitropropane
Nitrosamines
N-Nitrosodi-n-butylamine
N-Nitrosodiethanolamine
N-Nitrosodiethylamine
N-Nitrosodimethylamine
Nitrosodimethylamine
N-Nitrosodiphenylamine
p-Nitrosodiphenylamine
N-Nitrosodi-n-propylamine
N-Nitroso-N-ethylurea
N-Nitroso-N-methylurea
N-Nitrosomethylvinylamine
N-Nitrosomorpholine
N-Nitroso-N-methylurethane
N-Nitrosonornicotine
N-Nitrosopiperidine
N-Nitrosopyrrolidine
Nitrotoluene
m-Nitrotoluene
o-Nitrotoluene
p-Nitrotoluene
5-Nitro-o-toluidine
Norbormide
Octachloronaphthalene
Organorhodium complex (PMN-82-147)
Osmium oxide OsO4 (T-4)-
Osmium tetroxide
Ouabain
Oxamyl
Oxetane, 3,3-bis (chloromethyl)-
Oxirane
Oxydisulfoton
Ozone
Paraformaldehyde
Paraldehyde
Paraquat
Paraquat methosulfate
Parathion
Parathion-methyl
Paris green
PCBs

PCNB
Pentaborane
Pentachlorobenzene
Pentachloroethane
Pentachloronitrobenzene
PCP
Pentachlorophenol
Pentadecylamine
1,3-Pentadiene
Peracetic acid
Perchloroethylene
Perchloromethyl-mercaptan
Phenacetin
Phenanthrene
Phenol
Phenol, 2,2'-thiobis (4-chloro-6-methyl-)
Phenol, 3-(1-methyl-ethyl)-, methyl-carbamate
Phenoxarsine, 10,10'-oxydi
Phenyl dichloroarsine
p-Phenylenediamine
Phenylhydrazine hydrochloride
Phenylmercuric acetate
Phenylmercury acetate
2-Phenylphenol
Phenylsilatrane
Phenylthiourea
Phorate
Phosacetim
Phosfolan
Phosgene
Phosmet
Phosphamidon
Phosphine
Phosphonothioic acid, methyl-, 0-ethyl 0-(4-(methyl-thio)phenyl) ester
Phosphonothioic acid, methyl-, s-(2-(bis(1-methyl-ethyl)amino) ethyl)0-ethyl ester
Phosphonothioic acid, methyl-0-(4-nitrophenyl) 0-phenyl ester
Phosphoric acid, dimethyl 4-(methylthio) phenyl ester
Phosphoric acid
Phosphorothioic acid, 0,0-dimethyl-S-(2-methyl-thio) ethyl ester
Phosphorus
Phosphorus oxychloride
Phosphorus penta-chloride
Phosphorus pentoxide
Phosphorus trichloride
Phthalate esters
Phthalate anhydride
Physostigmine
Physostigmine, salicylate (1:1)
2-Picoline
Picric acid
Picrotoxin

Piperidine
Pirimifos-ethyl
Polybrominated biphenyls (PBBs)
Polychlorinated biphenyls
Polynuclear aromatic hydrocarbons
Potassium arsenate
Potassium arsenite
Potassium bichromate
Potassium chromate
Potassium cyanide
Potassium hydroxide
Potassium permanganate
Potassium silver cyanide
Promecarb
Propane, 1,2-dichloro-
1,3-Propane sultone
Propane sultone
Propargite
Propargyl alcohol
Propargyl bromide
Propiolactone, beta-
Propionaldehyde
Propionic acid
Propionic anhydride
Propionitrile
Propionitrile, 3-chloro-
Propiophenone, 4'-amino-
Propoxur
Propyl chloroformate
n-Propylamine
Propylene (Propene)
Propylene oxide
Propyleneimine
Di-n-propylnitrosamine
Prothoate
Pyrene
Pyrethrins
Pyridine
Pyridine, 2-methyl-5-vinyl-
Pyridine, 3-(1-methyl-2-pyrrolidinyl)-, (S)
Pyridine, 4-amino-
Pyridine, 4-nitro-, 1-oxide
Pyriminil
Quinoline
Quinone
Quintozene
Reserpine
Resorcinol
Saccharin (manufacturing)
Saccharin and salts
Safrote
Salcomine
Sarin
Selenious acid
Selenious acid, dithallium (1+) salt
Selenium

Selenium compounds
Selenium dioxide
Selenium oxychloride
Selenium sulfide
Selenourea
Semicarbazide hydrochloride
Silane, (4-aminobutyl) diethoxymethyl-
Silver
Silver compounds
Silver cyanide
Silver nitrate
Silvex (2,4,5-TP)
Sodium
Sodium arsenate
Sodium arsenite
Sodium azide (Na(N3))
Sodium bichromate
Sodium bifluoride
Sodium bisulfite
Sodium cacodylate
Sodium chromate
Sodium cyanide (Na(CN))
Sodium dodecyl-benzenesulfonate
Sodium fluoride
Sodium fluoroacetate
Sodium hydrosulfide
Sodium hydroxide
Sodium hypochlorite
Sodium methylate
Sodium nitrite
Sodium phosphate, dibasic
Sodium phosphate, tribasic
Sodium selenate
Sodium selenite
Sodium tellurite
Stannane, acetoxy-triphenyl-
Strontium chromate
Strychnine
Strychnine and salts
Strychnine, sulfate
Styrene
Styrene oxide
Sulfotep
Sulfoxide, 3-chloropropyl octyl
Sulfur dioxide
Sulfur monochloride
Sulfur phosphide
Sulfur tetrafluoride
Sulfur trioxide
Sulfuric acid
Sulfuric acid (fuming)
2,4,5-T acid
2,4,5-T amines
2,4,5-T esters
2,4,5-T salts
Tabun

Tellurium
Tellurium hexafluoride
TEPP
Terbufos
1,2,4,5-Tetrachlorobenzene
2,3,7,8-Tetrachlorodibenzo-p-dioxin (TCDD)
1,1,2,2-Tetrachloroethane
Tetrachloroethylene
2,3,4,6-Tetrachlorophenol
Tetrachlorvinphos
Tetraethyldithiopyrophosphate
Tetraethyl lead
Tetraethyl phosphate
Tetraethyltin
Tetramethyllead
Tetranitromethane
Thallic oxide
Thallium
Thallium compounds
Thallium (I) acetate
Thallium (I) carbonate
Thallium chloride
Thallium (I) nitrate
Thallium sulfate
Thallium (I) sulfate
Thallous carbonate
Thallous chloride
Thallous malonate
Thallous sulfate
Thioacetamide
Thiocarbazide
4,4'-Thiodianiline
Thiofanox
Thiomethanol
Thionazin
Thiophenol
Thiosemicarbazide
Thiourea
Thiourea, (2-chlorophenyl)-
Thiourea, (2-methylphenenyl)-
Thiourea, 1-naphthalenyl-
Thiram
Thorium dioxide
Titanium tetrachloride
o-Tolidine
Toluene
Toluenediamine
Toluene 2,4-diiso-cyanate
Toluene 2,6-diiso-cyanate
Toluenediisocyanate (mixed isomers)
o-Toluidine
p-Toluidine
o-Toluidine hydrochloride
Toxaphene
2,4,5-TP esters
Trans-1,4-dichloro-butene

Triamiphos
Triazoquone
Triazofos
Tribromethane
Trichlorfon
Trichloroacetyl chloride
Trichloroethylsilane
Trichloronate
Trichlorophenysilane
Trichloro(chloromethyl)silane
Trichloro(dichloro-phenyl)silane
1,2,4-Trichlorobenzene
1,1,1-Trichloroethane
1,1,2-Trichloroethane
Trichloroethylene
Trichlorofluoromethane [CFC-11]
Trichloromethanesulfenyl chloride
Trichloromonofluoro-methane
Trichlorophenol
2,3,4-Trichlorophenol
2,3,5-Trichlorophenol
2,3,6-Trichlorophenol
2,4,5-Trichlorophenol
2,4,6-Trichlorophenol
3,4,5-Trichlorophenol
Triethanolamine dodecylbenzene sulfonate
Triethoxsilane
Triethylamine
Trifluralin
Trimethylamine
1,2,4-Trimethylbenzene
Trimethylchlorosilane
Trimethylolpropane phosphite
Trimethyltin chloride
1,3,5-Trinitrobenzene
Triphenyltin chloride
Tris(2-chloroethyl) amine
Tris (2,3-dibromopropyl) phosphate
Trypan blue
Uracil mustard
Uranyl acetate
Uranyl nitrate
Urethane
Valinomycin
Vanadium (fume or dust)
Vanadium pentoxide
Vanadyl sulfate
Vinyl acetate monomer
Vinyl acetate
Vinyl bromide
Vinyl chloride
Vinylidene chloride
Warfarin
Warfarin sodium
Warfarin and salts (conc. > 0.3%)
m-Xylene

o-Xylene
p-Xylene
Xylene (mixed isomers)
Xyleonol
2,6-Xylidine
Xylylene dichloride
Zinc (fume or dust)
Zinc
Zinc compounds
Zinc acetate
Zinc ammonium chloride
Zinc borate
Zinc bromide
Zinc carbonate
Zinc chloride
Zinc cyanide
Zinc, dichloro(4,4-dimethyl-5 ((((methyl-amino) carbonyl)oxy) imino) pentane-nitrile)-,(T-4)-

Zinc fluoride
Zinc formate
Zinc hydrosulfite
Zinc nitrate
Zinc phenolsulfonate
Zinc phosphide
Zinc phosphide (conc. ≤ 10%)
Zinc phosphide (conc. > 10%)
Zinc silicofluoride
Zinc sulfate
Zineb
Zirconium nitrate
Zirconium potassium fluoride
Zirconium sulfate
Zirconium tetrachloride

NUCLEAR POWER

NUCLEAR ENERGY GLOSSARY

alpha particle: A relatively large, heavy, electrically charged radioactive particle consisting of two protons and two neutrons. Alpha particles slow down relatively quickly and are able to travel only short distances through air. They can not penetrate skin or even a sheet of paper. However, if a substance emitting alpha particles is ingested, they can cause serious damage.

atom: The smallest unit of matter that is recognizable as a chemical element. An atom contains a nucleus composed of protons (positively charged particles) and neutrons (neutral particles); the nucleus is circled by electrons (negatively charged particles). Normally, the number of protons equals the number of electrons, leaving the atom electrically neutral. [*See* ion]

atomic number: The number of protons in an element. It is constant for each element.

background radiation: Naturally occurring radiation that is always present in the environment. It is produced by cosmic rays, natural deposits of radioactive elements, building materials, etc.

becquerel: A measurement of nuclear disintegration of a radioactive material. One becquerel equals one decay (release of particle) per second.

beta particle: A particle with less mass and more speed than an alpha particle. They can penetrate skin but can be stopped by thin sheets of aluminum.

boiling-water reactor (BWR): A nuclear reactor that uses water as a coolant. The water circulates through the core and boils. The resulting steam turns a turbine to produce electricity.

boron: Chemical element that absorbs neutrons. It is used in control rods, which are raised or lowered in a reactor's core to regulate or stop nuclear fission.

breeder reactor: A nuclear reactor that produces fissionable material as a by-product. It produces as much fuel as (or more fuel than) it consumes.

cadmium: Chemical element that absorbs neutrons. It is used in control rods, which are raised or lowered in a reactor's core to regulate or stop nuclear fission.

CANDU reactor: Canadian Deuterium Uranium reactor; a heavy-water reactor that uses unenriched uranium. It can be refueled without being shut down.

chain reaction: A self-sustaining process in which the fission of one atom causes the fission of another or others, which causes more fission, etc.

containment: Nuclear reactor structures designed to prevent radiation from escaping.

control rods: Rods of neutron-absorbing material that can be raised or lowered in the core of a nuclear reactor to control or stop fission.

coolant: A liquid or gas that circulates through the core of a nuclear reactor to extract heat.

core: The area of a nuclear reactor where fission occurs. It contains fuel rods, control rods and a moderator (a substance, often the same as the coolant, used to slow neutrons).

critical: A term used to describe a fuel core that is undergoing a chain reaction. When a reactor reaches the point where the chain reaction becomes self-sustaining, it is said to have "gone critical."

critical mass: The minimum amount of radioactive material needed to sustain a chain reaction.

deuterium: A stable isotope of hydrogen in which the nucleus has both a neutron and a proton. (Ordinary hydrogen has only a proton in the nucleus.)

dose equivalent: A measure of exposure to radiation that considers both the amount of radiation and the type. The amount is multiplied by a "quality factor" related to the penetrating qualities of particular types of radiation. The unit of measurement is the sievert, the rem or the millirem.

electron: One of the components of an atom; a negatively charged particle that circles the nucleus.

enriched uranium: See uranium

fallout: The material that returns to Earth after a nuclear explosion.

fission: The splitting of atoms, which causes large amounts of energy to be released. It can occur naturally or it can be induced by bombarding an atom's nucleus with neutrons.

fuel cycle: The sequence of mining, refining, using, reprocessing and disposing of nuclear fuel.

fuel rod: Metal containers containing pellets of radioactive fuel. They are grouped in bundles called fuel assemblies in the core of the reactor.

fusion: The combining of nuclei, which causes large amounts of energy to be released.

gamma ray: A form of radiation, similar to an X-ray, which is released during nuclear reactions. Gamma rays can travel long distances and can penetrate some metals and concrete.

gas-cooled reactor: A nuclear reactor in which gas, such as carbon dioxide or helium, circulates around the core and serves as a coolant.

gray: A measurement of the absorbed dose of radiation. One gray is the dose of radiation that will cause one kilogram of material to absorb one joule of energy. Formerly, rads were used to measure absorbed radiation. One gray equals 100 rad.

half-life: The time required for half of the atoms in a sample of radioactive material to disintegrate. The same time is required for half of the remaining sample to decay, and for half of that remainder to decay, ad infinitum. Half-lives range from a fraction of a second to billions of years.

heavy-water reactor: A nuclear reactor that uses heavy water as a moderator and coolant. Heavy water (also known as deuterium oxide or D_2O) contains deuterium, a heavier isotope of hydrogen, instead of ordinary hydrogen.

high-level waste: The spent fuel from nuclear reactors, which remains deadly for many thousands of years.

intermediate-level waste: Material that has been directly contaminated by radioactive material, such as the metal cans that hold radioactive fuel.

ion: An atom to which electrons have been added or removed, resulting in an electrical charge. [See atom]

isotopes: Forms of an element with a differing number of neutrons. For example, all forms of uranium have 92 protons, but the number of neutrons varies. Two common isotopes are uranium-235 (92 protons and 143 neutrons) and uranium-238 (92 protons and 146 neutrons). [See atomic number, mass number, neutron, proton]

light-water reactor: Any reactor that uses ordinary water (H_2O) as a coolant. The water may be under increased pressure (a pressurized-water reactor) or not (a boiling-water reactor). Light-water reactors are the most common type in the United States. [See heavy-water reactor]

loss-of-coolant accident (LOCA): The most feared nuclear power accident, loss of coolant can lead to meltdown.

low-level waste: Any items that have had contact with radiation and are suspected of carrying low levels of radiation. Produced by medical and industrial use, and by nuclear power plants. Includes such items as protective clothing, disposable paper goods and the residues of treated waste water from nuclear plants.

mass number: The number of neutrons and protons in an atom of an element. Elements can have several isotopes, each with a different mass number. [See isotope]

megawatt: A unit of power; 1 million watts.

meltdown: A nuclear accident in which the fuel becomes so overheated that the fuel rods melt, releasing radioactive dust. The severity of the accident depends on the effectiveness of emergency cooling systems and the integrity of the containment system.

millirem: A measure of the effects of ionizing radiation on humans; one one-thousandth of a rem.

moderator: Material used in the core of a nuclear reactor to slow neutrons.

neutron: A particle with no electrical charge that is found in the nucleus of the atom. The number of neutrons in an element can vary, creating isotopes. [See isotope]

nuclear winter: A possible effect of a global nuclear war. Dust, smoke and soot in the atmosphere would obscure the sun, causing profound climate changes.

nucleus: The center of an atom. Contains one or more protons and neutrons, resulting in a positive charge. (Hydrogen, an exception, contains only a proton in its nucleus.)

permitted dose: A safety guideline indicating the maximum dose of radiation that an individual or population can receive over a given period of time. Because knowledge of immediate and potential effects of radiation is developing, the recommended permitted dose is subject to change.

plutonium: A transuranic element used as a fuel in nuclear reactors. [See transuranic elements]

pressure-tube graphite reactor: See RBMK

pressurized-water reactor (PWR): A light-water reactor in which the water that circulates around the core as coolant is under enough pressure that it does not boil. The pressurized water cools a second circuit of water, which turns to steam and is used to generate electricity.

proton: A positively charged particle found in the nucleus of the atom. The number of protons in an element (the atomic number) is constant.

PTRG: See RBMK

rad: A measurement formerly used to measure the absorbed dose of radiation. [See gray]

radiation sickness: Illness that results when radiation damages or kills cells. The severity of the illness depends on the type, extent and duration of exposure. Immediate symptoms include burns, central nervous system damage, nausea and vomiting. Radiation can also destroy the ability of bone marrow to produce blood cells, can destroy the cells lining the gastrointestinal tract, and can cause genetic mutations. Cell changes may result in cancer years after exposure.

radon gas: A colorless radioactive gas that is the largest component of background radiation. It is released by the decay of radioactive elements in soil and some building materials. Some buildings contain dangerously high levels of radon gas because of the surrounding geology, the materials used in construction or the ventilation characteristics of the building.

RBMK (graphite-moderator boiling-water reactor): A light-water reactor that uses graphite to slow neutrons in the core. It is a Soviet-designed reactor. (The acronym is derived from the Russian name.) Complex cooling circuits make maintenance difficult. It is the design used at Chernobyl. Also known as a pressure-tube graphite reactor (PTGR).

rem (roentgen equivalent man): A measure of radiation dose. It is based on the amount of radiation absorbed and the type of radiation. Low-level radiation is often measured in millirems.

scram: Rapid shutdown of a nuclear reactor, accomplished by moving control rods into the core to stop fission.

sievert: A measure of radiation dose. One sievert equals 100 rem. [*See* rem]

Synroc: A synthetic rock-like material under development in Australia. Some researchers claim that it could be a safe containment material for nuclear wastes.

transuranic elements: Elements that are heavier than uranium. They are produced artificially.

tritium: A radioactive isotope of hydrogen with one proton and two neutrons. (Ordinary hydrogen has no neutrons.)

uranium: The heaviest naturally occurring element (it has 92 protons). Naturally occurring uranium consists primarily of two isotopes: uranium-238 (about 99.3 percent) and uranium-235 (about 0.7 percent). Only uranium-235 can be used for fission in nuclear reactors. Because of this, naturally occurring uranium usually is enriched to increase the proportion of uranium-235 before it is used as fuel.

yellowcake: Uranium ore that has undergone initial purification. It is granular and mildly radioactive. It must be purified further before it can be used as nuclear fuel.

NUCLEAR ENERGY TECHNOLOGY IN BRIEF

The end process in nuclear and fossil-fuel power generating plants is the same—steam is generated, which turns a turbine, which produces electricity. The difference is in the source of power and the methods used to generate the steam. Where a fossil-fuel plant burns coal, oil or natural gas to produce the heat needed to produce steam, a nuclear plant "burns" radioactive fuel, usually uranium-235, by splitting its atoms to release energy.

The burning of fossil fuel releases heat and light. The "burning" of uranium releases heat and radiation. Fossil fuel produces ash, smoke and gases as waste products; uranium produces fragments of atoms, most of which are radioactive, and spent fuel, which is also radioactive. A primary difference between the two types of power generation, therefore, is in the danger of the by-products that result during and after their destruction. Another difference is in the inherent danger of the fuel itself.

Uranium is an unstable element, which means that the nuclei of its atoms break apart comparatively easily. As the nuclei break apart (a process called "fission"), particles and energy are released. The particles are the components of the nucleus and of the electrons that surround the nucleus. They include neutrons (electrically neutral particles), alpha particles (a combination of two protons and two neutrons), beta particles (electrons that are emitted in fast streams called beta rays) and gamma rays (waves of energy with great penetrating power, like X-rays, but with short wavelengths).

All uranium atoms have 92 protons. The number of neutrons varies, however. These variations are called isotopes. There are three naturally occurring isotopes of uranium: uranium-234 (92 protons + 142 neutrons), uranium-235 (92 protons + 143 neutrons) and uranium-238 (92 protons + 146 neutrons). Most naturally occurring uranium is more than 99 percent uranium-238. The remainder is primarily uranium-235, with traces of uranium-234.

Of the three isotopes, uranium-235 is the only one that undergoes fission readily. Most nuclear reactors use a form of uranium fuel in which the concentration of uranium-235 has been increased to about 3 percent. This process, called enrichment, can be extremely costly.

When a uranium-235 atom is struck by a neutron, other neutrons are released. If those neutrons strike other uranium-235 atoms, the process continues and is repeated. This is a chain reaction. If the reaction continues in geometric fashion, with each fission reaction causing numerous other reactions, the release of power becomes devastatingly explosive: an atomic bomb. The uranium that is used in atomic bombs is greatly enriched to make this possible. The uranium that is used in nuclear reactors does not contain enough uranium-235 to cause this type of explosion.

The danger at nuclear power plants is not a nuclear explosion, but release of radiation in a variety of ways, including leaks, sabotage, natural disasters, meltdown of the core and steam explosions that damage the containment structure. The buildings that contain the structures are designed to withstand severe force, to prevent the escape of radiation due to internal or external forces. The world's worst nuclear accident occurred on April 26, 1985, at the Chernobyl power plant in the Soviet Union, when the containment structure, which had been inadequately designed, ruptured.

The Chernobyl plant used graphite, which can burn at extremely high temperatures, in its core. Some experts have said that the design, which is not used in the United States, is inherently unsafe. One of the plant's reactors overheated after its emergency water-cooling system was turned off. The graphite, which is used to slow the nuclear reaction, began to burn. The reaction then went out of control, resulting in a power surge that caused the graphite to explode. That and a steam explosion blew the top off the reactor, spewing radiation into the air. A chemical explosion then caused further damage. The blast caused 31 deaths initially, but the total number of deaths attributed to the escaped radiation may not be known for years. The heaviest fallout was over the western Soviet Union and parts of Europe, but it spread across the Northern Hemisphere. The Soviet government has compiled a registry of 576,000 people who may be at risk for developing cancer and other diseases because of their exposure. Some estimates place the potential number at more than 4 million.

The largest nuclear accident in the United States occurred at the Three Mile Island reactor in Pennsylvania on March 28, 1979. In that case, however, the radiation was largely contained, which saved lives. The Three Mile Island accident occurred because of a partial meltdown of the reactor's core.

The chain reaction that occurs in nuclear reactors produces vast amounts of heat. If uncontrolled, the heat can be high enough to cause the fuel to melt, releasing radioactive dust. Reactors rely on a variety of safety measures to prevent a Loss-of-Coolant Accident (also called a LOCA), which could lead to a meltdown. If overheating occurs, there are other safety measures designed to control it and to prevent release of radiation and the rupture of the containment building. Some safety measures are designed to occur automatically. Others can be operated, or altered, by workers at the plant. Safety at nuclear plants, therefore, depends on their design and construction and on the ability of their crews.

At Three Mile Island, the accident began when the water used to cool the reactor core was inadvertently shut off. An automatic safety mechanism then shut down the reactor and opened a valve that released an emergency water supply. Operators, who did not understand what was happening, overrode the automatic system and shut off the emergency water supply. The mistake was discovered two hours later. By that time, however, the water level was low enough so that part of the core was uncovered and had begun to melt. Radioactive particles escaped into the containment building through an open valve and flowed into water storage tanks in an adjacent building. Some radioactive gases escaped, although the extent of the emission is debated. Most of the gases were contained within the building for more than a year. By that time, much of their radioactivity had dissipated and they could be released gradually into the atmosphere. The accident was blamed on poor operator training, faulty instrument systems, poor control-room design and a lack of communication within the industry, which prevented operators from learning from each other's experiences.

All reactors consist of a core of nuclear fuel, in pellet form, which is housed in metal tubes about 12 feet long called fuel rods or pins. The rods are arranged in groups called assemblies. Reactors can have hundreds of assemblies and tens of thousands of fuel rods.

The cores of nuclear reactors also contain control rods, which can be raised or lowered to speed up, slow down or stop nuclear fission. The rods contain material (usually boron or cadmium) that absorbs neutrons. When a plant is shut down, the control rods are in a position to absorb all of the neutrons that are being released by the fuel. When this happens, the chain reaction stops.

Each reactor also contains a moderator (a material used to slow neutrons) and a cooling agent, which is used to transfer the heat from reactor core to the turbine. Reactor types often are described by the types of coolants or moderators they use.

A Boiling-Water Reactor (BWR) uses water as a cooling agent. Water is pumped through the core, where it is turned to steam. The steam is then pumped out to turn a turbine. It is condensed and pumped back into the core as water. A Pressurized-Water Reactor (PWR) also uses water, but the water in the core is kept under high pressure, which prevents it from turning to steam. It is pumped out of the core to a boiler and back into the core. As the water in this pipe loop passes through the boiler, it heats another pipe that contains water at much lower pressure. The water in the second pipe loop turns to steam, which drives a turbine. The steam is then condensed, and the water is piped back to the boiler.

Heavy-Water Reactors use heavy water (a form of water in which a heavy isotope, deuterium, replaces the hydrogen atoms) as a moderator and coolant. They operate like a PWR, but they are able to use natural, rather than enriched, uranium. An example is the Canadian Deuterium Uranium (CANDU) reactor.

The Graphite-Moderated Boiling-Water Reactor is the type used in the Soviet Union. It is also known as a Pressure-Tube Graphite Reactor (PTGR) and by its Russian abbreviation, RBMK. The fuel assemblies are cooled by circulating water and are embedded in a graphite core.

High-Temperature Gas-Cooled Reactors (HTGRs) use helium as a coolant. The heated helium heats water in a pipe; the water turns to steam, which is used to drive a turbine.

Advanced Gas Reactors (AGRs) use carbon dioxide as a coolant.

Some reactors are designed so that they are dependent upon natural occurrences for their safety, rather than upon mechanical devices and human operators. These are sometimes called "inherently safe" reactors, although the label is subject to debate. One such design is the Process-Inherent Ultimately Safe Reactor (PIUS) from Sweden. It is a pressurized-water reactor that is immersed in borated water and contained in thick concrete walls. If the primary cooling system fails, the borated water automatically floods the core, which shuts down the reactor without operator intervention.

Breeder reactors differ from other reactors in that they produce as much or more fuel as they use. They use a core of uranium-235, which is surrounded by uranium-238. As the U-235 undergoes fission, the escaping neutrons strike the surrounding layer of U-238. That material, which is not useful as a nuclear fuel, is transformed into plutonium-239, which is useful. The plutonium-239 is removed periodically and fabricated into fuel pellets.

NUCLEAR ENERGY: FEDERAL FRAMEWORK AND CONTACTS

Although the Nuclear Regulatory Commission is the primary federal agency dealing with nuclear energy, many other agencies also are involved in overseeing the production, transportation, use and disposal of radioactive materials, or in handling emergencies. State agencies also are involved.

GOVERNMENTAL CONTACTS

Bureau of Land Management (Department of Interior): Develops and implements federal leasing programs dealing with uranium. Address: Main Interior Building, Washington, D.C. 20240, (202) 208-5717.

Defense Nuclear Facilities Safety Board: An independent board created by Congress to oversee and provide advice concerning defense nuclear facilities operated by the Department of Energy. Address: 625 Indiana Ave. NW, Washington, D.C. 20004, (202) 208-6400.

Department of Agriculture: In the event of an emergency, the DOA would test meat and poultry for contamination and provide information to farmers. Address: 14th St. and Independence Ave. SW, Washington, D.C. 20250, (202) 720-2791.

Department of Defense: The DOD coordinates research, development and procurement of nuclear weapons, in coordination with the Department of Energy. Address: Department of Defense, Atomic Energy, The Pentagon, Washington, D.C. 20301, (703) 545-6700.

Department of Energy: Develops nuclear energy and propulsion sources, provides uranium-enrichment services, develops and tests nuclear weapons, develops and implements policies concerning the use and reprocessing of nuclear materials, develops and licenses waste disposal facilities, and participates in international negotiations concerning nuclear nonproliferation. Headquarters is at 1000 Independence Ave. SW, Washington, D.C. 20585, (202) 586-5806 (press information), (202) 586-5575 (public information).

Department of Health and Human Services and Urban Development: In the event of a nuclear emergency, the department would provide food and shelter. Address: 200 Independence Ave. SW, Washington, D.C. 20201, (202) 690-6343 (press information), (202) 690-6867 (public information).

Department of Interior: In the event of an emergency, the department would measure fish and wildlife for contamination and would make decisions concerning federal lands and water projects. Address: Main Interior Bldg., 1849 C St. NW, Washington, D.C. 20240, (202) 208-3171. [See below, U.S. Geological Survey]

Department of Justice: The Emergency Programs Center deals with criminal activity involving nuclear materials. Address: 10th St. & Constitution Ave. NW, Washington, D.C. 20530, (202) 514-2000.

Department of State: Works with the Nuclear Regulatory Commission on issues involving nuclear imports and exports; monitors the Nuclear Nonproliferation Treaty; negotiates agreements with other countries concerning the safe operation of nuclear reactors. Address: 2201 C St. NW, Washington, D.C. 20520, (202) 647-4101.

Department of Transportation: Issues safety regulations concerning the transportation of hazardous materials. In the event of an emergency, the department would help evacuate residents, augmenting local services. Address: 400 7th St. SW, Washington, D.C. 20590; (202) 366-4461.

Energy Information Administration (Department of Energy): Analyzes and forecasts the availability, production, prices and transportation of nuclear fuel and the availability of nuclear power throughout the world. Address: 1707 H St. NW, Washington, D.C. Mailing address: 1000 Independence Ave. SW, Washington, D.C. 20585, (202) 586-8800.

Environmental Protection Agency: Conducts research concerning radiation hazards, sets exposure limits, establishes standards concerning use of radioactive materials, investigates violations, oversees federal compliance. Address: 401 M St. SW, Washington, D.C. 20460, (202) 260-4355 (press information), (202) 260-2080 (public information).

Federal Emergency Management Agency: Helps state and local governments prepare for and react to nuclear accidents of all types. Address: 500 C St. SW, Washington, D.C. 20472, (202) 646-4600.

National Transportation Safety Board: Investigates accidents concerning the transportation of hazardous materials. Address: 490 L'Enfant Plaza SW, Washington, D.C. 20594, (202) 382-0670.

Nuclear Regulatory Commission: Regulates commercial use of nuclear energy; reviews safety of proposed and existing nuclear reactors; licenses and inspects nuclear facilities; enforces standards set by the Environmental Protection Agency. The NRC fines utilities for rule violations based on the following guidelines: Severity Level I, $100,000; Severity Level II, $80,000; Severity Level III, $50,000; Severity Level IV, $15,000; Severity Level V, $5,000 (all penalties are per violation per day). Penalties can be increased or lowered 100 percent or 50 percent based on the utility's diligence. The Office of Governmental and Public Affairs serves as the public information office. Address: 11555 Rockville Pike, Rockville, MD. Mailing address: Washington, D.C. 20555, (301) 504-2240 (Office of Governmental and Public Affairs).

Nuclear Waste Technical Review Board: Independent board appointed by the President to evaluate development of nuclear waste disposal system by the Department of Energy. Address: 1100 Wilson Blvd., Arlington, VA 22209, (703) 235-4473.

Tennessee Valley Authority: Coordinates land-use programs in the Tennessee River Valley. Sells power to municipalities, federal installations, industry. Address: 1 Massachusetts Ave., Suite 300, Washington, D.C. 20444, (202) 479-4412.

U.S. Geological Survey (Department of Interior): Monitors geologic factors relating to nuclear reactor sites, test sites and disposal. Conducts research for other federal agencies. Address: 12201 Sunrise Valley Dr., Reston, VA 22092, (703) 648-6714, (703) 648-6960.

NONGOVERNMENTAL CONTACTS

American Nuclear Energy Council: Principal voice of the nuclear energy industry. Interests include legislation, licensing and waste disposal. Members include utilities that operate nuclear plants, manufacturers, contractors and mining and disposal companies. Address: 410 1st St. SE, Washington, D.C. 20003, (202) 484-2670.

American Physical Society: Society of scientists, educators and others that sponsors studies of topics such as reactor safety and energy use. Address: 335 E. 45th St., New York, NY 10017, (212) 682-7341.

Americans for Nuclear Energy: Promotes use of nuclear energy. Address: 2525 Wilson Blvd., Arlington, VA 22201, (703) 528-4430.

Nuclear Information and Resource Service: Information clearinghouse on nuclear power, waste and hazards. Address: 1424 16th St. NW, Washington, D.C. 20036, (202) 328-0002.

Public Citizen: Public interest group that opposes nuclear energy. Address: Critical Mass Energy Project, 215 Pennsylvania Ave. SE, Washington, D.C. 20003, (202) 546-4996.

Safe Energy Communication Council: Coalition of media, environmental and other groups that publicizes relative merits and hazards of nuclear and other forms of energy, and conservation. Address: 1717 Massachusetts Ave. NW, Washington, D.C. 20036, (202) 483-8491.

Union of Concerned Scientists: Concerned with energy policy and nuclear safety. Address: 26 Church St., Cambridge, MA 02238, (617) 547-5552.

U.S. Council for Energy Awareness: Members include nuclear utilities, industries, related organizations, government agencies and universities. Provides information on licensing, safety and waste disposal. Address: 1776 I St. NW, Washington, D.C. 20006, (202) 293-0770.

REFERENCES

The Greenpeace Book of the Nuclear Age, John May. New York: Pantheon Books, 1989.

Licensing Event Report Compilation, Nuclear Regulatory Commission, monthly. Available through Government Printing Office, Washington, D.C. 20402, (202) 783-3238.

The Journalist's Guide to Nuclear Energy, Edward Edelson. Washington, D.C.: U.S. Council for Energy Awareness, 1990. Available from the Council.

Monthly Operating Units Status Reports (also called the *Gray Book*), Nuclear Regulatory Commission, monthly. Available through Government Printing Office, Washington, D.C. 20402, (202) 783-3238.

Report to Congress on Abnormal Occurrences at Nuclear Facilities, Nuclear Regulatory Commission, quarterly. Available through Government Printing Office, Washington, D.C. 20402, (202) 783-3238.

NUCLEAR PLANT LOCATIONS AND TELEPHONE NUMBERS

The following nuclear power plants have received operating licenses, unless otherwise indicated. The plants that have operating licenses may or may not be in operation. Plants frequently are closed for repairs or maintenance. Even plants that are closed for long periods may retain operating licenses.

Alabama:

Reactors: Joseph M. Farley 1, 2
Location: Houston County
Type: pressurized-water reactor
Utility: Alabama Power Co.
P.O. Box 2641
Birmingham, AL 35291
(205) 250-1000

Reactors: Browns Ferry 1, 2, 3
Location: Decatur
Type: boiling-water reactor
Utility: Tennessee Valley Authority
400 W. Summit Hill Dr.
Knoxville, TN 37902
(615) 632-6000

Reactors: Bellefonte 1,2 (construction permits)
Location: Scottsboro
Type: pressurized-water reactor
Utility: Tennessee Valley Authority
400 W. Summit Hill Dr.
Knoxville, TN 37902
(615) 632-6000

Arizona:

Reactors: Palo Verde 1, 2, 3
Location: Wintersburg
Type: pressurized-water reactor
Utility: Arizona Public Service
P.O. Box 52034
Phoenix, AZ 85072-2034
(602) 250-1530

Arkansas:

Reactors: Arkansas Nuclear 1, 2
Location: Russellville
Type: pressurized-water reactor
* Operator: Entergy Operations, Inc.
Rt. 3, Box 137 G
Russellville, AR 72801-9399
(501) 964-5000

California:

Reactors: Diablo Canyon 1, 2
Location: Avila Beach
Type: pressurized-water reactor
Operator: Pacific Gas & Electric Co.
77 Beale St.
San Francisco, CA 94106
(415) 781-4211

Reactors: San Onofre 1, 2, 3
Location: San Clemente
Type: pressurized-water reactor
Operator: Southern California Edison Co.
    and San Diego Gas & Electric Co.
P.O. Box 800
Rosemead, CA 91770
(818) 302-1212

Connecticut:

Reactor: Haddam Neck
Location: Haddam Neck
Type: pressurized-water reactor
Operator: Connecticut Yankee Atomic Power Co.
362 Injun Hollow Rd.
East Hampton, CT 06424
(203) 267-2556

Reactors: Millstone 1, 2, 3
Location: Waterford
Type: Millstone 1, boiling-water reactor;
    Millstone 2, 3, pressurized-water reactors
Operator: Northeast Nuclear Energy Co. (operating subsidiary of Northeast Utilities)
P.O. Box 270
Hartford, CT 06141
(203) 447-1791

Florida:

Reactor: Crystal River 3
Location: Crystal River
Type: pressurized-water reactor
Operator: Florida Power Corporation
P.O. Box 219
Crystal River, FL 32623-0319
(904) 795-3145

Reactors: Turkey Point 3, 4
Location: Turkey Point
Type: pressurized-water reactors
Operator: Florida Power & Light Co.
9250 W. Flager St.
Miami, FL 33174
(305) 552-3552

Reactors: St. Lucie 1, 2
Location: St. Lucie County

Type: pressurized-water reactors
Operator: Florida Power & Light Co.
9250 W. Flager St.
Miami, FL 33174
(305) 552-3552

Georgia:

Reactors: Edwin I. Hatch 1, 2
Location: Baxley
Type: boiling-water reactor
Operator: Georgia Power Co.
P.O. Box 4545
Atlanta, GA 30302
(404) 526-6526

Reactors: Alvin W. Vogtle 1, 2
Location: Waynesboro
Type: pressurized-water reactor
Operator: Georgia Power Co.
P.O. Box 4545
Atlanta, GA 30302
(404) 526-6526

Illinois:

Reactors: Braidwood 1, 2
Location: Braidwood
Type: pressurized-water reactor
Operator: Commonwealth Edison Co.
P.O. Box 767
Chicago, IL 60690
(312) 294-4321

Reactors: Byron 1, 2
Location: Byron
Type: pressurized-water reactor
Operator: Commonwealth Edison Co.
P.O. Box 767
Chicago, IL 60690
(312) 294-4321

Reactors: Dresden 2, 3
Location: Morris
Type: boiling-water reactor
Operator: Commonwealth Edison Co.
P.O. Box 767
Chicago, IL 60690
(312) 294-4321

Reactors: LaSalle 1, 2
Location: Seneca
Type: boiling-water reactor
Operator: Commonwealth Edison Co.
P.O. Box 767
Chicago, IL 60690
(312) 294-4321

Reactors: Quad Cities 1, 2
Location: Cordova

Type: boiling-water reactor
Operator: Commonwealth Edison Co.
P.O. Box 767
Chicago, IL 60690
(312) 294-4321

Reactors: Zion 1, 2
Location: Zion
Type: pressurized-water reactor
Operator: Commonwealth Edison Co.
P.O. Box 767
Chicago, IL 60690
(312) 294-4321

Reactor: Clinton 1
Location: Clinton
Type: boiling-water reactor
Operator: Illinois Power Co.
P.O. Box 678
Clinton, IL 61727
(217) 935-8881

Iowa:

Reactor: Duane Arnold
Location: Palo
Type: boiling-water reactor
Operator: Iowa Electric Light & Power Co.
P.O. Box 351
Cedar Rapids, IA 52406
(319) 398-4406

Kansas:

Reactor: Wolf Creek 1
Location: Burlington
Type: pressurized-water reactor
Operator: Wolf Creek Nuclear Operating Corp.
P.O. Box 2908
Wichita, KS 67201
(316) 636-6700

Louisiana:

Reactor: River Bend 1
Location: St. Francisville
Type: boiling-water reactor
Operator: Gulf States Utilities Co.
P.O. Box 2951
Beaumont, TX 77704
(409) 838-6631

Reactor: Waterford 3
Location: Taft
Type: pressurized-water reactor
* Operator: Entergy Operations, Inc.
P.O. Box B
Killona, LA 70066
(504) 467-8211

Maine:

Reactor: Maine Yankee
Location: Wiscasset
Type: pressurized-water reactor
Operator: Maine Yankee Atomic Power Co.
Edison Drive
Augusta, ME 04330
(207) 622-4868

Maryland:

Reactors: Calvert Cliffs 1, 2
Location: Lusby
Type: pressurized-water reactor
Operator: Baltimore Gas & Electric Co.
Routes 2 & 4
P.O. Box 1535
Lusby, MD 20657
(301) 586-2200

Massachusetts:

Reactor: Pilgrim 1
Location: Plymouth
Type: boiling-water reactor
Operator: Boston Edison Co.
RFD #1, Rocky Hill Rd.
Plymouth, MA 02360
(508) 746-7900

Reactor: Yankee-Rowe
Location: Rowe
Type: pressurized-water reactor
Operator: Yankee Atomic Electric Co.
580 Main St.
Bolton, MA 01740-1398
(508) 779-6711

Michigan:

Reactor: Big Rock Point
Location: Charlevoix
Type: boiling-water reactor
Operator: Consumers Power Co.
212 West Michigan Ave.
Jackson, MI 49201
(517) 788-0550

Reactor: Palisades
Location: Covert
Type: pressurized-water reactor
Operator: Consumers Power Co.
212 West Michigan Ave.
Jackson, MI 49201
(517) 788-0550

Reactor: Fermi 2
Location: Newport
Type: boiling-water reactor
Operator: Detroit Edison Co.

2000 Second Ave.
Detroit, MI 48226
(313) 237-8000

Reactors: Donald C. Cook 1, 2
Location: Bridgman
Type: pressurized-water reactor
Operator: Indiana & Michigan Power Co.
1 Cook Place
Bridgeman, MI 49106
(616) 465-5901

Minnesota:

Reactor: Monticello
Location: Monticello
Type: boiling-water reactor
Operator: Northern States Power Co.
414 Nicollet Mall
Minneapolis, MN 55401
(612) 639-1234

Reactors: Prairie Island 1, 2
Location: Red Wing
Type: pressurized-water reactor
Operator: Northern States Power Co.
414 Nicollet Mall
Minneapolis, MN 55401
(612) 639-1234

Mississippi:

Reactor: Grand Gulf 1
Location: Port Gibson
Type: boiling-water reactor
* Operator: Entergy Operations, Inc.
P.O. Box 756
Port Gibson, MS 39150
(601) 437-2800

Missouri:

Reactor: Callaway
Location: Callaway County
Type: pressurized-water reactor
Operator: Union Electric Co.
P.O. Box 149
St. Louis, MO 63166
(314) 621-3222

Nebraska:

Reactor: Cooper
Location: Brownville
Type: boiling-water reactor
Operator: Nebraska Public Power District
P.O. Box 499
Columbus, NE 68602
(402) 564-8561

Reactor: Fort Calhoun
Location: Fort Calhoun
Type: pressurized-water reactor
Operator: Omaha Public Power District
444 S. 16th St. Mall
Omaha, NE 68102
(402) 636-2000

New Hampshire:

Reactor: Seabrook 1
Location: Seabrook
Type: pressurized-water reactor
Operator: Public Service Co. of New Hampshire
P.O. Box 330
Manchester, NH 03105
(603) 669-4000

New Jersey:

Reactor: Oyster Creek
Location: Lacey Township
Type: boiling-water reactor
Operator: GPU Nuclear Corp.
Oyster Creek Nuclear Station
P.O. Box 388
Forked River, NJ 08731
(609) 971-4020

Reactors: Salem 1, 2, Hope Creek 1
Location: Lower Alloways Creek Township
Type: Salem 1, 2, pressurized-water reactor;
    Hope Creek 1, boiling-water reactor
Operator: Public Service Electric & Gas Co.
80 Park Plaza
Newark, NJ 07101
(201) 430-7000

New York:

Reactor: Indian Point 2
Location: Buchanan
Type: pressurized-water reactor
Operator: Consolidated Edison Co. of New York
4 Irving Place
New York, NY 10003
(212) 460-4600

Reactor: Indian Point 3
Location: Buchanan
Type: pressurized-water reactor
Operator: Power Authority of the State of New
    York
150 Amsterdam Ave.
New York, NY 10023
(212) 468-6000

Reactor: Shoreham
Location: Brookhaven
Type: boiling-water reactor

Operator: Long Island Lighting Co.
175 East Old Country Rd.
Hicksville, NY 11801
(516) 933-4590

Reactor: James A. FitzPatrick
Location: Scriba
Type: boiling-water reactor
Operator: Power Authority of the State of New
    York
150 Amsterdam Ave.
New York, NY 10023
(212) 468-6000

Reactors: Nine Mile Point 1, 2
Location: Scriba
Type: boiling-water reactor
Operator: Niagara Mohawk Power Co.
300 Erie Boulevard West
Syracuse, NY 13202
(315) 474-1511

Reactor: Robert E. Ginna
Location: Rochester
Type: pressurized-water reactor
Operator: Rochester Gas & Electric Co.
89 East Avenue
Rochester, NY 14649
(716) 546-2700

North Carolina:

Reactors: Brunswick 1, 2
Location: Southport
Type: boiling-water reactor
Operator: Carolina Power & Light Co.
P.O. Box 10429
Southport, NC 28461
(919) 546-6111

Reactor: Shearon Harris 1
Location: New Hill
Type: pressurized-water reactor
Operator: Carolina Power & Light Co.
P.O. Box 10429
Southport, NC 28461
(919) 546-6111

Reactors: William McGuire 1, 2
Location: Cornelius
Type: pressurized-water reactor
Operator: Duke Power Co.
422 South Church St.
Charlotte, NC 28242-0001
(704) 373-4011

Ohio:

Reactor: Perry 1
Location: North Perry

Type: boiling-water reactor
Operator: Cleveland Electric Illuminating Co.
P.O. Box 5000
Cleveland, OH 44101
(216) 861-9000

Reactor: Perry 2 (construction permit)
Location: North Perry
Type: boiling-water reactor
Operator: Cleveland Electric Illuminating Co.
P.O. Box 5000
Cleveland, OH 44101
(216) 861-9000

Reactor: Davis-Besse 1
Location: Oak Harbor
Type: pressurized-water reactor
Operator: Toledo Edison Co.
300 Madison Avenue
Toledo, OH 43652
(419) 255-1530

Oregon:

Reactor: Trojan
Location: Rainier
Type: pressurized-water reactor
Operator: Portland General Electric Co.
121 Southwest Salmon St.
Portland, OR 97204
(503) 228-6322

Pennsylvania:

Reactors: Beaver Valley 1, 2
Location: Shippingport
Type: pressurized-water reactor
Operator: Duquesne Light Co.
P.O. Box 4
Shippingport, PA 15077
(412) 393-6000

Reactor: Three Mile Island 1
Location: Londonderry Township
Type: pressurized-water reactor
Operator: GPU Nuclear Corp.
Three Mile Island Station
P.O. Box 480
Middletown, PA 17057
(717) 948-8197

Reactors: Susquehanna 1, 2
Location: Berwick
Type: boiling-water reactor
Operator: Pennsylvania Power & Light Co.
2 North Ninth St.
Allentown, PA 19101
(215) 774-5151

Reactors: Peach Bottom 2, 3
Location: Peach Bottom Township
Type: boiling-water reactor
Operator: Philadelphia Electric Co.
2301 Market St.
Philadelphia, PA 19101
(215) 841-4000

Reactors: Limerick 1, 2
Location: Limerick Township
Type: boiling-water reactor
Operator: Philadelphia Electric Co.
2301 Market St.
Philadelphia, PA 19101
(215) 841-4000

South Carolina:

Reactor: H.B. Robinson 2
Location: Hartsville
Type: pressurized-water reactor
Operator: Carolina Power & Light Co.
P.O. Box 10429
Southport, NC 28461
(919) 546-6111

Reactors: Oconee 1, 2, 3
Location: Seneca
Type: pressurized-water reactor
Operator: Duke Power Co.
422 South Church St.
Charlotte, NC 28242-0001
(704) 373-4011

Reactors: Catawba 1, 2
Location: Clover
Type: pressurized-water reactor
Operator: Duke Power Co.
422 South Church St.
Charlotte, NC 28242-0001
(704) 373-4001

Reactor: Summer 1
Location: Jenkinsville
Type: pressurized-water reactor
Operator: South Carolina Electric & Gas Co.
Columbia, SC 29218
(803) 748-3000

Tennessee:

Reactors: Sequoyah 1, 2
Location: Soddy-Daisy
Type: pressurized-water reactor
Operator: Tennessee Valley Authority
400 W. Summit Hill Dr.
Knoxville, TN 37902
(615) 632-6000

Reactors: Watts Bar 1, 2 (construction permits)
Location: Spring City
Type: pressurized-water reactor
Operator: Tennessee Valley Authority
400 W. Summit Hill Dr.
Knoxville, TN 37902
(615) 632-6000

Texas:

Reactors: South Texas Project 1, 2
Location: Matagorda County
Type: pressurized-water reactor
Operator: Houston Lighting & Power Co.
P.O. Box 1700
Houston, TX 77251
(713) 228-9211

Reactor: Comanche Peak 1
Location: Somerville County
Type: pressurized-water reactor
Operator: Texas Utilities Electric Co.
P.O. Box 1002
Glenrose, TX 76048
(817) 897-8500

Reactor: Comanche Peak 2 (construction license)
Location: Somerville County
Type: pressurized-water reactor
Operator: Texas Utilities Electric Co.
P.O. Box 1002
Glenrose, TX 76048
(817) 897-8500

Vermont:

Reactor: Vermont Yankee
Location: Vernon
Type: boiling-water reactor
Operator: Vermont Yankee Nuclear Power Corp.
P.O. Box 157
Vernon, VT 05354
(802) 257-7711

Virginia:

Reactors: Surry 1, 2
Location: Surry
Type: pressurized-water reactor
Operator: Virginia Power Co.
P.O. Box 26666
Richmond, VA 23261
(804) 771-3000

Reactors: North Anna 1, 2
Location: Mineral
Type: pressurized-water reactor
Operator: Virginia Power Co.
P.O. Box 26666
Richmond, VA 23261
(804) 771-3000

Washington:

Reactor: Washington Nuclear 2
Location: Richland
Type: boiling-water reactor
Operator: Washington Public Power Supply System
P.O. Box 968
Richland, WA 99352
(509) 372-5000

Reactors: Washington Nuclear 1, 3 (construction licenses)
Location: Nuclear 1, Richland; Nuclear 3, Satsop
Type: pressurized-water reactor
Operator: Washington Public Power Supply System
P.O. Box 968
Richland, WA 99352
(509) 372-5000

Wisconsin:

Reactors: Point Beach 1, 2
Location: Two Creeks
Type: pressurized-water reactor
Operator: Wisconsin Electric Power Co.
P.O. Box 2962
Milwaukee, WI 53201
(414) 221-3333

Reactor: Kewaunee
Location: Carlton Township
Type: pressurized-water reactor
Operator: Wisconsin Public Service Corp.
P.O. Box 19002
Green Bay, WI 54307
(414) 433-1598

* Mailing addresses and phone numbers are for local plants. Central office is: Entergy Operations, Inc., P.O. Box 31995, Jackson, MS 39286-1995, (601) 984-9000.

AVIATION

HISTORY

For thousands of years, mankind dreamed of flying. In Greek mythology, **Daedalus** realized the dream for himself and his son, **Icarus,** by building wings of wax and feathers. Daedalus escaped captivity by flying. But Icarus, failing to heed his father's advice, fell to his death because he flew too close to the sun, causing the wings to melt.

The Daedalus myth embodies the two forces that have shaped mankind's quest for the air—the liberation of flying, and its sometimes awful cost.

Joseph Michel Montgolfier and **Jacques Etienne Montgolfier** were the first to make the dream of flight a reality. On June 5, 1783, the brothers conducted the first public, unmanned **balloon** flight at Annonay, near Lyons, France. Their linen and paper balloon, with a volume of 23,308 cubic feet, was buoyed by hot air. It rose more than 5,900 feet and flew one mile. On Nov. 21, 1783, a Montgolfier hot-air balloon was used for the first manned flight, from Paris to its suburbs. A month later, the French chemist **Jacques A.C. Charles** and an assistant flew in a hydrogen-filled balloon from Paris to Nesle, about 65 miles away. In 1793, **Jean Pierre Blanchard,** a French balloonist, made the first manned flight in the United States.

Hydrogen became the preferred gas for balloon flights because of its buoyancy. A balloon rises as long as the balloon (and everything that is attached to it) is lighter than the air that it displaces. Hot-air balloons rise because hot air is lighter (less dense) than cool air. As the air inside the balloon cools (and therefore becomes more dense), the balloon falls. Hydrogen does not need to be heated because it is lighter than air when both are at the same temperature. Helium, which became commercially available after World War I, was more expensive than hydrogen and did not have as much lifting power, so it never became a popular choice for balloon flights. Hydrogen has a serious disadvantage, however. Unlike helium, it is extremely flammable.

In the 18th and 19th centuries, balloons captured the imaginations of Americans and Europeans. Balloon flights, races and demonstrations became popular. **Jules Verne** captured the romantic allure of balloon flight in his science fiction works *Five Weeks in a Balloon* (1863) and *Around the World in 80 Days* (1873).

Balloons were not merely curiosities, however. As soon as manned flight became a reality, using them for military purposes, transportation and commerce became a possibility. In 1794, **Jean Marie Coutelle** became the first person to use a balloon for a military purpose when he conducted two four-hour surveillance flights for the French Army. In 1843, the first air transit company was formed in England, but it soon failed. Balloons underwent a major advance in 1852, when **Henri Giffard,** a French engineer, built and flew the first true **dirigible**—a balloon with a propulsion system and a steering mechanism. His airship was 144 feet long and 39 feet in diameter, powered by a steam engine. On Sept. 24, 1852, he flew from Paris to Trappe, France, at a speed of up to 6.7 miles per hour. Because he was able to steer his ship, he was not left entirely to the mercy of air currents, as earlier balloonists had been.

Two basic types of dirigibles were developed: the **rigid airship,** with an internal skeleton that determines it shape, and the nonrigid airship or **blimp,** which is flat until its internal chambers are filled with gas. From the late 1800s to the mid-1900s, the rigid airship gained prominence. Now, however, only blimps are used.

The leading builder of rigid dirigibles was the **Luftschiffbau Zeppelin** company of Germany. Its first dirigible took to the air in 1900. It was 419 feet long and was powered by two 16-horsepower engines. In the next 38 years, the company built 119 Zeppelins, most of which were produced for the German military during World War I. They were used for surveillance and to bomb London. Zeppelins proved to be of limited military value, however. They were slow moving, and the fact that they were filled with flammable gas made them good targets. About 40 were shot down while on air raids over London.

The most famous Zeppelin in the early 1930s was undoubtedly the *Graf Zeppelin,* which flew to the United States, the Arctic, the Middle East and South America, in addition to making a trip around the world. From 1934 to 1937 it provided scheduled passenger and mail service between Germany and Brazil. On May 6, 1937, its fame was eclipsed, however, when another Zeppelin, the *Hindenburg,* crashed and burned in Lakehurst, N.J. Thirty-five passengers and crew members died, as did one member of the ground crew. The awful spectacle of the crash, which was broadcast live on radio and captured by newsreel cameras, brought an end to the era of the dirigible, at a time when its future had seemed bright.

The *Hindenburg* was the world's first transatlantic commercial airliner. It was 804 feet long, 135 feet in diameter, contained 7 million cubic feet of hydrogen and could accommodate more than 70 passengers. It was powered by four 1,050-horsepower diesel engines and could travel at 82 miles per hour. The *Hindenburg* was also luxurious. It had an elegantly appointed dining room, a library and lounge, a grand piano, and promenades where passengers could stroll and look at the passing scenery through large windows. The trip across the North Atlantic was an elegant one, and fast by the standards of the time— only 50 to 60 hours. In 1936, the *Hindenburg* carried more than 1,300 passengers and several thousand pounds of cargo and mail on its regular trips between Germany and the United States.

During what should have been a routine landing on May 6, 1937, however, the *Hindenburg* ignited while it was being moored. There was speculation that the *Hindenburg* may have been sabotaged, but it was unsupported. The fire may have resulted from a spark caused by mooring. In any event, the *Hindenburg* was destroyed within a few minutes. The *Graf Zeppelin* was grounded (and scrapped three years later). The golden age of the dirigible had ended in tragedy.

Although rigid dirigibles are no longer in use, **blimps** are still familiar sights—particularly to viewers of televised sports, who see them hovering above playing fields, serving as broadcast sites. In fact, TV viewers got more than they bargained for when they tuned in to the third game of the World Series on Oct. 17, 1989. The blimp that was supposed to televise the game between the San Francisco Giants and Oakland A's was, instead, pressed into service to broadcast views of damage caused by an earthquake that rocked Northern California just as the game was about to begin.

Five manned blimps operate in the United States. Three are operated by the Goodyear Tire & Rubber Co., one by Metropolitan Insurance Co., and one by Fuji, the Japanese film manufacturer. All are filled with helium, which eliminates the danger of fire or explosion. Unmanned blimps are used by the U.S. Customs Service to detect drug smugglers trying to fly to the United States from Mexico. The 233-foot-long, helium-filled blimps are equipped with radar that can be used by ground crews to detect unscheduled aircraft. The blimps, called **aerostats**, are attached to the ground with inch-thick metal tethers.

Although blimps still have limited uses, and hot-air ballooning has undergone a rebirth to become a popular sport, the skies today are dominated by the descendants of a very strange invention that took to the air for the first time in 1903 near **Kitty Hawk,** N.C. While the Luftschiffbau Zeppelin company in Germany was busy perfecting the lighter-than-air ship, **Orville** and **Wilbur Wright** were testing the first successful heavier-than-air flight machine. Between 1900 and 1902 the brothers had refined the earlier work of **Otto Lilienthal, Octave Chanute** and **Percy Pilcher,** who had experimented with unpowered gliders but had found them difficult to maneuver and control. By 1902, the Wrights had learned how to control an engineless glider. The next year, they added an engine to their craft, which they called *Flyer I.*

The **Wright Flyer** (which is on display at the National Air and Space Museum, Smithsonian Institution, Washington, D.C.) was a biplane powered by a homemade 12-horsepower engine. On Dec. 17, 1903, Orville Wright lay in a prone position between the wings, opened the throttle and took to the air for the first time. His flight lasted 12 seconds and covered 120 feet. The brothers made four flights that day. A flight by Wilbur was the longest—852 feet in 59 seconds. Within two years, Orville Wright was able to keep their craft aloft for more than half an hour.

The Wright brothers were not alone in their quest for a powered heavier-than-air machine. Inventors around the world had been working on the same problem, with varying degrees of success. As a result, airplane development moved fairly rapidly. The **first airplane flight in Europe** took place in Paris in 1906, and Louis Blériot was able to cross the English Channel (26.6 miles) in 1909. In 1910, U.S. Navy Lt. Eugene Ely made the **first flight from a ship,** flying from the deck of the cruiser *Birmingham* at Hampton Roads, Va., to Norfolk, Va. The **first seaplane** was built in 1911. Two years later, the Russian inventor **Igor I. Sikorsky** built and flew the first four-engine plane.

The U.S. Army Signal Corps, which had established a balloon division in 1892, added airplanes in 1907. The U.S. used airplanes briefly during the **Mexican War** in 1916, and extensively during **World War I** (1914–18). World War I proved the usefulness of aircraft in combat, both for attack and for reconnaissance, and spurred the development of faster, more powerful and more reliable aircraft. At the start of the war, most planes could fly at about 70 miles per hour, at an altitude of about 14,000 feet. By the end of the war, the speed and altitude had doubled.

Prominent military planes of World War I included:

Country	Name	Type
France	Voisin 13	bomber
	Nieuport	fighter
	SPAD XIII	fighter
Germany	Gotha G IV	bomber
	Fokker D-VII	fighter
	Junkers J1	fighter
	Fokker DR-1	fighter

Country	Name	Type
Great Britain	Handley	bomber
	Vickers FB 27 Vimy	bomber
	Sopwith F1 Camel	fighter
	SE-5	fighter
Italy	Caproni	bomber

Americans flew French and British planes because the U.S. had few planes at the start of the war. During the war, the U.S. dramatically increased its production of planes. By the time the nearly 14,000 planes were completed, however, the war was over. **Baron Manfred von Richthofen** of Germany and **Capt. Edward V. Rickenbacker** of the United States became famous as fighter pilots. Richthofen (1892–1918) was credited with shooting down 80 Allied planes before he himself was shot down and killed on April 21, 1918. He became known as the Red Baron because he flew a red Fokker triplane. Rickenbacker (1890–1973) was the top American flying ace, having shot down 22 planes and four balloons.

World War I established a supply of airplanes and professionally trained pilots. After the war, some of those pilots were able to buy surplus aircraft inexpensively and become barnstormers—flyers who traveled the country performing aerial feats for paying audiences. They performed aerobatics, walked from wing to wing during flight, and even leaped from one plane to another in midair. Flying became a popular fascination.

The decade after World War I was a decade of firsts for aviation: the U.S. Post Office Department established the **first regular airmail service** (between Washington, D.C., and New York City) in 1918; the **first nonstop transatlantic flight** was completed by two British flyers, John Alcock and Arthur Whitten Brown, in 1919 when they flew from Ireland to Newfoundland in 16 hours and 12 minutes in a Vickers-Vimy bomber; the American flyers John A. Macready and Oakley Kelly made the **first nonstop transcontinental flight** in 1923, flying a single-engine Fokker T-2 from New York to San Diego in 26 hours and 50 minutes; the **first round-the-world flight** was completed by two U.S. Army planes that left Seattle on April 6, 1924, and returned 175 days later; the **first polar flight** was made by Arctic explorer **Richard E. Byrd,** acting as navigator, and pilot **Floyd Bennett,** who crossed the North Pole in a trimotor Fokker in 1926. It was a time of heroes. None stood taller than **Charles Augustus Lindbergh.**

Lindbergh was a young pilot flying a mail route between Chicago and St. Louis when he heard of a $25,000 prize that was being offered to the first person to fly solo across the Atlantic Ocean. Backed by St. Louis businessmen, he had a plane built for the flight. He called the Wright-powered Ryan monoplane the *Spirit of St. Louis.* On May 20, 1927, the unknown, 25-year-old pilot left Roosevelt Field, Long Island, N.Y. When he landed at Le Bourget Airport, Paris, 33½ hours later he was an international hero.

A month after he returned, he embarked upon a 22,000-mile, 82-city journey designed to promote aviation. Lindbergh, who had already received a tumultuous welcome in New York, was soon idolized, often to his embarrassment. Reporters wanted to find out if he had a girlfriend. They reported what he ate and what his eye color was. People wanted to touch him, to get his autograph, to give him presents. He wanted to talk about the future of aviation. At times, the message seemed to be lost, but it was not. People across the country felt that they knew Lindbergh. For the first time, someone they knew had flown across the Atlantic, around the nation and even to their hometown. Flight finally seemed more than a daring oddity.

In the 1930s, technological improvements in engines and improvements in design led to larger, faster and stronger planes. More records were set: In 1932 **Amelia Earhart,** flying a Pratt & Whitney Wasp-powered Lockheed Vega, became the **first woman to fly solo across the Atlantic Ocean;** in 1933, **Wiley Post** made the **first round-the-world solo flight** in a Lockheed Vega; in 1937, the German pilot Hanna Reitsch made the **first successful flight in a helicopter;** in 1939, transatlantic mail and passenger service was begun, and a **turbojet** was used for the first time by the Germans. In 20 years, aviation had gone from open-cockpit, barnstorming biplanes to the first helicopters and jets. It had also claimed some memorable lives. In 1935 **Wiley Post** and the humorist **Will Rogers** died in an airplane crash near Point Barrow, Alaska. Two years later, **Amelia Earhart** and her navigator, **Frederick J. Noonan,** disappeared after leaving New Guinea in an attempt to fly around the world at the equator. No wreckage or bodies were found, which led to speculation that they might have been taken prisoner by the Japanese.

Many of the engineering improvements of the 1930s were included in the Douglas DC-3, a twin-engine transport designed and built in the U.S., which made its first passenger flight in 1936. It cruised at 170 miles per hour and could carry 21 passengers. Previously, planes could carry only about 10 passengers. The DC-3 quickly became the leading airliner of the era and aided the growth of commercial air travel. In 1930, U.S. airlines carried 418,000 passengers. In 1940, that number had increased to 2.8 million. The growth of the airline market encouraged many technological developments, including improvements in navigation and air-to-ground communications.

World War II (1939–45) spurred the world's superpowers to refine conventional, propeller-driven, fixed-wing aircraft, and to develop new forms. The Axis and Allied countries built thousands of military aircraft during the war in a life-or-death battle for air superiority. At the start of the war, the best propeller-driven fighter planes could fly at about 300 miles per hour at 30,000 feet. By the end of the war, they could fly more than 400 miles per hour at 40,000 feet. Bombers and transports were capable of flying farther and carrying heavier loads. The development of radar helped the Royal Air Force (RAF) defend Great Britain against bombing raids made by the German Luftwaffe in 1940 and 1941.

In 1944, the German Messerschmitt Me 262 became the first jet plane to fly in combat. (The Germans had produced the first jet in 1939, and the Americans had produced one in 1942.) The Me 262 fighter could fly at nearly 550 miles per hour.

Prominent military planes of World War II included:

Country	Name	Type
Germany	Junkers Ju87 Stuka	bomber
	Junkers Ju88A-1	bomber
	Heinkel	bomber
	Dornier	bomber
	Messerschmitt Bf-109	interceptor, fighter
	Messerschmitt Bf-110	fighter
	Focke-Wulf Fw 190A-2	fighter
	Messerschmitt Me 262A-1a Schwalbe	jet fighter
	Junkers Ju-52	transport
Great Britain	Fairey Swordfish	carrier-borne bomber
	Vickers Wellington	bomber
	Handley Page Halifax	bomber
	De Havilland DH 98 Mosquito	bomber
	Avro Lancaster	bomber
	Hawker Hurricane	fighter
	Spitfire	fighter
	Gloster Meteor	jet fighter
Japan	Mitsubishi A6M-Zero-Sen	fighter, kamikaze aircraft

Country	Name	Type
U.S.	Consolidated B-24D Liberator	bomber
	Boeing B-17D Flying Fortress	bomber
	Boeing B-29 Super Fortress	bomber
	Curtiss P40E Warhawk	fighter
	Lockheed P-38 Lightning	long-range escort, aircraft/fighter
	Grumman F6F-3 Hellcat	carrier-borne fighter
	Vought F4U Corsair	fighter
	P-51 Mustang (renamed F-51)	escort fighter
	Douglas DC-3	transport
	Douglas DC-4	transport
	Lockheed Constellation	transport
	Curtiss C-46	transport
USSR	Ilyushin 11-2 Shturmovik (Stormavik)	fighter
	Mikoyan-Gurevich MiG-3	fighter-bomber

When the war ended, engineers continued to work to refine the primitive jet engines that had been hurriedly pressed into combat, and to develop planes that would be able to fly at a speed that seemed nearly unimaginable—faster than the speed of sound (760 miles per hour at sea level; 660 miles per hour at 40,000 feet). Jet planes of the era were not powerful enough or sturdy enough to break through the sound barrier; they were torn apart by shock waves as they approached Mach 1 (the speed of sound). Experimental rocket planes, which were more powerful than jets, were developed to do the job. On Oct. 14, 1947, U.S. Air Force Capt. **Charles E. "Chuck" Yeager** became the first human to fly faster than sound, piloting a Bell X-1 rocket plane. The pioneering years of supersonic aviation were chronicled in a best-selling book by Tom Wolfe, *The Right Stuff*, in 1979.

During the late 1940s, jet aircraft were also being refined, so that they too could fly at supersonic speeds.

Jet aircraft played a prominent role during the Korean War (1950–53) and, for the first time, helicopters were used extensively to transport supplies and wounded soldiers. At the end of the war, the United States produced the **first supersonic jet fighter,** the F-100 Super Sabre.

Prominent military aircraft of the Korean War era included:

Country	Name	Type
United States	Boeing B47-B Stratojet	jet bomber
	North American F-86A Sabre	jet interceptor, fighter
USSR	Mikoyan-Gurevich MiG-15	jet fighter

The Vietnam War (1957–75), which began only four years after the end of the Korean War, continued the drive for faster, sturdier and more maneuverable aircraft. Supersonic bombers, fighters and interceptors were used in combat. The jungle war also encouraged the refinement of vertical takeoff and landing aircraft (**VTOL**) and short takeoff and landing aircraft (**STOL**). Helicopters, which are VTOLs, were used not only for transport but also for attack. In 1969 the British introduced a fighter plane, the Hawker Siddeley Harrier, that combines vertical and short takeoff and landing capabilities (**V/STOL**). On takeoff, the exhaust of the jet engines is deflected downward, to lift the plane. In flight, the exhaust thrust is horizontal, to propel the plane forward.

Prominent military aircraft of the Vietnam War era included:

Country	Name	Type
France	Mirage 5	supersonic fighter
Great Britain	English Electric Canberra	jet bomber
	Hawker Siddeley Harrier	V/STOL tactical strike aircraft
United States	Boeing B-52G/H Stratofortress	bomber
	General Dynamics FB-111A	supersonic fighter, bomber
	Rockwell International B-1	supersonic bomber
	North American F100 Super Sabre	supersonic fighter
	McDonnell F4B Phantom	supersonic interceptor
	McDonnell Douglas F15A Eagle	supersonic fighter
	Fairchild A-10 Thunderbolt	fighter

Country	Name	Type
U.S. (*cont.*)	Lockheed U2A	high-altitude reconnaissance plane
	Boeing KC-135A Stratotanker	fuel carrier for mid-air refueling
	Lockheed C-130E Hercules	transport
	Lockheed SR-71	supersonic reconnaissance plane
	Bell AH-1G Huey Cobra	armed utility helicopter
USSR	Tupolev Tu V-G Backfire	supersonic bomber
	Mikoyan-Gurevich MiG-21F	supersonic fighter
	Mikoyan-Gurevich MiG 25 Foxbat	supersonic fighter, interceptor
	Mil Mi-8	transport helicopter
	Antonov An-22	transport

As military aviation improved and expanded, so too did commercial aviation. At the end of World War II, surplus transports were transformed into airliners and commercial planes. During the Korean War, commercial aviation followed the military into the jet age. In 1952, the British Overseas Airways Corporation (now British Airways) began the **first jet passenger service,** between London and Johannesburg, South Africa. The flight took 23 hours and 38 minutes, including stops. In 1958, BOAC became the first airline to provide jet service for passengers to the United States. Later that year, National Airlines started the **first domestic jet passenger service,** between New York City and Miami.

The supersonic planes that were produced during the Vietnam War also had their commercial counterparts. In 1968, the Soviet Union produced the **first commercial supersonic transport (SST),** the Tupolev Tu-144. It broke the sound barrier for the first time on June 5, 1969. The Tupolev Tu-144 began cargo service in 1975 and passenger service in 1977. Six years later it was withdrawn from service, after several crashes.

The **Concorde** SST began passenger service on Jan. 21, 1976, a joint effort of Air France and British Airways. The Concorde can fly at Mach 2 (approximately 1,350 miles per hour), far faster than the 550-miles-per-hour of other commercial jetliners. However, it is only allowed to fly that fast over water, where its loud sonic booms will not create a disturbance. When over land, it flies only slightly faster than other passenger jets. Speed regulations and high fuel costs have kept the Concorde from becoming popular.

By the 1980s, the sound barrier, which once had seemed nearly impervious, was broken daily by military and commercial aircraft. That does not mean that there were no milestones remaining for aviation, however. In 1986, **Richard Rutan** and **Jeana Yeager** made history when they completed the first nonstop flight around the world without refueling. They took off from Edwards Air Force Base in California on Dec. 14, 1986, and returned on Dec. 23, having traveled 25,000 miles in their ultralight plane, *Voyager.* The plane's 17 fuel tanks were so heavy on takeoff that the wing tips dragged along the

ground for 14,000 feet, damaging the stabilizers at each tip. Rutan called the journey aviation's "last plum," and it did symbolize the closing of a chapter of aviation history. But, as long as there is imagination and determination, there will be other chapters.

In 1990, when the Air Force retired the SR-71 reconnaissance plane, several records were shattered on the Blackbird's final flight. It flew coast-to-coast in 68 minutes, 17 seconds, shattering the old record of 3 hours, 38 minutes. And it set a new speed record of 2,242.48 mph, just to prove that it could be done.

"What kind of world would there be if there were no daring?" Rutan asked before his flight. What kind, indeed?

MILESTONES IN SPACE: UNMANNED FLIGHTS

Launch	Name	Country	Destination	Significance
10/4/57	Sputnik I	USSR	Earth orbit	First satellite to orbit Earth
11/3/57	Sputnik 2	USSR	Earth orbit	Contained the first living creature to be sent into space, the female dog Laika; her heartbeat, respiration and blood pressure were recorded to study the effects of space flight on living organisms; the satellite was not designed to return to Earth
1/31/58	Explorer 1	U.S.	Earth orbit	Detected Van Allen radiation belts; first US satellite
3/17/58	Vanguard	U.S.	Earth orbit	Established that Earth is oblate
9/12/59	Lunik II	USSR	Moon	First probe to reach Moon; crash-landed
10/4/59	Lunik III	USSR	Moon	First probe to photograph far side of Moon
4/1/60	Tiro I	U.S.	Earth orbit	First weather satellite
6/22/60	Transit I-B	U.S.	Earth orbit	First navigation satellite
8/12/60	Echo I	U.S.	Earth orbit	First communications satellite; metallic balloon off of which radio signals could be bounced
3/7/62	OSO I	U.S.	Earth orbit	Orbiting Solar Observatory
4/23/62	Ranger IV	U.S.	Moon	First U.S. probe to reach Moon
7/10/62	Telstar	U.S.	Earth orbit	First communications satellite to use electronic relays of signals; allowed television broadcasts between U.S. and Europe
8/27/62	Mariner II	U.S.	Venus	First probe to reach another planet and return information
6/26/63	Syncom II	U.S.	Earth orbit	First communications satellite to establish synchronous orbit to Earth (movement matches Earth's, so that it stays above same geographical point)
7/28/64	Ranger VII	U.S.	Moon	Returned detailed pictures of surface before crashing
11/28/64	Mariner IV	U.S.	Mars	Transmitted photos of Martian surface
4/6/65	Early Bird	U.S.	Earth orbit	First commercial satellite
11/26/65	A-1	France	Earth orbit	First satellite launched by country other than U.S. or USSR
1/31/66	Luna 9	USSR	Moon	Main vehicle crash lands; ejected capsule transmits photos to Earth
5/30/66	Surveyor I	U.S.	Moon	First soft landing on the Moon
3/31/66	Luna 10	USSR	Moon	First vehicle to orbit Moon
8/10/66	Lunar Orbiter 1	U.S.	Moon	First U.S. vehicle to orbit Moon

Launch	Name	Country	Destination	Significance
2/11/70	Ohsumi	Japan	Earth orbit	First satellite launched by Japan
4/24/70	"The East Is Red"	China	Earth orbit	First satellite launched by China; name not announced; broadcasts song, "The East Is Red."
8/17/70	Venera 7	USSR	Venus	First probe to return signals from Venus' surface
11/10/70	Luna 17	USSR	Moon	Carries roving vehicle, which travels about the Moon's surface and transmits pictures
12/12/70	Uhuru	U.S.	Earth orbit	First satellite-based X-ray telescope
5/28/71	Mars 3	USSR	Mars	First soft landing on Mars; equipment quickly stops functioning
5/30/71	Mariner 9	USSR	Mars	First probe to orbit another planet; transmits pictures
3/2/72	Pioneer 10	U.S.	Jupiter	First probe to study Jupiter; after leaving Jupiter, becomes first probe to leave the solar system (June 13, 1983)
7/23/72	Landsat I	U.S.	Earth orbit	First Earth resources satellite
3/6/73	Pioneer 11	U.S.	Saturn	First probe to approach Saturn
11/3/73	Mariner 10	U.S.	Venus, Mercury	Only probe to view Mercury
11/3/73	Venera 9	USSR	Venus	Returns first photos from surface of Venus
8/20/75	Viking 1	U.S.	Mars	First U.S. probe to soft-land on Mars; returns data until May 1983
8/20/77	Voyager 2	U.S.	Jupiter, Saturn, Uranus, Neptune	First probe to approach Uranus and Neptune
1/26/78	IUE	Int.	Earth orbit	Only astronomical satellite in geosynchronous orbit; still operating
5/20/78	Pioneer Venus 1	U.S.	Venus	First probe to orbit Venus
6/26/78	Seasat	U.S.	Earth orbit	Studies ocean currents and ice flow
12/13/78	HEAO-2	U.S.	Earth orbit	High-Energy Astronomy Observatory (Einstein Observatory); makes detailed X-ray images of the universe
2/24/79	P78-1	U.S.	Earth orbit	Studies solar radiation; intentionally shot down by U.S. Air Force 9/13/85 for training purposes
12/15/84	Vega 1	USSR	Halley's Comet	Studies comet; drops balloon into atmosphere of Venus; other Halley's Comet probes: Vega 2 by USSR on 12/21/84; Sakigake by Japan on 1/7/85; Giotto by European countries on 7/2/85; Suisei by Japan on 8/18/85
5/4/89	Magellan	U.S.	Venus	To map surface
10/18/89	Galileo	U.S.	Jupiter	To study moons, atmosphere
4/24/90	Hubble Space Telescope	U.S.	Earth orbit	First optical telescope to orbit Earth
7/3/92	SAMPEX	U.S.	Earth orbit	First of series of inexpensive satellites called Small Explorer Project. The Solar, Anomalous and Magnetospheric Particle Explorer (SAMPEX) studies cosmic rays.
9/25/92	Mars Observer	U.S.	Mars	Maps Mars surface in detail

MILESTONES IN SPACE: MANNED FLIGHTS

The Mercury Years: In the late 1950s and early 1960s, the U.S. and the USSR were in fierce competition, both in manned and in unmanned space flight. The Soviets had launched the first unmanned satellite (Sputnik 1) in 1957, marking the start of the Space Age. Less than four months later, the United States launched Explorer 1. In 1961, the USSR again captured world attention by launching the first manned flight. Less than a month later, Alan B. Shepard, Jr. became the first American in space. Still, Shepard's brief, 15-minute, suborbital flight was far less spectacular than Cosmonaut Yuri A. Gagarin's 1 hour 48 minute flight had been. In the space race, which sometimes seemed to be measured more by number of orbits than by scientific and technological significance, the United States seemed to be lagging.

The Mercury missions from 1961 to 1963 attempted to close the gap.

The Mercury program used one-person, bell-shaped capsules that were launched by Redstone or Atlas missiles. The capsules were tiny by later standards—only 9 feet 7 inches high from the heat shield at the bottom to the parachute deployment area, at the top. The astronaut reclined on a contoured couch, riding backward most of the time. He could control the capsule's position by firing thrusters, or he could allow them to fire automatically. Braking rockets slowed the capsule for re-entry. The capsules were further slowed by parachutes as they fell into the ocean.

Several unmanned flights tested the rockets and the capsule design. On Jan. 31, 1961, a Redstone rocket launched a chimpanzee, Ham, on a suborbital flight. He was safely recovered, setting the stage for the first U.S. manned flight on May 5, 1961.

Launch	Craft	Country	Duration	Crew	Significance
4/12/61	Vostok 1	USSR	1 hr. 48 min.	Yuri A. Gagarin	First manned space flight
5/5/61	Mercury 3	U.S.	15 min.	Alan B. Shepard, Jr.	First U.S. manned space flight; suborbital; space capsule was the Freedom 7
7/21/61	Mercury 4	U.S.	16 min.	Virgil I. "Gus" Grissom	Suborbital; capsule was Liberty Bell 7; after landing in ocean, hatch blew out prematurely; Grissom rescued by helicopter; capsule sank
8/6/61	Vostok 2	USSR	15 hrs. 18 min.	Gherman S. Titov	17 orbits of Earth
2/20/62	Mercury 6	U.S.	4 hrs. 55 min.	John H. Glenn, Jr.	First orbital flight by American; 3 orbits; in Friendship 7
5/24/62	Mercury 7	U.S.	4 hrs. 56 min.	M. Scott Carpenter	3 orbits in Aurora 7; capsule overshot splashdown area by 250 miles; located by search aircraft and recovered
8/11/62	Vostok 3	USSR	94 hrs. 24 min.	Andrian G. Nikolayev	With Vostok 4, was first paired space shot; craft came within 4 miles of each other
8/12/62	Vostok 4	USSR	70 hrs. 57 min.	Pavel R. Popovitch	[See Vostok 3]
10/3/62	Mercury 8	U.S.	9 hrs. 13 min.	Walter M. "Wally" Schirra, Jr.	In Sigma 7; splashdown only 4.6 miles from recovery ship
5/15/63	Mercury 9	U.S.	34 hrs. 20 min.	L. Gordon Cooper, Jr.	In Faith 7; last Mercury mission
6/14/63	Vostok 5	USSR	119 hrs. 6 min.	Valery F. Bikovsky	Passed within 3.1 miles of Vostok 6

Launch	Craft	Country	Duration	Crew	Significance
6/16/63	Vostok 6	USSR	70 hrs. 50 min.	Valentina V. Tereshkova	First woman in space
10/12/64	Voskhod 1	USSR	24 hrs. 17 min.	Vladimir M. Komarov, Konstantin P. Feokistov, Boris B. Yegorov	First multiperson crew

The Gemini Years: The Gemini program was designed as a transition between the Mercury program and flight to the Moon. Its goals were to test human endurance in space and to develop equipment and maneuvers that would be needed for lunar flight. Missions focused on rendezvous and docking maneuvers and on walks in space, officially known as Extravehicular Activity (EVA).

The Gemini capsules were enlarged versions of the bell-shaped Mercury capsules. Each was about 19 feet long and 10 feet wide. The cabin contained couches for two astronauts. (The name, Gemini, is Latin for "twins.") The Gemini spacecraft were lifted by Titan missiles, which were more powerful than those used in the Mercury program. The reentry process was a refined version of that developed in the Mercury program.

Launch	Craft	Country	Duration	Crew	Significance
3/18/65	Voskhod 2	USSR	26 hrs.	Aleksei A. Leonov, Pavel I. Belyayev	First walk in space (known as Extravehicular Activity or EVA); 10 minutes
3/23/65	Gemini 3	U.S.	4 hrs. 53 min.	Virgil I. "Gus" Grissom, John W. Young	First U.S. multiperson crew
6/3/65	Gemini 4	U.S.	97 hrs. 56 min.	James A. McDivitt, Edward H. White II	First U.S. EVA, by White
8/21/65	Gemini 5	U.S.	190 hrs. 56 min.	L. Gordon Cooper, Charles Conrad, Jr.	Simulated rendezvous; significantly increased length of time in space
12/4/65	Gemini 7	U.S.	330 hrs. 35 min.	Frank Borman, James A. Lovell, Jr.	Rendezvous with Gemini 6A; increased length of time in space, proving that Moon trip was physiologically possible
12/15/65	Gemini 6A	U.S.	25 hrs. 51 min.	Walter M. "Wally" Schirra, Jr., Thomas P. Stafford	Rendezvous with Gemini 7; Schirra piloted to within one foot of Gemini 7; first successful rendezvous in space
3/16/66	Gemini 8	U.S.	10 hrs. 42 min.	Neil A. Armstrong David R. Scott	Rendezvoused and docked with Agena rocket; malfunction of thrusters led to emergency landing in western Pacific Ocean
6/3/66	Gemini 9A	U.S.	72 hrs. 47 min.	Thomas P. Stafford, Eugene A. Cernan	More than 2 hours of EVA; unsuccessful docking maneuver
7/18/66	Gemini 10	U.S.	70 hrs. 47 min.	John W. Young, Michael Collins	Docked with Agena rocket
9/12/66	Gemini 11	U.S.	71 hrs. 17 min.	Charles Conrad, Jr., Richard F. Gordon, Jr.	Docked with Agena rocket

Launch	Craft	Country	Duration	Crew	Significance
11/11/66	Gemini 12	U.S.	94 hrs. 34 min.	James A. Lovell, Jr., Edwin A. Aldrin	5 hours of EVA; docked with Agena rocket; final Gemini mission

The Apollo Years: On May 25, 1961, President John F. Kennedy had pledged that the United States would put a man on the moon within a decade. The Apollo program accomplished that goal. On July 20, 1969, at 4:17:42 P.M. Eastern Daylight Time, Neil A. Armstrong and Edwin E. "Buzz" Aldrin, Jr., touched down on the Sea of Tranquility (MareTranquillitatis) in the Lunar Module Eagle and reported, "Houston, Tranquility Base here. The Eagle has landed." At 10:56:20 P.M. that day Armstrong became the first human to set foot on the lunar surface. He said, "That's one small step for [a] man, one giant leap for mankind." (NASA said the "a" was lost in transmission. Because of static on the tape, the fate of the "a" remains uncertain, although Armstrong has said that he intended to say it.) Armstrong and Aldrin planted an American flag, set up scientific experiments, took photographs and collected 53.61 pounds of rock and dirt samples. Armstrong, who was the last to return to the lunar module, spent 2 hours and 13 minutes on the moon's surface. Michael Collins remained in the Apollo capsule while Armstrong and Aldrin were on the moon.

Between July 1969 and December 1972, astronauts explored six lunar sites and collected hundreds of pounds of samples.

More than four years of related testing preceded the first manned Apollo flight on Oct. 11, 1968. Tragedy struck at the Kennedy Space Center in Florida during a flight simulation on Jan. 27, 1967, when a short-circuit caused a fire in the Apollo 1 Command Module. All three crew members died. Virgil I. "Gus" Grissom, Edward H. White II and Roger B. Chaffee were suffocated by the dense fumes from burning plastics in the cabin's interior. The plastics, which would have been fire-resistant in ordinary air, burned because of the pure oxygen atmosphere in the cabin.

The Apollo program used a three-man spacecraft, a two-man Lunar Excursion Module (LEM; also called a Lunar Module, or LM), and Saturn rockets. NASA launched 15 manned flights as part of the program, 11 of which were related to the lunar program. Six of the 11 made lunar landings. After the moon program was complete, four more flights were made—three of which transported astronauts to the Skylab space station in 1973 and 1974, and one of which was a joint flight with Soviet cosmonauts in 1975. [See Space Stations, below]

Launch	Craft	Country	Duration	Crew	Significance
4/23/67	Soyuz 1	USSR	26 hrs. 48 min.	Vladimir M. Komarov	Komarov died during re-entry when shroud lines of parachute became twisted
10/11/68	Apollo 7	U.S.	260 hrs. 8 min.	Walter M. Schirra, Donn F. Eisele, R. Walter Cunningham	Prolonged Earth orbit to test spaceworthiness of command module; crew developed colds
10/26/68	Soyuz 3	USSR	94 hrs. 51 min.	Georgi T. Beregovoi	Approached unmanned Soyuz 2 within 650 feet
12/21/68	Apollo 8	U.S.	147 hrs.	Frank Borman, James A. Lovell, Jr., William A. Anders	First manned craft to orbit Moon; crew read from Book of Genesis during 10 Moon orbits on Dec. 24, broadcast worldwide; scouted out landing sites

Launch	Craft	Country	Duration	Crew	Significance
1/14/69	Soyuz 4	USSR	71 hrs. 14 min.	Vladimir A. Shatalov	Docked with Soyuz 5; first linkage of two manned vehicles
1/15/69	Soyuz 5	USSR	72 hrs. 46 min.	Boris V. Volynov, Alexei S. Yeliseyev, Yevgeni V. Khrunov	Yeliseyev and Khrunov transferred to Soyuz 4 in practice of space rescue; Volynov landed alone
3/3/69	Apollo 9	U.S.	241 hrs. 1 min.	James A. McDivitt, David R. Scott, Russell L. Schweickart	Earth orbit; practiced docking with Lunar Module
5/18/69	Apollo 10	U.S.	192 hrs. 3 min.	Eugene A. Cernan, John W. Young, Thomas P. Stafford	Lunar Module tested in lunar orbit
7/16/69	Apollo 11	U.S.	165 hrs. 18 min.	Neil A. Armstrong, Michael Collins, Edwin E. "Buzz" Aldrin, Jr.	First lunar landing [for detailed description, *see above*, The Apollo Years]
10/11/69	Soyuz 6	USSR	118 hrs. 42 min.	Georgi S. Shonin, Valery N. Kubasov	First triple launch of manned ships (with Soyuz 7 and 8); performed welding experiments
10/12/69	Soyuz 7	USSR	118 hrs. 41 min.	Anatoly V. Filipchenko, Vladislav N. Volkov, Viktor V. Gorbatko	Triple space launch (with Soyuz 6 and 8); photographed Earth
10/13/69	Soyuz 8	USSR	118 hrs. 59 min.	Vladimir A. Shatalov, Aleksei S. Yeliseyev	Triple space launch (with Soyuz 6 and 7); performed rendezvous maneuver with Soyuz 7 but did not attempt docking
11/14/69	Apollo 12	U.S.	244 hrs. 36 min.	Charles Conrad, Jr., Richard F. Gordon, Jr., Alan L. Bean	Conrad and Bean landed on Ocean of Storms (Oceanus Procellarum) in LM Intrepid; two EVAs totaling 7 hrs. 50 min.; set up scientific instruments; hiked 0.5 mile to inspect Surveyor 3 spacecraft; collected 74.7 pounds of lunar samples
4/11/70	Apollo 13	U.S.	142 hrs. 55 min.	James A. Lovell, Jr., Fred W. Haise, Jr., John L. Swigert, Jr.	Moon landing canceled after oxygen tank exploded in Command Module, crippling power, life-support systems; returned safely
6/2/70	Soyuz 9	USSR	424 hrs. 59 min.	Andrian G. Nikolayev, Vitaly I. Sevastianov	Longest manned flight to date

Launch	Craft	Country	Duration	Crew	Significance
1/31/71	Apollo 14	U.S.	216 hrs. 42 min.	Alan B. Shepard, Jr., Stuart A. Roosa, Edgar D. Mitchell	Shepard and Mitchell landed on Fra Mauro formation of Moon; set up scientific instruments; towed cart to edge of crater; collected 94.3 pounds of samples; 9 hrs. 9 min. in EVAs
4/23/71	Soyuz 10	USSR	47 hrs. 46 min.	Vladimir A. Shatalov, Alexei S. Yeleseyev, Nikolai Rukavishnikov	Docked with Salyut 1, an unmanned space station
6/6/71	Soyuz 11	USSR	570 hrs. 22 min.	Georgi T. Dobrovolsky, Viktor I. Patsayev, Vladislav N. Volkov	Docked with and entered Salyut 1; crew members killed in reentry when pressure-equalizer valve in Command Module is jarred open
7/26/71	Apollo 15	U.S.	295 hrs. 22 min.	David R. Scott, Alfred M. Worden, James B. Irwin	Scott, Irwin landed on Moon's Appenine mountain front; used first surface vehicle, Lunar Roving Vehicle (LRV); traveled 18.6 miles in Rover; set up experiments, collected 173 pounds of soil and rocks
4/16/72	Apollo 16	U.S.	265 hrs. 51 min.	John W. Young, Thomas K. Mattingly II, Charles M. Duke, Jr.	Young and Duke explored lunar highlands with LRV, covered 16.8 miles, collected 210.8 pounds of samples
12/7/72	Apollo 17	U.S.	301 hrs. 52 min.	Eugene A. Cernan, Ronald E. Evans, Harrison H. Schmitt	Sixth and final moon landing; Cernan and Schmitt explored Moon's Taurus Mountain area; covered 22 miles in Rover, collected 242 pounds of rocks and soil cores; Schmitt became the first geologist in space

Space Stations: With the lunar phase of Apollo's missions completed, the focus of the U.S. space program shifted to developing a space station, a permanent base in Earth's orbit to which astronauts could commute. Space stations had been envisioned since the 1920s, when rocket technology made the concept of space travel possible. They had been seen as possible sites for research, defense, manufacturing and habitation. The Soviet Union had already launched its first station, Salyut 1, on April 19, 1971.

Several days after the successful launch of Salyut 1, three cosmonauts in Soyuz 10 docked with it, but did not enter. Two months later, the crew of Soyuz 11 successfully entered the space station, proving that humans could "commute" to space-based facilities. Their mission ended in tragedy, however, when a pressure valve in the cabin of Soyuz 11 was jarred open during re-entry. All three died. The USSR did not attempt another manned flight to a space station for two years.

The United States launched its first space station, Skylab, on May 14, 1973. In the following nine months, three successive crews visited the 118-foot-long station, spending a total of 171 days there. The first crew spent much of its time repairing damage that had been done during Skylab's ascent: two solar panels had been ripped off and one had been damaged. The second crew also made some repairs, conducting a record-setting four-hour EVA to deploy an external sunshade to keep temperatures within the station at about 75° F. (They had risen to 120° F.) The three crews also conducted research concerned with astronomy, physiology and the effects of weightlessness on life forms such as minnows, spiders and seedlings. They also took extensive photographs of Earth to be used in the study of volcanoes, earthquake faults, pollution, the atmosphere and natural resources.

Skylab was supposed to stay in orbit, 300 miles above Earth, until at least 1981, when it was to be refueled. Its orbit decayed more rapidly than had been predicted, however, and it began to fall to Earth. Its descent caused worldwide concern for months because of uncertainty concerning where it would land. On July 11, 1979, it disintegrated and burned as it entered the Earth's atmosphere. Debris was scattered over the Indian Ocean and uninhabited areas of Australia.

The Soviet Union launched seven Salyut space stations between 1971 and 1982, some of which remained in orbit for years. Some of the space stations were devoted primarily to scientific research and others to space technology and Earth observation, including reconnaissance. Cosmonauts made many trips to the stations, spending hundreds of days in space. The last Salyut space station, Salyut 7, was launched on Sept. 29, 1982, and is still in orbit.

On Feb. 20, 1986, the Soviet Union launched the Mir space station, which is designed to be permanently manned. Crews have already completed record-setting stays there, including a 366-day mission in 1988–89. In the 1980s the Soviet Union also began development of Buran, a reusable shuttle that would be used to reach Mir 2. Economic problems plagued the space program in the late 1980s, however, slowing development of Buran and of Mir 2. The slowdown also affected Kvant research modules, designed to be attached to Mir for specialized purposes. Because of this, the Mir station was abandoned for 132 days in 1989.

While the Soviets focused primarily on space station development, the United States has directed much of its attention to the Space Shuttle, a reusable spacecraft that is launched by rocket and returns to Earth by gliding down and landing on a runway. The Shuttle is designed to be a cost-effective method of transporting commercial and non-commercial payloads into space. The first shuttle, the *Columbia*, was launched on April 12, 1981, and made five voyages. Three more shuttles—*Challenger*, *Discovery* and *Atlantis*—made successful flights in the next four years.

Disaster struck on Jan. 28, 1986, when *Challenger*—which was on its 10th flight—exploded 73 seconds after takeoff. As stunned crowds watched, all six crew members were killed. Television and newspaper pictures relayed the grim sight around the world. Killed were: Commander Francis Scobee, Pilot Michael Smith, Mission Specialists Judith Resnick, Ellison Onizuka and Ronald McNair, and Payload Specialists Gregory Jarvis and Christa McAuliffe. Mrs. McAuliffe was an elementary school teacher who had been chosen for the trip in a nationwide competition. Her students, like others around the nation, were watching as *Challenger* exploded.

NASA suspended shuttle flights for nearly three years, until an investigation of the disaster was completed. A presidential commission placed the blame on a faulty O-ring seal between sections of one of the solid-fuel booster rockets. The commission also blamed NASA for poor management, rushed flight schedules and inadequate quality control. Congressional investigations indicated that NASA had known of the O-ring problem, which was aggravated by cold weather the day of the launch, but had failed to correct it. NASA underwent extensive management changes and the Shuttle program underwent a shift in focus. Pres. Ronald Reagan authorized a replacement for the *Challenger*, but he ordered NASA to get out of the business of transporting commercial payloads. After honoring old commitments and launching some scientific satellites, the Shuttle program would be directed toward Defense Department purposes and toward space-station assembly.

The United States is planning a permanently manned space station, Freedom, that would be an orbiting laboratory, port and service facility. The European Space Agency, Canada and Japan are joining the United States in planning Freedom. The joint effort is part of a cooperative trend that developed during the 1980s, when the U.S. and the USSR worked together on several missions and invited other nations to join them in space.

SKYLAB AND SALYUTS 3–6

Launch	Craft	Country	Duration	Crew	Significance
5/25/73	Skylab 2	U.S.	28 days	Charles Conrad, Jr., Joseph P. Kerwin, Paul J. Weitz	First manned Skylab launch; repaired unmanned Skylab, launched May 14
7/29/73	Skylab 3	U.S.	59 days	Alan L. Bean, Owen K. Garriot, Jack R. Lousma	Deployed thermal shield; conducted experiments
9/27/73	Soyuz 12	USSR	47 hrs. 16 min.	Vasily G. Lazarev, Oleg G. Makarov	First Soviet manned flight after Soyuz 11 tragedy
11/16/73	Skylab 4	U.S.	84 days	Gerald P. Carr, Edward G. Gibson, William R. Pogue	Conducted experiments, obtained physiological data on extended flights
12/18/73	Soyuz 13	USSR	7 days	Petr I. Klimuk, Valentin Lebedev	Conducted astrophysical and biological experiments
7/3/74	Soyuz 14	USSR	15 days	Pavel R. Popovich, Yuri P. Artyukhin	Entered Salyut 3 space station; photographed, studied Earth resources
8/26/74	Soyuz 15	USSR	2 days	Gennady Sarafanov, Lev Demin	Failure in automatic docking system prevented linkup with Salyut 3
12/2/74	Soyuz 16	USSR	5 days	Anatoly V. Filipchenko, Nikolai Rukavishnikov	Test flight for ASTP (Apollo-Soyuz Test Project)
1/10/75	Soyuz 17	USSR	30 days	Alexei A. Gubarev, Georgi M. Grechko	Docked with Salyut 4
4/5/75	Soyuz 18A	USSR	22 min.	Vasily G. Lazarev, Oleg G. Makarov	Stages of launch vehicle failed to separate; craft did not reach orbit; crew landed in Siberia
5/24/75	Soyuz 18B	USSR	63 days	Petr I. Klimuk, Vitaly I. Sevastyanov	Crew spent 62 days in Salyut 4
7/15/75	ASTP	U.S.	9 days	Thomas P. Stafford, Vance D. Brand, Donald K. Slayton	Apollo-Soyuz Test Project, the first mission with the USSR
7/15/75	Soyuz 19	USSR	6 days	Alexei A. Leonov, Valery N. Kubasov	Docked with ASTP
7/6/76	Soyuz 21	USSR	49 days	Boris V. Volynov, Vitaly Zholobov	Docked with Salyut 5; researched Earth resources
9/15/76	Soyuz 22	USSR	8 days	Valery F. Bykovsky, Vladimir Aksenov	Took photographs of Earth
10/14/76	Soyuz 23	USSR	2 days	Vyacheslav Zudov, Valery Rozhdestvensky	Electronic malfunctions of Soyuz 23 prevented docking with Salyut 5
2/7/77	Soyuz 24	USSR	18 days	Viktor G. Gorbatko, Yuri N. Glazkov	Docked with Salyut 5
10/9/77	Soyuz 25	USSR	2 days	Vladimir Kovalyonok, Valery Ryumin	Malfunction prevented docking with Salyut 6
12/10/77	Soyuz 26	USSR	96 days*	Yuri V. Romanenko, Georgi M. Grechko	Docked with Salyut 6; crew set endurance record
1/10/78	Soyuz 27	USSR	6 days*	Vladimir Dzhanibekov, Oleg G. Makarov	Docked with Salyut 6; after five days, crew returned on Soyuz 26

Launch	Craft	Country	Duration	Crew	Significance
3/2/78	Soyuz 28	USSR	8 days	Vladimir Remek, Alexei A. Gubarev	Docked with Salyut 6, spent 7 days there; Remek, a Czech, became first non-American, non-Soviet to fly in space
6/15/78	Soyuz 29	USSR	140 days*	Vladimir Kovalyonok, Aleksander Ivanchenko	Docked with Salyut 6; set new endurance record; crew returned on Soyuz 31
6/27/78	Soyuz 30	USSR	8 days	Pyotr I. Klimuk, Miroslaw Hermaszewski	Docked with Salyut 6; Hermaszewski was first Polish cosmonaut
8/25/78	Soyuz 31	USSR	8 days*	Valery F. Bykovsky, Sigmund Jahn	Docked with Salyut 6; Jahn was first East German cosmonaut
2/25/79	Soyuz 32	USSR	175 days*	Vladimir Lyakhov, Valery Ryumin	Docked with Salyut 6; set new endurance record
4/10/79	Soyuz 33	USSR	2 days	Nikolai Rukavishnikov, Georgi Ivanov	Engine failure caused early flight termination; Ivanov was first Bulgarian in space
6/6/79	Soyuz 34	USSR	73 days	Unmanned at launch	Docked with Salyut 6; used by Lyakhov and Ryumin to return to Earth
4/9/80	Soyuz 35	USSR	185 days*	Valery Ryumin, Leonid Popov	Transported crew to Salyut 6; crew returned on Soyuz 37
5/26/80	Soyuz 36	USSR	8 days*	Valery N. Kubasov, Bertalan Farkas	Transported crew to Salyut 6; crew returned in Soyuz 35; Farkas was first Hungarian in space
6/5/80	Soyuz T-2	USSR	4 days	Yuri Malyshev, Vladimir Aksenov	Test flight of modified Soyuz craft; docked with Salyut 6
7/23/80	Soyuz 37	USSR	8 days*	Viktor F. Gorbatko, Pham Tuan	Exchanged crews in Salyut 6; used by Soyuz 35 for return to Earth; Soyuz 37 crew remained 8 days, returned in Soyuz 36; Pham was first Vietnamese in space
9/18/80	Soyuz 38	USSR	8 days	Yuri V. Romanenko, Arnaldo Tamayo-Mendez	Docked with Salyut 6; Mendez was first black, first Cuban in space
11/27/80	Soyuz T-3	USSR	13 days	Leonard Kizim, Oleg G. Makarov, Genrodiy Strekalov	Docked with Salyut 6; repaired space station to extend its life
3/12/81	Soyuz T-4	USSR	75 days	Vladimir Kovalyonok, Viktor Savinykh	Docked with Salyut 6
3/22/81	Soyuz 39	USSR	8 days	Vladimir Dzhanibekov, Jugderemuduyn Gurragcha	Docked with Salyut 6; Gurragcha was first Mongolian in space
4/12/81	Shuttle	U.S.	2 days	John W. Young, Robert L. Crippen	First flight of shuttle *Columbia;* first landing of U.S. spacecraft on land
5/14/81	Soyuz 40	USSR	8 days*	Leonid Popov, Dumitru Prunariu	Docked with Salyut 6; Prunariu was first Romanian in space

* For some Soyuz flights, cosmonauts traveled to Salyut in one craft and returned in another. In those cases, the duration of the mission given is for the crew, not the craft.

THE SPACE SHUTTLE, SALYUTS 6 AND 7, AND MIR SPACE STATION

Launch	Craft	Country	Duration	Crew	Significance
11/12/81	Shuttle	U.S.	2 days	Joe H. Engle, Richard H. Truly	Reused *Columbia;* ended early due to fuel cell failure
3/22/82	Shuttle	U.S.	8 days	Jack R. Lousma, C. Gordon Fullerton	Third flight of *Columbia*
5/13/82	Soyuz T-5	USSR	211 days*	Anatoly Berezovoy, Valentin Lebedev	Docked with Salyut 7
6/24/82	Soyuz T-6	USSR	8 days*	Vladimir Dzhanibekoy, Jean-Loup Chrétien, Alexander Ivanchenkov	Mission with France; Chrétien was first French "spationaute"; docked with Salyut 7
6/27/82	Shuttle	U.S.	7 days	Thomas Mattingly II, Henry Hartsfield, Jr.	Fourth use of *Columbia*
8/16/82	Soyuz T-7	USSR	8 days*	Leonid I. Popov, Svetlana Savitskaya, Alexander Serebrov	Docked with Salyut 7; crew returned on Soyuz T-5
11/11/82	Shuttle	U.S.	5 days	Vance D. Brand, Robert F. Overmeyer, Joseph P. Allen, William B. Lenoir	Fifth use of *Columbia;* deployed 2 communications satellites into Earth orbit; first 4-person crew
4/4/83	Shuttle	U.S.	5 days	Paul J. Weitz, Karol J. Bobko, Donald H. Peterson, Story Musgrave	First flight of *Challenger;* deployed communications satellite; first shuttle EVA
4/20/83	Soyuz T-8	USSR	2 days*	Vladimir G. Titov, Gennadi M. Strekalov, Alexander A. Serebrov	Problem with maneuvering rocket on Soyuz T-8 prevented docking with Salyut 7
6/18/83	Shuttle	U.S.	6 days	Robert L. Crippen, Frederick H. Hauck, John M. Fabian, Sally K. Ride, Norman E. Thagard	Second *Challenger* flight; first 5-person crew; Ride was first American woman in space; deployed and retrieved West German satellite, using robot arm; deployed communications satellites for Canada and Indonesia
6/27/83	Soyuz T-9	USSR	150 days*	Vladimir Lyakhov, Alexander Aleksandrov	Docked with Salyut 7
8/30/83	Shuttle	U.S.	6 days	Richard Truly, Daniel Brandenstein, William Thornton, Guion Bluford, Jr., Dale Gardner	Third use of *Challenger;* launched satellite for India; Bluford was first black American in space
11/28/83	Shuttle	U.S.	10 days	John Young, Brewster Shaw, Jr., Robert Parker, Owen Garriott, Byron Lichtenberg, Ulf Merbold	Sixth use of *Columbia;* launched Spacelab, a reusable workshop and laboratory built by 10 European nations; crew included a West German scientist, Merbold

Launch	Craft	Country	Duration	Crew	Significance
2/3/84	Shuttle	U.S.	8 days	Vance Brand, Bruce McCandless, Robert Stewart, Ronald McNair, Robert Gibson	Fourth use of *Challenger*; successful test of jet-propelled backpacks for untethered EVAs; 2 satellites lost when their rockets fail; first landing at Kennedy Space Center
2/8/84	Soyuz T-10	USSR	237 days*	Leonard Kizim, Oleg Atkov, Vladimir Solovyov	Repaired propulsion system on Salyut 7; set new endurance record
4/2/84	Soyuz T-11	USSR	8 days*	Yuri Malyshev, Gennadi Strealov, Rakesh Sharma	Docked with Salyut 7; Sharma was first Indian in space
4/7/84	Shuttle	U.S.	8 days	Robert L. Crippen, Richard Scobee, Terry Hart, George Nelson, James van Hoften	Fifth use of *Challenger*; crew retrieved, repaired, redeployed Solar Maximum Mission research satellite using robotic arm; deployed Long Duration Exposure Facility containing 57 scientific experiments
7/18/84	Soyuz T-12	USSR	12 days*	Svetlana Savitskaya, Vladimir Djanibekov, Igor Volk	Docked with Salyut 7; Savitskaya was first woman to walk in space
8/30/84	Shuttle	U.S.	6 days	Henry W. Hartsfield, Jr., Michael L. Coates, Steven A. Hawley, Judith Resnick, Richard M. Mullane, Charles D. Walker	Two months earlier, flight had been aborted 2.6 seconds after engine start-up when fuel valve on new shuttle, *Discovery*, failed to open; first flight of *Discovery*; Walker was first person from private industry (McDonnell Douglas Corp.) on shuttle; launched 3 satellites
10/5/84	Shuttle	U.S.	7 days	Robert L. Crippen, Jon A. McBride, Kathryn D. Sullivan, Sally K. Ride, Marc Gameau, David C. Leestma, Paul D. Scully-Power	Sixth *Challenger* flight; Gameau was first Canadian in space; deployed satellites; largest crew to date
11/8/84	Shuttle	U.S.	7 days	Frederick H. Hauck, David M. Walker, Anna L. Fisher, Joseph P. Allen, Dale A. Gardner	Second use of *Discovery*; retrieved the 2 satellites that failed during 2/3/84 mission; returned them to Cape Canaveral for repair
1/24/85	Shuttle	U.S.	2 days	Thomas K. Mattingly, Loren J. Schriver, James F. Buchli, Ellison S. Onizuka, Gary E. Payton	Third use of *Discovery*; secret mission for Defense Department; satellite-boosting rocket tested successfully

Launch	Craft	Country	Duration	Crew	Significance
4/12/85	Shuttle	U.S.	6 days	Karol J. Bobko, Donald E. Williams, Jake Garn, Charles D. Walker, Jeffrey A. Hoffman, S. David Griggs, M. Rhea Seddon	Fourth use of *Discovery;* Garn was first Senator in space; communications satellite deployed but failed; *Discovery* nudged satellite with improvised hook in unsuccessful repair attempt
4/29/85	Shuttle	U.S.	7 days	Robert F. Overmeyer, Frederick D. Gregory, Don L. Lind, Taylor G. Wang, Lodewijk van der Berg, Norman Thagard, William Thornton	Seventh use of *Challenger;* carried second Spacelab, with 2 monkeys, 24 rats for experiments on motion sickness (sponsored by European nations)
6/6/85	Soyuz T-13	USSR	112 days*	Vladimir Dzhanibekov, Viktor Savinykh	Repaired Salyut 7, which had suffered power failure
6/17/85	Shuttle	U.S.	6 days	John O. Creighton, Shannon W. Lucid, Steven R. Nagel, Daniel C. Brandenstein, John W. Fabian, Salman al-Saud, Patrick Baudry	Fifth use of *Discovery;* Prince Sultan Salman al-Saud was first Saudi Arabian in space; deployed 3 communications satellites; deployed and retrieved Spartan X-ray deep-space telescope
7/29/85	Shuttle	U.S.	7 days	Roy D. Bridges, Jr., Anthony W. England, Karl G. Henize, F. Story Musgrave, C. Gordon Fullerton, Loren W. Acton, John-David F. Bartoe	Eighth use of *Challenger;* achieved orbit despite shutdown of one of 3 engines during ascent; carried Spacelab 2 (the third Spacelab) with instruments to measure magnetism in the solar system
8/28/85	Shuttle	U.S.	7 days	John M. Lounge, James D. van Hoften, William F. Fisher, Joe H. Engle, Richard O. Covey	Sixth use of *Discovery;* deployed 3 satellites; retrieved, repaired, and redeployed satellite
9/17/85	Soyuz T-14	USSR	65 days*	Vladimir Vasyutin, Alexander N. Valkov, Georgi M. Grechko	Brought supplies to Dzhanibekov and Savinykh in Salyut 7; Grechko and Dzhanibekov returned Sept. 26 in Soyuz T-13; Valkov and Savinykh returned early, on Nov. 21, after Vasyutin became ill
10/4/85	Shuttle	U.S.	2 days	Karol J. Bobko, Ronald J. Grabe, David C. Hilmers, William A. Pailes, Robert C. Stewart	First use of shuttle *Atlantis;* secret Defense Department mission

Launch	Craft	Country	Duration	Crew	Significance
10/30/85	Shuttle	U.S.	7 days	Henry W. Hartsfield, Jr., Steven R. Nagel, Bonnie J. Dunbar, Guion S. Bluford, Jr., Ernst Messerschmid, Reinhard Furrer, Wubbo J. Ockels	Ninth use of *Challenger;* carried Spacelab 1-D (fourth Spacelab) sponsored by West Germany; carried West German scientists to conduct Spacelab experiments
11/26/85	Shuttle	U.S.	7 days	Brewster H. Shaw, Jr., Bryan D. O'Conner, Charles Walker, Rudolfo Neri Vela, Jerri L. Ross, Sherwood C. Spring, Mary L. Cleave	Second use of *Atlantis;* Vela was first Mexican in space
1/28/86	Shuttle	U.S.	73 seconds	Francis R. Scobee, Michael J. Smith, Robert E. McNair, Ellison S. Onizuka, Judith A. Resnick, Gregory B. Jarvis, Christa McAuliffe	*Challenger,* on its 10th mission, exploded on takeoff, killing 6 astronauts and Christa McAuliffe, an elementary school teacher; future flights delayed pending investigation [for detailed description, see Space Stations, this chapter]
5/5/86	Soyuz T-15	USSR	125 days*	Vladimir Solovyov, Leonid Kizim	Docked with Mir, first space station designed to be permanently manned (Mir was launched 2/20/86); also docked with Salyut 7; welded a structure in space during EVA
2/7/87	Soyuz TM-2	USSR	326 days*	Yuri Romanenko, Alexander Laveykin	Docked with Mir
7/23/87	Soyuz TM-3	USSR	8 days*	Alexander Aleksandrov, Alexander Viktorenko, Muhammad Faris	Docked with Mir; Faris was first Syrian in space; Faris, Vitorenko and the ailing Laveykin (from Soyuz TM-2 mission) returned on TM-2
12/20/87	Soyuz TM-4	USSR	366 days*	Vladimir G. Titov, Musa Manarov, Anatoly Leuchenko	Docked with Mir; set endurance record
6/7/88	Soyuz TM-5	USSR	10 days*	Alexander Aleksandrov, Viktor P. Savinykh, Anatoly Y. Solovyov	Docked with Mir
8/29/88	Soyuz TM-6	USSR	9 days*	Vladimir Lyakhov, Valery Polyakov, Abdul Ahad Mohmand	Docked with Mir; Ahad was first Afghan in space; Ahad and Lyakhov returned in Soyuz TM-5 after one-day delay caused by computer problems and human error
9/29/88	Shuttle	U.S.	4 days	Mike Lounge, David Hilmers, Frederick Hauck, Pinky Nelson, Dick Covey	*Discovery* made first shuttle flight since *Challenger* disaster; launched communications satellite
11/26/88	Soyuz TM-7	USSR	152 days*	Alexander Volkov, Sergei Krikalev, Jean-Loup Chrétien	Docked with Mir; Mir was left empty for 132 days when all crew members returned to Earth

Launch	Craft	Country	Duration	Crew	Significance
12/2/88	Shuttle	U.S.	4 days	Robert L. Gibson, Jerry L. Ross, William M. Shepherd, Guy S. Gardner, Richard M. Mullane	Third use of *Atlantis;* launched secret military satellite
3/13/89	Shuttle	U.S.	4 days	Michael L. Coats, John E. Blanha, James F. Buchi, James P. Bagian, Robert C. Springer	*Discovery* deployed tracking and data-relay satellite; tested thermal control system for proposed Freedom space station
5/4/89	Shuttle	U.S.	4 days	David M. Walker, Ronald J. Grabe, Mary L. Cleave, Norman E. Thagard, Mark C. Lee	*Atlantis* deployed unmanned Magellan space probe toward Venus (Magellan due to arrive in 1990)
8/8/89	Shuttle	U.S.	6 days	Brewster H. Shaw, Jr., Richard N. Richards, David C. Leetsma, James Adamson, Mark Brown	*Columbia* mission for Defense Department
9/4/89	Soyuz TM-8	USSR	168 days*	Alexander Viktorenko, Alexander Serebrov	Reactivated Mir, left empty for 132 days as Soviet space program underwent budgetary problems; conducted experiments; carried U.S. research equipment for the first time
10/18/89	Shuttle	U.S.	6 days	Donald Williams, Michael McCulley, Ellen Baker, Franklin R. Chang-Diaz, Shannon W. Lucid	Deployed unmanned Galileo space probe toward Jupiter
11/22/89	Shuttle	U.S.	6 days	Frederick Gregory, John E. Blaha, F. Story Musgrave, Kathryn C. Thornton, Manley L. Carter, Jr.	*Discovery* mission for Defense Department
1/9/90	Shuttle	U.S.	10 days	Daniel C. Brandenstein, James D. Wetherbee, Bonnie J. Dunbar, G. David Low, Marsha Ivins	*Columbia* crew retrieved 11-ton Long-Duration Exposure Facility using robotic arm; the bus-sized lab had been in space 6 years
2/11/90	Soyuz TM-9	USSR	189 days*	Anatoli Solovyov, Alexander Balandin	Docked with Mir; replaced Soyuz TM-8 crew; U.S. and other countries paid to have research equipment on flight; cosmonauts had to repair damage before TM-9 could return to Earth

Launch	Craft	Country	Duration	Crew	Significance
2/28/90	Shuttle	U.S.	5 days	John O. Creighton, John H. Casper, David C. Hilmers, Richard M. Mullane, Pierre J. Thuot	*Atlantis* crew launched secret $500 million spy satellite for Defense Department
4/24/90	Shuttle	U.S.	6 days	Loren Shriver, Charles Bolden, Bruce McCandless, Steven Hawley, Kathryn Sullivan	After several launch delays, *Discovery* crew deployed $1.5 billion Hubble Space Telescope
8/1/90	Soyuz TM-10	USSR	9 days*	Gennady Manakov, Gennady Strekalov	Docked with Mir
10/6/90	Shuttle	U.S.	5 days	Richard N. Richards, Robert D. Cabana, Thomas D. Akers, Bruce E. Melnick, William M. Shepherd	*Discovery* crew deployed Ulysses spacecraft to explore sun's north and south poles
11/15/90	Shuttle	U.S.	6 days	Richard O. Covey, Frank L. Culbertson, Charles D. Gema, Carl J. Meade, Robert C. Springer	*Atlantis* mission for Defense Department
12/2/90	Shuttle	U.S.	10 days	Vance D. Brand, Guy S. Gardner, Jeffrey A. Hoffman, John M. Lounge, Robert A. R. Parker, Samuel T. Durrance, Ronald A. Parise	*Columbia* carried four telescopes for studies of ultraviolet and X-ray spectrums of the universe
12/2/90	Soyuz TM-11	USSR	8 days*	Viktor Afanasyev, Musa Manarov, Toyohiro Akiyama	Japanese journalist broadcast from space, returned after 8 days; Mir crew replaced
4/5/91	Shuttle	U.S.	6 days	Steven R. Nagel, Kenneth D. Cameron, Jay Apt, Linda M. Godwin, Jerry L. Ross	*Atlantis* crew put observatory into orbit
4/28/91	Shuttle	U.S.	8 days	Michael Coats, L. Blaine Hammond, Jr., Donald McMonagle, Gregory Harbaugh, Guion Bluford, Jr., Richard Hieb, Charles Lacy Veach	*Discovery* crew conducted tests to help Pentagon develop sensors for tracking missiles
5/8/91	Soyuz TM-12	USSR	9 days*	Anatoly Artsebarsky, Sergei Krikalev, Helen Sharman	Docked with Mir; British researcher (Sharman) returned after 9 days; Mir crew replaced
6/5/91	Shuttle	U.S.	9 days	Bryan O'Connor, Sidney Gutierrez, Tamara Jernigan, Millie Hughes-Fulford, James Bagian, F. Andrew Gaffney, M. Rhea Seddon	*Columbia* crew studied biological effects of weightlessness

Launch	Craft	Country	Duration	Crew	Significance
8/2/91	Shuttle	U.S.	9 days	John E. Blaha, Michael A. Baker, James C. Adamson, G. David Low, Shannon W. Lucid	*Atlantis* crew released $120 million Tracking and Data Relay Satellite
9/12/91	Shuttle	U.S.	5 days	John Creighton, Kenneth Reightler, Jr., James F. Buchli, Mark Brown, Charles "Sam" Gemar	*Discovery* crew launched $740 million Upper Atmosphere Satellite to study Earth's ozone layer
10/2/91	Soyuz TM-13	USSR	9 days*	Alexander Volkov, Toktar Aubakirov, Franz Viehboeck	Docked with Mir; Austrian researcher (Viehboeck) and Aubakirov returned after 9 days; Volkov replaced Mir cosmonaut Anatoly Artsebarsky
11/24/91	Shuttle	U.S.	7 days	Frederick Gregory, Story Musgrave, Terence "Tom" Henricks, James Voss, Mario Runco, Jr., Thomas Hennen	*Atlantis* crew returned from Defense Department mission three days early due to problem with navigation equipment
1/22/92	Shuttle	U.S.	8 days	Ronald Grabe, Stephen Oswald, William Readdy, Norman Thagard, David Hilmers, Roberta Bondar, Ulf Merbold	*Discovery* crew studied motion sickness, conducted experiments concerning biological effects of weightlessness. Crew included Canadian (Bondar) and German (Merbold)
3/17/92	Soyuz TM-14	Russia	9 days*	Alexander Viktorenko, Alexander Kalery, Klaus-Dietrich Flade	Viktorenko and Kalery replaced Mir cosmonauts Krikalev and Volkov. Krikalev had been orbiting 10 months, a stay lengthened due to the dissolution of the USSR
3/24/92	Shuttle	U.S.	9 days	Charles Bolden, Jr., Brian Duffy, David Leestma, Kathryn Sullivan, Michael Foale, Byron Lichtenberg, Dirk Frimout	*Atlantis* crew studied Earth's atmosphere magnetic field and the sun. Crew included a Belgian (Frimout), who is a physicist with the European Space Agency
5/7/92	Shuttle	U.S.	8 days	Daniel Brandenstein, Kevin Chilton, Richard Hieb, Bruce Melnick, Pierre Thuot, Kathryn Thornton, Thomas Akers	First flight for *Endeavour*, replacement for space shuttle *Challenger*. After initial failures, crew improvised plan to capture Intelsat-6 satellite for repair. Three astronauts grabbed satellite with their gloved hands, brought it into shuttle. It was released after repairs.

Launch	Craft	Country	Duration	Crew	Significance
6/25/92	Shuttle	U.S.	14 days	Richard N. Richards, Kenneth Bowersox, Bonnie Dunbar, Carl Meade, Ellen Baker, Lawrence DeLucas, Eugene Trinh	Longest shuttle mission to date. *Columbia* crew performed scientific experiments in preparation for establishment of space station.
7/27/92	Soyuz TM-15	Russia	14 days	Anatoly Solovyov, Sergei Avdeyev, Michel Tognini	Solovyov and Avdeyev replaced cosmonauts Alexander Viktorenko and Alexander Kalery on Mir. Tognini, a French researcher, returned to Earth with Viktorenko and Kalery
7/31/92	Shuttle	U.S.	8 days	Loren J. Shriver, Andrew M. Allen, Franco Malerba, Marsha Ivins, Jeffrey A. Hoffman, Franklin R. Chang-Diaz, Claude Nicollier	Attempt to release tethered satellite from *Atlantis* failed when an unreeling mechanism jammed. Crew successfully released scientific probe designed by European Space Agency, of which Nicollier (a Swiss) is a member.
9/12/92	Shuttle	U.S.	8 days	Robert L. Gibson, Curtis L. Brown, Mark C. Lee, Mamoru Mohri, Jay Apt, N. Jan Davis, Mae C. Jemison	*Endeavor* crew tested effects of weightlessness on tadpoles and insects. Davis and Lee were first married couple on a space flight. Jemison was first black woman in space.
10/22/92	Shuttle	U.S.	9 days	James D. Wetherbee, Michael A. Baker, Steven G. MacLean, Tamara E. Jernigan, William M. Shepherd, Charles L. Veach	*Columbia* crew deployed an Italian satellite to measure motion in the Earth's crust
12/2/92	Shuttle	U.S.	7 days	David M. Walker, Robert D. Cabana, Guion S. Bluford, Jr., James S. Voss, Michael R. Clifford	*Discovery* crew deployed spy satellite for Defense Department

* For some Soyuz flights, cosmonauts traveled to Salyut or Mir in one craft and returned in another. In those cases, the duration of the mission given is for the crew, not the craft. In some trips to the Mir space station, the Soyuz craft carried Soviet cosmonauts and foreign passengers. The cosmonauts replaced previous Mir crew members, staying for several months. The foreign passengers returned within days, accompanied by the members of the retiring Mir crew. In those cases, the duration given is for the foreign passenger.

TYPES OF AIRCRAFT

airplane: Any heavier-than-air craft.

airship: Any steerable, lighter-than-air craft that is buoyed by helium or hydrogen. *See* blimp, dirigible

amphibian aircraft: An airplane that can operate from land and water.

blimp: An airship that does not have a rigid frame. *See* airship

dirigible: Synonym for airship, q.v.

drone: A pilotless aircraft that is controlled from the ground; also known as a remotely piloted vehicle or RPV.

fan jet: *See* jet

floatplane: An aircraft that operates from the surface of water and is supported by floats; a type of seaplane.

flying boat: An aircraft that operates from the surface of water and floats on a waterproof hull; a type of seaplane.

glider: An aircraft that has no engine or only a small auxiliary engine.

helicopter: A powered aircraft that is lifted and propelled by one or more rotors; a type of VTOL, q.v.

jet: An airplane that uses one of a variety of types of jet engines. A jet engine produces a high-speed stream of gas, which propels the plane forward or is used to turn propellers, which propel the plane forward. In all jets, air is taken in, is mixed with fuel and is burned, producing a stream of exhaust. A jet differs from a rocket in that a jet draws in oxygen from the surrounding atmosphere in order to burn the fuel. A rocket carries its own oxygen supply, allowing it to operate outside of the earth's atmosphere.

The ramjet is the simplest form of jet engine: Air enters the engine, mixes with fuel, the fuel burns, and exhaust gases are expelled through a nozzle at the rear, which propels the craft forward. In a turbojet, a turbine within the engine compresses the incoming air before it enters the combustion chamber. Compressing the air increases the effect of the fuel combustion and increases the engine's thrust. In a fanjet (also known as a turbofan) some of the compressed air is used in the combustion chamber and some is expelled without being burned. Fanjets are quieter and more fuel-efficient than other jets, so they are widely used by airlines. In a turboprop engine, a turbine compresses the incoming air and turns a propeller. The propeller, not the exhaust, provides most of the thrust in a turboprop.

jumbo jet: Various models of the Boeing 747, a wide-body plane with two levels of passenger seating; some models can accommodate more than 500 passengers; other models are used as cargo planes.

ramjet: *See* jet

sailplane: Synonym for glider, q.v.

seaplane: A floatplane or flying boat, q.v.

SST: Supersonic transports (SSTs) are airplanes that travel faster than the speed of sound (660 mph at 36,000 feet altitude). The only one in commercial operation is the Concorde.

STOL aircraft: An aircraft designed for short takeoff and landing distances.

turbofan: *See* jet

turbojet: *See* jet

turboprop: *See* jet

ultralight: A lightweight, one-seat, single-engine aircraft flown for recreation; ultralights can weigh a maximum of 254 pounds and fly at a maximum speed of 55 mph.

V/STOL aircraft: An aircraft designed for vertical or short takeoff and landing distances.

VTOL aircraft: An aircraft designed for vertical takeoff and landing.

wide-body jet: An airplane with a wide fuselage, which allows more seats; typically, wide-body jets seat passengers nine or ten abreast, separated by two aisles; narrow-body airliners typically seat passengers six abreast, separated by one aisle.

COMMON COMMERCIAL AIRLINERS

Name (Builder country)	Type*
A300-600 (Airbus Industrie: joint European venture)	twin-engine, wide-body turbofan jet
A310 (Airbus Industrie: joint European venture)	twin-engine, wide-body turbofan jet
A320 (Airbus Industrie: joint European venture)	twin-engine turbofan jet
BAe 146 (British Aerospace: UK)	four-engine turbofan jet
Boeing 727 (Boeing Commercial Airplane Group: USA)	three-engine turbofan jet
Boeing 737 (Boeing Commercial Airplane Group: USA)	twin-engine turbofan jet
Boeing 747 (Boeing Commercial Airplane Group: USA)	four-engine jumbo turbofan jet (two passenger levels)

Boeing 757 (Boeing Commercial Airplane Group: USA)	twin-engine turbofan jet
Boeing 767 (Boeing Commercial Airplane Group: USA)	twin-engine, wide-body turbofan jet
Concorde (Aérospatiale/BAC: joint French-British venture)	four-engine supersonic jet
Convair CV-580 (Convair, General Dynamics: USA)	twin-engine turboprop
Dash-7 See DHC-7	
DC-8 (Douglas Aircraft Co.: USA)	four-engine turbofan jet
DC-9 (Douglas Aircraft Co.: USA)	twin-engine turbofan jet
DC-10 (Douglas Aircraft Co.: USA)	three-engine turbofan jet
DHC-6 Twin Otter (de Havilland Aircraft: Canada)	twin-engine, turboprop STOL
DHC-7 (de Havilland Aircraft: Canada)	four-engine, turboprop STOL
F27 (Fokker Aircraft: Netherlands)	twin-engine turboprop
F28 (Fokker Aircraft: Netherlands)	twin-engine turbofan jet
F100 (Fokker Aircraft: Netherlands)	twin-engine turbofan jet
Jetstream (British Aerospace: UK)	twin-engine turboprop
L100 (Lockheed Corp.: USA)	four-engine turboprop
L1011 Tristar (Lockheed Corp.: USA)	three-engine, wide-body turbofan jet
MD-11 (Douglas Aircraft Co.: USA)	three-engine turbofan jet
MD-80 (Douglas Aircraft Co.: USA)	twin-engine turbofan jet
Metro See SA 227AC	
SA 227AC (Fairchild Swearingen: USA)	twin-engine turboprop
Shorts Skyvan 360 (Short Brothers: UK)	twin-engine turboprop
TriStar See L1011	
Twin Otter See DHC-6	

* Twin-engine, turboprop planes (which get most of their power from their propellers, rather than from jet exhaust) are designed to carry relatively few passengers (usually fewer than 100) on short trips, frequently between cities. Other jets are designed for transcontinental or transoceanic flights. Some of the largest jet planes carry more than 500 passengers. (The passenger capacity of the planes varies greatly, depending on the seating arrangement and the percentage of space allotted to cargo and baggage.) A supersonic jet travels at a speed greater than the speed of sound. The Concorde is the only commercial supersonic jet. It carries approximately 130 passengers. STOLs are aircraft designed for short take-offs and landings.

U.S. MILITARY AIRCRAFT

U.S. military aircraft are identified by a code of letters and numbers. In 1962, the U.S. Department of Defense adopted a standard set of designations (called Mission, Design, Series Designators) for all military aircraft. Before that, an airplane might have one designation if owned by the Air Force and another if owned by the Navy.

Now each military aircraft has a three-part MDS designation: a letter prefix (usually one, two or three letters) that indicates the plane's use and status, a number that specifies the design of the aircraft, and a one-letter suffix that identifies the series of the aircraft's design. For example, an F-106B plane is a fighter, design number 106, series B (second series).

The letter prefix is easiest to decode if it is read from right to left. The letter closest to the design number usually indicates the plane's basic mission. The letter to the left of that letter (if there is one) indicates its modified mission, that is, a capability other than the basic one. The letter to the left of that letter (if there is one) indicates the plane's status.

Status Prefix	Modified Mission	Basic Mission
G - Permanently grounded	A - Attack	A - Attack
J - Special test (temporary)	C - Transport	B - Bomber
N - Special test (permanent)	D - Director	C - Transport
X - Experimental	E - Special electronic installation	E - Special electronic installation
Y - Prototype	F - Fighter	F - Fighter
Z - Planning	H - Search and rescue	O - Observation
	K - Tanker	P - Patrol
	L - Cold weather	R - Reconnaissance
	M - Multimission	S - Antisubmarine
	O - Observation	T - Trainer
	P - Patrol	U - Utility
	Q - Drone	X - Research
	R - Reconnaissance	
	S - Antisubmarine	
	T - Trainer	
	U - Utility	
	V - Staff	
	W - Weather	

There is one significant exception to the three-place letter designation arrangement. Some special types of aircraft, such as helicopters, have an additional letter between the design number and the basic mission letter. That letter indicates the type of aircraft. The designations are: G - Glider; H - Helicopter; S - Spaceplane; V - VTOL/STOL; Z - Lighter-than-air-vehicle.

Interpreting the designations of these aircraft is like interpreting the designations for any other aircraft, except for the added letter. For example, a CH-47C is a cargo helicopter, design number 47, series C (third series).

Often the same basic aircraft will be modified in several ways and be known by several MDS designators. The A-6 attack aircraft, for example, comes in the following versions: A-6A, EA-6A, JA-6A, NA-6A, A-6B, EA-6B, A-6C, KA-6D, A-6E and A-6F.

Fortunately, military aircraft usually are referred to by a minimum of numbers and letters. Often a one-letter prefix and a design number will suffice. For example, one of the workhorses of the Air Force is the F-4. It, like many other planes, is known also by a popular name—the Phantom.

U.S. MILITARY AIRCRAFT IN THE NEWS

Designation	Popular name	Comment
A-6	Intruder/Prowler	The Intruder was designed to be a carrier-borne attack bomber that could deliver nuclear or conventional weapons. It is equipped with electronic devices that enable it to locate targets in darkness and bad weather. The Intruder also has been adapted for other purposes. The EA-6 variation (known as the Prowler) is used for electronic surveillance. The KA-6 version of the Intruder is a tanker used for midair refueling. The A-6 carries a crew of two.
A-10	Thunderbolt	The Thunderbolt (nicknamed Warthog) is heavily armored and carries a seven-barrel gun capable of firing up to 4,200 rounds per minute. It is designed to attack armored vehicles. It carries only a pilot.
A-12	None	The A-12 is a carrier-based attack aircraft that carries a crew of two.
A-X	None	An experimental, carrier-borne attack plane proposed by the Navy as a replacement for the A-6. The Navy estimates that development would cost at least $10 billion. The first plane would not be ready until 2004.
B-1B	Lancer	The B-1B, which was designed to improve the payload and range abilities available with the B-52, can operate just below the speed of sound at low altitudes. Its low-level capability allows it to use terrain to hide from radar detection. At high altitudes it can operate at supersonic speeds. The plane has been plagued with problems ranging from fuel leaks to engine problems since it was introduced in 1986.

Designation	Popular name	Comment
B-2	Stealth bomber	The B-2 bomber has been the subject of considerable discussion, debate and revision since it was first proposed in the late 1970s. A prototype was flown for the first time in July 1989. A year later, the debate continued, as cost estimates soared. Those in favor of the bomber argued that the bat-wing plane would be nearly invisible to radar, providing extraordinary access to enemy targets. Opponents argued that the cost—which was estimated at more than $2 billion per plane (including development costs) in early 1992—was excessive. They argued that cruise missiles and other available weapons could do the same job at much lower cost, and that the plane was not as effective at eluding radar as had been hoped. Critics also said that the end of the Cold War diminished the need for the B-2. The bomber would use so-called stealth technology—swept-back wings, smooth contours and radar-absorbing materials—to minimize detection by radar. In 1991, 15 planes were completed or in production. In the 1992 defense budget, Congress rejected the administration's request to proceed with plans for five more.
B-52	Stratofortress	First deployed in 1959, the B-52 (nicknamed Buff) is still in wide use, although newer planes have diminished its importance. It can fly up to 7,500 miles at up to 595 mph.
C-5A	Galaxy	The Galaxy, the U.S. Air Force's largest cargo plane, is 222 feet from wing tip to wing tip, 247 feet long and 65 feet high. It can transport payloads up to 261,000 pounds with an unrefueled range at this payload of 3,430 miles and a cruise speed of approximately 560 mph. It can be refueled in flight.
C-17	None	The C-17 is being built as a replacement for the aging C-141. The wide-body will be able to carry massive cargo items, such as large tanks and helicopters that are now carried only by the C-5A. It will be able to land on runways shorter than those used by the C-5A. Like other proposed military aircraft, it has been the object of debate and cutbacks as cost projections have risen, the Cold War has ended, and the national economy has soured.
C-130	Hercules	The four-engine turboprop Hercules has been in use since the 1950s. It accommodates a crew of five and up to 92 troops. Many variations of the C-130 have been developed for specialized uses. With a full cargo load, the latest version can travel up to 2,356 miles at a cruising speed of approximately 345 mph.
C-141	Starlifter	The C-141 cruises at approximately 570 mph and has a range of 2,200 miles with maximum cargo load. It can be refueled in flight, increasing its range. It carries passengers, cargo or paratroopers.
CH-46	Sea Knight	Sea Knight helicopters are used by the Navy to resupply ships at sea, and by the Marines to transport troops. They have been involved in several crashes and have been grounded several times for investigation. Problems were found in the aft rotor transmission and in the linkage between the rotors and the forward engine.
CH-47	Chinook	The Chinook is a tandem-rotor transport helicopter with a rear loading ramp. It carries 3 crew members and 33 passengers.
CH-54A/B	Skycrane	The Skycrane is a helicopter with one lifting rotor and one tail rotor. The CH-54A can lift 20,000 pounds with a winch. The CH-54B lifts 25,000 pounds.
E-2C	Hawkeye	The Hawkeye is a carrier-based early-warning, command-and-control aircraft that carries a crew of five.
E-3	Sentry (AWACS)	The E-3 provides surveillance and command, control and communication information to assist commanders during battles. The plane carries a crew of 20, including 16 Airborne Warning and Control System (AWACS) specialists, who use advanced radar to locate and track airborne targets.

Designation	Popular name	Comment
F-4	Phantom	The Phantom, which has been an important fighter for many years, is being replaced in many units by the F-15 and F-16. It carries a crew of two, can fly at Mach 2 and has a range of 700 miles. It carries one multibarrel gun and can carry Sparrow, Shrike or Sidewinder missiles.
F-14	Tomcat	The F-14 is a carrier-based fighter that can be armed with a variety of air-to-air missiles and bombs. It has a crew of two: a pilot and a radar interceptor officer. It can fly at Mach 2.4 and has a combat radius of more than 900 miles when fully armed. It was introduced to service in 1972. Several upgraded models have been introduced since then.
F-15	Eagle	The F-15 is a pilot-only aircraft with a maximum speed of Mach 2.5. It is designed to fly long-range missions at night and in adverse weather. It carries air-to-air and air-to-surface munitions. (The F-15E model has two seats.)
F-16	Fighting Falcon	The F-16 is a long-range, Mach 2 aircraft that accommodates a pilot only. It carries air-to-air and air-to-surface missiles.
F-111A/D/E/F	None	The F-111 is a long-range, day or night fighter. It accommodates a crew of two, who are seated in an escape module. It can fly at Mach 2.5 and has a range of more than 2,925 miles with its internal fuel supply. It can carry two nuclear bombs internally and up to 25,000 pounds of bombs, rockets, missiles and fuel tanks externally.
F-117A	Stealth fighter	For many years, the F-117A was one of the military's best-kept secrets. It was finally unveiled in 1990, after a decade of rumors and clandestine flights, including a bombing mission over Panama. The F-117A is a single-seat, twin-engine, subsonic jet. Details of its performance capabilities have not been released. It uses stealth technology—a smooth shape and radar-absorbing composite materials—to help avoid radar detection. According to figures from the General Accounting Office, each F-117A costs $100 million, including development costs. The production cost, according to the Air Force, is $42.6 million per plane. Fifty-nine stealth fighters have been produced.
F/A-18A	Hornet	The Hornet is a carrier-based, supersonic fighter/attack aircraft. It can be catapult launched. It is a pilot-only aircraft (although trainer models can accommodate a crew of two). It can carry more than 17,000 pounds of ordnance, including air-to-air and air-to-ground missiles.
KC-135	Stratotanker	The Stratotanker is an aerial refueling tanker. It was used during the Vietnam War, proving the importance of aerial refueling in combat. It accommodates a crew of four or five and up to 80 passengers. It can fly 1,150 miles with 120,000 pounds of transfer fuel, at speeds up to 585 mph.
SR-71	Blackbird	The SR-71, which was retired in March 1990, is the fastest production aircraft ever built. It set several records on its final journey from California to Washington, D.C., where it became part of the collection of the Smithsonian Institution. It made the coast-to-coast trip in 68 minutes, 17 seconds, shattering the old record of 3 hours, 38 minutes. It also set a speed record of 2,242.48 mph. The SR-71 is a reconnaissance aircraft that flies at Mach 3 at 80,000 feet. It carries a crew of two. After 25 years of service, the plane was retired for budgetary reasons. Many of the photographic surveillance missions for which it was designed are now performed by satellites.
U-2R	None	The U-2R is a single-seat, high-flying jet glider used for reconnaissance. The original version, U-2, was given the "U" designation (for Utility) to hide its true mission. Its purpose was revealed in 1960 when a U-2 was shot down on a mission over the Soviet Union. The pilot, Francis Gary Powers, bailed out, was captured and was sentenced to 10 years in a Soviet prison. He was released after two years as part of a spy trade. Although spy satellites have taken over much of its work, the U-2R model was used extensively in the

Designation	Popular name	Comment
U-2R (*cont.*)		Persian Gulf War. It also is used for scientific research projects. It can fly at up to 90,000 feet, higher than any other U.S. plane. Pilots must wear pressurized space suits. It can reach speeds of more than 430 mph and flies 3,000 miles without refueling.
UH-60A	Black Hawk	The Black Hawk helicopter carries a crew of two or three, up to 14 troops, up to six litters, and internal or external cargo. It flies at up to 184 mph. Using internal fuel supplies, it has a range of 373 miles. External tanks can increase the range to 1,380 miles. Some H-60s are configured for night use (HH-60A, HH-60D) and are known as Night Hawks. Others have been adapted for use by the Navy (SH-60B, SH-60F, HH-60H, HH-60J) and are known as Sea Hawks. The VH-60D Night Hawk has been modified to transport the president, vice president and White House staff.
VC-25A	Air Force One	On Sept. 6, 1990, Pres. George Bush flew in the new Air Force One for the first time. The plane, a modified Boeing 747 that replaced a C-137, can fly 7,140 miles without refueling. In case of emergency, it can be refueled in midair. It carries 70 passengers (all in first-class-size seats) and a crew of up to 23. It is equipped with 19 televisions, 85 telephones, computers, a paper shredder, two galleys and freezer space for 2,000 meals. A private cabin for the president includes two couches that convert to twin beds. Its medical room is equipped for emergency surgery. A second VC-25A, which will also be designated Air Force One when the president is on board, was delivered in 1991, completing the replacement of the two C-137s that were the former Air Force Ones. The contracted cost of the jets was $266 million, but the actual cost reportedly ran closer to $400 million. Much of the cost overrun was absorbed by Boeing.

ASTRONOMY FACTS

STRUCTURE OF THE SOLAR SYSTEM

The **solar system** consists of the sun, nine planets and their moons, more than 1,000 comets and thousands of smaller bodies known as asteroids and meteoroids. The sun, a glowing sphere of gas at the center of the solar system, is by far the largest component. It is 860,000 miles in diameter (1.39 million km.), 109 times the size of Earth and nearly 10 times the size of the largest planet, Jupiter. The sun exerts a gravitational pull upon the other bodies in the solar system, controlling their motions.

The sun is not large when compared with other stars in the universe, however; it is classified as a dwarf star. Its size appears great to us because it is the closest star to Earth. The average distance between Earth and the sun is 92.96 million miles (149.591 million km.). This distance is often used as a unit of measurement to compare distances in space. It is called an Astronomical Unit.

Our solar system, with its one star, is a small part of our **galaxy**, the Milky Way. The galaxy contains about 100 billion stars, some of which may have planets orbiting them. Our galaxy, in turn, is but a small part of the observable **universe**.

Because of the vast distances in space, conventional linear measurements are of little use. Instead, distances often are expressed in terms of how many minutes, hours or years it would take a ray of light to travel the distance. Light travels at 186,000 miles per second. A **light-year** is the distance light travels in one year—5.88 million million miles or 9.46 million million kilometers.

Earth is about 8.3 light-minutes from the sun. It is about 3.8 light-years from the next closest star, Proxima Centauri (part of a three-star cluster, Alpha Centauri). The solar system is 11 light-hours in diameter. The galaxy is 100,000 light-years in diameter. The observable universe is about 30 billion light-years in diameter.

There are several theories concerning how the universe was formed. The most widely supported is the **Big Bang Theory.** According to this theory, the universe began as a ball of concentrated matter and energy that exploded between 13 billion and 20 billion years ago. The products of that explosion combined to form the bodies that make up the galaxies. According to that theory, the galaxies should continue to move apart, which has been shown to be the case.

The nine planets rotate around the sun. Seven of the planets have moons that, in turn, circle around them. The planets, in order from the sun, are Mercury, Venus, Earth, Mars, Jupiter, Saturn, Uranus, Neptune and Pluto.

ASTRONOMICAL BODIES

Alpha Centauri: This three-star cluster contains the stars nearest to our sun. The faint star Proxima Centauri is the closest in the group. It is 3.8 light-years away from Earth.

Andromeda galaxy: This galaxy is the only one that is visible without a telescope in the Northern Hemisphere. To the unaided eye, it appears as a tiny fuzzy glow. Through a telescope, it is seen as spiral-shaped, with about seven curving arms extending from a hub. It is more than 2 million light-years away.

asteroid: An asteroid is, in essence, a tiny planet—a small body that rotates around the sun. Tens of thousands of them have been identified, although none is visible to the unaided eye. There may be as many as 1 million. Most are clustered in a belt that lies between Jupiter and Saturn. The largest, Ceres, is about 625 miles in diameter.

black hole: *See* section entitled Astronomical Phenomena and Theories on page 270.

comet: A comet is a ball of frozen gases, dust and grit that travels around the sun, usually in an elongated orbit. As it nears the sun, the frozen ball (the nucleus) begins to vaporize and becomes surrounded by a cloud of gas and grit, which is known as the coma. When the comet comes closer to the sun, the size of the coma increases, and gases within it are pushed away from the sun by the pressure of the sun's radiation and by solar wind. These gases form the tail. The tail of a comet may be hundreds of millions of miles long.

About 10 comets are discovered every year. Although hundreds of comets have been identified, most cannot be seen without a telescope. A faint comet may be visible every three years or so, but a large, luminous comet is more of a rarity. Such a comet may be visible only a few times in a lifetime. A comet's apparent brightness depends upon its size and its position in relation to the sun and Earth. Comets become brighter as they approach the sun. If, at that point, their orbit brings them within good viewing range from Earth, they are particularly spectacular. To an observer, a comet appears to be a glowing sphere, followed by a luminous tail or tails. Because of its great distance from Earth, it appears stationary, although it is moving many thousands of miles per hour.

Comets with elliptical orbits appear at predictable intervals. Those with parabolic or hyperbolic orbits do not. The periodic comets vary greatly in their frequency of appearance. Encke's Comet, which appears every 3.3 years, has the shortest period. Many comets appear only after periods of 200 years or more.

The most famous comet is Halley's Comet, which returns about every 76 years. It was named for Edmund Halley (1656–1742), an English astronomer who observed it in 1682 and predicted its reappearance in 1759. He was the first to predict successfully the return of a comet. Halley's Comet last appeared in 1985–86, when it was best visible from the Southern Hemisphere.

Comets, because of their rarity and sometimes spectacular appearance, have often been imbued with mystical qualities. For centuries they have been regarded as harbingers of disaster. Mark Twain (1835–1910), who was born in a year when Halley's Comet was sighted, predicted that he would die the year that it reappeared. He did.

constellation: A constellation is a pattern formed by stars. Although the stars in the constellations may be quite distant from each other, to the viewer they appear to be related. Many of the 88 constellations are named for animals or for Greek and Roman mythological figures, which they are supposed to resemble. The patterns may, in fact, bear little resemblance to their namesakes. Still, they are useful as points of reference when locating astral bodies, particularly for amateur astronomers.

Mystics and sages of many cultures have imbued the constellations with meanings and powers from ancient times. Even today, astrologers believe that the motion of the planets through the 12 zodiac constellations affect human behavior and fortunes. The zodiac constellations are: Aries, Taurus, Gemini, Cancer, Leo, Virgo, Libra, Scorpius, Sagittarius, Capricornus, Aquarius and Pisces.

Some constellations are visible throughout the year. Others are visible only during certain seasons. In the Northern Hemisphere, the Big Dipper (Ursa Major), the Little Dipper (Ursa Minor), Cassiopeia (The Queen), Cepheus (The King) and Draco (The Dragon) are major constellations visible throughout the year. The tip of the handle of the Little Dipper is Polaris, the North Star, a bright star that is used in navigation because it is less than 1 degree away from polar north. Major spring constellations in the Northern Hemisphere include: Gemini (The Twins), Leo (The Lion), Bootes (The Herdsman) and Virgo (The Virgin). Major summer constellations include: Hercules, Lyra (The Lyre), Scorpius (The Scorpion), Sagittarius (The Archer), Cygnus (The Swan, also called the Northern Cross), Aquila (The Eagle), Sagitta (The Arrow) and Delphinus (The Dolphin). Major autumn constellations include: Pegasus (The Winged Horse), Andromeda, Perseus and Auriga (The Charioteer). Major winter constellations include: Orion (The Hunter), Taurus (The Bull), Canis Major (The Big Dog), Canis Minor (The Little Dog), Lepus (The Hare) and Columba (The Dove).

Some of the constellations of the Southern Hemisphere may be observed from far southern parts of the United States, such as southern Florida and Texas. The best known of these constellations is the Southern Cross, which points toward polar south.

Earth: Earth is the third planet from the sun, which is an average distance of 92.9 million miles away. Its diameter is 7,927 miles at the equator. It spins on its axis, like a tilted top, while it rotates around the sun. It spins once on its axis every 23 hours, 56 minutes and 4.09 seconds. It rotates around the sun once every 365 days, 5 hours, 48 minutes and 45.51 seconds.

The core of the planet Earth is a dense sphere of compressed, molten rock with a solid center. The core, about 4,200 miles in diameter, is estimated to have a temperature of 11,000° F. The core is covered by an 1,800-mile-thick layer of heavy rock, the mantle. The crust, which is about 25 miles thick, covers the mantle. Earth's surface area is approximately 196,949,970 sq. mi., about three-quarters of which is covered by water.

Earth is surrounded by its atmosphere—a layer of gases about 500 miles deep, held in place by Earth's gravity. The atmosphere becomes thinner as the distance from Earth increases. The atmosphere within 60 miles of Earth's surface is composed of approximately 78 percent nitrogen, 21 percent oxygen and 1 percent other gases, including argon and carbon dioxide and small amounts of neon, helium, krypton and xenon.

The atmosphere is divided into layers. The bottom layer, which extends from sea level to seven miles high, is the troposphere. The next layer, from seven to 30 miles, is the stratosphere. (The stratosphere is also sometimes called the ozonesphere.) The next layer, from 30 to 50 miles, is the mesosphere. The next, from 50 to 400 miles, is the thermosphere. Above the thermosphere is the exosphere. (The mesosphere, thermosphere and exosphere are known collectively as the ionosphere.) [*See* section entitled: Astronomical Phenomena and Theories on pages 270–272; Meteorology Glossary, page 273]

Evening Star: Venus is popularly called the Evening Star or the Morning Star, depending on when it appears in the sky. It is a planet, not a star, but it appears bright because of reflected light. At certain times in the year, when Mercury is visible just after sunset or just before sunrise, it is also called the Evening or Morning Star.

galaxy: A galaxy is a large, isolated group of stars held together by mutual gravitational attraction. Our galaxy is the Milky Way. [*See* Milky Way]

globular clusters: Globular clusters are large, spherical groups of stars at the edge of our galaxy. The brightest is faintly visible to the unaided eye. They can contain tens of thousands of stars.

Jupiter: Jupiter, the fifth planet from the sun, is the largest planet in the solar system. Its diameter is 88,700 miles at the equator. It rotates faster on its axis than any other planet, completing a rotation every 9 hours, 50 minutes and 30 seconds. The high-speed rotation causes it to be considerably flattened at each end. It travels around the sun once every 11.86 years.

Jupiter, like the other outer planets (Saturn, Uranus, Neptune and Pluto), is not at all like the inner planets (Mercury, Venus, Earth and Mars). Although it is gigantic, it is not nearly as dense as the inner, rocky planets. It is composed primarily of condensed, liquid and frozen gases. There may be a rocky core.

A thick layer of methane and ammonia clouds covers Jupiter's surface, obscuring it from Earth. The clouds form bands parallel to the equator. A prominent feature in the cloud layer, the Great Red Spot, is a storm thousands of miles wide that has been raging since at least 1665, when it was discovered. Jupiter also is surrounded by several faint rings.

Jupiter has 13 known moons. The two largest, Callisto and Ganymede, are each more than 3,125 miles in diameter, making them larger than Mercury and Pluto. (Ganymede, at nearly 3,300 miles, is the largest moon in the solar system.) Two other moons, Io and Europa, are large enough to be seen with field glasses.

Jupiter has been probed by four American spacecraft: Pioneers 10 and 11, which passed Jupiter in 1973 and 1974, and Voyagers 1 and 2 in 1979. The Galileo spacecraft, launched in 1989, is scheduled to arrive at Jupiter in 1995. An antenna problem could diminish the spacecraft's effectiveness.

Magellanic Clouds: The Magellanic Clouds are two small galaxies that orbit the Milky Way. They are the nearest galaxies to the Milky Way.

Mars: Mars, the fourth planet from the sun, is the third smallest in the solar system. Its diameter is 4,219 miles at the equator. It rotates on its axis once every 24 hours, 37 minutes and 23 seconds. It travels around the sun once every 687 days.

Mars is the most studied and best-known planet in the solar system, aside from Earth. Its thin atmosphere makes detailed observation possible with telescopes. In addition, U.S. and Soviet space probes have repeatedly investigated it. In 1976, the United States landed space probes on its surface for the first time. The probes, Vikings 1 and 2, sent television pictures from the Martian surface and used soil samples to search for signs of life. The tests, which showed some positive chemical indications of life, were inconclusive.

Mars resembles the other inner planets (Mercury, Venus and Earth) in that it is solid and rocky. (The outer planets—Jupiter, Saturn, Uranus, Neptune and Pluto—are largely frozen and liquefied gases.) Still, it would hardly be hospitable to life. Viking 1 recorded surface temperatures ranging from a high of − 6° F (in midsummer) to − 191° F. The surface has towering volcanoes (the tallest is 78,000 feet), gaping chasms and polar caps made of frozen carbon dioxide (dry ice). The flat areas are pockmarked by the craters of thousands of meteors, which are able to bombard the planet because of the thin atmosphere. The atmosphere is 95 percent carbon dioxide, 2.7 percent nitrogen and 1.6 percent argon.

Mars, which is visible to the unaided eye, has long been the object of fable. The Romans named the planet after their god of war because its reddish surface is the color of blood. (The planet's color is the result of iron oxide in the soil.) The two moons of Mars are named after the horses that pulled the god's chariot. The moons are Deimos (meaning "terror") and Phobos (meaning "fear").

In the 19th century astronomers observed what they believed to be canals on the Martian surface. This led to widespread belief that Mars was populated by intelligent creatures capable of building such structures. The Martian canals were actually optical illusions—unrelated dark spots linked only by the viewer's imagination.

Mercury: Mercury, the planet closest to the sun, is the second smallest planet in the solar system. (Pluto is the smallest.) Its diameter is 3,030 miles at the equator. It spins on its axis once every 58.6 days and travels around the sun once every 88 days.

It is a barren, alternately freezing and burning planet with virtually no atmosphere and no moons. It is extremely dense. Its rocky crust may cover a core of iron. Temperatures on the sunlit portion of the planet reach 950° F. Those on the dark side reach −346° F. Because Mercury turns so slowly on its axis, there is little opportunity for the day-night heating and cooling process that causes temperatures to moderate.

The U.S. Mariner 10 space probe provided detailed pictures of Mercury's surface in 1974 and 1975.

meteor, meteoroid, meteorite: Meteoroids are pieces of rocky debris in space. As they enter Earth's atmosphere they burn, causing streaks of light in the sky. Those streaks are meteors—also called falling stars or shooting stars. Meteors can be seen on any clear night, but they are most prevalent at certain times of the year, when Earth passes through meteoroid swarms. When meteors are frequent they are called meteor showers. Three heavy meteor showers are the Quadrantids in January (110 per hour), the Perseids in August (60 per hour) and the Geminids in December (50 per hour). Most meteoroids burn up before they reach Earth's surface. Those that actually hit the surface are called meteorites. They range from microscopic dust to chunks of stone or iron-nickel alloy weighing many tons.

Milky Way: The Milky Way is our galaxy. It is lens-shaped: round and thicker in the middle than at the edges. On a clear night, it appears as a milky band across the sky. That is because we are within the galaxy, looking through it lengthwise toward its edge.

Moon: A moon is a natural satellite of a planet.

Earth's moon is 2,160 miles in diameter, more than one-quarter the size of Earth and only about 350 miles smaller in diameter than Pluto. It rotates around the earth every 27.32 days. Because it also revolves on its axis once every 27.32 days, the same side is always toward Earth. (The side that we do not see is properly called the far side, not the dark side. Each side of the moon receives approximately 14 days of light followed by approximately 14 days of darkness). The moon is 226,000 to 252,000 miles from Earth, depending upon its position within its elliptical orbit.

Although the moon appears to shine like a star, it does not produce light. What we see from Earth is the sun's light reflected by the moon. For this reason, the moon appears to change shape throughout each 28-day cycle around Earth. At new moon, the moon is between the earth and the sun. Its lighted side is turned away from Earth. Therefore, it is not visible. As the relative positions change, parts of the illuminated moon can be seen from the earth. The phases are: new (not visible), crescent (a crescent showing), quarter (half of the side that is toward Earth illuminated), gibbous (nearly all of the side that is toward Earth illuminated) and full (all of the side that is toward Earth illuminated).

On July 20, 1969, at 4:17 P.M. EDT, U.S. astronaut Neil A. Armstrong became the first person to set foot on the moon. He was followed by Edwin E. Aldrin, Jr. The third member of the Apollo 11 crew, Michael Collins, stayed in the mother ship. By 1972, six two-man crews of astronauts had landed on the moon and brought back 842 pounds of rocks and soil.

The 1969 landing followed more than a decade of exploration by U.S. and USSR space probes. The first pictures of the far side of the moon were taken by the Soviet spacecraft Lunik 3 in 1959. They revealed an unseen side that was very like the near side.

The moon is marked by thousands of craters, some miles across, others smaller than one foot. There are also mountain ranges, peaks, rills (long crevices) and rays (light-colored streaks that radiate from craters). In addition, there are flat areas called maria (Latin for "seas"). Galileo believed them to be oceans when he named them in the 17th century, but there is no water on the moon. The maria appear to be solidified lava flows, billions of years old.

The moon has no atmosphere because its gravitational pull is not strong enough to keep a blanket of gases wrapped around it. The moon's gravity is one-sixth that of Earth, meaning that people and objects weigh only one-sixth as much on the moon as they do on Earth. High temperatures exceed 200° F; low temperatures are below −200° F.

nebula: A nebula is an interstellar cloud of dust and gas. When the cloud surrounds a central star, it is called a planetary nebula. Because nebulae and galaxies both appeared as hazy clouds in early telescopes, many galaxies were incorrectly labeled in the 18th, 19th and early 20th centuries.

Morning Star: *See* Evening Star

Neptune: Neptune, the eighth planet from the sun, has long been a source of mystery for astronomers. It was discovered in 1846, after mathematicians predicted its presence based on irregularities in Uranus's orbit, which could only be explained by the presence of another planet. Guided by the mathematical predictions, Johann Gottfried Galle of the Berlin Observatory first observed the planet on Sept. 23, 1846, one-half hour after he had begun looking for it. Still, its great distance from Earth—2.8 billion miles—made study difficult.

Mankind's knowledge of Neptune was substantially increased during the summer of 1989, when NASA's Voyager 2 became the first spacecraft to observe the planet. The spacecraft had traveled 12 years at an average speed of 42,000 miles per hour to reach Neptune. On the way it had also observed Jupiter, Saturn and Uranus. It viewed Neptune from June to October 1989 before heading out of the solar system.

Voyager 2 found six moons in addition to Triton and Nereid, which had been observed from Earth. It also found three complete rings around the planet, and a band of smaller, smoke-size particles between the lowest ring and the planet's surface.

Neptune, like Jupiter, Saturn and Uranus, is a gas giant. It appears blue because of a thick layer of methane gas. The planet's surface layers are believed to be frozen and liquid gases, centered around a molten, rocky core.

Neptune orbits the sun once every 164.8 years. It has an equatorial diameter of 30,775 miles and revolves once on its axis every 16 hours and 7 minutes.

neutron star: A neutron star is an aging star that has expended much of its energy. Its core has collapsed and its protons (positively charged particles) and electrons (negatively charged particles) have combined to form neutrons (uncharged particles). A neutron star is extremely dense: A star only a few miles in diameter may have a mass greater than the sun's. [See stars]

nova: Novae are stars that have suddenly brightened. Before telescopes were invented, the dim stars could not be seen and the novae appeared to be new stars. (*Nova* is Latin for "new.")

planet: A planet is a large, relatively cool body that revolves around a star. A smaller body with a regular path around the sun is called an asteroid. A star that revolves around another star is not a planet.

Pleiades: The Pleiades (also called the Seven Sisters) is an open cluster of hundreds of stars in the constellation Taurus (The Bull). Seven are visible to the unaided eye. It is visible in the winter in the Northern Hemisphere.

Pluto: Pluto is usually the planet farthest from the sun. Its orbit is so eccentric, however, that it sometimes crosses within Neptune's orbit. Pluto, which takes 247.7 years to circle the sun, has been closer to the sun than Neptune since 1980 and will continue to be so until 1999.

Because it is small—only about 1,500 miles in diameter—and at the edge of the solar system, relatively little is known about it.

Scientists do know, however, that it is unlike the other outer planets in the solar system, Jupiter, Saturn, Uranus and Neptune. Those planets are giants consisting largely of frozen and liquid gases. Pluto is believed to consist of ice and rock. Its only known moon, Charon, is about half Pluto's size. Charon and Pluto revolve on their axes at the same

rate, once every 6 days, 9 hours and 18 minutes. Because of the similarities, Pluto and Charon are often considered a double planet system.

Until recently, Pluto was believed to have little atmosphere. In June 1989, however, a group of M.I.T. astronomers using NASA equipment found evidence that Pluto has a substantial atmosphere. Its composition is unknown. Methane has been detected, but it may be a solid, a liquid or a gas. Other gases that may be present include argon, nitrogen, oxygen, carbon monoxide and neon.

Pluto is an average distance of 3.664 billion miles from the sun. It is, therefore, extremely cold. Temperatures never go above −415° F. It revolves on its axis once every 6 days, 9 hours and 18 minutes.

Pluto was discovered in 1930 by Clyde Tombaugh of the Lowell Observatory. Charon was discovered in 1978. Both appear only as tiny dots even through large telescopes.

Polaris: Polaris, the North Star, is used as a navigational aid because it is less than one degree from true north. It is the first star in the handle of the Little Dipper (Ursa Minor).

pulsar: A pulsar is a neutron star that rotates and emits radio signals. The signals are observed as regular pulses by radio telescopes. At one time the signals were believed to be the work of creatures from outer space. [See stars]

quasar: "Quasar" is a shortened form of the term "quasi stellar object." A quasar is an object in distant space that looks like a star but emits too much energy to be a star. Quasars may be centers of very distant galaxies.

satellite: A natural satellite is a celestial body that orbits a planet. The best-known example is Earth's moon. The natural satellites of other planets are commonly called moons.

An artificial satellite is an object launched by rocket and placed in orbit around Earth or another planet. The Soviet Union launched the first man-made satellite, Sputnik 1, on Oct. 4, 1957, beginning the Space Age. Less than four months later (Jan. 31, 1958), the United States launched Explorer 1. Since then, thousands of satellites have been launched. Today satellites have many scientific, military and commercial applications. They are used for research, communications, navigation, reconnaissance and weather prediction. Some satellites are geostationary, that is, they travel at a rate of speed equal to the rate of Earth's rotation, so they are always above the same point on Earth.

All man-made satellites have certain similarities. All include energy sources, altitude-control equipment, radio transmitters, radar to measure altitude, receivers used to communicate with their

Earth station, and devices that measure the satellite's condition. Power sources include solar cells, and backup batteries that store power when the satellite is not in sunlight. Nuclear power sources are also used.

Communications satellites relay radio signals around the globe. On land, microwave relay towers can receive radio signals, amplify them and transmit them to other towers 20 or 30 miles away. Using this method, about 100 relays are needed to cross the United States. Communications satellites operate in much the same way, but because they are in space, they can transmit signals across large areas of the globe. Radio, television and telephone transmissions are beamed at the satellites from Earth stations. The transmissions are then, in effect, bounced off the communications satellites and caught by receiving stations on other parts of the globe.

Navigation satellites broadcast a radio signal that can be used to determine positions on Earth. Because the position of the satellite is known, analysis of the signal can be used to determine the position of the receiver. The method, which is very accurate, is particularly useful for pinpointing ships at sea.

The first weather satellite was launched in 1960. Now such satellites are so common that nearly every television weather forecast includes at least one satellite photo of weather systems. Weather satellites are used to locate storm systems, jet streams and fronts, and to track hurricanes, typhoons and tropical storms. Infrared photos of ocean areas are useful for determining ocean temperature, which can have important shipping and fishing implications, as well as meteorological significance.

Research satellites are used as orbiting observatories, either to observe Earth from space, or to observe space from a better vantage point. Reconnaissance satellites, the so-called "spies in the sky," are used to gather information about other countries' military, industrial and agricultural strengths. Observation satellites, which use microwave, X-ray and infrared sensors, are used to monitor crops, mineral deposits, water resources and other environmental factors.

Saturn: Saturn, the sixth planet from the sun, is an average distance of 914 million miles away. It is the second largest planet (after Jupiter), with an equatorial diameter of 74,980 miles. It is the outermost planet that can be seen without a telescope. Saturn makes one trip around the sun every 29.46 years and rotates once on its axis every 10 hours, 39 minutes and 24 seconds. Saturn's distinguishing feature is its rings, which are more extensive than those of any other planet. They can be seen with a small telescope.

Saturn was first studied through a telescope by Galileo Galilei (1564–1642). Its great distance has made detailed observation difficult, however, even with modern equipment. Knowledge about Saturn was expanded greatly in 1979, when the U.S. space probe Pioneer 11 flew by the planet for the first time and relayed information to Earth. The flights of Voyagers 1 and 2 in 1980 and 1981 added even more detailed information. Still, there are many uncertainties concerning Saturn, its rings and its moons. More unmanned exploratory space missions are being planned, perhaps as early as 1996.

Like Jupiter, Saturn seems to consist of hydrogen, helium and small amounts of other gases in liquid, metallic and other forms. The planet probably has a rock core. Prior to the Voyager journeys, Saturn was believed to be surrounded by six rings composed of chunks of ice and rock. Closer observation showed that there are actually as many as 1,000 rings, and that they contain dark areas that look like spokes. Areas of several of the rings appear to be twisted.

Because the Voyager data are still being studied and interpreted, not all of the findings are conclusive. Saturn has at least 17 known moons, but the data may indicate as many as 23. Some of these satellites are jagged chunks of rock and ice only a few miles wide. Others are rounded and thousands of miles in diameter.

The largest moon—Titan—was studied extensively by Voyager 1, although a dense cloud layer obscures it from view. With a diameter of 3,200 miles, Titan is larger than the planets Mercury and Pluto. It is the second largest moon in the solar system. (Jupiter's Ganymede is the largest, with a diameter of nearly 3,300 miles.) It is the only moon that has a significant atmosphere—interesting to scientists, who see similarities between Titan and a frozen, primordial Earth.

Like Earth, Titan's atmosphere is primarily nitrogen. It also contains small amounts of methane, carbon monoxide, ethane, acetylene, ethylene and hydrogen cyanide. To scientists pondering the origins of life on Earth, the presence of hydrogen cyanide on Titan is particularly intriguing: It is a component of amino acids. Titan's chemistry may have similarities to that on Earth billions of years ago. There is at least one critical difference, however. Titan's great distance from the sun makes it so cold—several hundred degrees below 0° F—that further development of organic chemicals is unlikely.

stars: Stars are spheres of gas that shine by their own light. They are almost entirely hydrogen and helium. The light that they produce is the result of nuclear reactions in their centers, which give off light and produce surface temperatures of thousands of degrees Fahrenheit.

The nearest star, our sun, is 92.96 million miles away. The next closest star, Proxima Centauri, is about 300,000 times farther away. On a clear, starry night we can see several thousand stars without a telescope. This is only a tiny fraction of the billions of stars in our galaxy, the Milky Way.

Stars vary greatly in size. The smallest, neutron stars, may be no more than a few miles in diameter. The largest, the supergiant red stars, can be hundreds of times larger than the sun.

Although stars appear to be stationary because of their great distance from us, they are moving. The sun moves at about 12 miles per second toward the constellation Hercules. Other stars are traveling at much faster rates.

Star colors range from brilliant blue-white to red. Without a telescope we can discern the color of only the brightest stars.

It is useful to be able to compare stars based on their apparent brightness, which is a function of their actual brightness and their distance from us. In the second century B.C., the Greek astronomer Hipparchus established a system of rating stars' brightness that has been refined until the present day. He grouped the visible stars into six groups, from the brightest to the faintest, which he called magnitudes. The 20 brightest were in the first magnitude. The hundreds of stars that were barely visible to the unaided eye were in the sixth magnitude. We now use decimal designations (a star of 3.1 magnitude is slightly brighter than one of 3.2 magnitude, for example) and negative numbers, which allows for better differentiation among the brightest stars. (Sirius, the star that appears brightest, has a magnitude of −1.6, for example. The sun is magnitude −26.7.)

Stars are classified also by spectral type—that is, by the nature of the light that they emit. The classification system often is memorized by use of a mnemonic phrase: Oh, Be A Fine Girl, Kiss Me. The classes of stars, their colors and approximate surface temperatures are: Class O, blue-white, over 55,000° F; Class B, blue-white, 36,000° F; Class A, white, 20,000° F; Class F, yellowish white, 13,500° F; Class G, yellow, 11,000° F; Class K, orange, 7,500° F; Class M, red, 5,500° F. Each classification is further divided into 10 subsections, from 0 to 9. The sun, for example, is a G2 star.

More than 99 percent of all stars fall within these classifications. A few stars are hotter or cooler. They are classified as W stars if hotter and R, N or S if cooler. (The mnemonic device has been "re-fined" to include these groups: Wow! Oh, Be A Fine Girl, Kiss Me Right Now, Sweetie.)

Stars are born, they age and they die. Their life spans are so long, though, that most stars appear unchanged throughout a human lifetime. (The sun, for example, was formed about 5 billion years ago, and is expected to last another 5.5 billion years.) Scientists are able to compare stars, however, and note differences that denote an evolutionary process.

A star begins when gases combine in interstellar space, forming a nuclear furnace that emits enormous amounts of energy. When they expend their energy, they burn out—either in explosions or as cinders. During their life cycles stars change in size and luminosity. (Luminosity is the amount of energy released by a star in one second. It is an absolute measure, unlike magnitude, which is a measurement of perceived brightness.)

Most stars fall within a group known as the main sequence. These are stars that are burning their hydrogen supplies (in nuclear reactions, similar to the hydrogen bomb). Main sequence stars vary from large, hot, bright, blue stars (known as blue giants) to small, dim, cool, red stars (known as red dwarfs). The sun, a yellow star, is near the middle of the continuum.

Some stars, however, do not fall within the normal parameters. These are stars that have burned all of their hydrogen and are nearing the end of their lives. Red giants are very large stars (typically 100 times larger than the sun) that are relatively cool. Having depleted their hydrogen, they are burning their helium. Slowly, even these giants change: The helium burns, producing carbon and oxygen; the carbon and oxygen burns, producing silicon; the silicon burns, producing an iron core. Eventually the iron core will collapse. Astronomers believe that this happens with an enormous nuclear explosion that produces a sudden and dramatic increase in brightness, known as a supernova. Rather than being new stars (as the name seems to imply), supernovae are the dying gasps of stars that are burning out. Supernovae are extremely rare in our galaxy: the last was witnessed from Earth in 1987. It was the first since 1604.

When stars die, they leave rather remarkable remnants. The Crab Nebula, for example, is an expanding gas cloud in the constellation Taurus that was left by a supernova explosion visible on Earth in 1054. Near the center of the Crab Nebula is a pulsar, which is believed to be a type of neutron star (a remnant of a supernova explosion that is believed to consist of densely packed neutrons). [See neutron star] Pulsars emit regular pulses of electromagnetic radiation, primarily in the form of radio waves. They are believed to be rotating neutron stars, with the rate of rotation accounting for the regular pulse.

Some stars end their lives as white dwarfs. Their mass is not great enough to support the nuclear explosion of a supernova, so they merely burn out, contracting and becoming cooler. Slowly their energy is dissipated and they no longer glow. They then become black dwarfs (which cannot be seen).

Sun: The Greek astronomer Aristarchus of Samos was truly a man ahead of his time. In about 300 B.C. he argued that the sun, not Earth, was the center of the solar system. The notion was so ludicrous that it was soundly rejected for more than 1,800 years, until the Polish monk Nicholas Copernicus (1473–1543) revived and refined the theory. Gradually, astronomers began to accept the fact that Earth, which seems so stationary, is in fact on a constant journey through space, revolving around the sun with the other planets, asteroids and comets.

The sun, which is an average of 92.96 million miles from Earth (1 Astronomical Unit), is the source of much of our energy. Modern science has attempted to harness the sun's energy directly, through solar cells and batteries. This is only a small part of the sun's energy contribution to Earth, however. The sun's heat causes winds, an important energy source in some areas of the world and a vital energy source for early shipping and exploration. Its light permits photosynthesis, during which green plants produce carbohydrates from carbon dioxide. The carbohydrates are a food source for animals, and the source of other fuels as well. The fossil fuels (oil, coal and natural gas) are all the result of ancient photosynthesis. Wood is the product of modern photosynthesis.

Although the sun is the largest, most important body in the solar system, it does not have a very impressive position in the galaxy. It is 27,710 light-years from the center of the Milky Way, and it is only a middling star when compared with others. With an equatorial diameter of 865,000 miles and a surface temperature of 10,260° F, it is classified as a yellow dwarf. There are stars that are hundreds of times larger than the sun, and stars that are hundreds of times smaller. It is about 5 billion years old, and has about 5.5 billion years left.

The sun rotates on its axis but, because it is a sphere of gas, it does not rotate at the same rate throughout. Its equator rotates in about 25 days. Near its poles, rotation takes about 30 days. The rotation can be observed by charting the movement of sunspots, which are magnetic storms on the sun's surface.

The sun has four layers: the core, where hydrogen is converted to helium and temperatures reach 36 million degrees Fahrenheit; the photosphere, which is the surface of the sun that we see; the chromosphere, a pinkish layer of gases; and the corona, a halo of gases that can be seen during eclipses.

To avoid eye injury, the sun should never be viewed directly with the naked eye or with binoculars. It should be viewed only through special filters made for that purpose. Telescopes can project the sun's image on a sheet of paper. [*See* solar flares, solar wind, stars, sunspots]

Titan: *See* Saturn

Uranus: Uranus, the seventh planet from the sun, is a gas giant, like Jupiter, Saturn and Neptune. It is 32,168 miles in diameter at the equator and is an average of 1.782 billion miles from the sun. Unlike the other planets, it travels about the sun on its side, tipped at more than a 90-degree angle. Its poles, not its equator, face the sun. It revolves around the sun once every 84 years.

Uranus is only barely visible in the night sky. It was discovered on March 13, 1781, by Sir William Herschel, the patriarch of a prominent family of astronomers in England. He wished to name the planet in honor of King George III. Other astronomers wanted to name it Herschel. It was, instead, named after the mythological father of Saturn.

Its great distance from Earth has made detailed observation difficult. Knowledge of the planet was greatly increased in 1986, however, when Voyager 2 flew by and returned detailed photographs to Earth. Normally, a space probe would need 30 years to reach Uranus. Because of a fortunate and rare alignment of Saturn and Uranus, however, Voyager 2 was able to use Saturn's gravitational force to propel it toward Uranus and reach the planet in only 8.5 years. Scientists, who may not have another such opportunity in their lifetimes, are still interpreting the data that Voyager 2 collected.

Voyager 2 identified 10 new moons, bringing the total to 15. It also sent back mystifying portraits of the five known moons. One of them, Umbriel, seemed nearly featureless. The other four, however, appeared to be ragged, pockmarked orbs with deep crevices and mountains. The most interesting, Miranda, is only about 300 miles in diameter but contains steep gorges, massive cliffs and a terraced area that one scientist said looked like a stack of thin pancakes. It also has grooved areas that resemble racetracks. They are unlike anything seen in the solar system before.

Voyager 2 also studied Uranus's rings, and found a new one, bringing the total to 10. Previously, astronomers had believed that Uranus's rings consisted of dust, like Saturn's. Voyager's photographs showed, however, that the rings consist primarily of boulder-sized chunks of ice and rock. Scientists theorized that Uranus's unique magnetic field, which is tipped 55 degrees from its rotational poles, may act to sweep small particles out of the rings. (The magnetic fields of the other planets are within a few degrees of their north and south poles.)

Uranus's atmosphere contains hydrogen, helium and methane. Beneath that, there may be an ocean of water and methane, surrounding a small rocky core.

Venus: Venus, the second planet from the sun, is a terrestrial planet like Mercury, Earth and Mars. It is an average of 67.2 million miles from the sun. It rotates on its axis once every 243.01 Earth days and revolves around the sun once every 224.7 days. It is slightly smaller than Earth—7,517 miles in diameter at the equator. It has no moons.

At times, Venus is as close as 26 million miles from Earth, making it the closest planet. Its accessibility has made it a frequent target of space probes. It was the first planet to be viewed by a space probe, when the U.S. Mariner 2 flew by in 1962. Since then, numerous Soviet and American probes have explored the planet. In 1982, the Soviet probes Venera 13 and 14 were the first to land on Venus and transmit pictures from the surface. The U.S. Magellan probe, launched in May 1989, is providing a detailed map of the planet. By late 1991, it had mapped more than 90 percent of Venus's surface. As its mission continued, computers were being used to combine images taken from several angles, producing three-dimensional views of the planet.

Venus is sometimes considered Earth's sister planet because it is similar in size, composition and distance from the sun. Its heavy cloud layer, which shields the surface from view, allowed fanciful speculation about its surface. Some pictured it as a steamy, tropical, Earth-like place covered with great swamps and lumbering dinosaurs. The facts are quite different.

Although Venus is similar to Earth in many respects, it is also markedly dissimilar. The surface temperature is about 900° F, the atmosphere contains nearly no water and the atmospheric pressure is 90 times that of Earth. Its atmosphere is primarily carbon dioxide, with clouds of sulfuric acid at high levels. Even its direction of rotation is opposite from the Earth's, and from that of most other planets.

Scientists are particularly interested in one potential similarity between the planets, however. Venus appears to be a victim of the greenhouse effect. Its carbon dioxide atmosphere traps heat from the sun, like the glass in a giant greenhouse. Although the magnitude of the greenhouse effect on Venus is not comparable to that of Earth, scientists are curious about what effect it has had on Venus, and whether Venus was ever a more hospitable planet for life forms. [*See* Evening Star]

ASTRONOMICAL PHENOMENA AND THEORIES

aurora: Auroras are shimmering bands and ribbons of yellow, pink and green light that brighten the nighttime sky and may last for hours. They appear both as arcs above the horizon and as rays radiating from it. In northern latitudes, they are called the Northern Lights or Aurora Borealis. In southern latitudes, they are the Southern Lights or Aurora Australis. They are caused by atomic particles from the sun, which strike the thin gases in the upper atmosphere and produce a luminous effect. They are most frequent during periods of high sunspot activity, when the sun is releasing more charged particles.

Big Bang Theory: The Big Bang Theory is the most widely accepted scientific theory explaining the creation of the universe. According to the theory, the universe began about 13 billion to 20 billion years ago with a violent explosion, propelling matter outward in all directions. According to the theory, that movement is still going on, with all parts of the universe moving outward. This concept of an expanding universe has been supported by observations by telescopes, which indicate that other galaxies are moving away from us. The Hubble Telescope (named for the American astronomer Edwin R. Hubble, who discovered that the universe is expanding) will be used to learn more about the origins of the universe, and its expansion. The telescope was launched from a U.S. shuttle in April 1990.

eclipse: An eclipse occurs when one celestial body blocks the light from another body. A solar eclipse occurs when the moon comes between Earth and the sun, blotting out some or all of the sun's light. A lunar eclipse occurs when Earth is between the sun and the moon, and the moon passes through Earth's shadow, rather than passing above or below it.

There are three types of solar eclipses: total, partial and annular. When the moon passes between Earth and the sun, it casts a shadow on Earth, forming a dark spot that is no more than 170 miles in diameter. (The shadow is shaped like an inverted cone, with the point of the cone touching Earth.) Observers in the path of that dark spot, the umbra, witness a total solar eclipse. During a total eclipse, only the corona (the gas layer that surrounds the sun) can be seen. The sun itself is completely blocked; for up to 7.5 minutes, night seems to have fallen. Outside of the umbra is a much larger area, a circle about 4,000 miles in diameter, where some but not all of the sun's rays are blocked. This area is the penumbra. Observers in that area see a partial eclipse.

During an annular eclipse, the moon is so far from Earth that the point of its cone-shaped shadow does not touch Earth. During those eclipses, the sun is not completely blocked at any point on Earth. At the peak of an annular eclipse, a ring of sun remains visible around the moon.

Total solar eclipses for the remainder of the decade will be:

Date	Path
Nov. 3, 1994	Eastern Pacific Ocean, Peru, Chile, Bolivia, Paraguay, Brazil, Atlantic Ocean
Oct. 24, 1995	Iran, Afghanistan, Pakistan, India, Southeast Asia, Pacific Ocean
March 9, 1997	Mongolia, Siberia
Feb. 26, 1998	Eastern Pacific Ocean, Galápagos Islands, Panama, Colombia, Venezuela, Caribbean
August 11, 1999	Atlantic Ocean (east of Nova Scotia), Great Britain, central Europe, Middle East, India, Pakistan, Bay of Bengal

equinox: The equinox is the day that the sun's path crosses directly above Earth's equator. On that date, day and night are equally long. It occurs twice a year, marking the beginning of spring and fall. The vernal equinox occurs on or about March 21, and the autumnal equinox occurs on or about September 21. [*See* seasons, solstice]

expanding universe: *See* Big Bang Theory

greenhouse effect: *See* section entitled Meteorology Glossary on page 273

heliocentric theory: The heliocentric theory was proposed by Polish astronomer Nicholas Copernicus in the 16th century. It stated that the planets rotate around the sun, not around Earth. The theory was regarded as heresy and did not become accepted for 150 years. It replaced the Ptolemaic theory (named after the Greek astronomer Ptolemy, who lived around 150 A.D.), which stated that Earth is the center of the universe.

leap year: Leap year is a human invention designed to reconcile our calendars with the motion of the planet Earth. Modern calendars define a year as 365 days, yet Earth actually takes 365.256 days to complete a trip around the sun. We make up the difference by adding a day to February in every year whose last two digits are divisible by four. The only exception occurs in even century years—such as 1900 and 2000. Those years are leap years only if the entire number is divisible by four. Thus, 2000 is a leap year, but 1900 was not.

magnetic storms: Magnetic storms are disturbances in the magnetic field that surrounds Earth. They are associated with periods of high sunspot activity and solar flares, which change the amount of solar wind that reaches Earth. As this solar wind of charged particles "blows" against Earth's atmosphere, the magnetic field is temporarily distorted.

Radio transmissions are affected by magnetic storms because the transmissions are bounced off the ionosphere, a layer of Earth's atmosphere. The ionosphere contains charged particles and acts as a mirror to reflect radio waves back to Earth. Electrical changes in the ionosphere during magnetic storms cause distortions in this mirror. Changes can last from hours to days.

meteor showers: *See* meteors

seasons: Earth spins on its axis as it revolves around the sun. Each spin on its axis is one day. Each revolution around the sun is one year. If Earth were upright as it spins, the sun would always seem to be in the same position relative to Earth and there would be no seasons. Earth, however, is tilted at a 23.5-degree angle, which means that one hemisphere is pointed toward the sun while one is pointed away. When the Northern Hemisphere is pointed toward the sun, it receives more direct rays and gets warmer. That is summer. When the Northern Hemisphere is pointed away from the sun, the sun's rays hit at more of an angle, are less effective, and the Northern Hemisphere gets colder. That is winter. Seasons in the Northern and Southern Hemispheres are reversed. [*See* equinox, solstice]

shooting stars: *See* meteors

solar flare: Solar flares are fiery arms of charged particles that erupt from the surface of the sun near sunspots. They can extend hundreds of thousands of miles into space. They are associated with magnetic storms on Earth. [*See* magnetic storms]

solar wind: Solar wind is the stream of highly charged gas particles that extends from the sun. The wind extends hundreds of millions of miles into space. It was first detected in 1962.

solstice: The solstice is the day that the sun's path crosses Earth farthest from the equator. The solstices mark the first day of summer and of winter.

In the Northern Hemisphere, the summer solstice occurs on or about June 21. It is the longest day of the year. The winter solstice occurs on or about December 21. It is the shortest day of the year. In the Southern Hemisphere, the seasons are reversed. [*See* equinox, seasons]

sunspots: Sunspots are relatively dark spots on the sun that are cooler than the surrounding areas and have strong magnetic fields. They range in size from a few hundred miles to more than 50,000 miles in diameter. Sunspot activity waxes and wanes in cycles of approximately 11 years. Sunspot activity peaked in 1980, then declined and began increasing again, peaking in early 1990.

tides: All objects have gravity, a force that pulls other objects to them. The strength of that pull varies with the object's mass and its distance. Both the moon and the sun exert a gravitational pull upon Earth. Because the moon is so much closer, its pull is stronger. The moon's pull is the key determinant of tides.

The moon pulls hardest against the side of Earth that faces it. That causes the water on that side to bulge. It also pulls hard against Earth itself, causing Earth to pull away from the water on the opposite side and causing the water there to bulge.

The effect is two high tides, one on the side of Earth closest to the moon and one on the side farthest from the moon. As Earth turns on its axis, this bulge of water moves around the globe, producing a sequence of tides. Because Earth rotates once in approximately 24 hours, and there are two bulging high-tide areas on opposite sides of the globe at all times, the time between high tides is about 12 hours.

The moon travels on an elliptical orbit around Earth about once a month. Tides are higher than normal when the moon is at a point in its orbit that places it closest to Earth. They are lower than normal when the moon is farthest away.

The sun also influences the tides, but to a lesser degree because its gravitational pull is weaker. Twice a month, at new and full moon, the moon and the sun are aligned, with each pulling in the same direction. Tides then are unusually strong, with high tides being very high and low tides being very low. These are called spring tides. During the moon's first and last quarter, the moon and sun are at right angles, which means that their gravitational forces are working at cross-purposes. Tides then are quite mild. They are called neap tides.

METEOROLOGY GLOSSARY

acid rain: Acid rain is the common term for pollution caused when sulfur and nitrogen dioxides combine with atmospheric moisture to produce a rain, snow, or hail of sulfuric and nitric acids. Scientists have reported acid-rain damage to the environment of northern Europe and North America. Precipitation that sometimes is as acidic as vinegar has destroyed plant and animal life in lakes, damaged forests and crops, endangered coastal marine life, eroded structures, and contaminated drinking water. Some of the damage attributed to acid rain is a result of natural causes, but sulfur dioxide from oil and coal combustion and nitrogen oxides produced by automobile engines have greatly intensified the problem. Winds can carry the pollutants thousands of miles away from their source. Sulfur emissions from power plants in the United Kingdom contribute to acid deposits in Scandinavia. Canadian emissions contribute substantially to acid rain in the northwestern United States, and much of the sulfur falling in eastern Canada originates in the United States. Scientists agree that acid rain is harmful, but reports concerning its severity conflict. Further, the costs of control measures are formidable, and the question of who should pay them continues to arouse controversy.

adiabatic process: The process by which heat is maintained by a body of air despite changes in volume, pressure and external temperature.

advection: The horizontal movement of air or atmospheric properties; sometimes referred to as the horizontal component of convection.

air density: The density of air expressed in terms of its mass per unit of volume.

air mass: A large body of air having essentially uniform temperature and moisture. Air masses are identified according to the thermal properties of their source regions—tropical (T), polar (P) or arctic (A)—and their moisture is characterized as continental (c) or maritime (m). When the air mass travels over land warmer than the air mass itself, the air mass is unstable and the lower-case letter k is added to the end of the standard notation. When the air mass is warmer than the land, the air mass is stable and the lower-case letter w is added. The notation cPk, for example, would indicate an unstable continental polar air mass. The notation mTw would indicate a stable maritime tropical air mass.

altimeter: An instrument that determines the altitude of an object in relation to a fixed level.

altitude: Height expressed as distance above a reference plane, usually ground or mean sea level.

anemometer: An instrument used to measure wind speed.

anticyclone: An immense whirling mass of air that has high atmospheric pressure and a closed circulation pattern. Anticyclones are referred to as "highs" and may be warm or cold. Viewed from above, air in an anticyclone in the Northern Hemisphere moves clockwise; in the Southern Hemisphere, counterclockwise.

Arctic air: An air mass often extending to great height and bearing characteristics developed mostly in winter over icy and snow-covered Arctic surfaces.

atmosphere: The atmosphere comprises five gaseous layers about 500 miles deep, held in place by Earth's gravity. The bottom layer, extending from sea level to seven miles high, is the troposphere. At its outer edge, the troposphere includes a relatively thin layer, actually a series of layers, called the tropopause. The end of the tropopause marks the end of the troposphere and the start of the 30-mile deep stratosphere, or ozonesphere. The next outermost layer is the mesosphere, which is about 50 miles deep. Then the thermosphere extends for about 400 miles into the exosphere, which stretches into outer space. (*See* section entitled Astronomical Bodies, Earth on page 263)

atmospheric pressure: Also called barometric pressure. This is the weight of a column of air per unit area.

atmospherics: Static or disturbances produced in radio receivers by atmospheric phenomena such as storms.

auroras: Luminous, radiant bands or ribbons of light occurring mostly in high latitudes and centered over the earth's magnetic poles. The phenomenon is caused by electrical discharges in the ionized air 50 to 600 miles above the earth. In the Northern Hemisphere, these are generally referred to as Northern Lights, Aurora Borealis. In the Southern Hemisphere, they are the Southern Lights, Aurora Australis.

baguio: Filipino name for tropical cyclones. [*See* hurricane/typhoon]

bali: *See* winds (local)

barograph: A barometer that makes and records its readings continuously.

barometer: An instrument for measuring the pressure of the atmosphere. There are two kinds of barometers, aneroid and mercurial. An aneroid barometer reads atmospheric pressure on a metallic surface. The metal flexes and moves a pointer along a graduated scale. A mercurial barometer, which is the kind used by most weather stations, balances air pressure against the weight of a column of mercury in a graduated glass tube.

Beaufort scale: This is the scale of wind speeds developed by British Navy Admiral Sir Francis Beaufort in 1805 and modified for use by the National Weather Service.

Beaufort no.	Knots	Description	Effect
0	<1	Calm	Smoke rises vertically
1	1–3	Light air	Smoke drifts directionally
2	4–6	Light breeze	Leaves rustle, weather vane moves
3	7–10	Gentle breeze	Leaves and small twigs move; wind extends small flag
4	11–16	Moderate breeze	Small branches, dust, loose paper moves
5	17–21	Fresh breeze	Small, leaved trees begin to sway; waves with small crests form on inland waters
6	22–27	Strong breeze	Large branches move; umbrellas difficult to use
7	28–33	Moderate gale	Trees move; walking inconvenient
8	34–40	Fresh gale	Tree twigs break; walking is impeded
9	41–47	Strong gale	Slight structural damage, e.g. roofs, chimneys
10	48–55	Storm	Trees uprooted; major structural damage
11	55–63	Violent storm	Widespread major structural damage
12	>63	Hurricane	Broad devastation

blizzard: A violent storm characterized by dry, wind-driven snow and intense cold.

calm: The absence of wind or any apparent air motion.

ceiling: The distance between the surface of the earth and the lowest layer of clouds that cover more than half of the visible sky.

Celsius temperature: A temperature scale with zero degrees as the melting point of pure ice and 100 degrees as the boiling point of pure water at standard sea level atmospheric pressure. Celsius, or Centigrade, temperature is abbreviated as C.

clinometer: A weather observation instrument used, in conjunction with a ceiling light, to determine cloud height at night.

cloud: A mass of condensed water vapor formed by the cooling of air below its saturation point. There are two broad classifications of clouds: *cumulus*, puffy clouds formed by rising air currents, and *stratus*, sheet-like, layered clouds formed in the absence of vertical wind activity. Clouds are classified further according to their typical altitudes; *towering clouds* may reach as high as 75,000 feet with bases extending almost to earth; the bases of *high clouds* are about 20,000 feet above the earth; *middle clouds*, about 10,000 feet; *low clouds*, from near the earth's surface to about 6,000 feet.

altocumulus: White or light gray, sometimes wavy middle-level clouds that appear in layers or patches as rounded rolls or masses. These are usually water clouds, though the upper parts often carry ice crystals. Because of their shape, altocumulus clouds are often mistaken for cirrocumulus clouds, which generally are darker and somewhat smaller. Weather map abbreviation: Ac.

altostratus: Dense grayish or bluish middle-level clouds that usually appear as a sheet or veil over the sun. Weather map abbreviation: As.

cirrocumulus: High ice clouds in thin sheets or in layers of small globulous clouds. They sometimes appear as shadowless ripples such as those made by wind on sand, or scales on a fish. These clouds make a true "mackerel sky," which is rarely seen. More often, rolls of lower-level altocumulus clouds create a similar pattern. Weather map abbreviation: Cc.

cirrostratus: High, thin and gauze-like clouds of ice crystals. They form large luminous circles around the sun and moon. Weather map abbreviation: Cs.

cirrus: High, wispy or feathery clouds of ice crystals. They are often blown about into feathery strands called "mares' tails." Weather map abbreviation: Ci.

cumulonimbus: Towering white billowy clouds, thunderheads, with bases that may be so low as to almost touch the ground. Severe updrafts may push the tops of these clouds as high as 75,000 feet, where high winds forge their peaks into flat-topped, anvil-like formations. At their most violent, these clouds produce tornadoes. Weather map abbreviation: Cb.

cumulus: Low, white puffy clouds that constantly change shape in the rising warm air and disappear at night. They form at most any altitude and generally presage fair weather. Weather map abbreviation: Cu.

nimbostratus: True rain clouds, characteristically low and dark and often displaying sheets and streaks of rain extending to the ground. Weather map abbreviation: Ns.

stratocumulus: Irregular, low masses of variously shaded gray clouds spread out in a puffy or rolling layer. Weather map abbreviation: Sc.

stratus: Low, uniform, fog-like sheets of cloud ranging in color from light to dark gray. Weather map abbreviation: St.

coastal waters: This term refers to the waters within about 20 miles of the coast and includes bays, harbors and sounds.

cold front: A boundary between two air masses moving in such a way that colder air replaces warmer air. [*See* occlusion]

condensation level: The height at which a rising parcel or layer of air becomes saturated.

corona: A prismatically colored circle or arcs of a circle around the sun or moon. Typically, they are blue inside, red outside and composed of water droplets.

corposant: This luminous blue-green glow, more commonly known as St. Elmo's fire, actually is a discharge of electricity from the tips of protruding objects, such as ships' masts and yardarms, wings of aircraft, lightning rods, steeples, etc., that occurs in stormy weather. The phenomenon usually presages a turn to good weather. Early sailors attributed their good fortune in this regard to a divine presence. The word *corposant* is derived from the Portuguese *corpo santo*, meaning "holy body." [*See* St. Elmo's fire]

cyclone: *See* tornado, hurricane/typhoon

degree-day: The term describes one degree of deviation, on a single day, of the daily mean temperature from a given standard temperature, usually 65 degrees. The number of degrees above or below the standard temperature is recorded as degree-days. For example, a temperature of 59, six degrees below the standard temperature, would be described as six heating degree-days. A temperature of 71, six degrees above the standard temperature, would be recorded as six cooling degree-days. Degree-days are recorded cumulatively. The totals in a given year are used as indicators of heating or air-conditioning needs.

depression: An area of low pressure with winds under 39 mph.

dew: Water condensed on grass or ground cover that has a temperature above freezing but below the dew point temperature of air at its surface.

dew point: The temperature to which a sample of air must be cooled in order to become saturated with water.

Doldrums/Equatorial Doldrums: The belts of calm or of light, variable winds at the equator between the two tradewind belts. [*See* trade winds]

drifting snow: Snow particles lifted from the ground by the wind, but carried to a height of less than 6 feet.

dust devil: A small, vigorous but generally short-lived whirlwind made visible by the dust, sand and debris it picks up from the ground.

dust storm: A strong mass of dust-laden winds traveling at least 30 miles per hour and limiting visibility to a half-mile or less. Parts of the American Southwest see about 12 major dust storms each year. Dust storms are most prevalent in July and August, when surges of moist tropical air from the Pacific push up from the Gulf of California into Arizona. Squall lines pushing across arid land raise storms of dust that may stretch for hundreds of miles and rise as high as 14,000 feet above ground. [*See* winds (local): haboob]

earthquake: This trembling or shaking of the earth's crust is caused by the shifting and breaking of rock under great pressure below the earth's surface. Faulting of the crust and shifting of the huge plates on which it rests often is identified as the cause of earthquakes, but increasingly scientists consider the faulting a secondary occurrence and activity in the earth's mantle as primary. [*See* Mercalli scale, Richter scale, tsunami]

El Niño: This is the name given to a periodically disastrous warming of equatorial ocean water. Natives of the west coast of South America have been aware of the phenomenon for hundreds of years. They named the warming "The Child" because, like the infant Jesus, it arrives around Christmas and ends around Easter.

In some years, the ocean warming is hardly worthy of note. El Niño flows south from the equator, warming surface water along the coasts of southern Ecuador and northern Peru, but never upsetting major weather systems or substantially affecting the dominant northbound Peru, or Humboldt, current, which by luring large schools of fish to its rich nutrients brings relative prosperity to South American fisheries.

Every few years, the El Niño is abnormally intense and prolonged, lasting for more than a year, extending westward along the equator for more than 6,000 miles, disrupting weather in many equatorial countries and triggering havoc—from drought and dust storms, to torrential rains, storms, flooding and landslides. The El Niño of 1972–73 ruined Peru's anchovy fishery. Weather-related damage caused by El Niño conditions in 1982–83 was put at $6.5 billion, making the disaster one of the costliest in modern history.

Scientists know that El Niño amounts to a miniaturization of the Southern Oscillation, a massive seesawing of atmospheric pressure. The temperature change originates in the western Pacific, spreads eastward and oscillates back to the west. The phenomenon influences weather all over the world, but scientists are at a loss to explain precisely what creates the part of it known as El Niño or why the warming is more intense some years than others.

Fahrenheit temperature: A temperature scale with 32 degrees as the melting point of pure ice and 212 degrees as the boiling point of pure water at standard sea level atmospheric pressure.

flash flood: A sudden, violent flood, usually occurring after a heavy rain or rapid melting of heavy snow.

flash flood warning: A formal notice that flash flooding is imminent or in progress. People in the affected area should take precautions immediately.

flash flood watch: A formal alert that flash flooding is possible and people in the affected area should be ready to take additional precautions. A flash flood "watch" precedes a flash flood "warning."

fog: A layer or mass of minute water droplets or ice crystals suspended in the lower atmosphere and differing from a cloud only in that it is near the ground.

  advection fog: Fog resulting from the movement of warm, humid air over a cold surface. This sort of fog is most readily seen on the surface of lakes in the early morning.

  ground fog: Fog that conceals less than 0.6 of the sky and is not contiguous with the base of the clouds.

  ice fog: Fog composed of minute, suspended particles of ice; occurs at very low temperatures and may cause halo phenomena.

  radiation fog: This fog usually results when radiational cooling of the Earth's surface lowers the air temperature near the ground to or below its initial dew point on calm, clear nights.

  sea fog: This is a kind of advection fog that forms when warm air moves over a colder water surface.

  steam fog: Sometimes called sea smoke, this fog forms when cold air moves over relatively warm water or wet ground.

  upslope fog: Fog that forms when air flows upward over rising terrain and is cooled to or below its initial dew point.

funnel cloud: This is a violent, rotating column of air, extending as a pendant from a cumulonimbus cloud, but not touching the ground. A funnel cloud is often the start of a tornado, one of the most destructive atmospheric phenomena known.

gale: Winds are described as a gale when they are sustained within a range of 39 to 54 miles per hour.

greenhouse effect/global warming, cooling: "Greenhouse effect" is a popular, if inexact, term for the role that variable atmospheric constituents—water vapor, carbon dioxide, methane and, to a lesser degree, ozone—play in keeping the earth's surface warm. The earth's atmosphere, when it is clear, is nearly transparent to much of the sun's radiation, most of which is absorbed by the earth's surface, and then re-emitted. So-called "greenhouse gases" absorb much of that radiation and bounce it back to earth. In that fashion, the atmosphere acts as a blanket warming the planet.

The specter of global warming, the greenhouse effect, was first raised near the turn of the century by Swedish Nobel laureate Svante Arrhenius, and his reasoning has been the foundation for scientists' fears ever since. Throughout the world, scientists are concerned that global increases in the burning of fossil fuels have raised atmospheric carbon dioxide levels so much that the earth is getting uncharacteristically warmer. They warn that a temperature change of a few degrees would have a dramatic and worldwide impact. Precipitation patterns might be drastically altered, in many cases nearly reversed. The ice caps could melt, raising sea levels tens of feet, flooding coastlines and fertile deltas and altering the shape of the continents. For every foot of sea-level rise, 100 to 1,000 feet of coastline would be submerged. The situation is dramatically worsened by man's assault on the stratosphere's delicate ozone layer, which protects the earth from much of the sun's harmful radiation. Chlorofluorocarbons (CFCs) released by aerosols do not dissipate in the atmosphere, but interact with and destroy molecules of ozone, thus diminishing the layer and increasing the amount of radiation that reaches earth. [*See* ozone layer]

Scientists agree on the theoretical validity of greenhouse warming, but not on the extent of actual warming. And, indeed, the variables that complicate a forecast for Earth's future are great and numerous—from the extent of cloud cover and deforestation to the natural production of methane and the impact of ever-increasing industrialization, the "human volcano." Some scientists suggest that substantial increases in atmospheric pollutants actually have had a blocking effect on the sun's radiation, and that Earth really is cooling. The equally disastrous icy effect of that phenomenon, they suggest, is staved off by the increased carbon dioxide levels.

Scientists do believe that because the actions of

the atmosphere and oceans are inextricably linked, influencing each other's temperature, the warming of one should be reflected directly in the other. Early in 1991, the United States began testing underwater sound waves as a potential key to determining whether the earth's oceans are, in fact, warming. Scientists estimated they will need 10 years to conduct a proper experiment. Early in February 1992, the National Aeronautics and Space Administration released a report citing "alarming" levels of ozone-depleting chemicals over Europe, Canada and New England. A week later, on the eve of his announcement that he was running for reelection, President Bush ordered U.S. manufacturers of harmful chemicals, particularly CFCs, to stop production by the end of 1995.

gust: This sudden brief increase in wind usually is reported by meteorologists only when the variation between peaks and lulls is at least 10 knots.

hail: This form of summer-storm precipitation is composed of balls or irregularly shaped lumps of ice.

halo: A circle or arcs of a circle with the sun or moon at its center, whitish or prismatically colored, with red at the inside and blue outside; coloration is opposite that of a corona. [*See* corona]

harbor waves: Often mistaken for tsunamis, these are giant waves caused when a landslide falls into a confined body of water, such as a strait or bay. The largest wave ever recorded was a harbor wave. It was caused by an earthquake near a large geological fault at the mouth of Alaska's remote Lituya Bay. The earthquake, which registered 7.3 on the Richter scale, caused a landslide that dropped nearly 100 million tons of rock from a 3,000-foot hillside into the bay on July 9, 1958. The immense wave drenched hills on the opposite side of the bay to a height of 1,740 feet. [*See* tsunami]

haze: Bluish or yellowish tinged air composed of dust or salt particles so fine that they cannot be felt or seen individually by the naked eye, but which diminish visibility.

heavy snow: Meteorologists use the term to describe a rate of snowfall with visibility less than $5/16$ of a mile. Moderate snow restricts visibility to a distance ranging from $5/16$ to $5/8$ of a mile; light snow, if visibility is more than $5/8$ of a mile.

high: An area of high barometric pressure, with its attendant system of winds. A high-pressure system, which sometimes is referred to as an anticyclone, generally presages fair and stable weather.

high wind: Meteorologists normally use this reference when sustained winds are 39 miles per hour or more and are expected to persist for an hour or more.

Horse Latitudes: *See* trade winds

humidity: The water vapor content of air. Humidity may be expressed as specific humidity, relative humidity, or mixing ratio.

hurricane/typhoon: These are warm-core tropical cyclones with minimum sustained surface winds of 74 miles per hour; winds can be as high as 190 miles per hour. Hurricanes, which usually are 300 to 400 miles in diameter, usually diminish after about 10 days. All of these storms, which are among the most spectacular and destructive in nature, are born as tropical depressions in the oceans. They arise in the Doldrums near the equator, approximately between latitudes 5 and 20 degrees north and south. The surface temperature of the water there is 80 degrees Fahrenheit or more, and the sea and air are relatively calm. Slowly, the air becomes superheated. Opposing trade winds whirl around each other creating a cyclonic effect. The hot moist air begins to move in a lazy spiral, which rises and grows, spinning faster as it draws in more hot moist air. As hot moist air at the top of the spiral cools, huge rain clouds form. They are fed constantly by the hot moist air at the water's surface below. Surrounding air sweeps in rapidly until an immense and violent spinning wheel of wind and rain is formed. The comparatively calm center of a hurricane is referred to as its eye, a critical area of extremely low barometric pressure. The eye is responsible for one of the hurricane's most devastating effects, storm surge. The eye's low pressure causes the sea directly beneath it to rise measurably, creating a lethal moving hill of water that grows in height and breadth; it races to shore and crushes coastal areas. The storm diminishes after its source of hot moist air is depleted or cut off; this happens gradually over cold water or after landfall. When a tropical cyclone with sustained winds of more than 74 mph develops east of the international date line, it is called a hurricane. The word *hurricane* derives from the name of a West Indian god of storms, Huracán. West of the international date line, the same storm is known as a typhoon, a word that developed from *ta-feng*, which is Chinese for "violent winds." In Australia, a tropical cyclone is known as a Willy-Willy. In the Philippines, the storm is called a baguio. In the Indian Ocean, it is called a cyclone. The first published reference to a cyclone was made in 1844 in a book entitled *Handbook for Sailors*. The term means "coils of a snake." On the average, only one tropical depression in 10 becomes a tropical cyclone. [*See* hurricane/typhoon, hurricane categories, hurricane eye, hurricane season, hurricane tide, hurricane warning, tropical cyclone]

hurricane categories: The Saffir-Simpson scale ranks hurricanes from one to five, according to strength.

Only two category-five hurricanes have struck the United States since recordkeeping began in the 1930s. The first was a hurricane that hit the Florida Keys on Labor Day 1935 and killed 600 people. The second was Hurricane Camille, which wrecked the coast of Mississippi in 1969, killed 256 people and caused $1.4 billion in damage.

Category 1 The hurricane has a barometric pressure of 28.94 inches or more at its center and winds ranging from 74 to 95 miles per hour, is accompanied by a 4- to 5-foot storm surge and causes minimal damage.

Category 2 The storm has barometric pressure of 28.50 to 28.93 inches, has winds from 96 to 110 miles per hour, storm surges from 6 to 8 feet and causes moderate damage.

Category 3 The storm has barometric pressure of 27.91 to 28.49 inches, has winds from 111 to 130 miles per hour, storm surges from 9 to 12 feet and causes extensive damage.

Category 4 The storm has barometric pressure of 27.17 to 27.90 inches, has winds from 131 to 155 miles per hour, storm surges from 13 to 18 feet and causes extreme damage.

Category 5 The storm has barometric pressure less than 27.17 to 27.90 inches, has winds greater than 155 miles per hour, storm surges higher than 18 feet and causes catastrophic damage.

hurricane eye: This is a roughly circular, 5- to 20-mile area in the center of the storm, where winds generally are light and the sky often is partly cloudy.

hurricane seasons: Hurricanes in the Atlantic Ocean, Caribbean Sea and Gulf of Mexico are most prevalent from June through November, June through mid-November in the eastern Pacific, and June through October in the central Pacific.

hurricane warning: This is formal notification that one or more of the dangerous effects of a hurricane are expected in specified coastal areas in 24 hours or less: sustained winds of 74 miles per hour or more, or dangerously high water or a combination of dangerously high water and exceptionally high waves.

hurricane watch: An announcement for specific areas that a hurricane or hurricane conditions may threaten in a given time span. A hurricane "watch" precedes a hurricane "warning."

hygrometer: An instrument that measures the water vapor content of air.

ice crystals: A type of precipitation composed of unbranched crystals in the form of needles, columns, or plates.

ice storm: A highly damaging and treacherous winter storm condition that results when drizzle or rain freezes on objects as it strikes them.

ice storm warning: Formal notice that significant, and therefore dangerous, accumulations of ice are expected.

inversion: This is a reversal in the normal temperature lapse rate; the temperature rises with elevation instead of falling. [See smog]

isobar: A line of equal or constant barometric pressure.

jet streams: Generally horizontal, tube-shaped ribbons of wind about 300 miles wide, two miles deep and four miles high, at approximately the level of the Earth's tropopause, 7 to 10 miles above the ground. Jetstreams appear to form at the outer edge of the tropopshere, near overlaps in tropopause layers, where temperatures vary radically. Winds at the core of jet streams, which travel generally from west to east, are faster than at their outer perimeters, and may reach speeds of 250 miles per hour or more. Average speeds are 100 miles per hour in winter and 50 miles per hour in summer.

The existence of jet streams was unknown before World War II. American pilots bound for Japan reported difficulty controlling their bombers at about 30,000 feet because of fast-moving air currents. After the war, high-altitude aircraft and balloon flights confirmed the existence of jet streams. By the 1950s, scientists began to understand that jet streams influence the weather, controlling the development and movement of air masses in the lower atmosphere.

knot: A unit of speed equal to one nautical mile per hour, or about 1.15 statute miles per hour.

layer: This is a reference to any sky cover—clouds or other obscuring phenomena—whose bases are at approximately the same level.

lightning: Lightning is caused by the attraction of unlike electrical charges within a thundercloud, or between a thundercloud and the earth. When electrical pressure becomes high enough, charges of current are released by lightning. Initial lightning strokes take place within the cloud itself or between clouds. Visible lightning begins with "leader" strokes from the cloud, extending closer and closer to the ground. After ground contact, the leader strokes are followed immediately by return strokes, and the sequence is then repeated. What appears to the naked eye to be a single stroke of lightning actually is a series of repetitive strokes and returns that take place in less than one-tenth of a second. The sudden heat released by lightning causes the shock waves that we refer to as thunder. The temperature of a lightning bolt can be as hot as 50,000° F, which is roughly five times hotter than the surface of the sun. [See St. Elmo's fire]

low: An area of low barometric pressure with its attendant system of strong winds. Low-pressure systems, which sometimes are called depressions or cyclones, bring unstable weather, clouds and precipitation.

mackerel sky: *See* clouds: cirrocumulus

mean sea level: The average height of the surface of the sea during all tides. Throughout the United States, the term is used as a reference point to denote elevations.

Mercalli scale: Unlike the Richter scale, which measures the comparative magnitude of an earthquake, the Mercalli scale (commonly called the Modified Mercalli) measures an earthquake's intensity as it relates to people in a particular place. The rankings were devised in 1902 by Giuseppe Mercalli, an Italian geologist.

Intensity 0: Detected only by instruments.

Intensity 1: Detectable only in absolute stillness.

Intensity 2: Suspended objects are seen to move.

Intensity 3: Detectable indoors.

Intensity 4: Rattles windows; disturbs sleep.

Intensity 5: Generally noticed by everyone; windows, dishes may break.

Intensity 6: Detection unavoidable; chimneys crumble; walking is difficult.

Intensity 7: Damage is moderate; quake is noticeable even in moving cars.

Intensity 8: Weak structures are damaged.

Intensity 9: Weak structures are destroyed; fissures open in ground.

Intensity 10: All but strongest buildings are destroyed; ground fissures are severe, numerous.

Intensity 11: Most buildings fall; broad ground fissures.

Intensity 12: Destruction is total. Ground can be seen to move as a wave. [*See* earthquake, Richter scale]

microburst: *See* wind shear

monsoon: *See* winds (local): monsoon

National Hurricane Centers: These offices of the National Weather Service in Coral Gables, Fla., and Honolulu, Hawaii, are responsible for providing the United States with information on the development and track of tropical depressions, storms and hurricanes. The center in Miami is responsible for activity in the eastern Pacific Ocean, Atlantic Ocean, Gulf of Mexico and Caribbean Sea. The center in Honolulu is responsible for the Pacific Ocean north of the Equator from 140 west longitude to 180 degrees, the international date line.

nearshore waters: This is a reference to waters extending to five miles from shore.

occlusion: The front that is formed when a cold front overtakes a warm front and lifts the warm air above the earth's surface.

offshore waters: This is a reference to waters extending to about 250 miles from shore.

offshore winds: These are winds that blow from shore out over water.

onshore winds: These are winds that blow from the water toward shore.

ozone layer: This is the thin skin of ozone, an unstable oxygen (O_3), encircling the earth in the stratosphere about 25 miles away. The ozone layer shields the earth from the sun's harmful ultraviolet radiation. Research in the 1970s and 1980s showed that chlorofluorocarbon gases (CFCs), which are primary aerosol propellants and a component of refrigerants such as Freon, were slowly eroding the ozone layer. CFCs, scientists discovered, are broken down by ultraviolet light and release free atoms of chlorine, which react with and break up molecules of ozone. A single free chlorine atom starts a chain reaction that eventually can destroy thousands of ozone molecules.

The United States banned CFC aerosols in 1978, but their use continued in other countries. In 1986 researchers confirmed that ozone concentrations in the global stratosphere are decreasing. The greatest decreases have occurred over Antarctica, where an immense "ozone hole" develops in the stratosphere every spring.

Not all students of the phenomenon believe the CFCs are entirely to blame for the erosion of the protective layer. Some maintain that much of the chlorine in the stratosphere derives from common wood-rotting fungi that are widely distributed throughout the world. Others suggest that the formation of holes in the ozone layer is part of a natural, cyclical process tied to sunspot activity, one that has happened repeatedly since the beginning of time.

However, most researchers believe the problem is relatively new and man-made. The Montreal Protocol of 1987, an international treaty mandating a reduction in the use of CFCs, went into effect in 1989. The treaty called for an end to worldwide production of CFCs by the year 2000.

Early in February 1992, the National Aeronautics and Space Administration released a report citing "alarming" levels of ozone-depleting chemicals over Europe, Canada and New England. A week later President Bush ordered U.S. manufacturers to stop production of most ozone-depleting chemicals by the end of 1995.

Peter's lights: *See* St. Elmo's fire

polar air: An air mass with characteristics developed over high latitudes. Continental polar air (cP) has cold surface temperatures, low moisture content and great stability in its lower layers, especially when it is situated nearest its source regions. Polar air usually represents a shallower air mass than one described as Arctic. Maritime polar air (mP) initially possesses properties similar to those of continental polar air, but in passing over warmer water it becomes unstable and its moisture content rises.

polar easterlies, prevailing easterlies: These are cold easterly winds found north of the Arctic Circle and south of the Antarctic Circle.

prevailing westerlies: These are the broad and dominant winds that occupy the belt between 40 degrees and 60 degrees latitude, north and south, and account for the primarily west-to-east motion of the atmosphere. Were it not for repeated invasion by other wind systems, the prevailing westerlies would create generally stable and fair weather throughout the United States. At latitude 40 degrees south, the westerlies include the famed "Roaring Forties," cold, blustery west winds that sweep across the waters of the South Pacific.

psychrometer: An instrument that is used to determine the water vapor content of air.

Richter scale: This standardized, comparative measurement of an earthquake's magnitude was devised in 1935 by U.S. seismologist Charles F. Richter. The scale, which is based on seismographic readings, measures a quake's intensity at its source and assigns a ranking beginning with the number 1. The scale is open-ended and represents a logarithmic progression; every one-point increase on the scale marks a tenfold increase in magnitude. Thus, a magnitude 7 earthquake is 10 times more powerful than a magnitude 6 earthquake, 100 times more powerful than an earthquake that is ranked 5, and 1,000 times stronger than a magnitude 4 earthquake.

A quake measuring 1 on the scale is detectable only by instruments. A measurement of 2 or 3 indicates a release of energy roughly equal to that released by the burning of 75 to 125 gallons of gasoline. Such minor tremors occur hundreds of thousands of times annually all over the world. Earthquakes that rank 5 or higher are destructive. Major earthquakes usually are in the magnitude 7 range. The greatest earthquakes ever recorded probably ranked from about 8.7 to 8.9 on the Richter scale. [See earthquake, Mercalli scale; section entitled Earthquakes and Tsunamis on page 375]

ridge, ridge line: This is an elongated area of relatively high atmospheric pressure.

Roaring Forties: See prevailing westerlies

St. Elmo's fire: This luminous blue-violet glow, also known as corposant, appears as a corona around the tips of protruding objects, such as ships' masts and yardarms, wings of aircraft, lightning rods, steeples, etc., in stormy weather. The phenomenon is an ionization process known variously as point discharge, brush discharge or corona discharge. The "fire" occurs when, in a storm's very intense electrical field, the negatively charged base of a storm cloud attracts positively charged electricity from elevated ground points. Early Neapolitan sailors determined that good weather generally followed the occurrence of the discharge, which they took as a sign of divine intervention by their holy patron.

The name St. Elmo actually refers to St. Erasmus of Formiae, a 4th-century Roman Catholic bishop and martyr. (Formiae is in the Campagna, the plains outside Rome.) Church legend depicts him fearlessly preaching in a thunderstorm as lightning flashes nearby; hence his adoption as a patron saint of mariners. The name Erasmus evolved to Eramus, then Ermus, then Ermo and finally Elmo. Portuguese mariners many hundreds of years later adopted Friar Peter Gonzalez, a 12th-century saint, as their guardian and began calling the same atmospheric phenomenon "Peter's lights." The word *corposant*, which describes the St. Elmo's phenomenon, is derived from the Portuguese *corpo santo*, meaning "holy body."

sandstorm: A windstorm so laden with sand that visibility in the lowest 10 feet is reduced to between ⅝ and ⁵⁄₁₆ of a mile, usually in the face of winds of 30 miles per hour or more.

severe blizzard: A snowstorm with speeds of 45 miles per hour or more, great density of falling or blowing snow with visibility near zero and a temperature of 10 degrees or lower.

severe thunderstorm: Meteorologists commonly use two criteria to determine whether a thunderstorm warrants being called "severe": (1) sustained *winds* or gusts of 50 knots or more; (2) *hail* that is three-quarters of an inch or larger.

sleet/heavy sleet: The term generally describes round or irregularly shaped solid pellets of ice formed by the freezing of raindrops or the refreezing of melting snowflakes. Heavy sleet does not occur often. The term generally refers to fallen sleet that has accumulated to such a depth that it becomes a safety concern for motorists.

smog: Technically, the term is an elision, a combination of the words *smoke* and *fog*, and is generally taken to mean a form of natural or man-made air pollution, more often the latter. Salt particles from breaking waves, pollen and spores released by plants and carried on the wind, smoke from forest fires, wind-blown dust, and the ash and ejecta of active volcanoes all create or contribute to smog. In the Great Smoky Mountains of Tennessee, pine sap reacts naturally with sunlight and the damp surface air to produce a hydrocarbon type photochemical haze similar to the smog in big cities. Pollutants such as soot, dust, vehicular exhaust, ash, and factory-released chemicals all combine in the atmosphere and react with oxygen and water and each other to produce potentially more dangerous secondary pollutants. A report of high levels of polluting smog does not necessarily indicate an increase in pollution. Such a report may as often indicate that the polluted air is not being dispersed by turbulent winds. During a temperature inversion, warm air overlies cooler air and acts like a lid, preventing upward movement and dispersal of the foul air. The word *smog* is believed to have been used first in Europe in 1905, but then not again popularly until many years later when a reporter for the *Los Angeles Herald Examiner* combined the two words in a story about unhealthy weather conditions. His editor used "smog" in a headline, and the term caught on.

squall: This is a sudden increase of wind speed by at least 15 knots to a peak of 20 knots or more, and lasting for one minute or more. The duration of the peak wind speed marks the essential difference between a gust and a squall.

squall line: Any nonfrontal line or narrow band of active thunderstorms, with or without squalls.

stockman's advisory: This meteorological notice alerts the public that livestock exposed to the elements may need protection from certain combinations of impending cold, generally temperatures of 45 degrees or less, rain or snow, and winds of 25 miles per hour or more. The lower the temperature, the lower the wind speed may be to still qualify as an impending danger to livestock.

storm surge: *See* hurricane/typhoon

storm tide: Directional waves caused by a severe atmospheric disturbance.

stratosphere: *See* atmosphere

temperature inversion: *See* inversion, smog

thermograph: This is a thermometer that provides a continuous recording of temperature.

tidal wave: A huge wave that radiates outward from the epicenter of an earthquake. [*See* tsunami]

tornado: Tornadoes, or twisters, are the most violent localized storms on earth, generating winds that have been clocked as high as 280 miles per hour. These tightly wound vortexes of air are formed in the updrafts of severe thunderstorms and commonly appear as funnels extending earthward from the base of a storm cloud. "Families" of tornadoes, as many as six or eight distinct funnels extending from a single storm cloud, have been reported occasionally, and a single major storm system has been known to yield a series of separate tornadoes. Tornadoes usually rotate counterclockwise in the Northern Hemisphere and clockwise in the Southern Hemisphere. Typically, updrafts of warm air and downdrafts of air from the fast-moving jet stream conspire to start the storm mass rotating. As the winds rotate and gain speed, the atmospheric pressure of air at the core of the tornado drops, and pulls air into the base of the vortex from all directions. The air then spirals upward around the core until it merges with the airflow in the storm cloud at the upper end of the tornado. These two sequences of air flow give the tornado incalculable destructive capacity. A tornado may stand dead still or skip forward at speeds ranging to about 70 miles per hour. Influenced by the jet stream, tornadoes often take erratic paths, carving a swathe of destruction that may be as narrow as 50 feet or less, or as wide as almost three miles. Train cars weighing tons are derailed, lifted and moved. Cars and trucks are sent flying. Houses seem to explode. Bridges are rocked and felled. Trees are twisted and snapped like so many matchsticks. Debris is skyrocketed aloft; so are people, though most deaths and injuries attributed to tornadoes usually are caused by flying debris. Debris also is what gives a tornado its dark color. The United States is the world's tornado hot spot; an average of 800 are reported every year. Though tornadoes have struck most states at one time or another, they are most common in the great lowlands of the Mississippi, Missouri and Ohio River valleys. Here, moist warm air from the Gulf of Mexico collides with cool, dry air from the West, a convergence that breeds storms of immense power. The pattern of storms makes parts of Iowa, Nebraska, Kansas, Arkansas, Oklahoma, Mississippi, Alabama, Missouri, Indiana, Illinois, Ohio, Georgia and Texas the United States Tornado Belt. Within six of those states—Texas, Oklahoma, Missouri, Kansas, Iowa and Nebraska—is a geographical area of about 184,000 square miles where most of the nation's twisters occur, more than a third of all tornadoes that strike the U.S. every year. The area is known as "Tornado Alley," a swathe roughly 200 miles either side of a line extending approximately 460 miles from Abilene, Texas, to Omaha, Nebraska. Middle and late afternoons in April, May and June are the peak times for occurrences.

Tornado Alley: *See* tornado

Tornado Belt: *See* tornado

tornado warning: Meteorologists issue these formal notices when the formation of a tornado is very likely or the existence of one has been confirmed.

tornado watch: A meteorological notice that the public should be alert to the possibility of a tornado. A tornado "watch" precedes a tornado "warning."

trade winds: These two separate belts of dry, steady

winds are so named because they marked popular sailing routes for commercial trading vessels. They are found approximately between latitudes 5 degrees and 23 degrees, north and south. In the summer, the trades are subject to a seasonal shift of about 1,000 miles toward the pole in each hemisphere. They prevail northeasterly in the Northern Hemisphere, and southeasterly in the Southern Hemisphere.

The trade winds are separated on both sides of the equator by narrow belts of tropical calms, most commonly referred to as the equatorial doldrums, or simply, the Doldrums.

Two other zones of calm and variable winds separate the trade winds from the prevailing westerlies; these are known as the Horse Latitudes, though the origin of the name is uncertain. Sailing ships bound from Europe to the New World often were becalmed for days in the region, and ran out of food for the horses aboard ship. As the horses starved, or in order to lighten the ship's cargo to take advantage of what little wind there was, the horses often were thrown overboard. Another explanation attributes the name to the fact that by the time many sailors reached these latitudes, they had been advanced pay for their voyage, spent the money, and were said to be "paying off a dead horse."

tropical air: This is an air mass with characteristics developed over low altitudes. The principal type of tropical air is maritime tropical air (mT), very warm, humid air produced over the tropical and subtropical seas. Continental tropical air (cT) is produced over subtropical arid regions and is hot and very dry.

tropical cyclone: Any tropical disturbance which rotates counterclockwise in the Northern Hemisphere. A hurricane is a tropical cyclone and so, too, is a tropical storm or a tropical depression. A storm has winds between 39 mph and 74 mph, and a depression has winds under 39 mph. [See hurricane/typhoon]

tropical depression: This is a tropical cyclone, but one that represents either a relatively minor storm, a hurricane in the making, or a hurricane that has been downgraded after its power was spent. Regardless of its stage of development, for a storm to be classified as a tropical depression it must have maximum sustained winds of 38 miles per hour or less. [See hurricane/typhoon]

tropical storm: This term represents an intermediate level in the classification of a tropical cyclone. The maximum sustained winds in a tropical storm range from 39 to 73 miles per hour. [See hurricane/typhoon]

tropopause: See atmosphere

troposphere: See atmosphere

trough/trough line: An elongated area of relatively low atmospheric pressure.

tsunami: An immense wave caused by underwater volcanic eruptions, landslides or earthquakes. The name tsunami comes from the Japanese words tsu, for "port" and nami for "waves." These seismic occurrences are most common in the Pacific Ocean, with its volcano-ringed basin. One of history's greatest tsunamis was recorded in 1737 on the southern end of the Kamchatka Peninsula; the wave was 210 feet high when it reached shore. [See harbor wave]

twister: A colloquial term for tornado. [See tornado]

typhoon: See hurricane/typhoon

waterspout: A tornado over water.

will-o'-the-wisp: This is an eerie faint bluish or greenish light sometimes seen in swamps, moors, cemeteries and around burial vaults. The light is localized and may appear to be a tall, hovering candle flame. The phenomenon is caused by the spontaneous ignition of gases such as methane and phosphine produced by decaying organic matter.

Willy-Willy: An Australian name for a tropical cyclone. [See hurricane/typhoon]

wind: The flow of air parallel to the surface of the earth. Wind is caused by temperature differences. As air is warmed, it expands, becomes lighter and rises, and cooler air rushes in to fill the empty space. As the process continues, a steady air flow, or convection current, is created. Convection, the rotation of the earth and other factors create the planetary wind systems that circle the earth, bringing constant weather changes. A wind is named for the direction from which it blows. A southeasterly wind, for example, blows from the southeast.

winds, local: These are winds that contribute distinguishing features to the locales in which they prevail. Following is a selection:

bali: A powerful east wind that blows over eastern Java to the Java Sea.

barber: A strong cold wind in the northernmost sections of the United States and Canada, actually an ice fog, caused by sharply cold air flowing over warm water. Barber winds, which also are sometimes known as frost smoke, carry moisture that freezes on contact with hair.

belat or **belot:** A strong north or northwesterly wind that blows seaward through the southeast sections of Saudi Arabia from December through March. Belats are usually laden with dust and sand from the country's interior.

bise or **bize:** An exceptionally strong, dry and cold

northeast winter wind that blows through Switzerland and the French Alps. The wind is caused by high pressure over the Balkan Peninsula and low pressure over the adjoining Mediterranean. Other winds that originate in the same manner are the krivetz, nemere and kessava.

bohorok: A foehn-type, southerly mountain wind occurring in the winter half of the year in the Dutch East Indies, especially on Sumatra and Java. [*See* winds (local): foehn]

bora: When used generally, the word refers to a type of wind, also known as a "fall wind." Bora-type winds are formed in winter when a region of high pressure over a high, snow-covered plateau produces an intensely cold and dense air mass which eventually "falls over" an adjacent ridge and then flows violently downward toward the warmer seashore. The flow is strongest in the early morning when the air is coldest and most dense. Bora-type winds include mistrals, sno or elvegast winds, williwaws, reffolis and ciercos. When the term is used specifically, "bora" refers to the cold wind that blows southwesterly from mountainous interiors along the Adriatic Sea from Croatia to Albania and along the Black Sea southwest of the Caucasus Mountains.

borasca or **borasco:** Violent squalls accompanied by lightning and thunder, usually in the Mediterranean.

buran: Driving snow and bitter cold typify these much-feared northeast windstorms on the steppes of Russia and Siberia. Burans are much like blizzards in the United States and Canada.

Canterbury foehn: A foehn-type wind that blows through the region of prevailing westerlies known as the "Roaring Forties." The wind occurs with great frequency during the colder half of the year on the Canterbury Plains of South Island, New Zealand, where it brings clear skies and radiation fog. [*See* Roaring Forties, winds (local): foehn]

cat's paw: In the United States, a very slight breeze that causes ripples on a small portion of the surface of a body of water.

chergui: A dry and dusty east or southeast wind that blows into Morocco from the Sahara.

chibli or **ghibli:** These modified siroccos are responsible for the hottest weather ever recorded—136° F. at Al Aziziyah, Libya, Sept. 13, 1922. Already very humid, hot and dusty for having passed over warm water, these desert winds are made all the hotter by foehn activity, that is, by their descent down mountain slopes. [*See* winds (local): foehn; winds (local): sirocco, modified]

chili: A hot dry spring wind from the deserts of North Africa and Saudi Arabia that flows into southern and central areas of the Mediterranean. "Chili" is the name applied when the wind blows through Tripoli.

chinook: A foehn-type west wind that blows down the eastern slopes of the Rocky Mountains and adjacent plains in the United States and Canada during the colder half of the year. A chinook is warm, extremely dry and gusty, and may raise temperatures to as much as 100° F. within a few hours. The wind sometimes is called a "snow-eater" because it can cause snow to evaporate, preventing spring floods. [*See* winds (local): foehn]

cierco: A cold bora-type west wind in Spain's Ebro Valley, similar to France's mistral. [*See* winds (local): bora; winds (local): mistral]

etesians: The prevailing northerly and northwesterly summer winds that periodically wash the entire eastern Mediterranean and Aegean Sea areas with cool air.

fall wind: *See* winds (local): bora

foehn: Pronounced "fane," the word derives from *favonius*, Latin for "south wind." When *foehn* is used generally, that is, to indicate a type of wind, the word refers to wind that is created when air rises over a mountain and is appreciably warmed by adiabatic compression as it flows down the mountain's lee side. Foehns are always associated with clearing skies and excellent visibility. Foehn-type winds include bohoroks, chinooks, Canterbury foehns, double foehns, Greenland double foehns, Santa Anas, and zondas. When *foehn* is used as the specific name of a particular wind, the word usually is taken to mean the very warm, very dry wind that blows down out of the Swiss and Bavarian Alps into neighboring valleys and plains.

garvi or **gharbi:** A modified sirocco, a very warm, humid and dusty wind, blowing north off the Sahara Desert affecting weather along the Adriatic and Aegean Seas. Garvies usually bring heavy precipitation to the mountainous regions, and when the winds are laden with desert sand, they deliver "red rain." [*See* winds (local): sirocco, modified]

Greenland double foehn: A very strong and warm foehn-type wind on the east and west coasts of Greenland that blows seaward from the country's ice-covered high plateaus. [*See* winds (local): foehn]

haboob: This Arabic term meaning violent wind is the name given to extremely severe summer dust storms that form in the desert and plague Egypt and Northwest Africa. [*See* dust storms]

harmattan: The parching northeastern trade winds of the Western Sahara. Harmattan dominate weather in the Sahara Desert and are generally responsible for the dry warm weather throughout much of North and Northwest Africa. Clear skies usually accompany harmattan, but the dust they carry obscures atmospheric visibility.

Howling Fifties: Generally, the prevailing westerlies at latitudes 40 degrees to 50 degrees south. Nineteenth century sailors and whalers gave this belt of strong winds its impressionistic name. [*See* prevailing westerlies]

khamsin: These are hot, dry siroccos that blow into Egypt for about 50 days every year from late winter through early spring. Khamsin are southerly winds that carry fine, dry dust that sometimes is so dense as to create a false darkness at midday.

kessava: A very cold bise-type south wind that blows into Hungary and Yugoslavia's lower Danube from Yugoslavia's mountains in winter. [*See* winds (local): bise]

krivetz: The cold, dry bise-type wind that lashes Romania and Hungary in winter. [*See* winds (local): bise]

leveche: A very hot, dry and dusty wind that blows from the south and southeast into Spain. It is one of the many genuine siroccos that form in the deserts of Saudi Arabia and North Africa and influence weather along the Mediterranean. [*See* winds (local): sirocco, genuine]

maestral: The name of the summer winds that prevail in Italy. [*See* winds (local): etesians]

meltemia: Etesian-type winds that prevail from May to mid-September in Greece. [*See* winds (local): etesians]

mistral: Dry, cold and fierce bora-type wind that blows from north and central Europe across the plateaus and mountains of southeastern France down the Rhone River valley to the Mediterranean for about 100 days in winter and early spring. "Mistral" means master, and this cruel north wind can reach speeds of 80 miles per hour. [*See* winds (local): bora]

monsoon: The term derives from the Arabic word *mausim*, meaning "season," and though its most common use is in reference to torrential rains, *monsoon* more accurately defines the wind that brings such weather. Strictly speaking, the word describes the wind system of the Arabian Sea, which blows from the southwest for half of the year and the northeast for the other half, but generally *monsoon* is used to describe any annual climactic cycle with seasonal wind reversals that cause wet summers and dry winters. A winter monsoon is the result of high pressure over cold continents, producing offshore winds, that is, winds that blow from the interior to the sea. Such winds are very dry, clear and cold. In India, winter monsoons are gentle, northeasterly winds. They are northwest winds in Japan and northern China, and north winds off the coast of China between Hong Kong and Shanghai. In the north of China and the far east of Russia, winter monsoons are so strong and bitterly cold that they make the mountains impassable. A summer monsoon blows from the sea to a continent's interior, bringing very heavy rains. The biggest, most vigorous summer monsoons occur in Asia (particularly southern Asia), Africa and Australia. Storms are frequent and rainfall is abundant, as much as 200 inches or more per year. More than half of the world's population gets its water from monsoons.

nemere: A cold, northeasterly bise-type wind that accompanies blizzards in the Transylvanian Alps. [*See* winds (local): bise]

nor'easter: This is one of the best-known coastal storms of New England. Polar Atlantic air replaces polar Canadian air along the coast. The wind turns to the northeast. Clouds lower. Light rain or snow falls. The temperature rises from 15° to 20° F. Gales begin to blow.

norther: *See* winds (local): Texas norther

pampero: Polar air from the Antarctic produces these cold southerly and southwesterly winds in Uruguay and Argentina. The pamperos mean bad weather, cold fronts and squalls, and temperature drops of 20 to 30 degrees. They are called "dirty pamperos" when they occur with dust storms.

papagayo: A strong northwesterly wind occurring in colder weather in the Gulf of Papagayo and along the northwest coast of Costa Rica.

reffoli: The Italian name for peak gusts of bora-type winds. When used specifically, the term usually is taken as a reference to the extremely cold and gusty winter winds common across the Adriatic Sea in the Dalmatia section of western Yugoslavia. [*See* winds (local): bora]

Santa Ana: A hot, dry northerly or northwesterly foehn-type wind that blows from the Mojave Desert into the Los Angeles Basin. Santa Ana winds are winter phenomena that bring very warm weather to Southern California. [*See* winds (local): foehn]

sirocco, genuine: The dry, dusty and hot wind that blows east off the Arabian Desert into Syria and parts of Israel, Jordan and Egypt.

Leveches, harmattan, and chihili all are genuine siroccos.

sirocco, modified: Winds from a hot, dry desert region. Modified siroccos are turned very warm, humid and dusty by passage over the warm waters of the Mediterranean. They are primarily winter winds that blow off the Sahara Desert and north toward the coast of Africa and the southern peninsulas of Europe.

sharki: An occasional southeast wind that blows across the Persian Gulf.

simoon or **simmoom:** A hot, dry, dust-bearing sirocco that blows northward from the deserts of north-central Africa and into the southeast Mediterranean.

sno/elvegast winds: Cold, dry, bora-type winds that blow from Norway's interior toward its west coast in winter. [*See* winds (local): bora]

sonora: A warm west wind that blows across Arizona from California and Mexico.

southern or **southeast busters:** Strong, cold southerly winds in Australia that are caused by polar air from the Antarctic. They are tied to cold fronts and squalls and temperature drops of 20 to 30 degrees.

suhaili: A powerful southwest wind that carries heavy clouds and rain across the Persian Gulf.

tehuantepecer: Strong northerly winds produced by polar air from Alaska or Canada. Tehuantepecers occur in winter and early spring in Central America and the Gulf of Tehuantepec, Mexico. Having passed over the Gulf of Mexico, tehuantepecers are warmer and more moist than their counterparts, Texas northers.

Texas norther: Strong and gusty northerly winter winds produced by polar air from Alaska or Canada that sweeps down into the Great Plains. The winds usually accompany a huge, U-shaped cold front and are followed by rapidly clearing skies and an abrupt and severe drop in temperature.

tourments: The name usually given the blizzard winds that freeze travelers in the mountains of South America.

williwaws: Fast, violent, bora-type winds that rush down from steep, snow-covered mountain passes toward the coastal areas of Alaska. They also are encountered in Patagonia and as violent squalls in the Strait of Magellan, which separates Tierra del Fuego from mainland South America. [*See* winds (local): bora]

zonda: A foehn-type wind common in southern Chile in the band of prevailing westerlies known as the "Roaring Forties." In the spring, zondas blowing down the leeward side of the Andes Mountains and into western Argentina contribute to the dryness of the pampas. [*See* winds (local): foehn]

wind chill index: Also referred to as the wind chill factor, this is a calculation describing the combined effect of wind and cold temperatures on exposed skin. The higher the wind at a given temperature, the lower the wind chill reading. Wind speeds over 40 miles per hour have little additional cooling effect.

wind shear: A sudden shift in wind direction and/or speed. The phenomenon is often caused when a mass of cooled air rushes downward out of a thunderstorm in what is called a "microburst," hits the ground and rushes outward in all directions, creating horizontal winds with speeds of 100 miles per hour or more. Since 1964, microbursts have been cited as the cause of more than 30 airplane accidents in which 491 people were killed and 206 injured. At high altitude, a pilot often can recover from the precipitous drop in altitude that a microburst can cause, but an encounter during landing or takeoff can be disastrous. The plane first encounters a strong headwind from the microburst, which increases lift. The plane pitches up, and the pilot compensates by leveling off. But in a matter of seconds, the plane encounters a decreasing headwind, then a downdraft and then a strong tail wind. Suddenly, the plane is flying too low and does not have sufficient air speed to avoid a crash.

winter storm warning: A meteorological notification that severe winter weather conditions are imminent.

winter storm watch: A notification alerting the public to the possibility of severe winter weather conditions. A winter storm "watch" precedes a winter storm "warning."

SUGGESTED REFERENCE AND CONTACTS:

The Weather Almanac, edited by James A. Ruffner and Frank E. Bair. Detroit: Gale Research, Inc., 6th edition, 1991.

National Oceanic and Atmospheric Administration Weather Service, 1325 East-West Highway, Silver Spring, MD 20910 Station 18456, (301) 443-8910; (301) 713-0622 (public affairs). NOAA Weather Service is the primary source of meteorological data for the country, with separate offices in each of the 50 states. Headquarters in Silver Spring will field general questions, either directly or through reference to its regional offices. The service offers brochures on a wide variety of weather-related topics. The service also maintains a reference library in Rockville, Md., which can answer specific meteorological questions and inquiries. NOAA Library, E-OC4, 6009 Executive Blvd., Rockville, MD 20852, (301) 443-8287; (301) 443-8330 (reference desk).

Climate Analysis Center, 5200 Auth Road, Room 805, Camp Springs, MD 20746, (301) 763-8071. The center routinely fields questions from reporters and offers a broad range of national and international climatic information, including daily precipitation levels, temperatures and temperature extremes, all by specific locale, in addition to historical and comparative records on such meteorological phenomena as droughts. Much of the center's climatic information is available for a fee through its on-line computer database, the CAC Climate Dial-Up Service. For information about the service, call or write the Climate Analysis Center.

National Climatic Data Center, Federal Building, Asheville, NC 28801, (704) 259-0682. The center provides meteorological records for all U.S. locales, but data usually must be ordered. A fee is charged—$13 minimum. Call for instructions.

National Center for Atmospheric Research, P.O. Box 3000, Boulder, CO 80307, (303) 497-1183 for reference library service, (303) 497-8607 to arrange interviews with scientists through NCAR's information center. NCAR's work focuses on long-term climate changes and phenomena that may be tied to environmental problems such as depletion of the ozone layer, the greenhouse effect, and storm formation. NCAR's reference librarians answer reporters' inquiries. Upon request, NCAR's information center will prepare free packets of background reportage from newspapers and scientific magazines and journals.

National Severe Storms Forecast Center, Room 1728, 601 East 12th St., Kansas City, MO 64106, (816) 426-3427. The center's staff tracks tornadoes and severe thunderstorms throughout the United States, and will answer reporters' questions. The center maintains an extensive file of tornado occurrences dating back to 1953.

NOAA Weather Service Forecast Office, National Hurricane Center, 1320 South Dixie Highway, Coral Gables, FL 33146, (305) 666-4612. NOAA Weather Service Forecast Office, Central Pacific Hurricane Center, P.O. Box 29879, Honolulu, HI 96820, (808) 836-1831. The centers monitor the formation, strength and direction of hurricanes throughout the world. Center staffs will answer reporters' questions. The centers offer a free booklet summarizing hurricane activity from 1832 through 1979 and including annual supplementary reports since 1980.

United States Geological Survey, 907 National Center, Reston, VA 22092, (703) 648-4000 for general information, (703) 648-4302 for library reference service. The survey maintains extensive files of geological data for the United States, including records of earthquake activity. Reference library staff will accommodate public requests for specific information.

National Earthquake Information Center, P.O. Box 25046, MS 967, Denver, CO 80225, (303) 273-8500. From its headquarters in Golden, Colo., the NEIC monitors earthquake activity throughout the United States and the world. The center also maintains files of historical data and information on earthquakes, and will answer reporters' questions.

The U.S. Department of Agriculture Forest Service monitors avalanche activity in selected parts of the country. In addition to training highway and ski area personnel, the service provides public information concerning the danger and occurrence of avalanches in fall, winter and spring.

• Utah Avalanche Forecast Center, 337 North–2370 West, Salt Lake City, UT 84116, (801) 524-5304.

• Colorado Avalanche Information Center, 10230 Smith Road, Denver, CO 80239, (303) 371-1080.

• Northwest Avalanche Center, P.O. Box C15700, 7600 Sand Point Way Northeast, Seattle, WA 98115, (206) 526-6677.

FRONTIERS OF SCIENCE

AIDS

One of the most active topics of current medical research is the human immunodeficiency virus (HIV), which causes acquired immune deficiency syndrome (AIDS).

HIV attacks the body's disease-fighting cells, disabling the immune system and making the patient vulnerable to opportunistic infections and various forms of cancer. It can also attack cells in the central nervous system, causing neurological and psychological disturbances, including dementia. The virus, which is carried in body fluids, can be present for years before any ill effects are noticed. Thus, a person can be infected with the HIV virus and transmit it to others long before he or she has the infections, rare cancers and other problems that mark the onset of AIDS.

In the United States, more than 126,000 AIDS deaths were recorded between 1981 and 1991. By early 1992, the U.S. Centers for Disease Control reported more than 200,000 active AIDS cases and estimated that 1 million Americans are infected with the HIV virus. The World Health Organization estimated that 10 million to 12 million people are infected with the virus worldwide, and that the number may reach 30 million to 40 million by the end of the decade. At the Eighth International Conference on AIDS, held in Amsterdam July 19–24, 1992, the WHO estimate was criticized as being too low. The International AIDS Center at Harvard has estimated that as many as 110 million people could be infected by the year 2000. Africa is especially hard-hit. In 1992, the Harvard group estimated that 7 million people in sub-Saharan Africa carry the HIV virus and more than 1.3 million have AIDS. Virtually everyone who is infected with the HIV virus eventually suffers from AIDS.

The progression from carrying the HIV virus to suffering from AIDS is sometimes fast but often takes seven to 10 years. During that period, the person may have few or no symptoms. A flu-like illness may occur soon after infection, but may pass without notice. Lymph glands may become swollen, but may cause no discomfort. Despite the patient's apparent good health, he or she can transmit the virus.

The usual methods of transmission are sexual activity (homosexual or heterosexual), exposure to infected blood, and transmission from mother to baby during pregnancy or during birth. The danger of contracting AIDS through blood transfusions in the United States has been minimized since 1985, when

a screening test became available and was applied to all blood donations. In countries with lower standards of medical care, the danger remains substantial.

Drug addicts frequently become infected with HIV by sharing needles. In the process of injecting drugs, a small amount of blood is drawn into the needle. This blood is then injected into the next user. Health-care workers occasionally have been infected by sticking themselves accidentally with contaminated needles. In one case in Florida, an infected dentist was shown to have transmitted the virus to five patients. No cases have ever been documented to show that the virus can be transmitted through casual contact, such as hugging, talking or sharing living quarters. Public fear has caused many AIDS patients to be ostracized, however.

In the 1970s, doctors in the United States began to see a bewildering number of homosexual and bisexual men who were suffering from a variety of repeated, severe, often unusual infections and from rare forms of cancer. The patients invariably died. In 1981, AIDS was first formally described. Two years later, the T-cell lymphotropic virus that causes the syndrome was identified by Robert Gallo at the U.S. National Institutes of Health and by Luc Montagnier at France's Pasteur Institute. The virus apparently had been in existence for more than two decades, but had not been widespread enough to be detected. Its history has been traced at least to 1959, when a British sailor died of pneumonia and a series of overwhelming secondary infections that left medical experts perplexed. When his tissue samples were re-examined in 1990, they tested positive for AIDS. It is likely that he had been exposed to the virus several years before his death. The AIDS virus also has been found in a 1959 blood serum sample from Zaire.

In the United States, AIDS emerged primarily among homosexual and bisexual men. In fact, the correlation was so strong that some researchers proposed calling the new disease Gay-Related Immune Deficiency in 1982. In other parts of the world, however, the virus has been spread primarily through heterosexual contact. In fact, in late 1991 the World Health Organization estimated that 75 percent of the adults worldwide who had contracted the disease had done so through heterosexual contact. In the United States, only about 6 percent had contracted it through heterosexual contact.

The difference between the experience in the United States (and other industrialized countries) and elsewhere is not due to fundamental differences in the virus. It is due largely to social and behavioral differences. In countries in which female prostitution and polygamy are quite common, those practices have provided a more effective route of transmission than has homosexuality. High rates of sexually transmitted diseases, which can cause lesions that serve as gateways to the virus, also have abetted transmission among heterosexuals.

In the United States, homosexual contact is still the most frequent method of transmission, but intravenous drug use and heterosexual contact are increasingly common methods. In early 1992, the Centers for Disease Control estimated that 6 percent of AIDS patients in the United States had contracted the virus through heterosexual sex. Public awareness of the danger to heterosexuals was heightened when basketball superstar Magic Johnson announced on Nov. 7, 1991, that he was retiring from the game because he had tested positive for the HIV virus. (He subsequently decided to play in the 1992 Olympics.) He later said that he had never had homosexual experiences or used intravenous drugs, but that he had been intimate with many women before his marriage. He said he did not know who had infected him. His wife did not test positive for the virus.

Scientists have made rapid advances in understanding HIV, but they have been unable to develop a vaccine or a cure. The AIDS virus is particularly difficult to destroy because it lives largely in CD4 lymphocyte cells (also called T4 cells), which are critical to the body's ability to fight infection from viruses, parasites, bacteria and fungi. Once the virus invades the cells, it uses their genetic material to multiply and infect and destroy other cells. For this reason, a count of CD4 cells is often used as an indication of the progression of the disease.

AIDS (as opposed to HIV positivity) is diagnosed when a person who has the HIV virus develops certain conditions that are common among AIDS patients, such as rare pneumonias and cancers. On Jan. 1, 1993, the Centers for Disease Control has proposed that the definition should be changed to reflect a more quantifiable standard based on the number of CD4 cells in a cubic millimeter of blood. A new definition could shift thousands of people from the HIV-positive category to the AIDS category in the United States.

Although there is no cure for AIDS, the outlook for patients now is more hopeful than it was 10 years ago. The Food and Drug Administration has approved three drugs that can slow the progress of AIDS: azidothymidine (also known as AZT or zidovudine), dideoxycytidine (DDC) and didoxyinosine (DDI). In addition, drugs and treatments have been developed and refined to treat many of the opportunistic infections and cancers that plague AIDS pa-

tients. The infections include pneumocystis carinii pneumonia (PCP), caused by a protozoan that is normally tolerated by the body; toxoplasmosis (caused by a parasite); candidiasis ("yeast," "thrush"), a fungus that affects the mouth, esophagus and lungs; tuberculosis (both common and uncommon types); and infections caused by cytomegalovirus, herpes virus, histoplasmosis (fungus) and cryptococcus (fungus). Cancers include Kaposi's sarcoma (a tissue cancer that causes blue or brown skin discolorations), cancers of the lymph nodes and cancers of the tongue and rectum.

Researchers continue to seek a cure for AIDS and a vaccine that will prevent HIV infection. In the meantime, prevention is the best protection against AIDS. This includes practicing abstinence or avoiding sexual situations in which the risk of contracting the HIV virus is high. These situations include sex with partners whose lifestyles and personal histories are not well known, sex with many partners, sex with intravenous drug users (or with people who have used intravenous drugs in the past), sex with prostitutes and sex without a condom. Prevention also depends on drug addicts not sharing needles, on health-care workers using extreme caution when handling body fluids, and on blood banks screening all donations. For pregnant women who are HIV positive, there is no way to prevent the virus from passing to the fetus. About one-third of all babies born to infected mothers will develop the disease.

SUPERCONDUCTORS

When electricity flows through a conductor some energy is lost because the material resists the flow of electrons. The lost electrical energy is released as heat. In some applications, such as toasters, the heating is desirable. In many, however, it is not.

If electricity could flow through a wire without losing any of its energy, all of that wasted energy could be put to use, solving many of our energy problems. Electricity could be made when convenient and placed in storage loops, to be drawn upon when demand is high. It could be sent long distances across the country, rather than having to be used near where it is produced. And it could be used in innovative ways, such as high-speed trains that run on frictionless "rails" of electromagnetic energy.

Superconductors are materials that conduct electricity with no loss of energy. For 80 years, scientists have known that some metals become superconductors when they are cooled sufficiently. Unfortunately, the metals had to be cooled to exceedingly low temperatures—about 418 degrees below 0 degrees Fahrenheit. Cooling to this extent required liquid helium, which is difficult and expensive to produce. Commercial applications were, therefore, extremely limited.

Then, in 1986, scientists discovered ceramic materials that are superconductors at higher temperatures. (K. Alex Müller and J. George Bednorz received the Nobel Prize for Physics for the discovery in 1987.) Since the initial discovery, researchers have been developing forms that function at increasingly higher temperatures. Although the ceramics still require temperatures of several hundred degrees below 0 degrees Fahrenheit, the temperatures can be reached using liquid nitrogen (which boils at 321 degrees below 0 Fahrenheit). Because liquid nitrogen is cheaper and easier to obtain than liquid helium, commercial use is much more feasible.

The continued development of superconductors is likely to lead to other technological advances—including high-speed switching devices in supercomputers, a new generation of magnetic resonance imaging (MRI) equipment for use in medical diagnosis, and powerful magnetic force fields that will serve as "bottles" to contain particles in nuclear fusion reactors. The new superconductors could also offer some relief from energy problems by allowing more efficient production, storage and transmission.

NUCLEAR FUSION

Nuclear power plants currently use fission—splitting the nuclei of atoms—to produce energy. The process uses radioactive fuel, which is difficult and expensive to mine, process, transport and handle. It produces radioactive wastes, which are dangerous and expensive to handle and store.

Fusion, on the other hand, uses a common component of water as fuel and it produces much less radioactive waste than fission. Deuterium, a form of hydrogen that is easily removed from water, is the main fuel. It is sometimes combined with another form of hydrogen, tritium, to increase energy output. The atoms fuse, forming helium and releasing energy and mild radioactivity. If the power of nuclear fusion can be harnessed, it could offer a relatively clean, inexpensive, nearly inexhaustible energy source for the future.

Researchers have been working on the problem since the 1950s. Scientists at the Joint European Torus (Jet) reactor in Oxfordshire, England, produced the first significant amount of power from controlled nuclear fusion on Nov. 9, 1991. As important as the breakthrough was, however, it does not herald the advent of commercial fusion power. That goal may still be 50 years away. Jet researchers said that they produced 1.5 million to 2 million watts of electrical power in a two-second pulse. The energy that was produced was not great enough to offset the energy that was expended in producing it. It also was not great enough to cause a sustained reaction. A combination of international competition, cooperation and billions of dollars made the Jet breakthrough possible, and is likely to continue until an efficient fusion reactor is achieved.

Fusion draws its energy from joining the nuclei of atoms. When the nuclei combine, some of the energy that held the original nuclei together is released. The sun produces energy in the same way. Due to the sun's extremely high temperature (14 million degrees Centigrade at the core) and its crushing gravitational force, the nuclei of lightweight atoms fuse. The challenge for scientists is to create conditions that will cause, sustain and control the reaction on Earth.

Because the pressure within a fusion reactor does not approach that of the sun, the temperature must be far hotter. In the Jet experiment, the fuel was heated to 360 million degrees Centigrade by electric currents. Because no material on Earth is strong enough to contain such heat, it is confined in a "bottle" created by powerful magnetic fields. [See Superconductors]

In 1989, chemists at the University of Utah claimed to have created fusion at room temperature. The claim caused excitement among scientists around the world, hundreds of whom tried to reproduce the results. Interest dimmed when their efforts failed.

The Jet laboratory is a joint effort by 14 European nations. Scientists from Japan, the Soviet Union and the United States also have been working to gain preeminence in the field. In the United States, where research efforts are sponsored by the Department of Energy, Princeton University is the leading research center. Scientists at the Princeton Plasma Physics Laboratory have said that their research schedule has been delayed because of cuts in federal funding. A $5-billion international research project is under consideration. The International Thermonuclear Experimental Reactor would be sponsored by the United States, the Soviet Union, Japan and the members of the European Community.

SPACE

Astronomers stand poised at the edge of discoveries that are likely to challenge fundamental theories in the 1990s. Just as modern telescopes caused early astronomers to discard their vision of an Earth-centered cosmos, so advanced telescopes are likely to reveal new information that will demand new theories. The study of astronomy has advanced from what could be seen with the naked eye, to what could be seen with telescopes through the veil of the Earth's atmosphere, to what can be seen by an awe-inspiring array of Earth-bound and orbiting devices that "see" both visible and invisible radiation. And space probes, like the Galileo probe that revealed new views of Venus, have relayed pictures that have deepened our understanding of our own solar system.

New telescopes, many of which are expected to be completed in the 1990s, promise new visions for astronomers. Stargazers are accustomed to one view of the night sky—a twinkling, light-on-dark blanket. What they are seeing is electromagnetic radiation that falls within the wavelength range that the human eye can sense. What they don't see are all of the other wavelengths that are invisible to the human eye. These forms of radiation—including gamma rays, X-rays, ultraviolet radiation, infrared radiation and radio waves—provide a different picture for devices that can "see" them. Astronomers have already started to rethink some basic assumptions because of observations made with telescopes designed to detect these types of radiation, and because of extremely powerful optical telescopes that have been made possible because of improvements in technology.

One of the most surprising findings has been that the universe does not seem to be as homogeneous as was once imagined. The most widely held theory about the creation of the universe, the Big Bang Theory, holds that the universe began with a gigantic explosion, and that the universe has been expanding ever since. Under this theory, chance collisions would have created small clumps of gas molecules right after the explosion. Those clumps would have had more density, thus more gravitational attraction, than surrounding spaces. They would have drawn additional molecules to them, creating larger and larger structures. The result would be a universe with fairly evenly distributed clumps of matter. Instead, astronomers are finding evidence that the universe is quite different. Galaxies, rather than being randomly scattered, seem to form clumps about 400 million light-years apart. To explain forces that would produce such phenomena, scientists must question basic assumptions of astronomy and physics.

Observations with optical telescopes have led astronomers to infer, based on the movements of the stars and galaxies, that some unknown, unseen "dark matter" is pulling them. In fact, they estimate that 90 percent or more of the universe may be undetected. What is this "dark matter"? Why do X-ray detectors show gigantic amounts of radiation spewing from the center of some galaxies? How can the energy of quasars, the brightest objects in the cosmos, be explained? Their energy is greater than that produced by fusion, which powers the sun. But what is it? Could the energy be the result of a black hole, a

collapsed star that is so dense that even light cannot escape its gravitational pull? When the black hole vacuums in everything around it, does it release energy that we see as quasars?

Finding the answers to these questions is likely to be expensive. The Hubble Space Telescope, which was found to have a defective mirror after it was launched from the space shuttle in April 1990, cost $1.5 billion. The Gamma Ray Observatory, launched a year later, cost $600 million.

Even land-based telescopes are extraordinarily expensive. The Keck optical telescope in Hawaii will be the world's largest when it comes on line. A twin is scheduled to be in use by 1996. They will use 36 6-foot-wide mirrors that are so thin they would sag under their own weight. To maintain their accuracy, they must be electronically monitored and realigned every half-second. The technology they represent is monumental, and the information they may be able to reveal about the universe may be astounding. And each will cost more than $90 million.

Some extraordinary telescopes, with extraordinary price tags, are planned for the next 10 years. The Advanced X-ray Astrophysics Facility could be launched by 1997. It would study emissions from black holes, and cost the United States about $1.6 billion. The Space Infrared Telescope Facility could give us a view of the formation of stars and galaxies by the turn of the century—at a cost of about $1.3 billion.

Advances in astronomy in the 1990s will be tied not only to what is technologically and intellectually possible, but to what is economically and politically possible.

GENETICS

Genetics research may lead to new ways to predict, prevent and combat diseases in the next decade. Included will be not only the 4,000 conditions, such as cystic fibrosis, that are caused by a defect of a single gene, but also the myriad others that are caused by the interaction of several genes and environmental conditions. By the year 2000, genetic research and genetically engineered products may dramatically change the way medicine deals with such killers as cancer, heart disease and AIDS.

Many of the advances that make the current research possible have come within the last 20 years. In 1973, Paul Berg, a biochemist at Stanford University in California, developed a process that allowed him to take genes apart and reassemble them. (In 1980 he shared the Nobel Prize for Chemistry for his achievement.) This new ability to manipulate genetic structure opened a promising field—genetic engineering—that promised hardier plants, meatier cattle and new drugs that could attack diseases by altering molecular structure. It also raised the prospect that, with enough knowledge, we might be able to change the basic building blocks of life.

Human genetics are so complex, however, that solving even basic riddles has been time-consuming and expensive. Of the 100,000 genes that determine our physical structure, only about 2,000 have been precisely located. Charting their chemical structure has been an even more daunting task. A major research effort, the Human Genome Project, began tackling the job in 1990.

The project, under the guidance of the National Institutes of Health, is expected to take 15 years and cost $3 billion to complete. Its goal is to provide a detailed map of the human genome—all of our genetic material.

Our genetic material is contained in the nucleus of every cell. It is grouped in 23 pairs of chromosomes. (One member of each pair is inherited from each parent.) The chromosomes are strands of genes, made up of DNA (deoxyribonucleic acid). DNA is a molecule shaped like a twisted ladder, with pairs of bases on each side of the connecting rungs. The sequence of the pairs determines the cell's production of protein, out of which the body is made and with which the body functions. Scientists estimate that there are more than 3.3 billion pairs of bases. The Human Genome Project is attempting to identify the sequence of each of these pairs.

Some scientists have argued that the project is too ambitious, and that it will cost more and take longer than predicted. They argue that much of the sequencing may be of no real value, and that a less detailed map would be as useful and less costly. Advocates contend that we must unlock doors before we can dismiss them as being unimportant, and that a detailed map will provide the best foundation for future research. The success of the project, under the direction of Nobel laureate James D. Watson, depends in part on the success of technological improvements to speed the mapping process and in part on continued funding.

Other research projects are attempting to identify genes that cause specific diseases, and to design genetically engineered drugs to treat them. In recent years, scientists also have identified the location or approximate location of genes associated with juvenile diabetes, rheumatoid arthritis, melanoma and retinitis pigmentosa (a cause of blindness). A major medical breakthrough occurred in 1989, when scientists identified the gene responsible for cystic fibrosis, a debilitating disease that affects one in every 2,500 white infants born in the United States. (Infants of other races are affected less frequently.) The disease occurs when an infant inherits one cystic fi-

brosis gene from each parent. People who are known to be at risk of carrying the gene can now be tested, as can fetuses. If an efficient screening test can be developed, it might be used to identify the estimated 12 million Americans who carry one of the genes. Knowing more about the gene, and its particular defect, may someday enable scientists to correct the defect, or to improve treatment.

Cancer researchers are studying the ways in which our genetic inheritance predisposes us to certain cancers, and the way in which cancerous cells reproduce and cells in the human immune system fight them. By genetically altering immune system cells and producing them in mass quantities in laboratories, scientists may be able to produce supercharged immune cells to fight cancer. The dream is for a "magic bullet," cells that would fight only cancer cells and leave other cells unharmed. Because cancer cells vary so greatly, and genetic structure is so complex, that dream is still a long way off. Still, other advances offer new hope for cancer patients. Researchers are experimenting with genes that produce "tumor necrosis factor," a substance that kills tumor cells. Clinical trials with patients who have melanoma, a serious form of skin cancer, have produced promising results. Other researchers have tailor-made strands of DNA that may be useful in fighting cancer or screening for its presence. The gene that causes acute promyelocytic leukemia has been located, which has led to increased understanding of the disease. Genetic research linked to specific cancers, and to improved testing and treatment for those cancers, is going on at medical centers around the world.

Genetics research also holds promise for other diseases, including AIDS and adenosine deaminase (ADA) deficiency, a rare disease that severely weakens children's immune systems and leaves them vulnerable to life-threatening infections. In 1990, a four-year-old girl with ADA became the first person in history to receive new genes to correct a hereditary defect. She was given monthly doses of genetically engineered white blood cells that contained the gene she lacked. Although the full effect will not be known for years, her initial response was quite favorable.

Using the same type of technique, doctors one day may be able to bolster the immune systems of other types of patients, including those with AIDS. That, coupled with doses of genetically engineered drugs that invade viruses and kill them, could dramatically change the outlook for patients with many serious diseases.

Recent advances in molecular biology have opened new doors for medicine, and may unlock others. They have also raised important ethical questions, however, which remain to be answered. How far should science go in manipulating the building blocks of life? Should human genes be manipulated to prevent life-threatening diseases? Should they be altered for lesser reasons—to prevent nearsightedness, short stature, left-handedness—or for purely cosmetic reasons? In short, should we learn how to engineer the "perfect" baby? And, if we have the knowledge, should we use it?

Science is still a very long way from being able to present prospective parents with a genetic shopping list, so we may not have to deal with that question for a long time. But other issues may affect us in the next few years. If current research is successful, it may be possible to screen infants at birth for hundreds of genetically linked diseases. That information could be used to form a profile of susceptibility to specific types of cancers, heart disease, certain types of mental illnesses, kidney disease, diabetes and hundreds of other illnesses. Who should get that information? Should it be used to deny insurance or employment? If individuals know their risks, is it fair to keep that knowledge from potential insurers or employers? If science can predict a fatal illness, but cannot offer cure or prevention, should people know their fate? Should they have a choice? If costly new therapies are available to correct the identified genetic problem, who should bear the cost? And if a child requires a particular lifestyle to avert later disease, what should be done when parents do not comply?

The ethical questions may be as complex as the research itself.

PART SIX

ACCESS TO INFORMATION

FREEDOM OF INFORMATION LAWS

U.S. FREEDOM OF INFORMATION ACT

§552. Public information; agency rules, opinions, orders, records and proceedings

(a) Each agency shall make available to the public information as follows:

(1) Each Agency shall separately state and currently publish in the Federal Register for the guidance of the public

(A) descriptions of its central and field organization and the established places at which, the employees (and in the case of a uniformed service, the members) from whom, and the methods whereby, the public may obtain information, make submittals or requests, or obtain decisions;

(B) statements of the general course and method by which its functions are channeled and determined, including the nature and requirements of all formal and informal procedures available;

(C) rules of procedure, descriptions of forms available or the places at which forms may be obtained, and instructions as to the scope and contents of all papers, reports, or examinations;

(D) substantive rules of general applicability adopted as authorized by law, and statements of general policy or interpretations of general applicability formulated and adopted by the agency; and

(E) each amendment, revision, or repeal of the foregoing. Except to the extent that a person has actual and timely notice of the terms thereof, a person may not in any manner be required to resort to, or be adversely affected by, a matter required to be published in the Federal Register and not so published. For the purpose of this paragraph, matter reasonably available to the class of persons affected thereby is deemed published in the Federal Register when incorporated by reference therein with the approval of the Director of the Federal Register.

(2) Each agency, in accordance with published rules, shall make available for public inspection and copying

(A) final opinions, including concurring and dissenting opinions, as well as orders, made in the adjudication of cases;

(B) those statements of policy and interpretations which have been adopted by the agency and are not published in the Federal Register; and

(C) administrative staff manuals and instructions to staff that affect a member of the public; unless the materials are promptly published and copies offered for sale. To the extent required to prevent a clearly unwarranted invasion of personal privacy, an agency may delete identifying details when it makes available or publishes an opinion, statement of policy, interpretation, or staff manual or instruction. However, in each case the justification for the deletion shall be explained fully in writing. Each agency shall also maintain and make available for public inspection and copying current indexes providing identifying information for the public as to any matter issued, adopted, or promulgated after July 4, 1967, and required by this paragraph to be made available or published. Each agency shall promptly publish, quarterly or more frequently, and distribute (by sale or otherwise) copies of each index or supplements thereto unless it determines by order published in the Federal Register that the publication would be unnecessary and impracticable, in which case the agency shall nonetheless provide copies of such index on request at a cost not to exceed the direct cost of duplication. A final order, opinion, statement of policy, interpretation, or staff manual or instruction that affects a member of the public may be relied on, used, or cited as precedent by an agency against a party other than an agency only if

(i) it has been indexed and either made available or published as provided by this paragraph; or

(ii) the party has actual and timely notice of the terms thereof.

(3) Except with respect to the records made available under paragraphs (1) and (2) of this subsection, each agency, upon any request for records which (A) reasonably describes such records and (B) is made in accordance with published rules stating the time, place, fees (if any), and procedures to be followed, shall make the records promptly available to any person.

(4) (A)

(i) In order to carry out the provisions of this section, each agency shall promulgate regulations, pursuant to notice and receipt of public comment, specifying the schedule of fees applicable to the processing of requests under this section and establishing procedures and guidelines for determining when such fees should be waived or reduced. Such schedule shall conform to the guidelines which shall be promulgated, pursuant to notice and receipt of public comment, by the Director of the Office of Management and Budget and which shall provide for a uniform schedule of fees for all agencies.

(ii) Such agency regulations shall provide that (I) fees shall be limited to reasonable standard charges for document search, duplication, and review, when records are requested for commercial use; (II) fees shall be limited to reasonable standard charges for document duplication when records are not sought for commercial use and the request is made by an educational or noncommercial scientific institution, whose purpose is scholarly or scientific research; or a representative of the news media; and (III) for any request not described in (I) or (II), fees shall be limited to reasonable standard charges for document search and duplication.

(iii) Documents shall be furnished without any charge or at a charge reduced below the fees established under clause (ii) if disclosure of the information is in the public interest because it is likely to contribute significantly to public understanding of the operations or activities of the government and is not "primarily" in the commercial interest of the requester.

(iv) Fee schedules shall provide for the recovery of only the direct costs of search, duplication, or review. Review costs shall include only the direct costs incurred during the initial examination of a document for the purposes of determining whether the documents must be disclosed under this section and for the purposes of withholding any portions exempt from disclosure under this section. Review costs may not include any costs incurred in resolving issues of law or policy that may be raised in the course of processing a request under this section. No fee may be charged by any agency under this section (I) if the costs of routine collection and processing of the fee are likely to equal or exceed the amount of the fee; or (II) for any request described in clause (ii) (II) or (III) of this subparagraph for the first two hours of search time or for the first one hundred pages of duplication.

(v) No agency may require advance payment of any fee unless the requester has previously failed to pay fees in a timely fashion, or the agency has determined that the fee will exceed $250.

(vi) Nothing in this subparagraph shall supersede fees chargeable under a statute specifically providing for setting the level of fees for particular types of records.

(vii) In any action by a requester regarding the waiver of fees under this section, the court shall determine the matter de novo: **Provided,** That the court's review of the matter shall be limited to the record before the agency.

(B) On complaint, the district court of the United States in the district in which the complainant resides, or has his principal place of business, or in which the agency records are situated, or in the District of Columbia, has jurisdiction to enjoin the agency from withholding agency records and to order the production of any agency records improperly withheld from the complainant. In such a case the court shall determine the matter de novo, and may examine the contents of such agency records in camera to determine whether such records or any part thereof shall be withheld under any of the exemptions set forth in subsection (b) of this section, and the burden is on the agency to sustain its action.

(C) Notwithstanding any other provision of law, the defendant shall serve an answer or otherwise plead to any complaint made under this subsection within thirty days after service upon the defendant of the pleading in which such complaint is made, unless the court otherwise directs for good cause shown.

[(D) Repealed. Pub.L. 98-620, Title IV, §402(2), Nov. 8, 1984, 98 Stat. 3357.]

(E) The court may assess against the United States reasonable attorney fees and other litigation costs reasonably incurred in any case under this section in which the complainant has substantially prevailed.

(F) Whenever the court orders the production of any agency records improperly withheld from the complainant and assesses against the United States reasonable attorney fees and other litigation costs, and the court additionally issues a written finding that the circumstances surrounding the withholding raise questions whether agency personnel acted arbitrarily or capriciously with respect to the withholding, the Special Counsel shall promptly initiate a proceeding to determine whether disciplinary action is warranted against the officer or employee who was primarily responsible for the withholding. The Special Counsel, after investigation and consideration of the evidence submitted, shall submit his findings and recommendations to the officer or employee or his representative. The administrative authority shall take the corrective action that the Special Counsel recommends.

(G) In the event of noncompliance with the order of the court, the district court may punish for contempt the responsible employee, and in the case of a uniformed service, the responsible member.

(5) Each agency having more than one member shall maintain and make available for public inspection a record of the final votes of each member in every agency proceeding.

(6) (A) Each agency, upon any request for records made under paragraph (1), (2), or (3) of this subsection, shall

(i) determine within ten days (excepting Saturdays, Sundays, and legal public holidays) after the receipt of any such request whether to comply with such request and shall immediately notify the person making such request of such determination and the reasons therefor, and of the right of such person to appeal to the head of the agency any adverse determination; and

(ii) make a determination with respect to any appeal within twenty days (excepting Saturdays, Sundays, and legal public holidays) after the receipt of such appeal. If on appeal the denial of the request for records is in whole or in part upheld, the agency shall notify the person making such request of the provisions for judicial review of that determination under paragraph (4) of this subsection.

(B) In unusual circumstances as specified in this subparagraph, the time limits prescribed in either clause (i) or clause (ii) of subparagraph (A) may be extended by written notice to the person making such request setting forth the reasons for such extension and the date on which a determination is expected to be dispatched. No such notice shall specify a date that would result in an extension for more than ten working days. As used in this subparagraph, "unusual circumstances" means, but only to the extent reasonably necessary to the proper processing of the particular request

(i) the need to search for and collect the requested records from field facilities or other establishments that are separate from the office processing the request;

(ii) the need to search for, collect, and appropriately examine a voluminous amount of separate and distinct records which are demanded in a single request; or

(iii) the need for consultation, which shall be conducted with all practicable speed, with another agency having a substantial interest in the determination of the request or among two or more components of the agency having substantial subject-matter interest therein.

(C) Any person making a request to any agency for records under paragraph (1), (2), or (3) of this subsection shall be deemed to have exhausted his administrative remedies with respect to such request if the agency fails to comply with the applicable time limit provisions of this paragraph. If the Government can show exceptional circumstances exist and that the agency is exercising due diligence in responding to the request, the court may retain jurisdiction and allow the agency additional time to complete its review of the records. Upon any determination by an agency to comply with a request for records, the records shall be made promptly available to such person making such request. Any notification of denial of any request for records under this subsection shall set forth the names and titles or positions of each person responsible for the denial of such request.

(b) This section does not apply to matters that are:

(1) (A) specifically authorized under criteria established by an Executive order to be kept secret in the interest of national defense or foreign policy and (B) are in fact properly classified pursuant to such Executive order;

(2) related solely to the internal personnel rules and practices of an agency;

(3) specifically exempted from disclosure by statute (other than section 552b of this title), provided that such statute (A) requires that the matters be withheld from the public in such a manner as to leave no discretion on the issue, or (B) establishes particular criteria for withholding or refers to particular types of matters to be withheld;

(4) trade secrets and commercial or financial information obtained from a person and privileged or confidential;

(5) inter-agency or intra-agency memorandums or letters which would not be available by law to a party other than an agency in litigation with the agency;

(6) personnel and medical files and similar files the disclosure of which would constitute a clearly unwarranted invasion of personal privacy;

(7) records or information compiled for law enforcement purposes, but only to the extent that the production of such law enforcement records or information

(A) could reasonably be expected to interfere with enforcement proceedings, (B) would deprive a person of a right to a fair trial or an impartial adjudication, (C) could reasonably be expected to constitute an unwarranted invasion of personal privacy, (D) could reasonably be expected to disclose the identity of a confidential source, including a State, local, or foreign agency or authority or any private institution which furnished information on a confidential basis, and, in the case of a record or information compiled by criminal law enforcement authority in the course of a criminal investigation or by an agency conducting a lawful national security intelligence investigation, information furnished by a confidential source, (E) would disclose techniques and procedures for law enforcement investigations or prosecutions, or would disclose guidelines for law enforcement investigations or prosecutions, or would disclose guidelines for law enforcement investigations or prosecutions if such disclosure could reasonably be expected to risk circumvention of the law, or (F) be expected to endanger the life or physical safety of any individual;

(8) contained in or related to examination, operating, or conditions reports prepared by, on behalf of, or for the use of an agency responsible for the regulation or supervision of financial institutions; or

(9) geological and geophysical information and data, including maps, concerning wells. Any reason-

ably segregable portion of a record shall be provided to any person requesting such record after deletion of the portions which are exempt under this subsection.

(c) (1) Whenever a request is made which involves access to records described in subsection (b) (7) (A) and

(A) the investigation or proceeding involves a possible violation of criminal law; and

(B) there is reason to believe that (i) the subject of the investigation or proceeding is not aware of its pendency, and (ii) disclosure of the existence of the records could reasonably be expected to interfere with enforcement proceedings, the agency may, during only such time as that circumstance continues, treat the records as not subject to the requirements of this section.

(2) Whenever informant records maintained by a criminal law enforcement agency under an informant's name or personal identifier are requested by a third party according to the informant's name or personal identifier, the agency may treat the records as not subject to the requirements of this section unless the informant's status as an informant has been officially confirmed.

(3) Whenever a request is made which involves access to records maintained by the Federal Bureau of Investigation pertaining to foreign intelligence or counterintelligence, or international terrorism, and the existence of the records is classified information as provided in subsection (b) (1), the Bureau may, as long as the existence of the records remains classified information, treat the records as not subject to the requirements of this section.

(d) This section does not authorize withholding of information or limit the availability of records to the public, except as specifically stated in this section. This section is not authority to withhold information from Congress.

(e) On or before March 1 of each calendar year, each agency shall submit a report covering the preceding calendar year to the Speaker of the House of Representatives and President of the Senate for referral to the appropriate committees of the Congress. The report shall include

(1) the number of determinations made by such agency not to comply with requests for records made to such agency under subsection (a) and the reasons for each such determination;

(2) the number of appeals made by persons under subsection (a) (6), the result of such appeals, and the reason for the action upon each appeal that results in a denial of information;

(3) the names and titles or positions of each person responsible for the denial of records requested under this section, and the number of instances of participation for each;

(4) the results of each proceeding conducted pursuant to subsection (a) (4) (F), including a report of the disciplinary action taken against the officer or employee who was primarily responsible for improperly withholding records or an explanation of why disciplinary action was not taken;

(5) a copy of every rule made by such agency regarding this section;

(6) a copy of the fee schedule and the total amount of fees collected by the agency for making records available under this section; and

(7) such other information as indicates efforts to administer fully this section.

The Attorney General shall submit an annual report on or before March 1 of each calendar year which shall include for the prior calendar year a listing of the number of cases arising under this section, the exemption involved in each case, the disposition of such case, and the cost, fees, and penalties assessed under subsections (a) (4) (E), (F), and (G). Such report shall also include a description of the efforts undertaken by the Department of Justice to encourage agency compliance with this section.

(f) For purposes of this section, the term "agency" as defined in section 551(1) of this title includes any executive department, military department, Government corporation, Government controlled corporation, or other establishment in the executive branch of the Government (including the Executive Office of the President), or any independent regulatory agency.

STATE FREEDOM OF INFORMATION LAWS

Statutes guaranteeing access to specified public documents or entry to the meetings of publicly constituted groups vary from state to state.

In some measure, every state recognizes the public's right to inspect or acquire copies of legally disclosable public documents, generally those that do not violate an individual's right to privacy.

Most important, given the proliferation of computerized data in municipal offices throughout the country, most states now also acknowledge public records to include computer data. However, the form in which that material is available—whether on computer media, as printouts or as data merely subject to inspection—varies from state to state.

Most statutes that deal with computerized data specifically protect computer-storage and retrieval software as "trade secrets," thereby protecting the rights of software designers and owners, but making it potentially difficult, if not impossible, for requesters to actually access some of the public-records data they may be given.

Most states are constrained—by policy, regulation, statute or case law—to provide public data at a reasonable cost, thereby making it more difficult for agencies to use copying costs as a way to deny access to public information.

In every state, even those with quasijudicial bodies that hear denial-complaint cases, the courts are the ultimate redress for denial of information, but very few states make it easy for residents to pursue cases on their own.

Connecticut residents, for example, do not need to hire a lawyer in order to contest a refusal to release information; a quasijudicial body handles the matter, and its lawyers routinely represent complainants before the state's courts.

Throughout the nation, open-meeting statutes are similarly varied, and so is the states' willingness to improve public access to the workings of government.

The following list identifies state offices and commissions that deal with open-government statutes and may advise the public on the filing of information requests, complaints, or how to initiate legal action.

Alabama

Office of the Attorney General
Alabama State House
11 Union St.
Montgomery, AL 36130
(205) 242-7300

The Attorney General's office will answer questions about FOI regulations but will not interpret state statutes, which make no mention of computerized data in the public record. Neither do state statutes limit charges for copies of public records.

Alaska

Office of the Attorney General
P.O. Box K
Juneau, AK 99811-0300
(907) 465-3600

State statutes and regulations extend public access to records on computer media. Denial complaints must be pursued in court.

Arizona

Office of the Attorney General
1275 W. Washington St.
Phoenix, AZ 85007
(602) 542-4266

The state's public records law implies access to "printouts" of computerized records. Denial complaints must be pursued in court.

Arkansas

Consumer Protection Division
Attorney General's Office
200 Tower Building
323 Center St.
Little Rock, AR 72201
(501) 682-2341

The division will help a requester interpret open-government statutes. The division also provides copies of the state's Freedom of Information Act, which says the public is entitled to "any form" of disclosable data. Denial complaints must be pursued in court.

California

Office of the Attorney General
P.O. Box 94244-2550
Sacramento, CA 94244-2550
(916) 324-5437

The state's Public Records Act gives an agency discretion over the form in which data may be released. Denial complaints must be pursued in court.

Colorado

Attorney General's Office
110 16th St., Suite 1000
Denver, CO 80202
(303) 866-4500

No Colorado office or agency is directly charged with answering the public's questions about documents available under the state's Open Records Act. However, the Attorney General's staff is responsible for enforcement of the statutes. The ORA recognizes that computerized data are part of the public record. Redress for denial of records is through the courts.

Connecticut

Freedom of Information Commission
97 Elm St. Rear
Hartford, CT 06061
(203) 566-5682

Connecticut has one of the country's most progressive Freedom of Information statutes, as well as a standing quasijudicial commission empowered to interpret and enforce the law and to pursue court challenges in behalf of complainants. The state's FOI Act also stipulates that disclosable records be made available in computer-media form whenever an agency can reasonably do so.

Delaware

Office of the Attorney General
Department of Justice
Carvel State Office Building
820 N. French St.
Wilmington, DE 19801
(302) 577-2500

Two statutes, Delaware's Freedom of Information Act and Administrative Procedures Act, provide access to public information without regard to the form of data. Denial complaints must be pursued in court.

District of Columbia

Office of the Mayor
1350 Pennsylvania Ave. NW
5th Floor
Washington, D.C. 20004
(202) 727-2980

The district's Freedom of Information Act provides access to public information without regard to the form of data. Most cases are handled by the Mayor's legal counsel, which often is able to settle disputes out of court. Address letters to the attention of: F.O.I.A.

Florida

Office of the Attorney General
The Capitol
Tallahassee, FL 32399-1050
(904) 487-1963

The state's Public Records Act ensures access to public information without regard to the form of data. Florida also allows limited but direct access to public agency computers at the requester's expense. The Attorney General's office directs inquiries and requests for data to appropriate departments.

Georgia

State Law Library
State Judicial Building, Rm. 301
Atlanta, GA 30334
(404) 656-3468

Georgia statutes ensure access to public information without regard to the form of data, but the state has no agency to handle open-government complaints or questions. Copies of the Georgia open-records statute are available from the State Law Library. All cases must be pursued in court.

Hawaii

Office of Information Practices
426 Queens St., Rm. 201
Honolulu, HI 96813
(808) 586-1400

The state's Uniform Practices Act ensures access to all forms of disclosable public records. The Office of Information Practices hears denial complaints and issues written advisory opinions.

Idaho

Office of the Attorney General
State House Building, Rm. 210
Boise, ID 83720
(208) 334-2400

State statutes ensure access to all forms of disclosable public records. Denial complaints must be pursued in court. For $1, the Attorney General's office will provide a pamphlet explaining the law and the request process.

Illinois

Office of the Attorney General
500 South 2d St.
Springfield, IL 62706
(217) 782-9070

The state's Freedom of Information Act ensures access to all forms of disclosable public records. The Attorney General's office hears complaints and issues opinions.

Indiana

Oversight Commission on Public Records
402 W. Washington St.
Room W472
Indianapolis, IN 46204
(317) 232-3373

Indiana's Access to Public Records Act ensures availability of disclosable public records regardless of their form. The statute by itself, however, does not require agencies to release lists of names and addresses. The state's Oversight Commission on Public Records interprets the statute for requesters and complainants.

Iowa

Office of the Attorney General
Hoover Building, 2d Fl.
Des Moines, IA 50319
(515) 281-5164

The state's public records statute ensures access to all forms of disclosable public records. The Attorney General's office has compelled agencies to provide copies of data on computer media and at a reasonable cost; it also advises requesters on use of the public records statute.

Kansas

Office of the Attorney General
Kansas Judicial Building
301 W. 10th St., 2d Fl.
Topeka, KS 66612-1256
(913) 296-2215

The Attorney General's office interprets and enforces the state's Open Records Act, which includes computerized information in the definition of public records.

Kentucky

Office of the Attorney General
The Capitol
Frankfort, KY 40601
(502) 564-7600

The state's Open Records Act and court rulings have allowed requesters to copy any disclosable public information, including computerized data. A denial complaint may be taken directly to court or filed as an appeal with the Attorney General's office, which will rule in the matter.

Louisiana

Office of the Attorney General
Dept. of Justice
P.O. Box 94005
Baton Rouge, LA 70804
(504) 342-7013

The state's Public Records Act identifies computer data as part of the public record. Lawyers in the Attorney General's office will explain and interpret provisions of the statute for the public.

Maine

Office of the Attorney General
State House Station #6
Augusta, ME 04333
(207) 289-3661

The state's Freedom of Access Law clearly identifies computer data as part of the public record. The Attorney General's office fields FOI inquiries and directs requesters to appropriate state departments.

Maryland

Office of the Attorney General
501 St. Paul Pl.
Baltimore, MD 21202
(301) 333-4063

The state's Access to Public Records Act clearly puts computer data in the public domain. The Attorney General's office reviews straightforward records cases and makes informal rulings.

Massachusetts

Supervisor of Public Records
1 Ashburton Pl., Rm. 1719
Boston, MA 02108
(617) 727-2832

Records on computer media clearly are within the state's definition of public information. The Public Records Department fields denial complaints and rules whether records must be released.

Michigan

Office of the Attorney General
P.O. Box 30212
Lansing, MI 48913
(517) 373-1110

Although the state's Freedom of Information Act specifically includes computerized data in the definition of a public record, recent court rulings have not favored their release with the same alacrity as hard copy. The Attorney General's office answers general questions about the FOI Act, but denial complaints generally must go to court.

Minnesota

Office of the Attorney General
102 State Capitol
St. Paul, MN 55155
(612) 296-6196

The state's Government Data Practices Act covers computerized data, and court rulings have upheld the notion that information format does not affect data's status as a public record. The Attorney General's office will field basic questions, but redress for denial complaints is through the courts.

Mississippi

Office of the Attorney General
Opinion Division
P.O. Box 220
Jackson, MS 39201
(601) 359-3680

The state's Public Access to Records Act includes computer data as part of the public record, and a recent court ruling prevented an agency from recovering more than "actual costs" in satisfying a request for a computer tape. The Attorney General's office fields inquiries about provisions of the statute, but denial complaints generally go to court.

Missouri

Office of the Attorney General
P.O. Box 899
Jefferson City, MO 65102
(314) 751-1143

The state's Sunshine Law does not distinguish among forms of public records, though the statute specifically limits fees for computerized data. The Attorney General's office answers questions concerning applicability of the statute.

Montana

Office of the Attorney General
215 N. Sanders
Helena, MT 59620
(406) 444-2026

The state's Public Records Act does not differentiate among forms of public records, though other statutes do. The Attorney General's office handles inquiries and directs requesters to appropriate agencies.

Nebraska

Office of the Attorney General
2115 State Capitol
Lincoln, NE 68509
(402) 471-2682

The state's open records law acknowledges computerized data as public information, but sets no fees for copying. Nebraska residents may go to court to contest records denials or be represented by the Attorney General's office if the Attorney General deems the record in question to be public.

Nevada
Office of the Attorney General
198 S. Carson St.
Carson City, NV 89710
(702) 687-4170

The state's Open Records Law does not differentiate among public records, and the Attorney General has ruled that requests for computerized data must be weighed individually. The Attorney General's office fields inquiries about the statute and its applicability, but redress for records denials is through the courts.

New Hampshire
Office of the Attorney General
25 Capitol St.
Concord, NH 03301
(603) 271-3658

A recent amendment to the state's Right to Know Law gives agencies discretion over the form which copies of public records may take. Although the statute refers to records maintained in computers, it does not specifically identify computerized data as public information. The Attorney General's office publishes guidelines for use of the statute.

New Jersey
Deputy Attorney General's Office
Richard Hughes Justice Complex
CN 112
Trenton, NJ 08625
(609) 292-8740

The state's Right to Know Law does not define public records. In general, court rulings have dealt only with the disclosability of printouts of computerized data. However, a Public Advocate in the Attorney General's office intercedes in the public's behalf in denial-complaint cases, and often is able to resolve disputes outside of court action. The advocate's address is 25 Market St., CN 850, Trenton, NJ 08625, (609) 292-1889.

New Mexico
Office of the Attorney General
P.O. Drawer 1508
Santa Fe, NM 87504-1508
(505) 827-6000

The state's public records law does not identify computerized information as part of the public record, but court rulings have held that data format does not automatically exclude information from the purview of the statute. The Attorney General's office advises the public of its rights under the statute.

New York
Committee on Open Government
Department of State
162 Washington Ave.
Albany, NY 12231
(518) 474-2518

The state's Freedom of Information Law and attendant court rulings have put computerized data clearly within the scope of disclosable information. The Committee on Open Government hears denial complaints and issues advisory opinions.

North Carolina
Office of the Attorney General
P.O. Box 629
Raleigh, NC 27602
(919) 733-3377

The state's public records laws includes computerized data in their definition of public records. The Attorney General's office gives informal advice to requesters.

North Dakota
Office of the Attorney General
State Capitol
600 East Blvd.
Bismarck, ND 58505
(701) 224-2210

State statute does not define public records. The Attorney General's office routinely fields questions about the public records and open meetings statutes, and tries to help parties resolve differences without formal legal involvement.

Ohio
Office of the Attorney General
30 E. Broad St.
Columbus, OH 43215
(614) 466-4320

State statute specifically includes computerized data as part of the public record, and court rulings have reinforced availability. Agencies are required to make computer terminals available so that data can be scrutinized by the public. The Attorney General's office distributes copies of the public records statutes and offers advice to requesters.

Oklahoma
Office of the Attorney General
State Capitol, Rm. 112
Oklahoma City, OK 73105
(405) 521-3921

The state's Open Records Act includes computerized data in its definition of public records, and the Attorney General's office advises the public on use of the act.

Oregon

Office of the Attorney General
100 Justice Bldg.
Salem, OR 97310
(503) 378-4400

Computerized data is clearly within the scope of the state's public records statute, and court rulings have only reinforced the public's right to access. The Attorney General's office reviews and decides petitions for information from state agencies. Local district attorneys' offices mediate requests for municipal data.

Pennsylvania

Office of the Attorney General
Strawberry Sq.
Harrisburg, PA 17120
(717) 787-3391

Pennsylvania's Right to Know Law does not deal with public records in computerized form, and court rulings in general have held against the requesters of such information or given the agency discretion over the form in which data is to be released. The Attorney General's office fields questions about the statute.

Rhode Island

Office of the Attorney General
72 Pine St.
Providence, RI 02903
(401) 274-4400

Computerized data falls within the definition of public records in the state's Access to Public Records Act, and the Attorney General's office may intercede in a requester's behalf if it believes the information sought is a disclosable public record.

South Carolina

Public Information Office
P.O. Box 11549
Columbia, SC 29211
(803) 734-3970

Computerized information is public record, according to the state's Freedom of Information Act, and court rulings have affirmed its availability. The Public Information Office distributes copies of the FOIA, in addition to case rulings.

South Dakota

Office of the Attorney General
500 E. Capitol Ave.
Pierre, SD 57501-5070
(605) 773-3215

State statutes dealing with public records imply inclusion of computerized data as potentially disclosable information. The Attorney General's office serves less as a resource for requesters of information than for the state and municipal agencies from which the information is sought.

Tennessee

Office of the Attorney General
450 James Robertson Parkway
Nashville, TN 37243
(615) 741-3491

The state Open Records Act does not define public records, but other statutes seem to include computerized data among disclosable information. However, the same statutes also give agencies complete discretion over the form in which information is to be released. The Attorney General's office generally does not advise the public on any specific case. Primary redress for denial of information is through the courts.

Texas

Office of the Attorney General
P.O. Box 12548
Austin, TX 78701
(512) 463-2007

Court rulings and various Attorney General's opinions put computerized data within the public record. The Attorney General's office will rule in records disputes, but usually only at the request of a government agency.

Utah

Utah State Archives
State Archivist
State Capitol
Salt Lake City, UT 84114
(801) 538-3012

State statutes recognize computerized data as part of the public record, and the State Archives Office advises requesters on how to obtain document copies. Citizens may appeal request denials to the office's State Records Committee.

Vermont

Office of the Attorney General
State Office Bldg.
Montpelier, VT 05602
(802) 828-3171

State statutes seem to include computerized data in the public record. Laws require agencies to permit inspection of public records, but agencies must provide copies of data only if they happen to maintain copying devices. The Attorney General's office mediates records disputes.

Virginia

Office of the Attorney General
101 N. 8th St.
Richmond, VA 23219
(804) 786-2071

The state's Freedom of Information Act clearly identifies computer data as part of the public record, and the Attorney General's office tries to help the public deal with the statute's provisions.

Washington

Office of the Attorney General
Highways Licensing Building, 7th Fl.
Olympia, WA 98504
(206) 753-6200

State statutes include computer data as potentially disclosable public information. The Attorney General's office fields questions about the statutes.

West Virginia

Office of the Attorney General
E-26 State Capitol
Charleston, WV 25305
(304) 558-2021

Computerized information is part of the public record, and the Attorney General's office provides "informal guidance" on requests for data.

Wisconsin

Office of the Attorney General
P.O. Box 7857
Madison, WI 53707-7857
(608) 266-1221

Wisconsin law puts computerized information within the realm of disclosable data, and requires agencies to provide the public with the means to review and copy records, as long as new equipment is not required. In records disputes, the Attorney General's office may issue a written opinion in behalf of the requester.

Wyoming

Wyoming State Law Library
Supreme Court Bldg.
Cheyenne, WY 82002
(307) 777-7509

The state's Public Records Act makes computerized information a part of the public record, and specifically allows printouts of computer data. The law library distributes copies of the statute.

For additional contacts, *see* section entitled U.S. Press Groups and Associations on page 446.

DATABASES

For journalists and other nonfiction writers, information is the basic material required for production. Just as a spring maker has to know how and where to get the best wire at the best price, so a writer must know the most effective way to get current, reliable information at the lowest cost. At issue is not only the quality of the final product, but also productivity.

In the last few years, the growth of computer databases has changed how writers can do their basic research. In the near future, as more companies get into the computer data business and more government agencies make information available by computer, growth is likely to be exponential. For many writers, though, this seems like a brave, but not too friendly, new world. It need not be.

Writers use telephones all the time to set up interviews, call libraries, get information. Probably few of them can explain with great specificity how the contraption works, let alone how the signals are wrestled from one telephone company to another. How the telephone works is not important. Making it work is the issue. The same is true for computers that are linked to databases.

Linking a personal computer to a database is not an overwhelming task. The basic equipment that makes the process work is a modem, which allows computers to "talk" to each other over telephone lines. The modem, which is either built into the computer or can be purchased separately and attached with a cable, translates the computer's electronic language into a form that can be carried over telephone lines. The modem is connected to the phone line with a cable, in much the same way that an answering machine is connected. Modems usually are sold with the required cables.

The speed at which modems work varies. The speed, or baud rate, indicates how many bits of information can be transferred per second. For example, a 300-baud modem transfers 300 bits per second; a 2400-baud modem transfers 2400 bits per second. In general, the faster the better. A fast modem saves time and, for databases that charge by the minute, can save money.

A good 2400-baud modem often can be purchased for $200 or less. Prices range from about $60 to $400, depending on the features. Faster modems can cost considerably more. Whether they are worth the price depends on the volume of work that they will do, and the per-minute cost of connecting to the databases that you will be using. Nearly all modems are Hayes compatible, which means that they can communicate with Hayes modems and others that follow the same command sets. This has become the industry standard. Because your modem will be communicating with others, it is important that it be Hayes compatible.

To make the computer-modem connection work, one more thing is needed—a piece of software for the computer that allows it to work with the modem. Sometimes the software is included with the modem. It also can be purchased separately, or may be available for free or at very low cost from a computer club. Some commercial data companies produce their own communications software, which they provide when you apply for their service.

The software may be complicated from a technical point of view, but not from a user's point of view. When you start the computer, you need to be able to tell it that you want to use the modem. The software allows you to do that. When you use the software for the first time you need to type in a few pieces of information (like the baud rate and phone numbers of databases) to let it do its job. After that, the software does all the hard work for you.

The resources that are available through on-line databases are extraordinary: commercial news services, newspapers from around the nation and the world, scientific research papers, magazine articles, Department of State travel advisories, current stock market prices, laws and court decisions, encyclopedias, travel news, NASA archives and current news reports, government-compiled information about releases of toxic chemicals, Census Bureau information, corporate news, maps, weather, sports information . . . the options grow daily. In addition, on-line computer access can be used to send messages to other people, send text files to fax machines, make airline reservations and check flight status, exchange computer software and graphics, as a link between people with similar interests (who can "talk" together on the computer network or can leave information that may be of interest to others), play games (either against the computer or with others), pay bills and shop for everything from prescription drugs to cars.

There is, of course, a cost for all of this. The cost comes in many forms. It can include: a membership charge, per-minute charge (which can vary depending on the time of day), telephone line charge, surcharge for special databases and services, and charges for each information search. In the course of a month, data charges may amount to no more than the cost of a daily newspaper, or they can run into thousands of dollars.

Buying information from a database is no different from buying any other raw material. The issue is not cost. It is comparative cost. If the same information can be retrieved from a public library at minimal cost, then it makes sense to use the library. In addition to traditional reference sources, many libraries now have up-to-date information available on CD-ROMs (compact discs that store information). This allows libraries (with healthy budgets) to store and retrieve more current information than ever before. But what if the information you need is not available? Or what if getting that information is time-consuming? The time spent in research is an important cost of production that must be consid-

ered. And what if you would have to do extensive photocopying in the library? By using the computer, you already have the information available in workable form. Before using a database, it is important to consider the charges, the convenience and the time savings. Often, but not always, the cost of using a database will be money well spent.

There are two ways to contact databases—individually or through a vendor that serves as a gateway to many databases. Most databases are available through vendors. Some (particularly government databases) are available individually. Most writers probably will be able to get all of the information they want by subscribing to one large vendor or several small ones. Vendors' offerings change rapidly, so it's a good idea to get current information before subscribing.

When using a gateway vendor, you connect to a main directory and then tell the service where you want to go. Gateways are useful because they make hundreds of services available conveniently. Often the basic cost of the gateway service (whether a monthly charge, a per-minute charge or a combination of both) includes certain services and databases at no additional cost. To use other databases, additional fees may be charged on a per-minute or per-search basis.

SELECTED VENDORS

BRS: After Dark, Colleague, Search
BRS offers bibliographic citations, abstracts and (less frequently) full-text reports. It includes more than 150 databases dealing with business, medicine, science and technical information. BRS offers three products: Search (the most expensive, offers access to all databases), After Dark (easy to use, available nights and weekends, and less expensive than Search), and Colleague (a database for physicians).
BRS Information Technologies
Division of Maxwell Online
8000 Westpark Dr.
McLean, VA 22102

CompuServe
CompuServe, the largest vendor in the nation, opens the door to hundreds of special topic forums (where subscribers discuss special interests ranging from journalism to astronomy), an on-line shopping mall with more than 100 merchants, current stock market quotes, electronic mail and hundreds of databases (including full-text articles from the Associated Press wire service, newspapers and magazines). The IQuest database (a gateway within a gateway) opens the door to more than 900 additional databases.

CompuServe, Inc.
5000 Arlington Centre Blvd.
P.O. Box 20212
Columbus, OH 43220

DataTimes

DataTimes provides full texts of regional and international newspapers, Associated Press, Gannett News Service, press releases and business magazines. English translations of more than 100 daily Japanese-language newspapers also are available.

DataTimes
14000 Quail Springs Parkway
Suite 450
Oklahoma City, OK 73134

Dialog

Dialog offers access to about 400 databases. Business is covered extensively, but there are also substantial holdings in other areas, including law, medicine, science, technology and current events. It includes the full texts of more than 1,000 publications.

Dialog Information Service, Inc.
3460 Hillview Ave.
Palo Alto, CA 94304

Dow Jones News/Retrieval

News/Retrieval is one of the most complete business packages available. It combines the information of the Dow Jones news wires, the *Wall Street Journal*, *Barron's*, the Dow Jones stock quote retrieval system and specialized business publications and reports. In addition to company and industry data, analysis and news, there is world news, shopping, electronic mail and an on-line brokerage service.

Information Services Group
Dow Jones & Company, Inc.
P.O. Box 300
Princeton, NJ 08543

GEnie

GEnie, a product of General Electric Information Services, is a low-cost gateway that specializes in offering forums for people with similar interests. It also offers shopping, games, electronic mail and headline news. There is also a gateway to Dow Jones News/Retrieval.

GE Information Services
401 N. Washington St.
Rockville, MD 20850

Information America

Information America specializes in government and legal documents. It includes state and corporate limited-partnership records, state Uniform Commercial Code and lien filings and court records, among other offerings. You can also order state documents on-line.

Information America
600 West Peachtree St. NW
Atlanta, GA 30308

Mead Data Central: Lexis, Medis, Nexis

Mead Data Central offers three main services: Lexis (law), Medis (medicine) and Nexis (news). Nexis provides the full text of more than 700 newspapers, magazines, newsletters, government reports and newswires. Most of the files are available beginning with the early 1980s. Some go back as far as the late 1960s. The Lexis database covers federal and state law, court decisions and legal journals. It is cross-indexed with Nexis, so that news articles can be linked to legal issues. Medis includes medical journals, drug information, a cancer library and access to Medline, the National Library of Medicine's database.

Mead Data Central, Inc.
9393 Springboro Pike
P.O. Box 933
Dayton, OH 45401

NewsNet

NewsNet includes hundreds of U.S. and international business newsletters, worldwide wire services, business profiles, industry reports and stock market quotes.

NewsNet, Inc.
945 Haverford Rd.
Bryn Mawr, PA 19010

Prodigy

IBM and Sears teamed up to create this service, designed specifically for home use. Cost is low (in part because it carries commercial advertising). It includes some business information (stock market quotes, headline news, industry updates), but it specializes in lighter fare such as shopping, games, horoscopes and movie reviews. It also offers electronic mail and on-line banking, brokerage services and airline reservations.

Prodigy Services Company
Membership Services
445 Hamilton Ave.
White Plains, NY 10601

VU/TEXT

VU/TEXT, a subsidiary of Knight-Ridder, provides the full texts of dozens of daily newspapers and news services, including the *Chicago Tribune, Washington Post, Los Angeles Times, Philadelphia Inquirer* and Associated Press. It also offers extensive business and maritime information, as well as databases from Canada and Great Britain.

VU/TEXT Information Services Inc.
325 Chestnut St., Suite 1300
Philadelphia, PA 19106

Westlaw

Westlaw is the standard database of the legal profession. It is produced by West Publishing Co., the largest legal publisher. It includes the full text of federal and state court decisions, federal laws and regulations, information on special fields of law (such as tax, bankruptcy, antitrust, banking and international trade) and more than 400 legal periodicals.

West Publishing Co.
Customer Service
50 W. Kellogg Blvd.
P.O. Box 64779
St. Paul, MN 55164-9833

SELECTED DATABASES

Many databases are available from a variety of vendors. Their availability changes frequently. The best way to shop for computer information is to identify several vendors that carry the type of information in which you are interested, and then compare their offerings and their rates. The following databases are some of the thousands that are available.

- ABI/INFORM: indexes and abstracts of business articles.
- Academic American Encyclopedia: Grolier's on-line encyclopedia.
- American Banker: banking news and trends.
- AP News: AP wire report.
- BioBusiness: citations and abstracts on genetic engineering, pharmaceuticals, agriculture and food technology.
- Book Data: in-print and new book information from 600 U.S. and European publishers.
- Books in Print: in-print, out-of-print and new book information.
- Business Dateline: full-text business stories from regional business periodicals.
- Business Wire: full text of press releases on new products, legal action, financial information, personnel changes.
- Cendata: U.S. Bureau of Census on-line database.
- Computer Database: abstracts of articles from more than 100 computer-related publications.
- Daily Report for Executives: a daily summary of legal decisions affecting business from the Bureau of National Affairs.
- D&B—Dun's Financial Records: financial information on more than 750,000 public and private companies.
- Disclosure Online: information from Securities and Exchange Commission records for more than 12,000 companies.
- Infomat: summaries of more than 500 business newspapers and journals from around the world.
- Insider Trading Monitor: Securities and Exchange Commission information about trading by corporate insiders.
- Investext: full-text research reports on more than 11,000 large U.S. and foreign companies.
- M&A Filings: current information on mergers and acquisitions obtained from Security and Exchange Commission filings.
- Magazine Data Base Plus: full-text articles from consumer, business and science magazines.
- McGraw-Hill Publications On Line: complete text of articles published in more than 30 McGraw-Hill magazines and newsletters.
- Medline: the on-line database of the National Library of Medicine.
- Merck Index Online: information on agricultural products, pharmaceuticals, toxicology, environmental chemicals and related topics.
- Moody's Corporate News—U.S.: current information on publicly held companies.
- Moody's Corporate Profiles: descriptive and financial information about publicly traded companies.
- National Newspaper Index: combined index of the *New York Times, Wall Street Journal, Christian Science Monitor, Washington Post* and *Los Angeles Times.*
- Public Affairs Information Service (P.A.I.S.): bibliographic reference on public policy and public affairs.
- PR Newswire: daily press releases, primarily concerned with financial news but also including general interest news items.
- P.T.S.Prompt: abstracts and full text articles from business periodicals.
- Schoolmatch: information on U.S. public schools.
- Standard & Poor's Register—Biographical: one of many Standard & Poor's databases, this one provides information on more than 70,000 U.S. executives.
- Trademarkscan—Federal/State: information on all registered and pending trademarks.
- World Trade Statistics Database: government import/export information.

SUGGESTED REFERENCES:

Computer-Readable Databases, Kathleen Young Marcaccio, ed. Detroit: Gale Research, Inc., 6th edition, 1990.

Directory of Online Databases. New York: Cuadra/Elsevier, 1991.

Information Industry Directory, Bradley J. Morgan, editor. Detroit: Gale Research, Inc., 11th edition, 1991.

Online Access, 2271 N. Lincoln Ave., Chicago, IL 60614 (quarterly magazine).

PART SEVEN

TECHNICAL VOCABULARIES

COMPUTER TERMS

ADP: An abbreviation for Automatic Data Processing.

AI: An abbreviation for "artificial intelligence."

alphanumeric: Used to describe information composed of letters, symbols and numbers.

ALGOL: The general name of two algorithmic computer programming languages (ALGOL 60 and ALGOL 68) developed in the late 1950s and early 1960s and used primarily by mathematicians and scientists. ALGOL became the forerunner of such languages as Pascal.

algorithm: A sequence of precise instructions or procedures that leads to the logical solution of a problem.

analog computer: One of the two primary types of computers, an analog device translates the relationships between variables of a problem into comparable relationships between electrical quantities, such as current and voltage, and solves the original problem by solving the equivalent, or analog, that is set up in its circuitry. Modern, programmable computers are digital. [*See* digital computer]

array: A collection of data given one name and arranged so that each element can be located, examined and retrieved.

ASCII: An abbreviation for American Standard Code for Information Interchange, a uniform numerical code which represents characters as binary numbers for use in most digital computers.

assembler: A computer program that translates assembly language into machine, or binary, code so that it can be executed directly; sometimes used synonymously with the term *assembly language*. [*See* assembly language]

assembly language: Symbolically coded computer language in which each statement translates directly into a single machine-language statement. [*See* assembler, language level]

BASIC: An acronym for Beginners' All-Purpose Symbolic Instruction Code, an easily learned, interactive programming language; widely used with personal computers.

baud: A unit of measurement, expressed in bits per second, delineating the speed at which information is transferred from one computer to another. [*See* bit, byte]

binary: The two-digit numerical system used by most computers. It expresses all numbers as combinations of only two digits, 0 and 1. (The normal decimal system uses the digits 0 through 9.) Binary is uniquely suited to computers because each number can be represented by the "on" (1) and "off" (0) positions of electrical switches. The simplest calculator contains thousands of such switches in its microchips; computers contain millions.

bit: Shorthand for binary digit, the basic storage unit used by computers. [*See* binary]

bit-mapping: A method of graphic composition in which images are composed of arrays of tiny points, called pixels. [*See* pixels]

boot, reboot: The loading or reloading of basic operational instructions into a computer. A user who boots or reboots a computer starts or restarts the machine.

bps: Bits per second, an expression of data transmission rates between computers. [*See* baud]

bubble memory: *See* magnetic bubble memory

buffer: A controllable memory that temporarily stores data while the computer performs other functions.

bug: Jargon referring to any error or problem in a computer system.

byte: The amount of computer memory needed to store one alphabetic, numeric or symbolic character, usually 8 bits.

CAD: An acronym for computer-aided design, most commonly a reference to architectural or engineering design work in which a computer has been used to produce work which traditionally was executed by hand, such as drawings, layouts or site plans.

CAM: An acronym for computer-aided manufacturing, a reference to the use of computers in a manufacturing process.

cathode ray tube (CRT): Usually taken to mean a computer's display screen or monitor; sometimes called a VDT, video display terminal. The device itself is a vacuum tube, similar to a television screen, that focuses a stream of electrons on a fluorescent screen to produce lighted images.

CD-ROM: An abbreviation for Compact Disk-Read Only Memory, a compact disk with voluminous storage capacity, usually several hundred megabytes. A user can only retrieve data from a CD-ROM disk. Typical uses include storage of financial data, periodicals, indexes and encyclopedias.

central processing unit (CPU): The heart of a computer; the main circuitry that controls and executes all functions.

chip: The tiny bit of material, commonly silicon,

from which thousands of transistors and switches are formed into an integrated circuit that stores and processes information in a computer.

COBOL: An acronym for Common Business-Oriented Language, computer programming language, developed in 1959, specifically to process government and business data.

compiler: A computer program that translates sophisticated computer programming languages such as Pascal and FORTRAN into machine language, binary code, that a computer can use directly. [*See* binary]

core: The primary memory in a computer.

cps: An abbreviation for "characters per second."

CPU: *See* central processing unit

CRT: *See* cathode ray tube

cursor: A symbol, line or light on a computer's display screen that marks where a character will appear when the user starts typing.

database: A retrievable or usable collection of information compiled on computer storage media such as disks.

desktop publishing: The use of personal computers to design and print professional-quality publications.

digital computer: A computer that manipulates information in the form of discrete numbers. Most all-purpose, modern computers are digital. [*See* analog computers]

diskette: A thin, round, magnetic sheet on which data are stored for computer use. Diskettes used in personal computers are commonly referred to as "floppies" or "floppy disks," though many are encased in a shell of hard plastic. [*See* hard disk, optical disk]

disk drive: The mechanism that retrieves or writes information on a computer's sealed magnetic hard disk or on a floppy disk.

DOS: An acronym for "disk operating system," a widely used machine-language program installed in the read-only memory of many different computers as the firmware, or fixed software, enabling the central processing unit to load, store and manipulate data and programs on hard or floppy disks. The best-known DOS programs are MS-DOS and PC-DOS, both developed by Microsoft Inc. of Redmond, Washington. [*See* central processing unit, firmware, machine language]

dot matrix printer: A fast, inexpensive printer that uses patterns of dots to create printed characters.

dpi: Abbreviation for "dots per inch"; most commonly a reference to the resolution or clarity of a character printed on paper. A resolution of, for example, 250 dots per inch, indicates that the printing unit creates characters on a grid of black or white squares, each 1/250th of a square inch in area. The higher the number of dots, the greater the resolution of the printed character.

dumb terminal: A computer terminal that has no microprocessor and relies on its connection to a powerful mainframe computer for its ability to manipulate programs and data.

firmware: Machine-language programs stored in read-only memory form in computers so that the machines' central processing units can load, store and manipulate data and information.

floppy disk: *See* diskette

FORTRAN: An acronym for "formula translator," FORTRAN was the first major computer programming language, allowing mathematicians and scientists to describe their calculations by means of mathematical formulae. It was developed by IBM in 1954.

hard copy: A printout, on paper, of computer output.

hard disk: A sealed cartridge enclosing magnetic storage disks with high memory capacity. Hard disks may be completely enclosed within computers or added as separate, peripheral units. [*See* peripheral]

hardware: The physical parts of a computer, from terminals, integrated circuits and wiring to such peripheral units as printers and external drives.

input: Data fed into a computer for processing.

interpreter: A computer program that executes high-level language statements as quickly as it reads them. [*See* language (high-level)]

joystick: A computer device consisting of a handle that can be pointed in different directions that correspond to the movement of objects or a cursor on a computer's display screen.

K: Abbreviation for "kilobyte," a measurement unit indicating 1,024 bytes of computer storage capacity.

language level: A broad characterization of computer programming languages that reflects the extent to which a programmer must understand the inner workings of a computer. The more extensive an understanding of the computer that's required, the lower the classification.

language, high-level: Usually, languages that allow users to write computer programs without special knowledge of the computer itself, because each instruction directly corresponds to a set of machine-language instructions. Most often used in reference to such languages as BASIC, COBOL, FORTRAN and Pascal.

language, lower- or mid-level: Assembly language generally falls into this category because its use requires some knowledge and understanding of the computer's mechanical and operational composition. [*See* assembler, assembly language]

language, low-level: Most often a reference to pure machine language because the programming of it requires extensive knowledge of the computer's inner workings. [*See* machine language]

LAN: An acronym for "local area network," the linking of several computers in the same room or building, allowing them to share files or printers.

laptop: A compact, portable microcomputer.

laser printer: A high-quality printer that employs a laser beam to create an image and an electrostatic process to transfer the image to paper.

LCD/LED: LCD is an abbreviation for "liquid crystal display." LED is an abbreviation for "light-emitting diode." These are the two most common kinds of alphabetical and numerical displays on the screens of calculators, digital watches and laptop computers. The letters and numbers are formed from a basic pattern of seven small bars. In the LCD, the bars are made of liquid crystals that react to the computer-controlled flow of electrical current, creating specific numbers or characters. In LED units, the current flows to bars that serve as diodes, lighting up in display.

light pen: A computer input device that uses a light-sensitive stylus, wired to a computer terminal, to control images on a display screen.

machine language: Binary programming language in which each statement corresponds to a specific machine action.

magnetic bubble memory: A magnetic storage device that preserves data when a computer is turned off.

mainframe computer: A very large computer, usually occupying most of a large, air-conditioned room and capable of accommodating dozens or hundreds of users working simultaneously at "remote" terminals, computer workstations in other locations.

megabyte: Commonly referred to as "MB" or "meg," megabyte is a unit of storage capacity equal to 1,048,576 bytes. A single megabyte can store more than 1 million characters. [*See* bit, byte, kilobyte]

microcomputer: The smallest of the three general categories of computers, mainframe and minicomputers being larger. Microcomputers often are referred to as personal or desktop computers. The heart of a microcomputer's operation is a microprocessor, an integrated circuit imprinted on a single silicon chip, that decodes and executes all computer functions.

microprocessor: *See* microcomputer

minicomputer: An intermediate-size computer, typically one used by small or medium-size businesses or institutions.

modem: A contraction of "modulator/demodulator"; an electronic device that encodes computer data for transmission by telephone lines, microwaves, fiber optics or coaxial cable, allowing long-distance computer linkage.

mouse: A small, palm-size unit wired to a computer keyboard that allows a user to manipulate a cursor or symbol on a display screen and quickly execute a host of functions.

OCR: Abbreviation for "optical character reader" or "optical character recognition"; software-based system that allows printed pages to be "read" visually, character by character, and converts them to data that can be transmitted into a computer system, where the text can be edited. [*See* optical scanner]

optical disk: A high-density storage device with voluminous capacity, comparable to a CD-ROM. Since an optical disk stores information that is patterned on its surface by lasers, only a computer equipped with an optical disk drive can manipulate the data. [*See* CD-ROM, worm]

optical scanner: An electronic device that scans printed images and converts them to computer data. The scanned material, whether letters, numbers or pictures, are manipulated by the computer as graphics, unless the scanner has OCR capability. [*See* OCR]

parallel/serial data transmission: Most commonly, these are references to the manner in which printers are wired to computers. Parallel transmission involves the rapid and simultaneous transmission of several bits over different wires. Serial transmission, which is slower, involves the transmission of one bit at a time over a single wire.

Pascal: One of the most popular and widely used high-level programming languages; invented in 1961 and named after the French mathematician and philosopher, Blaise Pascal, inventor of the first successful mechanical calculator.

peripheral: Any auxiliary device, from keyboards and monitors to printers and magnetic storage devices, connected to a computer to allow additional functions or communication.

pixels: The tiny picture elements, actually a minute array of points, that make up an image on a computer's display screen.

RAM: *See* random access memory

random access memory (RAM): The main memory in most microcomputers that permits direct access to programs and data.

read-only memory (ROM): Computer memory containing firmware, operational data and programs, which can be activated but not altered by the computer user.

ROM: *See* read-only memory.

software: Programs and instructions for computers.

vaccine: A computer program that affords a measure

of protection against computer viruses. [*See* virus]

VDT: An abbreviation for "video display terminal." [*See* cathode ray tube]

virus: A self-replicating computer program designed to disrupt the operation of the computer. Vaccine programs are designed to detect and block computer viruses. [*See* vaccine]

worm: An acronym for "write once, read many"; used in reference to a kind of optical disk that allows the computer user to store information on the disk once, and then freely read, but not alter, the information.

BUSINESS TERMS

BANKING TERMS

accrued interest: Interest owed, but as yet unpaid.

adjustable-rate mortgage: A mortgage with interest rates that are periodically recalculated, usually at six-month or one-year intervals, against a money index or the lender's cost of funds. Such mortgages usually set a limit on the extent of change in the interest rate per year and over the life of the loan.

amortization: Dissolution or reduction of a debt by periodic payments covering interest and a portion of the principal.

appraisal: An estimate of property value, most commonly made for the purpose of using the property as collateral for a loan.

arbitrage: The purchase of currency, securities or commodities in one market and the nearly simultaneous resale of the same items in another market; an arbitrageur makes a profit on the price difference between the two markets.

assumable mortgage: A loan obligation allowing the buyer of property to take over payment of an existing mortgage.

automated teller machine (ATM): Computer terminal activated by a customer's magnetically encoded bank card or debit card in combination with a personal identification number. ATMs perform a host of routine transactions. [*See* bank card, debit card]

bank card: A general term applied to credit cards and debit cards. A credit card is tied to a preapproved line of credit. A debit card allows its holder convenient access to his own checking or savings account. [*See* debit card]

bank check: *See* cashier's check

bank draft: A check drawn by a bank against funds deposited to its account in another bank.

bank examiner: A representative of a federal or state bank supervisory authority who is empowered to review a bank's management, assets and compliance with state or federal regulations.

bank note: Technically, a bank note is any bank's written promise to pay a specified amount of money on demand, but the term comprises two broad categories:

(1) Non-interest-bearing Federal Reserve Notes issued by the Federal Reserve System's 12 member banks; the worth of the note is backed by the federal government. This is the common U.S. paper currency issued in face values ranging from $1 to $100. These are the only bank notes authorized by the government for general circulation. [*See* Federal Reserve Note, Federal Reserve System]

(2) Interest-bearing notes issued by banks, typically in denominations of $100,000 or more, and sold to institutional investors. These notes are the liabilities of the banks that issue them, that is, the notes are not secured either by deposit insurance or by any other company or institution.

bank run: A series of unexpected cash withdrawals due to a sudden decline in consumer confidence, such as fear of a bank closing.

bank statement: Generally taken as reference to the bank's periodic report on the status of a customer's checking account, showing all deposits recorded, checks paid, and fees paid for service in a specific time period, usually one month. The report includes the account balance and, generally, canceled checks.

bearer bond: A bond for which ownership is not registered or recorded by the issuer, thereby making the bond payable to anyone in possession of it. Bearer bonds are commonly called coupon bonds because the security includes detachable coupons, which the holder presents to the issuer for payment of interest semiannually. [*See* bond, municipal bond, registered bond, zero-coupon bond]

bond: An interest-bearing, usually negotiable, debt instrument signifying the promise of the issuer, generally a municipality or corporation, to pay the holder of the bond a specific amount of money on a specific date. Details of the bond agreement are contained in a written agreement called a bond indenture. Typically, the bond entitles its holder to semiannual payments of fixed-rate interest until the bond matures, at which time the holder is entitled to the bond's face value, or par value. Though there are many different kinds of bonds, each usually is one in a series issued for a specific purpose, often with the same security in common. [*See* bearer bond, municipal bond, registered bond, zero-coupon bond]

call report: The quarterly condition and income report that financial institutions are required to file with their primary supervisory agencies. State-chartered banks and trust companies file call reports with state banking agencies; state-chartered banks that are not members of the Federal Reserve System but are insured file with the Federal Deposit Insurance Corporation; state member banks file with Federal Reserve Banks, and national banks file call reports with the Office of the Comptroller of the Currency.

CAMEL rating: An acronym for "capital, asset, management, earnings and liquidity." CAMEL ratings are issued to banks by their supervisory agencies as indicators of the bank's soundness. The ratings, which are not disclosed to the public, rate the bank on a scale of 1 to 5, with 1 representing the soundest banks; a rating of 4 or 5 puts a bank on its supervisory agency's "watch list."

cashier's check: A check that a bank draws on itself, signed by a bank officer, authorizing payment of a specific amount of money.

certificate of deposit (CD): A time deposit account, typically at an interest rate that is fixed for the period of deposit, which may vary from 30 days to several years. A penalty normally is charged for early withdrawal.

certified check: A check stamped with the paying bank's certification that the check is drawn against account funds sufficient for coverage.

chattel mortgage: A loan that is secured by the borrower's pledge of personal property.

check: A bank draft, payable upon presentation, drawn on a checking account. [See draft]

check-kiting: An unlawful scheme that manipulates a check's clearance time between banks in order to establish, and draw from, a fictitious account balance.

clearings: The movement of checks from banks where they are deposited back to those on which they were written, so that funds may be routed accordingly. [See clearing house]

clearing house: Once deposited in a bank, checks are sent to a clearing house, a central collection site, for exchange with the banks against which the checks were drawn. Credits and debits are recorded, and funds are transferred accordingly.

closing: The meeting at which property is passed formally from one owner to another, usually within 30 to 60 days after the signing of a purchase agreement. The buyer, seller, banker or mortgage broker, and lawyers for all parties complete the transaction. Purchase price and all attendant fees are paid at the closing.

collateral: Specific property that a borrower pledges as security for repayment of a loan.

co-maker: A person who signs another borrower's promissory note in order to strengthen the borrower's security for the loan.

commercial paper: All short-term, negotiable instruments—in effect, promissory notes, issued by commercial firms and financial companies to finance current obligations.

compound interest: Interest that is added to the combination of principal and accrued interest.

construction mortgage: A short-term real estate loan to finance building costs; funds are released as progress payments at specific, prearranged intervals in construction. Typically, upon completion of the project, the loan is repaid with a long-term mortgage on the property.

conventional mortgage: A fixed or adjustable-rate loan, usually from a bank or savings and loan association, financing the purchase of real estate, and repayable in monthly installments over a period of 30 years or less. Typically, the mortgage is secured by the property itself, and not backed by the Federal Housing Administration or Veterans Administration.

cooperative bank: An organization that is owned by its members and makes loans and pays interest on pooled deposits. Credit unions and state-chartered savings associations are examples of cooperative banks.

coupon bond: See bearer bond

debit card: A bank card used to draw funds from a deposit account. There are two kinds of debit cards: bank-issued automated teller machine (ATM) debit cards, and national debit cards. Purchases made with national debit cards are charged directly to the card holder's checking or savings account.

demand deposit: Account funds that may be withdrawn at any time, without prior notice to the bank.

draft: A written payment order, actually a bill of exchange, directing a second party to pay a specified amount of money to a third party.

escrow: A written agreement placing money or property, in effect, with a second party for eventual delivery to a third party; money or property handled in this fashion is said to be "held in escrow." For example, a mortgagor (the borrower) often is required to pay the mortgagee (the lender), in addition to principal and interest on a mortgage loan, a monthly sum in anticipation of an annual property tax payment. The lender collects and deposits the additional sum in a separate bank account, called an escrow account, from which he is legally obligated to pay the borrower's tax bill when it is due.

escrow account: See escrow

Fannie Mae: The nickname of the Federal National Mortgage Association, which buys and sells mortgages on residential property.

Farmers Home Administration (FHA): A U.S. Department of Agriculture agency that administers a variety of loan programs for farmers.

FDIC: *See* Federal Deposit Insurance Corporation

Federal Deposit Insurance Corporation: The independent government agency responsible for insuring deposits of up to $100,000 in principal and interest at member commercial banks throughout the United States.

federal funds: In banking, federal funds are commercial-bank funds deposited at Federal Reserve Banks, including money that is in excess of the amount that the commercial bank is required by law to keep on hand to meet reserve requirements. Banks may lend federal money to each other overnight, to help the borrower meet its reserve requirements. [*See* federal funds rate, reserves]

federal funds rate: The interest rate that one commercial bank charges another for overnight use of federal funds to help the borrower bank meet its reserve requirements. Because the interest rate is set daily by market conditions, the federal funds rate is one of the most sensitive indicators of the direction of interest rates.

Federal Home Loan Mortgage Corporation: The publicly chartered corporation, nicknamed Freddie Mac, that buys residential mortgages from lending institutions, primarily savings and loans associations, and sells them as repackaged guaranteed securities on the open market.

Federal Housing Administration (FHA): An agency of the U.S. Department of Housing and Urban Development that administers loan, loan guarantee and loan insurance programs designed to make affordable housing more readily available.

Federal Reserve Bank: One of the 12 regional banks that make up the Federal Reserve System, providing central bank services and acting as depositories for member banks. Regional banks are located in New York, Boston, Cleveland, Philadelphia, St. Louis, Chicago, Atlanta, Richmond, Kansas City, Dallas, San Francisco and Minneapolis.

Federal Reserve Note: U.S. paper money; common, non-interest-bearing, circulating currency issued by the 12 U.S. Federal Reserve Banks in denominations ranging from $1 to $100. Federal Reserve Notes, the only government-authorized circulating bank notes, account for more than 99 percent of all U.S. paper money. Most of the remaining 1 percent comprises larger-denomination bills whose issuance was discontinued in 1969, bills with face values of $500, $1,000, $5,000, $10,000, and $100,000. The $100,000 bill, which bears a picture of President Woodrow Wilson, was authorized only for transactions between the Treasury Department and banks in the Federal Reserve System.

FHA: *See* Federal Housing Administration

float: Generally taken to mean the amount of money represented by debt instruments such as checks that have been written and deposited or written and mailed, but not yet credited.

FmHA: *See* Farmer's Home Administration

foreclosure: Legal action undertaken by a creditor to take possession of collateral securing a loan on which a debtor has defaulted.

401(k) plan: A savings plan allowing an employee to contribute as much as $7,000 a year in pretax salary to an investment pool managed by his employer. The funds are not taxable until they are withdrawn. Another term for 401 (k) plans is "salary reduction plans."

Freddie Mac: *See* Federal Home Loan Mortgage Corporation

Ginnie Mae: *See* Government National Mortgage Association

Government National Mortgage Association: An agency of the U.S. Department of Housing and Urban Development, nicknamed Ginnie Mae. The agency guarantees payments to investors in mortgage-backed securities; in a separate program, it provides low-interest loans used to finance low-income housing.

indenture: *See* bond

Individual Retirement Account (IRA): A personal retirement account allowing qualified investors to set aside a limited amount of tax-deferred annual income.

IRA: *See* Individual Retirement Account

junk bond: A bond issued by companies with below-investment-grade credit ratings but paying a high interest rate to investors willing to speculate.

Keogh plan: A pension account, specifically for employees of unincorporated businesses or self-employed individuals, allowing participants to set aside a limited amount of tax-deferred annual income.

kiting: *See* check-kiting

legal tender: Currency that is nationally recognized as lawful payment for debts. In the United States, legal tender is taken to mean all government-authorized circulating U.S. coins and paper money, primarily Federal Reserve Notes. [*See* Federal Reserve Notes]

letter of credit: A document that a commercial bank issues to a person or corporation signifying that the bank will cover payment of the customer's checks for a specified amount and period of time; most commonly used in international commerce.

maker: The party who signs a promissory note or writes a check or any other negotiable item, thereby assuming responsibility for payment.

maturity date: The calendar date on which the balance of any debt instrument is due and payable.

money market: An informal network of institutional investors and dealers who issue and trade short-term debt securities.

money order: A draft issued for a fee by post offices and financial institutions. The names of the payer and payee are imprinted on the money order.

mortgage: A legal instrument, a loan agreement, creating a lien upon property as security for payment of a specified debt.

mortgagee: The lender in a mortgage agreement.

mortgagor: The borrower in a mortgage agreement.

municipal bond: A formal debt security issued by a state or municipality to raise capital. [See bearer bond, bond, registered bond, zero-coupon bond]

negotiable order of withdrawal account: See NOW account

nonpar item: A check that a paying bank honors at less than its face, or par, value when the draft is presented for collection, deducting an exchange fee. Nearly all state-chartered banks treat checks as par items; banks that are members of the Federal Reserve system are required to do so. [See par item]

NOW account: NOW stands for "negotiable order of withdrawal." A checking account that pays interest.

origination fee: A lender's charge to a borrower covering the costs of issuing the loan.

overdraft: The amount by which a check exceeds the balance of the account against which it is drawn.

par item: A check that a paying bank honors at its face, or par, value. [See nonpar item]

par value: The face value of a financial instrument, such as a bond or promissory note, representing the sum that the borrower agrees to repay, not including interest.

passbook: Traditionally, the booklet issued by a bank to a savings account customer; the customer presents the passbook for recording of deposits, withdrawals and postings of interest; widely supplanted, given the growth of computerized bank systems, by statement savings accounts, in which transactions are recorded in a monthly statement that is mailed to a customer.

point: A one-time charge, equal to 1 percent of the mortgage principal; two points equals 2 percent of the principal, three points equals 3 percent, and so on. Points are assessed by the mortgagee (the lender) and paid at closing.

postdated check: A draft that is payable on a future date.

prepayment penalty: A fee paid by a mortgagor for paying off a mortgage before maturity; intended as a measure of compensation for the loss of future revenue by the mortgagee.

prime rate: The interest rate that banks charge to their biggest, most credit-worthy customers.

progress payments: See construction mortgage

promissory note: A written promise by the maker to pay a specific amount of money to the payee at a specific time.

registered bond: A bond for which the issuer records the owner's name, thereby restricting the security's negotiability. The endorsement of the registered-bond owner is required for transferal of ownership. [See bearer bond, bond]

reserves: Funds that banks set aside in anticipation of customers' withdrawals of demand and time deposits, as well as the legal reserves that banks are required to maintain in order to meet federal requirements.

reverse mortgage, reverse annuity mortgage: Typically, a mortgage that provides the mortgagor a monthly sum in return for the gradual accumulation of a debt to be paid at the end of the loan term; specifically designed for homeowners with high equity and little income.

right of rescission: A three-day cooling-off period in which a borrower may cancel a real estate secured loan.

salary reduction plan: See 401(k) plan

Sallie Mae: See Student Loan Marketing Association

S&Ls: See savings and loan institutions

savings and loan institutions: Also known as thrift institutions, thrifts or S&Ls, these federally or state chartered financial institutions use customer deposits to finance loans; by law, about 70 percent of an S&L's loan business must be in the form of home mortgages. The S&Ls' mandatory role as mortgage lenders is what distinguishes them among financial institutions.

securities: A general term referring to investments evidenced by documents signifying that the holder is an owner or creditor of a corporation or other property. Coupons, stock certificates, bonds and mortgages are examples.

service charge: A bank's charge to a customer for handling transactions in an account.

statement savings account: See passbook

Student Loan Marketing Association: A publicly traded corporation, commonly known as Sallie Mae, that uses the federal Guaranteed Student Loan Program and the Health Education Assistance Program to guarantee college education loans.

surety: A guarantee to repay a debt or fulfill a contractual obligation.

thrifts: See savings and loan associations

zero-coupon bond: A bond, literally with no coupons, that pays no periodic interest. The bond is sold at an appreciable discount of its face value, which is the sum the holder is paid when the bond matures. [*See* bearer bond, bond, municipal bond, registered bond]

SUGGESTED REFERENCES:

Dictionary of Banking Terms, Thomas P. Fitch. Hauppauge, N.Y.: Barron's Educational Services, 1990.
Dictionary of Finance and Investment Terms, John Downes and Jordan Goodman. Hauppauge, N.Y.: Barron's Educational Services, 3d. edition, 1991.
Encyclopedia of Banking and Finance, Glenn G. Munn and F. L. Garcia. Chicago: Bank Administration Institute of Chicago, 9th edition, 1991.
The Wall Street Journal Guide to Understanding Money & Markets. New York: Access Press, 1990.

INSURANCE TERMS

abandonment: An insured party's relinquishing of title to lost or damaged property in order to claim a total loss; title is given over to the insurer.

actual cash value: The value of property covered by insurance at the time a loss is incurred.

actuarial valuation: An actuary's assessment of the financial soundness of an investment instrument, most commonly a pension plan; funds must accumulate at a rate that will ensure benefits payments when they are due members of the plan.

adjustable life insurance: Coverage combining term and whole life insurance; size of premium, term of coverage and cash value vary. [*See* term insurance, whole life insurance]

all lines insurance: Life, health, property and liability insurance, all provided by a single policy.

automatic premium loan: A life insurance policy provision allowing the insurer to pay automatically any installment premium not paid by the end of the grace period; payment is made as a loan against the policy.

assigned risk: A risk for which coverage is legally required, despite its not being normally acceptable to insurers. Commonly used in reference to the extension of automobile liability insurance coverage, at a higher cost, to those who cannot otherwise obtain insurance (for example, motorists under the age of 21, or those with bad driving records).

binder: A preliminary agreement signifying insurance coverage until a formal policy can actually be written.

Blue Cross: An independent association providing members insurance protection against hospital care expenses.

Blue Shield: An independent association providing members protection against the costs of surgery, physicians' care and related expenses; works cooperatively with Blue Cross.

cash surrender value: The actual amount of money available to the insured upon surrender of a life insurance policy before its maturity date or before occurrence of the circumstance against which the policy holder is insured.

casualty insurance: Insurance that provides coverage against accidents and property damage; excludes life, fire and marine insurance.

coinsurance: An agreement by which two or more insurers share liability for a portion of losses; in health-care coverage, coinsurance provides that the insurer and the insured each share covered losses in a specified proportion.

commercial insurance: A general term that applies to most life and health insurance. Typically, the provider of commercial insurance may adjust the insured's rate as deemed necessary; the provider retains the option of whether to accept the insured's premium, thereby renewing coverage.

comprehensive health insurance: Coverage combining major and basic medical expense insurance protection in a single broad policy; commonly subject to payment of a deductible for some or all expenses. [*See* deductible]

constructive total loss: A determination that insured property is not worth repairing, though it has not been totally destroyed.

convertible term insurance: Term life insurance that can be converted to a permanent form of insurance without proof of insurability, if the change is made within a specified period of time.

decreasing term insurance: Term life insurance with a face value that gradually decreases while the premium remains constant.

deductible clause: A provision specifying an amount of money to be paid by the insured before the insurer makes any reimbursement for an insured loss. A $250 deductible on a homeowner's insurance policy, for example, would require the insured to pay the first $250 of a claim.

deferred annuity: An annuity providing for income payments to begin at some future date, such as in a specified number of years or at a specified age. Deferred annuities paid for with an annual premium are commonly known as retirement annuities. [*See* retirement annuities]

defined contribution plan: A tax-qualified retirement plan in which a contribution formula described in the plan determines permissible levels of contribution. Benefits that accrue to a participant vary with the amount of contributions and length of service under the plan.

disability benefit: A life insurance coverage provision stipulating that the insurer will waive payment of premiums during an insured's period of disability; also used in reference to benefits payable under disability income insurance coverage. [*See* disability income insurance]

disability income insurance: Health insurance providing periodic payments replacing income lost when the insured is unable to work due to sickness or injury.

endowment policy: A life insurance policy in which face and cash values are identical by the time the policy matures. The face value is payable upon the death of the insured or, if the insured is alive, upon maturity of the policy.

family income policy: Life insurance coverage providing the beneficiary with income payments for a specified time if the insured dies before the end of the coverage period, and the face amount of the policy at the end of the period.

group life insurance: Life insurance coverage extended to a group of people with a common interest or activity. One of the three major categories of life insurance; industrial and ordinary life are the others. Most group insurance is renewable term insurance that does not require proof of insurability.

Health Maintenance Organization (HMO): A health-care center offering a prepaid health care plan combining insurance and health-care services. HMOs stress preventative health care, early diagnosis and outpatient treatment.

homeowner's policy: A single insurance policy extending coverage to a homeowner for a broad variety of potential losses, from fire and theft to personal liability.

indemnity: Compensation for damages or losses.

industrial life insurance: Life insurance that is issued in small amounts, with premiums payable weekly or monthly to an agent who generally calls at the home of the policy holder. With ordinary life and group life insurance, one of three main categories of insurance.

legal reserve: The amount of money that an insurance company is required by law to have on hand each year to accommodate future claims and, as reflected in the increased age of the company's insureds, probable claims.

level premium: A life insurance premium that remains fixed for the duration of the contract.

limited policies: Health insurance policies that protect the insured only in the event of specific accidents or the occurrence of specific diseases; travel policies and so-called "dread-disease" policies are examples.

major medical expense insurance: Health insurance, often with large deductibles, providing coverage of most expenses up to a high limit.

medical expense insurance: Health insurance providing medical care coverage.

Medicaid: A national insurance program, established in 1965, providing hospitalization and medical care coverage for the poor, regardless of age; financed jointly by federal, state and local governments.

Medicare: A federal insurance program, established in 1966, providing hospitalization and medical care coverage for people age 65 and older.

Medigap: Nickname for Medicare Supplement Insurance, private health care coverage designed to fill in coverage gaps not met by Medicare.

mutual company: A life insurance company owned by its policy holders and managed by a board of directors chosen by them. Profits are returned to policy holders as dividends.

nonforfeiture option: A choice, extended to an insured person who discontinues premium payments, of whether to take the value of the policy as cash, extended term insurance, or reduced, paid-up insurance.

ordinary life insurance: One of the three chief categories of life insurance; group insurance and industrial insurance are the others. Ordinary life insurance, also referred to as whole life or straight life, includes whole life, endowment, universal, variable universal, and term life insurance. [*See* whole life insurance]

permanent life insurance: A general reference to any kind of life insurance, other than term insurance, that accrues cash value, and guarantees the insured coverage for as long as he pays the premium.

policy reserves: The amount of money an insurance company is required by law to hold in order to fulfill its policy obligations.

rated policy: Coverage issued at higher than normal premium rates; generally reflects either the hazardous occupation or impaired health of the insured.

renewable term insurance: Term insurance that is renewable at the end of the coverage term at the policy holder's option, without proof of insurability; the number of successive renewals is usually limited.

replacement-cost insurance: Insurance covering the cost of replacing damaged or stolen property.

term insurance: Generally the least expense kind of life insurance, providing a death benefit to beneficiaries for a stipulated period of time; typically, policies have no cash value, though they often are renewable or convertible to other kinds of insurance. [*See* convertible term insurance, renewable term insurance]

universal life insurance: Insurance affording permanent protection, flexible premiums and benefits, and cash value based on current interest rates and premiums paid.

waiver of premium: A provision whereby an insurer agrees to assume the insured's premium payments, thereby keeping his policy in full force; most common in cases of total and permanent disability.

whole life insurance: Insurance offering protection for the life of the insured at a specified premium, providing a fixed death benefit and increasing cash value that can be borrowed against.

SUGGESTED REFERENCES:

The Dictionary of Insurance, Lewis E. Davids. Lanham, Md.: Rowman & Littlefield Publishers, 1990.

The Insurance Almanac, edited by Donald E. Wolff. Englewood, N.J.: The Underwriter Printing and Publishing Co., 1990.

The Insurance Industry, An Information Sourcebook, Alan R. Weiner. Phoenix, Ariz.: Oryx Press, 1988.

REAL ESTATE AND ZONING TERMS

abandonment: This term is applied to the voluntary surrender of owned or leased property, without identification or designation of a successor as owner or tenant.

abatement: A reduction in amount. For example, a municipality that agrees to abate a company's taxes, agrees to reduce the debtor's burden.

abstract of title: A written history of proceedings, transactions or conditions that affect the title to a parcel of land.

abut: To touch or adjoin. One piece of property is said to abut another when part of their boundaries adjoin each other. The owners of such properties are said to be abutters.

accretion: The gradual addition of soil to land by natural processes. [*See* alluvium, avulsion]

adjacent: Nearby but not necessarily adjoining; generally used to describe the situation of properties in relation to each other.

adjoining: A reference to properties having boundaries in common; touching or contiguous.

administrator's deed: A deed conveying the property of someone who died without a will.

adverse possession: A means by which an individual legally acquires title to property by maintaining generally acknowledged, or "notorious," exclusive and continuous use of the property for a period of time prescribed by state law. Also referred to as "notorious possession."

alluvion: *See* alluvium

alluvium: Sand, clay or silt gradually deposited ashore by moving water. Soil that has accreted in this manner is considered part of the property on which it has been deposited; also referred to as "alluvion."

amortization: The use of periodic payments to retire debt.

appraisal: A formal opinion or estimate of property value.

appurtenance: An accessory that is physically outside a designated property but is considered a part of it; e.g., a right-of-way.

assessed valuation: Property value established for the purpose of taxation.

assessment: The tax or special payment due to a municipality or association.

assessment ratio: This term, expressed as a percentage, is used to differentiate between a property's assessed valuation and that portion on which a municipality actually computes its tax. If, for example, a city applies a 50 percent assessment ratio to its taxable property, then property with an assessed valuation of, say, $300,000 would be taxed as though its value were $150,000.

assumable mortgage: *See* section entitled Banking Terms on page 315

attachment: Legal seizure of property as a means of coercing payment of a debt.

attractive hazard (nuisance) doctrine: A legal principle requiring that property owners exercise reasonable care to protect the public from hazards posed by dangerous machines or amenities such as swimming pools.

avulsion: The sudden, natural transference of land from one person's property to another's without a formal change of ownership; used in reference to the loss of land due to changes in, for example, the course of a stream or river. [*See* accretion, alluvium]

balloon payment: A final loan payment—by prearrangement, one that is larger than any preceding installment—that usually pays off the loan balance.

betterment: An improvement to real estate, such as the addition of a building.

binder: A preliminary agreement securing the right of a buyer to purchase property according to specific terms within a specific period of time. A nominal sum of money usually accompanies the agreement as a sign of the buyer's good faith.

broker: A middleman or licensed agent who, for a commission, buys or sells property in behalf of others.

buffer zone: An area providing a physical transition between two properties used for contrasting, often conflicting, purposes; for example, a wooded area between a residential neighborhood and an industrial park.

certificate of occupancy: A document issued by a municipality to a builder or developer indicating that a building complies with local health, safety and building codes and therefore may be occupied.

chattel mortgage: *See* section entitled Banking Terms on page 315

closing: *See* section entitled Banking Terms on page 315

cloud on title: Term indicating the existence of a circumstance or an outstanding claim or encumbrance affecting the marketability of a property's title. [*See* encumbrance]

cluster housing: A method of subdivision in which separate housing units are situated in groups, leaving open spaces as common areas.

commission: Money paid for the services of a broker or real estate agent, usually a percentage of the property's sale price.

condemnation: A municipality's taking of private property for public use against the will of the property owner. In such cases, property owners are entitled by law to fair compensation. [*See* eminent domain]

condominium: An individually owned housing unit in a multiunit building wherein commonly used property such as stairs, sidewalks, swimming pools, etc. are owned jointly.

construction mortgage: *See* section entitled Banking Terms on page 315

contiguous: Touching. Properties with boundaries that touch each other at any point are said to be contiguous.

contour map: A topographical map with contour lines that indicate site elevations.

contract: A legally binding agreement between parties.

conversion: In real estate, most commonly used to describe a change in property use to a different use or form of ownership, such as the change of rental apartments to condominiums.

conventional mortgage: *See* section entitled Banking Terms on page 315

conveyance: The medium by which title to property is transferred from one party to another, most commonly a deed.

co-op: A type of apartment housing in which each tenant owns shares in a corporation that owns the apartment building.

covenant: A restriction written into a deed or mortgage to ensure compliance with an agreement concerning use or disposition of the property.

cul-de-sac: A form of subdivision in which houses are grouped around a closed turning area at the dead end of a street.

deed: A written document conveying title to real property.

deed restriction: A clause in a deed that specifically limits the use of property. [*See* covenant, encumbrance]

density: Intensity of land use; routinely used as a basis for zoning. Regulations, for example, may limit the number of multiunit dwellings that can be built per parcel of a specific size in a designated area.

depreciation: Decline in property value.

development rights: Literally, an owner's right to develop his property. In the past decade, many states and municipalities have purchased landowners' development rights as a way to ensure the preservation of open land, farmland or wooded areas.

easement: A right of one party to use the land or property of another, usually extended as a clause in a deed; for example, a right-of-way. [*See* deed restriction, encumbrance]

eminent domain: The right of a municipality or public utility to acquire property for public use.

encroachment: A land use, obstruction or building that intrudes upon or interferes with the use of another's property.

encumbrance: Any right to or interest in property that affects its value. [*See* covenant, deed restriction]

equity: The value of property after all mortgages and liens have been deducted. [*See* sweat equity]

escrow: *See* section entitled Banking Terms on page 315

escrow account: *See* section entitled Banking Terms on page 315

Fannie Mae: *See* section entitled Banking Terms on page 315

Federal Housing Administration: *See* section entitled Banking Terms on page 315

flood insurance: Insurance covering damage to property from natural flooding. Federally subsidized flood insurance is available to the owners of property situated in a flood plain, since such property usually is otherwise uninsurable. [*See* flood plain]

flood plain: A nearly flat land area along the course of a river or stream that is subject to flooding. The frequency of flooding is suggested by reference; the term "annual flood plain," for example, indicates a flood plain that is expected to flood once each year.

FmHA: *See* section entitled Banking Terms on page 315

Freddie Mac: *See* section entitled Banking Terms on page 315

Ginnie Mae: *See* section entitled Banking Terms on page 315

grandfather clause: A legal provision allowing a specific activity or land use to continue despite a new law or changes that would otherwise render the activity unlawful.

grantee: The buyer, the party to whom title to real property is conveyed.

grantor: The seller, the party who conveys title to real property to another.

HUD: The acronym of the U.S. Department of Housing and Urban Development, which administers numerous housing and community development programs.

indexing: An adjustment of interest rates on loans or mortgages according to a specified index or economic indicator.

interest: The charge a borrower pays to a lender for use of money.

joint tenancy: Property ownership by two or more people, each having separate and equal rights in any matter affecting disposition of the property, usually with the right of survivorship, meaning that in the event of one party's demise, ownership automatically accrues to a surviving owner.

lien: A legal claim by one party on the property of another as security for an unpaid debt. [*See* mechanic's lien]

littoral: A reference to land, or the right to use land, adjoining a body of water, as in littoral, or riparian, rights. [*See* riparian rights]

mechanic's lien: A legal claim by contractors, laborers or suppliers on the property of another as security for work or supplies.

metes and bounds: The boundaries of a piece of land, described with their terminal points and angles.

minimum lot restriction: The smallest, buildable lot size in a subdivision; usually specified by zoning regulations.

mortgage: *See* section entitled Banking Terms on page 315

mortgagee: *See* section entitled Banking Terms on page 315

mortgagor: *See* section entitled Banking Terms on page 315

nonconforming use: A property use that violates local zoning regulations but is held permissible because the use predates implementation of the regulations. In such cases, municipalities usually restrict expansion or substantial improvement of the property. [*See* planning commission, variance, zoning, zoning board]

nuisance: A use of property that is adjudged incompatible with the uses of neighboring property; for example, a junkyard in a residential neighborhood.

origination fee: *See* section entitled Banking Terms on page 315

percolation test: A test to determine a soil's capacity for drainage; required before installation of a septic system.

planned unit development: A form of development and zoning classification that allows greater flexibility in the design of subdivisions, making cluster housing possible, for example. [*See* cluster housing]

planning commission: An elected or appointed public body charged with overseeing growth and development of a municipality, usually in accordance with a master or general plan. Against such a backdrop, zoning becomes the specific means by which growth is controlled. [*See*, variance zoning, zoning board]

plat: A surveyor's map or chart of a lot, subdivision or community showing boundaries, buildings, improvements and easements.

point: *See* section entitled Banking Terms on page 315

prepayment penalty: *See* section entitled Banking Terms on page 315

quitclaim: A release of one's claim or title to property. [*See* quitclaim deed]

quitclaim deed: A deed that conveys any interest that the grantor may have; does not guarantee that the grantor, in fact, has an interest. For example, a buyer who receives a quitclaim deed for a piece of real estate receives only the rights that the seller had. There are no guarantees that the seller had a clear title, or that the buyer is getting a clear title.

raw land: Unimproved land, that is, without utilities, drainage, buildings, etc.

real property: Land and everything attached to it, extending into the sky above and to the center of the earth below.

Realtor: Though commonly used to describe anyone who sells real estate for a living, the term is applied accurately only to a person who is a member of a local real estate board that is affiliated with the National Association of Realtors. Realtor is a registered tradename and should be used in uppercase form.

redlining: Illegal refusal to write mortgages in neighborhoods identifiable by predominance of race, religion or ethnicity.

reverse mortgage, reverse annuity mortgage: *See* section entitled Banking Terms on page 315

right of survivorship: The right of a surviving joint owner to acquire the interest of a deceased joint owner. [*See* joint tenancy, tenancy by the entirety, tenancy in common]

riparian rights: A property owner's entitlement to use water on, under or adjacent to his land. The term is used mostly in the east. Comparable rights in the west are referred to as usufructory rights. Also sometimes referred to as littoral rights. [*See* usufructory rights]

setback: The distance from a boundary within which no building may be constructed.

special exception: *See* nonconforming use, planning commission, variance, zoning, zoning board

spot zoning: The rezoning of property for a use that is inconsistent or incompatible with that prescribed for surrounding properties. [*See* nonconforming use, planning commission, variance, zoning, zoning board]

steering: In real estate transactions, the unlawful, discriminatory act of influencing a client or prospective client to buy or sell property in a particular geographical location expressly for reasons of race, religion or ethnicity.

strip development: A form of commercial development that situates businesses side by side and, often, parallel to a thoroughfare to which each establishment has direct and specific access.

subdivision: A parcel of land divided into lots for development.

sweat equity: Value added to a property directly by the personal work of its owner.

tenancy by the entirety: Property ownership by husband and wife, each having an equal right of possession and survivorship, meaning that in the event of one party's demise, ownership automatically accrues to the surviving owner.

tenancy in common: Property ownership by two or more people, each having separate and equal rights in any matter affecting disposition of the property, but without the right of survivorship, meaning that in the event of one party's demise, ownership passes to a party or parties designated in the decedent's will.

title: Evidence, usually a certificate, certifying that the owner of property is the lawful possessor of it.

title company: A firm that examines title to real estate; may also insure title.

title search: An examination of public records to determine the ownership and encumbrances affecting real property.

tract house: A housing unit with a style and floor plan similar or identical to all others in the same development.

transfer tax: A fee paid to a municipality when title to property changes hands.

usufructory rights: Literally, a reference to one person's right to use the property of another. The term is most commonly used in reference to an owner's right to use water on, under or adjacent to his property. The water itself is considered publicly owned.

variance: A zoning authority's permission to use or alter property in a manner that is inconsistent with the property's zoning classification. Variances usu-

ally are granted when failure to do so would result in undue hardship for the property owner. Variances sometimes are referred to as "special exceptions," though some communities use both terms to identify distinctly different kinds of nonconforming land use. [*See* nonconforming use, planning commission, zoning]

warranty deed: A deed in which the seller guarantees conveyance of clear title to property and protection from any claims against it.

wetlands: Water-saturated lands, such as swamp or marsh; usually protected from development by local, state and federal environmental regulations.

zoning: The legal mechanism by which local governments regulate and control the use of privately owned property by designating acceptable uses, building and population densities and structural heights, all in accordance with the municipality's master, or general, plan for growth and development. [*See* planning commission, variance, zoning board]

Zoning Board, Zoning Board of Review: A quasi-judicial group of appointed or elected officials empowered to enforce a municipality's zoning ordinances [*See* planning commission, variance, zoning, zoning board of appeals]

Zoning Board of Appeals: A quasi-judicial group of appointed or elected officials empowered to hear appeals of rulings and decisions made by a municipality's zoning board or zoning board of review. [*See* planning commission, variance, zoning, zoning board]

SUGGESTED REFERENCES AND CONTACTS:

Dictionary of Real Estate Terms, Jack P. Friedman, Jack C. Harris and J. Bruce Lindeman. Hauppauge, N.Y.: Barron's Educational Services Inc., 1987.

The Real Estate Handbook, edited by Maury Seldin and James Boykin. Homewood, Ill.: Dow Jones-Irwin, 1990.

National Association of Realtors, Public Affairs Office, 777 14th St. NW, Washington, D.C. 20005-3271, (202) 383-1014.

National Association of Realtors, Public Relations Office, 430 N. Michigan Ave., Chicago, IL 60611-4084, (312) 329-8200.

The Nature Conservancy, 1815 North Lynn St., Arlington, VA 22209, (703) 841-5300, (800) 628-6860. With more than 600,000 members, this is the largest private organization in the United States devoted exclusively to the preservation of undeveloped land, especially sites that support endangered plants or animals. Since its founding in 1951, the Conservancy has acquired or placed in public trusts hundreds of thousands of acres. Conservancy chapters operate in every state. The organization has become the foremost authority on land preservation. Staff members routinely answer reporters' questions.

U.S. General Services Administration, 18th and F Streets NW, Washington, D.C. 20405, (202) 708-5082. The GSA controls all federally owned real estate, except park or forest lands or acreage for which the government has leased mineral or mining rights. Every year, the GSA submits its property inventories, which detail ownership, rentals and sales, to the House Committee on Government Operations and the Senate Appropriations Committee. The reports can be obtained from the U.S. General Services Administration and also are available from most government documents depository libraries. A free list of depository libraries is available from any of the country's Federal Information Centers.

National Register of Historic Places, National Park Service, U.S. Dept. of the Interior, 1100 L St. NW, Room 6111, Washington, D.C. 20005, (202) 343-9559. The staff of the National Register maintains the country's official list of historically important districts, sites, and buildings. Inclusion on the list can make designated properties eligible for tax credits, rehabilitation subsidies and, most commonly, protection from destruction or development. The process of evaluating a nominee for inclusion in the Register begins at the state government level, with the Historic Preservation Commission. The telephone numbers of state historic preservation commissions, or historical commissions, are listed in the government section of the telephone directory for each state capital.

MEDICAL TERMS

abortifacient: Anything used to cause an abortion. [*See* abortion]

abortion: The termination of a pregnancy before the fetus is viable. A spontaneous abortion (or miscarriage) may be caused by many reasons, including faulty embryonic development, abnormality of the placenta, trauma or endocrine imbalances. Abortions may also be induced, either for therapeutic or elective reasons. Abortions may be induced by the administration of drugs, by suction or by the injection of sterile hypertonic solutions (including saline solution) into the amniotic cavity, which causes the fetus to be expelled. Although induced abortion is legal in the United States, state laws regulating the practice differ. Some states define the fetus as viable at 20 weeks' gestation; others as late as 24 weeks.

abrasion: The scraping of the skin or a mucus membrane.

Achilles tendon: The thick strand of connective tissue that extends from the calf muscles to the heel bone. It enables the muscles to lift the heel while walking.

acquired immune deficiency syndrome: *See* AIDS

acupuncture: A technique, originated by the Chinese, which uses long, thin needles to treat certain disorders and to cause anesthesia. The needles are inserted into the skin at points that are believed to correspond neurologically to the region under treatment. The needles are twirled or are given a mild electric charge. It has been used as anesthesia for abdominal, thoracic and head and neck surgery.

agoraphobia: Literally meaning "fear of the marketplace," agoraphobia is a disorder that causes sufferers to feel overwhelming anxiety when in open areas (stores, crowds of people, when driving, etc.). Agoraphobics may suffer panic attacks, with rapid pulse, chest pain, difficulty breathing, dizziness, fear of dying and other symptoms. Treatment includes drugs, counseling, behavior modification and support groups.

AIDS (acquired immune deficiency syndrome): A deficiency in the immune system that is caused by the human immunodeficiency virus (HIV). The virus prevents the body from defending itself by disabling the T4 lymphocytes, allowing opportunistic infections, malignancies and neurological disease to develop. In the early stages, patients may experience transient viral symptoms. Often there are no early symptoms. The victim may remain asymptomatic for years, inadvertently infecting others with the virus. The HIV virus is carried in bodily fluids. It can be transmitted through heterosexual or homosexual contact, through shared needles used by drug users, through tainted blood or tissue donations, or from mother to child through the placenta. In the United States, it has been more prevalent among homosexuals than heterosexuals, but in other parts of the world (such as Haiti and the countries of Central Africa) it is commonly transmitted between heterosexuals. It has not been shown to be spread through casual contact, such as talking, coughing or hugging. AIDS patients are prone to numerous opportunistic infections and malignancies, including candidiasis (a fungal infection), pneumocystis carinii pneumonia and Kaposi's sarcoma. There is no cure, although treatment can ease symptoms and prolong life. Some patients live five years or more after diagnosis; about half die within 18 months. Zidovudine (often called AZT) is the drug most widely used to treat patients, but it is not a cure. [*See* section entitled AIDS on page 287; *See also* AZT in section entitled Common Prescription and Nonprescription Drugs on page 191]

allergen: A substance that causes an allergy. Common allergens include pollen, dust, fur, feathers, chemicals, insect venom, drugs, eggs, chocolate, milk, wheat and shellfish, although any substance can be an allergen. [*See* allergy]

allergy: An acquired sensitivity to a substance that does not adversely affect most people. An allergy may develop after only the second exposure to a substance, or after years of exposure. It is a disorder of the immune system, in which antibodies are produced to substances that are normally harmless. Reactions commonly affect the skin (eczema, contact dermatitis, hives) or the respiratory system (rhinitis, bronchial asthma). Severe allergic reactions can result in anaphylactic shock, which can cause death. [*See* anaphylactic shock]

alopecia: Baldness.

altitude sickness: A condition that occurs at high altitudes, where there is less oxygen in the air due to low atmospheric pressure. The oxygen deficiency can cause headaches, shortness of breath, impaired judgment, euphoria, lightheadedness, fainting or even death. Also called mountain sickness.

Alzheimer's disease: A chronic, progressive, organic mental disorder that causes loss of memory, impaired intellectual functioning, apathy, disorientation, and speech and gait disorders. Onset usually occurs between age 40 and 60. It affects more women than men.

amebic dysentery: A type of dysentery (inflammation of the mucous membrane of the intestinal tract) caused by infection with amoebae (one-celled animals found in soil and water). Many patients can have the infection (amebiasis) without symptoms. Others suffer diarrhea, weakness, nausea, vomiting and pain. The disease is transmitted through tainted food and drink.

amino acid: Any organic compound that is one of the building blocks out of which proteins are constructed. About 20 are used for human metabolism or growth. Some amino acids are produced by the human body; others must be supplied in food. The latter are called "essential." Protein foods that contain all of the essential amino acids are called complete proteins. Examples include milk, eggs and meat. Foods that contain some but not all of the essential amino acids are called incomplete proteins. Examples include vegetables and grains.

amniocentesis: Removal of a sample of fluid from the amniotic sac that surrounds the fetus to test for genetic and other abnormalities. A needle is inserted through the mother's abdomen to remove the fluid.

amyotrophic lateral sclerosis (ALS): A degenerative disease of unknown cause that affects the central nervous system, causing muscles to weaken and atrophy. It affects more men than women. Although there is no cure, some patients remain active for as many as 20 years after diagnosis. Also called Lou Gehrig's disease.

anaphylactic shock: A severe reaction to an allergen, often caused by drugs, foods or insect stings. Reaction to the allergen can be swift, beginning with difficulty in breathing and lowered blood pressure, and progressing to convulsions, unconsciousness and even death.

anemia: A condition in which blood is deficient in red blood cells, or in hemoglobin in the red blood cells, which decreases its ability to carry oxygen. Pallor, weakness, heart palpitations, dizziness and exhaustion can result. Anemia is a symptom of many diseases and nutritional deficiencies, and can be caused by severe blood loss.

anencephaly: Congenital absence of a brain and spinal cord.

aneurysm: A weakening in the wall of a blood vessel, usually an artery.

angina pectoris: Pain and a feeling of pressure on the chest caused by insufficient blood supply to the heart. Pain may spread to the left shoulder, left arm, back and jaw. It is treated with inhalation of amyl nitrate or use of nitroglycerin.

angiocardiogram: X-ray pictures taken of the heart and great blood vessels to determine their shape and condition. The vessel is injected with a radiopaque fluid, which shows up on the film.

anorexia: Loss of appetite.

anorexia nervosa: A psychological disorder that occurs most commonly in adolescent girls. It is characterized by an intense fear of becoming overweight, constant severe dietary restriction and an inaccurate body image. It can result in malnutrition, wasting, heart irregularities and death.

anthracosilicosis: A form of pneumonoconiosis caused by inhaling coal dust. [*See* pneumonoconiosis]

anthracosis: The accumulation of carbon in the lungs caused by inhaling smoke or coal dust. Also called black lung.

antibody: Any of a group of protein substances produced by the body in response to a foreign substance. Antibodies "recognize" and neutralize or destroy foreign substances, such as bacteria, toxins or foreign blood cells. This forms the basis for immunity. In certain disorders, called autoimmune diseases, the process is disturbed and the body produces antibodies against its own cells. [*See* autoimmune diseases]

anxiety attack: A psychological disturbance that results in an acute, intense feeling of anxiety. Episodes include panic and physical symptoms such as palpitations, shortness of breath, sweating and nausea.

aorta: The largest artery in the body, it carries oxygenated blood from the heart to the other major arteries.

Apgar score: An evaluation of an infant's physical condition one minute after birth (and sometimes again at five minutes after birth). Heart rate, respiration, muscle tone and response to stimuli and color are rated. Each factor is rated 0, 1 or 2. The system is named after its developer, Virginia Apgar, an American anesthesiologist (1909–74).

aphagia: Inability to swallow.

aphasia: Inability or impairment of the ability to communicate through speech, writing or signs. It is caused by a brain dysfunction, including stroke.

arrhythmia: An irregularity in the heartbeat caused by drugs, disease or physiology.

arsenic poisoning: A life-threatening condition caused by ingesting arsenic. Symptoms, which may occur within minutes or hours depending on how the poison is ingested, include a metallic taste and a garlic odor on the breath, burning gastrointestinal pain and vomiting. It can lead to convulsions, coma, paralysis and death.

arteriosclerosis: Thickening and loss of elasticity in the walls of the arteries.

arthritis: Inflammation of a joint, usually accompanied by pain and swelling. Causes include infections, metabolic disturbances and immunological disorders. Rheumatoid arthritis is a chronic systemic disease that is believed to result from a immunological defect that causes the body to attack its own tissue. There is no cure, but symptoms can be treated with drugs, surgery and physical therapy to provide some relief and to minimize the crippling effects of the disease. Onset usually occurs in middle age. In juvenile rheumatoid arthritis, onset occurs prior to age 16. Frequently there is total remission. Osteoarthritis, the most common form of arthritis, is common among the elderly although it can occur at earlier ages. It involves degeneration of a joint (particularly a weight-bearing joint), including degeneration of the cartilage and the formation of bone spurs.

arthroplasty: Surgery to reshape or reconstruct a diseased joint, or to replace it with an artificial joint.

artificial insemination: Mechanical introduction of sperm into the vagina, used to treat infertility.

asbestosis: A form of pneumonoconiosis caused by inhaling asbestos. [*See* pneumonoconiosis]

asphyxia: Lack of oxygen in the blood caused by the lungs' inability to deliver oxygen, due to either mechanical or chemical conditions. Causes include choking, inhalation of toxic gases or carbon monoxide, injuries, drowning, disease, cardiac deficiency, paralysis, electrocution and drugs.

aspiration pneumonia: Inflammation caused by inhaling foreign matter into the lungs.

asthma: Spasms and narrowing of the bronchial tubes, which causes shortness of breath and wheezing. Attacks may be brought on by infection, by allergy or by stress (including physical stress such as running).

atherosclerosis: A form of arteriosclerosis in which fatty deposits attach to the walls of arteries and impair blood flow.

atrial fibrillation: A disorder of the heart in which the contractions of the atria (the two upper chambers of the heart) are rapid and irregular, and are out of synchronism with the contractions of the ventricles (the two lower chambers).

autism: Psychological disorder in which attention is drawn inward. In infantile autism, the child becomes self-absorbed and unable to relate to others and engages in repetitive play and movements, often showing rage if interrupted.

autoimmune disease: Any disorder in which the immune system produces antibodies against the body's own tissues. Examples include rheumatoid arthritis, myasthenia gravis and scleroderma. [*See* antibody]

autonomic nervous system: The part of the nervous system that controls involuntary functions, such as glandular activity and heartbeat.

bariatrics: The branch of medicine dealing with weight control.

bedsore: *See* decubitus ulcer

Bell's palsy: A sudden paralysis of one side of the face, of unknown causes. The condition frequently subsides with no lasting effect.

bends: A painful condition that occurs when bubbles of nitrogren form in the blood and tissues because of a rapid reduction of pressure on the body. This often occurs when deep-sea divers ascend too rapidly. Patients are placed in a hyperbaric chamber, which re-creates the heaviest pressure to which they were exposed, and the pressure is gradually returned to normal, to give the body time to adapt normally to the change. Also called decompression sickness.

bipolar disorder: A psychological disorder in which the patient has both manic and depressive episodes. Also called manic-depressive disorder.

black lung disease: *See* anthracosis

blood count: A count of the red blood cells (erythrocytes) and white blood cells (leukocytes) and platelets in a cubic millimeter of whole blood. Also called a complete blood count or CBC. A blood sample is examined under a microscope to determine the number of cells. In a differential blood count, the number and subtypes of white blood cells are enumerated and the appearance of cells is evaluated.

blood groups: A method of classifying blood according to the presence or absence of certain proteins in the red blood cells. These proteins (antigens) are genetically determined and make some types of blood incompatible with others. Blood grouping is essential for transfusions. There are two types of grouping—the ABO grouping and the Rh factor. The groupings indicate which antigens are in the red blood cells. There are four ABO classifications: Type A, Type B, Type AB and Type O. The Rh factor (found originally in the Rhesus monkey) is present in about 85 percent of humans. People who have the factor are classified as Rh positive. Those who do not are Rh negative. This is important in pregnancy, when the mother's blood may be incompatible with the baby's, threatening its survival. It typically occurs when the infant is Rh-positive (having inherited the trait from its father) and the mother is Rh-negative.

blood pressure: A measurement of the force with which blood presses against the wall of a blood vessel, typically measured in an artery in the arm. The pressure is measured at two points: when the heart is contracting (systolic pressure) and when the heart is between contractions (diastolic pressure). For example, a blood pressure of 120/80 indicates a systolic pressure of 120 and a diastolic pressure of 80. In healthy young people, the systolic reading is typically 100 to 140; the diastolic reading is typically 60 to 90.

botulism: A rare, potentially fatal form of food poisoning caused by ingesting food containing botulinus toxins, produced by *Clostridium botulinum* bacteria. It usually arises from eating raw or improperly canned or processed food. (The toxins are destroyed at high temperatures.) It is most common in improperly processed meats and nonacid vegetables. It can cause cardiac and respiratory paralysis. An antitoxin should be administered as soon as the condition is suspected.

bradycardia: A slow heartbeat (under 60 beats per minute).

brain death: The total loss of all brain function. It is diagnosed by a lack of response to stimuli, absence of reflexes, absence of respiration, and an electroencephalogram that does not change in response to sound or pain stimuli. Life-support devices may keep the patient's body functioning, but death is inevitable. The legal definition of brain death varies from state to state. Typically, it must be confirmed by two electroencephalograms taken 12 to 14 hours apart.

brain stem: The central part of the brain that connects with the spinal cord; all of the brain except for the cerebrum and the cerebellum. It comprises the medulla oblongata, the pons and the midbrain.

bronchitis: An inflammation of the mucous membranes of the bronchial tubes (air passages to the lungs).

bulimia: Insatiable appetite. The term is usually used to indicate a psychological disorder in which the patient (typically an adolescent or young woman) engages in eating binges, followed by fasting or induced vomiting or diarrhea.

burns: Tissue injury that results from exposure to heat, sunlight, chemicals, electricity or radioactivity. They are classified according to their severity. First-degree burns are superficial, damaging only the outermost layer of the skin (the epidermis). They turn the skin red, but do not cause blisters. Second-degree burns extend to the next layer of the skin (the dermis), but do not destroy the skin's ability to regenerate. They cause blistering. Third-degree burns destroy the epidermis and dermis and extend into underlying tissue, destroying the ability to regenerate skin in the area. They leave an open wound.

bursitis: Inflammation of a bursa, a fluid-filled pouch that reduces friction between bones, tendons or ligaments. It commonly affects the shoulder, the elbow (tennis elbow) and the knee (housemaid's knee).

byssinosis: Pneumonoconiosis affecting cotton, flax and hemp workers; caused by inhaling dust containing bacteria, mold and fungi; also called brown lung. [*See* pneumonoconiosis]

cancer: An abnormal growth of cells, often forming a tumor. The cells tend to spread to other sites (metastasize), where they damage or destroy tissues or organs. There are two broad categories, carcinomas and sarcomas. Carcinomas begin in epithelial tissue (cells that cover the body, line cavities and passageways, and form the secreting parts of glands and ducts and parts of many sense organs). Sarcomas begin in connective tissue such as muscle and bone.

candida, candidiasis: Candida is a yeast-like fungus normally present in the mouth, the intestinal tract, the vagina and on the skin. Candidiasis is infection of the skin or mucous membranes by an overgrowth of candida, typically the *Candida albicans* variety. The infection may invade the blood stream.

carbon monoxide poisoning: Carbon monoxide (CO) is a colorless, odorless gas that is present in car exhaust and in fumes from gas heaters. It bonds with hemoglobin in the blood, preventing it from carrying oxygen to the tissues. Carbon monoxide poisoning symptoms can include headache, breathlessness, fatigue, dizziness, nausea and weakness. When concentration is sufficient, the skin becomes cherry red.

carcinogen: A substance that causes or increases the risk of cancer.

carcinoma: *See* cancer

cardiac arrest: Sudden stopping of the heart.

cardiac catheterization: A diagnostic procedure in which a tiny plastic tube is inserted into the heart through a blood vessel.

carpal tunnel syndrome: A painful wrist ailment that causes numbness, tingling, weakness and tenderness in the hand. It is caused when the carpal tunnel (a canal in the wrist that contains tendons and the median nerve) becomes inflamed and presses against the median nerve. It is associated with occupations that require repetitive hand movements, such as typing or playing the piano.

cataract: A clouding of the lens of the eye.

catatonia: A syndrome, usually associated with schizophrenia, in which the patient is unresponsive though conscious.

CAT scan: *See* computerized axial tomography

cerebellum: The part of the brain concerned with

coordination and control of voluntary muscular movement. Although it does not initiate movement, it controls posture, balance and coordination.

cerebral hemorrhage: The rupture of a blood vessel in the brain.

cerebral palsy: A term for a variety of conditions that include some lack of muscle control and result from damage to the brain during gestation, at birth or within the first three years. Symptoms range from mild to incapacitating.

cerebrovascular accident: *See* stroke

cerebrum: The largest part of the brain, it controls conscious activity. It is divided into right and left hemispheres, each of which is divided into lobes (frontal, parietal, occipital and temporal). The cerebrum is concerned with interpreting sensory impulses, initiating muscular activity, learning, reasoning, judgment, intelligence and emotions.

chicken pox: A highly contagious disease common among children caused by infection with a herpes virus. Symptoms include headache, fever and an itchy, bumpy rash that eventually scabs over. The incubation period is typically two to three weeks. After recovery, the herpes varicella-zoster virus remains dormant in nerve cells. It can reemerge in adults as herpes zoster, a painful nerve inflammation that results in blisters, commonly called "shingles."

Chinese restaurant syndrome: A reaction in individuals who are sensitive to monosodium glutamate, which is often used in Chinese cooking. Symptoms include headache, facial pressure, tingling, burning and chest pain.

chiropractic: A system of health care based on the belief that many physical ailments are caused by malalignment of the spinal column. Massage and manipulation are used in an attempt to improve alignment, and thereby improve nerve transmissions.

cholera: An acute, bacterial gastrointestinal infection causing severe vomiting and diarrhea. It can lead to dehydration and death. It is spread in food and water that has been contaminated by the feces of infected persons, making it a threat in areas of poor sanitation, such as underdeveloped nations and sites of natural disasters. It can be treated with antibiotics and replacement of lost fluids and nutrients. A vaccine is available.

cholesterol: Animal fat that is contained in foods (such as meat, eggs and dairy products) and is produced by the human body. Excess amounts can clog blood vessels and form gallstones.

chorionic villus sampling: A method of sampling the chorion (the outer layer of the embryonic sac) to determine whether the embryo is developing normally. A catheter is inserted into the cervix to obtain a sample. The procedure can be done early in pregnancy, before amniocentesis is possible.

chromosome: A thread-like structure in the nucleus of every cell that stores genetic information. It is composed of DNA (deoxyribonucleic acid) and protein. Human cells normally contain 23 pairs of chromosomes (one set of 23 is inherited from each parent). In females, the sex chromosomes match (both are X chromosomes). In males, they are different (one X and one Y chromosome). Genes, which carry the genetic information for specific traits, are located along each chromosome.

cirrhosis: A chronic liver condition in which healthy tissue is replaced by fibrous or fatty tissue, which interferes with blood flow and impairs function. Alcoholism is a major cause, but not the only cause.

cleft palate: A congenital defect in the roof of the mouth that forms a passageway between the mouth and the nasal cavities.

clubfoot: A congenital deformity of the foot which causes the bones to twist and the muscles and tendons to be stretched or shortened.

cold sore: A herpes simplex infection of the lips or face. Also called a "fever blister." [*See* herpes]

colic: Acute pain caused by abdominal spasms. In adults it may be caused by gall stones or kidney stones. In infants it can be caused by gas in the stomach or intestines, or by unknown causes.

colitis: An inflammation of the colon (the lower part of the large intestine) which can be episodic (e.g., irritable bowel syndrome) or chronic and progressive (including ulcerative colitis). Symptoms include pain, constipation or diarrhea, and bleeding.

colostomy: Surgical creation of an external opening to the colon, through which feces are excreted.

coma: A state of unconsciousness during which the patient cannot be roused by external stimuli. Some patients are aware of their surroundings and can hear what is being said, even though they do not respond to stimuli.

complete blood count (CBC): *See* blood count

computerized axial tomography (CAT): Using X-rays and a computer to produce a cross-sectional view of the body's soft tissue. It is frequently used in diagnostic brain studies. Also called computed tomography or CT.

congestive heart failure: A condition in which the heart fails to maintain adequate circulation, causing fluids to accumulate in the lungs, lower body and extremities. Symptoms include weakness and shortness of breath.

conjunctivitis: Inflammation of the conjunctiva (the

outer covering of the eye and the inner covering of the eyelid) caused by bacterial or viral infection, allergy or irritation. Also called pinkeye.

contraindication: Any symptom or condition indicating that a treatment that is suitable for other patients is not advisable in a particular patient because of the likelihood of unwanted effects.

contusion: A bruise.

convulsion: Sudden, involuntary muscle contractions, sometimes accompanied by loss of consciousness. Convulsions can be caused by many conditions, including epilepsy, meningitis, and poisoning. In children, convulsions frequently are caused by fever.

Cooley's anemia: *See* thalassemia

cornea: The transparent covering at the front of the eye.

coronary bypass: A shunt that allows blood to bypass an obstruction in an artery that supplies the heart muscle.

coronary thrombosis: Blockage of one of the arteries of the heart by a blood clot.

Coxsackie virus: A group of viruses responsible for a variety of illnesses, including meningitis and the common cold.

Crohn's disease: Chronic inflammation of the ileum (the lower portion of the small intestine). Also called ileitis, q.v.

cryosurgery: Application of extreme cold to destroy unwanted tissue. The surgery usually is performed with a probe through which liquid nitrogen circulates.

cyanide poisoning: A potentially fatal condition caused by inhaling or swallowing cyanide, which is present in the pits of certain fruits (such as apricots), in bitter-almond oil, in smoke and in industrial chemicals. Within a few seconds or minutes, the victim cries out and becomes unconscious. Death can come within five minutes.

cyanosis: A bluish or grayish skin color that results from a lack of oxygen in the blood.

cyst: A sac that contains fluid or solid material and is abnormal or caused by disease.

cystic fibrosis: An inherited disorder in which glands (particularly those of the pancreas, lungs and intestines) become overactive and secrete abnormally thick mucus. Chronic lung disease and inadequate food absorption frequently result. There is no cure, but effective treatment of symptoms can increase life span. Many patients now live to adulthood.

D and C: *See* dilatation and curettage

debridement: Removal of foreign material or dead or damaged tissue from a wound or burn.

decubitus ulcer: A skin sore often seen in elderly or immobilized patients. It is caused by prolonged pressure on one area, usually over a bony prominence such as a shoulder blade, buttocks or heel. Blood circulation to the area is restricted, which causes the tissue to die. If untreated, the sore can affect underlying tissue, causing deep ulcers that can become infected and become life-threatening. Prevention includes frequent turning of immobile patients, cushioning pressure points and the use of special mattresses. Also called bedsores or pressure sores.

defibrillation: Stopping fibrillation of the heart by the use of drugs or electrical stimulation. [*See* fibrillation]

delirium tremens: A complication of alcoholism that occurs when alcohol is withdrawn. Symptoms may include trembling, irritability, confusion, hallucinations, heartbeat irregularities and convulsions. It can cause death. It is also called the DTs.

deoxyribonucleic acid (DNA): A complex protein that is the basic component of genes. Its molecules are arranged in long chains that twine together and form a double helix. It carries a chemically coded message that determines heredity. [*See* gene]

depression: A mental state in which the sufferer feels dejected and shows a loss of interest in usually pleasurable pastimes. Symptoms include significant weight loss or gain, insomnia or excessive sleep, fatigue, feelings of worthlessness, inability to concentrate and recurrent thoughts of death or suicide. Situational (or reactive) depression is often self-limiting and follows a serious loss, such as a death in the family or the loss of a job. Endogenous depression, which is believed to have a biochemical basis, is not related to any immediate external event.

dermabrasion: The surgical process of removing scars, tattoos and fine wrinkles by removing the outer skin layer with sandpaper or wire brushes.

detoxification: Dealing with the physiologic effects of removing drugs from an addict (or alcohol from an alcoholic).

diabetes: Usually refers to diabetes mellitus, although the term also applies to diabetes insipidus, an uncommon metabolic disorder characterized by excessive thirst and urination. Diabetes mellitus is also characterized by excessive thirst and urination, but it also affects blood sugar levels, which can lead to serious complications. Diabetes mellitus is a common, chronic metabolic disorder caused by the partial or total lack of insulin production by the pancreas, or by the body's inability to use insulin effectively. (Insulin is a hormone that regulates how the body uses carbohydrates.) There are two types of diabetes mellitus: Type I or insulin-dependent diabetes (also called juvenile-onset diabetes), and Type II or non-insulin-dependent diabetes (also called adult-onset diabetes). Type I usually appears before age 25, is characterized by total or near total insulin deficiency and is often difficult to regulate. In Type II diabetes, which usually appears later in life, insulin production is low but not totally lacking. It can often be controlled by diet rather than by insulin injection.

dialysis: A process used to cleanse the blood when the kidneys are incapable of performing this function. In hemodialysis, the patient's blood is shunted through a mechanical filter, which removes impurities before returning the blood to the patient. In peritoneal dialysis, the blood is cleansed by flooding part of the abdominal cavity with warm, sterile chemical solutions. The solutions are added and drained through a permanent catheter.

dilatation and curettage: A minor surgical procedure in which the cervix is dilated and the lining of the uterus is scraped with a spoon-shaped instrument called a curette.

diphtheria: An acute, infectious bacterial disease that causes fever, severe sore throat and vomiting. It can be fatal to the very young, the very old and those who do not receive immediate treatment, including the administration of antitoxin and antibiotics. Childhood immunization confers immunity.

dissociative disorder: A psychological disorder in which childhood emotional trauma causes the patient to develop separate personality aspects, with confusion about identity. A patient may develop several personalities, of different ages, sexes and outlooks, who may or may not be aware of each other. Lapses of memory are common, as different personalities with different sets of memories come to the fore. Treatment includes psychotherapy, hypnosis and drugs.

diverticulitis: Inflammation of the diverticula (pouches in the wall of the colon).

DOA: Dead on arrival.

Down's syndrome: A congenital abnormality caused by the presence of an extra chromosome. It is characterized by moderate to severe retardation, a sloping forehead, oblique eyes, a short broad hand with only one crease in the palm, a flat nose, small stature, and bowel and heart abnormalities. The likelihood of the abnormality increases with the mother's age. It is also called Trisomy 21 (a reference to the extra chromosome that causes the syndrome). In the past it was called mongolism, a term which is no longer used.

dyskinesia: Any defect in the ability to make voluntary movements.

dyslexia: A term used to describe various reading and writing disabilities in people who can see and recognize letters.

dysphagia: Inability to swallow or difficulty in swallowing.

dysphasia: Speech impairment usually due to brain injury, tumor or stroke.

dysplasia: An abnormal change in the shape or size of cells.

echocardiography: The use of ultrasound to visualize the internal structure of the heart.

ectopic pregnancy: Implantation of the fertilized ovum outside the uterus, usually in one of the fallopian tubes.

edema: Swelling caused by an abnormal buildup of fluids in tissues or body cavities.

electrocardiogram: A record of the electrical impulses of the heart. Also known by its abbreviation, ECG, and by the abbreviation for the German spelling of the term, EKG.

electroconvulsive therapy: The use of electrical current to cause a brief convulsion. The electrical shock is applied to an anesthetized patient through electrodes placed on the forehead. It is used to treat severe depression. It is known by its abbreviation, ECT, and is sometimes called electroshock therapy or shock therapy.

electroencephalogram: A record of the electrical impulses of the brain used for diagnosis. It is known by its initials, EEG.

embolism: Blockage of a blood vessel by a blood clot, foreign object, tissue, or air or gas bubble. Also called a thromboembolism.

embryo: In human prenatal development, the stage from the second through the eighth week of gestation; the stage between the zygote and the fetus.

emphysema: A chronic lung disorder in which the small air sacks (alveoli) of the lungs become enlarged due to the breakdown of tissue between them. Lung function decreases and the patient becomes short of breath.

encephalitis: Inflammation of the brain, often due to viral infection. Equine encephalitis is transmitted from birds and wild animals to horses and man by mosquitoes.

endometriosis: A condition in which the lining of the uterus (the endometrium) grows outside of its normal location, causing pain during menstruation and coitus. It is a frequent cause of infertility, especially among childless women or those who have children late in life.

endorphin: Any of several chemicals produced in the brain that reduce pain and enhance pleasure.

endotracheal tube: A tube inserted into the nose or mouth, through the trachea, to maintain an open airway.

epilepsy: A neurological disorder caused by abnormal electrical discharges in the brain. It is characterized by recurrent convulsions, impaired consciousness and sensory phenomena. Epilepsy has a variety of causes, including brain tumor, trauma and disease. In many cases, however, no cause can be identified. Symptoms vary from nearly imperceptible alterations in consciousness in which patients become inactive for several seconds or minutes (petit mal seizures) to grand mal seizures, in which the patient loses consciousness, falls and undergoes muscle spasms.

erythrocytes: Red blood cells. They carry oxygen in the blood.

euthanasia: Deliberately causing death to relieve suffering.

Ewing's sarcoma: A malignant tumor that develops in bone marrow, usually in long bones or the pelvis.

farmer's lung: An allergic respiratory disorder caused by inhaling fungi from moldy hay.

fetal alcohol syndrome: Birth defects caused by the mother's alcohol consumption during pregnancy. Newborns may suffer from alcohol withdrawal symptoms. They may also suffer physical and mental impairments.

fetus: In human prenatal development, the stage between embryo and birth; the stage beginning at the start of the third month of gestation.

fibrillation: Rapid, incomplete, ineffective contractions of one or more of the chambers of the heart.

fibroid tumor: A benign tumor that contains fibrous tissue; also called a fibroma.

food poisoning: Any illness that results from ingesting tainted food. It includes eating poisonous foods (like mushrooms), foods that have been inadvertently poisoned (with insecticides or other chemicals) and foods that have been contaminated by bacteria or the toxins created by them. Bacteria commonly associated with food poisoning include *Clostridium botulinum*, *Salmonella*, and *Staphylococcus*. Symptoms vary according to the type of poisoning. They may include nausea, vomiting, diarrhea, paralysis, coma and death. [*See* botulism, salmonellosis]

forensic medicine: A branch of medicine that deals with legal issues, such as the cause of an unexplained or violent death.

fracture: A broken bone. Types include: blow-out (a fracture of the orbit of the eye, caused by a blow); compound (in which the skin is broken); greenstick (in which the bone splits and bends, but does not break completely); hairline (a minor fracture in which the bone remains in perfect alignment); simple or closed fracture (in which the skin is not broken); stress fracture (a fine hairline fracture, which may not be diagnosed for several weeks, often found in runners who run too much, too fast, on hard surfaces with improper shoes).

frostbite: Damage to skin and underlying tissues due to prolonged exposure to cold. Symptoms include tingling and redness, followed by paleness and numbness. The affected area should be rewarmed slowly to minimize tissue damage. Severe frostbite kills the tissue by stopping circulation. Dead tissue must be removed to prevent gangrenous infection. [*See* gangrene]

gangrene: Death of tissue, usually due to deficient blood supply. Painful in early stages, the body part then becomes cold and black and atrophies. The dead tissue (soft tissue and bone) must be removed to prevent the gangrene from spreading and to allow living tissue to heal. Infection is a constant threat.

gene: Part of a chromosome; the basic unit of heredity. Each gene, either individually or when combined with other genes, is responsible for an inherited characteristic. [*See* chromosome, deoxyribonucleic acid; *see also* section entitled Genetics on page 290]

German measles: *See* rubella

GI: Gastrointestinal

giardiasis: An intestinal infection caused by the *Giardia lamblia* protozoan, found in food and water contaminated by feces. Symptoms include diarrhea, nausea, vomiting and abdominal pain.

Gilles de la Tourette's syndrome: A rare neurological condition of unknown cause that begins in childhood and may continue for life. It is characterized by facial grimaces, tics, and involuntary grunts, shouts and upper-body movements. Some patients suffer from coprolalia, involuntary use of obscene or offensive language. It can often be controlled by drugs.

glaucoma: Disease in which increased pressure within the eye causes damage to the optic nerve. The disease can be controlled but not cured.

goiter: Enlargement of the thyroid gland. It may be caused by lack of iodine in the diet, by a tumor or by overactivity or underactivity of the thyroid gland.

gonorrhea: A common sexually transmitted bacterial disease. Symptoms include painful urination, inflammation and a yellow discharge from the penis or vagina. It can be cured by antibiotics. If untreated, it can damage the reproductive organs, the liver and the joints and can cause blindness.

gout: A painful joint inflammation caused by a genetic defect in uric acid metabolism, which causes crystals to accumulate in the joints. It commonly affects the big toe, although it can affect other joints as well. It can be controlled through diet and drug therapy.

grand mal: *See* epilepsy

Graves' disease: A condition caused by overactivity of the thyroid gland. It can be caused by lack of iodine in the diet or by unknown causes believed to be related to the immune system. The disorder causes enlarged thyroid (goiter), bulging eyeballs, abnormally rapid heartbeat, hand tremors, increased metabolism, vomiting, diarrhea, perspiration, irritability and anemia. Treatment includes drugs and/or removal of part or all of the thyroid gland, either surgically or by radiation. Also called exophthalmic goiter.

Guillain-Barré syndrome: A nerve inflammation causing pain and weakness, sometimes with paralysis of the extremities. It occurs after recovery from an infectious disease, or as a rare complication of immunization with influenza vaccine. Its cause is unknown. In most cases, recovery is complete.

hay fever: An allergic reaction to pollen from trees (in the spring), grasses (in the summer), weeds (in the fall) or other airborne allergens, such as animal dander and house dust mites. Symptoms include sneezing, running nose, nasal congestion and headache. [*See* allergen, allergy]

Health Maintenance Organization (HMO): A healthcare system in which members pay a fee that entitles them to comprehensive care, usually including both in-hospital and out-patient services. The HMO usually has member physicians and facilities, which patients must use. The HMO may also contract with other care providers for certain services.

heart-lung machine: A device used to maintain heart and lung functions during open-heart surgery so that the heart can be repaired. The machine pumps the blood, oxygenates it and removes carbon dioxide.

heart murmur: An abnormal heart sound. Some heart murmurs are harmless. Others indicate valve problems, constrictions or holes between heart chambers.

heat exhaustion: Weakness, dizziness, nausea and headache caused by overexposure to heat and depletion of body fluids and electrolytes (essential body chemicals). Skin is cold and clammy. Also called heat prostration. Treatment is rest, fluids, and removal from heat. [*See* heatstroke]

heatstroke: A severe, sometimes fatal, reaction to exposure to intense heat. Symptoms include high fever, rapid heartbeat, lack of sweating, headache, numbness, tingling and confusion. It may lead to delirium, convulsions and coma. Treatment includes cooling the patient, replacement of fluids and electrolytes (essential body chemicals) and sedation. Also called sunstroke. [*See* heat exhaustion]

Heimlich maneuver: An emergency technique developed by Dr. H.J. Heimlich to clear the windpipe (trachea) of someone who is choking. The choking victim is grasped from behind, with one hand forming a fist between the victim's navel and rib cage. The rescuer's free hand clasps the fist and thrusts upward quickly until the obstruction is forced out of the trachea.

hematoma: A mass of blood (usually clotted) in an organ, tissue or space.

hemodialysis: *See* dialysis

hemoglobin: An iron-containing pigment in red blood cells that carries oxygen from the lungs to body tissues.

hemophilia: A hereditary disease in which the ability of the blood to clot is disturbed. It is a genetically transmitted condition that occurs almost exclusively among males. Clotting factors can be removed from normal blood, concentrated and injected into hemophiliacs to prevent life-threatening bleeding. Contamination of these blood products has caused some hemophiliacs to be infected by the AIDS virus. [*See* AIDS]

hepatitis: Any liver inflammation; caused by viral or bacterial infections, chemicals, drugs, alcohol and parasites. Symptoms include loss of appetite, jaundice, headache, fever, pain and diarrhea. Viral hepatitis is caused by several viruses and can range from very mild to deadly. Hepatitis-A (caused by the type A virus) is usually mild. Hepatitis-B (caused by the type B virus) can be mild, but can also cause death because of extensive liver damage. Some people with hepatitis-B develop a chronic form of the disease. They can transmit the disease through blood and other body fluids. Blood donations must be tested for the presence of the hepatitis-B antigen. Intravenous drug users are at high risk. A vaccine is available for hepatitis-B.

herniated disc: A rupture of a disc between vertebrae of the spine. When the disc is displaced, there is no cushion between the vertebrae, which causes pain due to pressure on the spinal nerves. Also called a slipped disc.

herpes: One of a number of diseases caused by any of a group of herpes viruses. Herpes simplex is the cold sore. Herpes zoster is a nerve inflammation that results in a painful rash that follows the route of the nerve. It is caused by the same virus (herpes varicella zoster) that causes chicken pox in children. The virus can remain dormant from childhood and emerge years later. It is also known as shingles. Herpes genitalis is caused by a variant of the herpes simplex virus and is usually transmitted sexually. It causes recurrent, often painful, lesions on the skin and mucous membranes of the genital area. It is also called genital herpes. There is no cure. [*See* chicken pox, cold sore]

hiatal hernia: A common condition in which part of the stomach protrudes through the diaphragm, causing heartburn. Also called hiatus hernia.

high-density lipoprotein (HDL): A protein that is bound to fat and carries it in the blood (i.e., a lipoprotein). According to some studies, high HDL levels in the blood are associated with lower risk of coronary and vascular disorders. High-density lipoproteins contain more protein and less fat than the low-density lipoproteins.

HIV: *See* AIDS

Hodgkin's disease: A malignant disorder of the lymphatic system that causes enlarged lymph nodes, spleen and liver. It causes fever, chills, weight loss, night sweats and anemia. It occurs more often in males than females, and usually occurs between the ages of 15 and 35. Radiation and/or chemotherapy can bring about cure or long-term remission in many cases.

holistic medicine: A medical-care system built upon the belief that all areas of a person's life (physical, psychological, emotional, social, spiritual and economic) affect health and must be considered for effective treatment.

homeopathy: A medical-care system established in the late 18th century and still practiced today that attempts to cure on the theory that "like cures like." Drugs or other substances that would produce symptoms in healthy persons are used, in small amounts, to treat patients who already have those symptoms. For example, a feverish patient is given a small dose of a drug that raises body temperature.

Huntington's chorea: An inherited neurological disorder characterized by rapid involuntary movements (chorea) and mental deterioration. It usually begins between 30 and 50 years of age, growing progressively worse until the patient's death. Children have a 50 percent chance of inheriting the disease. There is no cure.

hypertension: High blood pressure. [*See* blood pressure]

hyperthermia: Extremely high body temperature.

hyperthyroidism: Overactivity of the thyroid gland, which causes an increased metabolic rate, goiter, weight loss and increased heart rate. [*See* goiter, Graves' disease]

hyperventilation: Air intake that is greater than needed due to breathing that is too frequent or too deep. It is associated with several breathing disorders (including asthma and emphysema) and with exercise, pain or anxiety. Symptoms include faintness, tingling of fingers and toes, and fainting. Breathing into a paper bag increases the level of carbon dioxide in the blood, thereby lowering the elevated level of oxygen and eliminating the symptoms.

hypotension: Low blood pressure. [*See* blood pressure]

hypothermia: Abnormally low body temperature (below 95° F.). Occurs most often in the elderly and the very young when exposed to severe cold weather. Sometimes induced during surgery to slow the metabolic rate and lower the need for oxygen.

hypothyroidism: Underactivity of the thyroid gland. Symptoms include obesity, dry skin and hair, low blood pressure and fatigue.

ICU: Intensive care unit.

ileitis: Inflammation of the ileum (the lower portion of the small intestine). Symptoms include pain and alternating diarrhea and constipation. The lining of the ileum can ulcerate and adhesions can form. Also called Crohn's disease. [*See* ileostomy]

ileostomy: Surgical creation of an external opening to the ileum (lower portion of the small intestine) through which feces are excreted. Used to treat inflammatory bowel diseases and cancer.

impetigo: A contagious bacterial skin disease that causes fluid-filled blisters, which crust. It is common in children.

infectious mononucleosis: An acute infection caused by the Epstein-Barr virus; it is not highly contagious. Symptoms include enlarged lymph nodes, fever, sore throat and fatigue. The spleen and liver often are enlarged. Rest is advised until the illness abates. Also called glandular fever or the kissing disease.

influenza: A contagious respiratory infection that begins abruptly. Symptoms include fever, chills, exhaustion, headache, muscle pain, cough and sore throat. Nausea, vomiting, diarrhea and lack of appetite are sometimes present. There are many strains of flu virus. Vaccination (or previous exposure) to one strain of virus does not offer protection against another variety. The disease usually subsides in about a week, but complications can be life-threatening, particularly to the very young, the very old and the infirm.

in situ: Localized.

insulin: A hormone secreted by the islets of Langerhans in the pancreas. It is essential for the metabolism of blood sugar (glucose). [*See* diabetes]

interferon: Protein formed when cells are exposed to a virus. It slows down the ability of the virus to multiply and spread. It is used in the treatment of AIDS and some cancers.

intubation: The process of inserting a tube into an opening, especially into the trachea (windpipe) to aid respiration.

in vitro: Literally, in glass (as in a test tube or laboratory dish). In vitro fertilization is the combining of an ovum and sperm outside the human body.

in vivo: In the living organism.

IV: Intravenous.

jaundice: A condition with yellowing of the skin and the whites of the eyes caused by excessive bile pigment (bilirubin) in the blood. It is a symptom of liver disease, obstruction of bile passageways and a type of anemia.

Kaposi's sarcoma: A malignant growth characterized by soft purplish or brownish spots on the skin. It eventually spreads to the lymph nodes and internal organs. It is often associated with Acquired Immune Deficiency Syndrome.

laceration: A wound with a jagged edge.

laparoscopy: Examination of the abdominal cavity with a lighted optical tube (laparoscope). The laparoscope is inserted through a small incision.

lead poisoning: A toxic condition caused by eating or inhaling materials containing lead. Acute lead poisoning can cause loss of appetite, vomiting, diarrhea, headache, paralysis, convulsions and coma. Chronic lead poisoning occurs when small amounts of lead are ingested over time (as when children chew on surfaces containing lead-based paint). The effects are cumulative and can include anemia, nerve damage, gastrointestinal disturbances and brain damage.

Legionnaires' disease: An acute, sometimes fatal, pneumonia with cough, chest pain, muscle pain, fever, chills and, sometimes, gastrointestinal symptoms. The disease can cause failure of major organs, including the heart. It can be treated with antibiotics. It is caused by *Legionella pneumophilia*, a bacterium that lives in moist places, such as humidified ventilation systems. The first outbreak was identified at an American Legion convention in Philadelphia in 1976, when 29 people who had stayed at the conference hotel died of the disease.

leprosy: A chronic, progressive bacterial disease of the skin and peripheral nervous system (sensory and motor nerves outside the brain and spinal cord). It can cause loss of feeling, weakness, paralysis and skin damage and raises a risk of secondary infections. Although patients previously were separated from society, this is not necessary with proper drug therapy, which eliminates the threat of contagion. Also called Hansen's disease.

leukemia: A chronic or acute form of cancer in which there are an abnormally high number of white blood cells. There are many types of leukemia. The prognosis for some forms is very good, due to chemotherapy and bone marrow transplants.

leukocyte: White blood cells. They fight infection.

low-density lipoproteins (LDL): A protein that is bound to fat and carries it in the blood (i.e., a lipoprotein). Low-density lipoproteins contain more fat and less protein than the high-density lipoproteins. [*See* high-density lipoproteins]

lupus: *See* systemic lupus erythematosus

Lyme arthritis: An inflammatory disease caused by bacteria and transmitted by the common deer tick. First identified in children in Lyme, Conn., it is now found in nearly every state. Within three to 30 days of being bitten by an infected tick, a patient often develops a red, circular rash with a light-colored center. There may also be flu-like symptoms, including fever, headache, malaise, joint aches and chills, which may last for several weeks if untreated. Neurological difficulties may follow—including meningitis, encephalitis, and partial paralysis. The heart can also be damaged. Months or years later, the patient may develop joint pain and swelling similar to rheumatoid arthritis. Antibiotics are effective when given in the initial stages of the disease. Early diagnosis can be difficult, however, because symptoms mimic other diseases and blood tests are not always conclusive in the disease's early stage. Also called Lyme disease.

lymph: Fluid, formed throughout the body, that bathes body tissues; it circulates through the lymphatic system, eventually entering the bloodstream. It is similar to blood, except that there are no red blood cells and the protein content is lower.

lymph node: Any of the small, bean-shaped structures that filter lymph, preventing particulate matter, especially bacteria, from entering the bloodstream. The nodes produce lymphocytes and monocytes, specialized cells that help the body fight disease. They may become enlarged during illness (a condition known as "swollen glands"). Also known as lymph glands.

lymphoma: A general term for several cancers that affect the lymphatic system. Examples include Hodgkin's disease and lymphatic leukemia. [*See* Hodgkin's disease]

malaria: An infectious disease, frequently found in tropical and subtropical regions, caused by several varieties of the plasmodium protozoan. It is transmitted from human to human by the anopheles mosquito and through blood transfusions and infected hypodermic needles. It causes headache, anemia, muscle aches and recurring periods of chills, followed by fever and sweats. Some varieties can cause meningitis, coma and death. Treatment includes chloroquinine and other drugs.

Travelers to infected regions should take antimalarial drugs before, during and after the trip.

malathion poisoning: Vomiting, nausea, abdominal cramps, weakness and breathing difficulties caused by inhaling or swallowing the insecticide malathion. In 1990, California approved the aerial spraying of malathion in populated areas to prevent the Mediterranean (Medfly) and Mexican fruit fly from ruining economically important crops. A state-sponsored study, undertaken because of citizens' concerns about long-term effects, concluded that the concentration used did not pose a substantial health risk.

Marfan's syndrome: An inherited condition that affects the connective tissue, bones, muscles and ligaments. It causes elongated limbs, fingers and head and can cause serious heart problems.

measles: A highly contagious viral disease that was once common among children but is now less common because of immunization. It causes high fever, sore throat, runny nose, cough, sensitivity to light, conjunctivitis, itching and a pinkish-orange rash. Complications can be life-threatening. They include encephalitis, pneumonia, serious ear infections and meningitis. Also known as rubeola.

Medicaid: A government program that provides medical care to the poor, using state and federal funds.

Medicare: Federally administered health insurance for those aged 65 and over. Part A, Hospital Insurance, covers some of the cost of hospitalization, inpatient services and home care. Part B, Supplementary Medical Insurance, is available for a monthly fee. It covers some of the cost of physician's fees, X-rays, laboratory tests and in-home medical equipment.

melanoma: The most serious form of skin cancer, it affects the pigment-forming cells of the skin (melanocytes). Tumors appear as black or brown moles or skin blemishes. New moles and changes in moles should be evaluated. When treated early, cure rate is high. Cure is less likely if the cancer spreads.

Ménière's disease: An inner-ear disease that causes recurrent dizzy spells, hearing loss, tinnitus (ringing in the ears), nausea and vomiting.

meningitis: An inflammation of the meninges (the membranes that enclose the brain and spinal cord) characterized by high fever, vomiting and headache. It can lead to convulsions and coma. Causes include bacterial, viral and fungal infections.

mental retardation: Below-average intellectual ability. There are wide variations in the intellectual abilities of the retarded, just as there are wide variations in the abilities of those who are not retarded. Classifications include: mildly retarded

(IQ 55–69), moderately retarded (IQ 40–54), severely retarded (IQ 25–39) and profoundly retarded (IQ 0–24). Mildly retarded people are considered educable; moderately retarded people are considered trainable.

mercury poisoning: A toxic condition caused by inhaling or swallowing mercury or mercury-containing products such as fungicides. Industrial contamination of water can taint fish with mercury. Acute poisoning causes vomiting, diarrhea and kidney disturbances that can be fatal. Chronic poisoning causes slurred speech, staggering, and teeth and gum problems.

metastasize: *See* cancer

microsurgery: Surgery performed using microscopes and miniaturized instruments to perform procedures on small structures not suited to conventional surgical techniques. Used on the eye, the brain, the spinal cord and to reattach small nerves and blood vessels in amputated fingers, toes and limbs.

migraine: Severe, recurring headaches of unknown cause that may be triggered by many factors, including allergy, menstruation and stress. The pain results from dilation of blood vessels surrounding the brain. Attacks may last for hours or days. They often include visual disturbances (such as flashing lights), dizziness, vomiting, and severe pain (usually on one side of the head).

mitral valve: A valve that permits blood to flow from the left atrium to the left ventricle of the heart and prevents backflow. Mitral valve prolapse is a common condition in which the valve does not close completely, allowing some backflow.

monoclonal antibody: An antibody that is produced in the laboratory and is effective against specific cells within the body. The antibody is re-created (cloned) from a single cell to create large quantities. Monoclonal antibodies are similar to antibodies produced by the body, but they can be produced in greater quantities and can be given to patients whose own immune systems cannot adequately fight the disease. Discovered in 1975, they are still in the developmental stage. They are used to aid diagnosis, to prevent tissue rejection and in some cancer therapies. Extensive research and development is ongoing. [*See* section entitled Genetics on page 290; *see also* AZT in section entitled Common Prescription and Nonprescription Drugs on page 191]

multiple personality: *See* dissociative disorder

multiple sclerosis: A progressive disease in which the covering of the nerve fibers of the brain and spinal cord deteriorates. It is characterized by periods of remission and exacerbation. Progress of the disease may be rapid (a few months) or slow (30 years or more). It can cause weakness, numbness, visual disturbances, difficulty in walking and dizziness. Severity of symptoms varies greatly.

mumps: A contagious viral disease characterized by swelling of the parotid glands (large salivary glands below and in front of each ear). It causes fever, headache, and earache. In adult males, it can also cause inflammation of the testes, which can cause sterility. Once a common childhood disease, vaccination has lessened its occurrence.

Munchausen's syndrome: A psychological condition that causes patients to feign physical illnesses, often quite dramatically and convincingly. When detected at one emergency room, they often go to another.

muscular dystrophy: A group of hereditary diseases characterized by progressive weakness and wasting of skeletal muscles. The most common form, Duchenne's muscular dystrophy, affects only males. Symptoms appear in early childhood and are progressive, often causing death by age 20. Other forms of the disease vary in severity and can affect children or adults of either sex.

mutagen: A physical or environmental agent that causes a mutation (change in genetic structure).

MRI: *See* nuclear magnetic resonance imaging

myasthenia gravis: A disease characterized by chronic fatigability and muscle weakness, especially involving the face and neck. Some cases are mild; others can cause death due to respiratory failure. Many patients have long periods of remission. It is caused by a chemical imbalance that affects nerve transmissions.

myocardial infarction (MI): Heart attack. Occurs when an area of heart muscle is damaged because of inadequate blood supply.

narcolepsy: A chronic ailment in which the patient has recurrent, sudden episodes of drowsiness or sleep, over which he has no control.

naturopathy: A system of medicine that relies on natural substances (such as herbs, fresh air and sunlight) rather than drugs to cure diseases.

neoplasm: An abnormal growth of new tissue (such as a tumor), whether it is malignant or benign.

neuroblastoma: A malignant tumor of embryonic nerve cells that occurs most often in children. It usually begins in an adrenal gland and spreads quickly.

neurofibromatosis: A congenital disease that causes multiple neurofibromas (nonmalignant tumors of the sheath that covers nerves). It also causes dark spots on the skin, and bone, muscle and organ abnormalities. It can also impair hearing and vision and can cause seizures. It is sometimes called Elephant Man's disease in reference to Joseph Merrick (1862–90), an Englishman who was severely disfigured by the disease and was exhibited as the Elephant Man. Most people with the disease have only mild symptoms.

neurosis: One of a number of psychological conditions in which the patient exhibits physical, emotional or behavioral symptoms but does not lose touch with reality (although actions may appear irrational). Neuroses can be characterized by depression, manic behavior, anxiety, obsessions, compulsions or phobias.

neurotransmitter: A chemical that affects the transmission of signals between nerves or from nerves to muscles.

NMR: *See* nuclear magnetic resonance imaging

nuclear magnetic resonance imaging: A diagnostic technique that uses electromagnetism to produce an image of internal structures such as the heart, blood vessels, brain and soft tissue. It is more accurate than X-rays for certain studies, but the equipment is expensive and it requires patients to lie still for prolonged periods. Also known as magnetic resonance imaging, MRI, NMR and NMRI.

obsessive-compulsive disorder: An uncontrollable need to repeat acts, rituals or thoughts.

occult blood: Blood that is not visible but can be detected by chemical tests or microscopic analysis.

oncology: The branch of medicine that deals with tumors.

opportunistic infection: Infections caused by organisms that usually are not troublesome. They result when a patient's physiology is altered, giving these organisms (usually fungi and bacteria) the opportunity to flourish. This can happen when antibiotics kill some microorganisms, allowing others to thrive. It also occurs among transplant patients who receive drugs to suppress their immune systems so that they won't reject the transplant. Opportunistic infections are common and life-threatening in AIDS patients.

osteoarthritis: The most common form of arthritis, occurring frequently in the elderly, and characterized by the deterioration of joints.

osteogenesis imperfecta: A genetic disorder that causes bones to be brittle and break easily. Severity varies greatly; the disease can be fatal or disabling, or it can improve significantly as the child matures. There is no cure.

osteomyelitis: An infection of the bone and bone marrow, usually caused by bacteria.

osteopathy: A therapeutic system that uses traditional medical therapy such as drugs and surgery, but also uses manipulation to align the body to achieve structural and functional balance.

ostomy: A surgical procedure in which an external opening is created for the removal of urine or feces.

pacemaker: A battery-operated device that is used to regulate heart rhythm by stimulating the heart to contract. Older models were affected by outside electrical and electromagnetic devices, such as microwave ovens.

palliative: Bringing relief, but not curing. For example, a disease that cannot be cured may be treated by palliative measures, such as painkillers.

paranoia: A condition in which persons have persistent and severe delusions of persecution, or have groundless jealousy.

paraplegia: Paralysis of both legs, sometimes with loss of sensation or motor function in the back and abdomen.

parathion poisoning: Abdominal pain, nausea, vomiting, headache, convulsions and/or breathing difficulties caused by inhaling or swallowing parathion, an agricultural insecticide.

Parkinsonism: A chronic, progressive neurological disease that causes tremor, shuffling gait, slowed speech, muscle rigidity and stooped posture. Also called Parkinson's disease, shaking palsy.

paternity test: A test that compares blood types to determine whether a man could have been the father of a particular child. The test can prove definitively that a man is not the father (if his blood type and the mother's could not have produced the child's). It cannot determine definitively that he is the father, since other men have the same blood type.

peritonitis: An inflammation of the peritoneum (the membrane that envelopes the abdominal organs).

pertussis: Acute, contagious respiratory disease that begins with cold symptoms and progresses to include coughing spasms, which end in characteristic whoops, often with vomiting. Vaccine is available. Also known as whooping cough.

petit mal: *See* epilepsy

phlebitis: Inflammation of the wall of a vein.

placebo effect: A beneficial change that occurs after a patient is given an ineffective substance (like distilled water or a sugar pill) that he believes to be effective. The change is attributed to the patient's expectations, rather than the physical properties of the substance. Placebos are used in drug testing, to compare the effect of the active drug, and are given to patients who want a drug that they don't need or shouldn't have.

plasma: The colorless, fluid part of blood and lymph composed of water, electrolytes, glucose, fats, protein and bile.

platelets: Blood cells that are essential to clotting.

pleurisy: Inflammation of the pleura (the membrane that covers the lungs and the inner surface of the chest).

pneumocystis carinii pneumonia: A potentially fatal form of pneumonia caused by the *Pneumocystis carinii* organism. It is uncommon, except among severely debilitated children and adults whose immunity has been compromised, particularly those with AIDS. [*See* pneumonia]

pneumonia: An inflammation of the lungs often caused by bacteria, viruses or chemical irritation. Aspiration pneumonia is caused by inhaling a foreign object into the lung. Treatment depends upon the cause.

pneumonoconiosis: A respiratory disorder caused by inhaling dust particles, often as a result of occupational exposure.

poliomyelitis: An infectious viral disease that affects the central nervous system. Symptoms range from slight flu-like symptoms to paralysis that leads to permanent disability or death. Once epidemic, the Sabin (oral) and Salk (injected) vaccines have greatly reduced the incidence of the disease. Years after recovery from the initial attack, the patient may experience new symptoms, known as post-poliomyelitis muscular atrophy.

progeria: A rare condition that causes premature aging in children or adolescents. Its cause is unknown.

psychogenic: Caused by the mind, not the body.

psychosis: A severe mental disorder in which the patient loses touch with reality and suffers impaired perceptions, thinking and responses. Symptoms include hallucinations and delusions. Hospitalization is often necessary.

psychosomatic: An adjective pertaining to the interrelation of the mind and body. Some illnesses with physical symptoms are said to be psychosomatic, in that they are caused by an emotional state.

pyelogram: An X-ray of the kidney and ureters (tubes that carry urine from the kidneys to the bladder).

quadriplegia: Paralysis of the arms and legs, usually including the trunk.

rabies: An acute viral disease of the central nervous system transmitted to humans by the saliva of an infected animal, usually through a bite. Bats, skunks, foxes, raccoons, dogs and cats are common carriers, although the virus can be transmitted by any warm-blooded mammal. Positive identification of the disease can be made studying brain tissue from the suspected carrier. Alternatively, the animal may be observed for 10 days to determine whether its behavior is characteristic of rabies. When the animal is not available, rabies treatment may be indicated as a precautionary measure. Incubation can range from one day to a year, but is typically about 10 days. Symptoms include fever, headache, muscle pain, spasms, excessive saliva, delirium, paralysis and coma. The larynx may go into spasm if the patient tries to swallow water, which is why rabies is sometimes called hydrophobia. If untreated, the disease is fatal. Vaccine and rabies immune globulin can prevent the disease if administered promptly.

radial keratotomy: A surgical procedure used to correct myopia (nearsightedness) by altering the shape of the cornea (the outer, transparent portion of the eye).

radiation sickness: Illness caused by exposure to ionizing radiation from radioactive substances, including nuclear bomb explosions and contamination in the workplace. Symptoms range from mild to life-threatening, depending on the amount and duration of exposure. Symptoms include nausea, vomiting, headache, diarrhea, hair loss, bleeding, sterility, fetal abnormalities, cataracts, disturbances in blood cell formation and the development of various cancers, including leukemia. Severe exposure can cause serious burns and rapid death. Also known as radiation syndrome.

repetitive strain injury (RSI): A phrase used to describe disabling inflammation and pain caused by repetitive hand and arm activities, often associated with an occupation. It is common among people who type for long periods on computers, and is also found among supermarket checkers, meat cutters and musicians. It includes carpal tunnel syndrome and other types of inflammation, such as tendinitis, tennis elbow and tenosynovitis (inflammation of the tendon and its sheath in the forearm). Symptoms include pain, tingling fingers, numbness and diminished motor abilities. A change in the work area, and taking frequent breaks, may prevent or ease the condition. It can be treated with anti-inflammatory drugs, injections, physical therapy and, in severe cases, by surgery. Severe cases can be disabling. [*See* carpal tunnel syndrome]

retina: The light-sensitive layer that lines the eye. It transmits visual impulses to the brain through the optic nerve.

Reye's syndrome: A syndrome of unknown cause that occurs primarily in children after a viral infection, particularly chicken pox or influenza. It is associated with taking aspirin, although the relationship is not understood. The syndrome causes abnormal brain function and infiltration of fat into internal organs, particularly the liver. It is often fatal.

rheumatic fever: An inflammatory disorder of unknown cause that occurs primarily in children and follows a streptococcal infection (usually of the throat). Symptoms include fever, joint pain, abdominal and chest pain, and a rash. Inflammation of the heart can cause permanent damage.

rheumatoid arthritis: *See* arthritis

Rh factor: *See* blood groups

rickets: Condition usually caused by a deficiency of vitamin D, which restricts absorption of calcium and phosphorus. It can also be caused by lack of calcium. It is most common in children, in whom it causes bone abnormalities. Prevention and treatment includes diet with proper levels of vitamin D, calcium and phosphorus, and exposure to ultraviolet light (either sunlight or artificial).

rickettsia: Microorganisms that live in ticks, lice, fleas and mites and are transmitted to humans, causing diseases such as Rocky Mountain spotted fever and typhus. [*See* Rocky Mountain spotted fever, typhus]

Rocky Mountain spotted fever: An infectious disease transmitted by the wood tick, occurring throughout North and South America. It causes fever, headache, muscle pain, confusion and a rash that appears first on the wrists and ankles.

rubella: A contagious viral disease that causes low fever, sore throat and a rash that begins on the face, spreads to the body, and fades quickly. The disease is usually mild. If contracted in early pregnancy, however, it can cause congenital defects. Rubella vaccine is usually given to children. Also called German measles.

salmonellosis: Food poisoning caused by eating food contaminated with a variety of *Salmonella* bacteria. Symptoms include nausea, vomiting, abdominal pain, fever and diarrhea. It can be life-threatening in the very young, the elderly and the infirm. In a small percentage of cases, it can cause arthritis. It is frequently transmitted on improperly cooked or handled meat, poultry, eggs, milk, fish and shellfish.

sarcoma: *See* cancer

scabies: A highly communicable skin disease caused by infection with the itch mite (*Sarcoptes scabiei*).

scarlet fever: An acute contagious disease caused by *Streptococcus* bacteria. Symptoms include fever, sore throat and a red rash. It usually occurs in children.

schizophrenia: An imprecise label for any of a variety of mental disorders in which the patient suffers from severe thought, perceptual and emotional disturbances and in which the perception of reality is grossly distorted. Symptoms can include apathy, delusions, hallucinations, catatonia (stupor), excessive activity, inappropriate activities and rambling speech. The cause is unknown, although genetic predisposition appears to be a factor.

scoliosis: An abnormal lateral curve of the spine.

scurvy: A disorder caused by a deficiency of vitamin C (ascorbic acid). It causes anemia, weakness, leg and joint pains and bleeding gums.

senile dementia: A progressive mental disorder of the aged, resulting from degenerative changes in the brain. Symptoms include loss of memory, confusion and irritability.

septicemia: A bacterial infection of the blood, usually resulting from the spread of infection from another site. Also called blood poisoning.

shock: A life-endangering, emergency situation in which blood flow from the extremities is insufficient to return adequate blood to the heart. This prevents the heart from maintaining adequate circulation, which limits oxygen levels in tissues and organs. Shock may be caused by hemorrhage, infection, drug reaction, trauma, poisoning, heart attack or dehydration. Symptoms include pale or blue skin, staring, dilated pupils, weak and rapid pulse, rapid and shallow breathing and low blood pressure.

sickle-cell anemia: A hereditary condition in which abnormal hemoglobin causes red blood cells to become sickle-shaped (rather than round) and fragile, resulting in anemia. It is most common among blacks and persons of Mediterranean descent. People who inherit the trait from only one parent may have few symptoms. Those who inherit it from both parents have chronic anemia, weakness, lethargy and joint pain. [See hemoglobin]

silicosis: A form of pneumonoconiosis caused by inhaling silica particles.

skin cancer: Most skin cancers fall into one of three types: basal cell, squamous cell or melanoma. The first two are rarely life-threatening. The third is quite serious. Basal cell cancers usually appear as hard, red translucent bumps in areas exposed to the sun. Squamous cell cancers are typically scaly patches that form crusts. They are also likely to appear on sun-damaged skin, but can occur anywhere. Melanomas usually appear as changes in existing moles, or as new moles; most are related to overexposure to sun. When melanomas are removed early, the cure rate is quite high. When they have spread, they are usually fatal.

smallpox: A highly contagious, viral disease that has been virtually eradicated because of worldwide vaccination programs. The virus is now believed to exist only as medical specimens in the U.S. and the USSR.

sphygmomanometer: The medical instrument used to measure blood pressure. It uses an inflatable cuff and a mercury-based scale.

spina bifida: A congenital defect in which vertebrae fail to close, which leaves the spinal cord unprotected. The condition can be quite mild, causing few or no symptoms, or it can cause paralysis if a large part of the spine is involved or the spinal cord protrudes.

STD: Sexually transmitted disease.

stroke: A sudden loss of consciousness or impaired motor functioning resulting from a blocked or ruptured blood vessel in the brain.

sudden infant death syndrome (SIDS): The unexpected, sudden death of a seemingly healthy infant, usually during sleep. Cause is unknown. In the United States, it is the leading cause of death among infants from 2 weeks to 1 year of age. Risk factors include prematurity, low birth weight and male sex. Also called cot death or crib death.

syncope: Fainting.

syphilis: An infectious disease transmitted through sexual contact or through the placenta. It can cause blindness or other congenital defects in newborns. In adults, its symptoms occur in three stages, over 15 years or more. In the first stage, a chancre appears two to four weeks after exposure. Symptoms in the second stage vary greatly, including nausea, vomiting, fever, joint pain and rash. They typically appear about six weeks after the first stage. In the third stage, there are benign tumors, which ulcerate and heal, often leaving scars. The heart, nervous system and lungs can be damaged, causing death. Penicillin is effective in treating the disease.

systemic lupus erythematosis (SLE): A chronic inflammatory disease that affects the skin, joints, kidneys, heart, blood vessels, nervous system and mucous membranes. It affects women more frequently than men and varies greatly in severity. Symptoms range from mild skin rashes (including a characteristic butterfly-shaped rash across the cheeks and the bridge of the nose) to crippling or life-threatening conditions. It is believed to be an autoimmune disease with an inherited component, but the exact cause and the mechanism that triggers symptoms is unknown. Periods of remission and relapse are common. Drugs are used to control symptoms. There is no cure. [See autoimmune disease]

tachycardia: Abnormally rapid heartbeat.

Tay-Sachs disease: An inherited disease that causes physical and mental degeneration and usually causes death by age 4. Symptoms begin at about 6 months of age and include blindness, mental and physical retardation, convulsions and spasticity. It occurs primarily among Ashkenazi Jews. (The gene must be inherited from both parents for the disease to develop.) There is no treatment.

tennis elbow: See bursitis

thalassemia: A hereditary form of leukemia most common among people of Mediterranean origin. Those who inherit genes for the disease from both parents (thalassemia major) have severe problems that begin in childhood, including severe anemia, enlarged heart and spleen, respiratory problems and retarded growth and development. It can be fatal. There is no cure. Also called Cooley's anemia. Those who inherit the gene from only one parent (thalassemia minor) have few or no symptoms. [*See* anemia, leukemia]

thromboembolism: *See* embolism

thrombosis: The formation or existence of a blood clot in a blood vessel. If the blood clot (thrombus) detaches, it becomes an embolism. [*See* embolism]

tic douloureux: *See* trigeminal neuralgia

toxic shock syndrome (TSS): A serious acute infection caused by the toxin created by some strains of the *Staphylococcus aureus* bacterium. Symptoms include high fever, red rash, vomiting and diarrhea, muscular pain, headache, disorientation and sore throat. It can lead to circulatory collapse and kidney and liver failure, which can be fatal. It occurs most often in menstruating women who use high-absorbency tampons, but it can affect anyone.

toxoplasmosis: An infection by the parasite *Toxoplasma gondii*. It can be contracted from cats, from litter boxes or by eating contaminated meat that has been poorly cooked. It usually causes mild symptoms (malaise, low fever, swollen glands). If contracted by pregnant women, it can cause fetal abnormalities, however.

Tourette's syndrome: *See* Gilles de la Tourette's syndrome

triage: A classification process used in military or emergency situations whereby patients are sorted according to their need for immediate care, so that those most in need are treated first.

trichinosis: Infestation with the roundworm *Trichinella spiralis*. It is transmitted through undercooked meat, particularly pork. Symptoms, which vary greatly in intensity, include nausea, diarrhea, abdominal pain, fever and muscle pain and stiffness. Encephalitis and meningitis may develop. After the roundworms become encysted in the muscles, symptoms fade over a period of several weeks.

trigeminal neuralgia: A condition resulting from pressure on or degeneration of the trigeminal nerve, which is involved in sensations and muscular actions of the face. It causes severe, stabbing pain, which usually follows a branch of the nerve along the angle of the jaw. Also called tic douloureux.

tuberculosis: A chronic infection caused by *Mycobacterium tuberculosis*. It commonly affects the lungs, but it may also affect the intestines, kidneys, nervous system, larynx, bones and skin. The infection is usually transmitted from an infected person or cow, or from drinking contaminated milk.

typhoid fever: A serious, sometimes fatal infection caused by the *Salmonella typhi* bacterium. It is transmitted by eating food or drinking water that has been contaminated by the urine or feces of infected people. Symptoms include high fever, headache, diarrhea, abdominal pain, delirium, cough, rose-colored spots and an enlarged spleen. Immunization confers immunity.

typhus: An infectious disease, rare in the United States, which is prevalent in areas of crowded, unsanitary living conditions and is caused by rickettsia microorganisms. It is transmitted by fleas and lice. Symptoms include malaise, headache, high fever, chills, rash, delirium and stupor. Mortality can be quite high in epidemics. When prompt treatment and adequate antibiotics are available, it can often be treated effectively. [*See* rickettsia]

ulcerative colitis: *See* colitis

URI: Upper respiratory infection.

X chromosome: The sex chromosome that is present in both sexes. Women have two X chromosomes. Men have one X and one Y chromosome. Abnormalities of this chromosome are associated with many sex-linked disorders, such as hemophilia.

SUGGESTED REFERENCES AND CONTACTS:

American Medical Directory, 4 vols., American Medical Association Staff. Chicago: American Medical Assn., 1990.

Directory of Medical Specialists, 1989–1990, 3 vols. Wilmette, Ill.: Marquis Who's Who/Macmillan Directory Div., 24th revised edition, 1989.

Medical & Health Information Directory, vol. 1, *Organizations, Agencies and Institutions* (1989), vol. 2, *Publications, Libraries and Other Information Services* (1990), vol. 3, *Health Services* (1990).

Merck Manual. Rahway, N.J.: Merck & Co. Inc., 15th ed., 1987.

Physician's Desk Reference, edited by E. R. Barnhart. Oradell, N.J.: Medical Economics Books, 44th edition, 1990.

Physician's Desk Reference for Nonprescription Drugs, edited by E. R. Barnhart. Oradell, N.J.: Medical Economics Books, 11th edition, 1990.

Health Database Plus: A computer database with full-text articles and synopses from consumer and professional publications concerning health, nutrition and fitness; available through CompuServe; surcharge and fee for viewing articles.

MEDLARS: National Library of Medicine's computer databases; includes databases on AIDS, bioethics, cancer, chemicals, toxicology, hazardous substances, toxic chemical releases, etc. Available through MEDLARS Management Section, National Library of Medicine, Bethesda, MD 20894, (800) 638-8480, fax (301) 496-0822.

MEDLINE, the National Library of Medicine's bibliographic computer database, is provided by Beth

Israel Hospital, 330 Brookline Ave., Boston, MA 02115, (800) 722-2075; it is available through CompuServe.

NORDServices/Rare Disease Database: A computer database maintained by the National Organization for Rare Disorders, P.O. Box 8923, New Fairfield, CT 06812, (203) 746-6518, a nonprofit group concerned with identification and cure of rare diseases. Provides information on rare and "orphan" diseases.

Physicians Data Query: A computer database published by National Cancer Institute, available through BRS Information Technologies and CompuServe. Comprises four databases: Consumer Cancer Information File contains information for laypeople on more than 80 cancer types; Professional Cancer Information File contains current information for professionals; Directory File contains names and addresses of institutions with National Cancer Institute centers and a physician directory with names and phone numbers of 12,000 specialists; Protocol File contains more than 1,000 protocols for cancer treatment, with contact information.

IQuest Medical Info Center: A comprehensive group of medical computer databases including citations, abstracts and full-text articles from journals, books, government publications and other sources. Available through DIALOG Information Services, BRS Information Technologies, Data-Star, CompuServe; surcharge and charge for articles.

AIDS Articles from Comprehensive Core Medical Library: A computer database of full-text articles from medical references, texts and journals; published by BRS Information Technologies; available through CompuServe.

HealthNet: A computer database of general medical and health information for laypeople; available through CompuServe.

Alcoholics Anonymous World Services, Inc., P.O. Box 459, Grand Central Station, New York, NY 10163, (212) 870-3400. Refers people to local chapters, has statistics and a pamphlet package available.

Alzheimer's Disease and Related Disorders Association, Inc., 70 E. Lake St., Suite 600, Chicago, IL 60601, (312) 335-8700; information hot line, (800) 621-0379. Has publications, video kits, handbooks, statistic sheets, article reprints and will answer questions.

American Anorexia Bulimia Association, Inc., 418 East 76th St., New York, NY 10021, (212) 734-1114. Information and referral service; publishes a quarterly newsletter and a bibliography.

American Cancer Society, 1599 Clifton Road NE, Atlanta, GA 30329-4251, (404) 320-3333, (800) ACS-2345. Has information on any type of cancer, including research, detection, treatment and statistics. Will also locate information.

American Dental Association, 211 E. Chicago Ave., Chicago, IL 60611, (312) 440-2500. Information on new and traditional treatments, statistics; spokespersons available.

American Diabetes Association, Inc., National Service Center, 1660 Duke St., Alexandria, VA 22314, (703) 549-1500. Provides information on diabetes and related diseases.

American Heart Association, 7320 Greenville Ave., Dallas, TX 75231, (214) 373-6300. Spokespersons available for questions on specific topics; pamphlets and brochures available.

American Lung Association, 1740 Broadway, New York, NY 10019, (212) 315-8700. Information on lungs, lung cancer, emphysema and other conditions (colds, hay fever, etc.); statistics and brochures available.

American Medical Association, 515 State St., Chicago, IL 60610, (312) 464-4818. A membership organization of physicians, it does research for doctors; will provide credentials of a specific doctor.

Arthritis Foundation, 1314 Spring St. NW, Atlanta, GA 30309, (404) 872-7100. Brochures, statistics, photos available; spokespersons available to comment on general and specific topics.

Asthma and Allergy Foundation of America, 1717 Massachusetts Ave. NW, Suite 305, Washington, D.C. 20036, (202) 466-7643. Pamphlets, statistics, list of doctors available; spokespersons available.

Cancer Information Service, Boy Scout Bldg., Rm. 340, 9000 Rockville Pike, Bethesda, MD 20892, (800) 4CA-NCER. Collects and distributes educational materials to organizations, health care providers and the public.

Centers for Disease Control, Office of Public Affairs, 1600 Clifton Road NE, Bldg. 1, Rm. 2167, Atlanta, GA 30333, (404) 639-3286; AIDS hotline: (800) 458-5231. Information available on a number of diseases, including AIDS. Fact sheets, reprints available.

Cystic Fibrosis Foundation, 6931 Arlington Rd., Bethesda, MD 20814, (800)-FIGHTCF. Has pamphlets, brochures, biannual newspaper; makes referrals to 70 branch offices.

Division of Sexually Transmitted Diseases, Centers for Disease Control, Atlanta, GA 30333, (800) 227-8922 (hotline). Gives information on diseases and sends packets of literature.

Epilepsy Foundation of America, 4351 Garden City Dr., Landover, MD 20785, (800) 332-1000. Information, referrals, publications, statistics available. The National Epilepsy Library, (800) 332-4050, can also answer questions.

Food and Drug Administration Press Office, 15-A05, 5600 Fishers Lane, Rockville, MD 20857, (301) 443-4177, (301) 443-3285. Reprints of consumer magazine articles, publications list, information sheets available.

High Blood Pressure Information Center, 4733 Bethesda Ave., Suite 530, Bethesda, MD 20814, (301) 951-3260. Provides information to consumers and health-care professionals.

March of Dimes Birth Defects Foundation, 1275 Mamaroneck Ave., White Plains, NY 10605, (914) 428-7100. Provides pamphlets, brochures, fact sheets, annual report, statistics, referrals to local chapters; spokespersons available.

Muscular Dystrophy Association, 3561 East Sunset Dr., Tucson, AZ 85718, (602) 529-2000. Provides brochures, statistics, research information.

National Arthritis and Musculo-Skeletal and Skin Diseases Information Clearinghouse, Box AMS, Rockville Pike, Bethesda, MD 20892, (301) 495-4484. Distributes information to those involved in public, professional or patient education.

National Association of Anorexia Nervosa & Associated Disorders, Box 7, Highland Park, IL 60035, (708) 831-3438 (hotline). Provides crisis counseling, consumer advocacy, information on research, statistics.

National Clearinghouse for Alcohol and Drug Information, P.O. Box 2345, Rockville, MD 20852, (301) 468-2600. Provides publications; has recent information on illegal drug and alcohol use.

National Clearinghouse on Child Abuse and Neglect, P.O. Box 1182, Washington, D.C. 20013, (800) 394-3366. Collects and distributes information.

National Council on Alcoholism, 12 West 21st St., New York, NY 10010, (212) 206-6770. Provides information on alcoholism; makes referrals to local chapters.

National Diabetes Information Clearinghouse, Box NDIC, 9000 Rockville Pike, Bethesda, MD 20892. Collects and distributes educational materials; list of publications available.

National Digestive Diseases Information Clearinghouse, Box NDDIC, 9000 Rockville Pike, Bethesda, MD 20892, (301) 468-6344. Provides printed information on digestive diseases.

National Foundation for Ileitis and Colitis, 444 Park Avenue S., New York, NY 10016, (212) 685-3440. Provides brochures and books; people available to answer questions.

National Health Information Center, P.O. Box 1133, Washington, D.C., 20013-1133, (703) 522-2590, (800) 336-4797. Helps the public locate health information; makes referrals to appropriate agencies for specific information.

National Hemophilia Foundation, 110 Greene St., Suite 303, New York, NY 10012, (212) 219-8180. People available to answer basic questions; statistics available.

National Institutes of Health, 9000 Rockville Pike, Bethesda, MD 20892-0001, (301) 496-4000. Comprises 14 institutes spanning all areas of health. Pamphlets, publications, statistics, spokespersons available:

- National Cancer Institute, Bldg. 31, NIH, (301) 496-5615.
- National Heart, Lung and Blood Institute, Bldg. 31, NIH, (301) 496-5166.
- National Eye Institute, Bldg. 31, NIH, (301) 496-2234.
- National Institute on Aging, Bldg. 31, NIH, (301) 496-9265.
- National Institute of Allergy and Infectious Diseases, Bldg. 31, NIH, (301) 496-2263.
- National Institute of Arthritis and Musculoskeletal and Skin Diseases, Bldg. 31, NIH, (301) 496-4353.
- National Institute of Child Health and Human Development, Bldg. 31, NIH, (301) 496-3454.
- National Institute on Deafness and Other Communication Disorders, 9000 Rockville Pike, Bethesda, MD 20892, (301) 496-7243; (TDD number: (301) 496-6596).
- National Institute of Dental Research, 9000 Rockville Pike, Bethesda, MD 20892, (301) 496-3571.
- National Institute of Diabetes and Digestive and Kidney Diseases, Bldg. 31, NIH, (301) 496-5877.
- National Institute of Environmental Health Sciences, Research Triangle Park, NC 27709, (919) 541-3212.
- National Institute of General Medical Sciences, (Genetics), 5333 Westbard Ave., Bethesda, MD 20892, (301) 496-7301.
- National Institute of Mental Health, 5600 Fishers Lane, Rockville, MD 20857, (301) 443-4513.
- National Institute of Neurological Disorders and Stroke, Bldg. 31, NIH, (301) 496-9746.

National Kidney Foundation, 30 East 33rd St., New York, NY 10016, (800) 441-1280. Makes referrals to regional offices.

National Mental Health Association, 1021 Prince St., Alexandria, VA 22314-2971, (703) 684-7722. Provides brochures, answers questions, directs to other sources.

National Multiple Sclerosis Society, 205 E. 42nd St., 3d Fl., New York, NY 10017, (212) 986-3240. Medical staff answers questions.

National Society to Prevent Blindness, 500 E. Remington Rd., Schaumburg, IL 60173, (708) 843-2020, (800) 331-2020. Pamphlets, brochures, catalog, statistics available; answers basic questions on vision, eye health, safety.

National Spinal Cord Injury Association, 600 West

Cummings Park, Suite 2000, Woburn, MA 01801, (617) 935-2722. Books, information packages, statistics available (rush service available: fax (617) 932-8369); questions answered or referred.

National Sudden Infant Death Syndrome Clearinghouse, 8201 Greensborrow Dr., Suite 600, McLean, VA 22102-3810, (703) 821-8955. Provides information to public and health-care professionals; bibliographic database available.

Office on Smoking and Health Technical Information Center, 5600 Fishers Lane, Park Building, Rm. 1-16, Rockville, MD 20857, (301) 217-7272.

Printed information, answers to questions available.

Planned Parenthood Federation of America, Inc., 810 Seventh Ave., New York, NY 10019, (212) 541-7800. Pamphlets, brochures, fact sheets available; questions answered; spokespersons available.

United Cerebral Palsy Associations, Inc., 7 Pennsylvania Plaza, Suite 804, New York, NY 10001, (800) USA-1UCP. Provides literature, answers questions, makes referrals to local chapters.

For more sources of information, *see* Part One: Government; Part Six: Access to Information.

ARCHITECTURAL TERMS AND U.S. HOUSING STYLES

abacus: In Greco-Roman architecture, a horizontal slab set on, or forming, the flat, uppermost part of the capital of a column. The abacus supports the entablature—architrave, frieze and cornice—of a structure. [*See* architrave, capital, column, cornice, entablature, frieze]

abutment: A solid masonry mass, traditionally one that receives the thrust of an arch, supporting such structures as bridges or overpasses.

Adam (housing style): Commonly referred to as Federal style, houses of this type flourished along the New England seacoast from about 1780 to 1840. They represent a refinement and embellishment of the Georgian style, which had dominated American colonial architecture for about 80 years. Typically, Adam-style houses are side-gabled or hip-roofed, two or three stories tall, and box-like, usually with multipaned windows and shutters balanced precisely around elaborate front-door surrounds that include a semicircular light. Named after the Adam brothers—John, James, William and, particularly, Robert—influential London architects.

Adobe (housing style): *See* Pueblo

A-frame (housing style): A Contemporary folk style popular in the late 1940s and the 1950s that employed one or more severely vertical letter "A"s as the frame of the structure. Typically, a vacation home.

American Mansard (housing style): *See* Second Empire

apse: A nearly semicircular or polygonal space, typically housing an altar, at the terminus of an axis in the classic floor plan of a church.

arcade: A series of arches supported by piers or columns and forming a gallery or passageway, commonly lined with shops on both sides.

architrave: The lowest horizontal member of an entablature, which rests on the capital of a column. [*See* abacus, architrave, column, cornice, entablature, frieze]

ashlar: A building stone squared true on all faces.

atrium: In Greco-Roman architecture, an open central court or hall; a forecourt in early Christian churches.

baluster: One of a row of closely spaced vertical supports for a railing. [*See* balustrade]

balustrade: A railing system; a handrail and its supporting balusters. [*See* baluster]

banister/bannister: A corruption of baluster, generally taken to mean baluster or balustrade. [*See* baluster, balustrade]

Beaux-Arts (housing style): Landmarks and mansions in this grand, classical Eclectic Period style were built in the country's affluent urban and industrial areas between approximately 1885 and 1930. They are distinguished by flat, low-pitched or mansard roofs; symmetrically arranged pilasters, columns, or both; light-colored masonry construction with lavishly decorative stonework. The name derives from France's École des Beaux-Arts, the most prestigious and influential architectural school of the day. [*See* Eclectic Period]

bi-level: *See* split-level

brick row house: *See* brownstone

brownstone: A general reference to the four- and five-story, flat-roofed, connected row houses that sprang up as a housing solution in the cities of the Northeast from the mid-1800s to the turn of the century. The name derives from the reddish brown sandstone of which they commonly were built, though the name often is used generically to mean any row house; also known as brick row houses and eastern town houses; often Italianate in style. [*See* Italianate]

bungalow: A simple, often one-story, cottage-like house popular throughout the early 1900s. Sometimes called California bungalow. [*See* Craftsman]

buttress: A projecting support built into or against the exterior of a masonry wall; a primary feature of Gothic architecture.

California bungalow: *See* Craftsman

campanile: A bell tower, whether attached to a church or free-standing.

cantilever: A projecting bracket used primarily to carry the weight of a cornice or the protruding eaves of a building.

Cape Cod (housing style): One of the most enduring of early American Folk Period styles, capes date to about 1700, originally with 1½ stories, a center chimney, a steeply pitched gable roof and no dormers. Wood shingles, used for roofing and siding, were allowed to weather gray. [*See* Folk Period]

capital: The top part of a column, including, in classical architecture, its abacus, on which rests the entablature of a structure. [*See* abacus, entablature]

Carpenter Gothic (housing style): *See* Stick Style

catslide roof: A long, steeply sloping roof; generally a reference to the stylized rear roof of a Saltbox Colonial, which drops sharply from the ridgepole of a 2½- or 3-story house to the top of the first floor. [*See* Saltbox]

Chalet (housing style): *See* Swiss Chalet

chancel: The sanctuary of a church, the space around the altar usually restricted to clergy.

Châteauesque (housing style): Like the Beaux-Arts style which was its contemporary in the Eclectic Period, Châteauesque construction was reserved for the stone landmarks and mansions of the wealthy. As the term implies, French Gothic châteaux were the style's primary influence, hence examples display a soaring vertical emphasis—spires, turrets, tall chimneys, steeply pitched hipped roofs and gables built through the cornice line. [*See* Eclectic Period]

clerestory: The uppermost part of a room's interior built high enough to loom over adjacent rooftops and fitted with windows to admit light.

cloister: A covered walk surrounding a court; traditionally, linking a church to monastery buildings.

Colonial Period (housing style): Housing styles from this broad period (1600 to about 1825) are among the most enduring and often repeated in U.S. history. The original period encompasses Adam, Dutch Colonial, Early Classical Revival, French Colonial, Georgian and Spanish Colonial styles—nearly all of which have been recreated as centennial or revival forms.

Colonial Revival (housing style): This rather amorphous, long-lived category of housing, which dominated U.S. residential construction from about 1880 to the 1950s, harks back to a broad variety of prototypical styles, most notably Adam and Georgian, and reflects a renewed appreciation of U.S. architectural heritage. The category encompasses at least nine different original styles, and individual houses often display the influence of more than one of them. Prominent, covered front doorways employing columns, pilasters or pediments are a common distinguishing feature. [*See* Eclectic Period]

colonnade: A row of columns in which each is equidistant from the other.

column: An upright, often decorative pillar consisting of a cylindrical or polygonal shaft, base and a crown known as a capital; traditionally used to support an entablature though often, in modern architecture, an ornamentation. [*See* capital, entablature, orders]

Composite: *See* orders: Composite

Contemporary (housing style): Post-1940s housing that generally defies traditional forms; favored by many architect-designers from the early 1950s through the 1960s. Characterized by flat or low-pitched roofs, eaves with very wide overhangs and, often, nontraditional, asymmetrical windows. [*See* Modern Period]

corbel: A projection built into a wall or protruding from its face, commonly bracket-shaped and used to support a cornice or overhang; often decorative as well as functional.

Corinthian: *See* orders: Corinthian

cornice: A projecting, horizontal molding along the top of a wall. In classical architecture, the cornice is the uppermost, horizontal member of an entablature; below it, in descending order, sit the frieze and architrave. [*See* architrave, entablature, frieze]

Craftsman (housing style): An Eclectic-period style that originated in Southern California and enjoyed great popularity from about 1905 to 1930. Most commonly referred to as bungalows or California bungalows, these are compact, often one-story, cottage-like houses with low-pitched gabled or hipped roofs. Front porches and side- or front-gabled styles predominate. [*See* Eclectic Period]

cupola: A short, light, roofed tower built on a roof, traditionally for use as a belfry, lighthouse or lookout; almost strictly decorative today.

Doric: *See* orders: Doric

dormer: A roofed housing addition jutting out perpendicularly from a sloping roofline; commonly used in reference to a kind of squared-off, roof-high addition to the back of Cape Cod–style houses; sometimes referred to as eye-dormers when they are small, center-windowed and protruding, often in pairs.

Dutch Colonial (housing style): A Colonial-period, 1- to 2-story house, moderate in size, with a gambrel roof distinguished by eaves that flare outward. Main entrance doors originally were divided in half horizontally; popular from the early 1600s to about 1840. [*See* Colonial Period]

Early Classical Revival (housing style): Colonial-period houses in this Roman-influenced style were built from about 1770 to 1840, but limited in number. Thomas Jefferson was its best-known proponent. One- and 2-story examples predominated. They were distinguished by careful symmetry and dominant, roof-high front porticoes, usually with Tuscan columns, supporting a centered gable. [*See* Colonial Period]

Early Georgian (housing style): Often referred to as Williamsburg Georgian to distinguish it from the more ornate Georgian style that prevailed in the Colonial period from about the late 1700s to the early 1800s. Typical Early Georgian houses, built in the United States in the early 1700s, had two or three stories and were characterized by their rectangular, nearly box-like shape, double-hung, small-pane windows and, at each end, two tall chimneys. [*See* Colonial Period]

Eastern town house (housing style): *See* brownstone

Eastlake (housing style): A forerunner of the Stick Style house, this ornate 19th-century style is characterized by an open front porch, tower or turret, gable roof and rich, carved or lathe-turned ornamentation; named after the English architect Charles Lock Eastlake, who pioneered the Tudor Revival.

Eclectic Period (housing style): One of the broadest categories of U.S. houses, encompassing a host of different and sharply varying styles: Beaux Arts, Chateauesque, Colonial Revival, Craftsman, French Eclectic, International, Italian Renaissance, Mission, Modernistic, Monterey, Neoclassical, Prairie, Pueblo Revival, Spanish Eclectic and Tudor, all were popular from about 1880 to 1940.

Elizabethan (housing style): *See* Tudor

entablature: In Greco-Roman architecture, the three horizontal beams or members—architrave, frieze and cornice—set on the capitals of columns to form a structure. [*See* architrave, capital, column, cornice, frieze]

eaves: The lower edges of a sloping roof, projecting beyond the face of a wall.

Exotic Revivals (housing styles): Few examples of these Romantic-period houses remain today. Three styles were built from about 1835 to 1890: Oriental, Swiss Chalet and Egyptian. Oriental forms, which reflected European interests of the same period, featured embellishments such as ogee, scallop-edged arches around windows, doors and entrance ways, and onion-shaped, Turkish, domes atop cube-shaped Italianate or Greek Revival houses. Egyptian forms were elaborations of the same cube-shaped structure, distinguished primarily by huge stick-bundle columns as part of a front portico. [*See* Swiss Chalet, Romantic Period]

eye-dormer: *See* dormer

fascia: Most commonly taken to mean the long board or strip of siding that covers the ends of rafters atop a house wall immediately below the eaves of a roof. [*See* eaves]

Federal (housing style): A popular though broad and somewhat imprecise reference to Adam-style houses, an English-influenced development in American Colonial Period housing that flourished from about 1785 to 1835, after the Georgian architectural era. [*See* Adam, Colonial Period]

Folk Period (housing style): The oldest category of housing, extending from the Native American styles that predominated for many thousands of years before the European settlement of the U.S. to about 1900, overlapping simple Pre-Railroad styles (1850 to about 1910) and National-era houses (1850 to about 1895).

Folk Victorian (housing style): These Victorian-period houses, built from about 1870 to at least 1910, represented a popular attempt to bring the period's lacy ornamentation, spindlework and cut-out embellishments to simple, gable-front or gable-end folk houses. [*See* Victorian Period]

French Colonial (housing style): Colonial-period houses in this manner reflect France's influence in America through the 18th century and, in the New Orleans area, into the 19th century as late as 1860. Housing forms are generally divided into urban and rural. Urban styles feature side-gabled buildings with overhanging, flared eaves. Houses often were built at the edge of a sidewalk, and each room usually had its own exterior doorway. Houses in this style often featured ground-floor shops and upper-story residences, somewhat block-shaped and distinguished by fine wrought-iron, second-floor balconies. Rural styles featured steeply pitched hip roofs and long front porches with a system of wooden columns supporting the roof edge; another set of columns, often masonry, supports the porch floor. [*See* Eclectic Period]

French Eclectic (housing style): *See* French Provincial

French Provincial (housing style): Sometimes referred to as French Eclectic, 1½- to 2½-story houses of this type sprouted throughout the country in the Eclectic period from about 1915 to 1945; characterized by a high, steeply pitched hip roof, often with upward-flaring eaves. Siding is most commonly brick, stone or stucco; windows are symmetrically arranged, and upper-story windows, with curved crowns, often intersect the cornices of the roof. [*See* Eclectic Period]

frieze: Commonly, a decorative band atop an interior wall below the cornice, or horizontal molding serving as a cornice. In classical architecture, the middle horizontal member of an entablature. It is situated below the cornice and above the architrave. [*See* architrave, cornice, entablature]

gable: The vertical, often triangular, sections of end walls in a building that has a double-sloping, peaked roof, specifically the wall section extending from the eaves to the roof's peak.

gambrel roof: A roof with two pitches, or slopes, on each of two sides. The upper roofs pitch gently, the lower roofs steeply; in Great Britain, the style of roof is known generically as mansard. [*See* American Mansard]

gargoyle: A spout projecting from a rain gutter to carry water downward and away from a building. In medieval architecture, gargoyles were simple cylindrical projections of lead or stone. As architecture became more ornate, so did gargoyles. By the Gothic period, from about the year 1200, gargoyles were being carved into ornate and commonly fantastic images, hence the use of the word today to describe grotesque or monstrous features.

gazebo: An airy and small summer house set on a terrace or near a garden so as to afford a pleasant view. Usually rather ornate.

Georgian (housing style): From about 1700 to 1780, the predominant Colonial Period architectural style throughout the American colonies. Typical houses are one or two stories high, two, sometimes three rooms deep, and box-like; side-gabled, gambrel- and hip-roofed styles were most common. Multipaned windows are usually arranged in symmetrical rows around a paneled front door capped with an elaborate crown and a row of transom lights and flanked by pilasters. Cornices are commonly decorated with dentil molding. [*See* Colonial Period]

gingerbread: The heavily stylized and often lacy ornamentation (spindlework, balusters, turnings and carvings) commonly found in some Victorian houses, notably Queen Anne, Stick and Gothic Revival styles.

Gothic: The dominant architectural style in western Europe from about 1250 to 1550; evolved from Byzantine and Romanesque forms in France; characterized by fine masonry and woodworking and, particularly, the use of the pointed arch, ribbed vaults and exterior flying buttresses to create structurally lighter buildings.

Gothic Revival (housing style): A Romantic-period housing style that originated in the Northeast in 1840 and enjoyed considerable popularity for about 40 years; characterized by steeply pitched side-gabled roofs and equally steep cross gables, both with ornate vergeboards, boards fastened beneath the eaves as inverted vees (some with cross-bracing), providing a decorative frame for the gables. Open, one-story, full-width front porches are common, as are Gothic-influenced windows. [*See* Romantic Period]

Greek Revival (housing style): A dominant U.S. housing style from about 1830 to 1860, most of the Romantic period. Houses were typically 2 to 2½ stories tall, two rooms deep with a low-pitched hipped or side-gabled roof. All cornice lines are distinguished by classically derived frieze-and-architrave trim bands. Entry- or full-width porch is most commonly supported by prominent columns, usually Doric. [*See* Tudor]

half-timber: *See* Elizabethan house

High-Victorian Italianate (housing style): These ornate, lavishly decorated houses flourished from about 1850 to 1875, part of the Romantic period. They are characterized by symmetrically arranged bay windows, most often with three different kinds of window arches, all flanking an ornate entrance

way featuring an entablature supported by columns. [*See* Romantic Period]

hip/hipped roof: A roof that slopes upward from all four sides of a building.

International (housing style): This unadorned, determinedly functional style evolved in the Eclectic period from the work of famous European architects in the mid-1920s, and continues to influence American architecture today. International Style houses are characterized by smooth, uniform exterior wall surfaces, flat roofs (sometimes at multiple levels and cantilevered), and continuous windows, often floor-to-ceiling in style. [*See* Eclectic Period]

Ionic: *See* orders: Ionic

Italianate (housing style): This Romantic-period style was a primary and pervasive influence in U.S. architecture from about 1840 to at least 1885. The purest form is a 2- or 3-story cube of stone or stucco with a simple hipped roof, widely overhanging eaves supported by decorative corbels, pilastered front entranceway or portico with columns, quoins and long, vertical windows with arched crowns. Some examples include a cupola. Many forms, inspired by rambling Italian villas, incorporate part of a square or multisided tower into the structure. [*See* Romantic Period]

Italian Renaissance (housing style): Moderately popular from about 1890 to 1935, these Eclectic-period houses most commonly are square or rectangular, two stories high, with a simple, low-pitched hip roof, typically of tile. Eaves are closed but wide and supported by decorative corbels. Exterior walls often are stucco or masonry veneer, and first-floor windows employ an arched crown. [*See* Eclectic Period]

lintel: A horizontal beam, supported by posts, used to support the weight over a window or door; referred to as post-and-lintel construction.

log cabins/houses: In the U.S., houses built of logs date to the Delaware Valley of the 1630s. Swedish, Finnish, German and Swiss settlers developed and refined log-house and log-cabin construction techniques throughout the American frontier. In the 1970s, modern production, construction and insulation techniques contributed to a rebirth in the popularity of log houses that continues today, particularly in rural or wooded settings. [*See* Folk Period]

loggia: A roofed gallery, traditionally with an arcade or colonnade, open on at least one side. [*See* arcade, colonnade]

mansard: *See* American Mansard

Minimal Traditional (housing style): A simple Modern-period house that flourished from 1935 to about 1950, primarily as tract housing. Typically, these forerunners of Ranch-style houses are one-story, with a low- or moderately pitched roof, a large chimney and short eaves. [*See* Modern Period]

Mission (housing style): An Eclectic-period style that owes its design to the landmark Hispanic missions of the American Southwest. These tile-roofed, stucco houses evolved in California in the late 1880s, often incorporating towers and, more commonly, arched roof and front porch parapets. [*See* Eclectic Period]

Midland (housing style): These Folk-period houses, mostly three-room, often center-chimney, log homes, were built by the European settlers of the mid-Atlantic colonies. Expansions sometimes included a shed-roof porch and adjoining room. [*See* Folk Period]

minaret: A high tower, part of or beside a mosque, with a gallery or balcony from which a muezzin calls the faithful to prayer.

Modern Period (housing style): This rather amorphous category has been used to describe most U.S. housing forms developed since about 1940: Contemporary, Ranch, Minimal Traditional, Shed, and Split-Level.

Monterey (housing style): Characterized by two stories, featuring a long balcony and a low-pitched gabled roof, this Eclectic-period housing style revived Spanish architectural influences and united them with a typically Colonial, or massed, floor plan, in which rooms were grouped together at least two deep. [*See* Eclectic Period]

narthex: An enclosed vestibule or anteroom at the entrance to a church.

National (housing style): This category represents not so much a unique style of house as it does a change in building technique and an expansion in the geographical occurrence of specific Folk-period houses that were already well established by the start of the period in 1850. In the next 40 years, as the railroads spread westward and south throughout the nation, varieties of building materials became more readily available everywhere. Building styles, determined in part by the availability of materials, were no longer restricted to specific geographical areas. The sod houses of the prairies and the log homes of the midlands quickly gave way to framed and braced, wood-sheathed houses. [*See* Folk Period]

Native American (housing style): This is a broad category that encompasses a variety of original housing styles developed by American Indians from the Pacific to the Atlantic in the centuries that preceded European settlement—from domed wigwams and conical tepees to arch-roofed long-houses, rectangular plank houses and flat-roofed adobe houses. [*See* Folk Period]

nave: The principal interior section of a church, extending from the main entrance or narthex, down the main aisle to the chancel, or sanctuary; used primarily by the congregation.

Neoclassical (housing style): Houses in this Eclectic-period style, immensely fashionable from the late 1890s until about 1950, were dominated by roof-high front porticoes supported by Corinthian or Ionic columns. The form employs elements of Early Classical Revival, Greek Revival, Adam and Georgian styles. [*See* Eclectic Period]

Neoeclectic (housing style): Houses in this post-1940s period have, since about the mid-1960s, presented a grab bag of modernistic adaptations and interpretations (hence use of the prefix "Neo") of several historic styles, from Mansard, Victorian and Colonial, to Tudor, Mediterranean, and Classical Revival.

Octagon (housing style): Relatively few original examples still exist in this Romantic-period style, which owes its 20-year spate of popularity (1850–70), mostly to promotion by New Yorker Owen S. Fowler. These eight-sided houses usually were two stories high with low-pitched hip roofs and wide overhanging eaves supported by decorative corbels. [*See* Romantic Period]

ogee: A double curve that resembles the letter S, formed by joining a concave and convex line. In architecture, the term commonly describes the profile of certain moldings or the shape of some arches.

orders: In classical Greco-Roman architecture, a reference to the principal styles of columns with their bases, capitals and entablatures. The three Greek orders are named for the three areas of Greece where they originated: Doric (Doris), Ionic (Ionia), Corinthian (Corinth). The two Roman orders are Composite and Tuscan.

    Doric: The oldest and sturdiest of the orders, these columns are fluted, massive and simple, having a plain capital and no formal base.

    Ionic: A fluted column but more slender than the Doric; easily distinguished by its scroll-shaped capital.

    Corinthian: The most slender and ornate of the three Greek columns, the Corinthian order is easily known by its decorative capital of delicately carved acanthus leaves.

    Composite: This Roman order column represents a development of the Greek Corinthian style. Called composite because the style incorporates the scroll-shaped capital of the Ionic column with the ornate acanthus-leafs carving that distinguished the capital of the Corinthian.

Tuscan: A Roman order modeled after the Greek Doric, but even simpler in form, having no flutes. [*See* capitals, columns, entablature]

pagoda: A temple or sacred building, often pyramidal or tower-like, comprising several roofed stories, each of which curves upward.

Palladian: An architectural manner based on strict classical Roman forms; named for Andrea Palladio (1508–80), an Italian Renaissance architect whose work influenced European architecture for more than 200 years after his death. Today the term is most commonly used to describe a popular style of window that has evolved from the classical Palladian form: a large window with a rounded arch at its top and two narrower, shorter windows on either side; the side windows are flanked by pilasters and capped with entablatures on which the arch of the central window rests.

pediment: In Greco-Roman architecture, the triangular, gable end of a roof above the horizontal cornice; also the crown of a monument or part of a facade; commonly part of a decorative scheme incorporated in the molding atop windows and doors or fine cabinetry. When the pediment encloses a complete triangle, the pediment is referred to as pointed. If the area is semicircular, the pediment is called curved. Commonly, the pediment is identifiable but open at its top and said to be a broken pediment.

pier: In architecture, a solid mass of concrete or masonry supporting the thrust of an arch or a vertical load.

pilaster: A flat column or support, often having a capital and base, and built into the face of a wall; commonly used as a decorative, simulated pillar flanking entrance ways and fireplace hearths.

Plains (housing style): Houses in this Folk-period style were made of the building materials that were most commonly available—sometimes stone, more commonly sod—which was cut into bricks and used to make thick walls. Sod also was used as roofing over a frame of poles or planks. Some houses of the period were, in effect, dugouts or half-dugouts, built into small hills or embankments.

plinth: A rectangular or square slab beneath the base of a column or pier. A number of slabs laid together to form a base for a wall is referred to as a plinth course.

portico: An open, roofed structure supported by columns or piers; commonly attached to a building as a porch.

post and lintel: *See* lintel

Postmedieval English (housing style): Houses built from about 1600 to the first half of the 18th century were the first in the Colonial period, and as such they directly reflected the style best known to early English settlers. Two-story houses with steeply pitched, side-gabled roofs, very large chimneys and diamond-pane windows were characteristic. [*See* Colonial Period]

Prairie (housing style): A uniquely American, Eclectic-period design, this short-lived style (1900–20) evolved in Chicago from the famous Prairie School of architecture pioneered by such architects as Frank Lloyd Wright, Louis Sullivan, and Charles E. White, Jr. The style radically deemphasized the box-like designs that were the standard in American architecture, opting instead for a more sweeping, horizontally oriented form, featuring low-pitched, commonly hipped, roofs, wide eaves and rows of windows. [*See* Eclectic Period]

Pueblo (housing style): A housing style that enjoyed a resurgence of popularity in the early 1900s, Adobe, or Pueblo, derives from early dwellings in the American Southwest. Houses are made from bricks and mortar of sun-dried adobe clays, or of material that simulates adobe. Vigas, roof beams that extend visibly through outside walls, give the house its characteristic appearance. [*See* Eclectic Period]

Queen Anne (housing style): A distinctively ornate Victorian-period style that dominated American architecture from about 1880 to 1910. Decorative spindlework, patterned siding, steeply pitched but irregularly shaped, sometimes pyramidal, roofs and a dominant front gable are characteristics of the style. The term "Queen Anne" often is applied to any similarly ornate American house of the period. [*See* Victorian Period]

quoin: In masonry construction, a quoin is a hard stone or brick used, usually in one vertical course on both sides of a corner, as decorative reinforcement.

Ranch (housing style): No Modern-period style is more thoroughly equated with suburban growth, newfound mobility and the rise of the American middle class than this rambling, one-story form that prospered from about 1935 to 1975. Typical examples incorporate a garage, low-pitched hipped or cross-gabled roof with moderate-to-wide eaves. [*See* Modern Period]

Richardsonian Romanesque (housing style): Named after Boston architect Henry Hobson Richardson, this Victorian-period style uses masonry exclusively and is limited primarily to a relatively small number of commercial and public buildings. Most examples include round towers with conical roofs, rounded arches over windows, entrance and porch roof supports. [*See* Victorian Period]

Romantic Period (housing style): A general reference to a variety of 19th-century U.S. housing styles that were developed from earlier forms. The period is generally taken to encompass Exotic Revival, Greek Revival, Gothic Revival, Italianate and Octagonal; all were popular between 1820 and the late 1880s.

Saltbox (housing style): A common New England traditional-style house from the early 1700s. It is typically 2½ stories high with a catslide roof that allows a 1½-room-deep floor plan. [*See* catslide roof, Folk Period]

Second Empire (housing style): An ornate Victorian-period style that flourished from about 1855–85, emulating architectural designs popular at the time in France, the reign of Napoleon III. Characterized chiefly by any of five different styles of mansard roof, all of which have a double slope on all four sides. The lower roofs are vertical, or nearly vertical, and commonly feature several gable-style dormers. [*See* Romantic Period]

Shed (housing style): A post-1940s Modern-style house common since about 1960 emphasizing geometric shapes; dominant feature is a series of shed roofs, often slanting in different directions. [*See* Modern Period, shed roof]

shed roof: A roof having only one sloping side.

Shingle (housing style): These uniquely American, high-style Victorian-period houses, built from about 1880 to 1900, used wood shingles to unify the surfaces of irregularly shaped, typically rambling, houses that were an amalgam of Queen Anne, Richardsonian Romanesque and Colonial Revival influences. [*See* Colonial Revival, Queen Anne, Richardsonian Romanesque, Victorian Period]

Spanish Colonial (housing style): Colonial-period houses of this style were ubiquitous throughout the American Southwest from at least 1600 well into the 19th century. Typically, these houses were stucco over adobe or rock and one story high with flat or low-pitched, side-gabled roofs of half-cylindrical tiles. [*See* Colonial Period]

Spanish Eclectic or Spanish Colonial Revival (housing style): These Eclectic-period houses generally were built from about 1915 to 1940 in many parts of the South and Southwest, in virtually any locale where Spanish Colonial-style houses had flourished. Red-tiled, low-pitched roofs and stucco siding are distinguishing characteristics. Stylistic embellishments borrow from a broad range of historic Spanish architecture. [*See* Eclectic Period]

Split-level (housing style): A Modern-period housing style popular since the late 1950s featuring a two-level living area with a front entrance situated above the lower level but below the upper level. Viewed from its front, such a house commonly appears to be a bit more than one story high, but from the back, two. [*See* Modern Period]

Stick (housing style): A dramatically decorated and stylized Victorian-period house characterized by high, steep roofs; carved, complex silhouettes; ornate windows and doors; gingerbread trim; exposed framing timbers; and, especially, patterned exterior walls. Sometimes referred to as Carpenter Gothic, Stick Style houses—popular from about 1860 to 1890—represent a transition between Gothic Revival and Queen Anne styles. [*See* Victorian Period]

stucco: A textured exterior plaster finish of portland cement, lime, sand and water.

Swiss Chalet (housing style): A 1½- to 2½-story house with a gable front, several large windows, a second-story porch or balcony with a decorative balustrade of cutout spindles and decorative natural exterior woodwork. The style first presented itself in the U.S. from 1835 to about 1890, during the Romantic period; usually classified as an Exotic Revival. [*See* Romantic Period]

Tidewater South (housing style): These Folk-period houses, built from about 1700 to 1850 in the coastal regions of the American South, usually were side-gabled, one-story dwellings, linear in orientation and, especially among later examples, featuring a full-width, open-front, shed-roofed front porch. [*See* Folk Period]

tracery: Ornamental bars or ribs forming a geometrical or curvilinear pattern in a screen, panel or, traditionally, in the upper part of a Gothic window.

transept: The horizontal, or transverse, section in the classical, cruciform layout of a church.

Tudor (housing style): An Eclectic-period style popular from about 1890 to 1940 generally based on medieval English architecture and encompassing styles that range from small stylized cottages to grand manors; characterized by steeply pitched roofs and gable fronts or prominent cross-gables; also typical are decorative false half-timbering, tall narrow windows and a massive chimney capped with decorative chimney pots. [*See* Eclectic Period]

turret: A small tower, usually one that is built into a corner or other structural angle of a fortress or castle.

Tuscan: *See* orders: Tuscan

vault: An arched ceiling or roof, usually of masonry, with a broad range of structural and decorative complexity, from barrel vaults to stylized rib vaults.

veranda: An open porch, usually roofed and often partially enclosed; usually adjacent or attached to a house or outbuilding.

vestibule: An anteroom or small foyer.

vestry: A church room in which vestments and liturgical objects are kept.

Victorian Period (housing style): A general reference that actually encompasses a variety of ornate styles: Folk Victorian, Queen Anne, Richardsonian Romanesque, Second Empire, Shingle, and Stick; all were fashionable in the U.S. from about 1860 to the turn of the century, the latter years of British Queen Victoria's reign.

vigas: Wooden roof beams that project through the exterior walls of Adobe or Pueblo Revival houses.

wainscot: A decorative and protective wood facing affixed as panels on the lower portion of an interior wall.

Williamsburg Georgian (housing style): *See* Early Georgian

SUGGESTED REFERENCES AND CONTACTS:

A Field Guide to American Houses, Virginia and Lee MacAlester. New York: Alfred A. Knopf, Inc., 1990.

A History of Architecture, Sir Banister Fletcher, edited by John Musgrave. Stoneham, Mass.: Butterworth Publishing (subsidiary of Reed Publishing), 1987.

National Register of Historic Places, National Park Service, U.S. Dept. of the Interior, 1100 L St. NW, Room 6111, Washington, D.C. 20005, (202) 343-9559. The staff of the National Register maintains the country's official list of historically important districts, sites, and buildings. Inclusion on the list can make designated properties eligible for tax credits, rehabilitation subsidies and, most commonly, protection from destruction or development. The process of evaluating a nominee for inclusion in the Register begins at the state government level, with the Historic Preservation Commission. The telephone numbers of state historic preservation commissions, or historical commissions, are listed in the government section of the telephone directory for each state capital.

PHOTOGRAPHY TERMS

ASA: A film-speed rating system devised by the now-defunct American Standards Association, gradually being replaced by the ISO system. [*See* ISO]

aperture: A camera's lens opening; size is indicated by f-stop numbers. [*See* f-stop numbers]

BCPS: An abbreviation for Beam Candle Power Seconds, a numerical measurement of light output from a flash unit.

bleed: An image extending to the edge of the paper on which it is printed.

blocking out: The process of painting parts of a negative with an opaque liquid so as to block out light and make them appear white on the print. The effect is to isolate an image on the negative; often used in commercial work.

box camera: Introduced in 1888 by American manufacturer George Eastman, the box camera employed a single-element, fixed-focus lens, and gelatin-based roll film. It was the first popular camera. [*See* fixed-focus lens]

bracketing: A common shooting technique designed to make an acceptable exposure a certainty. A photographer takes several frames of the same subject from the same vantage point but at different exposures.

B-setting: Shutter-ring letter indicating the proper setting for a time exposure; the shutter opens when the release is pressed and closes when it is released; has largely replaced T- (for time) settings.

cable release: A flexible cable attached to a camera's shutter release that allows a photographer to take a picture without otherwise touching the camera; useful in making time exposures, which could suffer from slight camera movement.

camera obscura: The concept behind this precursor of the modern camera, which evolved as an artist's drawing aid, dates to Aristotle more than 300 years before Christ, though the term itself did not appear until about the 11th century. The earliest camera obscura was a dark room with a small hole, or aperture, in one wall, through which passing light played an inverted image of the scene outside onto a blank wall or screen. By the 15th century, lenses were fitted to the aperture, and over the next three centuries the use of canopies made the camera obscura portable. Artists used them to trace scenic designs and establish realistic perspectives for their work.

color negative film: *See* color print film

color positive film: *See* color slide film

color print film: Color film that produces a negative image; also called color negative film.

color slide film: Color film that produces a positive image; also called color positive, color reversal, or transparency film.

contact print: A print that is the same size as the negative; usually made as a convenient way to check the prospective quality of prints.

cropping: Eliminating undesirable parts of a picture, either in the shooting itself, in the way the subject is framed, or in the printing or reproduction, by image selection or enlargement.

daguerreotype: A photographic print made in the manner introduced in 1839 by French physicist and painter Louis Jacques Mandé Daguerre (1787–1851). Daguerreotyping was the world's first commercial photographic process. Daguerre created a permanent image by making a single exposure on a highly polished, silver-coated plate of copper that had been exposed to iodine vapors, creating a light-sensitive layer of silver iodide. The copper plate was then exposed to vapors of warmed mercury and "fixed" with sodium thiosulfate or sodium chloride. The resultant photographs, daguerreotypes, heralded the popularization of photography as an art form. Though Daguerre's process made him the best-known of all historic photographers, it is his partner, Joseph Nicéphore Niépce (1765–1833), who generally is credited as the inventor of photography. Niépce, also a French chemist and physicist, made the first paper negative in 1816. By 1826, using an emulsion of light-sensitive hydrocarbon known as bitumen of Judea, he was able to fix a permanent positive image, a view of his own estate at Gras, France, on a pewter plate. The photograph survives today. Niépce became Daguerre's partner in 1829, but died in 1833, while the two men were trying to devise a commercially acceptable photographic process. The daguerreotype evolved six years later.

definition: A general term most often used to indicate the sharpness and clarity of images in a negative or print or the ability of a lens to produce such detail.

depth of field: The part of a photograph that is in sharpest focus; specifically, the distance between in-focus objects at the extremes of foreground and background.

diaphragm: The aperture mechanism, which controls the size of the lens opening; adjusted by f-stop.

DIN: Abbreviation for *Deutsche Industrie Norm* (German Standards Organization), which set a European standard for film speeds; being replaced by the ISO system. [*See* ISO]

disc camera: A small automatic camera that uses a thin, wheel-shaped film cartridge, usually providing 15 exposures.

distance symbols: Symbols on the focus control of simple cameras that serve as focus guides.

emulsion: The light-sensitive chemical coating, usually silver halides in gelatin, on acetate or paper.

exposure: A term used variously as a synonym for "photograph" or for the length of time that a specific intensity of light is allowed to act on film.

exposure meter: A hand-held or built-in camera device that reads, or measures, the intensity of light falling on or reflected from a subject and translates the reading into f-stops and shutter speeds.

exposure setting: The combination of f-stop and shutter speed.

film cartridge: Prepacked, quick-loading and light-tight plastic film container used in pocket and subminiature cameras.

film cassette: Light-tight metal or plastic film container used in 35mm cameras.

film speed: A numerical system (ISO/ASA) indicating a film's relative sensitivity to light. The higher the number, the more light-sensitive the film.

fish-eye lens: An extreme wide-angle lens that produces a round, usually distorted, picture.

fixed-focus lens: A lens focused on a fixed point so that most subjects, from about 6 feet to infinity, can be photographed clearly.

flash synchronization: The timing of the light burst from a flash bulb or electronic flash unit in relation to the speed of a camera's shutter. Camera controls must be set to differentiate shutter response times for one of these two artificial-light sources. Since light from a flash bulb reaches its peak of brightness more slowly than does light from an electronic flash, the actual opening of the camera's shutter must be delayed accordingly; usually accomplished with a setting of *M* for bulb flash, *X* for electronic.

focal length: The distance between the optical center of a camera's lens when the camera is focused on infinity and the focal plane, that is, the flat film surface in a loaded camera. The longer the focal length, the bigger the image the lens will produce, that is, the closer it will appear in the film frame. Telephoto lenses are examples of lenses with long focal lengths.

f-stop numbers: Numbers on a camera lens indicating aperture sizes. The bigger the number, the smaller the aperture and, therefore, the less light admitted to the camera. Each change of number usually represents a halving or doubling of aperture size. An aperture setting of f/8, for example, admits half as much light as an f/5.6 setting, and twice as much as a setting of f/11.

grain: The sandy or pebbly appearance of some photographs; most obvious in high-speed films, enlargements or films that have been overdeveloped. Most noticeable in even, midtone areas of a print.

guide numbers: A system of numbers, varying with film speed, film type and light source, used to provide correct exposure when using a flash attachment.

high-key: Term used to describe a photograph in which light tones dominate and midtones and shadows are few. [*See* low-key]

high-speed film: Film that is exceptionally light-sensitive; usually rated at least ISO/ASA 400; referred to as fast film.

holography: Complex system of photography employing laser beams to create three-dimensional images.

hot shoe: A flash-attachment holder built into a camera and connected to a flash synchronization and shutter system.

hyperfocal point: The nearest point to the camera that is acceptably sharp when the lens is focused on infinity. Used in simple, fixed-focus lens systems. [*See* infinity]

infinity: The point, or distance from the camera, beyond which no further focusing is required in order to keep the photographic subject, usually the broad panorama, in reasonably sharp focus; indicated on a camera lens by the symbol ∞.

infra-red light: Though invisible to the human eye, these light rays beyond the end of the electromagnetic spectrum can be recorded on specially sensitized films, producing black-and-white or color images that record heat, as well as light, intensities.

instant camera: A self-processing camera, such as a Polaroid, that produces its own color or black-and-white prints.

IR/R setting: A mark on many cameras indicating where to set focus in order to shoot infra-red film.

ISO: Abbreviation for the International Standardization Organization, which devised a numerical film-speed rating system taking the place of ASA and DIN numbers throughout the world, actually by incorporating both numbers. For example, an ISO rating of 100/21° indicates an ASA number of 100 and a DIN rating of 21°.

joule: A unit of measurement, equal to one watt-second, used to gauge the amount of light generated by an electronic flash. [*See* watt-second]

lens: The glass or plastic optical element in a camera that bends image-bearing light into focus on film.

low-key: Term describing a photograph in which dark tones dominate and highlights are few. [*See* high-key]

microflash: A very fast electronic flash used in the photographing of high-speed subjects, such as bullets.

miniature camera: Usually taken to mean any camera that uses film smaller than 35mm.

mirror lens: A lens that uses a curved mirror, or set of mirrors, that reflect light; most often used to gain very long focal lengths in a relatively short lens.

montage: A picture that is a composite of several photographs.

motor drive: A camera feature or accessory which, when the shutter is depressed, automatically advances film and shoots from one to six frames per second.

negative: Developed film in which light and dark areas appear reversed.

orthochromatic: Term describing a film emulsion that is sensitive to blue and green light, but not red.

panchromatic: Term describing a film emulsion that is sensitive to all visible colors of the light spectrum, though not uniformly.

panning: Common photographic technique used to connote a sense of motion or speed. A camera, its shutter held open at a slow speed, is moved with the subject, thereby blurring the background but keeping the subject in focus.

photocell: A light-sensitive cell of selenium or cadmium sulfide used in the metering systems of cameras or exposure meters.

photogrammetry: The process of making exact measurements from photographs; for example, maps from aerial photographs.

pinhole camera: A rudimentary camera, actually a simple box wherein light passes through a tiny hole, instead of a lens, and forms an image on film at the back of the box.

polarizing filter: A lens filter that has the effect of darkening blue skies in color photographs and diminishing reflection from most shiny surfaces.

Polaroid: The registered tradename of the famous instant camera employing a one-step photographic process known as the Land process, after its inventor Edwin H. Land. Black-and-white Polaroid film was first marketed in 1948, the color process in 1963.

rangefinder: An optical device, often coupled with a camera's lens, used for focusing. Viewed through a coupled rangefinder, photographic subjects usually appear as split images; adjusting the lens aligns the images, indicating the subject is in focus.

red-eye: A common problem in flash photography, occurring when the light source is too close to the lens; manifests itself as a decided pink or red cast in the eyes of a photographed subject; caused by the sudden burst of light on the subject's retinas. Moving the light source away from the camera lens generally solves the problem.

reflex cameras: Cameras in which a retractable mirror, situated behind the lens, reflects photographic images onto a ground glass for viewing. Single-lens reflex cameras, the most popular of modern cameras, allow viewing and image-making through one lens. The mirror moves out of the way during exposure, allowing light to reach the film.

retouching: After-treatment carried out on a negative or print, in the form of local chemical reduction, local dye or pencil additions or air-brushing. The purpose is to remove blemishes on the negative or print, or to treat particular subject areas to improve the final effect.

reversal film: *See* color slide film

safelight: Used with special filters in a darkroom to provide illumination that does not damage or expose photographic paper or film.

shutter: The mechanical screen that covers the film. When the shutter opens, light strikes the film for a controlled period of time, creating an exposure. [*See* aperture, shutter speed]

shutter speed: Literally, the speed of the shutter, measured in fractions of a second; each setting indicates the exact length of time the shutter will be open, admitting light onto the camera's film.

single-lens reflex camera: *See* reflex cameras

slide: A transparency mounted in cardboard, plastic or glass for use in a projector.

SLR: *See* reflex cameras

standard/normal lens: A lens with a focal length approximately equal to the diagonal measurement of the film with which it is used; for example, a 35mm or 50mm lens on a camera using 35mm film.

stop: The aperture of a lens, as in "f-stop."

stopping down: The act of changing f-stops to reduce lens aperture size, thus decreasing the amount of light entering the camera and increasing the depth of field; for example, "stopping down" from f/8 to f/11.

strobe: Reference to an electronic flash unit.

telephoto lens: A lens with a longer focal length and narrower angle of view than a standard or normal lens; for example, a 135mm lens on a 35mm camera has the effect of enlarging a photo subject, that is, bringing it closer to the camera. [*See* focal length]

through-the-lens: Often abbreviated as TTL, the term generally refers to a light-metering or flash system built into a camera and keyed to the amount of light that passes through the lens.

transparency: Black-and-white or color film that produces a positive image on the film itself, one that can be viewed directly as light passes through it.

T-setting: *See* B-setting

watt-second: A unit of power equal to the energy released by one watt for one second; the equivalent of one joule; both terms are used to gauge the amount of light generated by an electronic flash.

wide-angle lens: A lens that has the effect of widening the photographer's angle of view; for example, a 28mm lens on a 35mm camera.

zoom lens: A specially designed lens that allows the photographer to vary focal lengths and, therefore, the relative closeness of the subject, while keeping the subject in focus.

SUGGESTED REFERENCES:

Eyes of Time: Photojournalism in America, Marianne Fulton. Boston: Bulfinch Press (Little, Brown & Co.), 1989.

The Photographer's Handbook, John Hedgecoe. New York: Alfred A. Knopf, Inc., 2d edition, 1988.

LEGAL TERMS

affidavit: A sworn, voluntary, written statement of facts. [*See* deposition]

amicus curiae: Literally, a friend of the court; someone who is not a party to the legal action at hand but who voluntarily provides information to the court, either to help clarify a complex matter or to protect the volunteer's own interests.

arraignment: In criminal law, the process of calling a defendant before a court, stating the charge against the defendant, asking whether the defendant is guilty or not guilty, and entering the defendant's plea.

array: The entire group of people summoned to court as potential jurors; often used as a synonym for panel. [*See* venire]

attorney: In its broadest sense, one who has been legally authorized to act in another's behalf. One who has such power is said to have the power of attorney. The word is also commonly used as a synonym for "lawyer," but someone who is acting as an attorney for another need not be a lawyer.

certiorari: A writ of review or inquiry that asks an appellate court to review the work of a lower court. [*See* writ; *see also* section entitled Supreme Court of the United States on page 61]

challenge: In jury selection, an objection by the prosecution or defense to the seating of a particular juror, or to the composition of the group from which jurors are being selected. [*See* challenge for cause, peremptory challenge]

challenge for cause: In jury selection, a challenge for which some reason is given. [*See* challenge, peremptory challenge]

chattel mortgage: A mortgage on personal property. Frequently encountered as a lien to ensure payment or performance. [*See* lien]

common-law marriage: A marriage that is not created by the ordinary legal procedure but rather by an agreement to marry, followed by cohabitation. Both persons must be able legally to enter a marriage contract. Not all states recognize common-law marriage, so care must be taken when using the term.

de facto: Existing in fact. [*See* de jure]

de jure: By right or law. [*See* de facto]

demur: To take exception to the legal basis of a pleading, or to the facts stated.

demurrer: A plea for dismissal by a defendant who claims that even if the stated facts are true, they are not sufficient for legal action or are so legally flawed that they will not stand in a court of law.

deposition: Testimony of a witness in response to interrogatories. The testimony is not taken in court, but it is written down and authenticated so that it may be used in court. The term is not a synonym for affidavit, which refers to a voluntary statement. [*See* affidavit, interrogatories]

discovery, bill of: A request by the plaintiff for necessary facts or documents held by the defendant.

dismissal: An order by a judge or court that ends a suit, action, criminal charge, etc., without a trial. A dismissal may be granted for procedural reasons or because the prosecution or plaintiff has not presented a case that merits continuing to trial. [*See* dismissal with prejudice]

dismissal with prejudice: A dismissal in which the decision to drop is based on the merits of the case. This bars future actions on the same claim. [*See* dismissal]

double jeopardy: Prosecution twice for the same crime or transaction; specifically prohibited by the U.S. Constitution. [*See* section entitled U.S. Constitution and Amendments on page 49]

dram shop act: A statute that allows a plaintiff who was injured by someone who was intoxicated to take civil action against people who contributed to the intoxication. Commonly used against saloonkeepers and liquor store owners.

duces tecum: Literally, bring with you. [*See* subpoena duces tecum]

escheat: Reversion of property to the state, due to the lack of a legal heir.

et ux: *See* uxor

exception: In addition to its common meaning, an objection to the action taken by a court in overruling an objection. It notes disagreement with the decision and implies an intention to seek reversal of that decision at a later time.

ex parte: From one party only.

fiduciary: As a noun, one entrusted to act in good faith on another's behalf. As an adjective, having the characteristics of a trust. [*See* section entitled Banking Terms on page 315]

grand jury: A jury of inquiry impaneled to review criminal complaints, hear evidence presented by a prosecutor and decide whether the evidence is sufficient to issue indictments. [*See* indictment, petit jury]

habeas corpus: Literally, you have the body; a writ that seeks to bring a party or, in civil actions, a cause before a particular court or judge. [*See* habeas corpus ad faciendum et recipiendum, habeas corpus ad subjiciendum, writ]

habeas corpus ad faciendum et recipiendum: A writ

LEGAL TERMS 359

used in civil cases to move the cause from a lower court to a higher court for disposition. [*See* habeas corpus, writ]

habeas corpus ad subjiciendum: When people refer to a writ of habeas corpus, this is usually the legal document to which they are referring. The writ commands a person who is detaining someone else, a law enforcement agency, for example, to produce the person identified in the writ for whatever purpose the court specifies. Historically, such writs evolved as protection against unlawful arrest and protracted detention by the government. [*See* habeas corpus, writ]

indictment: A written accusation presented by a grand jury charging that a named individual has committed a punishable offense. [*See* grand jury, information, true bill]

in extremis: Gravely ill without hope of recovery; near death.

information, criminal: An accusation of criminal activity having the same effect as an indictment. A criminal information differs from an indictment only in that it is made by a prosecutor instead of a grand jury. Local law and practice determine when a criminal information must or may be issued instead of an indictment. [*See* indictment]

in forma pauperis: As a pauper; a litigant in such condition cannot be charged for court costs.

interrogatories: Written questions that are drawn up by one party and served on an adversary, who must respond under oath. [*See* deposition]

lessee: Someone who holds a lease; commonly, a tenant.

lessor: Someone who conveys a lease; commonly, a landlord.

libel: Publication that causes injury to reputation. [*See* Libel on page 411]

mens rea: Wrongful purpose or criminal intent.

nolle prosequi: A formal statement by the plaintiff in a civil case or the prosecutor in a criminal case that he will not proceed with all or part of the case, counts or defendants. In effect, it removes some or all of the case from prosecution or litigation. Sometimes used as a verb, as in: The charges against one of the defendants were nolled.

nolo contendere: Literally, I do not wish to contest [it]. In criminal law, a plea by which the defendant chooses not to contest the charge against him. It has the same effect as a guilty plea, although it is not an admission of guilt. It cannot be used as proof of guilt or liability in any civil suit arising from the same circumstance that spawned the criminal charge.

no true bill: In criminal law, a finding by a grand jury that there is not enough evidence to justify indictment.

obiter dictum: Literally, something said in passing; incidental comments; statements in a legal decision that do not bear upon the question under consideration.

obligee: A person to whom a debt or service is owed under contract. [*See* obligor]

obligor: A person who is obligated to perform a debt or service under a contract, or who is liable for a tort. [*See* obligee, tort]

parole: Conditional release of a prisoner after part of his court-imposed term of imprisonment has been completed; may be revoked if convict fails to follow conditions set forth in parole agreement. [*See* probation]

parol evidence: Evidence that is oral or verbal, including court testimony.

peremptory challenge: During the process of jury selection in criminal law, the right to exclude a specified number of potential jurors without showing cause. [*See* challenge]

perjury: Lying under oath, whether in court, in an affidavit or in a deposition.

petit jury: A jury that hears evidence in civil or criminal trials and decides questions of guilt or civil liability; it is called a petit jury to distinguish it from a grand jury, which deals with pretrial proceedings. [*See* grand jury]

power of attorney: The legal authority granted by a person empowering another to act in the person's behalf or as the person's legal representative. [*See* attorney]

prima facie: Literally, on first appearance. [*See* prima facie case, prima facie evidence]

prima facie case: A case in which a plaintiff's or prosecutor's initial evidence is sufficient grounds for continuance of legal action.

prima facie evidence: Evidence that, on its face, is presumed to be true and is sufficient to establish a fact or case unless disproven.

probation: A court-ordered sentence that allows someone convicted of an offense to avoid incarceration, under the condition of good behavior and usually with supervision. A defendant, for example, may be sentenced to six months in prison and one year probation instead of a more lengthy prison term. [*See* parole]

pro bono: Literally, for the good (a shortened form of pro bono publico, for the public good). Used to describe professional work undertaken by lawyers in the public interest, without compensation.

pro se: Literally, for himself; in his own behalf. Frequently used to describe persons who represent themselves in court.

quitclaim deed: A conveyance of realty that transfers any title, interest or claim that the grantor may have in the property; it does not guarantee that the grantor has a clear or valid title. [*See* warranty deed]

res: Literally, a thing; used to refer to items and issues that are the subject of legal action; also refers to the legal actions themselves. [*See* res ipsa loquitur, res judicata]

res adjudicata: *See* res judicata

res ipsa loquitur: Literally, the thing speaks for itself; a presumption that the defendant was negligent, based on proof that the means for the injury was within his control, and that the injury was not one that would have occurred normally without negligence on the part of the defendant. [*See* res]

res judicata: An issue that has been authoritatively and finally settled by a court decision. Often misspelled res adjudicata. [*See* res]

seriatim: Separately. Five people may be tried for commission of a felony, for example, but if tried seriatim, each would be tried separately.

sine die: Literally, without a day; without setting a date for a further meeting; a final adjournment.

subpoena: Literally, under penalty; a writ requiring a witness to appear at a specified time before a specified court. [*See* subpoena duces tecum]

subpoena duces tecum: A subpoena that requires the summoned party to bring documents, evidence, etc. [*See* subpoena; *see also* Libel on page 411]

sui generis: Literally, of its own kind; unique; a Latin term found often in legal decisions to indicate a singular set of events.

sui juris: Literally, of one's own right; possessing full legal and social rights; able to handle one's own affairs; encountered often in reference to competency.

tort: A civil wrong or injury that does not involve contractual rights. Torts include injury to a person, to his reputation, to his feelings or to his property. Libel is an example of a tort.

true bill: In criminal practice, a finding by a grand jury that there is enough evidence to justify indictment. [*See* indictment]

uxor: Wife; frequently found in land records in the phrase *et uxor*, which follows a man's name and means "and wife." Sometimes shortened to *et ux*.

venue: The geographical place in which an action is brought for trial, and from which jurors are chosen. Commonly encountered when a defendant requests a change of venue; that is, a change in the place of the trial. Such requests often are based on the claim that pretrial publicity may have biased potential jurors in a particular area.

venire: The process of assembling an array of potential jurors. [*See* array]

voir dire: A preliminary examination of a witness or juror during which the person's competency to testify or to sit in judgment is examined. Challenges may be made. [*See* challenge]

warranty deed: A conveyance of realty in which the grantor guarantees that he has clear title, free of any encumbrances or liens, to the property he is transferring. It differs from a quitclaim deed in that it specifies the interests of the grantor and guarantees that those interests are transferred with the property. [*See* quitclaim deed]

writ: A legal document issued by a court that commands performance of a specified act, or that grants authority for an act. [*See* habeas corpus, habeas corpus ad faciendum et recipiendum, habeas corpus ad subjiciendum]

SUGGESTED REFERENCES:

Black's Law Dictionary, Henry Campbell Black et al. Saint Paul, Minn.: West Publishing Co., 6th edition, 1990.

The Guide to American Law: Everyone's Legal Encyclopedia, vols. 1–12. Saint Paul, Minn.: West Publishing Co., 1985, updated by supplements.

Law Dictionary, Steven H. Gifis. Hauppauge, N.Y.: Barron's Educational Series Inc., 2d edition, 1984.

You and the Law, Consumer Guide Editors. New York: NAL/Dutton division of Penguin USA, 1991.

Lexis, a full-text computer database covering federal and state laws, legal journals and reference sources; provided by Mead Data Central, 9393 Springboro Pike, P.O. Box 933, Dayton, OH 45401, (513) 865-6800.

Westlaw, a collection of computer databases that includes full texts of state and federal court decisions, federal regulations and legal periodicals; provided by West Publishing Co., 50 W. Kellogg Blvd., St. Paul, MN 55164-9833, (800) 937-8529.

PART EIGHT

MATHEMATICS

PERCENTS AND INTEREST

Percents: Percents tell how many out of one hundred. They are fractions in which the % symbol represents 1/100. For this reason, it is necessary to convert percentages to fractions before doing most mathematical functions. Percentages can converted by making 100 the divisor, or by moving the decimal point two places to the left. Thus, 80% can be expressed as 80/100 (which is equivalent to 4/5) or .80.

Percentiles: Percentages should not be confused with percentiles, which divide a variable into 100 equal groupings. For example, a student might answer 80 percent of the questions on a standardized test correctly. (That is, 80 out of every 100.) That performance might place the student in the 90th percentile of all students who took the test. (That is, when the performance of all students was divided into 100 equal parts, his performance placed him in the 90th grouping. Of every 100 students who took the test, on average, 89 scored below him and 10 scored above him.)

Finding a percentage: Multiply the number by the percent, expressed in hundredths. For example: Suppose that 35 percent of the state's 180 municipal planners oppose proposed legislation. To find how many oppose it, multiply the number of planners by the percent, expressed in hundredths or as a fraction:

$$180 \times .35 = 63$$

or

$$180 \times 35/100 = 63$$

Finding what percent one number, A, is of another, B: Divide A by B and convert the resulting fraction to a percent. For example, if 63 out of 180 municipal planners oppose proposed legislation, what percentage oppose it?

It may help to phrase percent problems in a consistent way, so that the phrasing helps to set up the equation. This is especially useful in complicated problems. In this case, the phrase would be: 63 is what percent of 180? The phrase "of 180" indicates that this is the number that is being used as the comparison value. It is the divisor.

$$63/180 = .35 \qquad .35 = 35\%$$

The larger number is not always the divisor. For example, if 2,500 people attended a convention this year, and only 2,000 attended last year, how does this year's turnout compare with last year's? The question can be phrased: 2,500 is what percent of 2,000? The "of" word represents the divisor.

$$2,500/2,000 = 1.25 \qquad 1.25 = 125\%$$

Finding the whole when a percent is given: The easiest way to find the number in the whole is to find the number that represents 1 percent, and then multiply that by 100. For example, if 9 of the directors of a company voted for a proposal, and that is only 18 percent of the directors, how many directors are there?

$$18\% = 9$$

To find what 1 percent equals, divide both sides by 18.

$$18\%/18 = 9/18$$

$$1\% = .50$$

If 1% equals .50, then we can find 100 percent by multiplying both sides of the equation by 100.

$$100 \times 1\% = 100 \times .50$$

$$100\% = 50$$

Finding percentage increases or decreases: The process for finding a percentage increase or decrease is the same as for finding what percentage one number is of another, with this warning: You must make sure that you are dealing with the portion that represents only the increase or decrease.

For example, if 2,500 people attended this year's convention, and 2,000 attended last year's, what percentage increase does that represent? We want to know how the increase—500—compares with last year's total. The question can be phrased: What percentage is 500 of 2,000? The "of" word is the divisor.

$$500/2,000 = .25 \qquad .25 = 25\%$$

The increase is 25%. As we saw in the earlier problem, 2,500 is 125% of 2,000. If we had wanted to, we could have obtained the percentage increase from that equation by subtracting 100% from 125%. The result is the same.

Decreases are figured in the same way. For example, if 2,250 people sign up for next year's convention, how much of a decrease will that be from this year's total of 2,500? Because we are interested in the amount of decrease—250—we can phrase the question: 250 is what percent of 2,500? The "of" word is the divisor.

$$250/2,500 = .10 \qquad .10 = 10\%$$

Figuring multiple discounts: Percents are often used to indicate a price discount. When there is only one discount, the problem is straightforward. For example, a computer normally sells for $2,500 but is on sale for 20 percent less.

$$\$2,500 \times .20 = \$500$$
$$\$2,500 - \$500 = \$2,000$$

When there are multiple discounts, these each must be figured in succession. For example, a 20 percent discount followed by a 10 percent discount is not the same as a 30% percent discount. In the computer example, if there is an additional 10% discounted because of a coupon, the second discount is:

$$\$2,000 \times .10 = \$200$$

This amount is subtracted from the $2,000 that resulted from the first discount.

$$\$2,000 - \$200 = \$1,800$$

The price of the $2,500 computer, after a 20% discount and a 10% discount, is $1,800. (If there had been a 30% discount from the original price, the selling price would have been $1,750.)

A convenient way to find the final price when there are multiple discounts is to subtract each discounted percentage from 100, and then multiply each of the fractional answers by the whole price. In the computer example, the first sale price was 80 percent of the original price, and the second sale price was 90 percent of the first.

$$\$2,500 \times 80\% \times 90\% = X$$
$$\$2,500 \times .80 \times .90 = \$1,800$$

Figuring simple interest: Percentages often are used to indicate the rate of return on principal over time. The amount of interest earned can be found by multiplying the principal times the rate times the length of time (usually expressed in years).

$$\text{Interest} = \text{Principal} \times \text{Rate} \times \text{Time}$$

For example, if someone lends a friend $2,000 for a year at a 5% rate of interest, what will the interest be?

$$\text{Interest} = \$2,000 \times .05 \times 1$$
$$\text{Interest} = \$100$$

Figuring compound interest: Compound interest differs from simple interest in that it is added to the principal at points throughout the payment period, rather than just at the end. When the interest is added to the principal, it begins to earn interest. Thus, identical rates produce greater return if they are compounded than if they are not. The interest may be compounded daily, weekly, monthly, quarterly, yearly or at any other intervals.

For example, a member of a credit union places $2,000 in a one-year savings account that earns 6% interest. If that interest is not compounded, at the end of the year, the member will have earned $120 in interest ($120 = $2,000 × .06 × 1).

If the interest is compounded quarterly (that is, the credit union adds earned interest to the principal every quarter of a year), the member will earn more money.

At the end of the first quarter:

$$\text{Interest} = \$2,000 \times 6\% \times .25 \text{ year}$$
$$\text{Interest} = \$2,000 \times .06 \times .25$$
$$\text{Interest} = \$30$$

At the end of the second quarter:

$$\text{Interest} = (\$2,000 + \$30) \times .06 \times .25$$
$$\text{Interest} = \$30.45$$

At the end of the third quarter:

$$\text{Interest} = (\$2,030 + \$30.45) \times .06 \times .25$$
$$\text{Interest} = \$30.91$$

At the end of the fourth quarter:

$$\text{Interest} = (\$2,060.45 + \$30.91) \times .06 \times .25$$
$$\text{Interest} = \$31.37$$

Total interest equals:

$$\$30 + 30.45 + 30.91 + 31.37 = \$122.73$$

Because the calculations are so cumbersome, it is usually easier to use a compound interest table to figure interest return (on an investment, for example) or charges (on a car loan, for example). The tables are available at banks, libraries and office supply stores.

Rule of 72: This gives the approximate time required for a sum of money to double at a given rate of compound interest. To find the approximate number of years, divide 72 by the interest rate.

For example, if money is placed in a savings account at 6.75% interest, how long before the money will double?

$$\text{Approximate Years} = 72/\% \text{ interest}$$
$$\text{Approximate Years} = 72/6.75$$
$$\text{Approximate Years} = 10.67$$

PROPORTIONS

Proportions are simple equations that indicate relationships between numbers. There is a constant ratio between the numbers in a proportion. For example: $5/10 = 7.5/15$. This would be read: 5 is to 10 as 7.5 is to 15. The ratio on both sides of the equation is 1:2.

Usually, problems involving proportions require solving the equation for a missing number. For example: A photo is 3 inches wide by 5 inches tall. When the width is increased to 4.5 inches, how tall will it be? We know that the new and the old photos will be proportionate in size—that is, the ratio between the height and width is constant—so we can set up a proportion equation and solve for the missing number, X. Setting up the equation can sometimes be simplified by saying the relationship aloud, then translating the equation into mathematical symbols. For example:

The old width is to the old height as the new width is to the new height.

Old width/old height = new width/new height

$$3 \text{ in.}/5 \text{ in.} = 4.5 \text{ in.}/X$$

The equation can then be solved by cross-multiplying and dividing:

$$(5)(4.5) = (3) X$$
$$(5)(4.5)/3 = X$$
$$22.5/3 = X$$
$$7.5 = X$$

The new height is 7.5 inches.

The unknown number can be in any of the four positions of the equation. The process for solving each problem can be written in general terms, using letters to indicate the positions of the numbers:

$$A_1/B_1 = A_2/B_2$$

X may be in any of the four positions.

Sometimes factors in a problem are related by inverse proportion—that is, as one factor increases, another decreases a corresponding amount.

For example: The amount of a certain atmospheric gas decreases at a constant rate as altitude increases. If the concentration is 10 parts per million at 1,000 feet, what is the concentration at 2,000 feet? Because the relationship is inverse, the ratio between the heights is the reverse of the ratio between the parts per million of gas.

We could state this as: The old height is to the new height as the new gas concentration is to the old gas concentration.

old height/new height = new gas/old gas

$$1,000/2,000 = X/10$$
$$1/2 = X/10$$
$$10 (1/2) = X$$
$$X = 5$$

In general terms, we could state this as:

$$A_1/A_2 = B_2/B_1$$

The unknown variable, X, can be in any position.

COMMON MATHEMATICAL FORMULAS

Acceleration:

acceleration = (final velocity − initial velocity)/time

Area of a rectangle, square:

area = length × width

Area of a triangle:

area = 1/2 × base × height

Area of a cube:

area = square of the length of one side × 6

Area of a sphere:

area = square of the diameter × pi [pi = 3.1416]

Area of a circle:

area = square of the radius × pi [pi = 3.1416]

Circumference of a circle:

circumference = diameter × pi [pi = 3.1416]

Force (Newton's Second Law):

force = mass × acceleration

Momentum:

momentum = mass × velocity

Power:

power = work/time

Velocity:

velocity = distance × time

Volume of a cube:

volume = the length of one side cubed

Volume of a pyramid:

volume = area of the base × height × 1/3

Volume of a cylinder:

volume = area of base × height

Volume of a sphere:

volume = radius cubed × 4/3 × pi [pi = 3.1416]

Volume of a cone:

volume = area of base × height × 1/3

Volume of a rectangular solid:

volume = length × width × height

Weight:

weight = mass × force of gravity [32.2 feet/sec.^{2}]

Work:

work = force × distance

TEMPERATURE

Celsius

The international system used for measuring temperature. Water freezes at 0° C. and boils at 100° C. (Also called "Centigrade," although "Celsius" is preferred.) Named for Anders Celsius, the Swedish astronomer who devised the system in 1942. Absolute zero (the coldest possible temperature) is −273.15° C. Normal body temperature is 37° C.

Kelvin

A scale of temperature similar in structure to the Celsius scale, but with the zero-point at absolute zero (the coldest possible temperature). There are no negative temperatures. Water freezes at 273.15° K and boils at 373.15° K. Normal body temperature is 310.15° K.

Fahrenheit

The temperature scale in common use in the United States. The zero-point is set at the lowest temperature that its creator (G.D. Fahrenheit) could achieve in his laboratory. Water freezes at 32° F. and boils at 212° F. Absolute zero is −459.7° F. Normal body temperature is 98.6° F.

TEMPERATURE CONVERSIONS:

Celsius to Fahrenheit:
Multiply the Celsius temperature by 9. Divide the result by 5. Add 32.

$$F = 9/5 \ C + 32$$

Celsius to Kelvin:
Add 273.15.

$$K = C + 273.15$$

Fahrenheit to Celsius:
Subtract 32 from the Fahrenheit temperature. Multiply the result by 5. Divide by 9.

$$C = 5/9 \ (F - 32)$$

Kelvin to Celsius:
Subtract 273.15.

$$C = K - 273.15$$

WEIGHTS AND MEASURES

METRIC MEASURES:

Most of the world uses the metric system of measurement, which is built upon units of 10. It is also known as the International System (*Système Internationale* or *SI*). Common prefixes, abbreviations and their meanings are:

Giga-	G	billion
Mega-	M	million
Kilo-	K	thousand
Hecto-	h	hundred
Deka-	da	ten
Deci-	d	one-tenth
Centi-	c	one-one hundredth
Milli-	m	one-one millionth
Micro-	μ	one-one-millionth
Nano-	n	one-one billionth

linear:

1 centimeter (cm) = 10 millimeters (mm)
1 decimeter (dm) = 10 centimeters
1 meter (m) = 10 decimeters = 100 centimeters
1 dekameter (dkm) = 10 meters (m)
1 hectometer (hm) = 10 dekameters
1 kilometer (km) = 10 hectometers = 1,000 meters

area:

1 square centimeter (cm^2) = 100 square millimeters (mm^2)
1 square meter (m^2) = 10,000 square centimeters
1 are (a) = 100 square meters
1 hectare (ha) = 100 ares = 10,000 square meters
1 square kilometer (km^2) = 100 hectares (ha) = 1,000,000 square meters

volume:

1 centiliter (cl) = 10 milliliters (ml)
1 deciliter (dl) = 10 centiliters
1 liter (l) = 10 deciliters = 1,000 milliliters
1 dekaliter (dal) = 10 liters
1 hectoliter (hl) = 10 dekaliters = 100 liters
1 kiloliter (kl) = 10 hectoliters = 1,000 liters

cubic:

1 cubic centimeter (cm^3) = 1,000 cubic millimeters (mm^3)
1 cubic decimeter (dm^3) = 1,000 cubic centimeters
1 cubic meter (m^3) = 1,000 cubic decimeters = 1 stere

weight:

1 centigram (cg) = 10 milligrams (mg)
1 decigram (dg) = 10 centigrams = 100 milligrams
1 gram (g) = 10 decigrams = 1,000 milligrams
1 dekagram (dkg) = 10 grams
1 hectogram (hg) = 10 dekagrams = 100 grams
1 kilogram (kg) = 10 hectograms = 1,000 grams
1 metric ton (t) = 1,000 kilograms

CUSTOMARY U.S. MEASURES:

Although the U.S. Metric Conversion Act of 1975 was designed to encourage voluntary conversion to the metric system, the United States continues to use its customary measuring system, which is derived from the British Imperial System of the Colonial Period. Within this system, there are several methods of fluid and weight measurements.

Fluids are measured according to the customary liquid measure system (gills, pints, quarts and gallons) or the apothecaries' fluid measure (minims, drams, fluid ounces, pints, quarts and gallons). The apothecaries' fluid measure is used primarily for the compounding and dispensing of liquid drugs.

Weight is measured according to the avoirdupois system (grains, drams, ounces, pounds, hundredweights, tons, long tons), the troy weight system (grains, pennyweights, troy ounces, troy pounds) or the apothecaries' weight system (grains, scruples, apothecaries' drams, apothecaries' ounces, apothecaries' pounds). The avoirdupois system is the common one. Troy weights are used to weigh gems and precious metals. Apothecaries' weights are used primarily in the compounding and dispensing of drugs. The grain is equal in all three systems. The troy ounce and pound and the apothecaries' ounce and pound are equivalent.

In addition, some units of measure pertain to specific products or are defined by national or international convention. For example, one cord of wood is 128 cubic feet (4 feet by 4 feet by 8 feet). In most cases, one barrel is 31.5 gallons, but one petroleum barrel is 42 gallons. Ships' cargo is measured in shipping tons, a measure of volume (not weight) equivalent to 40 cubic feet. The internal capacity of ships is measured in register tons, a measure of volume (not weight) equivalent to 100 cubic feet.

linear:

1 foot (ft) = 12 inches (in)
1 yard (yd) = 3 feet

1 rod (rd), pole or perch = 5½ yards
1 furlong (fur) = 220 yards = 40 rods
1 statute or land mile (mi) = 8 furlongs = 5,280 feet
1 international nautical mile = 6,076.11549 feet

area:

1 square foot (ft^2) = 144 square inches (in^2)
1 square yard (yd^2) = 9 square feet
1 square rod (rd^2) = 30¼ square yards
1 acre = 4,840 square yards = 43,560 square feet = 160 square rods
1 mile square (mi^2) = 640 acres = 1 section (of land)
1 township = 36 sections = 36 square miles = 6 miles square

cubic:

1 cubic foot (ft^3) = 1,728 cubic inches (in^3)
1 bulk barrel = 5.8 cubic feet
1 cubic yard (yd^3) = 27 cubic feet
1 cord (wood) = 128 cubic feet
1 ton (shipping) = 40 cubic feet
1 register ton = 100 cubic feet

liquid:

1 pint (pt) = 28.875 cubic inches (in^3) = 4 gills (gi)
1 quart (qt) = 57.75 cubic inches = 2 pints
1 gallon (gal) = 4 quarts = 8 pints = 32 gills
1 barrel = 31.5 gallons
1 petroleum barrel = 42 gallons

Apothecaries' Fluid Measure: (used in dispensing drugs)

1 fluid dram (fl dr) = 0.2256 cubic inches (in^3) = 60 minims (min.)
1 apothecaries' fluid ounce (fl oz. ap) = 1.8047 cubic inches = 8 fluid drams
1 apothecaries' pint (pt ap) = 16 apothecaries' fluid ounces
1 apothecaries' quart (qt ap) = 32 apothecaries' fluid ounces = 2 apothecaries' pints
1 apothecaries' gallon (gal ap) = 128 apothecaries' fluid ounces = 4 apothecaries' quarts

dry:

1 quart (qt) = 2 pints (pt) = 67.2006 cubic inches (in^3)
1 peck (pk) = 8 quarts = 16 pints
1 bushel (bu) = 4 pecks = 32 quarts

avoirdupois weight:

1 dram (dr) = 27¹¹/₃₂ grains
1 ounce (oz.) = 16 drams
1 pound (lb) = 16 ounces
1 hundredweight (cwt) = 100 pounds
1 ton (t) = 2,000 pounds = 20 hundredweights

1 gross (or long) hundredweight = 112 pounds
1 gross or long ton = 20 gross or long hundredweights = 2,240 pounds

troy weight: (used in measuring precious metals)

1 pennyweight (dwt) = 24 grains
1 ounce troy (oz. t) = 20 pennyweights
1 pound troy (lb t) = 12 ounces troy

Apothecaries' Weight: (used in dispensing drugs)

1 scruple (s ap) = 20 grains
1 dram apothecaries' (dr ap) = 3 scruples
1 ounce apothecaries' (oz. ap) = 8 drams apothecaries'
1 pound apothecaries' (lb ap) = 12 ounces apothecaries'

Gunter's or Surveyor's Chain Measure:

1 link (li) = 7.92 inches
1 rod (rd) = 25 links = 16½ feet
1 chain (ch) = 4 rods = 100 links = 66 feet
1 statute or land mile (mi) = 80 chains (ch) = 320 rods (rd) = 5,280 feet (ft)

cooking:

1 tablespoon = 3 teaspoons
1 cup = 16 tablespoons
1 pint = 2 cups
1 quart = 2 pints
1 gallon = 4 quarts

MISCELLANEOUS MEASURES:

ampere: Unit of electric current (analogous to other units of flow, such as gallons per second). It is equal to the current produced by one volt of electrical force acting through the resistance of one ohm.

astronomical unit (A.U.): A unit of length used in astronomy; equals the mean distance between the earth and the sun, about 93 million miles.

balthazar: 8 magnums of champagne.

board foot (fbm): 144 cubic inches of wood (12 inches by 12 inches by 1 inch).

bolt: 40 yards of cloth.

British thermal unit (Btu): The heat needed to raise the temperature of one pound of water by 1° F.

caliber: The diameter of the bore of a gun. Expressed in hundredths of an inch (e.g., .22 or .30), thousandths of an inch (e.g., .357) or in millimeters (e.g., the 5.56mm M16 rifle, 105mm howitzer). In naval usage, the caliber is the relationship between the length of the gun's barrel and its diameter. For example, a gun with a 250-inch-long barrel, with a 5-inch bore, is a 50-caliber gun.

calorie: A unit used to express the heat output of an organism, or the energy value of food; also called the kilocalorie. It is equal to 1,000 gram calories. A gram calorie is the amount of heat needed to raise the temperature of one gram of water from 14.5° to 15.5° C at sea level.

carat (c): A unit of weight for gem stones; 200 milligrams.

decibel (dB): A measure of the relative intensity of sound. One decibel is the smallest difference that can be discerned by the human ear. Intensity varies exponentially: A 20 dB sound is 10 times louder than a 10 dB sound; a 30 dB sound is 100 times louder than a 10 dB sound; a 40 dB sound is 1,000 times louder than a 10 dB sound. A whisper is about 10 dB; normal conversation about 30 dB; a noisy office about 60 dB; normal traffic about 70 dB; heavy traffic about 90 dB; a jet plane at takeoff about 100 dB. At 120 dB, noise is painful.

fifth: 0.8 quarts (0.75706 liters) of liquor; one-fifth of a gallon.

foot-pound (ft.-lb.): A measure of work; the work done by a one-pound force when applied a distance of one foot.

gauge: A measure of the bore of a shotgun. The higher the gauge, the smaller the diameter: 6 gauge = 23.34mm bore; 10 gauge = 19.67mm; 12 gauge = 18.52mm; 14 gauge = 17.60mm; 16 gauge = 16.81mm; 20 gauge = 15.90mm. Also used in some occupations to express a specific system of measurement. For example, the width of railroad tracks, the thickness of wire or thin metals, and the fineness of knitted fabrics all are expressed in gauges.

gross: 12 dozen (144).

hand: 4 inches; used to measure horses.

horsepower: The power needed to lift 550 pounds one foot in one second (or 33,000 pounds one foot in one minute). Equals 746 watts.

jeroboam: 6.4 pints (1.6 magnums or 0.8 gallons) of champagne or brandy.

jigger: 1.5 ounces of liquor.

karat: A unit for measuring the fineness of gold. It indicates how many parts of alloy are in 24 parts of gold. Thus, 24-karat gold is pure gold; 18-karat gold is 6 parts alloy and 18 parts gold.

kilowatt: 1,000 watts.

kilowatt-hour (kwh): The measure commonly used to express output or consumption of electricity; measures the flow and the force of the current over time.

knot: One nautical mile per hour.

light-year: The distance light travels in one year in a vacuum; 5,878,000,000,000 miles (5.88 trillion miles).

Mach: A measurement of aircraft speed in relation to the speed of sound (1,088 feet per second at sea level at 32° F). A plane flying at Mach 1 is flying at the speed of sound; at Mach 2, at twice the speed of sound.

magnum: A large bottle of wine equivalent to about 50 ounces; equals 2.49797 standard bottles of wine.

methuselah: 4 magnums of champagne.

nebuchadnezzar: 10 magnums of champagne.

ohm (Ω): The unit used to measure the electrical resistance of a conductor; the resistance offered to a 1-ampere flow being driven by 1 volt of force.

parsec: A unit of measure for interstellar space; equals 3.26 light-years (19.2 trillion miles).

pi: The ratio between the circumference of a circle and its diameter; 3.14159265+.

pica (p): A typographic measure; 1/6 inch; 12 points.

point (pt): A typographic measure; 1/72 inch. Also a measure of the weight of a gemstone: 0.01 carat.

pony: 0.75 ounce of liquor. It is half a jigger.

ream: 500 sheets of paper.

rehoboam: 3 magnums of champagne.

salmanazar: 6 magnums of champagne.

shot: 1 ounce of liquor.

stone: British measure of weight: 14 pounds.

volt (v): Measure of electrical force (analogous to the force of a stream of water). It is the force that causes a current of 1 ampere to flow through a conductor with a resistance of 1 ohm.

watt (w): Unit of power (electrical, mechanical or thermal). In electrical power, the product of the voltage and the amperage; measures both the force of the current and the rate of the current.

wine bottle (standard): 0.800633 quart (0.7576778 liter).

CONVERSIONS:

To Convert from:	To:	Multiply by:
acres	feet, square	43,560
acres	miles, square	0.001562
acres	hectares	0.4046856
acres	kilometers, square	0.004046856
acres	meters, square	4046.856
BTU	horsepower-hour	0.0003931
BTU	kilowatt-hour	0.002928
BTU/hour	watts	0.2931
bushels	pecks	4
centimeters	inches	0.3937
centimeters	feet	0.03281
centimeters	meters	0.01
centimeters, square	square meters	0.0001
degrees, Celsius	degrees, F.	9/5 and add 32
degrees, Fahrenheit	degrees, C.	subtract 32 and multiply by 5/9
fathoms	feet	6
feet	miles (nautical)	0.0001645
feet	miles (statute)	0.0001894
feet	centimeters	30.48
feet	meters	0.3048
feet	kilometers	0.0003048
feet per second	miles per hour	0.6818
feet, cubic	inches, cubic	1,728
feet, cubic	meters, cubic	0.0283
feet, cubic	liters	28.316847
feet, square	centimeters, square	929.0304
feet, square	meters, square	0.09290304
furlongs	feet	660
furlongs	miles	0.125
gallons, British Imperial	gallons, U.S.	1.20095
gallons, U.S. liquid	quarts, U.S. liq.	4
gallons, U.S. liquid	liters	3.78541
gallons, U.S. liquid	meters, cubic	0.00378541
grains	grams	0.0648
grams	ounces, avd.	0.03527396
grams	pounds, avd.	0.00220462
grams	ounces, troy	0.03215075
grams	pounds, troy	0.00267923
hectares	acres	2.47105
hectares	kilometers, square	0.01
hectares	meters, square	10,000
horsepower	watts	745.7
hours	days	0.04167
inches	millimeters	25.4
inches	centimeters	2.54
inches	meters	0.0254
inches, cubic	milliliters	16.387064
inches, cubic	liters	0.016387064
inches, square	centimeters, square	6.4516
inches, square	meters, square	0.00064516
kilograms	ounces, troy	32.15075
kilograms	pounds, avd.	2.2046
kilograms	tons, metric	0.001
kilometers	miles	0.6214
kilometers, square	hectares	100
kilowatts	horsepower	1.341
knots	nautical miles/hour	1
knots	statute miles/hour	1.151
liters	gallons (U.S.)	0.2642
liters	pecks	0.1135
liters	pints (dry)	1.8162
liters	pints (liquid)	2.1134
liters	quarts (dry)	0.9081
liters	quarts (liquid)	1.0567
liters	milliliters	1000
liters	meters, cubic	0.001
meters	feet	3.280840
meters	yards	1.093613
meters	miles	0.0006214
meters	millimeters	1000
meters	centimeters	100
meters	kilometers	0.001
meters, cubic	feet, cubic	35.31467
meters, cubic	liters	1000
meters, cubic	tons, register	0.353147
metric tons	tons (long)	0.9842
metric tons	tons (short)	1.1023
miles, nautical	kilometers	1.852
miles, nautical	miles, statute	1.1516
miles, square	hectares	258.9998
miles, square	kilometers, square	2.589998
miles, statute	feet	5,280
miles, statute	miles, nautical	0.8684
miles, statute	centimeters	160934.4
miles, statute	meters	1609.344
miles, statute	kilometers	1.609344
miles per hour	feet per minute	88
ounces, avd.	grams	28.349523
ounces, avd.	kilograms	0.028349523
ounces, avd.	pounds, avd.	0.0625
ounces, troy or apoth.	ounces, avd.	1.09714
ounces, troy or apoth.	pounds, troy or apoth.	0.083333
ounces, troy or apoth.	grams, troy or apoth.	31.10348
pecks	bushels	0.25
pints, dry	quarts, dry	0.5
pints, liquid	quarts, liquid	0.5
pints, liquid	milliliters	473.176473
pints, liquid	liters	0.473176473
pounds, avd.	ounces, avd.	16
pounds, avd.	grams	453.59237
pounds, avd.	kilograms	0.45359237
pounds, avd.	tons, metric	0.000453592
pounds, avd.	tons, avd.	0.0005
pounds, apoth. or troy	ounces, apoth. or troy	12

To Convert from:	To:	Multiply by:
pounds, apoth. or troy	grams, apoth. or troy	373.2417
quarts British Imperial	quarts, U.S.	1.20095
quarts, dry/liquid	pints, dry/liquid	2
quarts, dry	liters	1.101221
quarts, U.S. liquid	quarts, Brit. Imp.	0.832674
quarts, U.S. liquid	gallons, U.S. liq.	0.25
quarts, liquid	milliliters	946.352946
quarts, liquid	liters	0.946352946
stones (British)	pounds, avd.	14
tons	pounds	2,000
tons	kilograms	907.185
tons	tons, metric	0.907185
tons, long	pounds	2,240
tons, long	kilograms	1016.047
tons, long	tons, metric	1.016047
tons, register	feet, cubic	100
tons, register	meters, cubic	2.831685
watts	BTU/hour	3.4129
watts	horsepower	0.001341
yards	feet	3
yards	inches	36
yards	miles	0.0005682
yards	centimeters	91.44
yards	meters	0.9144
yards, cubic	liters	764.555
yards, cubic	meters, cubic	0.764555
yards, square	meters, square	0.836127

ROMAN NUMERALS:

I=1; II=2; III=3; IV=4; V=5; VI=6; VII=7; VIII=8; IX=9; X=10; XI=11; XIX=19; XX=20: XXX=30; XL=40; L=50; LX=60; LXX=70; LXXX=80; XC=90; C=100; CC=200; CCC=300; CD=400; D=500; DC=600; DCC=700; DCCC=800; CM=900; M=1,000. A line over any numeral indicates that the numeral is multiplied by 1,000.

The Roman number system is an additive system, with an important exception. Whenever a symbol of lesser value is to the left of a symbol of greater value, you subtract the lesser value from the greater.

For example:

$$IV=4 \ (V-I=5-1)$$

$$VI=6 \ (V+I=5+1)$$

$$MCMXCII=M+(M-C)+(C-X)+I+I=1,000+$$
$$(1,000-100)+(100-10)+1+1=1992$$

PART NINE

DISASTERS, U.S. AND FOREIGN

EARTHQUAKES AND TSUNAMIS

(The Richter scale, which measures the magnitude of earthquakes, did not come into official use until after 1935. Official estimates for earlier earthquakes are extrapolated from extent of damage, size of geographical impact, and survivors' accounts. All death tolls are approximate. For more information, *see* earthquake, harbor waves, Richter scale, tsunami in section entitled Meteorology Glossary on page 273.)

WORST U.S. EARTHQUAKES

The five worst earthquakes in U.S. history, ranked by deaths:

San Francisco, Calif.: April 18, 1906; 503 dead.
Dutch Harbor, Unimak Island, Alaska: April 1, 1946; 190 dead.
Long Beach, Calif.: March 10, 1933; 120 dead.
Anchorage, Alaska: March 27, 1964; 117 dead.
Loma Prieta, Calif.: Oct. 17, 1989; 67 dead.

Number 1: San Francisco, California
April 18, 1906: Seismologists estimate that the most disastrous earthquake in U.S. history had a magnitude equivalent to 8.25 on the Richter scale. The immense upheaval occurred at 5:12 A.M. Pacific Time along the huge geological fracture that came to be known as the San Andreas Fault. Nearly 5 square miles, including more than 28,000 buildings, in 512 downtown city blocks, were destroyed. What the quake didn't destroy, fires did. Live electrical wires, gas leaking from ruptured lines, and hot stoves toppled by the tremors started huge fires all over the city. Hayes Street and much of the city's business district were destroyed in the "Ham-and-Eggs" fire, so called because the blaze erupted when a woman tried to cook breakfast on a stove whose flue had been damaged by the quake. Stymied by broken water mains that deprived them of much of the city's 80-million-gallon water reservoir, firefighters blew up buildings in the path of the inferno. Instead of robbing the fire of fuel, they inadvertently fed it. Burning airborne debris from the explosions touched off another fire that leveled Chinatown. The conflagration raged for three days and nights. Estimates of the death toll from the earthquake and fires have ranged from 452 to well over 800. Authorities fixed the death toll at 503. More than 400 were injured. More than 300,000 people were left homeless, huddled in tent cities. Thousands of others had fled the city by rail car. Nearly three quarters of San Francisco had to be rebuilt at a cost of about $229 million. The cost to repair such damage today would be on the order of $3 billion.

Number 2: Dutch Harbor, Unimak Island, Alaska
April 1, 1946: A powerful earthquake registering 7.2 on the Richter scale ripped the sea floor at a depth of about 15,000 feet in the Aleutian Deep, a great chasm south of the Shumagin Islands off Dutch Harbor and Unimak Island in the Alaska Peninsula. The quake caused immense tsunamis that swept a 4,000-mile expanse of the Aleutian Islands, Hawaiian Islands and the West Coast of North America. In Hawaii, Hilo was hardest hit. Shore areas were belted by waves ranging from 5 to 50 feet high and traveling at more than 300 miles per hour. About 5,000 people were left homeless. Deaths totaled 190.

Number 3: Long Beach, California
March 10, 1933: A powerful tremor estimated at 6.3 on the Richter scale shook Southern California from Ventura to San Diego shortly before 6 P.M. The epicenter of the quake was about three miles southwest of Newport Beach in an offshore fault from which minor shocks had emanated for years. Long Beach and Compton sustained the most severe damage, totaling about $50 million. Deaths and injuries resulted primarily from panic and shoddily built houses. More than 130 aftershocks followed the initial tremor. Fires erupted in Long Beach as the aftershocks continued. Martial law was declared. About 4,000 U.S. Marines and Navy personnel joined American Legion volunteers to patrol the stricken city and help in rescue operations. At least 4,150 people were injured; 123 people killed.

Number 4: Anchorage, Alaska
March 27, 1964: The most violent earthquake ever directly recorded in North America struck Anchorage on a Good Friday. The quake measured from 8.3 to nearly 8.6 on the Richter scale, making it more powerful than the great San Francisco earthquake, the equal of two quakes that rocked remote Yakatanga, Alaska, in 1899, and a rival of the fabled quakes that ripped New Madrid, Mo., in the 19th century. The Anchorage earthquake tore up 30 city blocks of the state's largest city, killed at least 117 people, left thousands homeless and as much as 75 percent of the city in ruin with more than $300 million in damage. More destruction stretched in an arc for 500 miles. The waterfronts of Valdez, Seward, Homer, Cordova, Kodiak Island, Chenega, and Seldovia were wracked by immense harbor

waves and tsunamis created by the earthquakes. The waves roared across the Pacific and flooded Port Alberni, 35 miles inland on Vancouver Island, Canada. Four children on a beach in Depoe, Oreg., were swept away. About 150 stores were destroyed and at least 12 people died when the tsunamis hit Crescent City, Calif. They struck Hawaii and lashed the coast of Japan, more than 4,000 miles away. Ground waves generated by the quake were felt in Seattle, Wash., Houston, Tex., and Cape Canaveral, Fla. Aftershocks attributed to the earthquake were reported for almost 18 months. Seismologists studied the Alaska earthquake and its impact for years, and they concluded that no other single earthquake in modern history had reshaped so much of the earth's surface. Substantial upheavals or depressions directly linked to the quake extended for 100,000 square miles.

Number 5: Loma Prieta, California

Oct. 17, 1989: At 5:04 P.M. Pacific Time, millions of Americans had their televisions tuned in to the third baseball game in the World Series between the Oakland Athletics and the San Francisco Giants. During warm-ups, 16 minutes before the start of the game, the pictures broadcast from San Francisco's Candlestick Park began to shake. Much of America was watching an earthquake.

The epicenter of the quake was to the southeast in Loma Prieta in the Santa Cruz Mountains, along the San Andreas Fault. The magnitude of the earthquake ranged from 6.9 to 7.1 on the Richter scale. The main shock lasted only 15 seconds, but it was followed by hundreds of aftershocks.

The baseball game was quickly postponed and about 58,000 people were safely evacuated from the ballpark. Sections of downtown Santa Cruz, Calif., were destroyed. A building collapsed in San Francisco. Fires erupted there, in Berkeley and in Oakland. A part of the two-tier Nimitz Freeway's upper deck collapsed. Seven Northern California counties were declared disaster areas. The World Series resumed on Oct. 27, and a day later the Oakland Athletics completed a sweep of the Giants. The A's celebrated, but with taste and modesty. No champagne was poured. No fireworks were lighted. The national pastime had been shocked into perspective. The Federal Emergency Management Agency suggested that if the earthquake had been as severe as the one that hit San Francisco in 1906, the death toll would have been on the order of 11,000 people. As it was, the earthquake killed 67 people and caused more than $5.6 billion in damage, making the Loma Prieta quake one of the costliest in U.S. history.

OTHER U.S. EARTHQUAKES

Boston, Massachusetts

Nov. 18, 1775: Just before dawn, a series of tremors shook the cultural center of Colonial America. The quake, which was felt from South Carolina to Nova Scotia, destroyed numerous houses, toppled about 1,500 chimneys, knocked the historic gilded cricket from its perch atop Faneuil Hall's weathervane, but no deaths were reported. The 3.5-minute quake brought immediate warnings of divine retribution for man's wickedness. More importantly, the quake aroused the scientific curiosities of John Winthrop IV, a Harvard University mathematics and philosophy professor, and Great Britain's John Mitchell, a Cambridge University science lecturer and church rector. The two men developed insights into the nature and origins of earthquakes and set the stage for the development of seismology as a science.

New Madrid, Missouri

Dec. 16, 1811, to Feb. 7, 1812: The greatest series of earthquakes in eastern North America struck the sparsely populated town of New Madrid in the winter of 1811–12. New Madrid sits on a geological fault 3 to 12 miles deep extending diagonally from northeastern Arkansas to just north of Cairo, Ill. Major earthquakes with hundreds of aftershocks struck on Dec. 16, 1811; Jan. 23, 1812; and Feb. 7, 1812. Some seismologists have estimated the magnitude of the earthquakes to have been as high as 8.7 on the Richter scale. The sequence, which killed 10 people, destroyed two towns to the south of New Madrid, Big Prairie and Little Prairie, Mo. In northwestern Tennessee, the quakes created Reelfoot Lake. The bottom of Reelfoot Swamp sank during the quakes. Water from Reelfoot Creek flowed into the resulting cavity, filling the new lake to a width of 5 miles and a length of 18 miles.

With such a cataclysm in their background, many residents of New Madrid panicked when independent climatologist Iben Browning predicted there was at least a 50-50 chance that another quake would rock the town around Dec. 3, 1990. A quake measuring 4.5 on the Richter scale did cause relatively minor damage to the region on Sept. 26, 1990; but come Dec. 3, with a ghoulish public spotlight turned directly on New Madrid, nothing happened.

Owens Valley, California

March 26, 1872: No estimate was made for the magnitude of this earthquake, which left 60 people dead.

Charleston, South Carolina

Aug. 31, 1886: A quake with a Richter equivalent of 7 killed 83 people.

Yakatanga, Alaska
Sept. 3, 1899: Though it was estimated to be the equivalent of 8.3 on the Richter scale, no deaths were linked to this potent quake.

Yakatanga, Alaska
Sept. 10, 1899: An immense quake with an estimated magnitude of 8.6 on the Richter scale ripped the landscape for tens of thousands of miles, but no deaths were reported.

Pleasant Valley, Nevada
Oct. 2, 1915: A mighty quake with an estimated magnitude of 7.8 on the Richter scale shook a wide but sparsely populated area, but no deaths were reported.

Helena, Montana
June 27, 1925: No deaths reported from a quake estimated at 6.8 on the Richter scale.

Mt. Livermore, Texas
Aug. 16, 1931: No deaths reported from a quake estimated at 6.4 in Richter magnitude.

Cedar Mountain, Nevada
Dec. 20, 1932: No deaths reported from a quake with an estimated Richter magnitude of 7.3.

Great Salt Lake, Utah
May 12, 1934: No deaths were reported from a quake with an estimated magnitude of 6.6 on the Richter scale.

Helena, Montana
October–November 1936: No magnitude was estimated for a quake here that killed 2 people.

Imperial Valley, California
May 18, 1940: A quake measuring 7.1 on the Richter scale killed 9 people.

Bakersfield, California
July 21, 1952: A quake measuring 7.7 on the Richter scale killed 12 people.

Frenchman's Station, Nevada
Dec. 16, 1954: An earthquake measuring 7.1 on the Richter scale; no deaths reported.

Lituya Bay, Alaska
July 9, 1958: A quake measuring 7.9 on the Richter scale occurred near the mouth of the remote bay. Three deaths were reported. The quake created a mammoth landslide that triggered a world-record harbor wave. [See harbor wave in section entitled Meteorology Glossary on page 273]

Hebgen Lake, Montana
Aug. 17, 1959: An earthquake measuring 7.1 on the Richter scale; 28 dead.

Los Angeles, California
Feb. 9, 1971: Southern California's San Fernando Valley and the metropolitan Los Angeles area were rocked by a violent temblor that registered 6.5 on the Richter scale. The quake centered about 25 miles south of the San Andreas Fault. Freeways buckled. Five highway overpasses dropped. The walls in two wings of a Veterans Administration Hospital in Sylmar collapsed, killing at least 40 people. About a mile away, Olive View Sanitarium caved in, killing at least three more people. Aftershocks continued for more than a week; one of them had a magnitude of 5.7. When the tally was taken, nearly 3,200 buildings had been damaged or destroyed. Damage exceeded $1 billion. About 900 people had been injured. At least 64 were dead—and most of Southern California was asleep at the time. The earthquake came at dawn.

Hawaiian Islands
April 26, 1973: A quake measuring 6.2 on the Richter scale; no deaths reported.

Near Islands, Alaska
Feb. 2, 1975: A quake measuring 7.6 on the Richter scale; no deaths reported.

Hawaiian Islands
Nov. 29, 1975: A quake measuring 7.2 on the Richter scale; no deaths reported.

Hollister, California
Aug. 6, 1979: An earthquake centered near Hollister, about 100 miles south of San Francisco, shook a sparsely populated region of northern California along the Calaveras Fault. The tremor measured 5.9 on the Richter scale.

Coalinga, California
May 2, 1983: An earthquake weighing in at from 6.1 to 6.5 on the Richter scale destroyed eight blocks of the downtown business district in Coalinga, a town in central California's Fresno County. The quake, which injured about 50 people and caused more than $31 million in damage, was felt from Sacramento in the north to Los Angeles in the south.

Hamilton, California
May 7, 1983: A tremor of 4.9 in Richter magnitude was reported along the Calaveras Fault near Hamilton.

San Jose, California
April 24, 1984: A powerful quake measuring 6.2 on the Richter scale wrecked houses, fractured a bridge and left 25 people injured along the Calaveras Fault 12 miles southeast of San Jose in northern California. The quake caused more than $10 million in damage. No deaths were reported.

Northeastern Ohio
Jan. 31, 1986: No deaths were linked to a quake that registered 4.9 on the Richter scale.

San Francisco Bay area, California
March 29–31, 1986: Two earthquakes shook the San Francisco Bay area late in March 1986. The first quake, on March 29, was relatively mild, 4 on the Richter scale; the second quake, on March 31, was not; it registered 5.3 to 5.6 on the Richter scale. No deaths were reported, and damage was moderate. The quake was centered near Fremont, southeast of San Francisco.

Palm Springs, California
July 8 and 13, 1986: Two earthquakes along the Banning Fault, at the southern end of the San Andreas Fault, injured about 40 people and caused nearly $6 million in damage.

Whittier, California
Oct. 1, 1987: A quake measuring 5.9 on the Richter scale rocked metropolitan Los Angeles, killed at least six people and left dozens injured. The center of the quake was in suburban Whittier, where 30 buildings collapsed. Damages throughout the area ran to more than $213 million. The tremor, which was felt throughout Southern California and 275 miles to the east in Las Vegas, focused seismologists' attention on an undiscovered geological fault that runs beneath part of Los Angeles.

Imperial Valley, California
Nov. 23–24, 1987: Two big tremors shook Southern California near the town of Westmoreland, 90 miles east of San Diego. The first, on Nov. 23, measured 6.3 on the Richter scale; the second came 12 hours later on Nov. 24 and measured 6. Two people were killed.

Pasadena, California
Dec. 3, 1988: An earthquake measuring 5 on the Richter scale occurred near Pasadena, but no deaths were associated with it.

Ferndale, California
April 25, 1992: An earthquake registering 6.9 on the Richter scale occurred north of San Francisco near the small coastal towns of Ferndale, Eureka and Petrolia, causing an estimated $60 million in damage but no deaths and about 100 injuries.

Yucca Valley, California
June 28, 1992: Two powerful earthquakes jolted Southern California. The first, at 4:58 A.M. near Landers and Joshua Tree, measured 7.4 on the Richter scale, making it the most powerful quake in the state in nearly 40 years. The second quake, which registered 6.5, came at 8:05 A.M. about 20 miles away near Big Bear Lake. One death was attributed to the quake. About 350 people were injured. Damage ran to $16 million. Two months earlier, on April 22, the same part of Southern California had been struck by an earthquake measuring 6.1. Numerous injuries, no deaths and minor property damage were reported.

WORST FOREIGN EARTHQUAKES

China
The most populous nation on earth has lost more lives to single earthquakes than any other country on earth—more than 2.2 million people.

Earthquakes claimed 23,000 victims in Shanxi in 1036; 100,000 in Chihli (Hopeh) in 1290; another 100,000 in Beijing in 1731; more than 180,000 in Kansu in 1920; 200,000 in Nan-Shan in 1927; 70,000 in Kansu in 1932; 3,000 in eastern China in 1969; 10,000 in Yunnan Province in 1970; about 300 in Liaoning Province in 1975; more than 730 in Yunnan Province in 1988; about 30 people near the Shanxi-Hebei border in 1989, and another 126 in Qinghai Province in 1990.

The death toll of 687,186 that China suffered from those disasters in the span of 954 years still does not equal the losses from either of its two other great earthquakes.

The "Great China Quake" of January-February 1556 probably was the most destructive in history. Historians have estimated that the earthquake killed more than 800,000 people in Honan, Shansi and Shensi provinces. Hundreds of thousands of people were killed outright; many thousands more died of starvation and disease in the aftermath.

On July 28, 1976, China again suffered an earthquake of catastrophic magnitude. A great quake measuring from 8 to 8.2 on the Richter scale struck Tientsin and Tangshan, leveling all buildings in Tangshan for 20 sq. mi. Death toll estimates ranged as high as 750,000.

Assam State, India
Two of the most powerful earthquakes in modern history were recorded in Assam State in mountainous northeastern India, 53 years apart. On June 12, 1897, a quake with an estimated strength of 8.7 on the Richter scale sent tremors over 1.75 million sq. mi. and destroyed all buildings for 3,000 sq. mi., leaving 1,542 people dead. On Aug. 15, 1950, another earthquake of exactly the same magnitude, 8.7, struck the region again, killing another 1,500 people.

Honshu, Japan
The greatest single natural shock in history may have been the March 3, 1933, earthquake off Honshu's Sanriku District in Japan. The quake created 75-foot-high tsunamis that sank about 8,000 ships and killed 3,000 people. The earthquake's estimated magnitude

was put at what is still the highest level ever reached on the Richter scale: 8.9.

On the other hand, no official magnitude estimates ever were made of the earthquake that struck the same region about 37 years earlier. On June 15, 1896, a long series of immense offshore shocks sent 100-foot-high tsunamis roaring ashore at estimated speeds of up to 500 miles an hour. More than 10,000 houses were swept away. More than 9,000 people were injured and 27,000 killed.

MAJOR FOREIGN EARTHQUAKES SINCE 1950

Northwestern Turkey
March 18, 1953: 7.2 on Richter scale; 1,200 dead.

Northern Afghanistan
June 10–17, 1956: Series of earthquakes; 7.7 on Richter scale; about 2,000 dead.

Northern Iran
July 2, 1957: 7.4 on Richter scale; 2,500 dead.

Agadir, Morocco
Feb. 29, 1960: 5.8 on Richter scale; tsunami and fires destroyed most of coastal city; nearly 20,000 dead.

Concepción, Chile
May 21–30, 1960: Series of onshore and offshore earthquakes as high as 8.3 on the Richter scale and resulting tsunamis killed 5,700 in Chile; tsunamis from the same earthquakes reached Hawaii and Japan, killing 199 people.

Northwestern Iran
Sept. 1–2, 1962: 7.1 on Richter scale; 12,403 dead.

Skoplje, Yugoslavia
July 26, 1963: 6 on Richter scale; nearly 2,000 dead.

Iran
Aug. 31, 1968: Quake in Khurasan Province; 7.8 on Richter scale; 12,000 dead; 100,000 homeless.

Northern Peru
May 30, 1970: 7.7 on Richter scale; entire villages in the Andes swept away; 67,000 dead.

Managua, Nicaragua
Dec. 23, 1972: 6.2 on Richter scale; 10,000 dead; more than 200,000 homeless.

Northern Pakistan
Dec. 28, 1974: 6.3 on Richter scale; 5,200 dead.

Guatemala City, Guatemala
Feb. 4, 1976: 7.5 on Richter scale; 23,000 dead; more than a million homeless in Guatemala and Honduras.

Indonesia
June 26, 1976: 7.2 on Richter scale; 9,000 dead.

Mindanao, Philippines
Aug. 17, 1976: Offshore earthquake measuring 7.8 on Richter scale resulted in tsunami; 8,000 dead.

Muradiye, Turkey, near Mt. Ararat
Nov. 24, 1976: 7.9 on Richter scale; 5,000 dead.

Bucharest, Romania
March 4, 1977: 7.2 on the Richter scale; 1,541 dead.

Tabas, Iran
Sept. 16, 1978: 7.7 on Richter scale; city was razed and scores of nearby cities and towns were damaged; 25,000 dead.

Al Asnam, Algeria
Oct. 10, 1980: Two quakes, 7.5 and 6.5 on Richter scale; 4,500 dead.

Southern Italy
Nov. 23, 1980: 7.2 on Richter scale; nearly 5,000 dead; more than 200,000 homeless; about $20 billion in damage.

Southeastern Iran
June 11, 1981: 6.6 on Richter scale; 8,000 dead.

Northern Yemen
Dec. 13, 1982: 6 on Richter scale; 3,000 dead.

Off Honshu, Japan
May 26, 1983: Earthquake off west coast of Japan's main island; 8.1 on Richter scale; tsunamis left at least 81 dead.

Erzurum, Kars Provinces, Eastern Turkey
Oct. 30, 1983: 7.1 on Richter scale; more than 1,300 dead.

Uzbekistan, Turkmenistan and Tadzhikistan, Soviet Union
March 20, 1984: 7.1 on Richter scale; although the quake shook 250,000 sq. mi. of earth from Gazli, which had been nearly leveled by an earthquake in 1976, to northeastern Iran, Soviet authorities reported only about 100 injuries and no deaths.

Central Chile
March 3, 1985: 7.4 on Richter scale; at least 100 killed; 8,000 homeless in Santiago alone.

Mexico City, Mexico
Sept. 19–20, 1985: Two successive quakes measuring 8.1 and 7.3 on Richter scale; widespread damage; 8,000 dead; more than 30,000 homeless.

Northeastern Ecuador
March 5–6, 1987: 7.3 on Richter scale; 4,000 dead.

Soviet Armenia
Dec. 7–8, 1988: 6.9 on Richter scale; 60,000 dead.

Caspian Sea off Iran
June 21, 1990: 7.3. to 7.7 on Richter scale; 40,000 dead.

Cabanatuan, near Manila, Philippines
July 16, 1990: 7.7 on Richter scale; 1,621 dead.

Afghanistan
Feb. 1, 1991: 6.8 on Richter scale; more than 1,000 dead in Afghanistan; about 200 dead in Pakistan.

Hindu Kush Mountains, Northwestern Pakistan and Northeastern Afghanistan
Feb. 1, 1991: 6.8 on Richter scale; more than 1,000 dead in Afghanistan; about 200 dead in Pakistan.

Georgia, Soviet Union
April 29, 1991: A quake of 7.2 on Richter scale; more than 100 dead, some in landslides resulting from aftershocks; tens of thousands homeless.

Managua, Nicaragua
Sept. 2, 1992: Tidal waves triggered by a 7 earthquake 75 miles off the coast of Nicaragua, killed about 100 people, injured about 150 others and left thousands of families homeless.

Turkey
March 13–15, 1992: Two earthquakes, one near Erzincan measuring 6.2 on the Richter scale, the other measuring 6 near Tunceli, killed several hundred people in the country's mountainous eastern region.

Northern Europe
April 13, 1992: The strongest earthquake in nearly two centuries struck Roermond, the Netherlands, near the borders of Germany and Belgium. The quake, measuring 5.8 on the Richter scale, killed one person and injured at least 40 others.

Cairo, Egypt
Oct. 12, 1992: An earthquake registering 5.9 on the Richter scale toppled buildings 20 miles southwest of Cairo, killing at least 450 people and injuring about 4,000.

Indonesia
Dec. 12, 1992: A powerful earthquake in the Flores Sea 19 miles off the east coast of Indonesia wracked the island and sent immense tidal waves hurtling ashore, killing nearly 2,500 people, injuring hundreds and leaving thousands more homeless. The quake registered 6.8 on the Richter scale.

FIRES

WORST U.S. FIRES

The five worst fires in U.S. history, ranked according to deaths:

1 Peshtigo, Wisc.: Oct. 9, 1871; 1,152 dead.
2 Minnesota: Oct. 12, 1918; 800–1,000 dead.
3 Iroquois Theater, Chicago: Dec. 30, 1903; 603 dead.
4 Cocoanut Grove, Boston: Nov. 28, 1942; 492 dead.
5 Hinkley, Minn.: Sept. 1, 1894; 418 dead.

Number 1: Peshtigo, Wisconsin
The best-known fires in U.S. history occurred in San Francisco and Chicago, but the all-time worst took place in the bustling lumber town of Peshtigo, Wisc., early in October 1871. The states of the Great Plains were reeling in a drought. Scant rainfall all summer had left the deep woods tinder-dry. In mid-September, small fires ignited in the forest around Marinette. They kindled more fires, and gradually they formed a single conflagration deep in the forest. The fire grew, consuming everything in its path, mounting in intensity and fury until it became an immense whirling storm that swept into Peshtigo on Oct. 8 and incinerated the town. People were burned to death where they stood. Some killed themselves first. Hundreds of people managed to save themselves by jumping into the Peshtigo River. A day later, heavy rains drenched the region. The holocaust had scorched more than 2,400 sq. mi. of forest and caused more than $3 million in damage. Much of Chicago on the same day had been burned flat in the most destructive fire in American history—more than $200 million in damage and nearly 300 people killed. Days passed before the world discovered that the death toll from the Peshtigo firestorm had been far worse; at least 1,152 people had been killed.

Number 2: Minnesota
Much of Minnesota went without rain for nearly half of 1918, and for much of that time small underground fires simmered throughout the peat bogs and dense underbrush in the northern part of the state. Some underground fires were common in the dry season, but these were extensive and particularly long-lived. When, on Oct. 12, the north country was swept by a 60-mile-an-hour gale, the smoldering fires were swept into an inferno that raged across the landscape from Bemidji to Two Harbors then halfway to Duluth and Minneapolis. Nearly 400 residents of the resort town of Moose Lake were trapped and burned to death. Just north of Duluth, scores of people died trying to row or swim to safety in Pike Lake. The holocaust swept the lakes area, killing hundreds more and threatening Duluth, which was spared by a shift of the wind that diverted the firestorm. Nearly 560 deaths were confirmed, but dozens more people were missing and never accounted for. The unofficial death toll ranged to about 800.

Number 3: Chicago
The worst theater fire in U.S. history occurred in a 38-day-old Chicago theater that was advertised as "absolutely fireproof." The matinee showing of the farce *Mr. Bluebeard*, starring Eddie Foy, packed 1,830 people into the new Iroquois Theater at Randolph and Dearborn streets on Dec. 30, 1903. More than 200 patrons were standing in the aisles and near the exits when an electric arc floodlamp spit sparks into the stage scenery and started a fire. Powder extinguishers were useless. There was no water conveniently at hand. No pumps. The sprinkler system was unfinished. Curtains, chairs and all the scenery were flammable. The flames leaped through the theater. The cast fled. Foy narrowly escaped. The audience panicked. Hundreds of victims were trapped in the galleries and balconies as the entire theater erupted in flame. The dead were removed to nearby Thompson's Restaurant, 603 people in all.

Number 4: Boston
The worst fire in New England history, and one of the worst in the nation, occurred at a packed nightclub in Boston, Mass., Nov. 28, 1942. The capacity of the popular Cocoanut Grove on Tremont Street was about 500 people. On the night of the fire, more than 1,000 patrons were jammed into the main floor of the club and its three bars. In the basement Melody Lounge, a patron unscrewed a light fixture to create a more mellow atmosphere. A busboy struck a match so he could see to replace the bulb. He dropped the match. An artificial palm tree caught fire. The blaze spread quickly. The crowd panicked. As the entire club was swept with flame, its walls and ceilings ablaze, dozens of people were trampled. Many were overcome with smoke and gases from the club's burning furnishings. About a hundred victims were trapped by doors that opened inward. The death toll was 492.

Number 5: Hinkley, Minnesota
Small forest and peat fires ravaged the parched north woods of Michigan, Wisconsin and Minnesota in the last two weeks of August, 1894, the end of a long dry summer marked by scorching temperatures and no

rainfall. Brush fires were normal for the season, but the fires of 1894 did not burn themselves out. Instead, gusting winds fanned the blazes into an immense conflagration that swept through the north country, incinerating everything in its path. Entire towns in all three states were ravaged or destroyed. Hardest hit was the small town of Hinkley, Minn., about 70 miles from St. Paul. The fire raged through the deep woods surrounding Hinkley and engulfed the town. People tried to save themselves by jumping into ponds and the Grindstone River, but the drought had left the water too shallow to provide safety for hundreds of people. Hundreds of Hinkley residents escaped by jumping aboard two trains that passed through the flaming town. At least 413 people died in Hinkley alone; scores more died the same day in area towns touched by the fire.

OTHER MAJOR U.S. FIRES

New Jersey
June 30, 1900: Cargo on Pier Number 3 on Hoboken's North River waterfront caught fire, and in minutes the blaze spread to three Lloyd Line ships crowded with sightseers. Many were trapped below decks; 326 dead; 250 injured.

California
April 18, 1906: Much of San Francisco destroyed by fires that erupted after major earthquake; at least 452 dead. [See Earthquakes, page 375]

Ohio
March 4, 1908: Lake View Elementary School fire in Cleveland suburb of Collinwood; 176 dead.

New York
March 25, 1911: Triangle Shirtwaist Factory; 146 dead.

Ohio
April 21, 1930: Ohio State Penitentiary in Columbus; 317 dead; 231 injured.

Mississippi
April 23, 1940: Dance hall in Natchez; 198 dead.

Connecticut
July 6, 1944: Ringling Brothers and Barnum and Bailey Circus tent was set afire by an arsonist; 168 dead; 682 injured.

Georgia
Dec. 7, 1946: Atlanta's Winecoff Hotel, the worst hotel fire in U.S. history; 119 dead; 90 injured.

Illinois
April 5, 1949: Hospital fire in Effingham; 77 dead.

Missouri
Feb. 17, 1957: Nursing home in Warrenton; 72 dead.

Illinois
Dec. 1, 1958: Chicago parochial school; 93 dead.

New York
Dec. 16, 1960: Fire on aircraft carrier Constellation killed 50 workmen in Brooklyn naval shipyard.

New York
June 30, 1974: Discotheque in Port Chester; 24 dead.

Kentucky
May 28, 1977: Supper club in Southgate; 165 dead.

Nevada
Nov. 21, 1980: MGM Grand Hotel in Las Vegas; 84 dead.

New York
Dec. 4, 1980: Stouffer Inn fire in Harrison, N.Y.; 26 dead.

Puerto Rico
Dec. 31, 1986: Dupont Plaza Hotel; 96 dead.

Yellowstone National Park
August–September 1988: More than 1.2 million acres burned.

New York
March 25, 1990: Happy Land social club in the Bronx borough of New York City was set afire by arsonist; 87 dead.

North Carolina
Sept. 3, 1991: Frying-vat accident at Imperial Food Products chicken-processing plant, Hamlet, N.C.; 25 dead; at least 40 injured.

California
Oct. 19, 1991: High winds rekindled a small brush fire into a huge conflagration that swept through more than 1,700 acres of wooded hills outside Oakland and Berkeley, killing 24 people, injuring 148 others, destroying more than 3,000 homes and causing more than $5 billion in damage by week's end, making the blaze the most costly in U.S. history.

VOLCANIC AND GAS EXPLOSIONS

West Indies
May 7, 1902: La Soufrière, "The Sulfur Pit," on the island of St. Vincent, exploded, killing more than 1,500 people.

Martinique
May 8, 1902: Mount Pelée erupted with an explosion heard for 300 miles. The eruption was one of the most devastating of the century. The volcano rained lava, ash, and flaming gas on the busy port of St. Pierre, burying or incinerating nearly everything within 10 sq. mi.; estimates of the death toll ranged from 29,000 to 36,000.

Martinique
Aug. 30, 1902: Mt. Pelée erupted, killing at least 2,000 people.

Guatemala
Oct. 24, 1902: Mt. Santa Maria erupted, killing 6,000.

Italy
April 18, 1906: Mt. Vesuvius erupted, killing nearly 200 people.

Philippines
Jan. 30, 1911: Taal volcano on Luzon near Manila erupted, destroying at least 13 villages and killing 1,335 people.

United States
June 6, 1912: Mt. Katmai in remote eastern Alaska erupted, laying waste to 50 sq. mi. of rugged terrain. Thereafter, the area was dubbed The Valley of 10,000 Smokes. The eruption spewed so much volcanic dust that the world's atmosphere was turned hazy for the summer and the average temperature dropped 13 degrees.

Indonesia
May 1919: Mt. Kelut on Java erupted after 18 years of dormancy; a lake that had formed in its immense crater was destroyed; avalanche of mud and water descended on valley; at least 5,500 people killed.

Italy
1929: Mt. Vesuvius erupted, damaging villages with flows of lava; several hundred people killed.

Indonesia
March 13–28, 1931: Merapi volcano on Java erupted, killing at least 1,300 people.

Turkey
May 4, 1935: Mt. Ararat erupted after a major earthquake; at least 400 people killed.

Mexico
April 15, 1941: Mt. Colima erupted; earthquakes, fires killed at least 300 people.

Italy
March 18–24, 1944: Mt. Vesuvius erupted, burying nearby towns and villages in lava and ash; at least 100 killed.

Mexico
June 10, 1944: Parícutin, a new volcano growing since February 1943, buried two towns with lava; at least 3,500 dead.

New Guinea
Jan. 15–21, 1951: Mt. Lamington buried countryside in thick dust and hot volcanic gas, killing as many as 5,000 people.

Philippines
Dec. 4, 1951: Gas cloud spewed from Mt. Hibokhibok, killing more than 500 people.

Soviet Union
March 20, 1956: Mt. Bezymianny on the Kamchatka Peninsula erupted in one of the most powerful explosions in recent history; 0.5 cubic mile of volcanic debris was dropped throughout remote region; no deaths reported.

Philippines
Sept. 28, 1956: Taal volcano on Luzon near Manila erupted, killing about 350 people.

Chile
May 21–30, 1960: Extraordinary earth-plate shifting stirred earthquakes and volcanic activity; six long-dormant volcanoes exploded; three new volcanoes were created; tsunamis swamped towns, villages and cities. More than 100,000 were left homeless. At least 5,700 people were killed.

Indonesia
March 17–21, 1963: Mt. Agung on Bali erupted, burying nearby towns and villages; more than 200,000 homeless; at least 1,584 dead.

Costa Rica
July 29, 1968: Mt. Arenal exploded; at least 80 people killed.

Iceland
Jan. 23, 1973: Eruption through a fissure outside the town of Vestmannaeyjar on Heimaey Island created a new 735-foot volcano in the shadow of long-dormant Mt. Helgafell. Heimaey's 5,500 residents were evacuated as lava from the new volcano burned

some houses and tephra, a black volcanic ash, buried many others; one death was reported.

Zaire
Jan. 10, 1977: Mt. Nyiragongo erupted, killing more than 70 people.

Indonesia
Feb. 20, 1979: Mt. Sinila on Java erupted, spewing poisonous gases that killed more than 175 people.

United States
May 18, 1980: Mt. St. Helens in the Cascades of Washington erupted for first time in 123 years. Largest eruption in U.S. history blew out one side of the volcano, ruining 232 sq. mi. and killing at least 60 people.

Mexico
March 28, April 3–4, 1982: El Chichón erupted; nearly 2,000 killed.

Cameroon
Aug. 16, 1984: A carbon dioxide bubble, possibly the result of underground volcanic activity, surfaced from beneath Lake Monoun and killed about 40 people in the lake area.

India
Dec. 3, 1984: Methyl isocyanate gas escaped from a Union Carbide plant in Bhopal, killing at least 1,700 people and injuring 200,000.

Colombia
Nov. 13, 1985: A massive eruption of long-dormant Navado del Ruiz melted the ice cap atop the 17,822-foot mountain, creating huge mudslides, or lahars, that buried towns and villages northwest of Bogotá; at least 22,940 people killed; thousands more left homeless.

Cameroon
Aug. 21, 1986: An immense bubble of carbon dioxide gas, possibly the result of deep volcanic activity, exploded to the surface of Lake Nyos, killing at least 1,700 people.

Indonesia
Feb. 10, 1990: Mt. Kelut on Java erupted, burying houses in ash; no deaths reported.

Japan
June 3, 1991: Mt. Unzen, 30 miles east of Nagasaki on Kyushu, exploded in its first major eruption in nearly two centuries; at least 38 people were killed, including Maurice and Katia Krafft, French scientists known internationally for their documentary film work on volcanic eruptions.

Philippines
June 12–15, 1991: Mt. Pinatubo, about 55 miles northwest of Manila, erupted and spewed ash, rock and volcanic debris as high as 19 miles into the atmosphere. The explosion forced the evacuation of more than 20,000 U.S. Navy and Air Force personnel from Clark Air Force Base and Subic Bay Naval Base. At least 200 people were killed. Many were crushed in their houses, which collapsed from the weight of fallen volcanic ash. At least 100,000 Filipinos were left homeless.

Guadalajara, Mexico
April 22, 1992: Fifteen explosions from a buildup of gas in the sewers of Mexico's second largest city ripped apart 26 blocks of the Reforma District, killing at least 212 people and injuring more than 1,000.

TORNADOES

Nowhere in the world do tornadoes occur with greater frequency than in the United States, where an average of about 800 twisters a year are reported. Tornadoes are the most violent localized storms in the world, carrying winds that have been clocked at up to 280 miles an hour. Though tornadoes have struck most states, they are most common in the lowlands of the Mississippi, Missouri and Ohio river valleys, where moist warm air from the Gulf of Mexico collides with cool, dry air from the West and breeds storms of immense power. Parts of six states—Texas, Oklahoma, Missouri, Kansas, Iowa and Nebraska—are infamous as "Tornado Alley." The nickname applies to a geographical area of roughly 184,000 sq. mi. where more than a third of the nation's twisters occur every year. [See tornado in Chapter entitled: Meteorology Glossary on page 273]

Tornadoes tend to travel in a northeasterly direction, but they move erratically and unpredictably. Often they hop and skip from one spot to another, but sometimes their path is straight and continuous. The longest recorded unbroken tornado path in history was carved on May 26, 1917, from Louisiana to Indiana, 293 miles.

It is a myth that tornadoes don't strike the same place twice. Countless towns and cities in the United States have suffered through numerous tornado disasters, some only minutes and hours apart; others, years. In some places, tornadoes have even been a regular event. The small town of Codell, Kan., for example, was hit by a tornado at approximately the same time of day every May 20 for three consecutive years: 1916, 1917, and 1918.

Texas has the greatest number of tornadoes every year, an average of 123. The state's record for reported tornadoes is 232, set in 1967. From 1953 to 1988, Texas also had the highest number of annual tornado deaths, 12. Oklahoma had the record for annual occurrences per square mile: 7.62 tornadoes for every 10,000 sq. mi. Florida was next with 7.49. But the state with the record for tornado deaths in that time period per 10,000 sq. mi. is nowhere near the traditionally vulnerable states of the Central Plains and the South. It's on the East Coast: Massachusetts, with 120 deaths per 10,000 sq. mi.

For tornado-related deaths in the second half of the 20th century, no year has been worse than 1953, when twisters ravaged three sections of the country, killing at least 515 people.

On May 11, 1953, a single tornado savaged downtown Waco, Tex., killing at least 116 people.

On June 8, 1953, six tornadoes tore through southeastern Michigan and northern Ohio; Flint, Mich., was devastated; 139 people were killed.

On June 9, 1953, New England suffered its worst tornado in 75 years. Ninety-four people were killed in Worcester, Mass. Thousands in the region were left homeless.

On Dec. 5, 1953, a tornado wiped out seven blocks of downtown Vicksburg, Mo., and damaged or destroyed nearly 600 homes, killing 38 people.

The year's total of 421 tornadoes was only moderate compared with some of the annual totals reported since; 1,046 tornadoes in 1982, for example. Higher annual numbers are due, in part, to improved reporting systems. Even so, the death toll of 515 people in 1953 is far and away the record.

WORST U.S. TORNADOES SINCE 1900

The five worst tornadoes in this century, ranked by deaths:

1 Missouri, Illinois, Indiana: March 18, 1925; 689 dead.
2 Mississippi, Alabama, Georgia: April 2–7, 1936; 455 dead.
3 Southern, Midwestern states: April 3, 1974; 350 dead.
4 Arkansas, Tennessee, Missouri, Mississippi, Alabama and Kentucky: March 21–22, 1952; 343 dead.
5 Iowa, Indiana, Illinois, Ohio, Michigan, Wisconsin: April 11, 1965; 272 dead.

Number 1: Missouri, Illinois, Indiana

The deadliest twister in U.S. history was the great Tri-State Tornado of March 18, 1925. This massive tornado, just one of eight that developed that day in the nation's center, was bred from an immense thunderstorm in the Ohio River Valley. Few survivors reported seeing the tornado in its traditional funnel-shaped form. In many locales, the storm was so close to the ground that there was no room for a long, swirling vortex to develop. The storm was reported, instead, as a huge boiling black cloud that swept the ground with violence. The tornado struck first at Annapolis in the western part of Reynolds County, Mo., and carved a 219-mile continuous path of destruction east-northeast across Missouri, Illinois and Indiana, finally dissipating about 16 miles beyond Princeton, Ind. The great tornado lasted 3 hours and 18 minutes. In that time, it devastated parts of 35 cities and towns. Hardest hit was Murphysboro, Ill., where 152 city blocks were destroyed, about 60 percent of the city; 234 people were killed, and at least 800 more were injured. By the time the tornado was spent, it had killed 689 people, more by far than have been killed by any other single tornado this century. The actual toll probably was considerably higher, since scores of apparent tornado victims never were found. Nearly 2,000 people were injured, and more than 15,000 were left homeless. Property damage ran to $16.6 million.

Number 2: Mississippi, Georgia

A series of tornadoes between April 2 and April 7, 1936, tore through North Carolina, South Carolina, Georgia, Mississippi, Arkansas, and Tennessee. Shortly before 9 P.M. April 5, a tornado slashed a 400-yard-wide path through about 20 residential miles of Tupelo, Miss., killing 216 people, injuring more than 700 others; damages were more than $3 million. A day later, on April 6 at 8:37 A.M., two distinctly separate tornadoes appeared to the west of Gainesville, Ga. As they reached the city, they converged into one tornado and cut a four-block-wide path through the heart of the business district. In the tornado's wake 203 people were dead; 934 had been injured. Roughly 750 houses had been leveled, and 200 were severely damaged. Property losses were put at more than $13 million. The tornado emerged on the other side of Gainesville as two separate funnels and moved on for another 40 miles. When the April 2–7 outbreaks were over, a total of 455 people had been killed, at least 1,800 injured.

Number 3: South, Midwest

The biggest series of tornadoes in U.S. history savaged 13 states in the South and Midwest and reached into parts of Canada in a 16-hour, 10-minute rampage April 3 and April 4, 1974. At least 148 separate tornadoes tore northeast across 2,598 sq. mi., wreaking devastation in parts of Alabama, Georgia, Louisiana, Kentucky, Missouri, Virginia, West Virginia, Tennessee, Indiana, Illinois, Ohio, North Carolina, Michigan, and Ontario Province. About 350 people were killed, nearly 5,500 injured. Damage was estimated at about $1 billion. Brandenburg, Ky., and Xenia, Ohio, were hardest hit.

Number 4: Arkansas, Tennessee

A series of 31 tornadoes ravaged Alabama, Arkansas, Kentucky, Mississippi, Missouri and Tennessee March 21 and 22, 1952. Three-hundred and forty-three deaths were confirmed. At least 1,409 people were injured. About 3,600 homes were damaged or destroyed. Property losses were more than $15.3 million. Arkansas and Tennessee suffered the most extensive damage and loss of life; 13 twisters were reported in each state; 313 people died in those two states alone, accounting for more than 91 percent of the storms' death toll. The towns of Judsonia, Ark., and Henderson, Tenn., were demolished.

Number 5: Midwest

Thirty-seven tornadoes and about 50 thunderstorms rolled through six Midwestern states—Iowa, Indiana, Illinois, Michigan, Wisconsin and Ohio—on Palm Sunday April 11, 1965. Indiana was hit hardest; 22 communities were torn apart. Russiaville and Alto, Ind., were nearly leveled. Families of twisters wracked Goshen, Fort Wayne, Elkhart, Dunlap, Lebanon, Marion and Kokomo. Damage was estimated at $235 million. At least 272 people were killed and about 5,000 injured by the tornadoes. Dozens more people died days later in Minnesota, Wisconsin, Iowa and Illinois in floods brought in with the torrential rains that were part of the storms' onslaught.

HURRICANES AND TYPHOONS

Hurricanes were not always given people's names. In the 1800s, only the worst storms earned titles. The names generally referred to a person, place or ship associated with the storm, or the year in which it occurred. The practice of personifying hurricanes began in 1953 when meteorologists began assigning women's names to hurricanes. Feminists pressured the World Meteorological Organization to give men equal treatment in 1979. The names have alternated from male to female ever since.

The WMO issues its name lists every year. The names are listed alphabetically in a six-year cycle. A separate list of names is issued for hurricanes in the Atlantic. Hawaiian names are given to hurricanes that develop in an area about 1,000 miles on either side of the Hawaiian Islands. Hurricanes originating off the coasts of Mexico and Central America are given Spanish names.

The names of the most devastating storms are used only once and then retired.

Hurricanes are called typhoons when they occur west of the International Dateline.

WORST U.S. HURRICANES SINCE 1900

The five worst U.S. hurricanes in this century, ranked by deaths:

1. Galveston, Tex.: Sept. 8, 1900; 6,000 to 10,000 dead.
2. Lake Okeechobee, Fla., and Puerto Rico: Sept. 10–17, 1928; 4,000 dead, 1,836 in Florida alone.
3. Gulf Coast, from Texas to Florida: Sept. 14–17, 1919; 772 dead.
4. New England and Long Island: Sept. 21–22, 1938; 680 dead.
5. Coastal Louisiana, Mississippi and Texas: June 27, 1957; 550 dead.

Number 1: Galveston, Texas

At dawn Sept. 8, 1900, a powerful hurricane swept the prosperous and populous city of Galveston, Tex., leaving in its wake the worst carnage of any weather disaster in U.S. history. Winds of more than 120 miles an hour and waves that surged to 20 feet swamped and devastated the unprotected island city and then moved on to the Texas mainland, where at least 4,000 people fell victim. In Galveston, more than 2,600 houses were battered beyond repair or ripped from their foundations. More than 6,000 people were killed. Another 5,000 were injured. About 10,000 were left homeless. When Clara Barton and a small staff of Red Cross volunteers reached Galveston a week later, the air was still fetid with the stench from thousands of corpses that had been burned on funeral pyres.

Number 2: Lake Okeechobee, Florida

A massive Atlantic hurricane from about Sept. 10 to 17, 1928, ravaged part of the Dominican Republic, Guadeloupe, the islands of the Lesser Antilles, the Bahamas and Puerto Rico and then ripped into southern Florida. The ferocious storm leveled 21 miles of mud dikes surrounding Lake Okeechobee, Fla., loosing tons of water on hapless victims who were swept away, crushed by collapsing buildings or struck by rocketing debris. When the storm was over, more than 4,000 people were dead; 1,876 of the victims were Floridians.

Number 3: Gulf Coast, from Texas to Florida

One of the biggest hurricanes of the 20th century also was one of the slowest-moving. The storm formed off Santo Domingo about Sept. 2, 1919, and slowly moved through the West Indies to the Bahamas, then gradually cut west into the Florida Straits and lashed Key West, causing more than $2 million in damage. In the Gulf of Mexico off the Dry Tortugas, the hurricane caught and capsized 10 ships. One of them was the *Valbanera*, a Spanish steamer that went to the bottom with 488 people aboard. The storm spent itself on the coast of Texas, ripping with a fury into Corpus Christi, where 16-foot tides added to the devastation. The hurricane caused more than $20 million in damage to the Texas coast, and left at least 284 people dead, raising the death total to 772.

Number 4: New England and Long Island

The highest hurricane winds ever recorded in North America, 190 miles an hour, were part of the great hurricane that wracked Long Island and New England on Sept. 21, 1938. The region had little warning of the impending calamity. New Jersey was sideswiped. Long Island's South Shore took a direct hit. Communications went, and the National Weather Service had no modern storm-tracking equipment at the time. There was no way to warn New England of the storm's onslaught and the threat posed by 20- and 30-foot storm surges. Parts of Connecticut were hit hard. Rhode Island was savaged. The great storm spent itself inland, but not without wreaking devastation throughout parts of Massachusetts, Vermont and New Hampshire. Nearly a quarter of a million trees were snapped and broken like matchsticks. The hurricane was the worst storm to hit New England in more than a century. The death toll in the region was at least 680. Property damage ran to more than $400 million. Nearly 60,000 people were left homeless.

Number 5: Coastal Louisiana, Mississippi, Texas

Meteorologists saw Hurricane Audrey coming. They watched the storm grow in the Gulf of Mexico, and warned coastal residents of Louisiana, Mississippi, and Texas that they should evacuate low-lying areas. Some did, but many did not. The small, intense hurricane picked up speed in the 12 hours before landfall on June 27, 1957. Audrey hit Cameron, La., the hardest, ripping up trees, smashing and splintering nearly 40,000 homes and washing corpses away in a 12-foot storm surge. At least 534 people died, most of them in Cameron.

MAJOR HURRICANES, CYCLONES AND TYPHOONS SINCE 1950

Hurricane Carol
Aug. 30, 1954: New England and Long Island hit; 60 dead; more than 1,000 injured; $461 million in damage.

Hurricane Edna
Sept. 2–14, 1954: Widespread destruction in New England and New York; 21 dead; $40 million in damage.

Hurricane Hazel
Oct. 5–18, 1954: Three towns in Haiti destroyed; 410 dead; coastal cities and towns from South Carolina to New York wracked; 99 dead; another 85 people in Canada died in hurricane-related floods.

Hurricanes Connie and Diane
Aug. 18–19, 1955: Combined storms raged from North Carolina to New England causing worst floods in southern New England history; 184 dead; more than $1 billion in damage.

Typhoon Ida
Sept. 27–28, 1958: Central Honshu, south of Tokyo, Japan, hit hard; 928 dead or missing.

Typhoon Sarah
Sept. 17–19, 1959: Japan and South Korea struck; more than 2,000 dead.

Typhoon Vera
Sept. 26–27, 1959: Worst storm in Japan's history killed at least 5,000 people on Honshu; left 1.5 million homeless.

East Pakistan (Bangladesh) Cyclones
Oct. 10 and 31, 1960: Two cyclones with terrific storm surges killed a total of more than 10,000 people in Bay of Bengal region.

Hurricane Donna
Sept. 4–12, 1960: Entire Eastern Seaboard from Florida to New England was raked by a single broad-front storm with 145 mile-per-hour winds gusting to 180; 115 dead in Antilles; another 50 on mainland U.S.; damage ran to $500 million.

Hurricane Carla
Sept. 3–15, 1961: Texas Gulf Coast cities devastated; 46 dead; $408 million in damage.

Hurricane Hattie
Oct. 31, 1961: Most of Belize, British Honduras, destroyed; more than 300 dead.

East Pakistan (Bangladesh) Cyclone
May 28–29, 1963: Cyclone from Bay of Bengal, related storms and surges killed at least 22,000.

Hurricane Flora
Sept. 30–Oct. 9, 1963: Haiti, Cuba, and Dominican Republic struck; more than 6,000 dead.

Hurricane Cleo
Aug. 20–Sept. 5, 1964: Torrential rain, winds of up to 110 miles per hour whipped Haiti, Guadeloupe, Southern Florida and Eastern Virginia; 214 dead in the Caribbean; 3 dead on U.S. mainland.

Hurricane Dora
Aug. 28–Sept. 16, 1964: Fierce storm headed east, inland from northeastern Florida to southern Georgia with 125-mile-per-hour winds and torrential rain; five dead; $250 million in damage.

Typhoon Gloria
Sept. 11–12, 1964: Taiwan hit; 330 dead.

East Pakistan (Bangladesh) Cyclones
May 11–12 and June 1–2, 1965: Two successive cyclones with immense storm surges savaged Bay of Bengal region, killing as many as 47,000 people.

Hurricane Alma
June 4–10, 1966: Honduras and the southeastern United States were lashed with high winds, torrential rains; 51 dead.

Hurricane Betsy
Sept. 7–12, 1965: Winds ranging from 136 to 165 miles per hour devastated the Bahamas, Southern Florida and Louisiana, causing more than $1.4 billion in damage; 75 dead.

Hurricane Inez
Sept. 24–30, 1966: Cuba, Guadeloupe and Haiti ravaged; more than 3,600 dead.

Typhoon Billie
July 9, 1967: Japan's Honshu and Kyushu were hit; 347 dead; 2,000 homeless.

Hurricane Beulah
Sept. 5–22, 1967: Caribbean islands, Mexico, and Brownsville, Tex., areas ravaged by winds of up to 109 miles per hour and torrential rains; storm spawned numerous tornadoes; 328 coastal towns were damaged or destroyed; 58 dead; damage exceeded $1 billion.

Hurricane Camille
Aug. 17–19, 1969: One of the most powerful storms ever to hit the U.S. mainland ripped into seven states, from Louisiana to Virginia, with winds of up to 200 miles per hour; widespread damage totaled more than $1.5 billion; at least 256 people killed despite the largest evacuation in U.S. history.

Hurricane Celia
July 23–Aug. 5, 1970: 160-mile-per-hour winds lashed Texas coast; Corpus Christi was ruined; property damage exceeded $453 million; 11 dead.

East Pakistan (Bangladesh) Cyclone
Nov. 12, 1970: The single most devastating storm of the century, an immense Bay of Bengal cyclone and devastating surges, killed nearly 500,000 people in the low-lying Ganges River Delta area.

India Cyclone
Nov. 1, 1971: Cyclone and storm surge killed at least 10,000 people in Orissa state.

Hurricane Agnes
June 14–23, 1972: After her birth in the Caribbean, Agnes crossed Florida on June 19 and caused torrential rains from the Carolinas to Pennsylvania and New York, where flooding reached record levels. At least 117 people dead; 50 in Pennsylvania alone. Damages ran to more than $2.1 billion.

Hurricane Fifi
Sept. 19–20, 1974: Honduras savagely battered; more than 6,000 dead.

Hurricane Tracy
Dec. 24–25, 1974: 90 percent of Darwin, Australia, was destroyed; at least 49 dead.

Hurricane Eloise
Sept. 13–24, 1975: Florida and Southern Alabama sustained damage amounting to nearly $500 million; 21 dead.

Hurricane Belle
Aug. 6–10, 1976: Southern New England, New Jersey and New York sustained about $100 million in damage; five dead.

India Cyclone
Nov. 21, 1977: Cyclone and resultant storm surge assaulted state of Andhra Pradesh; death toll estimates ranged from more than 3,000 to nearly 10,000.

Hurricane David
Aug. 29–Sept. 7, 1979: Caribbean and Eastern Seaboard of the United States; 5 dead in United States, but more than 1,200 in Dominica, Puerto Rico, Haiti and the Dominican Republic.

Hurricane Frederic
Sept. 4–14, 1979: Caribbean and U.S. Gulf Coast; this second of two back-to-back hurricanes did more than $2.3 billion in damage to Alabama, Mississippi, and Florida. The storm hit the U.S. mainland at the entrance to Mobile Bay, Ala., Sept. 12 with 144 mile-per-hour winds, but only five people died.

Hurricane Allen
Aug. 4–11, 1980: Caribbean islands, coastal Texas; 272 dead.

Hurricane Alicia
Aug. 18, 1983: Galveston and Houston areas battered; 17 dead; massive damage.

Typhoon Ike
Sept. 2, 1984: Southern Philippines ravaged; 1,363 dead.

Hurricane Juan
Oct. 26–Nov. 6: Coastal regions of southeastern United States; 97 dead.

Bangladesh Cyclone
May 25, 1985: Cyclone in Bay of Bengal hit coastal areas; as many as 10,000 dead.

Hurricane Gilbert
Sept. 10–17, 1988: One of the most violent and powerful hurricanes ever recorded in the Western Hemisphere; record low pressure of 26.22 inches of mercury and winds of up to 185 miles per hour; devastated Jamaica, the Cayman Islands, and Mexico's Yucatán Peninsula; more than 400 killed; 750,000 homeless; nearly $5 billion in damage; $50 million of that in Texas, where Gilbert spawned 29 damaging tornadoes.

Hurricane Hugo
Sept. 16–22, 1989: Extensive damage in Caribbean and along southeast coast of United States; Charleston, S.C., devastated; 504 dead. Damages amounted to nearly $4.3 billion, making the storm one of the most costly in U.S. history.

Hurricane Bob
Aug. 19, 1991: Heavy rains and winds of up to 125 miles per hour hit the Eastern Seaboard from Cape Hatteras to Nova Scotia. At least 16 deaths were blamed on the hurricane. Damages were $780 million.

Hurricane Andrew
Aug. 23–26, 1992: Although other hurricanes have taken a greater toll in lives, none has been more

costly than Andrew. With winds gusting to more than 150 mph, Andrew struck the Bahamas Aug. 23, swept savagely across the southern tip of Florida Aug. 24, and spent itself in the bayous of southern Louisiana Aug. 26. When it was over, at least 52 people had been killed, and scores injured; 111,000 homes had been destroyed; more than 200,000 people were homeless. Damage was estimated at more than $20 billion—$30 billion, counting the cost of massive private and federal relief efforts.

Hurricane Iniki

Sept. 11, 1992: Hurricane Iniki, which means "sharp" or "piercing" in Hawaiian, roared across the western edge of Hawaii, devastating the rich tropical island of Kauai. Winds were clocked at 130 mph with gusts to nearly 160 mph. The storm left three people dead, nearly 100 others injured and more than 8,000 people homeless. Damage was estimated at more than $1 billion.

FLOODS

FIVE WORST FLOODS IN U.S. HISTORY

The five worst floods in U.S. history, ranked by deaths:

1 Galveston, Tex.: Sept. 8, 1900; 6,000 to 10,000 dead.
2 Johnstown, Pa.: May 31, 1889; at least 2,209 dead.
3 Ohio and Indiana: March 28, 1913; 732 dead.
4 California: March 12–13, 1928; 350 dead.
5 Ohio and Mississippi river valleys: January and February 1937; at least 250 dead.

Number 1: Galveston, Texas

At the turn of the century, nothing but luck stood between prosperous Galveston, Tex., and the waters of the Gulf of Mexico. When a hurricane bearing winds of more than 120 miles an hour swept the low-lying island city on Sept. 8, 1900, Galveston was quickly cut off from the Texas mainland, inundated and swamped. Tidal waves washed away one building foundation after another. Houses crumpled and collapsed. Victims were trapped, crushed or washed to sea. On the mainland, the storm claimed at least 4,000 victims, but Galveston was even harder hit. More than 6,000 people died there. Another 5,000 were injured. Carnage was so extensive that to prevent the spread of disease, thousands of corpses were burned on pyres. In the next two years, most of the city's houses were rebuilt on raised foundations, and a giant rock wall—17 feet high, 16 feet wide and 3.3 miles long—was built between Galveston and the sea. Another hurricane struck Galveston in 1915, but this time fewer than 12 people were lost to the storm.

Number 2: Johnstown, Pennsylvania

The membership of Andrew Carnegie, Andrew Mellon, Henry Frick and other prestigious industry leaders in the exclusive South Fork Fishing and Hunting Club included control of one of the largest man-made lakes in the country, 700-acre Lake Conemaugh in Johnstown, Pa. A huge and poorly maintained earthen dam created the lake in the 1850s from the waters of the Little Conemaugh River. The property was turned over to the exclusive club in 1880. Two days of rain late in May 1889 raised the lake's water perilously high. At 3:10 P.M. May 31, the earthworks 400 feet above unsuspecting Conemaugh Valley gave way. More than 20 million tons of water was unleashed on the valley in a raging torrent. The flood swept away South Fork, Mineral Point, Woodvale, East Conemaugh, and Gautier Mills. When the deluge roared into Johnstown, 14 miles from the broken dam, it carried with it thousands of tons of debris and bodies from the shattered towns in the valley. A 30-acre mountain of debris piled up at a stone bridge in the city and erupted in flames. The flood waters roiled until morning, and when they receded the valley lay in ruin. Nearly 8,000 workmen needed three months to clear the wreckage and bury the flood's victims. At least 2,209 people had been killed; about 800 of them were buried unnamed in a single mass grave; another 1,000 people were missing.

Number 3: Ohio and Indiana

Three days of heavy rain swelled the Miami, Mad, Muskingum, Scioto, Wabash, White and Ohio rivers to overflowing late in March 1913. Throughout the Ohio River Basin, waterways broke their banks and levees and flooded vast areas of Ohio, Illinois and Indiana. Cities and towns throughout Ohio were particularly hard hit. The flooding was without precedent, and it caught the region by surprise. Telephone lines were toppled immediately. Houses were flooded and broken apart. Entire towns and cities were inundated. In downtown Dayton, Ohio, scores of bodies floated and churned in the floodwaters as they raged past residents who had been stranded on higher ground. Families clung to chimneys and rooftops. At least 732 people died in the floods, which extended for more than 1,000 miles. In Ohio alone, more than 175,000 people were left homeless. Many more thousands were left homeless in Indiana and Illinois. Damages throughout the stricken region exceeded $147 million.

Number 4: California

Torrential rains in California's San Francisquito Valley raised the waters at St. Francis Dam in Santa Paula, 45 miles north of Los Angeles, to such a height in March 1928 that magnified pressure opened cracks and caused leaks in several parts of the 205-foot-high concrete barrier. On March 12, William Mulholland, the Chief Engineer of the Los Angeles City Water Works, inspected his two-year-old creation and decided that it was secure. At midnight of that day, the dam gave way, unleashing 12.4 billion gallons of water on the unsuspecting valley. A massive 120-foot wave roared from the dam, carrying 500,000 cubic feet of water per second, emptying the reservoir in an hour, shattering all in its path and quickly drowning at least 350 people. Investigators later determined that the dam's foundation was defective. The huge barrier had been built on a porous base that was part sandy conglomerate, part mica schist. Worse, the massive structure was situated on a fault line.

Number 5: Ohio and Mississippi River Valleys

After 25 days of unrelenting heavy rain in the Ohio and Mississippi river valleys early in 1937, the Scioto and Ohio rivers overflowed their banks late in January and slowly but inexorably flooded parts of 182 counties in 12 states. Officially, the victims of the flood numbered 137, but the death toll was complicated. Many victims were missing, and many others died not from floodwaters but from fires and explosions set off by broken gas mains, downed power lines and toppled stoves. The true death toll was nearer the 250 mark. More than 13,000 homes had been destroyed. More than 8 million acres were flooded. Damages ran to more than $418 million.

OTHER MAJOR U.S. FLOODS

Oregon

June 14, 1903: Willow Creek overflowed, flooding Heppner, Oreg.; 247 dead.

Mississippi River Valley

April 1927: Widespread flooding killed 313 people, caused $285 million in damage.

Florida

Sept. 10–16, 1928: Lake Okeechobee, swollen by hurricane, inundated southern Florida; 2,000 were killed.

New England

Sept. 23, 1938: Flooding in New York and New England after hurricane caused $350 million in damage; 500 dead.

Hawaii

April 1, 1946: Tsunami hit Hilo, Hawaii, with such force that railroad tracks were wrapped around trees; 179 dead.

Kansas and Missouri

July 1951: Flooding of Kansas River at Kansas City, Mo., and Topeka and Lawrence, Kans., caused first $1-billion flood loss in U.S. history; 41 dead.

New England

Aug. 17–19, 1955: Severe flooding from rains of Hurricane Diane killed 190 people. Damage was put at $1.8 billion.

Virginia

Aug. 19, 1969: Nelson County. Backlash of Hurricane Camille dropped an average of 18 inches of rain in six hours, 1.2 trillion gallons of water, which caused widespread flooding; at least 125 dead.

South Dakota

June 9, 1972: Canyon Lake Dam broke, flooding Rapid City; 200 people dead.

Colorado

July 31, 1976: Flash flood in Big Thompson Canyon killed more than 100 people.

Texas

Aug. 1–8, 1978: After weeks of drought, the north and west central parts of the state were swamped by torrential rains and flooding; 26 people died.

Northern California

Jan. 3–6, 1982: Violent rain storms soaked the clay hills of five counties, causing devastating mudslides that destroyed houses, buried roads, killed 31 people and caused more than $300 million in damage. Santa Cruz, Marin, Sonoma, Contra Costa and San Mateo counties were hardest hit.

Midwest

March 13–20, 1982: Relentless downpours and the sudden thawing of heavy snows swelled a dozen rivers in Indiana, Ohio and Michigan to overflowing, causing the worst flooding in 69 years. Seven people were killed. Tens of thousands of people were forced from their homes. Allen County, Indiana, was declared a federal disaster area.

Connecticut

June 6, 1982: The southern part of the state was swamped by up to 11 inches of rainfall, causing flooding in four counties that washed out roads, dams and bridges, damaged more than 5,000 homes, killed 12 people and caused at least $276 million in damage. New London, New Haven, Middlesex and Fairfield counties were hardest hit.

Mississippi Valley

Dec. 2–9, 1982: A week of powerful storms and heavy downpours caused flooding throughout parts of Illinois, Missouri and Arkansas, killing 22 people and causing at least $600 million in property damage.

California

Jan. 23–30, 1983: Four severe rainstorms along the California coast caused flooding that killed 11 people, forced more than 2,000 people from their homes, damaged more than 3,100 homes and businesses, and caused more than $70 million in damage.

Appalachia

May 6–8, 1984: Torrential rains caused flooding throughout Tennessee, Kentucky, West Virginia and northern Alabama. At least 10 people drowned, and more than 6,000 had to be evacuated from their homes.

Oklahoma

May 27, 1984: More than a foot of overnight rain caused the worst flooding in Tulsa's history, killing 13 people, injuring at least 80 and forcing more than 3,000 people from their homes. Damages ran in excess of $150 million.

Western States

Feb. 14–20, 1986: Unusually moist air from the Pacific Ocean and unseasonably warm weather created a six-day series of intense storms that left northern California, Utah, Oregon, Montana, Wyoming, Nevada, Idaho, Colorado and British Columbia reeling from snow, rain, avalanches and floods. At least 17 people were killed and more than 33,000 were driven from their homes.

Southwest, Gulf Coast

April 15–May 15, 1990: Three days of torrential April rain touched off the worst, most widespread flooding in 80 years throughout 117 counties in Texas, Oklahoma, Louisiana and Arkansas, which were already sodden from an unusually wet spring. Thirteen people were killed. Property and crop damage was nearly $1 billion.

Texas

Dec. 18–26, 1991: Heavy rainstorms caused flooding throughout eastern Texas; at least 15 people were killed, and homes, livestock and farmland sustained millions of dollars worth of damage.

Southern California

Feb. 9–15: Storms dropped 15 inches of rain, causing the worst flooding in decades. Damage, which exceeded $23 million, was heaviest in Los Angeles and Ventura counties. Twelve people were killed.

Illinois

April 13, 1992: About 250 million gallons of water from the Chicago River poured through a crack in a maze of utility tunnels below Chicago's central business district, the "Loop." Parts of the subway, City Hall and dozens of other buildings were flooded. Damage was estimated at more than $1 billion. No deaths or injuries were reported.

MAJOR FOREIGN FLOODS

China

Aug. 6–7, 1951: Flooding after a typhoon in Manchuria killed at least 4,800 people.

Great Britain

Aug. 15–16, 1952: East and West Lyn rivers overflowed from torrential rains, swamping Lynmouth; 84 dead.

Netherlands

Feb. 1, 1953: Relentless hurricane winds raised sea level, breaking dozens of dikes and flooding more than 500,000 acres; 1,835 people killed.

Japan

June 27, 1953: Extensive flooding in Kyushu left 1 million people homeless and killed 684; floods renewed July 17, 1953, killing another 638 people.

China

Aug. 1, 1954: Yangtze Rivers overflowed, forcing evacuation of 10 million people; 40,000 were killed.

East Pakistan (Bangladesh)

Oct. 31, 1960: Tidal waves in the aftermath of an immense cyclone ravaged the country's coast, destroying 900,000 homes; 10,000 were killed.

Germany

Feb. 16, 1962: Dikes broke near Hamburg; flooding killed 343 people, left 500,000 homeless.

South Vietnam

November–December 1964: Typhoons Iris and Joan drenched the Mekong River Delta; massive floods killed at least 5,000 people.

Italy

Nov. 3–4, 1966: Month-long rains caused flooding throughout the country. At least 113 people were killed, 35 in Florence where the Arno overflowed its banks, causing millions of dollars in damage to art treasures.

Brazil

Jan. 23, 1967: Flooding in Rio de Janeiro and São Paulo killed at least 620 people.

China

April 23, 1969: Extraordinary flood tides from immense storms in Shantung Province killed hundreds of thousands of people.

East Pakistan (Bangladesh)

Nov. 12, 1970: Tidal waves from immense cyclone devastated Ganges River Delta; at least 300,000 reported dead; another 100,000 missing.

North Vietnam

Aug. 30, 1971: Heavy flooding swept the country; death toll estimates reached 100,000.

Bangladesh

August 1974: Widespread flooding after summer monsoon rains caused more than $2 billion in property damage; at least 2,500 died.

India

June–September 1978: Flooding from unusually heavy summer monsoons devastated northern parts of the country; more than 1,200 dead.

Bangladesh

August–September 1985: Severe flooding left 25 million homeless; more than 1,000 dead.

Bangladesh
August–September 1987: Massive flooding in the northern part of the country killed more than 1,000 people.

Bangladesh
Sept. 6, 1988: Unusually heavy summer rains caused major floods throughout the country; more than 28 million people homeless; more than 400 dead.

Pakistan
Sept. 17, 1992: Three days of torrential monsoon rains caused the Indus River to overflow, devastating three provinces in the northern and eastern parts of the country, killing more than 2,000 people and leaving more than 100,000 others homeless.

AVIATION DISASTERS

WORST AIR DISASTERS

The five worst air disasters, ranked according to deaths:

1 March 27, 1977: Canary Islands; 582 killed.
2 Aug. 12, 1985: Tokyo, Japan; 520 killed.
3 March 3, 1974: Paris, France; 346 killed.
4 June 23, 1985: off Ireland; 329 killed.
5 Aug. 19, 1980: Saudi Arabia; 301 killed.

Number 1: Canary Islands
March 27, 1977: The worst aviation disaster in history occurred on the lone runway of Los Rodeos Airport at Santa Cruz de Tenerife in the Canary Islands at 4:40 P.M. The airstrip was cloaked in fog, and communications among the pilots of two Boeing 747 jumbo jets and traffic control were confused. Neither of the planes had been scheduled for a stop at Los Rodeos. The flights had been successfully diverted from scheduled landings at Las Palmas, 65 miles away, because a terrorist bomb had exploded in the airport there. One of the aircraft, a Pan American Airways charter flight carrying 394 people from Los Angeles, was already back on the 11,155-foot airstrip taxiing to a parking turnoff to await takeoff. The pilots of the other plane, a KLM Royal Dutch Airlines flight with 249 people aboard, thought the runway had already been cleared, and the KLM jet was accelerating for flight. As it loomed out of the fog at 165 miles per hour, the Pan Am jet turned to avoid collision, but the KLM jet struck it broadside. The planes erupted in a ball of fire. Everyone on the KLM flight was killed. Only 61 people on the Pan Am flight survived; 333 died. The death toll of 582 far outstripped loss of life in any other aviation disaster.

Number 2: Tokyo
Aug. 12, 1985: The worst single-plane disaster in aviation history was the loss of 520 people aboard a Japan Air Lines Boeing 747 jumbo jet making a 50-minute hop from Tokyo to Osaka. Control problems developed 13 minutes after the plane had left Tokyo's Haneda Airport. The pilot asked four times for permission to turn back. Twenty-nine minutes later, after 42 minutes in flight, he got permission for an emergency landing. By then, it was too late. The aircraft, which had been damaged before in accidents, had lost its vertical stabilizer. Other parts of the jumbo jet's tail disintegrated. The plane lost altitude and crashed into Mt. Ogura 70 miles northwest of Tokyo. Only four of the 524 people aboard the aircraft survived.

Number 3: Paris
March 3, 1974: Turkish Airlines Flight 981, a McDonnell Douglas DC-10, plummeted into Ermenonville Forest near Mortefontaine, France, nine minutes after takeoff from Orly Airport in Paris. The aircraft's cargo door had blown open. A similar, though less disastrous, DC-10 crash less than two years earlier had dramatized a safety problem with the cargo-door latches, but next to nothing had been done about it. When the cargo door blew off, Flight 981 was traveling 475 miles per hour at 12,500 feet. The sudden, violent decompression sucked six people out of the jet and buckled the floor of the passenger area, severing cables critical to control of the plane. The aircraft dove straight to the ground; 346 people died; only four bodies were found intact.

Number 4: Southeast of Ireland
June 23, 1985: A terrorist's bomb was the probable cause of an explosion that ripped apart an Air India Boeing 747 jumbo jet 31,000 feet over the Atlantic Ocean southeast of Cork, Ireland. The plane was en route from Toronto, Canada, to Bombay, India. The flight made a stopover in Montreal, and then crossed the Atlantic. The flight was about 45 minutes away from a scheduled stop in London when it vanished from air controllers' radar screens with no prior hint of difficulties. All of the 22-member crew and most of the passengers were Indian. Eighty-six of the passengers were children. All 329 people aboard the jet were killed. Sikh extremists were suspected of sabotaging the aircraft, though Sikh leaders publicly deplored the loss.

Number 5: Saudi Arabia
Aug. 19, 1980: Fire struck a Saudi Arabian Airlines jet, a Lockheed L-1011 Tristar, out of Riyadh, Saudi Arabia. The flight was en route from Karachi, Pakistan, to Jidda, Saudi Arabia. The aircraft stopped briefly in Riyadh. Shortly after takeoff, the pilot radioed that he was turning back for an emergency landing. A fire had broken out, apparently after a Moslem pilgrim had lighted a portable butane stove to brew tea. When the plane landed, it was already in flames. Sixteen crew members and 285 passengers were trapped inside. Neither they nor emergency firefighters were able to open any of the aircraft's 12 emergency exits. All 301 people aboard the Tristar were killed.

OTHER NEWSWORTHY AIR CRASHES

Sept. 17, 1908
Lt. Thomas E. Selfridge, 26, became the first fatality in the history of powered flight when plane he was flying with Orville Wright crashed in Fort Meyer, Va. Wright was badly injured.

July 2, 1912
First U.S. dirigible, *Akron*, exploded 2,000 feet above Atlantic City, N.J.; 5 died.

July 21, 1919
Dirigible *Wing Fool* crashed into skylight of Chicago bank; 13 died.

Aug. 24, 1921
British dirigible *ZR-2* broke up on maiden voyage near Hull, England; 62 died.

Feb. 21, 1922
U.S. dirigible *Roma* exploded and crashed in Hampton, Va.; 34 died.

Oct. 30, 1930
World's largest airship, the British *R-101*, crashed in Beauvais, France; 47 died.

April 14, 1933
U.S. dirigible *Akron*, the second by that name, was swamped in a thunderstorm, and plunged into Atlantic Ocean off New Jersey; 73 died.

May 6, 1937
German dirigible *Hindenburg* exploded while mooring in Lakehurst, N.J.; 36 died. The cause of the explosion was never clear, but the disaster spelled the end of the dirigible's use in commercial aviation.

Aug. 23, 1944
U.S. Air Force B-24 bomber crashed into school in Freckelton, England, and burns; 76 were killed, including 51 children.

July 28, 1945
U.S. B-25 bomber smashed into 78th and 79th floors of Empire State Building, New York City; 14 died, 10 in building.

Dec. 16, 1951
Airliner dove into Elizabeth River, Elizabeth, N.J., shortly after departure from Newark; 56 died.

Jan. 22, 1952
Airliner crashed into houses in Elizabeth, N.J.; 30 died, including seven on ground.

Feb. 11, 1952
Airliner crashed in Elizabeth, N.J.; third plane crash in same locale in less than two months; 33 died, including four on ground.

June 18, 1953
U.S. Air Force Globemaster plane crashed near Tokyo, Japan; 129 died.

Nov. 1, 1955
United Air Lines DC-6B exploded and crashed after a passenger's son planted bomb to collect insurance money; 44 were killed.

June 30, 1956
United Airlines Douglas DC-7 and TWA Lockheed Super-Constellation jet collided over Grand Canyon in Arizona; 128 were killed.

Dec. 16, 1960
United Airlines DC-8 and TWA jet collided over Staten Island, New York; 136 were killed, including at least six on the ground.

Feb. 15, 1961
Sabena Airlines Boeing 707 crashed near Brussels, Belgium; 73 died, including 18 members of U.S. Olympic figure skating team.

Sept. 10, 1961
President Airlines DC-6 crashed near Shannon Airport in Ireland; 83 people died.

March 4, 1962
Caledonian Airlines DC-7C crashed in jungle in Cameroon shortly after takeoff; 111 died.

June 3, 1962
Air France Boeing 707 crashed after takeoff from Orly Airport in Paris, France; 130 died.

June 22, 1962
Air France Boeing 707 crashed during storm-forced emergency landing on Guadeloupe in the West Indies; 113 died.

Nov. 29, 1963
Trans-Canada Air Lines jet crashed 20 miles north of Montreal, Canada; 118 died.

May 20, 1965
Pakistani Boeing 707 crashed in Cairo, Egypt; 124 died.

Jan. 24, 1966
Indian Boeing 707 crashed into Mont Blanc in French Alps; 117 were killed.

Feb. 4, 1966
Japanese jetliner crashed into Tokyo Bay; 133 died.

March 5, 1966
British Boeing 707 caught fire and crashed into base of Mt. Fuji in Japan; 124 died.

Dec. 24, 1966
U.S. military transport plane crashed near Binh Thai in South Vietnam; 129 died.

April 20, 1967
Swiss airliner crashed at Nicosia, Cyprus, after being struck by lightning; 126 died.

Feb. 16, 1968
First manslaughter charges were lodged against commercial airline pilots in connection with crash in Taiwan; 22 were killed in crash.

March 16, 1969
Viasa DC-9 crashed in suburb of La Coruba, Venezuela, after pilot was shot by gunman; 155 died—84 on the plane and 71 on the ground.

Aug. 9, 1969
DC-9 and plane piloted by student collided near Indianapolis, Ind.; 83 were killed.

July 3, 1970
Charter airliner crashed at Barcelona, Spain; 112 died.

July 5, 1970
Air Canada DC-8 crashed near Toronto, Canada, after two engines and part of wing fall off; 109 were killed.

July 30, 1971
Midair collision of Japanese Boeing 727 and Japanese fighter over Morioka, Japan; 162 died.

Sept. 4, 1971
Alaskan Airlines Boeing 727 crashed east of Juneau, Alaska; 109 died.

June 18, 1972
British airliner crashed shortly after takeoff from Heathrow Airport outside London, England; 118 were killed.

Aug. 14, 1972
East German-chartered Ilyushin jet crashed outside of Berlin just after takeoff; 156 died.

Oct. 13, 1972
Soviet Ilyushin-62 jet airliner crashed trying to land at Moscow's international airport; 176 died.

Dec. 3, 1972
Spanish-chartered Convair 990A crashed just after taking off from Tenerife in Canary Islands; 155 were killed.

Dec. 8, 1972
United Air Lines Boeing 737 plowed into houses near Chicago's Midway Airport; 45 died.

Dec. 29, 1972
Eastern Airlines Lockheed Tri-Star jet crashed into Everglades in Florida; 101 died.

Jan. 22, 1973
Jordanian Boeing 707 crashed in thick fog in Nigeria while carrying pilgrims returning from Mecca; 176 died.

April 10, 1973
British European Airways jet crashed during attempted landing at Basel, Switzerland; 104 died.

July 11, 1973
Brazilian jetliner crashed south of Orly Airport in Paris; 122 died.

April 27, 1974
Pan Am Boeing 708 crashed into mountain on Bali, Indonesia; 107 died.

Dec. 4, 1974
DC-8 en route to Mecca, Saudi Arabia, crashed in Sri Lanka during rainstorm; 191 died.

April 4, 1975
U.S. Air Force Galaxy C-5A transport jet crashed on takeoff from Saigon during airlift of 2,000 Vietnamese orphans to United States; 172 were killed.

June 24, 1975
Eastern Airlines Boeing 727 crashed on approach to New York's Kennedy International Airport during electrical storm; 113 died.

Aug. 3, 1975
Charter Boeing 727 crashed into Atlas Mountains near Agadir, Morocco; 188 died.

Aug. 20, 1975
Czechoslovakian Airlines jetliner crashed south of Damascus, Syria; 126 died.

Sept. 10, 1976
British Airways jet and Yugoslavian chartered DC-9 collided in midair near Zagreb, Yugoslavia; 176 died.

Sept. 19, 1976
Turkish airliner crashed into mountainside during premature landing near Isparta in southwestern Turkey; 155 died.

Nov. 19, 1977
Portuguese airliner overshot runway at Funchal, Madeira, and burst into flames; 130 died.

Jan. 1, 1978
Air India jumbo jetliner exploded shortly after takeoff from Bombay, India, and plunged into sea; 213 died.

Sept. 25, 1978
Pacific Southwest Airlines Boeing 727 jetliner and private plane collided over San Diego, Calif.; 144 died.

Nov. 15, 1978
Chartered Icelandic jet crashed just short of runway at Sri Lanka's Colombo airport; 183 died.

Dec. 23, 1978
Alitalia jet crashed near Palermo, Sicily; 109 died.

May 25, 1979
American Airlines plane crashed at Chicago's O'Hare International Airport; 275 died.

Aug. 11, 1979
Two Soviet jetliners collided in the Ukraine; 173 people killed.

Nov. 26, 1979
Pakistan International jet crashed into mountains north of Jidda, Saudi Arabia, shortly after takeoff; 156 died.

Nov. 28, 1979
Air New Zealand DC-10 jetliner on sightseeing flight crashed into Mt. Erebus in Antarctica; 257 were killed.

Jan. 21, 1980
Iranian Airlines Boeing 727 crashed in mountains north of Tehran, Iran; 128 people died.

March 14, 1980
Polish Ilyushin-62 jet crash landed at Warsaw airport; 97 people died, including 22 members of an American amateur boxing team.

April 25, 1980
British Boeing 727 crashed into mountain during approach to Santa Cruz de Tenerife airport in the Canary Islands; 146 died.

July 7, 1980
Soviet TU-154 jetliner crashed after takeoff from Kazakhstan; 183 died.

Aug. 22, 1981
Taiwanese jet exploded in midair over Sanyi, Taiwan; 110 died.

Dec. 1, 1981
Chartered Yugoslavian DC-9 smashed into mountain near airport in Corsica; 180 died.

Jan. 13, 1982
Air Florida Boeing 727 jet caught in snowstorm crashed into bridge over Potomac River shortly after takeoff from Washington National Airport, Washington, D.C.; 78 died, including four victims in cars on the bridge.

April 26, 1982
Chinese jet crashed near Guilin in South China; 112 people died.

June 8, 1982
Brazilian Boeing 727 jet crashed in mountains near Fortaleza; 137 died.

July 9, 1982
Pan American Airways Boeing 727 jetliner crashed into residential neighborhood in Kenner, La., shortly after takeoff from New Orleans International Airport; 154 people died, including eight victims on the ground.

Sept. 1, 1983
Soviet fighter plane shot down South Korean airliner, which was off course in Soviet airspace; 269 were killed.

Nov. 27, 1983
Colombian jetliner crashed near Spain's Madrid airport; 183 died.

Feb. 19, 1985
Spanish jetliner crashed into mountain near Bilbao, Spain; 148 died.

Aug. 2, 1985
U.S. Delta jet crashed in a storm near Dallas–Fort Worth Airport; 134 died.

Dec. 12, 1985
Chartered Arrow Air jet crashed at Gander, Newfoundland; 256 were killed; 248 of the victims were U.S. soldiers coming home after tours of duty in the Middle East.

March 31, 1986
Mexican jet crashed in mountains near Mexico City; 166 died.

May 9, 1987
Soviet jetliner crashed just after takeoff from Warsaw, Poland; 183 died.

Aug. 16, 1987
Northwest Airlines jetliner disintegrated in a fireball near Detroit, Mich., airport; 156 died.

Aug. 28, 1988
Italian jets collide during air show and crash into spectators in Ramstein, West Germany; 50 were killed and over 500 wounded.

July 3, 1988
Iranian airbus was shot down after flying too close to U.S. Navy ship engaged in combat with Iranian gunboats in Persian Gulf; 290 died.

Dec. 21, 1988
A Libyan terrorist bomb exploded aboard Pan Am Boeing 747 near Lockerbie, Scotland; 270 were killed, including 11 on ground.

June 7, 1989
Surinam DC-8 jetliner crashed near Surinam's Paramaribo Airport; 168 died.

July 19, 1989
United Airlines DC-10 crashed in Sioux City, Iowa, while landing with disabled hydraulic system; 111 died.

Sept. 19, 1989
French DC-10 flying from the Congo to Chad to Paris exploded over Niger; 171 died.

Oct. 21, 1989
Honduran jetliner, a Boeing 727, crashed into mountain in Las Mesitas, Honduras, while preparing to land in Tegucigalpa; 131 killed.

Oct. 2, 1990
Hijacked Chinese jetliner, a Boeing 737, crashed in Guangzhou during landing; at least 132 people killed; 50 injured.

May 26, 1991
Austrian jetliner, a Boeing 767-300, exploded and crashed 120 miles northwest of Bangkok, Thailand; 223 people killed.

July 11, 1991
McDonnell Douglas DC-8 charter jet crashed about a half-mile from King Abdel-Aziz International Airport in Jidda, Saudi Arabia. The pilot had reported a fire in the plane's landing gear and tried to return shortly after takeoff. The plane was carrying Nige-rian Moslems home from a pilgrimage; 261 people killed.

Jan. 20, 1992
An Air France Airbus A-320 jet on a domestic flight from Lyon to Strasbourg crashed into a fog- and snow-covered ridge in the Vosges Mountains, killing 87 of the 96 passengers and crew on board.

July 31, 1992
A Chinese airliner, a Soviet-made Yakovlev-42, exploded in flames during takeoff from Nanjing, killing at least 100 people.

July 31, 1992
A Thai Airways jetliner crashes during a heavy rainstorm in Nepal's Himalayas, killing all 113 passengers and crew aboard.

Oct. 4, 1992
An El Al Boeing 747-200 cargo jet crashed into a 10-story apartment complex in Duivendrecht, a suburb of Amsterdam, shortly after takeoff from Schiphol Airport in the Netherlands. At least 250 people, four of them aboard the jet, were killed in the crash.

MARINE DISASTERS

WORST MARINE DISASTERS IN U.S. WATERS

The five worst marine disasters in U.S. waters, ranked according to deaths:

1 April 27, 1865: *Sultana;* 1,547 dead.
2 May 29, 1914: *Empress of Ireland;* 1,024 dead.
3 June 15, 1904: *General Slocum;* 1,021 dead.
4 July 24, 1915: *Eastland;* 812 dead.
5 Sept. 8, 1934; *Morro Castle;* 134 dead.

Number 1: Sultana

April 27, 1865: The huge Mississippi River steamboat *Sultana,* en route to Cincinnati from New Orleans, stopped in Vicksburg, Miss., on April 25, just 16 days after the end of the Civil War. The relatively new 720-ton sidewheeler was designed to carry about 376 people. The ship already was carrying about a hundred travelers, as well as livestock and a staff and crew of about 80 people. The captain of the *Sultana* disregarded the ship's capacity, and took on about 2,400 new passengers, bedraggled Union Army soldiers frantic to return to their homes in the North. Many were amputees and recently released prisoners of war. By the time the *Sultana* pulled away from the dock in Vicksburg, the ship was riding perilously low in the water. The overloaded steamboat docked in Memphis April 26 to take on more coal; one of the ship's boilers had been malfunctioning for nearly the entire trip. Refueled, the *Sultana* resumed her journey. At about 2 A.M. April 27, as the steamboat chugged through a small group of islands known as the Hens and Chickens, the malfunctioning boiler exploded and the ship erupted in flames. Sleeping passengers were crushed by falling debris, scalded or burned to death. Hundreds drowned in the Mississippi. The official death toll, long debated, is 1,547.

Number 2: Empress of Ireland

May 29, 1914: The elegant Canadian Pacific cruise ship *Empress of Ireland,* carrying 1,024 passengers and crew, was two days out of Quebec en route to Liverpool when it was swallowed by thick fog in the St. Lawrence River (between the United States and Canada) near Rimouski, New Brunswick. As the early-morning fog engulfed the *Empress,* its captain spotted the Norwegian collier *Storstad* bearing his way downriver. Both ships sounded warning signals, but neither stopped. The collier rammed the liner amidships and kept going. The *Empress* listed as tons of water flooded the ship's hull, trapping sleeping passengers. The luxury liner sank to the riverbottom in 14 minutes; 1,024 people went to their graves.

Number 3: General Slocum

June 15, 1904: More than 1,400 picnickers, most of them German immigrants from St. Mark's School in the Bronx, boarded the 250-foot excursion steamboat *General Slocum* in New York's East River. A fresh coat of white paint hid extensive rot throughout the ship. Safety equipment was either missing or faulty; fire hoses were rotted; so were life preservers, and many of them were filled with iron bars to raise their weight to the legal requirement. Worse, the ship was manned by an ill-trained crew of 23 men under the command of a captain already known for his recklessness and poor seamanship, 61-year-old William H. Van Shaick. About 300 yards off Manhattan's 130th Street, fire broke out on the *General Slocum.* The origin of the blaze is unclear, either the ship's galley or a paint locker. A stiff wind quickly spread the flames. Passengers and most of the crew panicked. Inexplicably, Capt. Van Shaick turned the huge vessel into the East River and headed for North Brother Island. With passengers dying or huddled screaming on the ship's stern as flames licked at them, the *General Slocum* crashed into the island's shore. Van Shaick and most of the crew jumped ship. The excursion boat burned to its waterline. Bodies littered the shore. Van Shaick later was charged with manslaughter and negligence and sentenced to 10 years in prison, but was pardoned in 1908. The Justice Department indicted the manufacturer of the iron-weighted life preservers, Nonpareil Cork Works. But 1,021 passengers aboard the *General Slocum* were dead; most of the victims were women and children.

Number 4: S.S. Eastland

July 24, 1915: At the docks in the Chicago River, throngs of passengers boarded the packet S.S. *Eastland,* a St. Joseph–Chicago Steamship Company riverboat sharply and publicly criticized for design and structural faults that made the vessel unseaworthy. The ship's passengers were Western Electric Company employees bound for an annual picnic. The *Eastland* was built to accommodate 2,500 people, but at least 3,500 were allowed to board. Still at the dock, the packet began listing to port. Engineers emptied one ballast tank after another in futile efforts to right the ship. It capsized, and water flooded in belowdecks. Hundreds of passengers drowned inside the vessel. Hundreds more died beneath the hull. Twenty years later, an Illinois court ruled that the ship's engineers had mishandled the ballast tanks, and that the steamship company was blameless; 812 passengers died.

Number 5: Morro Castle

Sept. 8, 1934: The Ward Line luxury liner *Morro Castle*, beset with violent labor trouble, a mutinous crew and a history of narcotics and immigrant smuggling, was en route from Havana to New York when fire broke out during a fierce gale off the New Jersey coast. The ship's skipper, Capt. Robert R. Wilmott, had been found dead the day before, apparently the victim of a heart attack. Chief Mate William F. Warms was in command. He panicked, ordered the *Morro Castle* ahead at full speed, which only turned the blaze into an inferno. Warms finally weighed anchor and ordered the liner abandoned. Eban S. Abbot, chief engineer, and most of the crew jumped ship, leaving passengers to fend for themselves. Scores of travelers burned to death in their cabins. Others died of smoke inhalation. Some drowned trying to swim to safety. Later that morning, the charred hulk of the ship drifted to shore at Asbury Park, N.J. The death toll was 134. Warms was sentenced to two years in jail; Abbot, four.

FAMOUS MARINE DISASTERS

The Titanic

The sinking of the British White Star luxury liner *Titanic* in the frigid waters of the North Atlantic, April 15, 1912, is among the best-known marine disasters in history. The *Titanic* was widely publicized as one of the world's greatest ships, an unsinkable 45,000-ton, 882.5-foot colossus, and this was its maiden voyage, a slow and elegant journey from Southampton, England, to New York. Among the passengers who went down with the *Titanic* were some of the most influential people in the world: New York millionaire Isidor Straus, Col. John Jacob Astor, Jr., Benjamin Guggenheim and George D. Widener. The *Titanic*'s captain was E. J. Smith, the White Star Line's most experienced and respected skipper. Five days into the uneventful voyage, shortly before midnight Sunday April 14, the *Titanic* struck an iceberg off Newfoundland's Grand Banks. The ship's starboard bow plates buckled from the impact, and the sea rushed into the gigantic ship. The *Titanic* carried 16 wooden lifeboats and four canvas rafts, an inadequate complement of safety equipment for 2,207 people—a crew of 700 and 1,507 passengers. As rescue ships sped to the aid of the rapidly sinking *Titanic*, women and children boarded the life rafts first, bidding agonized farewells to loved ones who stayed behind. Many families refused to be separated and stayed together aboard ship. At about 2:15 A.M. April 15, the *Titanic* sank, taking about 1,500 people, including Captain Smith, to their deaths. Official estimates of the death toll have ranged from 1,490 to 1,517.

The Lusitania

The British Cunard Line steamer *Lusitania*, en route from New York to Liverpool, England, with 1,901 people aboard, was 10 miles off Ireland's Old Head of Kinsale May 7, 1915, when it was sunk, struck fore and aft by torpedoes from a German submarine. On May 1, the German Embassy in Washington, D.C., had warned all civilian vessels to stay out of the war zone surrounding Great Britain. Still, the deaths of 1,198 civilian passengers, 128 of them U.S. citizens, shocked the world and enraged the United States. Though Pres. Woodrow Wilson did not declare war against Germany and its Austrian-Hungarian allies until 1917, two years later, U.S. sentiment against Germany had been crystallized, in part, by the sinking of the *Lusitania*. Thereafter, U.S. neutrality had been more of a hollow formality than fact.

The Maine

Since 1895, the Cuban government had weathered persistent rebellion against Spanish rule. U.S. sympathies, fueled by the blatantly sensationalistic reporting of William Randolph Hearst's *New York Journal* and Joseph Pulitzer's *New York World*, lay with the rebels. The two powerful newspapers, meanwhile, were locked in a battle for circulation. They used inflammatory reporting, gimmicks and comics in their competition. One of the most popular comic strips of the day was the *World*'s "Yellow Kid." The *Journal* lured the strip away from its competition. In the fray, the name of the comic became synonymous with the quality of the two newspapers' reportage, particularly as it applied to Spanish influence in the Western Hemisphere and, specifically, to the trouble in Cuba; hence, the term "yellow journalism." In January 1898, when Cubans loyal to Spain rioted against U.S. involvement and threatened U.S. citizens, the United States sent the battleship *Maine* into Havana Harbor. At 9:40 P.M. Feb. 15, an explosion ripped the battleship apart; 260 men went down with the *Maine*. The New York press publicly and stridently blamed Spain, crying "Remember the Maine," though there is little conclusive evidence that Spain was responsible for the underwater mine that sank the *Maine*. A little more than two months later, on April 25, Congress declared war on Spain. The Spanish-American War lasted less than four months. An armistice was signed on Aug. 12. Cuba became free, but under U.S. guidance. Spain ceded Puerto Rico and Guam to the United States, and surrendered the Philippines for $20 million.

Untold thousands have perished aboard ships throughout peacetime history, but some of the greatest maritime losses are relatively unknown:

- 6,000 people died Jan. 27, 1949, when a Chinese liner and collier collided off the south coast of China.
- More than 1,500 Soviet seamen died when the battleship *Novorossiisk* sank in the Black Sea during military maneuvers in October 1955.

FOREIGN MARINE DISASTERS SINCE 1950

April 26, 1952

The U.S. Navy destroyer-minesweeper *Hobson* was struck amidships and sunk by the large U.S. Navy aircraft carrier *Wasp* during maneuvers in the middle of the Atlantic. The skipper of the *Wasp* turned his ship to accommodate landing aircraft. The move went unnoticed by the flanking *Hobson;* 176 died.

Jan. 9, 1953

South Korean passenger steamer *Chang Tyong-Ho* was capsized and sunk by a huge tsunami off Pusan; 249 died.

Jan. 31, 1953

The stern doors of the British channel ferry *Princess Victoria* were ripped open and damaged during a gale. The vessel foundered and sank near Mew Island, off Belfast, Northern Ireland; 121 people died.

May 26, 1954

An explosion and fire rocked U.S. Navy aircraft carrier *Bennington* while launching planes in maneuvers 75 miles off Newport, R.I.; 107 died.

Sept. 26, 1954

Japanese train ferry *Toya Maru* capsized and sank during typhoon in Tsugaru Strait off Hakodate; 1,172 died.

July 26, 1956

Italian luxury liner *Andrea Doria* sank off Nantucket Island, Mass., after collision July 25 with Swedish liner *Stockholm* in dense fog; 1,654 aboard the *Andrea Doria* were rescued; 52 died.

July 14, 1957

Russian fishing ship *Eshghabad* struck a reef between Baku and Salyan and sank during a violent storm on the Caspian Sea; 270 died.

March 1, 1958

Turkish ferry *Uskudar* broke up during a gale on Izmit Bay in the Sea of Marmara; 350 died.

Jan. 30, 1959

The 2,800-ton Danish passenger freighter *Hans Hedtoft* struck an iceberg 37 miles south of Cape Farewell, Greenland, and sank on her maiden voyage; 95 died.

May 8, 1959

A Nile River excursion boat, the *Dandarah*, capsized 10 miles north of Cairo; about 200 died.

April 8, 1961

The 5,030-ton British passenger ship *Dara* exploded and burned in the Persian Gulf off Dubai. The ship had been sabotaged; 236 died.

July 8, 1961

Portuguese steamer *Save* ran aground, exploded and sank at the mouth of the River Linde, Mozambique; 259 died.

Jan. 4, 1963

Indonesian ferry *Djandji Radjan* caught fire and sank in North Sumatra's Toba Lake; 105 died.

April 10, 1963

U.S. Navy nuclear submarine *Thresher* broke up at 8,400 feet during test dives in the Atlantic 220 miles east of Cape Cod, Mass.; 129 died.

May 4, 1963

A double-decker ferry overloaded with Moslem pilgrims capsized and sank in the Upper Nile River about 300 yards off Maghagha, Egypt; 221 died.

Aug. 17, 1963

Three-hundred-ton Japanese ferryboat *Midori Maru* foundered off Okinawa in East China Sea; 128 died.

Dec. 22, 1963

Fire broke out in the hairdressing salon aboard the Greek cruise ship *Lakonia*, which burned about 180 miles off Madeira, Portugal; 128 died.

April 10, 1964

A motor launch from Iran sank in Persian Gulf; 113 died.

July 23, 1964

The *Star of Alexander*, a United Arab Republic freighter, exploded at the dock in Bone, Algeria, as 2,000 tons of ammunition was being unloaded; more than 100 died.

May 23, 1965

River ferry capsized in Shire River near Liwonde, Malawi; 150 died.

Dec. 12, 1966

A 16-ton refrigerator trailer broke loose aboard the Greek ferry *Heraklion* during a storm in the Aegean Sea. The loose cargo tore a hole in the ferry, which sank with 281 aboard; 241 died.

July 29, 1967

An auxiliary gas tank fell from a fighter jet as it was launched from the U.S. aircraft carrier *Forrestal* during daily air strikes against North Vietnam. The ship caught fire and ignited bombs; 134 died.

Aug. 10, 1967
Steamboat capsized in severe storm on Romania's Lake Tel; 153 died.

May 21, 1968
U.S. Navy nuclear submarine *Scorpion* imploded at 2,000 feet and sank to 10,000 feet below the surface of the Atlantic 400 miles southwest of São Miguel in the Azores; faulty pipe joints and an inadequate deballasting system were blamed; 99 died.

Oct. 10, 1968
Ferryboat sank off Mindanao in the Philippines; death toll ranged to 500.

June 2, 1969
Australian aircraft carrier *Melbourne* collided with U.S. destroyer *Frank E. Evans* 650 miles southwest of Manila in South China Sea. The *Evans* was cut in half; 74 died.

June 21, 1969
A barge carrying 150 Portuguese troops capsized in Zambezi River 190 miles north of Beira in Mozambique; 108 died.

July 5, 1970
Indian ferry capsized in Krushna River; 150 died.

Dec. 15, 1970
Shifting cargo sank 62-ton South Korean ferry *Namyong-Ho* in Korea Strait 50 miles off Korea's southern coast; about 300 died.

Feb. 21, 1973
Burmese ferryboat and Japanese freighter collided in Rangoon Harbor; more than 200 died.

May 10, 1973
Overloaded Bangladesh motor launch, the *Swamasaore*, sank in Padma River; at least 300 died.

Sept. 26, 1974
Soviet destroyer burst into flames and sank in Black Sea; more than 200 died.

Aug. 3, 1975
Two excursion boats collided in West River near Canton, China; nearly 500 died.

Nov. 10, 1975
The 729-foot ore carrier *Edmund Fitzgerald* sank in a storm on Lake Superior in the worst marine disaster on the Great Lakes in nearly two decades; 29 died.

April 4, 1978
Typhoon in Bay of Bengal swamped fleet of cargo ships; more than 1,000 died.

Nov. 22, 1978
Fishing boat overloaded with Vietnamese refugees sank off coast of Malaysia; 200 died.

April 20, 1980
Bangladesh ferry sank on Padma River near Dacca; at least 230 died.

April 22, 1980
Oil tanker and a ferry collided near Maestre de Campo, an island in the Philippines; 116 died.

Jan. 6, 1981
Brazilian steamer *Novo Amapa* sank in Amazon River near Macapa, Brazil; 260 died.

Jan. 27, 1981
Indonesian liner *Tamponas II* burned and sank in Java Sea; 580 died.

Sept. 19, 1981
Riverboat *Sobral Santos* capsized and sank in Amazon River near Obidos, Brazil; at least 300 died.

May 25, 1983
Egyptian Nile River steamboat *10th of Ramadan* sank in Lake Nasser; 357 died.

June 5, 1983
On Volga River at Ulyanovsk, Soviet ship hit railway bridge; 240 died.

April 20, 1986
Bangladesh ferry sank in Dhaleswari River; at least 600 died.

May 25, 1986
Bangladesh ferry sank in Meghna River; at least 450 died.

Aug. 31, 1986
Soviet passenger liner *Admiral Nakhimov* sank after colliding with Soviet freighter *Pyotr Vasev* in Black Sea; 398 died.

March 6, 1987
British ferry *Herald of Free Enterprise* sank in North Sea off Belgian coast; death toll estimates ranged to 188.

July 5, 1987
A barge crossing Luapala River between Zambia and Zaire sank; 390 died.

Dec. 20, 1987
Filipino passenger ferry *Doña Paz* sank after colliding with tanker *Victor* in waters south of Manila; death toll estimates range as high as 3,000.

July 6, 1988
Explosion and fire on Occidental Petroleum oil rig off coast of Scotland; 166 died.

Aug. 6, 1988
Indian passenger ferry capsized in the Ganges River near Manihari Ghat in Bihar state; at least 400 died.

March 8, 1989
A fishing boat jammed with Vietnamese refugees sank after colliding with the propeller of the *Nissei Maru,* a Japanese supertanker; 130 died.

April 19, 1989
Explosion in a gun turret aboard U.S.S. *Iowa;* 47 died.

Sept. 10, 1989
A Romanian pleasure boat collided with a Bulgarian barge on the Danube River and sank; 161 died.

Nov. 3, 1989
The U.S. gas-drilling ship *Seacrest* capsized in a typhoon off the coast of Thailand; 93 died.

April 6, 1990
Gale winds sank a passenger ferry in Myanmar's Gyaing River; more than 200 died.

April 7, 1990
Fire sank the Danish ferry *Scandinavian Star* in the North Sea; at least 176 died.

April 10, 1991
An Italian automobile ferry, the *Moby Prince,* rammed the tanker *Agip Abruzzo,* lying at anchor in thick fog outside Livorno Harbor. The ferry exploded and sank; at least 140 died.

Dec. 15, 1991
An Egyptian ferry, the *Salem Express,* en route from Jiddah, Saudi Arabia, to Safaga, Egypt, struck a coral reef in the Red Sea and quickly sank six miles from its destination; at least 460 people drowned.

OIL SPILLS

The severity of damage caused by an oil spill is always difficult to ascertain. The U.S. Coast Guard categorizes as "major" any oil spill of more than 100,000 gallons, but such categorization is misleading. Damage actually depends on the kind of oil that is spilled, how quickly containment and clean-up efforts begin, weather conditions, tides and currents, proximity of wildlife and waterfowl, and locale, generally. Thus, the impact of a 50,000-gallon oil spill in an ecologically sensitive area may be potentially more disastrous than a 500,000-gallon spill in open ocean.

Major Oil Spills
Following is a list of major oil spills, ranked according to gallons lost.

1 February 1983: Blowout in the Nowruz oil field, Persian Gulf; 176.4 million gallons.
2 June 3, 1979: Blowout at Ixtoc 1, an exploratory offshore drilling rig 50 miles off Mexico's Yucatán Peninsula in the Gulf of Mexico; 176.4 million gallons.
3 July 19, 1979: Collision of *Atlantic Empress* and *Aegean Captain,* off Trinidad and Tobago; 88.2 million gallons.
4 Aug. 6, 1983: Fire aboard the Spanish supertanker *Castillo de Beliver,* off Cape Town, South Africa, destroyed and broke up the ship; 73.5 million gallons.
5 March 16, 1978: Supertanker *Amoco Cadiz* grounded off Portsall, France, broke in two; 65.6 million gallons.
6 Dec. 19, 1989: Explosion aboard Iranian supertanker *Kharg-5* off the Canary Islands; spillage estimates ran as high as 37 million gallons.
7 March 18, 1967: *Torrey Canyon* grounded off Land's End, England; nearly 35 million gallons.
8 Dec. 19, 1972: *Sea Star* ruptured in collision in Gulf of Oman; 33.8 million gallons.
9 May 12, 1976: Tanker *Urquiola* grounded off La Coruña, Spain; 29.4 million gallons.
10 Feb. 25, 1977: Fire aboard the *Hawaiian Patriot* in the northern Pacific; 29.1 million gallons.
11 Dec. 3, 1992: The Greek tanker *Aegean Sea* ran aground and broke apart in the fishing grounds off La Coruña, Spain, creating a slick that stretched for 20 square miles; 23.8 million gallons.
12 March 20, 1970: Tanker *Othello* damaged in collision in Tralhavet Bay, Sweden; roughly 23.5 million gallons.
13 June 13, 1968: Hull of tanker *World Glory* gave out off coast of South Africa; 13.5 million gallons.
14 April 11, 1991: Supertanker *Haven* exploded in Gulf of Genoa in the Mediterranean Sea; spillage estimates ran as high as 12.6 million gallons.
15 March 24, 1989: *Exxon Valdez* grounded in Prince William Sound, Alaska; 10.9 million gallons—the largest oil spill in U.S. waters.
16 Nov. 1, 1979: Liberian tanker *Burmah Agate* sank after collision with Liberian freighter *Mimosa* in Galveston Bay, Texas; 10.7 million gallons.
17 Nov. 5, 1969: Hull of the *Keo* failed off the coast of Massachusetts; 8.8 million gallons.
18 Nov. 4, 1969: Storage tank ruptured in Sewaren, N.J.; 8.4 million gallons.
19 April 22, 1977: Well blowout in the Ekofisk oil field on the North Sea; 8.2 million gallons.
20 Dec. 15, 1976: *Argo Merchant* grounded off Nantucket, Mass.; 7.7 million gallons.
21 Oct. 15, 1967: Ship's anchor snagged and broke pipeline in West Delta, La.; 6.7 million gallons.
22 Nov. 30, 1971: Tanker broke up in heavy seas off Japan; 6.3 million gallons.

23 April 10, 1991: Automobile ferry *Moby Prince* collided with anchored tanker *Agip Abruzzo* near Livorno Harbor, Italy, causing explosion on tanker and an oil leak; 6.2 million gallons.

24 June 8 and 9, 1990: Norwegian tanker *Mega Borg* exploded and burned southeast of Galveston, Tex., in Galveston Bay; 3 million gallons.

25 Jan. 25, 1991: Iraqi saboteurs opened release valves at Kuwait's Sea Island Terminal, a supertanker loading dock, dumping oil into Persian Gulf; 1.2 million gallons.

26 Jan. 2, 1988: Ashland Oil Co. diesel fuel storage tank on the Monongahela River in Pittsburgh, Pa., ruptured; 750,000 gallons.

27 Jan. 2, 1990: Gash in Exxon Corp. refinery pipeline in Arthur Kill shipping channel of New York Harbor; 567,000 gallons.

28 July 28, 1990: Two oil barges collided with Greek tanker *Shinoussa* in Galveston Bay, off Texas City, Tex.; 500,000 gallons.

29 April 27, 1988: Drain valve accidentally opened at a Shell Oil Co. refinery in Martinez, Calif., on San Francisco Bay; 500,000 gallons.

30 June 23, 1989: Greek tanker *World Prodigy* grounded on reef off Newport, R.I., in Narragansett Bay; 420,000 gallons.

31 Feb. 7, 1990: *American Trader*, a tanker leased by British Petroleum Oil Shipping Co., U.S.A., ran over its own anchor two miles off Huntington Beach, Calif., and opened gash in a storage hold; nearly 400,000 gallons.

32 June 24, 1989: Uruguayan tanker *Presidente Rivera* hit rock in Delaware River off Claymont, Del.; 310,000 gallons.

33 June 23, 1989: Panamanian freighter *Rachel B* collided with oil barge in Houston Ship Channel of Galveston Bay; 250,000 gallons.

34 Jan. 31, 1969: A leak from an offshore oil rig in the Santa Barbara Channel six miles off the coast of California created a massive slick and destroyed marine life along 30 miles of the state's coast; 235,000 gallons.

35 March 6, 1990: Oil barge exploded in Arthur Kill shipping channel of New York Harbor; 200,000 gallons.

36 July 22, 1991: Japanese fish-processing ship *Tenyo Maru* sank 22 miles off coast of Washington after collision with Chinese ship *TuoHai;* at least 100,000 gallons spilled, fouling beaches along coast of Washington's Olympic National Park.

37 Aug. 19, 1989: Leak in Royal Dutch/Shell Co. pipeline at Bromborough, England, fouled the River Mersey; 44,100 gallons.

NUCLEAR ACCIDENTS

The attribution of deaths to nuclear accidents is limited and arbitrary, at best. Fatalities may be caused by explosions and fires, sudden and clear exposure to radioactive materials or prolonged exposure to contaminants over varying lengths of time. Exposures also may be only contributing factors to death, and therefore less readily discernible.

Chalk River, Ontario, Canada

Dec. 12, 1952: Human error during a low-power test at the NRX nuclear reactor at Chalk River about 100 miles from Ottawa in Ontario, Canada, resulted in leakage of radioactive contaminants, and destruction of the reactor's core, but no apparent injuries. On May 23, 1958, a faulty switch at the new 200-MW NRU nuclear power plant on Chalk River triggered leakage of radiation-contaminated coolant. Most damage was confined to the building. No injuries were reported, but no follow-up studies were conducted on the plant employees responsible for cleanup after the accidents.

Chelyabinsk-40, Soviet Union

December 1957–January 1958: A chemical explosion at Chelyabinsk-40, a plutonium production plant on Lake Kyzyltash near the industrial towns of Kyshtym and Kasli in the Central Urals Mountains of the Soviet Union, spread massive amounts of radioactive material over 14 lakes and at least 30 communities within 625 sq. mi. of the nuclear facility. Thousands of people were evacuated and relocated. The government burned their homes, buried the land on which they stood and turned much of it into a military training ground. The incident was long suspected by Western scientists, but not confirmed by Soviet authorities until late in 1988.

Windscale/Sellafield, Great Britain

Oct. 10, 1957: A burst fuel cartridge caused a fire in one of two plutonium production reactors at a site called Windscale in Sellafield on the coast of Cumbria, north of Liverpool, Great Britain. Water used to cool three tons of burning uranium billowed radioactive contaminants over the countryside. Farmers, villagers and Windscale workers were exposed to high levels of radioactivity. Nearly 40 deaths and more than 250 cases of cancer were traced directly to the incident. The owner of the plant, British Nuclear Fuels Limited, changed Windscale's name to Sellafield in 1981. Critics charged that the move was an effort to disassociate Windscale from its long record of lethal mishaps. In fact, troubles at the site had continued for more than a decade. On Sept. 26, 1973, a steam explosion had vented radioactive gas throughout the 10 stories of the site's Head End Plant, where spent uranium oxide fuels were being reprocessed. At least 100 workers were contaminated. The plant was shut down and, four years later, permanently closed. A formal investigation of Windscale later disclosed as many as 194 safety incidents up to 1977. In February 1979 had come the disclosure that highly radioactive waste had been leaking from storage at the plant for at least three years. In November 1983, radioactive debris and a heavily contaminated oil slick was discovered. A succession of accidents in 1986 brought renewed investigations and calls for the closing of Sellafield. By the turn of the decade, Sellafield was being used mostly for underwater storage of spent fuel rods, but even that use has been problematic. Critics say that the rods have contaminated local waters.

Rocky Flats, Colorado

Sept. 11, 1957: A fire at Dow Chemical's Rocky Flats, Colorado, plutonium production plant spewed contaminated smoke throughout the countryside northwest of Denver. Another fire broke out at the same site on May 11, 1969, and caused millions of dollars in damage and a six-month shutdown. Soil near the plant was heavily contaminated. The problem was worsened by leakage of contaminated oil from storage drums. The government was later forced to buy thousands of acres of contaminated, unusable land adjoining the plant, which had been operated under contract with the Atomic Energy Commission.

Idaho Falls, Idaho

Jan. 3, 1961: A sudden pressure release during maintenance of the core of an experimental nuclear reactor, the Stationary Low-Power Reactor in Idaho Falls, Idaho, killed three technicians and contaminated the plant. By midsummer 1962, the building had been razed and the 892-sq.-mi. plant site decontaminated and turned over to other uses.

Fermi Reactor, Detroit

Oct. 5, 1966: Part of the core of the Enrico Fermi nuclear breeder reactor outside Detroit, Mich., melted down after a cooling system malfunction, but contamination was contained. The plant was closed until 1970. During start-up, coolant leaked from a burst pipe and again contaminated the building. The Fermi reactor was closed permanently in 1972.

Lucens Vad, Switzerland

Jan. 21, 1969: Radiation was released by a cooling system malfunction in an underground nuclear reactor. Radioactive contamination was sealed off in a cavern.

Monticello, Minnesota

Nov. 19, 1971: Nearly 50,000 gallons of radiation-contaminated waste water was dumped into the Mississippi River after overflowing from the Northern States Power Company's nuclear reactor in Monticello, Minn.

Browns Ferry, Alabama

March 22, 1975: An accidental fire lowered the temperature of cooling water at the core of the Browns Ferry nuclear reactor near Decatur, Ala., to the danger point, and meltdown was narrowly averted. The fire was caused when a workman used a lighted candle to check for air-pressure leaks. The fire was one of a series of accidents that have put the Browns Ferry installation among the top 10 most accident-prone power plants in the United States.

Beloyarsk Reactor, Soviet Union

Dec. 30–31, 1978: An electrical short circuit started a fire at the Baloyarsk fast-breeder reactor near Sverdlovsk. The fire raged through the plant, threatening meltdown. About 1,200 firefighters got the blaze under control and narrowly averted an unprecedented disaster.

Erwin, Texas

Aug. 7, 1979: A secret government nuclear fuel plant near Erwin, Tex., leaked enriched uranium, exposing about 1,000 people to dangerous levels of contamination.

Soddy-Daisy, Tennessee

Feb. 11, 1981: More than 100,000 gallons of radiation-contaminated coolant leaked from the Tennessee Valley Authority's Sequoyah 1 nuclear plant when a workman mistakenly opened a containment valve. Leakage was restricted to the plant's containment building, but eight workers were exposed.

Wakasa Bay, Japan

March 8, 1981: A tank storing tons of radiation-contaminated waste water at JAPCO's Tsuruga I nuclear reactor overflowed, contaminating the waters of Wakasa Bay. The plant's owners kept the leak secret. At least 56 workers were contaminated trying to clean up the tainted water. Investigation disclosed that numerous leaks had occurred previously. JAPCO paid heavy fines.

Rochester, New York

Jan. 25, 1982: Small amounts of radioactive steam were spewed into the air outside the Rochester Gas & Electric Company's Robert E. Ginna reactor in Rochester, N.Y. A corroded pipe carrying high-pressure coolant water through a steam generator had ruptured.

Gore, Oklahoma

Jan. 6, 1986: At Kerr-McGee's Sequoyah Fuels Corporation, a uranium processing plant near Gore, Okla., a container of 29,500 pounds of radioactive uranium hexafluoride burst when it was improperly heated. One employee was killed. The plant's air-conditioning system picked up fumes from the explosion and spread them into the company's lunchroom. More than 100 employees were treated at local hospitals for breathing problems. At least 34 victims were temporarily hospitalized.

Three Mile Island, Pennsylvania

March 28, 1979: The worst nuclear accident in U.S. history occurred at one of two nuclear reactors on Three Mile Island in the Susquehanna River near Harrisburg, Pa. The plants were operated by Metropolitan Edison Company (Met Ed) and owned by the General Public Utility Company. Part of the reactor's core melted as a result of technological and human errors, and radioactive gases were spewed into the atmosphere. Official reports of the incident cited negligible harm from the fallout. Critics point ominously to abnormally high infant mortality rates in the area around Three Mile Island, as well as dramatic increases in cancer death rates. Some scientists and researchers, however, have insisted that the true impact of the incident has never been clear and may never be known.

Chernobyl, Soviet Union

April 26, 1986: History's worst known nuclear accident occurred in the Soviet Union, at one of four high-power nuclear reactors in Chernobyl, on the Pripyat River about 60 miles from Kiev in the Ukraine. The accident happened during a scheduled shutdown. Operators violated safety procedures. Two explosions—the first of steam caused by a power burst, the second of hydrogen gas—ripped through Unit 4. It took 10 days for workers to bring the plant's burning reactor core under control and prevent further contamination of the environment. Two technicians died outright, victims of the explosions. Twenty-nine firefighters and plant employees suffered fatal radiation burns trying to contain the disaster. About 135,000 people were evacuated from the cities and towns surrounding Chernobyl. For weeks, abnormal levels of radiation were reported throughout most of Europe. The potential death toll linked to fallout from the Chernobyl incident is horrifying. Dr. Vladimir Chernousenko, the nuclear physicist who supervised the emergency teams charged with controlling the disaster, estimated that there would be from 5,000 to 7,000 deaths from Chernobyl-related cancers or radiation poisoning, but that the health of as many as 35 million people was affected by the disaster.

PART TEN

THE JOURNALIST'S NOTEBOOK

LIBEL

Libel is a publication (words or image) that defames a living person. It may defame him by holding him up to public scorn, hatred, contempt or ridicule, or by impugning his ability in his trade, job or profession. (Spoken defamation is slander. The differentiation between the two is less important today than historically because of Supreme Court decisions and the growth of the broadcast media.)

There are four threshold elements for libel:

1 Defamation. The plaintiff must prove that he was defamed.
2 Identification. The plaintiff must be identifiable, but does not have to have been identified by name. The context may provide enough information to identify him. As a consequence, a defamatory statement made about a small group may libel everyone in the group. For example, a statement that members of a certain quartet are known to take drugs libels all members of the quartet because the reputation of each is harmed (each is identified as a possible drug user). A statement that members of the Army take drugs does not libel all soldiers because the group is so large that the statement does not identify any particular person.
3 Publication. The statement (or image) does not have to appear in the mass media to be published. Publication occurs when someone other than the author and the subject sees the material. It can occur when a writer shows material to a co-worker, even though the material never appears in the press.
4 Falsity. The plaintiff must be able to prove that what was published was false. Publication of the truth, no matter how disagreeable, is not libelous.

The plaintiff must also show some degree of fault on the part of the defendant. The standard of fault varies, depending on the public or private status of the defendant and the public or private nature of the issues involved. The Supreme Court has been defining and refining this standard since 1964. [See Major Supreme Court Libel Decisions, below] In some cases, a plaintiff must merely show that the defendant was negligent. In other cases, he must show that the defendant acted with "actual malice," which the Supreme Court has defined as publication with knowledge that the information was false or "with reckless disregard of whether it was false or not." In general, public officials and public figures must show malice. (Not everyone who is in the public eye is a public figure, however. The Supreme Court has been narrowing the definition in recent years.) States are free to set their own standards, as long as they are within the constitutional guidelines established by the Supreme Court.

A court may award two types of damages in libel cases—actual and punitive. Actual damages include compensation for out-of-pocket expenses, injury to reputation, humiliation, mental anguish and suffering. Punitive damages, which are awarded to a plaintiff to punish a defendant, are often many times larger than actual damages. Punitive damages are awarded only when there is a finding of actual malice.

Cartoons, drawings, photographs, captions, headlines, letters to the editor, editorials, advertisements, direct quotations, memos, letters and signs can all be libelous. Anyone who spreads a libel may be held accountable and liable for damages. If a libel appears in a newspaper, for example, the reporter, all of the editors who handled the story, the production staff and the publisher may all be held liable. In practice, however, most plaintiffs look for the defendants with the "deep pockets," that is, with the most money.

There are three major defenses to a libel claim:

1 Truth. Truth is the only absolute defense for libel. Although the burden of proof is on the plaintiff, the defendant must be able to refute the plaintiff's assertion. This can be difficult in cases in which a writer has promised to keep a source confidential. The Supreme Court has ruled that minor, inconsequential inaccuracies do not defeat a defense of truth.
2 Privilege. There are two types of privilege, absolute and qualified. Absolute privilege means that a person has immunity from a libel lawsuit. Absolute privilege applies to many public officials when they are performing their official duties. For example, members of Congress enjoy absolute privilege during debates on the floor of Congress. They can say anything they wish during official Congressional proceedings, without fear of reprisal. Local, state and federal officials enjoy the privilege during official legislative proceedings. Senior members of the executive branch of federal and state governments have absolute privilege when conducting official business, as do persons participating in public court

proceedings. The range of the privilege varies from state to state, depending on how courts and legislatures have interpreted the concept of "official" business and "senior" executives. The news media have a qualified privilege to report on proceedings and documents that involve absolute privilege. (If the news media did not have such protection, they could not report what officials said or did, for fear of libel claims.) The qualified privilege protects the media against libel claims as long as the media provide a fair and accurate account of the governmental proceedings and records. A biased account, or one that contains inaccuracies, is not privileged. Although privilege is clear in some contexts (a Senate hearing, for example), it is subject to interpretation in others. In police matters, for example, what type of report is official? In general, police records that are public (such as arrest and booking records) are subject to absolute privilege. Police records that are not public, such as working case files, are not. In court cases, public records are subject to absolute privilege. Sealed records, or unofficial notes, probably are not.

3 Fair comment. A statement of opinion about the performance of a person who places himself in the public spotlight (a performer, a sports star, a politician, etc.) is protected from a libel claim. Without the protection, there could be no unfavorable arts reviews or political commentaries. The Supreme Court has held, however, that not all parts of an opinion piece need be privileged. Although opinion is privileged, a factual error stated within an opinion piece can be subject to a libel claim. [See Milkovich v. Lorain Journal Co., et al., below]

Mitigating factors are the last line of defense against a libel action. Although they cannot defeat a complaint, they may limit the size of the damage award. Many state statutes specify factors to be considered in determining damage awards. They include:

1 Retraction and correction. Publishing a retraction or correction within a reasonable time period may limit the amount of punitive or actual damages that may be awarded.

2 Proof of previous bad reputation. If the plaintiff's reputation was so bad to begin with that it could not be further sullied, a damage award may be reduced or eliminated. The bad reputation and the libel must be closely related. A bad reputation in one area does not necessarily affect other areas.

3 Reliance on a usually reliable source. Showing that the report was based on a usually reliable source will defeat a claim of actual malice. It may mitigate a claim of negligence.

4 Anything that the defendant can do to show regret or lack of malice, or that the harm done was not as great as was claimed.

Major Supreme Court Libel Decisions

New York Times Co. v. L. B. Sullivan, 376 U.S. 254, 11 L.Ed.2d 686, 84 S.Ct. 710 (1964). Set a new standard of fault in libel cases concerning public officials, in order to safeguard the free flow of information required by the First Amendment. Held that a public official had to show not only that the defamatory information published about him was wrong, but also that it had been published with "actual malice." Justice William J. Brennan, Jr., writing for the court, said, "The constitutional guarantees require, we think, a federal rule that prohibits a public official from recovering damages for a defamatory falsehood relating to his official conduct unless he proves that a statement was made with 'actual malice'—that is, with knowledge that it was false or with reckless disregard of whether it was false or not."

Curtis Publishing Co. v. Wallace Butts, Associated Press v. Edwin A. Walker, 388 U.S. 130, 18 L.Ed.2d 1094, 87 S.Ct. 1975 (1967). Created a new category for libel plaintiffs: public figures. Held that a public figure is one who attracts public interest, either because of his job or because he thrusts himself into public issues. (The public figures in these cases were a college athletic director and a former Army general who was politically active.) The court ruled that public figures, like public officials, had to show more than the mere inaccuracy of a defamatory publication in order to succeed in a libel suit. The court held that public figures could win only "on a showing of highly unreasonable conduct constituting an extreme departure from the standards of investigation and reporting." In effect, the decision extended the New York Times v. Sullivan standard to public figures.

Phil A. St. Amant v. Herman A. Thompson, 390 U.S. 727, 20 L.Ed.2d 262, 88 S.Ct. 1323 (1968). Defined the "reckless disregard" standard of New York Times v. Sullivan. Held that "reckless conduct is not measured by whether a reasonably prudent man would have published" the information, but by whether the defendant "entertained serious doubts as to the truth of his publication."

George A. Rosenbloom v. Metromedia, Inc., 403 U.S. 29, 29 L.Ed.2d 296, 91 S.Ct. 1811 (1971). Extended the "actual malice" standard of New York Times v. Sullivan to include private individuals who are caught up in issues or events that are of public interest.

Elmer Gertz v. Robert Welch, Inc., 418 U.S. 323, 41

L.Ed.2d 789, 94 S.Ct. 2997 (1974). A pivotal case in the development of libel law, Gertz v. Welch retreated from the standard set by Rosenbloom v. Metromedia. The court began to increase the ability of a private person to recover damages for libel. Held that the criterion for applying the actual malice standard should be the public or private status of the plaintiff, not the public's interest in the issue being discussed. The court specified three classes of public figures: the involuntary public figure (who has public interest thrust upon him through no action of his own), the famous person who is a public figure for "all purposes and in all contexts," and the limited public figure, who "voluntarily injects himself or is drawn into a particular controversy." The court held that a person may be a public figure in some contexts and a private figure in others. In this case, the court decided that Elmer Gertz, a prominent lawyer, was a public figure in some context, but not in the context in which he was defamed. The court found that, as a private figure, he would not have to prove actual malice in order to recover actual damages, although he would have to show some degree of fault. The ruling specified that awards for actual damages could take into account out-of-pocket expenses, damage to reputation, humiliation, mental anguish and suffering. In order to recover punitive damages, the court ruled, a private plaintiff would have to prove actual malice.

Time, Inc. v. Mary Alice Firestone, 424 U.S. 448, 47 L.Ed.2d 154, 96 S.Ct. 958 (1976). Held that well-known figures are not necessarily public figures. In this case, which involved inaccurate reporting of the grounds for a divorce, the court ruled that the well-known plaintiff (Mary Alice Firestone) was not a public figure because she did not seek to put her divorce in the public eye.

Ilya Wolston v. Reader's Digest Association, Inc., 443 U.S. 157, 61 L.Ed.2d 450, 99 S.Ct. 2701 (1979). Narrowed the definition of "public figure." The court held that Ilya Wolston, who had refused to appear before a grand jury and had been convicted of criminal contempt of court 20 years before the defamatory publication, was not a public figure because he had not chosen to inject himself into any controversy.

Dun & Bradstreet, Inc. v. Greenmoss Builders, Inc., 472 U.S. 749, 86 L.Ed.2d 593, 105 S.Ct. 2939 (1985). Held that a private person, defamed about a matter that does not concern the public, does not have to show actual malice in order to recover punitive damages. (This is distinguished from Gertz, in which a private person defamed about a matter of public concern was required to show actual malice in order to recover punitive damages).

Philadelphia Newspapers, Inc. v. Maurice S. Hepps, 475 U.S. 767, 89 L.Ed.2d 783, 106 S.Ct. 1558 (1986). Shifted the burden of proof for private persons engaged in matters of public concern who are defamed by the media. Held that the plaintiff has the burden of showing that a defamatory statement was false before he can recover damages. (Previously, the defendant had to prove that the statement was true.) This reversed a 200-year-old common law practice. The court ruled that requiring the defendant to prove the truth of the defamation would have a "chilling effect" on the free speech guaranteed by the First Amendment.

Hustler Magazine and Larry C. Flint v. Jerry Falwell, 485 U.S. 46, 99 L.Ed.2d 41, 108 S.Ct. 876 (1988). The issue before the Supreme Court was not libel (which had been rejected as a claim by a lower court) but another tort—intentional infliction of emotional distress—which had been claimed as an alternative method of collecting damages for an injurious publication. The court rejected the claim. Jerry Falwell, a nationally known minister, had sued *Hustler* Magazine because of an ad parody that depicted him in a cartoon as a drunk who had had an incestuous affair with his mother in an outhouse. At the bottom of the page was written, "Ad parody. Not to be taken seriously." The Supreme Court said that Falwell, a public figure, could not collect damages for intentional infliction of emotional distress without showing in addition that the publication contained a false statement of fact made with "actual malice," as would have been required in a libel case. To require otherwise, one court said, would have had a chilling effect on satire and political cartoons, which historically have been an important form of free expression.

Milkovich v. Lorain Journal Co., et al., 58 Law Week 4846, 110 S.Ct. 2695 (1990). The court drew a distinction between pure opinion, which cannot be libelous, and a statement of opinion that contains a false statement of fact, which can be libelous. In Gertz, the court had stated that, "under the First Amendment there is no such thing as a false idea. However pernicious an opinion may seem, we depend for its correction not on the conscience of judges and juries but on the competition of other ideas." If an opinion can not be false, then it cannot be libelous, because libel requires falsehood. In this case, however, the court ruled that a false allegation contained within a statement of opinion is not protected. The plaintiff in the case had sued a sports columnist who had accused him of lying under oath. A lower court ruled that the column was an expression of opinion and, therefore, not libelous. The Supreme Court ruled that the columnist's opinions could not be held to be libelous, but that the coach's veracity was an issue of fact, not opinion. As an issue of fact, the court ruled, it could be the basis for a libel suit.

REFERENCES:

Major Principles of Media Law, Wayne Overbeck. New York: Harcourt Brace Jovanovich College Publishers, 1991.

Mass Communication Law, Cases and Comment, Donald M. Gillmor and Jerome A. Barron. New York: West Publishing Co., 5th edition, 1990.

The Writer's Legal Companion, Brad Bunnin. New York: Addison-Wesley Publishing Co., 1988.

PRIVACY LAW

Privacy, unlike libel, is a fairly new legal issue. An 1890 *Harvard Law Review* article by Samuel D. Warren and Louis D. Brandeis (who later became a Supreme Court justice) contended that there should be such a right. "The press," they wrote, "is overstepping in every direction the obvious bounds of propriety and of decency. Gossip is no longer the resource of the idle and of the vicious, but has become a trade, which is pursued with industry as well as effrontery."

Gradually, state courts began to accept that there is a right to privacy, but their interpretation of that right varied greatly. Privacy issues are still governed largely by state law, either through statute or precedent. For that reason, it is important to consult a lawyer who is familiar with privacy issues in a particular jurisdiction.

Privacy lawsuits typically fall into one of four categories:

1) Intrusion into a person's physical seclusion, solitude or private affairs.

This is more concerned with a reporter's or photographer's conduct than with the content of what is produced. It occurs when journalists cross an imaginary line between newsgathering and snooping, either physically or electronically. The line varies from court to court. The celebrity of the subject is often a factor in determining where the line is drawn, although courts have ruled that even extraordinarily famous people have some rights in this area.

For example, in Galella v. Onassis (487 F.2d 986, 2d cir., 1973) the Court of Appeals for the Second Circuit upheld a ruling against a freelance photographer who had specialized in photographing Jacqueline Kennedy Onassis and her family. The trial court had found (in a case that combined lawsuits brought by Ron Galella and Onassis) that when Galella had tried to take photographs "the children were caused to bang into glass doors, school parents were bumped, passage was blocked, flashbulbs affected vision, telephoto lenses were used to spy, the children were imperiled in the water, a funeral was disturbed, plaintiff [Galella] pursued defendant [Onassis] into the lobby of a friend's apartment building, plaintiff trailed defendant through the City hour after hour, plaintiff chased defendant by automobile, plaintiff and his assistants surrounded defendant and orbited while shouting, plaintiff snooped into purchases of stockings and shoes, flashbulbs were suddenly fired on lonely black nights—all accompanied by Galella jumping, shouting and acting wildly." The trial court ordered Galella to stay 150 feet away from Onassis and 225 feet from her children. The appeals court upheld the lower court's decision but reduced the distances to 25 feet and 30 feet. In 1982, the trial court found that Galella had repeatedly violated the restraining order and ordered him to pay $10,000 to Onassis.

2) Disclosure of embarrassing private facts.

This differs from libel in that the facts that have been revealed are true. The plaintiff alleges that the facts, while true, were embarrassing and should not have been made public. Typically, defendants reply that the facts were newsworthy and, therefore, fair game. If the media could be restrained from publishing newsworthy private information merely because it embarrassed the subject, investigative journalism could not be practiced and the public would suffer.

Although courts' definitions of "newsworthy" varies, the standards chosen have been fairly broad. More often they have dealt with the public's interest in a topic, rather than its need to know about a topic. In 1976, for example, a federal district court in California ruled in Virgil v. Time Inc. (424 F. Supp. 1286, D.C.Cal) that Mike Virgil, a surfer, could not recover damages from Time, Inc., for an article that had appeared in *Sports Illustrated*. The article said, among other things, that Virgil had eaten spiders, that he had extinguished cigarettes in his mouth, and that he had tried to injure himself while working on construction jobs so that he could collect unemployment compensation and go surfing. The court said that Virgil could not recover for invasion of privacy because the story was newsworthy.

Courts have also ruled in favor of the media when the embarrassing information that was disclosed was from court records that were properly obtained. In 1975, the Supreme Court overruled the verdict of a Georgia court against a broadcaster who had published the name of a rape victim. The reporter had obtained the name from a court record. The Supreme Court ruled that the use was permitted, as long as the information was lawfully obtained from official records. Four years later, in Smith v. Daily Mail (443 U.S. 97, 1979), the court voided a West Virginia law that imposed criminal sanctions for publishing the names of juvenile offenders. (The names had been lawfully obtained by monitoring police radio broadcasts and talking to witnesses.) The court ruled that a state cannot impose criminal sanctions against the media for disseminating the names of juvenile offenders, even when that information does not come from official sources. It did not rule out civil lawsuits, however.

In other cases, however, courts have ruled against the media. Some courts, particularly those in California, have ruled that publication of long-forgotten, once-newsworthy indiscretions can be an invasion of privacy. In Melvin v. Reid (112 C.A. 285, 1931), for example, a California Appellate Court ruled in favor of the plaintiff. She had been a prostitute and had been charged with murder and acquitted. She had then moved, married and made new friends who did not know of her past. Years later, a movie focused on her earlier life, and used her maiden name in the advertising. The court ruled that she had a right to sue for invasion of privacy. State courts have upheld the right to sue in such cases, although trial courts have often ruled against plaintiffs, based on the facts of the case.

3) Portraying someone in a false light.

In false-light cases, a subject is portrayed in a way that does not accurately represent him. The portrayal need not be unflattering, although that is often the case. The facts may be literally true, as long as they convey an inaccurate impression.

Photo captions can be particularly vulnerable areas, especially if they are misplaced. For example, if a caption about a burglary suspect is incorrectly placed under a photo of a local businessperson, the businessperson has been portrayed in a false (and quite unflattering) light. Even if captions are placed correctly, they can convey the wrong message. For example, a caption focusing on beer-drinking at an outdoor concert could give a false impression of the nondrinkers in the accompanying photograph.

False-light cases can also involve reporting, however. In Time Inc. v. Hill (385 U.S. 374, 1967), the Supreme Court considered a case concerning a *Life* magazine article. The James J. Hill family had been taken hostage in its home by escaped convicts in 1952. Their experience prompted Joseph Hayes to write a novel, which became a stage play and a movie. The fictionalized account differed from the actual event in several ways. The convicts were brutal in the fictional account, for example, but not to the Hills. A *Life* review of the play stated that the play reflected the Hills' experience. The Hills sued, claiming that the article portrayed them in a false light. The trial court awarded the family $30,000. The Supreme Court reversed that decision, however, after applying a standard of fault similar to that used in the New York Times v. Sullivan libel case [*see* chapter entitled Libel on page 411]. The court said that persons who were involved in a "matter of public interest" would have to show that the falsehood was publishing knowingly or with reckless disregard for the truth. The Hills were not able to meet that burden of proof.

The court upheld an invasion-of-privacy ruling against a newspaper in 1974 because, it said, the newspaper was guilty of "reckless untruth" and "calculated falsehoods." That case, Cantrell v. Forest City Publishing (419 U.S. 245, 1974), resulted from a follow-up story concerning the family members of a victim of a bridge collapse. A *Cleveland Plain Dealer* reporter visited the victim's home several months after his death. The widow was not at home, so they interviewed the children. The resulting story, which focused on the family's poverty, contained several inaccuracies, including statements indicating that the widow had been interviewed. The court upheld a $60,000 judgment against the newspaper, saying that it had published "knowing or reckless falsehoods."

4) Appropriation.

Unlike other types of privacy actions, this type does not usually involve people who shun publicity. It involves the unauthorized commercial use of a person's name, likeness or persona—considerations that often affect the famous. For this reason, it is sometimes referred to as infringement of the plaintiff's "right of publicity."

The media can publish news stories and photos without fear of infringing on anyone's right of publicity—no matter how famous the subject. Courts have ruled that this fulfills an information function that is protected under the First Amendment. What is not protected is unauthorized commercial use, such as in advertising or product endorsements.

Courts have ruled that a person has a right to the publicity value not only of his name and likeness, but also of other identifying aspects. In Carson v. Here's Johnny (698 F.2d 831, 1983), a federal court found in favor of Johnny Carson, although Carson had not been identified by name. Here's Johnny Portable Toilets Inc. had used the "Here's Johnny" phrase which is associated with the comedian, and had called their product "the world's foremost commodian." The court ruled that the phrase was identifiable enough because it was firmly linked to Carson in the minds of millions of television viewers.

Two primary defenses for invasion-of-privacy lawsuits have emerged:

1 Newsworthiness. The newsworthiness of a subject is of critical importance in lawsuits concerning disclosure of embarrassing private facts. It can also be important in false-light cases in determining whether a plaintiff can recover damages. (The Supreme Court has held that plaintiffs in cases involving a "matter of public interest" must show that the publication was made with knowledge that it was false or with reckless disregard for the truth.)
2 Consent. This is the key defense in misappropriation cases. To be a successful defense, however,

the consent must be in a form that is legally enforceable. That is, there must be proof of a valid contract (written proof is by far best) and the consent given must be broad enough to encompass the use. Consent given for one type of use does not confer the rights to all uses. Release forms used by commercial photographers, film makers and others should specify the contract terms (what both sides will gain and what they will do) and the permitted uses.

Privacy rights often are discussed in two contexts that are quite different from the ones usually encountered by writers. Those contexts include the Constitutional right to make private decisions, and the right to be free from governmental snooping.

One of the landmark cases involving the right to make private decisions was Roe v. Wade (410 U.S. 113, 1973), in which the Supreme Court ruled that in the early months of pregnancy abortion is a private matter between a woman and her physician, and that states cannot invade that private choice by prohibiting abortions. A similar rationale had been used in Griswold v. Connecticut (381 U.S. 479, 1965), when the court struck down a Connecticut law that banned the use of contraceptives, citing the private right of married couples to make such decisions for themselves.

The Privacy Act of 1974 (U.S. Code 1982 Title 5, §552q) recognizes a person's "right to be left alone" and prohibits the federal government from indiscriminate snooping. It gives citizens the right to inspect federal records maintained on them, to challenge errors and to prevent improper distribution. It forbids federal agencies to accumulate personal information that is not related to the agency's mission. Many states have enacted similar laws.

REFERENCES:

Major Principles of Media Law, Wayne Overbeck. New York: Harcourt Brace Jovanovich College Publishers, 1991.

Mass Communication Law, Cases and Comment, Donald M. Gillmor and Jerome A. Barron. New York: West Publishing Co., 5th edition, 1990.

The Writer's Legal Companion, Brad Bunnin. New York: Addison-Wesley Publishing Co., 1988.

QUICK GUIDE TO COPYRIGHT

A copyright is actually a group of rights pertaining to literary, musical, artistic and other intellectual works. The copyright owner has the exclusive rights to:

1 Reproduce the work in copies or recordings.
2 Prepare derivative works (such as arrangements, dramatizations or translations).
3 Distribute copies or recordings to the public.
4 Perform or display the work publicly.

The owner may retain all rights or may transfer all or some of them. Publishing contracts normally specify which rights are transferred. For example, an agreement that buys "first North American rights" purchases the right of first publication in North America. All other rights—including the rights to adapt as a stage play, to republish and to publish in other parts of the world—remain with the author.

The author is usually the owner of the copyright. If the work was created as a "work for hire," however, the author's employer may own the copyright. If a work is created as part of an employment arrangement, the work belongs to the employer. A common example of "work for hire" occurs in the newspaper industry. Newspapers, not staff reporters, own the copyright on news stories. Freelancers are presumed to be on their own, not creating "works for hire," unless a contract specifies otherwise. (The line between freelancer and employee can sometimes be difficult to draw, however.)

The Copyright Revision Act of 1976 (Title 17 of the United States Code) applies to all works created after the law went into effect on Jan. 1, 1978. Before that, a combination of laws applied, including the Copyright Act of 1909 and a variety of state laws based on common law (traditional legal practices derived from British law).

Under the 1976 law, a copyright begins when the work is created and extends for the life of the author and 50 years past his death. (In the case of co-authors, it extends 50 years past the life of the last surviving author.) When a work is published anonymously, with a pseudonym or as a work for hire, the copyright extends for 75 years from the date of publication or 100 years from its creation, whichever comes first.

For works copyrighted before Jan. 1, 1978, the duration rules are different. Under the 1909 law, works could be copyrighted for 28 years from the date of publication and could be renewed for 28 years. The new law created several formulas to adjust the duration of those copyrights that were already in effect.

Because of the number of variables involved, it is best to consult a lawyer concerning the status of material copyrighted under the old law.

A copyright is created when the work is created, that is, when it is in a fixed, tangible form. The work need not be published. The copyright exists regardless of whether a notice of copyright has been included on the work, and whether the work has been registered with the U.S. Copyright Office. There are good reasons for including a notice of copyright and for registering the work, however.

The notice of copyright serves to alert others of your property rights in the material. Although you have the rights regardless of whether you include the notice, you may not be able to collect damages if someone inadvertently misappropriates your work because there was no warning. Once you inform the person of your copyright, you can prevent future misuse.

A copyright notice requires only three elements:

1 The © symbol, the word "Copyright" or the abbreviation "Copr.";
2 The year that the work was first published (or created, if it has not yet been published);
3 The name of the owner.

It should be placed at a prominent place in the work, such as the first or last page.

Registration is a simple process that serves two important functions:

1 It serves as a public record.
2 It preserves your right to collect statutory damages and lawyers' fees in a lawsuit for copyright infringement.

Although registration is not a requirement for a copyright, it is required before a lawsuit can be filed for infringement. The filing can be made after the infringement occurs. In that case, however, the law restricts the liability of the person who misappropriated the material. The copyright owner may only collect actual damages and the infringer's profits from the misuse. The owner can also have the remaining copies impounded and can receive an injunction preventing the infringer from using and distributing the material in the future. If the copyright had been registered before the infringement, the copyright owner would also be able to seek reimbursement for reasonable lawyers' fees and statutory damages. Statutory damages can be important when the amount of actual damages is small or difficult to prove. The usual range of statutory damages is between $500 and $20,000, although they may be higher or lower in extraordinary circumstances.

To register a copyright, you must file a registration form, pay a $20 fee and submit one or two copies of the work for deposit in the Library of Congress. (Alternatives are available for work that is bulky, such as statues, or extremely costly, such as limited-edition volumes.) A free information packet and forms are available from the U.S. Copyright Office, Library of Congress, Washington, D.C. 20559, (202) 479-0700 (information).

The registration form used varies with the type of work:

Form TX	Published and unpublished nondramatic literary works
Form PA	Published and unpublished works in the performing arts
Form SR	Sound recordings
Form VA	Visual arts
Form RE	Copyright renewal under the old law
Form GR/CP	Registration of a group of contributions to periodicals; must be used with Form TX or PA.

Many forms of intellectual and artistic expression can be copyrighted, including magazine articles, poems, musical works, books, motion pictures, sound recordings, choreography and computer programs. There are some limitations, however.

1 A copyrighted work must be original. That does not mean that the work must break new ground, as a patented invention must. The work may resemble other similar works, as long as it is a new creation and does not misappropriate other copyrighted material. Collections, such as anthologies, may have their own copyright, representing the complete work, even though individual items retain their separate copyrights. (The creator of the anthology must, of course, obtain permission from the copyright owners to use the material.)
2 It must be in a fixed, tangible form. A spontaneous speech or performance may not be copyrighted (although the recording of such a speech or performance may be).
3 Works of the U.S. government cannot be copyrighted.
4 Names, short phrases, slogans and titles cannot be copyrighted (although they may be protected by trademark).
5 Works that are in the public domain cannot be copyrighted. When a copyright expires, the work enters the public domain. It may not then be copyrighted anew. Also, if the creator of the work

does not claim copyright privileges, the work enters the public domain and cannot be copyrighted by someone else.
6 Facts and ideas cannot be copyrighted. A copyright covers the form of expression, not the content. If this were not the case, the first news organization that reported that man had walked on the moon could have precluded all other news organizations from using that information.

Copyright law does not require permission for all uses of copyrighted material. Congress recognized that some uses are "fair use" because they are socially desirable and are not unfair to the copyright owner. They do not require permission.

Applying the "fair use" concept in individual cases can be difficult and is open to judicial interpretation. In general, however, courts consider four criteria when determining if a use was fair:

1 The purpose and character of the use. Nonprofit, educational uses are given more leeway than uses for economic gain.
2 The nature of the copyrighted work. The more socially important the work, the more leeway courts are likely to grant. For example, use of an important political thesis would probably be given more leeway than use of a work that was purely entertainment-oriented.
3 The amount of the work used in relation to the whole of the copyrighted work. Using small amounts of a large work is probably permissible. The problem is in defining "small." The more material is used, the greater the danger.
4 The effect of the use on the market for, or value of, the copyrighted work.

The proliferation of electronic copying apparatus for printed material, video tapes, movies, sound recordings, computer programs, and computerized information has made reproduction an important issue for copyright owners. The 1976 law and subsequent court interpretations have established some guidelines for when reproduction is permissible and when it is not, although the issue is still murky. In general, limited reproduction of a copyrighted work is permissible if it is for private, educational or journalistic use. For example, a library patron may photocopy pages from an encyclopedia for his own use. A teacher may photocopy and distribute to students a news story, an essay, a poem or a book passage. (The teacher may not, however, routinely use photocopies of copyrighted materials instead of requiring students or the school to purchase the material.) Consumers may videotape television programs so that they may view them at a more convenient time, but not for commercial use. A computer user may make, for his own use, a backup copy of software that he has purchased (but he may not distribute copies of the software).

This area of copyright law is evolving rapidly, especially in relation to computer databases, which have revolutionized how intellectual property is distributed and reproduced.

CONTACTS AND REFERENCES:

U.S. Copyright Office, Library of Congress, Washington, D.C. 20559, (202) 707-3000 (information).

Major Principles of Media Law, Wayne Overbeck. New York: Harcourt Brace Jovanovich College Publishers, 1991.

Patents, Copyrights and Trademarks, Frank H. Foster and Robert L. Shook. New York: John Wiley & Sons, 1989.

The Writer's Legal Companion, Brad Bunnin. New York: Addison-Wesley Publishing Co., 1988.

SOCIETY OF PROFESSIONAL JOURNALISTS CODE OF ETHICS

The Society of Professional Journalists, Sigma Delta Chi, believes the duty of journalists is to serve the truth.

We believe the agencies of mass communication are carriers of public discussion and information, acting on their Constitutional mandate and freedom to learn and report the facts.

We believe in public enlightenment as the forerunner of justice, and in our Constitutional role to seek the truth as part of the public's right to know the truth.

We believe those responsibilities carry obligations that require journalists to perform with intelligence, objectivity, accuracy, and fairness.

To these ends, we declare acceptance of the standards of practice here set forth:

I. RESPONSIBILITY:

The public's right to know of events of public importance and interest is the overriding mission of the mass media. The purpose of distributing news and enlightened opinion is to serve the general welfare. Journalists who use their professional status as representatives of the public for selfish or other unworthy motives violate a high trust.

II. FREEDOM OF THE PRESS:

Freedom of the press is to be guarded as an inalienable right of people in a free society. It carries with it the freedom and the responsibility to discuss, question, and challenge actions and utterances of our government and of our public and private institutions. Journalists uphold the right to speak unpopular opinions and the privilege to agree with the majority.

III. ETHICS:

Journalists must be free of obligation to any interest other than the public's right to know the truth.

1 Gifts, favors, free travel, special treatment or privileges can compromise the integrity of journalists and their employers. Nothing of value should be accepted.
2 Secondary employment, political involvement, holding public office, and service in community organizations should be avoided if it compromises the integrity of journalists and their employers. Journalists and their employers should conduct their personal lives in a manner that protects them from conflict of interest, real or apparent. Their responsibilities to the public are paramount. That is the nature of their profession.
3 So-called news communications from private sources should not be published or broadcast without substantiation of their claims to news values.
4 Journalists will seek news that serves the public interest, despite the obstacles. They will make constant efforts to assure that the public's business is conducted in public and that public records are open to public inspection.
5 Journalists acknowledge the newsman's ethic of protecting confidential sources of information.
6 Plagiarism is dishonest and unacceptable.

IV. ACCURACY AND OBJECTIVITY:

Good faith with the public is the foundation of all worthy journalism.

1 Truth is our ultimate goal.
2 Objectivity in reporting the news is another goal that serves as the mark of an experienced professional. It is a standard of performance toward which we strive. We honor those who achieve it.
3 There is no excuse for inaccuracies or lack of thoroughness.
4 Newspaper headlines should be fully warranted by the contents of the articles they accompany. Photographs and telecasts should give an accurate picture of an event and not highlight an incident out of context.
5 Sound practice makes clear distinction between news reports and expressions of opinion. News reports should be free of opinion or bias and represent all sides of an issue.
6 Partisanship in editorial comment that knowingly departs from the truth violates the spirit of American journalism.
7 Journalists recognize their responsibility for offering informed analysis, comment, and editorial opinion on public events and issues. They accept the obligation to present such material by individuals whose competence, experience, and judgment qualify them for it.

8 Special articles or presentations devoted to advocacy or the writer's own conclusions and interpretations should be labeled as such.

V. FAIR PLAY:

Journalists at all times will show respect for the dignity, privacy, rights, and well-being of people encountered in the course of gathering and presenting the news.

1 The news media should not communicate unofficial charges affecting reputation or moral character without giving the accused a chance to reply.
2 The news media must guard against invading a person's right to privacy.
3 The media should not pander to morbid curiosity about details of vice and crime.
4 It is the duty of news media to make prompt and complete correction of their errors.

5 Journalists should be accountable to the public for their reports and the public should be encouraged to voice its grievances against the media. Open dialogue with our readers, viewers, and listeners should be fostered.

VI. PLEDGE:

Adherence to this code is intended to preserve and strengthen the bond of mutual trust and respect between American journalists and the American people.

The Society shall—by programs of education and other means—encourage individual journalists to adhere to these tenets, and shall encourage journalistic publications and broadcasters to recognize their responsibility to frame codes of ethics in concert with their employees to serve as guidelines in furthering these goals.

Adopted 1926; revised 1973, 1984, 1987.

TRADEMARKS AND TRADE NAMES

HOW TO USE THEM

Trademarks may be any devices—from words, single letters and symbols, to brands, slogans, songs, sounds, or designs—that manufacturers or dealers use to distinguish their products from those of their competitors. Though many companies use their trade names as trademarks, the two terms are not synonymous. Trade names are the proper names by which products are commonly identified.

Companies have an interest in maintaining their trademarks as their own. If their trademarks slip into generic use, they have lost an important means of identification. For this reason, many companies closely monitor the use of such words. They run advertisements in trade publications, and aggressively monitor misuse of their trademarks. This defense of the trademark is an important part of maintaining control over it, should there ever be a court challenge.

Federal law protects even those trademarks that have not been formally registered with the U.S. Patent and Trademark Office. Generally, the manufacturer who first uses a trademark in commerce is protected. A key part of that protection is assurance that others may not use the trade name of a specific product generally.

A writer is not supposed to use the trade name Band-Aid, for example, as a general reference to plastic bandages, Sheetrock as a universal reference to wallboard, Xerox as a synonym for photocopy, Jeep for off-road or four-wheel-drive vehicle, Kleenex for facial tissue, Loafer for a moccasin-like shoe—although everyday speech often makes no such distinctions.

In time, many successful trade names have become part of the vernacular. The words zipper, nylon, linoleum and thermos are examples. They now are listed in lowercase form in dictionaries and may be used generically with impunity. That is because the manufacturers of those products relinquished or lost proprietary control.

The interests of trademark owners often conflict with those of writers, however, who may wish to use a common trade name—Loafer, for example—in a generic sense for the sake of readability.

The U.S. Trademark Association, a not-for-profit organization that has promoted the interests of trademark owners since 1878, cautions that trademarks are proper adjectives, not nouns, and as such should not be pluralized. "He ordered two Sankas," would be incorrect on two counts. "He ordered two Sanka decaffeinated coffees," would be preferable, according to the USTA, especially since the sentence also includes a generic description of the product. Similarly, trademarks should not be treated as verbs, according to the USTA. Uses such as, "They Simonized their van" or "He Xeroxed the page" would be incorrect.

The USTA also suggests that trademarks not be used in the possessive form unless the trademark itself is possessive; for example, Levi's jeans and McDonald's restaurants.

Writers also are exhorted not to drop the "s" from trademarks ending in "s" in order to turn the trademark into a singular form. "She took a cookie from a Baggie," would be incorrect. The USTA would prefer: "She took a cookie from a Baggies plastic bag." The association favors complete capitalization of all trademarks, so "She took a cookie from a BAGGIES plastic bag" would be even better. "Other alternatives for distinguishing trademarks," according to the USTA Media Guide, "include italic, boldface, or different-color type."

While few general-circulation publications agree to such deferential treatment, most do try to ensure fair treatment. The stylebooks and publication policies of many newspapers and magazines advise writers not to use trade names gratuitously, and to use them only when they are pertinent and appropriate to the story, or when there is no reasonable generic synonym. Many trade names fall into this latter category: Laundromat, Wiffle ball, Velcro and Frisbee are examples.

Further, the style of most publications dictates that only the first letter of a trade name be capitalized. Thus the trade name "AstroTurf," as it is registered with the U.S. Patent and Trademark Office, generally becomes "Astroturf." It follows that some trade names that also serve as trademarks usually lose some of their peculiar characteristics in general-circulation print; "Bac*Os," for example, generally becomes Bacos; "SpaghettiOs" becomes Spaghettios; "Chee·tos" becomes Cheetos.

SUGGESTED REFERENCES:

- *Brands and Their Companies 1990*; also, *Companies and Their Brands 1990*, edited by Donna Wood. Detroit: Gale Research Inc., 8th edition. To order, call (800) 877-4253. The two-volume *Brands and Their Companies 1990* is the single most complete reference on the subject. It alphabetically lists more than 210,000 trademarks and trade names and then cites the roughly 40,000 companies associated with them. The two-volume companion, *Companies and Their Brands 1990*, provides essentially the same information, but alphabetizes by name and address the more than 40,000 companies and then cites the trademarks and trade names of their products.

- DIALOG, 3450 Hill View Ave., Palo Alto, CA 94304, (800) 334-2564 for marketing. DIALOG's Trademark Research Center offers access to two databases containing information on all trademarks and trade names active in the United States. The "Trademarkscan Federal" database identifies the owners, and their registration numbers, of all textual and numeric U.S. trademarks and trade names; the database is updated every week. The "Trademarkscan State" database provides information on all noncorporate, textual-numeric trademarks and trade names used by the 50 states and Puerto Rico; the database is updated every two weeks.

SUGGESTED CONTACTS:

The U.S. Trademark Association, 6 East 45th St., New York, NY 10017, (212) 986-5880. The association routinely answers all inquiries concerning use and ownership of trademarks and trade names. For a nominal fee, the USTA will fill requests for its Media Guide and Trademark Checklist.

U.S. Patent and Trademark Office, Crystal Plaza 2, 2011 Jefferson Davis Highway, Arlington, VA 22202, (703) 557-4636. More than 680,000 trademarks are registered with the U.S. Patent and Trademark Office, which maintains a search library and records of all active registrations and pending applications. The library is open to the public Monday through Friday from 8 A.M. to 5:30 P.M.

50 BASIC REFERENCE WORKS

1 *American Medical Association Encyclopedia of Medicine*, Charles B. Clayman, M.D., ed.; Random House, 1989.

2 *An Encyclopedia of World History* (2 vols.), William L. Langer; Houghton Mifflin, 5th edition, 1973.

3 *Bartlett's Familiar Quotations*, John Bartlett; Little, Brown & Co., 16th edition, 1992.

4 *Benét's Reader's Encyclopedia: The Classic and Only Encyclopedia of World Literature in a Single Volume;* HarperCollins Inc., 3d edition, 1987.

5 *Black's Law Dictionary*, Henry Campbell Black et al.; West Publishing Co., 6th edition, 1991.

6 *Book of the States;* The Council of State Governments, published biennially.

7 *Books in Print;* R. R. Bowker, annual with serial updates.

8 *Chase's Annual Events;* Contemporary Books, published annually.

9 *Computer-Readable Databases*, Kathleen Young Marcaccio, ed.; Gale Research Inc., 6th edition, 1990.

10 *County and City Data Book;* U.S. Government Printing Office, revised periodically.

11 *Current Biography;* H. W. Wilson, published annually.

12 *The HarperCollins Dictionary of American Government and Politics*, Jay M. Shafritz; HarperCollins Publishers, 1992.

13 *Editorials On File;* Facts On File Inc., published annually.

14 *Encyclopaedia Britannica* (32 vols.); Encyclopaedia Britannica, Inc., 15th edition, 1987; annual updates.

15 *Encyclopedia of Associations* (3 vols.), Deborah M. Burek, ed.; Gale Research Inc., 25th edition, 1990.

16 *Facts On File;* Facts On File Inc., published biweekly, bound annually.

17 *Gale Directory of Publications and Broadcast Media*, Donald P. Boyden and John Krol, eds.; Gale Research Inc., 122d edition, with updates.

18 *Guinness Book of Records, 1992*, E. Donald McFarlan, ed.; Facts On File Inc., published annually.

19 *Harper Dictionary of Contemporary Usage*, William Morris and Mary Morris; HarperCollins Inc., 2d edition, 1985.

20 *Harper Dictionary of Foreign Terms*, HarperCollins Inc., 3d edition, 1987.

21 *Harper's English Grammar*, John Opdyke; HarperCollins Inc., 1983.

22 *Historical Statistics of the United States: Colonial Times to 1970;* U.S. Government Printing Office, 1975.

23 *Hotel & Motel Redbook;* American Hotel and Motel Association, annual.

24 *Keesing's Record of World Events*, Roger East, ed.; Longman Group UK Limited, published annually with serial updates.

25 *McGraw-Hill Encyclopedia of Science and Technology* (20 vols.); McGraw-Hill, 6th edition, 1987, updated annually.

26 *Moody's Industrial Manual;* Moody's Investors Service, published annually with updates.

27 *National Geographic Atlas of the World*, National Geographic Society Staff; 6th edition, 1990.

28 *The New Columbia Encyclopedia*, William H. Harris and Judith S. Levey, eds.; Columbia University Press, 4th edition, 1975.

29 *New York Public Library Book of Chronologies;* Prentice-Hall Press, 1990.

30 *Oxford Dictionary of Art*, Ian Chilbers and Harold Osborne, eds.; Oxford University Press, 1988.

31 *Oxford Dictionary of Music*, Michael Kennedy; Oxford University Press, 1985.

32 *Physician's Desk Reference*, Edward R. Barnhart; Medical Economics, published annually.

33 *Physician's Desk Reference for Nonprescription Drugs;* Van Nostrand Reinhold, published annually.

34 *Politics in America 1992*, Phil Duncan, ed.; Congressional Quarterly Inc., published annually.

35 *Rand McNally Road Atlas*, Rand McNally Staff; 1992.

36 *Standard and Poor's Register of Corporations, Directors and Executives* (3 vols.); Standard and Poor's, published annually.

37 *Statistical Abstract of the United States;* U.S. Government Printing Office, published annually.

38 *Statistical and Metropolitan Area Date Book;* U.S. Government Printing Office, published annually.

39 *The Careful Writer: A Modern Guide to English Usage*, Theodore M. Bernstein; Macmillan, 1977.

40 *The Encyclopedia of American Facts & Dates*, Gorton Carruth; HarperCollins Inc., 8th edition, 1987.

41 *The Information Please Sports Almanac,* Mike Mererole, ed.; Houghton Mifflin Co., published annually.

42 *The National Directory of Addresses and Telephone Numbers;* General Information Inc., 1990.

43 *The New Roget's Thesaurus in Dictionary Form;* Berkley Publications, 1991.

44 *The Sports Encyclopedia of North America* (50 vols.); Academic International, 1987.

45 *The World Factbook,* U.S. Central Intelligence Agency; U.S. Government Printing Office, published annually.

46 *United Nations Statistical Yearbook;* United Nations, published annually.

47 *Washington Information Directory;* Congressional Quarterly Inc., published annually.

48 *Webster's Ninth New Collegiate Dictionary;* Merriam-Webster, 9th edition, 1983.

49 *Who's Who, 1992* (2 vols.); St. Martin's Press.

50 *Writer's Market;* Writer's Digest Books, published annually.

UNINTENDED INSULTS

Writers should not be afraid to use plain, commonly accepted language in their work. They should not resort to anemic phrases, contrivances and euphemisms to describe the human condition, regardless of popular pressure to comply with the politically correct attitude of the day.

Sloppiness and imprecision often result in writing that is inadvertently offensive and, regardless of intent, an insult is an insult. Writers must remember to consider people as individuals first. Their sex, race, religion, nationality, or physical or mental attributes do not define them, and any reference to such characteristics may be wholly inappropriate and, depending on circumstances, offensive as well. For example, if a musician wins an award, there is no reason to describe him as epileptic or diabetic or paraplegic. If a pilot can no longer fly, however, a reference to her epilepsy or diabetes or paralysis may be essential.

Some potential insults are easy to spot: "The real estate agent, a former beauty queen, set a record for sales this year." Others, however, are more subtle: "The baby was born with a severe birth defect." The intent may be only to describe a pertinent medical condition. The effect, however, may be to label the infant defective, which parents are likely to find demeaning.

Writers also must take care not to insult people by minimizing their grief. When a plane crashes, it is callous to write that "only" one person died. Any death is tragic.

The best advice is: Be careful; be fair. If you are in doubt about the correctness, fairness or accuracy of a reference, ask the subject. If you are hesitant to ask the subject for fear of giving offense, don't use the word or words; when in doubt, as the saying goes, leave it out.

Here are a few words and phrases that predictably require caution:

abnormal: Should be used only when referring to variance from a mathematical norm. The word should not be used as a synonym for *unusual* or *rare*. For example, "He had an abnormal voice." [*See* normal]

alcoholic, alcoholism: Alcoholism is a disease, not a moral state. Therefore, do not say that a person is an admitted alcoholic or a self-confessed alcoholic. Say that he acknowledges that he has the disease. An alcoholic who no longer drinks is not a "reformed alcoholic," which carries a moral implication. Say that he is a "recovering alcoholic." The fact that a person is a recovering alcoholic is not always pertinent to a story. If it isn't, don't mention it.

Amazon: Offensive when used in any reference to women; taken to mean tall, buxom and predatory.

Asian, Asiatic, Asian-American: The words *Asian* and *Asiatic* are not synonymous with the term *Asian-American*. The first two refer literally to a person or thing from Asia. *Asian-American* is a general reference to someone or something more accurately described as Korean-American, Japanese-American, etc.

bi: An offensive slang reference to someone who is bisexual.

birth defect: The term may not be offensive when used to describe a class of medical conditions, but may be offensive when applied to a particular person. Children should never be described as defective. When writing about individuals, use "born with . . ."

black: *See* colored

blind: There are many degrees of visual impairment. Don't say "blind" unless you are referring to someone who is completely without sight; some people prefer the word *sightless*.

boy: Males over 18 years of age are men.

Canuck: An unacceptable and disparaging term for Canadians.

Chinaman: An offensive racial slur against a Chinese person or a Chinese-American.

cleaning lady, cleaning woman: Use "cleaner," "housekeeper."

coed: May be used as an adjective, as a shortened form of coeducational; for example: "The school became coed in 1978." However, *coed* should not be used as a noun to describe a female college student. Use *student*.

colored: Widely regarded as unacceptable in the United States, except in the title of the National Association for the Advancement of Colored People. "People of color," however, may be acceptable in many areas and in certain sociological contexts to refer to non-Caucasians. Context and local custom should determine use. The word "colored" may carry specific legal meaning in some countries, such as South Africa. In general, use *black* or *Negro* or *African-American*.

• In sentences that contain parallel constructions, make sure that equivalent forms are used. For example: "A white man and a black woman are being sought by police"; "A Caucasian man and a Negro woman are being sought by police." Not: "A white man and a Negro woman are being sought by police." And not: "A man and a Negro woman are being sought by police."

• As of this writing, the term *African-American* was gaining increased popularity and acceptance, but remained the focus of considerable debate. The careful writer will stay attuned to such changes in the vernacular, and use them when appropriate. When in doubt as to preference, ask.

• Race should be mentioned only when it is pertinent to the story—for example, when a person is receiving an award for racial awareness, or when a politician is courting a particular racial group, or when a criminal is being sought and a full description is in the public interest. Some writers assume that all nonwhites need to be identified by race, merely because they are not white. This assumption is demeaning in the extreme.

confined to a wheelchair: The phrase connotes a degree of immobility that some people may find inappropriate, given their ability to participate in the workplace and community. Say instead "uses a wheelchair."

cracker: An old reference to lawless people; now taken to mean a low-born, racist white Southerner. [*See* regional or geographic insults]

crippled: *Disabled* is preferable.

deaf: Do not assume that everyone with a significant hearing impairment is deaf. Use *hearing-impaired* unless you are certain that the individual is totally without hearing. [*See* deaf and dumb]

deaf and dumb: Do not assume that a person who cannot hear cannot speak. Many deaf or hearing-impaired people can speak. Also, a person who cannot speak is "mute," not dumb. A person who has difficulty speaking is "speech-impaired," or may have "a speech impediment."

diabetic: Use only if the physical condition is pertinent to the story. The types and severity of diabetes vary significantly. Do not assume disability.

dialect: Use sparingly and with caution, and only in direct quotations. Many people speak many forms of English in many ways. Because there is no standard accent, it is appropriate to draw attention to speech patterns only when they are a significant part of the story. Reproducing a person's dialect merely to show his or her ethnic background is offensive. Ethnic background frequently is not pertinent. If it is pertinent, make the connection clear.

divorcée: When marital status is pertinent to the story, care should be taken to use neutral terms. *Divorcée*, a term that applies only to women, has developed a derogatory connotation. Use *divorced* to indicate the marital status of either sex.

Down's syndrome: Down's syndrome is a physical condition, present at birth, resulting from a chromosomal abnormality. It can have many effects, including heart problems, digestive-tract problems and retardation. The degree of retardation varies widely. Do not assume the type or degree of disability. [*See* mongoloid]

dwarf: May be used in a medical context when referring to someone who is diagnosed as having dwarfism. In general, however, use "little person," which is the reference preferred by the national organization formed to protect their interests, Little People of America. [*See* midget]

epileptic: Use only if the physical condition is pertinent to the story. Epilepsy has several causes and forms. Some people experience the grand mal seizures that are commonly associated with the condition, but many do not. Under no condition is it appropriate to refer to an epileptic "fit."

ex-: Use caution when using the prefix *ex-*. The person's former status may not be germane to the present situation.

female: Beware of stereotyping. Identifying a person as a "female executive," a "female civil engineer" or a "lady lawyer" is inappropriate unless you would feel compelled to use the words *male* or *gentleman* in the same context. Male stereotyping should also be avoided. Examples include "male kindergarten teacher," "male nurse," "male secretary." Do not define people as oddities merely because of their gender. If a person's gender is germane to the story, make the importance clear.

former: *See* ex-

gender-specific suffixes: Most are now considered offensive and inappropriate; for example, actress, aviatrix, executrix or executress, comedienne, starlet, etc.

gentlemen's agreement: Use "informal" or "verbal agreement."

ghetto blaster: An offensive and stereotypical reference to a large portable stereo or "boom box."

girl: Females over 18 years of age are women.

golden-ager: Construed by some to be a condescending, euphemistic attempt to disguise a normal stage of human life. Some also object to "senior citizen" on the same grounds, although the use of that term has become widespread and widely accepted. Use "the old," "the aged," "the elderly" when referring to a group. When referring to an individual, it is better to use a specific age; someone who is 70 may not consider himself old. *Retired* is not a synonym for *old*.

greenhorn: Derogatory reference to a person who has recently immigrated to the United States.

Guido: This is an Italian male first name. When used as a common noun, it is an inappropriate and derisive reference to Italian-American men.

gyp: Derogatory in all uses; derived from *gypsy;* use *cheat* instead.

gypsy: Use *vagrant, wanderer, itinerant,* etc., to avoid its literal, ethnic meaning.

handicap/handicapped: Use *disability* or *disabled,* references generally preferred by national organizations representing disabled people. Do not use *disabled* as a noun, e.g., "He works with the disabled." Do not use "differently abled" or "physically challenged" to describe someone with a physical impairment or disability. Such terms are patronizing and condescending. Nor should a writer be too quick to refer to someone with a handicap as necessarily "heroic," "courageous," "inspiring," "special," or a "victim." And writers should not presume that disabled people necessarily "overcome" anything or succeed "in spite of" their disabilities. All such terms, when used automatically, reflect simplistic presumptions on the part of the writer.

he/she: Though a well-intentioned attempt to neutralize the sexist effect of male and female pronouns, "he/she" is an extremely awkward construction that detracts from clarity. Rewording the sentence to use plural pronouns may be more graceful. For example: "When a driver must renew his license, he must go to the Department of Motor Vehicles." Rephrased: "When drivers must renew their licenses, they must go to the Department of Motor Vehicles."

hick: An opprobrious reference to someone who lives in a rural area; generally taken to imply backwardness or lack of sophistication. [*See* regional or geographical insults]

hillbilly: Specifically, a disparaging reference to residents of mountainous regions of the southeastern United States; taken to indicate lack of sophistication and ignorance. [*See* regional or geographic insults]

Hispanic: Appropriate when used to describe civil-rights issues that pertain to persons with Hispanic surnames; inappropriate when used as an umbrella term to describe people of widely varying ethnic, geographic and cultural backgrounds; use more precise terms: Mexican-American, Caribbean, South American, Cuban-American, Spanish, etc.

holy roller: Offensive; use the proper name of the religious denomination, or "fundamentalist," "evangelist," etc., depending upon religious belief.

honky: Offensive; a disparaging reference to white people.

hot-blooded: Derogatory and stereotypical when used in reference to people of Latin American, South American or Mediterranean ancestry.

housewife: Offensive in many contexts because it equates women with household duties.

idiot: As a medical term, used to describe a person who requires constant custodial care and whose mental age does not exceed three years. Colloquially, its use is cruel. If it is being used in its medical sense, that use should be specified. For example: "After psychiatric testing, six of the patients were classified as idiots, requiring custodial care for the rest of their lives." [*See* retarded]

imbecile: As a medical term, used to describe a person who requires supervision to perform daily tasks and whose mental age is between three and seven years. Colloquially, its use is cruel. If it is being used in its medical sense, that use should be specified. For example: "Hospital personnel knew that as an imbecile she would need help accomplishing the most basic of tasks." [*See* retarded]

Indian: Properly used to describe someone from the Asian country of India. The term was applied inappropriately to Native Americans by Columbus, who thought he had landed in Asia. There is no reason to perpetuate a 500-year-old error. Use "Native American" or "American Indian," depending on regional preference. Many American Indians prefer to be identified with their particular tribe, rather than with a broad, disparate group. For example, Choctaw, Algonquin, Apache, Navajo, etc. Using the word *Indian* after a tribal name is redundant.

Indian file: Use "single file."

Indian giver: Offensive in all uses.

inner city: This term stereotypically implies ethnicity, poverty, crime and squalid living conditions. [*See* regional or geographical insults]

Jap: An offensive reference to a person of Japanese descent.

JAP: An acronym for Jewish American Princess. The term is stereotypical and offensive.

Jew: Use of the word, in singular or plural forms, by itself may be taken as offensive; "Jewish person" or "Jewish people" often is preferred. The word is never to be used as a verb.

lady: An attempt to put a soft edge on what is most often a gratuitous reference to gender. Worse, in most references the word is condescending and patronizing. [*See* female]

Latin lover: An offensive ethnic stereotype.

live-in boyfriend, girlfriend: Salacious, judgmental and almost always inappropriate. If all you mean is that two particular people live together, then say so. If you need to know their exact relationship, ask. If you don't ask, you've no right to presume the sexual relationship that clearly is implied by the use of such terms.

maiden name: Use "birth name" or "given name."

mad: Use "angry," if that is your meaning; use "mentally ill," if that is your meaning.

male: Men are as entitled as women to language that

is free of gratuitous reference and stereotyping. Examples include "male kindergarten teacher," "male nurse," "male secretary." If a person's gender is germane to a story, make the importance clear. [*See* female]

man and wife: Men and women should be treated with equal deference. Appropriate parallel constructions are "man and woman" or "husband and wife."

middle-aged: May be useful when referring to groups. When referring to an individual, however, a precise age is better. A 38-year-old man may or may not consider himself middle-aged.

midget: Use "little person." [*See* dwarf]

Miss: Most publications have their own styles regarding use of titles. In general, however, when titles are used people should be allowed to use the title of their choice, as long as the title is accurate. [*See* Mrs., Ms]

mongoloid: People born with Down's syndrome sometimes have facial characteristics that, in the past, caused them to be referred to as "mongoloid." This is not appropriate, and it is derogatory to Mongols as well. The proper reference uses the words "Down's syndrome," the choice of national organizations formed for the benefit of such people. [*See* Down's syndrome]

Mr.: *See* Mrs.

Mrs.: Most publications have their own styles for referring to men and women. In general, however, equal treatment is desirable. Women should be called *Miss, Ms,* or *Mrs.* only in cases in which men are called *Mr.* Regardless of the publication's policy, however, care should be taken not to refer to a woman by only her husband's name, for example, "Mr. and Mrs. John Smith." Women, like men, have first names. Use John and Mary Smith on first reference, and Mr. and Mrs. Smith on second, if your publication uses such titles.

Ms: Most publications have their own rules regarding use of *Ms.* In general, however, when titles are used people should be allowed to use the title of their choice, as long as the title is accurate. [*See* Mrs.]

mute: Do not assume that someone who is deaf or hearing-impaired cannot speak.

nigger: Offensive. Sometimes used colloquially, in a nonoffensive context, among blacks. In almost all cases, use of the term is inflammatory and should be avoided. If using in a direct quotation, make sure that the context is clear.

normal: Best used in mathematical contexts only. When used to describe human conditions or behaviors, it is often demeaning. The writer should not presume to know what is "normal" for all human beings in all circumstances. Do not use as a synonym for *frequent, common, usual, accepted* or *proper.* [*See* abnormal]

Okie: Originally, in the 1930s this term referred to poor migrant families from the Dust Bowl states, specifically Oklahoma, but it came to be taken as a reference to poor rural people. [*See* regional or geographical insults]

people of color: *See* colored

PR: Offensive acronym reference to Puerto Rican.

pro-abortion: The semantics of the abortion debate have strong emotional and political content. Care must be taken not to use terms that convey unintended bias. People may favor legal access to abortion, while viewing the necessity of abortion as extremely unpalatable. For this reason, many prefer to be referred to as "pro-choice." They prefer to be associated with a positive concept (choice) rather than a negative one (abortion). In a similar sense, people who are opposed to legal access to abortion may prefer to be associated with a positive stance (pro-life) rather than a negative one (anti-abortion). As a result, opposing sides of the debate both prefer to refer to themselves in positive terms—pro-choice vs. pro-life. This is in contradiction to the pro- and anti- labels that apply to most opponents. Regardless of which term you use, be aware that both have political and public relations ramifications: Anyone opposed to "pro-choice" is, by implication, against freedom of choice. Similarly, anyone who disagrees with a "pro-life" stance can be considered "anti-life."

pro-choice: *See* pro-abortion

provincial: Offensive when used to imply a lack of sophistication. [*See* regional or geographical insults]

queen: Offensive when used to describe a homosexual. May be used colloquially among homosexuals. When using in a direct quotation, make sure that the context is clear.

queer: Offensive when used as a noun synonymous with homosexuals, unless the term is used colloquially among homosexuals.

reb: Short for *rebel,* an insulting reference to people who live in the American South; hark back to the Civil War. [*See* regional or geographical insults]

regional or geographical insults: Depending on context, virtually any reference that implies character traits supposedly distinctive within specific geographical boundaries may be construed as insulting or pejorative. Such terms are most offensive when used as disparaging or simplistic descriptions by someone not a member of the same group. Two New England residents, for example, may inoffensively refer to each other as Yankees, but the same appellation applied to either person by someone from the South may cause hard feelings.

retarded: There are many types and degrees of retardation, and people who have this condition vary as widely as people who do not. The term should not be used as an all-encompassing label.

Scotch: Should not be used as a synonym for *frugal*.

senior citizen: *See* golden-ager

spastic/spaz: *Spaz* is always derogatory. *Spastic* should never be used casually, as a synonym for *clumsy*. Its medical meaning refers to a state of spasm, or to a type of paralysis that can accompany several physical conditions, including cerebral palsy. "Spastic" is not a synonym for "person with cerebral palsy."

WASP: Offensive and stereotypical; an acronym for White Anglo-Saxon Protestant.

wheelchair-bound: *See* confined to a wheelchair

working mother: This assumes that women who do not work outside the home do not work. It also assumes that mothers who hold paying jobs are inherently different from fathers who hold paying jobs. Use "woman who works outside the home" if the reference is pertinent.

Yankee: A glib reference to Northerners, specifically residents of New England. [*See* regional or geographical insults]

U.S. LABOR UNIONS WITH 25,000 OR MORE MEMBERS

AFL-CIO
(American Federation of Labor–Congress of Industrial Organizations)
815 16th St. NW
Washington, D.C. 20006
(202) 637-5000
President: Lane Kirkland

The AFL-CIO is a voluntary organization of U.S. labor unions that represents the interests of its members before Congress and the government.

Actors' Equity Association (AFL-CIO)
165 W. 46th St.
New York, NY 10036
(212) 869-8530
President: Ron Silver
Membership: 40,000

Amalgamated Clothing and Textile Workers Union (AFL-CIO)
815 16th St. NW
Washington, D.C. 20006
(202) 628-0214
President: Jack Sheinkman
Headquarters: 15 Union Square
New York, NY 10003
(212) 242-0700
Membership: 272,000

Amalgamated Transit Union (AFL-CIO)
5025 Wisconsin Ave. NW
Washington, D.C. 20016
(202) 537-1645
President: James La Sala
Membership: 160,000

American Association of Classified School Employees
1050 17th St. NW
Washington, D.C. 20036
(202) 429-9725
President: Dorothy Burke
Membership: 150,000

American Association of University Professors
1012 14th St. NW
Washington, D.C. 20005
(202) 737-5900
President: Barbara Bergman
Membership: 43,000

American Federation of Government Employees (AFL-CIO)
80 F St. NW
Washington, D.C. 20001
(202) 737-8700
President: John Sturdivant
Membership: 215,000

American Federation of Grain Millers (AFL-CIO)
4949 Olson Memorial Highway
Minneapolis, MN 55422
(612) 545-0211
President: Robert W. Willis
Membership: 28,500

American Federation of Musicians of the United States and Canada (AFL-CIO)
1501 Broadway
New York, NY 10036
(212) 869-1330
President: J. Martin Emerson
Membership: 207,000

American Federation of State, County and Municipal Employees (AFL-CIO)
1625 L St. NW
Washington, D.C. 20036
(202) 429-1100
President: Gerald W. McEntee
Membership: 1,200,000

American Federation of Teachers (AFL-CIO)
555 New Jersey Ave. NW
Washington, D.C. 20001
(202) 879-4415
President: Albert Shanker
Membership: 770,000

American Federation of Television and Radio Artists (AFL-CIO)
5480 Wisconsin Ave.
Chevy Chase, MD 20815
(301) 657-2560
President: John Hall
Headquarters: 260 Madison Ave.
New York, NY 10016
(212) 532-0800
Membership: 67,000

American Nurses' Association
1101 14th St. NW
Washington, D.C. 20005
(202) 554-4444
President: Lucille A. Joel
Headquarters: 2420 Pershing Road
Kansas City, MO 64108
(202) 554-4444
Membership: 196,000

American Postal Workers Union (AFL-CIO)
1300 L St. NW
Washington, D.C. 20005
(202) 842-4200
President: Moe Biller
Membership: 365,000

**Associated Actors and Artists
of America** (AFL-CIO)
165 W. 46th St.
New York, NY 10036
(212) 869-0358
President: Theodore Bikel
Membership: 95,000

Association of Flight Attendants (AFL-CIO)
1625 Massachusetts Ave. NW
Washington, D.C. 20036
(202) 328-5400
President: Susan Bianchi-Sand
Membership: 26,000

Bakery, Confectionery, and Tobacco Workers' International Union (AFL-CIO)
10401 Connecticut Ave.
Kensington, MD 20895
(301) 933-8600
President: John DeConcini
Membership: 135,000

Brotherhood of Locomotive Engineers
(AFL-CIO)
400 N. Capitol St. NW
Washington, D.C. 20001
(202) 347-7936
President: Larry D. McFather
Headquarters: 1370 Ontario St.
Cleveland, OH 44113
(216) 241-2630
Membership: 55,722

**Brotherhood of Maintenance
of Way Employees** (AFL-CIO)
400 N. Capitol St. NW
Washington, D.C. 20001
(202) 638-2135
President: Mac Fleming
Headquarters: 12050 Woodward Ave.
Detroit, MI 48203
(313) 948-1010
Membership: 65,000

California School Employees Association
2045 Lundy Ave.
(Mailing address: P.O. Box 640)
San Jose, CA 95131
(408) 263-8000
President: Bill Ellis
Membership: 83,750

Communications Workers of America
(AFL-CIO)
1925 K St. NW
Washington, D.C. 20006
(202) 434-1100
President: Morton Bahr
Membership: 700,000

**Federation of Nurses
and Health Professionals** (AFL-CIO)
555 New Jersey Ave. NW
Washington, D.C. 20001
(202) 879-4491
President: Albert Shanker
Membership: 30,000

Fraternal Order of Police
520 S. High St.
Columbus, OH 43215
(614) 221-0180
President: Dewey R. Stokes
Membership: 203,000

Graphic Communications International Union
(AFL-CIO)
1900 L St. NW
Washington, D.C. 20036
(202) 462-1400
President: James J. Norton
Membership: 143,747

**Glass, Molders, Pottery, Plastics
and Allied Workers International Union**
(AFL-CIO)
608 E. Baltimore Pike
(Mailing address: P.O. Box 607)
Media, PA 19063
(215) 565-5051
President: James E. Hatfield
Membership: 88,000

**Hotel Employees and Restaurant
Employees International Union** (AFL-CIO)
1219 28th St. NW
Washington, D.C. 20007
(202) 393-4373
President: Edward T. Hanley
Membership: 293,000

International Air Line Pilots Assn. (AFL-CIO)
1625 Massachusetts Ave. NW
Washington, D.C. 20036
(703) 689-2270
President: Randolph Babbitt
Membership: 42,000

International Alliance of Theatrical Stage Employees and Moving Picture Machine Operators of the United States and Canada (AFL-CIO)
1515 Broadway
New York, NY 10036
(212) 730-1770
President: Alfred W. DiTolla
Membership: 60,000

International Assn. of Bridge, Structural and Ornamental Iron Workers (AFL-CIO)
1750 New York Ave. NW
Washington, D.C. 20006
(202) 383-4800
President: Jake West
Membership: 143,000

International Association of Fire Fighters (AFL-CIO)
1750 New York Ave. NW
Washington, D.C. 20006
(202) 737-8484
President: Alfred K. Whitehead
Membership: 142,000

International Association of Machinists and Aerospace Workers (AFL-CIO)
1300 Connecticut Ave. NW
Washington, D.C. 20036
(202) 857-5200
President: George J. Kourpias
Membership: 750,000

International Brotherhood of Boilermakers, Iron Ship Builders, Blacksmiths, Forgers and Helpers (AFL-CIO)
2722 Merrilee Dr.
Fairfax, VA 22031
(703) 560-1493
President: Charles W. Jones
Headquarters: 753 State Ave.
Kansas City, KS 66101
(913) 371-2640
Membership: 98,000

International Brotherhood of Electrical Workers (AFL-CIO)
1125 15th St. NW
Washington, D.C. 20005
(202) 833-7000
President: John J. Barry
Membership: 790,000

International Brotherhood of Painters and Allied Trades of the United States and Canada (AFL-CIO)
1750 New York Ave. NW
Washington, D.C. 20006
(202) 637-0700
President: William A. Duval
Membership: 157,500

International Brotherhood of Teamsters, Chauffeurs, Warehousemen and Helpers of America (AFL-CIO)
25 Louisiana Ave. NW
Washington, D.C. 20001
(202) 624-6800
President: Ron Carey
Membership: 1,600,000

International Chemical Workers Union (AFL-CIO)
1126 16th St. NW
Washington, D.C. 20036
(202) 659-3747
President: Frank D. Martino
Headquarters: 1655 W. Market St.
Akron, OH 44313
(216) 867-2444
Membership: 50,000

International Federation of Professional and Technical Engineers (AFL-CIO)
8701 Georgia Ave.
Silver Spring, MD 20910
(301) 565-9016
President: James E. Sommerhauser
Membership: 25,000

International Ladies Garment Workers' Union (AFL-CIO)
815 16th St. NW
Washington, D.C. 20006
(202) 347-7417
President: Jay Mazur
Headquarters: 1710 Broadway
New York, NY 10019
(212) 265-7000
Membership: 175,000

International Longshoremen's and Warehousemen's Union (AFL-CIO)
1133 15th St. NW
Washington, D.C. 20005
(202) 463-6265
President: James R. Herman
Headquarters: 1188 Franklin St.
San Francisco, CA 94109
(415) 775-0533
Membership: 50,000

International Longshoremen's Assn.
(AFL-CIO)
815 16th St. NW
Washington, D.C. 20006
(202) 628-4546
President: John Bowers
Headquarters: 17 Battery Pl.
New York, NY 10004
(212) 425-1200
Membership: 110,000

International Union, Allied Industrial Workers of America (AFL-CIO)
3520 Oklahoma Ave.
Milwaukee, WI 53215
(414) 645-9500
President: Dominick D'Ambrosio
Membership: 65,000

International Union, Aluminum, Brick and Glass Workers (AFL-CIO)
3362 Hollenberg Dr.
Bridgeton, MO 63044
(314) 739-6142
President: Ernie J. LaBaff
Membership: 46,000

International Union of Bricklayers and Allied Craftsmen (AFL-CIO)
815 15th St. NW
Washington, D.C. 20005
(202) 783-3788
President: John T. Joyce
Membership: 106,000

International Union Electronic, Electrical, Salaried, Machine and Furniture Workers (AFL-CIO)
1126 16th St. NW
Washington, D.C. 20036
(202) 296-1200
President: William H. Bywater
Membership: 180,000

International Union of Operating Engineers (AFL-CIO)
1125 17th St. NW
Washington, D.C. 20036
(202) 429-9100
President: Frank Hanley
Membership: 329,000

International Union, United Automobile, Aerospace and Agricultural Implement Workers of America (UAW) (AFL-CIO)
1757 N St. NW
Washington, D.C. 20036
(202) 828-8500
President: Owen F. Bieber

Headquarters: 8000 E. Jefferson Ave.
Detroit, MI 48214
(313) 926-5000
Membership: 922,000

International Union, United Plant Guard Workers of America
25510 Kelly Rd.
Roseville, MI 48066
(313) 772-7250
President: Henry E. Applen
Membership: 28,000

International Woodworkers of America
(AFL-CIO)
25 Cornell Ave.
Gladstone, OR 97027
(503) 656-1475
President: Wilson J. Hubbell
Membership: 27,000

Laborers' International Union of North America (AFL-CIO)
905 16th St. NW
Washington, D.C. 20006
(202) 737-8320
President: Angelo Fosco
Membership: 500,000

Maryland Classified Employees Association
7127 Rutherford Rd.
Baltimore, MD 21207
(301) 298-8800
President: Joel Dan Lehman
Membership: 28,000

National Assn. of Letter Carriers (AFL-CIO)
100 Indiana Ave. NW
Washington, D.C. 20001
(202) 393-4695
President: Vincent R. Sombrotto
Membership: 314,214

National Education Association
1201 16th St. NW
Washington, D.C. 20036
(202) 833-4000
President: Keith Geiger
Membership: 2,000,000

National Federation of Federal Employees (AFL-CIO)
1016 16th St. NW
Washington, D.C. 20036
(202) 862-4400
President: Sheila Velazco
Membership: 45,000

**National Marine Engineers'
Beneficial Association** (AFL-CIO)
444 N. Capitol St. NW
Washington, D.C. 20001
(202) 347-8585
President: C. E. DeFries
Membership: 40,000

National Rural Letter Carriers' Assn.
(AFL-CIO)
1448 Duke St.
Alexandria, VA 22314
(703) 684-5545
President: Vernon H. Meier
Membership: 77,288

National Treasury Employees Union
1730 K St. NW
Washington, D.C. 20006
(202) 783-4444
President: Robert M. Tobias
Membership: 75,900

The Newspaper Guild (AFL-CIO)
8611 2nd Ave.
Silver Spring, MD 20910
(301) 585-2990
President: Charles Dale
Membership: 34,000

**Office and Professional Employees
International Union** (AFL-CIO)
815 16th St. NW
Washington, D.C. 20006
(202) 393-4464
President: John Kelly
Headquarters: 265 W. 14th St.
New York, NY 10011
(212) 675-3210
Membership: 135,000

**Oil, Chemical and Atomic Workers
International Union** (AFL-CIO)
1126 16th St. NW
Washington, D.C. 20036
(703) 876-9300
President: Joseph M. Misbrener
Headquarters: 255 Union Blvd.
Lakewood, CO
(Mailing address: P.O. Box 2812
Denver, CO 80201)
(303) 987-2229
Membership: 110,000

**Operative Plasterers' and Cement Masons'
International Association
of the United States
and Canada** (AFL-CIO)
1125 17th St. NW
Washington, D.C. 20036
(202) 393-6569
President: Robert J. Holton
Membership: 50,000

**Retail Wholesale and Department
Store Union** (AFL-CIO)
30 E. 29th St.
New York, NY 10016
(212) 684-5300
President: Lenore Miller
Membership: 200,000

Screen Actors Guild (AFL-CIO)
5480 Wisconsin Ave.
Chevy Chase, MD 20815
(301) 657-2560
President: John McGuire
Headquarters: 7065 Hollywood Blvd.
Hollywood, CA 90028
(213) 465-4600
Membership: 73,000

**Seafarers International Union
of North America** (AFL-CIO)
5201 Auth Way
Camp Springs, MD 20746
(301) 899-0675
President: Michael Sacco
Membership: 80,000

Service Employees International Union
(AFL-CIO)
1313 L St. NW
Washington, D.C. 20005
(202) 898-3200
President: John J. Sweeney
Membership: 925,000

**Sheet Metal Workers'
International Association** (AFL-CIO)
1750 New York Ave. NW
Washington, D.C. 20006
(202) 783-5880
President: Edward J. Carlough
Membership: 150,000

State Employees Assn. of North Carolina
P.O. Drawer 27727
Raleigh, NC 27611
(919) 833-6436
Executive Director: Dr. Robert A. Berlam
Membership: 53,000

Transportation Communications International Union (AFL-CIO)
815 16th St. NW
Washington, D.C. 20006
(202) 783-3660
President: Richard I. Kilroy
Headquarters: 3 Research Place
Rockville, MD 20850
(301) 948-4910
Membership: 110,000

Transport Workers Union of America
(AFL-CIO)
80 West End Ave.
New York, NY 10023
(212) 873-6000
President: John E. Lawe
Membership: 85,000

UAW: *See* International Union, United Automobile, Aerospace and Agricultural Implement Workers of America

United Assn. of Journeymen and Apprentices of the Plumbing and Pipe Fitting Industry of the United States and Canada
(AFL-CIO)
901 Massachusetts Ave. NW
Washington, D.C. 20001
(202) 628-5823
President: Marvin J. Boede
Membership: 330,000

United Brotherhood of Carpenters and Joiners of America (AFL-CIO)
101 Constitution Ave. NW
Washington, D.C. 20001
(202) 546-6206
President: Sigurd Lucassen
Membership: 600,000

United Electrical, Radio and Machine Workers of America
1800 Diagonal Rd.
Alexandria, VA 22314
(703) 684-3123
President: John H. Hovis, Jr.
Headquarters: 535 Smithfield St.
Pittsburgh, PA 15222
(412) 471-8919
Membership: 80,000

United Farm Workers of America
P.O. Box 62-LaPaz
Keene, CA 93570
(805) 822-5571
President: Cesar E. Chavez
Membership: 30,000

United Food and Commercial Workers International Union (AFL-CIO)
1775 K St. NW
Washington, D.C. 20006
(202) 223-3111
President: William H. Wynn
Membership: 1,250,000

United Garment Workers of America
(AFL-CIO)
4207 Lebanon Rd.
Hermitage, TN 37076
(615) 889-9221
President: Earl W. Carroll
Membership: 25,000

United Mine Workers of America (AFL-CIO)
900 15th St. NW
Washington, D.C. 20005
(202) 842-7200
President: Richard L. Trumka
Membership: 150,000

United Paperworkers International Union
(AFL-CIO)
Headquarters: 3340 Perimeter Hill Drive
Mailing address: P.O. Box 1475
Nashville, TN 37202
(615) 834-8590
President: Wayne E. Glenn
Membership: 220,000

United Rubber, Cork, Linoleum and Plastic Workers of America (AFL-CIO)
87 S. High St.
Akron, OH 44308
(216) 376-6181
President: Milan Stone
Membership: 100,000

United Steelworkers of America (AFL-CIO)
815 16th St. NW
Washington, D.C. 20006
(202) 638-6929
Headquarters: 5 Gateway Center
Pittsburgh, PA 15222
(412) 562-2400
Membership: Lynn R. Williams

United Transportation Union (AFL-CIO)
227 Massachusetts Ave. NE
Washington, D.C. 20002
(202) 347-0900
President: Fred A. Hardin
Headquarters: 14600 Detroit Ave.
Cleveland, OH 44107
(216) 228-9400
Membership: 95,000

United Union of Roofers, Waterproofers and Allied Workers (AFL-CIO)
1125 17th St. NW
Washington, D.C. 20036
(202) 638-3228
President: Earl J. Kruse
Membership: 25,573

United Workers Union of America (AFL-CIO)
815 16th St. NW
Washington, D.C. 20006
(202) 347-8105
President: James Joy, Jr.
Membership: 58,000

WRITING AND GRAMMAR TIPS FOR JOURNALISTS

Red Smith, a Pulitzer Prize winner and a dazzling writer, described journalism this way: "The essential thing is to report the facts; if there is time for good writing as well, that's the frosting on the cake." Journalistic writing is functional. Each story must have a point that is expressed clearly in terms the reader can understand; it must answer any questions it raises.

Write simple short sentences. When short sentences are witty, they sparkle. When angry, they snap. Even dull ones are clear. Simple sentences are important. They command attention:

"I shall return." (Gen. Douglas MacArthur)

"Let them eat cake." (attributed to Marie Antoinette)

"Veni, vidi, vici." (Julius Caesar)

"Ich bin ein Berliner." (John F. Kennedy)

Long, wordy sentences utilizing technological, bureaucratic or socioeconomic vocabularies are often the province of writers who are enamored of their ability, be it inherited or innate, to relate complex thoughts in equally complex terms, relying upon multisyllabic words and a multitude of clauses to impress rather than illuminate.

What follows are some useful guidelines for good journalism and a run through some common grammatical pitfalls.

You can't write what you didn't notice.
Good journalism is not merely something that happens at a typewriter or computer terminal. Reporting always comes first. That means getting the facts and remembering that they come in many forms.

What people do or say is a fact—and so is the way they sit and move, the way they speak and eat. The color of their rooms, the temperature of their offices, the odor of their jail cells are facts, too; if they aren't in your notes, they probably won't be in your story. So begin by learning to take accurate and careful notes.

Find the people.
Stories of human emotion and drama often are easy to write. But much of what a journalist must write lies elsewhere. By the time most reporters have covered their third budget hearing they have used up all of their natural exuberance for the topic.

Charter revision stories, sewer commission articles and the school beat are not dazzling by nature, but good journalists don't save good writing for good stories. It is often the boring, but important, stories that most need to be written well.

The best way to do that is to find the people. The news in a story is always about people, no matter the topic. Sometimes it takes some searching to find them.

If a story begins: "The Sewer Commission voted last night to delay action on a proposal that would have extended sewer lines to the northwest corner of town," you have told your readers what happened. If, instead, you write: "Homeowners in the northwest corner of town will have to wait at least another year for sewer lines," you have said what the story means to people.

If, the next day, you go to the northwest corner of town and see that some backyards have bubbling ponds of sewage, and you speak with someone who tells you that guests at a garden wedding couldn't smell the roses because the wind shifted, then you have found the people again.

In covering education, look to schoolchildren and teachers to explain the impact of any action. In state finance, consider taxpayers, or state workers, or people receiving state services, or all three. When the topic is business, find the meaning to employees or entrepreneurs, managers or consumers. If the story is about international trade, report what it means to business owners, workers, travelers, diplomats, politicians. When there is a breakthrough in theoretical physics, talk to researchers, teachers and scholars.

No matter what the issue, look for the people.

SAAAWP: Shun Acronyms And Abbreviations When Possible.
Some abbreviations defy comprehension, and some acronyms are merely cute; too many simply get in the reader's way.

Your publication's stylebook must be your guide, but ideally the use of acronyms and abbreviations would be limited to those so commonly known that they can stand alone: SALT for Strategic Arms Limitation Talks; MADD for Mothers Against Drunk Driving; FBI for Federal Bureau of Investigation; CIA for Central Intelligence Agency; NAACP, for National Association for the Advancement of Colored People; etc. But rare is the reporter who hasn't had to write a story involving some organization with a precious and contrived title.

The names of local groups such as CLOUDY, Community Leaders Opposing Unlawful Drugs for Youth, for example, demand clear, first-reference definition. Thereafter, a generic reference—"group," "organization," or "association"—usually is preferable to the acronym.

To write, read.

It is no accident that most good writers also are voracious readers of newspapers, magazines and books. They are always eager for a new fact, a new idea, for bits of detail or explanations that shed light on life's complexities and offer insight into the human condition.

Writers also read for knowledge of their craft. There is much to be learned from the work of others, from examining and reexamining structure, use of detail, development, effective dialog, the movement of a narrative.

Writers should also read to gain a sense of what their peers are doing.

Get out of the way of your story.

Few things are more distracting and annoying to a reader than a writer's gratuitous intrusion into the story. Use of the first person is sometimes justifiable, necessary and even desirable—for example, in columns, essays and reportage in which the reporter has unavoidably become a legitimate part of the news. Most first-person reporting outside of those forms is misguided and superficial. At worst, it is a hallmark of laziness, for it usually takes the place of legitimate research, interviewing and reporting. At best, it is a presumptuous and egotistical attempt to "personalize" the story: The writer is supposed to be every reader's good friend. Either way, first-person reportage usually presumes that reporters are more important than the information they have to deliver, and as interesting as the stories they have to tell.

Listen to what you're writing.

Good writing is meant to be read, and that means it also is meant to be heard. Even when writers read their work to themselves they must listen to what is being said and how. Good writers invariably have a finely tuned inner ear. They have a sense of the sounds that words make when they are properly arranged and ring true to purpose. To the extent that circumstances allow, determined writers will write and rewrite and rewrite until every sentence, paragraph and page sounds right.

He said, she said.

Novices often announce their inexperience by trying too hard to vary forms of attribution. They suspect they lack creativity if they have to use "said" more than once in a story. As a result, their stories are fraught with contrivances ranging from the simple ("he added," "he continued," "he explained") to the ungainly ("she stated," "she opined," "she asserted") to the superfluous ("he averred," "he chortled").

There is nothing wrong with using "he said" or "she said" repeatedly. Readers expect it. They take in the attribution without fastening on it or stumbling over it. The reader remains free to focus on the information in the sentence.

Don't be cute.

Written dialect or regional or ethnic speech patterns demand extraordinary care; even when used successfully and accurately, they may seem self-consciously folksy, condescending or mocking. Such attempts at verisimilitude are often simply impractical: If the reader must pause or reread a paragraph to decipher what is being said, then the writer has failed.

Be ruthless.

Readers are unforgiving, and so must writers be with their own work. Write as though someone out there, despite your hours of legwork, interviewing, research, writing and rewriting, is eager for an excuse to say, "So what?"

When you finish a piece, ask yourself if it is as good as you can make it under the circumstances, and be honest.

Have you finished the reporting?

Have you explained the facts clearly and presented them in a logical, organized manner?

Have you anticipated the reader's questions and answered them?

Is attribution clear?

Have you chosen the best way to tell the story?

Have you told the story accurately, fairly and well?

Have you made your point as effectively as possible?

Have you treated people in your story fairly?

Does everything in the story have a purpose, or have you used certain words and phrases simply because you like the sound of them?

Would you be proud to have your name on this story?

Take care of your tools.

Good grammar, correct punctuation, proper sentence structure, accurate spelling, an understanding of common word usage and the principles of composition are among the writer's most valuable tools. No professional disregards or treats them frivolously, but no professional pursues technical perfection for the sake of itself, either. If a story is grammatically and stylistically correct, but self-conscious, stilted and sophomoric, the writer has undermined the entire effort. Effective reporters, writers and editors heed the rules of grammar and the dictates of style partly out of professional pride, but mostly out of sheer practicality. Properly used, the rules help keep language crisp, clear and precise; they enable writers to say exactly what they mean in terms that readers can understand. That is the point.

Grammar

AGREEMENT

The most common grammatical mistakes writers make evolve from confusion over agreement, whether between subject and verb or pronoun and antecedent. Subjects and verbs must agree in number and person, regardless of whether parenthetical constructions or phrases separate them in a sentence:

A limousine, as well as a driver, was hired for the prom; not *"were* hired for the prom." The key to quickly identifying the parenthetical construction is the presence of such introductory words as "as well as," "together with," "like," "with," and "in addition to."

More than one subject joined by "and" usually requires a plural verb: A limousine and driver were hired for the prom.

If the two subjects refer to the same person or thing, a singular verb is required: My friend and confidante was among the missing; not *"were* among the missing."

When "each" or "every" precedes two subjects joined by "and," a singular verb is required: Each of the boys and girls was missing a front tooth; not *"were* missing a front tooth."

His prized assortment of knives, bayonets and pistols was stolen; not " . . . *were* stolen." The subject of the sentence is "assortment." The word is a collective noun, but the context clearly indicates that it is meant to be considered as a single unit. If the context of the sentence indicates that the collective noun subject is meant to indicate separate entities, the noun is treated as a plural, and requires a plural verb. For example: The judiciary were treated as pawns of the administration.

Artistic, musical and literary works require singular verbs: "The Elements of Style" is a classic guide to English usage.

Pronouns must agree with their antecedents in number, person and gender. Meaning determines whether collective noun antecedents take singular or plural pronouns. When the context of the sentence indicates that the collectivity is to be considered as a unit, a singular pronoun is required.

The baseball team won its first home game; not " . . . *their* first home game."

The audience clasped their hands over their ears; not " . . . *its* hands over *its* ears."

When "one" is the antecedent, the pronoun that follows is always "one": Under the circumstances, one has no way of knowing what one would do; not " . . . what *he, she, you* or *they* would do."

Most indefinite pronouns—words such as "either," "neither," "each," "anything," "everybody," "everyone," "nothing," "somebody"—take the singular.

Each of the cars spun its wheels; not " . . . *their* wheels."

Either is right.

"All," "none," "some" or "any" may be singular or plural, depending on the meaning conveyed by the nouns or pronouns to which they refer.

All of the class is out sick today.

All of the women are club members.

When one part of a subject is singular and the other is plural and they are joined by "or" or "nor," the verb agrees with the closest subject.

Neither the director nor the actors were any good.

Neither the actors nor the director was any good.

AVOIDING SEXISM

Gender differences between subjects require a careful grammatical response.

Neither John nor Sally would do his or her part.

Most editors would accept this slightly awkward sentence, if there were no easy way to recast it.

The pronoun "their" would be incorrect, because it implies an antecedent that is clearly plural.

The pronoun "his" or "her" alone would be inappropriate at best, sexist at worst.

In general, when the gender of the subject is unspecified, avoid defaulting to the masculine. Don't write: A good carpenter takes care of his tools . . . her tools . . . his or her tools. Better to make the subject of the sentence plural, and write: Good carpenters take care of their tools.

CONSISTENCY WITHIN A SENTENCE

Don't write: As he drove along the highway, you could see for miles. Make it read: As he drove along the highway, he could see for miles.

FORMS OF WHO, WHOM

The correct form of the pronoun depends upon its case, which is determined by the way the pronoun is used in a sentence. The nominative form, "who," is used if the pronoun is used as a form of subject. The objective form, "whom," is used if the pronoun is used as a form of object.

Writers and editors often trip over constructions such as the following:

I'll speak to whoever is home.

"Whoever" is the correct choice because it is in the nominative case as the subject of the clause "whoever is home"; the entire clause is used as the direct object of the preposition, "to." The most common error is to choose "whomever" on the grounds that the pronoun alone is the direct object of the verb "speak" or the object of the preposition "to."

Marry whomever you desire.

"Whomever" is the correct pronoun because it is in the objective case as the indirect object of the verb "desire" (transposed: you desire whomever . . .). The entire clause, ". . . whomever you desire," serves as direct object of the verb "marry."

THAT, WHICH, WHO

"That" may refer to either persons or things, and it is properly used to introduce a clause that is essential to the meaning of a sentence.

The car that her husband bought was too expensive.

Clearly, the point of the sentence is that her husband spent too much money for a particular car.

"Which" usually refers to a thing, and it is not properly used to introduce a clause that is not essential to the meaning of a sentence. In fact, the pronoun and the phrase it introduces usually can be deleted without destroying the sentence's meaning.

The car, which her husband bought, was too expensive.

The point here is that the car was too expensive, regardless of who made the purchase. The fact that her husband bought the vehicle is presented as nonessential information that can be deleted without losing the point of the sentence.

"Who" is used exclusively in reference to persons or, arbitrarily, to inanimate objects treated in contexts as living things.

Davy Crockett, who was elected to Congress, made his name on the Tennessee frontier.

Ole' Betsy, the flintlock rifle who was Davy's trusted friend and companion, had helped him through many brushes with death.

PARALLELISM

Ideas of comparable value and purpose in a sentence must be balanced grammatically.

Incorrect: He liked to jog or sprint and running.

Change to: He liked to jog, sprint and run.

Incorrect: Computers may be used for composition, page design, or solving problems.

Change to: Computers may be used for composition, page design or problem-solving.

DANGLING MODIFIERS

These awkward constructions usually are produced in haste, not in ignorance. They always are an embarrassment to the writer.

Walking down the avenue, the Empire State Building looked beautiful.

Any number of possibilities would be preferable:

As he walked down the avenue, he thought the Empire State Building looked beautiful.

From the avenue, the Empire State Building looked beautiful.

EXPLETIVES

Expletives usually waste time and space, which are always at a premium among nonfiction writers. When they are not needed for emphasis, expletives should be deleted and the sentence recast.

There was a car accident at Grover and Cleveland streets early today that killed two persons.

Change to: A car accident at Grover and Cleveland streets killed two persons early today.

It is her intention to present the petitions to the Board of Selectmen tomorrow night.

Change to: She intends to present the petitions to the Board of Selectmen tomorrow night.

TENSES

Writing that is riddled with inconsistent, arbitrary or out-of-sequence tenses is annoying and confusing.

As a rule, stories should be grounded in a single tense—past, present or future. Parts of the story should deviate from the chosen tense only when it is necessary and appropriate to do so. It is appropriate, for example, to shift from present tense to past, when writing of historical matters.

". . . I hate to admit it, but I've done this before," Charlie says.

By 1985 he was snorting cocaine four times a day. He had a $2,000-a-week habit.

"I thought everything was great," he says, "but I can see now that I was in pitiful shape."

VOICE

In a well-written sentence, action moves briskly from subject to verb to object; this is active voice. The reader nearly runs through the story.

Active: She threw the ball.

Passive: The ball was thrown by her.

Active: The City Council last night reviewed a proposal to turn Main Street into a shopping mall.

Passive: A proposal to turn Main Street into a shopping mall was reviewed by the City Council last night.

MIXED METAPHORS

Metaphors are figures of speech that imply comparison or identity. They are useful devices, but they can also be trite, cliché-ridden and disastrous.

"Our campaign is on the launching pad," Mayor McCarthy said, "and the goalposts are in sight."

(If you invite this man to a football game, tell him to leave his rocket home.)

The medical examiner tried to unravel the chain of events that had mired the murder victim in a sea of trouble.

(In one sentence, the writer has created three contradictory images: Someone is trying to unravel a chain, which is a neat trick; someone is stuck, but not in a swamp, bog or quicksand, while getting killed, though not necessarily by drowning.)

AFFECT, EFFECT

Writers often err in the use of these two words.

"Affect" is most commonly used as a verb meaning to influence or have a bearing on.

The earthquake affected people in three states.

Sometimes "affect" is used as a verb meaning pretending to have, assuming artificially.

She was afraid, but she affected a confident smile.

"Effect" is most commonly used as a noun meaning result.

Officials didn't know the effect of the disaster until it was too late.

On those relatively few occasions when "effect" is used as a verb, it means to accomplish or bring about.

The incident effected a major change in her attitude.

Commonly Misspelled Words

abscess
accede
accommodate
accumulate
admissible
adviser
advisory
aesthetic
affidavit
afterward
albino, albinos
align
allege
allot
allotted
allotting
all right
alter (to change)
altar (church platform)
amok
anemia

anemic
anoint
appall
athlete's foot
baccalaureate
balloon
banana
barbiturate
bazaar (a fair)
bellwether
besiege
bettor
bizarre (unusual)
bona fide
broccoli
caliber
Caribbean
changeable
changeover
chaperon
chauffeur
cigarette
Cincinnati
commitment
compatible
competent
consensus
consistent
consul
contagious
contemptible
courtroom
crisis, crises (pl.)
criterion, criteria (pl.)
defendant
definitely
demagogue
dependent
descendant
dialogue
diarrhea
dilemma
diphtheria
disastrous
dissension
doughnut
drought
drunkenness
eighth
embarrass
en route
epidemiology
espresso
exaggerate
exercise
exhilarating

exorbitant
exorcise
feud
filibuster
fiord
fluorescent
fulfill
gaiety
gauge
glamorous
glamour
goodbye
government
grammar
guerrilla
harass
harassment
hearsay
hemorrhage
hemorrhoid
hindrance
hitchhike
incredible
indestructible
indict
indispensable
innocuous
inoculate
irresistible
judgment
kibbutz, kibbutzim
kindergarten
largess
liaison
lightning
likable
limousine
liquefy
manageable
marshal
memento, mementos
millennium
minuscule
mischievous
mustachioed
occasion
occurred
occurrence
ophthalmologist
parallel
paraphernalia
penicillin
permissible
personnel
Philippines
picnicking

pinscher
pompon
potato, potatoes
precede
predominantly
privilege
prostate gland
questionnaire
queue
raccoon
rarefy
reconnaissance
re-elect
renowned
rescission
resistible
restaurateur
rock 'n' roll
roommate
saboteur
sacrilegious
scurrilous
seize
serviceable
sheriff
siege
sizable
sleight of hand
soliloquy
sophomore
strait-laced
subpoena
supersede
tobacco, tobaccos
trafficking
travelogue
Tucson (Arizona)
ukulele
vacuum
vice versa
villain
weird
wield
wondrous

SUGGESTED REFERENCES:

The Associated Press Stylebook and Libel Manual. New York: Addison-Wesley Publishing Co., revised edition, 1992.

The Careful Writer: A Modern Guide to English Usage, Theodore M. Bernstein. New York: Atheneum, 1977.

The Elements of Style, William Strunk, Jr., and E. B. White. New York: Macmillan Publishing Co., 1979.

The Little, Brown Handbook, H. Ramsey Fowler and Jane E. Aron. Glenview, Ill.: Scott, Foresman and Company, 4th edition, 1989.

The Transitive Vampire: A Handbook of Grammar for the Innocent, the Eager, and the Doomed, Karen Elizabeth Gordon. New York: Times Books, 1984.

The Well-Tempered Sentence: A Punctuation Handbook for the Innocent, the Eager, and the Doomed, Karen Elizabeth Gordon. New York: Ticknor & Fields, 1983.

U.S. PRESS GROUPS AND ASSOCIATIONS

For help with Freedom of Information issues:

The Reporters Committee
for Freedom of the Press
1735 I Street NW, Suite 504
Washington, D.C. 20006
(202) 466-6313

This is one of the best-informed and most helpful organizations in the country on access issues generally, and Freedom of Information issues specifically. The Reporters Committee maintains a 24-hour hot line for advice on FOI filings. Telephone: (800) 336-4243.

The Committee also publishes some of the most practical, informative, and useful booklets available anywhere, as well as an authoritative quarterly magazine, *The News Media and the Law*.

One of the Committee's booklets, *How to Use the Federal FOI Act*, is widely regarded as the single most useful guide to the act.

A series of booklets, *Tapping Officials' Secrets: The Door to Open Government in . . .* , offers a complete explanation of FOI and open-meeting statutes in each of the 50 states. Booklets are available per state or as *A State Open-Government Compendium*, a single volume covering the entire country.

Investigative Reporters and Editors, Inc.
100 Neff Hall
School of Journalism
University of Missouri
Columbia, MO 65211
(314) 882-2042

IRE is to good reporting what the Reporters Committee for Freedom of the Press is to FOI and access issues: expert and generously helpful. The organization is unflinchingly devoted to support and guidance for reporters.

Two IRE editors, John Ullmann and Steve Honeyman, produce *The Reporter's Handbook*, a unique, serious and authoritative guide to the paper chase. The book, in its third edition, is available from St. Martin's Press, 175 Fifth Ave., New York, NY 10010.

Society of Professional Journalists
Box 77
Greencastle, IN 46135-0077
(317) 653-3333

SPJ National FOI Committee
c/o USA Today
1000 Wilson Blvd.
Arlington, VA 22229
(703) 276-3732

With numerous chapters throughout the country, the SPJ is the largest association of professional journalists in the country. The SPJ follows FOI issues at all levels of government, and annually publishes an excellent, up-to-date national report. For copies of the FOI Report, write SPJ, 53 West Jackson Blvd., Suite 731, Chicago, IL 60604.

Other Press Organizations:

The Alicia Patterson Foundation
1001 Pennsylvania Ave. NW
Suite 1250
Washington, D.C. 20004
(301) 951-8512

American Newspaper Publishers Association and Foundation (ANPA)
The Newspaper Center
Box 17407
Dulles Airport
Washington, D.C. 20041
(703) 648-1000

American Press Institute
11690 Sunrise Valley Dr.
Reston, VA 22091
(703) 620-3611

American Society of Magazine Editors
575 Lexington Ave.
New York, NY 10022-6102
(212) 752-0055

American Society of Newspaper Editors
Box 17004
Washington, D.C. 20041
(703) 648-1144

Asian American Journalists Association
1765 Sutter St., Suite 1000
San Francisco, CA 94115
(415) 346-2051

(The) Associated Church Press
Box 162
Ada, MI 49301-0162
(616) 676-1190

Associated Press Broadcasters, Inc.
1825 K Street NW
Suite 615
Washington, D.C. 20006
(202) 955-7200

Association of Black Communicators
333 Communications Building

University of Tennessee
Knoxville, TN 37996
(615) 974-4291

Black Press Archives and Gallery of Distinguished
Newspaper Publishers
Moorland-Spingam Research Center
Howard University
Washington, D.C. 20059
(202) 806-7239

California Newspaper
   Publishers Association
Box 1530
La Jolla, CA 92038-1595
Copley Newspapers
(916) 443-5991
(619) 454-0411

Catholic Press Association
   of the United States and Canada
119 North Park Ave.
Rockville Centre, NY 11570
(516) 766-3400

(The) Dow Jones Newspaper Fund, Inc.
P.O. Box 300
Princeton, NJ 08543-0300
(609) 452-2820

(The) Freedom Forum
1101 Wilson Blvd.
Arlington, VA 22209
(703) 528-0800

(The) Fund for Investigative Journalism, Inc.
1755 Massachusetts Ave. NW
Room 504
Washington, D.C. 20036
(202) 462-1844

Gannett Center for Media Studies
Columbia University
2950 Broadway
New York, NY 10027
(212) 280-8392

Hearst, William Randolph, Foundation Journalism
   Awards Program
90 New Montgomery St.
Suite 1212
San Francisco, CA 94105
(415) 543-6033

Institute for Public Relations
   Research and Education
3800 South Tamiami Trail
Suite N
Sarasota, FL 34239-6913
(813) 955-5577

Inter-American Press Association Scholarship Fund
   Inc.
2911 NW 39th St.
Miami, FL 33142-5148
(305) 376-3522

International Newspaper
   Financial Executives
P.O. Box 16573
Dulles Airport
Washington, D.C. 20041
(703) 648-1160

International Society
   of Weekly Newspaper Editors
South Dakota State University
Box 2235
Brookings, SD 57007-0596
(605) 688-4171

Magazine Publishers of America
575 Lexington Ave.
New York, NY 10022-6102
(212) 752-0055

National Association
   of Black Journalists
Box 17212 Dulles Airport
Washington, D.C. 20041
(703) 648-1270

National Association
   of Broadcasters
1771 N Street NW
Washington, D.C. 20036-2891
(202) 429-5300

National Association
   of Hispanic Journalists
1193 National Press Building NW
Washington, D.C. 20045
(202) 662-7145

National Association
   of Science Writers
Box 294
Greenlawn, NY 11740
(516) 757-5664

National Conference
   of Editorial Writers
6223 Executive Blvd.
Rockville, MD 20852
(301) 984-3015

National Federation
   of Press Women, Inc.
Box 99
Blue Springs, MO 64013
(816) 229-1666

National Newspaper Association
1627 K St. NW
Suite 400
Washington, D.C. 20006
(202) 466-7200

National Press
   Photographers Association
3200 Croasdaile Drive
Suite 306
Durham, NC 27705
(919) 383-7246

Native American Journalists Association
230 10th Ave. South, Suite 301
Minneapolis, MN 55415
(612) 376-0441

(The) Newspaper Guild
8611 Second Ave.
Silver Springs, MD 20910
(301) 585-2990

New England Newspaper Association
70 Washington St.
Salem, MA 01970
(508) 744-8940

New England Press Association
Suite 280-HN
360 Huntington Ave.
Boston, MA 02115
(617) 437-5610

Media Institute
3017 M Street NW
Washington, D.C. 20007
(202) 298-7512

Nieman Foundation
One Francis Ave.
Cambridge, MA 02138
(617) 495-2237

(The) Poynter Institute
   for Media Studies
801 Third St. South
St. Petersburg, FL 33701
(813) 821-9494

(The) Pulliam Journalism Fellowship
The News
Box 145
Indianapolis, IN 46206
(317) 633-1240

Public Relations Society of America, Inc.
33 Irving Pl.
New York, NY 10003-2376
(212) 995-2230

Radio-Television News Directors Association
1000 Connecticut Ave. NW
Suite 615
Washington, D.C. 20036
(202) 659-6510

Scripps Howard Foundation
1100 Central Trust Tower
Cincinnati, OH 45202
(513) 977-3035

Sigma Delta Chi Foundation
P.O. Box 77
(16 S. Jackson St.)
Greencastle, IN 46135
(317) 653-3333

Southern Newspaper Publishers
   Association and Foundation
P.O. Box 28875
Atlanta, GA 30358
(404) 256-0444

Suburban Newspapers of America
401 N. Michigan Ave.
Chicago, IL 60611-4267
(312) 644-6610

Washington Journalism Center
2600 Virginia Ave. NW
Suite 502
Washington, D.C. 20037
(202) 337-3603

Women in Communications
2101 Wilson Blvd.
Suite 417
Arlington, VA 22201
(703) 528-4200

PART ELEVEN

QUICK CENSUS FIGURES

CRIMES BY TYPE—SELECTED LARGE CITIES: 1991

| City | Total Pop. | Total Crimes | Violent Crimes | | | | Property Crimes | | | |
			Murder	Forci-ble rape	Rob-bery	Aggra-vated assault	Arson	Bur-glary	Lar-ceny/ theft	Motor vehicle theft
Baltimore, Md.	748,099	85,669	304	701	10,770	7,257	601	16,230	39,213	10,593
Chicago, Ill.	2,811,478	320,332[1]	925	NA[2]	43,783	42,237	2,069	52,234	131,688	47,396
Dallas, Tex.	1,028,362	156,456	500	1,208	11,254	13,449	1,527	31,513	71,920	25,085
Detroit, Mich.	1,036,246	128,604	615	1,427	13,569	12,651	1,524	26,059	44,019	28,740
Houston, Tex.	1,665,756	182,185	608	1,213	13,883	10,947	1,877	39,726	73,769	40,162
Indianapolis, Ind.	489,392	36,291	95	561	2,001	4,415	286	8,732	14,970	5,231
Los Angeles, Calif.	3,558,516	351,200	1,027	1,966	3,977	47,104	4,976	57,460	130,234	68,655
Memphis, Tenn.	619,981	63,835	169	653	4,504	3,492	698	16,580	24,357	13,382
New York, N.Y.	7,350,023	684,054	2,154	2,892	98,512	66,832	1,993	112,015	256,473	139,977
Philadelphia, Pa.	1,596,699	111,132	440	904	13,921	7,216	1,993	21,460	40,880	24,318
Phoenix, Ariz.	995,895	99,577	128	480	3,448	6,954	405	24,219	47,338	16,605
San Antonio, Tex.	955,905	118,501	208	698	3,778	2,889	1,015	24,941	70,559	14,413
San Diego, Calif.	1,133,681	97,038	167	472	5,331	7,860	257	17,088	44,645	21,218
San Francisco, Calif.	739,039	69,779	95	400	7,020	4,645	429	10,604	34,679	11,907
Washington, D.C.	598,000	64,575	482	214	7,265	6,704	256	12,403	29,119	8,132

1. Total does not include figures for forcible rape.
2. Chicago's reporting of statistics on forcible rape did not meet federal criteria, and were excluded.
Source: U.S. Federal Bureau of Investigation, *Crime in the United States, 1992.*

CRIME RATES BY STATE AND REGION: 1991 (OFFENSES KNOWN TO POLICE PER 100,000 POPULATION)

| Region, State | Total violent crime | Violent Crimes | | | | Total pro-perty crime | Property Crimes | | |
		Murder[1]	Forcible rape	Robbery	Aggra-vated assault		Bur-glary	Larceny— theft	Motor vehicle theft
U.S.	**758.1**	**9.8**	**42.3**	**272.7**	**433.3**	**5,139.7**	**1,252.0**	**3,171.0**	**630.0**
Northeast	752.1	8.4	28.9	351.7	363.1	4,403.4	1,010.2	2,598.2	795.0
Middle Atlantic	829.2	9.9	28.5	419.0	371.8	4,397.9	977.8	2,597.7	822.5
East North Central	704.3	8.9	50.2	262.6	382.6	4,777.3	1,056.0	3,151.3	570.0
West North Central	456.6	5.4	34.0	129.4	287.8	4,265.1	990.6	2,918.4	356.2
South Atlantic	851.0	11.4	43.7	285.6	510.3	5,734.3	1,508.3	3,665.2	560.8
East South Central	630.9	10.4	40.8	149.1	430.5	4,056.1	1,196.2	2,464.7	395.1
West South Central	805.9	14.2	50.4	253.7	487.6	6,312.5	1,653.0	3,871.2	788.2
Mountain	543.7	6.5	46.4	287.5	497.6	5,581.2	1,323.7	3,522.2	790.9
Pacific	945.4	10.7	47.2	345.4	542.0	5,656.2	1,350.7	3,409.5	896.0
Alabama	844.2	11.5	35.6	152.8	644.4	4,521.4	1,268.6	2,889.5	363.4
Alaska	613.9	7.4	91.8	113.2	401.6	5,087.7	979.3	3,574.6	533.9
Arizona	670.7	7.8	42.4	165.7	454.8	6,734.9	1,607.5	4,266.3	861.1
Arkansas	593.3	11.1	44.6	135.6	401.9	4,581.7	1,226.5	3,013.8	341.4
California	1,089.9	12.7	42.4	411.3	623.5	5,682.7	1,397.8	3,246.0	1,038.9
Colorado	559.3	5.9	47.0	107.4	398.9	5,514.8	1,158.3	3,930.0	426.4
Connecticut	539.7	5.7	29.2	224.4	280.5	4,824.4	1,191.1	2,837.6	795.7

Region, State	Total violent crime	Violent Crimes				Total property crime	Property Crimes		
		Murder[1]	Forcible rape	Robbery	Aggravated assault		Burglary	Larceny—theft	Motor vehicle theft
Delaware	714.3	5.4	86.5	214.7	407.6	5,155.1	1,127.6	3,652.4	375.1
District of Columbia	2,453.3	80.6	35.8	1,215.6	1,121.4	8,314.7	2,074.4	4,879.9	1,360.4
Florida	1,184.3	9.4	51.7	399.8	723.4	7,362.9	2,005.8	4,573.5	783.6
Georgia	738.2	12.8	42.3	268.2	415.0	5,775.2	1,514.7	3,629.2	611.3
Hawaii	241.8	4.0	33.0	86.9	117.9	5,728.6	1,234.4	4,158.1	336.0
Idaho	290.3	1.8	28.9	20.7	238.9	3,905.5	826.0	2,901.2	178.3
Illinois	1,039.2	11.3	40.0	456.1	531.8	5,092.9	1,120.0	3,317.5	655.3
Indiana	505.3	7.5	41.3	116.0	340.5	4,312.5	977.1	2,870.6	464.8
Iowa	303.3	2.0	20.9	45.0	235.4	3,830.7	832.5	2,827.5	170.7
Kansas	499.6	6.1	44.8	138.4	310.3	5,034.7	1,306.7	3,377.1	351.0
Kentucky	438.0	6.8	35.4	83.1	312.7	2,920.3	796.6	1,909.1	214.6
Louisiana	951.0	16.9	40.9	278.9	614.3	5,473.5	1,411.5	3,488.6	573.4
Maine	132.1	1.2	21.9	22.7	86.3	3,635.6	902.5	2,569.8	163.3
Maryland	956.2	11.7	45.9	407.1	491.5	5,253.1	1,157.6	3,364.7	730.8
Massachusetts	736.1	4.2	32.1	194.6	505.2	4,586.2	1,167.1	2,500.5	918.7
Michigan	803.1	10.8	78.7	243.3	470.3	5,335.0	1,186.2	3,469.1	679.7
Minnesota	316.0	3.0	39.8	98.0	175.3	4,180.2	853.6	2,963.2	363.4
Mississippi	389.1	12.8	46.3	116.3	213.7	3,831.7	1,331.9	2,213.5	286.3
Missouri	763.0	10.5	34.0	251.1	467.4	4,652.6	1,253.3	2,840.9	558.5
Montana	139.9	2.6	19.8	18.6	98.9	3,508.3	523.6	2,778.3	206.3
Nebraska	334.6	3.3	28.1	54.0	249.2	4,019.5	726.6	3,080.4	212.6
Nevada	677.0	11.8	66.0	312.5	286.7	5,621.7	1,403.9	3,565.5	652.3
New Hampshire	119.3	3.6	29.9	33.0	52.8	3,328.5	735.4	2,372.9	220.3
New Jersey	634.8	5.2	29.1	293.1	307.3	4,796.5	1,015.7	2,854.9	925.9
New Mexico	834.8	10.5	52.4	120.3	651.6	5,844.6	1,723.0	3,775.3	346.3
New York	1,163.9	14.2	28.2	622.1	499.4	5,080.7	1,132.5	2,944.3	1,003.9
North Carolina	658.4	11.4	34.6	178.0	434.4	5,230.3	1,692.3	3,238.7	99.3
North Dakota	65.4	1.1	18.3	8.0	38.0	2,728.5	372.8	2,229.0	126.8
Ohio	561.8	7.2	52.5	215.2	287.0	4,471.2	1,055.2	2,915.6	500.4
Oklahoma	583.7	7.2	50.9	128.9	396.7	5,085.0	1,478.2	3,050.1	556.6
Oregon	506.3	4.6	53.4	150.1	298.2	5,248.8	1,176.0	3,598.4	474.4
Pennsylvania	450.0	6.3	28.7	193.9	221.1	3,108.6	719.6	1,907.4	481.5
Rhode Island	462.0	3.7	30.9	122.9	304.5	4,577.4	1,127.5	2,655.8	794.1
South Carolina	972.5	11.3	58.9	171.1	731.2	5,206.7	1,454.9	3,364.7	387.1
South Dakota	182.2	11.0	39.7	18.8	122.0	2,897.0	589.8	2,192.3	114.9
Tennessee	725.9	8.4	46.4	212.9	455.6	4,640.7	1,365.0	2,662.1	613.6
Texas	840.1	15.3	53.4	286.5	484.9	6,979.0	1,802.4	4,232.3	944.3
Utah	286.8	2.9	45.6	55.1	183.1	5,320.8	840.2	4,239.6	241.0
Vermont	116.8	2.1	30.5	11.8	72.3	3,838.4	1,020.1	2,673.9	144.4
Virginia	373.2	9.3	29.9	137.6	196.4	4,234.2	783.1	3,112.5	338.6
Washington	522.6	4.2	70.3	145.5	302.5	5,781.5	1,235.5	4,101.5	444.5
West Virginia	191.0	6.2	23.0	43.3	118.5	2,472.4	666.8	1,630.7	174.9
Wisconsin	277.0	4.8	25.4	119.0	127.7	4,188.9	751.6	3,000.9	436.4
Wyoming	310.2	3.3	25.9	17.2	263.9	4,078.7	692.2	3,232.0	154.6

1. Includes nonnegligent manslaughter.
Source: U.S. Federal Bureau of Investigation, *Crime in the United States, 1992.*

DEATHS FROM MOTOR VEHICLE ACCIDENTS, BY STATE: 1972–1990*

Region, State	1972[1]	1975	1980	1985	1986	1987	1988	1989	1990
U.S.	**56,528**	**46,032**	**53,476**	**46,159**	**48,140**	**48,290**	**48,900**	**47,100**	**46,300**
Alabama	1,356	1,087	1,054	1,005	1,180	1,185	1,023	1,025	1,095
Alaska	64	120	91	124	98	90	97	84	95
Arizona	858	713	983	942	1,073	925	944	884	863
Arkansas	750	577	607	580	624	658	610	648	604
California	5,300	4,414	5,860	5,294	5,523	5,774	5,381	5,105	5,173
Colorado	746	621	783	628	657	615	497	522	543
Connecticut	444	404	584	449	448	464	486	406	378
Delaware	130	129	164	119	160	152	165	118	143
District of Columbia	100	91	79	96	86	82	63	75	55
Florida	2,570	2,067	2,967	2,968	2,925	2,805	3,090	3,016	2,951
Georgia	1,940	1,420	1,558	1,462	1,604	1,618	1,660	1,632	1,563
Hawaii	164	153	195	134	124	134	149	147	175
Idaho	324	291	345	268	273	263	257	238	243
Illinois	2,216	1,816	1,985	1,594	1,633	1,835	1,862	1,748	1,589
Indiana	1,578	1,139	1,213	1,045	1,077	1,127	1,104	973	1,044
Iowa	904	714	662	478	446	508	566	511	459
Kansas	678	531	615	500	519	534	483	426	442
Kentucky	1,114	885	865	749	829	883	840	782	850
Louisiana	1,136	993	1,261	1,011	987	867	923	857	912
Maine	252	235	264	224	218	217	256	190	212
Maryland	852	686	822	766	796	815	794	750	726
Massachusetts	1,042	895	933	761	773	748	726	700	607
Michigan	2,236	1,811	1,817	1,605	1,666	1,730	1,704	1,633	1,563
Minnesota	1,052	798	900	657	608	601	615	605	568
Mississippi	976	629	796	691	785	812	720	728	751
Missouri	1,500	1,105	1,239	1,005	1,205	1,085	1,103	1,052	1,096
Montana	408	294	339	233	240	223	198	181	212
Nebraska	504	385	406	259	311	296	261	296	262
Nevada	290	236	388	297	274	244	286	307	343
New Hampshire	172	155	192	198	181	174	168	190	158
New Jersey	1,352	1,099	1,130	986	1,059	1,094	1,051	890	886
New Mexico	588	556	617	561	539	525	487	538	499
New York	3,140	2,277	2,717	2,121	2,183	2,495	2,237	2,239	2,183
North Carolina	2,026	1,560	1,588	1,553	1,727	1,577	1,587	1,464	1,383
North Dakota	206	183	184	117	120	113	104	81	112
Ohio	2,336	1,652	1,976	1,581	1,609	1,831	1,748	1,700	1,550
Oklahoma	792	748	1,006	781	725	669	641	655	646
Oregon	774	582	698	605	649	642	677	630	578
Pennsylvania	2,320	2,102	2,162	1,817	1,968	2,069	1,932	1,877	1,646
Rhode Island	144	140	142	124	155	140	125	100	84
South Carolina	1,148	837	895	943	1,077	1,087	1,033	996	983
South Dakota	312	216	238	142	152	156	147	151	153
Tennessee	1,526	1,280	1,280	1,219	1,372	1,298	1,266	1,081	1,172
Texas	3,714	3,472	4,378	3,825	3,701	3,330	3,395	3,361	3,243
Utah	354	285	370	335	370	307	297	303	270
Vermont	126	124	131	117	105	112	128	116	89
Virginia	1,256	1,069	1,111	1,021	1,141	1,075	1,069	999	1,073
Washington	836	804	1,048	786	763	865	785	781	825

Region, State	1972[1]	1975	1980	1985	1986	1987	1988	1989	1990
West Virginia	578	499	583	461	470	503	460	468	481
Wisconsin	1,148	943	1,009	777	769	831	813	817	763
Wyoming	196	210	246	145	163	107	155	127	125

* Data reflect date of death, not date of accident. Data reflect state where death occurred.
1. Peak year for deaths from motor vehicle accidents.
Source: National Center for Health Statistics.

INFANT MORTALITY RATES BY STATE[1]

State	Total		State	Total	
	1988	1989		1988	1989
U.S.	**10.0**	**9.8**			
			Missouri	10.1	9.9
Alabama	12.1	12.1	Montana	8.7	11.3
Alaska	11.6	9.2	Nebraska	9.0	7.9
Arizona	10.7	9.2	Nevada	8.4	8.1
Arkansas	10.7	10.2	New Hampshire	8.3	8.0
California	8.6	8.5			
			New Jersey	9.9	9.3
Colorado	9.6	8.7	New Mexico	10.0	8.5
Connecticut	8.9	8.8	New York	10.8	10.6
Delaware	11.8	11.8	North Carolina	12.5	11.3
District of Columbia	23.2	22.9	North Dakota	10.5	8.0
Florida	10.6	9.8			
			Ohio	9.7	9.9
Georgia	12.6	12.3	Oklahoma	9.0	8.5
Hawaii	7.2	8.3	Oregon	8.6	8.9
Idaho	8.8	9.7	Pennsylvania	9.9	10.2
Illinois	11.3	11.7	Rhode Island	8.2	10.2
Indiana	11.0	10.2			
			South Carolina	12.6	12.8
Iowa	8.7	8.3	South Dakota	10.1	9.6
Kansas	8.0	8.8	Tennessee	10.8	10.8
Kentucky	10.7	9.2	Texas	9.0	9.2
Louisiana	11.0	11.4	Utah	8.0	8.0
Maine	7.9	7.4			
			Vermont	6.8	6.9
Maryland	11.3	10.3	Virginia	10.4	10.0
Massachusetts	7.9	7.7	Washington	9.0	9.2
Michigan	11.1	11.1	West Virginia	9.0	9.4
Minnesota	7.8	7.1	Wisconsin	8.4	9.1
Mississippi	12.3	11.6	Wyoming	8.9	9.4

1. Deaths per 1,000 live births. Represents deaths of infants under 1 year old, exclusive of fetal deaths. Excludes deaths of nonresidents of the United States.
Source: Bureau of the Census.

HISTORICAL STATISTICS: U.S. PROFILE

	1800	1900	1980	1990
Demographics				
Population[1] (1,000)	5,308	76,212	226,542	248,710
Per square mile of land (Persons)	6.1	25.6	64.0	70.3
White (1,000)	4,306	66,900	188,372	199,686
Black and other (1,000)	1,002	9,312	38,170	49,024
Median age (Years)	16.7[2]	22.9	30.0	32.3
Homicide rate (per 100,000)	NA	1.2	10.7	9.4
Vital Statistics				
Birth rate[3]	NA	32.3	15.9	16.7
Death rate[3]	NA	17.8	8.8	8.6

	1800	1900	1980	1990
Education				
School enrollment, public (1,000)	6,872[4]	15,503	40,987	40,526
Expenditures per pupil (Dollars)	NA	17	2,230	4,639
Communication/transportation				
Households with TV sets (1,000)	NA	89[5]	76,000	93,100
Post offices (Number)	903	76,668	30,326	28,959
Motor vehicle factory sales (1,000)	NA	4	8,067	9,769
Money supply/prices/business				
Commercial banks (Number)	NA	12,427	14,434	12,509
Consumer price index (CPI-Urban)	51	25	82.4	130.7
Concerns in business (1,000)	204[6]	1,174	2,780	5,804[7]
Business failure rate per 10,000 concerns listed (Rate)	242[6]	92	42	98[7]
Other economics				
Exports of goods and services (Mil. dol.)	107	1,686	342,485	394,044.9
Imports (Mil. dol.)	108	1,179	333,360	495,042.0
Balance of trade (Mil. dol.)	−2	507	1,533	−100,997.1
Federal Government expenditures (Mil. dol.)	11	521	590,900	1,251,850
Public debt (Mil. dol.)	83	1,263	907,700	3,233,300

1. 1800, as of August 4; 1900, June 1; 1980, April 1; and 1990, July 1.
2. 1820 data.
3. Rate per 1,000 population for specified group.
4. 1870 data.
5. 1946 data.
6. 1857 data.
7. 1988 data.
Source: Bureau of the Census.

RACE AND HISPANIC ORIGIN FOR THE UNITED STATES AND STATES: 1990

States	Total	White	Black	American Indian Eskimo, or Aleut	Asian or Pacific Islander	Other Race	Hispanic Origin[1]
U.S.	**248,709,873**	**199,686,070**	**29,986,060**	**1,959,234**	**7,273,662**	**9,804,847**	**22,354,059**
Alabama	4,040,587	2,975,797	1,020,705	16,506	21,797	5,782	24,629
Alaska	550,043	415,492	22,451	85,698	19,728	6,674	17,803
Arizona	3,665,228	2,963,186	110,524	203,527	55,206	332,785	688,338
Arkansas	2,350,725	1,944,744	373,912	12,773	12,530	6,766	19,876
California	29,760,021	20,524,327	2,208,801	242,164	2,845,659	3,939,070	7,687,938
Colorado	3,294,394	2,905,474	133,146	27,776	59,862	168,136	424,302
Connecticut	3,287,116	2,859,353	274,269	6,654	50,698	96,142	213,116
Delaware	666,168	535,094	112,460	2,019	9,057	7,538	15,820
District of Columbia	606,900	179,667	399,604	1,466	11,214	14,949	32,710
Florida	12,937,926	10,749,285	1,759,534	36,335	154,302	238,470	1,574,143
Georgia	6,478,216	4,600,148	1,746,565	13,348	75,781	42,374	108,922
Hawaii	1,108,229	369,616	27,195	5,099	685,236	21,083	81,390
Idaho	1,006,749	950,451	3,370	13,780	9,365	29,783	52,927
Illinois	11,430,602	8,952,978	1,694,273	21,836	285,311	476,204	904,446
Indiana	5,544,159	5,020,700	432,092	12,720	37,617	41,030	98,788
Iowa	2,776,755	2,683,090	48,090	7,349	25,476	12,750	32,647
Kansas	2,477,574	2,231,986	143,076	21,965	31,750	48,797	93,670

States	Total	White	Black	American Indian Eskimo, or Aleut	Asian or Pacific Islander	Other Race	Hispanic Origin[1]
Kentucky	3,685,296	3,391,832	262,907	5,769	17,812	6,976	21,984
Louisiana	4,219,973	2,839,138	1,299,281	18,541	41,099	21,914	93,044
Maine	1,227,928	1,208,360	5,138	5,998	6,683	1,749	6,829
Maryland	4,781,468	3,393,964	1,189,899	12,972	139,719	44,914	125,102
Massachusetts	6,016,425	5,405,374	300,130	12,241	143,392	155,288	287,549
Michigan	9,295,297	7,756,086	1,291,706	55,638	104,983	86,884	201,596
Minnesota	4,375,099	4,130,395	94,944	49,909	77,886	21,965	53,884
Mississippi	2,573,216	1,633,461	915,057	8,525	13,016	3,157	15,931
Missouri	5,117,073	4,486,228	548,208	19,835	41,277	21,525	61,702
Montana	799,065	741,111	2,381	47,679	4,259	3,635	12,174
Nebraska	1,578,385	1,480,558	57,404	12,410	12,422	15,591	36,969
Nevada	1,201,833	1,012,695	78,771	19,637	38,127	52,603	124,419
New Hampshire	1,109,252	1,087,433	7,198	2,134	9,343	3,144	11,333
New Jersey	7,730,188	6,130,465	1,036,825	14,970	272,521	275,407	739,861
New Mexico	1,515,069	1,146,028	30,210	134,355	14,124	190,352	579,224
New York	17,990,455	13,385,255	2,859,055	62,651	693,760	989,734	2,214,026
North Carolina	6,628,637	5,008,491	1,456,323	80,155	52,166	31,502	76,726
North Dakota	638,800	604,142	3,524	25,917	3,462	1,755	4,665
Ohio	10,847,115	9,521,756	1,154,826	20,358	91,179	58,996	139,696
Oklahoma	3,145,585	2,583,512	233,801	252,420	33,563	42,289	86,160
Oregon	2,842,321	2,636,787	46,178	38,496	69,269	51,591	112,707
Pennsylvania	11,881,643	10,520,201	1,089,795	14,733	137,438	119,476	232,262
Rhode Island	1,003,464	917,375	38,861	4,071	18,325	24,832	45,752
South Carolina	3,486,703	2,406,974	1,039,884	8,246	22,382	9,217	30,551
South Dakota	696,004	637,515	3,258	50,575	3,123	1,533	5,252
Tennessee	4,877,185	4,048,068	778,035	10,039	31,839	9,204	32,741
Texas	16,986,510	12,774,762	2,021,632	65,877	319,459	1,804,780	4,339,905
Utah	1,722,850	1,615,845	11,576	24,283	33,371	37,775	84,597
Vermont	562,758	555,088	1,951	1,696	3,215	808	3,661
Virginia	6,187,358	4,791,739	1,162,994	15,282	159,053	58,290	160,288
Washington	4,866,692	4,308,937	149,801	81,483	210,958	115,513	214,570
West Virginia	1,793,477	1,725,523	56,295	2,458	7,459	1,742	8,489
Wisconsin	4,891,769	4,512,523	244,539	39,387	53,583	41,737	93,194
Wyoming	453,588	427,061	3,606	9,479	2,806	10,636	25,751

The data for race represent self-classification by people according to the race with which they most closely identify. Persons identified their race by classifying themselves in one of the categories listed, i.e., White, Black, American Indian, Eskimo, Aleut, Chinese, Filipino, Japanese, Asian Indian, Korean, Vietnamese, Hawaiian, Samoan, Guamanian, Other API, or Other race. In cases where persons did not identify with any of the given race categories they were directed to identify as "Other API" ("API" means Asian or Pacific Islander) or "Other race." Persons of Spanish/Hispanic origin or descent are those who classify themselves in one of the specific Hispanic origin categories listed on the Census form—for example, Mexican, Puerto Rican, or Cuban—as well as those who indicated that they were of other Spanish/Hispanic origin.

1. Spanish origin and race are distinct; thus, persons of Spanish/Hispanic origin may be of any race.

Source: Bureau of the Census.

STATE SCHOOL EXPENDITURES, PER CAPITA INCOME

Region, State	School expenditures per pupil[1], 1988–89 (dol.)	Personal income per capita 1988–89 (dol.)	Ranking, support of public education	School expenditures per pupil[1], 1989–90 (dol.)	Personal income per capita 1989–90 (dol.)	Ranking, support of public education
U. S.	**$4,541**	**$16,489**	—	**$4,890**	**$17,592**	—
Alabama	3,182	12,851	1) N.J.	3,314	14,826	1) N.J.
Alaska	7,543	19,079	2) N.Y.	7,252	21,761	2) N.Y.
Arizona	3,751	14,970	3) Alaska	3,853	16,297	3) Conn.
Arkansas	2,698	12,219	4) Conn.	3,272	14,218	4) D.C.
California	4,075	18,753	5) D.C.	4,598	20,795	5) Alaska
Colorado	4,633	16,463	6) Mass.	4,580	18,794	6) R.I.
Connecticut	7,261	23,059	7) R.I.	7,934	25,358	7) Mass.
Delaware	5,506	17,661	8) Pa.	5,848	20,039	8) Md.
District of Columbia	6,219	21,389	9) Del.	7,407	24,181	9) Del.
Florida	4,669	16,603	10) Wyo.	5,051	18,586	10) Wis.
Georgia	4,143	15,260	11) Md.	4,456	16,944	11) Pa.
Hawaii	4,034	16,753	12) Wis.	4,504	20,254	12) Maine
Idaho	2,946	12,665	13) Vt.	3,037	15,160	13) Vt.
Illinois	4,513	17,575	14) Ore.	4,853	20,303	14) Wyo.
Indiana	3,858	14,924	15) Maine	4,126	16,864	15) N.H.
Iowa	4,260	14,662	16) Va.	4,590	17,249	16) Minn.
Kansas	4,404	15,759	17) Fla.	4,706	17,986	17) Ore.
Kentucky	3,655	12,822	18) Colo.	3,824	14,929	18) Miss.
Louisiana	3,308	12,292	19) Minn.	3,457	14,391	19) Fla.
Maine	4,845	15,106	20) Mich.	5,577	17,200	20) Va.
Maryland	5,391	19,487	21) N.H.	5,887	21,864	21) Ill.
Massachusetts	6,118	20,816	22) Ill.	6,170	22,642	22) Kan.
Michigan	4,576	16,552	23) Kan.	5,073	18,346	23) Wash.
Minnesota	4,582	16,674	24) Wash.	5,114	18,731	24) Calif.
Mississippi	2,917	11,116	25) Iowa	3,151	12,735	25) Iowa
Missouri	3,838	15,452	26) Mont.	4,226	17,494	26) Colo.
Montana	4,259	12,866	27) Ga.	4,147	15,110	27) Hawaii
Nebraska	3,732	14,774	28) Ohio	3,874	17,221	28) Ga.
Nevada	3,887	17,511	29) Calif.	4,387	19,416	29) Ohio
New Hampshire	4,563	19,434	30) Hawaii	5,149	20,789	30) Nev.
New Jersey	7,571	21,994	31) N.M.	8,439	24,968	31) N.C.
New Mexico	3,973	12,488	32) Nev.	4,180	14,228	32) Mo.
New York	7,561	19,305	33) N.C.	8,094	21,975	33) N.M.
North Carolina	3,872	14,304	34) Ind.	4,386	16,203	34) Mont.
North Dakota	3,411	12,833	35) Texas	3,581	15,255	35) W. Va.
Ohio	4,139	15,536	36) Mo.	4,394	17,473	36) Ind.
Oklahoma	3,212	13,323	37) W. Va.	3,484	15,444	37) Texas
Oregon	4,845	14,885	38) Ariz.	5,085	17,156	38) Neb.
Pennsylvania	5,520	16,233	39) Neb.	5,670	18,672	39) Ariz.
Rhode Island	5,939	16,892	40) Ky.	6,523	18,841	40) Ky.
South Carolina	3,560	12,926	41) S.C.	3,731	15,099	41) S.C.
South Dakota	3,329	12,755	42) N.D.	3,312	15,872	42) N.D.
Tennessee	3,305	13,873	43) S.D.	3,503	15,798	43) Tenn.
Texas	3,842	14,586	44) La.	4,056	16,759	44) Okla.
Utah	2,571	12,193	45) Tenn.	2,733	14,083	45) La.
Vermont	5,115	15,302	46) Okla.	5,418	17,436	46) Ala.
Virginia	4,744	17,675	47) Ala.	5,000	19,746	47) S.D.
Washington	4,334	16,473	48) Idaho	4,638	18,858	48) Ark.
West Virginia	3,822	11,735	49) Miss.	4,146	13,747	49) Miss.
Wisconsin	5,259	15,524	50) Ark.	5,703	17,503	50) Idaho
Wyoming	5,462	15,676	51) Utah	5,281	16,398	51) Utah

1. Current expenditures per pupil in average daily attendance.
Source: Bureau of the Census.

MARRIAGES AND DIVORCES: 1960–90

Year	Marriages[1]		Divorces	
	Number (1,000)	Rate per 1,000 pop.	Number (1,000)	Rate per 1,000 pop.
1960	1,523	8.5	393	2.2
1965	1,800	9.3	479	2.5
1970	2,159	10.6	708	3.5
1975	2,153	10.0	1,036	4.8
1980	2,390	10.6	1,189	5.2
1981	2,422	10.6	1,213	5.3
1982	2,456	10.6	1,170	5.0
1983	2,446	10.5	1,158	4.9
1984	2,477	10.5	1,169	5.0
1985	2,413	10.1	1,190	5.0
1986	2,407	10.0	1,178	4.9
1987	2,403	9.9	1,166	4.8
1988	2,389	9.7	1,183	4.8
1989	2,405	9.6	1,163	4.7
1990	2,448	9.8	1,175	4.7

1. Beginning in 1980, includes nonlicensed marriages registered in California.
Source: National Center for Health Statistics.

WOMEN IN CIVILIAN LABOR FORCE: 1960–90

Female Labor Force as Percent of Female Population

Year	Total (1,000)	Total	Single	Married	Widowed or Divorced
1960	23,240	37.7	58.6	31.9	41.6
1965	26,200	39.3	54.5	34.9	40.7
1970	31,543	43.3	56.8	40.5	40.3
1975	37,475	46.3	59.8	44.3	40.1
1980	45,487	51.5	64.4	49.8	43.6
1981	46,696	52.1	64.5	50.5	44.6
1982	47,755	52.6	65.1	51.1	44.8
1983	48,503	52.9	65.0	51.8	44.4
1984	49,709	53.6	65.6	52.8	44.7
1985	51,050	54.5	66.6	53.8	45.1
1986	52,413	55.3	67.2	54.9	45.6
1987	53,658	56.0	67.4	55.9	45.7
1988	54,742	56.6	67.7	56.7	46.2
1989	56,030	57.4	68.0	57.8	47.0
1990	56,554	57.5	68.4[1]	59.0[1]	48.1[1]

1. Preliminary figures.
Source: U.S. Bureau of Labor Statistics.

EDUCATION

	Unit	1980	1985	1990
School enrollment[1]	Mil.	58.3	57.3	59.8
Elementary (K–8)	Mil.	28.2	28.4	29.5
Secondary (grades 9–12)	Mil.	18.0	16.6	16.7
Higher education	Mil.	12.1	12.3	13.6
School expenditures, total[2]	$Bil.	270.9	297.3	358.7
Elementary/secondary	$Bil.	168.7	179.4	215.5
Colleges/Universities	$Bil.	102.2	118.0	143.2
Average salary, public school teachers[2,3]	$Thous.	16.0	23.6	31.2

EDUCATIONAL ATTAINMENT

	Unit	1980	1985	1989
Adults[4]				
Years completed:				
High school	Pct.	66.5	73.9	76.9
College	Pct.	16.2	19.4	21.1

1. Includes kindergarten.
2. For school year ending June the following year.
3. Elementary and secondary schools only.
4. Persons 25 years old and over.
Source: Bureau of the Census.

PART TWELVE

RELIGION

MAJOR DENOMINATIONS

BAHÁÍ

Bahá'í was founded in 1863 by Mirza Husayn 'Ali Nuri, who took the name Baha'Ullah (Splendor of God). It teaches that God's will is expressed through prophets or manifestations, that all prophets are spiritually one, that revelations are progressive, that mankind is united, that men and women are equal, that science and religion are in harmony, and that the human soul is immortal. It promotes universal education, world peace and world government. The faith has spread to more than 250 countries, including the United States and Canada.

BUDDHISM

Buddhism was founded in Northern India in the 6th century B.C. by Siddhartha Gautama, who became known as the Buddha (Enlightened One). It is practiced throughout East and Southeast Asia. Although accurate numbers are elusive because many people combine Buddhist beliefs with other religions, the number of Buddhists worldwide has been estimated at more than 300 million. The Buddha achieved enlightenment (Nirvana) through meditation, and established a community of monks to follow his example and encourage others. Buddhism teaches that Nirvana can be reached through meditation and good moral and religious behavior. It also maintains that people are reincarnated, and that their lives are happy or sad depending on their actions (karma) in a previous life. Buddhist beliefs center around the Four Noble Truths: that all living beings must suffer, that desire and self-importance causes suffering, that achievement of Nirvana ends suffering, and that Nirvana can be attained by meditation and righteous actions, thoughts and attitudes. There are two main divisions: Theravada (Way of the Elders, also called Hinayana Buddhism), and Mahayana (Great Vehicle). The Theravada, which is the more conservative, is common in Sri Lanka, Myanmar and Thailand. The Mahayana is dominant in Taiwan, Korea, Japan and some areas of Tibet. A third form, Tibetan Buddhism, is dominant in most of Tibet. Traditionally, Buddhist monks spurned worldly goods and begged for food and financial support. In Southeast Asia, they still beg daily.

CHRISTIANITY

Christianity has about a billion adherents, whose beliefs center on the teachings of Jesus Christ. Christians believe that Jesus was both human and divine, and that he was born into the world to redeem humanity from the effects of sin. They believe that through his death on a cross he made it possible for people to enter heaven. Christian doctrine teaches that Christ rose from the dead and that he will return to judge the living and the dead. Christians believe that there is one god. Most believe that God exists as an inseparable trinity: God the Father (the creator), God the Son (Jesus Christ, the redeemer), and God the Holy Spirit (the sanctifier). They believe in life after death, and in heaven and hell. The basic text of Christianity is the Bible, which includes both the Old Testament (the Hebrew Bible) and the New Testament, a collection of early Christian writings.

In 1054, the Christian churches underwent their first split, or schism, between Western and Eastern churches. The Western Church, which used Latin in its liturgies, believed in the supremacy of the bishop of Rome (the Pope) over all other patriarchs and bishops. The Eastern Orthodox Church, which emphasized Greek, disputed that contention. During the Reformation in the 16th century, the churches of the West underwent further divisions when religious dissenters challenged what they saw as various abuses within the Roman Catholic Church. This led to the creation of many Protestant denominations and sects. The harsh sectarianism that followed has been eased somewhat by an ecumenical movement that began among Protestants in the early 1900s and was joined by Roman Catholics in the 1960s. Most Christian churches observe Sunday as the Sabbath. Major religious holidays are Christmas, which commemorates the birth of Jesus, and Easter, which celebrates his resurrection from the dead. Although practices differ widely, two common sacraments are baptism (a ceremonial cleansing that initiates members into a church) and the Eucharist (a religious ceremony including prayer, reflection and a ceremonial meal of bread and wine that is believed to unite the faithful with Christ).

Armenian Church

The Armenian Church is similar to the Orthodox Catholic Church (q.v.) in most beliefs and practices, but it espouses the Monophysite doctrine that Jesus Christ was divine, not human, while on earth. In this way it differs from other Christian churches. It shares this belief with the Coptic, Ethiopian and Jacobite churches. The Armenian Church, which is also known as the Armenian Apostolic or Gregorian church, is the church of most Armenians.

Church of Jesus Christ of Latter-Day Saints (Mormonism)

The church was founded by Joseph Smith in Fayette, N.Y., in 1830. Smith, whom the church regards as a prophet, said that he had his first vision of God in 1820, at age 15. He said that God told him that the Gospel of Jesus Christ needed to be restored, and that Smith would be used for this purpose. As the church grew, so did opposition. Nonmembers objected to the local political influence of the church (whose members often voted as a bloc), and were enraged by the rumor that Smith had secretly approved of polygamy. Smith was killed by a mob in Carthage, Ill., in 1844. Members, who had already moved several times due to opposition, moved again, this time following the new leader of the church, Brigham Young, to the area of Utah's Great Salt Lake. The headquarters is now in Salt Lake City, Utah. Polygamy was practiced by some members of the church, but was banned in 1890. (Some dissenters continue to practice plural marriage, but the practice is not approved by the church.) The Mormons, as Christians, believe in one three-person god, and in Jesus Christ as redeemer. Their beliefs center around the Bible and the *Book of Mormon*, which they view as a supplementary work revealed to them by Smith. According to Smith, a heavenly messenger directed him to some gold-colored plates engraved with hieroglyphics. His translation of the plates became the *Book of Mormon*. The book describes the history and religious beliefs of a group of people who lived between 600 B.C. and 421 A.D. and migrated from Jerusalem to America. Two other books—*Doctrine and Covenants* and the *Pearl of Great Price*—are also regarded as scriptural revelations made to Smith. Mormons believe that God continues to make revelations to believers, and to church leaders. In 1978, for example, the church rescinded its ban against allowing black men to become priests because of divine revelation. Mormons baptize members at age 8 or older, when they are thought to be old enough to be accountable for their actions. They also believe that the dead can be baptized vicariously. Because of this belief, they emphasize the study of genealogy, so that families can be traced and ancestors can be baptized. They believe that a marriage that has been sanctified by the church lasts forever, not merely until death. Members are encouraged to tithe the church. There are about 4 million Mormons in the United States, mostly in the western states, and another 3 million in 100 other countries. There are several Mormon splinter groups, which separated from the mainstream over the selection of Brigham Young as the successor to Joseph Smith. They believe that Smith's descendants should have succeeded him.

The largest of these groups is the Reorganized Church of Jesus Christ of the Latter-Day Saints, which has about 192,000 members. Its headquarters is in Independence, Mo.

Jehovah's Witnesses

Jehovah's Witnesses believe that they were founded by Jehovah and that, as servants of God, are part of a tradition that dates back 6,000 years. They, therefore, do not consider themselves to be Protestants, whom they believe they predate. Their beginning as a group dates to the late 1800s, when Charles T. Russell of Pennsylvania established the Watch Tower Bible and Tract Society as the legal agency of the church. The church itself is not incorporated. Jehovah's Witnesses believe that the Bible offers practical guidance for daily living, that Satan was expelled from heaven in 1914, that the second coming of Christ is imminent, that a "grand tribulation" is due and will end in the Battle of Armageddon, and that Jesus will then rid the world of its wicked ways and rule for 1,000 years. They believe that 144,000 true believers will go to heaven to live with Jesus, and that billions of others (both living and dead) who do not go to heaven but who are capable of redemption will live on Earth, which will have become a paradise. They will then, through their actions, have the chance to earn the right to join Jesus in heaven. Some, who have been wicked, will not rise from the grave and will cease to exist. Because they believe that theirs is the true religion, they feel they have an obligation to proselytize. They seek out people in their homes and in public places, distribute literature and seek to make conversions. All Jehovah's Witnesses are ministers, they believe, although they serve in different ways. They believe that the titles "Reverend" or "Father" should be reserved for God; they do not use the terms to refer to mortal religious leaders. Those who serve in an active ministerial capacity in the church usually maintain secular jobs because they are not paid. Children are encouraged to preach. Although Jehovah's Witnesses do not oppose national government, they believe that saluting a nation's flag is worshipping an image and therefore violates the First Commandment. The United States Supreme Court has upheld their religious right to refuse to salute the flag. They also refuse to serve in the military. They are not pacifists, but they believe that only God, not man, can rightfully proclaim war. They believe that has not happened for several thousand years. They refuse blood transfusions, based on a biblical admonition against consuming blood. They believe that woman's role is to complement man, not to lead him, in part because Eve was created from Adam. Male elders preside over local congregations. Witnesses attend five meetings a week, in buildings often called Kingdom Halls, to prepare them for their ongoing outreach work. There are approximately 770,000 Witnesses in the United States and 2.3 million worldwide.

Eastern Orthodox Church

The Eastern Orthodox Church is actually a group of self-governing Christian churches that are joined by common beliefs and liturgy. It is also known as the Greek Orthodox Church and the Orthodox Catholic Church. It evolved from the same religious tradition as the Roman Catholic Church. In the 4th century, the Christian church was organized around five geographical centers or patriarchies: Rome (the presiding church), Constantinople, Alexandria, Antioch and Jerusalem. Each church center developed its own liturgical style, structure and doctrines. Through the centuries, the differences caused by geography, languages, culture and politics deepened between the church centered in Rome (the Western Rite) and those centered elsewhere (the Eastern Rite). Eventually the Eastern churches rejected the concept that the Pope, the bishop of Rome, was the ultimate divine authority. Although the Great Schism was a gradual process, a key date was 1054, when Pope Leo IX excommunicated Michael Cerularius, patriarch of Constantinople, the leader of the Eastern churches. Cerularius excommunicated the papal legate, Cardinal Humbert. In successive centuries the gulf between the Roman Catholic and Orthodox churches widened, despite periodic attempts at reconciliation. The ecumenical movement that began in the 1960s has begun to narrow the gap. After a historic meeting in 1964 (the first such meeting in 500 years), Pope Paul VI and Patriarch Athenagoras I issued a joint declaration removing the excommunications, and moving the Roman Catholic and the Orthodox churches closer together. The Eastern Orthodox Church is the major Christian church in the Middle East and Eastern Europe. The separate churches that comprise the Eastern Orthodox Church include the Church of Greece, the Church of Cyprus, the Serbian Eastern Orthodox Church, the Bulgarian Eastern Orthodox Church, the Romanian Eastern Orthodox Church, the Ukrainian Orthodox Church and the Russian Orthodox Church, among others. Each church is free to elect its own head and bishops. To the extent that there is central leadership, the role traditionally has fallen to the Patriarch of Constantinople. (The church does not use the city's modern name, Istanbul.) He is recognized as a "first among equals." He acts as a chairman of bishops, but has no singular authority. The Orthodox Church recognizes the same sacraments as the Roman Cath-

olic Church and venerates the Virgin Mary. Married men may become priests, but bishops and monks are not allowed to marry. There are about 4 million members of the Orthodox Church in the United States and between 100 million and 200 million worldwide.

Protestantism

Protestantism encompasses many churches with differing beliefs, rituals and organizations. They are united by a belief in Jesus Christ as God, and in rejection of the Roman Catholic Church's belief in the divine authority of the Pope.

• Adventist Churches

Members of Adventist churches believe that Christ's return to Earth is imminent. Although Christians in many separate denominations may share this belief, there are several churches in which the belief is a basic tenet. The foremost is the Seventh-Day Adventist Church, which has about 1.5 million members worldwide, nearly half of whom live in the United States. Seventh-Day Adventists observe Saturday as the Sabbath. Other Adventist churches observe the Sabbath on Sunday. Modern Adventist belief dates from the early 1800s. William Miller, an American preacher, taught that, based on his interpretation of biblical prophecy, Christ would return between March 1843 and March 1844 and cleanse the Earth with fire. When the dates passed he lost many followers. Others faulted his method of calculation but maintained the belief that Christ will soon reappear.

• Anglican Communion

The Anglican Communion is a group of independent churches derived from the Church of England. In the United States, the largest member is the Episcopal Church (q.v.). The bishops of the various churches meet every 10 years at the Lambeth Conference at Lambeth in London, under the leadership of the Archbishop of Canterbury. The group has no legal power, but exerts some moral authority and is a symbol of unity among the churches. Churches in the Anglican Communion include: the Church of England; the Church of Ireland; the Episcopal Church in Scotland; the Church of Wales; the Anglican Church of Canada; the Episcopal Church (United States); the Church of India, Pakistan, Burma and Sri Lanka; the Church of the Province of South Africa; the Church of England in Australia and Tasmania; the Church of the Province of New Zealand; the Church of the Province of the West Indies; Chung Hua Sheng Kung Hui (China); Nippon Sei Kwai (Japan); the Church of the Province of West Africa; the Church of the Province of Central Africa; the Church of the Province of East Africa; the Church of the Province of Uganda and Rwanda and Burundi; and the Episcopal Church of Brazil.

• **Baptist Church**

The Baptist Church was founded in England by John Smyth in 1609. Baptists believe that committed adults, not infants, should be baptized and that the Bible is the fundamental authority in matters of faith, religious doctrine and morality. There is great variety in modern Baptist belief, with many constituent churches (conventions) being decidedly conservative and others quite liberal. Baptist churches have produced both opponents and leaders of the Ecumenical Movement. The reason for the disparity can be found in the scriptural orientation of the faith (which has led some groups toward a traditional, conservative stance) and in its emphasis on personal belief, freedom of conscience and autonomy of local churches (which has allowed others to follow a more liberal path). The Baptist churches constitute the largest family of Protestant believers in the United States with more than 28 million members. Some of the larger bodies within the church include the Southern Baptist Convention; the National Baptist Convention, U.S.A., Inc.; the National Baptist Convention of America; the American Baptist Churches in the U.S.A.; and Baptist Bible Fellowship, International.

• **Christian Church (Disciples of Christ)**

The official name of the church is Christian Church (Disciples of Christ), but local congregations often use just "Christian Church." Others may call themselves the "Church of Christ." The church originated in Kentucky and western Pennsylvania in the early 1800s. It sought to eliminate the divisiveness that separated many Protestant denominations. There is no official church dogma, except for belief in Jesus Christ. Members are free to determine their own beliefs, based on scripture, and to act according to their own consciences. Some members interpret the Bible literally; others view it as a broad spiritual guide that was not meant to be precisely construed. It admits as a member anyone who professes belief in Jesus Christ. The church has no prescribed worship ritual, although most Sunday services include hymns, readings and responses, the Lord's Prayer, a sermon and a Communion service. The church has ministers, but no bishops. Lay persons hold important roles in the church and often preside at worship services. The General Assembly, which meets every two years, includes clergy and laypersons. It is a democratic organization that deals with church problems and considers moral issues. Members and congregations are free to accept or reject the assembly's moral stance. The church, which has about 1.6 million members, is the largest religious movement to have originated in the United States. There have been two separations from the church in this century, with the separating churches retaining quite similar names and most of the beliefs of the original church. In 1906, a group objected to the use of musical instruments in worship services. It withdrew to become the Churches of Christ. More recently, some conservative groups have gradually pulled away from the church and have formed the Christian Churches. Because the names are plural forms of common names for the Christian Church (Disciples of Christ), the groups often are confused.

• **Church of Christ, Scientist (Christian Science)**

The Church of Christ, Scientist, was founded by Mary Baker Eddy in 1879. The church emphasizes divine healing. Its main teachings come from the Bible and from *Science and Health with Key to the Scriptures* by Mrs. Eddy. The church defines health in spiritual, not physical, terms. It teaches that disease can be conquered by spiritual understanding. The healing process may be assisted by the prayers of a Christian Science practitioner, a person trained in spiritual healing and approved by the Mother Church in Boston. The practitioner may be miles away from the patient. (The church sanctions the use of medical doctors to assist at childbirth, and to set broken bones surgically, if the patient cannot heal the fracture by spiritual means alone.) The church has no clergy. Church services are led by readers elected by church members. Mind, Spirit, Soul, Principle, Life, Truth and Love are used as synonyms for God when capitalized.

• **Episcopal Church**

The Episcopal Church in the United States is part of the Anglican Communion, a group of independent churches derived from the Church of England. It was established shortly after the American Revolution, when Americans who were members of the Church of England cut their religious ties with Great Britain. The new church retained much of its Anglican heritage, but added insistence on the separation of church and state. Worship is based on the Book of Common Prayer and the Bible. Like other Anglican churches, it retains the sacraments and creeds of the Catholic Church (from which it separated during the Reformation), but rejects the authority of the Pope and emphasizes the authority of the Bible. It has 2.7 million members.

• **Lutheran Church**

The Lutheran Church evolved from the work of Martin Luther (1483–1546), a Roman Catholic priest who broke from that church over disputes concerning its teachings and practices, including the sale of indulgences. His central message was that salvation is granted by God alone, not by the actions of man. His beliefs were derived from his study of the Bible, which remains the central scriptural text for Lutherans. Lutheran principles were elucidated in the Augsberg Confession, written in 1530, and in subsequent writings, called confessions, which were collected in the *Book of Concord* in 1580. Those works remain important statements of Lutheran principles. The church, which was born out of fervent doctrinal concern, places more emphasis on doctrine than many other Protestant churches. The worship service retains much of the structure of the Roman Catholic service, which Luther adapted. It recognizes two sacraments, baptism (of babies) and the Lord's Supper (communion). Church governance takes different forms in different countries. In Europe, most Lutheran churches are led by bishops. In North America, most churches follow a democratic structure; delegates represent local churches at periodic conferences that determine church policy. In the United States, there are two main branches of the church, the Evangelical Lutheran Church in America (which has about 5.3 million members) and the more conservative Lutheran Church—Missouri Synod (with about 2.6 million members). Lutheranism has about 70 million adherents worldwide, many of whom are in Germany, Denmark, Finland, Iceland, Norway and Sweden.

- **Mennonite Churches**

Menno Simons, a 16th-century Dutch reformer, founded the Mennonite Church. He was an Anabaptist whose writings and leadership united his followers under his name. He retained the basic tenets of the Anabaptist Church: that only those who have repented their sins and committed themselves to Jesus should be baptized, that there should be freedom of choice in religion, that Christians should refrain from using force, that Christians should not swear oaths and that worldliness should be avoided. Because they refused to swear oaths of loyalty, serve as police or join the military, they were viewed as subversives and were persecuted. They fled Europe for North America, where most now live. There are more than 10 Mennonite denominations in the United States, with a total of about 240,000 members. The largest group is the Mennonite Church, with about 90,000 members. The next largest group, the Old Order Amish Church, has about 60,000 members. The Amish follow the teachings of Jacob Amman, a Swiss bishop who left the Mennonite Church in 1693 because he found it to be too liberal and worldly. The Amish

follow a simple lifestyle that focuses on worship and family values, rather than worldly possessions and ostentation. They avoid modern technology, using horses instead of tractors and cars. Men wear beards and plain, dark clothes. Women wear plain bonnets, dresses and shawls. They speak a German-English dialect known as Pennsylvania Dutch. They are centered around Lancaster County, Penn., Holmes County, Ohio, and Elkhart County, Ind.

- **Methodist Church**

The Methodist Church began as the outgrowth of a reform movement led by the Anglican cleric John Wesley (1703–91). Wesley did not intend for his followers to leave the Church of England. Instead, he wanted to establish groups within the church that would devote more personal effort to their religion, setting aside regular times for group prayer and Bible study, and spending more time in individual prayer. The members of these societies were so disciplined and methodical about their religious studies that others derisively called them Methodists. As the Methodist movement spread, particularly in the United States, its followers gradually separated from the Church of England. In 1795, the church declared that its ministers no longer had to be ordained by the Church of England. The Methodist Church continues to share the basic values of churches in the Anglican Communion (q.v.). It emphasizes personal religious experience, and urges members to address social problems as part of their religious life. There are about 38 million Methodists worldwide, many of whom are in the British Isles. In the United States, there are about 13 million church members. The major divisions of the Methodist Church in the United States include the United Methodist Church (9 million members), the African Methodist Episcopal Church (2 million members), the African Methodist Episcopal Zion Church (1 million members) and the Christian Methodist Episcopal Church (700,000 members). The African Methodist Episcopal Church, the African Methodist Episcopal Zion Church and the Christian Methodist Episcopal Church are predominantly black churches.

- **Presbyterian Church**

Presbyterianism refers to a form of church government, rather than to a creed. "Presbyterian" derives from the Greek word *presbyteros*, meaning "elder." The church has a representative form of government, in which elders, who are chosen from the clergy and the laity, make decisions at all levels. There are four governing levels in the church: the session (for the local congregation), the presbytery (representing a group of congregations), the synod (representing a group of presbyteries), and the general assembly (representing the whole church within a nation). The session consists of the local minister or pastor and lay elders. It is assisted by deacons, who direct charitable work, and trustees, who direct financial and legal affairs. All offices are elective. In the presbytery, the synod and the general assembly, the clergy and the laity are equally represented. The church is based on the work of John Calvin (1509–64), a French-Swiss reformer who asked Christians to reject the government style of the Roman Catholic Church and return to a form common in the 1st century A.D. Calvinism was brought to Scotland by John Knox, who led a Protestant uprising in 1559 and established the first Presbyterian Church there. In 1690, the Presbyterian Church of Scotland became the established church. There are about 50 million Presbyterians worldwide, and about 3.2 million in the United States. The largest Presbyterian body in the United States is the Presbyterian Church (U.S.A.), which has about 3 million members.

• Salvation Army

The Salvation Army was founded in London in 1865 by William Booth, a Methodist minister. It has more than 400,000 members in the United States and 2.5 million worldwide. Its members express their Christian faith through nondenominational acts of charity. The church provides many social services, including emergency assistance, alcoholism and drug abuse rehabilitation, counseling, day care, summer camps and homeless shelters. It is organized in military fashion: The general (in London) is the top official; ministers are officers with military rank; parishioners are soldiers. All members may wear the Army's uniform.

• Unitarian Universalist Association

The Unitarian Universalist Association was formed in 1961 when the Unitarian and Universalist churches united. Its distinguishing beliefs are expressed in its name. Unitarianism is the belief that God exists as one being (the Father), not a trinity. Universalism is the belief that a loving god will save all souls, not just those that repent or follow a particular code. Although Unitarian Universalism was an outgrowth of Protestant religious belief, many members do not consider themselves Christians because they do not believe that Jesus was divine. (Jesus is revered as an inspirational human.) Other members consider themselves liberal Christians. The church is nondogmatic. It maintains that lessons can be learned from many religions and many religious texts. It asserts that members should be able to form their own religious views, based on reason and innate moral abilities. It has more than 170,000 members in the United States.

• United Church of Christ

The United Church of Christ was formed in 1957 when the Congregational Christian Churches and the Evangelical and Reformed Church merged. The church is distinguished from other Protestant denominations in that the basic unit is the local church. Each church has autonomy; no higher authority can direct its actions. Local churches are in voluntary affiliation with regional and national groups. They determine the form of their liturgy. They confer membership, usually based on baptism and confirmation or a profession of faith. All members of local churches automatically become members of the United Church of Christ. Elected delegates attend a biennial General Synod, which guides the church's national and international work, elects officers (president, secretary, director of finance and treasurer) and makes recommendations. Local churches are expected to hold the General Synod's decisions and advice "in highest regard," but are not obligated to follow it. The church traces its beginnings to the Pilgrims, who were the first Congregationalists in America. It supported the abolition of slavery, has allowed the ordination of women for more than a century and has been active in ecumenical efforts. There are about 1.7 million followers in the United States.

Religious Society of Friends (Quakers)

The Religious Society of Friends was established by George Fox in England in the mid-1600s. Fox rejected traditional religious hierarchy, elaborate church rituals and rigid doctrine. He preached that God's spirit is in everyone, and that it could be found by quiet contemplation and reading of the Bible. Fox's followers received the Quaker nickname because of his admonition to "tremble at the word of the Lord." It was originally a term of derision. Quakers were persecuted and killed in England and America because they rejected popular religious forms, refused to swear oaths (which they believed was forbidden in the Bible) and believed in nonviolence, which led them to reject military service. Although many Quakers have refused to serve in wars, they are not uniform in their refusal to do so. For some, the decision has been based on weighing two negatives: fighting or allowing unjust conditions to continue. Although Quakers believe in pacifism, those who have made other choices, based on conscience, are not necessarily excluded from membership. Quakers have been very active in promoting peace and social welfare. Fox's concept of Inner Light is still central to Quaker beliefs. Traditional Quaker Meetings for

Worship have no formal structure. Friends gather at an appointed time and contemplate God in silence. When one is moved to pray, read from the Bible or preach aloud, one does so. Friends who are especially good preachers are recorded by the group as ministers. The recording serves to identify talented preachers, and to encourage them to use and develop their gifts. There is no ordained ministry. Many groups continue to follow the traditional practices, although there is great variation. Some groups have structured worship meetings, led by a pastor, with many of the elements of Protestant worship services. Those groups sometimes call themselves Friends Churches. Quakers conduct business in a series of Meetings for Business. Local groups hold monthly meetings; districts (encompassing several localities) hold quarterly meetings; regions (encompassing several districts) hold yearly meetings. Issues are considered and points of view are presented. There is no voting and no compromise process. The goal is to find true answers, based on scripture, precedent and prayerful contemplation. A clerk records "the sense of the meeting" when consensus appears to have been reached. It is then read to the group. If it is correct, the issue has been resolved. If no consensus has been reached, the matter is delayed until consensus is possible. Historically, emphasis on plain dress and plain speech has been a distinctive feature. The customs are no longer widespread, although they are maintained in some areas, particularly during Services for Worship. The plain-dress custom originated as a protest against conspicuous consumption. Clothes are gray or black, with no trimming or frills. Women wear plain dresses and sometimes wear sugar-scoop bonnets. Men wear plain, broad-brimmed hats and suits with no lapels or useless buttons. The plain-language custom dates from 17th-century England, when the Quakers chose to use the common "thee" and "thou" instead of "you" in addressing one person, to distinguish themselves from the aristocracy. They also rejected the common names of the days and months because of what they regarded as pagan origins. They substituted a simple numbering system. "Sunday" became "First-day," for example. "January" became "First-month." Today some Quakers reject the plain-language custom as being separatist. For others, it is part of their identity. Many who use it do so only among Friends or within the family. There are about 200,000 Quakers worldwide, about half of whom are in the United States.

Roman Catholic Church

The Roman Catholic Church is the largest Christian church in the world. It has 900 million followers, more than 20 percent of the world's population. It is the largest religious denomination in the United States, with 53 million members. It claims direct descent from the church formed by Jesus Christ's disciple, Peter. Popes are viewed as Peter's successors. Because their power is believed to come from God, they are believed to be infallible when making certain official pronouncements concerning doctrine. They are elected by the College of Cardinals, a group of bishops who have been elevated to the status of cardinal and serve for life. Roman Catholics, like other Christians, believe that Jesus is one of God's three forms: the Father, the Son (Jesus) and the Holy Spirit. They believe that through his life, death and resurrection he brought the hope of salvation to the world. They believe that he will come again to judge the living and the dead, and that those who have been forgiven from sin will live forever in heaven. Most Protestant denominations recognize only baptism and the Lord's Supper (communion) as sacraments (religious experiences that convey special grace). The Roman Catholic Church recognizes seven: baptism, communion (Holy Eucharist), penance (confession), confirmation, matrimony, holy orders (ordination into the priesthood) and anointing of the sick (also called extreme unction or last rites). Children are baptized as infants, receive communion and go to confession for the first time when elementary-school age, and are confirmed as adolescents. Confession has traditionally been conducted in a confessional, a private booth in which the priest is separated from the penitent by a screen. The penitent kneels in his side of the confessional, recounts his sins, prays, expresses regret and willingness to change, and asks forgiveness. The priest offers counsel, prayers and God's absolution. He directs the penitent to do penance in order to be forgiven. (Usually, the priest advises that certain prayers be said.) Confession may also be conducted face to face. There is also a group penance rite, in which sins are not confessed aloud. Catholics pray to many saints, most notably the Virgin Mary, but do not worship the saints as gods. They ask the saints to intercede with God on their behalf. The Second Vatican Council (1962–65), a conference of bishops called by Pope John XIII, brought about significant changes in the church, including the translation of the Mass from Latin into the vernacular. Since the council, the church has played an increasing role in the Ecumenical Movement.

CONFUCIANISM

Confucianism was founded by Confucius, a Chinese philosopher, in the 6th and 5th centuries B.C. He emphasized the importance of li (proper behavior) and jen (sympathetic attitude). He also believed in heaven and in the worship of ancestors, which his followers extended to include the worship of Confucius in the 2d century B.C. Confucianism has declined in importance in China since the Communist revolution, although it still has more than 5 million followers.

CULTS

There is no single definition of what constitutes a religious cult. Cults are characterized by a sense of community, intense shared belief and divergence from mainstream religious views or practices. They emphasize devotion—to the espoused doctrine, to the group, and, often, to the cult's leaders—and personal religious experience. Cults often are ephemeral. Although the term *cult* has a negative connotation, many mainstream religious denominations sprang from similar beginnings. Cults may develop within an established church, or they may have no connection with an established religion. In the United States, interest in cults escalated in the late 1960s and 1970s when many disillusioned young people were attracted to them. In a turbulent era, cults promised a sense of community, commitment, harmony and spiritual calm. Some cults have been accused of brainwashing members into submissive service and causing them to reject their families in favor of the "family" of the cult. This has led friends and relatives to forcefully separate members from cults and attempt to "deprogram" them. Deprogrammers believe that they are saving helpless cult members from robotic, slave-like existences in which cult leaders control their thoughts and lives. Cult leaders believe that members are being harassed because of their religious beliefs. Some cults have established legal defense funds to fight deprogramming efforts in court. Whether a religious group is a "cult" is often a matter of perspective. The views from the inside and the outside are quite different. Still, groups that are often considered cults in the United States are the Unification Church, the Church Universal and Triumphant and the Hare Krishnas. The Rev. Sun Myung Moon, a Korean Presbyterian minister, founded the Unification Church in 1954. It spread to the United States in the 1960s, and Moon moved its headquarters to Tarrytown, N.Y. His followers, called "Moonies," believe him to be the new Messiah. He has been accused of financial improprieties, and in 1982 was convicted of tax evasion. The Church Universal and Triumphant was founded by Elizabeth Clare Prophet, who is known as Guru Ma. Prophet claims that she receives "dictations" from Jesus and other spiritual beings directing her and her followers to prepare for the end of the world, which will come soon in the form of a nuclear holocaust. Her followers have built a substantial underground headquarters in Montana. They attempt to avert calamities by "decreeing," rapidly repeating rhythmic chants. The Hare Krishna movement began in the United States in 1965. It is a Hindu sect, properly known as the International Society for Krishna Consciousness. Its followers chant "Hare Krishna" (O Lord Krishna) as part of their devotion, and actively seek converts. The most notorious cult in recent history was the People's Temple, led by James Warren "Jim" Jones (1931–78). Jones founded the group in Indianapolis in the 1950s and moved to California in 1965. Jones preached social and racial equality, began programs to help the poor and was even named chairman of the San Francisco Housing Authority in 1976. He was also accused of exerting improper influence over members, extorting money from them, encouraging sexual promiscuity and directing beatings of members who failed to follow his commands. After his tactics were revealed in the press, he and hundreds of cult members fled to Guyana and established the community of Jonestown. In November 1978, California Congressman Leo Ryan visited Jonestown to investigate allegations that members were being held as virtual slaves. On Nov. 18, Ryan and four members of his entourage were murdered by Jones's forces as they attempted to leave Guyana. Jones then led nearly all of the residents of Jonestown, more than 900 people, in a mass suicide. Some were forced to drink cyanide-laced fruit drink, but most appeared to have done so willingly.

HINDUISM

Hinduism encompasses a vast variety of beliefs, practices and rituals. Its oldest written works, the Vedas, are about 3,000 years old, and the practice of Hinduism predates those writings. Its diversity of belief, which is in contrast to many Western religions, may also be a reason for its longevity and its widespread practice. In India alone, there are more than 300 million Hindus. Worldwide, the number is about 450 million. Most Hindus are polytheists, although individuals and groups may revere different gods in different ways. There are many deities, including Brahma (the creator), Shiva (the destroyer), Vishnu (the preserver, who is worshipped in several incarnations, one of which is Krishna), Lakshmi (goddess of prosperity), Hanuman (the monkey god), Skanda (god of war), and Ganesha (the elephant-headed god who brings good fortune). There are also many things that are sacred to Hindus, although the choices vary widely from individual to individual and group to group. They include the sun, moon, some trees, bovines, monkeys, peacocks, cobras, tigers, horses, rivers (especially the Ganges) and mountains. Astrology is widely practiced. Yoga is used to control the mind and sense organs, as an aid to meditation. A common thread in Hinduism is a belief in reincarnation, castes and karma. According to Hindu belief, a person is born into a certain caste (social class) based on his good or bad deeds (karma) in a past life. Through meditation and a righteous life, he may advance to another caste in his next life, or may even achieve god-like status and be freed from future incarnations. Traditionally, caste lines were strict and carried with them rigid social restrictions. This has been modified somewhat, but class differences are still felt. There are five main castes. In descending order of social worth, they are: Brahmans (priests and scholars), Kshatriyas or Rajanyas (temporal rulers), Vaishyas (merchants and artisans), Sudras (servants) and Panchamas (also called "untouchables" or "fifths"). There are many divisions within each caste, and classifications are subject to dispute. Although the untouchables were once shunned, India's constitution declared that "untouchability is abolished" in 1950.

ISLAM

The Islamic religious movement was initiated in Arabia by the prophet Mohammed between 610 and 632 A.D. It is estimated to have between 600 million and 900 million followers. Islam is the dominant religion in all Arab and non-Arab Middle East nations (except Israel) and has adherents in other parts of Asia, Africa, Europe and the United States. Muslims (sometimes spelled "Moslems") worship one god, Allah, who is revealed to them in their fundamental sacred text, the Koran. Muslims believe that they are linked to Jews and Christians as children of Abraham. They recognize Abraham as a "Muslim before Mohammed." They also recognize the Torah, the Psalms of David and the Gospel of Jesus. They see the Koran as the perfection of these earlier works, and Islam as the true faith. Muslims do not worship Mohammed, and many vehemently oppose the notion that he "founded" the religion, viewing him more as a messenger of Allah. Islam encompasses religious, ethical, social and cultural aspects. It provides guidelines and rules that apply to all aspects of life. The sharia (sacred laws that govern individuals and structure society) has four sources. In descending order of importance, they are: the Koran; tradition, which derives from the sunna (customs) of Moham-

med; qiyas, the application of past principles to new questions; and ijma, the consensus of believers. The basic duties of Muslims are known as the "five pillars" of Islam. They are: shahada (professing faith in Allah and in Mohammed as his messenger), salat (prayers performed five times a day while facing Mecca, Mohammed's birthplace), zakat (the giving of alms), sawm (fasting during the daylight hours in the month of Ramadan, the ninth month of the Muslim year), and hajj (making at least one pilgrimage to Mecca, if possible). Muslims assemble for congregate worship in mosques on Fridays and they participate in two large festivals each year: Id al-Fitr, which celebrates the end of the Ramadan fast, and Is al-Adha, a festival commemorating Abraham's willingness to sacrifice his son. There are two major branches of Islam: the Sunnites and the Shiites. The Sunnites, by far the majority, follow the traditional practices (sunna) of Mohammed and are the mainstream group. The Shiites, who split from the Sunnites after Mohammed's death due to disagreement about his rightful successor, have been further divided by disputes among themselves concerning subsequent successors. They are in the majority in Iran, but not in other Arab countries.

JUDAISM

Judaism, which developed among wandering Semitic tribes about 2000 B.C., now has about 18 million followers worldwide. Judaism was the first religion to teach belief in one god. It teaches that God provides for all people, but that he entered into a special covenant with the ancient Israelites, making them his "chosen people," those chosen to bring his message to the world. Judaism teaches that God promised the Israelites his care and protection, if they would follow his word. Judaism teaches that the Messiah is coming. The basic scripture of Judaism is the Hebrew Bible (the Old Testament, to Christians). The first five books (Torah or Pentateuch) are particularly important because they contain God's revelations to Moses at Sinai (including the Ten Commandments), which have become the basis for Jewish law. The laws of the Torah were later elaborated and clarified by elders in the Oral Torah, which survives in written form as the Mishnah and Talmud. Modern Judaism encompasses many viewpoints and varying degrees of adherence to ancient beliefs and rituals. There are three main communities: Orthodox, Reform and Conservative. Orthodox Jews view the rules of the Torah and the Oral Torah as the word of God, and therefore absolutely binding. Among these are dietary rules, which prohibit the eating of some foods, including pigs and shellfish, and the mixing of meat and dairy products. There are several groups among Orthodox Jews, who differ in some beliefs and ceremonies. They include the Hasidim, the Mitnaggedim, the Sephardim and the Ashkenazim. The Reform movement began in 1818, when a group of Jews in Hamburg, Germany, instituted a number of changes, including translating the Hebrew prayers into German. The movement emphasized the ethical content of the Torah over the specific rules. Despite vehement opposition, the movement grew. Eventually dietary restrictions were removed, confirmation for boys and girls replaced the traditional male Bar Mitzvah, and women were allowed to worship with men in synagogues. Conservative Judaism seeks a middle ground between the Orthodox and Reform movements. The Jewish sabbath is observed from sunset Friday to sunset Saturday, traditionally by worship, reflection and rest. The Sabbath observance traditionally begins and ends with ceremonies in the home. Men wear a fringed shawl (tallith) during prayer, and a head covering ("yarmulke" in Yiddish) is common. The Jewish religious calendar includes 12 lunar months, totaling 354 days. Six times in 19 years an additional month is added to adjust the calendar. The year starts with the High Holy Days, 10 days of reflection and penitence known as the Days of Awe and Reverence. The first day is Rosh Hashanah, the Jewish New Year. The 10 days end with Yom Kippur, the Day of Atonement. Yom Kippur is observed with a 24-hour fast, reflection and repentance for sins. The Torah also prescribes three joyous festivals: Passover, Shavuot and Sukkot. Passover, which originated as a thanksgiving ceremony at the beginning of the planting season, is celebrated for a week. It is marked with a seder (meal and worship service) in the home and with worship services. Shavuot is observed seven weeks later, at the time of the first harvest, and commemorates the giving of the Torah to Moses at Mount Sinai. Sukkot begins five days after Yom Kippur and is observed for a week. In traditional communities, meals are taken outside in a sukkah, a roofless shed decorated with the fruits of the harvest. Chanukah (also spelled "Hanukkah") and Purim are festive holidays that were added to the Jewish calendar after the Torah. Chanukah, an eight-day Festival of Lights, commemorates the rededication of the temple in Jerusalem in 165 B.C. According to legend, there was only enough oil to allow the Eternal Light in the temple to burn for one day. Through a miracle, it burned for eight. The holiday is marked by lighting a menorah (candelabrum). One candle is lit the first night, and a candle is added each night throughout the holiday. Because the holiday falls near the Christian celebration of Christmas, it has come to include gift-giving. Purim commemorates the rescue of the Persian Jews by Queen Esther.

CONTACTS AND REFERENCES:

Cult Awareness Network, 2421 W. Pratt Blvd., Suite 1173, Chicago, IL 60645, (312) 267-7777. Provides information packets on specific cults or on general cult issues, such as child abuse and deceptive recruitment. Compiles statistics. Experts and former cult members on staff will speak with reporters.

- Adventists:
  Advent Christian Church, P.O. Box 23152, Charlotte, NC 28227, (704) 545-6161.
- Anglican Communion:
  The Archbishop of Canterbury, Lambeth Palace, London, SE1 7JU, England.
- Armenian Apostolic Church:
  Armenian Apostolic Church of America, 138 East 39th St., New York, NY 10016, (212) 689-7810.
- Bahá'í:
  National Spiritual Assembly, 1233 Central, Evanston, IL 30201, (708) 869-9039.
- Baptist churches:
  Baptist World Alliance International Office, 6733 Curran St., McLean, VA 22101, (703) 790-8980.
  Southern Baptist Convention, 901 Commerce St., Suite 750, Nashville, TN 37203, (615) 228-6292.
  National Baptist Convention of America, 1327 Pierre Ave., Shreveport, LA 71103, (318) 221-3701.
  American Baptist Churches in the U.S.A., P.O. Box 851, Valley Forge, PA 19482-0851, (215) 768-2000.
  Baptist Bible Fellowship International, P.O. Box 191, Springfield, MO 65801, (417) 862-5001.
- Buddhists:
  Buddhist Churches of America, 1710 Octavia St., San Francisco, CA 94109, (415) 776-5600.
- Christian churches:
  National Council of Churches of Christ in the U.S.A., 475 Riverside Dr., New York, N.Y. 10115, (212) 870-2200.
- Christian Science:
  The First Church of Christ, Scientist, 175 Huntington Ave., Boston, MA 02115, (617) 450-2000.
- Church Universal and Triumphant:
  Church Universal and Triumphant, Box A, Corwin Springs, MT 59021, (406) 848-7441.
- Disciples of Christ:
  Christian Church, 222 S. Downey Ave., P.O. Box 1986, Indianapolis, IN 46206, (317) 353-1491.
- Eastern Orthodox Church:
  The Orthodox Church in America, P.O. Box 675, Syosset, NY 11791, (516) 922-0550.
  Greek Orthodox Archdiocese of North and South America, 8–10 East 79th St., New York, NY 10021, (212) 570-3500.

- Episcopal Church:
  Episcopal Church, 815 Second Ave., New York, NY 10017, (212) 867-8400; 1-800-334-7626.
- Hare Krishnas:
  International Society of Krishna Consciousness, 1030 Grand Ave., San Diego, CA 92109, (619) 272-8334.
- Islam:
  The Islamic Center of Washington, 2552 Massachusetts Ave. NW, Washington, D.C. 20008, (202) 332-8343.
- Jehovah's Witnesses:
  Jehovah's Witnesses, 124 Columbia Heights, Brooklyn, NY 11201; (718) 625-3600.
- Judaism:
  Union of Orthodox Jewish Congregations of America, 45 West 36th St., New York, NY 10018, (212) 563-4000.
  Union of American Hebrew Congregations [Reform], 838 Fifth Ave., New York, NY 10021, (212) 249-0100.
  United Synagogue of America [Conservative], 155 Fifth Ave., New York, NY 10010, (212) 533-7800.
- Lutheran churches:
  The American Association of Lutheran Churches, 10800 Lyndale Ave. S., Suite 124, Minneapolis, MN 55420, (612) 884-7784.
  Evangelical Lutheran Church in America, 8765 W. Higgins Rd., Chicago, IL 60631, (312) 380-2700.
  Lutheran Church–Missouri Synod International Center, 1333 S. Kirkwood Rd., St. Louis, MO 63122, (314) 965-9000.
- Mennonite Church:
  Mennonite Church, 421 S. Second St., Suite 600, Elkhart, IN 46516, (219) 294-7131.
- Methodist churches:
  The United Methodist Church, Council of Bishops, 1100 West 42d St., Indianapolis, IN 46208, (317) 924-1321.

  African Methodist Episcopal Church, 208 Auburn Ave. NE, Atlanta, GA 30303, (404) 524-8279.
  African Methodist Episcopal Zion Church, 3753 Springhill Ave., Mobile, AL 36608.
  Christian Methodist Episcopal Church, 2805 Shoreland Dr., Atlanta, GA 30331, (404) 752-7800.
- Mormons:
  Church of Jesus Christ of Latter-Day Saints, 50 East North Temple St., Salt Lake City, UT 84150, (801) 240-1000.
- Old Order Amish Church:
  Old Order Amish Church, Der Neue Amerikanische Calendar, c/o Raber's Book Store, 2467 CR 600, Baltic, OH 43804.
- Presbyterian Church:
  Presbyterian Church, 100 Witherspoon St., Louisville, KY 40202, (502) 569-5360.
- Quakers:
  Religious Society of Friends [Conservative], 710 E. Lake Dr., Greensboro, NC 27401.
  Religious Society of Friends [Unaffiliated Meetings], Alaska Yearly Meeting, P.O. Box 687, Kotzebue, AK 99752.
- Roman Catholic Church:
  National Conference of Catholic Bishops [Roman Catholic Church], 3211 Fourth St. NE, Washington, D.C. 20017, (202) 541-3000.
- Salvation Army:
  Salvation Army, 799 Bloomfield Ave., Verona, N.J. 07044, (201) 857-8822.
- Unification Church:
  Unification Church of America, 481 Eighth Ave., New York, NY 10001, (212) 947-1115.
- Unitarian-Universalist Association:
  Unitarian-Universalist Association, 25 Beacon St., Boston, MA 02108, (617) 742-2100.
- United Church of Christ:
  United Church of Christ, 700 Prospect Ave. E., Cleveland, OH 44115, (216) 736-2100.

U.S. RELIGIOUS AFFILIATIONS

MEMBERSHIP OF U.S. RELIGIOUS GROUPS*

Group	Year Reported	Membership
African Methodist Episcopal Church	1981	2,210,000
African Methodist Episcopal Zion Church	1991	1,200,000
American Baptist Association	1986	250,000
American Baptist Churches in the U.S.A.	1990	1,535,971
Antiochian Orthodox Christian Archdiocese of North America	1989	350,000
Apostolic Catholic Assyrian Church of the East, N. A. Diocese	1989	120,000
Armenian Apostolic Church of America	1991	150,000
Armenian Church of America, Diocese of	1979	450,000
Assemblies of God	1990	2,181,502
Baptist Bible Fellowship, International	1986	1,405,900
Baptist General Conference	1991	134,717
Baptist Missionary Association of America	1990	229,166
Christian and Missionary Alliance	1990	279,207
Christian Brethren (a.k.a. Plymouth Brethren)	1984	98,000
Christian Church (Disciples of Christ)	1990	1,039,692
Christian Churches and Churches of Christ	1988	1,070,616
Christian Congregation	1990	109,919
Christian Methodist Episcopal Church	1983	718,922
Christian Reformed Church in North America	1990	226,163
Church of God	1978	75,890
Church of God (Anderson, Ind.)	1990	205,884
Church of God (Cleveland, Tenn.)	1990	620,393
Church of God in Christ	1991	5,499,875
Church of God in Christ, International	1982	200,000
Church of God of Prophecy	1991	72,904
Church of the Lord Jesus Christ of Latter-Day Saints	1990	4,267,000
Church of the Brethren	1990	148,253
Church of the Nazarene	1991	573,834
Churches of Christ	1990	1,683,346
Community Churches, International Council of	1991	250,000

Group	Year Reported	Membership
Congregational Christian Churches, National Association of	1991	90,000
Conservative Baptist Association of America	1989	210,000
Coptic Orthodox Church	1990	165,000
Cumberland Presbyterian Church	1990	98,891
Episcopal Church	1990	2,446,050
Evangelical Covenant Church	1990	89,735
Evangelical Free Church of America	1991	192,352
Evangelical Lutheran Church of America	1990	5,240,739
Evangelical Presbyterian Church	1991	52,645
Free Methodist Church of North America	1990	74,313
Free Will Baptists, National Association of	1990	197,206
Friends United Meeting	1990	54,945
Full Gospel Fellowship of Churches and Ministers, International	1985	65,000
General Association of Regular Baptist Churches	1990	168,068
General Baptists (General Association of)	1990	74,156
Greek Orthodox Archdiocese of North and South America	1977	1,950,000
Independent Fundamental Churches of America	1991	78,174
International Church of the Foursquare Gospel	1990	199,385
Jehovah's Witnesses	1991	858,367
Jews[1]	1990	5,981,000
Liberty Baptist Fellowship	1990	180,000
Lutheran Church—Missouri Synod	1990	2,602,849
Mennonite Church	1990	92,517
National Baptist Convention of America	1956	2,668,799
National Baptist Convention, U.S.A., Inc.	1991	7,800,000
National Primitive Baptist Convention, Inc.	1975	250,000
North American Old Roman Catholic Church	1986	62,611
Old Order Amish Church	1989	70,650
Orthodox Church in America	1978	1,000,000
Pentecostal Church of God, Inc.	1990	91,300
Pentecostal Holiness Church, International	1989	119,073

Group	Year Reported	Membership	Group	Year Reported	Membership
Polish National Catholic Church of America	1960	282,411	Seventh-day Adventist Church	1990	717,446
			Southern Baptist Convention	1990	15,038,409
Presbyterian Church in America	1990	223,935	Triumph the Church and Kingdom of God in Christ (International)	1972	54,307
Presbyterian Church (U.S.A.)	1990	3,788,009			
Primitive Baptists	1960	72,000			
Progressive National Baptist Convention, Inc.	1991	2,500,000	Ukrainian Orthodox Church in the U.S.A.	1966	87,745
Reformed Church in America	1990	326,850	Unitarian Universalist Association	1991	141,315
Reorganized Church of Jesus Christ of Latter-Day Saints	1990	189,524	United Church of Christ	1990	1,599,212
Roman Catholic Church	1990	58,568,015	United Methodist Church	1989	8,904,824
Romanian Orthodox Episcopate of America	1990	65,000	United Pentecostal Church, International	1991	500,000
Russian Orthodox Church Outside of Russia	1955	55,000	Wesleyan Church	1990	110,561
			Wisconsin Evangelical Synod	1990	420,039
Salvation Army	1990	445,991			
Serbian Eastern Orthodox Church in the U.S.A. and Canada	1986	67,000			

* Represents information reported by religious bodies with memberships of 50,000 or more. Not all groups define membership in the same way.

[1] This number represents Jews as a religious, ethnic and social community, whether or not they belong to a synagogue or temple. An estimated 3.75 million Jews are members of synagogues and temples of the Orthodox, Conservative and Reformed branches.

Source: Yearbook of American and Canadian Churches 1992, Kenneth Bedell and Alice M. Jones, ed., Abingdon Press, Nashville, 1992.

RELIGIOUS ROGUES

(Unless otherwise noted, dates in parentheses indicate the year in which the scandal was brought to public attention.)

The Rev. Edward W. Hall and Eleanor Mills (1922)

The married pastor of Hall's Episcopal Church in New Brunswick, N.J., and the wife of the church's sexton were found brutally murdered in DeRussey's Lane, one of the town's secluded trysting spots. No suspects were arrested, but in 1926, the *New York Daily Mirror* published scandalous stories that prompted charges against the pastor's widow, Mrs. Frances Hall; her two brothers, Henry and William Stevens; and their cousin, Henry Carpender. The sensational trial was covered by reporters from throughout the country. The memory of a supposed eyewitness to the murders was discredited, and Mrs. Hall and the Stevens brothers were found not guilty. Charges against Carpender were dropped. The case was never solved.

The Rev. Charles Edward Coughlin (1926–42)

America's first "radio" priest was the pastor of the Shrine of the Little Flower in Royal Oak, Mich. Father Coughlin stirred thousands of listeners with impassioned sermons against the spread of socialism and communism, but gradually turned into an unbridled and leading defender of fascism, a vicious anti-Semite and a propagandist for Nazism. He was finally silenced in May of 1942 by the FBI, which invoked provisions of the Espionage Act of 1917.

Claudius Vermilye, Jr. (1977)

The former Episcopal minister and founder of Boys' Farm Inc., a shelter for troubled youngsters near Winchester, Tenn., was found guilty of state charges of illicit homosexual activities and distribution of pornographic materials. Homosexual orgies at Boys' Farm were filmed, and copies sold for "donations" to the farm.

Daniel and Philip Berrigan (1965–1981)

The Berrigan brothers, both Roman Catholic priests, rose to public prominence during the movement against the Vietnam War. The Rev. Daniel Berrigan was among the first popular figures to protest U.S. escalation of the war in 1965. In 1967, he was arrested in an antiwar demonstration at the Pentagon. The Rev. Philip Berrigan, meanwhile, was arrested with three other persons for pouring animal blood on draft records at the Customs House in Baltimore, Md. ("The Baltimore Four"). In 1968, the two brothers were sent to prison after burning draft records in Catonsville, Md., with seven other protesters ("The Catonsville Nine"). While in prison in 1971, Philip Berrigan was indicted and tried with six others for conspiring to kidnap Presidential foreign policy adviser Henry A. Kissinger and destroy the heating systems in federal buildings ("The Harrisburg Seven"). The jury deadlocked in favor of acquittal, and the government later dropped all charges. In 1980, the Berrigans and six others broke into a General Electric Company missile guidance systems plant near Philadelphia, damaged missile nose cones and destroyed records ("The Plowshares Eight"). The brothers were sentenced to prison again in 1981.

The Rev. Billy James Hargis (1974)

The popular evangelist president of American Christian College and leader of the Church of the Christian Crusade, a zealous radio and television campaign against the evils of modern society and the encroachment of communism, was discredited by revelations that he engaged in extramarital bisexual affairs. He resigned the college presidency in October 1974, but later tried to recant his admission of impropriety, saying he was victimized by a "liberal plot."

Rabbi Bernard Bergman (1976)

Rabbi Bernard Bergman of New York, a wealthy and well-known nursing home owner, was sent to prison after pleading guilty to fraud and theft charges arising from misuse of public funds intended for the care of indigent patients.

The Rev. Sun Myung Moon (1982)

The Rev. Sun Myung Moon, leader and founder of the Unification Church (formally the Holy Spirit Association for the Unification of World Christianity), was fined and, after long unsuccessful court appeals, imprisoned for 18 months for income tax evasion and conspiracy to obstruct justice.

The Rev. Gilbert Gauthe, Jr. (1985)

The Rev. Gilbert Gauthe, Jr., a Roman Catholic priest in Vermilion Parish, Louisiana, was publicly charged with molesting young boys, most of them altar boys with whom he was associated. Publicity surrounding Gauthe's case focused attention on the question of church liability for the actions of its priests. Similar cases were pressed in Idaho, Rhode Island and Wisconsin. Gauthe was defrocked in 1983 and sentenced to 20 years in prison.

The Rev. Jim Bakker (1987)

The Rev. Jim Bakker, a nationally popular Pentecostal evangelist, admitted to adultery with a former

New York church secretary named Jessica Hahn, to whom he then paid hush money. Bakker's admission was made in the face of an impending news story about the dalliance. He resigned as head of the PTL (Praise the Lord) Network, which spread his ministry to more than 13 million cable television viewers. Word of Bakker's indiscretion was widely rumored to have been leaked by evangelist Jimmy Swaggart, a rival for control of Bakker's multimillion-dollar empire. Bakker later was sentenced to prison for fraud and conspiracy in connection with his handling of PTL funds.

The Rev. Jimmy Swaggart (1988)

On Feb. 21, 1988, the Rev. Jimmy Swaggart, the popular Pentecostal evangelist with the Assemblies of God, publicly confessed to "moral failure" and asked his huge congregation to forgive him. The confession came three days after a scandal had erupted. Rival television evangelist Marvin Gorman had supplied church officials with photos of Swaggart in the company of a prostitute, later identified as Debra Murphree. Gorman was seeking revenge for Swaggart's having earlier exposed him for similar infidelities. Gorman, who was defrocked by the Assemblies of God, sued Swaggart for defamation and later won. In March 1988, the church hierarchy banned Swaggart from the pulpit for a year, but he successfully defied the order, and instead returned to his television ministry May 22, 1988. Swaggart's reign as a popular evangelist was about over, however, for he later was caught with another prostitute, this time by police.

James R. Porter (1992)

Frank Fitzpatrick, a private investigator from Cranston, R.I., and eight other people, publicly charged in May 1992 that in childhood, years earlier, they had been sexually molested by a former Roman Catholic priest. They identified the man as James R. Porter, who served as a priest in four Southeastern Massachusetts parishes from 1960 until 1974, when he left the priesthood; he later married. Porter's accusers charged that his superiors, officials of the Diocese of Fall River, Mass., had, in effect, sanctioned the priest's behavior by transferring him to a different parish whenever problems surfaced. In the months that followed the allegations, 55 other people joined the accusers, saying they, too, had been molested by Porter. On Dec. 3, 1992, the Diocese of Fall River reached an out-of-court settlement with the 68 victims, reportedly for more than $5 million. On Dec. 11, 1992, a Minneapolis, Minn., jury found Porter guilty of six counts of sexually molesting his children's teenage babysitter in 1987. He was freed on bail to await sentencing.

PART THIRTEEN

GETTING AROUND

TRAVEL TIPS

PASSPORTS, VISAS, IMMUNIZATIONS

Passports: Passports are valid for 10 years when issued to people 18 and older. They are valid for five years for those under 18. Passports are issued through many large post offices, some state and federal courthouses and 13 U.S. passport agencies (see below). Processing takes two to four weeks. Turnaround is likely to be quickest between August and December, when volume of requests is lowest. Passports may be renewed at any time.

The fee is $55 for people 18 and older, $30 for those under 18. There is an additional $10 processing charge the first time a passport is sought, or if the applicant must appear in person. An applicant must appear in person if he is applying for the first time, if he is renewing a passport that is more than 12 years old, if he is replacing a lost or stolen passport or if he was under 16 years old when he received his previous passport.

To secure a passport, the following must be provided:

1 Proof of citizenship, such as a certified birth certificate, expired passport or certificate of naturalization.
2 Two identical 2-inch-by-2-inch identification photos taken within the previous six months. They may be in color or black and white.
3 Proof of identity that contains a physical description of the applicant and his or her signature. A driver's license or military identification card may be used.
4 The fee, in a check or money order payable to Passport Services.
5 A completed application.

If a passport is needed immediately due to an emergency, it can be sought in person at one of the 13 U.S. passport agencies in major cities. The applicant should plan to arrive early in the day with all of the necessary application materials (see above), plus proof of departure date (such as an airline ticket) and proof of emergency (such as a telegram).

The locations of the U.S. Passport Agencies are:

Boston: John F. Kennedy Building, Government Center, Rm. E123, Boston, MA 02203.
Chicago: Kluczynski Office Building, 230 S. Dearborn St., Rm. 380, Chicago, IL 60604.
Honolulu: New Federal Building, 300 Ala Moana Blvd., P.O. Box 50185, Honolulu, HI 96850.
Houston: One Allen Center, 500 Dallas St., Houston, TX 77002.
Los Angeles: Federal Building, 11000 Wilshire Blvd., Los Angeles, CA 92061.
Miami: Federal Office Building, 51 Southwest 1st Ave., Miami, FL 33130.
New Orleans: Postal Services Bldg., 701 Loyal Ave., T-12005, New Orleans, LA 70113.
New York: Rockefeller Center, International Bldg., 630 Fifth Ave., New York, NY 10020.
Philadelphia: Federal Building, 600 Arch St., Rm. 4426, Philadelphia, PA 19106.
San Francisco: 525 Market St., San Francisco, CA 94105.
Seattle: Federal Building, 915 2d Ave., Seattle, WA 98174.
Stamford, CT: One Landmark Square, Broad and Atlantic streets, Stamford, CT 06901.
Washington, D.C.: 1425 K St. NW, Washington, D.C. 20524.

The Passport Services Office of the Department of State operates a telephone information line in Washington, D.C., that provides detailed passport information and routes callers to other information pertinent to traveling abroad. Topics include: obtaining passports, reporting their loss or theft, obtaining a report of birth or death for a U.S. citizen abroad and travel advisories. The telephone number is (202) 647-0518. It is available 24 hours a day.

The Citizens Emergency Center of the Department of State operates a telephone information line in Washington, D.C., that provides travel advisories about specific countries, as well as information on how to obtain help concerning the death, arrest or welfare of an American abroad, and information on ordering publications concerning foreign travel. The telephone number is (202) 647-5225. It is available 24 hours a day.

U.S. citizens are not required to carry a passport to enter Canada, Mexico or many countries in South or Central America. Because all countries do require positive proof of citizenship, however, obtaining a passport may simplify travel in many countries. Other forms of identification that are often acceptable are: birth certificate, certificate of naturalization, certificate of citizenship, valid driver's license or government identification card. Because travel regulations are subject to change, it is best to check with a knowledgeable travel agent or with the foreign country's embassy or consulate before making final plans.

Visas: A visa is an authorization issued by a foreign government that allows a traveler to enter the country. The visa is added to the U.S. passport and must be shown on arrival. Some countries allow travelers to obtain visas immediately after arrival, but this often causes difficulty and delays. Visas always should be obtained before traveling to the foreign country. Because visa requirements can change frequently, it is best to check with a knowledgeable travel agent or with the foreign country's embassy or consulate before making final plans. [*See* chapter entitled International Government on page 3] There are also agencies that will obtain visas and passports for travelers for a fee. In some cases, they offer same-day service. The fees vary depending on the complexity of the documents and the speed required. One such firm, Visa Advisors, provides a computer database of visa and passport information available through the Compuserve network. [*See* section entitled Databases on page 304] Travel agents often can recommend reputable visa agencies. Visa Advisors is located at 1930 18th St. NW, Washington, D.C. 20009 (202) 797-7976, fax (202) 667-6708.

Many countries have passport and visa requirements that vary depending on the length and the nature of the visit. Business travelers often are required to obtain documentation different from that required of vacationers. Travelers staying for long periods of time (often more than 30, 60 or 90 days) may also need special permission. Some countries waive their visa requirement for travelers who are merely passing through an airport en route to another country. Others require full documentation.

Other Requirements: Some countries require only positive proof of citizenship. Others demand passports and visas and have a host of other requirements. Some require visitors to prove that they have enough money to pay for their stay, that they have a ticket for an ongoing flight, that they have met certain health requirements, or that they have not visited an unfriendly nation in the recent past. In lieu of visas, some countries issue visitor's passes through their airlines.

Because requirements can be quite complex, can change rapidly and can differ considerably from country to country, it is important to know specific current regulations before leaving the United States. A knowledgeable travel agent, a commercial visa agency or the foreign country's embassy or consulate can provide up-to-date information. [*See* chapter entitled International Government on page 3]

Because the United States shares borders with Mexico and Canada, and enjoys stable relationships with them, travel requirements for those countries are relatively simple and subject to little change.

U.S. citizens traveling to Canada must show proof of nationality. Acceptable proof includes a birth certificate with valid driver's license, voter's registra-

U.S. TIME ZONES

Eastern (Noon)	Central (11 A.M.)	Mountain (10 A.M.)	Pacific (9 A.M.)	Alaskan (8 A.M.)	Aleut (7 A.M.)
Connecticut	Alabama	Arizona	California	Alaska	Hawaii
Delaware	Arkansas	Colorado	Idaho*		
District of	Florida*	Idaho*	Nevada		
Columbia	Illinois	Kansas*	Oregon*		
Florida*	Indiana*	Montana	Washington		
Georgia	Iowa	Nebraska*			
Indiana*	Kansas*	New Mexico			
Kentucky*	Kentucky*	North Dakota*			
Maine	Louisiana	Oregon*			
Maryland	Minnesota	South Dakota*			
Massachusetts	Mississippi	Texas*			
Michigan	Missouri	Utah			
New Hampshire	Nebraska*	Wyoming			
New Jersey	North Dakota*				
New York	Oklahoma				
North Carolina	South Dakota*				
Ohio	Tennessee*				
Pennsylvania	Texas*				
Rhode Island	Wisconsin				
South Carolina					
Tennessee*					
Vermont					
Virginia					
West Virginia					

An asterisk (*) denotes states with more than one time zone.

tion card with valid driver's license, naturalization certificate or passport. A visa is required for stays of three months or longer. (A passport is required if citizens are not traveling directly from the United States.)

For travel to Mexico, U.S. citizens must show proof of nationality and a tourist card (which is available from airlines, embassies, consulates, Mexican tourist offices and at border crossings). Acceptable proofs of nationality include a passport, birth certificate, voter's registration card with current photo identification, naturalization certificate, baptismal certificate with place of birth, or military identification. Yellow fever vaccination is required if traveling from an infected area. Malaria pills are recommended in some areas.

Immunizations: Countries may require international certificates of vaccination against yellow fever and cholera before permitting entry. Smallpox vaccination is not required. Visitors to some countries may be advised to take malaria pills, to receive certain immunizations or to take other precautions to prevent sickness. Health information is subject to rapid change. It should be checked before each trip when visiting countries with poor sanitation or health care. Information is available from embassies and consulates [See chapter entitled International Government on page 3], from travel agents, from state health departments, from physicians and from the local office of the U.S. Public Health Service (listed in the government section of telephone books under the Department of Health and Human Services). The following publication of the Department of Health and Human Services can also be helpful: *Health Information for International Travel*, Superintendent of Documents, U.S. Government Printing Office, Washington, D.C. 20402, $4.75.

WORLD TIME ZONES

(Using Eastern Standard Time as a reference)

Country	Time difference in hours
Afghanistan	+9.5
Algeria	+6
Angola	+6
Argentina	+2
Australia	+15
Austria	+6
Bahrain	+8
Bangladesh	+11
Belgium	+6
Belize	−1
Bolivia	+1
Botswana	+7
Brazil*	+2

Country	Time difference in hours
Brunei	+13
Bulgaria	+7
Burkina Faso	+5
Burundi	+7
Cameroon	+6
Canada	Similar to U.S.
Central African Republic	+6
Chad	+6
Chile	+1
China (PRC)	+13
Colombia	0
Commonwealth of Independent States (CIS)*	+8
Congo	+6
Costa Rica	−1
Cuba	0
Cyprus	+7
Czechoslovakia	+6
Denmark	+6
Ecuador	0
Egypt	+7
El Salvador	−1
Ethiopia	+8
Fiji	+17
Finland	+7
France	+6
Gabon	+6
Gambia	+5
Germany	+6
Ghana	+5
Greece	+7
Guadeloupe	+1
Guam	+15
Guatemala	−1
Guinea	+5
Guyana	+2
Haiti	0
Honduras	−1
Hong Kong	+13
Hungary	+6
Iceland	+5
India	+10.5
Indonesia*	+12
Iran	+8.5
Iraq	+8
Ireland	+5
Israel	+7
Italy	+6
Ivory Coast	+5
Japan	+14
Jordan	+7
Kenya	+8
Kiribati	+17
Korea, South	+14
Kuwait	+8
Lebanon	+7
Lesotho	+7
Liberia	+5
Libya	+7
Luxembourg	+6
Madagascar	+8
Malawi	+7
Malaysia*	+13
Mali	+5

Country	Time difference in hours
Marshall Islands	+17
Mauritania	+5
Mauritius	+9
Mexico*	+1
Micronesia	+16
Mongolia	+13
Morocco	+5
Mozambique	+7
Myanmar	+11 .5
Namibia	+7
Nepal	+10.5
Netherlands	+6
Netherlands Antilles	+1
New Zealand	+17
Nicaragua	−1
Niger	+6
Nigeria	+6
North Mariana Islands	+15
Norway	+6
Oman	+9
Pakistan	+10
Panama	0
Papua New Guinea	+15
Paraguay	+2
Peru	0
Philippines	+13
Poland	+6
Portugal	+5
Qatar	+8
Romania	+7
Saudi Arabia	+8
Senegal	+5
Sierra Leone	+5
Singapore	+13
Somalia	+8
South Africa	+7
Spain	+6
Sri Lanka	+10.5

Country	Time difference in hours
Sudan	+7
Sweden	+6
Switzerland	+6
Syria	+7
Taiwan	+13
Tanzania	+8
Thailand	+12
Togo	+5
Tunisia	+6
Turkey	+7
Uganda	+8
United Arab Emirates	+9
United Kingdom	+5
Uruguay	+2
Vatican City	+6
Venezuela	+1
Yemen	+8
Yugoslavia	+6
Zaire	+6
Zambia	+7
Zimbabwe	+7

* Countries marked with an asterisk encompass more than one time zone. The time differences indicated are for the following major cities: in Brazil, Rio de Janeiro; Indonesia, Jakarta; Malaysia, Kuala Lumpur; Mexico, Mexico City; Commonwealth of Independent States, Moscow.

International Date Line

The international date line approximately follows the 180th meridian, zigzagging to accommodate political boundaries. Alaska (including the Aleutian Islands), Hawaii and American Samoa are on the eastern side of the line. Asia and Australia are to the west. The date advances one day when crossing from east to west. The date is set back one day when crossing from west to east.

AIRLINES

SELECTED DOMESTIC AND INTERNATIONAL AIRLINES OPERATING IN THE U.S.

The following telephone numbers are for passenger information and flight reservations:

Aer Lingus	1-800-223-6537
Aerolineas Argentinas	1-800-333-0276
Aeromexico	1-800-237-6639
Aero Peru	1-800-777-7717
Air Canada	1-800-776-3000
Air France	1-800-237-2747
Air India	1-800-223-7776
Air Jamaica	1-800-523-5585
Air New Zealand	1-800-262-1234
Air Sedona	1-800-535-4448
Air Wisconsin Inc.	1-800-424-9050
Aloha Airlines	1-800-367-5250
Alaska Airlines	1-800-426-0333
Alia Royal Jordanian Airlines	1-800-223-0470
Alitalia	1-800-223-5730
All Nippon Air	1-800-235-9262
ALM Antillean Airlines	1-800-327-7230
American Airlines	1-800-433-7300
America West Airlines	1-800-247-5692
Australian Airlines	1-800-922-5122
Austrian Airlines	1-800-843-0002
Avensa Airlines	1-800-428-3672
Bahamas Air	1-800-222-4262
British Airways	1-800-247-9297
Canadian Airlines	1-800-426-7000
Cathay Pacific Airways	1-800-233-2742
Cayman Airways	1-800-422-9626
Continental Airlines	1-800-231-0856
Corporate Airlines	1-800-272-6262
Czechoslovak Airlines	1-800-223-2365
Delta Airlines	1-800-221-1212
Ecuatoriana Airlines	1-800-327-7478
Egyptair	1-800-334-6787
El Al Israel Airlines	1-800-223-6700
Garuda Indonesia Airways	1-800-342-7832
Guyana Airways	1-800-242-4210
Haiti Trans Air	1-800-432-4248
Hawaiian Airlines	1-800-367-5320
Horizon Air Industries	1-800-547-9308
Iberia Air Lines of Spain	1-800-432-1231
Icelandair	1-800-223-5500
Japan Airlines	1-800-525-3663
Kenya Airlines	1-800-343-2506
KLM Royal Dutch Airlines	1-800-367-6893, 1-800-882-4452
Korean Air	1-800-438-5000
LACSA Airline of Costa Rica	1-800-225-2272
Las Vegas Airlines	1-800-634-6851
Lufthansa German Airline	1-800-645-3880
Malaysian Airline System	1-800-421-8641
Malev Hungarian Airlines	1-800-262-5380, 1-800-223-6884
Mexicana Airlines	1-800-531-7921
Midwest Express	1-800-452-2022
Mohawk Airlines	1-800-252-2144
Northwest Airlines	1-800-225-2525
Olympic Airways	1-800-223-1226
Pacific Coast Airline	1-800-426-5400
Pakistan International Airlines	1-800-221-2552
PanAm Express	1-800-245-7678
Philippine Airlines	1-800-435-9725
Polish Airlines LOT	1-800-223-0593
Qantas Airways	1-800-227-4500
Royal Air Maroc	1-800-344-6726
Royal Jordanian Airline	1-800-223-0470
Royal Nepal Airline	1-800-922-7622
Scandinavian Airlines	1-800-221-2350
Singapore Airlines	1-800-742-3333
Skywest Airlines	1-800-453-9417
South African Airways	1-800-722-9675
Southwest Airlines	1-800-531-5601
Swissair	1-800-522-6906, 1-800-221-4750
TACA International Airlines	1-800-535-8780
Thai Airways International	1-800-426-5204
Trans African Airline	1-800-527-3807
Transbrasil Airlines	1-800-872-3153
Trans World Airlines	1-800-221-2000
United Airlines	1-800-241-6522
USAir	1-800-428-4322
Varig Brazilian Airlines	1-800-468-2744
WestAir Airlines	(209) 294-6915
Yemen Airways	1-800-257-1133
Zambia Airways	1-800-223-1136

TOP 20 U.S. AIRPORTS

Mailing addresses and telephone numbers are for airport administration. For information concerning flights, contact individual airlines. Number in parentheses indicates relative ranking by annual passenger volume.

Dallas–Fort Worth International Airport (2)
P.O. Drawer DFW
DFW Airport, TX 75261
(214) 574-8888

Detroit Metropolitan Wayne County Airport (12)
L.C. Smith Terminal
Mezzanine Level
Detroit, MI 48242
(313) 942-3550

Greater Pittsburgh International Airport (18)
Pittsburgh, PA 15231
(412) 472-3500

Hartsfield Atlanta International Airport (4)
Aviation Commissions Office
Atlanta, GA 30320
(404) 530-6600

Honolulu International Airport (10)
Department of Transportation
Visitor Information Program
Honolulu, HI 96819
(808) 836-6413

Houston Intercontinental Airport (20)
Aviation Department
P.O. Box 60106
Houston, TX 77205
(713) 230-3000

J.F. Kennedy International Airport (5)
Building 141
Jamaica, Queens, NY 41130
(718) 656-4520

La Guardia Airport (9)
Flushing, NY 11371
(718) 476-5000

Lambert–St. Louis International Airport (15)
P.O. Box 10212
St. Louis, MO 63145
(314) 426-8000

Logan International Airport (11)
Aviation Director
East Boston, MA 02128
(617) 561-1818

Los Angeles International Airport (3)
1 World Way
Los Angeles, CA 90045
(310) 646-5252

McCarran International Airport (19)
5757 Wayne Newton Blvd.
Las Vegas, NV 89119
(702) 739-5211

Miami International Airport (8)
P.O. Box 592075
Miami, FL 33159
(305) 876-7515

Minneapolis–St. Paul International Airport (16)
4300 Glumack Drive
St. Paul, MN 55111-3010
(612) 726-5555

Newark International Airport (13)
Newark, NJ 07114
(201) 961-6000

O'Hare International Airport (1)
P.O. Box 66142
Chicago, IL, 60666
(312) 686-2200

Orlando International Airport (17)
1 Airport Blvd.
Orlando, FL 32827-4399
(407) 825-2001

San Francisco International Airport (6)
San Francisco, CA 94128
(415) 761-0800

Sky Harbor International Airport (14)
City of Phoenix, Aviation Department
3400 East Sky Harbor Blvd.
Phoenix, AZ 85034
(602) 273-3300

Stapleton International Airport (7)
8100 East 32nd Ave.
Denver, CO 80207
(303) 398-3844

AIR MILES FROM NEW YORK

AIR MILES FROM NEW YORK CITY TO MAJOR FOREIGN CITIES

Acapulco	2,260
Amsterdam	3,639
Antigua	1,783
Aruba	1,963
Athens	4,927
Barbados	2,100
Bermuda	771
Bogotá	2,487
Brussels	3,662
Buenos Aires	5,302
Caracas	2,123
Copenhagen	3,849
Curaçao	1,993
Frankfurt	3,851
Geneva	3,859
Glasgow	3,211
Hamburg	3,806
Kingston	1,583
Lima	3,651
Lisbon	3,366
London	3,456
Madrid	3,588
Manchester	3,336
Mexico City	2,086
Milan	4,004
Nassau	1,101
Oslo	3,671
Paris	3,628
Reykjavik	2,600
Rio de Janeiro	4,816
Rome	4,280
St. Croix	1,680
San Juan	1,609
Santo Domingo	1,560
Tel Aviv	5,672
Zurich	3,926

AIR MILES FROM NEW YORK CITY TO OTHER MAJOR U.S. CITIES

Albuquerque	1,810
Atlanta	747
Baltimore	170
Boston	188
Chicago	711
Denver	1,628
Detroit	483
Kansas City, Mo.	1,097
Los Angeles	2,446
Memphis	953
Miami	1,095
Nashville	758
New Orleans	1,173
Omaha	1,144
Philadelphia	83
Phoenix	2,142
Portland	2,455
St. Louis	873
Salt Lake City	1,972
San Francisco	2,568
Seattle	2,419
Washington, D.C.	204

FOREIGN CURRENCIES

Country	Currency
Afghanistan	afghani
Albania	lek
Algeria	dinar
Andorra	French franc, Spanish peseta
Antigua	E. Caribbean dollar
Argentina	austral
Australia	dollar
Austria	schilling
Bahamas	dollar
Bahrain	dinar
Bangladesh	taka
Barbados	dollar
Belau	dollar
Belgium	franc
Belize	dollar
Benin	franc (CFA*)
Bhutan	ngultrum
Bolivia	peso
Bophuthatswana	S. African rand
Botswana	pula
Brazil	cruzado
Brunei	dollar
Bulgaria	lev
Burkina Faso	franc (CFA*)
Burundi	franc
Cambodia	riel
Cameroon	franc (CFA*)
Canada	dollar
Cape Verde	escudo
Central Africa	franc (CFA*)
Chad	franc (CFA*)
Chile	peso
China	yuan
Ciske	S. African rand
Colombia	peso
Commonwealth of Independent States	ruble
Comoros	franc (CFA*)
Congo	franc (CFA*)
Costa Rica	colon
Cuba	peso
Cyprus	pound
Czechoslovakia	koruna
Denmark	krone
Djibouti	franc
Dominica	E. Caribbean dollar
Dominican Republic	peso
Ecuador	sucre
Egypt	pound
El Salvador	colon
Equatorial Guinea	ekuele
Ethiopia	birr
Fiji	dollar
Finland	markka
France	franc
Gabon	franc (CFA*)

Country	Currency
Gambia	dalasi
Germany	mark
Ghana	cedi
Greece	drachma
Grenada	E. Caribbean dollar
Guatemala	quetzal
Guinea	syli
Guinea Bissau	peso
Guyana	dollar
Haiti	gourde
Honduras	lempira
Hungary	forint
Iceland	krone
India	rupee
Indonesia	rupiah
Iran	rial
Iraq	dinar
Ireland	pound
Israel	shekel
Italy	lira
Ivory Coast	franc (CFA*)
Jamaica	dollar
Japan	yen
Jordan	dinar
Kenya	shilling
Kiribati	Australian dollar
Korea, North	won
Korea, South	won
Kuwait	dinar
Laos	kip
Lebanon	pound
Lesotho	loti
Liberia	dollar
Libya	dinar
Liechtenstein	Swiss franc
Luxembourg	franc
Madagascar	franc
Malawi	kwacha
Malaysia	ringgit
Maldives	rupee
Mali	franc (CFA*)
Malta	pound
Marshall Islands	dollar
Mauritania	ouguiya
Mauritius	rupee
Mexico	peso
Micronesia	dollar
Monaco	French franc
Mongolia	tugrik
Morocco	dirham
Mozambique	metical
Myanmar	kyat
Namibia	S. African rand
Nauru	Australian dollar
Nepal	rupee
Netherlands	guilder
New Zealand	dollar

Country	Currency
Nicaragua	cordoba
Niger	franc (CFA*)
Nigeria	naira
Norway	krone
Oman	rial
Pakistan	rupee
Panama	balboa
Papua New Guinea	kina
Paraguay	guarani
Peru	inti
Philippines	peso
Poland	zloty
Portugal	escudo
Qatar	riyal
Romania	lei
Rwanda	franc
St. Kitts	E. Caribbean dollar
St. Lucia	E. Caribbean dollar
St. Vincent	E. Caribbean dollar
San Marino	Italian lira
São Tomé and Príncipe	dobra
Saudi Arabia	riyal
Senegal	franc (CFA*)
Seychelles	rupee
Sierra Leone	leone
Singapore	dollar
Solomon Islands	dollar
Somalia	shilling
South Africa	rand
Spain	peseta
Sri Lanka	rupee
Sudan	pound
Suriname	guilder
Swaziland	lilangeni
Sweden	krona
Switzerland	franc
Syria	pound
Taiwan	new Taiwan dollar
Tanzania	shilling
Thailand	baht
Togo	franc (CFA*)
Tonga	dollar

Country	Currency
Transkei	S. African rand
Trinidad and Tobago	dollar
Tunisia	dinar
Turkey	lira
Tuvalu	Australian dollar
Uganda	shilling
United Arab Emirates	dirham
United Kingdom	pound sterling
Uruguay	peso
Vanuatu	vatu
Vatican City	lira
Venda	S. African rand
Venezuela	bolivar
Vietnam	dong
W. Samoa	tala
Yemen, North	rial
Yemen, South	dinar
Yugoslavia	dinar
Zaire	zaire
Zambia	kwacha
Zimbabwe	dollar

* Colonies Française d'Afrique

BRITISH CURRENCY

British currency is based on the pound sterling. Coinage is called pence, with 100 pence adding up to one pound (£1). Coin denominations are one pence, two pence, five pence, 10 pence, 20 pence, 50 pence and the new £1 and £5 coins.

Paper currency begins with the £5 note and follows with £10, £20, and £50.

In slang, £1 is often referred to as "a quid;" £5 as 5 quid or a "fiver"; £10 as 10 quid or a "tenner."

Some terms for coins, now obsolete, include a halfpenny or "ha' penny;" "tuppence" or "tuppenny" for two pence; "thruppence" or "thrupenny" for three pence. A "shilling" was equal to about 12 pence, and a "bob" was equal to a shilling.

PART FOURTEEN

POPULAR CULTURE

TRENDS: 1960 TO 1992

The Sixties

The Federal Drug Administration sanctions birth-control pills in 1960; they go on sale in the United States a year later.

The first of Hugh Hefner's Playboy Clubs opens in Chicago this year.

The U.S. Circuit Court of Appeals rules in 1960 that *Lady Chatterley's Lover*, by D.H. Lawrence, is not obscene, clearing the way for distribution in the United States.

A year later, Henry Miller's *Tropic of Cancer* and *Tropic of Capricorn* are published in the United States.

Ebbets Field, home of the once-sacred Brooklyn Dodgers, is demolished (Feb. 23, 1960); the team is moving to Los Angeles.

In Texas, a 27-year-old black man is beaten and hung upside down from an oak tree with "KKK" carved into his chest (March 7, 1960).

Caryl Chessman loses a highly publicized 12-year-old fight to block his execution for rape, robbery and kidnapping, and dies in San Quentin's gas chamber (May 2, 1960).

Elvis Presley finishes a two-year hitch in the Army in 1960 and starts making a long string of movies. His songs still sell and his movies still draw, but critics generally say the films run the gamut from mediocre to bad—except for *Flaming Star*, which premiers in 1960.

The musical *The Fantasticks* opens at the Sullivan Street Playhouse in New York City (May 3, 1960). The production will run longer than any other musical in history.

Floyd Patterson becomes the first man to regain a lost heavyweight championship boxing title; he knocks out Sweden's Ingemar Johansson in five rounds (June 20, 1960). He flattens Johansson again the following year (March 13, 1961), this time in six rounds, to defend the title. He defends the crown again later in the year (Dec. 4, 1961), knocking out Tom McNeeley in four rounds. In 1962, Patterson loses the title in a single round to a tall, punishing heavyweight named Sonny Liston (Sept. 25). Liston beats Patterson a second time, again in the first round, of a rematch (July 22, 1963). Liston seems indestructible, but a lot of attention is being paid to a fast, brash and promising kid from Louisville, Ky., an Olympian named Cassius Clay. Clay works his way through Archie Moore and moves closer to a title shot at Liston.

Teflon-coated cookware and felt-tip markers debut in 1960. So does the United States' 50-star flag (July 4), signifying Hawaii's admission to the Union less than a year earlier (Aug. 21, 1959).

"M Squad," a popular police drama starring Lee Marvin as Lt. Frank Ballinger, ends a three-year run on television (Sept. 13, 1960).

One of the most popular shows on television in 1960 is "Rocky and His Friends." The prime-time cartoon show, which premiered in the fall of 1959, features the adventures of Rocket J. Squirrel, Bullwinkle Moose, Boris Badenov and femme fatale Natasha Fataly, not to mention Peabody and Sherman, Dudley Doright of the Mounties, his heroine Nell Fenwick, and the evil Snidely Whiplash. Edward Everett Horton is narrator of the show's pun-filled "Fractured Fairy Tales."

The popularity of Rocky and Bullwinkle begets another prime-time cartoon show in the fall of 1960, "The Flintstones," featuring Fred and Wilma Flintstone and Barney and Betty Rubble. The characters are Stone-Age extensions of Jackie Gleason's wildly successful 1955 hit sitcom "The Honeymooners."

"The Andy Griffith Show" introduces America to rural Mayberry in the fall of 1960, and that same season "Mr. Ed," a smart palomino horse, starts talking to viewers and his owner Wilbur.

Two of the most popular and enduring Western movies of the decade debut in 1960: John Wayne's *The Alamo*, and John Sturges' *The Magnificent Seven*. Movie buffs use the cast of "the Seven" as a favorite question for years after: Yul Brynner, Steve McQueen, Charles Bronson, Robert Vaughn, James Coburn, Horst Buchholz and . . . and . . . Brad Dexter. Eli Wallach played the villain.

Walt Disney's movie *Swiss Family Robinson* is the biggest box office draw of 1960—$20.2 million. The year's big movies also include *The Apartment, Butterfield 8, Elmer Gantry, Never on Sunday, Spartacus, Exodus* and Alfred Hitchcock's *Psycho*, which puts the Bates Motel on the horror map forever and, at least for a time, upsets the calm with which America takes showers.

Republican Vice-Pres. Richard M. Nixon agrees to a series of four public debates with his challenger for the presidency, Democratic Sen. John F. Kennedy of Massachusetts. In the fall of 1960, roughly 70 million Americans tune their televisions in to what becomes popularly known as The Great Debates. Kennedy's use of television in the campaign represents a milestone for the new medium, and it plays a major role in his election victory.

Casey Stengel, since 1949 the inimitable manager

of the New York Yankees and one of baseball's most colorful characters, is fired (Oct. 18, 1960).

Chrysler Corporation announces that the DeSoto will no longer be manufactured, ending 32 years of production (Nov. 18, 1960).

Big trampolines are fun and popular in the early 1960s, but by the middle of the decade numerous injuries have forced the fad into decline.

California feels like a mecca, a place where the sun and the surf are always up, the Beach Boys are always young, women are supposed to be as fast and sleek as new cars, it's cool to own a woodie, and even cooler to shoot California's piers, though much too dangerous; pier roulette wipes out quickly. Surfing does not. It spreads, albeit palely, to the East Coast. In places where there's water but no surf, round wooden disks called pypoboards suffice, even if a towline is necessary.

Ernest Evans, Jr., better known as Chubby Checker, popularizes Hank Ballard's 1959 dance song "The Twist." The tune makes it to the top of the pop music charts twice, and the dance reaches the height of its popularity in 1962.

1962 is the midway mark in a four-year national fever for new dances that include the Mashed Potato, Loco-Motion, Frug, Monkey and Funky Chicken, not to mention a rock reincarnation of the 1911 Turkey Trot; others are the Slauson, Swim, Jerk, Freddie and Shaggy Dog. Dance clubs are popular. Twisting is chic at New York's Peppermint Lounge, Studio 54, and Roseland ballroom. In Los Angeles, the Whiskey á Go-Go is hot. Killer Joe Piro teaches the dance to social royalty: Leonard Bernstein, Truman Capote, the Duke and Duchess of Windsor and Lee Radziwill, sister of First Lady Jacqueline Kennedy. In the White House, Jackie hosts her own Twist party. Soon thereafter the dance's popularity begins to wane, but not Jackie's. Her puffed-out bouffant hair style, big buttons and pillbox hats set the fashion trend for women.

Librium is marketed by Roche Laboratories in 1960, and a year later Hoffmann-LaRoche introduces Valium; anxiety is chased from coast-to-coast. The Food and Drug Administration approves Red Dye Number 2 as a food additive (1960), and declares the popular miracle drug Krebiozen ineffective against cancer (1963); Red Dye Number 2 will be declared carcinogenic 16 years later.

In the early 1960s, Xerox creeps into the language as a synonym for photocopy, but only in the vernacular; 32 years later, Xerox still guards its trademark.

College students in Canada and California race beds.

Popular fashion begins to reflect the rise of folk music; more men are wearing beards and sandals.

The Latin American song and dance Bossa Nova is briefly popular. So is the Watusi. So is Vaughn Meader's album *The First Family*, a 1962 best-seller that wins a Grammy Award for its good-hearted impersonations of the "Bahston" crowd that's taken over the White House.

In supermarkets, freeze-dried foods start to appear, but they're a novelty.

Chess wonder Bobby Fischer is fascinating. He's a teenager and has been the U.S. champion since 1957. Though notoriously idiosyncratic, Fischer is a source of Cold War national pride, not to mention a boon to the marketers of chess sets. Fischer will hold the U.S. title until 1961, lose it to Larry Evans for a year, regain it in 1962, reign through 1968, then beat Soviet whiz Boris Spassky for the World Chess Championship in 1972. Fischer is the first American to win the world crown; he will wear it through 1975.

FCC Chairman Newton N. Minow complains publicly that television programming caters too much to the nation's whims and not enough to its needs. He calls television "a vast wasteland" (May 9, 1961). Many people seem to agree, but most keep watching "Art Linkletter's House Party," "Leave It to Beaver" and "The Adventures of Ozzie and Harriet."

Soviet ballet dancer Rudolf Nureyev defects to the United States in 1961 and makes his U.S. and Paris debut in 1962 to world acclaim.

Satirical 20-page coloring books arrive in 1961 and leave in 1963, but not before *The Executive Coloring Book* has sold more than 1 million copies at $9.98 apiece. The book has clones, coloring books for architects and psychiatrists. There also is one that pokes fun at JFK, and another that takes on his archenemy, Soviet leader Nikita Khrushchev.

To ease back pain, JFK often sits in a rocking chair, which is enough to send rockers shooting to popularity throughout the country.

Physical fitness, especially among school children, is a topic of national concern; so is civil preparedness, fallout shelters (until 1962), joining the new Peace Corps, and the size of the rightist John Birch Society, which in 1961 claims to have more than 60,000 members.

ABC-TV's "Wide World of Sports" premiers in 1961 (April 29); so do "Ben Casey, M.D." and "Doctor Kildare." Johnny Carson replaces Jack Paar as host of NBC's "Tonight Show" (Oct. 1); he will hold the spot as one of America's premier comedians and entertainers for the next three decades. "The Dick Van Dyke Show" starts a five-year run in 1961.

New York Yankees' slugger Roger Maris breaks George Herman "Babe" Ruth's home-run record. Maris hits home run number 61 (Oct. 1, 1961). Critics point out that in his record-breaking 1927 season,

Ruth hit 60 long-balls in 154 games, while it took the irascible Mr. Maris 162 games to hit 61.

In response to the rising popularity of small import cars such as the Volkswagen Beetle, Volvo, and Renault, American automakers have been producing more compact cars. Ford has its Falcon model; Studebaker, the Lark; American Motors, the Rambler; Plymouth, the Valiant and, until young lawyer Ralph Nader invents modern consumer advocacy with publication of his book *Unsafe at Any Speed* (1965), Chevrolet has its Corvair.

Folk music rises, along with middle-class affluence, civil-rights protests, anger over segregation, U.S. bungling in the affairs of Fidel Castro's socialist experiment in Cuba—which includes assassination attempts—and increasing U.S. involvement in Vietnam. Bob Dylan, Joan Baez, and Peter, Paul and Mary are becoming popular by 1962.

The Philadelphia Warriors' Wilt Chamberlain becomes the first professional basketball player to score 100 points in a game—before 4,124 fans in Hershey, Pa., against the New York Knicks with 36 goals and 28 foul shots (March 2, 1962). The final score is 169 to 147.

Ernesto Che Guevera, martyr for Castro's populist cause, is outrageously popular among antiwar activists; and eventually so is Ho Chi Minh and Mao Zedong, whose "little red book" of quotations becomes radically chic in the United States.

Country and Western music star Patsy Cline is killed when her small airplane crashes in the woods of Camden, Tenn. (March 5, 1963). Pilot Randy Hughes and two of Cline's co-stars at the Grand Ole Opry, Hawkshaw Hawkins and Cowboy Copas, also are killed. In the years that follow, Cline's music makes her one of the best-selling international recording artists of all time, selling an average of 750,000 records per year well into the 1990s.

"Freedom rider" and "sit-in" reach the vernacular early in the decade. Folk "hootenannies" reach television. "Like" slips into the language, as in: "Like, later."

James Baldwin warns of racial violence in his book *The Fire Next Time* in 1963, the same year that "The Beverly Hillbillies" becomes the most-watched weekly television show, and sports' first instant replay is telecast during the Dec. 7 Army–Navy football game in Philadelphia.

In 1963, piano hacking, Op Talk, Mondo and College haircuts and love chains made of folded chewing-gum wrappers are regional rages for all of several weeks. Metracal, nondairy creamers, diet soft drinks and Weight Watcher foods are becoming part of the national diet.

The U.S. Post Office carves the nation into 43,000 parts in 1963 and identifies each with its own ZIP code, for Zone Improvement Plan. ZIP codes will help the Post Office improve efficiency by using machines to sort the mail.

"Have Gun Will Travel," one of the most popular weekly Westerns on television, goes off the air (Sept. 21, 1963) after five seasons.

Rock 'n' roll's great songwriter and singer Sam Cooke is shot to death in a Los Angeles motel room by Bertha Lee Franklin (Dec. 11, 1964).

Kodak introduces the Instamatic camera and cartridge film in 1964; Ed Sullivan introduces the Beatles (Feb. 15) during their first wild tour of the country; Mick Jagger and The Rolling Stones reintroduce hard and sexy rock to the Top 40 listings, and Rudi Gernreich introduces the topless bathing suit, which people mostly talk about. What they actually shop for are stylish new bellbottom jeans and slacks, white boots, poor-boy sweaters, "mod" haircuts, Nehru jackets, pointed "winkle-picker" shoes and boots, and "mop-top" haircuts.

Lava Lites debut; by the end of the 1960s they'll light up rooms all over America . . . sort of. Electric carving knives are popular new gadgets, and so are electric toothbrushes, Lee Iacocca's Ford Mustangs, Plymouth Barracudas, Pontiac Firebirds and Chevrolet Camaros.

Kennedy's assassination Nov. 22, 1963, one of the most tragic events in modern U.S. history, also is one of the most formative in the history of television. CBS newsman and anchor Walter Cronkite—one of the most trusted men in America then and now—interrupts the daytime soap opera "As the World Turns" to tell the nation the news from Dallas. For the next 56 hours, CBS covers the assassination and subsequent on-camera killing of Lee Harvey Oswald live—without the benefit of today's videotape, satellite links, microwave relays and direct-from-the-scene minicams. Through the aftermath of the tragedy and JFK's burial, as much as 96 percent of America watches the three major networks—not just for news but also for solace, a way to comprehend and deal with the magnitude of the events.

After Kennedy is assassinated, the presidency falls to Texan Lyndon Baines Johnson. Ten-gallon cowboy hats start showing up atop unlikely heads in New York City, Los Angeles and Washington, D.C., but their fashionability outside of the American West is about as brief as LBJ's. Although President Johnson declares war on poverty, signs the landmark Civil Rights Act into law (July 2), sets his Great Society program of sweeping social legislation into action, and First Lady Lady Bird Johnson campaigns aggressively to beautify America, the coarse Texan still becomes one of the most reviled presidents in modern history. Vietnam spells his downfall. President Eisenhower first put U.S. forces in Southeast Asia; JFK increased the numbers; LBJ escalates the policy and the draft of the nation's youth. Full-time college students and weekenders for the National Guard are deferred from service. The burden of military duty falls inordinately to noncollegians, the poor, and minorities.

Cassius Marcellus Clay takes his shot at heavyweight boxing champion Sonny "The Bear" Liston and makes it good (Feb. 25, 1964) when Liston refuses to fight a seventh round. Clay has the title, and though it's tainted, he proves to be one of the most controversial and electrifying figures in sports, and one of the smartest boxers in history. His cockiness and rhyming banter earn him the nickname "The Louisville Lip." He proclaims himself "The Greatest," and proves it in the ring time after time. He beats Liston in a rematch (May 25, 1965), this time as Muhammad Ali, minister of Islam. One minute and 42 seconds into the first round, Ali lifts Liston off his feet and onto the mat with a decisive punch that is so hard and fast that only photographs prove he actually threw it. Ali goes on to beat Floyd Patterson, George Chuvalo, Henry Cooper, Brian London, Karl Mildenberger, Cleveland Williams, Ernie Terrell and Zora Folley. In 1967 the World Boxing Association strips him of his title for refusing to be drafted into the Army. For his antiwar stance, Ali is cursed in some circles, lionized in others. The government convicts him of draft evasion, fines him $10,000 and sentences him to five years in prison (June 20, 1967). The conviction is later overturned (June 28, 1971).

Jug band music flourishes briefly in San Francisco and Boston; its big names are Dave Van Ronk and Jimmy Kweskin.

Guitars have been showing up in Roman Catholic churches, where the song "Michael" now seems more common than "Ave Maria." Folk masses are popular. The Roman Catholic Church stops using Latin as its liturgical language (Nov. 23, 1964).

Actor Clint Eastwood becomes a certified box office smash and an international movie idol in 1964 with *A Fistful of Dollars*, the first in a series of Westerns directed by Italian film maker Sergio Leone. Eastwood reprises his tough, no-name gunfighter role the following year with *For a Few Dollars More*, and then again the next year with *The Good, the Bad and the Ugly*. The movies are callously, but commonly, referred to as "Spaghetti Westerns."

"The Twilight Zone" has been popular on television since its premier (Oct. 2, 1959). Horror movie actor Boris Karloff's weekly television show "Thriller" goes off the air in the summer of 1962 after a two-year run. "The Outer Limits" is a two-year TV hit (Sept. 16, 1963 to Jan. 16, 1965). "The Addams Family" premiers later (Sept. 18, 1964), "The Munsters" debuts the same month (Sept. 29), as does "Gilligan's Island" (Sept. 26, 1964). Critics quickly proclaim the show one of the dumbest, most cliché-infested television sitcoms in history; naturally, "Gilligan's Island" becomes a smash hit, lasts for three full seasons and its reruns continue approximately forever.

"My Mother the Car," "Hogan's Heroes," "Get Smart!" and "The Man from U.N.C.L.E." are big TV shows in 1965, and ever-increasing numbers of Americans are watching programs in color.

Kids from Queens to California are trying out skateboards.

Cigarette-smoking is becoming less cool as its links to heart disease and lung cancer become clearer. Manufacturers must put health warnings on cigarette packs, thanks to a new law signed by LBJ (July 15, 1965).

Sonny and Cher (Salvatore Phillip Bono and Cherilyn Sakisian LaPierre) are popular with the middle class. Charlie Brown, Snoopy and the whole *Peanuts* crowd seem popular with most everyone.

James Brown is the number one soul singer in the country.

Toe rings are briefly popular in the middle of the decade, but not for as long as communes, psychedelic trips, black lights, Day-Glo colors and, among women, ironed-straight, very long hair. Wire-frame and octagonally cut eyeglasses, as well as glassless eyeglasses, and floor-length granny dresses, are fashionable, not to mention elkskin moccasins.

Scantily clad, platform go-go dancers are the rage of nightclubs in the mid-sixties. Leg decorations are considered sexy. The miniskirt, created by British fashion designer Mary Quant, becomes popular in mid-sixties America. By the end of the '60s, miniskirts are being worn with Courréges boots and maxi-length coats.

Wham-O popularizes the Super Ball (1965), about the time that computer dating comes in.

Pierced ears become fashionable about 1966.

Pass/fail grading takes hold in the nation's colleges and universities, especially as it becomes clear to students and sympathetic faculty that flunking out means a trip to Vietnam.

"Wild, Wild West," "Green Acres," and "Bewitched" are popular television shows. "My Favorite Martian" ends a popular three-season run in the fall of 1966.

Cleveland Browns' fullback Jim Brown proves himself to be one of the greatest football players of this decade or any other. In nine seasons, he leads the National Football League in rushing eight times, is All-Pro eight times and the League's MVP three times. He retires in 1965 with a career rushing record of 12,312 yards and 756 points, including 106 touchdowns. Brown leaves the gridiron for the silver screen. He stars with tough guy Lee Marvin and a celebrity cast in *The Dirty Dozen*, a wildly popular 1967 war movie and the best of several adventure movies in which Brown will appear.

Iron crosses start showing up as patches, decorations and jewelry, supposedly less as a mark of Nazism and anti-Semitism than as a callous insult to the Establishment.

With five seconds left in the seventh game of the National Basketball Association's Eastern Division finals and the Boston Celtics down one point to the Philadelphia 76ers, Boston's John Havlicek steals the ball, tips it to teammate Sam Jones, who scores, and the Celtics win. The Celtics' gravel-voiced radio announcer Johnny Most immortalizes the moment when he screams "Havlicek stole the ball!" Boston goes on to win the league championship against the Los Angeles Lakers and take the NBA title for the seventh straight year. Boston's all-time record string of championship title wins continues through 1966, and ends at eight.

The Northeastern United States and parts of Canada are plunged into darkness by the biggest power blackout in history (Nov. 9, 1965).

Freeze-dried coffee is new in 1966. Low-calorie foods are taking off in popularity.

As of its debut on weekly television (Jan. 13, 1966), "Batman" is one of the biggest hits of the decade. Adam West plays the caped crusader in broad, silly fashion, and Burt Ward chirps as Robin. A big cast of Hollywood celebrities appear as characters based on the classic comic-book stories. To name just a few: Burgess Meredith, Penguin; Julie Newmar, Catwoman; Liberace, Evil Fingers; Frank Gorshin, Riddler; Otto Preminger, Mr. Freeze. The show lasts until March 14, 1968.

"Mission: Impossible" has an immense following almost from its premier in 1966, but its long-term popularity is dwarfed by enthusiasm for "Star Trek." "Star Trek" runs for four seasons (Sept. 8, 1966, until Sept. 2, 1969), but the adventures of the starship U.S.S. *Enterprise* may last forever in syndication, videos, paperback books and movies.

Paper clothing is faddish from 1966 until about 1968, or until it disintegrates. Singles bars come on in 1967; so do titillating knee watches; waterbeds debut a year later.

A startlingly thin, 17-year-old British fashion model called Twiggy (a.k.a. Leslie Hornby) becomes the focus of androgynous high fashion in 1967. Her "look" is a moddish political statement, which the public tires of after a year; on the other hand, unisex styles and look-alike couples are fashionable in 1968, so go figure.

Ornamental chains are big in the late sixties. In 1967 and 1968, it's also fashionable for women to dress like 1930s gangster Bonnie Parker, in a beret and long skirt—thanks to the controversial popularity of *Bonnie and Clyde*, starring Faye Dunaway and Warren Beatty. Bonnie and Clyde meet their violent end in a long, bloody ambush filmed in brutal slow-motion by Arthur Penn.

Turtleneck jerseys and sweaters also are big in the late 1960s. So are odd pets such as wolves, ocelots, monkeys and de-scented skunks. Yogurt-making machines are big for a while, and more Americans are getting fitness-conscious. Riding a bicycle to work becomes trendy.

Vince Lombardi's Green Bay Packers of the National Football League play the Kansas City Chiefs of the American Football League in the first in a series of new post-season football games destined for immense promotion, popularity and, very often, lopsided victories: The Super Bowl. The Packers beat the Chiefs 35–10 in Super Bowl I (Jan. 15, 1967).

Baseball's 1967 Boston Red Sox, led by left-fielder Carl Yastrzemski, take the American League Pennant long after everyone in baseball counts them out. Yaz is a triple-crown winner this year—.326 batting average, 121 runs batted in, 44 home runs. He is one of the very few men in major league history to win a triple crown (and, as of the start of the 1993 baseball season, the *last* one to do it), but even he can't chase the notoriously bad karma that seems to surround the Sox. The franchise hasn't won a World Series since 1918, and the St. Louis Cardinals see to it that the string isn't ended by Boston's "Impossible Dream Team." The Cards beat the BoSox four games to three.

One quest does come to an end in 1967. After four televised years of being unjustly blamed and pursued for killing his wife, Dr. Richard Kimball finally catches up with the elusive one-armed murderer in the final episode of the popular weekly television drama "The Fugitive." Kimball is exonerated on August 29—before one of the largest viewing audiences in television history.

After eight years of making generally bad movies, eight years in which he took a distant back seat to the Beatles, Rolling Stones, folk and folk-rock music, Elvis Presley makes one of the most startling comebacks in memory. Suddenly he seems as fresh, irreverently powerful and evocative in black leathers as he was in the 1950s, even though the stage is a television special and the time is 1968. He goes back to recording for the first time in more than 13 years.

Military fatigues or flak jackets or black combat boots or any combination thereof are fashionable as the decade winds to a close. For "hawks," pro-war youth, the garb is uniform. For "doves," antiwar protesters, such dress is a kind of sport, though the two groups are easy to distinguish; the establishment types usually are too neat and stickers that say "America: Love It Or Leave It" may be plastered on their bumpers.

The modern "Children's Crusade," the social and political campaign against the Vietnam War, scores its biggest victory with President Johnson's televised announcement (March 31, 1968) that he will not seek reelection.

As the decade draws to a close, the Baby Boom generation's heroes, its leaders and galvanizers, have all been murdered: John F. Kennedy (Nov. 22, 1963), Malcolm X (Feb. 21, 1965), Dr. Martin Luther King, Jr. (April 4, 1968), Bobby Kennedy (June 5, 1968). The generation is set adrift spiritually, emotionally, politically and symbolically, and it will reel in self-absorption and ennui for two decades.

A sense of the nation's deepening turmoil and schizophrenia is captured in its attitude toward movie actor John Wayne, a cinema hero since the 1940s. The indomitable Duke is still fighting lung cancer. He had been a cigarette smoker, but for all anyone knows, the disease could have been exacerbated by radiation exposure during the filming of a 1956 turkey called *The Conquerors*. The star had worked less than 150 miles from Yucca Flat, Nev., where the government had secretly exploded at least 11 atomic bombs. The movie's director, Dick Powell, nearly 40 of his crew members and virtually all of Wayne's co-actors (except William Conrad, who later starred as TV's "Cannon")—from Agnes Moorehead and Pedro Armendariz to Susan Hayward—died of cancer. But in 1968, the Duke flies his patriotic colors high with *The Green Berets*. Antiwar protesters widely rebuke him and everything he stands for—the same values with which they were raised. A year later, when the actor trades the battlefield for the familiar Western range in *True Grit*, John Wayne becomes a hero again—and earns the first Oscar of his long career.

One of the most popular movies of 1969 is *Easy Rider*, wherein druggies Peter Fonda and Dennis Hopper cross America while heavily weighing its violence and bigotry. The movie seems to confirm the worst fears of America's alienated youth; some see it as a condemnation of escapism and drug use; others see it as an excoriation of American values; many see it as both. The movie's rock sound track is popular long after *Easy Rider* is recognized as a period piece.

"The Brady Bunch" airs on television the same year, 1969, and *The Wild Bunch* reaches the silver screen. Sam Peckinpah's landmark Western raises cinematic violence to a gritty new high.

The Vietnam War continues to play in America's living rooms the way no U.S. war in history ever did. Footage broadcast by network television news is taking the knee-jerk glory out of war and bringing the horror of it home.

Huge anti–Vietnam War rallies are held in dozens of cities throughout the nation (Oct. 15, 1969). Thousands of young men and women who are fighting for their country in a foreign land the way their parents did in World War II and the Korean War now come home to find themselves, their efforts, and their values reviled by antiwar protesters who consider themselves equally patriotic for having stood against the war.

Republican Vice-Pres. Spiro T. Agnew labels protest leaders "an effete core of impudent snobs."

More than 400,000 youths from all over the country show up at Max Yasgur's farm in the Catskills near Bethel, N.Y., for the Woodstock Music and Art Fair (Aug. 15–17, 1969). Bad weather and folk and rock music prevail. Part of the nation is appalled by proof that a so-called "counter-culture" really does exist in America, and part applauds that the peace-and-love notion seems to hold for a weekend.

See-through fashions show themselves in 1969.

America and the world watches as U.S. astronaut Neil A. Armstrong becomes the first man to set foot on the moon; Edwin E. "Buzz" Aldrin, Jr. follows (July 20, 1969). Earth suddenly seems small, more fragile; the universe, incomprehensibly vast. Mankind loses its innocence. Civilization now has parameters. Film at 11.

The Department of Health, Education and Welfare bans cyclamates, widely used artificial sweeteners (Oct. 18, 1969).

"Rowan and Martin's Laugh-In," a fast-paced weekly comedy show, is so popular between 1968 and 1970 that many of its staccato-paced one-liners quickly slip into the vernacular: "You bet your bippy," "Here comes the judge" and "Sock it to me! Sock it to me! Sock it to me!"

President Nixon signs a national draft lottery bill into law (Nov. 26). The first "Washington Roulette" numbers are drawn Dec. 1.

The FDA eases the cyclamate ban (Dec. 20), but it still applies to soft drinks; Fresca never tastes quite the same again.

The Seventies

By 1970, long hair for men peaks in popularity. Dress codes, to the extent that they exist at all anymore in high schools, colleges and universities, sanction the new style.

Most major cities now have massage parlors; many of them are legitimate.

Increasing concern about pollution prompts the first Earth Day observance around the country (April 22, 1970), and starts to move environmentalists nearer the front of mainstream popular causes.

Smile-face buttons show up for the first time in public in the very early '70s. So do "earth shoes," which have soles that are thick in the front and thin at the back—to improve posture, according to their Danish originator.

With its April 1970 issue, *Penthouse* breaks the general-circulation magazine taboo against showing pubic hair.

Hot pants are fashionable in 1970, but are mostly gone by 1972. Platform shoes, which rose in fashion late in the '60s, are still popular at the turn of the decade but fall flat as the '70s progress.

"Monday Night Football" debuts on ABC television (September 1970), and is an immediate and lasting success.

Congress creates the Public Broadcasting System (Sept. 29, 1970).

Paul McCartney sues to break up the Beatles (Dec. 31, 1970).

Women's liberation gains momentum, strength and power as a movement in the early '70s.

Early in the decade, Vice-President Agnew refers to the media as "the nattering nabobs of negativism," and accuses liberal Democrats of "pusillanimous pussyfooting."

Thousands march in New York City for gay rights (June 27, 1971).

Bob Dylan, George Harrison, Ravi Shankar, Eric Clapton, Leon Russell and some of their friends hold a surprise concert (Aug. 1, 1971) in New York's Madison Square Garden to raise money for refugees from Bangladesh, which declared independence from Pakistan late in April.

Acupuncture pricks the public consciousness for the first time in 1971; official acceptance of its usefulness is very slow and begrudging, but its advocates persist—all the way into the 1990s.

In 1972, rainbow decals, stickers and jewelry become another way to formalize harmless sentiment: "Have a Nice Day! Take time to smell the flowers."

Animated pornography is popular in 1972 with release of the movie *Fritz the Cat*.

Burt Reynolds turns up naked in a *Cosmopolitan* magazine centerfold.

Hot-tubs are big in the 1970s, early on the West Coast, later in the East. So is hang-gliding, yoga, est, transcendental meditation, paranoia (We know your mantra), puka shell necklaces, tank tops, leisure suits (especially in polyester) and, mostly among young men, running naked in public, or streaking.

Movie actress and peace activist Jane Fonda re-

turns from a visit to Hanoi, North Vietnam, declaring that the Vietnamese are not her enemy (July 28, 1972). Veterans' groups will never forgive her, even after she apologizes about 18 years later.

Swimmer Mark Spitz wins a record seven Olympic gold medals (Sept. 4, 1972).

ABC-TV's reporter Jim McKay for "Wide World of Sports" earns accolades and broad recognition for live, continuous coverage and commentary on terrorism at the Munich Olympics (Sept. 5 and 6, 1972).

HBO (Home Box Office) goes on the air with its first cable-television program, a National Hockey League game (Nov. 8, 1972).

Baseball's American League adopts the designated hitter as an experimental change in the game (Jan. 11, 1973).

Vice-President Agnew resigns in disgrace (Oct. 10, 1973). He is caught up in a bribery scandal, but trades a no-contest plea to income tax evasion for the dropping of other charges.

For upwardly nubile men and women in the summer of 1974, G-string "thongs" and string bikinis are fashionable.

Monster trucks, powerful pickup trucks on immense tires capable of rolling over most any obstacle, grab a lot of attention in Missouri in 1974, and their popularity spreads throughout the country. Magazines, fan clubs and public shows devoted to the "sport" will be popular into the 1990s.

Digital watches show up in 1974, become popular fast and remain so through the 1980s, partly for their precision and partly for their high-tech look; but because of their predominance the children of Baby Boomers will be slow to learn how to tell time.

The great Hank Aaron, now with the Atlanta Braves, breaks Babe Ruth's career home-run record with round-tripper number 715 (April 8, 1974) in a game in Atlanta against the Los Angeles Dodgers.

Thanks to a California advertising whiz named Gary Dahl, who realizes that Americans grow weary of caring for their household cats, dogs and canaries, rocks are finally domesticated in November 1975, just in time for Christmas, in fact. Over the next several months, more than 5 million pet rocks are sold, at about $5 each. (That's roughly $25 million gross, of which about $4.75 million went to Dahl.)

Prototypical mid-seventies American consumers might feed their pet rocks pâté, which all of a sudden is an equally fashionable hors d'oeuvre. Anyone with a pet rock and pâté in the mid-seventies also is apt to be wearing a mood ring and spending some time caring for an array of exotic indoor plants, which may be suspended in macramé hangers.

Household plants get talked to now, too, because it is becoming clear they respond to "vibes," good or bad, part of the growing interest in biofeed-back.

One of those plants may be a four- to eight-foot tall leafy, herbaceous annual called *Cannabis sativa*, or marijuana, which is cool to "do," extraordinarily popular, supposed to be better for you than alcohol and somehow doesn't qualify as cigarette smoking, which is slowly continuing its fall from favor.

Big-name designers get into blue-jean wars by the middle of the decade, and the body count is as staggering as the prices. Hundreds of thousands of jeans are being sold every week in the United States at prices ranging to about $50, and Europe is clamoring for as many as it can get. There is a big secondary market everywhere for second-hand jeans.

(Used goods won't be referred to as "pre-owned" until some time after the Arab oil embargo in the winter of '73–'74. Car dealers introduce the euphemism in order to preserve the status and respectability of overpriced, oversized, second-hand gas-guzzlers.)

Pie "killing" is big in 1975, unless you're one of the victims surprised by having a cream pie thrown in your face.

By 1976, CB radios are hot as a two-dollar pistol, good buddy. It seems everyone's got a handle, as well as instant membership in a huge, amorphous and mobile fraternity. The fad's fun for a few years, but becomes a cliché early in the 1980's, so it's ten-four, forever. Do you copy?

Personal classified advertisements such as "Swinging SWF seeks fun with SWM" make their debut in the mainstream. So does "The Gong Show" (June 1976).

Personal computers are introduced by the Apple and Tandy corporations.

Bobbed or wedged-shaped hairdos for women, à la Olympic gold-medal figure skater Dorothy Hamill, sweep the nation (1976).

July 4, 1976, is the nation's 200th birthday, and the federal government helps cities and towns throughout the country set up special bicentennial commissions to organize and promote special events, commemorations and displays of civic and ethnic heritage. The birthday milestone itself is celebrated unabashedly coast-to-coast with the ringing of bells at 2 P.M., huge parades, gigantic fireworks displays, the arrival in Valley Forge, Pa., of six wagon trains that had come cross-country and, at the National Archives in Washington, D.C., a vigil of 76 hours to mark the signing of the Declaration of Independence. Most people will remember the country's bicentennial year for spectacular tours by dozens of full-rigged sailing ships, "Tall Ships," replicas and training vessels from around the world.

The Fonz, leather-jacketed '50s motorcycle rider

Arthur Fonzarelli played by actor Henry Winkler on television's long-running sitcom "Happy Days" (1974–84), is one of the most popular figures in America; "Eeay."

In 1977, The Sex Pistols and similarly outrageous musical groups in Great Britain unveil punk rock.

Liquid protein diets and yogurt are big this year; walking is, too, but jogging is bigger.

Pres. Jimmy Carter's brother, Billy, markets his own brew, Billy Beer, and it's a popular novelty for a while.

Volkswagen stops producing the once-ubiquitous Beetle in 1977.

Hackey Sacks, small kickable beanbags invented in 1972 by an injured ex-football player as a means of leg exercise, are showing up on college campuses by the middle of the decade, and grow in popularity straight through the 1980s.

Director George Lucas scores big in 1977 with the movie *Star Wars*. "May the force be with you" becomes a favorite salutation. Toys, action figures, virtually anything associated with the hit movie—and its sequels through 1987—are hot sellers, to the tune of more than $2.5 billion over the 10-year period.

The ABC-TV special "Roots," based on a novel by Alex Haley, sets an all-time record as the most popular dramatic presentation on network television (Jan. 23–31, 1977); as many as 100 million Americans watch the final episode. The success of "Roots" marks renewed controversy over European enslavement of Africans, heralds the potential of televised miniseries and stimulates widespread interest in genealogy.

Long, tossled manes à la actress Farrah Fawcett are fashionable this year.

The 1977 movie *Saturday Night Fever*, starring John Travolta as dancer Tony Manero, sweeps the popular young actor (Vinnie Barbarino of television's "Welcome Back, Kotter") to international stardom and ushers in a national craze for disco music and dancing. The movie's soundtrack album, dominated by the singing of The Bee Gees, becomes one of the best-selling record albums of all time (11 million copies, according to the Recording Industry Association of America, but Fleetwood Mac's *Rumours* album also is released in 1977, and it will surpass sales of *Saturday Night Fever* by 2 million copies). Roller disco follows later in the decade, but as disco fades with the turn of the decade, roller-skating rinks are still enjoying a mild rebirth in popularity.

Elvis Aron Presley, the 42-year-old "King of Rock 'n' Roll," is found dead in his mansion, Graceland, in Memphis, Tenn. (Aug. 16, 1977). Fans around the world are shocked by the news. Scandal follows when the autopsy tests reveal extensive drug abuse. Presley's promoters and the handlers of his estate turn Graceland into a shrine; tens of thousands of visitors still pay homage every year, and Elvis impersonators dot stages all over the country. Supermarket tabloids for the next 15 years tout sightings of Elvis in locales all over the nation.

Campus toga parties, popular at fraternities and sororities in the 1960s, are rejuvenated by sophomoric hijinks in *National Lampoon's Animal House,* which premiers in the summer of 1978 to huge crowds.

"Dallas" premiers on television (April 2, 1978). It takes about two years, but the nighttime soap opera gradually becomes the most popular show on television, and J.R. Ewing (Larry Hagman) the man most of America loves to hate.

Superman, the guy America loves to love, is popular again after 1978, when actor Christopher Reeve stars as the Man of Steel in the first, and best, of four *Superman* movies.

The popularity of "Space Invaders" in 1978 shows that video games are rapidly getting more sophisticated, but a 1974 fantasy role-playing game called Dungeons and Dragons has legions of devotees. D&D's popularity continues through the turn of the decade.

Jim Henson's Muppets are particularly big from the middle of the decade on. Miss Piggy gets an Academy Award nomination as best actress in 1979 for her role in that year's hit *The Muppet Movie;* she loses to Sally Field for *Norma Rae,* but does so with rare grace.

Sony's Walkman tape players make music ever more portable in 1979. Light Walkman earphones will adorn heads through the 1980s.

The Eighties

A popular bumper sticker captured the essence of the 1980s: "The one who dies with the most toys wins." The decade is marked by an emphasis on consumerism. Financial planning becomes a key to personal well-being. Perriér mineral water, American Express cards, derisively referred to as "Yuppie Green Cards," BMW cars ("Beemers"), Saabs, Volvos, Mercedes-Benzes, and town houses are common status symbols.

Actor Henry Winkler, Arthur The Fonz Fonzarelli, from television's "Happy Days" sitcom donates his trademark leather jacket to the Smithsonian Institution in 1980. The timing is appropriate. 1950s greasers are out; preppies are in from the start, officially so with the popularity of *The Official Preppy Handbook* late in 1980.

Chocolate-chip cookies become faddish this year, and they are a staple of new cookie shops everywhere. On the West Coast, bars specializing in mineral water are popular for a while.

Reusable, peelable Post-It™ notes, originated by 3M Corporation, show up about 1980 and quickly prove about as indispensable to office work as notepads and paper clips.

"The Gong Show" goes off the air in 1980, and Ted Turner's Cable News Network comes on. At first, all-news CNN makes slow but steady inroads into the viewing domain occupied exclusively by the three major networks. In the next 10 years, CNN will grab a major share of the national viewing audience, partly by steadily beefing up its news reporting, and partly because America's television-watching habits are changing. With the steady expansion of cable television, the proliferation of channels, the growth of video cassette recorders and the rising popularity of remote-control "channel grazing," TV viewers have much more control over what they watch on television. The major networks are vulnerable.

By 1980, many factors have conspired to make the Western look very fashionable all over the country. In some measure, it followed Georgia peanut farmer Jimmy Carter's rise to the presidency in 1977: old-fashioned blue jeans rolled up at the cuff, gingham checked shirts, expensive cowboy boots, hats and bolo ties. The steadily rising popularity of Larry Hagman's nasty J.R. Ewing on "Dallas" adds to the push. As former movie actor and California Gov. Ronald Reagan rides to the presidency, the look gains a little more ground. When John Travolta dons the duds for the popular movie *Urban Cowboy* in 1980, the change is complete. Demand for Western apparel is high and rising until about 1982.

Meanwhile, in 1981, jelly beans replace peanuts as presidential, and therefore eminently marketable, fads.

More than 400,000 fans turn out for a reunion concert by Paul Simon and Art Garfunkel in New York City's Central Park (Sept. 19, 1981).

Colorful, plastic Rubik's Cube puzzles, courtesy of Hungarian inventor Erno Rubik, are in Christmas stockings all over the world in 1981.

MTV carves itself a lasting niche in cable television packages everywhere.

Pac-Man video games grip the country like fever.

IBM makes its bid for dominance in the burgeoning personal computer market.

Society's ever-quickening pace, two-job households, and changes in housing patterns all have conspired to boost the timeless appeal of house cats as favorite pets. By the 1990s, cats will far outstrip dogs as the nation's pet pet.

E.T. "the Extra-terrestrial" makes a collect phone call on the hearts of American moviegoers in 1982.

Also in 1982, the cast of "Saturday Night Live," particularly John Belushi, makes "deely-bobbers" popular gag headware.

BMX bicycles make parents groan that another two-wheeled fad has arrived.

Jane Fonda burns up the fitness market with home-workout videos.

Little blue people called Smurfs are considered adorable, collectible (as figurines), and eminently watchable in cartoons.

The Gannett newspaper syndicate publishes *USA Today* (Sept. 15, 1982), with the intention of building a national circulation ... which it does rather quickly. The daily newspaper specializes in short news items, splashy graphics and extensive color. Critics of the newspaper call it "McPaper," the journalistic equivalent of fast food, but the sucker sells ... and sells ... and sells. By 1990 *USA Today* will have a daily paid circulation of 1,347,450, making it second in circulation only to the *Wall Street Journal*, which by then sells 1,857,131 copies a day.

Michael Jackson releases *Thriller* in 1982, and the album gives him a lasting spot in the rock-celebrity firmament. *Thriller* sells more than 20 million copies, making it *the* biggest-selling album in history.

Sony turns television personally portable by marketing its small Watchman set in 1982.

"Cheers" premiers Sept. 30, 1982, and becomes one of the longest-running situation comedies on television.

The last episode of "M*A*S*H" airs on CBS (Sept. 19, 1983). More than 124 million viewers watch the finale to 11 seasons; the show debuted Sept. 17, 1972.

Interior Secretary James Watt is to the Reagan administration what Agriculture Secretary Earl Butz was to the Ford administration: a social and political disaster. Watt, who has drawn the anger of everyone from environmentalists to rock fans, is forced to resign (Oct. 9, 1983) after noting publicly that the membership of a federal commission should be palatable because it comprises "a black, a woman, two Jews and a cripple."

The most popular child playthings in 1983 are Cabbage Patch Dolls. After this holiday season consumers will be much farther down the road to accepting an annual dose of raincheck slips and gotta-have-it-pandemonium as the price of a status Christmas gift.

California-speak is slipping into teens' national consciousness. Words and phrases such as "fer sher," "grody," "ex-suh-lent," "gnarly," "tubular," "dude," are increasingly common; "grody to the max."

In 1983, the recording industry and electronics manufacturers are pushing compact discs and players.

At the box office, *Flashdance* is one of 1983's biggest hits. Jennifer Beales as the movie's welder-dancer heroine prompts one of the '80s biggest fashion trends: torn, scoop-neck, short-sleeve sweatshirt, worn off the shoulder over leotards or tank tops and very tight pants with leg-warmers.

Young black men in the Bronx and Brooklyn bring break dancing to public attention. The movements, refined for more than a decade among agile street performers, are fast, artful, acrobatic and pretzel-bending. Most of America can only watch.

Slam dancing, punkish body-contact set to music, is around for a while, too, but doesn't last much longer than the bumps and bruises it causes.

By the end of 1983, the biggest adult game in town is a Canadian import, a board game called Trivial Pursuit. Mania for the game will continue through 1984 and then settle in as a fixture among board games.

Most credit cards have decorative little holograms on them now, and *Newsweek* declares 1984 the year of the Young Urban Professional, a.k.a. Yuppie.

Minivans are starting to redefine standard transit for the middle class American family; they pick up where wood-grain Ford Country Squire station wagons left off.

Television commercials for Wendy's restaurants feature Clara Peller, who turns "Where's the beef?" into a popular question.

Big-time, showboat wrestling comes of age by the mid-1980s. The likes of old stuntmen like Killer Kowalski and Haystack Calhoun suddenly seem tame beside Hulk Hogan, Rowdy Roddy Piper, Andre the Giant, Sargeant Slaughter and Captain Lou Albano. By the end of the decade, the new generation of showmen is at the heart of a multibillion-dollar industry.

Demographers and sociologists in 1984 are talking about the aging of the U.S. population; "the graying of America" is the way they put it. Baby Boomers are having difficulty dealing with care for their aging parents.

The demand for *Star Wars* action figures and play sets is so great by Christmas of 1984 that when Kenner Company can't produce them fast enough, the public proves willing to accept boxed coupons assuring delivery of the toy in six weeks.

Masters of the Universe action figures, Cabbage Patch dolls, Teddy Ruxpin (a talking teddy bear), and Transformer figures account for more than $1.4 billion in retail toy sales in 1985.

The record-store space occupied by cassette audio tapes, which pushed big selections of long-playing record albums all but out of most music stores by about 1980, are being squeezed hard by compact discs. By the end of the decade, CDs will have nearly taken over.

Cocaine is chic throughout the ranks of new achievers in the moneyed upper middle class, and less-expensive crack cocaine surfaces among the urban poor.

Four-wheel-drive vehicles are growing in popularity by 1985. Manly stubble is, too—thanks to "Miami Vice" star Don Johnson, Mel Gibson, Bruce Springsteen, Harrison Ford and men's fashion advertisements by everyone from Gap to Giorgio Armani.

Running shoes are comfortable, fashionable, expensive and here to stay by 1985. Along city streets women wear them with dresses to and from work. Teen-agers wear them everywhere; Adidas, Avia, and especially Reebok and Nike, which boast adjustable air-cushioned models, emerge as status names.

Garrison Keillor's American Radio Company public-radio variety show from Minnesota moves nearer the cultural mainstream in the mid-1980s as homespun humor and news from the fictional Lake Woebegone capture the imagination of listeners from coast to coast.

Social consciousness is made more respectable by pop musicians who sponsor huge concerts for African relief and drought-stricken U.S. farmers. The proceeds from their best-known joint effort, a song called "We Are the World," earns more than $30 million.

The Coca-Cola Company makes one of the biggest marketing moves of 1985 by announcing it is abandoning its traditional formula (April 23, 1985) for the famous soft drink. Consumers don't approve, and in July the company resumes production of the old drink; but it's sold now as "Coca-Cola Classic."

The Houston Astros' Nolan Ryan becomes the first major league baseball pitcher to strike out 4,000 batters (July 11, 1985).

High-stakes profit-taking and wheeling-and-dealing has become exciting and more fashionable than ever in the business world of the mid-1980s. Corporate raiding, hostile takeovers, leveraged buyouts, and mergers and acquisitions dominate the financial news pages. "Downsizing" becomes the common euphemism for stripping a company of its profitable assets and selling them. "Outplacement" counseling is what tens of thousands of fired ("terminated, furloughed or excessed") employees sorely need.

Mexican beer, especially Corona with a twist of lime tucked into the bottle's long neck, is fashionable in 1986. So are flavored seltzers. Ground turkey becomes a health-conscious, low-cholesterol alternative to sausage, pastrami and, for some, even hamburger.

Inexpensive, folding cardboard sun screens become commonplace behind car windshields, and rear windows become a favorite spot for signs, particularly small school-bus-yellow models. The fad

starts with motorist advisories such as "Children on board" and gravitates to "Mother-in-law in trunk" and "Don't you hate these signs?"

The nation celebrates the 100th birthday of the Statue of Liberty (July 3–6, 1986) with a parade of tall ships in New York harbor and more than 40,000 pieces of fireworks, the largest display in history. The weekend gala marks the end of a three-year, $70 million restoration of the statue. One of the biggest hits of the celebration is a series of performances by about 200 Elvis impersonators.

World oil prices decline in 1986, and gasoline prices stabilize, allowing America to resume its long love affair with big cars.

Andrew Wyeth, arguably America's favorite (but until 1986 somewhat retiring) artist, causes a stir with the disclosure of more than 200 paintings, some of them nudes, of a Pennsylvania neighbor named Helga. They are reprinted in a popular coffee-table tome, and the originals travel in exhibition.

The latest in fashionable mainstream footwear is "walkers," walking shoes marketed as such.

Physical fitness is part of the 1980s philosophy of being one's own best friend. Most anyone who can afford the time and club membership fees is working out on resistance machines, jogging, fast-walking, or exercising aerobically. Tanning salons catch on for a few years in the middle of the decade, but their popularity fades as the 1980s progress; the risks from prolonged exposure prove worrisome.

Depression is described as the common cold of the 1980s, but no longer is there stigma attached to psychotherapy. Among the middle class in the 1980s, having a regular therapist is about as common as having a regular dentist.

Laid-back "New Age" music and attitudes emphasizing personal harmony, oneness with the universe, and the influence of crystals gain numerous disciples in the 1980s, especially in the upper middle class.

A slick but vacuous computer-imaged character called Max Headroom is popular, but briefly; not enough K.

The Boston Celtics' top draft pick, University of Maryland basketball star Len Bias, collapses and dies of cocaine poisoning (June 19, 1986), and national attention turns to drug abuse among athletes.

The Budweiser Brewing Company puts a smallish but macho dog named Spuds MacKenzie in its commercials, and he's a big hit.

Tie-dyed T-shirts edge back from the 1960s and Grateful Dead concerts into modest fashion.

The term "couch potato" has been around a while, but this year use of the term becomes common.

Spiked hair is popular.

Apple's Macintosh computers, *the* machine for the

non-computer person, carves huge inroads into the burgeoning market.

Glenn Close and Michael Douglas in the movie *Fatal Attraction* curdle national taste for casual sex, not to mention rabbit stew. The movie reflects the nation's increasing preference for fidelity in monogamous relationships. The new propriety is part political; as personal affluence swells throughout the middle class under Pres. Ronald Reagan, the country has been turning steadily to the right. The new attitude also becomes something of a practicality in the face of the international spread of AIDS. Condoms are touted as the main line of defense, and drug stores stop hiding them. Meanwhile, magazines such as *Playboy, Playgirl* and *Penthouse* move behind the counter, and customers who seek them are apt to get copies handed to them either face-down or in a discreet brown wrapper.

Traditional right-leaning democratic values are winning throughout the world. Political turmoil in Africa is the result of movement toward self-determination and democratization. Communist regimes world-wide seem to be cracking; the economics of communism simply have not worked. The Soviet Union's President Mikhail Gorbachev is the darling of the West. Traditional U.S. and Soviet tensions steadily diminish as Gorbachev moves his country toward reform.

By 1987, vicious attacks by pit bulls are getting the publicity once reserved for German shepherds, St. Bernards, and Dobermans; Rotweilers will be next.

Vincent Van Gogh's *Irises* commands nearly $54 million at auction this year.

"Dinks" (double income, no kids) joins "Yuppie" as part of the vernacular.

The stock market posts its biggest decline since 1914. Nearly 600 million shares are traded in a 508-point drop ("Black Monday," Oct. 19, 1987) that spells investment losses of more than $500 billion.

In 1988, the country is briefly scared by a report from the National Academy of Sciences in January that says an odorless, invisible, naturally occurring gas called radon may be seeping into house foundations and contributing substantially to as many as 13,000 lung-cancer deaths per year. Radon-detection kits and radon-detecting companies hit the market quickly.

The animated clay-figure California Raisins delight television watchers, boost raisin consumption, repopularize Marvin Gaye's 1968 hit single "I Heard It Through the Grapevine," and win rave reviews throughout the advertising industry.

Hot-air ballooning is noticeably popular, and so is kite-flying.

Seats for *The Phantom of the Opera* are sold out for about a year by the time it opens on Broadway in January; advance ticket sales total about $17 million.

A vitamin-A-based drug called Retin-A is touted in a January issue of the prestigious *Journal of the American Medical Association* as an effective treatment for some skin wrinkles.

Chicago Bears running back Walter Payton ends 13 seasons in the National Football League (January 1988) with an all-time rushing record: 16,726 yards.

Superman turns 50 (March 1988).

Northwest Airlines bans cigarette-smoking on most domestic flights, becoming the first major U.S. carrier to do so (March 1988). Federal regulations go into effect a month later, banning cigarette smoking on all flights of less than two hours.

Sonny (Salvatore Phillip) Bono, the less flamboyant half of the now-defunct Sonny and Cher sixties song team, is elected mayor of Palm Springs, Calif. (April 1988).

The American League's Baltimore Orioles set a major league baseball record by losing their first 21 games of the 1988 season.

Coleco Corp., which reaped windfall profits on sales of the faddish Cabbage Patch Dolls and Trivial Pursuit board games in the middle of the decade, announces it is millions of dollars in debt (April 1988) and will lay off more than a third of its managerial staff at headquarters in Connecticut.

Garfield the cat is one of the decade's most popular cartoon characters, and in 1988 he shows up stuck to the inside of car windows . . . along with flattened stuffed felines from the not-too-subtle anti-cat crowd.

Harvard University is issued the first patent (April 1988) for a "transgenic non-human mammal," a genetically altered, cancer-prone mouse to be used in research.

Fax machines are in vogue as the hottest new telecommunication tool and toy, and competition among manufacturers has made them more affordable.

In the summer of 1988, Sony markets a portable videotape player called the Video Walkman.

The Edmonton Oilers of the National Hockey League win their fourth Stanley Cup championship in five years by sweeping the Boston Bruins in four games (May 1988).

Who Framed Roger Rabbit? is a runaway hit at the box office, and an object of adoration among lovers of animation.

Consumer Reports magazine causes a stir by reporting (June 1988) that Suzuki's popular four-wheel-drive Samurai is considered "not acceptable" because it's likely to tip over in a sharp turn; the company denies the reports, and some Suzuki dealers around the country set up (stationary) displays in which Samurais seem balanced on two wheels.

Controversial New York Yankees owner George Steinbrenner fires baseball manager Billy Martin for the fifth time (June 1988), and replaces him with Lou Pinella.

In Lansing, Mich., the last of Hugh Hefner's 22 Playboy Clubs in the United States closes (July 31, 1988).

New York real estate billionaire Donald Trump buys one of the world's most spectacular yachts, Saudi arms dealer Adnan Khasoggi's 282-foot *Nabila*, for $29 million. Trump spends another $8.5 million on renovations and renames the yacht *Trump Princess*.

The oldest ballpark in the National League, Chicago's Wrigley Field, gets lights this year. The park was built in 1914, and became home to the Chicago Cubs two years later, but no game was played there at night until Aug. 8, 1988; 39,012 fans were on hand.

Movie director Martin Scorsese raises religious hackles all over the country with *The Last Temptation of Christ* (August 1988), in which actor Willem Dafoe portrays an introspective Jesus Christ with a measure of lust for Mary Magdalene.

Canadian Ben Johnson wins an Olympic gold medal by running the 100-meter dash in a world-record 9.79 seconds, but he is later stripped of the medal after failing a test for anabolic steroids (September 1988). Nine months later, he will admit to having used steroids since 1981.

The Roman Catholic Church announces (October 1988) that scientific tests show the Shroud of Turin, which was believed to have wrapped the body of Jesus Christ, dates only to 1280 A.D., and not to the crucifixion.

Elvis is sighted at a laundromat in Michigan.

"Trash TV"—sensational news, talk and information shows such as Morton Downey Jr.'s "A Current Affair" and "Hard Copy"—tease, titillate and push the bounds of good judgment, taste and fairness, not to mention accuracy, to new limits. Many talk shows lapse into the same category: Geraldo Rivera's, Sally Jessy Raphael's, Phil Donahue's and, sometimes, Oprah Winfrey's.

In most major metropolitan areas, billiard parlors start to make a comeback in 1988.

So does Republican presidential candidate George Herbert Walker Bush. He seems somewhat wimpish at first, but the public perception changes to fiesty after a contentious interview with CBS newsman Dan Rather. The GOP campaign is sleazy and demagogic, appealing to racial fears and biases and a nameless dread over the specter of liberalism. But in the face of it, Massachusetts Governor Michael Dukakis's Democratic presidential campaign falters and founders. Bush is swept into office, with Indiana Senator J. Danforth Quayle right behind him as Vice-President.

Quayle is caricatured relentlessly as vapid and inconsequential. By 1991, the Vice-President will be such an obscure figure that booksellers will capitalize on the phenomenal popularity of *Where's Waldo?* books by selling one that asks seekers "Where's Dan?"

Inexpensive "slap-wrap" bracelets debut late in 1989 and by 1991 are as ubiquitous among teen-age women as stirrup pants and long sweaters.

By the end of the decade, animal-rights activists have made the cosmetological testing of animals and the wearing of natural furs somewhat less acceptable than cigarette-smoking in public.

Nintendo games, which have been around since 1985, are the most popular video toys in America by 1989. In three different incarnations, the Mario Brothers are the most sought-after game characters.

In 1989, mass murderer Ted Bundy is executed in Florida state prison. He is believed responsible for the murders of between 30 and 100 young women throughout the country between 1974 and 1979 (January 24).

Short ponytails and rattails and, for men *and* women, "big hair," teased and puffed for height, are popular styles. So are tall, angular crew cuts such as flattops, spikes, Barts (for Bart Simpson), and fades, very many with distinctive head lines, from initials to logos.

The Rand Corporation reports that although the gap in wages between men and women has narrowed substantially in the last two decades, women still earn only about 65 percent of the wages men would be paid for the same jobs (February 8).

Iran's Ayatollah Ruhollah Khomeini offers a reward of $3 million to any Iranian who kills British writer Salman Rushdie for blaspheming against the prophet Mohammed in the author's new novel, *The Satanic Verses* (February 14). A $1 million bounty will be paid if Rushdie's executioner is not an Iranian. Rushdie goes into hiding.

The Dallas Cowboys' legendary coach Tom Landry, who in 29 National Football League seasons made the Cowboys one of the winningest teams in history (20 winning seasons in a row), is fired (March 1989) after the team's ownership changes hands.

Mazda's classy little roadster, the Miata, is one of the most sought-after cars of the year.

Two electrochemists, Dr. B. Stanley Pons of the University of Utah and Dr. Martin Fleischman of the University of Southampton, England, stun scientists throughout the world by announcing (March 23, 1989) they have created cold nuclear fusion. Scientists are skeptical and critical, and by fall the claim is debunked.

The Italian Historical Society of America holds ceremonies in New York (April 9, 1989) honoring Antonio Meucci for inventing the telephone in 1871, five years before Alexander Graham Bell patented and commercialized the invention.

After a gang of six teen-agers beat and rape a 28-year-old woman jogging in New York City's Central Park (April 19, 1989), the word "wilding" slithers into the vernacular to describe random violence during a brutal rampage.

Basketball's all-time leader in points scored (38,387), center Kareem Abdul-Jabbar, ends his 20-year career with the Los Angeles Lakers of the National Basketball Association (June 13, 1989).

With sales falling precipitously, the apple-growing industry announces it will no longer use the chemical Alar as a ripener and preservative (May 1989). The action is taken after the Environmental Protection Agency says it will ban Alar in the wake of a CBS-TV "60 Minutes" segment linking the substance to cancer.

Lethal Weapon II, wherein Mel Gibson and Danny Glover reprise their roles as buddy cops, is a box-office smash, and Batmania grips the country this summer with the premier of *Batman*, starring Michael Keaton, Kim Basinger and, as the Joker, Jack Nicholson.

The West's growing admiration for China and its young nationals who have embraced rock 'n' roll, Christianity and democratic reform, dies in Beijing's Tienanmen Square when Communist troops kill hundreds, perhaps thousands, of demonstrators (June 4, 1989).

The National Gay and Lesbian Task Force announces that violence against gays, "gay bashing," from killings to verbal and physical assaults, is on the increase throughout the nation (July 1989).

The controversial musical *Oh, Calcutta!*, which features complete nudity, ends its 20-year run at New York City's Edison Theater (Aug. 6, 1989).

The Texas Rangers' Nolan Ryan becomes the first major league baseball pitcher to strike out 5,000 batters (Aug. 22, 1989).

"Charlie Hustle," Cincinnati Reds' great Pete Rose, is banned from professional baseball and declared ineligible for the Baseball Hall of Fame for betting activities (Aug. 24, 1989). A year later, he will serve a five-month jail term for tax evasion.

After 18 years as one of the leading players in professional tennis, Chris Evert announces her retirement (Sept. 5, 1989).

Art Shell, Football Hall of Fame defensive tackle for the Los Angeles Raiders, takes over his old team and becomes the first black head coach in the National Football League in nearly 60 years.

Secretariat, winner of the 1973 Triple Crown and one of the most famous race horses in history, is put down (Oct. 4, 1989), suffering from a hoof disease.

A group of Hollywood film experts declares Martin Scorsese's 1980 black-and-white film *Raging Bull*, in which actor Robert De Niro portrays boxer Jake LaMotta, the best movie of the decade (Oct. 5, 1989).

America's hungry for oat bran and lower cholesterol.

After the 28-year-old Berlin Wall separating Communist East Germany from Democratic West Germany is breached (Nov. 9, 1989), intrepid marketers start peddling souvenir pieces of it around the world.

They, however, are no match for the Teenage Mutant Ninja Turtles—Donatello, Raphael, Michelangelo and Leonardo. They chomp pizza, speak in Valley-Girl-Surfer fashion ("Kowabunga, Dude"), are wildly popular in movies, television cartoon shows, clothing, computer games, comic books and action figures, to the tune of more than $600 million in 1989 alone.

The great music conductor and composer Leonard Bernstein refuses to accept the National Medal of Arts (November 1989). Bernstein is protesting the fact that the National Endowment for the Arts has bowed to public sentiment against support for homosexually oriented artistic expression.

People magazine names 59-year-old actor Sean Connery the sexiest man alive (December 1989).

Elvis is sighted in Detroit.

The Nineties

Nearly 36 million Americans under the age of 65 have neither public nor private health insurance. The total of 35.7 million people represents an increase from 34.4 million in 1989, a change to 16.6 percent of the population in 1990, compared with 16.1 percent in 1989.

Liberation's pendulum swings quietly and rather briefly toward men early in the 1990s. The nation's most visible proponent is poet Robert Bly, whose book *Iron John* becomes a best-seller. After a decade in which men's role in modern society was tenderly nebulous at best, men in the 1990s are urged to put their mothers far behind and find their more primal selves.

The three greatest tenors in the world—Luciano Pavarotti, Plácido Domingo and José Carreras—join renowned conductor Zubin Mehta in Rome for a concert that draws world acclaim (July 7, 1990).

Ken Burns' stirring 11-hour documentary series "The Civil War" airs on PBS (Sept. 23–27, 1990), and is hailed as one of public television's finest moments.

Harvard University graduate student Edward L. Widmer discovers a clipping from the *New York Morning News* of Oct. 21, 1845, reporting the results of a "time-honored game of Base" played a day earlier at the Elysian Fields in Hoboken, N.J. Reports in early October of 1990 indicate that the modern game of baseball was not invented by either Abner Doubleday or Alexander J. Cartwright and was not first played in 1846, but that baseball, instead, evolved years earlier from a number of different enthusiasts.

As the pace and expense of modernity hastens, mail-order shopping is bigger than ever by the 1990s. Spiegel, L'eggs, Fingerhut, Lillian Vernon, L.L. Bean, J. Crew, Lands' End, Orvis, Eddie Bauer and the like all do immense catalog business. For real convenience, millions of Americans find television the handiest mall of all. Cable television's Home Shopping Channel and QVC (for Quality, Value and Convenience) draw stay-at-home credit card shoppers by the millions.

Walt Disney Studios has four of the top ten best-selling children's home videos in 1990: *Dumbo, Cinderella, Winnie the Pooh: New Found Friends*, and (at number one) *Bambi*.

A number of surveys suggest that the public's attitude towards sex and sexual experience has grown more conservative as the 1990s get underway, and fear of AIDS is only part of the reason. Promiscuity is considered seamy, a general sign of low-life activity. Monogamy is seen as infinitely more desirable.

Telephone pagers, "beepers," are part of standard daily dress for "with it" teenagers in the Northeast, especially in New York. The trend is part fashion, part fractiousness (drug dealers use beepers for business), and part practical function; beepers make it easier for friends and parents to keep track of wearers.

For the first time in 81 years, the Chicago White Sox play their home-opening baseball game (April 18, 1991) in a glittering new stadium replacing Comisky Park, the oldest ball park in the major leagues. The historic event is marred by a humiliating 16-0 loss to the Detroit Tigers.

Ever-popular romance novels are directly reflecting themes now dear to the hearts of Baby Boomers. One plot after another revolves either around a preoccupation with parenting, or the biological pressure on single career women to start families before it is too late.

Rap rock star M.C. Hammer drops the M.C. from his public name as his popularity soars with "Too Legit To Quit."

The Oakland Athletics' Rickey Henderson sets baseball's all-time base stealing record in the fourth inning of a 7-4 win over the New York Yankees (May 1, 1991). He steals third base and goes ahead of former St. Louis Cardinals 12-year record-holder Lou Brock with career-steal number 939.

Fat-wheeled and sturdy "mountain bikes" have far outstripped the wildly popular, 10-speed racing bikes that have dominated the market for two decades. Mountain bikes account for nearly two thirds of the 10 million bicycles sold every year in the U.S. and more than one half of the 15 million bicycles sold annually in Europe.

Movie director Oliver Stone stirs anger and bitter debate with the release of *JFK*, a provocative dramatization of the theory that the U.S. government conspired to assassinate Pres. John F. Kennedy because he intended to curb American involvement in Vietnam. The movie prompts sharp calls for release of the government's sealed files on the case. The Justice Department balks, citing national security.

Paul Reubens, best known as movie star and kid-show host ("Pee-Wee's Playhouse") Pee-Wee Herman, is arrested for masturbating in an adult-movie theater in Sarasota, Fla. (July 26, 1991). His fans are generally open-minded and supportive, but his career seems doomed.

The cover of August 1991's *Vanity Fair* magazine sports a controversial, startling nude photo of pregnant actress Demi Moore.

Ben Bradlee gives up executive editorship of the *Washington Post* (Aug. 1, 1991), ending his 26-year, 23-Pulitzer Prize reign as one of the nation's most aggressive and respected newspaper editors.

In Oracle, Ariz., four men and four women enter a 3.15-acre glass and steel enclosure called Biosphere 2 (Earth is Biosphere 1), for a two-year experiment in survivalism and ecological correctness (Sept. 26, 1991). The biosphere includes 3,800 species of plants and animals; five distinct ecosystems: ocean, rain forest, desert, savanna and marsh; living quarters and a farm. Many scientists dismiss the project as frivolous, unregimented and a waste of $150 million.

Rollerblades, in-line skates originally used to train hockey players out of season, are popular as sport and wherever teenagers have to navigate an expanse of pavement.

In October 1991, millions of television viewers watch the U.S. Senate confirmation hearings on the nomination of Judge Clarence Thomas to the U.S. Supreme Court. University of Oklahoma law professor Anita F. Hill charges that she was sexually harassed by Thomas. The hearings galvanize national attention to the issue.

A New York Times/CBS poll released Oct. 11, 1991, indicates that four of every 10 women have encountered some form of sexual harassment at work. Fully one third of the victims didn't report the incidents because they feared for their jobs, which, by the way, pay them an average of less than 60 cents for every $1 earned by men.

In the fall of 1991, Puma USA introduces its Disc System sneaker to the $5.5-billion-a-year world of high-tech, expensive athletic footwear. Following on the heels of Nike's Air shoes and Reebok's Pumps, Disc System sneakers, which retail for about $125, have a dial-system closure instead of Velcro flaps or laces, but seem destined to join other mechanical-closure shoes, such as the "Snap-Jacks" of the 1950s, in profound obscurity.

More than 30 percent of American households own a Nintendo set now; more than 30 million units are in play.

Late in 1991, the 500th anniversary of Christopher Columbus's voyages to the New World are celebrated, but with considerable ambivalence, for though his discoveries opened the West, they also heralded the visitation of disease, oppression and colonization upon the native peoples of the Americas.

Thirty-three states and the District of Columbia have lotteries by fall of 1991, and Americans are spending more than $20 billion a year on them.

Baseball's 1991 World Series between the Minnesota Twins and the Atlanta Braves is the most exciting in years. The series, which Minnesota wins in seven games, is lauded as the best in years, good for the national pastime, good for the country. The event is marred, however, by Atlanta fans who yell war cries and make tomahawk-chop gestures on national television, offending many Native Americans.

Eleven-year-old Macauley Culkin has millions of dollars in the bank after starring in *Home Alone* in 1991 and signing on for a sequel.

Basketball great Earvin "Magic" Johnson tells a stunned nation on Nov. 7, 1991, that he has contracted the HIV virus that is a precursor of AIDS, which now infects more than 1.5 million people around the world. Johnson quits professional basketball, but vows to play in the 1992 Olympics. He instantly becomes a spokesman and national champion in the fight against AIDS.

Voters in Louisiana return the governorship to Edwin Edwards in November balloting, but his opponent, ex-Ku Klux Klansman David Duke, gets national exposure for his populist but doomed campaign for the presidency.

Michael Jackson's long-awaited new album *Dangerous* is released to long overnight lines Nov. 25, 1991.

Author Salman Rushdie makes a surprise public appearance in New York City. He has been in hiding since Feb. 14, 1989, when Iran's Ayatollah Ruhollah Khomeini put a bounty on his life for writing the book *The Satanic Verses*. Rushdie surfaces to deliver a speech to an audience at Columbia University's Graduate School of Journalism Dec. 11, 1991, honoring the First Amendment and Supreme Court Justice William J. Brennan, Jr. "Free speech is life itself," Rushdie says. "Free speech is the whole thing, the whole ball game."

A Gallup poll at the end of 1991 indicates that more Americans than ever are praying with great regularity—91 percent of women and 85 percent of men now pray.

Elvis is sighted in Los Angeles, but fails to keep a national tabloid's promise that he will return Jan. 1, 1992.

Scents from the 1960s—musk oils, sandalwood and patchouli—are back on fragrance counters all over the country and enjoying renewed favor.

President Bush's popularity by the start of election year 1992 slides precipitously as the nation reels from high unemployment and recession.

In January 1992, President Bush and beleaguered American industrial leaders travel to Japan in a frustrating effort to convince leaders of the world's strongest economy that they should buy more American goods and services—America seems to be whining. To compound matters, President Bush gets sick at a banquet in his honor and retches on a Japanese dignitary. Relations between the two nations become strained shortly thereafter when Japanese political leaders charge that U.S. corporate executives are vastly overpaid and U.S. workers lack education and a work ethic. In response, "Japan bashing" becomes popular for the winter. American auto workers smash a Japanese-made car while television news cameras roll. For a while, "Buy American" takes on renewed patriotic fervor.

The U.S. Postal Service announces (Jan. 9, 1992) that Elvis will appear on a postage stamp as part of a new "Legends of Music" series of commemoratives in 1993. The service initiates a national public opinion survey asking fans to choose between two Elvis images, one as a young rocker, the other in his later years. Not surprisingly, in June the young rocker version wins.

The national Centers for Disease Control reports outbreaks of drug-resistant tuberculosis in 13 states (Jan. 23, 1992).

Though not a new stunt, Velcro wall-jumping is increasingly popular in metropolitan-area night spots. Contestants in Velcro jumpsuits execute a forward half-somersault off a small trampoline to land upside down as far up a padded Velcro wall as possible. Late night comedian David Letterman performed a version of Velcro wall-jumping on national television in the mid-1980s.

Former heavyweight boxing champion Mike Tyson is sentenced to six years in prison (March 26, 1992) after being convicted of raping a beauty pageant contestant. Bail is denied, but as Tyson heads for jail in Indiana his lawyers, led by Harvard law professor Alan M. Dershowitz, begin the appeals process.

Rock 'n' roll is taking a back seat to Country Western music, which for several years has been moving steadily closer to the mainstream of popular taste. Baby Boomers have grown weary of Golden Oldies tunes from the 1950s. As they slow down for forty-something reflection, Country Western, with its penchant for heartbreak, disillusionment and true-blue American values, seems more to their liking. Singers Garth Brooks and Reba McEntire are icons. So is singer, guitarist and songwriter Bonnie Raitt, whose songs and intricate arrangements smoothly bridge the distance between rock and country.

More Americans than ever are including vitamin supplements in their daily diet, from B6 and E and C to calcium, lecithin and niacin. Though many researchers increasingly lend credibility to the practice, others, such as Dr. Victor Herbert, a professor of medicine at Mount Sinai Medical School in New York City, insist that if daily diet is proper, "taking supplements just gives you expensive urine."

Chrysler, Ford and General Motors begin unveiling small emission-free cars and vans powered by improved batteries, but costs per vehicle run as high as $125,000.

Arthur Ashe, former U.S. Open and Wimbledon champion and a pioneer in sports and social issues, announces that he has had the deadly HIV virus for more than three years. Ashe contracted AIDS from a blood transfusion during surgery in 1988, but had managed to keep his illness a secret. He made the disclosure (April 8, 1992) because USA Today seemed to be on the verge of breaking the story. The circumstances surrounding the disclosure draw bitter criticism of the press, and cause considerable soul-searching throughout the industry.

After exhausting appeals of her conviction for tax fraud and despite public rallies in her support, Leona Helmsley begins a four-year sentence for tax fraud (April 16, 1992). The 71-year-old self-styled queen of the Helmsley hotel empire becomes prisoner No. 15113-054 at a federal prison in Lexington, Ky. She becomes eligible for parole on Aug. 13, 1993.

Author Joyce Carol Oates' novel Black Water causes a stir upon release in May 1992. The book, an account of a young woman's drowning presented from the victim's perspective, is unabashedly based on the 1969 death of Mary Jo Kopechne in a car driven by Sen. Edward M. Kennedy (D-Mass.). The novel draws considerable praise, but strident condemna-tion as well, because it is "faction," a popular work that blurs the distinction between facts and fiction.

By spring, the hottest consumer collectibles anywhere are limited-edition Swatches, fashionable Swiss-made wristwatches calculated to skyrocket several hundred times their retail value. The watches range from $40 each. Designer versions have sold at auction for more than $30,000.

Men's neckties are wider now; so are sport and suit jacket lapels. Platform shoes and sandals, some with cork soles (shades of the early 1970s), are making a modest comeback in women's fashion. "Retro" dressing, donning fashions from the 1950s, 1960s and 1970s, is a popular fad in metropolitan nightspots, and among teenagers in some places, wearing clothes backwards is catching on.

Stephen Sondheim, the award-winning lyricist and composer, refuses to accept the 1992 National Medal of Arts award from the National Endowment for the Arts, which he says is becoming "a conduit and symbol of censorship and repression . . ." (May 8, 1992).

At the spring close of the formal 1991–92 television season, "The Cosby Show," "Who's the Boss?," "Night Court," "Matlock" and "The Golden Girls" all make their final bows on network television.

The season finale of "Murphy Brown" (May 18, 1992) causes a week-long national flap when the sitcom's star, played by Candice Bergen, has a baby out of wedlock. Vice-President Dan Quayle cites the popular show as further evidence that "family values" have faltered throughout the United States, and that the decline is at the root of the nation's problems. White House spokesman Marlin Fitzwater quickly agrees but minutes later notes that the sitcom episode did seem "pro-life," and that it did also seem to honor single parents. President Bush vaguely supports Quayle, who stands by his comments, but the administration seems chagrined by the whole affair.

Alexander and Alexandra are "in" names for 1990s newborns.

The federal Centers for Disease Control reports (May 21, 1992) that Americans are giving up cigarettes in record numbers. Between 1987 and 1990 cigarette smoking decreased more than twice as fast as it did in the 20 years from 1965 to 1985.

Comedian Johnny Carson calls it quits after a 30-year reign as host of "The Tonight Show" (May 22, 1992). Carson succeeded Jack Paar on Oct. 1, 1962. Jay Leno is Carson's successor. Top competitor Arsenio Hall vows to beat Leno in the ratings.

Whimsical tote bags in the shape of fish, cats, dogs and reptiles are fashionable in the spring of 1992.

New York magazine reports (June 8, 1992) that despite the surging AIDS epidemic and a decade-long national turn toward the moralistic right—or perhaps as a backlash against those influences—indiscriminate sex among both heterosexuals and homosexuals is reaching revolutionary proportions at private nightclubs and bars.

Michael Keaton reprises his starring role as the caped crusader in *Batman Returns*, the first of the 1992 summer's big box-office hits. The movie is widely panned as plotless and pointless, but it pulls in $46 million in its first June weekend and more than three times that by summer's end. Meanwhile, Clint Eastwood's elegiac Western *Unforgiven* opens in August and is an immediate box-office and critical success. So is *The Last of the Mohicans* in September.

"Ledge" haircuts are popular among teenage males; the top is worn long and the sides are shorn close. Baggy pants are popular. Radically teased "tall" or "mall" hair among women is becoming passé in the summer of 1992, falling to more natural-looking styles. Skirts are fashionably short.

In 1992, the Baby Boom generation shows a preoccupation with its descent into middle age. A television sitcom called "Middle Ages" slips into prime-time fall popularity. Gail Sheehy's book *The Silent Passage* and Germaine Greer's *The Change* elevates concern with the problems of menopause to best-seller status.

A five-volume set of Elvis Presley's 1950s hits is released in the summer of 1992 and by mid-August, the 15th anniversary of his death, sells more than 500,000 copies. Sales boost Presley's gold record total to 110, more than double that of his closest competitor, The Beatles, whose song sales tallied 41 gold records.

Rap music, not rock 'n' roll, is at the center of pop culture in the United States by 1992. It is fast, dissonant, intricate and as high-pressured and chaotic as life in the 1990s. The music reflects deep and divisive racial anger and frustration. Rap also is the first inherently rebellious and establishment-threatening new music since rock 'n' roll to have mass, color-blind appeal among the nation's youth. More and more young men on college campuses around the country wear visored caps turned backward, defying the norm of dress, just as the new music itself defies traditional pop-music forms. Rap draws from reggae and calypso styles of the West Indies. In the late 1970s and through the 1980s, rap and its hybrids became the province of rebellious inner-city youth, but by 1992 the music has legions of devotees in Mexico, Japan, the Soviet republics, France, Great Britain, West Africa, India, China and Eastern Europe.

By 1992, more than half of all American households have telephone answering machines.

Country and Western singer Billy Ray Cyrus sweeps the summer music charts with a hit single called "Achy Breaky Heart." The song, and its promoter Mercury Records, launch Achy Breaky dancing, a 22-step line dance based on the Texas two-step, as a dance sensation.

U.S. athletes bring home a total of 108 medals, 37 of them gold, from the XXV Summer Olympic Games in Barcelona, Spain (July 25–Aug. 9). The total ranks second to the 112 medals won by athletes from the 12 former republics of the Soviet Union competing as the "Unified Team."

The basketball team fielded by the United States is a focus of attention and some controversy. The Olympians are a "Dream Team" of National Basketball Association players who are allowed to compete in Barcelona despite the professional experience of all of them but Christian Laettner, who has graduated from Duke University in May and a month later has been the first-round draft pick of the Minnesota Timberwolves. Laettner joins Olympic teammates Charles Barkley, Philadelphia 76ers; Larry Bird, Boston Celtics; Clyde Drexler, Portland Trail Blazers; Patrick Ewing, New York Knickerbockers; Earvin "Magic" Johnson, Los Angeles Lakers; Michael Jordan and Scottie Pippin, Chicago Bulls; Karl Malone and John Stockton, Utah Jazz; Chris Mullen, Golden State Warriors and David Robinson, San Antonio Spurs.

Not surprisingly, the Dream Team goes undefeated, trouncing all of its opponents by an average margin of 43.8 points per game. Critics say the Dream Team undermined the true competitiveness of the traditionally amateur international event and, to that extent, made the basketball games boring. Fans seem unfazed. The game is uniquely American; the team stellar, the play hard. So the gold medal is a lock from the start; what of it? In a symbolic way, the Dream Team elevates American basketball prowess to new heights on the international stage. Perhaps most importantly, the Dream Team reminds anyone who is paying attention that while baseball may be the hallowed American pastime, it is no longer the pantheon from which the culture draws its heroes.

In a guest spot on the "Arsenio Hall" show (Aug. 10, 1992), Earvin "Magic" Johnson announces that he *may* return to professional basketball despite his having contracted the HIV virus.

A nagging back injury forces Boston Celtics' superstar forward Larry Bird to announce his retirement from professional basketball (Aug. 18, 1992) after 13 seasons, 10 of them as an All-Star. With extraordinary athleticism and galvanic play, Bird and his arch-rival Magic Johnson did more than any other players in the 1980s to revitalize professional basketball.

More than 2.3 million fax machines are in use across the United States by August 20, 1992.

"Brain Gyms," private clubs where patrons use therapies and equipment designed for instant mental relaxation, crop up in metropolitan areas around the world.

Expensive prescription nicotine transdermal patches, expected to be a billion-dollar industry by the end of the year, are now the most popular stop-smoking aids in the United States.

Vice-President Dan Quayle and about 14 million other television viewers tune in for the one-hour season premier of "Murphy Brown" (Sept. 21, 1992). Quayle takes his lumps but complains that his remarks had been widely misinterpreted.

Magic Johnson resigns from President Bush's Council on AIDS (Sept. 25, 1992) after Bush rejects the group's request for more funds. Johnson says Bush has generally ignored the council's recommendations. Four days later (Sept. 29), Johnson announces that he will return to the Los Angeles Lakers for the 1992–93 professional basketball season. He will be paid about $14 million to play from 50 to 60 games, making him the highest paid athlete in history.

Singer, actress and sex symbol Madonna (Ciccone) moves from mainstream titillation to calculated effrontery (and the top of the best-seller lists) with the release (Oct. 21, 1992) of a Mylar-enclosed, $50 Warner book of darkly erotic photographs titled *Sex*.

Magic Johnson retires from professional basketball again (Nov. 2), this time for good. His status as the nation's best-known AIDS victim has caused too much controversy among fellow N.B.A. players. "I'm not having fun," he says. "I can't be Magic."

In the Nov. 3, 1992, general election, Arkansas Gov. Bill Clinton and Tennessee Sen. Albert Gore beat Pres. George Bush and Vice-Pres. Dan Quayle decisively, ending 12 years of Republican rule. Clinton promises to focus like "a laser beam" on the nation's troubled economy. Meanwhile, he says, he will take fast action against Congressional perquisites, the ban against homosexuals in the military and abortion-rights restrictions.

Chess grandmaster Bobby Fischer may still be idiosyncratic, irascible and irreverent, but he's still also one of the best chess players in the world. He proves it by again beating Boris Spassky, 10 games to 5 (Nov. 5, 1992) in a 30-game, two-month exhibition match in Belgrade, Yugoslavia.

Legendary stock-car driver Richard Petty, winner of 200 races and world champion 7 times, finishes his farewell 35th season safely, but with his car in flames at the Hooters 500 at Atlanta Motor Speedway in Georgia (Nov. 15, 1992).

Director Spike Lee's long-awaited, 3-hour and 19-minute movie, *Malcolm X* premiers (Nov. 18, 1992) to huge crowds and critical acclaim. In a culture that has been starved of its heroes, the blunt-talking, well-educated black Muslim leader, played by Denzel Washington, seems right for the times; a flawed visionary who will try to do the right thing, or die trying. Malcolm X was assassinated Feb. 21, 1965.

On the same day that *Malcolm X* premiers (Nov. 18, 1992), DC Comics allows the villain Doomsday to kill 54-year-old Superman. The venerable Man of Steel had gotten as hackneyed and predictable as the heroic standard he immortalized; his sales were down, too. Spectators and comic buffs queue up at magazine counters all over the country for their copies of issue No. 75, which comes sealed in plastic. Some copies include a black in-memorium armband. Superman's creators assure the skeptical public that Krypton's favorite son will not be resurrected . . . this year.

America's favorite British gentleman, Alistair Cooke, says, "So good night and goodbye" to loyal viewers of PBS's "Masterpiece Theater" (Nov. 29, 1992), leaving the award-winning show he has hosted since 1971.

The creators and executive producers of "Cheers," one of the highest-rated weekly comedy shows on television, tell NBC (Dec. 7, 1992) that the show's 271st episode, to air in May 1993, will be its last. By the end of the 1992 season, "Cheers" had won 26 Emmy Awards and received more nominations, 111, than any other show in history.

Comedian David Letterman accepts $16 million (Dec. 8, 1992) to move his quirky late-night television show from NBC to CBS in a 1993 ratings assault on the 11:30 P.M. time-slot occupied by competitors Jay Leno and Arsenio Hall.

Chess grandmaster Bobby Fischer is indicted (Dec. 15, 1992) for violating the United Nations Security Council's economic sanctions against Yugoslavia.

The U.S. Census Bureau reports (Dec. 29, 1992) that sharp increases in immigration and growth in the West has pushed the nation's population to a new high of 256.6 million.

AWARD WINNERS

ACADEMY AWARDS
Academy of Motion Picture Arts and Sciences

The Oscar, the annual award of the Academy of Motion Picture Arts and Sciences, in Beverly Hills, Calif., is the best known and most celebrated award in the United States for achievement in cinema. The first awards were made in 1928 at a small banquet for about 250 people. Today, Oscars are awarded in more than 20 categories during a televised ceremony in early spring that is watched by nearly 30 percent of the households in America.

BEST PICTURE OF THE YEAR

1927–28	Wings
1928–29	The Broadway Melody
1929–30	All Quiet on the Western Front
1931–32	Grand Hotel
1932–33	Cavalcade
1934	It Happened One Night
1935	Mutiny on the Bounty
1936	The Great Ziegfeld
1937	The Life of Emile Zola
1938	You Can't Take It With You
1939	Gone With the Wind
1940	Rebecca
1941	How Green Was My Valley
1942	Mrs. Miniver
1943	Casablanca
1944	Going My Way
1945	The Lost Weekend
1946	The Best Years of Our Lives
1947	Gentleman's Agreement
1948	Hamlet
1949	All the King's Men
1950	All About Eve
1951	An American in Paris
1952	The Greatest Show on Earth
1953	From Here to Eternity
1954	On the Waterfront
1955	Marty
1956	Around the World in 80 Days
1957	The Bridge on the River Kwai
1958	Gigi
1959	Ben-Hur
1960	The Apartment
1961	West Side Story
1962	Lawrence of Arabia
1963	Tom Jones
1964	My Fair Lady
1965	The Sound of Music
1966	A Man for All Seasons
1967	In the Heat of the Night
1968	Oliver!
1969	Midnight Cowboy
1970	Patton
1971	The French Connection
1972	The Godfather
1973	The Sting
1974	The Godfather, Part II
1975	One Flew Over the Cuckoo's Nest
1976	Rocky
1977	Annie Hall
1978	The Deer Hunter
1979	Kramer vs. Kramer
1980	Ordinary People
1981	Chariots of Fire
1982	Gandhi
1983	Terms of Endearment
1984	Amadeus
1985	Out of Africa
1986	Platoon
1987	The Last Emperor
1988	Rain Man
1989	Driving Miss Daisy
1990	Dances With Wolves
1991	The Silence of the Lambs

ACTOR

(Best Performance by an Actor in a Leading Role)

1927–28	Emil Jannings, The Way of All Flesh and The Last Command
1928–29	Warner Baxter, In Old Arizona
1929–30	George Arliss, Disraeli
1930–31	Lionel Barrymore, A Free Soul
1931–32	Wallace Beery, The Champ
1932–33	Charles Laughton, The Private Life of Henry VIII
	Fredric March, Dr. Jekyll and Mr. Hyde
1934	Clark Gable, It Happened One Night
1935	Victor McLaglen, The Informer
1936	Paul Muni, The Story of Louis Pasteur
1937	Spencer Tracy, Captains Courageous
1938	Spencer Tracy, Boys Town
1939	Robert Donat, Goodbye, Mr. Chips
1940	James Stewart, The Philadelphia Story
1941	Gary Cooper, Sergeant York
1942	James Cagney, Yankee Doodle Dandy
1943	Paul Lukas, Watch on the Rhine
1944	Bing Crosby, Going My Way
1945	Ray Milland, The Lost Weekend

1946	Fredric March, *The Best Years of Our Lives*
1947	Ronald Colman, *A Double Life*
1948	Laurence Olivier, *Hamlet*
1949	Broderick Crawford, *All the King's Men*
1950	Jose Ferrer, *Cyrano de Bergerac*
1951	Humphrey Bogart, *The African Queen*
1952	Gary Cooper, *High Noon*
1953	William Holden, *Stalag 17*
1954	Marlon Brando, *On the Waterfront*
1955	Ernest Borgnine, *Marty*
1956	Yul Brunner, *The King and I*
1957	Alex Guinness, *The Bridge on the River Kwai*
1958	David Niven, *Separate Tables*
1959	Charlton Heston, *Ben-Hur*
1960	Burt Lancaster, *Elmer Gantry*
1961	Maximilian Schell, *Judgment at Nuremberg*
1962	Gregory Peck, *To Kill a Mockingbird*
1963	Sidney Poitier, *Lilies of the Field*
1964	Rex Harrison, *My Fair Lady*
1965	Lee Marvin, *Cat Ballou*
1966	Paul Scofield, *A Man for All Seasons*
1967	Rod Steiger, *In the Heat of the Night*
1968	Cliff Robertson, *Charly*
1969	John Wayne, *True Grit*
1970	George C. Scott, *Patton*
1971	Gene Hackman, *The French Connection*
1972	Marlon Brando, *The Godfather*
1973	Jack Lemmon, *Save the Tiger*
1974	Art Carney, *Harry and Tonto*
1975	Jack Nicholson, *One Flew Over the Cuckoo's Nest*
1976	Peter Finch, *Network*
1977	Richard Dreyfuss, *The Goodbye Girl*
1978	Jon Voight, *Coming Home*
1979	Dustin Hoffman, *Kramer vs. Kramer*
1980	Robert De Niro, *Raging Bull*
1981	Henry Fonda, *On Golden Pond*
1982	Ben Kingsley, *Gandhi*
1983	Robert Duvall, *Tender Mercies*
1984	F. Murray Abraham, *Amadeus*
1985	William Hurt, *Kiss of the Spider Woman*
1986	Paul Newman, *The Color of Money*
1987	Michael Douglas, *Wall Street*
1988	Dustin Hoffman, *Rain Man*
1989	Daniel Day-Lewis, *My Left Foot*
1990	Jeremy Irons, *Reversal of Fortune*
1991	Anthony Hopkins, *The Silence of the Lambs*

ACTRESS

(Best Performance by an Actress in a Leading Role)

1927–28	Janet Gaynor, *Seventh Heaven; Street Angel;* and *Sunrise*
1928–29	Mary Pickford, *Coquette*
1929–30	Norma Shearer, *The Divorcee*
1930–31	Marie Dressler, *Min and Bill*
1931–32	Helen Hayes, *The Sin of Madelon Claudet*
1932–33	Katharine Hepburn, *Morning Glory*
1934	Claudette Colbert, *It Happened One Night*
1935	Bette Davis, *Dangerous*
1936	Luise Rainer, *The Great Ziegfeld*
1937	Luise Rainer, *The Good Earth*
1938	Bette Davis, *Jezebel*
1939	Vivien Leigh, *Gone With the Wind*
1940	Ginger Rogers, *Kitty Foyle*
1941	Joan Fontaine, *Suspicion*
1942	Greer Garson, *Mrs. Miniver*
1943	Jennifer Jones, *The Song of Bernadette*
1944	Ingrid Bergman, *Gaslight*
1945	Joan Crawford, *Mildred Pierce*
1946	Olivia de Havilland, *To Each His Own*
1947	Loretta Young, *The Farmer's Daughter*
1948	Jane Wyman, *Johnny Belinda*
1949	Olivia de Havilland, *The Heiress*
1950	Judy Holliday, *Born Yesterday*
1951	Vivien Leigh, *A Streetcar Named Desire*
1952	Shirley Booth, *Come Back Little Sheba*
1953	Audrey Hepburn, *Roman Holiday*
1954	Grace Kelly, *The Country Girl*
1955	Anna Magnani, *The Rose Tattoo*
1956	Ingrid Bergman, *Anastasia*
1957	Joanne Woodward, *The Three Faces of Eve*
1958	Susan Hayward, *I Want to Live!*
1959	Simone Signoret, *Room at the Top*
1960	Elizabeth Taylor, *Butterfield 8*
1961	Sophia Loren, *Two Women*
1962	Anne Bancroft, *The Miracle Worker*
1963	Patricia Neal, *Hud*
1964	Julie Andrews, *Mary Poppins*
1965	Julie Christie, *Darling*
1966	Elizabeth Taylor, *Who's Afraid of Virginia Woolf?*
1967	Katharine Hepburn, *Guess Who's Coming to Dinner*
1968	Katharine Hepburn, *The Lion in Winter* Barbra Streisand, *Funny Girl*
1969	Maggie Smith, *The Prime of Miss Jean Brodie*
1970	Glenda Jackson, *Women in Love*
1971	Jane Fonda, *Klute*
1972	Liza Minnelli, *Cabaret*
1973	Glenda Jackson, *A Touch of Class*
1974	Ellen Burstyn, *Alice Doesn't Live Here Anymore*
1975	Louise Fletcher, *One Flew Over the Cuckoo's Nest*
1976	Faye Dunaway, *Network*
1977	Diane Keaton, *Annie Hall*
1978	Jane Fonda, *Coming Home*
1979	Sally Field, *Norma Rae*

1980	Sissy Spacek, *Coal Miner's Daughter*
1981	Katharine Hepburn, *On Golden Pond*
1982	Meryl Streep, *Sophie's Choice*
1983	Shirley MacLaine, *Terms of Endearment*
1984	Sally Field, *Places in the Heart*
1985	Geraldine Page, *The Trip to Bountiful*
1986	Marlee Matlin, *Children of a Lesser God*
1987	Cher, *Moonstruck*
1988	Jodie Foster, *The Accused*
1989	Jessica Tandy, *Driving Miss Daisy*
1990	Kathy Bates, *Misery*
1991	Jodie Foster, *The Silence of the Lambs*

BEST SUPPORTING ACTOR

1936	Walter Brennan, *Come and Get It*
1937	Joseph Schildkraut, *The Life of Emile Zola*
1938	Walter Brennan, *Kentucky*
1939	Thomas Mitchell, *Stagecoach*
1940	Walter Brennan, *The Westerner*
1941	Donald Crisp, *How Green Was My Valley*
1942	Van Heflin, *Johnny Eager*
1943	Charles Coburn, *The More the Merrier*
1944	Barry Fitzgerald, *Going My Way*
1945	James Dunn, *A Tree Grows in Brooklyn*
1946	Harold Russell, *The Best Years of Our Lives*
1947	Edmund Gwenn, *Miracle on 34th Street*
1948	Walter Huston, *The Treasure of the Sierra Madre*
1949	Dean Jagger, *Twelve O'Clock High*
1950	George Sanders, *All About Eve*
1951	Karl Malden, *A Streetcar Named Desire*
1952	Anthony Quinn, *Viva Zapata!*
1953	Frank Sinatra, *From Here to Eternity*
1954	Edmond O'Brien, *The Barefoot Contessa*
1955	Jack Lemmon, *Mister Roberts*
1956	Anthony Quinn, *Lust for Life*
1957	Red Buttons, *Sayonara*
1958	Burl Ives, *The Big Country*
1959	Hugh Griffith, *Ben-Hur*
1960	Peter Ustinov, *Spartacus*
1961	George Chakiris, *West Side Story*
1962	Ed Begley, *Sweet Bird of Youth*
1963	Melvyn Douglas, *Hud*
1964	Peter Ustinov, *Topkapi*
1965	Martin Balsam, *A Thousand Clowns*
1966	Walter Matthau, *The Fortune Cookie*
1967	George Kennedy, *Cool Hand Luke*
1968	Jack Albertson, *The Subject Was Roses*
1969	Gig Young, *They Shoot Horses, Don't They?*
1970	John Mills, *Ryan's Daughter*
1971	Ben Johnson, *The Last Picture Show*
1972	Joel Grey, *Cabaret*
1973	John Houseman, *The Paper Chase*
1974	Robert De Niro, *The Godfather, Part II*
1975	George Burns, *The Sunshine Boys*
1976	Jason Robards, *All the President's Men*

1977	Jason Robards, *Julia*
1978	Christopher Walken, *The Deer Hunter*
1979	Melvyn Douglas, *Being There*
1980	Timothy Hutton, *Ordinary People*
1981	John Gielgud, *Arthur*
1982	Louis Gossett, Jr., *An Officer and a Gentleman*
1983	Jack Nicholson, *Terms of Endearment*
1984	Haing S. Ngor, *The Killing Fields*
1985	Don Ameche, *Cocoon*
1986	Michael Caine, *Hannah and Her Sisters*
1987	Sean Connery, *The Untouchables*
1988	Kevin Kline, *A Fish Named Wanda*
1989	Denzel Washington, *Glory*
1990	Joe Pesci, *Goodfellas*
1991	Jack Palance, *City Slickers*

BEST SUPPORTING ACTRESS

1936	Gale Sondergaard, *Anthony Adverse*
1937	Alice Brady, *In Old Chicago*
1938	Fay Bainter, *Jezebel*
1939	Hattie McDaniel, *Gone With the Wind*
1940	Jane Darwell, *The Grapes of Wrath*
1941	Mary Astor, *The Great Lie*
1942	Teresa Wright, *Mrs. Miniver*
1943	Katina Paxinou, *For Whom the Bell Tolls*
1944	Ethel Barrymore, *None But the Lonely Heart*
1945	Anne Revere, *National Velvet*
1946	Anne Baxter, *The Razor's Edge*
1947	Celeste Holm, *Gentleman's Agreement*
1948	Claire Trevor, *Key Largo*
1949	Mercedes McCambridge, *All the King's Men*
1950	Josephine Hull, *Harvey*
1951	Kim Hunter, *A Streetcar Named Desire*
1952	Gloria Grahame, *The Bad and the Beautiful*
1953	Donna Reed, *From Here to Eternity*
1954	Eva Marie Saint, *On the Waterfront*
1955	Jo Van Fleet, *East of Eden*
1956	Dorothy Malone, *Written on the Wind*
1957	Miyoshi Umeki, *Sayonara*
1958	Wendy Hiller, *Separate Tables*
1959	Shelley Winters, *The Diary of Anne Frank*
1960	Shirley Jones, *Elmer Gantry*
1961	Rita Moreno, *West Side Story*
1962	Patty Duke, *The Miracle Worker*
1963	Margaret Rutherford, *The V.I.P.'s*
1964	Lila Kedrova, *Zorba the Greek*
1965	Shelley Winters, *A Patch of Blue*
1966	Sandy Dennis, *Who's Afraid of Virginia Woolf?*
1967	Estelle Parsons, *Bonnie and Clyde*
1968	Ruth Gordon, *Rosemary's Baby*
1969	Goldie Hawn, *Cactus Flower*
1970	Helen Hayes, *Airport*
1971	Cloris Leachman, *The Last Picture Show*
1972	Eileen Heckart, *Butterflies Are Free*

1973 Tatum O'Neal, *Paper Moon*
1974 Ingrid Bergman, *Murder on the Orient Express*
1975 Lee Grant, *Shampoo*
1976 Beatrice Straight, *Network*
1977 Vanessa Redgrave, *Julia*
1978 Maggie Smith, *California Suite*
1979 Meryl Streep, *Kramer vs. Kramer*
1980 Mary Steenburgen, *Melvin and Howard*
1981 Maureen Stapleton, *Reds*
1982 Jessica Lange, *Tootsie*
1983 Linda Hunt, *The Year of Living Dangerously*
1984 Peggy Ashcroft, *A Passage to India*
1985 Anjelica Huston, *Prizzi's Honor*
1986 Dianne Wiest, *Hannah and Her Sisters*
1987 Olympia Dukakis, *Moonstruck*
1988 Geena Davis, *The Accidental Tourist*
1989 Brenda Fricker, *My Left Foot*
1990 Whoopi Goldberg, *Ghost*
1991 Mercedes Ruehl, *The Fisher King*

BEST DIRECTOR (AND ASSISTANT DIRECTOR)

(An award for assistant director was given from 1932 to 1937.)

1927–28 Frank Borzage, *Seventh Heaven*
 Lewis Mileston, *Two Arabian Nights*—Comedy Direction
1928–29 Frank Lloyd, *The Divine Lady*
1929–30 Lewis Milestone, *All Quiet on the Western Front*
1930–31 Norman Taurog, *Skippy*
1931–32 Frank Borzage, *Bad Girl*
1932–33 Frank Lloyd, *Cavalcade*
 Charles Barton, Scott Beal, Charles Dorian, Fred Fox, Gordon Hollingshead, Dewey Starkey, William Tumme—Assistant Directors
1934 Frank Capra, *It Happened One Night*
 John Waters, *Viva Villa*—Assistant Director
1935 John Ford, *The Informer*
 Clen Beauchamp and Paul Wing, *Lives of a Bengal Lancer*—Assistant Directors
1936 Frank Capra, *Mr. Deeds Goes to Town*
 Jack Sullivan, *The Charge of the Light Brigade*—Assistant Director
1937 Leo McCarey, *The Awful Truth*
 Robert Webb, *In Old Chicago*—Assistant Director
1938 Frank Capra, *You Can't Take It with You*
1939 Victor Fleming, *Gone With the Wind*
1940 John Ford, *The Grapes of Wrath*
1941 John Ford, *How Green Was My Valley*
1942 William Wyler, *Mrs. Miniver*
1943 Michael Curtiz, *Casablanca*

1944 Leo McCarey, *Going My Way*
1945 Billy Wilder, *The Lost Weekend*
1946 William Wyler, *The Best Years of Our Lives*
1947 Elia Kazan, *Gentleman's Agreement*
1948 John Huston, *The Treasure of the Sierra Madre*
1949 Joseph L. Mankiewicz, *A Letter to Three Wives*
1950 Joseph L. Mankiewicz, *All About Eve*
1951 George Stevens, *A Place in the Sun*
1952 John Ford, *The Quiet Man*
1953 Fred Zinnemann, *From Here to Eternity*
1954 Elia Kazan, *On the Waterfront*
1955 Delbert Mann, *Marty*
1956 George Stevens, *Giant*
1957 David Lean, *The Bridge on the River Kwai*
1958 Vincente Minnelli, *Gigi*
1959 William Wyler, *Ben-Hur*
1960 Billy Wilder, *The Apartment*
1961 Robert Wise, Jerome Robbins, *West Side Story*
1962 David Lean, *Lawrence of Arabia*
1963 Tony Richardson, *Tom Jones*
1964 George Cukor, *My Fair Lady*
1965 Robert Wise, *The Sound of Music*
1966 Fred Zinnemann, *A Man for All Seasons*
1967 Mike Nichols, *The Graduate*
1968 Sir Carol Reed, *Oliver!*
1969 John Schlesinger, *Midnight Cowboy*
1970 Franklin J. Schaffner, *Patton*
1971 William Friedkin, *The French Connection*
1972 Bob Fosse, *Cabaret*
1973 George Roy Hill, *The Sting*
1974 Francis Ford Coppola, *The Godfather, Part II*
1975 Milos Forman, *One Flew Over the Cuckoo's Nest*
1976 John G. Avildsen, *Rocky*
1977 Woody Allen, *Annie Hall*
1978 Michael Cimino, *The Deer Hunter*
1979 Robert Benton, *Kramer vs. Kramer*
1980 Robert Redford, *Ordinary People*
1981 Warren Beatty, *Reds*
1982 Richard Attenborough, *Gandhi*
1983 James L. Brooks, *Terms of Endearment*
1984 Milos Forman, *Amadeus*
1985 Sydney Pollack, *Out of Africa*
1986 Oliver Stone, *Platoon*
1987 Bernardo Bertolucci, *The Last Emperor*
1988 Barry Levinson, *Rain Man*
1989 Oliver Stone, *Born on the Fourth of July*
1990 Kevin Costner, *Dances With Wolves*
1991 Jonathan Demme, *The Silence of the Lambs*

BEST SONG

1934 "Continental," from *The Gay Divorcee*, by Con Conrad (music), Herb Magidson (lyrics)

1935 "Lullaby of Broadway," from *Gold Diggers of 1935*, by Harry Warren (music), Al Dubin (lyrics)

1936 "The Way You Look Tonight," from *Swing Time*, by Jerome Kern (music), Dorothy Fields (lyrics)

1937 "Sweet Leilani," from *Waikiki Wedding*, by Harry Owens

1938 "Thanks for the Memory," from *The Big Broadcast of 1938*, by Ralph Raininger (music), Leo Robin (lyrics)

1939 "Over the Rainbow," from *The Wizard of Oz*, by Harold Arlen (music), E. Y. Harburg (lyrics)

1940 "When You Wish Upon a Star," from *Pinocchio*, by Leigh Harline (music), Ned Washington (lyrics)

1941 "The Last Time I Saw Paris," from *Lady Be Good*, by Jerome Kern (music), Oscar Hammerstein II (lyrics)

1942 "White Christmas," from *Holiday Inn*, by Irving Berlin

1943 "You'll Never Know," from *Hello, Frisco, Hello*, by Harry Warren (music), Mack Gordon (lyrics)

1944 "Swinging on a Star," from *Going My Way*, by James Van Heusen (music), Johnny Burke (lyrics)

1945 "It Might As Well Be Spring," from *State Fair*, by Richard Rodgers (music), Oscar Hammerstein II (lyrics)

1946 "On the Atchison, Topeka and Santa Fe," from *The Harvey Girls*, by Harry Warren (music), Johnny Mercer (lyrics)

1947 "Zip-A-Dee-Doo-Dah," from *Song of the South*, by Allie Wrubel (music), Ray Gilbert (lyrics)

1948 "Buttons and Bows," from *The Paleface*, by Jay Livingston, Ray Evans (music and lyrics)

1949 "Baby It's Cold Outside," from *Neptune's Daughter*, by Frank Loesser

1950 "Mona Lisa," from *Captain Carey, USA*, by Ray Evans, Jay Livingston (music and lyrics)

1951 "In the Cool, Cool, Cool of the Evening," from *Here Comes the Groom*, by Hoagy Carmichael (music), Johnny Mercer (lyrics)

1952 "High Noon (Do Not Forsake Me, Oh My Darlin)," from *High Noon*, by Dimitri Tiomkin (music), Ned Washington (lyrics)

1953 "Secret Love," from *Calamity Jane*, by Sammy Fain (music), Paul Francis Webster (lyrics)

1954 "Three Coins in the Fountain," from *Three Coins in the Fountain*, by Jule Styne (music), Sammy Cahn (lyrics)

1955 "Love Is a Many-Splendored Thing," from *Love Is a Many-Splendored Thing*, by Sammy Fain (music), Paul Francis Webster (lyrics)

1956 "Whatever Will Be, Will Be" ("Que Sera, Sera"), from *The Man Who Knew Too Much*, by Ray Evans, Jay Livingston (music and lyrics)

1957 "All the Way," from *The Joker Is Wild*, by James Van Heusen (music), Sammy Cahn (lyrics)

1958 "Gigi," from *Gigi*, by Frederick Loewe (music), Alan Jay Lerner (lyrics)

1959 "High Hopes," from *A Hole in the Head*, by James Van Heusen (music), Sammy Cahn (lyrics)

1960 "Never on Sunday," from *Never on Sunday*, by Manos Hadjidakis

1961 "Moon River," from *Breakfast at Tiffany's*, by Henry Mancini (music), Johnny Mercer (lyrics)

1962 "Days of Wine and Roses, from *Days of Wine and Roses*, by Henry Mancini (music), Johnny Mercer (lyrics)

1963 "Call Me Irresponsible," from *Papa's Delicate Condition*, by James Van Heusen (music), Sammy Cahn (lyrics)

1964 "Chim Chim Cher-ee," from *Mary Poppins*, by Richard M. Sherman and Robert B. Sherman (music and lyrics)

1965 "The Shadow of Your Smile," from *The Sandpiper*, by Johnny Mandel (music), Paul Francis Webster (lyrics)

1966 "Born Free," from *Born Free*, by John Barry (music), Don Black (lyrics)

1967 "Talk to the Animals," from *Doctor Doolittle*, by Leslie Bricusse

1968 "The Windmills of Your Mind," from *The Thomas Crown Affair*, by Michel Legrand (music), Alan and Marilyn Bergman (lyrics)

1969 "Raindrops Keep Fallin' on My Head," from *Butch Cassidy and the Sundance Kid*, by Burt Bacharach (music) and Hal David (lyrics)

1970 "For All We Know," from *Lovers and Other Strangers*, by Fred Karlin (music), Robb Royer and James Griffin a.k.a. Robb Wilson and Arthur James (lyrics)

1971 "Theme from Shaft," from *Shaft*, by Isaac Hayes

1972 "The Morning After," from *The Poseidon Adventure*, by Al Kasha, Joel Hirschhorn (music and lyrics)

1973 "The Way We Were," from *The Way We Were*, by Marvin Hamlisch (music), Alan and Marilyn Bergman (lyrics)

1974 "We May Never Love Like This Again," from *The Towering Inferno*, by Al Kasha, Joel Hirschhorn (music and lyrics)

1975 "I'm Easy," from *Nashville*, by Keith Carradine

1976 "Evergreen," from *A Star Is Born*, by Barbra Streisand (music), Paul Williams (lyrics)

1977 "You Light Up My Life," from *You Light Up My Life*, by Joseph Brooks

1978 "Last Dance," from *Thank God It's Friday*, by Paul Jabara

1979 "It Goes Like It Goes," from *Norma Rae*, by David Shire (music), Norman Gimbel (lyrics)

1980 "Fame," from *Fame*, by Michael Gore (music), Dean Pitchford (lyrics)

1981 "Arthur's Theme" ("Best That You Can Do"), from *Arthur* by Burt Bacharach, Carole Bayer Sager (music and lyrics)

1982 "Up Where We Belong," from *An Officer and a Gentleman*, by Jack Nitzsche and Buffy Sainte-Marie (music), Will Jennings (lyrics)

1983 "Flashdance . . . What a Feeling," from *Flashdance*, by Giorgio Moroder (music), Keith Forsey and Irene Cara (lyrics)

1984 "I Just Called to Say I Love You," from *The Woman in Red*, by Stevie Wonder

1985 "Say You, Say Me," from *White Nights*, by Lionel Richie

1986 "Take My Breath Away," from *Top Gun*, by Giorgio Moroder (music), Tom Whitlock (lyrics)

1987 "The Time of My Life," from *Dirty Dancing*, by Frank Previte, John DeNicola, and Donald Markowitz

1988 "Let the River Run," from *Working Girl*, by Carly Simon

1989 "Under the Sea," from *The Little Mermaid*, by Howard Ashman and Alan Menken

1990 "Sooner or Later," from *Dick Tracy*, by Stephen Sondheim

1991 "Beauty and the Beast," from *Beauty and the Beast*, by Howard Ashman

EMMY AWARDS
Academy of Television Arts and Sciences

The Emmy is the highest annual honor bestowed by the National Academy of Television Arts and Sciences in New York. In 1949, when the academy publicly presented its first six award statuettes, there were fewer than 200,000 television sets in the United States; by 1990, there were roughly 200 million. The Emmy Awards had grown, too. Scores of awards are presented every September in a special program that is watched by millions of viewers. The following list is a selection of the awards presented in connection with prime-time programs.

1948 Most Popular TV Program: "Pantomime Quiz Time" (KTLA)
Outstanding TV Personality: Shirley Dinsdale (and her puppet Judy Splinters) (KTLA)
Best Film Made for Television: *The Necklace* on "Your Show Time" (NBC)
Special Award: Louis McManus, for his design of the Emmy

1949 Best Live Show: "The Ed Wynn Show" (CBS)
Best Kinescope Show: "Texaco Star Theater" (NBC)
Outstanding Live Personality: Ed Wynn (CBS)
Outstanding Kinescope Personality: Milton Berle (NBC)
Best Film Made for TV: *The Life of Riley* (NBC)

1950 Best Dramatic Show: "Pulitzer Prize Playhouse" (ABC)
Outstanding Personality: Groucho Marx (NBC)
Best Actor: Alan Young (CBS)
Best Actress: Gertrude Berg (CBS)

1951 Best Dramatic Show: "Studio One" (CBS)
Best Comedy Show: "The Red Skelton Show" (CBS)
Best Actor: Sid Caesar (NBC)
Best Actress: Imogene Coca (NBC)

1952 Best Dramatic Program: "Robert Montgomery Presents" (NBC)
Best Situation Comedy: "I Love Lucy" (CBS)
Best Actor: Thomas Mitchell
Best Actress: Helen Hayes

1953 Best Dramatic Program: "The U.S. Steel Hour" (ABC)

Best Situation Comedy: "I Love Lucy" (CBS)

Best Male Star of Regular Series: Donald O'Connor, "Colgate Comedy Hour" (NBC)

Best Female Star of Regular Series: Eve Arden, "Our Miss Brooks" (CBS)

1954   Best Dramatic Series: "The U.S. Steel Hour" (ABC)

Best Situation Comedy Series: "Make Room for Daddy" (ABC)

Best Actor Starring in a Regular Series: Danny Thomas, "Make Room for Daddy" (ABC)

Best Actress Starring in a Regular Series: Loretta Young, "The Loretta Young Show" (NBC)

1955   Best Dramatic Series: "Producers' Showcase" (NBC)

Best Comedy Series: "The Phil Silvers Show" (CBS)

Best Actor (Continuing Performance): Phil Silvers, "The Phil Silvers Show" (CBS)

Best Actress (Continuing Performance): Lucille Ball, "I Love Lucy" (CBS)

1956   Best Single Program of the Year: "Requiem for a Heavyweight" on "Playhouse 90" (CBS)

Best Series (Half Hour or Less): "The Phil Silvers Show" (CBS)

Best Series (One Hour or More): "Caesar's Hour" (NBC)

Best Continuing Performance by an Actor in a Dramatic Series: Robert Young, "Father Knows Best" (NBC)

Best Continuing Performance by an Actress in a Dramatic Series: Loretta Young, "The Loretta Young Show" (NBC)

1957   Best Single Program of the Year: "The Comedian" on "Playhouse 90" (CBS)

Best Dramatic Series With Continuing Characters: "Gunsmoke" (CBS)

Best Comedy Series: "The Phil Silvers Show" (CBS)

Best Continuing Performance by an Actor in a Leading Role in a Dramatic or Comedy Series: Robert Young, "Father Knows Best" (NBC)

Best Continuing Performance by an Actress in a Leading Role in a Dramatic or Comedy Series: Jane Wyatt, "Father Knows Best" (NBC)

1958–59   Most Outstanding Single Program of the Year: "An Evening With Fred Astaire" (NBC)

Best Dramatic Series (One Hour or Longer): "Playhouse 90" (CBS)

Best Dramatic Series (Less Than One Hour): "Alcoa-Goodyear Theatre" (NBC)

Best Comedy Series: "The Jack Benny Show" (CBS)

Best Actor in a Leading Role (Continuing Character) in a Dramatic Series: Raymond Burr, "Perry Mason" (CBS)

Best Actress in a Leading Role (Continuing Character) in a Dramatic Series: Loretta Young, "The Loretta Young Show" (NBC)

Best Actor in a Leading Role (Continuing Character) in a Comedy Series: Jack Benny, "The Jack Benny Show" (CBS)

Best Actress in a Leading Role (Continuing Character) in a Comedy Series: Jane Wyatt, "Father Knows Best" (CBS and NBC)

1959–60   Outstanding Program Achievement in the Field of Humor: "The Art Carney Special" (NBC)

Outstanding Program Achievement in the Field of Drama: "Playhouse 90" (CBS)

Outstanding Performance by an Actor in Series (Lead or Support): Robert Stack, "The Untouchables" (ABC)

Outstanding Performance by an Actress in Series (Lead or Support): Jane Wyatt, "Father Knows Best" (CBS)

1960–61   Program of the Year: *Macbeth*, on "The Hallmark Hall of Fame" (NBC)

Outstanding Program Achievement in the Field of Humor: "The Jack Benny Show" (CBS)

Outstanding Program Achievement in the Field of Drama: *Macbeth*, on "The Hallmark Hall of Fame" (NBC)

Outstanding Performance by an Actor in Series (Lead): Raymond Burr, "Perry Mason" (CBS)

Outstanding Performance by an Actress in Series (Lead): Barbara Stanwyck, "The Barbara Stanwyck Show" (NBC)

1961–62   Program of the Year: "Victoria Regina," on "The Hallmark Hall of Fame" (NBC)

Outstanding Program Achievement in the Field of Humor: "The Bob Newhart Show" (NBC)

Outstanding Program Achievement in the Field of Drama: "The Defenders" (CBS)

Outstanding Continued Performance by an Actor in Series (Lead): E. G. Marshall, "The Defenders" (CBS)

Outstanding Continued Performance by an Actress in Series (Lead): Shirley Booth, "Hazel" (NBC)

1962–63   Program of the Year: "The Tunnel" (NBC)

Outstanding Program Achievement in the Field of Humor: "The Dick Van Dyke Show" (CBS)

Outstanding Program Achievement in the Field of Drama: "The Defenders" (CBS)

Outstanding Continued Performance by an Actor in Series (Lead): E. G. Marshall, "The Defenders" (CBS)

Outstanding Continued Performance by an Actress in Series (Lead): Shirley Booth, "Hazel" (NBC)

1963–64   Program of the Year: "The Making of the President 1960" (ABC)

Outstanding Program Achievement in the Field of Comedy: "The Dick Van Dyke Show" (CBS)

Outstanding Program Achievement in the Field of Drama: "The Defenders" (CBS)

Outstanding Continued Performance by an Actor in Series (Lead): Dick Van Dyke, "The Dick Van Dyke Show" (CBS)

Outstanding Continued Performance by an Actress in Series (Lead): Mary Tyler Moore, "The Dick Van Dyke Show" (CBS)

1964–65   Outstanding Achievements in Entertainment: "The Dick Van Dyke Show" (CBS); "The Magnificent Yankee," on "The Hallmark Hall of Fame" (NBC); My Name Is Barbra" (CBS)

Outstanding Individual Achievements in Entertainment (Actors and Performers): Lynn Fontanne, "The Magnificent Yankee," on "The Hallmark Hall of Fame" (NBC); Barbra Streisand, "My Name Is Barbra" (CBS); Dick Van Dyke, "The Dick Van Dyke Show" (CBS)

1965–66   Outstanding Drama Series: "The Fugitive" (ABC)

Outstanding Comedy Series: "The Dick Van Dyke Show" (CBS)

Outstanding Continuing Performance by an Actor in a Leading Role in a Drama Series: Bill Cosby, "I Spy" (NBC)

Outstanding Continued Performance by an Actress in a Leading Role in a Drama Series: Barbara Stanwyck, "The Big Valley" (ABC)

Outstanding Continued Performance by an Actor in a Leading Role in a Comedy Series: Dick Van Dyke, "The Dick Van Dyke Show" (CBS)

Outstanding Continued Performance by an Actress in a Leading Role in a Comedy Series: Mary Tyler Moore, "The Dick Van Dyke Show" (CBS)

1966–67   Outstanding Drama Series: "Mission: Impossible" (CBS)

Outstanding Comedy Series: "The Monkees" (NBC)

Outstanding Continued Performance by an Actor in a Leading Role in a Drama Series: Bill Cosby, "I Spy" (NBC)

Outstanding Continued Performance by an Actress in a Leading Role in a Drama Series: Barbara Bain, "Mission: Impossible" (CBS)

Outstanding Continued Performance by an Actor in a Leading Role in a Comedy Series: Don Adams: "Get Smart" (NBC)

Outstanding Continued Performance by an Actress in a Leading Role in a Comedy Series: Lucille Ball, "The Lucy Show" (CBS)

1967–68   Outstanding Drama Series: "Mission: Impossible" (CBS)

Outstanding Comedy Series: "Get Smart" (NBC)

Outstanding Continued Performance by an Actor in a Leading Role in a Drama Series: Bill Cosby, "I Spy" (NBC)

Outstanding Continued Performance by an Actress in a Leading Role in a Drama Series: Barbara Bain, "Mission: Impossible" (CBS)

Outstanding Continued Performance by an Actor in a Leading Role in a Comedy Series: Don Adams: "Get Smart" (NBC)

Outstanding Continued Performance by an Actress in a Leading Role in a Comedy Series: Lucille Ball, "The Lucy Show" (CBS)

1968–69   Outstanding Drama Series: "NET Playhouse" (NET)

Outstanding Comedy Series: "Get Smart" (NBC)

Outstanding Continued Performance by an Actor in a Leading Role in a Drama Series: Carl Betz, "Judd for the Defense" (ABC)

Outstanding Continued Performance by an Actress in a Leading Role in a Drama Series: Barbara Bain, "Mission: Impossible" (CBS)

Outstanding Continued Performance by an Actor in a Leading Role in a Comedy Series: Don Adams, "Get Smart" (NBC)

Outstanding Continued Performance by an Actress in a Leading Role in a Comedy Series: Hope Lange, "The Ghost and Mrs. Muir" (NBC)

1969–70 Outstanding Drama Series: "Marcus Welby, M.D." (ABC)

Outstanding Comedy Series: "My World and Welcome to It" (NBC)

Outstanding Continued Performance by an Actor in a Leading Role in a Drama Series: Robert Young, "Marcus Welby, M.D." (ABC)

Outstanding Continued Performance by an Actress in a Leading Role in a Drama Series: Susan Hampshire, "The Forsyte Saga" (NET)

Outstanding Continued Performance by an Actor in a Leading Role in a Comedy Series: William Windom, "My World and Welcome to It" (NBC)

Outstanding Continued Performance by an Actress in a Leading Role in a Comedy Series: Hope Lange, "The Ghost and Mrs. Muir" (NBC)

1970–71 Outstanding Drama Series: "The Senator" (NBC)

Outstanding Comedy Series: "All in the Family" (CBS)

Outstanding Continued Performance by an Actor in a Leading Role in a Drama Series: Hal Holbrook, "The Senator" (NBC)

Outstanding Continued Performance by an Actress in a Leading Role in a Drama Series: Susan Hampshire, "The First Churchills," on "Masterpiece Theatre" (PBS)

Outstanding Continued Performance by an Actor in a Leading Role in a Comedy Series: Jack Klugman, "The Odd Couple" (CBS)

Outstanding Continued Performance by an Actress in a Leading Role in a Comedy Series: Jean Stapleton, "All in the Family" (CBS)

1971–72 Outstanding Drama Series: "Elizabeth R," on "Masterpiece Theatre" (PBS)

Outstanding Comedy Series: "All in the Family" (CBS)

Outstanding Continued Performance by an Actor in a Leading Role in a Drama Series: Peter Falk, "Columbo" (NBC)

Outstanding Continued Performance by an Actress in a Leading Role in a Drama Series: Glenda Jackson, "Elizabeth R," on "Masterpiece Theatre" (PBS)

Outstanding Continued Performance by an Actor in a Leading Role in a Comedy Series: Carroll O'Connor, "All in the Family" (CBS)

Outstanding Continued Performance by an Actress in a Leading Role in a Comedy Series: Jean Stapleton, "All in the Family" (CBS)

1972–73 Outstanding Drama Series: "The Waltons" (CBS)

Outstanding Comedy Series: "All in the Family" (CBS)

Outstanding Continued Performance by an Actor in a Leading Role in a Drama Series: Richard Thomas, "The Waltons" (CBS)

Outstanding Continued Performance by an Actress in a Leading Role in a Drama Series: Michael Learned, "The Waltons" (CBS)

Outstanding Continued Performance by an Actor in a Leading Role in a Comedy Series: Jack Klugman, "The Odd Couple" (CBS)

Outstanding Continued Performance by an Actress in a Leading Role in a Comedy Series: Mary Tyler Moore, "The Mary Tyler Moore Show" (CBS)

1973–74 Outstanding Drama Series: "Upstairs, Downstairs," on "Masterpiece Theatre" (PBS)

Outstanding Comedy Series: "M*A*S*H" (CBS)

Best Lead Actor in a Drama Series: Telly Savalas, "Kojak" (CBS)

Best Lead Actress in a Drama Series: Michael Learned, "The Waltons" (CBS)

Best Lead Actor in a Comedy Series: Alan Alda, "M*A*S*H" (CBS)

Best Lead Actress in a Comedy Series: Mary Tyler Moore, "The Mary Tyler Moore Show" (CBS)

1974–75 Outstanding Drama Series: "Upstairs, Downstairs," on "Masterpiece Theatre" (PBS)

Outstanding Comedy Series: "The Mary Tyler Moore Show" (CBS)

Outstanding Lead Actor in a Drama Series: Robert Blake, "Baretta" (ABC)

Outstanding Lead Actress in a Drama Series: Jean Marsh, "Upstairs, Downstairs," on "Masterpiece Theatre" (PBS)

Outstanding Lead Actor in a Comedy Series: Tony Randall, "The Odd Couple" (ABC)

Outstanding Lead Actress in a Comedy Series: Valerie Harper, "Rhoda" (CBS)

1975–76 Outstanding Drama Series: "Police Story" (NBC)

Outstanding Comedy Series: "The Mary Tyler Moore Show" (CBS)

Outstanding Lead Actor in a Drama Series: Peter Falk, "Columbo" (NBC)

Outstanding Lead Actress in a Drama Series: Michael Learned, "The Waltons" (CBS)

Outstanding Lead Actor in a Comedy Series: Jack Albertson, "Chico and the Man" (NBC)

Outstanding Lead Actress in a Comedy Series: Mary Tyler Moore, "The Mary Tyler Moore Show" (CBS)

1976–77 Outstanding Drama Series: "Upstairs, Downstairs," on "Masterpiece Theatre" (PBS)

Outstanding Comedy Series: "The Mary Tyler Moore Show" (CBS)

Outstanding Lead Actor in a Drama Series: James Garner, "The Rockford Files" (NBC)

Outstanding Lead Actress in a Drama Series: Lindsay Wagner, "The Bionic Woman" (ABC)

Outstanding Lead Actor in a Comedy Series: Carroll O'Connor, "All in the Family" (CBS)

Outstanding Lead Actress in a Comedy Series: Beatrice Arthur, "Maude" (CBS)

1977–78 Outstanding Drama Series: "The Rockford Files" (NBC)

Outstanding Comedy Series: "All in the Family" (CBS)

Outstanding Lead Actor in a Drama Series: Edward Asner, "Lou Grant" (CBS)

Outstanding Lead Actress in a Drama Series: Sada Thompson, "Family" (ABC)

Outstanding Lead Actor in a Comedy Series: Carroll O'Connor, "All in the Family" (CBS)

Outstanding Lead Actress in a Comedy Series: Jean Stapleton, "All in the Family" (CBS)

1978–79 Outstanding Drama Series: "Lou Grant" (CBS)

Outstanding Comedy Series: "Taxi" (ABC)

Outstanding Lead Actor in a Drama Series: Ron Leibman, "Kaz" (CBS)

Outstanding Lead Actress in a Drama Series: Mariette Hartley, "The Incredible Hulk" (CBS)

Outstanding Lead Actor in a Comedy Series: Carroll O'Connor, "All in the Family" (CBS)

Outstanding Lead Actress in a Comedy Series: Ruth Gordon, "Taxi" (CBS)

1979–80 Outstanding Drama Series: "Lou Grant" (CBS)

Outstanding Comedy Series: "Taxi" (ABC)

Outstanding Lead Actor in a Drama Series: Ed Asner, "Lou Grant" (CBS)

Outstanding Lead Actress in a Drama Series: Barbara Bel Geddes, "Dallas" (CBS)

Outstanding Lead Actor in a Comedy Series: Richard Mulligan, "Soap" (ABC)

Outstanding Lead Actress in a Comedy Series: Cathryn Damon, "Soap" (ABC)

1980–81 Outstanding Drama Series: "Hill Street Blues" (NBC)

Outstanding Comedy Series: "Taxi" (ABC)

Outstanding Lead Actor in a Drama Series: Daniel J. Travanti, "Hill Street Blues" (NBC)

Outstanding Lead Actress in a Drama Series: Barbara Babcock: "Hill Street Blues" (NBC)

Outstanding Lead Actor in a Comedy Series: Judd Hirsch, "Taxi" (ABC)

Outstanding Lead Actress in a Comedy Series: Isabel Sanford, "The Jeffersons" (CBS)

1981–82 Outstanding Drama Series: "Hill Street Blues" (NBC)

Outstanding Comedy Series: "Barney Miller" (ABC)

Outstanding Lead Actor in a Drama Series: Daniel J. Travanti, "Hill Street Blues" (NBC)

Outstanding Lead Actress in a Drama Series: Michael Learned, "Nurse" (CBS)

Outstanding Lead Actor in a Comedy Series: Alan Alda, "M*A*S*H" (CBS)

Outstanding Lead Actress in a Comedy Series: Carol Kane, "Taxi" (ABC)

1982–83   Outstanding Drama Series: "Hill Street Blues" (NBC)

Outstanding Comedy Series: "Cheers" (NBC)

Outstanding Lead Actor in a Drama Series: Ed Flanders, "St. Elsewhere" (NBC)

Outstanding Lead Actress in a Drama Series: Tyne Daly, "Cagney & Lacey" (CBS)

Outstanding Lead Actor in a Comedy Series: Judd Hirsch, "Taxi" (NBC)

Outstanding Lead Actress in a Comedy Series: Shelley Long, "Cheers" (NBC)

1983–84   Outstanding Drama Series: "Hill Street Blues" (NBC)

Outstanding Comedy Series: "Cheers" (NBC)

Outstanding Lead Actor in a Drama Series: Tom Selleck, "Magnum P.I." (CBS)

Outstanding Lead Actress in a Drama Series: Tyne Daly, "Cagney & Lacey" (CBS)

Outstanding Lead Actor in a Comedy Series: John Ritter, "Three's Company" (ABC)

Outstanding Lead Actress in a Comedy Series: Jane Curtin, "Kate & Allie" (CBS)

1984–85   Outstanding Drama Series: "Cagney & Lacey" (CBS)

Outstanding Comedy Series: "The Cosby Show" (NBC)

Outstanding Lead Actor in a Drama Series: William Daniels, "St. Elsewhere" (NBC)

Outstanding Lead Actress in a Drama Series: Tyne Daly, "Cagney & Lacey" (CBS)

Outstanding Lead Actor in a Comedy Series: Robert Guillaume, "Benson" (ABC)

Outstanding Lead Actress in a Comedy Series: Jane Curtin, "Kate & Allie" (CBS)

1985–86   Outstanding Drama Series: "Cagney & Lacey" (CBS)

Outstanding Comedy Series: "The Golden Girls" (NBC)

Outstanding Lead Actor in a Drama Series: William Daniels, "St. Elsewhere" (NBC)

Outstanding Lead Actress in a Drama Series: Sharon Gless, "Cagney & Lacey" (CBS)

Outstanding Lead Actor in a Comedy Series: Michael J. Fox, "Family Ties" (NBC)

Outstanding Lead Actress in a Comedy Series: Betty White, "The Golden Girls" (NBC)

1986–87   Outstanding Drama Series: "L.A. Law" (NBC)

Outstanding Comedy Series: "The Golden Girls" (NBC)

Outstanding Lead Actor in a Drama Series: Bruce Willis, "Moonlighting" (ABC)

Outstanding Lead Actress in a Drama Series: Sharon Gless, "Cagney & Lacey" (CBS)

Outstanding Lead Actor in a Comedy Series: Michael J. Fox, "Family Ties" (NBC)

Outstanding Lead Actress in a Comedy Series: Rue McClanahan, "The Golden Girls" (NBC)

1987–88   Outstanding Drama Series: "thirtysomething" (ABC)

Outstanding Comedy Series: "The Wonder Years" (ABC)

Outstanding Lead Actor in a Drama Series: Richard Kiley, "A Year in the Life" (NBC)

Outstanding Lead Actress in a Drama Series: Tyne Daly, "Cagney & Lacey" (CBS)

Outstanding Lead Actor in a Comedy Series: Michael J. Fox, "Family Ties" (NBC)

Outstanding Lead Actress in a Comedy Series: Beatrice Arthur, "The Golden Girls" (NBC)

1988–89   Outstanding Drama Series: "L.A. Law" (NBC)

Outstanding Comedy Series: "Cheers" (NBC)

Outstanding Lead Actor in a Drama Series: Carroll O'Connor, "In the Heat of the Night" (NBC)

Outstanding Lead Actress in a Drama Series: Dana Delany, "China Beach" (ABC)

Outstanding Lead Actor in a Comedy Series: Richard Mulligan, "Empty Nest" (NBC)

Outstanding Lead Actress in a Comedy Series: Candice Bergen, "Murphy Brown" (CBS)

1989–90   Outstanding Drama Series: "L.A. Law" (NBC)

Outstanding Comedy Series: "Murphy Brown" (CBS)

Outstanding Lead Actor in a Drama Series: Peter Falk, "Columbo" (ABC)

Outstanding Lead Actress in a Drama Series: Patricia Wettig, "thirtysomething" (ABC)

Outstanding Lead Actor in a Comedy Series: Ted Danson, "Cheers" (NBC)

Outstanding Lead Actress in a Comedy Series: Candice Bergen, "Murphy Brown" (CBS)

1990–91   Outstanding Drama Series: "L.A. Law" (NBC)

Outstanding Comedy Series: "Cheers" (NBC)

Outstanding Lead Actor in a Drama Series: James Earl Jones, "Gabriel's Fire" (ABC)

Outstanding Lead Actress in a Drama Series: Patricia Wettig, "thirtysomething" (ABC)

Outstanding Lead Actor in a Comedy Series: Burt Reynolds, "Evening Shade" (CBS)

Outstanding Lead Actress in a Comedy Series: Kirstie Alley, "Cheers" (NBC)

1991–92   Outstanding Drama Series: "Northern Exposure" (CBS)

Outstanding Comedy Series: "Murphy Brown" (CBS)

Outstanding Lead Actor in a Drama Series: Christopher Lloyd, "Avonlea" (Disney Channel)

Outstanding Lead Actress in a Drama Series: Dana Delany, "China Beach" (ABC)

Outstanding Lead Actor in a Comedy Series: Craig T. Nelson, "Coach" (ABC)

Outstanding Lead Actress in a Comedy Series: Candice Bergen, "Murphy Brown" (CBS)

GRAMMY AWARDS
National Academy of Recording Arts and Sciences

Since 1959, the National Academy of Recording Arts and Sciences in Burbank, Calif., has honored outstanding musical and technical achievement in recording. More than 60 Grammys, miniature gramophones, are presented in a nationally televised awards ceremony every February.

Year	Record of the Year	Album of the Year
1958	Domenico Modugno "Nel Blu Dipinto di Blu" ("Volare")	Henry Mancini *The Music from Peter Gunn*
1959	Bobby Darin "Mack the Knife"	Frank Sinatra *Come Dance with Me*
1960	Percy Faith "Theme from a Summer Place"	Bob Newhart *Button-Down Mind*
1961	Henry Mancini "Moon River"	Judy Garland *Judy at Carnegie Hall*
1962	Tony Bennett "I Left My Heart in San Francisco"	Vaughn Meader *The First Family*
1963	Henry Mancini "The Days of Wine and Roses"	Barbra Streisand *The Barbra Streisand Album*
1964	Stan Getz; Astrud Gilberto "The Girl from Ipanema"	Stan Getz; Astrud Gilberto *Getz/Gilberto*
1965	Herb Alpert & the Tijuana Brass "A Taste of Honey"	Frank Sinatra *September of My Years*
1966	Frank Sinatra "Strangers in the Night"	Frank Sinatra *A Man and His Music*
1967	5th Dimension "Up, Up and Away"	The Beatles *Sgt. Pepper's Lonely Hearts Club Band*
1968	Simon & Garfunkel "Mrs. Robinson"	Glen Campbell *By the Time I Get to Phoenix*
1969	5th Dimension "Aquarius/Let the Sunshine In"	Blood, Sweat & Tears *Blood, Sweat & Tears*
1970	Simon & Garfunkel "Bridge over Troubled Water"	Simon & Garfunkel *Bridge over Troubled Water*
1971	Carole King "It's Too Late"	Carol King *Tapestry*

Year	Record of the Year	Album of the Year
1972	Roberta Flack "The First Time Ever I Saw Your Face"	George Harrison; Ravi Shankar; Bob Dylan et al. *Concert for Bangladesh*
1973	Roberta Flack "Killing Me Softly with His Song"	Stevie Wonder *Innervisions*
1974	Olivia Newton-John "I Honestly Love You"	Stevie Wonder *Fulfillingness' First Finale*
1975	Captain & Tennille "Love Will Keep Us Together"	Paul Simon *Still Crazy After All These Years*
1976	George Benson "This Masquerade"	Stevie Wonder *Songs in the Key of Life*
1977	The Eagles "Hotel California"	Fleetwood Mac *Rumours*
1978	Billy Joel "Just the Way You Are"	Various Artists *Saturday Night Fever*
1979	The Doobie Brothers "What a Fool Believes"	Billy Joel *52nd Street*
1980	Christopher Cross "Sailing"	Christopher Cross *Christopher Cross*
1981	Kim Carnes "Bette Davis Eyes"	John Lennon/Yoko Ono *Double Fantasy*
1982	Toto "Rosanna"	Toto *Toto IV*
1983	Michael Jackson "Beat It"	Michael Jackson *Thriller*
1984	Tina Turner "What's Love Got to Do with It?"	Lionel Richie *Can't Slow Down*
1985	USA for Africa "We Are the World"	Phil Collins *No Jacket Required*
1986	Steve Winwood "Higher Love"	Paul Simon *Graceland*
1987	Paul Simon "Graceland"	U2 *The Joshua Tree*
1988	Bobby McFerrin "Don't Worry, Be Happy"	George Michael *Faith*
1989	Bette Midler "Wind Beneath My Wings"	Bonnie Raitt *Nick of Time*
1990	Phil Collins "Another Day In Paradise"	Quincy Jones *Back on the Block*
1991	Natalie Cole with Nat "King" Cole "Unforgettable"	Natalie Cole with Nat "King" Cole *Unforgettable*

TONY AWARDS (ANTOINETTE PERRY AWARDS)

League of American Theatres and Producers

The Tony Awards, presented every June by the American Theater Wing in New York, recognize outstanding achievement in American theater. The award depicts the masks of tragedy and comedy on one side and a profile of Antoinette Perry, the Tony's namesake, on the other. Perry was a Broadway actress, producer, director, and head of the American Theater Wing until her death in 1946. The Tony Awards were established and first presented a year later.

PLAY

1948 *Mister Roberts*, Thomas Heggen and Joshua Logan based on novel by Thomas Heggen
1949 *Death of a Salesman*, Arthur Miller
1950 *The Cocktail Party*, T. S. Eliot
1951 *The Rose Tattoo*, Tennessee Williams
1952 *The Fourposter*, Jan de Hartog
1953 *The Crucible*, Arthur Miller
1954 *The Teahouse of the August Moon*, John Patrick
1955 *The Desperate Hours*, Joseph Hayes
1956 *The Diary of Anne Frank*, Francis Goodrich and Albert Hackett
1957 *Long Day's Journey into Night*, Eugene O'Neill
1958 *Sunrise at Campobello*, Dore Schary
1959 *J.B.*, Archibald MacLeish
1960 *The Miracle Worker*, William Gibson
1961 *Becket*, Jean Anouilh, translated by Lucienne Hill
1962 *A Man for All Seasons*, Robert Bolt
1963 *Who's Afraid of Virginia Woolf?*, Edward Albee
1964 *Luther*, John Osborne
1965 *The Subject Was Roses*, Frank Gilroy
1966 *Marat/Sade*, Peter Weiss, English version by Geoffrey Skelton
1967 *The Homecoming*, Harold Pinter
1968 *Rosencrantz and Guildenstern Are Dead*, Tom Stoppard
1969 *The Great White Hope*, Howard Sackler
1970 *Borstal Boy*, Frank McMahon
1971 *Sleuth*, Anthony Shaffer
1972 *Sticks and Bones*, David Rabe
1973 *That Championship Season*, Jason Miller
1974 *The River Niger*, Joseph A. Walker
1975 *Equus*, Peter Shaffer
1976 *Travesties*, Tom Stoppard
1977 *The Shadow Box*, Michael Cristofer
1978 *Da*, Hugh Leonard

1979	*The Elephant Man*, Bernard Pomerance
1980	*Children of a Lesser God*, Mark Medoff
1981	*Amadeus*, Peter Shaffer
1982	*The Life and Adventures of Nicholas Nickleby*, David Edgar
1983	*Torch Song Trilogy*, Harvey Fierstein
1984	*The Real Thing*, Tom Stoppard
1985	*Biloxi Blues*, Neil Simon
1986	*I'm Not Rappaport*, Herb Gardner
1987	*Fences*, August Wilson
1988	*M. Butterfly*, David Henry Hwang
1989	*The Heidi Chronicles*, Wendy Wasserstein
1990	*The Grapes of Wrath*, John Steinbeck
1991	*Lost in Yonkers*, Neil Simon
1992	*Dancing at Lughnasa*, Brian Friel

MUSICAL

1949	*Kiss Me, Kate*
1950	*South Pacific*
1951	*Guys and Dolls*
1952	*The King and I*
1953	*Wonderful Town*
1954	*Kismet*
1955	*The Pajama Game*
1956	*Damn Yankees*
1957	*My Fair Lady*
1958	*The Music Man*
1959	*Redhead*
1960	*Fiorello*
1961	*Bye, Bye, Birdie*
1962	*How to Succeed in Business Without Really Trying*
1963	*A Funny Thing Happened on the Way to the Forum*
1964	*Hello, Dolly!*
1965	*Fiddler on the Roof*
1966	*Man of La Mancha*
1967	*Cabaret*
1968	*Hallelujah, Baby!*
1969	*1776*
1970	*Applause*
1971	*Company*
1972	*Two Gentlemen of Verona*
1973	*A Little Night Music*
1974	*Raisin*
1975	*The Wiz*
1976	*A Chorus Line*
1977	*Annie*
1978	*Ain't Misbehavin'*
1979	*Sweeney Todd*
1980	*Evita*
1981	*42nd Street*
1982	*Nine*
1983	*Cats*
1984	*La Cage aux Folles*
1985	*Big River*

1986	*The Mystery of Edwin Drood*
1987	*Les Miserables*
1988	*The Phantom of the Opera*
1989	*Jerome Robbins' Broadway*
1990	*City of Angels*
1991	*The Will Rogers Follies*
1992	*Crazy for You*

ACTOR (DRAMATIC)

1969	James Earl Jones, *The Great White Hope*
1970	Fritz Weaver, *Child's Play*
1971	Brian Bedford, *The School for Wives*
1972	Cliff Gorman, *Lenny*
1973	Alan Bates, *Butley*
1974	Michael Moriarty, *Find Your Way Home*
1975	John Kani, *Sizwe Banzi*
	Winston Ntshona, *The Island*
1976	John Wood, *Travesties*
1977	Al Pacino, *The Basic Training of Pavlo Hummel*
1978	Barnard Hughes, *Da*
1979	Tom Conti, *Whose Life Is It Anyway?*
1980	John Rubinstein, *Children of a Lesser God*
1981	Ian McKellen, *Amadeus*
1982	Roger Rees, *The Life and Adventures of Nicholas Nickelby*
1983	Harvey Fierstein, *Torch Song Trilogy*
1984	Jeremy Irons, *The Real Thing*
1985	Derek Jacobi, *Much Ado About Nothing*
1986	Judd Hirsch, *I'm Not Rappaport*
1987	James Earl Jones, *Fences*
1988	Ron Silver, *Speed the Plow*
1989	Philip Bosco, *Lend Me a Tenor*
1990	Robert Morse, *Tru*
1991	Nigel Hawthorne, *Shadowlands*
1992	Judd Hirsch, *Conversations With My Father*

ACTRESS (DRAMATIC)

1947	Ingrid Bergman, *Joan of Lorraine*
	Helen Hayes, *Happy Birthday*
1948	Judith Anderson, *Medea*
	Katharine Cornell, *Antony and Cleopatra*
	Jessica Tandy, *A Streetcar Named Desire*
1949	Martita Hunt, *The Madwoman of Chaillot*
1950	Shirley Booth, *Come Back, Little Sheba*
1951	Uta Hagen, *The Country Girl*
1952	Julie Harris, *I Am a Camera*
1953	Shirley Booth, *Time of the Cuckoo*
1954	Audrey Hepburn, *Ondine*
1955	Nancy Kelly, *The Bad Seed*
1956	Julie Harris, *The Lark*
1957	Margaret Leighton, *Separate Tables*
1958	Helen Hayes, *Time Remembered*
1959	Gertrude Berg, *A Majority of One*
1960	Anne Bancroft, *The Miracle Worker*

1961 Joan Plowright, *A Taste of Honey*
1962 Margaret Leighton, *Night of the Iguana*
1963 Uta Hagen, *Who's Afraid of Virginia Woolf?*
1964 Sandy Dennis, *Any Wednesday*
1965 Irene Worth, *Tiny Alice*
1966 Rosemary Harris, *The Lion in Winter*
1967 Beryl Reid, *The Killing of Sister George*
1968 Zoe Caldwell, *The Prime of Miss Jean Brodie*
1969 Julie Harris, *Forty Carats*
1970 Tammy Grimes, *Private Lives*
1971 Maureen Stapleton, *Gingerbread Lady*
1972 Sada Thompson, *Twigs*
1973 Julie Harris, *The Last of Mrs. Lincoln*
1974 Colleen Dewhurst, *A Moon for the Misbegotten*
1975 Ellen Burstyn, *Same Time, Next Year*
1976 Irene Worth, *Sweet Bird of Youth*
1977 Julie Harris, *The Belle of Amherst*
1978 Jessica Tandy, *The Gin Game*
1979 Constance Cummings, *Wings*
      Carole Shelley, *The Elephant Man*
1980 Phyllis Frelich, *Children of a Lesser God*
1981 Jane Lapotaire, *Piaf*
1982 Zoe Caldwell, *Medea*
1983 Jessica Tandy, *Foxfire*
1984 Glenn Close, *The Real Thing*
1985 Stockard Channing, *Joe Egg*
1986 Lily Tomlin, *The Search for Signs of Intelligent Life in the Universe*
1987 Linda Lavin, *Broadway Bound*
1988 Joan Allen, *Burn This*
1989 Pauline Collins, *Shirley Valentine*
1990 Maggie Smith, *Lettice & Lovage*
1991 Mercedes Ruehl, *Lost in Yonkers*
1992 Glenn Close, *Death and the Maiden*

ACTOR (MUSICAL)

1948 Paul Hartman, *Angel in the Wings*
1949 Ray Bolger, *Where's Charley?*
1950 Ezio Pinza, *South Pacific*
1951 Robert Alda, *Guys and Dolls*
1952 Phil Silvers, *Top Banana*
1953 Thomas Mitchell, *Hazel Flagg*
1954 Alfred Drake, *Kismet*
1955 Walter Slezak, *Fanny*
1956 Ray Walston, *Damn Yankees*
1957 Rex Harrison, *My Fair Lady*
1958 Robert Preston, *The Music Man*
1959 Richard Kiley, *Redhead*
1960 Jackie Gleason, *Take Me Along*
1961 Richard Burton, *Camelot*
1962 Robert Morse, *How to Succeed in Business Without Really Trying*
1963 Zero Mostel, *A Funny Thing Happened on the Way to the Forum*
1964 Burt Lahr, *Foxy*

1965 Zero Mostel, *Fiddler on the Roof*
1966 Richard Kiley, *Man of La Mancha*
1967 Robert Preston, *I Do! I Do!*
1968 Robert Goulet, *The Happy Time*
1969 Jerry Orbach, *Promises, Promises*
1970 Cleavon Little, *Purlie*
1971 Hal Linden, *The Rothschilds*
1972 Phil Silvers, *A Funny Thing Happened on the Way to the Forum*
1973 Ben Vereen, *Pippin*
1974 Christopher Plummer, *Cyrano*
1975 John Cullum, *Shenandoah*
1976 George Rose, *My Fair Lady*
1977 Barry Bostwick, *The Robber Bridegroom*
1978 John Cullum, *On the Twentieth Century*
1979 Len Cariou, *Sweeney Todd*
1980 Jim Dale, *Barnum*
1981 Kevin Kline, *The Pirates of Penzance*
1982 Ben Harvey, *Dreamgirls*
1983 Tommy Tune, *My One and Only*
1984 George Hearn, *La Cage aux Folles*
1985 Category eliminated
1986 George Rose, *The Mystery of Edwin Drood*
1987 Robert Lindsay, *Me and My Girl*
1988 Michael Crawford, *The Phantom of the Opera*
1989 Jason Alexander, *Jerome Robbins' Broadway*
1990 James Naughton, *City of Angels*
1991 Jonathan Pryce, *Miss Saigon*
1992 Gregory Hines, *Jelly's Last Jam*

ACTRESS (MUSICAL)

1948 Grace Hartman, *Angel in the Wings*
1949 Nanette Fabray, *Love Life*
1950 Mary Martin, *South Pacific*
1951 Ethel Merman, *Call Me Madam*
1952 Gertrude Lawrence, *The King and I*
1953 Rosalind Russell, *Wonderful Town*
1954 Dolores Gray, *Carnival in Flanders*
1955 Mary Martin, *Peter Pan*
1956 Gwen Verdon, *Damn Yankees*
1957 Judy Holliday, *Bells Are Ringing*
1958 Thelma Ritter, *New Girl in Town*
      Gwen Verdon, *New Girl in Town*
1959 Gwen Verdon, *Redhead*
1960 Mary Martin, *The Sound of Music*
1961 Elizabeth Seal, *Irma la Douce*
1962 Anna Maria Alberghetti, *Carnival*
      Diahann Carroll, *No Strings*
1963 Vivien Leigh, *Tovarich*
1964 Carol Channing, *Hello, Dolly!*
1965 Liza Minnelli, *Flora, The Red Menace*
1966 Angela Lansbury, *Mame*
1967 Barbara Harris, *The Apple Tree*
1968 Patricia Routledge, *Darling of the Day*
      Leslie Uggams, *Hallelujah, Baby!*
1969 Angela Lansbury, *Dear World*

1970 Lauren Bacall, *Applause*
1971 Helen Gallagher, *No, No, Nanette*
1972 Alexis Smith, *Follies*
1973 Glynis Johns, *A Little Night Music*
1974 Virginia Capers, *Raisin*
1975 Angela Lansbury, *Gypsy*
1976 Donna McKechnie, *A Chorus Line*
1977 Dorothy Loudon, *Annie*
1978 Liza Minnelli, *The Act*
1979 Angela Lansbury, *Sweeney Todd*
1980 Patti LuPone, *Evita*
1981 Lauren Bacall, *Woman of the Year*
1982 Jennifer Holliday, *Dreamgirls*
1983 Natalia Makarova, *On Your Toes*
1984 Chita Rivera, *The Rink*
1985 Category eliminated
1986 Bernadette Peters, *Song and Dance*
1987 Maryann Plunkett, *Me and My Girl*
1988 Joanna Gleason, *Into the Woods*
1989 Ruth Brown, *Black and Blue*
1990 Tyne Daly, *Gypsy*
1991 Lea Salonga, *Miss Saigon*
1992 Faith Prince, *Guys and Dolls*

SPECIAL AWARDS

1947 Dora Chamberlain
Mr. and Mrs. Ira Katzenberg
Jules Leventhal
P. A. MacDonald
Burns Mantle
Arthur Miller
Vincent Sardi, Sr.
Kurt Weill
1948 Vera Allen
Paul Beisman
Joe E. Brown
Robert Dowling
Experimental Theatre, Inc.
Rosamond Gilder
June Lockhart
Mary Martin
Robert Porterfield
James Whitmore
1949 No award
1950 Maurice Evans
American Theatre Wing's hospital
volunteer program (presented by Eleanor
Roosevelt)
1951 Ruth Green
1952 Charles Boyer
Judy Garland
Edward Kook
1953 Equity Community Theatre
Danny Kaye
Beatrice Lillie

1954 No award
1955 Proscenium Productions
1956 The Theatre Collection of the New York
Public Library
The Threepenny Opera
1957 American Shakespeare Festival
Jean-Louis Barrault French Repertory
1958 Mrs. Martin Beck
New York Shakespeare Festival
1959 John Gielgud
Howard Lindsay and Russel Crouse
1960 John D. Rockefeller 3d
James Thurber and Burgess Meredith,
A Thurber Carnival
1961 David Merrick
The Theatre Guild
1962 Brooks Atkinson
Richard Rodgers
Franco Zeffirelli
1963 Alan Bennett
Irving Berlin
Peter Cook
W. McNeil Lowry
Jonathan Miller
Dudley Moore
1964 Eva Le Gallienne
1965 Gilbert Miller
Oliver Smith
1966 Helen Menken (posthumously)
1967 No award
1968 APA-Phoenix Theatre
Pearl Bailey
Carol Channing
Maurice Chevalier
Marlene Dietrich
Audrey Hepburn
David Merrick
1969 Leonard Bernstein
Carol Burnett
Rex Harrison
The National Theatre Company of
Great Britain
The Negro Ensemble Company
1970 Noël Coward
Alfred Lunt and Lynn Fontanne
New York Shakespeare Festival
Barbra Streisand
1971 Ingram Ash
Elliot Norton
Playbill
Roger L. Stevens
1972 *Fiddler on the Roof*
Ethel Merman
Richard Rodgers
The Theatre Guild–American Theatre Society

1973   Actors' Fund of America
        John Lindsay
        Shubert Organization
1974   *A Moon for the Misbegotten*
        Actors' Equity Association
        Candide
        Peter Cook and Dudley Moore, *Good Evening*
        Harold Friedlander
        Bette Midler
        Liza Minnelli
        Theatre Development Fund
        John F. Wharton
1975   Al Hirschfeld
        Neil Simon
1976   Richard Burton, *Equus*
        Thomas H. Fitzgerald, The Arena Stage
        Mathilda Pincus, Circle in the Square
1977   Equity Library Theatre
        Barry Manilow
        National Theatre for the Deaf
        Diana Ross
        Mark Taper Forum Theatre, Los Angeles
        Lily Tomlin
1978   Long Wharf Theatre
1979   American Conservatory Theater
        Walter F. Diehl
        Henry Fonda
        Eugene O'Neill Memorial Theater Center
1980   Actors Theatre of Louisville
        Goodspeed Opera House
        Mary Tyler Moore
1981   Lena Horne
        Trinity Square Repertory Company, Providence, R.I.
1982   The Actors' Fund of America
        The Guthrie Theatre
1983   Oregon Shakespearean Festival Association
        The Theatre Collection, Museum of the City of New York
1984   Peter Feller
        Al Hirschfeld—Brooks Atkinson Award
        San Diego Old Globe Theatre
        La Tragedie de Carmen
1985   Yul Brynner
        Edwin Lester
        New York State Council on the Arts
        Steppenwolf Theater
1986   American Repertory Theatre
1987   George Abbott
        Jackie Mason
        San Francisco Mime Troupe
1988   South Coast Repertory Company, Costa Mesa, Calif.
1989   Hartford Stage Company
1990   Alfred Drake
1991   Yale Repertory Theater

1992   Goodman Theater of Chicago
        The Fantasticks, world's longest-running musical, which began its 33d consecutive season off-Broadway May 3

COUNTRY MUSIC ASSOCIATION AWARDS

These awards, given annually since 1967 by the Country Music Association in Nashville, Tenn., are the most coveted in the country music recording industry. Awards are made by vote of the association's membership. Selections are based on the 12-month period from July 1 of the preceding year through June 30 of the year in which the award is presented. Winners are announced on a nationally broadcast television show in October and presented with a bullet-shaped trophy.

ALBUM OF THE YEAR

1966–67   *There Goes My Everything*, Jack Greene
1967–68   *Johnny Cash at Folsom Prison*, Johnny Cash
1968–69   *Johnny Cash at San Quentin Prison*, Johnny Cash
1969–70   *Okie from Muskogee*, Merle Haggard
1970–71   *I Won't Mention It Again*, Ray Price
1971–72   *Let Me Tell You About a Song*, Merle Haggard
1972–73   *Behind Closed Doors*, Charlie Rich
1973–74   *A Very Special Love Song*, Charlie Rich
1974–75   *A Legend in My Time*, Ronnie Milsap
1975–76   *Wanted—The Outlaws*, Waylon Jennings, Willie Nelson, Tompall Glaser, Jessie Colter
1976–77   *Ronnie Milsap Live*, Ronnie Milsap
1977–78   *It Was Almost Like a Song*, Ronnie Milsap
1978–79   *The Gambler*, Kenny Rogers
1979–80   *Coal Miner's Daughter*, Original Motion Picture Soundtrack
1980–81   *I Believe in You*, Don Williams
1981–82   *Always on My Mind*, Willie Nelson
1982–83   *The Closer You Get*, Alabama
1983–84   *A Little Good News*, Anne Murray
1984–85   *Does Fort Worth Ever Cross Your Mind*, George Strait
1985–86   *Lost in the Fifties Tonight*, Ronnie Milsap
1986–87   *Always and Forever*, Randy Travis
1987–88   *Born to Boogie*, Hank Williams, Jr.
1988–89   *Will the Circle Be Unbroken, Vol. II*, Nitty Gritty Dirt Band
1989–90   *Pickin' on Nashville*, Kentucky Head-Hunters
1990–91   *No Fences*, Garth Brooks
1991–92   *Ropin' the Wind*, Garth Brooks

ENTERTAINER OF THE YEAR

1966–67	Eddy Arnold
1967–68	Glen Campbell
1968–69	Johnny Cash
1969–70	Merle Haggard
1970–71	Charley Pride
1971–72	Loretta Lynn
1972–73	Roy Clark
1973–74	Charlie Rich
1974–75	John Denver
1975–76	Mel Tillis
1976–77	Ronnie Milsap
1977–78	Dolly Parton
1978–79	Willie Nelson
1979–80	Barbara Mandrell
1980–81	Barbara Mandrell
1981–82	Alabama
1982–83	Alabama
1983–84	Alabama
1984–85	Ricky Skaggs
1985–86	Reba McEntire
1986–87	Hank Williams, Jr.
1987–88	Hank Williams, Jr.
1988–89	George Strait
1989–90	George Strait
1990–91	Garth Brooks
1991–92	Garth Brooks

FEMALE VOCALIST OF THE YEAR

1966–67	Loretta Lynn
1967–68	Tammy Wynette
1968–69	Tammy Wynette
1969–70	Tammy Wynette
1970–71	Lynn Anderson
1971–72	Loretta Lynn
1972–73	Loretta Lynn
1973–74	Olivia Newton-John
1974–75	Dolly Parton
1975–76	Dolly Parton
1976–77	Crystal Gayle
1977–78	Crystal Gayle
1978–79	Barbara Mandrell
1979–80	Emmylou Harris
1980–81	Barbara Mandrell
1981–82	Janie Frickie
1982–83	Janie Frickie
1983–84	Reba McEntire
1984–85	Reba McEntire
1985–86	Reba McEntire
1986–87	Reba McEntire
1987–88	K. T. Oslin
1988–89	Kathy Mattea
1989–90	Kathy Mattea
1990–91	Tanya Tucker
1991–92	Mary Chapin-Carpenter

MALE VOCALIST OF THE YEAR

1966–67	Jack Greene
1967–68	Glen Campbell
1968–69	Glen Campbell
1969–70	Merle Haggard
1970–71	Charley Pride
1971–72	Charley Pride
1972–73	Charlie Rich
1973–74	Ronnie Milsap
1974–75	Waylon Jennings
1975–76	Ronnie Milsap
1976–77	Ronnie Milsap
1977–78	Don Williams
1978–79	Kenny Rogers
1979–80	George Jones
1980–81	George Jones
1981–82	Ricky Skaggs
1982–83	Lee Greenwood
1983–84	Lee Greenwood
1984–85	George Strait
1985–86	George Strait
1986–87	Randy Travis
1987–88	Randy Travis
1988–89	Ricky Van Shelton
1989–90	Clint Black
1990–91	Vince Gill
1991–92	Vince Gill

SINGLE OF THE YEAR

1966–67	"There Goes My Everything," Jack Greene
1967–68	"Harper Valley P.T.A.," Jeannie C. Riley
1968–69	"A Boy Named Sue," Johnny Cash
1969–70	"Okie From Muscogee," Merle Haggard
1970–71	"Help Me Make It Through the Night," Sammi Smith
1971–72	"The Happiest Girl in the Whole U.S.A.," Donna Fargo
1972–73	"Behind Closed Doors," Charlie Rich
1973–74	"Country Bumpkin," Cal Smith
1974–75	"Before the Next Teardrop Falls," Freddy Fender
1975–76	"Good Hearted Woman," Waylon Jennings and Willie Nelson
1976–77	"Lucille," Kenny Rogers
1977–78	"Heaven's Just a Sin Away," The Kendalls
1978–79	"The Devil Went Down to Georgia," Charlie Daniels Band
1979–80	"He Stopped Loving Her Today," George Jones
1980–81	"Elvira," Oak Ridge Boys
1981–82	"Always on My Mind," Willie Nelson
1982–83	"Swingin'," John Anderson

1983–84 "A Little Good News," Anne Murray
1984–85 "Why Not Me," The Judds
1985–86 "Bop," Dan Seals
1986–87 "Forever and Ever, Amen," Randy Travis
1987–88 "18 Wheels and a Dozen Roses," Kathy Mattea
1988–89 "I'm No Stranger to the Rain," Keith Whitley
1989–90 "When I Call Your Name," Vince Gill
1990–91 "Friends in Low Places," Garth Brooks
1991–92 "Achy Breaky Heart," Billy Ray Cyrus

SONG OF THE YEAR

(*An Award for Songwriting*)
1966–67 "There Goes My Everything," Dallas Frazier
1967–68 "Honey," Bobby Russell
1968–69 "Carroll County Accident," Bob Ferguson
1969–70 "Sunday Morning Coming Down," Kris Kristofferson
1970–71 "Easy Loving," Freddie Hart
1971–72 "Easy Loving," Freddie Hart
1972–73 "Behind Closed Doors," Kenny O'Dell
1973–74 "Country Bumpkin," Don Wayne
1974–75 "Back Home Again," John Denver
1975–76 "Rhinestone Cowboy," Larry Weiss
1976–77 "Lucille," Roger Bowling, Hal Bynum
1977–78 "Don't It Make My Brown Eyes Blue," Richard Leigh
1978–79 "The Gambler," Don Schlitz
1979–80 "He Stopped Loving Her Today," Bobby Braddock, Curly Putnam
1980–81 "He Stopped Loving Her Today," Bobby Braddock, Curly Putnam
1981–82 "Always on My Mind," Johnny Christopher, Wayne Carson, Mark James
1982–83 "Always on My Mind," Johnny Christopher, Wayne Carson, Mark James
1983–84 "Wind Beneath My Wings," Larry Henley, Jeff Silbar
1984–85 "God Bless the USA," Lee Greenwood
1985–86 "On the Other Hand," Paul Overstreet, Don Schlitz
1986–87 "Forever and Ever, Amen," Paul Overstreet, Don Schlitz
1987–88 "80s Ladies," K. T. Oslin
1988–89 "Chiseled in Stone," Max D. Barnes, Vern Gosdin
1989–90 "Where've You Been," Jon Vezner, Don Henry
1990–91 "When I Call Your Name," Tim Dubois, Vince Gill
1991–92 "Look at Us," Max D. Barnes, Vince Gill

VOCAL GROUP OF THE YEAR

1966–67 The Stoneman Family
1967–68 Porter Wagoner and Dolly Parton
1968–69 Johnny Cash and June Carter
1969–70 The Glaser Brothers
1970–71 The Osborne Brothers
1971–72 The Statler Brothers
1972–73 The Statler Brothers
1973–74 The Statler Brothers
1974–75 The Statler Brothers
1975–76 The Statler Brothers
1976–77 The Statler Brothers
1977–78 The Oak Ridge Boys
1978–79 The Statler Brothers
1979–80 The Statler Brothers
1980–81 Alabama
1981–82 Alabama
1982–83 Alabama
1983–84 The Statler Brothers
1984–85 The Judds
1985–86 The Judds
1986–87 The Judds
1987–88 Highway 101
1988–89 Highway 101
1989–90 Kentucky HeadHunters
1990–91 Kentucky HeadHunters
1991–92 Diamond Rio

MISS AMERICA

Since 1921, through the change and turmoil of seven decades and despite various scandals and the rise of feminism, the Miss America Pageant in Atlantic City, N.J., has remained the premier beauty contest in the United States. The annual September spectacle is watched by about 60 million television viewers. The contestants, women from the age of 17 to 26 from all 50 states, still are judged on their looks in a swimsuit, but the point system by which they are judged has been changed substantially. Where once beauty and talent were primary, the swimsuit competition now accounts for only about 15 percent of a contestant's score. Poise and grace in evening gowns also counts 15 percent; talent is 40 percent, and 30 percent is based on intelligence. The winner of the contest receives a $30,000 scholarship and is paid about $150,000 to make personal appearances throughout the nation in behalf of the Miss America Organization. Emcee Bert Parks hosted the annual gala for 25 years, from 1954 to 1979, and then again in 1990 for the selection of Miss America 1991.

1921   Margaret Gorman (District of Columbia)
1922–23 Mary Campbell (Ohio)
1924   Ruth Malcolmson (Pennsylvania)

1925	Fay Lamphier (California)
1926	Norma Smallwood (Oklahoma)
1927	Lois Delaner (Illinois)
1933	Marion Bergeron (Connecticut)
1935	Henrietta Leaver (Pennsylvania)
1936	Rose Coyle (Pennsylvania)
1937	Bette Cooper (New Jersey)
1938	Marilyn Meseke (Ohio)
1939	Patricia Donnelly (Michigan)
1940	Frances Marie Burke (Pennsylvania)
1941	Rosemary LaPlanche (California)
1942	Jo-Caroll Dennison (Texas)
1943	Jean Bartel (California)
1944	Venus Ramey (District of Columbia)
1945	Bess Myerson (New York)
1946	Marilyn Buferd (California)
1947	Barbara Jo Walker (Tennessee)
1948	BeBe Shopp (Minnesota)
1949	Jacque Mercer (Arizona)
1951	Yolanda Betbeze (Alabama)
1952	Colleen Kay Hutchins (Utah)
1953	Neva Jane Langley (Georgia)
1954	Evelyn Ay (Pennsylvania)
1955	Lee Ann Meriwether (California)
1956	Sharon Kay Ritchie (Colorado)
1957	Marian McKnight (South Carolina)
1958	Marilyn Van Derbur (Colorado)
1959	Mary Ann Mobley (Mississippi)
1960	Lynda Lee Mead (Mississippi)
1961	Nancy Ann Fleming (Michigan)
1962	Maria Beale Fletcher (North Carolina)
1963	Jacquelyn Mayer (Ohio)
1964	Donna Axum (Arkansas)
1965	Vanda Kay Van Dyke (Arizona)
1966	Deborah Irene Bryant (Kansas)
1967	Jane Jayroe (Oklahoma)
1968	Debra Barnes (Kansas)
1969	Judith Ford (Illinois)
1970	Pamela Eldred (Michigan)
1971	Phyllis George (Texas)
1972	Laurie Lee Schaefer (Ohio)
1973	Terry Meeuwsen (Wisconsin)
1974	Rebecca King (Colorado)
1975	Shirley Cothran (Texas)
1976	Tawney Godin (New York)
1977	Dorothy Benham (Minnesota)
1978	Susan Perkins (Ohio)
1979	Kylene Barker (Virginia)
1980	Cheryl Prewitt (Mississippi)
1981	Susan Powell (Oklahoma)
1982	Elizabeth Ward (Arkansas)
1983	Debra Sue Maffett (California)
1984	Vanessa Williams (New York) (resigned July 23, 1984)
	Suzette Charles (New Jersey)
1985	Sharlene Wells (Utah)

1986	Susan Akin (Mississippi)
1987	Kellye Cash (Tennessee)
1988	Kaye Lani Rae Rafko (Michigan)
1989	Gretchen Elizabeth Carlson (Minnesota)
1990	Debbye Turner (Missouri)
1991	Marjorie Vincent (Illinois)
1992	Carolyn Suzanne Sapp (Hawaii)

NOBEL PRIZES
Nobel Foundation

The Nobel Prizes are the world's most distinguished annual awards for achievements in the arts and sciences and in pursuit of international peace. The awards were established and endowed by the will of Alfred Bernhard Nobel, the Swedish chemist who, in 1866, invented dynamite. His mixture of nitroglycerine and inert filler vastly improved the stability and safety of explosives, but Nobel grew increasingly concerned about his legacy. He left most of his fortune in trust as a fund from which annual prizes would be given to those whose work resulted in "the greatest benefit to mankind." Nobel's will established awards in five areas: physics, chemistry, physiology or medicine, literature, and peace. The awards were first made in 1901. The Nobel Memorial Prize in Economics was added in 1969 and endowed by the Central Bank of Sweden. The Royal Swedish Academy of Sciences names recipients of the awards in economics, chemistry and physics. The Royal Caroline Medico-Chirurgical Institute names winners of the prize for physiology or medicine. The Swedish Academy decides winners of the prize for literature. The Norwegian Nobel Committee, appointed by Norway's parliament, determines the winner of the peace prize. The Nobel Foundation in Stockholm administers all six awards, which are announced in October.

NOBEL PRIZE FOR LITERATURE

1901	Rene F. A. Sully Prudhomme (France)
1902	Theodor Mommsen (Germany)
1903	Bjornstjerne Bjornson (Norway)
1904	Frederic Mistral (France)
	Jose Echegaray (Spain)
1905	Henryk Sienkiewicz (Poland)
1906	Giosuè Carducci (Italy)
1907	Rudyard Kipling (Great Britain)
1908	Rudoll Eucken (Germany)
1909	Selma Lagerlof (Sweden)
1910	Paul Heyse (Germany)
1911	Maurice Maerterlinck (Belgium)
1912	Gerhart Hauptmann (Germany)
1913	Rabindranath Tagore (India)
1914	No award

1915	Romain Rolland (France)
1916	Verner von Heidenstam (Sweden)
1917	Karl Gjellerup (Denmark)
	Henrik Pontoppidan (Denmark)
1918	No award
1919	Carl Spitteler (Switzerland)
1920	Knut Hamsun (Norway)
1921	Anatole France (France)
1922	Jacinto Benavente (Spain)
1923	William Butler Yeats (Ireland)
1924	Wladyslaw Reymont (Poland)
1925	George Bernard Shaw (Great Britain)
1926	Grazia Deledda (Italy)
1927	Henri Bergson (France)
1928	Sigrid Undset (Norway)
1929	Thomas Mann (Germany)
1930	Sinclair Lewis (U.S.)
1931	Erik Axel Karlfeldt (Sweden)
1932	John Galsworthy (Great Britain)
1933	Ivan Bunin (stateless, living in France)
1934	Luigi Pirandello (Italy)
1935	No award
1936	Eugene O'Neill (U.S.)
1937	Roger Martin du Gard (France)
1938	Pearl Buck (U.S.)
1939	F. E. Sillanpaa (Finland)
1940–43	No award
1944	Johannes V. Jensen (Denmark)
1945	Gabriela Mistral (Chile)
1946	Hermann Hesse (Switzerland)
1947	Andre Gide (France)
1948	T. S. Eliot (Great Britain)
1949	William Faulkner (U.S.)
1950	Bertrand Russell (Great Britain)
1951	Par Lagerkvist (Sweden)
1952	Francois Mauriac (France)
1953	Winston Churchill (Great Britain)
1954	Ernest Hemingway (U.S.)
1955	Halldor Laxness (Iceland)
1956	J. R. Jimenez (Spain)
1957	Albert Camus (France)
1958	Boris Pasternak (USSR) (declined the prize)
1959	Salvatore Quasimodo (Italy)
1960	Saint-John Perse (France)
1961	Ivo Andric (Yugoslavia)
1962	John Steinbeck (U.S.)
1963	Giorgos Seferiades (Greece)
1964	Jean-Paul Sartre (France) (declined the prize)
1965	Mikhail Sholokhov (USSR)
1966	Shmuel Y. Agnon (Israel)
	Nelly Sachs (German living in Sweden)
1967	Miguel A. Asturias (Guatemala)
1968	Yasunari Kawabata (Japan)
1969	Samuel Beckett (Ireland)

1970	Alexander Solzhenitsyn (USSR)
1971	Pablo Neruda (Chile)
1972	Heinrich Boll (Federal Republic of Germany)
1973	Patrick White (Australia)
1974	Eyvind Johnson (Sweden)
	Harry Martinson (Sweden)
1975	Eugenio Montale (Italy)
1976	Saul Bellow (U.S.)
1977	Vicente Aleixandre (Spain)
1978	Isaac B. Singer (U.S.)
1979	Odysseus Elytis (Greece)
1980	Czeslaw Milosz (Poland/U.S.)
1981	Elias Canetti (Great Britain)
1982	Gabriel Garcia Marquez (Colombia)
1983	William Golding (Great Britain)
1984	Jaroslav Siefert (Czechoslovakia)
1985	Claude Simon (France)
1986	Wole Soyinka (Nigeria)
1987	Joseph Brodsky (USSR)
1988	Naguib Mahfouz (Egypt)
1989	Camilo José Cela (Spain)
1990	Octavio Paz (Mexico)
1991	Nadine Gordimer (South Africa)
1992	Derek Walcott (U.S.)

NOBEL PEACE PRIZE

1901	Jean-Henri Dunant of Switzerland, founder of the International Committee of the Red Cross; Frédéric Passy, founder of a French peace society.
1902	Elie Ducommun of Switzerland, Director of the Permanent International Peace Bureau; Charles A. Gobat of Switzerland, Secretary-General of the Inter-Parliamentary Union.
1903	Sir William R. Cremer of Great Britain, founder of the International Arbitration League.
1904	Institute of International Law.
1905	Baroness Bertha S. F. von Suttner of Austria, author of antiwar novel, *Lay Down Your Arms.*
1906	Theodore Roosevelt, U.S. President, for his role in mediating the Russo-Japanese War.
1907	Ernesto T. Moneta of Italy, founder of the Lombard League of Peace; Louis Renault of France, for his work at the Hague Peace conferences.
1908	Klas P. Arnoldson, founder of the Swedish Peace and Arbitration League; Fredrik Bajer of Denmark, a writer and peace activist.
1909	Auguste M. F. Beernaert, Prime Minister of Belgium and a peace activist; Paul

H. B. B. d'Estournelles de Constant (Baron de Constant de Rebecque), for his work for voluntary arbitration.

1910 Permanent International Peace Bureau.

1911 Tobias M. C. Asser of the Netherlands, a founder of the Institute of International Law; Alfred H. Fried, an Austrian journalist, for founding peace publications.

1912 Elihu Root, U.S. Secretary of State.

1913 Henri Lafontaine of Belgium, President of the Permanent International Peace Bureau.

1914–16 No award.

1917 International Committee of the Red Cross, Geneva, Switzerland.

1918 No award.

1919 Thomas Woodrow Wilson, U.S. President, for his role in establishing the League of Nations.

1920 Léon Victor A. Bourgeois of France, for drafting the framework of the League of Nations.

1921 Karl H. Branting, pacifist Prime Minister of Sweden; Christian L. Lange of Norway, a founder of the Inter-Parliamentary Union.

1922 Fridtjof Nansen, a Norwegian scientist, explorer, statesman and the League of Nations' high commissioner for refugees.

1923–24 No award.

1925 Sir Austen Chamberlain, British Foreign Secretary, for his work on the Locarno Pact, guaranteeing the demilitarized status of the Rhineland and its borders; Charles G. Dawes, U.S. Vice-President, for the Dawes Plan, providing for reduction of German reparation payments after World War I.

1926 Aristide Briand of France and Gustav Stresemann of Germany, creators of the Locarno Pact, which guaranteed the demilitarized status of the Rhineland and its borders.

1927 Ferdinand Buisson, a French human rights advocate; Ludwig Quidde, a German peace activist.

1928 No award.

1929 Frank B. Kellogg, U.S. Secretary of State and a creator of the Kellogg-Briand Pact of 1928, under which 62 nations renounced war.

1930 L. O. Nathan Söderblom of Sweden, an archbishop and a leader in the ecumenical movement.

1931 Jane Addams of the U.S., President of the Women's International League for Peace and Freedom; Nicholas M. Butler of the U.S., promoter of the Kellogg-Briand Pact of 1928, under which 62 nations renounced war.

1932 No award.

1933 Sir Norman R. L. Angell (a.k.a. Ralph Lane) of Great Britain, author of the antiwar book *The Great Illusion*.

1934 Arthur Henderson of Great Britain, President of the League of Nations World Disarmament Conference in 1932.

1935 Carl von Ossietzky, a German journalist and pacifist.

1936 Carlos Saavedra Lamas, Argentina's Secretary of State and President of the League of Nations.

1937 Lord Edgar Algernon R. G. Cecil of Great Britain, for his work to establish the League of Nations.

1938 Nansen International Office for Refugees of Geneva, Switzerland.

1939–43 No award.

1944 International Committee of the Red Cross of Geneva, Switzerland.

1945 Cordell Hull, U.S. Secretary of State, for his work in helping to create the U.N.

1946 Emily G. Balch, an American leader of an international women's peace movement; John R. Mott of the U.S., leader of the Christian ecumenical movement.

1947 The Friends Service Council (Great Britain) and The American Friends Service Committee (U.S.), Quaker groups.

1948 No award.

1949 Lord John Boyd Orr, a British nutritionist, for his work to ease world hunger.

1950 Ralph Bunche of the U.S., for his work as mediator of the Middle East war.

1951 Léon Jouhaux of France, for his work to improve the conditions of the working class.

1952 Albert Schweitzer, a French missionary and surgeon, for his work among the ill in Africa.

1953 George C. Marshall, an American general and developer of the Marshall Plan, which provided a recovery plan for European nations after World War II.

1954 Office of the United Nations' High Commissioner for Refugees, Geneva.

1955–56 No award.

1957 Lester B. Pearson, Canada's Secretary of State, for his work to resolve the Suez Canal crisis.

1958   Georges Pire of Belgium, a Dominican priest, for his leadership of l'Europe du Coeur au Service du Monde, a relief group for refugees.

1959   Philip J. Noel-Baker of Great Britain, for his work toward peace through disarmament.

1960   Albert J. Luthuli of South Africa, President of the African National Congress, for his peaceful resistance to apartheid.

1961   Dag Hammarskjöld, Sweden, U.N. Secretary-General, for his work for peace in the Congo.

1962   Linus C. Pauling, a U.S. chemist who warned about the dangers of radioactive fallout.

1963   International Committee of the Red Cross and the League of Red Cross Societies, both of Geneva, Switzerland.

1964   Martin Luther King, Jr., a clergyman and a leader of the American civil-rights movement.

1965   United Nations Children's Fund (UNICEF).

1966–67   No award.

1968   René Cassin of France, President of the European Court for Human Rights.

1969   International Labour Organization, a U.N. agency in Geneva, Switzerland, for its work to improve working and social conditions.

1970   Norman E. Borlaug, a U.S. agriculture scientist who developed high-yield grains used to ease world hunger.

1971   Willy Brandt, Chancellor of the Federal Republic of Germany, for his work toward East-West détente.

1972   No award.

1973   Henry A. Kissinger, U.S. Secretary of State, and Le Duc Tho, Foreign Minister of the Democratic Republic of Vietnam, for negotiating the Vietnam ceasefire. Mr. Le declined the award.

1974   Seán MacBride of Ireland, U.N. commissioner for Namibia and President of the International Peace Bureau; Eisaku Sato, Prime Minister of Japan, for his campaign against nuclear weapons.

1975   Andrei Sakharov, a physicist from the Soviet Union, for his work for human rights.

1976   Mairead Corrigan and Betty Williams of Northern Ireland, founders of Northern Ireland Peace Movement.

1977   Amnesty International, a human-rights group.

1978   Menachem Begin, Prime Minister of Israel, and Anwar el-Sadat, President of Egypt, for negotiating the Israeli-Egyptian peace agreement.

1979   Mother Teresa, a Catholic nun working for the poor in Calcutta, India.

1980   Adolfo Pérez Esquivel, an Argentine architect, sculptor and human-rights leader.

1981   Office of the United Nations High Commissioner for Refugees, Geneva, Switzerland.

1982   Alva Myrdal of Sweden and Alfonso García Robles of Mexico for their work on disarmament.

1983   Lech Walesa, leader of the Solidarity trade union federation in Poland.

1984   Desmond M. Tutu, Bishop of Johannesburg, South Africa, and a leader of the antiapartheid movement.

1985   International Physicians for the Prevention of Nuclear War, peace organization headed by Soviet and American doctors.

1986   Elie Wiesel, U.S. writer and Nazi death-camp survivor, in recognition of his work concerning the Holocaust.

1987   Oscar Arias Sánchez, president of Costa Rica, in recognition of his peace plan for Central America.

1988   United Nations Peace-Keeping Forces.

1989   The Dalai Lama, exiled religious and political leader of Tibet, in recognition of his nonviolent opposition to Chinese domination.

1990   Mikhail Gorbachev, President of the Soviet Union, instrumental in movement toward greater freedom in Eastern Europe.

1991   Aung San Suu Kyi, Burmese leader under house arrest since 1989 for uniting opposition forces in nonviolent struggle against military rule; she was recognized for offering "one of the most extraordinary examples of civil courage in Asia in recent decades."

1992   Rigoberta Menchu, an outspoken leader in the fight for native Indian rights in Guatemala, where guerrillas have fought military repression for more than 30 years. The country's civil war left Menchu an orphan. She recounted her experiences in a 1983 book, *I,*

Rigoberta, which won international acclaim.

NOBEL PRIZE FOR CHEMISTRY

1901 Jacobus H. van't Hoff (Germany).
1902 Hermann E. Fischer (Germany).
1903 Svante A. Arrhenius (Sweden).
1904 Sir William Ramsay (Great Britain).
1905 Johann F. W. A. von Baeyer (Germany).
1906 Henri Moissan (France).
1907 Eduard Buchner (Germany).
1908 Lord Ernest Rutherford (Great Britain).
1909 Wilhelm Ostwald (Germany).
1910 Otto Wallach (Germany).
1911 Marie Curie (France).
1912 Victor Grignard (France); Paul Sabatier (France).
1913 Alfred Werner (Switzerland).
1914 Theodore W. Richards (U.S.) of Harvard University.
1915 Richard M. Willstätter (Germany).
1916 No award.
1917 No award.
1918 Fritz Haber (Germany).
1919 No award.
1920 Walter H. Nernst (Germany).
1921 Frederick Soddy (Great Britain).
1922 Francis W. Aston (Great Britain).
1923 Fritz Pregl (Austria).
1924 No award.
1925 Richard A. Zsigmondy (Germany).
1926 The (Theodor) Svedberg (Sweden).
1927 Heinrich O. Wieland (Germany).
1928 Adolf O. R. Windaus (Germany).
1929 Sir Arthur Harden (Great Britain); Hans K. A. von Euler-Chelpin (Sweden).
1930 Hans Fischer (Germany).
1931 Carl Bosch (Germany); Friedrich Bergius (Germany).
1932 Irving Langmuir (U.S.) of General Electric Co.
1933 No award.
1934 Harold C. Urey (U.S.) of Columbia University.
1935 Frédéric Joliot-Curie (France); Irène Joliot-Curie (France).
1936 Petrus J. W. Debye (Netherlands, working in Germany).
1937 Sir Walter N. Haworth (Great Britain); Paul Karrer (Switzerland).
1938 Richard Kuhn (Germany).
1939 Adolf F. J. Butenandt (Germany).
1940–42 No award.
1943 George de Hevesy (Hungary, working in Sweden).

1944 Otto Hahn (Germany).
1945 Artturi J. Virtanen (Finland).
1946 James B. Sumner (U.S.) of Cornell University; John H. Northrop (U.S.) and Wendell M. Stanley (U.S.), both of the Rockefeller Institute for Medical Research.
1947 Sir Robert Robinson (Great Britain).
1948 Arne W. K. Tiselius (Sweden).
1949 William F. Giauque (U.S.) of the University of California, Berkeley.
1950 Otto P. H. Diels (West Germany); Kurt Alder (West Germany).
1951 Edwin M. McMillan (U.S.) and Glenn T. Seaborg (U.S.), both of University of California, Berkeley.
1952 Archer J. P. Martin (Great Britain); Richard L. M. Synge (Scotland).
1953 Hermann Staudinger (West Germany).
1954 Linus C. Pauling (U.S.) of California Institute of Technology.
1955 Vincent du Vigneaud (U.S.) of Cornell University.
1956 Sir Cyril N. Hinshelwood (Great Britain); Nikolaj Semenov (USSR).
1957 Alexander Todd (Great Britain).
1958 Frederick Sanger (Great Britain).
1959 Jaroslav Heyrovsky (Czechoslovakia).
1960 Willard F. Libby (U.S.) of the University of California, Los Angeles.
1961 Melvin Calvin (U.S.) of the University of California, Berkeley.
1962 Sir John C. Kendrew (Great Britain); Max F. Perutz (Great Britain).
1963 Karl Ziegler (West Germany); Giulio Natta (Italy).
1964 Dorothy Crowfoot Hodgkin (Great Britain).
1965 Robert Burns Woodward (U.S.) of Harvard University.
1966 Robert S. Mulliken (U.S.) of the University of Chicago.
1967 Manfred Eigen (West Germany); Ronald G. W. Norrish (Great Britain); George Porter (Great Britain).
1968 Lars Onsager (U.S.) of Yale University.
1969 Sir Derek H. R. Barton (Great Britain).
1970 Luis F. Leloir (Argentina).
1971 Gerhard Herzberg (Canada).
1972 Christian B. Anfinsen (U.S.) of National Institutes of Health; Stanford Moore (U.S.), William H. Stein (U.S.), both of Rockefeller University.
1973 Geoffrey Wilkinson (Great Britain).
1974 Paul J. Flory (U.S.) of Stanford University.

1975   Sir John Warcup Cornforth (Australia and Great Britain); Vladimir Prelog (Switzerland).

1976   William N. Lipscomb, Jr., (U.S.) of Harvard University.

1977   Ilya Prigogine (Belgium).

1978   Peter D. Mitchell (Great Britain).

1979   Herbert C. Brown (U.S.) of Purdue University; Georg Wittig (West Germany).

1980   Paul Berg (U.S.) of Stanford University; Walter Gilbert (U.S.) of Biological Laboratories; Frederick Sanger (Great Britain).

1981   Kenichi Fukui (Japan); Roald Hoffman (U.S.) of Cornell University.

1982   Aaron Klug (Great Britain).

1983   Henry Taube (U.S.) of Stanford University.

1984   Robert Bruce Merrifield (U.S.) of Rockefeller University.

1985   Herbert A. Hauptman (U.S.) of the Medical Foundation of Buffalo; Jerome Karle, U.S. Naval Research Laboratory.

1986   Dudley R. Herschbach (U.S.) of Harvard University; Yaun T. Lee (U.S.) of University of California, Berkeley.

1987   Charles L. Pedersen (U.S.) of DuPont Laboratory; Jean-Marie Lehn (France); Donald J. Cram (U.S.) of University of California, Los Angeles.

1988   Johann Deisenhofer (U.S.) of the Howard Hughes Medical Institute; Robert Huber and Hartmut Michel (West Germany).

1989   Thomas R. Cech (U.S.) of the University of Colorado; Sidney Altman (U.S.) of Yale University.

1990   Elias James Corey (U.S.) of Harvard University.

1991   Richard R. Ernst (Switzerland) of the Swiss Federal Polytechnic Institute.

1992   Rudolph A. Marcus (Canada) of the California Institute of Technology, Pasadena.

NOBEL PRIZE FOR PHYSICS

1901   Wilhelm C. Röntgen (Germany).

1902   Hendrik A. Lorentz (Netherlands); Pieter Zeeman (Netherlands).

1903   Antoine Henri Becquerel (France); Pierre Curie (France); Marie Curie (France).

1904   Lord Rayleigh (John W. Strutt) (Great Britain).

1905   Philipp E. A. Lenard (Germany).

1906   Sir Joseph J. Thomson (Great Britain).

1907   Albert A. Michelson (U.S.) of the University of Chicago.

1908   Gabriel Lippmann (France).

1909   Guglielmo Marconi (Italy); Carl F. Braun (Germany).

1910   Johannes D. van der Waals (Netherlands).

1911   Wilhelm Wien (Germany).

1912   Nils G. Dalén (Sweden).

1913   Heike Kamerlingh-Onnes (Netherlands).

1914   Max von Laue (Germany).

1915   Sir William Henry Bragg (Great Britain); Sir William Lawrence Bragg (Great Britain).

1916   No award.

1917   Charles G. Barkla (Great Britain).

1918   Max K. E. L. Planck (Germany).

1919   Johannes Stark (Germany).

1920   Charles E. Guillaume (Switzerland).

1921   Albert Einstein (Germany).

1922   Niels Bohr (Denmark).

1923   Robert A. Millikan (U.S.) of California Institute of Technology.

1924   Karl M. G. Siegbahn (Sweden).

1925   James Franck (Germany); Gustav Hertz (Germany).

1926   Jean B. Perrin (France).

1927   Arthur H. Compton (U.S.) of the University of Chicago; Charles T. R. Wilson (Great Britain).

1928   Sir Owen W. Richardson (Great Britain).

1929   Prince Louis-Victor de Broglie (France).

1930   Sir Chandrasekhara Venkata Raman (India).

1931   No award.

1932   Werner Heisenberg (Germany).

1933   Erwin Schrödinger (Austria, working in Germany); Paul A. M. Dirac (Great Britain).

1934   No award.

1935   Sir James Chadwick (Great Britain).

1936   Victor F. Hess (Austria); Carl D. Anderson (U.S.) of California Institute of Technology.

1937   Clinton J. Davisson (U.S.) of Bell Telephone Laboratories; Sir George P. Thomson (Great Britain).

1938   Enrico Fermi (Italy).

1939   Ernest O. Lawrence (U.S.) of the University of California, Berkeley.

1940–42   No award.

1943   Otto Stern (U.S.) of Carnegie Institute of Technology (Carnegie Mellon University).

1944	Isador I. Rabi (U.S.) of Columbia University.
1945	Wolfgang Pauli (Austria), working at Princeton University.
1946	Percy W. Bridgman (U.S.) of Harvard University.
1947	Sir Edward V. Appleton (Great Britain).
1948	Lord Patrick M. S. Blackett (Great Britain).
1949	Hideki Yukawa (Japan).
1950	Cecil F. Powell (Great Britain).
1951	Sir John D. Cockcroft (Great Britain); Ernest T. S. Walton (Ireland).
1952	Felix Block (U.S.) of Stanford University; Edward M. Purcell (U.S.) of Harvard University.
1953	Frits (Frederik) Zernike (Netherlands).
1954	Max Born (Great Britain); Walter Bothe (Germany).
1955	Willis E. Lamb (U.S.) of Stanford University; Polykarp Kusch (U.S.) of Columbia University.
1956	William Shockley (U.S.) of Semiconductor Laboratory of Beckman Instruments, Inc.; John Bardeen (U.S.) of the University of Illinois; Walter H. Brattain (U.S.) of Bell Telephone Laboratories.
1957	Tsung-Dao Lee (China), working at Columbia University, New York; Chen Ning Yang (China), working at Institute for Advanced Study, Princeton, N.J.
1958	Pavel A. Cerenkov (USSR); Il'ja M. Frank (USSR); Igor J. Tamm (USSR).
1959	Emilio G. Segrè (U.S.) of the University of California, Berkeley; Owen Chamberlain (U.S.) of the University of California, Berkeley.
1960	Donald A. Glaser (U.S.) of the University of California, Berkeley.
1961	Robert Hofstadter (U.S.) of Stanford University; Rudolf L. Mössbauer (Germany), working in Germany and at the California Institute of Technology.
1962	Lev D. Landau (USSR).
1963	Eugene P. Wigner (U.S.) of Princeton University; Maria Goeppert-Mayer (U.S.) of University of California, La Jolla; J. Hans D. Jensen (West Germany).
1964	Charles Townes (U.S.) of M.I.T.; Nikolai G. Basov (USSR); Aleksandre M. Prochorov (USSR).
1965	Sin-Itiro Tomonaga (Japan); Julian Schwinger (U.S.) of Harvard University; Richard P. Feynman (U.S.) of California Institute of Technology.
1966	Alfred Kastler (France).
1967	Hans A. Bethe (U.S.) of Cornell University.
1968	Luis W. Alvarez (U.S.) of University of California, Berkeley.
1969	Murray Gell-Mann (U.S.) of California Institute of Technology.
1970	Hannes Alfvén (Sweden); Louis Neel (France).
1971	Dennis Gabor (Great Britain).
1972	John Bardeen (U.S.) of University of Illinois; Leon N. Cooper (U.S.) of Brown University; Robert John Schrieffer (U.S.) of the University of Pennsylvania.
1973	Leo Esaki (Japan) of IBM Thomas J. Watson Research Center in New York; Ivar Giaever (U.S.) of General Electric Co.; Brian D. Josephson (Great Britain).
1974	Sir Martin Ryle (Great Britain); Antony Hewish (Great Britain).
1975	Aage Bohr (Denmark); Ben Mottelson (Denmark); James Rainwater (U.S.) of Columbia University.
1976	Burton Richter (U.S.) of Stanford Linear Accelerator Center; Samuel C. C. Ting (U.S.) of M.I.T.
1977	Philip W. Anderson (U.S.) of Bell Laboratories; Sir Nevill F. Mott (Great Britain); John H. van Vleck (U.S.) of Harvard University.
1978	Pjotr L. Kapitsa (USSR); Arno A. Penzias (U.S.) and Robert W. Wilson (U.S.), both of Bell Laboratories.
1979	Sheldon L. Glashow (U.S.) of Harvard University; Abdus Salam (Pakistan); Steven Weinberg (U.S.) of Harvard University.
1980	James W. Cronin (U.S.) of the University of Chicago; Val L. Fitch (U.S.) of Princeton University.
1981	Nicholaas Bloembergen (U.S.) of Harvard University; Arthur L. Schawlow (U.S.) of Stanford University; Kai M. Siegbahn (Sweden).
1982	Kenneth G. Wilson (U.S.) of Cornell University.
1983	Subrahmanyan Chandrasekhar (U.S.) of the University of Chicago; William H. Fowler (U.S.) of California Institute of Technology.
1984	Carlo Rubbia (Italy) and Simon van der Meer (Netherlands), both working in Geneva, Switzerland.

1985   Klaus von Klitzing (West Germany).

1986   Ernest Ruska (West Germany); Gerd Binnig (West Germany); Heinrich Rohrer (Switzerland).

1987   George Bednorz (Switzerland) and K. Alex Müller (Switzerland), both of IBM's Zurich Research Laboratory.

1988   Leon M. Lederman (U.S.) of Fermi National Accelerator Laboratory; Melvin Schwartz (U.S.) of Digital Pathways, Inc.; Jack Steinberger (Switzerland).

1989   Norman F. Ramsey (U.S.) of Harvard University; Hans G. Demelt (U.S.) of the University of Washington; Wolfgang Paul (West Germany).

1990   Jerome Friedman (U.S.) and Henry Kendall (U.S.), both of M.I.T., and Richard Taylor (Canada), working at Stanford University.

1991   Pierre-Gilles de Gennes (France) of the Collège de France, Paris.

1992   George Charpack (France) of the École Supérieure de Physique et Chemie, Paris.

NOBEL PRIZE IN ECONOMIC SCIENCES

1969   Ragnar Frisch (Norway); Jan Tinbergen (Netherlands).

1970   Paul A. Samuelson (U.S.) of M.I.T.

1971   Simon Kuznets (U.S.) of Harvard University.

1972   Sir John R. Hicks (Great Britain); Kenneth J. Arrow (U.S.) of Harvard University.

1973   Wassily Leontief (U.S.) of Harvard University.

1974   Gunnar Myrdal (Sweden); Friedrich A. von Hayek (Great Britain).

1975   Leonid Kantorovich (USSR); Tjalling C. Koopmans (U.S.) of Yale University.

1976   Milton Friedman (U.S.) of the University of Chicago.

1977   Bertil Ohlin (Sweden); James E. Meade (Great Britain).

1978   Herbert A. Simon (U.S.) of Carnegie-Mellon University.

1979   Theodore W. Schultz (U.S.) of the University of Chicago; Sir Arthur Lewis (Great Britain).

1980   Lawrence R. Klein (U.S.) of the University of Pennsylvania.

1981   James Tobin (U.S.) of Yale University.

1982   George J. Stigler (U.S.) of the University of California.

1983   Gerard Debreu (U.S.) of the University of California, Berkeley.

1984   Sir Richard Stone (Great Britain).

1985   Franco Modigliana (U.S.) of M.I.T.

1986   James M. Buchanan, Jr., (U.S.) of Center for Study of Public Choice.

1987   Robert M. Solow (U.S.) of M.I.T.

1988   Maurice Allais (France).

1989   Trygve Haavelmo (Norway).

1990   Harry M. Markowitz (U.S.) of the City University of New York; Merton Miller (U.S.) of the University of Chicago; William Sharpe (U.S.), formerly of the University of Washington and Stanford University.

1991   Ronald Coase (U.S.) of the University of Chicago.

1992   Gary Becker (U.S.) of the University of Chicago.

NOBEL PRIZES IN PHYSIOLOGY OR MEDICINE

1901   Emil A. von Behring (Germany), for his work on serum therapy, especially as applied to diphtheria.

1902   Sir Ronald Ross (Great Britain), for his work on malaria.

1903   Niels R. Finsen (Denmark), for his contribution to the treatment of diseases, particularly lupus vulgaris.

1904   Ivan P. Pavlov (Russia), for research on the physiology of digestion.

1905   Robert Koch (Germany), for discoveries concerning tuberculosis.

1906   Camillo Golgi (Italy) and Santiago Ramón y Cajal (Spain), for work on the structure of the nervous system.

1907   Charles L. A. Laveran (France), for work on the role of protozoa in causing diseases.

1908   Il'ja I. Mecnikov (Russia) and Paul Ehrlich (Germany), for their work on immunity.

1909   Emil T. Kocher (Switzerland), for work on the physiology, pathology and surgery of the thyroid.

1910   Albrecht Kossel (Germany), for contributions to the knowledge of cell chemistry.

1911   Allvar Gullstrand (Sweden), for research on the dioptrics of the eye.

1912   Alexis Carrel (France), working at Rockefeller Institute for Medical Research in New York, for work on vascular sutures and transplantation of blood vessels and organs.

1913   Charles R. Richet (France), for his work on anaphylaxis.

1914   Robert Bárány (Austria), for research on the vestibular apparatus.

1915–18	No award.
1919	Jules Bordet (Belgium), for discoveries concerning immunity.
1920	Schlack A. S. Krough (Denmark), for discovering the capillary motor regulating mechanism.
1921	No award.
1922	Sir Archibald V. Hill (Great Britain), for discovery concerning heat production in the muscle; Otto F. Meyerhof (Germany), for discovering the fixed relationship between oxygen consumption and the metabolism of lactic acid in muscles.
1923	Sir Frederick B. Banting (Canada) and John J. R. Macleod (Canada), for discovering insulin.
1924	Willem Einthoven (Netherlands), for discovering the electrocardiogram mechanism.
1925	No award.
1926	Johannes A. G. Fibiger (Denmark), for discovering Spiroptera carcinoma.
1927	Julius Wagner-Jauregg (Austria), for discovering the value of malaria inoculation in the treatment of dementia paralytica.
1928	Charles J. H. Nicolle (France), for work concerning typhus.
1929	Christiaan Eijkman (Netherlands), for discovering the antineuritic vitamin; Sir Frederick G. Hopkins (Great Britain), for discovering growth-stimulating vitamins.
1930	Karl Landsteiner (Austria), working at Rockefeller Institute for Medical Research in New York, for discovering human blood groups.
1931	Otto H. Warburg (Germany), for discovering the nature and action of the respiratory enzyme.
1932	Sir Charles S. Sherrington (Great Britain) and Lord Edgar D. Adrian (Great Britain), for discoveries concerning the functions of neurons.
1933	Thomas H. Morgan (U.S.) of the California Institute of Technology, for discoveries concerning the role of chromosomes in heredity.
1934	George H. Whipple (U.S.) of Rochester University, George R. Minot (U.S.) of Harvard University and William P. Murphy (U.S.) of Harvard University, for discoveries concerning liver therapy for anemia.
1935	Hans Spemann (Germany), for discoveries concerning embryonic development.
1936	Sir Henry H. Dale (Great Britain) and Otto Loewi (Austria), for discoveries concerning the chemical transmission of nerve impulses.
1937	Albert Szent-Györgyi von Nagyrapolt (Hungary), for discoveries concerning biological combustion processes, especially concerning vitamin C and the catalysis of fumaric acid.
1938	Corneille J. F. Heymans (Belgium), for discoveries concerning the regulation of respiration.
1939	Gerhard Domagk (Germany), for discovering the antibacterial effects of prontosil.
1940–42	No award.
1943	Henrik C. P. Dam (Denmark), for discovering vitamin K; Edward A. Doisy (U.S.) of St. Louis University, for discovering the chemical nature of vitamin K.
1944	Joseph Erlanger (U.S.) of Washington University and Herbert S. Gasser (U.S.) of Rockefeller Institute for Medical Research, for discoveries concerning the differentiated functions of single nerve fibers.
1945	Sir Alexander Fleming (Great Britain), Sir Ernst B. Chain (Great Britain) and Lord Howard W. Florey (Great Britain), for discovering penicillin.
1946	Hermann J. Muller (U.S.) of Indiana University, for discovering mutations caused by X-ray irradiation.
1947	Carl F. Cori (U.S.) and Gerty T. Cori (U.S.), both of Washington University, for discoveries concerning the catalytic conversion of glycogen; Bernardo A. Houssay (Argentina), for discoveries concerning the role of the hormone of the anterior pituitary lobe in metabolizing sugar.
1948	Paul F. Müller (Switzerland), for discovering the effectiveness of DDT against several arthropods.
1949	Walter R. Hess (Switzerland), for discovering the interbrain; Antonio Caetano de Abreu F. E. Moniz (Portugal), for discovering the therapeutic use of leucotomy in treating certain psychoses.
1950	Edward C. Kendall (U.S.) of the Mayo Clinic, Tadeus Reichstein (Switzerland) and Philip S. Hench (U.S.) of the

Mayo Clinic, for discoveries concerning the hormones of the adrenal cortex.

1951   Max Theiler (Union of South Africa), working at the Laboratories Division of Medicine and Public Health, Rockefeller Foundation, New York, for discoveries concerning yellow fever.

1952   Selman A. Waksman (U.S.) of Rutgers University, for discovering streptomycin, the first antibiotic effective against tuberculosis.

1953   Sir Hans A. Krebs (Great Britain), for discovering the citric acid cycle; Fritz A. Lipmann (U.S.) of Harvard Medical School and Massachusetts General Hospital, for discovering co-enzyme A and its importance.

1954   John F. Enders (U.S.) of Harvard Medical School and the Research Division of Infectious Diseases, Children's Medical Center, Thomas H. Weller (U.S.) of the Research Division of Infectious Diseases, Children's Medical Center, and Frederick C. Robbins (U.S.) of Western Reserve University, for discovering the ability of poliomyelitis viruses to grow in cultures of various tissues.

1955   Axel H. T. Theorell (Sweden) for discoveries concerning the oxidation of enzymes.

1956   André F. Cournand (U.S.) of the Cardio-Pulmonary Laboratory, Columbia University Division, Bellevue Hospital, Werner Forssmann (Germany) and Dickinson W. Richards (U.S.) of Columbia University, for discoveries concerning heart catheterization and pathological changes of the circulatory system.

1957   Daniel Bovet (Italy) for discoveries concerning synthetic compounds that inhibit the action of certain body substances, especially as they affect the vascular system and skeletal muscles.

1958   George W. Beadle (U.S.) of the California Institute of Technology and Edward L. Tatum (U.S.) of Rockefeller Institute for Medical Research, for discovering that genes act by regulating chemical events; Joshua Lederberg (U.S.) of Wisconsin University, for discoveries concerning genetic recombination and organization of genetic material in bacteria.

1959   Severo Ochoa (U.S.) of New York University College of Medicine and Arthur Kornberg (U.S.) of Stanford University, for discoveries concerning the synthesis of ribonucleic acid (RNA) and deoxyribonucleic acid (DNA).

1960   Sir Frank M. Burnet (Australia) and Sir Peter B. Medawar (Great Britain), for discovering acquired immunological tolerance.

1961   Georg von Békésy (U.S.) of Harvard University, for discoveries concerning stimulation within the cochlea.

1962   Francis H. C. Crick (Great Britain), James D. Watson (U.S.) of Harvard University and Maurice H. F. Wilkins (Great Britain) for discoveries concerning the structure of nucleic acids and information transfer.

1963   Sir John C. Eccles (Australia), Sir Alan L. Hodgkin (Great Britain) and Sir Andrew F. Huxley (Great Britain), for discoveries concerning excitation and inhibition of the nerve cell membrane.

1964   Konrad Bloch (U.S.) of Harvard University and Feodor Lynen (West Germany) for discoveries concerning cholesterol and fatty-acid metabolism.

1965   François Jacob (France), André Lwoff (France) and Jacques Monod (France) for discoveries concerning genetic control of enzyme and virus synthesis.

1966   Peyton Rous (U.S.) of Rockefeller University, for discovering tumor-inducing viruses; Charles B. Huggins (U.S.) of Ben May Laboratory for Cancer Research, the University of Chicago, for discoveries concerning hormone treatment of prostate cancer.

1967   Ragnar Granit (Sweden), Haldan K. Hartline (U.S.) of Rockefeller University and George Wald (U.S.) of Harvard University, for discoveries concerning physiological and chemical processes in the eye.

1968   Robert W. Holley (U.S.) of Cornell University, Har G. Khorana (U.S.) of the University of Wisconsin, and Marshall W. Nirenberg (U.S.) of the National Institutes of Health, for discoveries concerning the genetic code and protein synthesis.

1969   Max Delbrück (U.S.) of the California Institute of Technology, Alfred D. Hershey (U.S.) of Carnegie Institution of Washington and Salvador Luria (U.S.)

of M.I.T., for discoveries concerning the genetic structure and replication of viruses.

1970   Sir Bernard Katz (Great Britain), Ulf von Euler (Sweden) and Julius Axelrod (U.S.) of the National Institutes of Health, for discoveries concerning transmitters in nerve terminals.

1971   Earl W. Sutherland, Jr., (U.S.) of Vanderbilt University, for discoveries concerning the actions of hormones.

1972   Gerald M. Edelman (U.S.) of Rockefeller University and Rodney R. Porter (Great Britain), for discoveries concerning the chemical structure of antibodies.

1973   Karl von Frisch (West Germany), Konrad Lorenz (Austria) and Nikolaas Tinbergen (Great Britain), for discoveries concerning individual and social behavior patterns.

1974   Christian de Duve (Belgium), working at Rockefeller University in New York, Albert Claude (Belgium), and George E. Palade (U.S.) of Yale University School of Medicine, for discoveries concerning cell structure and function.

1975   David Baltimore (U.S.) of M.I.T., Renato Dulbecco (U.S.) of Imperial Cancer Research Fund Laboratory in London, England, and Howard M. Temin (U.S.) of the University of Wisconsin, for discoveries concerning the interaction of tumor viruses and the genetic material of the cell.

1976   Baruch S. Blumberg (U.S.) of the Institute for Cancer Research and D. Carleton Gajdusek (U.S.) of the National Institutes of Health, for discoveries concerning the origin and dissemination of infectious diseases.

1977   Rogert Guillemin (U.S.) of the Salk Institute and Andrew V. Schally (U.S.) of the Veterans Administration Hospital in New Orleans, for discoveries concerning peptide hormone production of the brain; Rosalyn Yalow (U.S.) of the Veterans Administration Hospital, Bronx, for developing radioimmunoassays of peptide hormones.

1978   Werner Arber (Switzerland), Daniel Nathans (U.S.) and Hamilton O. Smith (U.S.), both of Johns Hopkins School of Medicine, for discoveries concerning enzymes and molecular genetics.

1979   Allan M. Cormack (U.S.) of Tufts University and Sir Godfrey N. Hounsfield (Great Britain), for developing computer-assisted tomography (CAT scans).

1980   Baruj Benacerraf (U.S.) of Harvard Medical School, Jean Dausset (France) and George D. Snell (U.S.) of Jackson Laboratory, for discoveries concerning cell structure and the regulation of immunological reactions.

1981   Roger W. Sperry (U.S.) of the California Institute of Technology, for discoveries concerning the specialization of cerebral hemispheres; David H. Hubel (U.S.) of Harvard Medical School and Torsten N. Wiesel (Sweden), working at Harvard Medical School, for discoveries concerning visual information processing.

1982   Sune K. Bergström (Sweden), Bengt I. Samuelsson (Sweden) and Sir John R. Vane (Great Britain), for discoveries concerning prostaglandins and related substances.

1983   Barbara McClintock (U.S.) of Cold Spring Harbor Laboratory, for discovery of mobile genetic elements.

1984   Niels K. Jerne (Denmark), George J. F. Köhler (West Germany) and César Milstein (Great Britain and Argentina), for discoveries concerning the immune system and the production of monoclonal antibodies.

1985   Michael S. Brown (U.S.) and Joseph L. Goldstein (U.S.), both of the University of Texas Health Science Center, for discoveries concerning regulation of cholesterol metabolism.

1986   Stanley Cohen (U.S.) of Vanderbilt University and Rita Levi-Montalcini (Italy and U.S.), for discoveries concerning growth factors.

1987   Susumu Tonegawa (U.S.) of M.I.T., for genetic discovery concerning antibodies.

1988   Sir James W. Black (Great Britain), Gertrude B. Elion (U.S.) and George H. Hitchings (U.S.), both of Wellcome Research Laboratories, for discoveries concerning drug treatment.

1989   J. Michael Bishop (U.S.) and Harold E. Varmus (U.S.), both of University of California Medical School, for discovering that normal genes can cause cancer when they malfunction due to changes caused by chemical carcinogens.

1990   Joseph E. Murray (U.S.) of Brigham and Women's Hospital in Boston and E. Donnall Thomas (U.S.) of Fred Hutchinson Cancer Research Center in Seattle, for advances in kidney and bone marrow transplants, respectively.

1991   Erwin Neher (Germany) of the Max-Planck-Institute for Biophysical Chemistry, Göttingen, and Bert Sakmann (Germany) of the Max-Planck-Institute for Medicine Research, Heidelberg, for research in cellular mechanisms underlying several diseases.

1992   Edmond Fischer and Edwin Krebs (U.S.), professors emeritus of the University of Washington, Seattle, for their discovery of one of the basic processes of human cell regulation.

PULITZER PRIZES

The Pulitzer Prizes are among the United States' most distinguished awards for achievements in music and letters; in journalism there is no higher honor. The awards are named after Joseph Pulitzer, one of the country's most famous newspaper publishers. Pulitzer was born in Mako, Hungary, April 10, 1847. He bought the *St. Louis Dispatch* and merged it with the *St. Louis Post* in 1878 to create a new, more successful and aggressive newspaper, the *St. Louis Post-Dispatch*. Five years later, in 1883, Pulitzer bought the *New York World* and turned it into one of the most powerful daily newspapers in America. He founded the Graduate School of Journalism at Columbia University in New York in 1903, and endowed the school and created the Pulitzer Prizes in his will; he died Oct. 29, 1911. The awards have been made annually every spring since 1917.

BIOGRAPHY OR AUTOBIOGRAPHY

1917   *Julia Ward Howe*, by Laura E. Richards and Maude Howe Elliott, assisted by Florence Howe Hall

1918   *Benjamin Franklin, Self-Revealed*, by William Cabell Bruce

1919   *The Education of Henry Adams*, by Henry Adams

1920   *The Life of John Marshall*, 4 vols., by Albert J. Beveridge

1921   *The Americanization of Edward Bok*, by Edward Bok

1922   *A Daughter of the Middle Border*, by Hamlin Garland

1923   *The Life and Letters of Walter H. Page*, by Burton J. Hendrick

1924   *From Immigrant to Inventor*, by Michael Idvorsky Pupin

1925   *Barrett Wendell and His Letter*, by M. A. DeWolfe Howe

1926   *The Life of Sir William Osler*, 2 vols., by Harvey Cushing

1927   *Whitman*, by Emory Holloway

1928   *The American Orchestra and Theodore Thomas*, by Charles Edward Russell

1929   *The Training of an American. The Earlier Life and Letters of Walter H. Page*, by Burton J. Hendrick

1930   *The Raven*, by Marquis James

1931   *Charles W. Eliot*, by Henry James

1932   *Theodore Roosevelt*, by Henry F. Pringle

1933   *Grover Cleveland*, by Allan Nevins

1934   *John Hay*, by Tyler Dennett

1935   *R. E. Lee*, by Douglas S. Freeman

1936   *The Thought and Character of William James*, by Ralph Barton Perry

1937   *Hamilton Fish*, by Allan Nevins

1938   *Pedlar's Progress*, by Odell Shepard; *Andrew Jackson*, 2 vols., by Marquis James

1939   *Benjamin Franklin*, by Carl Van Doren

1940   *Woodrow Wilson, Life and Letters*, Vols. VII and VIII, by Ray Stannard Baker

1941   *Jonathan Edwards*, by Ola Elizabeth Winslow

1942   *Crusader in Crinoline*, by Forrest Wilson

1943   *Admiral of the Ocean Sea*, by Samuel Eliot Morison

1944   *The American Leonardo: The Life of Samuel F. B. Morse*, by Carlton Mabee

1945   *George Bancroft: Brahmin Rebel*, by Russell Blaine Nye

1946   *Son of the Wilderness*, by Linnie Marsh Wolfe

1947   *The Autobiography of William Allen White*, by William Allen White

1948   *Forgotten First Citizen: John Bigelow*, by Margaret Clapp

1949   *Roosevelt and Hopkins*, by Robert E. Sherwood

1950   *John Quincy Adams and the Foundations of American Foreign Policy*, by Samuel Flagg Bemis

1951   *John C. Calhoun: American Portrait*, by Margaret Louise Coit

1952   *Charles Evans Hughes*, by Merlo J. Pusey

1953   *Edmund Pendleton 1721–1803*, by David J. Mays

1954   *The Spirit of St. Louis*, by Charles A. Lindbergh

1955   *The Taft Story*, by William S. White

1956 *Benjamin Henry Latrobe*, by Talbot Faulkner Hamlin

1957 *Profiles in Courage*, by John F. Kennedy

1958 *George Washington*, by Southall Freeman, and Vol. VII, written by John Alexander Carroll and Mary Wells Ashworth after Dr. Freeman's death in 1953.

1959 *Woodrow Wilson, American Prophet*, by Arthur Walworth

1960 *John Paul Jones*, by Samuel Eliot Morison

1961 *Charles Sumner and the Coming of the Civil War*, by David Donald

1962 No award

1963 *Henry James*, by Leon Edel

1964 *John Keats*, by Walter Jackson Bate

1965 *Henry Adams*, by Ernest Samuels

1966 *A Thousand Days*, by Arthur M. Schlesinger, Jr.

1967 *Mr. Clemens and Mark Twain*, by Justin Kaplan

1968 *Memoirs*, by George F. Kennan

1969 *The Man From New York: John Quinn and His Friends*, by Benjamin Lawrence Reid

1970 *Huey Long*, by T. Harry Williams

1971 *Robert Frost: The Years of Triumph, 1915–1938*, by Lawrence Thompson

1972 *Eleanor and Franklin*, by Joseph P. Lash

1973 *Luce and His Empire*, by W. A. Swanberg

1974 *O'Neill, Son and Artist*, by Louis Sheaffer

1975 *The Power Broker: Robert Moses and the Fall of New York*, by Robert Caro

1976 *Edith Wharton: A Biography*, by R. W. B. Lewis

1977 *A Prince of Our Disorder: The Life of T. E. Lawrence*, by John E. Mack

1978 *Samuel Johnson*, by Walter Jackson Bate

1979 *Days of Sorrow and Pain: Leo Baeck and the Berlin Jews*, by Leonard Baker

1980 *The Rise of Theodore Roosevelt*, by Edmund Morris

1981 *Peter the Great: His Life and World*, by Robert K. Massie

1982 *Grant: A Biography*, by William S. McFeely

1983 *Growing Up*, by Russell Baker

1984 *Booker T. Washington: The Wizard of Tuskegee, 1901–1915*, by Louis R. Harlan

1985 *The Life and Times of Cotton Mather*, by Kenneth Silverman

1986 *Louise Bogan: A Portrait*, by Elizabeth Frank

1987 *Bearing the Cross: Martin Luther King, Jr., and the Southern Christian Leadership Conference*, by David J. Garrow

1988 *Look Homeward: A Life of Thomas Wolfe*, by David Herbert Donald

1989 *Oscar Wilde*, by Richard Ellman

1990 *Machiavelli in Hell*, by Sebastian de Grazia

1991 *Jackson Pollack: An American Saga*, by Stephen Naifeh and Gregory White Smith

1992 *Fortunate Son: The Healing of a Vietnam Vet*, by Lewis B. Puller, Jr.

DRAMA

1917 No award

1918 *Why Marry*, by Jesse Lynch Williams

1919 No award

1920 *Beyond the Horizon*, by Eugene O'Neill

1921 *Miss Lulu Bett*, by Zona Gale

1922 *Anna Christie*, by Eugene O'Neill

1923 *Icebound*, by Owen Davis

1924 *Hell-Bent for Heaven*, by Hatcher Hughes

1925 *They Knew What They Wanted*, by Sidney Howard

1926 *Craig's Wife*, by George Kelly

1927 *In Abraham's Bosom*, by Paul Green

1928 *Strange Interlude*, by Eugene O'Neill

1929 *Street Scene*, by Elmer L. Rice

1930 *The Green Pastures*, by Marc Connelly

1931 *Alison's House*, by Susan Glaspell

1932 *Of Thee I Sing*, by George S. Kaufman, Morrie Ryskind and Ira Gershwin

1933 *Both Your Houses*, by Maxwell Anderson

1934 *Men in White*, by Sidney Kingsley

1935 *The Old Maid*, by Zoe Akins

1936 *Idiot's Delight*, by Robert E. Sherwood

1937 *You Can't Take It With You*, by Moss Hart and George S. Kaufman

1938 *Our Town*, by Thornton Wilder

1939 *Abe Lincoln in Illinois*, by Robert E. Sherwood

1940 *The Time of Your Life*, by William Saroyan

1941 *There Shall Be No Night*, by Robert E. Sherwood

1942 No award

1943 *The Skin of Our Teeth*, by Thornton Wilder

1944 No award

1945 *Harvey*, by Mary Chase

1946 *State of the Union*, by Russel Crouse and Howard Lindsay

1947 No award

1948 *A Streetcar Named Desire*, by Tennessee Williams

1949 *Death of a Salesman*, by Arthur Miller

1950 *South Pacific*, by Richard Rodgers, Oscar Hammerstein 2d and Joshua Logan

1951 No award

1952 *The Shrike*, by Joseph Kramm

1953 *Picnic*, by Wiliam Inge

1954 *The Teahouse of the August Moon*, by John Patrick

1955 *Cat on a Hot Tin Roof*, by Tennessee Williams

1956 *Diary of Anne Frank*, by Albert Hackett and Frances Goodrich

1957 *Long Day's Journey into Night*, by Eugene O'Neill

1958 *Look Homeward, Angel*, by Ketti Frings

1959 *J.B.*, by Archibald MacLeish

1960 *Fiorello!*, book, Jerome Weidman, George Abbott; music, Jerry Bock; lyrics, Sheldon Harnick

1961 *All the Way Home*, by Tad Mosel

1962 *How to Succeed in Business Without Really Trying*, by Frank Loesser and Abe Burrows

1963 No award

1964 No award

1965 *The Subject Was Roses*, by Frank D. Gilroy

1966 No award

1967 *A Delicate Balance*, by Edward Albee

1968 No award

1969 *The Great White Hope*, by Howard Sackler

1970 *No Place to Be Somebody*, by Charles Gordone

1971 *The Effect of Gamma Rays on Man-in-the Moon Marigolds*, by Paul Zindel

1972 No award

1973 *That Championship Season*, by Jason Miller

1974 No award

1975 *Seascape*, by Edward Albee

1976 *A Chorus Line*, conceived, choreographed, directed by Michael Bennett; book by James Kirkwood, Nicholas Dante; music by Marvin Hamlisch; lyrics by Edward Kleban

1977 *The Shadow Box*, by Michael Cristofer

1978 *The Gin Game*, by Donald L. Coburn

1979 *Buried Child*, by Sam Shepard

1980 *Talley's Folly*, by Lanford Wilson

1981 *Crimes of the Heart*, by Beth Henley

1982 *A Soldier's Play*, by Charles Fuller

1983 *'Night, Mother*, by Marsha Norman

1984 *Glengarry Glen Ross*, by David Mamet

1985 *Sunday in the Park With George*, music and lyrics by Stephen Sondheim, book by James Lapine

1986 No award

1987 *Fences*, by August Wilson

1988 *Driving Miss Daisy*, by Alfred Uhry

1989 *The Heidi Chronicles*, by Wendy Wasserstein

1990 *The Piano Lesson*, by August Wilson

1991 *Lost in Yonkers*, by Neil Simon

1992 *The Kentucky Cycle*, by Robert Shennkan

MUSIC

1943 William Schuman, for Secular Cantata No. 2, A Free Song.

1944 Howard Hanson, for Symphony No. 4, Opus 34

1945 Aaron Copland, for *Appalachian Spring*, a ballet written for and presented by Martha Graham and group

1946 Leo Sowerby, for The Canticle of the Sun

1947 Charles Ives, for Symphony No. 3

1948 Walter Piston, for Symphony No. 3

1949 Virgil Thomson, for his music for the film *Louisiana Story*

1950 Gian-Carlo Menotti, for his music in *The Consul*

1951 Douglas S. Moore, for Giants in the Earth

1952 Gail Kubik, for Symphony Concertante

1953 No award

1954 Quincy Porter, for Concerto for Two Pianos and Orchestra

1955 Gian-Carlo Menotti, for *The Saint of Bleecker Street* (opera)

1956 Ernst Toch, for Symphony No. 3

1957 Norman Dello Joio, for Meditations on Ecclesiastes

1958 Samuel Barber, for *Vanessa*, an opera in four acts, libretto by Gian-Carlo Menotti

1959 John LaMontaine, for Concerto for Piano and Orchestra

1960 Elliott Carter, for Second String Quartet

1961 Walter Piston, for his Symphony No. 7

1962 Robert Ward, for *The Crucible*, an opera in three acts, libretto by Bernard Stambler, based on the play by Arthur Miller

1963 Samuel Barber, for Piano Concerto No. 1

1964 No award

1965 No award

1966 Leslie Bassett, for Variations for Orchestra

1967 Leon Kirchner, for his Quartet No. 3

1968 George Crumb, for his orchestral suite, Echoes of Time and the River

1969 Karel Husa, for his String Quartet No. 3

1970 Charles Wuorinen, for Time's Encomium

1971 Mario Davidovsky, for Synchronisms No. 6 for Piano and Electronic Sound (1970)

1972 Jacob Druckman, for Windows

1973 Elliott Carter, for String Quartet No. 3

1974 Donald Martino, for chamber music, Notturno

1975 Dominick Argento, for From the Diary of Virginia Woolf, for medium voice and piano

1976 Ned Rorem, for Air Music

1977 Richards Wernick, for Visions of Terror and Wonder

1978 Michael Colgrass, for Déjà Vu for Percussion Quartet and Orchestra

1979 Joseph Schwantner, for Aftertones of Infinity

1980 David Del Tredici, for In Memory of a Summer Day, a work for soprano solo and orchestra
1982 Roger Sessions, for Concerto for Orchestra
1983 Ellen Taaffe Zwilich, for Symphony No. 1 (Three Movements for Orchestra)
1984 Bernard Rands, for Canti del Sole for tenor and orchestra
1985 Stephen Albert, for Symphony, River Run
1986 George Perle, for Wind Quintet IV
1987 John Harbison, for The Flight into Egypt
1988 William Bolcom, for 12 New Etudes of Piano
1989 Roger Reynolds, for Whispers Out of Time
1990 Mel Powell, for Duplicates: A Concerto for Two Pianos and Orchestra
1991 Shulamit Ran, for Symphony
1992 Wayne Peterson, for The Face of the Night, the Heart of the Dark

FICTION

(Until 1947, the prize was called the Pulitzer Prize for the Novel)
1917 No award
1918 His Family, by Ernest Poole
1919 The Magnificent Ambersons, by Booth Tarkington
1920 No award
1921 The Age of Innocence, by Edith Wharton
1922 Alice Adams, by Booth Tarkington
1923 One of Ours, by Willa Cather
1924 The Able McLaughlins, by Margaret Wilson
1925 So Big, by Edna Ferber
1926 Arrowsmith, by Sinclair Lewis
1927 Early Autumn, by Louis Bromfield
1928 The Bridge of San Luis Rey, by Thornton Wilder
1929 Scarlet Sister Mary, by Julia Peterkin
1930 Laughing Boy, by Oliver LaFarge
1931 Years of Grace, by Margaret Ayer Barnes
1932 The Good Earth, by Pearl S. Buck
1933 The Store, by T. S. Stribling
1934 Lamb in His Bosom, by Caroline Miller
1935 Now in November, by Josephine Winslow Johnson
1936 Honey in the Horn, by Harold L. Davis
1937 Gone With the Wind, by Margaret Mitchell
1938 The Late George Apley, by John Phillips Marquand
1939 The Yearling, by Marjorie Kinnan Rawlings
1940 The Grapes of Wrath, by John Steinbeck
1941 No award
1942 In This Our Life, by Ellen Glasgow
1943 Dragon's Teeth, by Upton Sinclair
1944 Journey in the Dark, by Martin Flavin

1945 A Bell for Adano, by John Hersey
1946 No award
1947 All the King's Men, by Robert Penn Warren
1948 Tales of the South Pacific, by James A. Michener
1949 Guard of Honor, by James Gould Cozzens
1950 The Way West, by A. B. Guthrie, Jr.
1951 The Town, by Conrad Richter
1952 The Caine Mutiny, by Herman Wouk
1953 The Old Man and the Sea, by Ernest Hemingway
1954 No award
1955 A Fable, by William Faulkner
1956 Andersonville, by MacKinlay Kantor
1957 No award
1958 A Death in the Family, by James Agee
1959 The Travels of Jaimie McPheeters, by Robert Lewis Taylor
1960 Advise and Consent, by Allen Drury
1961 To Kill a Mockingbird, by Harper Lee
1962 The Edge of Sadness, by Edwin O'Connor
1963 The Reivers, by William Faulkner
1964 No award
1965 The Keepers of the House, by Shirley Ann Grau
1966 Collected Stories, by Katherine Anne Porter
1967 The Fixer, by Bernard Malamud
1968 The Confessions of Nat Turner, by William Styron
1969 House Made of Dawn, by N. Scott Momaday
1970 Collected Stories, by Katherine Anne Porter
1971 No award
1972 Angle of Repose, by Wallace Stegner
1973 The Optimist's Daughter, by Eudora Welty
1974 No award
1975 The Killer Angels, by Michael Shaara
1976 Humboldt's Gift, by Saul Bellow
1977 No award
1978 Elbow Room, by James Alan McPherson
1979 The Stories of John Cheever, by John Cheever
1980 The Executioner's Song, by Norman Mailer
1981 A Confederacy of Dunces, by John Kennedy Toole
1982 Rabbit Is Rich, by John Updike
1983 The Color Purple, by Alice Walker
1984 Ironweed, by William Kennedy
1985 Foreign Affairs, by Alison Lurie
1986 Lonesome Dove, by Larry McMurtry
1987 A Summons to Memphis, by Peter Taylor
1988 Beloved, by Toni Morrison
1989 Breathing Lessons, by Anne Tyler
1990 The Mambo Kings Play Songs of Love, by Oscar Hijuelos
1991 Rabbit at Rest, by John Updike
1992 A Thousand Acres, by Jane Smiley

GENERAL NONFICTION

1962   *The Making of the President 1960*, by Theodore H. White

1963   *The Guns of August*, by Barbara W. Tuchman

1964   *Anti-Intellectualism in American Life*, by Richard Hofstadter

1965   *O Strange New World*, by Howard Mumford Jones

1966   *Wandering Through Winter*, by Edwin Way Teale

1967   *The Problem of Slavery in Western Culture*, by David Briar Davis

1968   *Rousseau and Revolution*, 10th and final volume of *The Story of Civilization*, by Will Durant and Ariel Durant

1969   *So Human an Animal*, by René Jules Dubos; *The Armies of the Night*, by Norman Mailer

1970   *Ghandhi's Truth*, by Erik H. Erikson

1971   *The Rising Sun*, by John Toland

1972   *Stilwell and the American Experience in China, 1911–1945*, by Barbara W. Tuchman

1973   *Children of Crisis*, vols. II and III, by Robert Coles

1974   *The Denial of Death*, by Ernest Becker

1975   *Pilgrim at Tinker Creek*, by Annie Dillard

1976   *Why Survive Being Old in America?* by Robert N. Butler

1977   *Beautiful Swimmers*, by William W. Warner

1978   *The Dragons of Eden*, by Carl Sagan

1979   *On Human Nature*, by Edward O. Wilson

1980   *Gödel, Escher, Bach: An Eternal Golden Braid*, by Douglas R. Hofstadter

1981   *Fin-de-Siècle Vienna: Politics and Culture*, by Carl E. Schorsky

1982   *The Soul of a New Machine*, by Tracy Kidder

1983   *Is There No Place on Earth for Me?* by Susan Sheehan

1984   *The Social Transformation of American Medicine*, by Paul Starr

1985   *The Good War: An Oral History of World War Two*, by Studs Terkel

1986   *Move Your Shadow: South Africa, Black and White*, by Joseph Lelyveld; *Common Ground: A Turbulent Decade in the Lives of Three American Families*, by J. Anthony Lucas

1987   *Arab and Jew: Wounded Spirits in a Promised Land*, by David K. Shipler

1988   *The Making of the Atomic Bomb*, by Richard Rhodes

1989   *A Bright Shining Lie: John Paul Vann and America in Vietnam*, by Neil Sheehan

1990   *And Their Children After Them*, by Dale Maharidge and Michael Williamson

1991   *The Ants*, by Bert Holldobler and Edward O. Wilson

1992   *The Prize: The Epic Quest for Oil, Money and Power*, by Daniel Yergin

HISTORY

1917   *With Americans of Past and Present Days*, by His Excellency J. J. Jusserand, French ambassador to the United States

1918   *A History of the Civil War, 1861–1865*, by James Ford Rhodes

1919   No award

1920   *The War with Mexico*, 2 vols., by Justin H. Smith

1921   *The Victory at Sea*, by William Sowden Sims in collaboration with Burton J. Hendrick

1922   *The Founding of New England*, by James Truslow Adams

1923   *The Supreme Court in United States History*, by Charles Warren

1924   *The American Revolution: A Constitutional Interpretation*, by Charles Howard McIllwain

1925   *A History of the American Frontier*, by Frederic L. Paxson

1926   *The History of the United States*, by Edward Channing

1927   *Pickney's Treaty*, by Samuel Flagg Bemis

1928   *Main Currents in American Thought*, 2 vols., by Vernon Louis Parrington

1929   *The Organization and Administration of the Union Army, 1861–1865*, by Fred Albert Shannon

1930   *The War of Independence*, by Claude H. Van Tyne

1931   *The Coming of the War: 1914*, by Bernadotte E. Schmitt

1932   *My Experiences in the World War*, by John J. Pershing

1933   *The Significance of Sections in American History*, by Frederick J. Turner

1934   *The People's Choice*, by Herbert Agar

1935   *The Colonial Period of American History*, by Charles McLean Andrews

1936   *The Constitutional History of the United States*, by Andrew C. McLaughlin

1937   *The Flowering of New England*, by Van Wyck Books

1938   *The Road to Reunion, 1856–1900*, by Paul Herman Buck

1939   *A History of American Magazines*, by Frank Luther Mott

1940   *Abraham Lincoln: The War Years*, by Carl Sandburg

1941 *The Atlantic Migration, 1607–1860*, by Marcus Lee Hansen

1942 *Reveille in Washington*, by Margaret Leech

1943 *Paul Revere and the World He Lived In*, by Esther Forbes

1944 *The Growth of American Thought*, by Merle Curti

1945 *Unfinished Business*, by Stephen Bonsal

1946 *The Age of Jackson*, by Arthur Meier Schlesinger, Jr.

1947 *Scientists Against Time*, by James P. Baxter III

1948 *Across the Wide Missouri*, by Bernard DeVoto

1949 *The Disruption of American Democracy*, by Roy Franklin Nichols

1950 *Art and Life in America*, by Oliver W. Larkin

1951 *The Old Northwest, Pioneer Period 1815–1840*, by R. Carlyle Buley

1952 *The Uprooted*, by Oscar Handlin

1953 *The Era of Good Feelings*, by George Dangerfield

1954 *A Stillness at Appomattox*, by Bruce Catton

1955 *Great River: The Rio Grande in North American History*, by Paul Horgan

1956 *Age of Reform*, by Richard Hofstadter

1957 *Russia Leaves the War: Soviet-American Relations, 1917–1920*, by George F. Kennan

1958 *Banks and Politics in America*, by Bray Hammond

1959 *The Republican Era: 1869–1901*, by Leonard D. White, with the assistance of Jean Schneider

1960 *In the Days of McKinley*, by Margaret Leech

1961 *Between War and Peace: The Potsdam Conference*, by Herbert Feis

1962 *The Triumphant Empire, Thunder-Clouds in the West*, by Lawrence H. Gibson

1963 *Washington, Village and Capital, 1800–1878*, by Constance McLaughlin Green

1964 *Puritan Village: The Formation of a New England Town*, by Sumner Chilton Powell

1965 *The Greenback Era*, by Irwin Unger

1966 *Life of the Mind in America*, by Perry Miller

1967 *Exploration and Empire: The Explorer and the Scientist in the Winning of the American West*, by William H. Goetzmann

1968 *The Ideological Origins of the American Revolution*, by Bernard Bailyn

1969 *Origins of the Fifth Amendment*, by Leonard W. Levy

1970 *Present at the Creation: My Years in the State Department*, by Dean Acheson

1971 *Roosevelt, The Soldier of Freedom*, by James MacGregor Burns

1972 *Neither Black Nor White*, by Carl N. Degler

1973 *People of Paradox: An Inquiry Concerning the Origins of American Civilization*, by Michael Kammen

1974 *The Americans: The Democratic Experience*, by Daniel J. Boorstin

1975 *Jefferson and His Time, vols. I–V*, by Dumas Malone

1976 *Lamy of Santa Fe*, by Paul Horgan

1977 *The Impending Crisis*, by David M. Potter (a posthumous publication); manuscript finished by Don E. Fehrenbacher

1978 *The Visible Hand: The Managerial Revolution in American Business*, by Alfred D. Chandler, Jr.

1979 *The Dred Scott Case*, by Don E. Fehrenbacher

1980 *Been in the Storm So Long*, by Leon F. Litwack

1981 *American Education: The National Experience, 1783–1876*, by Lawrence A. Cremin

1982 *Mary Chestnut's Civil War*, edited by C. Vann Woodward

1983 *The Transformation of Virginia, 1740–1790*, by Rhys L. Isaac

1984 No award

1985 *Prophets of Regulation*, by Thomas K. McCraw

1986 *. . . The Heavens and the Earth: A Political History of the Space Age*, by Walter A. McDougall

1987 *Voyagers to the West: A Passage in the Peopling of America on the Eve of the Revolution*, by Bernard Bailyn

1988 *The Launching of Modern American Science 1846–1876*, by Robert V. Bruce

1989 *Parting of the Waters: America in the King Years, 1954–63*, by Taylor Branch; *Battle Cry of Freedom: The Civil War Era*, by James M. McPherson

1990 *In Our Image: America's Empire in the Philippines*, by Stanley Karnow

1991 *A Midwife's Tale: The Life of Martha Ballard, based on her diary, 1785–1812*, by Laurel Thatcher Ulrich

1992 *The Fate of Liberty: Abraham Lincoln and Civil Liberties*, by Mark E. Neely, Jr.

POETRY

(This award was established as a permanent category in 1922. Awards were made in 1918 and 1919, provided by gifts from the Poetry Society.)

1918 *Love Songs*, by Sara Teasdale (award provided by the Poetry Society)

1919 *Old Road to Paradise*, by Margaret Widdemer (award provided by the Poetry

Society); *Corn Huskers*, by Carl Sandburg (award provided by the Poetry Society)

1922   *Collected Poems*, by Edwin Arlington Robinson

1923   *The Ballad of the Harp-Weaver; A Few Figs from Thistles; Eight Sonnets in American Poetry, 1922; A Miscellany*, by Edna St. Vincent Millay

1924   *New Hampshire: A Poem with Notes and Grace Notes*, by Robert Frost

1925   *The Man Who Died Twice*, by Edwin Arlington Robinson

1926   *What's O'Clock*, by Amy Lowell

1927   *Fiddler's Farewell*, by Leonora Speyer

1928   *Tristram*, by Edwin Arlington Robinson

1929   *John Brown's Body*, by Stephen Vincent Benét

1930   *Selected Poems*, by Conrad Aiken

1931   *Collected Poems*, by Robert Frost

1932   *The Flowering Stone*, by George Dillon

1933   *Conquistador*, by Archibald MacLeish

1934   *Collected Verse*, by Robert Hillyer

1935   *Bright Ambush*, by Audrey Wurdemann

1936   *Strange Holiness*, by Robert P. Tristram Coffin

1937   *A Further Range*, by Robert Frost

1938   *Cold Morning Sky*, by Marya Zaturenska

1939   *Selected Poems*, by John Gould Fletcher

1940   *Collected Poems*, by Mark Van Doren

1941   *Sunderland Capture*, by Leonard Bacon

1942   *The Dust Which Is God*, by William Rose Benét

1943   *A Witness Tree*, by Robert Frost

1944   *Western Star*, by Stephen Vincent Benét

1945   *V-Letter and Other Poems*, by Karl Shapiro

1946   No award

1947   *Lord Weary's Castle*, by Robert Lowell

1948   *The Age of Anxiety*, by W. H. Auden

1949   *Terror and Decorum*, by Peter Viereck

1950   *Annie Allen*, by Gwendolyn Brooks

1951   *Complete Poems*, by Carl Sandburg

1952   *Collected Poems*, by Marianne Moore

1953   *Collected Poems 1917–1952*, by Archibald MacLeish

1954   *The Waking*, by Theodore Roethke

1955   *Collected Poems*, by Wallace Stevens

1956   *Poems—North & South*, by Elizabeth Bishop

1957   *Things of This World*, by Richard Wilbur

1958   *Promises: Poems 1954–1956*, by Robert Penn Warren

1959   *Selected Poems 1928–1958*, by Stanley Kunitz

1960   *Heart's Needle*, by W. D. Snodgrass

1961   *Times Three: Selected Verse from Three Decades*, by Phyllis McGinley

1962   *Poems*, by Alan Dugan

1963   *Pictures from Breughel*, by William Carlos Williams

1964   *At the End of the Open Road*, by Louis Simpson

1965   *77 Dream Songs*, by John Berryman

1966   *Selected Poems*, by Richard Eberhart

1967   *Live or Die*, by Anne Sexton

1968   *The Hard Hours*, by Anthony Hecht

1969   *Of Being Numerous*, by George Oppen

1970   *Untitled Subjects*, by Richard Howard

1971   *The Carrier of Ladders*, by William S. Merwin

1972   *Collected Poems*, by James Wright

1973   *Up Country*, by Maxine Kumin

1974   *The Dolphin*, by Robert Lowell

1975   *Turtle Island*, by Gary Snyder

1976   *Self-Portrait in a Convex Mirror*, by John Ashbery

1977   *Divine Comedies*, by James Merrill

1978   *Collected Poems*, by Howard Nemerov

1979   *Now and Then*, by Robert Penn Warren

1980   *Selected Poems*, by Donald Justice

1981   *The Morning of the Poem*, by James Schuyler

1982   *The Collected Poems*, by Sylvia Plath

1983   *Selected Poems*, by Galway Kinnell

1984   *American Primitive*, by Mary Oliver

1985   *Yin*, by Carolyn Kizer

1986   *The Flying Change*, by Henry Taylor

1987   *Thomas and Beulah*, by Rita Dove

1988   *Partial Accounts: New and Selected Poems*, by William Meredith

1989   *New and Collected Poems*, by Richard Wilbur

1990   *The World Doesn't End*, by Charles Simic

1991   *Near Changes*, by Mona Van Duyn

1992   *Selected Poems*, by James Tate

Pulitzer Prizes for Journalism

EDITORIAL CARTOONING

1922   Rollin Kirby, *New York World*

1923   No award

1924   Jay Norwood Darling, *Des Moines Register & Tribune*

1925   Rollin Kirby, *New York World*

1926   D. R. Fitzpatrick, *St. Louis Post-Dispatch*

1927   Nelson Harding, *Brooklyn Daily Eagle*

1928   Nelson Harding, *Brooklyn Daily Eagle*

1929   Rollin Kirby, *New York World*

1930   Charles R. Macauley, *Brooklyn Daily Eagle*

1931   Edmund Duffy, *The Baltimore Sun*

1932   John T. McCutcheon, *Chicago Tribune*

1933   H. M. Talburt, *Washington Daily News*

1934   Edmund Duffy, *The Baltimore Sun*

1935   Ross A. Lewis, *Milwaukee Journal*

1936   No award

1937 C. D. Batchelor, *New York Daily News*
1938 Vaughn Shoemaker, *Chicago Daily News*
1939 Charles G. Werner, *Daily Oklahoman*
1940 Edmund Duffy, *The Baltimore Sun*
1941 Jacob Burck, *Chicago Times*
1942 Herbert L. Block ("Herblock"), NEA Service
1943 Jay Norwood Darling, *Des Moines Register & Tribune*
1944 Clifford K. Berryman, *The Evening Star*, (Washington, D.C.)
1945 Sergeant Bill Mauldin, United Feature Syndicate, Inc.
1946 Bruce Alexander Russell, *Los Angeles Times*
1947 Vaughn Shoemaker, *Chicago Daily News*
1948 Reuben L. Goldberg, *New York Sun*
1949 Lute Pease, *Newark* (N.J.) *Evening News*
1950 James T. Berryman, *The Evening Star* (Washington, D.C.)
1951 Reg Manning, *Arizona Republic*
1952 Fred L. Packer, *New York Mirror*
1953 Edward D. Keukes, *Cleveland Plain Dealer*
1954 Herbert L. Block ("Herblock"), *Washington Post & Times Herald*
1955 Daniel R. Fitzpatrick, *St. Louis Post-Dispatch*
1956 Robert York, *Louisville Times*
1957 Tom Little, *Nashville Tennessean*
1958 Bruce M. Shanks, *Buffalo Evening News*
1959 William H. (Bill) Mauldin, *St. Louis Post-Dispatch*
1960 No award
1961 Carey Orr, *Chicago Tribune*
1962 Edmund S. Valtman, *The Hartford* (Conn.) *Times*
1963 Frank Miller, *Des Moines Register*
1964 Paul Conrad, *The Denver Post*
1965 No award
1966 Don Wright, *Miami News*
1967 Patrick P. Oliphant, *Denver Post*
1968 Eugene Gray Payne, *Charlotte* (N.C.) *Observer*
1969 John Fischetti, *Chicago Daily News*
1970 Thomas F. Darcy, *Newsday* (N.Y.)
1971 Paul Conrad, *Los Angeles Times*
1972 Jeffrey K. MacNelly, *Richmond News-Leader*
1973 No award
1974 Paul Szep, *The Boston Globe*
1975 Gary Trudeau, Universal Press Syndicate
1976 Tony Auth, *The Philadelphia Inquirer*
1977 Paul Szep, *The Boston Globe*
1978 Jeffrey K. MacNelly, *Richmond News-Leader*
1979 Herbert L. Block ("Herblock"), *The Washington Post*
1980 Don Wright, *The Miami News*
1981 Mike Peters, *Dayton Daily News*
1982 Ben Sargent, *The Austin American-Statesman*

1983 Richard Locher, *Chicago Tribune*
1984 Paul Conrad, *Los Angeles Times*
1985 Jeff MacNelly, *Chicago Tribune*
1986 Jules Feiffer, *The Village Voice* (New York City)
1987 Berke Breathed, The Washington Post Writers Group
1988 Doug Marlette, *Atlanta Constitution* and *Charlotte Observer*
1989 Jack Higgins, *Chicago Sun-Times*
1990 Tom Toles, *The Buffalo News*
1991 Jim Borgman, *The Cincinnati Enquirer*
1992 Signe Wilkinson, *Philadelphia Daily News*

COMMENTARY

1970 Marquis W. Childs, *St. Louis Post-Dispatch*
1971 William A. Caldwell, *The Record* (Hackensack, N.J.)
1972 Mike Royko, *Chicago Daily News*
1973 David S. Broder, *The Washington Post*
1974 Edwin A. Roberts, Jr., *National Observer*
1975 Mary McGrory, *Washington Star*
1976 Walter Wellesley ("Red") Smith, *The New York Times*
1977 George F. Will, The Washington Post Writers Group
1978 William Safire, *The New York Times*
1979 Russell Baker, *The New York Times*
1980 Ellen H. Goodman, *The Boston Globe*
1981 Dave Anderson, *The New York Times*
1982 Art Buchwald, Los Angeles Times Syndicate
1983 Claude Sitton, *Raleigh News & Observer*
1984 Vermont Royster, *The Wall Street Journal*
1985 Murray Kempton, *Newsday* (N.Y.)
1986 Jimmy Breslin, *New York Daily News*
1987 Charles Krauthammer, The Washington Post Writers Group
1988 Dave Barry, *Miami Herald*
1989 Clarence Page, *Chicago Tribune*
1990 Jim Murray, *Los Angeles Times*
1991 Jim Hoagland, *The Washington Post*
1992 Anna Quindlen, *The New York Times*

CRITICISM

1970 Ada Louise Huxtable, *The New York Times*
1971 Harold C. Schonberg, *The New York Times*
1972 Frank Peters, Jr., *St. Louis Post-Dispatch*
1973 Ronald Powers, *Chicago Sun-Times*
1974 Emily Genauer, Newsday Syndicate
1975 Roger Ebert, *Chicago Sun-Times*
1976 Alan M. Kriegsman, *The Washington Post*
1977 William McPherson, *The Washington Post*
1978 Walter Kerr, *The New York Times*
1979 Paul Gapp, *Chicago Tribune*
1980 William A. Henry III, *The Boston Globe*

1981 Jonathan Yardley, *The Washington Star*
1982 Martin Bernheimer, *Los Angeles Times*
1983 Manuela Hoelterhoff, *The Wall Street Journal*
1984 Paul Goldberger, *The New York Times*
1985 Howard Rosenberg, *Los Angeles Times*
1986 Donal Henahan, *The New York Times*
1987 Richard Eder, *Los Angeles Times*
1988 Tom Shales, *The Washington Post*
1989 Michael Skube, *Raleigh News & Observer*
1990 Allan Temko, *San Francisco Chronicle*
1991 David Shaw, *Los Angeles Times*
1992 No award

EDITORIAL WRITING

1917 *New York Tribune*
1918 *Louisville Courier Journal*
1919 No award
1920 Harvey E. Newbranch, *Evening World Herald* (Omaha, Neb.)
1921 No award
1922 Frank M. O'Brien, *New York Herald*
1923 William Allen White, *Emporia* (Kans.) *Gazette*
1924 *Boston Herald.* A special prize was awarded to the widow of Frank I. Cobb, *New York World,* in recognition of his editorial writing and service.
1925 *Charleston* (S.C.) *News and Courier*
1926 Edward M. Kingsbury, *The New York Times*
1927 F. Lauriston Bullard, *Boston Herald*
1928 Grover Cleveland Hall, *Montgomery* (Ala.) *Advertiser*
1929 Louis Isaac Jaffe, *Norfolk Virginian-Pilot*
1930 No award
1931 Charles S. Ryckman, *Fremont* (Neb.) *Tribune*
1932 No award
1933 *Kansas City* (Mo.) *Star*
1934 E. P. Chase, *Atlantic* (Iowa) *News-Telegraph*
1935 No award
1936 Felix Morley, *The Washington Post;* George B. Parker, Scripps-Howard Newspapers
1937 John W. Owens, *The Baltimore Sun*
1938 William Wesley Waymack, *Des Moines Register & Tribune*
1939 Ronald G. Callvert, *Portland Oregonian*
1940 Bart Howard, *St. Louis Post-Dispatch*
1941 Reuben Maury, *New York Daily News*
1942 Geoffrey Parsons, *New York Herald Tribune*
1943 Forrest W. Seymour, *Des Moines Register & Tribune*
1944 Henry J. Haskell, *Kansas City* (Mo.) *Star*
1945 George W. Potter, *Providence Journal-Bulletin*
1946 Hodding Carter, *Delta Democrat-Times* (Greenville, Miss.)
1947 William H. Grimes, *The Wall Street Journal*
1948 Virginius Dabney, *Richmond Times-Dispatch*

1949 John H. Cider, *Boston Herald;* Herbert Elliston, *The Washington Post*
1950 Carl M. Saunders, *Jackson* (Mich.) *Citizen Patriot*
1951 William Harry Fitzpatrick, *New Orleans States*
1952 Louis LaCoss, *St. Louis Globe Democrat*
1953 Vermont Connecticut Royster, *The Wall Street Journal*
1954 Don Murray, *Boston Herald*
1955 Royce Howes, *Detroit Free Press*
1956 Lauren K. Soth, *Des Moines Register & Tribune*
1957 Buford Boone, *Tuscaloosa* (Ala.) *News*
1958 Harry S. Ashmore, *Arkansas Gazette*
1959 Ralph McGill, *Atlanta Constitution*
1960 Lenoir Chambers, *Norfolk Virginian-Pilot*
1961 William J. Dorvillier, *San Juan* (Puerto Rico) *Star*
1962 Thomas M. Storke, *Santa Barbara News Press*
1963 Ira B. Harkey, Jr., *Pascagoula Chronicle*
1964 Hazel Brannon Smith, *Lexington* (Miss.) *Advertiser*
1965 John R. Harrison, *Gainesville Daily Sun*
1966 Robert Lasch, *St. Louis Post-Dispatch*
1967 Eugene Patterson, *Atlanta Constitution*
1968 John S. Knight, Knight Newspapers
1969 Paul Greenberg, *Pine Bluff Commercial*
1970 Philip L. Geyelin, *The Washington Post*
1971 Horace G. Davis, Jr., *Gainesville Sun*
1972 John Strohmeyer, *Bethlehem* (Pa.) *Globe-Times*
1973 Roger B. Linscott, *Berkshire Eagle* (Pittsfield, Mass.)
1974 F. Gilman Spencer, *Trentonian* (Trenton, N.J.)
1975 John Daniell Maurice, *Charleston* (W.V.) *Daily Mail*
1976 Philip P. Kerby, *Los Angeles Times*
1977 Warren L. Lerude, Foster Church and Norman F. Cardoza, *Reno Evening Gazette* and *Nevada State Journal*
1978 Meg Greenfield, *The Washington Post*
1979 Edwin M. Yoder, Jr., *The Washington Star*
1980 Robert L. Bartley, *The Wall Street Journal*
1981 No award
1982 Jack Rosenthal, *The New York Times*
1983 Editorial Board of *The Miami Herald*
1984 Albert Scardino, *The Georgia Gazette* (Savannah)
1985 Richard Aregood, *The Philadelphia Daily News*
1986 Jack Fuller, *Chicago Tribune*
1987 Jonathan Freedman, *San Diego Tribune*
1988 Jane Healy, *Orlando Sentinel*
1989 Lois Wille, *Chicago Tribune*

1990 Thomas J. Hylton, *The Mercury* (Pottstown, Pa.)

1991 Ron Casey, Harold Jackson, Joey Kennedy, *The Birmingham* (Ala.) *News*

1992 Maria Henson, *Lexington* (Ky.) *Herald Leader*

EXPLANATORY JOURNALISM

1985 Jon Franklin, *The Baltimore Evening Sun*, for his seven-part series "The Mind Fixers," on molecular psychiatry.

1986 *The New York Times* staff, for a six-part series on the Strategic Defense Initiative.

1987 Jeff Lyon and Peter Gorner, *Chicago Tribune*, for their series on the promise of gene therapy.

1988 Daniel Hertzberg, James B. Stewart, *The Wall Street Journal*, for stories about the panic the day after the Oct. 19, 1987, stock market crash, and for stories about insider trading.

1989 David Hanners (reporter), William Snyder (photographer) and Karen Blessen (artist), *Dallas Morning News*, for a 12-page section on the crash of a corporate jet.

1990 David A. Vise, Steve Coll, *The Washington Post*, for stories about the Securities and Exchange Commission.

1991 Susan C. Faludi, *The Wall Street Journal*, for reporting on the human toll of the leveraged buyout of Safeway Stores Inc.

1992 Robert S. Capers, Eric S. Lipton, *The Hartford Courant*, for their series explaining the flaw in a mirror crucial to the Hubble Space Telescope.

FEATURE WRITING

(Citations not included prior to 1980.)

1979 Jon D. Franklin, *The Baltimore Evening Sun*, for an account of brain surgery.

1980 Madeleine Blais, *The Miami Herald*, for "Zepp's Last Stand."

1981 Teresa Carpenter, *The Village Voice* (New York City), for a story about three murders. The award originally was presented to Janet Cooke of *The Washington Post* for a story about an 8-year-old heroin addict. The *Post* relinquished the award when it learned that parts of the story were fabricated and that the main character was a "composite."

1982 Saul Pett, The Associated Press, for an article profiling the federal bureaucracy.

1983 Nan Robertson, *The New York Times*, for the story of her struggle with toxic shock syndrome.

1984 Peter Mark Rinearson, *The Seattle Times*, for his story about the new Boeing 757 jetliner.

1985 Alice Steinbach, *The Baltimore Sun*, for her account of a blind boy's world.

1986 John Camp, *St. Paul Pioneer Press and Dispatch*, for his five-part series examining the life of an American farm family faced with the worst agricultural crisis since the Depression.

1987 Steve Twomey, *The Philadelphia Inquirer*, for profile of life aboard an aircraft carrier.

1988 Jacqui Banaszynski, *St. Paul Pioneer Press and Dispatch*, for a series concerning the life and death of a prominent political activist who died of AIDS.

1989 David Zucchino, *Philadelphia Inquirer*, for a series on the lives of blacks in South Africa.

1990 Dave Curtin, *Colorado Springs Gazette Telegraph*, for an account of a family's struggle to recover after its members were severely burned in an explosion that devastated their home.

1991 Sheryl James, *St. Petersburg* (Fla.) *Times*, for stories about the impact of a mother's abandonment of her newborn child.

1992 Howell Raines, *The New York Times*, for a reminiscence about Grady Hutchinson, his family's housekeeper.

MERITORIOUS PUBLIC SERVICE

(Citations not included prior to 1980.)

1917 No award

1918 *The New York Times*

1919 *Milwaukee Journal*

1920 No award

1921 *Boston Post*

1922 *New York World*

1923 *Memphis Commercial Appeal*

1924 *New York World*

1925 No award

1926 *Columbus* (Ga.) *Enquirer Sun*

1927 *Canton* (Ohio) *Daily News*

1928 *Indianapolis Times*

1929 *New York Evening World*

1930 No award

1931 *Atlanta Constitution*

1932 *Indianapolis News*

1933 *New York World-Telegram*

1934 *Medford* (Ore.) *Mail Tribune*

1935 *The Sacramento Bee*

1936 *The Cedar Rapids Gazette*

1937 *St. Louis Post-Dispatch*

1938 *The Bismarck* (N.D.) *Tribune*

1939 *The Miami Daily News*

1940 *Waterbury* (Conn.) *Republican & American*
1941 *St. Louis Post-Dispatch*
1942 *Los Angeles Times*
1943 *Omaha World-Herald*
1944 *The New York Times*
1945 *Detroit Free Press*
1946 *Scranton* (Pa.) *Times*
1947 *Baltimore Sun*
1948 *St. Louis Post-Dispatch*
1949 *Nebraska State Journal*
1950 *Chicago Daily News* and *St. Louis Post-Dispatch*
1951 *The Miami Herald* and *Brooklyn* (N.Y.) *Eagle*
1952 *St. Louis Post-Dispatch*
1953 *Whiteville* (N.C.) *News Reporter* and *Tabor City* (N.C.) *Tribune*
1954 *Newsday* (N.Y.)
1955 *Columbus* (Ga.) *Ledger* and *Sunday Ledger-Enquirer*
1956 *Watsonville* (Calif.) *Register-Pajaronian*
1957 *Chicago Daily News*
1958 *Arkansas Gazette* (Little Rock, Ark.)
1959 *Utica* (N.Y.) *Observer-Dispatch* and *The Utica Daily Press*
1960 *Los Angeles Times*
1961 *Amarillo* (Tex.) *Globe-Times*
1962 *Panama City* (Fla.) *News-Herald*
1963 *Chicago Daily News*
1964 *St. Petersburg* (Fla.) *Times*
1965 *Hutchinson* (Kans.) *News*
1966 *The Boston Globe*
1967 *The Louisville* (Ky.) *Courier-Journal* and *The Milwaukee Journal*
1968 *The Riverside* (Calif.) *Press-Enterprise*
1969 *Los Angeles Times*
1970 *Newsday* (N.Y.)
1971 *The Winston-Salem Journal and Sentinel*
1972 *The New York Times*
1973 *The Washington Post*
1974 *Newsday* (N.Y.)
1975 *The Boston Globe*
1976 *Anchorage Daily News*
1977 *The Lufkin* (Tex.) *News*
1978 *The Philadelphia Inquirer*
1979 *Point Reyes Light*, a California weekly
1980 Gannett News Service, for its series on financial contributions to the Pauline Fathers.
1981 *Charlotte* (N.C.) *Observer*, for its series on brown lung.
1982 *The Detroit News*, for series by Sydney P. Freedberg and David Ashenfelter exposing U.S. Navy's cover-up of circumstances surrounding deaths of seamen aboard ship.
1983 The *Jackson* (Miss.) *Clarion-Ledger*, for its

successful campaign supporting the governor in his legislative battle to reform Mississippi's public school system.
1984 *The Los Angeles Times*, for an in-depth examination of Southern California's growing Latino community.
1985 *The Fort Worth Star-Telegram* for Mark J. Thompson's reporting disclosing deaths of 250 U.S. servicemen due to a design problem in helicopters built by Bell Helicopter.
1986 *The Denver Post*, for an in-depth study of "missing children," which revealed that most are in custody disputes or are runaways.
1987 *The Pittsburgh Press*, for reporting by Andrew Schneider and Matthew Brelis that revealed the inadequate medical screening of airline pilots and led to reforms.
1988 *Charlotte* (N.C.) *Observer*, for revealing misuse of funds by the PTL television ministry.
1989 *Anchorage Daily News*, for series revealing the high rate of alcoholism and suicide among native Alaskans.
1990 *The Philadelphia Inquirer*, for reporting by Gilbert M. Gaul that showed that the American blood industry operates with little governmental supervision or regulation.
1991 *The Des Moines Register*, for Jane Shorer's reporting identifying a rape victim, with the woman's consent; stories forced reconsideration of whether newspapers should conceal rape victims' identities.
1992 *The Sacramento Bee*, for Tom Knudson's series of stories on the pollution, overdevelopment and overpopulation of the Sierra Nevada mountain range. *The Washington* (N.C.) *Daily News*, for revealing that the city water supply was contaminated with carcinogens.

CORRESPONDENCE

(From 1929 to 1947, the Correspondence category recognized the achievements of Washington and foreign correspondents).
1929 Paul Scott Mowrer, *Chicago Daily News*
1930 Leland Stowe, *New York Herald Tribune*
1931 H. R. Knickerbocker, *The Philadelphia Public Ledger* and the *New York Evening Post*
1932 Walter Duranty, *The New York Times*, and Charles G. Ross, *St. Louis Post-Dispatch*
1933 Edgar Ansel Mowrer, *Chicago Daily News*
1934 Frederick T. Birchall, *The New York Times*
1935 Arthur Krock, *The New York Times*

1936 Wilfred C. Barber, *Chicago Tribune*
1937 Anne O'Hare McCormick, *The New York Times*
1938 Arthur Krock, *The New York Times*
1939 Louis P. Lochner, Associated Press
1940 Otto D. Tolischus, *The New York Times*
1941 Group Award to recognize the service of American reporters in the war zones of Europe, Asia and Africa
1942 Carlos P. Romulo, *Philippines Herald*
1943 Hanson W. Baldwin, *The New York Times*
1944 Ernest Taylor Pyle, Scripps-Howard Newspaper Alliance
1945 Harold V. (Hal) Boyle, Associated Press
1946 Arnaldo Cortesi, *The New York Times*
1947 Brooks Atkinson, *The New York Times*

INTERNATIONAL REPORTING

(Citations not included prior to 1980. From 1942 to 1947 the category was called Telegraphic Reporting [International].)

1942 Laurence Edmund Allen, Associated Press
1943 Ira Wolfert, North American Newspaper Alliance, Inc.
1944 Daniel DeLuce, Associated Press
1945 Mark S. Watson, *Baltimore Sun*
1946 Homer William Bigart, *New York Herald Tribune*
1947 Eddy Gilmore, Associated Press
1948 Paul W. Ward, *Baltimore Sun*
1949 Price Day, *Baltimore Sun*
1950 Edmund Stevens, *Christian Science Monitor*
1951 Keyes Beech, *Chicago Daily News;* Homer Bigart, *New York Herald Tribune;* Marguerite Higgins, *New York Herald Tribune;* Relman Morin, Don Whitehead, Associated Press; and Fred Sparks, *Chicago Daily News,* for their reporting of the Korean War.
1952 John M. Hightower, Associated Press
1953 Austin C. Wehrwein, *Milwaukee Journal*
1954 Jim G. Lucas, Scripps-Howard Newspapers
1955 Harrison E. Salisbury, *The New York Times*
1956 William Randolph Hearst, Jr., Kingsbury Smith, Frank Coniff, International News Service
1957 Russell Jones, United Press
1958 *The New York Times*
1959 Joseph Martin and Philip Santora, *New York Daily News*
1960 A. M. Rosenthal, *The New York Times*
1961 Lynne Heinzerling, Associated Press
1962 Walter Lippmann, New York Herald Tribune Syndicate
1963 Hal Hendrix, *Miami News*

1964 Malcolm W. Browne, Associated Press; and David Halberstam, *The New York Times*
1965 J. A. Livingston, *Philadelphia Bulletin*
1966 Peter Arnett, Associated Press
1967 R. John Hughes, *Christian Science Monitor*
1968 Alfred Friendly, *The Washington Post*
1969 William Tuohy, *Los Angeles Times*
1970 Seymour M. Hersh, Dispatch News Service, Washington, D.C.
1971 Jimmie Lee Hoagland, *The Washington Post*
1972 Peter R. Kann, *The Wall Street Journal*
1973 Max Frankel, *The New York Times*
1974 Hedrick Smith, *The New York Times*
1975 William Mullen, reporter, and Ovie Carter, photographer, *Chicago Tribune*
1976 Sydney H. Schanberg, *The New York Times*
1977 No award
1978 Henry Kamm, *The New York Times*
1979 Richard Ben Cramer, *The Philadelphia Inquirer*
1980 Joel Brinkley, reporter, and Jay Mather, photographer, *The Louisville Courier-Journal,* for stories from Cambodia.
1981 Shirley Christian, *Miami Herald,* for her reporting from Central America.
1982 John Darnton, *The New York Times,* for his reporting from Poland.
1983 Thomas L. Friedman, *The New York Times,* and Loren Jenkins, *The Washington Post,* for their individual reporting of the Israeli invasion of Beirut and its tragic aftermath.
1984 Karen Elliot House, *The Wall Street Journal,* for her interviews with Jordan's King Hussein which correctly anticipated the problems that would confront the Reagan administration's Middle East peace plan.
1985 Josh Friedman and Dennis Bell, reporters; Ozier Muhammad, photographer, *Newsday* (N.Y.), for their series on hunger in Africa.
1986 Lewis M. Simons, Pete Carey and Katherine Ellison, *San Jose* (Calif.) *Mercury News,* for their series documenting massive transfers of wealth abroad by President Marcos, direct impact on political developments in the Philippines and the United States.
1987 Michael Parks, *Los Angeles Times,* for coverage of South Africa.
1988 Thomas L. Friedman, *The New York Times,* for coverage of Israel.
1989 Bill Keller, *The New York Times,* for coverage of the Soviet Union; Glenn Frankel, *The Washington Post,* for coverage of the Palestinian uprising.
1990 Nicholas D. Kristof, Sheryl Wu Dunn, *The New York Times,* for coverage of the move-

ment toward democracy, and its suppression, in China.

1991   Caryle Murphy, *The Washington Post*, for dispatches from occupied Kuwait while in hiding from Iraqi authorities; Serge Schmemann, *The New York Times*, for coverage of the reunification of Germany.

1992   Patrick J. Sloyan, *New York Newsday*, for his reporting on the Persian Gulf war.

NATIONAL REPORTING

(Citations not included prior to 1980. From 1942 to 1947 the category was called Telegraphic Reporting [National].)

1942   Louis Stark, *The New York Times*

1943   No award

1944   Dewey L. Fleming, *The Baltimore Sun*

1945   James B. Reston, *The New York Times*

1946   Edward A. Harris, *St. Louis Post-Dispatch*

1947   Edward T. Folliard, *The Washington Post*

1948   Bert Andrews, *New York Herald Tribune*

1949   C. P. Trussell, *The New York Times*

1950   Edwin O. Guthman, *Seattle Times*

1951   No award

1952   Anthony Leviero, *The New York Times*

1953   Don Whitehead, Associated Press

1954   Richard Wilson, *Des Moines Register & Tribune*

1955   Anthony Lewis, *Washington Daily News*

1956   Charles L. Bartlett, *Chattanooga Times*

1957   James Reston, *The New York Times*

1958   Relman Morin, Associated Press; Clark Mollenhoff, *Des Moines Register & Tribune*

1959   Howard Van Smith, *Miami News*

1960   Vance Trimble, Scripps-Howard Newspaper Alliance

1961   Edward R. Cony, *The Wall Street Journal*

1962   Nathan G. Caldwell and Gene S. Graham, *Nashville Tennessean*

1963   Anthony Lewis, *The New York Times*

1964   Merriman Smith, United Press International

1965   Louis M. Kohlmeier, *The Wall Street Journal*

1966   Haynes Johnson, *Washington Evening Star*

1967   Stanley Penn and Monroe Karmin, *The Wall Street Journal*

1968   Howard James, *Christian Science Monitor*

1969   Robert Cahn, *Christian Science Monitor*

1970   William J. Eaton, *Chicago Daily News*

1971   Lucinda Franks and Thomas Powers, United Press International

1972   Jack Anderson, syndicated columnist

1973   Robert Boyd and Clark Hoyt, Knight Newspapers

1974   James R. Polk, *Washington Star-News;* Jack White, *Providence Journal and Evening Bulletin*

1975   Donald L. Barlett and James B. Steele, *The Philadelphia Inquirer*

1976   James Risser, *Des Moines Register*

1977   Walter Mears, The Associated Press

1978   Gaylord D. Shaw, *Los Angeles Times*

1979   James Risser, *Des Moines Register*

1980   Bette Swenson Orsini and Charles Stafford, *St. Petersburg* (Fla.) *Times*, for their investigation of the Church of Scientology.

1981   John M. Crewdson, *The New York Times*, for his coverage of illegal aliens and immigration.

1982   Rick Atkinson, *The Kansas City Times*, for the excellence of his reporting and writing on stories of national import.

1983   *The Boston Globe*, for its special report on the nuclear arms race.

1984   John Noble Wilford, *The New York Times*, for reporting on a wide variety of scientific topics.

1985   Thomas J. Knudson, *The Des Moines Register*, for his series of articles on the dangers of farming.

1986   Arthur Howe, *The Philadelphia Inquirer*, for reporting on massive deficiencies in the processing of tax returns, which prompted changes in IRA procedures; Craig Flournoy and George Rodrigue, *The Dallas Morning News*, for their investigation of subsidized housing in East Texas which uncovered patterns of racial discrimination in public housing across the United States.

1987   *The Miami Herald* staff, for persistent coverage of the U.S. Iran-Contra connection. *The New York Times* staff, for coverage of the aftermath of the *Challenger* explosion, which included stories that identified flaws in shuttle design and program administration.

1988   Tim Weiner, *The Philadelphia Inquirer*, for a series on secret Pentagon budget items that cover military research and weapons production.

1989   Donald L. Barlett, James B. Steele, *The Philadelphia Inquirer*, for a series on loopholes in the Tax Reform Act of 1986.

1990   Ross Anderson, Bill Dietrich, Mary Ann Gwinn and Eric Nalder, *The Seattle Times*, for coverage of the *Exxon Valdez* oil spill.

1991   Marjie Lundstrom, Rochelle Sharpe, Gannett News Service, for reporting that medical examiners' errors allow hundreds of child-abuse-related deaths to go undetected each year.

1992   Jeff Taylor, Mike McGraw, *The Kansas City*

(Mo.) Star, for their critical examination of the U.S. Department of Agriculture; Nat S. Finney, *Minneapolis Tribune;* Nathan K. Kotz, *The Des Moines Register* and *Minneapolis Tribune*

GENERAL NEWS REPORTING

(This category was created in 1985.)

1985 Thomas Turcol, *The Virginian-Pilot and Ledger-Star* (Norfolk, Va.), for city hall coverage that exposed the corruption of an economic development official.

1986 Edna Buchanan, *Miami Herald*, for police-beat reporting.

1987 Editorial staff, *Akron Beacon Journal*, for deadline coverage of the attempted take-over of Goodyear Tire and Rubber Co. by a European financier.

1988 Editorial staff, *The Alabama Journal*, for a series about the high rate of infant mortality in the state; editorial staff, *The Eagle-Tribune* (Lawrence, Mass.), for a series that revealed the shortcomings of the state's prison furlough system.

1989 Editorial staff, *The Courier-Journal* (Louisville, Ky.), for coverage of a school bus accident in which 27 people died.

1990 Editorial staff, *San Jose* (Calif.) *Mercury News*, for coverage of the earthquake of Oct. 17, 1989, and its aftermath.

1991 Editorial staff, *Miami* (Fla.) *Herald*, for profiles of local cult leader, his followers and their connection to several area murders.

1992 Editorial staff, *New York Newsday*, for spot news reporting of the derailment of a New York City subway train.

REPORTING

(The Reporting category was in use from 1917 to 1952. It included local, national and international reporting. A separate Correspondence category was added in 1929 to recognize foreign and national correspondents.)

1917 Herbert Bayard Swope, *New York World*
1918 Harold A. Littledale, *New York Evening Post*
1919 No award
1920 John J. Leary, Jr., *New York World*
1921 Louis Seibold, *New York World*
1922 Kirke L. Simpson, Associated Press
1923 Alva Johnson, *The New York Times*
1924 Magner White, *San Diego Sun*
1925 James W. Mulroy and Alvin H. Goldstein, *Chicago Daily News*
1926 William Burke Miller, *Louisville Courier-Journal*

1927 John T. Rogers, *St. Louis Post-Dispatch*
1928 No award
1929 Paul Y. Anderson, *St. Louis Post-Dispatch*
1930 Russell D. Owen, *The New York Times*
1931 A. B. MacDonald, *Kansas City* (Mo.) *Star*
1932 W.C. Richards, D. D. Martin, J. S. Pooler, F. D. Webb and J. N. W. Sloan, *Detroit Free Press*
1933 Francis A. Jamieson, Associated Press
1934 Royce Brier, *San Francisco Chronicle*
1935 William H. Taylor, *New York Herald Tribune*
1936 Lauren D. Lyman, *The New York Times*
1937 John J. O'Neill, *New York Herald Tribune;* William L. Laurence, *The New York Times;* Howard W. Blakeslee, Associated Press; Gobind Behari Lal, Universal Service; and David Dietz, Scripps-Howard, for science coverage at the tercentenary of Harvard University.
1938 Raymond Sprigle, *Pittsburgh Post-Gazette*
1939 Thomas Lunsford Stokes, Scripps-Howard Newspaper Alliance
1940 S. Burton Heath, *New York World-Telegram*
1941 Westbrook Pegler, *New York World-Telegram*
1942 Stanton Delaplane, *San Francisco Chronicle*
1943 George Weller, *Chicago Daily News*
1944 Paul Schoenstein and Associates, *New York Journal-American*
1945 Jack S. McDowell, *San Francisco Call-Bulletin*
1946 William Leonard Laurence, *The New York Times*
1947 Frederick Woltman, *New York World-Telegram*
1948 George E. Goodwin, *Atlanta Journal*
1949 Malcolm Johnson, *New York Sun*
1950 Meyer Berger, *The New York Times*
1951 Edward S. Montgomery, *San Francisco Examiner*
1952 George De Carvalho, *San Francisco Chronicle*

SPOT NEWS PHOTOGRAPHY

(Citations not included prior to 1980. Prior to 1968, spot news and feature photographs were judged together in the photography category.)

1968 Rocco Morabito, *Jacksonville Journal*
1969 Edward T. Adams, Associated Press
1970 Steve Starr, Associated Press, Albany, N.Y., Bureau
1971 John Paul Filo, *Valley News Dispatch*, Tarentum and New Kensington, Pa.
1972 Horst Fass and Michel Laurent, Associated Press
1973 Hyunh Cong Ut, Associated Press

1974   Anthony K. Roberts, a freelance photographer from Beverly Hills, Calif.

1975   Gerald H. Gay, *The Seattle Times*

1976   Stanley Forman, *Boston Herald American*

1977   Neal Ulevich, Associated Press, and Stanley Forman, *Boston Herald American*

1978   John H. Blair, United Press International

1979   Thomas J. Kelly III, *The Pottstown* (Pa.) *Mercury*

1980   A photographer for United Press International (unnamed), for "Firing Squad in Iran."

1981   Larry C. Price, *Fort Worth Star Telegram*, for photographs from Liberia.

1982   Ron Edmonds, The Associated Press, for coverage of the Reagan assassination attempt.

1983   Bill Foley, The Associated Press, for his series of pictures of the victims and survivors of the massacre in the Sabra Camp in Beirut.

1984   Stan Grossfeld, *The Boston Globe*, for his series of photographs revealing the effects of war on the people of Lebanon.

1985   Photography staff of *The Register* (Santa Ana, Calif.), for coverage of the Olympic Games.

1986   Carol Guzy and Michel duCille, *The Miami Herald*, for photographs of the devastation caused by Nevado del Ruiz volcano in Colombia.

1987   Kim Komenich, *San Francisco Examiner*, for his photographic coverage of the fall of Ferdinand Marcos.

1988   Scott Shaw, *The Odessa* (Tex.) *American*, for photos of the infant Jessica McClure being rescued from a well.

1989   Ron Olshwanger (amateur, photo published in *St. Louis Post-Dispatch*), for photo of a firefighter giving mouth-to-mouth resuscitation to a child.

1990   Photo staff, *The Tribune* (Oakland, Calif.), for photographs of Oct. 17, 1989, earthquake.

1991   Gregory Marinovitch, The Associated Press, for a series of photos of a group of people stabbing and burning a man believed to be a Zulu Inkatha supporter.

1992   Boris Yurchenko, Liu Heung-Shing, Olga Shalygin, Alexander Zemlianichenko and Czarek Sokolowski, The Associated Press, for photos of the attempted coup in Russia and the collapse of the regime.

FEATURE PHOTOGRAPHY

(Citations not included prior to 1980. Prior to 1968, spot news and feature photographs were judged together in the Photography category.)

1968   Toshio Sakai, United Press International

1969   Moneta Sleet, Jr., *Ebony*

1970   Dallas Kinney, *Palm Beach Post*

1971   Jack Dykinga, *Chicago Sun-Times*

1972   Dave Kennerly, United Press International

1973   Brian Lanker, *Topeka Capital-Journal*

1974   Slava Veder, Associated Press

1975   Matthew Lewis, *The Washington Post*

1976   Photo staff, *The Louisville Courier-Journal and Times*

1977   Robin Hood, *Chattanooga News-Free Press*

1978   J. Ross Baughman, The Associated Press

1979   Staff photographers of the *Boston Herald American*

1980   Erwin H. Hagler, *Dallas Times Herald*, for a series on the Western cowboy.

1981   Taro M. Yamasaki, *Detroit Free Press*, for photographs of Jackson, Mich., State Prison.

1982   John H. White, *Chicago Sun-Times*, for consistently excellent work.

1983   James B. Dickman, *Dallas Times Herald*, for his photographs of life and death in El Salvador.

1984   Anthony Suau, *The Denver Post*, for a series of photographs depicting starvation in Ethiopia and for a single photograph of a woman at her husband's graveside on Memorial Day.

1985   Stan Grossfeld, *The Boston Globe*, for his series of photographs of the famine in Ethiopia and for photographs of illegal aliens on the Mexican border; Larry C. Price, *The Philadelphia Inquirer*, for his series of photographs from Angola and El Salvador.

1986   Tom Gralish, *The Philadelphia Inquirer*, for his series of photographs of Philadelphia's homeless.

1987   David Peterson, *The Des Moines Register*, for photographs depicting the shattered dreams of American farmers.

1988   Michel duCille, *The Miami Herald*, for a series of photos showing how crack cocaine dominated the lives of poor people in a public housing project.

1989   Manny Crisostomo, *Detroit Free Press*, for a 12-page section on life in a Detroit high school.

1990   David C. Turnley, *Detroit Free Press*, for photographs of political uprisings in China and Eastern Europe.

1991   William Snyder, *Dallas Morning News*, for pictures of living conditions of ill and orphaned Romanian children.

1992   John Kaplan, *Monterey* (Calif.) *Herald* and *Pittsburgh Post-Gazette* of Block Newspapers, for photo essays depicting the lives of 21-year-olds across the United States.

PHOTOGRAPHY

1942   Milton Brooke, *Detroit News*

1943   Frank Noel, Associated Press

1944   Frank Filan, Associated Press, and Earle L. Bunker, *World-Herald* (Omaha, Neb.)

1945   Joe Rosenthal, Associated Press

1946   No award

1947   Arnold Hardy, amateur photographer of Atlanta, Ga., for his photo of girl leaping to her death in hotel fire; distributed by the Associated Press.

1948   Frank Cushing, *Boston Traveler*

1949   Nathaniel Fein, *New York Herald Tribune*

1950   Bill Crouch, *Oakland Tribune*

1951   Max Desfor, Associated Press

1952   John Robinson and Don Ultang, *Des Moines Register & Tribune*

1953   William M. Gallagher, *Flint* (Mich.) *Journal*

1954   Mrs. Walter M. Schau, San Anselmo, Calif., an amateur, for a photograph of a rescue at Redding, Calif. The picture was published in the *Akron* (Ohio) *Beacon Journal* and distributed nationally by the AP.

1955   John L. Gaunt, Jr., *Los Angeles Times*

1956   *New York Daily News*, for excellent news photographs in 1955.

1957   Harry A. Trask, *Boston Traveler*

1958   William C. Beall, *Washington* (D.C.) *Daily News*

1959   William Seaman, *Minneapolis Star*

1960   Andrew Lopez, United Press International

1961   Yasushi Nagao, Mainichi, Tokyo

1962   Paul Vathis, Associated Press, Harrisburg, Pa.

1963   Hector Rondon, *La Republica* (Caracas, Venezuela)

1964   Robert H. Jackson, *Dallas Times-Herald*

1965   Horst Faas, Associated Press

1966   Kyoichi Sawada, United Press International

1967   Jack R. Thornell, Associated Press, New Orleans

SPECIALIZED OR BEAT REPORTING

(This category originated in 1985.)

1985   Randall Savage and Jackie Crosby, *Macon Telegraph and News*, for their examination of academics and athletics at the University of Georgia and the Georgia Institute of Technology.

1986   Andrew Schneider and Mary Pat Flaherty, *The Pittsburgh Press*, for investigating violations and failures in the organ-transplant system in the United States.

1987   Alex S. Jones, *The New York Times*, for "The Fall of the House of Bingham," a report of a newspaper family's bickering and how it led to the sale of a media empire.

1988   Walt Bogdanich, *The Wall Street Journal*, for a series on faulty testing at medical laboratories.

1989   Edward Humes, *The Orange County* (Calif.) *Register*, for stories on the causes of nighttime crashes of Marine Corps helicopters.

1990   Tamar Stiebe, *Albuquerque Journal*, for reporting that linked a rare blood disorder to an over-the-counter dietary supplement, L-tryptophan.

1991   Natalie Angier, *The New York Times*, for compelling science reporting.

1992   Deborah Blum, *The Sacramento Bee*, for reporting on ethical problems posed by scientific experimentation on animals.

INVESTIGATIVE REPORTING

(This category originated in 1985.)

1985   William K. Marimow, *The Philadelphia Inquirer*, for revealing that city police dogs had attacked more than 350 people. Lucy Morgan and Jack Reed, *St. Petersburg Times*, for reporting on Pasco County Sheriff John Short, which revealed his department's corruption and led to his removal from office by voters.

1986   Jeffrey A. Marx and Michael M. York, *Lexington* (Ky.) *Herald-Leader*, for their series that exposed cash payoffs to University of Kentucky basketball players.

1987   Daniel R. Biddle, H. G. Bissinger and Fredric N. Tulsky, *The Philadelphia Inquirer*, for their series that revealed transgressions in the Philadelphia court system and led to federal and state investigations; John Woestendiak, *The Philadelphia Inquirer*, for outstanding prison-beat reporting, which included proving the innocence of a man convicted of murder.

1988   Dean Baquet, William Gaines, Ann Marie Lipinski, *Chicago Tribune*, for a series revealing how City Council members wasted public funds and placed their private interests over public interests.

1989   Bill Dedman, *Atlanta Journal and Constitution*, for a series on racial discrimination *in the loan practices of local banks and savings-and-loan institutions.*

1990   Louis Kilzer, Chris Ison, *Star Tribune*, Minneapolis-St. Paul, for exposing a network of local residents who had links to the St. Paul fire department and who profited from fires.

1991   Joseph T. Hallinen, Susan M. Headden, *The Indianapolis Star*, for their series on medical malpractice.

1992   Lorraine Adams, Dan Malone, *The Dallas Morning News*, for their reporting on civil rights violations by law-enforcement officials throughout Texas.

SPECIAL LOCAL REPORTING

(This category existed for one year.)

1984   Kenneth Cooper, Joan FitzGerald, Jonathan Kaufman, Norman Lockman, Gary McMillan, Kirk Scharfenberg, and David Wessel, *The Boston Globe*.

LOCAL INVESTIGATIVE/SPECIALIZED REPORTING

(This category existed from 1964 to 1983.)

1964   James V. Magee and Albert V. Gaudiosi, reporters, and Frederick A. Meyer, photographer, *Philadelphia Bulletin*

1965   Gene Goltz, *The Houston Post*

1966   John Anthony Frasce, *Tampa Tribune*

1967   Gene Miller, *Miami Herald*

1968   J. Anthony Lukas, *The New York Times*

1969   Albert L. Delugach and Denny Walsh, *St. Louis Globe-Democrat*

1970   Harold Eugene Martin, *The Montgomery Advertiser* and *The Alabama Journal*

1971   William Jones, *Chicago Tribune*

1972   Timothy Leland, Gerald M. O'Neill, Stephen A. Kurkjian and Ann DeSantis, *Boston Globe*

1973   Editorial staffs, The Sun Newspapers of Omaha

1974   William Sherman, *New York Daily News*

1975   Editorial staff, *The Indianapolis Star*

1976   Editorial staff, *Chicago Tribune*

1977   Acel Moore and Wendell Rawls, Jr., *The Philadelphia Inquirer*

1978   Anthony R. Dolan, *The Stamford* (Conn.) *Advocate*

1979   Gilbert M. Gaul and Elliot G. Jaspin, *Pottsville* (Penn.) *Republican*

1980   Stephen A. Kurkjian, Alexander B. Hawes, Jr., Nils Bruze, Joan Vennochi, and Robert M. Porterfield, *The Boston Globe*

1981   Clark Hallas and Robert B. Lowe, *The Arizona Daily Star*

1982   Paul Henderson, *The Seattle Times*

1983   Loretta Tofani, *The Washington Post*

REPORTING, NO EDITION TIME

(This category for nondeadline, investigative reporting existed from 1953 to 1963.)

1953   Edward J. Mowery, *New York World-Telegram & Sun*

1954   Alvin Scott McCoy, *Kansas City* (Mo.) *Star*

1955   Roland Kenneth Towery, *Cuero* (Tex.) *Record*

1956   Arthur Daley, *The New York Times*

1957   Wallace Turner and William Lambert, *Portland Oregonian*

1958   George Beveridge, *The Evening Star* (Washington, D.C.)

1959   John Harold, *Scranton Tribune* and *The Scrantonian*

1960   Miriam Ottenberg, *The Evening Star* (Washington, D.C.)

1961   Edgar May, *Buffalo Evening News*

1962   George Bliss, *Chicago Tribune*

1963   Oscar Griffin, Jr., *Pecos* (Tex.) *Independent and Enterprise*

SPECIAL AWARDS AND CITATIONS

1930   William P. Dapping, *The Auburn* (N.Y.) *Citizen*, for reporting of the outbreak at Auburn prison during December 1929.

1938   *Edmonton* (Alberta) *Journal*, for editorial leadership in defense of freedom of the press in the province of Alberta, Canada.

1941   *The New York Times*, for the educational value of its foreign news report.

1944   Richard Rodgers and Oscar Hammerstein II, for *Oklahoma!*.

1945   The cartographers of the American press whose maps of the war fronts helped clarify and increase public information on the progress of the war.

1947   Columbia University and the Graduate School of Journalism, for their efforts to maintain and advance the high standards governing the Pulitzer Prize awards. *St. Louis Post-Dispatch*, for its adherence to the ideals of its founder and for its constructive leadership in the field of American journalism.

1948   Dr. Frank Diehl Fackenthal, for interest and service.

1951   Cyrus L. Sulzberger, *The New York Times*, for his exclusive interview with Archbishop Stepinac.

1952   Max Kase, *New York Journal-American*, for his exclusive exposures of bribery and other forms of corruption in basketball;

Kansas City (Mo.) *Star* for coverage of the regional flood of 1951 in Kansas and northwestern Missouri.

1953   *The New York Times*, for the section of its Sunday newspaper edited by Lester Markel and headed "Review of the Week."

1957   Kenneth Roberts, for his historical novels.

1958   Walter Lippman, nationally syndicated columnist of the *New York Herald Tribune*, for the wisdom, perception and high sense of responsibility with which he has commented for many years on national and international affairs.

1960   Garrett Mattingly, for *The Armada*.

1961   *The American Heritage Picture History of the Civil War.*

1964   Gannett Newspapers, for their program "The Road to Integration," an example of the use of a newspaper group's resources to complement the work of its individual newspapers.

1973   James Thomas Flexner, for *George Washington*, vols. 1–4.

1976   Prof. John Hohenberg, for administration of the Pulitzer Prizes and for his achievements as a teacher and journalist.

1977   Alex Haley, for *Roots*.

1978   Richard Lee Strout for distinguished commentary from Washington over many years as staff correspondent for *The Christian Science Monitor* and contributor to *The New Republic;* E. B. White, for his letters, essays, and the full body of his work.

1982   Milton Babbit, for his life's work as a distinguished and seminal American composer.

1984   Theodor Seuss Geisel, "Dr. Seuss," for his special contribution over nearly half a century to the education and enjoyment of America's children and their parents.

1985   William Schuman, for more than half a century of contribution to American music as a composer and educational leader.

1987   Joseph Pulitzer, Jr., for his extraordinary services to American journalism and letters during his 31 years as chairman of the Pulitzer Prize Board and for his accomplishments as an editor and publisher.

1992   Art Spiegelman, for his "Maus" chronicles, the history of an Auschwitz survivor told in comic book form; Byron Price, Director of the Office of Censorship, for creating and administering the newspaper and radio codes; Mrs. William Allen White, for service as a member of the advisory board of the Graduate School of Journalism, Columbia University.

NEWSPAPER HISTORY AWARD

(Given only once.)

1918   Minna Lewinson and Henry Beetle Hough, for their history of the services rendered to the public by the American press during the preceding year.

PART FIFTEEN

SPORTS

PROFESSIONAL TEAMS: SUGGESTED CONTACTS

BASEBALL

BASEBALL TEAMS, SUGGESTED CONTACTS:
Office of the Commissioner
350 Park Ave., Floor 17
New York, NY 10022
(212) 339-7800

American League

American League of Professional Baseball Clubs
350 Park Ave.
New York, NY 10022
(212) 339-7600

Baltimore Orioles
Memorial Stadium
Baltimore, MD 21218
(410) 685-9800

Boston Red Sox
Fenway Park
24 Yawkey Way
Boston, MA 02215
(617) 267-9440

California Angels
P.O. Box 2000
Anaheim, CA 92803
(714) 937-6700

Chicago White Sox
324 W. 35th Street
Chicago, IL 60616
(312) 924-1000

Cleveland Indians
Cleveland Municipal Stadium
Cleveland, OH 44114
(216) 861-1200

Detroit Tigers
2121 Trumbull St.
Detroit, MI 48216
(313) 962-4000

Kansas City Royals
1 Royals Way
Kansas City, MO 64129
(816) 921-2200

Milwaukee Brewers
County Stadium
201 S. 46th St.
Milwaukee, WI 53214
(414) 933-1818

Minnesota Twins
Metrodome Stadium
501 Chicago Ave. S.
Minneapolis, MN 55415
(612) 375-7444

New York Yankees
Yankee Stadium
Bronx, NY 10451
(212) 293-6000

Oakland Athletics
P.O. Box 2220
Oakland, CA 94621
(415) 638-4900

Seattle Mariners
100 S. King St.
Seattle, WA 98104
(206) 628-3555

Texas Rangers
P.O. Box 1111
Arlington, TX 76004
(817) 273-5222

Toronto Blue Jays
300 The Esplanade W.
Suite 3200
Toronto, ON M50-383
(416) 341-1000

National League

National League of Professional Baseball Clubs
350 Park Ave., 18th Floor
New York, NY 10022
(212) 339-7700

Atlanta Braves
521 Capitol Ave. SW
Atlanta, GA 30312
(404) 522-7630

Chicago Cubs
Wrigley Field
1060 Addison St. W.
Chicago, IL 60613
(312) 404-2827

Cincinnati Reds
100 Riverfront Stadium
Cincinnati, OH 45202
(513) 421-4510

Colorado Rockies
1700 Broadway
Denver, CO 80290
(303) 292-0200

Florida Marlins
100 Northeast 3rd Ave.
Fort Lauderdale, FL 33301
(305) 779-7070

Houston Astros
8400 Kirby Drive
Houston, TX 77054
(713) 799-9500

Los Angeles Dodgers
1000 Elysian Park Ave.
Los Angeles, CA 90012
(213) 224-1530

Montreal Expos
4549 Pierre-de-Coubertin St.
Montreal, PQ H1V-3P2
(514) 253-3434

New York Mets
Shea Stadium
Flushing, NY 11368
(718) 507-6387

Philadelphia Phillies
Veterans Stadium
Broad St. & Pattison Ave.
Philadelphia, PA 19148
(215) 463-6000

Pittsburgh Pirates
Three Rivers Stadium
600 Stadium Circle
Pittsburgh, PA 15212
(412) 323-5000

Saint Louis Cardinals
Busch Memorial Stadium
250 Stadium Plaza
Saint Louis, MO 63102
(314) 421-3060

San Diego Padres
9449 Friars Road
San Diego, CA 92108
(619) 283-7294

San Francisco Giants
Candlestick Park
San Francisco, CA 94124
(415) 468-3700

BASKETBALL

BASKETBALL TEAMS, SUGGESTED CONTACTS:
National Basketball Association
Olympic Tower
645 5th Ave., 15th Floor
New York, NY 10022
(212) 826-7000

Eastern Conference

Atlanta Hawks
1 CNN Center NW
S. Tower Suite 405
Atlanta, GA 30335
(404) 827-3800

Boston Celtics
Boston Garden
150 Causeway St.
Boston, MA 02114
(617) 523-6050

Charlotte Hornets
1 Hive Drive
Charlotte, NC 28217
(704) 357-0252

Chicago Bulls
908 N. Michigan Ave.
Suite 1600
Chicago, IL 60611
(312) 943-5800

Cleveland Cavaliers
Coliseum
2923 Streetsboro Road
Richfield, OH 44286
(216) 659-9100

Detroit Pistons
3777 Lapeer Road
Auburn Hills, MI 48057
(313) 377-0100

Indiana Pacers
300 E. Market St.
Indianapolis, IN 46204
(317) 263-2100

Miami Heat
Miami Arena
721 N.W. 1st Ave.
Miami, FL 33136
(305) 577-4328

Milwaukee Bucks
1001 N. 4th St.
Milwaukee, WI 53203
(414) 227-0500

New Jersey Nets
Brendan Byrne Arena
East Rutherford, NJ 07073
(201) 935-8888

New York Knicks
2 Pennsylvania Plaza
New York, NY 10001
(212) 465-6000

Philadelphia 76ers
The Spectrum
Broad St. & Pattison Ave.
Philadelphia, PA 19148
(215) 339-7600

Washington Bullets
Capitol Center
1 Harry S. Truman Drive
Landover, MD 20785
(301) 773-2255

Western Conference

Dallas Mavericks
Reunion Arena
777 Sports St.
Dallas, TX 75207
(214) 988-0117

Denver Nuggets
P.O. Box 4658
Denver, CO 80204
(303) 893-6700

Golden State Warriors
Oakland Coliseum Arena
Nimitz Freeway
Oakland, CA 94621
(415) 638-6300

Houston Rockets
10 Greenway Plaza
Houston, TX 77046
(713) 627-0600

Los Angeles Clippers
Los Angeles Sports Arena
3939 S. Figueroa St.
Los Angeles, CA 90037
(213) 748-8000

Los Angeles Lakers
The Forum
3900 W. Manchester Blvd.
Inglewood, CA 90305
(310) 419-3100

Minnesota Timberwolves
730 Hennepin Ave.
Suite 500
Minneapolis, MN 55403
(612) 337-3865

Orlando Magic
1 Magic Place
Orlando, FL 32801
(407) 649-3200

Phoenix Suns
2910 N. Central
Phoenix, AZ 85012
(602) 379-7900

Portland Trail Blazers
700 N.E. Multnomah St.
Suite 600
Portland, OR 97232
(503) 234-9291

Sacramento Kings
1 Sport Parkway
Sacramento, CA 95834
(916) 928-6900

San Antonio Spurs
600 E. Market St.
Suite 102
San Antonio, TX 78205
(512) 554-7787

Seattle SuperSonics
190 Queen Anne Ave.
N. Seattle, WA 98109
(206) 281-5850

Utah Jazz
5 Triad Center
Suite 500
Salt Lake City, UT 84101
(801) 575-7800

FOOTBALL

FOOTBALL TEAMS, SUGGESTED CONTACTS:
National Football League
410 Park Ave.
New York, NY 10022
(212) 758-1500

American Football Conference

Eastern Division

Buffalo Bills
1 Bills Drive
Orchard Park, NY 14127
(716) 648-1800

Indianapolis Colts
7001 W. 56th St.
Indianapolis, IN 46254
(317) 297-7000

Miami Dolphins
2269 N.W. 199th St.
Miami, FL 33056
(305) 620-5000

New England Patriots
Rt. 1, Foxboro Stadium
Foxboro, MA 02035
(508) 543-8200

New York Jets
598 Madison Ave.
New York, NY 10022
(516) 538-6600

Central Division

Cincinnati Bengals
200 Riverfront Stadium
Cincinnati, OH 45202
(513) 621-3550

Cleveland Browns
1085 W. 3rd St.
Cleveland, OH 44114
(216) 891-5000

Houston Oilers
6910 Fannin St.
Houston, TX 77030
(713) 797-9111

Pittsburgh Steelers
Three Rivers Stadium
300 Stadium Circle
Pittsburgh, PA 15212
(412) 323-1200

Western Division

Denver Broncos
13655 Broncos Park
Englewood, CO 80112
(303) 649-9000

Kansas City Chiefs
1 Arrowhead Drive
Kansas City, MO 64129
(816) 924-9300

Los Angeles Raiders
332 Center St.
El Segundo, CA 90245
(310) 322-3451

San Diego Chargers
Jack Murphy Stadium
9449 Friars Road
San Diego, CA 92108
(619) 280-2111

Seattle Seahawks
11220 N.E. 53rd St.
Kirkland, WA 98033
(206) 827-9777

National Football Conference

Eastern Division

Dallas Cowboys
1 Cowboys Parkway
Irving, TX 75063
(214) 556-9900

New York Giants
Giants Stadium
East Rutherford, NJ 07073
(201) 935-8111

Philadelphia Eagles
Veterans Stadium
Broad St. & Pattison Ave.
Philadelphia, PA 19148
(215) 463-2500

Phoenix Cardinals
P.O. Box 888
Phoenix, AZ 85001
(602) 379-0101

Washington Redskins
13832 Redskin Drive
Herndon, VA 22071
(703) 478-8900

Central Division

Chicago Bears
250 N. Washington Road
Lake Forest, IL 60045
(708) 295-6600

Detroit Lions
1200 Featherstone Road
Pontiac, MI 48057
(313) 335-4131

Green Bay Packers
1265 Lombardi Ave.
Green Bay, WI 54304
(414) 496-5700

Minnesota Vikings
9520 Viking Drive
Eden Prairie, MN 55344
(612) 828-6500

Tampa Bay Buccaneers
1 Buccaneer Place
Tampa, FL 33607
(813) 870-2700

Western Division

Atlanta Falcons
Suwanee Road & I-85
Suwanee, GA 30174
(404) 945-1111

Los Angeles Rams
2327 Lincoln Ave.
Anaheim, CA 92801
(714) 535-7267

New Orleans Saints
1500 Poydras St.
New Orleans, LA 70112
(504) 733-0255

San Francisco 49ers
4949 Centennial Blvd.
Santa Clara, CA 95054
(408) 562-4949

HOCKEY

HOCKEY TEAMS, SUGGESTED CONTACTS:
National Hockey League
650 5th Ave., 33rd Floor
New York, NY 10019
(212) 398-1100

1155 Metcalfe St., Rm. 960
Montreal, PQ H3B-2W2
(514) 288-9220

Campbell Conference

Norris Division

Chicago Blackhawks
Chicago Stadium
1800 W. Madison
Chicago, IL 60612
(312) 733-5300

Detroit Red Wings
Joe Louis Arena
600 Civic Center Dr.
Detroit, MI 48226
(313) 396-7600

Minnesota North Stars
Met Center
7901 Cedar Ave.
Bloomington, MN 55425
(612) 853-9333

Saint Louis Blues
5700 Oakland Ave.
Saint Louis, MO 63110
(314) 781-5300

Tampa Bay Lightning
1 Mack Center
501 East Kennedy Blvd.
Suite 175
Tampa, FL 33602
(813) 226-0000

Toronto Maple Leafs
Maple Leaf Gardens
60 Carton St.
Toronto, ON M5B-1L1
(416) 977-1641

Smythe Division

Calgary Flames
P.O. Box 1540 Station M
Calgary, AB T2P-3B9
(403) 261-0475

Edmonton Oilers
Northlands Coliseum
7424 118th Ave.
Edmonton, AB T5B-4M9
(403) 474-8561

Los Angeles Kings
The Forum
3900 W. Manchester Blvd.
Inglewood, CA 90306
(310) 419-3160

Vancouver Canucks
Pacific Coliseum
100 N. Renfrew St.
Vancouver, BC V5K-3N7
(604) 254-5141

Winnipeg Jets
15-1430 Maroons Road
Winnipeg, MB R3G-0L5
(204) 982-5387

Wales Conference

Adams Division

Boston Bruins
Boston Garden
150 Causeway St.
Boston, MA 02114
(617) 227-3206

Buffalo Sabres
Memorial Auditorium
140 Main St.
Buffalo, NY 14202
(716) 856-7300

Hartford Whalers
1 Civic Center Plaza
Hartford, CT 06103
(203) 728-3366

Montreal Canadiens
Montreal Forum
2313 Saint Catherine St. W.
Montreal, PQ H3H-1N2
(514) 932-2582

Ottawa Senators
c/o Terrace Investment Ltd.
301 Moodie Drive
Nepean, ON K2H-9C4
(613) 726-0540

Quebec Nordiques
2205 Ave. de Colisee
Quebec City, PQ G1L-4W7
(418) 529-8441

Patrick Division

New Jersey Devils
Brendan Byrne Arena
50 Rt. 120 N.
East Rutherford, NJ 07073
(201) 935-6050

New York Islanders
Nassau Coliseum
Uniondale, NY 11553
(516) 794-4100

New York Rangers
Madison Square Garden
7th Ave. & 32nd St.
New York, NY 10001
(212) 465-6741

Philadelphia Flyers
The Spectrum
Broad St. & Pattison Ave.
Philadelphia, PA 19148
(215) 465-4500

Pittsburgh Penguins
Civic Arena
300 Auditorium Place
Pittsburgh, PA 15219
(412) 642-1800

Washington Capitols
Capitol Center
1 Harry S. Truman Drive
Landover, MD 20785
(301) 386-7000

PROFESSIONAL SPORTS

MAJOR LEAGUE BASEBALL
American League

East Division

Toronto Blue Jays
Boston Red Sox
Detroit Tigers
Milwaukee Brewers
New York Yankees
Baltimore Orioles
Cleveland Indians

West Division

Minnesota Twins
Chicago White Sox
Texas Rangers
Oakland Athletics
Seattle Mariners
Kansas City Royals
California Angels

National League

East Division

Pittsburgh Pirates
St. Louis Cardinals
Philadelphia Phillies
Chicago Cubs
New York Mets
Montreal Expos
Florida Marlins

West Division

Atlanta Braves
Los Angeles Dodgers
San Diego Padres
San Francisco Giants
Cincinnati Reds
Houston Astros
Colorado Rockies

THE WORLD SERIES

Every October, the winners of the pennants in major
league baseball's American and National leagues
play each other in the American pastime's annual
fall classic. In 1903, 1919, 1920, and 1921 the series
was a best-of-nine-games contest. In every other
year, the first team to win four games has become
champion.

1903: Boston Red Sox (AL) 5
Pittsburgh Pirates (NL) 3
1904: No series
1905: New York Giants (NL) 4
Philadelphia Athletics (AL) 1
1906: Chicago White Sox (AL) 4
Chicago Cubs (NL) 2
1907: Chicago Cubs (NL) 4
Detroit Tigers (AL) 0
1908: Chicago Cubs (NL) 4
Detroit Tigers (AL) 1
1909: Pittsburgh Pirates (NL) 4
Detroit Tigers (AL) 3
1910: Philadelphia Athletics (AL) 4
Chicago Cubs (NL) 1
1911: Philadelphia Athletics (AL) 4
New York Giants (NL) 2
1912: Boston Red Sox (AL) 4
New York Giants (NL) 3
1913: Philadelphia Athletics (AL) 4
New York Giants (NL) 1
1914: Boston Braves (NL) 4
Philadelphia Athletics (AL) 0
1915: Boston Red Sox (AL) 4
Philadelphia Phillies (NL) 1
1916: Boston Red Sox (AL) 4
Brooklyn Dodgers (NL) 1
1917: Chicago White Sox (AL) 4
New York Giants (NL) 2
1918: Boston Red Sox (AL) 4
Chicago Cubs (NL) 2
1919: Cincinnati Reds (NL) 5
Chicago White Sox (AL) 3
1920: Cleveland Indians (AL) 5
Brooklyn Dodgers (NL) 2
1921: New York Giants (NL) 5
New York Yankees (AL) 3
1922: New York Giants (NL) 4
New York Yankees (AL) 0
1923: New York Yankees (AL) 4
New York Giants (NL) 2
1924: Washington Senators (AL) 4
New York Giants (NL) 3
1925: Pittsburgh Pirates (NL) 4
Washington Senators (AL) 3
1926: St. Louis Cardinals (NL) 4
New York Yankees (AL) 3
1927: New York Yankees (AL) 4
Pittsburgh Pirates (NL) 0
1928: New York Yankees (AL) 4
St. Louis Cardinals (NL) 0

1929: Philadelphia Athletics (AL) 4
Chicago Cubs (NL) 1
1930: Philadelphia Athletics (AL) 4
St. Louis Cardinals (NL) 2
1931: St. Louis Cardinals (NL) 4
Philadelphia Athletics (AL) 3
1932: New York Yankees (AL) 4
Chicago Cubs (NL) 0
1933: New York Giants (NL) 4
Washington Senators (AL) 1
1934: St. Louis Cardinals (NL) 4
Detroit Tigers (AL) 3
1935: Detroit Tigers (AL) 4
Chicago Cubs (NL) 2
1936: New York Yankees (AL) 4
New York Giants (NL) 2
1937: New York Yankees (AL) 4
New York Giants (NL) 1
1938: New York Yankees (AL) 4
Chicago Cubs (NL) 0
1939: New York Yankees (AL) 4
Cincinnati Reds (NL) 0
1940: Cincinnati Reds (NL) 4
Detroit Tigers (AL) 3
1941: New York Yankees (AL) 4
Brooklyn Dodgers (NL) 1
1942: St. Louis Cardinals (NL) 4
New York Yankees (AL) 1
1943: New York Yankees (AL) 4
St. Louis Cardinals (NL) 1
1944: St. Louis Cardinals (NL) 4
St. Louis Browns (AL) 2
1945: Detroit Tigers (AL) 4
Chicago Cubs (NL) 3
1946: St. Louis Cardinals (NL) 4
Boston Red Sox (AL) 3
1947: New York Yankees (AL) 4
Brooklyn Dodgers (NL) 3
1948: Cleveland Indians (AL) 4
Boston Braves (NL) 2
1949: New York Yankees (AL) 4
Brooklyn Dodgers (NL) 1
1950: New York Yankees (AL) 4
Philadelphia Phillies (NL) 0
1951: New York Yankees (AL) 4
New York Giants (NL) 2
1952: New York Yankees (AL) 4
Brooklyn Dodgers (NL) 3
1953: New York Yankees (AL) 4
Brooklyn Dodgers (NL) 2
1954: New York Giants (NL) 4
Cleveland Indians (AL) 0
1955: Brooklyn Dodgers (NL) 4
New York Yankees (AL) 3
1956: New York Yankees (AL) 4
Brooklyn Dodgers (NL) 3

1957: Milwaukee Braves (NL) 4
New York Yankees (AL) 3
1958: New York Yankees (AL) 4
Milwaukee Braves (NL) 3
1959: Los Angeles Dodgers (NL) 4
Chicago White Sox (AL) 2
1960: Pittsburgh Pirates (NL) 4
New York Yankees (AL) 3
1961: New York Yankees (AL) 4
Cincinnati Reds (NL) 1
1962: New York Yankees (AL) 4
San Francisco Giants (NL) 3
1963: Los Angeles Dodgers (NL) 4
New York Yankees (AL) 0
1964: St. Louis Cardinals (NL) 4
New York Yankees (AL) 3
1965: Los Angeles Dodgers (NL) 4
Minnesota Twins (AL) 3
1966: Baltimore Orioles (AL) 4
Los Angeles Dodgers (NL) 0
1967: St. Louis Cardinals (NL) 4
Boston Red Sox (AL) 3
1968: Detroit Tigers (AL) 4
St. Louis Cardinals (NL) 3
1969: New York Mets (NL) 4
Baltimore Orioles (AL) 1
1970: Baltimore Orioles (AL) 4
Cincinnati Reds (NL) 1
1971: Pittsburgh Pirates (NL) 4
Baltimore Orioles (AL) 3
1972: Oakland Athletics (AL) 4
Cincinnati Reds (NL) 3
1973: Oakland Athletics (AL) 4
New York Mets (NL) 3
1974: Oakland Athletics (AL) 4
Los Angeles Dodgers (NL) 1
1975: Cincinnati Reds (NL) 4
Boston Red Sox (AL) 3
1976: Cincinnati Reds (NL) 4
New York Yankees (AL) 0
1977: New York Yankees (AL) 4
Los Angeles Dodgers (NL) 2
1978: New York Yankees (AL) 4
Los Angeles Dodgers (NL) 2
1979: Pittsburgh Pirates (NL) 4
Baltimore Orioles (AL) 3
1980: Philadelphia Phillies (NL) 4
Kansas City Royals (AL) 2
1981: Los Angeles Dodgers (NL) 4
New York Yankees (AL) 2
1982: St. Louis Cardinals (NL) 4
Milwaukee Brewers (AL) 3
1983: Baltimore Orioles (AL) 4
Philadelphia Phillies (NL) 1
1984: Detroit Tigers (AL) 4
San Diego Padres (NL) 1

1985: Kansas City Royals (AL) 4
St. Louis Cardinals (NL) 3
1986: New York Mets (NL) 4
Boston Red Sox (AL) 3
1987: Minnesota Twins (AL) 4
St. Louis Cardinals (NL) 3
1988: Los Angeles Dodgers (NL) 4
Oakland Athletics (AL) 1
1989: Oakland Athletics (AL) 4
San Francisco Giants (NL) 0
1990: Cincinnati Reds (NL) 4
Oakland Athletics (AL) 0
1991: Minnesota Twins (AL) 4
Atlanta Braves (NL) 3
1992: Toronto Blue Jays (AL) 4
Atlanta Braves (NL) 2

The Cy Young Award

Since 1967, given annually to the best pitcher in each league. From 1956 to 1966, a single award went to the best pitcher in both leagues.

1956: Don Newcombe, Brooklyn Dodgers (NL)
1957: Warren Spahn, Milwaukee Braves (NL)
1958: Bob Turley, New York Yankees (AL)
1959: Early Wynn, Chicago White Sox (AL)
1960: Vernon Law, Pittsburgh Pirates (NL)
1961: Whitey Ford, New York Yankees (AL)
1962: Don Drysdale, Los Angeles Dodgers (NL)
1963: Sandy Koufax, Los Angeles Dodgers (NL)
1964: Dean Chance, Los Angeles Angels (AL)
1965: Sandy Koufax, Los Angeles Dodgers (NL)
1966: Sandy Koufax, Los Angeles Dodgers (NL)
1967: Jim Lonborg, Boston Red Sox (AL);
Mike McCormick, San Francisco Giants (NL)
1968: Dennis McLain, Detroit Tigers (AL);
Bob Gibson, St. Louis Cardinals (NL)
1969: Mike Cuellar, Baltimore Orioles, and
Dennis McLain, Detroit Tigers (tied in AL);
Tom Seaver, New York Mets (NL)
1970: Jim Perry, Minnesota Twins (AL);
Bob Gibson, St. Louis Cardinals (NL)
1971: Vida Blue, Oakland Athletics (AL);
Ferguson Jenkins, Chicago Cubs (NL)
1972: Gaylord Perry, Cleveland Indians (AL);
Steve Carlton, Philadelphia Phillies (NL)
1973: Jim Palmer, Baltimore Orioles (AL);
Tom Seaver, New York Mets (NL)
1974: Catfish Hunter, Oakland Athletics (AL);
Mike Marshall, Los Angeles Dodgers (NL)
1975: Jim Palmer, Baltimore Orioles (AL);
Tom Seaver, New York Mets (NL)
1976: Jim Palmer, Baltimore Orioles (AL);
Randy Jones, San Diego Padres (NL)
1977: Sparky Lyle, New York Yankees (AL);
Steve Carlton, Philadelphia Phillies (NL)

1978: Ron Guidry, New York Yankees (AL);
Gaylord Perry, San Diego Padres (NL)
1979: Mike Flanagan, Baltimore Orioles (AL);
Bruce Sutter, Chicago Cubs (NL)
1980: Steve Stone, Baltimore Orioles (AL);
Steve Carlton, Philadelphia Phillies (NL)
1981: Rollie Fingers, Milwaukee Brewers (AL);
Fernando Valenzuela, Los Angeles Dodgers (NL)
1982: Pete Vuckovich, Milwaukee Brewers (AL);
Steve Carlton, Philadelphia Phillies (NL)
1983: LaMarr Hoyt, Chicago White Sox (AL);
John Denny, Philadelphia Phillies (NL)
1984: Willie Hernandez, Detroit Tigers (AL);
Rick Sutcliffe, Chicago Cubs (NL)
1985: Bret Saberhagen, Kansas City Royals (AL);
Dwight Gooden, New York Mets (NL)
1986: Roger Clemens, Boston Red Sox (AL);
Mike Scott, Houston Astros (NL)
1987: Roger Clemens, Boston Red Sox (AL);
Steve Bedrosian, Philadelphia Phillies (NL)
1988: Frank Viola, Minnesota Twins (AL);
Orel Hershiser, Los Angeles Dodgers (NL)
1989: Bret Saberhagen, Kansas City Royals (AL);
Mark Davis, San Diego Padres (NL)
1990: Bob Welch, Oakland Athletics (AL);
Doug Drabek, Pittsburgh Pirates (NL)
1991: Roger Clemens, Boston Red Sox (AL);
Tom Glavine, Atlanta Braves (NL)
1992: Dennis Eckersley, Oakland Athletics (AL);
Greg Maddux, Chicago Cubs (NL)

Baseball's Top 20 All-Time Home-Run Hitters (By end of 1992 season)

1)	Hank Aaron	755
2)	Babe Ruth	714
3)	Willie Mays	660
4)	Frank Robinson	586
5)	Harmon Killebrew	573
6)	Reggie Jackson	563
7)	Mike Schmidt	548
8)	Mickey Mantle	536
9)	Jimmie Foxx	534
10)	Willie McCovey	521
11)	Ted Williams	521
12)	Ernie Banks	512
13)	Eddie Mathews	512
14)	Mel Ott	511
15)	Lou Gehrig	493
16)	Stan Musial	475
17)	Willie Stargell	475
18)	Dave Winfield	460
19)	Carl Yastrzemski	452
20)	Dave Kingman	442

PROFESSIONAL BASKETBALL
National Basketball Association

EASTERN CONFERENCE

Atlantic Division

Boston Celtics
Philadelphia 76ers
New York Knicks (Knickerbockers)
Washington Bullets
New Jersey Nets
Miami Heat

Central Division

Chicago Bulls
Detroit Pistons
Milwaukee Bucks
Atlanta Hawks
Indiana Pacers
Cleveland Cavaliers
Charlotte Hornets

WESTERN CONFERENCE

Midwest Division

San Antonio Spurs
Utah Jazz
Houston Rockets
Orlando Magic
Dallas Mavericks
Denver Nuggets
Minnesota Timberwolves

Pacific Division

Portland Trail Blazers
Los Angeles Lakers
Phoenix Suns
Golden State Warriors
Seattle SuperSonics
Los Angeles Clippers
Sacramento Kings

NBA Champions

The winners of each conference vie for the title in an annual best-of-seven games matchup.

1946–47: Philadelphia 4
Chicago 1
1947–48: Baltimore 4
Philadelphia 2
1948–49: Minneapolis 4
Washington 2
1949–50: Minneapolis 4
Syracuse 2
1950–51: Rochester 4
New York 3
1951–52: Minneapolis 4
New York 3
1952–53: Minneapolis 4
New York 1
1953–54: Minneapolis 4
Syracuse 3
1954–55: Syracuse 4
Ft. Wayne 3
1955–56: Philadelphia 4
Ft. Wayne 1
1956–57: Boston 4
St. Louis 3
1957–58: St. Louis 4
Boston 2
1958–59: Boston 4
Minneapolis 0
1959–60: Boston 4
St. Louis 3
1960–61: Boston 4
St. Louis 1
1961–62: Boston 4
Los Angeles 3
1962–63: Boston 4
Los Angeles 2
1963–64: Boston 4
San Francisco 1
1964–65: Boston 4
Los Angeles 1
1965–66: Boston 4
Los Angeles 3
1966–67: Philadelphia 4
San Francisco 2
1967–68: Boston 4
Los Angeles 2
1968–69: Boston 4
Los Angeles 3
1969–70: New York 4
Los Angeles 3
1970–71: Milwaukee 4
Baltimore 0
1971–72: Los Angeles 4
New York 1
1972–73: New York 4
Los Angeles 1
1973–74: Boston 4
Milwaukee 3
1974–75: Golden State 4
Washington 0
1975–76: Boston 4
Phoenix 2
1976–77: Portland 4
Philadelphia 2
1977–78: Washington 4
Seattle 3

1978–79: Seattle 4
Washington 1
1979–80: Los Angeles 4
Philadelphia 2
1980–81: Boston 4
Houston 2
1981–82: Los Angeles 4
Philadelphia 2
1982–83: Philadelphia 4
Los Angeles 0
1983–84: Boston 4
Los Angeles 3
1984–85: Los Angeles 4
Boston 2
1985–86: Boston 4
Houston 2
1986–87: Los Angeles 4
Boston 2
1987–88: Los Angeles 4
Detroit 3
1988–89: Detroit 4
Los Angeles 0
1989–90: Detroit 4
Portland 1
1990–91: Chicago 4
Los Angeles 1
1991–92: Chicago 4
Portland 2

ALL-TIME NBA LEADERS

MOST POINTS SCORED

Boldface indicates players still active in major teams of the NBA at the start of the 1992–93 season.

	Years	Games	Points	Avg.
Kareem Abdul-Jabbar	20	1,560	38,387	24.6
Wilt Chamberlain	14	1,045	31,419	30.1
Elvin Hayes	16	1,303	27,313	21.0
Moses Malone	16	1,246	27,016	21.7
Oscar Robertson	14	1,040	26,710	25.7
John Havlicek	16	1,270	26,395	20.8
Alex English	15	1,193	25,613	21.5
Jerry West	14	932	25,192	27.0
Adrian Dantley	15	955	23,177	24.3
Elgin Baylor	14	846	23,149	27.4
Larry Bird	13	897	21,791	24.3
Hal Greer	15	1,122	21,586	19.2
Walt Bellamy	14	1,043	20,941	20.1
Bob Pettit	11	792	20,880	26.4
George Gervin	10	791	20,708	26.2
Robert Parish	16	1,260	20,634	16.4
Dominique Wilkins	10	762	19,975	26.2
Walter Davis	15	1,033	19,521	18.9
Bernard King	13	842	19,432	23.1

	Years	Games	Points	Avg.
Dolph Schayes	16	1,059	19,249	18.2
Bob Lanier	14	959	19,248	20.1
Gail Goodrich	14	1,031	19,181	18.6
Reggie Theus	13	1,026	19,015	18.5
Michael Jordan	8	589	19,000	32.3
Chet Walker	13	1,032	18,831	18.2
Bob McAdoo	14	852	18,787	22.1

SCORING AVERAGE

	Years	Games	Points	Avg.
Michael Jordan	8	589	19,000	32.3
Wilt Chamberlain	14	1,045	31,419	30.1
Elgin Baylor	14	846	23,149	27.4
Jerry West	14	932	25,192	27.0
Bob Pettit	11	792	20,880	26.4
Dominique Wilkins	10	762	19,975	26.2
George Gervin	10	791	20,708	26.2
Karl Malone	7	570	14,770	25.9
Oscar Robertson	14	1,040	26,710	25.7
Kareem Abdul-Jabbar	20	1,560	38,387	24.6
Larry Bird	13	897	21,791	24.3
Adrian Dantley	15	955	23,177	24.3
Pete Maravich	10	658	15,948	24.2
Patrick Ewing	7	520	12,293	23.6
Charles Barkley	8	610	14,184	23.3
Rick Barry	10	794	18,395	23.2
Bernard King	13	842	19,432	23.1
Hakeem Olajuwan	8	594	13,575	22.9
Paul Arizin	10	713	16,266	22.8
George Mikan	9	520	11,764	22.6
Chris Mullin	7	520	11,536	22.2
Bob McAdoo	14	852	18,787	22.1
David Thompson	8	509	11,264	22.1
Julius Erving	11	836	18,364	22.0
Moses Malone	16	1,246	27,016	21.7
Alex English	15	1,193	25,613	21.5
Terry Cummings	10	768	16,364	21.3
Mark Aguirre	11	833	17,542	21.1
Kiki Vandeweghe	12	769	15,726	20.4

MOST FIELD GOALS MADE

	Years	FGA	FGM	Pct.
Kareen Abdul-Jabbar	20	28,307	15,837	.559
Wilt Chamberlain	14	23,497	12,681	.540
Elvin Hayes	16	24,272	10,976	.452
Alex English	15	21,036	10,659	.507
John Havlicek	16	23,900	10,513	.440
Oscar Robertson	14	19,620	9,508	.485
Moses Malone	16	18,916	9,307	.492
Jerry West	14	19,032	9,016	.474
Elgin Baylor	14	20,171	8,693	.431
Larry Bird	13	17,334	8,591	.496

MOST FREE THROWS MADE

	Years	FTA	FTM	Pct.
Moses Malone	16	10,910	8,395	.769
Oscar Robertson	14	9,185	7,694	.838
Jerry West	14	8,801	7,160	.814
Dolph Schayes	16	8,273	6,979	.844
Adrian Dantley	15	8,351	6,832	.818
Kareem Abdul-Jabbar	20	9,304	6,712	.721
Bob Pettit	11	8,119	6,182	.761
Wilt Chamberlain	14	11,862	6,057	.511
Elgin Baylor	14	7,391	5,763	.780
Lenny Wilkins	15	6,973	5,394	.774

MOST ASSISTS

	Years	Games	Assists	Avg.
Magic Johnson	12	874	9,921	11.4
Oscar Robertson	14	1,040	9,887	9.5
Isiah Thomas	11	842	7,991	9.4
Maurice Cheeks	14	1,066	7,285	6.8
Lenny Wilkens	15	1,077	7,211	6.7
Bob Cousy	14	924	6,955	7.5
Guy Rodgers	12	892	6,917	7.8
Nate Archibald	13	876	6,476	7.4
John Lucas	14	928	6,454	7.0
Reggie Theus	13	1,026	6,453	6.3

MOST REBOUNDS

	Years	Games	Rebounds	Avg.
Wilt Chamberlain	14	1,045	23,924	22.9
Bill Russell	13	963	21,620	22.5
Kareem Abdul-Jabbar	20	1,560	17,440	11.2
Elvin Hayes	16	1,303	16,279	12.5
Moses Malone	16	1,246	15,894	12.8
Nate Thurmond	14	964	14,464	15.0
Walt Bellamy	14	1,043	14,241	13.7
Wes Unseld	13	984	13,769	14.0
Jerry Lucas	11	829	12,942	15.6
Bob Pettit	11	792	12,849	16.2

MOST GAMES PLAYED

	Years	Career Span	Number
Kareem Abdul-Jabbar	20	1970–89	1,560
Elvin Hayes	16	1969–84	1,303
John Havlicek	16	1963–78	1,270
Robert Parish	16	1977–	1,260
Paul Silas	16	1965–80	1,254
Moses Malone	16	1977–	1,246
Alex English	15	1977–91	1,193
Hal Greer	15	1959–73	1,122
Jack Sikma	14	1978–91	1,107
Dennis Johnson	14	1977–90	1,100

PROFESSIONAL FOOTBALL
The Super Bowl

I:	1966	Green Bay Packers (NFL) 35
		Kansas City Chiefs (AFL) 10
II:	1967	Green Bay Packers (NFL) 33
		Oakland Raiders (AFL) 14
III:	1968	New York Jets (AFL) 16
		Baltimore Colts (NFL) 7
IV:	1969	Kansas City Chiefs (AFL) 23
		Minnesota Vikings (NFL) 7
V:	1970	Baltimore Colts (AFC) 16
		Dallas Cowboys (NFC) 13
VI:	1971	Dallas Cowboys (NFC) 24
		Miami Dolphins (AFC) 3
VII:	1972	Miami Dolphins (AFC) 14
		Washington Redskins (NFC) 7
VIII:	1973	Miami Dolphins (AFC) 24
		Minnesota Vikings (NFC) 7
IX:	1974	Pittsburgh Steelers (AFC) 16
		Minnesota Vikings (NFC) 6
X:	1975	Pittsburgh Steelers (AFC) 21
		Dallas Cowboys (NFC) 17
XI:	1976	Oakland Raiders (AFC) 32
		Minnesota Vikings (NFC) 14
XII:	1977	Dallas Cowboys (NFC) 27
		Denver Broncos (AFC) 10
XIII:	1978	Pittsburgh Steelers (AFC) 35
		Dallas Cowboys (NFC) 31
XIV:	1979	Pittsburgh Steelers (AFC) 31
		Los Angeles Rams (NFC) 19
XV:	1980	Oakland Raiders (AFC) 27
		Philadelphia Eagles (NFC) 10
XVI:	1981	San Francisco 49ers (NFC) 26
		Cincinnati Bengals (AFC) 21
XVII:	1982	Washington Redskins (NFC) 27
		Miami Dolphins (AFC) 17
XVIII:	1983	Los Angeles Raiders (AFC) 38
		Washington Redskins (NFC) 9
XIX:	1984	San Francisco 49ers (NFC) 38
		Miami Dolphins (AFC) 16
XX:	1985	Chicago Bears (NFC) 46
		New England Patriots (AFC) 10
XXI:	1986	New York Giants (NFC) 39
		Denver Broncos (AFC) 20
XXII:	1987	Washington Redskins (NFC) 42
		Denver Broncos (AFC) 10
XXIII:	1988	San Francisco 49ers (NFC) 20
		Cincinnati Bengals (AFC) 16
XXIV:	1989	San Francisco 49ers (NFC) 55
		Denver Broncos (AFC) 10
XXV:	1990	New York Giants (NFC) 20
		Buffalo Bills (AFC) 19
XXVI:	1991	Washington Redskins (NFC) 37
		Buffalo Bills (AFC) 24

ALL-TIME NFL LEADERS

Names in boldface indicate players still active at the end of 1990–91 NFL season.

PASSING YARDAGE

	Years	Attempts	Comple- tions	Pct.	Yard- age
Fran Tarkenton	18	6,467	3,686	57.0	47,003
Dan Fouts	15	5,604	3,297	58.8	43,040
Johnny Unitas	18	5,186	2,830	54.6	40,239
Joe Montana	12	4,579	2,914	63.6	34,998
Jim Hart	19	5,076	2,593	51.1	34,665
John Hadl	16	4,687	2,363	50.4	33,513
Ken Anderson	16	4,475	2,654	59.3	32,838
Sonny Jurgensen	18	4,262	2,433	57.1	32,224
John Brodie	17	4,491	2,469	55.0	31,548
Dan Marino	8	4,181	2,480	59.3	31,416
Norm Snead	15	4,353	2,276	52.3	30,797
Joe Ferguson	18	4,519	2,369	52.4	29,817
Roman Gabriel	16	4,498	2,366	52.6	29,444
Len Dawson	19	3,741	2,136	57.1	28,711
Phil Simms	11	3,969	2,164	54.5	28,519
Steve DeBerg	14	4,179	2,376	56.9	28,490
Y. A. Tittle	15	3,817	2,118	55.5	28,339
Ron Jaworski	16	4,117	2,187	53.1	28,190
Terry Bradshaw	14	3,901	2,025	51.9	27,989
Ken Stabler	15	3,793	2,270	59.8	27,938
Craig Morton	18	3,786	2,053	54.2	27,908
Joe Namath	13	3,762	1,886	50.1	27,663
George Blanda	26	4,007	1,911	47.7	26,920
Steve Grogan	16	3,593	1,879	52.3	26,886
Bobby Layne	15	3,700	1,814	49.0	26,768

TOUCHDOWN PASSES

	Years	TD	Intercept.
Fran Tarkenton	18	342	266
Johnny Unitas	18	290	253
Sonny Jurgensen	18	255	189
Dan Fouts	15	254	242
John Hadl	16	244	268
Joe Montana	12	242	123
Dan Marino	8	241	136
Len Dawson	19	239	183
George Blanda	26	236	277
John Brodie	17	214	224
Terry Bradshaw	14	212	210
Y. A. Tittle	15	212	221
Jim Hart	19	209	247
Roman Gabriel	15	201	149
Ken Anderson	16	197	160
Norm Snead	15	196	253
Joe Ferguson	18	196	209
Bobby Layne	15	196	243

	Years	TD	Intercept.
Ken Stabler	15	194	222
Bob Griese	14	192	172
Sammy Baugh	16	187	203
Dave Krieg	11	184	136
Craig Morton	18	183	187
Steve Grogan	16	182	208
Ron Jaworski	16	179	164

RECEIVING

	Years	No.	Yards	Avg.	TD
Steve Largent	14	819	13,089	16.0	100
Charlie Joiner	18	750	12,146	16.2	65
Art Monk	11	730	9,935	13.6	52
Ozzie Newsome	13	662	7,980	12.1	47
Charley Taylor	13	649	9,110	14.0	79
James Lofton	13	642	11,963	18.6	61
Don Maynard	15	633	11,834	18.7	88
Raymond Berry	13	631	9,275	14.7	68
Harold Carmichael	14	590	8,985	15.2	79
Fred Biletnikoff	14	589	8,974	15.2	76
Harold Jackson	16	579	10,372	17.9	76
Lionel Taylor	10	567	7,195	12.7	45
Wes Chandler	11	559	8,966	16.0	56
Stanley Morgan	14	557	10,716	19.2	72
J. T. Smith	13	544	6,974	12.8	35
Lance Alworth	11	542	10,266	18.9	85
Kellen Winslow	10	541	6,741	12.5	45
John Stallworth	14	537	8,723	16.2	63
Roy Green	12	522	8,496	16.3	66
Bobby Mitchell	11	521	7,954	15.3	65

RUSHING YARDAGE

	Years	Carries	Yards	Avg.	TD
Walter Payton	13	3,838	16,726	4.4	110
Tony Dorsett	12	2,936	12,739	4.3	77
Jim Brown	9	2,359	12,312	5.2	106
Franco Harris	13	2,949	12,120	4.1	91
Eric Dickerson	8	2,616	11,903	4.6	86
John Riggins	14	2,916	11,352	3.9	104
O. J. Simpson	11	2,404	11,236	4.7	61
Ottis Anderson	12	2,499	10,101	4.0	80
Earl Campbell	8	2,187	9,407	4.3	74
Jim Taylor	10	1,941	8,597	4.4	83
Joe Perry	14	1,737	8,378	4.8	53
Larry Csonka	11	1,891	8,081	4.3	64
Marcus Allen	9	1,960	7,957	4.1	75
Gerald Riggs	9	1,911	7,940	4.2	58
Freeman McNeil	10	1,704	7,604	4.5	36
Mike Pruitt	11	1,844	7,378	4.0	51
James Brooks	10	1,515	7,347	4.8	47
Leroy Kelly	10	1,727	7,274	4.2	74
George Rogers	7	1,692	7,176	4.2	54
Roger Craig	8	1,686	7,064	4.2	50

ALL-PURPOSE RUNNING

	Years	Rush	Rec.	Ret.	Total
Walter Payton	13	16,726	4,538	539	21,803
Tony Dorsett	12	12,739	3,554	33	16,326
Jim Brown	9	12,312	2,499	648	15,459
Franco Harris	13	12,120	2,287	215	14,622
O. J. Simpson	11	11,236	2,142	990	14,368
Bobby Mitchell	11	2,735	7,954	3,389	14,078
James Brooks	10	7,347	3,274	3,088	13,709
Eric Dickerson	8	11,903	1,725	15	13,643
John Riggins	14	11,352	2,090	−7	13,435
Steve Largent	14	83	13,089	224	13,396
Greg Pruitt	12	5,672	3,069	4,521	13,262
Ottis Anderson	12	10,101	3,021	29	13,151
Ollie Matson	14	5,173	3,285	4,426	12,884
Timmy Brown	10	3,862	3,399	5,423	12,684
Lenny Moore	12	5,174	6,039	1,238	12,451
Don Maynard	15	70	11,834	475	12,379
Charlie Joyner	18	22	12,146	199	12,367
Leroy Kelly	10	7,274	2,281	2,775	12,330
Floyd Little	9	6,323	2,418	3,432	12,173
Abner Haynes	8	4,630	3,535	3,900	12,065

INTERCEPTIONS

	Years	No.	Yards	TD
Paul Krause	16	81	1,185	3
Emlen Tunnell	14	79	1,282	4
Dick "Night Train" Lane	14	68	1,207	5
Ken Riley	15	65	596	5
Dick LeBeau	13	62	762	3
Dave Brown	15	62	698	5

PROFESSIONAL HOCKEY
National Hockey League
CAMPBELL CONFERENCE

Norris Division

Chicago Blackhawks
St. Louis Blues
Detroit Red Wings
Minnesota North Stars
Toronto Maple Leafs

Smythe Division

Los Angeles Kings
Calgary Flames
Edmonton Oilers
Vancouver Canucks
Winnipeg Jets

WALES CONFERENCE

Adams Division

Boston Bruins
Montreal Canadiens
Buffalo Sabres
Hartford Whalers
Quebec Nordiques

Patrick Division

Pittsburgh Penguins
New York Rangers
Washington Capitals
New Jersey Devils
Philadelphia Flyers
New York Islanders

The Stanley Cup

1894	Montreal A.A.A.
1895	Montreal Victorias
1896	Winnipeg Victorias
1897	Montreal Victorias
1898	Montreal Victorias
1899	Montreal Victorias
1900	Montreal Shamrocks
1901	Winnipeg Victorias
1902	Montreal A.A.A.
1903	Ottawa Silver Seven
1904	Ottawa Silver Seven
1905	Ottawa Silver Seven
1906	Montreal Wanderers
1907	Kenora Thistles/Jan.
1907	Montreal Wanderers/March
1908	Montreal Wanderers
1909	Ottawa Senators
1910	Montreal Wanderers
1911	Ottawa Senators
1912	Quebec Bulldogs
1913	Quebec Bulldogs
1914	Toronto Blueshirts
1915	Vancouver Millionaires
1916	Montreal Canadiens
1917	Seattle Metropolitans
1918	Toronto Arenas
1919	No champion
1920	Ottawa Senators
1921	Ottawa Senators
1922	Toronto St. Patricks
1923	Ottawa Senators
1924	Montreal Canadiens
1925	Victoria Cougars
1926	Montreal Maroons
1927	Ottawa Senators
1928	New York Rangers
1929	Boston Bruins
1930	Montreal Canadiens
1931	Montreal Canadiens
1932	Toronto Maple Leafs
1933	New York Rangers
1934	Chicago Black Hawks

1935	Montreal Maroons
1936	Detroit Red Wings
1937	Detroit Red Wings
1938	Chicago Black Hawks
1939	Boston Bruins
1940	New York Rangers
1941	Boston Bruins
1942	Toronto Maple Leafs
1943	Detroit Red Wings
1944	Montreal Canadiens
1945	Toronto Maple Leafs
1946	Montreal Canadiens
1947	Toronto Maple Leafs
1948	Toronto Maple Leafs
1949	Toronto Maple Leafs
1950	Detroit Red Wings
1951	Toronto Maple Leafs
1952	Detroit Red Wings
1953	Montreal Canadiens
1954	Detroit Red Wings
1955	Detroit Red Wings
1956	Montreal Canadiens
1957	Montreal Canadiens
1958	Montreal Canadiens
1959	Montreal Canadiens
1960	Montreal Canadiens
1961	Chicago Black Hawks
1962	Toronto Maple Leafs
1963	Toronto Maple Leafs
1964	Toronto Maple Leafs
1965	Montreal Canadiens
1966	Montreal Canadiens
1967	Toronto Maple Leafs
1968	Montreal Canadiens
1969	Montreal Canadiens
1970	Boston Bruins
1971	Montreal Canadiens
1972	Boston Bruins
1973	Montreal Canadiens
1974	Philadelphia Flyers
1975	Philadelphia Flyers
1976	Montreal Canadiens
1977	Montreal Canadiens
1978	Montreal Canadiens
1979	Montreal Canadiens
1980	New York Islanders
1981	New York Islanders
1982	New York Islanders
1983	New York Islanders
1984	Edmonton Oilers
1985	Edmonton Oilers
1986	Montreal Canadiens
1987	Edmonton Oilers
1988	Edmonton Oilers
1989	Calgary Flames
1990	Edmonton Oilers
1991	Pittsburgh Penguins
1992	Pittsburgh Penguins

NHL Most Valuable Player: The Hart Trophy

1924	Frank Nighbor, Ottawa
1925	Billy Burch, Hamilton
1926	Nels Stewart, Montreal Maroons
1927	Herb Gardiner, Montreal Canadiens
1928	Howie Morenz, Montreal Canadiens
1929	Roy Worters, New York Americans
1930	Nels Stewart, Montreal Maroons
1931	Howie Morenz, Montreal Canadiens
1932	Howie Morenz, Montreal Canadiens
1933	Eddie Shore, Boston
1934	Aurel Joliat, Montreal Canadiens
1935	Eddie Shore, Boston
1936	Eddie Shore, Boston
1937	Babe Siebert, Montreal Canadiens
1938	Eddie Shore, Boston
1939	Toe Blake, Montreal Canadiens
1940	Ebbie Goodfellow, Detroit
1941	Bill Cowley, Boston
1942	Tom Anderson, New York Americans
1943	Bill Cowley, Boston
1944	Babe Pratt, Toronto
1945	Elmer Lach, Montreal Canadiens
1946	Max Bentley, Chicago
1947	Maurice Richard, Montreal Canadiens
1948	Buddy O'Connor, New York Rangers
1949	Sid Abel, Detroit
1950	Chuck Rayner, New York Rangers
1951	Milt Schmidt, Boston
1952	Gordie Howe, Detroit
1953	Gordie Howe, Detroit
1954	Al Rollins, Chicago
1955	Ted Kennedy, Toronto
1956	Jean Beliveau, Montreal Canadiens
1957	Gordie Howe, Detroit
1958	Gordie Howe, Detroit
1959	Andy Bathgate, New York Rangers
1960	Gordie Howe, Detroit
1961	Bernie Geoffrion, Montreal Canadiens
1962	Jacques Plante, Montreal Canadiens
1963	Gordie Howe, Detroit
1964	Jean Beliveau, Montreal Canadiens
1965	Bobby Hull, Chicago
1966	Bobby Hull, Chicago
1967	Stan Mikita, Chicago
1968	Stan Mikita, Chicago
1969	Phil Esposito, Boston
1970	Bobby Orr, Boston
1971	Bobby Orr, Boston
1972	Bobby Orr, Boston
1973	Bobby Clarke, Philadelphia
1974	Phil Esposito, Boston

1975	Bobby Clarke, Philadelphia
1976	Bobby Clarke, Philadelphia
1977	Guy Lafleur, Montreal
1978	Guy Lafleur, Montreal
1979	Bryan Trottier, New York Islanders
1980	Wayne Gretzky, Edmonton
1981	Wayne Gretzky, Edmonton
1982	Wayne Gretzky, Edmonton
1983	Wayne Gretzky, Edmonton
1984	Wayne Gretzky, Edmonton
1985	Wayne Gretzky, Edmonton
1986	Wayne Gretzky, Edmonton
1987	Wayne Gretzky, Edmonton
1988	Mario Lemieux, Pittsburgh
1989	Wayne Gretzky, Los Angeles
1990	Mark Messier, Edmonton
1991	Brett Hull, St. Lawrence
1992	Mark Messier, New York Rangers

NHL All-Time Leaders

Boldface indicates players still active in major teams of the NHL at the start of the 1992–93 season.

CAREER SCORING POINTS

	Years	Games	Goals	Assists	Points
Wayne Gretzky	13	999	749	1,514	2,263
Gordie Howe	26	1,767	801	1,049	1,850
Marcel Dionne	18	1,348	731	1,040	1,771
Phil Esposito	18	1,282	717	873	1,590
Stan Mikita	22	1,394	541	926	1,467
Bryan Trottier	17	1,238	520	890	1,410
John Bucyk	23	1,540	556	813	1,369
Guy Lafleur	17	1,126	560	793	1,353
Gilbert Perreault	17	1,191	512	814	1,326
Alex Delvecchio	24	1,549	456	825	1,281
Jean Ratelle	21	1,281	491	776	1,267
Norm Ullman	20	1,410	490	739	1,229
Jean Beliveau	20	1,125	507	712	1,219
Bobby Clarke	15	1,144	358	852	1,210
Peter Stastny	12	892	427	754	1,181
Bobby Hull	16	1,063	610	560	1,170
Denis Savard	12	883	407	735	1,142
Mark Messier	13	930	427	714	1,141
Bernie Federko	14	1,000	369	761	1,130
Mike Bossy	10	752	573	553	1,126
Darryl Sittler	15	1,096	484	637	1,121
Dale Hawerchuk	11	870	433	683	1,116
Paul Coffey	12	873	318	796	1,114
Frank Mahovlich	18	1,181	533	570	1,103
Michel Goulet	13	970	509	569	1,078
Denis Potvin	15	1,060	310	742	1,052
Dave Taylor	15	1,030	421	626	1,047
Henri Richard	20	1,256	358	688	1,046
Jari Kurri	10	754	474	569	1,043
Rod Gilbert	18	1,065	406	615	1,021

GOALS

	Years	Games	Number
Gordie Howe	26	1,767	801
Wayne Gretzky	13	999	749
Marcel Dionne	18	1,348	731
Phil Esposito	18	1,282	717
Bobby Hull	16	1,063	610
Mike Bossy	10	752	573
Guy Lafleur	17	1,126	560
John Bucyk	23	1,540	556
Maurice Richard	18	978	544
Stan Mikita	22	1,394	541
Mike Gartner	13	1,005	538
Frank Mahovlich	18	1,181	533
Bryan Trottier	17	1,238	520
Gilbert Perreault	17	1,191	512
Michel Goulet	13	970	509
Jean Beliveau	18	1,125	507
Lanny McDonald	16	1,111	500
Jean Ratelle	21	1,281	491
Norm Ullman	20	1,410	490
Darryl Sittler	15	1,096	484
Jari Kurri	10	754	474
Alex Delvecchio	24	1,549	456
Rick Middleton	14	1,005	448
Rick Vaive	13	876	441
Glenn Anderson	12	900	437
Yvan Cournoyer	16	968	428
Steve Shutt	13	930	424
Dave Taylor	15	1,030	421
Bill Barber	12	903	420
Garry Unger	16	1,105	413

ASSISTS

	Years	Games	Number
Wayne Gretzky	13	999	1,514
Gordie Howe	26	1,767	1,049
Marcel Dionne	18	1,348	1,040
Stan Mikita	22	1,394	926
Bryan Trottier	17	1,238	890
Phil Esposito	18	1,281	873
Bobby Clarke	15	1,144	852
Alex Delvecchio	24	1,549	825
Gilbert Perreault	17	1,191	814
John Bucyk	23	1,540	813
Guy Lafleur	17	1,126	793
Jean Ratelle	21	1,281	776
Bernie Federko	14	1,000	761
Larry Robinson	20	1,384	750
Denis Potvin	15	1,060	742

COLLEGIATE SPORTS

NCAA BASKETBALL

NCAA teams, suggested contact:

National Collegiate Athletic Association
6201 College Blvd.
Overland Park, KS 66211
(913) 339-1906

National Collegiate Athletics Association Division IA Basketball Schools

Air Force Academy, "Falcons", Colorado Springs, Colo.; Akron, University of, "Zips", Akron, Ohio; Alabama State University, "Hornets", Montgomery, Ala.; Alabama, University of, "Crimson Tide", Tuscaloosa, Ala.; Alabama at Birmingham, University of, "Blazers"; Alcorn State University, "Braves", Lorman, Miss.; American University, "Eagles", Washington, D.C.; Appalachian State University, "Mountaineers", Boone, N.C.; Arizona, University of, "Wildcats", Tucson, Ariz.; Arizona State University, "Sun Devils", Tempe, Ariz.; Arkansas State University, "Indians", State University, Ark.; Arkansas at Fayetteville, University of, "Razorbacks"; Arkansas at Little Rock, University of, "Trojans"; Army, U.S. Military Academy, "Cadets", West Point, N.Y.; Auburn University, "Tigers", Auburn, Ala.; Austin Peay State University, "Governors", Clarksville, Tenn.

Ball State University, "Cardinals", Muncie, Ind.; Baylor University, "Bears", Waco, Tex.; Bethune-Cookman College, "Wildcats", Daytona Beach, Fla.; Boise State University, "Broncos", Boise, Idaho; Boston College, "Eagles", Chestnut Hill, Mass.; Boston University, "Terriers", Boston, Mass.; Bowling Green State University, "Falcons", Bowling Green, Ohio; Bradley University, "Braves", Peoria, Ill.; Brigham Young University, "Cougars", Provo, Utah; Brooklyn College, City University of New York, "Kingsmen", Brooklyn, N.Y.; Brown University, "Bruins", Providence, R.I.; Bucknell University, "Bison", Lewisburg, Pa.; Buffalo, State University of New York at, "Bulls"; Butler University, "Bulldogs", Indianapolis, Ind.

California, University of, "Golden Bears", Berkeley, Calif.; California at Irvine, University of, "Anteaters"; California at Los Angeles, University of, "Bruins"; California at Santa Barbara, University of, "Gauchos"; California State University at Fullerton, "Titans"; California State University at Northridge, "Matadors"; California State University at Sacramento, "Hornets"; Campbell University, "Fighting Camels", Buies Creek, N.C.; Canisius College, "Golden Griffins", Buffalo, N.Y.; Centenary College of Louisiana, "Gentlemen", Shreveport, La.; Central Connecticut State University, "Blue Devils", New Britain, Conn.; Central Florida, University of, "Knights", Orlando, Fla.; Central Michigan University, "Chippewas", Mt. Pleasant, Mich.; Charleston, College of, "Cougars", Charleston, S.C.; Charleston Baptist College, "Buccaneers", Charleston, S.C.; Chicago State University, "Cougars", Chicago, Ill.; Cincinnati, University of, "Bearcats", Cincinnati, Ohio; The Citadel—The Military College of South Carolina, "Bulldogs", Charleston, S.C.; Clemson University, "Tigers", Clemson, S.C.; Cleveland State University, "Vikings", Cleveland, Ohio; Coastal Carolina College, "Chanticleers", Conway, S.C.; Colgate University, "Red Raiders", Hamilton, N.Y.; Colorado State University, "Rams", Fort Collins, Colo.; Colorado, University of, "Buffaloes", Boulder, Colo.; Columbia University, "Lions", New York, N.Y.; Connecticut, University of, "Huskies", Storrs, Conn.; Coppin State College, "Eagles", Baltimore, Md.; Cornell University, "Big Red", Ithaca, N.Y.; Creighton University, "Bluejays", Omaha, Nebr.

Dartmouth College, "Big Green", Hanover, N.H.; Davidson College, "Wildcats", Davidson, N.C.; Dayton, University of, "Flyers", Dayton, Ohio; DePaul University, "Blue Demons", Chicago, Ill.; Delaware, University of, "Blue Hens", Newark, Del.; Delaware State College, "Hornets", Dover, Del.; Detroit, University of, "Titans", Detroit, Mich.; Drake University, "Bulldogs", Des Moines, Iowa; Drexel University, "Dragons", Philadelphia, Pa.; Duke University, "Blue Devils", Durham, N.C.; Duquesne University, "Dukes", Pittsburgh, Pa.

East Carolina University, "Pirates", Greenville, N.C.; Eastern Illinois University, "Panthers", Charleston, Ill.; Eastern Kentucky University, "Colonels", Richmond, Ky.; Eastern Michigan University, "Eagles", Ypsilanti, Mich.; East Tennessee State University, "Buccaneers", Johnson City, Tenn.; Eastern Washington University, "Eagles", Cheney, Wash.; Evansville, University of, "Purple Aces", Evansville, Ind.

Fairfield University, "Stags", Fairfield, Conn.; Fairleigh Dickinson University at Teaneck-Hackensack, "Knights", Teaneck, N.J.; Florida, University of, "Gators", Gainesville, Fla.; Florida A&M University, "Rattlers", Tallahassee, Fla.; Florida International University, "Golden Panthers", Miami, Fla.; Florida State University, "Seminoles", Tallahassee, Fla.; Fordham University, "Rams", Bronx,

N.Y.; Fresno State College, "Bulldogs", Fresno, Calif.; Furman University, "Paladins", Greenville, S.C.

George Mason University, "Patriots", Fairfax, Va.; George Washington University, "Colonials", Washington, D.C.; Georgetown University, "Hoyas", Washington, D.C.; Georgia, University of, "Bulldogs" or "Dawgs", Athens, Ga.; Georgia Southern University, "Eagles", Statesboro, Ga.; Georgia State University, "Crimson Panthers", Atlanta, Ga.; Georgia Institute of Technology, "Yellow Jackets", Atlanta, Ga.; Gonzaga University, "Bulldogs" or "Zags", Spokane, Wash.; Grambling State University, "Tigers", Grambling, La.

Hartford, University of, "Hawks", West Hartford, Conn.; Harvard University, "Crimson", Cambridge, Mass.; Hawaii of Manoa, University of, "Rainbows", Honolulu, Hawaii; Hofstra University, "Flying Dutchmen", Hempstead, N.Y.; Holy Cross, College of the, "Crusaders", Worcester, Mass.; Houston, University of, "Cougar" or "Cougars", Houston, Tex.; Howard University, "Bison", Washington, D.C.

Idaho, University of, "Vandals", Moscow, Idaho; Idaho State University, "Bengals", Pocatello, Idaho; Illinois at Urbana-Champaign, University of, "Fighting Illini", Champaign, Ill.; Illinois at Chicago, University of, "Flames"; Illinois State University, "Redbirds", Normal, Ill.; Indiana University at Bloomington, "Hoosiers"; Indiana State University, "Sycamores", Terre Haute, Ind.; Iona College, "Gaels", New Rochelle, N.Y.; Iowa, University of, "Hawkeyes", Iowa City, Iowa; Iowa State University, "Cyclones", Ames, Iowa.

Jackson State University, "Tigers", Jackson, Miss.; Jacksonville University, "Dolphins", Jacksonville, Fla.; James Madison University, "Dukes", Harrisonburg, Va.

Kansas, University of, "Jayhawks", Lawrence, Kans.; Kansas State University, "Wildcats", Manhattan, Kans.; Kent State University, "Golden Flashes", Kent, Ohio; Kentucky, University of, "Wildcats", Lexington, Ky.

La Salle University, "Explorers", Philadelphia, Pa.; Lafayette College, "Leopards", Easton, Pa.; Lamar University, "Cardinals", Beaumont, Tex.; Lehigh University, "Engineers", Bethlehem, Pa.; Liberty University, "Flames", Lynchburg, Va.; Long Beach State University, "49ers", Long Beach, Calif.; Long Island University at Brooklyn, "Blackbirds", Brooklyn, N.Y.; Louisiana State University, "Fighting Tigers", Baton Rouge, La.; Louisiana Tech University, "Bulldogs", Ruston, La.; Louisville, University of, "Cardinals", Louisville, Ky.; Loyola Marymount University, "Lions", Los Angeles, Calif.; Loyola University of Chicago, "Ramblers", Chicago, Ill.; Loyola College, "Greyhounds", Baltimore, Md.

Maine, University of, "Black Bears", Orono, Maine; Manhattan College, "Jaspers", Riverdale, N.Y.; Marist College, "Red Foxes", Poughkeepsie, N.Y.; Marquette University, "Warriors", Milwaukee, Wis.; Marshall University, "Thundering Herd", Huntington, W.Va.; Maryland, University of, "Terrapins", College Park, Md.; Maryland at Baltimore County, University of, "Retrievers", Baltimore, Md.; Maryland at Eastern Shore, University of, "Hawks", Princess Anne, Md.; Massachusetts, University of, "Minutemen", Amherst, Mass.; McNeese State University, "Cowboys", Lake Charles, La.; Memphis State University, "Tigers", Memphis, Tenn.; Mercer University at Macon, "Bears", Macon, Ga.; Miami, University of, "Hurricanes", Coral Gables, Fla.; Miami University, "Redskins", Oxford, Ohio; Michigan, at Ann Arbor, University of, "Wolverines"; Michigan State University, "Spartans", East Lansing, Mich.; Middle Tennessee State University, "Blue Raiders", Murfreesboro, Tenn.; Minnesota, University of, "Golden Gophers", Minneapolis, Minn.; Mississippi, University of, "Rebels" or "Ole Miss", Oxford, Miss.; Mississippi State University, "Bulldogs", Starkville, Miss.; Mississippi Valley State University, "Delta Devils", Itta Bena, Miss.; Missouri, University of, "Tigers", Columbia, Mo.; Missouri at Kansas City, University of, "Kangaroos"; Monmouth College, "Hawks", West Long Branch, N.J.; Montana, University of, "Grizzlies", Missoula, Mont.; Montana State University, "Bobcats", Bozeman, Mont.; Morehead State University, "Eagles", Morehead, Ky.; Morgan State University, "Bears", Baltimore, Md.; Mount Saint Mary's College, "Mountaineers", Emmitsburg, Md.; Murray State University, "Racers", Murray, Ky.

Navy, U.S. Naval Academy, "Midshipmen", Annapolis, Md.; Nebraska, University of, "Cornhuskers", Lincoln, Nebr.; Nevada, University of, "Wolf Pack", Reno, Nev.; Nevada at Las Vegas, University of, "Runnin' Rebels"; New Hampshire, University of, "Wildcats", Durham, N.H.; New Mexico, University of, "Lobos", Albuquerque, N.M.; New Mexico State University, "Aggies", Las Cruces, N.M.; New Orleans, University of, "Privateers", New Orleans, La.; New York at Buffalo, State University of, "Bulls"; Niagara University, "Purple Eagles", Niagara, N.Y.; Nicholls State University, "Colonels", Thibodaux, La.; North Carolina, University of, "Tar Heels", Chapel Hill, N.C.; North Carolina Agricultural and Technical State University, "Aggies", Greensboro, N.C.; North Carolina State University, "Wolfpack", Raleigh, N.C.; North Carolina at Asheville, University of, "Bulldogs"; North Carolina at Charlotte, University of, "49ers"; North Carolina at Greensboro, University of, "Spartans"; North Carolina at Wilmington, University of, "Seahawks";

North Texas, University of, "Mean Green", Denton, Tex.; Northeastern Illinois University, "Golden Eagles", Chicago, Ill.; Northeast Louisiana University, "Indians", Monroe, La.; Northeastern University, "Huskies", Boston, Mass.; Northern Arizona University, "Lumberjacks", Flagstaff, Ariz.; Northern Illinois University, "Huskies", De Kalb, Ill.; Northern Iowa, University of, "Panthers", Cedar Falls, Iowa; Northwestern University, "Wildcats", Evanston, Ill.; Northwestern State University of Louisiana, "Demons", Natchitoches, La.; Notre Dame, University of, "Fighting Irish", South Bend, Ind.

Ohio University, "Bobcats", Athens, Ohio; Ohio State University, "Buckeyes", Columbus, Ohio; Oklahoma, University of, "Sooners", Norman, Okla.; Oklahoma State University, "Cowboys", Stillwater, Okla.; Old Dominion University, "Monarchs", Norfolk, Va.; Oregon, University of, "Ducks", Eugene, Oreg.; Oregon State University, "Beavers", Corvallis, Oreg.

Pacific, University of the, "Tigers", Stockton, Calif.; Pan American University, "Broncs", Edinburg, Tex.; Penn State University, "Nittany Lions", University Park, Pa.; Pennsylvania, University of, "Quakers", Philadelphia, Pa.; Pepperdine University–Seaver College, "Waves", Malibu, Calif.; Pittsburgh, University of, "Panthers", Pittsburgh, Pa.; Portland, University of, "Pilots", Portland, Oreg.; Prairie View A&M University, "Panthers", Prairie View, Tex.; Princeton University, "Tigers", Princeton, N.J.; Providence College, "Friars", Providence, R.I.; Purdue University, "Boilermakers", West Lafayette, Ind.

Radford University, "Highlanders", Radford, Va.; Rhode Island, University of, "Rams", Kingston, R.I.; Rice University, "Owls", Houston, Tex.; Richmond, University of, "Spiders", Richmond, Va.; Rider College, "Broncs", Lawrenceville, N.J.; Robert Morris College, "Colonials", Coraopolis, Pa.; Rutgers University, "Scarlet Knights", New Brunswick, N.J.

St. Bonaventure University, "Bonnies", St. Bonaventure, N.Y.; St. Francis College, "Terriers", Brooklyn Heights, N.Y.; St. Francis College, "Red Flash", Loretto, Pa.; St. John's University, "Redmen", Jamaica, N.Y.; St. Joseph's University, "Hawks", Philadelphia, Pa.; St. Louis University, "Billikens", St. Louis, Mo.; St. Mary's College of California, "Gaels", Moraga, Calif.; St. Peter's College, "Peacocks", Jersey City, N.J.; Sam Houston State University, "Bearkats", Huntsville, Tex.; Samford University, "Bulldogs", Birmingham, Ala.; San Diego, University of, "Toreros," San Diego, Calif.; San Diego State University, "Aztecs", San Diego, Calif.; San Francisco, University of, "Dons", San Francisco, Calif.; San Jose State University, "Spartans", San Jose, Calif.; Santa Clara University, "Broncos", Santa Clara, Calif.; Seton Hall University, "Pirates",

South Orange, N.J.; Siena College, "Saints", Loudonville, N.Y.; South Alabama, University of, "Jaguars", Mobile, Ala.; South Carolina, University of, "Gamecocks", Columbia, S.C.; South Carolina State University, "Bulldogs", Orangeburg, S.C.; South Florida, University of, "Bulls", Tampa, Fla.; Southeastern Louisiana University, "Lions", Hammond, La.; Southeastern Missouri State University, "Indians", Cape Girardeau, Mo.; Southern California, University of, "Trojans", Los Angeles, Calif.; Southern Illinois University at Carbondale, "Salukis"; Southern Methodist University, "Mustangs", Dallas, Tex.; Southern Mississippi, University of, "Golden Eagles", Hattiesburg, Miss.; South Utah State College, "Thunderbirds", Cedar City, Utah; Southern University–Baton Rouge, "Jaguars", Baton Rouge, La.; Southwest Missouri State University, "Bears", Springfield, Mo.; Southwest Texas State University, "Bobcats", San Marcos, Tex.; Southwestern Louisiana, University of, "Ragin' Cajuns", Lafayette, La.; Stanford University, "Cardinal", Palo Alto, Calif.; Stephen F. Austin University, "Lumberjacks", Nacogdoches, Tex.; Stetson University, "Hatters", DeLand, Fla.; Syracuse University, "Orangemen", Syracuse, N.Y.

Temple University, "Owls", Philadelphia, Pa.; Tennessee at Chattanooga, University of, "Moccasins"; Tennessee at Knoxville, University of, "Volunteers"; Tennessee State University, "Tigers", Nashville, Tenn.; Tennessee Technological University, "Golden Eagles", Cookeville, Tenn.; Texas at Austin, University of, "Longhorns"; Texas at El Paso, University of, "Miners"; Texas A&M University, "Aggies", College Station, Tex.; Texas Christian University, "Horned Frogs", Fort Worth, Tex.; Texas Southern University, "Tigers", Houston, Tex.; Texas Tech University, "Red Raiders", Lubbock, Tex.; Texas at Arlington, University of, "Mavericks"; Texas at San Antonio, University of, "Roadrunners"; Toledo, University of, "Rockets", Toledo, Ohio; Towson State University, "Tigers", Towson, Md.; Tulane University, "Green Wave", New Orleans, La.; Tulsa, University of, "Golden Hurricane", Tulsa, Okla.

Utah, University of, "Utes", Salt Lake City, Utah; Utah State University, "Aggies", Logan, Utah.

Valparaiso University, "Crusaders", Valparaiso, Ind.; Vanderbilt University, "Commodores", Nashville, Tenn.; Vermont, University of, "Catamounts", Burlington, Vt.; Villanova University, "Wildcats", Villanova, Pa.; Virginia, University of, "Cavaliers", Charlottesville, Va.; Virginia Commonwealth University, "Rams", Richmond, Va.; Virginia Military Institute, "Keydets", Lexington, Va.; Virginia Polytechnic University and State University, "Hokies" or "Gobbler", Blacksburg, Va.

Wagner College, "Seahawks", Staten Island, N.Y.;

Wake Forest University, "Demon Deacons", Winston-Salem, N.C.; Washington, University of, "Huskies", Seattle, Wash.; Washington State University, "Cougars", Pullman, Wash.; Weber State College, "Wildcats", Ogden, Utah; West Virginia University, "Mountaineers", Morgantown, W.Va.; Western Carolina University, "Catamounts", Cullowhee, N.C.; Western Illinois University, "Leathernecks", Macomb, Ill.; Western Kentucky University, "Hilltoppers", Bowling Green, Ky.; Western Michigan University, "Broncos", Kalamazoo, Mich.; Wichita State University, "Shockers", Wichita, Kans.; William and Mary, College of, "Indians", Williamsburg, Va.; Winthrop College, "Eagles", Rock Hill, S.C.; Wisconsin, University of, "Badgers", Madison, Wis.; Wisconsin at Green Bay, University of, "Phoenix"; Wright State University, "Raiders", Dayton, Ohio; Wyoming, University of, "Cowboys", Laramie, Wyo.

Xavier University, "Musketeers", Cincinnati, Ohio

Yale University, "Bulldogs" or "Elis", New Haven, Conn.; Youngstown State University, "Penguins", Youngstown, Ohio

DIVISION IA FINAL FOUR WINNERS

1961	Cincinnati 70, Ohio State 65
1962	Cincinnati 71, Ohio State 59
1963	Loyola (Ill.) 60, Cincinnati 58
1964	UCLA 98, Duke 83
1965	UCLA 91, Michigan 80
1966	UTEP 72, Kentucky 65
1967	UCLA 79, Dayton 64
1968	UCLA 78, N. Carolina 55
1969	UCLA 92, Purdue 72
1970	UCLA 80, Jacksonville 69
1971	UCLA 68, Villanova 62
1972	UCLA 81, Florida State 76
1973	UCLA 87, Memphis State 66
1974	N.C. State 76, Marquette 64
1975	UCLA 92, Kentucky 85
1976	Indiana 86, Michigan 68
1977	Marquette 67, N. Carolina 59
1978	Kentucky 94, Duke 88
1979	Michigan State 75, Indiana State 64
1980	Louisville 59, UCLA 54
1981	Indiana 63, N. Carolina 50
1982	N. Carolina 63, Georgetown 62
1983	N.C. State 54, Houston 52
1984	Georgetown 84, Houston 75
1985	Villanova 66, Georgetown 64
1986	Louisville 72, Duke 69
1987	Indiana 74, Syracuse 73
1988	Kansas 83, Oklahoma 79
1989	Michigan 80, Seton Hall 79
1990	UNLV 103, Duke 73
1991	Duke 72, Kansas 65
1992	Duke 71, Michigan 51

NCAA FOOTBALL

NCAA teams, suggested contact:
National Collegiate Athletic Association
6201 College Blvd.
Overland Park, KS 66211
(913) 339-1906

National Collegiate Athletic Association Division I A Football Schools

Air Force Academy, "Falcons", Colorado Springs, Colo.; Akron, University of, "Zips", Akron, Ohio; Alabama, University of, "Crimson Tide", Tuscaloosa, Ala.; Arizona, University of, "Wildcats", Tucson, Ariz.; Arizona State University, "Sun Devils", Tempe, Ariz.; Arkansas at Fayetteville, University of, "Razorbacks"; Army, U.S. Military Academy, "Cadets", West Point, N.Y.; Auburn University, "Tigers", Auburn, Ala.

Ball State University, "Cardinals", Muncie, Ind.; Baylor University, "Bears", Waco, Tex.; Boston College, "Eagles", Chestnut Hill, Mass.; Boston University, "Terriers", Boston, Mass.; Bowling Green State University, "Falcons", Bowling Green, Ohio; Brigham Young University, "Cougars", Provo, Utah

California, University of, "Golden Bears", Berkeley, Calif.; California at Los Angeles, University of, "Bruins"; California State University at Fullerton, "Titans"; Central Michigan University, "Chippewas", Mt. Pleasant, Mich.; Cincinnati, University of, "Bearcats", Cincinnati, Ohio; Clemson University, "Tigers", Clemson, S.C.; Colorado, University of, "Buffaloes", Boulder, Colo.; Colorado State University, "Rams", Fort Collins, Colo.

Duke University, "Blue Devils", Durham, N.C.

East Carolina University, "Pirates", Greenville, N.C.; Eastern Michigan University, "Eagles", Ypsilanti, Mich.

Florida, University of, "Gaters", Gainesville, Fla.; Florida State University, "Seminoles", Tallahassee, Fla.; Fresno State College, "Bulldogs", Fresno, Calif.

Georgia, University of, "Bulldogs" or "Dawgs", Athens, Ga.; Georgia Institute of Technology, "Yellow Jackets", Atlanta, Ga.

Hawaii at Manoa, University of, "Rainbows", Honolulu, Hawaii; Houston, University of, "Cougar" or "Cougars", Houston, Tex.

Illinois at Urbana-Champaign, University of, "Fighting Illini"; Indiana University at Bloomington, "Hoosiers"; Iowa, University of, "Hawkeyes", Iowa City, Iowa; Iowa State University, "Cyclones", Ames, Iowa

Kansas, University of, "Jayhawks", Lawrence, Kans.; Kansas State University, "Wildcats", Manhattan, Kans.; Kent State University, "Golden Flashes", Kent, Ohio; Kentucky, University of, "Wildcats", Lexington, Ky.

Long Beach State University, "49ers", Long Beach, Calif.; Louisiana State University, "Fighting Tigers", Baton Rouge, La.; Louisiana Tech University, "Bulldogs", Ruston, La.; Louisville, University of, "Cardinals", Louisville, Ky.

Maryland, University of, "Terrapins" or "Terps", College Park, Md.; Memphis State University, "Tigers", Memphis, Tenn.; Miami, University of, "Hurricanes", Coral Gables, Fla.; Miami University, "Redskins", Oxford, Ohio; Michigan at Ann Arbor, University of, "Wolverines"; Michigan State University, "Spartans", East Lansing, Mich.; Minnesota, University of, "Golden Gophers", Minneapolis, Minn.; Mississippi, University of, "Rebels" or "Ole Miss", Oxford, Miss.; Mississippi State University, "Bulldogs", Starkville, Miss.; Missouri, University of, "Tigers", Columbia, Mo.

Navy, U.S. Naval Academy, "Midshipmen", Annapolis, Md.; Nebraska, University of, "Cornhuskers", Lincoln, Nebr.; Nevada at Las Vegas, University of, "Runnin' Rebels"; New Mexico, University of, "Lobos", Albuquerque, N.M.; New Mexico State University, "Aggies", Las Cruces, N.M.; North Carolina, University of, "Tar Heels", Chapel Hill, N.C.; North Carolina State University, "Wolfpack", Raleigh, N.C.; Northern Illinois University, "Huskies", De Kalb, Ill.; Northwestern University, "Wildcats", Evanston, Ill.; Notre Dame, University of, "Fighting Irish", South Bend, Ind.

Ohio University, "Bobcats", Athens, Ohio; Ohio State University, "Buckeyes", Columbus, Ohio; Oklahoma, University of, "Sooners", Norman, Okla.; Oklahoma State University, "Cowboys", Stillwater, Okla.; Oregon, University of, "Ducks", Eugene, Oreg.; Oregon State University, "Beavers," Corvallis, Oreg.

Pacific, University of the, "Tigers", Stockton, Calif.; Penn State University, "Nittany Lions", University Park, Pa.; Pittsburgh, University of, "Panthers", Pittsburgh, Pa.; Purdue University, "Boilermakers", West Lafayette, Ind.

Rice University, "Owls", Houston, Tex.; Rutgers University, "Scarlet Knights", New Brunswick, N.J.

San Diego State University, "Aztecs", San Diego, Calif.; San Jose State University, "Spartans", San Jose, Calif.; South Carolina, University of, "Gamecocks", Columbia, S.C.; Southern California, University of, "Trojans", Los Angeles, Calif.; Southern Methodist University, "Mustangs", Dallas, Tex.; Southern Mississippi, University of, "Golden Eagles", Hattiesburg, Miss.; Southwestern Louisiana, University of, "Ragin' Cajuns", Lafayette, La.; Stanford University, "Cardinal", Palo Alto, Calif.;

Syracuse University, "Orangemen", Syracuse, N.Y.

Temple University, "Owls", Philadelphia, Pa.; Tennessee at Knoxville, University of, "Volunteers"; Texas at Austin, University of, "Longhorns"; Texas at El Paso, University of, "Miners"; Texas A&M University, "Aggies", College Station, Tex.; Texas Christian University, "Horned Frogs", Fort Worth, Tex.; Texas Tech University, "Red Raiders", Lubbock, Tex.; Toledo, University of, "Rockets", Toledo, Ohio; Towson State University, "Tigers", Towson, Md.; Tulane University, "Green Wave", New Orleans, La.; Tulsa, University of, "Golden Hurricane", Tulsa, Okla.

Utah, University of, "Utes", Salt Lake City, Utah; Utah State University, "Aggies", Logan, Utah

Vanderbilt University, "Commodores", Nashville, Tenn.; Virginia, University of, "Cavaliers", Charlottesville, Va.; Virginia Polytechnic University and State University, "Hokies" or "Gobbler", Blacksburg, Va.

Wagner College, "Seahawks", Staten Island, N.Y.; Wake Forest University, "Demon Deacons", Winston-Salem, N.C.; Washington, University of, "Huskies", Seattle, Wash.; Washington State University, "Cougars", Pullman, Wash.; West Virginia University, "Mountaineers", Morgantown, W.Va.; Western Michigan University, "Broncos", Kalamazoo, Mich.; Wisconsin, University of, "Badgers", Madison, Wis.; Wyoming, University of, "Cowboys", Laramie, Wyo.

National Collegiate Athletic Association Division IAA Football Schools

Alabama State University, "Hornets", Montgomery, Ala.; Alcorn State University, "Braves", Lorman, Miss.; Appalachian State University, "Mountaineers", Boone, N.C.; Arkansas State University, "Indians", State University, Ark.; Austin Peay State University, "Governors", Clarksville, Tenn.

Bethune-Cookman College, "Wildcats", Daytona Beach, Fla.; Boise State University, "Broncos", Boise, Idaho; Boston University, "Terriers", Boston, Mass.; Brown University, "Bruins", Providence, R.I.; Bucknell University, "Bison", Lewisburg, Pa.

Central Florida, University of, "Knights", Orlando, Fla.; The Citadel—The Military College of South Carolina, "Bulldogs", Charleston, S.C.; Colgate University, "Red Raiders", Hamilton, N.Y.; Columbia University, "Lions", New York, N.Y.; Connecticut, University of, "Huskies", Storrs, Conn.; Cornell University, "Big Red", Ithaca, N.Y.; Creighton University, "Bluejays", Omaha, Nebr.

Dartmouth College, "Big Green", Hanover, N.H.;

Delaware, University of, "Blue Hens", Newark, Del.; Delaware State College, "Hornets", Dover, Del.

Eastern Illinois University, "Panthers", Charleston, Ill.; Eastern Kentucky University, "Colonels", Richmond, Ky.; Eastern Michigan University, "Eagles", Ypsilanti, Mich.; East Tennessee State University, "Buccaneers", Johnson City, Tenn.; Eastern Washington University, "Eagles", Cheney, Wash.

Florida A&M University, "Rattlers", Tallahassee, Fla.; Fordham University, "Rams", Bronx, N.Y.; Fresno State College, "Bulldogs", Fresno, Calif.; Furman University, "Paladins", Greenville, S.C.

Georgia Southern University, "Eagles", Statesboro, Ga.; Grambling State University, "Tigers", Grambling, La.

Harvard University, "Crimson", Cambridge, Mass.; Holy Cross, College of the, "Crusaders", Worcester, Mass.; Houston, University of, "Cougar" or "Cougars", Houston, Tex.; Howard University, "Bison", Washington, D.C.

Idaho, University of, "Vandals", Moscow, Idaho; Idaho State University, "Bengals", Pocatello, Idaho; Illinois State University, "Redbirds", Normal, Ill.; Indiana State University, "Sycamores", Terre Haute, Ind.

Jackson State University, "Tigers", Jackson, Miss.; James Madison University, "Dukes", Harrisonburg, Va.

Lafayette College, "Leopards", Easton, Pa.; Lehigh University, "Engineers", Bethlehem, Pa.; Liberty University, "Flames", Lynchburg, Va.

Maine, University of, "Black Bears", Orono, Maine; Marshall University, "Thundering Herd", Huntington, W.Va.; Massachusetts, University of, "Minutemen", Amherst, Mass.; McNeese State University, "Cowboys", Lake Charles, La.; Middle Tennessee State University, "Blue Raiders," Murfreesboro, Tenn.; Mississippi Valley State University, "Delta Devils", Itta Bena, Miss.; Montana, University of, "Grizzlies", Missoula, Mont.; Montana State University, "Bobcats", Bozeman, Mont.; Morehead State University, "Eagles", Morehead, Ky.; Morgan State University, "Bears", Baltimore, Md.; Murray State University, "Racers", Murray, Ky.

Nevada, University of, "Wolf Pack", Reno, Nev.; New Hampshire, University of, "Wildcats", Durham, N.H.; Nicholls State University, "Colonels", Thibodaux, La.; North Carolina Agricultural and Technical State University, "Aggies", Greensboro, N.C.; North Texas, University of, "Mean Green", Denton, Tex.; Northeast Louisiana University, "Indians", Monroe, La.; Northeastern University, "Huskies",

Boston, Mass.; Northern Arizona University, "Lumberjacks", Flagstaff, Ariz.; Northern Iowa, University of, "Panthers", Cedar Falls, Iowa; Northwestern State University of Louisiana, "Demons", Natchitoches, La.

Pennsylvania, University of, "Quakers", Philadelphia, Pa.; Prairie View A&M University, "Panthers", Prairie View, Tex.; Princeton University, "Tigers", Princeton, N.J.

Rhode Island, University of, "Rams", Kingston, R.I.; Richmond, University of, "Spiders", Richmond, Va.

Sam Houston State University, "Bearkats", Huntsville, Tex.; Samford University, "Bulldogs", Birmingham, Ala.; South Carolina State University, "Bulldogs", Orangeburg, S.C.; Southeastern Missouri State University, "Indians", Cape Girardeau, Mo.; Southern Illinois University at Carbondale, "Salukis"; Southern University–Baton Rouge, "Jaguars", Baton Rouge, La.; Southwest Missouri State University, "Bears", Springfield, Mo.; Southwest Texas State University, "Bobcats", San Marcos, Tex.; Stephen F. Austin University, "Lumberjacks", Nacogdoches, Tex.

Tennessee at Chattanooga, University of, "Moccasins"; Tennessee State University, "Tigers", Nashville, Tenn.; Tennessee Technological University, "Golden Eagles", Cookeville, Tenn.; Texas Southern University, "Tigers", Houston, Tex.; Towson State University, "Tigers", Towson, Md.

Villanova University, "Wildcats", Villanova, Pa.; Virginia Military Institute, "Keydets", Lexington, Va.

Weber State College, "Wildcats", Ogden, Utah; Western Carolina University, "Catamounts", Cullowhee, N.C.; Western Illinois University, "Leathernecks", Macomb, Ill.; Western Kentucky University, "Hilltoppers", Bowling Green, Ky.; William and Mary, College of, "Indians", Williamsburg, Va.

Yale University, "Bulldogs" or "Elis", New Haven, Conn.; Youngstown State University, "Penguins", Youngstown, Ohio

National College Football Champions (Since 1940)

The nation's championship college football team is selected each year by press association polls. The Associated Press polls sports writers around the country. United Press International polls college football coaches. The results are accepted by the National Collegiate Athletic Association. When the polls disagree, the selection of each is listed; UPI's choice is listed second.

1940	Minnesota
1941	Minnesota
1942	Ohio State
1943	Notre Dame
1944	Army
1945	Army
1946	Notre Dame
1947	Notre Dame
1948	Michigan
1949	Notre Dame
1950	Oklahoma
1951	Tennessee
1952	Michigan State
1953	Maryland
1954	Ohio State, UCLA
1955	Oklahoma
1956	Oklahoma
1957	Auburn, Ohio State
1958	Louisiana State
1959	Syracuse
1960	Minnesota
1961	Alabama
1962	S. California
1963	Texas
1964	Alabama
1965	Alabama, Michigan State
1966	Notre Dame
1967	S. California
1968	Ohio State
1969	Texas
1970	Texas, Nebraska
1971	Nebraska
1972	S. California
1973	Notre Dame, U. of Alabama
1974	Oklahoma, S. California
1975	Oklahoma
1976	Pittsburgh
1977	Notre Dame
1978	Alabama, S. California
1979	Alabama
1980	Georgia
1981	Clemson
1982	Penn State
1983	Miami
1984	Brigham Young
1985	Oklahoma
1986	Penn State
1987	Miami
1988	Notre Dame
1989	Miami
1990	Colorado, Georgia Tech
1991	Washington, Miami
1992	Alabama

FOOTBALL BOWL GAMES
Rose Bowl (Pasadena, California)

Jan. 1, 1960   Washington 44, Wisconsin 8
Jan. 2, 1961   Washington 17, Minnesota 7
Jan. 1, 1962   Minnesota 21, UCLA 3
Jan. 1, 1963   S. California 42, Wisconsin 37
Jan. 1, 1964   Illinois 17, Washington 7
Jan. 1, 1965   Michigan 34, Oregon State 7
Jan. 1, 1966   UCLA 14, Michigan State 12
Jan. 2, 1967   Purdue 14, S. California 13
Jan. 1, 1968   S. California 14, Indiana 3
Jan. 1, 1969   Ohio State 27, S. California 16
Jan. 1, 1970   S. California 10, Michigan 3
Jan. 1, 1971   Stanford 27, Ohio State 17
Jan. 1, 1972   Stanford 13, Michigan 12
Jan. 1, 1973   S. California 42, Ohio State 17
Jan. 1, 1974   Ohio State 42, S. California 21
Jan. 1, 1975   S. California 18, Ohio State 17
Jan. 1, 1976   UCLA 23, Ohio State 10
Jan. 1, 1977   S. California 14, Michigan 6
Jan. 2, 1978   Washington 27, Michigan 20
Jan. 1, 1979   S. California 17, Michigan 10
Jan. 1, 1980   S. California 17, Ohio State 16
Jan. 1, 1981   Michigan 23, Washington 6
Jan. 1, 1982   Washington 28, Iowa 0
Jan. 1, 1983   UCLA 24, Michigan 14
Jan. 2, 1984   UCLA 45, Illinois 9
Jan. 1, 1985   USC 20, Ohio State 17
Jan. 1, 1986   UCLA 45, Iowa 28
Jan. 1, 1987   Arizona State 22, Michigan 15
Jan. 1, 1988   Michigan State 20, USC 17
Jan. 2, 1989   Michigan 22, S. California 14
Jan. 1, 1990   USC 17, Michigan 10
Jan. 1, 1991   Washington 46, Iowa 34
Jan. 1, 1992   Washington 34, Michigan 14
Jan. 1, 1993   Michigan 38, Washington 31

Orange Bowl (Miami)

Jan. 1, 1960   Georgia 14, Missouri 0
Jan. 2, 1961   Missouri 21, Navy 14
Jan. 1, 1962   Louisiana State 25, Colorado 7
Jan. 1, 1963   Alabama 17, Oklahoma 0
Jan. 1, 1964   Nebraska 13, Auburn 7
Jan. 1, 1965   Texas 21, Alabama 17
Jan. 1, 1966   Alabama 39, Nebraska 28
Jan. 2, 1967   Florida 27, Georgia Tech 12
Jan. 1, 1968   Oklahoma 26, Tennessee 24
Jan. 1, 1969   Penn State 15, Kansas 14
Jan. 1, 1970   Penn State 10, Missouri 3
Jan. 1, 1971   Nebraska 17, Louisiana State 12
Jan. 1, 1972   Nebraska 38, Alabama 6
Jan. 1, 1973   Nebraska 40, Notre Dame 6
Jan. 1, 1974   Penn State 16, Louisiana State 9

Jan. 1, 1975   Notre Dame 13, Alabama 11
Jan. 1, 1976   Oklahoma 14, Michigan 6
Jan. 1, 1977   Ohio State 27, Colorado 10
Jan. 2, 1978   Arkansas 31, Oklahoma 6
Jan. 1, 1979   Oklahoma 31, Nebraska 24
Jan. 1, 1980   Oklahoma 24, Florida State 7
Jan. 1, 1981   Oklahoma 18, Florida State 17
Jan. 1, 1982   Clemson 22, Nebraska 15
Jan. 1, 1983   Nebraska 21, Louisiana State 20
Jan. 2, 1984   Miami 31, Nebraska 30
Jan. 1, 1985   Washington 28, Oklahoma 17
Jan. 1, 1986   Oklahoma 25, Penn State 10
Jan. 1, 1987   Oklahoma 42, Arkansas 8
Jan. 1, 1988   Miami 20, Oklahoma 14
Jan. 2, 1989   Miami 23, Nebraska 3
Jan. 1, 1990   Notre Dame 21, Colorado 6
Jan. 1, 1991   Colorado 10, Notre Dame 9
Jan. 1, 1992   Miami, Fla. 22, Nebraska 0
Jan. 1, 1993   Florida State 27, Nebraska 14

Sugar Bowl (New Orleans)

Jan. 1, 1960   Mississippi 21, Louisiana State 0
Jan. 2, 1961   Mississippi 14, Rice 6
Jan. 1, 1962   Alabama 10, Arkansas 3
Jan. 1, 1963   Mississippi 17, Arkansas 13
Jan. 1, 1964   Alabama 12, Mississippi 7
Jan. 1, 1965   Louisiana State 13, Syracuse 10
Jan. 1, 1966   Missouri 20, Florida 18
Jan. 1, 1967   Alabama 34, Nebraska 7
Jan. 1, 1968   Louisiana State 20, Wyoming 13
Jan. 1, 1969   Arkansas 16, Georgia 2
Jan. 1, 1970   Mississippi 27, Arkansas 22
Jan. 1, 1971   Tennessee 34, Air Force 13
Jan. 1, 1972   Oklahoma 40, Auburn 22
Dec. 31, 1972   Oklahoma 14, Penn State 0
Dec. 31, 1973   Notre Dame 24, Alabama 23
Dec. 31, 1974   Nebraska 13, Florida 10
Dec. 31, 1975   Alabama 13, Penn State 6
Jan. 1, 1977   Pittsburgh 27, Georgia 3
Jan. 2, 1978   Alabama 35, Ohio State 6
Jan. 1, 1979   Alabama 14, Penn State 7
Jan. 1, 1980   Alabama 24, Arkansas 9
Jan. 1, 1981   Georgia 17, Notre Dame 10
Jan. 1, 1982   Pittsburgh 24, Georgia 20
Jan. 1, 1983   Penn State 27, Georgia 23
Jan. 2, 1984   Auburn 9, Michigan 7
Jan. 1, 1985   Nebraska 28, Louisiana State 10
Jan. 1, 1986   Tennessee 35, Miami, Fla. 7
Jan. 1, 1987   Nebraska 30, Louisiana State 15
Jan. 1, 1988   Syracuse 16, Auburn 16
Jan. 2, 1989   Florida State 13, Auburn 7
Jan. 1, 1990   Miami 33, Alabama 25
Jan. 1, 1991   Tennessee 23, Virginia 22
Jan. 1, 1992   Notre Dame 39, Florida 28
Jan. 1, 1993   Alabama 34, Miami, Fla. 13

Cotton Bowl (Dallas)

Jan. 1, 1960	Syracuse 23, Texas 14
Jan. 2, 1961	Duke 7, Arkansas 6
Jan. 1, 1962	Texas 12, Mississippi 7
Jan. 1, 1963	Louisiana State 13, Texas 0
Jan. 1, 1964	Texas 28, Navy 6
Jan. 1, 1965	Arkansas 10, Nebraska 7
Jan. 1, 1966	Louisiana State 14, Arkansas 7
Dec. 31, 1966	Georgia 24, S. Methodist 9
Jan. 1, 1968	Texas A&M 20, Alabama 16
Jan. 1, 1969	Texas 36, Tennessee 13
Jan. 1, 1970	Texas 21, Notre Dame 17
Jan. 1, 1971	Notre Dame 24, Texas 11
Jan. 1, 1972	Penn State 30, Texas 6
Jan. 1, 1973	Texas 17, Alabama 13
Jan. 1, 1974	Nebraska 19, Texas 3
Jan. 1, 1975	Penn State 41, Baylor 20
Jan. 1, 1976	Arkansas 31, Georgia 10
Jan. 1, 1977	Houston 30, Maryland 21
Jan. 1, 1978	Notre Dame 38, Texas 10
Jan. 1, 1979	Notre Dame 35, Houston 34
Jan. 1, 1980	Houston 17, Nebraska 14
Jan. 1, 1981	Alabama 30, Baylor 2
Jan. 1, 1982	Texas 14, Alabama 12
Jan. 1, 1983	S. Methodist 7, Pittsburgh 3
Jan. 1, 1984	Georgia 10, Texas 9
Jan. 1, 1985	Boston College 45, Houston 28
Jan. 1, 1986	Texas A&M 36, Auburn 16
Jan. 1, 1987	Ohio State 28, Texas A&M 12
Jan. 1, 1988	Texas A&M 35, Notre Dame 10
Jan. 2, 1989	UCLA 17, Arkansas 3
Jan. 1, 1990	Tennessee 31, Arkansas 27
Jan. 1, 1991	Miami, Fla. 46, Texas 3
Jan. 1, 1992	Florida State 10, Texas A&M 2
Jan. 1, 1993	Notre Dame 28, Texas A&M 3

Gator Bowl (Jacksonville, Florida)

Jan. 2, 1960	Arkansas 14, Georgia Tech 7
Dec. 31, 1960	Florida 13, Baylor 12
Dec. 30, 1961	Penn State 30, Georgia Tech 15
Dec. 29, 1962	Florida 17, Penn State 7
Dec. 28, 1963	N. Carolina 35, Air Force 0
Jan. 2, 1965	Florida State 36, Oklahoma 19
Dec. 31, 1965	Georgia Tech 31, Texas Tech 21
Dec. 31, 1966	Tennessee 18, Syracuse 12
Dec. 30, 1967	Penn State 17, Florida State 17
Dec. 28, 1968	Missouri 35, Alabama 10
Dec. 27, 1969	Florida 14, Tennessee 13
Jan. 2, 1971	Auburn 35, Mississippi 28
Dec. 31, 1971	Georgia 7, N. Carolina 3
Dec. 30, 1972	Auburn 24, Colorado 3
Dec. 29, 1973	Texas Tech 28, Tennessee 19
Dec. 30, 1974	Auburn 27, Texas 3
Dec. 29, 1975	Maryland 13, Florida 0

Dec. 27, 1976	Notre Dame 20, Penn State 9
Dec. 30, 1977	Pittsburgh 34, Clemson 3
Dec. 29, 1978	Clemson 17, Ohio State 15
Dec. 28, 1979	N. Carolina 17, Michigan 15
Dec. 29, 1980	Pittsburgh 37, S. Carolina 9
Dec. 28, 1981	N. Carolina 31, Arkansas 27
Dec. 30, 1982	Florida State 31, West Virginia 1
Dec. 30, 1983	Florida 14, Iowa 6
Dec. 28, 1984	Oklahoma State 21, S. Carolina 14
Dec. 30, 1985	Florida State 34, Oklahoma 23
Dec. 27, 1986	Clemson 27, Stanford 21
Dec. 31, 1987	Louisiana State 30, S. Carolina 13
Jan. 1, 1989	Georgia 34, Michigan State 27
Dec. 30, 1989	Clemson 27, West Virginia 7
Jan. 1, 1991	Michigan 35, Mississippi 3
Dec. 29, 1991	Oklahoma 48, Virginia 14
Dec. 31, 1992	Florida 27, N.C. State 10

Heisman Memorial Trophy Winners (Since 1940)

The Heisman Memorial Trophy honors the nation's top collegiate football player. Presented annually by the Downtown Athletic Club of New York City, the award is one of the most prestigious and coveted prizes in collegiate sports.

1940	Tom Harmon, Michigan
1941	Bruce Smith, Minnesota
1942	Frank Sinkwich, Georgia
1943	Angelo Bertelli, Notre Dame
1944	Leslie Horvath, Ohio State
1945	Felix Blanchard, Army
1946	Glenn Davis, Army
1947	Johnny Lujack, Notre Dame
1948	Doak Walker, S. Methodist
1949	Leon Hart, Notre Dame
1950	Vic Janowicz, Ohio State
1951	Dick Kazmaier, Princeton
1952	Billy Vessels, Oklahoma
1953	Johnny Lattner, Notre Dame
1954	Alan Ameche, Wisconsin
1955	Howard Cassady, Ohio State
1956	Paul Hornung, Notre Dame
1957	John Crow, Texas A&M
1958	Pete Dawkins, Army
1959	Billy Cannon, Louisiana State
1960	Joe Bellino, Navy
1961	Ernie Davis, Syracuse
1962	Terry Baker, Oregon State
1963	Roger Staubach, Navy
1964	John Huarte, Notre Dame
1965	Mike Garrett, S. California
1966	Steve Spurrier, Florida
1967	Gary Beban, UCLA
1968	O. J. Simpson, S. California

1969	Steve Owens, Oklahoma
1970	Jim Plunkett, Stanford
1971	Pat Sullivan, Auburn
1972	Johnny Rodgers, Nebraska
1973	John Cappelletti, Penn State
1974	Archie Griffin, Ohio State
1975	Archie Griffin, Ohio State
1976	Tony Dorsett, Pittsburgh
1977	Earl Campbell, Texas
1978	Billy Sims, Oklahoma
1979	Charles White, S. California
1980	George Rogers, S. Carolina
1981	Marcus Allen, S. California
1982	Hershel Walker, Georgia
1983	Mike Rozier, Nebraska
1984	Doug Flutie, Boston College
1985	Bo Jackson, Auburn
1986	Vinnie Testaverde, Miami
1987	Tim Brown, Notre Dame
1988	Barry Sanders, Oklahoma State
1989	Andre Ware, Houston
1990	Ty Detmer, Brigham Young
1991	Desmond Howard, Michigan
1992	Gino Torretta, Miami, Fla.

INDEX